LIBRARY SUBSCRIPTION AGENCY

INDEX TO FAIRY TALES, 1949 - 1972

Including

Folklore, Legends & Myths,
In Collections

By

Norma Olin Ireland

Author of Index to Women; Index to Full Length
Plays (1944-1964); Index to Scientists, etc.

F. W. FAXON COMPANY, INC.
Westwood, Massachusetts
1973

International Standard Book Number 0-87305-101-7

Library of Congress Card Number 26-11491

Printed in the United States of America

DEDICATION

To the memory of my husband, Dave, who left me on September 18, 1970, but who saw the beginning of this book and encouraged me, as always. As he was my chief constructive critic, I have immeasurably missed his corrections and suggestions. He loved the "Little People" and read many of the Irish and Scottish tales with great enjoyment.

TABLE OF CONTENTS

FOREWORD

This work was compiled, at the request of the Publishers, to continue *Index to fairy tales* (and Supplements 1 and 2), by Mary Huse Eastman, now deceased. The second Supplement indexed fairy tales through 1948, so we began our compilation with the year 1949 and have brought it up to date, to the publication date of this volume.

It is never easy to continue another's publication and especially one as popular and useful as Miss Eastman's. We have found it necessary, however, to make certain changes to conform with the pattern of our own previous indexes. We shall mention these innovations below, as they pertain to the various phases of the index discussed.

Scope and Arrangement

This Index is necessarily a very large volume as it covers a twenty-three span of years, including not only fairy tales, but also folklore, legends and myths of all countries of the world. 406 books have been indexed, under title and subject, with authors included only when specifically mentioned in the collection. Stories in collections *only* are included, not individual-story books.

We have included a few older titles which have come out in new additions, or were not included in the earlier indexes. An example is the *My Book House* set, as a great many stories therein are not found elsewhere and there have been some additions. Variant titles are cross-referenced only if mentioned in the books indexed; Eastman has a very complete list of variants and should be referred to, if needed.

Our first innovation is the comprehensive subject indexing of stories. The decision to do this was made after discussion with children's librarians who expressed a desire for such a "break-down", to facilitate the location of stories by some elusive subject within the story or when the title was forgotten, or unknown.

We have included not only fairy tales, but also folklore, legends and myths because of the overlapping in library collections as well as in individual books. All entries are combined into a single alphabet, unlike the Eastman books, as we feel that such an arrangement is easier to use.

Arrangement is by word, not letter, as this is the most useful arrangement for this type of index. Then alphabetization is letter by letter, to end of word, or sentence. If first word of title is similar or directly related to subject, then that title is omitted under the subject classification, as redundant. We follow the American Library Association Rules in arrangement, e.g. if words are the same, then arrange by author, subject and title, in that order. In the case of names, proper names first, geographical names, then subjects.

The *title* entry is the main entry, as is typical for this type of index. Symbols are used to locate stories, as found in "List of Collections analyzed".

Punctuation marks are disregarded in alphabetization (commas, apostrophes, etc.) and thus we have *Boys* (as subject) arranged before Boy's . . . (as title), but elisions are arranged as they are printed and not as if spelled out: *an'* for instance, before *and.* Capitalization is used sparingly, as in library practice – for proper names, first word of title, inverted headings.

Subject Headings

We have tried to choose subject headings which would be simple and easy to use and yet enable users to locate special, unusual subjects as well. Cross-references are liberally included, but not to excess, but we have avoided duplication as much as possible. But sometimes there is a "fine-line" difference and then both headings are used. Occasionally early names of countries are used when the stories pertained to the earlier years of these countries, e.g. Persia. We have endeavored to correlate our headings with those of the Eastman indexes insofar as possible, but of course have necessarily included hundreds of new ones because of our comprehensive subject-indexing. We have tried to analyze stories according to the *importance* of subjects (not always every subject) and towards that purpose we have personally read most every one of these stories – to our great enjoyment!

Acknowledgments

We wish to acknowledge the help and cooperation of several individuals and libraries, without whose assistance this book could never have been *completed*:

Mrs. Barbara Hayes, of Fallbrook, for *many months of typing and checking assistance,* always with *good humor, patience* and *perseverance.*

Mrs. Geraldine Bauer, Librarian of the Fallbrook branch of the San Diego Co. Library, for *interlibrarian loans, and other co-operation.*

Mrs. Helen Robbins, Children's Librarian of the Oceanside Public Library, for *constantly supplying "hard-to-find" and new books.*

Mrs. Beatrice Chambers, Reference Librarian of the San Diego Co. Library, for her *interlibrary loan assistance.*

California State Library and all other contributing libraries in the state, who "combed" their shelves for our benefit.

We hope this index will be helpful to all types of libraries: public school, college and university – the latter for use in their classes in folklore. It is a "popular" type of index, however, and we have made no scholarly break-down of folk-motifs in stories.

It has been no small job, considering the wealth of published collections; we have done our best to index all of the material available to us, as accurately as is humanly possible.

(Mrs.) Norma Olin Ireland
2237 Brooke Road
Fallbrook, California, 92028

X

AARDEMA – STORY
Aardema, Verna. Tales from the story hat. Illus. by Elton Fax. N. Y., Coward-Mc-Cann, 1960. 72p

AARDEMA – TALES
Aardema, Verna. Tales for the third ear from Equatorial Africa. Illus. by Ib Ohlsson. N. Y., E. P. Dutton & Co., Inc., 1969. 96p

ALEGRIA – THREE
Alegria, Ricardo E. The three wishes. A collection of Puerto Rican folktales. Trans. by Elizabeth Culbert. Illus. by Lorenzo Homar. N. Y., Harcourt, Brace & World, Inc., 1969. 128p

ALEXANDER – PEBBLES
Alexander, Frances. Pebbles from a broken jar. Fables and hero stories from old China. Indianapolis, The Bobbs-Merrill Co., c. 1963, 1967. 29p

ALGER. *see* LEODHAS

ALMEDINGEN – KNIGHTS
Almedingen, E. M. The knights of the golden table. Illus. by Charles Keeping. Phil., J. B. Lippincott, 1964. 191p

ALMEDINGEN – RUSS.
Almedingen, E. M. Russian folk and fairy tales. Illus. by Simon Jeruchim. N. Y., G. P. Putnam's Sons, c. 1957, 1963. 192p

ANDERSON – BOY
Anderson, Paul. The boy and the blind storyteller. Illus. by Yong Hwan Kim. N. Y., Wm. R. Scott, Inc., 1964. 94p

APPIAH – ANANSE
Appiah, Peggy. Ananse the spider. Tales from an Ashanti village. Illus. by Peggy Wilson. N. Y., (Random House) Pantheon Books, 1966. 152p

ARBUTHNOT – TIME
Arbuthnot, May Hill, comp. Time for fairy tales, old and new. Rev. ed. Illus. by John Averill (and others). N. Y., Scott, 1961. 431p

ARKHURST – SPIDER
Arkhurst, Joyce Cooper. The adventures of spider. West African folk tales. Illus. by Jerry Pinkney. Boston, Little, Brown & Co., 1964. 58p

ARNOTT – AFRICAN
Arnott, Kathleen. African myths and legends. Illus. by Joan Kiddell-Monroe. N. Y., H. Z. Walck, c. 1962, 1963. 211p

ARNOTT – TALES
Arnott, Kathleen. Tales of Temba. Traditional African stories. Illus. by Tom Feelings. N. Y., Henry Z. Walck, Inc., 1967. 144p

ASBJORNSEN – EAST
Asbjornsen, Peter and E. Moe Jorgen. East of the sun and west of the moon, and other tales. Illus. by Tom Vroman. N. Y., The MacMillan Co., c. 1963. 139p

ASBJORNSEN – NORW.
Asbjornsen, Peter and E. Moe Jorgen. Norwegian folk tales. Illus. by Erik Werenskiold and Theodor Kittelsen. Trans. by Pat Shaw Iversen and Carl Norman. N. Y., Viking, 1960. 188p

AULAIRE – NORSE
  Aulaire, Ingri (Mortenson) d' and Edgar Parin d' Aulaire. Norse gods and giants. Garden City, N. Y., Doubleday & Co., Inc., 1967. 161p

AUNG – KINGDOM
  Aung, Maung Htin and Helen G. Trager. A kingdom lost for a drop of honey. And other Burmese folktales. Illus. by Paw Oo Thet. N. Y., Parents' Magazine Press, 1968. 96p

AYRE – SKETCO
  Ayre, Robert. Sketco the raven. Illus. by Philip Surrey. Toronto, MacMillan Co., 1961. 183p

BAKER – GOLDEN
  Baker, Augusta. The golden lynx, and other tales. Illus. by Johannes Troyer. Phil., J. B. Lippincott Co., 1960. 160p

BAKER – TALKING
  Baker, Augusta. The talking tree. Fairy tales from 15 lands. Illus. by Johannes Troyer. Phil., J. B. Lippincott Co., 1955. 255p

BALDWIN – FAVOR.
  Baldwin, James. Favorite tales of long ago. Illus. by Lili Rethi. N. Y., Aladdin Books, 1955. 150p

BAMBERGER – FIRST
  Bamberger, Richard. My first big story-book. Trans. by James Thin. Illus. by Emanuela Wallenta. Irvington-on-Hudson, N. Y., Harvey House, Inc., 1960. 220p

BARASH – GOLDEN
  Barash, Asher. A golden treasury of Jewish tales. Trans. by Murray Roston. N. Y., Dodd, Mead & Co., c. 1965, 1966. 167p

BARBEAU – GOLDEN
  Barbeau, Marius and Michael Hornyansky. The Golden phoenix, and other French-Canadian fairy tales. N. Y., Henry Z. Walck, Inc., 1958. 144p

BARLOW – LATIN
  Barlow, Genevieve. Latin American tales. From the Pampas to the Pyramids of Mexico. Illus. by Wm. M. Hutchinson, Rand McNally & Co., 1966. 144p

BATCHELOR – SUPER.
  Batchelor, Julie Forsyth, and Claudia DeLys. Superstitious? Here's why! Illus. by Erik Blegvad. N. Y., Harcourt, Brace & Co., 1954. 129p

BECHSTEIN – FAIRY
  Bechstein, Ludwig. Fairy tales of Ludwig Bechstein. Trans. by Anthea Bell. Illus. by Irene Schreiber. N. Y., Abelard – Schuman, c. 1966, 1967. 205p

BELPRE – TIGER
  Belpre, Pura. The tiger and the rabbit, and other tales. Illus. by Tomie de Paola. Phil., J. B. Lippincott Co., 1965. 127p

BELTING – CAT
  Belting, Natalia M. Cat tales. Illus. by Lee Summers. N. Y., Holt, 1959. 95p

BELTING – EARTH
  Belting, Natalia. The earth is on a fish's back: tales of beginnings. Illus. by Esta Nesbitt. N. Y., Holt, 1965. 91p

BELTING – ELVES
>Belting, Natalia. Elves and ellefolk. Tales of the Little People. Illus. by Gordon Laite. N. Y., Holt, Rinehart and Winston, 1961. 96p

BELTING – LONG
>Belting, Natalia M. The long-tailed bear, and other Indian legends. Illus. by Louis F. Carey. Indianapolis, Bobbs-Merrill Co., 1961. 96p

BELTING – STARS
>Belting, Natalia M. The stars are silver reindeer. Illus. by Esta Nesbitt. N. Y., Holt, Rinehart & Winston, 1966. n.p.

BELTING – THREE
>Belting, Natalia. Three apples fell from heaven. Unfamiliar legends of the trees. Illus. by Anne Marie Jauss. Indianapolis, The Bobbs-Merrill Co., Inc., 1953. 158p

BENTON. see SHEEHAN

BERGER – BLACK
>Berger, Terry. Black fairy tales. Illus. by David Omar White. N. Y., Atheneum Pub., 1969. 137p

BERRY – MAGIC
>Berry, Erick. The magic banana and other Polynesian tales. Illus. by Nicholas Amorosi. N. Y., The John Day Co., 1968. 126p

BIRCH – CHINESE
>Birch, Cyril. Chinese myths and fantasies. Illus. by Ivan Kiddell-Monroe. N. Y., Henry Z. Walck, Inc., 1961. 200p

BLOCK – UKRAIN
>Block, Marie Halun, trans. Ukrainian folk tales from the original collections of Ivan Rudchenko and Maria Lukiyaninko. Illus. by J. Hnizdovsky. N. Y., Coward, McCann, Inc., 1964. 76p

BONNET – CHINESE
>Bonnet, Leslie. Chinese folk and fairy tales. Illus. by Maurice Brevannes. N. Y., G. P. Putnam's Sons, 1958. 191p

BORSKI – GOOD
>Borski, Lucia Merecka, comp. and trans. Good sense and good fortune, and other Polish folk tales. Illus. by Erica Gorecka-Egan. N. Y., David McKay Co., Inc., 1970. 83p

BOUCHER – MEAD
>Boucher, Alan, trans. Mead moondaughter and other Icelandic folk tales. Illus. by Karolina Larusdotlir. Phil., Chilton Book Co., 1967. 180p

BOWES – BIRD
>Bowes, Anne LaBastille. Bird kingdom of the Mayas. Illus. by Anita Benarde. Princeton, N. J., Van Nostrand Co., Inc., c. 1967. 80p

BRENNER – BOY
>Brenner, Anita. The boy who could do anything and other Mexican folk tales. N. Y., Wm. R. Scott, Inc., 1958. 136p

BRIGGS – PERS.
>Briggs, Katherine Mary. The personnel of fairyland. A short account of the fairy people of Great Britain for those who tell stories to children. Illus. by Jane Moore. Cambridge, Mass., Robert Bentley, 1953, 1955. 228p

BRO – HOW
Bro, Margueritte Harmon. How the mouse deer became king. Illus. by Joseph Low. Garden City, N. Y., Doubleday, 1966. 127p

BROWN – AROUND
Brown, Shirley. Around the world stories to tell to children. Illus. by Angela Conner. N. Y., Franklin Watts, Inc., 1962. 140p

BUCK – FAIRY
Buck, Pearl S. Fairy tales of the Orient. Illus. by Jeanyee Wong. N. Y., Simon & Schuster, 1965. 320p

BUDBERG – RUSSIAN
Budberg, Moura and Anabel Williams-Ellis, trans. Russian fairy tales. Illus. by Sarah Nechamkin. N. Y., Frederick Warne & Co., Inc., c. 1965, 1967. 272p

BUDD – FULL
Budd, Lillian. Full moons. Indian legends of the seasons. Illus. by George Armstrong. Chicago, Rand McNally & Co., 1971. 79p

BUEHR – SEA
Buehr, Walter. Sea Monsters. Illus. by the author. N. Y., W. W. Norton, 1966. 92p

BULATKIN – EURASIAN
Bulatkin, I. F. Eurasian folk and fairy tales. Illus. by Howard Simon. N. Y., Criterion, 1965. 128p

BURNETT – RACKETTY
Burnett, Frances Hodgson. Racketty-Packetty house, and other stories. Illus. by Harold Berson. N. Y., Charles Scribner's Sons, 1961. 190p

BURTON – MAGIC
Burton, W. F. P. The magic drum. Tales from Central Africa. Illus. by Ralph Thompson. N. Y., Criterion Books, 1961. 127p

CAMPBELL – MAORI
Campbell, Alistair. Maori legends. Some myths and legends of the Maori people. Illus. by Robin White. Wellington, Seven Seas Pub. Co., 1969. 60p

CARLSON – TALKING
Carlson, Natalie Savage. The talking cat and other stories of French Canada. Illus. by Roger Duvoisin. N. Y., Harper & Brothers, 1952. 87p

CARPENTER – AFRICAN
Carpenter, Frances. African wonder tales. Illus. by Joseph Escourido. Garden City, N. Y., Doubleday & Co., 1963. 215p

CARPENTER – DOGS
Carpenter, Frances. Wonder tales of dogs and cats. Illus. by Ezra Jack Keats. N. Y., Doubleday & Co., Inc., 1955. 255p

CARPENTER – ELEPHANT'S
Carpenter, Frances. The elephant's bathtub. Wonder tales from the Far East. Illus. by Hans Guggenheim. Garden City, N. Y., Doubleday & Co., Inc., 1962. 219p

CARPENTER – HORSES
Carpenter, Frances. Wonder tales of horses and heroes. Illus. by William D. Hayes. Garden City, N. Y., Doubleday & Co., Inc., 1952. 238p

CARPENTER – SHIPS
Carpenter, Frances. Wonder tales of seas and ships. Illus. by Peter Spier. Garden City, N. Y., Doubleday & Co., Inc., 1959. 285p

CARPENTER – SOUTH
Carpenter, Frances. South American wonder tales. Illus. by Ralph Creasman. Chicago, Follett Pub. Co., 1969. 192p

CATHON – PERHAPS
Cathon, Laura E. and Thusnelda Schmidt. Perhaps and perchance. Tales of nature. Illus. by Anne Marie Jauss. N. Y., Abington Press, 1962. 260p

CHAFETZ – THUNDER.
Chafetz, Henry. Thunderbird and other stories. Illus. by Ronni Solbert. N. Y., Pantheon, 1964. 41p

CHAPPELL – THEY
Chappell, Warren. They say stories. Illus. by Warren Campbell. N. Y., Alfred A. Knopf, 1960. 79p

CHILD – CASTLES
Child Study Assoc. of America. Castles and dragons. Illus. by William du Bois. N. Y., Crowell, 1958. 299p

COBBLE – WEMBI
Cobble, Alice D. Wembi, the singer of stories. Illus. by Doris Hallas. St. Louis, Mo., The Bethany Press, 1959. 128p

COLUM – STONE
Colum, Padraic. The stone of Victory, and other tales . . . Illus. by Judith Gwyn Brown. N. Y., McGraw-Hill Book Co., 1966. 119p

COOPER – FIVE
Cooper, Lee. Five fables from France. Illus. by Charles Keeping. N. Y., Abelard-Schuman, 1970. 87p

COTHRAN – MAGIC
Cothran, Jean, ed. The magic calabash. Folk tales from America's islands and Alaska. Illus. by Clifford N. Geary. N. Y., David McKay Co., Inc., 1956. 88p

COTHRAN – WITH
Cothran, Jean, ed. With a wig, with a wag, and other American folk tales. Illus. by Clifford N. Geary. N. Y., David McKay Co., Inc., 1954. 95p

COURLANDER – FIRE
Courlander, Harold and Wolf Leslau. The fire on the mountain: and other Ethiopian stories. Illus. by Robert W. Kane. N. Y., Holt, Rinehart & Winston, 1950. 141p

COURLANDER – HAT
Courlander, Harold. The hat-shaking dance. And other Ashanti tales from Ghana, with Albert Kofi Prempeh. Illus. by Enrico Arno. N. Y., Harcourt, Brace & World, Inc., 1957. 115p

COURLANDER – KANT.
Courlander, Harold. Kantchil's lime pit. Illus. by Robert W. Kane. N. Y., Harcourt, Brace, 1950. 150p

COURLANDER – KING'S
Courlander, Harold. The king's drum and other African stories. Illus. by Enrico Arno. N. Y., Harcourt, Brace & World, Inc., 1962. 125p

COURLANDER – OLODE
Courlander, Harold with Ezekiel A. Eshugbayi. Olode the hunter, and other tales from Nigeria. Illus. by Enrico Arno. N. Y., Harcourt, 1968. 153p

COURLANDER – PEOPLE
Courlander, Harold. People of the short blue corn. Tales and legends of the Hopi Indians. N. Y., Harcourt Brace, Jovanovich, Inc., 1970.189p

COURLANDER – PIECE
Courlander, Harold. The piece of fire and other Haitian tales. Illus. by Beth and Joe Krush. N. Y., Harcourt, Brace & World, Inc., 1964. 128p

COURLANDER – RIDE see U. N. – RIDE

COURLANDER – TERRA.
Courlander, Harold. Terrapin's pot of sense. Illus. by Elton Fax. N. Y., Henry Holt & Co., 1957. 125p

COURLANDER – TIGER'S
Courlander, Harold. The tiger's whisker, and other tales and legends from Asia and the Pacific. Illus. by Enrico Arno. N. Y., Harcourt, Brace, 1959. 152p

CREANGA – FOLK
Creanga, Ion. Folk tales from Roumania. Trans. by Mabel Nandris. Illus. by Iza Constantinonici-Hein. London, Routledge and Kegan Paul, c. 1952, 1953. 170p

CREDLE – TALL
Credle, Ellis. Tall tales from the high hills, and other stories. Illus. by Richard Bennett., N. J., Nelson, 1957. 156p

CUMMINGS – FAIRY
Cummings, E. E. Fairy tales. Illus. by John Eaton. N. Y., Harcourt, Brace & World, Inc., c. 1950, 1965. 39p

CURCIJA – HEROES
Curcija-Prodanovic, Nada. Heroes of Serbia. Folk ballads. Illus. by Dusan Ristic. N. Y., Henry Z. Walck, Inc., 1964. 178p

CURCIJA – YUGOSLAV
Curcija-Prodanovic, Nada. Yugoslav folk-tales. Illus. by Joan Kiddell-Monroe. (Oxford myths and legends). N. Y., Henry Z. Walck, Inc., 1957. 210p

CURRY – DOWN
Curry, Jane Louise. Down from the lonely mountain. California Indian tales. Illus. by Enrico Arno. N. Y., Harcourt, Brace & World, Inc., 1965. 128p

DAVIS – LION'S
Davis, Russell and Brent Ashabranner. The lion's whiskers. Tales of high Africa. Illus. by James G. Teason. Boston, Little, Brown & Co., 1959. 191p

DAVIS – TEN
Davis, Russell and Brent Ashabranner. Ten thousand desert swords. The epic story of a great Bedouin tribe. Illus. by Leonard Everett Fisher. Boston, Little, Brown & Co., 1960. 155p

DE LA IGLESIA – CAT
De La Iglesia, Marie Elena. The cat and the mouse and other Spanish tales. Illus. by Joseph Low. N. Y., (Random House) Pantheon Books, 1966. unp.

DELEEUW. see LEEUW

DE REGNIERS – GIANT
De Regniers, Beatrice Schenk. The giant book. Illus. by William Lahey Cummings. N. Y., Atheneum Pub., 1966. 188p

DELARUE – FRENCH
Delarue, Paul. French fairy tales. Illus. by Warren Chappell. N. Y., Alfred A. Knopf, c. 1956, 1968. 117p

DEUTSCH – FAR. *see* DEUTSCH – TALES

DEUTSCH – MORE
Deutsch, Babette and Avrahm Yarmolinsky. More tales of faraway folk. Iilus. by Janina Domanska. N. Y., Harper & Row, Pub., 1964. 93p

DEUTSCH – TALES
Deutsch, Babbette and Avrahm Yarmolinsky. Tales of faraway folk. Illus. by Irena Lorentowicz. N. Y., Harper & Row, 1952. 68p

DOBBS – MORE
Dobbs, Rose. More once-upon-a-time stories. Illus. by Flavia Gag. N. Y., Random House, 1961. 96p

DOBBS – ONCE
Dobbs, Rose. Once upon a time. Twenty cheerful tales to read and tell. Illus. by Flavia Gag. N. Y., Random House, Inc., 1950. 117p

DOWNING – RUSSIAN
Downing, Charles. Russian tales and legends. Illus. by Joan Kiddell-Monroe. (Oxford myths and legends). London, Oxford Univ. Press, 1957. 231p

DUDDINGTON – RUSS.
Duddington, Natalie, trans. Russian folk tales. Illus. by Dick Hart. N. Y., Funk & Wagnalls, 1967. 144p

DURHAM – TIT
Durham, Mae. Tit for tat, and other Latvian folk tales. Illus. by Harriet Pincus. N. Y., Harcourt, Brace & World, 1967. 126p

EDMONDS – OOKA
Edmonds, I. G. Ooka the wise. Tales of old Japan. Illus. by Sanae Yamazaki. Indianapolis, Boobs-Merrill Co., 1961. 96p

EDMONDS – TRICKSTER
Edmonds, I. G. Trickster tales. Illus. by Sean Morrison. Phil., J. B. Lippincott Co., 1966. 147p

EELLS – SPAIN
Eells, Elsie Spicer. Tales of enchantment from Spain. Illus. by Maud and Miska Petersham. N. Y., Dodd, Mead & Co., 1950. 173p

EKREM – TURKISH
Ekrem, Selma. Turkish fairy tales. Illus. by Lila Bayrack. Princeton, N. J., D. Van Nostrand Co., Inc., 1964. 117p

ELLIOT – SINGING
Elliot, Geraldine. The singing chameleon. A book of African stories based on local customs, proverbs and folk-lore. Phil., Dufour Editions, 1963. 169p

ELLIOT – WHERE
Elliot, Geraldine. Where the leopard passes. A book of African folk tales. Illus. by Sheila Hawkins. N. Y., Schocken Books, 1949. 133p

FARJEON – LITTLE
Farjeon, Eleanor. The little bookroom. Illus. by Edward Ardozzone. London, Oxford Univ. Press, 1956. 302p

FARJEON – SILVER
Farjeon, Eleanor. The silver curlew. Illus. by Ernest H. Shepard. N. Y., The Viking Press, c. 1953, 1968. 192p

FEINSTEIN – FOLK
Feinstein, Alan S. Folk tales from Siam. Illus. by Pat Pibulsonggram. N. Y., A. S. Barnes & Co., 1969. 90p

FELTON – NEW
Felton, Harold W. New tall tales of Pecos Bill. Illus. by Wm. Moyers. Englewood Cliffs, N. J., Prentice-Hall, c. 1958, 1963. 164p

FELTON – TRUE
Felton, Harold W. True tall tales of Stormalong: sailor of the Seven Seas. Illus. by Joan Sandin. Englewood Cliffs, N. J., Prentice-Hall, 1968. 64p

FELTON – WORLD'S
Felton, Harold W. The world's most truthful man. Tall tales told by Ed Grant in Maine. N. Y., Dodd, Mead & Co., 1961. 151p

FILLMORE – SHEPHERD'S
Fillmore, Parker. The shepherd's nosegay stories from Finland and Czechoslovakia. Ed. by Katherine Love. Illus. by Enrico Arno. N. Y., Harcourt, Brace & Co., 1958. 192p

FINLAY – FOLK
Finlay, Winifred. Folk tales from the North. Illus. by Victor Ambrus. N. Y., Franklin Watts, Inc., c. 1968, 1969. 127p

FISHER – STORIES
Fisher, Anne B. Stories California Indians told. Illus. by Ruth Robbins. Berkeley, Calif., Parnassus Press, 1957. 110p

FOSTER – STONE
Foster, Ruth. The stone horsemen. Tales from the Caucasus. Illus. by Judith Gwyn Brown. Indianapolis, Bobbs-Merrill Co., 1965. 86p

GAER – FABLES
Gaer, Joseph. The fables of India. Illus. by Randy Monk. Boston, Little, Brown & Co., 1955. 176p

GARNER – GOBLINS
Garner, Alan, Ed. A cavalcade of goblins. Illus. by Kreptyna Turska. N. Y., Henry Z. Walck, Inc., 1969. 227p

GARNIER – LEGENDS
Garnier, Charles-Marie. Legends of Ireland. Trans. and adapted by Leslie Vyse. Illus. by Jean Giannini. Cleveland, the World Pub. Co., 1968. 190p

GHOSE – FOLK
Ghose, Sudhin N. Folk tales and fairy stories from further India. Illus. by Shrimati E. Carlile. N. Y., A. S. Barnes & Co., Inc., 1966. 145p

GILLHAM – BEYOND
Gillham, Charles E. Beyond the Clapping Mountains. Eskimo stories from Alaska. Illus. by author. N. Y., The MacMillan Co., 1947. 134p

GILSTRAP – SULTAN'S
   Gilstrap, Robert and Irene Estabrook. The sultan's fool, and other North African tales. Illus. by Robert Greco. N. Y., Henry Holt & Co., 1958. 95p

GINSBURG – MASTER
   Ginsburg, Mirra, trans. and ed. The master of the winds, and other tales from Siberia. Illus. by Enrico Arno. N. Y., Crown Publishers, Inc., 1970. 158p

GORHAM – REAL
   Gorham, Michael. Real book of American tall tales. Illus. by Herbert Danska. Garden City, N. Y., Garden City Books, 1952. 192p

GRAHAM – BEGGAR
   Graham, Gail B. The beggar in the blanket and other Vietnamese tales. Illus. by Brigitte Bryan. N. Y., Dial Press, 1970. 96p

GRAY – INDIA'S
   Gray, J. E. B. India's tales and legends. Illus. by J. E. B. Gray. N. Y., Henry Z. Walck, 1961. 230p

GRAY – MAINLY
   Gray, Nicolas Stuart. Mainly in moonlight. Ten stories of sorcery and the supernatural. Illus. by Charles Keeping. N. Y., Meredith Press, 1965. 181p

GREEN – BIG
   Green, Margaret, comp. and ed. The big book of animal fables. Illus. by Janusz Grabianski. N. Y., Franklin Watts, Inc., 1965. 240p

GREEN – GREEKS
   Green, Roger Lancelyn. Tales of the Greeks and Trojans. Illus. by Janet and Anne Grahame Johnstone. London, Purnell & Sons, Ltd., 1963. 77p

GREEN – LEPRECHAUN
   Green, Kathleen. Leprechaun tales. Illus. by Victoria de Larrea. Phila., J. B. Lippincott Co., 1968. 127p

GREEN – TALES
   Green, Roger Lancelyn. Tales of ancient Egypt. Illus. by Elaine Raphael. N. Y., Henry Z. Walck, Inc., 1968. 216p

GREY – SOUTH (1)
   Grey, Eve. Legends of the South Seas. Book one. Illus. by Tambi Larsen. Honolulu, Hawaii, Island Import Co., 1954. 31p

GREY – SOUTH (2)
   Grey, Eve. Legends of the South Seas. Book two. Illus. by Tambi Larsen. Honolulu, Hawaii, Island Import Co., 1954. 31p

GRINGHUIS – GIANTS
   Gringhuis, Dirk. Giants, dragons, and gods. Constellations and their folklore. Illus. by Dirk Gringhuis. N. Y., Meredith Press, 1968. 76p

GUIRMA – TALES
   Guirma, Frederic. Tales of Mogho. African stories from Upper Volta. N. Y., The MacMillan Co., 1971. 113p

HACK – DANISH
   Hack, Inge. Danish fairy tales. Illus. by Harry and Ilse Toothill. Chic., Follett Pub. Co., 1964. 194p

HAMPDEN – GYPSY
Hampden, John. The gypsy fiddle, and other tales told by the gypsies. Illus. by Robin Jacques. N. Y., World Pub., Co., 1969. 160p

HARDENDORFF – FROG'S
Hardendorff, Jeanne B. The frog's saddle horse and other tales. Illus. by Helen Webber. Phil., J. B. Lippincott Co., 1968. 157p

HARDENDORFF – TRICKY
Hardendorff, Jeanne B. Tricky Peik, and other picture tales. Illus. by Tomie de Paola. Phil., J. B. Lippincott, 1967. 122p

HARMAN – TALES
Harman, Humphrey. Tales told near a crocodile; stories from Nyanza. Illus. by George Ford. N. Y., The Viking Press, 1967. 185p

HARRIS – ONCE
Harris, Christie. Once upon a totem; woodcuts by John Frazer Mills. N. Y., Atheneum Pub., 1963. 148p

HASKETT – GRAINS
Haskett, Edythe. Grains of pepper. Folktales from Liberia. Illus. by Edythe Haskett. N. Y., The John Day Co., 1967. 120p

HATCH – MORE
Hatch, Mary Cottam. More Danish tales. Illus. by Edgun. N. Y., Harcourt, Brace & Co., 1949. 237p

HAUFF – CARAVAN
Hauff, Wilhelm. The caravan. Trans. from the German by Alma Overholt. Illus. by Burt Silverman. N. Y., Thomas Y. Crowell Co., 1964. 220p

HAUFF – FAIRY
Hauff, Wilhelm. Fairy tales of Wilhelm Hauff. Trans. by Anthea Bell. Illus. by Ulrik Schramm. N. Y., Abelard-Schuman, 1969. 222p

HAVILAND – CZECH.
Haviland, Virginia. Favorite fairy tales, told in Czechoslovakia. Illus. by Trina Schart Hyman. Boston, Little, Brown & Co., 1966. 90p

HAVILAND – ENGLAND
Haviland, Virginia. Favorite fairy tales told in England. Retold by Joseph Jacobs. Illus. by Bettina. Boston, Little, Brown & Co., 1959. 88p

HAVILAND – FRANCE
Haviland, Virginia. Favorite fairy tales told in France. Illus. by Roger Duvoisin. Boston, Little, Brown & Co., 1959. 92p

HAVILAND – GERMANY
Haviland, Virginia. Favorite fairy tales told in Germany; retold from the Brothers Grimm. Illus. by Susanne Suba. Boston, Little, Brown & Co., 1959. 85p

HAVILAND – GREECE
Haviland, Virginia. Favorite fairy tales told in Greece. Illus. by Nonny Hogrogian. Boston, Little, Brown & Co., 1970. 90p

HAVILAND – IRELAND
Haviland, Virginia. Favorite fairy tales told in Ireland. Illus. by Artur Marokvia. Boston, Little, Brown & Co., 1961. 91p

HAVILAND – ITALY
Haviland, Virginia. Favorite fairy tales told in Italy. Illus. by Evaline Ness. Boston, Little, Brown & Co., 1965. 90p

HAVILAND – JAPAN
Haviland, Virginia. Favorite fairy tales told in Japan. Illus. by George Suyeoka. Boston, Little, Brown & Co., 1967. 89p

HAVILAND – NORWAY
Haviland, Virginia. Favorite fairy tales told in Norway. Retold from Norse folklore. Illus. by Leonard Weisgard. Boston, Little, Brown & Co., 1961. 88p

HAVILAND – POLAND
Haviland, Virginia. Favorite fairy tales told in Poland. Illus. by Felix Hoffmann. Boston, Little, Brown & Co., 1963. 90p

HAVILAND – RUSSIA
Haviland, Virginia. Favorite fairy tales told in Russia. Illus. by Herbert Danska. Boston, Little, Brown & Co., 1961. 86p

HAVILAND – SCOTLAND
Haviland, Virginia. Favorite fairy tales told in Scotland. Illus. by Adrienne Adams. Boston, Little, Brown & Co., 1963. 92p

HAVILAND – SPAIN
Haviland, Virginia. Favorite fairy tales told in Spain. Illus. by Barbara Cooney. Boston, Little, Brown & Co., 1965. 87p

HAVILAND – SWEDEN
Haviland, Virginia. Favorite fairy tales told in Sweden. Illus. by Ronni Solbert. Boston, Little, Brown & Co., 1966. 92p

HAYES – INDIAN
Hayes, William D. Indian tales of the desert people. Illus. by Wm. D. Hayes. N. Y., David McKay Co., Inc., 1957. 111p

HAZELTINE – HERO
Hazeltine, Alice I. ed. Hero tales from many lands. Illus. by Gordon Laite. N. Y., Abington Press, 1961. 475p

HEADY – JAMBO
Heady, Eleanor B. Jambo, Sungura. Tales from East Africa. Illus. by Robert Frankenberg. N. Y., W. W. Norton, 1965. 95p

HEADY – TALES
Heady, Eleanor B. Tales of the Nimipoo, from the land of the Nez Perce Indians. Illus. by Eric Carle. N. Y., The World Publishing Co., 1970. 125p

HEADY – WHEN
Heady, Eleanor B. When the stones were soft; East African fireside tales. Illus. by Tom Feelings. N. Y., Funk & Wagnall Co., Inc., 1968. 94p

HEARN – JAPANESE
Hearn, Lafcadio and others. Japanese fairy tales. Illus. by "Kay". N. Y., Liveright Pub. Corp., 1953. 132p

HITCHCOCK – KING
Hitchcock, Patricia. The king who rides a tiger, and other folk tales from Nepal. Illus. by Lillian Sader. Berkeley, Calif., Parnassus Press, 1966. 133p

HODGES – SEREND.
Hodges, Elizabeth Jamison. Serendipity tales. Illus. by Jane Atkin Corwin. N. Y., Atheneum Pub., 1966. 179p

HOKE – WITCHES
Hoke, Helen, ed. Witches, witches, witches. Pictures by W. R. Lohse. N. Y., Franklin Watts, Inc., 1958. 230p

HOLDING – SKY
Holding, James. The sky-eater and other South Sea tales. Illus. by Charles Keeping. N. Y., Abelard-Schuman, 1965. 124p

HOLLADAY – BANTU
Holladay, Virginia. Bantu tales. Illus. by Rocco Negri. N. Y., Viking Press, 1970. 95p

HOPE-SIMPSON – CAVAL.
Hope-Simpson, Jacynth. A cavalcade of witches. Illus. by Krystyna Turska. N. Y., Henry Z. Walck, Inc., 1967. 226p

HOSFORD – THUNDER
Hosford, Dorothy. Thunder of the gods. Illus. by Claire and George Louden. N. Y., Holt, Rinehart & Winston, 1952. 115p

HSIEH – CHINESE
Hsieh, Tehayi, trans. and ed. Chinese village folk tales. Boston, Bruce Humphries, Inc., 1948. 74p

HTIN – KINGSOM. see AUNG – KINGDOM

HUME – FAVORITE
Hume, Lotta. Favorite children's stories from China and Tibet. Illus. by Lo Koon-chiu. Rutland, Vt., Chas. E. Tuttle Co., 1962, 1965. 119p

ILLYES – ONCE
Illyes, Gyula. Once upon a time. Forty Hungarian folk-tales. Hungary, Corvina Press, 1964. 286p

INS-SOB – FOLK
Ins-Sob, Zong. Folk tales from Korea. London, Routledge & Kegan Paul Ltd., 1952. 257p

IRVING – TALES
Irving, Wash. Wash. Irving's tales of the Alhambra . . . by Robert C. Goldston. Indianapolis, Bobbs-Merrill, 1962. 153p

IVES – TALES
Ives, Burl. Burl Ives' tales of America. Illus. by Helen Borten. Cleveland, The World Pub. Co., 1954. 305p

JABLOW – MAN
Jablow, Alta & Carl Withers. The man in the moon; sky tales from many lands. Illus. Peggy Wilson. N. Y., Holt, 1969. 131p

JACOBS – EUROPE.
Jacobs, Joseph. European folk and fairy tales. Illus. by John D. Batten. N. Y., G. P. Putnam's Sons, 1916. (restored and retold) 264p

JACOBS – MORE
Jacobs, Joseph. More English fairy tales. Illus. by John D. Batten. N. Y., G. P. Putnam's Sons, n. d. 268p

JACOBSON – FIRST
Jacobson, Helen. The first book of mythical beasts. Illus. by Lewis Zacks. N. Y., Watts, 1960. 69p

JACOBSON – LEGEND.
Jacobson, Helen. The first book of legendary beings. Pictures by Lewis Zacks. N. Y., Franklin Watts, Inc., 1962. 53p

JAGENDORF – GHOST
Jagendorf, Moritz A. The ghost of Peg-Leg Peter; and other stories of old New York. Illus. by Lino S. Lipinski. N. Y., The Vanguard Press, Inc., n. d. 125p

JAGENDORF – GYPSIES
Jagendorf, Moritz A. & C. H. Tillhagen. The gypsies' fiddle. Illus. by Hans Helweg. N. Y., The Vanguard Press, 1956. 186p

JAGENDORF – KING
Jagendorf, Moritz A. & R. S. Boggs. The king of the mountains. A treasury of Latin American folk stories. Illus. by Carybe. N. Y., The Vanguard Press, 1960. 313p

JAGENDORF – MERRY
Jagendorf, Moritz A. The merry men of Gotham. Illus. by Shane Miller. N. Y., The Vanguard Press, 1950. 150p

JAGENDORF – NEW
Jagendorf, Moritz A. New England bean-pot; Amer. folk stories to read and to tell. Illus. by Donald McKay. N. Y., The Vanguard Press, 1948. 272p

JAGENDORF – SAND
Jagendorf, Moritz A. Sand in the bag, and other folk stories of Ohio, Indiana, and Illinois. Introduction by Wm. T. Utter. Illus. by John Moment. N. Y., The Vanguard Press, Inc., 1952. 192p

JAGENDORF – UPSTATE
Jagendorf, Moritz A. Upstate, downstate. Folk stories of the Middle Atlantic States. Illus. by Howard Simon. N. Y., The Vanguard Press, 1949. 299p

JAMES – MYTHS
James, T. G. H. Myths and legends of ancient Egypt. Illus. by Brian Melling. N. Y., Grosset & Dunlap, 1971. 159p

JENNINGS – BLACK
Jennings, Gary. Black magic, white magic. Illus. by Barbara Begg. N. Y., The Dial Press, 1964. 177p

JEWETT – WHICH
Jewett, Eleanore. Which was witch? Tales of ghosts and magic from Korea. Illus. by Taro Yashima, pseud. N. Y., The Viking Press, 1953. 160p

JOHNSON – HARPER
Johnson, Sally Patrick. The Harper book of princes. Illus. by Janina Domanska. N. Y., Harper & Row, Pub., 1964. 330p

JOHNSON – PRINC.
Johnson, Sally Patrick. The princesses. Illus. by Beni Montresor. N. Y., Harper & Row, 1962. 318p

JOHNSON – WHAT
Johnson, Clifton. What they say in New England, and other American folklore. Illus. by Clifton Johnson. An introduction by Carl Withers. N. Y., Columbia Univ. Press, 1963. 289p

JONES – SCAND.
Jones, Gwyn. Scandinavian legends and folk-tales. Illus. by Joan Kiddell-Monroe. (Oxford myths and legends). London, Oxford Univ. Press, 1956. 222p

JONES – WELSH
Jones, Gwyn. Welsh legends and folk-tales. Illus. by Joan Kiddell-Monroe. London, Oxford Univ. Press, 1955. 230p

JORDAN – BURRO
Jordan, Philip. The burro Benedicto; and other folktales and legends of Mexico. N. Y., Coward-McCann, Inc., 1960. 92p

JUDA – WISE
Juda, L. The wise old man. Turkish tales of Nasreddin Hodja. Edinburgh, Thomas Nelson & Sons, Ltd., 1963. 112p

KAPLAN – SWEDISH
Kaplan, Irma. Swedish fairy tales. Chicago, Follett Pub. Co., c. 1953, 1967. 229p

KAULA – AFRICAN
Kaula, Edna Mason. African village folktales. Illus. by the author. N. Y., World Pub., Co., 1968. 155p

KELSEY – ONCE
Kelsey, Alice Geer. Once the Mullah; Persian folk tales. Illus. by Kurt Werth. N. Y., Longmans, 1954. 137p

KOREL – LISTEN
Korel, Edward. Listen and I'll tell you. Illus. by Quentin Blake. Phil., J. B. Lippincott Co., 1962. 122p

KRUEGER – SERPENT
Krueger, Kermit. The serpent prince. Folk tales from Northeastern Thailand. Illus. by Yoko Mitsumashi. N. Y., World Pub. Co., 1969. 159p

KRYLOV – 15
Krylov, Ivan Andreevich. 15 Fables of Krylov. Trans. by Guy Daniels. Illus. by David Pascal. N. Y., The Macmillan Co., 1965. 39p

LA FONTAINE – FABLES
La Fontaine, Jean de. The fables of La Fontaine. Adapted by Richard Scarry. Garden City, N. Y., Doubleday & Co., Inc., 1963. 60p

LANG – OLIVE
Lang, Andrew. Olive fairy book. Illus. by Anne Vaughan. N. Y., David McKay Co., 1950. 236p

LANG – VIOLET
Lang, Andrew, coll. & ed. Violet fairy book. Illus. by Dorothy Lake Gregory. N. Y., David McKay Co., Inc., 1951, 1963. 233p

LARSON – PALACE
Larson, Jean Russell. Palace in Bagdad. Illus. by Marianne Yamaguchi. N. Y., Chas. Scribner's Sons. 1966. 95p

LAURITZEN – BLOOD
Lauritzen, Jonreed. Blood, banners and wild boars. Tales of early Spain. Illus. by Gil Miret. Boston, Little, Brown & Co., 1967. 151p

LAWSON – STRANGE
Lawson, Marie Abrams. Strange sea stories. Legends, lore, and superstitions of the mysterious waters. N. Y., The Viking Press, 1955. 192p

LEACH – HOW
Leach, Maria. How the people sang the mountains up. How and why stories. Illus. by Glen Rounds. N. Y., The Viking Press, 1967. 159p

LEACH – LUCK
Leach, Maria. The luck book. Illus. by Kurt Werth. Cleveland, The World Pub. Co., 1964. 112p

LEACH – NOODLES
Leach, Maria. Noodles, nitwits, and numskulls. Drawings by Kurt Werth. Cleveland, The World Pub. Co., 1961. 95p

LEACH – RAINBOW
Leach, Maria. The rainbow book of American folk tales and legends. N. Y., The World Pub. Co., 1958. 319p

LEACH – SOUP
Leach, Maria. The soup stone: The magic of familiar things. Illus. by Mamie Harmon. N. Y., Funk & Wagnalls Co., 1954. 160p

LEEKLEY – KING
Leekley, Thomas B. King Herla's quest, and other medieval stories from Walter Map. Illus. by Johannes Troyer. N. Y., The Vanguard Press, 1956. 127p

LEEKLEY – RIDDLE
Leekley, Thomas B. The Riddle of the black knight, and other tales and fables based on the Gesta Romanorum. Illus. by Johannes Troyer. N. Y., The Vanguard Press, 1957. 176p

LEEKLEY – WORLD
Leekley, Thomas B. The world of Manabozho. Tales of the Chippewa Indians. Illus. by Yeffe Kimball. N. Y., The Vanguard Press, Inc., 1965. 128p

LEEUW – INDO.
Leeuw, Adele de. Indonesian legends and folk tales. Illus. by Ronni Solbert. N. Y., Thomas Nelson & Sons, 1961. 160p

LEEUW – LEGENDS
Leeuw, Adele de. Legends and folk tales of Holland. Illus. by Paul Kennedy. N. Y., Thomas Nelson & Sons, 1963. 157p

LEODHAS – BY
Leodhas, Sorche Nic. By loch and by lin; tales from Scottish ballads. Illus. by Vera Bock. N. Y., Holt, Rinehart & Winston, 1969. 130p

LEODHAS – CLAYMORE
Leodhas, Sorche Nic. Claymore and kilt. Tales of Scottish kings and castles. Illus. by Leo and Diane Dillin. N. Y., Holt, Rinehart & Winston, 1967. 157p

LEODHAS – GAELIC
Leodhas, Sorche Nic. Gaelic ghosts. Illus. by Nonny Hogrogian. N. Y., Holt, Rinehart & Winston, 1963. 110p

LEODHAS – GHOSTS
Leodhas, Sorche Nic. Ghosts go haunting. Illus. by Nonny Hogrogian. N. Y., Holt, Rinehart & Winston, 1965. 128p

LEODHAS – HEATHER
Leodhas, Sorche Nic. Heather and broom. Tales of the Scottish Highlands. Illus. by Consuelo Joerns. N. Y., Holt, Rinehart & Winston, 1960. 128p

LEODHAS – SEA
Leodhas, Sorche Nic. Sea-spell and moor-magic. Tales of the Western Isles. Illus. by Vera Bock. N. Y., Holt, Rinehart & Winston, 1968. 207p

LEODHAS – THISTLE
Leodhas, Sorche Nic. Thistle and thyme. Tales and legends from Scotland. Illus. by Evaline Ness. N. Y., Holt, Rinehart & Winston, 1962. 143p

LEODHAS – TWELVE
Leodhas, Sorche Nic. Twelve great black cats; and other eerie Scottish tales. Illus. by Vera Bock. N. Y., E. P. Dutton & Co., Inc., 1971. 175p

LIN – MILKY
Lin, Adet. The milky way, and other Chinese folk tales. Illus. by Enrico Arno. N. Y., Harcourt, Brace & World, Inc., 1961. 92p

LINES – NURSERY
Lines, Kathleen. Nursery stories. Illus. by Harold Imes. N. Y., Franklin Watts, Inc., 1960. 127p

LINES – TALES
Lines, Kathleen. Tales of magic and enchantment. Illus. by Alan Howard. London, Faber & Faber, 1966. 288p

LITTLEDALE – GHOSTS
Littledale, Freya. Ghosts and spirits of many lands. Illus. by Stefan Martin. Garden City, N. Y., Doubleday & Co., Inc., 1970. 167p

LOWE – LITTLE
Lowe, Patricia Tracey. The little horse of seven colors, and other Portuguese folk tales. From translations from the Portuguese by Anne Marie Jauss. N. Y., The World Pub., Co., 1970. 124p

LUM – ITALIAN
Lum, Peter. Italian fairy tales. Illus. by Harry and Ilse Toothill. Chicago, Follett Pub. Co., 1963. 194p

MAAS – MOON
Maas, Selve. The moon painters, and other Estonian folk tales. Illus. by Laszlo Gal. N. Y., The Viking Press, 1971. 143p

McALPINE – JAPAN.
McAlpine, Helen and William. Japanese tales and legends. Illus. by Joan Kiddell-Monroe. (Oxford myths and legends). N. Y., Henry Z. Walck, Inc., 1959. 212p

MacFARLANE – TALES
MacFarlane, Iris. Tales and legends from India. Illus. by Eric Thomas. N. Y., Franklin Watts, Inc., 1965. 136p

McHARGUE – BEASTS
McHargue, Georgess. The beasts of never; a history of natural and unnatural of monsters mythical & magical. Illus. by Frank Bozzo. Indianapolis, Bobbs-Merrill, 1968. 112p

MacMANUS – BOLD
MacManus, Seumas. The bold heroes of Hungry Hill, and other Irish folk tales. Illus. by Jay Chollick. N. Y., Pellegrini and Cudahy, 1951. 207p

MacMANUS – HIBERIAN
MacManus, Seumas. Hiberian Nights. Introduced by Padraic Colum. Illus. by Paul Kennedy. N. Y., Macmillan, 1963. 263p

MacMILLAN – GLOOS.
Macmillan, Cyrus. Glooskap's country, and other Indian tales. Illus. by John A. Hall. N. Y., Oxford Univ. Press, 1956. 273p

McNEILL – DOUBLE
McNeill, James. The double knights. More tales from round the world. Illus. by Theo Dimson. N. Y., Henry Z. Walck, Inc., 1964. 128p

McNEILL – SUNKEN
McNeill, James. The sunken city, and other tales from round the world. Illus. by Theo Dimson. N. Y., Henry Z. Walck, Inc., 1959. 160p

MAHER – BLIND
Maher, Ramona. The blind boy and the loon; and other Eskimo myths. Illus. N. Y., The John Day Co., 1969. 158p

MANNING – BEASTS
Manning-Sanders, Ruth. A book of magical beasts. Illus. by Raymond Briggs. N. Y., Thomas Nelson, Inc., 1970. 244p

MANNING – DAMIAN
Manning-Sanders, Ruth. Damian and the dragon. Modern Greek folk-tales. N. Y., Roy Publishers, Inc., 1965. 190p

MANNING – DEVILS
Manning-Sanders, Ruth. A book of devils and demons. Illus. by Robin Jacques. N. Y., E. P. Dutton & Co., Inc., 1970. 124p

MANNING – DRAGONS
Manning-Sanders, Ruth. A book of dragons. Illus. by Robin Jacques. N. Y., E. P. Dutton & Co., Inc., 1964, 1965. 128p

MANNING – DWARFS
Manning-Sanders, Ruth. A book of dwarfs. Illus. by Robin Jacques. N. Y., E. P. Dutton & Co. Inc., 1963. 128p

MANNING – ENGLISH
Manning-Sanders, Ruth. Stories from the English and Scottish ballads. Illus. by Trevor Ridley. N. Y., E. P. Dutton & Co., Inc., 1968. 148p

MANNING – GHOSTS
Manning-Sanders, Ruth. A book of ghosts and goblins. Illus. by Robin Jacques. N. Y., E. P. Dutton & Co., Inc., 1968. 127p

MANNING – GIANNI
Manning-Sanders, Ruth. Gianni and the ogre. Illus. by William Stobbs. N. Y., E. P. Dutton & Co., Inc., c. 1970, 1971. 192p

MANNING – GIANTS
Manning-Sanders, Ruth. A book of giants. Illus. by Robin Jacques. London, Methuen & Co., Ltd., c. 1962, 1963. 125p

MANNING – GLASS
Manning-Sanders, Ruth. The glass man and the golden bird. Hungarian folk and fairy tales. Illus. by Victor G. Ambrus. N. Y., Roy Publishers, Inc., 1968. 194p

MANNING – JONNIKIN
Manning-Sanders, Ruth. Jonnikin and the flying basket; French folk and fairy tales. Illus. by Victor G. Ambrus. N. Y., E. P. Dutton & Co., Inc., 1969. 152p

MANNING – MERMAIDS
Manning-Sanders, Ruth. A book of mermaids. Illus. by Robin Jacques. N. Y., E. P. Dutton & Co., Inc., 1968. 128p

MANNING – PETER
   Manning-Sanders, Ruth. Peter and the Pishkies. Cornish folk and fairy tales. Illus. by Raymond Briggs. N. Y., Roy Publishers, Inc., 1958. 215p

MANNING – PRINCES
   Manning-Sanders, Ruth. A book of princes and princesses. Illus. by Robin Jacques. N. Y., E. P. Dutton & Co., Inc., c. 1969, 1970. 127p

MANNING – RED
   Manning-Sanders, Ruth. The red king and the witch. Gypsy folk and fairy tales. Illus. by Victor G. Ambrus. N. Y., Roy Publishers, Inc., 1964. 175p

MANNING – WITCHES
   Manning-Sanders, Ruth. A book of witches. Illus. by Robin Jacques. N. Y., E. P. Dutton & Co., Inc., c. 1965, 1966. 126p

MANNING WIZARDS
   Manning-Sanders, Ruth. A book of wizards. Illus. by Robin Jacques. N. Y., E. P. Dutton & Co., Inc., c. 1966, 1967. 126p

MAR – CHINESE
   Mar, S. Y. Lu. Chinese tales of folklore. Illus. by Howard Simon. N. Y., Criterion Books, 1964. 160p

MARGOLIS – IDY
   Margolis, Ellen. Idy, the fox chasing cow, and other stories. Illus. by Kurt Werth. Cleveland, Ohio, World Pub. Co., 1962. 64p

MARKS – SPANISH
   Marks, John. Spanish fairy tales. Illus. by Roberta Moynihan. N. Y., Alfred A. Knopf, 1958. 181p

MARMUR – JAPAN.
   Marmur, Mildred, trans. Japanese fairy tales. Illus. by Benvenuti. N. Y., Golden Press, 1960. 66p

MARRIOTT – AMER.
   Marriott, Alice and Carol K. Rachlin. American Indian mythology. N. Y., Thomas Y. Crowell, Co., 1968. 211p

MARTIN – COYOTE
   Martin, Fran. Nine tales of coyote. Illus. by Dorothy McEntee. N. Y., Harper & Bros., 1950. 60p

MARTIN – NINE
   Martin, Fran. Nine tales of raven. Pictures by Dorothy McEntee. N. Y., Harper & Bros., 1951. 60p

MASEY – STORIES
   Masey, Mary Lou. Stories of the steppes. Kazakh folktales. Illus. by Helen Basilevsky. N. Y., David McKay Co., Inc., 1968. 142p

MATSON – LONGHOUSE
   Matson, Emerson N. Longhouse Legends. Illus. by Lorence Bjorklund. Camden, N. J., Thomas Nelson & Sons, 1968. 128p

MAYNE – GIANTS
   Mayne, William. William Mayne's book of giants. Illus. by Raymond Briggs. N. Y., E. P. Dutton Co., Inc., 1969. 215p

MAYNE – HEROES
Mayne, William. William Mayne's book of heroes. Stories and poems. Illus. by Krystyna Turska. N. Y., E. P. Dutton & Co., Inc., 1967. 230p

MEHDEVI – BUNGLING
Mehdevi, Alexander. Bungling Pedro and other Majorcan tales. Illus. by Isabel Bodor. N. Y., Alfred A. Knopf, 1970. 119p

MEHDEVI – PERSIAN
Mehdevi, Anne Sinclair. Persian folk and fairy tales. Illus. by Paul E. Kennedy. N. Y., Alfred A. Knopf, 1965. 117p

MELZACK – DAY
Melzack, Ronald. The day Tuk became a hunter, and other Eskimo stories. Illus. by Ronald Melzack. N. Y., Dodd, Mead & Co., 1968. 92p

MICHAEL – PORTUGUESE
Michael, Maurice and Pamela. Portuguese fairy tales. Illus. by Harry and Ilse Toothill. Chicago, Follett Pub. Co., 1965. 185p

MILLER – MY BOOK. see MY BOOK HOUSE

MINCIELI – OLD
Mincieli, Rose Laura. Old Neopolitan fairy tales. Selected and retold from Il Pentamerone. Illus. by Beni Montresor. N. Y., Alfred A. Knopf, 1963. 123p

MINCIELI – TALES
Mincieli, Rose Laura. Tales, merry and wise. Illus. by Kurt Werth. N. Y., Holt, Rinehart & Winston, 1958. 128p

MONTGOMERIE – 25
Montgomerie, Norah. Twenty-five fables. N. Y., Abelard-Schuman, 1961. 60p

MONTROSE – WINTER
Montrose, Anne. The winter flower and other fairy tales. Illus. by Mircea Vasiliu. N. Y., The Viking Press, 1964. 143p

MOONEY. see SCHEER – CHEROKEE

MORAY – FAIR
Moray, Ann. A fair stream of silver. Love stories from Celtic lore. N. Y., William Morrow & Co., 1965. 207p

MORRIS – UPSTAIRS
Morris, James. The upstairs donkey, and other stolen stories. Illus. by Pauline Baynes. N. Y., Pantheon Books, 1961. 127p

MOZLEY – ARABY
Mozley, Charles. The first book of tales of ancient Araby. N. Y., Franklin Watts, Inc., 1960. 66p

MOZLEY – EGYPT
Mozley, Charles. The first book of tales of ancient Egypt. N. Y., Franklin Watts, Inc., 1960. 69p

MULLER – SWISS
Muller-Guggenbuhl, Fritz. Swiss-alpine folk-tales. Trans. by Katherine Potts. Illus. by Joan Kiddell-Monroe. London, Oxford Univ. Press, 1958. 225p

MY BOOK HOUSE
My Book House. Miller, Olive Beaupre, ed. Through fairy halls of My Book House. Lake Bluff, Ill., The Book House for Children, Pub., c. 1920, 1965. v. 1-12

NAHMAD – PEASANT
Nahmad, H. M. The peasant and the donkey. Tales of the Near and Middle East. Illus. by William Papas. N. Y., Henry Z. Walck, 1968. 159p

NAHMAD – PORTION
Nahmad, H, M., trans. A portion in paradise, and other Jewish folktales. N. Y., W. W. Norton & Co., Inc., 1970. 170p

NIC LEOHDAS see LEODHAS

NORLEDGE – ABORIGINAL
Norledge, Mildred. Aboriginal legends from eastern Australia. The Richmond-Mary River region. Illus. by Denis Burton. Sydney, A. H. & A. W. Reed, 1968. 62p

NYBLOM – WITCH
Nyblom, Helena. The witch of the woods. Fairy tales from Sweden. Illus. by Nils Christian Hald. Trans. by Holger Lundbergh, N. Y., Alfred A. Knopf, 1968. 211p

NYE – MARCH
Nye, Robert. March has horse's ears and other stories. Illus. by Dorothy Maas. N. Y., Hill and Wang, 1966. 88p

O'FAOLAIN – IRISH
O'Faolain, Eileen. Irish sagas and folk-tales. Illus. by Joan Kiddell-Monroe. (Oxford myths and legends). N. Y., Henry Z. Walck, Inc., 1954. 245p

OMAN – ESKIMO
Oman, Lela. Eskimo legends. Nome, Alaska, Nome Publishing Co., 1956. 66p. pap.

O'SULLIVAN – FOLK
O'Sullivan, Sean. Folktales of Ireland. Chicago, The Univ. of Chicago Press, 1966. 321p

PALMER – DRAGONS
Palmer, Robin. Dragons, unicorns and other magical beasts. Illus. by Don Bolognese. N. Y., Henry Z. Walck, Inc., 1966. 95p

PALMER – FAIRY
Palmer, Robin and Pelagie Doane. Fairy elves. A dictionary of the Little People with some old tales and verses about them. Illus. by Pelagie Doane. N. Y., Henry Z. Walck, Inc., 1964. 92p

PALMER – JOURNEY
Palmer, Geoffrey and Noel Lloyd. Journey by broomstick. Illus. by Rowel Friers. N. Y., Roy Publishers, Inc., 1966. 160p

PARKER – AUSTRALIAN
Parker, K. Langloh. Australian legendary tales. Selected and edited by H. Drake-Brockman. Illus. by Elizabeth Durack, N. Y., The Viking Press, 1966. 255p

PERRAULT – CLASSIC
Perrault's classic French fairy tales. Illus. by Janusz Grabianski. N. Y., Meredith Press, 1967. 224p

PERRAULT – COMPLETE
Perrault, Charles. Perrault's complete fairy tales; trans. from the French by A. E. Johnson and others. Illus. by W. Heath Robinson. N. Y., Dodd, 1961. 183p

PERRAULT – FAMOUS
Perrault, Charles. Famous fairy tales; pictures by Charles Mozley; trans. by Sarah Chokla Gross. N. Y., Franklin Watts, 1959. 192p

PICARD – CELTIC
Picard, Barbara Leonie. Celtic tales; legends of tall warriors of old enchantments. Illus. by John G. Galsworthy. N. Y., Criterion Books, c. 1964, 1965. 159p

PICARD – FAUN
Picard, Barbara Leonie. The faun and the woodcutter's daughter. Illus. by Charles Stewart. N. Y., Criterion Books, 1964. 255p

PICARD – GERMAN
Picard, Barbara Leonie. German hero-sagas and folk-tales. Illus. by Joan Kiddell-Monroe. (Oxford myths and legends). N. Y., Henry Z. Walck, Inc., 1958. 196p

PICARD – HERO
Picard, Barbara Leonie. Hero-tales from the British Isles. Illus. by John G. Galsworthy. N. Y., Criterion Books, 1963. 159p

PICARD – LADY
Picard, Barbara Leonie. The lady of the linden tree. Illus. by Charles Stewart. N. Y., Criterion Books, 1962. 214p

PICARD – MERMAID
Picard, Barbara Leonie. The mermaid and the simpleton. Illus. by Philip Gough. N. Y., Criterion Books, 1970. 254p

PICARD – STORIES
Picard, Barbara Leonie. Stories of King Arthur and his knights, with wood engravings by Roy Morgan. London, Oxford Univ. Press, 1955. 292p

PICARD
Picard, Barbara Leonie. Tales of the British people. Illus. by Eric Fraser. N. Y., Criterion Books, Inc., 1961. 159p

PILKINGTON – SHAM.
Pilkington, F. M. Shamrock and spear. Tales and legends from Ireland. Illus. by Leo and Diane Dillon. N. Y., Holt, Rinehart & Winston, 1966. 178p

PILKINGTON – THREE
Pilkington, F. M. The three sorrowful tales of Erin. Illus. by Victor Ambrus. N. Y., Henry Z. Walck, 1966. 232p

PONSOT – RUSSIAN
Ponsot, Marie, trans. Russian fairy tales. Illus. by Benvenuti. N. Y., Golden Press, 1960. 64p

PRATT – MAGIC
Pratt, Davis & Elsa Kula. Magic animals of Japan. Berkeley, Calif., Parnassus Press, 1967. unp.

PRIDHAM – GIFT
Pridham, Radost. A gift from the heart. Folk tales from Bulgaria. Cleveland, Ohio, The World Publishing Co., c. 1966, 1967. 156p

PROTTER – CHILD.
Protter, Eric. Children's treasury of folk and fairy tales. Great Neck, N. Y., Channel Press, Inc., 1961. 211p

PUGH – TALES
Pugh, Ellen. Tales from the Welsh hills. Illus. by Joan Sandin. N. Y., Dodd, Mead & Co., 1968. 143p

RANKE – GERMANY
Ranke, Kurt, ed. Folktales of Germany. Trans. by Lotte Ranke. Chicago, The Univ. Of Chicago Press, 1966. 257p

RASKIN – TALES
Raskin, Joseph and Edith. Tales our settlers told. Illus. by William Sauts Bock. N. Y., Lothrop, Lee and Shepard, 1971. 96p

REED – TALK
Reed, Gwendolyn. The talkative beasts. Myths, fables, and poems of India. Photographs by Stella Snead. N. Y., Lothrop, Lee and Shepard Co., 1969. 94p

REEVES – ENGLISH
Reeves, James. English fables and fairy stories. Illus. by Joan Kiddell-Monroe. London, Oxford Univ. Press, 1954. 234p

REEVES – THREE
Reeves, James. Three tall tales. Illus. by Edward Ardizzone. N. Y., Abelard-Schuman. 1964. n.p.

REGNIERS. *see* DE REGNIERS

ROBERTSON – FAIRY
Robertson, Dorothy Lewis. Fairy tales from Viet Nam. Illus. by W. T. Mars. N. Y., Dodd, Mead & Co., 1968. 95p

ROBERTSON – PHILIP.
Robertson, Dorothy Lewis. Fairy Tales from the Philippines. Illus. by Howard M. Burns. N. Y., Dodd, Mead & Co., 1971. 129p

ROSS – BLUE
Ross, Eulalie Steinmetz. The blue rose. A collection of stories for girls. N. Y., Harcourt, Brace & World, Inc., 1966. 185p

ROSS – BURIED
Ross, Eulalie Steinmetz. The buried treasure and other picture tales. Illus. by Josef Cellini. Phil., J. P. Lippincott Co., 1958. 187p

ROSS – MEXICO
Ross, Patricia Fent. In Mexico they say. Illus. by Henry C. Pitz. N. Y., Alfred A. Knopf, 1942. 211p

RUDOLPH – MAGIC
Rudolph, Marguerita. The magic egg, and other folk stories of Rumania. Illus. by Wallace Tripp. Boston, Little, Brown & Co., 1971. 71p

RUSHMORE – DANCING
Rushmore, Helen and Wolf Robe Hunt. The dancing horses of Acoma, and other Acoma Indian stories. Illus. by Wolf Robe Hunt. Cleveland, Ohio, The World Pub. Co., 1963. 164p

SAKADE – JAPAN.
Sakade, Florence, ed. Japanese children's favorite stories. Illus. by Yoshisuke Kurosaki. Rutland, Vt., Chas. E. Tuttle Co., 1958. 120p

SAVORY – ZULU
Savory, Phyllis. Zulu fireside tales. N. Y., Hastings House, 1961. 64p

SAWYER – DIETRICH
Sawyer, Ruth & Emmy Molles. Dietrich of Berne and the dwarf King Laurin. Hero tales of the Austrian Tyrol. Illus. by Frederick T. Chapman. N. Y., The Viking Press, 1963. 190p

SCHEER – CHEROKEE
Scheer, George F. ed. Cherokee animal tales. Illus. by Robert Frankenberg. N. Y., Holiday House, Inc., 1968. 80p

SCHOOLCRAFT – FIRE
Schoolcraft, Henry Rowe. The fire plume. Legends of the American Indians. Ed. by John Bierhorst. Pictures by Alan E. Cober. N. Y., The Dial Press, Inc., 1969. 90p

SECHRIST – ONCE
Sechrist, Elizabeth Hough. Once in the first times; folk tales from the Philippines. Illus. by John Sheppard. Phil., Macrae Smith Co., c. 1949, 1969. 213p

SEKI – FOLKTALES
Seki, Keigo. Folktales of Japan. Trans. by Robert J. Adams. Chicago, The Univ. of Chicago Press, 1963. 221p

SERWER – LET'S
Serwer, Blanche Luria. Let's steal the moon. Jewish tales, ancient and recent. Illus. by Trina Schart Hyman. Boston, Little, Brown & Co., 1970. 88p

SHAPIRO – HEROES
Shapiro, Irwin. Heroes in American folklore. Illus. by James Daugherty and Donald McKay. N. Y., J. Messner, 1962. 256p

SHAPIRO – TALL
Shapiro, Irwin. Tall tales of America. Illus. by Al Schmidt. Poughkeepsie, N. Y., Guild Press, Inc., 1958. 124p

SHEAHAN – HENRY
Sheahan, Henry Beston. Henry Beston's fairy tales. N. Y., Aladdin Books, 1952. 352p

SHEPPARD – SCOT.
Sheppard-Jones, Elisabeth. Scottish legendary tales. Illus. by Paul Hogarth. Edinburgh, Thomas Nelson & Sons, Ltd., 1962. 180p

SHEPPARD – WELSH
Sheppard-Jones, Elisabeth. Welsh legendary tales. Illus. by Paul Hogarth. Edinburgh, Thomas Nelson & Sons, Lts., 1959. 182p

SHERLOCK – ANANSI
Sherlock, Philip M. Anansi, the spider man; Jamaican folk tales. Illus. by Marcia Brown. N. Y., Thomas Y. Crowell Co., 1954. 112p

SHERLOCK – IGUANA'S
Sherlock, Philip. The iguana's tail. Crick crack stories from the Caribbean. Illus. by Gioia Fiammenghi. N. Y., Thomas Y. Crowell, 1969. 98p

SHERLOCK – WEST
Sherlock, Philip. West Indian folk-tales. Illus. by Joan Kiddell-Monroe. N. Y., Henry Z. Walck, Inc., 1966. 151p

SIDDIQUI – TOON.
Siddiqui, Ashraf and Marilyn Lerch. Toontoony pie, and other tales from Pakistan. Illus. by Jan Fairservis. Cleveland, Ohio, The World Pub. Co., 1961. 158p

SIDEMAN – WORLD'S
  Sideman, Belle Becker, ed; The world's best fairy tales. A Reader's Digest anthology.
  Illus. by Fritz Kredel. Pleasantville, N. Y., The Reader's Digest Assoc., 1967. 832p

SINGER – WHEN
  Singer, Isaac Bashevis. When Shlemiel went to Warsaw and other stories. Trans. by
  the author and Elizabeth Shub. Illus. by Margot Zemach. N. Y., Farrar, Straus &
  Giroux, 1968. 116p

SINGER – ZLATEH
  Singer, Isaac Bashevis. Zlateh the goat, and other stories; pictures by Maurice
  Sendak. N. Y., Harper & Row, 1966. 90p

SLOANE – FOLK.
  Sloane, Eric. Folklore of American weather. N. Y., Duel, Sloan & Pearce, 1963. 63p

SPELLMAN – BEAUT.
  Spellman, John W., ed. The beautiful blue jay and other tales of India. Illus. by
  Jerry Pinckney. Boston, Little, Brown & Co., 1967. 101p

SPICER – DEVILS
  Spicer, Dorothy Gladys. 13 devils. Illus. by Sofia. N. Y., Coward-McCann, Inc.,
  1967. 127p

SPICER – GHOSTS
  Spicer, Dorothy Gladys. 13 ghosts. Illus. by Sofia. N. Y., Coward-McCann, Inc.,
  1965. 128p

SPICER – GIANTS
  Spicer, Dorothy Gladys. 13 giants. Illus. by Sofia. N. Y., Coward-McCann, Inc.,
  1966. 127p

SPICER – GOBLINS
  Spicer, Dorothy Gladys. 13 goblins. Illus. by Sofia. N. Y., Coward-McCann, Inc.,
  1969. 128p

SPICER – KNEELING
  Spicer, Dorothy Gladys. The kneeling tree; and other folktales from the Middle
  East. N. Y., Coward-McCann, Inc., 1971. 127p

SPICER – LONG
  Spicer, Dorothy Gladys. Long ago in Serbia. Illus. by Linda Ominsky. Phil., The
  Westminster Press, 1968. 159p

SPICER – OWL'S
  Spicer, Dorothy Gladys. The owl's nest. Folktales from Friesland. Illus. by Alice
  Wadowski-Bak. N. Y., Coward-McCann, Inc., 1968. 125p

SPICER – 13. see SPICER – GIANTS

SPICER – WITCHES
  Spicer, Dorothy Gladys. 13 witches, 2 wizards, the devil and a pack of goblins. Illus.
  by Sofia. N. Y., Coward-McCann, Inc., 1963. 95p

STOCKTON – TING
  Stockton, Frank R. Ting-a-ling tales. Illus. by Richard Floethe. N. Y., Charles
  Scribner's Sons, 1955. 161p

STOUTENBURG – AMER.
  Stoutenburg, Adrien. American tall tales. Illus. by Richard M. Powers. N. Y., The
  Viking Press, 1966. 112p

STOUTENBURG – CROC.
Stoutenburg, Adrien. The crocodile's mouth; folk-song stories. N. Y., The Viking Press, 1966. 64p

STOUTENBURG – FEE
Stoutenburg, Adrien. Fee, Fi, Fo, Fum. Friendly and funny giants. Illus. by Rocco Negri. N. Y., The Viking Press, 1969. 127p

STRONG – FAVORITE
Strong, Joanna. Favorite folktales and fables. Illus. by Hubert Whatley. N. Y., Hart Pub. Co., 1950. 96p

SUN –LAND
Sun, Ruth Q. Land of seagull and fox. Illus. by Ho Thanh Duc. Rutland, Vt., Charles E. Tuttle Co., 1967. 135p

SUTCLIFF – HIGH
Sutcliff, Rosemary. The high deeds of Finn MacCool. Illus. by Michael Charlton. N. Y., E. P. Dutton & Co., Inc., 1967. 189p

TAFT – PROFILE
Taft, Lewis A. Profile of old New England. Yankee legends, tales and folk-lore. Illus. (photographs). N. Y., Dodd, Mead & Co., 1965. 271p

TASHJIAN – ONCE
Tashjian, Virginia A. Once there was and was not. Armenian tales retold. Based on stories by H. Toumanian. Illus. by Nonny Hogrogian. Boston, Little, Brown & Co., 1966. 85p

TASHJIAN – THREE
Tashjian, Virginia A. Three apples from heaven; Armenian tales retold. Illus. by Nonny Hogrogian. Boston, Little, Brown & Co., 1971. 76p

THOMPSON – HAWAII.
Thompson, Vivian L. Hawaiian myths of earth, sea, and sky. Illus. by Leonard Weisgard. N. Y., Holiday House, 1966. 84p

THOMPSON – LEGENDS
Thompson, Vivian L. Hawaiian legends of tricksters and riddlers. Illus. by Sylvie Selig. N. Y., Holiday House, Inc., 1969. 103p

THOMPSON – ONE
Thompson, Stith. One hundred favorite folktales. Drawings by Franz Altschuler. Bloomington, Ind., Indiana University Press, 1968. 439p

TOLKIEN – READER
Tolkien, J. R. R. The Tolkien reader. N. Y., Ballantine Books, 1966. In 4 parts: 24p, 122p, 79p, 64p, pap.

TOOR – GOLDEN
Toor, Frances. The golden carnation, and other stories told in Italy. Illus. by Anne Marie Jauss. N. Y., Lothrop, Lee & Shepard Co., 1960. 190p

TOOZE – MONKEY
Tooze, Ruth. Three tales of monkey. Ancient folk tales from the Far East. Illus. by Rosalie Petrash. N. Y., The John Day Co., 1967. 72p

TOOZE – THREE
Tooze, Ruth. Three tales of turtle. Ancient folk tales from the Far East. Illus. by Rosalie Petrash Schmidt. N. Y., The John Day Co., 1968. 64p

TOOZE – WONDER.
Tooze, Ruth. The wonderful wooden peacock flying machine; and other tales of
Ceylon. Illus. by Rosalie Petrash Schmidt. N. Y., The John Day Co., 1969. 126p

TRACEY – LION
Tracey, Hugh. The lion on the path, and other African stories. Illus. by Eric Byrd.
Music transcribed by Andrew Tracey. N. Y., Frederick A. Praeger, 1968. 127p

TUDOR – TASHA
Tudor, Tasha. The Tasha Tudor book of fairy tales. Illus. by Tasha Tudor. N. Y.,
Platt & Munk, Pub., 1961. 92p

TURNBULL – FAIRY
Turnbull, Lucia. Fairy tales of India. Illus. by Hazel Cook. N. Y., Criterion Books,
Inc., 1959. 170p

UCHIDA – DANCING
Uchida, Yoshiko. The dancing kettle, and other Japanese folk tales. Illus. by Richard
C. Jones. N. Y., Harcourt, Brace & Co., 1949. 174p

UCHIDA – MAGIC
Uchida, Yoshiko. The magic listening cap; more folk tales from Japan. Illus. by
Yoshiko Uchida. N. Y., Harcourt, Brace & Co., 1955. 146p

UCHIDA – SEA
Uchida, Yoshiko. The sea of gold, and other tales from Japan. Illus. by Marianne
Yamaguchi. N. Y., Charles Scribner's Sons, 1965. 136p

U. N. – RIDE
The United Nations Women's guild. Ride with the sun. An anthology of folk tales
and stories from the United Nations. Ed. by Harold Courlander. Illus. by Roger
Duvoisin. N. Y., Whittlesey House, 1955. 296p

UNTERMEYER – FIRE
Untermeyer, Louis. The firebringer and other great stories. Fifty-five legends that
live forever. Illus. by Mae Gerhard. N. Y., M. Evans & Co., Inc., 1968. 255p

URE – RUMANIAN
Ure, Jean. Rumanian folk tales. Illus. by Charles Mozley. N. Y., Franklin Watts,
Inc., 1960. 194p

VANSITTART – DARK
Vansittart, Peter. The dark tower. Tales from the past. Illus. by Margery Gill. N. Y.,
Thomas Y. Crowell Co., 1965. 135p

VITTORINI – OLD
Vittorini, Domenico. Old Italian tales. Illus. by Katheryn L. Fligg. N. Y., David
McKay Co., Inc., 1958. 110p

VO-DINH – TOAD
Vo-Dinh. The toad is the emperor's uncle. Animal folk-tales from Vietnam. Illus.
by Vo-Dinh. N. Y., Doubleday & Co., 1970. 143p

WALKER – DANCING
Walker, Barbara K. The dancing palm tree and other Nigerian folktales. Woodcuts by
Helen Siegl. N. Y., Parents' Magazine Press, 1968. 112p

WALKER – ONCE
Walker, Barbara K. Once there was and twice there wasn't. Illus. by Gordon Kibbee.
N. Y., Follett Pub. Co., 1968. 128p

WALKER – WATER.
Walker, Barbara K. Watermelons, walnuts and the wisdom of Allah, and other tales of the Hoca. Illus. by Harold Berson. N. Y., Parents' Magazine Press, 1967. 71p

WESTWOOD – MEDIEVAL
Westwood, Jennifer. Medieval tales. N. Y., Coward-McCann, Inc., 1968. 147p

WHEELER – HAWAII.
Wheeler, Post. Hawaiian wonder tales. Illus. by Jack Matthew. N. Y., The Beechhurst Press, 1953. 232p

WILLIAMS – FAIRY
Williams-Ellis, Amabel. Fairy tales from the British Isles. Illus. by Pauline Diana Baynes. N. Y., Frederick Warne & Co., 1960. 344p

WILLIAMS – LOST
Williams, Brad and Choral Pepper. Lost legends of the West. N. Y., Holt, Rinehart & Winston, 1970. 192p

WILLIAMS – OLD
Williams-Ellis, Amabel. Old world and new world fairy tales. Illus. by William Stobbs. N. Y., Frederick Warne & Co., Inc., 1966. 357p

WILLIAMS – ROUND
William-Ellis, Amabel. Round the world fairy tales. Illus. by William Stobbs. N. Y., Frederick Warne & Co., Inc., c. 1963, 1966. 302p

WILLIAMS-ELLIS. see WILLIAMS

WILSON – GREEK
Wilson, Barbara Ker. Greek fairy tales. Illus. by Harry Toothill. Chicago, Follett Pub. Co., 1966. 229p

WILSON – IRELAND
Wilson, Barbara Ker. Fairy tales of Ireland. Illus. by G. W. Miller. N. Y., Dutton, 1959. n. p.

WILSON – SCOTTISH
Wilson, Barbara Ker. Scottish folk-tales and legends. Illus. by Joan Kiddell-Monroe. (Oxford myths and legends). N. Y., Henry Z. Walck, Inc., 1954. 207p

WITHERS – I SAW
Withers, Carl. I saw a rocket walk a mile. Nonsense tales, chants, and songs from many lands. Illus. by John E. Johnson. N. Y., Holt, Rinehart & Winston, 1965. 160p

WITHERS – WORLD
Withers, Carl. A world of nonsense; Strange and humorous tales from many lands. Illus. by John E. Johnson. N. Y., Holt, Rinehart & Winston, 1968. 118p

WYATT – GOLDEN
Wyatt, Isabel. The golden stag and other folk tales from India. Illus. by Anne Marie Jauss. N. Y., David McKay Co., 1962. 117p

WYNDHAM – CHINA
Wyndham, Robert. Tales the people tell in China. Illus. by Jay Yang. N. Y., Julian Messner, 1971. 92p

WYNDHAM – RUSS.
Wyndham, Lee. Russian tales of fabulous beasts and marvels. Illus. by Charles Mikolaycak. N. Y., Parents Education Press, 1969. 96p

WYNDHAM – TALES
    Wyndham, Lee. Tales the people tell in Russia. Illus. by Andrew Antal. N. Y., Julian Messner, 1970. 95p

YOUNG – HOW
    Young, Blanche Cowley, comp. How the Manx cat lost its tail, and other Manx folk stories. Illus. by Nora S. Unwin. N. Y., David McKay Co., Inc., 1959. 114p

ZAGLOUL – BLACK
    Zagloul, Ahmed and Zane Zagloul. The black prince, and other Egyptian folk tales. Illus. by Beverly Armstrong. Garden City, N. Y., Doubleday & Co., 1971. 161p

INDEX TO FAIRY TALES

A

A, B, C, kitty's in the snow I see!
MY BOOK HOUSE v. 1 p120.

Abbots and abbeys
The affable lion
The carefree monastery
Collen
The courage of Mairi
The drowned bells of the abbey
The emperor's questions
The gardener, the abbot and the king
The Inchcape rock
King John and the abbot
King John and the Abbot of
Canterbury
The little book
Old Nick's bridge
Ramiro II, the monk
The singing bell
Sir Richard at the lee and the abbot
The spirit's drum
The thoughtless abbot

Abdune and the friendly snake
ZAGLOUL — BLACK p97-102

Abe Lincoln in Indiana
JAGENDORF — SAND p75-79

The abominable snowman
JACOBSON — FIRST p61-62

"Abominable snowmen"
The hairy man from the forest
A San and the Wang Liang
A trio of lost monsters

Aborigines
The crane who taught the birds to
dance and make corroboree
The eel, the man, and the cave
The head-hunters
How people got fire
How the black snake got its fangs
The kaola bear and the tribal laws
The man who could see everything
The origin of the platypus
The possums, the man, and the tree
The two dogs—Burrajahnee and
Inneroogun
—Tribes—Dyraaba
Dhungura-ngarian: where the
pelican danced
The drifting canoe

The old women who were turned
into birds
The people who lived near a
mountain
The place of the death adders
The satin bird
The three brothers
The ti-trees
The two boys and the sacred
carpet snake
The witch who lived in a cave
The young man and the giant
The young man and the kangaroo

—Tribes—Githerbal
The bean trees that are sacred to
the witches
The haunted lagoon
He who lives in a mountain
How the little black wren got its
red feathers
Nooloigah and the fire
Nooloigah who caused his brother
to die
The spirit of the water hole
The woman and the sacred Bora
ring

About devils
SPICER — DEVILS p6.

About Elizabeth Eliza's piano
ARBUTHNOT — TIME p360.

About Eskimo stories
MELZACK — DAY p9-10

About ghosts
SPICER — GHOSTS p6.

About goblins
SPICER — GOBLINS p7-8

About Jan the Prince, Princess Wonderface and the flamebird
HAVILAND — POLAND

About Majorcan tales
MEHDEVI — BUNGLING p3-5

About Sinbad's other wonderful journeys
MOZLEY — ARABY p55.

About the Cherokee
SCHEER — CHEROKEE p9-21

1

About the good American witch
    HOKE — WITCHES p101-111

About the gypsies
    JAGENDORF — GYPSIES p9-14

About the hedgehog who became prince
    HAVILAND — POLAND p3-12

About the legendary beings
    JACOBSON — LEGEND p1-3

About the magic animals
    PRATT — MAGIC unp.

About the mythical beasts
    JACOBSEN — FIRST p9-35

About this book
    PERRAULT — FAMOUS (preface)

About witches, enchantments, and spells
    SPICER — WITCHES p9.

Above the wind, with the wind, or below
    the wind?
    NYE — MARCH p84-88

Abraham Lincoln, 1809-1865
    MY BOOK HOUSE v. 5 p128.

Absalom (Biblical)
    Solomon and the four winds

The absent-minded king
    ROBERTSON — PHILIP. p91-95

The absent-minded tailor
    CATHON — PERHAPS p36-41

Absent-mindedness
    Air castles
    Doll's daydream
    The happy milkmaid
    The hunter of Perak
    The scholar of Kosei

Abu-Zahra, Nadia
    The clever bride of Tunisia

Abu-Zahra, Nadia
    The tale of a proverb

Abu Zaid seeks a horse and finds a wife
    DAVIS — TEN p114-127

Abu Zaid the Hilali
    DAVIS — TEN p37-47

Abunuwas the trickster
    COURLANDER — TIGER'S p90-99

Abunuwas, the wit
    U.N. — RIDE p85-91

Abuse. See Cruelty

Abyssinia. See Africa—Ethiopia

Acacia trees
    The tale of the two brothers

Accidents
    "Measure twice, cut once"

The accomplished and strange teakettle
    BUCK — FAIRY P89-91

According to tradition
    GRAY — MAINLY p91-108

Account rendered
    JUDA — WISE p34-42

Accumulative stories. See Repetitive
    rhymes and stories

Achilles
    The anger of Achilles
    The boy Achilles
    The slaying of Hector
    The unhappy island

Achiles and Polyxena
    GREEN — GREEKS p32-33

The acorn and the pumpkin
    MY BOOK HOUSE v. 7 p132-133

The acorn maidens
    LEACH — RAINBOW p281

Acorns
    Carry an acorn
    The frog with the golden key
    The giant who took a long time to
    grow
    Longshanks, girth, and keen
    The magic acorn
    A message in a bottle
    The son of strength

    , Golden
    Dummling

Acrobats
Hwan and Dang

Action
BATCHELOR – SUPER. p84-95

Actors and actresses
The brave actor
The story of Nosschoy Datta of Ujjain
Tale of the good, gay lady

Adam and Eve (Biblical)
Atam and Im
It's all the fault of Adam
A son of Adam
The tree from Adam's grave
Why donkeys have long ears
Why God made the dog

Adam Bell, Clym of the Clough, and
William of Cloudesley
MANNING – ENGLISH p30-43
MAYNE – HEROES p45-59

Adares, King of Arabia
NAHMAD – PORTION p78-80

Adcock, Fleur
A game

The adder and the fox
GAER – FABLES p30-33

Addison, Joseph
Providence

Addison, Joseph
In the days of Queen Anne

The aderna bird
SECHRIST – ONCE p131-135

Adirondack skeeters
JAGENDORF – UPSTATE p37-39

The adjutant-bird
WILLIAMS – ROUND p274-278

Admirals
Young midshipman David Farragut

Adrian and Bardus
GREEN – BIG p201-205

The advantages of learning
MORRIS – UPSTAIRS p99-104

Adventure
Four brothers who were both wise
and foolish
The giant who loved adventure
The girl with the rose-red slippers
The peasant and the workman
The story of the Greek princess
The story of the shipwrecked sailor
The strange adventure of Baron
Münchausen
Surprising adventures of Don Quixote
of La Mancha
The taking of Joppa
The treasure thief
The voyage of Maelduin

Adventure in plaindealing
JAGENDORF – UPSTATE p286-292

An adventure with a bear
FELTON – WORLD'S p115-120

The adventures of a water baby
MY BOOK HOUSE v. 3 p211-224

The adventures of Alexander Selkirk
MY BOOK HOUSE v. 9 p41-65

The adventures of Billy Macdaniel
MANNING – DWARFS p95-103

The adventures of Bona and Nello
BAKER – GOLDEN p101-110

The adventures of Ciad
MacMANUS – HIBERIAN p60-73

The adventures of Florian
SHEAHAN – HENRY p43-63

The adventures of General Tom Thumb
MY BOOK HOUSE v. 8 p155-171

The adventures of Iain Direach
WILSON – SCOTTISH p121-136

The adventures of Kahukura and Te
Kanawa, the Little People of Polynesia
BELTING – ELVES p66-69

The adventures of Little Peachling
BUCK – FAIRY p138-140

The adventures of Magboloto
SECHRIST – ONCE p67-75

The adventures of Manawyddan
PICARD – CELTIC p21-35

The adventures of Nera
GARNER – GOBLINS p92-97

The adventures of Nomvula
SAVORY — ZULU p14-19

The adventures of Pengo: 1. Pengo and
the giants; 2. Pengo and the span
high man
MANNING — GLASS p159-173

The adventures of Perseus
MY BOOK HOUSE v. 9 p140-150

The adventures of Silvervit and Lillvacker
KAPLAN — SWEDISH p108-141

The adventures of Sinuhe
GREEN — TALES p159-169

The adventures of Tom Bambadil, and
other verses from the Red Book
TOLKIEN — READER (part 4) p5-78

Adventuring: white man on the warpath
IVES — TALES p97-113

The adventurous winnower
VITTORINI — OLD p19-23

Advice
The fox and the bird
Good advice
Good advice, a guinea a piece
Grandfather's advice
A mother's advice
The old crow teaches the young corw
The rats in council
Shinga-mamba
The snake chief
The three words of advice
The tinner, the dog, the Jew, and the
cake
Where to lay the blame
A wise man on a camel

The advice that cost a thousand ryo
SEKI — FOLKTALES p160-163

Aeneas
The sack of Troy
The wanderings of Aeneas

Aeneas . . . His wanderings
UNTERMEYER — FIRE. p53-59

Aes Sidhes. *See* **Sidhe** (Sidhean)

Aesir
Asgard and the Aesir gods
The creation of man
The creation of the world
The death of Balder
The first gods and giants
Heimdall, the watchman of Asgard
Idunn's apples of youth
Njord, Frey and Freya
Odin, the all-father
Odin's eight-legged steed
Ragnarokk, the destiny of the gods
The theft of Thor's hammer
Thor and the jotun Aegir
Yggdrasil, the world tree

Aesop
Fables and fabulists

Aesop's Fables
The ass and the pet dog
At the lion's cave
Belling the cat
The boaster
The boy and the nuts
The boy who cried wolf
The bundle of sticks
The cat and the hen
The city mouse and the country
mouse
The crow and the pitcher
The crow and the water jug
The dancing monkeys
The dog in the manger
The donkey and the boar
The donkey and the lap dog
The foolish dog and his reflection
The fox and the crane
The fox and the crow
The fox and the grapes
The fog and the stork
A fox in hiding
The goat and the wolf
The goat in the well
The hare and the tortoise
Just his luck
The lark and her young ones
The lion and the mouse
The lion and the woodcutter
The lizards and the stag
The man and the boy and the donkey
The milkmaid and her pail
The oak and the reed
One good turn deserves another
The puffed-up frog
The raven and the fox
The shepherd's boy
The town mouse and the country
mouse
The travellers and the bear

Aesop's Fables (*Continued*)

The two crabs
The wind and the sun
The wolf and the crane
The wolf and the watch-dog
The wolf in sheep's clothing

Afanas'yev, A.N.
The czar's frog daughter
The two friends

Afancs (imaginary animals)
The oxen and the afanc

Afar in the desert
MY BOOK HOUSE v. 8 p36-37

The affable lion
SPICER – KNEELING p107-121

Affection. *See* **Friendship; Love**

Afghanistan
The hare and the tiger
How the dotty Afghan woodman died
One mean trick deserves another
The silver on the hearth

Afghans
Moti

Africa
The babbling reed-warbler
The barrel of water
The battle of the animals
The beautiful feathers
The bird of the valley
The bird with the most beautiful song
The bragging bat
The brave man of Golo
The cannibal and his sweet singing
bird
The cat who came indoors
The cerval's secret name
The chief above and chief below
The chief of the Guernsi
The clever little jackal
The delicate daughter
Dog couldn't be cured
The donkeys ask for justice
The elephant hunters
The end of the evening
The famine and the fruit tree
A father-in-law and his son-in-law
The feast
The first zebra
The fisherman
Four very skillful people

Frog's wives make ndiba pudding
The giant who played with pygmies
The giraffe hunters
The girl and the crocodile
The girl on the hill
The girl on the rock
The girl who forgot her hoe
The golden lion
Grandfather tells some tales
The grandmother and the crocodile
The greedy spider
The hemp smoker and the hemp
grower
How chameleon became King of the
animals
How frog lost his tail
How poverty was revealed to the king
of Adja
How the Milky Way began
The hunter and his talking leopard
The hyena's egg
Improbable tales from Africa
The injured lion
Jirimpimbira
Kalulu and the elephant
Kalulu and the leopard
Kamiyo of the river
The kindly ant-bear
The kindly ghost
The king of Sedo
The king's drum
A leg for the lion
The lemur and the shrew
Liberia–land of promise
The light in the house
Lion and the woman
Lion, chameleon, and chicken
The lion on the path
The lion's share
Little fish and big fish
Long memories
Magic bird
The magic herdboy
The man who turned into a hyena
Mapandangare, the great baboon
The message from the moon
The mighty warrior in hare's house
The muula tree
Nawasi goes to war
Nyangara, the python
The panther in the pit
The past and the future
The poor herdsman and his sons, the
Little People of Africa
Rabbit and lion
Rabbit and tortoise
Rabbit at the water hole
Rabbit, elephant and hippopotamus
The race
The rain-god's daughter
The rain makers

6

Africa (*Continued*)

The ram and the leopard
Ruda, the quick thinker
Sakunaka, the handsome young man
The search: who gets the chief's
 daughter?
The sky god's daughter
Sleep, sleep, my little one!
The snake king
The snake who bit a girl
A song for the new chief
The song of Gimmile
The spider and the lizard
The stone lute
The swallowing monster
Temba becomes a warrior
Temba wins a bride
Temba's bag of salt
Temba's magic boat
Temba's monkey friends
Three fast men
The three gluttons and the hunter
The three sisters and the cannibals
Three skillful men
Three sons of a chief
The tortoise and the monkey
The tortoise and the osprey
Tortoise triumphant
The tree with the difficult name
Tsimbarume, the hardened bachelor.
The tug of war
Two friends: how they parted
The water sprite
The wedding of the hawk
Why the chameleon shakes his head
The wise old camel
The woman and the mouse
The yam child

—Algeria
  See also Africa—Tribes—Kabyle
  The jinni's magic flute
  Omar's big lie
  The sultan's fool

—Angola. *See* Africa—Tribes—Loanda;
Africa—Tribes—Mbaka

—Assam
  The ant and the frog
  How men learned about evil
  The moon raised the sky
  The rooster and the sun

—Basutoland
  Bobo, black dog, and the cannibal
   woman
  Polo, the snake-girl

—Belgian Congo. *See* Africa—Congo

—Cameroons
  See also Africa—Tribes—Bamum

Child, I must sweep the hut today
, Central
  The bachelors and the python
  The bat who belonged to no one
  The blacksmith lion and the
   conceited goat
  The boy who cut everything to
   pieces
  The buffalo who made undue
   demands
  Buya marries the tortoise
  The children who could do without
   their elders
  The courting of the bat, the spider
   and the beetle
  The friendship of the tortoise and
   the eagle
  He who is feared by all
  The honey gatherer's three sons
  How baby wart hog saved his
   father's life
  How the rabbit made enemies by
   trying to be too friendly
  A husband for the chief's daughter
  The inseparable friends
  The lazy man and the water spirit
  The leopard and the bushbuck buy
   a dream
  The leopard and the bushbuck go
   hunting
  The leopard and the rabbit go
   courting
  The leopard builds a house for
   the bushbuck
  The little black men and the
   honeybees
  Look behind as well as before
  The magic drum
  The man who always helped the
   needy
  The man who tried to catch the
   night
  The most useful tree in the world
  Mother of the forest
  Open your beak, my little bird
  The pattern on tortoise's back
  Pemba and the python and the
   friendly rat
  The rabbit grows a crop of money
  The rabbit steals the elephant's
   dinner
  The rabbit takes his revenge on
   the elephant
  Shinga-mamba
  The small red feather
  Teaching baby crab to walk
  Three unscrupulous men
  The tortoise and the reedbuck
   run a race
  Two hunters
  Why the sendji rat has no tail

Africa (*Continued*)

—Congo
  See also Africa—Tribes—Bakongo;
  Africa—Tribes—Bandimba; Africa—
  Tribes—Bushong; Africa—Tribes—
  Mongo
    The antelope and the spider
    The bat and the eagle
    The bat and the turtle
    The boy who turned himself into
      a peanut
    He washed the monkey's face
    The hen's house
    How the parrots helped the
      women
    How the porcupine fooled the
      elephant
    How the turtle fooled the leopard
    Intole the giant
    The leopard and the tortoise
    The louse and the fingernail
    The man who became a chimpanzee
    The man who had no wife
    The man who refused help
    Mboyo and the giants
    Mboyo the hunter
    The meat hungry man and the
      grave digger
    The monkey and the banana
    Musakalala, the talking skull
    The proud bokungu tree
    The snake and the toad
    The tortoise and the crocodile
    The turtle, the hippo, and the
      elephant
    Wembi, the singer of stories
    What the lemur is saying at night
    Who should get the neck ring?
    Why the dog lost his wife

, East
  See also Africa—Tribes—Swahili
    The baboon and the hare
    The baobab tree
    The bean pot
    The bee tree
    The cattle egret
    Colored coats
    The greedy hyena
    How the hare learned to swim
    The lion's threats
    The little crow
    A lot of silence makes a great noise
    Men of different colors
    Mumbele and the goats
    The Namashepani
    The nandi bear
    The ostrich chicks
    The pots that sang
    The rainbow
    The rug maker

    The scarecrow
    The silent maiden
    The sky people
    Son of the long one
    The talking house
    The trap
    Trust your friends
    The tug of war
    Wanja's choice
    Why cats live with women
    Why dogs live with men
    Why the hyrax has no tail
    The wonderful tree

—Egypt. *See* Egypt

, Equatorial
    Ananse and the king's cow
    Gizo's counting trick
    Hyena and the oil with flies on it
    Ikpoom
    Kindai and the ape
    Little sister and the Zimwi
    The lonely lioness and the ostrich
      chicks
    The long one
    Ol-Ambu and He-of-the-long sleep-
      ing-place

—Ethiopia
  See also Africa—Tribes—Amhara;
  Africa—Tribes—Falasha
    The ancient land of Ethiopia
    The battle of Eghal Shillet
    The contrary woman
    Dinner with the tota
    The donkey who sinned
    The donkeys ask for justice
    The farmer of Babbia
    Fire and water, truth and falsehood
    The fire on the mountain
    The game board
    The goat well
    The goats who killed the leopard
    The golden earth
    The Habasha and the king of kings
    The hero of Adi Nifas
    How Abunawas was exiled
    The jackal's lawsuit
    The judgement of Hailu
    The judgment of the wind
    Justice
    The light in the house
    The lion and the hare go hunting
    Lion and the woman
    The marriage of the mouse
    May it not happen
    The messenger donkey
    Ojje Ben Onogh
    Se-Osiris and the sealed letter
    Sleep, sleep, my little one!
    The story in the sealed book
    The storyteller

8

Africa—Ethiopia (*Continued*)

Tecle's goat
The wonder child
The woodcutter of Gura

—Gambia. See Africa—Tribes—Fulnai

—Ghana
   See also Africa—Tribes—Akan;
   Africa—Tribes—Ashanti
   All light comes from the sun
   All stories are Anansi's
   Ananse and his visitor, turtle
   Anansi and the elephant exchange
      knocks
   Anansi and the elephant go
      hunting
   Anansi borrows money
   Anansi plays dead
   Anansi steals the palm wine
   Anansi, the oldest of animals
   Anansi's hat-shaking dance
   Anansi's rescue from the river
   The coming of the yams
   The elephant's tail
   How the lizard lost and regained
      his farm
   Ikpoom
   The liars' contest
   Nyame's well
   Okraman's medicine
   Osebo's drum
   The planting party
   The porcupine's hoe
   The sword that fought by itself
   Two feasts for Anansi
   Why wisdom is found everywhere

—Gold Coast
   The bride who melted away
   Why ants carry large bundles
   The young hunter and the Juju man

, High
   See also Africa—Ethiopia; Africa—
   Tribes—Amhara; Africa—Tribes—
   Gallas; Africa—Tribes—Guragies;
   Africa—Tribes—Shankilla; Africa—
   Tribes—Somalis
   The ancient land of Tigre
   The ant and the tower to God
   The bob-tailed monkey and the
      king's honey
   The brave prince
   Digit the midget
   The fight with crazy man
   Four good men
   The gift and the giver
   Gift for the lazy
   The gold-lined donkey
   How God helped Mammo

The hyena man
King Firdy the Just
King Solomon and the Queen of
   Sheba
The king's black curtain
Know your own strength
The lion's share
The lion's whiskers
Live alone; die alone
The long walk
The man with a lion head in a can
A most generous host
The only people
The peace between the leopard and
   the antelope
The prize
Saint Gabre Manfas and his animals
The smiling innkeeper
The snake in the bottle
The talkative turtle
The three suitors
To outleap a rabbit
The ungrateful snake
We kill the snake god
The wise judge

—Kenya
   The mighty warrior in hare's house
   Tutu bird

   —Kamba
      Sun and moon and the pretty
         girl

   —Masai
      The moon's face

—Lake Nyanza
   Arap Sang and the cranes
   Bukango and the crocodiles
   The hyena's medicine man
   The king of the frogs
   Moi and the red bull
   Omganda and the gold
   Onsongo and the Masai cattle
   Podhu and Aruwa
   Thunder, elephant and Dorobo
   The year of Nyangondhu's cattle
   The year of the feast at Simbi
   The year of the monkeys of Ramogi

—Liberia
   See also Africa—Tribes—Jabo;
   Africa—Tribes—Kpelli; Africa—
   Tribes—Loma; Africa—Tribes—
   Temme; Africa—Tribes—Vai
   All about the tail of the leopard
   The anger of Sande-Nyana
   The beginning of spirit societies
   Catfish and his terrible end
   The clever question
   The Dicot tree and the deer
   Disobedient Hawa
   Hare makes a fool of leopard

Africa—Liberia (*Continued*)

He danced fine-o
How a man became unwitched
How a Wuuni ate nine evil spirits
How dog came to live with man
How hare asked for wisdom
How monkey king became a slave
How Pakayana the spider got his
  small waist
How people became different
How Sima humbugged a crocodile
Koi and the kola nuts
The lady and the devil
Liberia—land of promise
Liberian proverbs
The lizard and the catfish
Pakpai and Boto
Tema's promise to the white bird
Think on four wives
The three who made Ku
Tola and the sea monster
Two ways to count to ten
Why some animals live with man
Why yams and cassava hide in the
  ground
Zolo Dumah and the priest

—Morocco. *See* Morocco

—Mount Kibo
The poor herdsman and his sons,
  the Little People of Africa

—Mozambique
Chameleon finds—

—Nigeria. *See* Africa—Tribes—Fulani;
  Africa—Tribes—Hausa; Africa—Tribes
  —Ibio; Nigeria

—Nile River
The golden lotus
Isis and Osiris
Khnemu of the Nile

—North
Ali and the camels
Allah will provide
The brainy rabbit
The handkerchief
The happy man
The language of the birds
The miser's wife
The sloogeh dog and the stolen
  aroma
The sultan's fool
The thousand pieces of gold
The unusual excuse
The wise goat

—Rhodesia
See also Africa—Tribes—Bemba
The drums call the village to dance

Kalulu and his money farm

—Senegal
See also Africa—Tribes—Fulani;
  Africa—Tribes—Wolof
Bomba, the brave

—Senegambia
The careless master

—South
See also Africa—Tribes—Hottentot;
  Africa—Tribes—Xhosa; Africa—
  Tribes—Zulu
The bird that would not stay dead
The ghost-bird
How animals got their beautiful
  coats
In unity is strength
The lost spear
Monkeys in the sausage tree

—Southeast
Lion and honey badger

—Sudan
The battle between the birds and
  the beasts
The colts in the pumpkin
The monkeys and the little red
  hats
Monkeys in the sausage tree
Ruda, the quick thinker

—Swaziland
The injured lion

—Tanganyika. *See* Africa—Tribes—
  Chaga; Africa—Tribes—Kamba;
  Africa—Tribes—Sukumu

—Tanzania
How frog lost his tail
Lion, chameleon, and chicken
The mighty warrior in hare's house
The rain makers

—Tribes

  —Abaluya
  Omganda and the gold

  —Adama
  Nawasi goes to war

  —Akan
  The man who learned the
    language of the animals
  Spider and squirrel

  —Altai
  The bat

  —Amhara
  The Amharas: rulers of high
    Africa
  The bob-tailed monkey and
    the king's honey

Africa—Tribes—Amhara (*Continued*)

Digit the midget
The gold-lined donkey
Lion and the woman
Lion bones and the Gardula
  magicians
A most generous host
The smiling innkeeper
The snake in the bottle
To outleap a rabbit

—Ashanti
All stories are Anansi's
Ananse and his visitor, turtle
Anansi and the elephant ex-
  change knocks
Anansi and the elephant go
  hunting
Anansi borrows money
Anansi plays dead
Anansi steals the palm wine
Anansi, the oldest of animals
Anansi's hat-shaking dance
Anansi's rescue from the river
The coming of the yams
The elephant's tail
How the lizard lost and regained
  his farm
How wisdom came to man
The liar's contest
Nyame's well
Okraman's medicine
Osebo's drum
The planting party
The porcupine's hoe
The sky god's daughter
A song for the new chief
The sword that fought by itself
Two feasts for Anansi
Why ants carry large bundles
Why spider has a little head and
  a big behind
Why wisdom is found every-
  where

—Baganda
The blacksmith's dilemma
How chameleon became king
  of the animals
Why rabbit has a short tail

—Bakongo
Frog's wives make ndiba pudding
The hunter and his talking
  leopard
Two friends; how they parted

—Baluba
The tug of war

—Bambuti
The bird with the most
  beautiful song

—Bamum
The feast

—Bandimba
The prince who wanted the
  moon

—Bantu
See also Africa—Tribes—
Baganda

—Bantu
The black-handed monkey
The cannibal who ate too fast
The cannibal's drum
The dwarfs of the ant hill
The frog and the moon
Hare and the hyena
How frog lost his tail
How the bat caught friendship
  with the moon
In unity is strength
Kabundi's eye
The leopard and the antelope
The leopard's tricks
The leopard's wine
Lion and honey badger
Lion, chameleon, and chicken
The lion, the leopard, and the
  antelope
The man and the mango trees
The monkeys' feast
The seven-headed giant
The singing drum and the
  mysterious pumpkin
Tortoise and the lizard
Tshiama, the snake's daughter
Tshikashi Tshikulu and the
  woman
Tug of war
The two white stones
The weasel and his mother
The worthless man of poverty

—Bemba
The pattern on tortoise's back
The stone lute
Why the chameleon shakes
  his head

—Bushmen
The battle of the animals

—Bushong
Why the dog is the friend of
  man

—Chaga
The calabash children
The rain makers

Africa—Tribes (*Continued*)

—**Danakil**
The fight with crazy man
Know your own strength
The only people

—**Denkas**
Don't beat your dog

—**Ekoi**
Why the bush-fowl calls at
dawn and why flies buzz

—**Ewe**
The wedding of the hawk

—**Falasha**
Falasha: the mystery people
The gift and the giver
King Solomon and the Queen
of Sheba

—**Fulani**
The discontented fish
Fereyel and Debbo Engal the
witch
Goto, king of the land and
the water
Hare and the corn bins
Why the buzzard eats the
rooster's children

—**Gallas**
The brave prince
Four good men
The Gallas: mounted warriors
of high Africa
King Firdy the Just
The light in the house
The long walk
A most generous host
The wise judge

—**Gardula**
Lion bones and the Gardula
magician

—**Gindo**
The song of Gimmile

—**Guernsi**
The chief of the Guernsi

—**Guragies**
The ant and the tower to God
Gift for the lazy
The Guragies: workmen of high
Africa
Live alone; die alone

—**Hausa**
The brave man of Golo
Hallabau's jealousy
The rubber man
Spider and the lion
The tale of the superman

A test of skill
Three sons of a chief
Warthog and hornbill

—**Haweia**
Nawasi goes to war

—**Hottentot**
The bungled message
The message from the moon

—**Ibibio**
Thunder and lightning
Why the bat flies at night
Why the sun and moon live in
the sky

—**Ikom**
Why the crab has no head or
how the first river was made

—**Jabo**
The fisherman

—**Kabyle**
The first tears
How mankind learned to make
bread

—**Kaffa**
River child

—**Kamba**
The children who lived in a
tree-house

—**Kazakh**
The forty whoppers
A Sherlock Holmes of the
Steppes

—**Kpelli**
Nansii and the eagle

—**Kuki**
How men learned about evil

—**Loanda**
A father-in-law and his son-in-
law

—**Loma**
Twins of gold and silver

—**Mandingo**
The hunters and the antelope
Who was most skillful?

—**Masai**
The brawl between sun and
moon
The giraffe hunters
The mighty warrior in hare's
house
Onsongo and the Masai cattle

—**Mashona**
The hemp smoker and the
hemp grower

Africa—Tribes—Mashona (*Continued*)

Kalulu and his money farm
—**Mbaka**
The past and the future
—**Mendi**
Three fast men
—**Mmoatia**
The search: who gets the chief's daughter?
—**Mongo**
What the squirrel saw
—**Mpongwes**
Why chicken lives with man
—**'Msuto**
The story of the shining princess
—**Nanai**
The strongest
—**Nandhi**
Moi and the red bull
—**Nenetz**
The cuckoo
—**Nyanja**
Tortoise and the baboon
—**Pygmy**
The bird with the most beautiful song
The giant who played with pygmies
King Herla'a quest
The little black men and the honeybees
—**Samoyed.** *See* **Africa—Tribes—Nenetz**
—**Shangani**
The rabbit prince
The serpent's bride
—**Shankilla**
The peace between the leopard and the antelope
The Shankilla
The ungrateful snake
We kill the snake god
—**Somali**
The man with a lion head in a can
The Somalis: wizards of lion country
The talkative turtle
The three suitors

—**Sukumu**
How a young man became a chief
—**Swahili**
Little sister and the Zimwi
A lot of silence makes a great noise
The monkey and the shark
The monkey's heart
Snake magic
—**Swazi**
Baboon skins
The beauty and the beast
The enchanted buck
The fairy bird
The fairy frog
The moss green princess
The three little eggs
—**Temme**
How a boy got a baboon
—**Tiv**
Spider's web
—**Udmurt**
The greedy rich man
—**Vai**
The big tree and the big bird
—**Votyak**
The greedy rich man
—**Wolof**
The king of Sedo
—**Xhosa**
Afar in the desert
The magic horns
The snake chief
—**Yakut**
The girl in the moon
—**Yaos**
Why lion lives in the forest
Why people keep dogs
—**Yoruba**
The magic drum
—**Zulu**
The adventures of Nomvula Fenisana
The ghost-bird
How animals got their beautiful coats
How baboons came into the world
The hyena and the moon
The injured lion
The love of Kenelinda
Makhandu Mahlanu or The five heads

13

Africa—Tribes—Zulu (*Continued*)

The marriage feast
Nabulela
Nkalimeva
Ntunjambili
The river maiden
The son of the tortoise
The song of the doves
The two brothers
Unanana and the elephant
The wicked Mazimuzimu

—Tripoli
Ali and the camels

—Tunisia
The clever bride of Tunisia
The language of the birds

—Uganda
The blacksmith's dilemma
How chameleon became king of
the animals
How dog outwitted shepherd

, West
Ananse and his visitor, turtle
Bomba, the brave
The boom-boom-y beast
The duel of the cat and the
mouse
How spider got a bald head
How spider got a thin waist
How spider helped a fisherman
How the world got wisdom
Kalulu and his money farm
Kindai and the ape
Koi and the kola nuts
Madame giraffe
The proud camel and the rude
monkey
The six horsemen
Swën-Naba; king of the warlocks
Tim for wealth and happiness
Tricksy rabbit
Warthog and hornbill
Wend' Yamba
When the rooster was king of the
cats
Who can break a bad habit?
Why spider lives in ceilings
Why spiders live in dark corners
Wikki, the weaver

—Mogho
Kuluile, the dancing girl
Magic and friendship
Naba Zid-Wende
The war of the animals
against the birds

—Zambia
The pattern on tortoise's back

—Zanzibar
Goso the teacher

African child rhymes
MY BOOK HOUSE v. 1 p146-147

The African hunter and the forbidden
room
MORRIS — UPSTAIRS p65-70

Agamemnon
The anger of Achilles
How Agamemnon came home
Iphigenia . . . The transported sacrifice
The wounded archer

Agates
The secret of Kaboniyan

Agayk and the strangest spear
EDMONDS — TRICKSTER p21-29

Age. *See* Birthdays; Old age; Time; Youth

The age of the animals
WITHERS — WORLD p79.

The age of the partridge
GAER — FABLES p159-161

The aged father
INS-SÖB — FOLK p186-187

The aged infant
JONES — WELSH p175-181

Agreement (Acquiescence)
Freddy and his fiddle

Agreements (Bargaining; Pacts)
See also Devils
The anger bargain
Bouki rates a horse
Finger never says 'Look here'; it
says 'Look yonder'
How the gypsy sold his horse
Keep cool
King O'Toole and his goose
The man who lost his shadow
Ooka and the barbered beast
The rat who made one bargain too
many
The rich landowner and his worker
St. Francis and the wolf
The two bridegrooms
Two different interpretations of the
same pact

Agricola
  The tale of the sons of Cathmor

Agriculture. *See* Country life; Farmers;
Ploughs and ploughing

Ah Tcha the sleeper
  HOKE – WITCHES p5-14

Ahmes, Queen
  The great Queen Hatshepsut

Ahuehuetes trees (cyprus)
  Bird Cu

Aileel and Ailinda
  SHEAHAN – HENRY p129-146

The Ailp king's children
  WILSON – SCOTTISH p148-155

The Ailpein bird, the stolen princess,
  and the brave knight
  LEODHAS – HEATHER p15-33

Aiming too high
  GREEN – BIG p144-145

Ainsel
  WILSON – SCOTTISH p95-98

Ainsworth, Harrison
  Lancashire – fiction

Air
  The children of Lir

Air castles
  WITHERS – WORLD p23.

The airplane
  MY BOOK HOUSE v.1 p194.

Airplanes. *See* Aviation

Airy-go-round
  ARBUTHNOT – TIME p384-389

Akiba and the daughter of Kalba Sabbu'a
  NAHMAD – PORTION p120-122

Alabama
  Devil in church
  Fire, a story of the Alabama Indians
  Reform meeting
  Stackalee

Why rabbit has a short tail

Alabama
  LEACH – RAINBOW p63-64

Aladdin
  The idle boy
  New lamps for old
  The princess
  The slave of the lamp
  The slave of the ring
  Underground palace

Aladdin. *See* The idle boy; New lamps for
  old; The princess; The slave of the
  camp; The slave of the ring; The underground palace

Aladdin and his wonderful lamp
  See also Aladdin and the wonderful
  lamp
  BROWN – AROUND p53-66

Aladdin and the princess
  MOZLEY – ARABY p16-18

Aladdin and the wonderful lamp
  ARBUTHNOT – TIME p152-159
  MOZLEY – ARABY p12-20
  SIDEMAN – WORLD'S p502-524

Alas!
  MANNING – DAMIAN p129-138

Alaska
  See also Eskimos
  The bear woman
  The boastful Alaskans
  The cranberry feast
  The creek of whale oil
  Dance, raven, dance
  The enchanted sky
  The extraordinary black coat
  How the foxes became red
  How thunder and lightning came to
  be
  How Yehl, the hero, freed the beam-
  ing maiden
  Kunikdjuaq, a bear story of the Inuit
  Kutlee-Seek-Vik (where the bird skin
  was cooked)
  Lights of the caribou
  Nathlook: Susie my name
  The return of the land-otter
  The sea serpent
  The spirit of slumber
  Whale of a tale
  Whistle the winds

–Kotzebue
  Aye-Mee and the mermaid
  A legend of Kotzebue

The Albahaca plant
BELPRE – TIGER p89-94

Albania
The servant lass

Albatrosses
A wizard of the twilight

Alberich and the dwarfs
JACOBSON – LEGEND. p20-23

Alberto and the monsters
SECHRIST – ONCE p204-213

The alchemist
WESTWOOD – MEDIEVAL p81-86

Alchemy
The advantages of learning
The lady who put salt in her coffee

Alchemy: the magic science
JENNINGS – BLACK p56-66

Alcoholism
The drunkard and the opium-eater
Eight leaves of story (2) The sigh of
Gwyddno Long-Shank
The flooding of the Lower Hundred
The hermit and the devil
The kind pixy
The musicians
Salt
The staff of Oranmirgan
The warning of the frogs

Alcott, Louisa May
Little Gulliver
The witch's curse

Alcott, Louisa May
Life in Concord

Aldar-Kos and the greedy rich
MASEY – STORIES p65-72

Alden, Raymond MacDonald
The knights of the silver shield

Alder trees
The creation of man

Ale. See Beer

Alertness
The boy hero of Harlem
Jamie Watt and the giant in the tea-
kettle
The little rooster and the little hen
Policeman Joe
The twelve dancing princesses
Wee Robin's Christmas song

Aleutian Islands
The men fashion the frames of their
kayaks

Alexander and Bucephalus
BALDWIN – FAVOR. p85-87

Alexander of Macedon at the gates of
Paradise
NAHMAD – PORTION p150-151

Alexander the Great
Diogenes the wise man
The Gordian knot, the destiny of
Alexander
A horse afraid of his shadow

Alfonso, the Chaste, King
Bernardo and the red knight

Alfred, King
King Alfred and the cakes

Alger, Leclaire G.
Courage
Names
The penalty of greatness

Algeria. See Africa–Algeria

Ali and the camels
GILSTRAP – SULTAN'S p9-17

Ali Baba and the forty thieves
LINES – TALES p171-186
MOZLEY – ARABY p21-37
SIDEMAN – WORLD'S p85-100

Ali Sundos
ZAGLOUL – BLACK p11-28

"Alice in Wonderland" and "Through
the looking glass"
Jabberwocky
A mad tea party

Aliosha's visit to the bald mountain
ALMEDINGEN – KNIGHTS p59-71

Alison Gross
  MANNING – BEASTS p61-64
  MANNING – ENGLISH p70-73
  VANSITTART – DARK p30-32

All about Columbus
  MY BOOK HOUSE v. 5 p112.

All about the tail of the leopard
  HASKETT – GRAINS p103-106

All around the cobbler's bench
  MY BOOK HOUSE v. 1 p107.

All change
  JACOBS – EUROPE. p13-18

All creatures great and small
  CATHON – PERHAPS p43-99

All in green, went my love riding
  GARNER – GOBLINS p126-127

All light comes from the sun
  JABLOW – MAN p83-85

All my lambkins and all my bear cubs
  NYBLOM – WITCH p121-131

All Saint's Day
  Saint Martin and the honest man

All stories are Anansi's
  COURLANDER – HAT p3-12

All the cats consulted
  MY BOOK HOUSE v. 1 p85.

All things beautiful
  CATHON – PERHAPS p253.

All things bright and beautiful
  CATHON – PERHAPS p8-42

All things wise and beautiful
  CATHON – PERHAPS p215-253

Allah
  Ishallah
  Watermelons, walnuts and the wisdom
    of Allah
  The wisdom of Allah

Allah will provide
  GILSTRAP – SULTAN'S p81-87

Allegiance. *See* **Loyalty**

Allen, Ethan
  Giant of the Green Mountains
  Green Mountain hero

Alleyne, Leonora
  The frog
  The husband of the rat's daughter

Alligators and crocodiles
  Anansi an' de cherries
  Anansi and fish country
  Anansi and the alligator eggs
  Anansi and the crabs
  Aruman, a hero of Java
  The beginning of the Narran Lake
  The biggest crocodile in the world
  The boy who was lost
  The bride who melted away
  Buh rabbit's big eat
  Bukango and the crocodiles
  The case of the mouse-deer and the
    crocodile's eggs
  The crab, the crocodile and the jackal
  The crocodile's daughter
  The crocodile's mouth
  Crocodile's share
  The dilemma of a pious man
  Dreamland opens here
  The girl and the crocodile
  Gizo's counting trick
  The grandmother and the crocodile
  Ha! Tío rabbit is bigger
  How Sima humbugged a crocodile
  The jackal and the crocodile
  The jackal and the fig tree
  The king of the frogs
  Koi and the kola nuts
  The luck of the sea and the luck of
    the mountain
  The magic crocodile
  Malati and the prince
  The monkey and the crocodile
  Monkey-lord and crocodile
  The monkey's heart
  The number of spots
  One against a hundred
  The ostrich and the crocodile
  The prince and the Three Fates
  The quarrel
  The rabbit and the crocodile
  A school for crocodiles
  A search for the magic lake
  Three tales of the mouse-deer
  The tortoise and the crocodile
  The ungrateful crocodile
  War between the crocodiles and
    Kantchil
  The white hare and the crocodiles
  Why crocodile does not eat hen
  Why no one ever carries the alligator
    down to the water

Alligators and crocodiles (*Continued*)

Why rabbit has a short tail
Why the crocodile hates man
The wise monkey

Allingham, William
The fairy shoemaker
Song of the leprechaun or fairy
  shoemaker

All's well that ends well
JAGENDORF – SAN p173-177

The almanacks
SLOANE – FOLK. p16-19

Almedingen, E. M.
ALMEDINGEN – KNIGHTS p191.

The almond bough
PICARD – LADY p41-62

Almond trees
The cavallino
The knight of the almond blossoms
The legend of the almond tree

Aloneness. *See* **Loneliness**

Along the Monongahela
JAGENDORF – UPSTATE p178-180

The Alp that disappeared
MÜLLER – SWISS p29-32

Alphabet
See also **Writing**
How the letter X got into the alphabet
The Kris of Adji Saka

Alps (mountains)
The brave cowman
The bull of Uri
Charles the Bold of Burgundy
Charles the Great and the snake
Death a prisoner
Dwarf stories
The fairy grotto
The father's steps
Four tales of how the devil was out-
  witted
Fridolin
The Frisian ride
The frontier contest
Giant pear and giant cow
The groschen hole in the Murz Valley

How the Kuhreihen began
Ida of Toggenburg
The judge of Bellinzona
The key maiden of Tegerfelden
The knife
The knight of La Sarraz
The lost cows
The martyr of Thebes
Meinrad and the ravens
The mermaid of Zug
Nidelgret
The ring of Hallwil
The singing fir-tree
The snake crown
Sturdy Hans
The three languages
The three ravens
Tredeschin
Verena and the jug
William Tell and the founding of the
  Swiss Confederation

Altaics (Asian people)
The bat
The miserly frog
Sartak-Pai
Why dog has a fur coat and woman
  has seven tempers

Altars
The golden altar of the Church of St.
  Joseph
The rain god's reprisal

Altitude
The eagle and the wren

Alvarado, Diego de
When Boquerón spoke

Amasis, Pharaoh
The girl with the rose-red slippers

Amazons
The woman tribe

Ambassador from Chi
COURLANDER – TIGER'S p43-45

Ambassadors. *See* **Diplomats**

Amber
The magic amber

Ambition
Aiming too high
The circus man

Ambition (*Continued*)

The cobbler astrologer and the forty
thieves
Dick Whittington and his cat
Down by the River Avon
London streets
Sir Beaumains, the kitchen knight
Tortoise and Babarinsa's daughters
The wonderland of an artist's workshop

The ambitious maiden
MONTGOMERIE – 25 p41-43

Amelungs
Dietrich of Bern

Amen-em-het, Pharaoh
The adventures of Sinuhe
The story of the shipwrecked sailor

Amen-Ra. *See* **Ra**

America
See also names of American countries;
**Colonial life and customs; Eskimos;
Indians; Tall tales**
Adventuring: white man on the war-
path
A bauchan in the family
Beautiful doll
Bigfoot Wallace
Bowleg Bill
Captain Samuel Samuels
Davy Crockett
Davy Crockett, the yaller blossom o'
the forest
Febold Feboldson
From a wayfarer's notebook: eighteenth
century
From a wayfarer's notebook: nineteenth
century
From a wayfarer's notebook: seventeenth
century
Gabriel, blow your horn!
The ghost and Hans Van Duin
Gib Morgan
He died hard
The heroine of the Mohawk Valley
High John the conqueror
Jacob Heard and the golden horse
Joe Magarac
John Henry
John Tabor, whaler
Johnny Appleseed
Love and war
Love story
The man who started it all and the
man who couldn't forget

Mike Fink
Minstrel making
Mr. X and the loyalty oath
Of gold and men
Of sea-going snakes
Of silver and men
A passel of real lies
Paul Bunyan
Pecos Bill
The privateer turned patriot
Queen of the Comstock
Real stuff
A red berry and two hills of snow
Remembered
Sam Patch
The Scotty who knew too much
Seán Palmer's voyage to America
with the fairies
The secret room
Smolligosters, etc.
Stormalong
The story of a princess
A trail of tall tales
An unsung heroine
The unwilling pirate
Wintering with Paul Bunyan

, **Discovery of**
Foretelling the future
Leif the Lucky . . . What he
discovered
The spell-song

American family westward
IVES – TALES p191-208

American Indian songs
MY BOOK HOUSE v. 1 p80-81

An American miner's song
MY BOOK HOUSE v. 2 p23

American rhymes
MY BOOK HOUSE v. 1 p82-117

The American saga
TAFT – PROFILE p3-12

The Amharas: rulers of high Africa
DAVIS – PION'S p29-32

Amin and the ghul
WILLIAMS – ROUND p73-80

Amizemus (cannibals)
The beautiful feathers

Among the chickens
JUDA – WISE p49-53

Amphisbaenes (imaginary animals)
The double-headed snake of Newbury

Amulets
The sacred amulet

Anabaptists
Lady Eaton's curse

Anangarati and the men of four castes
GRAY – INDIA'S p220-223

Ananse and his visitor, turtle
KAULA – AFRICAN p25-31

Ananse and the king's cow
AARDEMA – TALES p9-18

Anansi an' de cherries
WILLIAMS – OLD p113-117

Anansi and bicycle
WILLIAMS – ROUND p197-203

Anansi and candlefly
SHERLOCK – WEST p97-104

Anansi and fish country
SHERLOCK – ANANSI p70-75

Anansi and five
WILLIAMS – ROUND p204-207

Anansi and snake the postman
SHERLOCK – WEST p71-76

Anansi and the alligator eggs
SHERLOCK – ANANSI p84-93

Anansi and the crabs
SHERLOCK – ANANSI p95-103

Anansi and the elephant exchange knocks
COURLANDER – HAT p63-69

Anansi and the elephant go hunting
COURLANDER – HAT p38-45

Anansi and the old hag
SHERLOCK – ANANSI p26-29

Anansi and the plantains
SHERLOCK – ANANSI p64-69

Anansi and turtle and pigeon
SHERLOCK – ANANSI p31-34

Anansi asks a favor. *See* Tiger story,
Anansi story

Anansi borrows money
COURLANDER – HAT p55-58

Anansi hunts with tigers
SHERLOCK – WEST p118-124

Anansi play with fire, Anansi get burned
JAGENDORF – KING p171-176

Anansi plays dead
COURLANDER – HAT p20-24

Anansi steals the palm wine
COURLANDER – HAT p77-79

Anansi stories
All stories are Anansi's
Bandalee
Born a monkey, live a monkey
Brother Breeze and the pear tree
Dry-bone and Anansi
From tiger to Anansi
How Kwaku Ananse destroyed a
kingdom
How Kwaku Ananse won a kingdom
with a grain of corn
How the lizard lost and regained his
farm
How wisdom came to man
Ikpoom
Introduction: From sun-spirit to
spider-man
Kisander
The kling kling bird
Kwaku Ananse and the donkey
Kwaku Ananse and the greedy lion
Kwaku Ananse and the rain maker
Kwaku Ananse and the whipping cord
The liars' contest
Mancrow, bird of darkness
Mr. Wheeler
The quarrel
The sea-mammy
The sky god's daughter
Ticky-picky boom-boom
Tiger in the forest, Anansi in the web
Tiger story, Anansi story
Two feasts for Anansi
Who was Anansi?
Why ants carry large bundles
Why Kwaku Ananse stays on the ceil-
ing
Why rabbit have short tail
Why wisdom is found everywhere
Why women won't listen
Work-let-me-see
Yung-Kyung-Pyung

Anansi, the oldest of animals
COURLANDER – HAT p9-12

20

Anansi's hat-shaking dance
COURLANDER — HAT p13-17

Anansi's old riding-horse
SHERLOCK — WEST p105-111

Anansi's rescue from the river
COURLANDER — HAT p59-62

Ancestry
The fox, the hare, and the toad have
an argument
The geese
The two owls and the sparrow

Anchors
The three clever brothers

The ancient land of Ethiopia
COURLANDER — FIRE p1-5

The ancient land of Tigre
DAVIS — LION'S p150-153

And I dance mine own child
FARJEON — LITTLE p216-243

. . . and the magic they made
JENNINGS — BLACK p38-55

And upon the fourth bray
JUDA — WISE p87-93

Andersen, Hans Christian
The buckwheat
The children and the bear
The emperor's new clothes
The flying trunk
It's perfectly true!
The jumping contest
Little Claus and Big Claus
Little fir tree
The little girl and the new dress
The little match-girl
The little mermaid
The nightingale
Ole shut-eyes, the sandman
The princess on the pea
The real princess
The red shoes
The snow-queen
The steadfast tin soldier
The swineherd
Thumbelina
The tinder box
The wild swans

Anderson, Hans Christian
JOHNSON — PRINC. p307.

The ugly duckling

Anderson, Paul
ANDERSON — BOY p94.

Andrew and the mermaid
SHEPPARD — SCOT. p150-154

Andrew Moir and the seal-people
MORAY — FAIR p91-120

Androcles (Androclus) and the lion
BALDWIN — FAVOR. p73-77
JACOBS — EUROPE p107-109

Andromeda
The boastful queen

The angakok and the mother of seals
CARPENTER — SHIPS p37-46

The angel
DOWNING — RUSSIAN p187-189

Angelica
The powers of plants and trees to
protect against witches

Angels
The best wish
Chanina and the angels
The flying angel
The giant and the mite
How stars and fireflies were made
King David and the angel of death
Leviathan and the fox
The little fox
Prince Llewellyn and the red-haired
man
The prophet Elijah and the angel of
death
The proud king
Rabbi Joseph Della Reina
The robe
Robert of Sicily . . . The proudest king
The shepherd's crown
Sungold
The tale of Columba and the angel
The three wishes
The tree from Adam's grave
The weeping willow

Anger
See also Temper
Ask a foolish question
The birds' St. Valentine day

Anger (*Continued*)

The crowza stones
The first strawberries
Frithjof, the Viking
The jurga
The little sticky rice basket
Master and man
The messenger
Old pipes and the dryad
The poor and the rich
The rich landowner and his worker
Richard Feverel and the hay-rick
The rooster and the sultan
The three precepts

The anger bargain
THOMPSON − ONE p369-376

The anger of Achilles
GREEN − GREEKS p26-27

The anger of Sande-Nyana
HASKETT − GRAINS p98-100

Anglo-Saxons
Beowulf
Hereward the wake
How Beowulf delivered Heorot

The angry baron
DURHAM − TIT p85-89

Angus
MAYNE − GIANTS p55-62

Ani, the mother who was too proud
BOWES − BIRD p40-44

Aniello
MANNING − WIZARDS p9-21

Animal and bird stories
GREY − SOUTH (1) p4.

Animal captor persuaded to talk. *See*
The fox and the cock

Animal crackers
MY BOOK HOUSE v. 1 p162

The animal languages
RANKE − GERMANY p115-117

The animal musicians
ALEGRIA − THREE p9-14

Animal races. *See* **Races, Athletic**

Animal trainers. *See* **Animals−Training**

The animal wife
THOMPSON − ONE p143-147

Animals
All creatures great and small
Author's note
Bahram and the snake prince
The barrel of water
The bat's choice
The battle
The battle between the birds and the
beasts
The battle of the animals
Beauty and the beast
The birth of the River Emajogi
The birth years
The black swans
The bragging bat
Buh mouse testifies
Buh rabbit's human weakness
Buh rabbit's tight necktie
The cerval's secret name
Chameleon finds −
The crested curassow
The earthquake
The escape of the animals
The famine and the fruit tree
The farmyard
The first zebra
The flight of the animals
The flight with the Wendigo
The foolish, timid, little hare
The friendly animals
"General" Dog and his army
Glooskap's country
The golden deer
How animals brought fire to man
How bat won the ball game
How coyote became a friend to man
How it came about that there is a sun
and a moon
How night was let loose and all the
animals came to be
How Papantha got its patron saint
How the world was made (1)
I stand in the pulpit and preach
I went to the animal fair
Ingratitude is the way of the world
Insects and other critters
The King of Araby's daughter
Krencipal and Krencipalka
The lad and his animals
The lonely lioness and the ostrich
chicks
The long-nosed princess
The long one
The meeting
The muula tree
The number of spots
Over in the meadow
Pán Kotsky

Animals (*Continued*)

The Panchatantra
The quest for Olwen (4) Fulfilling
    the tasks (2) The oldest animals
The rain makers
The rarest animal of all
The Red Etin
Reform meeting
The Rehepapp and Vanapagan
The river that was stolen
Saint Gabre Manafas and his animals
Sindhu
The spiteful nanny goat
The tale of bat
Temba's bag of salt
Terrapin's pot of sense
Tiny Perry
Tlacuache the saint
Tricksy rabbot
The troll's daughter
Two friends: how they parted
The walk around the island
The war between the lion and the
    cricket
The war of the animals against the
    birds
The well
What is a fable?
Why animals are afraid of fire
Why bat flies alone
Why some animals live with man
Why the animals have no fire
Why there is both day and night
The witch
The woman of Llyn-y-fan (2) The
    parting
The youth and the dog dance
The youth who made friends with
    the beasts and the birds

—Age
The age of the animals
Anansi, the oldest of animals

—Color
Colored coats
How the foxes became red

—Fur
How animals got their beautiful
    coats
The rabbit and the crocodile

—Homes
Why the animals live where they
    do

, Imaginary
See also names of imaginary
    animals
The abominable snowman
About the legendary beings

About the magic animals
About the mythical beasts
Atlantes and the hippogriffs
The beast with a single horn
Beasts of the zodiac
Bird of the sun
Centaurs
Cerberus
The chimera
Chinese dragons
The Derbyshire ram
Dictionary of magical beasts
Dragons
Fact or fancy?
Ganesha
Guardians of hidden treasure
The horny-goloch
How to catch a unicorn
Jabberwocky
Japanese dragons
King of the serpents
The lion and the unicorn
Medusa
The minotaur
The monster of Loch Ness
Monsters and ghosts
Mythical beast of the sea
Mythical beasts in heraldry
The nandi bear
The Nemean lion
Orthrus
Other legendary beings
Part animal, part human
River child
Saint George and the dragon
Satyrs
Scylla and Charybdis
The sleepless dragon
Smolligosters, etc.
Some mythical beasts of today
Some namesakes of the dragon
Sphinxes
The terrible family
Tiamat
The untamable unicorn

—Kings
How chameleon became king of
    the animals
Kantjil brings the elephants to heel
Kantjil interprets a dream
King All-tusk
King Kantjil's kingdom expands
The king of the animals

—Language
The animal languages
The animal musicians
Brother Anansi and Sir Peacock

The curious wife
The Da-Tang crabs
Diggory

Animals—Language (*Continued*)

The donkey, the ox, and the
    farmer
Hans the tailor and the talking
    animals
Irraweka, mischief-maker
Jabuty, the strong
The language of animals
The magic ruby
The man who learned the language
    of the animals
May it not happen
The sand-carrier crab
The shepherd who understood the
    language of the animals
The shepherd with the curious wife
The song of the animals
The speech of beasts
The tale of the little sausage and
    the little mouse
Why the bear sleeps all winter
Why the fish do not speak

, Longest
From tiger to Anansi

—Mothers
The game mother
Mrs. Tabby Gray
Mother of the forest

—Paws
Clever-clever-clever

—Training
The hyena man
In Coney Island by the sea

, Winged
How the animals made wings for
    bat and flying squirrel
Winged wonders

Animals
    BATCHELOR — SUPER. p34-43

The animals go on trial
    SECHRIST — ONCE p64-66

The animals' paradise
    GREEN — BIG p138-139

Animals, people and the moon
    JABLOW — MAN p27-55

The animals' quarrel
    MASEY — STORIES p118-121

Anis (birds)
Ani, the mother who was too proud

Anklets
The bat and the eagle
Golden bracelets, golden anklets
Jackal or tiger?
Why the dog lost his wife

Annam. *See* **Vietnam**

Annie Christmas
    LEACH — RAINBOW p48-49

Annie goes to the cabbage field
    MY BOOK HOUSE v. 1 p129

Anpu and Bata
    THOMPSON — ONE p36-44

Answer to a child's question
    MY BOOK HOUSE v. 2 p142

The ant and the frog
    WITHERS — I SAW p115-118

The ant and the grasshopper
    ARBUTHNOT — TIME p202

The ant and the tower to God
    DAVIS — LION'S p132-135

The ant and the yellow jacket
    HEADY — TALES p32-34

The ant in search of her leg
    ALEGRÍA — THREE p40-43

The ant, the lamb, the cricket, and the
    mouse
    BRENNER — BOY p19-20

Antar the hero
    HAZELTINE — HERO p332-346

Anteaters
The kindly ant-bear
The right time to laugh
The sky people
When a man is foolish
The Wi-oombeens and Piggi-billa

The antelope and the spider
    COBBLE — WEMBI p43-45

The antelope skin
    COURLANDER — OLODE p29-31

Antelopes
Afar in the desert
The decision
The hunters and the antelope
The leopard and the antelope

Apples–Golden (*Continued*)

The golden castle that hung in
  the air
How Jack sought the golden apples
Katie Woodencloak
The king of England and his three
  sons
The king's vine
The little mouse
Little one eye, little two eyes and
  little three eyes
Magic apples
The nine peahens and the golden
  apples
An old king and his three sons of
  England
One-eye, two-eyes, and three-eyes
Peahens and golden apples
The princess on the glass hill
Simple and the princess
The sun, the moon and the star of
  morning
Sungold and the remarkable cow
The three golden apples
The white snake
Yiankos

  –Juice
Au Sung meets Kim Lee
Spring flood

  –Seeds
Johnny Appleseed
Old Johnny Appleseed
Rainbow walker/Johnny Apple-
  seed

The apples of Iduna
  HOSFORD – THUNDER p85-91

"Apples of youth"
The apples of Iduna
Idunn's apples of youth
Loki . . . The apples of youth

Appleseed, Johnny
Johnny Appleseed
Old Johnny Appleseed
Rainbow walker/Johnny Appleseed

Appreciation. See Gratitude

Apprentices
The devil's apprentice
The faithless apprentice
The handsome apprentice
Master and pupil
Ooka and the terrible-tempered
  tradesman
The sign at the smithy door
The spider specter of the pool
The tailor's apprentice . . . And the
  bear
The wandering apprentice

Apricots
The absent-minded tailor
The canary that liked apricots

April
MY BOOK HOUSE v. 6 p97.

The Arabe duck
  HARDENDORFF – TRICKY p45-50

Arabia (includes Arabian Nights)
See also **Arabians; Iraq**
About Sinbad's other wonderful
  journeys
Abunuwas the trickster
Adares, King of Arabia
Aladdin and his wonderful lamp
Aladdin and the princess
Ali Baba and the forty thieves
Antar the hero
The ape and the two cats
Bird of the sun
The blue belt
The blue palm tree
The blue parrot
The Caliph stork, told by Selim
  Baruch, the stranger
Caravan
The cat and the prophet
The clever bride of Tunisia
The doe and the lioness
Down to Arabia
An emir and two thieves
The faithful Morgiana
Fareedah's carpet
The fisherman and the genie
The golden lamb
The golden lion
Hani the simple
The happy man
The horse without a master
Juha and the dispute over a goat
Juha at the banquet
The king and the two owls
The king who tried to cheat destiny
A lie for a lie
Little Mukra
The magic carpet
The magic horse
The magician returns
Moon pearls
The pilgrim and the judge

Arabia (*Continued*)

Recollections of the Arabian Nights
Saint Michael and the idle husband
Scheherazade
Sinbad and the Roc
Sinbad the sailor
The spotted rug
The story of Caliph stork
The story of little Mukra
The story of the talking bird
The tale of a proverb
The teacher and his pupil
Three times lucky
The twice-blessed Arab
The weeping willow
The would-be wizard
Zohair and the witch

—Tribes—**Bani Hilal** (Bedouins)
Abu Zaid seeks a horse and finds
  a wife
Abu Zaid the Hilali
Bani Hilal; A tribe is born
The banishment of Diab
A battle and a wedding
A blessing and a curse
Father fights son in the tribe of
  Hilal
The horse without a master
The price of a curse
Rescue from the fire worshippers
The return of Diab
Son of the south wind
The sons of Hilal; fact and legend
The wonderful mare Khadra

Arabians
The golden-headed fish
He wins who waits
Kabadaluk: The little Arab boy
Kralyevich Marko and the Arab
The legend of the Arabian magician
The sick Doytchin

Arachne
  ARBUTHNOT — TIME p216-217

Arachne . . . The eternal spinner
  UNTERMEYER — FIRE. p38-40

Aram and the shepherd
  TASHJIAN — THREE p17-21

Arap Sang and the cranes
  HARMAN — TALES p109-117

Arawn
  PUGH — TALES p61-81

Arbitration. *See* **Judges and Justice**

Arbutus
Legend of the arbutus

Archaeology
A few lost bones
Lost arts
North Salem's Irish? ruins

Archangels. See Angels

Archbishops
The enchanted mule

The archbishop's mule
  MICHAEL — PORTUGUESE p84-91

The archer, William Tell
  UNTERMEYER — FIRE. p38-40

Archery
See also **Arrows;** etc.
Adam Bell, Clym of the Clough and
  William of Cloudesley
Bajan Budiman, the sharpshooter
The bold little bowman
Borrowed arrows
The bow, the deer, and the talking
  bird
The death of Balder
The dream
Dunay
The emperor's magic bow
The frog
The giant archer of the sky
The great bear
Great heart and the three tests
The greatest archer
How coyote became a friend to man
How the cock got his red crown
How the turkey got his beard
The hunters and the antelopes
I-know-not-what of I-know-not-where
Kalulu and the elephant
The king and his seven sons
Kralyevich Marko and Alil-Aga
The legend of William Tell
The lion who listened to a jackal
The little pet Rani
The magic calabash
The magic carpet
Mancrow, bird of darkness
The monkey and the banana
Nasreddin Hoca and the third shot
A prince went hunting
Princess Maring, the huntress
The queen's care
Rama . . . The bow that could not be
  bent
The robber baron . . . And the bat
Shah Meram and Sade Sultan

Archery (*Continued*)

The sheriff's shooting match
The story of William Tell
The three brothers
Ugly boy
Vassillissa the wise
Why there is thunder and lightning
William of Cloudslee
William Tell and the founding of the
  Swiss Confederation
The wonder ship and ship's crew
The wonderful talking bowl
The wounded archer
Young hunter

Archery
  JUDA – WISE p54-59

Architects
  The princess and the thief
  The thief and the king's treasure

Architecture. *See* Builders and building

Arctic
  See also Eskimos; North Pole
  The Eskimo widow . . . And her
    strange son
  How Peary reached the North Pole

Are fat people happy?
  BATCHELOR – SUPER. p66.

Are fish buffaloes?
  WITHERS – WORLD p50.

Are pins lucky?
  BATCHELOR – SUPER. p117-118

Are there such women?
  BORSKI – GOOD p78-81

Areca trees and nuts
  The beginning of good conversation
  Three who couldn't be parted

Argentina
  See also Indians of Latin America–
    Toba
  The fox who wanted to whistle
  The girl and the puma
  The great bird in the carob trees
  How spider taught women to weave
  Kakui, bird of the night
  The lazy fox
  The little black book of magic
  The sad, sorry sister

–Pampas
  Don't make a bargain with a fox
  The eternal wanderer of the Pampas
–Patagonia
  The enchanted palace

Argonauts
  The sleepless dragon

Arguments. *See* Quarreling

Arimasians (people)
  Guardians of hidden treasure

Aristophanes
  The birds' convention

Aristotle and the three sons
  GARNIER – LEGENDS p27-30

Arithmetic. *See* Mathematics

Arizona
  Children of cloud
  Corn moon
  How crane saved coyote
  How fire was brought from lightning
  Lost arts
  The lost lover of Pearl Hart
  The lost payroll at Wickenburg
  Man-eagle
  Navahchoo
  Tobacco woman and corn spirit
  The turquoise stones
  Wampum eater and the canal
  Why coyote is the color of the ground
  Why the world is the way it is

–Crooked Mountain
  The evil spirits of Crooked Moun-
    tain
  The legend of Crooked Mountain

–San Francisco Peaks
  The world beyond

–Superstition Mountain
  Of gold and men

Arizona
  LEACH – RAINBOW p64-67

Arkansas
  Davy Crockett, the yaller blossom o'
    the forest
  The man who hung his powder horn
    on the moon

–Ozarks
  Blood on his forehead

Arkansas
  LEACH – RAINBOW p67-70

The Arkansas fiddler
  STOUTENBURG – CROC. p35-39

Arks. *See* Noah's ark

Armadillos
  The lazy fox

The armadillos
  LEACH – RAINBOW p298-299

Armadillo's story
  SHERLOCK – IGUANA'S p76-97

Armenia
  Aram and the shepherd
  Badikan and Khan Boghu
  The beardless, the lame and the
    one-eyed thief
  The clever thieves
  The enormous genie
  The foolish man
  The frog and the stork
  The gift of gold
  The goat
  The hare's kidneys
  He wins who waits
  Heart and mind
  The horsefly
  Horses of the thunder
  The king and the shepherd
  The lazy man
  Master and man
  The master and the servant
  The miller-king
  Nazar the brave
  The nightingale Hazaran
  The rich landowner and his worker
  A rupee earned
  Shrovetide
  The story of Zoulvisia
  The talking fish
  The white snake

Armies
  See also Battles; Soldiers; Warriors
  The bird of the golden land
  Cnut and Edmund
  Donal O'Donnell's standing army
  "General" Dog and his army
  King Johnny
  Pappa Greatnose
  Pen and four foolish ministers

The armless maiden
  THOMPSON – ONE p314-419

Armor. *See* Girdles; Shields and shield-makers; Swords; etc.

Arms
  The girl without arms

Arnold, Benedict
  Giant of the Green Mountains

Arnold Winkelried
  BALDWIN – FAVOR. p45-48

Arnott, Kathleen
  Fereyel and Debbo Engal the witch

Arnsy Maull, the conjureman
  JAGENDORF – UPSTATE p159-164

Around the corner
  WITHERS – I SAW p37.

Arrogance. *See* Pride

The arrow chain
  JABLOW – MAN p35-38

Arrows
  Borrowed arrows
  The borrowing of 100,000 arrows
  The daughter of the dwarf
  The demon giant of Mount Ariake
  The frog
  Kalekeā and his wish
  The king and his seven sons
  Ko-pa-ta, the gambling god
  The legend of William Tell
  The mouse hole
  The old man and his sons
  One hundred thousand arrows
  Orphan boy
  Red king and green king
  The sea knight
  Why there is thunder and lightning

The arrows that became trees
  BELTING – THREE p136-141

Arson
  The father's steps
  Richard Feverel and the hay rick

Art, King of Leinster
  O'SULLIVAN – FOLK. p97-117

30

Art
  See also **Painters and paintings;
  Sculptors and sculpture; etc.**
  The boy who made a dream come
  true
  Lost arts
  The wonderland of an artist's work-
  shop

The art of reading
  GREEN – BIG p208.

Arthur, King
  Beaumains . . . The knightly kitchen-
  boy
  The bride-price for Olwen
  The coming of Arthur
  The death of Uwaine
  The dream of Ronabbway
  The end of Arthur
  The fair maid of Astolat
  Galahad . . . The holy grail
  Gareth and Linette
  Gawaine and the green knight
  Geraint and Enid
  Geraint and the knight of the
  sparrow-hawk
  The healing of Urre
  How Arthur gained Excalibur
  How Galahad came to Arthur's court
  How Guenevere went a-maying
  How Percival came to Arthur's court
  How Tristram fought against the
  knight from Ireland
  How Trystan won Esyllt
  King Arthur . . . The shield and the
  hammer
  The knight with the two swords
  Lancelot and Elaine
  Lancelot and Galahad
  Lancelot and Gawaine
  Lancelot and Guenever
  Lancelot of the lake
  The marriage of Arthur
  The marriage of Gawaine
  The poisoned apple
  The quest for Olwen
  The quest for Olwen (1) The destiny
  The quest for Olwen (2) At Arthur's
  court
  The quest for Olwen (4) Fulfilling the
  tasks
  The quest for Olwen (4) Fulfilling the
  tasks 2/ The oldest animals
  The quest for Olwen (4) Fulfilling the
  tasks 3/ The lame ant
  The quest for Olwen (4) Fulfilling the
  tasks 4/ The beard of Dillus the
  bearded

The quest for Olwen (4) Fulfilling
  the tasks 6/ The tusk of Ysgithyrwyn
The quest for Olwen (4) Fulfilling
  the tasks 7/ The hunting of the
  otherworld bear
The quest for Olwen (5) Bulhwch
  marries Olwen
The quest of the Holy Grail
Rhitta of the beards
St. Cadog and King Arthur
The siege of joyous Gard
Sir Beaumains, the kitchen knight
Sir Gawain, and the green knight
Sir Perceval
The story of Tom Thumb
The sword in the stone
Tarn Wethelan
The treachery of Morgan LeFay
Tristram and Isolt
Uwaine and the Lady of the fountain
The Welshman and the hazel staff
Where Arthur sleeps

Arthur, King of Britain
  PICARD – HERO p11-29

The artificial earthquake
  SECHRIST – ONCE p91-93

Artists
  See also **Painters and Paintings;** etc.
  The blackbird's song
  The boy who drew cats
  The boy who had to draw cats
  The ivory box
  Leaf by Niggle
  The maker of maps

Aruman, a hero of Java
  MY BOOK HOUSE v. 6 p202-208

As I went to Bonner
  MY BOOK HOUSE v. 1 p29.

As it fell upon a day
  MY BOOK HOUSE v. 1 p148.

As many as –
  LEACH – NOODLES p57-58

As Tommy Snooks and Bessie Brooks
  MY BOOK HOUSE v. 1 p46

As you like it
  MY BOOK HOUSE v. 10 p165-174

Asbjörnsen, Peter Christian
  The ash lad and the good helpers
  The ash lad who made the princess
  say "You're a liar"
  The bear and the fox who made a bet

Asbjörnsen, Peter Christian (*Continued*)

The boy with the beer keg
The boys who met the trolls in the
  Hedal woods
Butterball
The charcoal burner
The cock and the fox
The companion
The devil and the bailiff
East of the sun and west of the moon
The fox as shepherd
The giant who had no heart in his
  body
The golden bird
The golden castle that hung in the air
"Good day, fellow!" "Axe handle!"
The hare who had been married
The house mouse and the country
  mouse
The key in the distaff
Little Freddie with his fiddle
Not driving and not riding
The old woman against the stream
The parson and the sexton
The princess on the Glass Hill
The princess who always had to have
  the last word
The princess whom nobody could
  silence
The ram and the pig who went into
  the woods to live by themselves
The seventh father of the house
Soria Moria castle
The squire's bride
The tabby who was such a terrible
  glutton
Taper-Tom who made the princess
  laugh
Three billy goats gruff
The three princesses in the mountain-
  in-the-blue
The twelve wild ducks
White-bear-King-Valemon
Why the sea is salt

Asbjörnsen, Peter Christian
  ASBJÖRNSEN – EAST p137.
  SIDEMAN – WORLD'S p830.

  The Norwegian folk tales and their
  illustrators

Asgard
  How Odin brought the mead to Asgard
  In the beginning
  The world of the gods

Asgard and the Aesir gods
  AULAIRE – NORSE p36-37

The ash lad and the good helpers
  ASBJÖRNSEN – NORW. p170-177

The ash lad who had an eating match
with the troll
  ASBJÖRNSEN – NORW. p81-83

The ash lad who made the princess say
"You're a liar"
  ASBJÖRNSEN – NORW. p17-19

Ash sweeper and the wishing wand
  BECHSTEIN – FAIRY p145-153

Ash trees
  The creation of man
  Lucky Rose Tuttle
  Maid Lena
  Yggdrasil, the world tree

Ashes
  Ashypelt
  La Cenerentola
  The old man of the flowers
  Soria Moria castle

Ashiwi (people)
  To feed my people: The coming of
  corn

Ashoremashika
  WALKER – DANCING p35-41

Ashputtel
  CHILD – CASTLES p109-125

Ashypelt
  HAMPDEN – GYPSY p51-56

Asia
  See also names of countries
  The bat
  The jackal who tried to copy the
  lion

  –Steppes
    See also Russia–Steppes
    A clever judge

Ask a foolish question
  SERWER – LET'S p30-37

Ask Mr. Bear
  ARBUTHNOT – TIME p257-259

Asmund, Authun, and Odd
  JONES – SCAND. p140-142

Aspen trees
  Boys with golden stars
  The Indian Cinderella

Aspinwall, Alicia
A quick-running squash

The ass and the pet dog
MONTGOMERIE – 25 p28-29

The ass gets the better of the wolf
WILSON – GREEK p40-41

The ass in the lion's skin
GAER – FABLES p157-159

The ass in the tiger skin
MONTGOMERIE – 25 p34-35

The ass that lays money
THOMPSON – ONE p248-251

The ass that was flayed
GAER – FABLES p80-81

The assembling of the fays
MY BOOK HOUSE v. 6 p17.

Asses. *See* **Donkeys**

Assipattle and the giant sea serpent
HAVILAND – SCOTLAND p71-92

The ass's promise
GHOSE – FOLK p54-55

The astrologer
DE LA IGLESIA – CAT unp.

The astrologer and the physician
BORSKI – GOOD p68-71

Astrology
The chief astrologer
The cobbler astrologer and the forty
thieves
The crab
Deidre and the sons of Usna
Giants, dragons, and gods
The golden casket
Katcha and the devil
The miller's four sons
The mountain of hope
Prince Sneeze
The soothsayers

Astronomy
See also names of constellations,
planets, etc.
The thoughtless abbot

Asuras
The making of the earth
Prahlada

At Arthur's court. *See* The quest for
Olwen

At Christmas
HOPE-SIMPSON – CAVAL. p211.

At Christmas play and make good cheer
MY BOOK HOUSE v. 2 p217.

At the lion's cave
GREEN – BIG p129.

At the pike's command
ALMEDINGEN – RUSS. p95-104

At the wedding of Miss Jenny Wren
MY BOOK HOUSE v. 1 p125.

Atalanta . . . The fleet-footed runner
UNTERMEYER – FIRE. p25-28

Atalanta's race
ARBUTHNOT – TIME p225-226

Atalanta's race; a contest for love or
death
STRONG – FAVORITE p75-79

Atam and Im
LEACH – RAINBOW p278-279

Atheists
The haunted mine
The white mule from the other world

Athene (goddess)
Arachne . . . The eternal spinner

Athletes and athletics
See also **Acrobats;** names of types of
athletics; **Races; Athletic**
Riddler on the hill
Thor . . . How the thunderer was
tricked
Twins in the sky

A-tishoo!
MANNING – GIANNI p141-144

A-tisket, a-tasket
MY BOOK HOUSE v. 1 p89.

Atlantes and the hippogriff
JACOBSON – FIRST p37-39

Atlantis
The sea serpent

Atlantis
LAWSON – STRANGE p6.

Atlas
The three golden apples

Atonement. *See* **Penitence; Punishment; Regret**

Attila the conqueror
HAZELTINE – HERO p68-87

Atwater, Richard and Florence
Troubles with a penguin

Au Sung meets Kim Lee
ANDERSON – BOY p9-36

Aucassin and Nicolette
WESTWOOD – MEDIEVAL p99-109

Aucassin and Nicolette . . . Their difficult
romance
UNTERMEYER – FIRE. p198-206

The audacious kitten
MANNING – BEASTS p26-28

The August moon
McALPINE – JAPAN. p176-178

Augustine the thief
MEHDEVI – BUNGLING p69-83

Aükele and the water-of-life
WHEELER – HAWAII. p21-48

Aulaire, Edgar Parin D'
AULAIRE – NORSE p161.

Aulaire, Ingri Mortenson
AULARIE – NORSE p161.

The auld cailleach's curse
LEODHAS – TWELVE p71-87

Aung, Maung Htin
AUNG – KINGDOM p96.

"Aunt Effie's rhymes"
The clucking hen

Aunt Karin's chest
NYBLOM – WITCH p160-176

Aunt Misery
LOWE – LITTLE p64-66

Aunt Piety
BIRCH – CHINESE p113-122

Auntie, where are you going?
MY BOOK HOUSE v. 1 p128.

Aunts
The bird which laid diamonds
The golden twins
The great-aunt
The magic lute
The skunk in Tante Odette's oven
The talking cat
The three aunts
The wtich aunts

Aurora Borealis
The ice ship in the hot sea
Lights of the caribou
The milky way
The passing of Glooskap
The singing man

Austin, Mary
The fire bringer

Australia
See also **Aborigines**
The babymakers
Beereeun the miragemaker
The beginning of the Narran Lake
Biggoon and the little duck
Bilba and Mayra
The black-breasted magpie
The black swans
Bohra hunts the dark
Bohra the kangaroo
The Bora of Baiame
Bubber the giant brown-and-yellow-
snake
The dancing bird
The dark guest
Deegeenboya the soldier bird
Dinewan the emu and Goomble-
gubbon the turkey
Dinewan the emu and Wahm the crows
The dogs of Bahloo
Eerin the small gray owl
The finding of the Eleanba Wunda
The firemakers
The frog heralds
The frog that swallowed the ocean
The galah and Oola the lizard
Gaya-dari the platypus
Gheeger Gheeger the cold west wind
The goodoo of Wirreebilla
Goola-willeels the topknot pigeons

34

Australia (*Continued*)

Goolay-yali the pelican
Gooloo the magpie and the waroogas
Gwai-nee-bu the redbreast
How mussels were brought to the
creeks
How the sun was made
The iguana and the black snake
The iguana's poison bag
A legend of the flowers
Maya-mayi the seven sisters
Mrs. Wallaby Jones
The Moha Moha
The Mopoke and the moon
Mullian-ga the morning star
Narahdarn the bat
No flowers
Piggi-billa the porcupine
The rain bird
The rainmaker Wirinun
The right time to laugh
The southern cross
The stone frogs
The wagtail and the rainbow
Wahn the crow Wirinun
Wallu-barl the bark lizard
Wayamba the turtle
Wayamba the turtle and Woggoon the
turkey
Weedah the mockingbird
Where the frost comes from
The Wi-oombeens and Piggi-billa
The wonders seen by Wurrunna
Wurrunna's trip to the sea

−**Arnhem Land**
The river flows full through the
sky land

, **East**
The bean trees that are sacred to
the witches
The crane who taught the birds to
dance and make corroberee
Dhungura-ngarian: where the peli-
can danced
The drifting canoe
The eel, the man, and the cave
The haunted lagoon
He who lives in a mountain
How people got fire
How the black snake got its fangs
How the little black wren got its
red feathers
The kaola bear and the tribal laws
The man who could see everything
Nooligah and the fire
Nooligah who caused his brother
to die
The old women who were turned
into birds

The origin of the platypus
The people who lived near a
mountain
The place of the death adders
The possums, the man, and the
tree
The satin bird
The spirit of the waterhole
The three brothers
The ti-trees
The two boys and the sacred carpet
snake
The two dogs−Burrajahnee and
Inneroogun
The witch who lived in a cave
The woman and the sacred Bora
ring
The young man and the giant
The young man and the kangaroo

−**Euahlayis**
How the sun was made

−**Gumaity**
How crane got his long beak

Austria
The duty that was not paid
The hermit and the devil
How Urseli became a princess
It's already paid
The luck boy of Toy Valley
Momus the mocker
The Nuremberg stove
Once in, never out again

−**Salzburg**
The penitent governor

−**Tyrol**
The birch twig
The boyhood of a hero
The crowning of a king
The devil and the seamstress
Dietrich defends the snow queen
Dietrich is knighted
Emperor of Rome
King Adder
King Laurin goes awooing
The making of a hero
The skull
Swift-as-the-wind, Hold fast
and Hard-as-iron

Authors
A boy in Russia
Fjords and mountain peaks
Old Noll
A Spanish hero
The ugly duckling

, **American**
Life in Concord

Authors, American (*Continued*)

The lonely boy
A rover in the Catskills
'Way down South in Dixie

, English
The boy of Newstead Abbey
The little girl of Griff House
London streets
Watching Vanity Fair go by

, Scottish
The Laird of Abbotsford

Author's note
VO-DINH — TOAD p9-13

Authun and the bear
JONES — SCAND. p143-152

Automobiles
See also types of automobiles
The big street in the big city

Autumn
Beaver moon
The boy in the land of shadows
Harvest moon
Hunters' moon
November's party
Rainbow and the autumn leaves
The scarlet maple

Autumn
BUDD — FULL p50-65

Aviation
Good or bad?
Wilbur Wright and Orville Wright

Avocados
Brother Breeze and the pear tree

Awake, O north wind
MY BOOK HOUSE v. 2 p79.

Awls
Old Mother Twitchett

Axes
Boots and his brothers
The cerval's secret name
Changing luck
The clumber pup
The do-all ax
The honest woodman
I don't know where and I don't know
what
Iwa the crafty one
The King of Araby's daughter
Little Rosa and Long Leda
The man who was only three inches
tall
The master-maid
Paul Bunyan swings his axe
Paul Bunyan's cornstalk
The peasant and the watermen
The shepherd's nosegay
Sir Gawain and the green knight
Sky bright axe/ Paul Bunyan
The tale of the tail of a bear

, Golden
The golden axe

Aye-Mee and the mermaid
OMAN — ESKIMO p27-32

Azaleas
Indian legends of shrubs in our
gardens

B

Baa, baa, black sheep
  MY BOOK HOUSE v. 1 p29.

Baba Yaga
  WILLIAMS – ROUND p81-89
  WYNDHAM – TALES p76-87

Baby Yaga and the little girl with the
kind heart
  HOKE – WITCHES p19-30
  HOPE-SIMPSON – CAVAL. p62-74

Babbit, Ellen C.
  Why the bear sleeps all winter

The babbling reed-warbler
  ELLIOT – WHERE p10-15

The babe Moses
  MY BOOK HOUSE v. 3 p156-160

Babe Ruth, the home-run of baseball
  MY BOOK HOUSE v. 7 p144a-144b

Babel, Tower of
  He who bound the dragons of chaos

Babies
  The aged infant
  Betty Stogs and the Little People
  Betty Stogs' baby
  The child of death
  The copper pan
  Dance, little baby, dance up high!
  Fate and the faggot gatherer
  Fenisana
  The five swallow sisters
  The girl without arms
  Golden bracelets, golden anklets
  The golem and the bridal pair
  The hound Gelert
  How many days has my baby to play?
  How raven found the daylight
  How the coconut tree came to be
  The invisible baby
  The king and brahmin's child
  A kiss from the beautiful Fiorita
  The legend of Llangorse Lake
  The leopard and the antelope
  Little Stormy
  The magic mountain
  Manstin, the rabbit
  The mistress of fire
  Momotaro
  Momotaro, the peach boy

The monkey nursemaid
Naming the baby
The princess of light
Pwyll and Pryderi (2) The birth of
  Pryderi
Rock-a-bye, baby
Sleep, baby, sleep
The snail Choja
The snake prince
Soonjmaya
Storks and babies
The story of Zal
The tale the crofter told
The test
The Three Fates
The three golden hairs of Grandad Sol
The three wishes
Ubazakura
Which is the greater?
Why lions live in the forest
The wonder of Skoupa
Written in the stars

The baboon and the hare
  HEADY – JAMBO p54-59

Baboon skins
  BERGER – BLACK p124-134

Baboons
  The ant and the tower to God
  Dinner with the tota
  Fenisana
  How a boy got a baboon
  How baboons came into the world
  The hunter's child
  I went to the animal fair
  The jackals and the tiger
  The jackal's lawsuit
  Mapandangare, the great baboon
  The marriage feast
  Old Noah
  Rabbit at the water hole
  Rabbit, elephant, and hippopotamus
  Tortoise and the baboon

Babrius
  Good advice

Baby bye, here's a fly
  MY BOOK HOUSE v. 1 p90.

The baby camel
  MASEY – STORIES p12-15

Baby carriages
   The invisible baby

The baby mosque
   KELSEY – ONCE p95-99

The baby that was sold
   WILLIAMS – OLD p278-284

The babymakers
   PARKER – AUSTRALIAN p49-55

Babylon
   He who bound the dragons of Chaos
   How many miles to Babylon?
   The lost gift
   Pyramus and Thisbe . . . The mulberry
   tree
   Shadrack, Meshack, and Abednego
   . . . The fiery furnace
   Tiamat

Bacchus
   The golden touch; the king who
   worshipped gold

The bachelors and the python
   BURTON – MAGIC p75-77

Bacon, Josephine Daskam
   The sleepy song

Bacon, Peggy
   About the good American witch

Bacon
   The mill at the bottom of the sea
   Why the sea is salt

The bad baronets
   HOPE-SIMPSON – CAVAL. p91-94

The bad boy and the good dog
   CARPENTER – DOGS p95-100

Bad luck cannot be arrested. *See* Good
luck and bad luck

Bad luck put into the bag
   LEACH – LUCK p37-40

The bad prince
   FEINSTEIN – FOLK p68-72

The bad-tempered wife
   DURHAM – TIT p11-16

The badger and the boatmen
   PRATT – MAGIC unp.

The badger and the magic fan
   SAKADE – JAPAN p73-77

Badgers
   The accomplished and strange tea-
   kettle
   Cliff dweller
   The crackling mountain
   The dancing teapot
   Glooskap's country
   The good fortune kettle
   The good-luck teakettle
   The hare, badger, monkey, and otter
   Kachi Kachi mountain
   The magic teakettle
   Mainly in moonlight
   A message in a bottle
   The quail and the badger
   Reynard the fox
   Three-fingered Ike's story
   Trust your friends

The badger's gratitude
   BUCK – FAIRY p91-95

Badikan and Khan Boghu
   NAHMAD – PEASANT p68-76

Baffin Island
   Udleqdjun in the sky

The bag of lies
   PRIDHAM – GIFT p124-129

Bagdad
   The Caliph stork, told by Selim
   Baruch, the stranger
   Day dreaming
   The fortunes of Säid
   The half-pint jinni
   Palace in Bagdad
   The royal geese
   Sindbad the sailor
   The story of Caliph stork
   The tale of Caliph stork
   Three silly schoolmasters

Baglan, Saint
   Eight leaves of story (3) Baglan the
   builder

Baglan the builder. *See* Eight leaves of
story (3) Baglan the builder

Bagpipes
   Gathering song of Donuil Dhu
   The house that lacked a bogle
   The maid of the waves

Bagpipes (*Continued*)

The meal mill at Eathie
Old pipes and the dryad
The Pied Piper of Hamelin
The piper of Sutherland
The ploughboy poet
The silver chanter of the MacCrimmons
There was a piper had a cow
The young piper, the Little People of
Ireland

Bags. *See* **Sacks**

Bahamas
Jack who could do anything
Smart working man, foolish boss man
Why elephant & whale live where
they do

Bahmoo and the frog
WILLIAMS – OLD p99-105

Bahmoo rides the wrong frog
JAGENDORF – KING p139-141

Bahram and the snake prince
MEHDEVI – PERSIAN p3-21

Bahri of the beauty spot
EKREM – TURKISH p53-60

Bailey, Carolyn Sherwin
The chipmunk who chattered too
much
How maple sugar came
The little rabbit who wanted red wings
The nutcracker and sugardolly stories
The story of Li'l Hannibal

Bailey, Margery
Bergamot

Bailiffs
The bridge of St. Cloud
The devil and the bailiff
"Good day, fellow!" "Axe handle!"

Bain, Robert Nisbet
The straw ox
Thomas Berennikov

Bajan Budiman, the sharpshooter
COURLANDER – KANT. p123-128

Baker, Augusta
The horned woman

Baker, Elizabeth W.
Sonny-boy Sim

Baker, Margaret
The guinea pig's tail

Bakers
See also **Bread; Cakes.** etc.
Blow, wind, blow, and go, mill, go!
The cat and the mouse
A dozen is thirteen
The enchanted island
The four abdallahs
The great scare
Ingratitude is the way of the world
Max and Moritz
The old witch
Pat-a-cake, pat-a-cake, baker's man!
Rub-a-dub-dub
The son of the baker of Barra
The story of big Paul Bunyan
The three bugganes, II, III
Who am I?
The woman who flummoxed the
fairies

The baker's daughter
WILLIAMS – FAIRY p103-105

A (The) baker's dozen
JAGENDORF – UPSTATE p28-33
RASKIN – TALES p9-13

The baker's neighbor
HARDENDORFF – FROG'S p29-39

The Bakki brothers
BOUCHER – MEAD p68-73

Balaton, Lake of
The tale of the Balaton

Balconies
The flying angel

The bald old man
INS-SOB – FOLK p191

Bald pate
See also Baldpate
MANNING – RED p23-30

Balder, the god of light
AUCLAIRE – NORSE p54-55

Baldness
Anansi and the old hag
Arap Sang and the cranes
Baldpate
The bettle's hairpiece
The boy who would eat lobsters
A father-in-law and his son-in-law
How spider got a bald head

Baldness (*Continued*)

In Coney Island by the sea
Keloğlan and God's greatness
Keloğlan and the lucky exchanges
Keloğlan and the magic hairs
Keloğlan and the magician
Keloğlan and the ooh-genie
Keloğlan and kindhearted
Madschun
Melisande
The wrong man

Baldpate
HAMPDEN – GYPSY p147-154

Baldur the bright
GARNER – GOBLINS p201-208

Baldwin, James
A cause of war
A Roland for an Oliver
A young prince named Siegfried

Bali (island)
A boy in the island of Bali
The messenger

Baliol, John (Toom-Tabard), King of Scotland
The tale of the riddle sent to Bruce

Ball games
See also types of ball-games
The games of Tlachtli
How bat won the ball game
How the animals made wings for bat and flying squirrel

The ballad of east and west
MY BOOK HOUSE v. 9 p129-133

The ballad of Lord Lovell
JOHNSON – WHAT p154-155

Ballads
See also **Folk songs**
Alison Gross
Earl Mar's daughter
The gay goss-hawk
Kempe Owyne
The Lochmaben harper
The sheriff complains to the king
The tale of Bonnie Baby Livingston
The tale of Dick o' the cow
The tale of Lang Johnnie Mor
The tale of the Earl of Mar's daughter
The tale of the famous flower of Servingmen
The tale of the heir of Linne
The tale of the knight and the shepherd lass
The tale of the lay of the Amadhain Mhor
The tale of the lay of the Smithy
The tale of the Lochmaben harper
Young Charlotte

, **American**
John Henry, the big steel-drivin' man
Old Noah

, **British**
Adam Bell, Clym of the Clough, and William of Cloudesley
Alison Gross
Childe Rowland
The crafty farmer
The heir of Linne
Introduction (MANNING – ENGLISH)
King Estmere
King Orfeo
Tam Lin
Thomas the rhymer

, **English**
The birth of Robin Hood
The king and Robin Hood
Little John and the Sheriff of Nottingham
Robin Hood and Sir Richard at the lee
Robin Hood and the monk
The sheriff's shooting match
Sir Richard at the lee and the abbot
A tale of Robin Hood
There are twelve months
When woods awake
Young Bekie

, **Scottish**
Hind horn
Hynd horn
The young Lord of Lorn

–**Yugoslavian**
Marko, the champion of Serbian liberty

Ballet. *See* **Dancers & Dancing**

Balloons
The daring prince
That is why he was always called Pooh
What's the news of the day

Balls
John the bear
The little white cat
The man who sold magic
The red-maned horse
Roll it, bowl it
Sally's blue ball
The task of Prince Kurumamochi
The task of the chief councillor
Otomo-no-Miyuki
The white cat

, Copper
The well o' the world's end

, Golden
The boy who taught the fairies
tears
Elidorus in fairyland
The frog prince
The golden ball
The grateful prince
The silent princess
The wild man

, Magic
The lady's quest
The magic ball
The white sword of light

, Silver
The three silver balls

Balsam trees
The origin of the balsam tree
The stone of victory

Balys, Jonas, trans.
A ghost at the door

Bamboo Trees
The black cat of Cotabato
The child in the bamboo tree
Datu Omar and the fairy
From tiger to Anansi
How Master Thumb defeated the sun
How the pig got his snout
Legend of the first Filipinos
The moon raised the sky
The old man who cut bamboo
The princess of light
The three sons
Tiger lily and the dragon
The turtle prince

Banana Trees
Fire magic and the mud hen
The magic banana
The old humpback
Pakpai and Boto
Three magic charms
The three sons

The turtle and the monkey share a
tree
Why the bananas belong to the monkey

Bandalee
SHERLOCK — ANANSI p47-57

Bandits
See also **Thieves and thievery**
The caravan ends
Dumb Juan and the bandits
Eppelin of Gailingen
The horse and the eighteen bandits
How three pilgrims called Ilya to the
rescue of Kiev
Ilya of Murom and Nightingale the
robber
Jesse James
Karl the Great and the robber
Kernel
The lads who met the highwaymen
The lost payroll at Wickenburg
The magician and the bandits
Panch Villa's lost head
Railroad Bill
The rescue of Fatima, told by Lezah
The robber baron . . . and the bat
The tale of Dick o' the cow
The three journeys of Ilya of Murom
Vassily and Curly Head the brigand

Bang-whang-whang
MY BOOK HOUSE v. 1 p185.

Bangs, John Kendrick
The little elf

Bani Hilal: A tribe is born
DAVIS — TEN p3-11

Banishment. *See* **Exile**

The banishment of Diab
DAVIS — TEN p93-113

The banishment of Rāma
GRAY — INDIA'S p96-107

Bankers
Grasp all, lose all
A long-bow story
Upa and her admirers

Banks with binks
LEACH — SOUP p31-32

Bannerman, Helen
Little Black Sambo

Bannockburn
MY BOOK HOUSE v. 10 p29.

Bannocks
    The fox and the little bannock
    The three sons of Gorla
    The wee bannock

Banquets. *See* **Dinners; Feasts**

Banshees
    The three banshees
    The three brothers and the treacle
        toffee

The banshee's birthday treat
    GREEN – LEPRECHAUN p96-101

The banyan deer
    ARBUTHNOT – TIME p151-152
    ROSS – BURIED p81-87

Banyan trees
    The age of the partridge
    Chu Cuoi's trip to the moon
    The crow in the banyan tree
    The mongoose, the owl, the cat and
        mouse
    The mouse surrounded
    The old man and his fishing line
    The traveller and the tiger

The baobab tree
    HEADY – WHEN p59-61

Baobab trees
    The children who lived in a tree house
    A test of skill

Baptisms
    See also **Christenings**
    Anansi and the crabs
    Fairy caskets
    Young Paul

Baptistries
    The marvelous doors, the Little People
        of Italy

Barbados
    The house that strong boy built

Barbers
    First adventures
    The fortune of the poet's son
    Goat's ears
    I am not from Sarajevo
    The jackal, the barber and the Brahmin
        who had seven daughters
    The jackal with the torn nose

The king and the barber
    King March has horse's ears
    The king who wanted a beautiful wife
    The magic mirror
    March has horse's ears
    March's ears
    Ooka and the barbered beast
    The puss's tail
    The story of the haunted jars
    The three brothers
    Toontoony and the barber
    Tsar Trajan's ears
    An unhappy lord
    The wrong man

Bardiello
    MANNING – GIANNI p31-42

Bards. *See* **Minstrels**

Bargaining. *See* **Agreements**

Barges
    Life in Concord
    The rescue of Fatima, told by Lezah

Barham, Richard Harris
    The hand of glory

Bark. *See* **Trees–Bark**

Barker's knee
    MANNING – PETER p183-193

Barley
    The beardless one
    Hantsjc and the remarkable beast

Barney, Joshua
    A boy on the high seas

Barns
    Cheating the devil
    The stone owl's nest

Barnum, Phineas T.
    The adventures of General Tom Thumb
    The circus man
    The greatest show on earth

The barnyard
    MY BOOK HOUSE v. 1 p114-115

Barons & baronets
    The angry baron
    The bad baronets
    The devil and the pit

Barons and baronets (*Continued*)

Fiddler John and the devil
A game of dice
The hairs of the baron's head
The man who sold magic
The nightingale
The peasant and the baron
Scandalous affairs of a baronet and
a tavern maid
Tit for tat
The werewolf

The baron's haughty daughter
RANKE – GERMANY p127-129

Barques
The three waves

Barr, Mathias
Moon, so round and yellow

The barrel decree
BARASH – GOLDEN p69-71

The barrel of water
ELLIOT – WHERE p122-127

The barrel-organ
FARJEON – LITTLE p116-119

Barrels
From Brownie to boggart
The golden bird
Let's steal the moon
Willie's bad night

The barren stones
SPICER – LONG p70-71

Barter. *See* **Agreements**

Baruch, Dorothy
The elevator

Baš Čelik
CURCIJA – YUGOSLAV p184-210

Baseball
Babe Ruth, the home-run of baseball
Casey at the bat
Casey's comeback

Bash Tchelik
GARNER – GOBLINS p63-75

The bashful prince
MICHAEL – PORTUGUESE p105-111

Basia, the babbler
BORSKI – GOOD p41-45

The basilisk, king serpent
McHARGUE – BEASTS p45-51

Basilisks
King of the serpents

The basket-maker's donkey
HAMPDEN – GYPSY p97-99

Baskets & basket-weavers
Dwarf stories
How coyote brought back people
after the flood
Jonnikin and the flying basket
The king of the wood
The little sticky rice basket
The magic peas
The leprechaun in the basket
Old Bluebeard
Three magic charms
The three wishes
The tongue-cut sparrow
Upa and her admirers

Baskets in a little cart
MANNING – DRAGONS p95-102

Bass viols
Diddle, diddle on a bass viol

Bassoons
A musical visit to fairyland

Bast (cat goddess)
The cat of Bubastis

Bastianelo
HAVILAND – ITALY p55-66

The bat
DEUTSH – MORE p7-10

The bat and the eagle
COBBLE – WEMBI p109-111

The bat and the turtle
COBBLE – WEMBI p51-53

Bat, bat, come under my hat
MY BOOK HOUSE v. 1 p45.

The bat who belonged to no one
BURTON – MAGIC p52-53

Baths
The elephant's bathtub
The giant beanstalk
The goblins at the bath house
The miller and the fairies

Batim the horse
HAMPDEN – GYPSY p89-95

Bats
The battle of the birds and the fish
The bragging bat
The courting of the bat, the spider
and the beetle
The crystal bowl
The friendly frog
How bat won the ball game
How the animals made wings for
bat and flying squirrel
How the bat caught friendship
with the moon
It's perfectly true!
Kantjil brings the elephants to heel
The legend of the Prince Ahmed
Al Kamel
A lesson for the bat
Narahdarn the bat
The right time to laugh
The tale of bat
Tippity Witchit's Hallowe'en
Why bat flies alone
Why the bat flies at night

Bats
MY BOOK HOUSE v. 1 p211.

The bat's choice
BULATKIN – EURASIAN p111-113

The battle
MANNING – GIANNI p95-102

A battle and a wedding
DAVIS – TEN p28-36

The battle at White Cliff house
RUSHMORE – DANCING p35-50

The battle between the birds and the
beasts
CARPENTER – AFRICAN p87-92

A battle nobody won
THOMPSON – HAWAII p15-19

The battle of Eghal Shillet
See also Nawasi goes to war
COURLANDER – FIRE p121-126

The battle of Gavra
SUTCLIFF – HIGH p170-178

The battle of Ichi-no-Tani
McALPINE – JAPAN. p54-65

The battle of Kossovo
CURCIJA – HEROES p29-54

The battle of Mishar
CURCIJA – HEROES p171-173

The battle of Nembro Wood
LAURITZEN – BLOOD p88-108

The battle of Roncesvalles
MAYNE – HEROES p127-143

The battle of the animals
KAULA – AFRICAN p101-109

The battle of the birds and the fish
GREY – SOUTH (1) p18-23

The battle of the buffaloes
LEEUW – INDO. p135-139

The battle of the bulls
O'FAOLÁIN – IRISH p84-87

The battle of the firefly and the apes
MY BOOK HOUSE v. 3 p59-61

The battle of the frogs and the mice
MY BOOK HOUSE v. 4 p104-112

The battle of the Nile
JOHNSON – WHAT p160.

The battle on the Isle of Camphor
GAER – FABLES p105-107

Battle songs
Bannockburn

The battle that tilted the sea
HOLDING – SKY p24-38

The battle with Skuld. See King Hrolf
and the bear's son

Battle with the Sockdolager
FELTON – NEW p59-76

Battles
Adam Bell, Clym of the Clough, and
William of Cloudesley
Arnold Winkelried
Beowulf and Grendel
Bernardo and the red knight
The brave three hundred
Cnut and Edmund
The country of the mice
Cuchulain, the hound of Ulster

Battles (*Continued*)

Dearmid and Grania
The death of Roland
The defeat of the Fomorians
The fall of Serbia
Fionn's journey to Lochlan
The first attack
General Chang's strategy
The ghost of Haniesh MacDonald,
  the fool of the family
Gudrun
The holy relic of Bannockburn
The hostel of the quicken
The house of the rowan tree
Ivo Senkovich and Aga of Ribnik
Kian and the children of Tuireann
King Hrolf and the bear's son
The knights of the silver shield
The last battle
Lyonnesse
The maiden of Kossovo
Marko, the champion of Serbian
  liberty
Njord, Frey and Freya
Old Meg, the witch
The origin of the balsam tree
Prince Murko's journey
Prince Prigio and the firedrake
The pursuit of the hard man
Queen Crane
Ragnar Lodbrok and his sons
Ragnarokk, the destiny of the gods
Rāma's conquest of Rāvana
The Ramayana
Revolt
The riddle of the black knight
Rustem and his rose-colored steed
The sack of Troy
Saxons
The silver penny
Sir Bevis of Hampton
The tale of a foolish brother and of a
  wonderful bush
Thor's combat with Rungnir
The three teeth of the king
The Valkyries and Valhalla
The victory of the buffalo
The war between the lion and the
  cricket
Yellow hair: George Armstrong
  Custer
Young Conall of Howth

A bauchan in the family
LEODHAS – SEA p179-200

Baucis and Philemon
ARBUTHNOT – TIME p226-227

Baucis and Philemon . . . The reward of
hospitality
UNTERMEYER – FIRE. p95-98

Baum L. Frank
The wizard of Oz. The cowardly lion

Bay leaf
The powers of plants and trees to
  protect against witches

The bay-tree maiden
MANNING – DAMIAN p61-66

Bayamey (god)
The frog that swallowed the ocean

Bazaars
A dinar for a donkey
Donkey, mind your mother!
The quivering needle

Be careful!
LEACH – LUCK p93-94

Be careful what you say
CURČIJA – YUGOSLAV p120-122

Beaches
The devil's apprentice
The fisherman and his soul
King Canute on the seashore
Little sister and the Zimwi
The sand-carrier crab
A sea-song from the shore
When I was down beside the sea
The white horse of Volendam

The beacon light
MINCIELI – TALES p101-106

Beads
The first mosquito
How kingfisher got his necklace
How the moon and the stars came to
  be
Overhead on a salt marsh
Podhu and Aruwa
The secret of Kaboniyan
Three unscrupulous men

Beagle, Peter S.
TOLKIEN – READER p xvi

Beals, Katherine M.
The mignonette fairy

The bean pot
HEADY – JAMBO p34-38

46

The bean tree
   MANNING – GIANNI p119-126

The bean trees that are sacred to the witches
   NORLEDGE – ABORIGINAL p19.

Beans
   Anansi's hat-shaking dance
   The ass's promise
   The flying Dutchman
   Giacco and his bean
   The giant beanstalk
   The hare, badger, monkey and otter
   How bean got his stripe
   Jack and the beanstalk
   Kalulu and the elephant
   King Bean
   The king who was a gentleman
   Naba Zid-Wende
   Straw, bean, and coal
   The straw, the coal and the bean
   The three gluttons and the hunter
   Three times and out

The bear and the fox who made a bet
   ASBJÖRNSEN – NORW. p120-121

The bear and the wild cat
   CREDLE – TALL p27-29

The bear and the two rascals
   LA FONTAINE – FABLES p12-13

Bear, fox and man
   RANKE – GERMANY p19-20

Bear Hunt. *See* Dreams

The bear in the black hat
   CREDLE – TALL p55-63

The bear in the coach
   WILLIAMS – FAIRY p169.

The bear-maiden. *See* Little bear

The bear says north
   FILLMORE – SHEPHERD'S p69-71

The bear went over the mountain
   WITHERS – I SAW p42-43

The bear woman
   OMAN – ESKIMO p56-63

The beardless one
   MANNING – DAMIAN p155-164

The beardless, the lame, and the one-eyed thief
   NAHMAD – PEASANT p45-52

Beards
   Bluebeard
   The crumb in the beard
   Foolish kings
   The green-bearded king
   The king and the wise man
   King Kojata
   Kokata
   Old Bluebeard
   The quest for Olwen (4) Fulfilling the tasks 4/ The Beard of Dillus the bearded
   Rhitta of the beards
   Ruddy-my-beard
   The silly fellow who sold his beard

Bears
   An adventure with a bear
   All my lambkins and all my bear cubs
   Authun and the bear
   The big warm dog
   The blue belt
   The boy and the water-sprite
   Buh fox's number nine shoes
   Brave rabbit and bug with the golden wings
   The bun
   The canoe in the rapids
   The cat and the fox
   The cat on the dovrefell
   Chi and Yi
   The children and the bear
   Clever–clever–clever
   The coyote and the bear
   The cranberry feast
   Dan-Gun, first King of Korea
   Daughter and stepdaughter
   The day Tuk became a hunter
   Dream behind bars
   East of the sun and west of the moon
   Ermine and the hunter
   The escape of the animals
   The Eskimo widow . . . And her strange son
   The farmer, the bear, and the fox
   Fire, a story of the Alabama Indians
   The fishnet and the bear
   Five in a glove
   The flight with the Wendigo
   Fox and raven steal the moon
   The fox and the bear
   The fox and the hare
   The fox as shepherd
   From a moral alphabet
   The gardener and the bear
   A girl and a stepmother

Bears (*Continued*)

Goldilocks and the three bears
The good son
The grizzly and the rattlesnake men
A horned goat
How and why: Why the bear waddles
  when he walks
How Brer Rabbit met Brer Tar-Baby
How chipmunk got his stripes
How death came into the world (2)
How Sketco tricked the grizzly
How the birds came to have their
  many colors
How the long-tailed bear lost his tail
How the robin's breast became red
The hunger time
The hunting cat
Ivan the fool
The jackal and the bear
John the bear
Johnny and Tommy and the bear
Johnny-cake
Kagssagssuk, the homeless boy who
  became a strong man
Kunikdjuaq, a bear story of the Inuit
The lily and the bear
Little bear
The little house
Lucky Rose Tuttle
The man who rode the bear
The marriage of Tom and the vixen
The mermaid and the boy
Mr. Samson cat
Mittens the cat
More south than south, more north
  than north
Mowgli's brothers
The Nandi bear
Netchillik and the bear
The Northern lights
The nut branch
Of a tailor and a bear
The old bear in the tree
Old Johnny Appleseed
An old Korean story
Old wall eyes
The old woman and the bear
One day, one night
The one who wasn't afraid
Pecos Bill, the cowboy
Pleiades
Pooh goes visiting and gets into a
  tight place
Preziosa, the she-bear
(The) quartet
The rabbit and the bear
Rabbit and the grain buyers
Rabbit and the Indian chief
Radowid
Rainbow and the autumn leaves

The raven and the grizzly bear
The red swan
The Rehepapp and Vanapagan
Reynard the fox
Roommates
Scrapefoot
The she-bear
The snow-queen
Snow-white
Snow-white and Rose-red
Sonny-boy Sim
The stars above: Pursuit of the bear
The story of the three bears
The straw ox
The strong boy
The struggle between the wolf and
  the fox
The tailor's apprentice . . . And the
  bear
The teddy bears' picnic
"That is why he was always called
  Pooh"
The theft of fire
The three bears
To your good health
The travellers and the bear
Two brothers
Udleqdjun in the sky
Uncle Ed is chased by a bear
Uncle Mitya's horse
The ungrateful bear
Wahconah
The water-sprite and the bear
The waters beneath: the great river
  monster
The white bear
White-bear-King-Valemon
Whitebear Whittington
Why bear sleeps all winter
Why bears eat meat
Why grizzly bears walk on all fours
Why the bear cannot play the kantele
Why the bear is stumpy-tailed
Why the bear sleeps all winter
Why there are four seasons in the year
Winnie-the-Pooh
The woman who raised a bear as a son
The woodman and the fox
The wren and the bear
—**Skins**
  The hideless bear
  A most peculiar bear hide
  Uncle Ed's unusual bear hide

—**Tails**
  The fish thief
  How the long-tailed bear lost his
    tail
  Reynard and Bruin
  Why the bear has a stumpy tail
  Why the bear is stumpy-tailed
  Why the bear's tail is short

The bears
   HEADY – TALES p67-74

The bear's head
   LEEKLEY – WORLD p58-63

Bears in the sky
   GRINGHUIS – GIANTS p27-38

The bear's son comes to court. *See* King
Hrolf and the bear's son

The beast
   GARNER – GOBLINS p209.

The beast with a single horn
   JACOBSEN – FIRST p28-29

Beasts. *See* **Animals: Monsters: etc.**

Beasts of the zodiac
   JACOBSEN – FIRST p64-65

Beatrice
   The man who lived in the world of
   dreams

Beatrice . . . And the statue
   UNTERMEYER – FIRE. p243-251

Beaumains . . . The knightly kitchen-boy
   UNTERMEYER – FIRE. p182-188

The beautiful blue jay
   SPELLMAN – BEAUT. p3-7

Beautiful doll
   IVES – TALES p65-70

The beautiful feathers
   ARNOTT – TALES p85-93

The beautiful princess
   MICHAEL – PORTUGUESE p712-178

The beautiful weaver and the golden shell
   TOOR – GOLDEN p143-150

A beautiful young woman as the head of
the family
   HSIEH – CHINESE p58-62

Beauty
   The adventures of Iain Direach
   All things beautiful
   All things bright and beautiful
   Baboon skins

The beardless one
The chafers and the dove
The cow maiden
The crow-Peri
Cupid and Psyche . . . The trial of love
The daughter of the dwarf
The delicate daughter
The eagle and the owl
Echo and Narcissus: the chattering
   nymph and the proud youth
The enchanted castle in the sea
Endymion . . . The sleeping shepherd
The fairy of Hawili Falls
The first of May
Flash-of-the-paddle and Listener-to-
   the-heavenly voice
The flower of beauty
For the love of a woman
The foretelling
Frey and Gerd, the jotun maiden
The gift to the hummingbird
The golden horse
Granny Shelock
He wins who waits
How Sigurd awoke Brynhild
I don't know where and I don't know
   what
The innkeeper's daughter
Kabadaluk: the little Arab boy
Kilmeny
The King of Araby's daughter
The king who wanted a beautiful wife
Lady Eleanore's mantle
The lady of the linden tree
The land beyond the fire
Lazy bout of a plant
The loathly lady
The lucky serving maid
The maiden who did not get her wish
Mellitot and Iolanda
Oraggio and Bianchinetta
The peacock bridegroom
The peacock, the turkey and the
   goose
The plain princess
The proud princess
The return of Diab
Ricky of the tuft
Ricky with a tuft
Riquet with the quiff
The seven proud sisters
The seven Simons
The sleeping beauty
The sleeping beauty in the wood
Socrates . . . The cup of hemlock
Sweet peas and Grecian urns
Swift things are beautiful
The tale of a Pakistan parrot
The tale of Bonnie Baby Livingston
The tale of the famous flower of
   Servingmen

Beauty (*Continued*)

Teen-ager
Tehi Tegi
The ugly duckling
Unanana and the elephant
The welcome
The white dove of the city of the
swinging gate
Why no one lends his beauty

The beauty and her gallant
MANNING – GHOSTS p101-102

Beauty and the beast
See also The serpent and the grape-
grower's daughter
ARBUTHNOT – TIME p105-113
BAMBERGER – FIRST p67-71
BERGER – BLACK p55-67
HAVILAND – FRANCE p38-59
JACOBS – EUROPE. p34-41
PERRAULT – COMPLETE p115-134
SIDEMAN – WORLD'S p275-299

Beaver moon
BUDD – FULL p61-65

Beavers
The flood
Frogs in the moon
The giant who loved adventure
Glooskap's country
Hiawatha's childhood
How beaver got his fine fur
How the beaver came to build their
homes in the water
Other island
Rabbit and the Indian chief

–**Tails**
How the beaver lost the hair on
his tail

Bech, the ambitious quail
BOWES – BIRD p19-23

Bechstein, Ludwig
Fish with the rolls
The kitten and the knitting needles
The never never land
The old wizard and the children

Bechstein, Ludwig
BECHSTEIN – FAIRY p203-205

The beckoning cat
PRATT – MAGIC unp.

Becky's garden
JAGENDORF – NEW p67-71

The bed
BELPRÉ – TIGER p33-35

The bedbug, the louse, and the flea
INS-SOB – FOLK p36.

Bedding in one's ear
SEKI – FOLKTALES p197.

Bedouins. *See* **Arabia–Tribes–Bani Hilal**

The bed's stead
LEACH – SOUP p38-41

Beds
The duped giant
Getting out of bed right
The lost prince
Other people's beds
Saint Margery Daw
The wonderful bed

Beside visit. *See* Deaf men and their
answers

The bee-hunter and the oozie
AUNG – KINGDOM p66-70

The bee man and the boundary man
JAGENDORF – NEW p195-201

The bee on the cap
ĆURĆIJA – YUGOSLAV p110-111

The bee, the harp, the mouse and the
bum-clock
HAVILAND – IRELAND p3-25

The bee, the mouse and the bum-clock
MY BOOK HOUSE v. 2 p155-162

The bee tree
HEADY – JAMBO p29-33

Beech trees
The giant of the brown beech wood
The King of Araby's daughter
A message in a bottle
The whispering giant

The beef tongue of Orula
U.N. – RIDE p257-258

The beekeeper and the bewitched hare
LEODHAS – THISTLE p106-118

Beer
The boy with the beer keg
The girl and the crocodile

50

Beer (*Continued*)

The heather beer
Ra and his children
The secret of heather-ale
Six sillies
The tale of the two brothers

Beereeun the miragemaker
PARKER – AUSTRALIAN p192-200

Bees
The ant and the yellow jacket
The battle of the animals
The brook song
The butterfly's ball
Eight leaves of story (3) Baglan the
  builder
The fairyland of science
The fly and the bee
The fruits of health
The goat who couldn't sneeze
Grandfather tells some tales
The honeybee bride
The hornets and the honeybees
How confusion came among the
  animals
How doth the little busy bee
How the bee got his bumble
The imposter
Johnny and the three goats
Kantjil and the monkey business
The king who was a gentleman
A legend of the flowers
The little black men and the honey-
  bees
Lyonesse
The man who bought a dream
The mermaid and the boy
Mogo, Pogo, and Wogo
The nutcracker and the sugardolly stories
The old woman and the thief
Over in the meadow
The rooster and the sultan
The sad, sorry sister
The servant who took the place of his
  master
The skinned goat
The song of the bee
The story of big Paul Bunyan
Sum-m, sum-m, sum-m!
"That is why he was always called
  Pooh"
Three tests for the prince
Tiger story, Anansi story
The wicked Mazimuzimu
The wise king and the little bee
–Wings
  The beardless one

The bees
CATHON – PERHAPS p85.

The bees and the drones
GREEN – BIG p178-179

Bees in the bonnets in New Jersey
JAGENDORF – UPSTATE p112-116

Beeswax
How the first horse was made

The beetle and a drop of honey
TURNBULL – FAIRY p136-150

The beetle and the paca
CARPENTER – SOUTH p108-113

Beetles
The adventures of a water baby
The bee, the mouse, and the bum-clock
The butterfly's ball
The courting of the bat, the spider and
  the beetle
The fairyland of science
The flea
How the Brazilian beetles got their
  gorgeous coats
Thumbelina
The unsmiling princess
The wise ant
The young gentleman and the tiger

The beetle's hairpiece
COURLANDER – PEOPLE p46-49

The beggar and the rice
WITHERS – I SAW p119.

The beggar in the blanket
GRAHAM – BEGGAR p11-21

Beggars
Any more food?
The armless maiden
The baker's daughter
The best wish
The blue belt
A boy and a beggar
Brothers and friends
The cat and the dog
The cats
The fortunate shoemaker
Goblin gold
Godfather death
The good judge
Graadonner
Graylegs
Hind horn

Beggars (*Continued*)

The Hoca and Allah's son-in-law
How Flint-face lost his name
How the miser turned into a monkey
The insatiable beggar
Judge not the vessel
The kind caliph and the horse thief
The king and the shoemaker
King Frost and the snow maiden
King Hilary and the beggarman
The king on trial
The Lake of Zangzĕ
The legend of the Narcissus
The lucky beggar
The lucky serving maid
The magic berries
The magician's heart
The man from Paradise
The man with the bag
Marko the rich and Vassili the luckless
An old story of the three sworn brothers
One roll of bread
The proud princess
Rattle-rattle-rattle and chink-chink-chink
The rich man's dinner party
Rich woman, poor woman
Saint Margery Daw
The shoemaker's dream
The soldier and the knapsack
The story of Tom Thumb
The tale of the Gaberlunzie man
The three brothers and the black hen
The three wishes
Three wonderful beggars
Tit for tat
Tsarino's greatest treasure
The two beggars
Up and down the minaret

The beggar's prophecy
SPICER – OWL'S p56-73

The beginning
SLOANE – FOLK. p11-15

The beginning of good conversation
SUN – LAND p31-36

The beginning of spirit societies
HASKETT – GRAINS p71-74

The beginning of the Fians
WILSON – SCOTTISH p175-177

The beginning of the Narran Lake
PARKER – AUSTRALIAN p27-30

The beginning of the Serbian uprising against the Turks
CURCIJA – HEROES p161-170

The beginning of the world and the making of California
CURRY – DOWN p9-21

Behn, Harry
Spring flowers

Behold the fig tree
MY BOOK HOUSE v. 2 p78.

Belena
MORAY – FAIR p134-148

A Belgian morning
MY BOOK HOUSE v. 2 p141.

Belgium
How the finch got her colors
Mr. Louse and Mrs. Louse
The soup stone

Belief
HOPE-SIMPSON – CAVAL. p143-144

Beling, Mabel Ashe
This hound hath loved me

Bell, Corydon
The first strawberries
The origin of Indian pipes

The bell of Atri
BALDWIN – FAVOR. p49-57

The bell of Monte Pino
PROTTER – CHILD. p81-87

Bell ringers
Aileel and Ailinda

Bellerophon . . . The winged horse
UNTERMEYER – FIRE. p17-20

Belling the cat
ARBUTHNOT – TIME p206.
MY BOOK HOUSE v. 2 p35-36

Belloc, Hilarie
From a moral alphabet

Bells
Big clock-tick tock!
Charles the Great and the snake
The children of Lir
The Christian bell
Chucho, who's afraid?

52

Bells (*Continued*)

Constantes and the dragon
Dick Whittington and his cat
The drowned bells of the abbey
Eight leaves of story (6) The Sun of
 Llanfabon
Esben and the witch
Four tales of how the devil was out-
 witted
Gay go up and gay go down
The ghost of Peg-Leg Peter
The golden buffalo
The great bell
The groach of the Isle of Lok
Hark, the Christmas bells are ringing
The holy cat of Tibet
How Tepozton hung the bells
I heard the bells on Christmas day
The Inchcape rock
Jingle bells, jingle bells
Keel-Wee, a Korean Rip Van Winkle
The king who ate chaff
The magic bell
Mirabella
The missing fog bell
The pheasants and the bell
The revenge of the serpent
The singing bell
The singing fir-tree
Sir Michael Scott
Stealing the bell
The swans of Ballycastle
Tall Peter and Short Peter
They hide a bell
Thomas the rhymer
The tree with the difficult name
The trials of Ting Ling
The voice of the bell
The Welshman and the hazel staff
The wild dog and the king's son
The witch of Lok Island

, **Christian**
 The children of Lir

, **Church**
 The little milleress

, **Golden**
 Diggory
 The terrible Olli

, **Silver**
 Diggory
 Mary, Mary, quote contrary
 The silver bell

The bells
 MY BOOK HOUSE v. 7 p71.

Bells on her toes
 LEACH – SOUP p78-85

Belts
 The blue belt
 Dummling
 The first mosquito
 The magic belt
 Prince Loaf
 The princess of Tomboso
 The untidy mermaid

, **Skin**
 The cowherd with the belt of skin
 The speckled bull

Benches
 Banks with binks
 Stretching the bench

Bendebukk
 ILLYÉS – ONCE p115-124

Benét, Rosemary and Stephen
 Abraham Lincoln, 1809-1865
 Wilbur Wright and Orville Wright

Benét, William Rose
 How to catch unicorns

Benevolence. *See* **Charity**

Benito the faithful
 SECHRIST – ONCE p156-167

Benizara and Kakezara
 SEKI – FOLKTALES p130-134

Bennett, Richard
 Shawneen and the gander

Beorhtnoth's death. *See* The homecoming
 of Beorhtnoth Beorhthelm's son

Beowulf
 See also The World's great epics
 How Beowulf delivered Heorot

Beowulf
 PICARD – TALES p51-71

Beowulf and Grendel
 LINES – TALES p187-198

Beowulf conquers Grendel
 HAZELTINE – HERO p88-99

Beowulf . . . The fight with Grendel
 UNTERMEYER – FIRE. p144-147

Beowulf fights a battle with the sea
 CARPENTER – SHIPS p183-190

Beppo Pipetta and his knapsack
LUM — ITALIAN p1-13

Bequests. *See* **Gifts; Inheritance**

Bergamot
HOKE — WITCHES p221-230

Berlioz, Hecter
The song of the flea

Bernardo and the red knight
LAURITZEN — BLOOD p64-87

Berries
The brown cow
The fairy tree of Doolas Woods
Kupti and Imani
The little white cat
The princess and the dwarf
The three wishes
The white cat

Bertall, illus.
The strangest thing in the world

Beside the fire
O'FAOLAIN — IRISH p179-180

The best devil in the land
JAGENDORF — UPSTATE p117-118

Best foot forward
BATCHELOR — SUPER. p88-89

The best wish
U.N. — RIDE p131-136
WILLIAMS — ROUND p120-129

Beston, Henry
The lost half-hour

The bet between Matjan and Gadja
COURLANDER — KANT. p47-51

Betel
The beginning of good conversation
The bet between Matjan and Gadja
The poor weaver and the princess
Three who couldn't be parted

Bethlehem
Get up, little horsey

Betrayal
See Also **Disloyalty; Traitors**
Bech, the ambitious quail

The bewitched court
The children of Lir
The death of Diarmaid
The emperor's magic bow
The fox and the wolf
The golden deer
The hunter and the hind
Julius Caesar . . . The Ides of March
King Bean
The lad who returned from Faerye
Ruba and the stork
The sky beings: thunder and his
helpers
Zolo Dumah and the priest

The betrayal
GAER — FABLES p107-108

Bets. *See* **Wagers**

Better not whistle!
BATCHELOR — SUPER. p20-22

Betty Stogs and the Little People
BRIGGS — PERS. p60-61

Betty Stogs' baby
MANNING — PETER p17-21

The bewitched court
SPICER — WITCHES p88-93

Bewitched cream
JOHNSON — WHAT p163.

Bezoar stones
Magic and medicine

Bhartrihari
Why?

Bible
See Also Names of characters in the
Bible
The babe Moses
Behold the fig tree
The boy Samuel
Bring me a light
The dangers of sorcery
Daniel in the lion's den
David and Goliath
David, the shepherd boy
The devil and the Good Book
The giant who rode on the ark
Gideon, the warrior
God hath made me to laugh
How the devil fetched the mayor
It is God that hath made us
The jewel
Joseph and his brethren

Bible (*Continued*)

The lass that lost the laird's daughter
Mary and the Christ-child
Noah's ark
Old Noah
The sky at night
Song of Solomon
Songs of joy from the Bible
Spring songs from the Bible
Wind bloweth where it listeth
The witch of Endor

Bicycles
Anansi and bicycle
Cadwalader's goat

Bidpai (East Indian fables)
The flying turtle
The Panchatantra
The partridge and the crow
The tyrant who became a just ruler

Big, big lies!
WITHERS – WORLD p90-100.

The big, big rabbit
WITHERS – I SAW p76.

The big black umbrella
LEACH – RAINBOW p199-202

Big bus, stop!
MY BOOK HOUSE v. 1 p173.

The big cabbage and the big kettle
WITHERS – I SAW p71.

The big cat and the big rat
O'SULLIVAN – FOLK p189-191

The big Chinese drum
WITHERS – WORLD p30.

Big clock–tick, tock!
my book house v. 1 p72.

The big engine
MY BOOK HOUSE v. 1 p179-180

Big fox and little fox
MONTGOMERIE – 25 p11-13

Big ghost, little ghost–Who's scared of a ghost?
JAGENDORF – UPSTATE p203-206

A big head has a big headache
CHAPPELL – THEY p19-24

Big Hermel
PICARD – GERMAN p189-197

Big Matsiko
MANNING – DAMIAN p41-53

Big men. *See* Giants

Big mosquitoes
WITHERS – WORLD p86.

The big mudhole
CREDLE – TALL p9-15

The big prescription
ĆURČIJA – YUGOSLAV p61.

The big pumpkin and the big kettle
WITHERS – WORLD p28.

The big street in the big city
MY BOOK HOUSE v. 1 p170-172

The big tree and the big bird
WITHERS – I SAW p142.

The big umbrella and the little rubbers
MY BOOK HOUSE v. 1 p190-191

The big warm dog
LEACH – RAINBOW p258-260

Bid winds
JOHNSON – WHAT p225-227

Big women. *See* Amazons; Giants

Bigfoot Wallace
IVES – TALES p209-222

The biggest crocodile in the world
KRUEGER – SERPENT p75-89

Biggoon and the little duck
WILLIAMS – ROUND p259-264

Bilba and Mayra
PARKER – AUSTRALIAN p122-123

Billy Beg and his (the) bull
SIDEMAN – WORLD'S p409-423
HAVILAND – IRELAND p39-60

Billy Beg and the sassafras switch
YOUNG – HOW p49-62

Billy B's adventure
BRIGGS – PERS. p172-174

Billy, Billy, come and play
MY BOOK HOUSE v. 1 p47.

Billy boy
JOHNSON – WHAT p158-159

The billy goat and the king
LANG – OLIVE p85-89

The billy goat and the sheep
BLOCH – UKRAIN. p19-23

Billy the Kid
LEACH – RAINBOW p171-174

Binoculars
George and the field glasses

Birch trees
Baba Yaga and the little girl with the
kind heart
Christening the baby in Russia
Cold, son of wind and snow
The fool and the birch-tree
The little birch tree
Three princes and their beasts

, **Leaves**
The wood fairy

The birch twig
BAMBERGER – FIRST p171-173

The bird and the buffalo
CARPENTER – ELEPHANT'S p91-99

The bird and the man
DURHAM – TIT p90-91

Bird Cu
BARLOW – LATIN p138-144

Bird language
DUDDINGTON – RUSS. p83-86

Bird-men
The golden apples of Loch Erne

Bird of power
MARRIOTT – AMER. p177-183

The bird of seven colors
ALEGRIA – THREE p25-30

The bird of the golden land
O'FAOLAIN – IRISH p219-231

Bird of the sun
JACOBSON – FIRST p33-34

The bird of the valley
TRACEY – LION p34-38

The bird on the roof
ALEXANDER – PEBBLES p26.

The bird that told tales
CARPENTER – ELEPHANT'S p58-65

The bird that would not stay dead
CARPENTER – AFRICAN p179-186

The birds which laid diamonds
EELLS – SPAIN p45-56

The bird with the most beautiful song
KAULA – AFRICAN p110-117

Birdling
SHEAHAN – HENRY p214-228

Birds
See also Names of birds; **Superstitions
–Birds**
The Ailpein bird, the stolen princess,
and the brave knight
Anansi and the alligator eggs
Animal and bird stories
Answer to a child's question
Ashputtel
At the wedding of Miss Jenny Wren
The bad prince
Bajan Budiman, the sharpshooter
Baldpate
Bas Celik
The bat's choice
The battle between the birds and the
beasts
The battle of the animals
The battle of the birds and the fish
The big tree and the big bird
The blind king and the magic bird
Brian and the fox
The pride-price for Olwen
The carnation youth
The cattle egret
Cenerentola
La Cenerentola
Chimpanzee's story
Chourilo's little comb
The crane who taught the birds to
dance and make corroboree
The crested curassow
The cuckoo and the clock
The dancing bird
The dancing water, singing apple, and
speaking bird
The donkey lettuce
Each little bird that sings
The eagle and the wren
Earl Mar's daughter

Birds (*Continued*)

The eight leaves of story (4) A harp
 on the water
The English nobleman, the diplomat,
 and the great crested bustard
The fairy bird
The feathers from the bird Venus
The fish with bent noses
Flint bird
Georgic and Merlin
The giant okab
Glooskap's country
The golden snuff-box
The great fish
Gwai-nee-bu the redbreast
Hear how the birds
The house that ate mosquito pie
How a bird turned the world upside
 down
How bat won the ball game
How Glooskap made the birds
How monkey king became a slave
How the animals made wings for bat
 and flying squirrel
How the ptarmigans learned to fly
How yams got their eyes
In spring the birds do sing
The jurga
Kela and the giant bird Halulu
The king of the birds
The king of the mountains
The king on trial
A kiss from the beautiful Fiorita
The kling kling bird
The land of youth
The last of the giants
A little bird sits in the willow
The little bird that found the pea
The little bird's rice
The little duck
The long-eared cat and the vulture
The long-nosed princess
Lost and found
Madschun
The magic banana
The magic calabash
The magic melons
The magician Palermo
The man without a heart
Mancrow, bird of darkness
Maui and the death goddess
Mr. Noy
Mother of the forest
The mouse, the bird and the sausage
Musk and amber
Odd Olle
The old man who cut bamboo
Once I saw a little bird
Open your beak, my little bird
Orphan boy

Over in the meadow
The palace of the night
The palace of the white cat
Phoenix, bird of the sun
The poor man's son, the dwarfs, and
 the birds
The pretty bird
The prince and the birds
The prince and the vizier's son
Prince Finn the fair
Princess Janina and the troll
 Bradalba
Princess September
The queen's necklace
The quest for Olwen (4) Fulfilling the
 tasks 2/ The oldest animals
The rabbit prince
The rain bird
The Rāmāyana
The return of Diab
Saint Gabre Manfas and his animals
The serpent
Shah Meram and Sade Sultan
The silver bell
Sindhu
The six brothers
The sleigh ride
The small red feather
Stone patience and knife patience
The story of Zal
The storyteller
The straight and narrow way
The summer birds
The sweetest song in the woods
The tale of bat
Tema's promise to the white bird
The three languages
The three oranges
The tobacco fairy from the blue hills
The turquoise stones
The two princesses
The war of the animals against the
 birds
The Warau people discover the earth
Wawanosh
What does little birdie say?
When Mrs. Bird wants Mr. Bird
Whence came the birds?
While other birds at will may go
The white bride and the black bride
Why animals are afraid of fire
Why bat flies alone
Why cats always wash themselves after
 eating
Why the evergreen trees never lose
 their leaves
Why the waringen tree is holy
The wind-demon
The wise bird and the hunter; an old
 Hebrew fable
The witch

Birds (*Continued*)

With and without
The wonder-tree
The wren
The yellow-haired witch
The youth and the dog dance
The youth who made friends with the
beast and the birds

−**Colors**
The babbling reed-warbler
The beautiful blue jay
How crane got his long legs
How the birds came to have their
many colors
How the cardinal got his red
feathers
How the finch got her colors
How turkey got his white tail
Little red bird
The raven paints the birds for war
The thunder man
Why the crane's feathers are brown
and otter doesn't feel the cold
Why crows are black
Why the birds are different colors

, **Golden**
The adventures of Florian
The glass man and the golden bird
The gold bird
The golden bird
Japanese dragons
Tropsyn

−**Imaginary**
Garuda
Sirens

−**Language**
The antmolly birds
The bird that told tales
The bow, the deer, and the talking
bird
The boy and the birds
The dancing water, the singing
apple, and the speaking bird
The donkey, the ox and the farmer
John the true
The king and the two owls
The language of the birds
The legend of Eilean Donan castle
The magic ruby
The story of the talking bird
The stupid hunter and the crafty
bird
The three languages
The three ravens

−**Nests**
The children's sea
The magic oysters
The magpie's nest

Mrs. Mag and her nest
The son of the hen-wife
Two birds and their nest

−**Skin**
Kutlee-Seek-Vik

−**Songs**
The beautiful blue jay
The bird and the man
The bird with the most beautiful
song
The blackbird's song
The cardinal's concert
The donkey and the nightingale
The eagle and the lark
The finch with the golden voice
Hansel and Grethel
How loon learned his call
In spring the birds do sing
The juniper
The magpie's nest
The mysterous path
Shon Shenkin
The song-bird and the healing
waters
A song of the railroad men
Swans
The twilight
The two step-sisters
Wee robin's Christmas song

, **Underground**
The great bird in the carob tree

, **White**
The white bird sister

Birds
BATCHELOR − SUPER. p28-33

The birds' convention
MY BOOK HOUSE v. 2 p142.

Birds of a feather
MY BOOK HOUSE v. 1 p55.

Birds-of-the-night
Kakui, bird of the night

Birds' St. Valentine day
MY BOOK HOUSE v. 3 p198-203

Birth
Nathlook: Susie, my name
The old man who said "Why"

The birth and boyhood of Finn
SUTCLIFF − HIGH p9-17

The birth of Japan
McALPINE − JAPAN. p3-22

The birth of Oisin
    SUTCLIFF — HIGH p57-69

The birth of Pryderi
    See also Pwyll and Pryderi (2)
    LINES — TALES p198-204

The birth of Robin Hood
    MANNING — ENGLISH p105-109

The birth of the islands
    McALPINE — JAPAN. p10-15

The birth of the River Emajogi
    MAAS — MOON p44-46

The birth years
    PRATT — MAGIC unp.

Birthday luck
    LEACH — LUCK p41-43

The birthday of the Infanta
    JOHNSON — PRINC. p96-117

Birthdays
    The banshee's birthday treat
    A converted thief
    Rocking-horse land
    The silver ship
    The son of the baker of Barra

Birthmarks
    The innkeeper of Moscow
    Kayuta, the drop star

Bisans (spirits)
    The princess in the camphor tree

Bishops
    The king and the bishop
    A legend of Saint Nicholas
    The mousetower
    Our Lady of Guadalupe
    Shiny tales of Vincennes

Biting Marion
    MY BOOK HOUSE v. 1 p174-176

The bitter withy
    VANSITTART — DARK p68-70

Björnson, Björnstjerne
    Oeyvind and Marit, a story of Norway

Björnsen, Björnstjerne
    Fjords and mountain peaks

The black art
    O'SULLIVAN — FOLK. p226-227

Black Bartelmy
    LEACH — RAINBOW p268-271

The black-bearded Brownies of
    Boneberg
    SPICER — GHOSTS p101-111

The black bodach
    SHEPPARD — SCOT. p43-49

The black-breasted magpie
    PARKER — AUSTRALIAN p205-
    209

The black bull of Norroway
    ARBUTHNOT — TIME p24-27
    JACOBS — MORE p20-27
    WILLIAMS — FAIRY p89-95

Black cat
    BATCHELOR — SUPER. 34-36

The black cat of Cotabato
    ROBERTSON — PHILIP. p81-90

The black cat of the witch-dance-place
    HOKE — WITCHES p194-196

Black clouds at midnight
    REED — TALK. p47.

Black Colin of Loch Awe
    WILSON — SCOTTISH p56-65

The black dog of the wild forest
    MANNING — RED p139-145

The black giant of Luckless River
    SPICER — GIANTS p118-127

The black-handed monkey
    HOLLADAY — BANTU p78-79

The black pool
    KRUEGER — SERPENT p37-43

The black prince
    ZAGLOUL — BLACK p109-124

Black Roderic
    SHEPPARD — SCOT. p99-103

Black Sam Bellamy
    TAFT — PROFILE p201-213

The black spider
  MICHAEL – PORTUGUESE p1-8

The black stone
  MARKS – SPANISH p147-162

The black swans
  PARKER – AUSTRALIAN p168-173

The black thief. *See* 1. King Conal's horses. 2. The three enchanted maidens 3. The thirteen enchanted cats 4. The faithless apprentice 5. The three giants

The black woodpecker
  RANKE – GERMANY p150.

"Black woodsman" (devil)
  Tom Walker and the devil

Blackbeard
  The treasure under the tree

Blackberries
  Moorachug and Meenachug

The blackbird
  CATHON – PERHAPS p165.

The blackbird and the pine needle
  EKREM – TURKISH p113-116

Blackbirds
  Anansi an ' de cherries
  The Birds' St. Valentine day
  The blackbird
  The cold May night
  The giant archer of the sky
  The magpie's nest
  The sea-mammy
  Sing a song of sixpence
  The squirrel went out to cut the hay
  Tam and Tessa
  There were two blackbirds
  Tobacco woman and corn spirit
  Tutu birds

  –Eggs
    The wishing chair of the Lord of Errigal

The blackbird's song
  PICARD – FAUN p193-205

"Blackfellows"
  The dogs of Bahloo
  Mullian-ga the morning star
  The rain bird

Weedah the mockingbird
  The Wi-oombeens and Piggi-billa

The blacksmith
  MY BOOK HOUSE v. 4 p159-160

The blacksmith and the devil
  MANNING – DEVILS p76-86

The blacksmith and the horseman
  O'SULLIVAN – FOLK. p253-254

The blacksmith in the moon
  JABLOW – MAN p7-9

The blacksmith lion and the conceited goat
  BURTON – MAGIC p125-126

Blacksmiths
  Aileel and Ailinda
  Arawn
  The chase of Slieve Gallion
  The clever lad from Skye
  Conchobar and Teeval
  The crow and the sparrow
  Cuchulainn and the smith's wife
  The devil to pay
  The dragon who lost his fire
  The fairies and the smith
  The Fians asleep in the Great Rock
  The giant's causeway
  The golden chain
  The green-skinned princess
  The crimson purse
  The gypsy and the snake
  The handsome apprentice
  Hasty porridge in the boiling water
  How Celebes got its name
  How Fionn found his sword
  John the bear
  John the blacksmith destroys the wasps
  Jonathan Moulton and the devil
  Journey by broomstick
  Kalevala, land of heroes
  The laird's lass and the gobba's son
  The little fish and (the) big fish
  The little gray pony
  The lord of gold
  The man who was only three inches tall
  The master-smith
  The moon painters
  O will you shoe our pony, pray?
  Olaf Goddardson and the sword Macabuin
  Olaf the mermaid's son
  One-eyed Likho
  Revenge of the tin god
  A rupee earned

60

Blacksmiths (*Continued*)

Sif's golden hair
The sign at the smithy door
The Sing-Bonga beheld men
The smith and the faeries
The snake monster
The spider specter of the pool
The stone crusher of Banjang
The tale of the lay of the smithy
The three brothers
The three traveling artisans
The tiny, tiny man
Volund the smith
Wayland Smith
The wee red man
Why women won't listen
Wind and wave and wandering flame
The witch's shoes
The young giant

The blacksmiths
COURLANDER – PIERCE p84-88

The blacksmith's dilemma
ARNOTT – AFRICAN p119-123

The blackstairs mountain
MANNING – WITCHES p123-127

Bladders
(The) little bull calf

Blake, William
Laughing song
Nurse's song

Blame
The bee-hunter and the Oozie
The devil and our Lord
Where to lay the blame
Why the rabbit's nose twitches

Blanche's high-flying Halloween
HOKE – WITCHES p45-55

Blankets
The colonel's blanket
Two novices who behaved like a pair
of otters
Why the sun is brighter than the moon

A blessing and a curse
DAVIS – TEN p147-155

"Blessing of the animals"
The burro Benedicto

Blessings
At the pike's command

Dates to Cairo
Father fights son in the tribe of Hilal
The golden horse
Juanito and the princess
The mop servant
Mother's day
The queen of the planets
The Red Etin
Riches or happiness?
The seven-year blessing
The seven years of blessing
The singing bell
Snake magic
Vassilissa the beautiful
The white lady of Pumphul

Blessings on thee, dog of mine
MY BOOK HOUSE v. 1 p143.

Blind
Au Sung meets Kim Lee
The bashful prince
The beautiful blue jay
The blue belt
Cum and Koompang
Damian and the dragon
The dutiful daughter
The fairy child
A father-in-law and his son-in-law
Four good men
The golden-headed fish
The griffon
Hoichi the earless
How Au Sung repaid Kim Lee
How Maui obtained the magic jawbone
Johnny and the witch-maidens
The kelpie
Khalid and Aantar
The Korean goblins
The little lion dog and the blue
prince
The Lochmaben harper
The lost sun, moon, and stars
The magical tune
The man who was only three inches
tall
Manstin, the rabbit
Mellitot and Iolanda
An old Korean story
Old man moon
The raccoon and the old men
Rapunzel
The rich Per Muller
The robber baron . . . and the bat
Sindhu
The smiling innkeeper
The tale of a Pakistan parrot
The theft of fire
True and untrue
Two hunters
Why mole's front paws are bent

Blind (*Continued*)

The young piper, the Little People of Ireland

The blind boy and the loon
MAHER – BLIND p17-30

The blind king and the magic bird
MICHAEL – PORTUGUESE p179-185

The blind man and the deaf man
BAKER – GOLDEN p80-88

The blind man and the devils
INS-SÖB – FOLK p59-62

The blind man, the deaf man and the donkey
PALMER – FAIRY p45-49

The blind men and the elephant
BALDWIN – FAVOR. p104-106
LEACH – NOODLES p54.

The blinded giant
JACOBS – MORE p92-93

The blizzard of '98
CREDLE – TALL p40-42

Blizzards
The master of the winds
Minute pudding
More south than south, more north than north
Old Surly and the boy
Roommates
The silver ship

Block Island. *See* **Rhode Island–Block Island**

Blocks
Building with blocks
O I'll build a square with my pretty red blocks
What are you able to build with your blocks?

Blodeuedd and the slaying of Llew
SHEPPARD – WELSH p63-68

Blonde, brunette or redhead
BATCHELOR – SUPER. p60-62

Blood
Ashoremashika
Blue Beard

The bone that testified
Faithful John
Moon of blood
The mosquitoes
The princess with the twelve pair of golden shoes
The secret room
The serpent

Blood on his forehead
LITTLEDALE – GHOSTS p135-138

The bloodless battle of the elm
JAGENDORF – GHOST p64-71

Blow, wind, blow, and go, mill, go!
MY BOOK HOUSE v. 1 p31.

Blowing
The foggy stew
The giant and the Rumanian
The wonder ship and ship's crew

Blue Beard
See also **Bluebeard**
PERRAULT – COMPLETE p78-87
PERRAULT – FAMOUS p73-90
SIDEMAN – WORLD'S p637-644

The blue belt
ASBJÖRNSEN – EAST p53-71
THOMPSON – ONE p267-278

The blue cap
WILSON – SCOTTISH p33-37

The blue cat
CARPENTER – ELEPHANT'S p159-165

The blue centaur
CARPENTER – HORSES p47-57

The blue dog
JAGENDORF – UPSTATE p293-299

The blue flame
BECHSTEIN – FAIRY p103-105

The blue foal
CARPENTER – HORSES p193-204

The blue jackal
GAER – FABLES p69-71
GREEN – BIG p216-219

Blue jays
The beautiful blue jay
The miller and the blue jay
The theft of dawn
Two birds and their nest

The blue lake
BAKER — TALKING p138-178

Blue legs
RUSHMORE — DANCING p126-178

The blue lotus flower
TOOZE — WONDER. p77-82

The blue men of the Minch
SHEPPARD — SCOT. p173-175

The blue palm tree
BELTING — THREE p131-135

The blue parrot
LANG — OLIVE p10-24

Blue Ridge Mountains
The bear and the wildcat
The bear in the black hat
The big mudhole
The blizzard of '98
The fighting rams
The goat that went to school
How pa learned to grow hot peppers
Janey's shoes
The lake that flew
The man who rode the bear
Old Blueheard
Old Plott
The perambulatin' pumpkin
The popcorn patch
The pudding that broke up the preaching
Saved by a turkey
The self-kicking machine
The short horse
Surprise for the black bull
A tall turnip
The voice in the jug

The blue rose
ROSS — BLUE p138-148

Blue-tits (birds)
The clever blue tit and the fox

The blue virgin
JAGENDORF — KING p229-232

Blue water
RUSHMORE — DANCING p73-87

Bluebeard
See also Blue Beard
Old Bluebeard
The tale of the Fäderäevisch

Bluebeard
PERRAULT — CLASSIC p39-51

Bluebirds
The beauty and her gallant
The growing rock
How the finch got her colors
The last word of a bluebird as told to a child
Over in the meadow
What does little birdie say?
Why coyote is the color of the ground

Bluffing
Donal O'Ciaran from Connaught
Masoy and the ape
The monkey, the tiger, and the jackal family
Salakhbai and the fox
A slip of the tongue
Stan Bolovan
The valiant tailor

Boarding houses
Queen of the Comstock

Boars. *See* **Hogs**

The boaster
MY BOOK HOUSE v. 3 p175.

The boastful Alaskans
WITHERS — WORLD p30.

The boastful gnat
WILSON — GREEK p212-213

The boastful queen
GRINGHUIS — GIANTS p50-58

The boastful tortoise
LIN — MILKY p11-15

Boastfulness. *See* **Braggarts**

Boat races
Along the Monongahela
The little prairie hen and the big Indiana
Princess Maring, the huntress

The boat that would not move
CARPENTER — SHIPS p227-235

The boatman he's a lucky man!
MY BOOK HOUSE v. 1 p97.

Boatmen
The badger and the boatmen

Boatmen (*Continued*)
The king and his seven sons
Maine's best boatman
Mike Fink
Mister Luck and Mister Industry
The patridge and his drum
River roarer/Mike Fink
The vixen and the boatmen

Boatmen's songs
The boatman he's a lucky man!
When Uncle Henry was a little tiny
boy

Boats
See also **Boat races. Ships and shipbuilding; Types of** boats, e.g. **Barges, Canoes,** etc.
The adjutant bird
Bombadil goes boating
Chug-chug along the O-hi-o
Commodore Vanderbilt's first boat
The cowskin boat
The dancing princesses
David Copperfield and little Emily
Doctor Lee and little Aran
Fairy workmen
The harbor
The haunted boat
How Master Thumb defeated the sun
Ivashko and the witch
Little Firenko
The little footprints
The little prairie hen and the big Indiana
The little white cat
Look, see the boat!
The magic mortar
Marking the boat to locate the sword
My boat
My boat (anonymous)
The ogress in the stone boat
Paper boats
The people of Mols
The river of lantern land
Seán Palmers voyage to America with the fairies
The skipper and the dwarfs
Stormy lifts anchor
Stormy sets sail
The story of the fairy boat
Temba's magic boat
The twelve dancing princesses
The voyage of Maelduin
Wainamoinen finds the lost-words
Where go the boats?
The white cat
The witch in the stone boat

, **Golden**
The golden boat

The bob-tailed monkey and the king's honey
DAVIS – LION'S p32-44

Bobby Shafto's gone to sea
MY BOOK HOUSE v. 1 p44.

Bobo, black dog, and the cannibal women
CARPENTER – DOGS p101-110

The bobtail monkey
SAKADE – JAPAN. p113-120

Bodisat (Bodhisattva)
The age of the partridge
The ass in the lion's skin
The crow in the rose-apple tree
The flight of the animals
The foolish jackal
The fox in saint's clothing
The golden deer
The golden goose
The greedy cow
A handful of peas
The Jatakas
The king and the monkey
The lion who listened to a jackal
The monkey king's bridge
The monkey's heart
The otters and the fox
The outwitted hunter
The peacock's mistake
The tiger and the goats
The ungrateful lion

Bodor, Isabel
MEHDEVI – BUNGLING p119.

Bog
The dishonest tailor

The boggart
BRIGGS – PERS. p131-132
LITTLEDALE – GHOSTS p35-38

Boggarts
From brownie to boggart
The hairy boggart
The hairy boggart's field
Yallery Brown

Boggs, R. S.
The eternal wanderer of the Pampas

Bogies
Gwarwyn-a-Throt
The little red bogie-man

Bogles. *See* Ghosts

The bogles from the howff
LEODHAS – HEATHER p113-128

Bohemia
See also Czechoslovakia
The greedy tailor
How the carrot-counter got his name
King Svatopluk and the three sticks
Kristina and the devil
The magic walking-stick
The mouse hole
Stone soup in Bohemia
The three golden hairs

A Bohemian evening
MY BOOK HOUSE v. 2 p140.

Bohra hunts the dark
PARKER – AUSTRALIAN p136-137

Bohra the kangaroo
PARKER – AUSTRALIAN p133-135

Boiled wheat for a bountiful harvest
WALKER – WATER. p68-72

Bokungu trees
The proud bokungu tree

Bola Bola
LOWE – LITTLE p41-43

The bold heroes of Hungry Hill
MacMANUS – BOLT p3-18
MacMANUS – HIBERIAN p212-223

The bold little bowman
WYATT – GOLDEN p85-92

Bolivia
The coming of Asin
The great white condor
Greed in heaven, growth on earth
The king of the mountains
–Andes Mountains
The hero in the village

The boll weevil
STOUTENBURG – CROC. p26-29

Bomba, the brave
CARPENTER – AFRICAN p169-178

Bombadil goes boating
TOKIEN – READER (part 4) p17-23

Bonaventure, Berthon
The miller's three sons

The bone that testified
BARASH – GOLDEN p33-35

Bones
The cat, the dog, and death
The clever weaver
The faery and the kettle
The giant bones
The griffon
The holy relic of Bannockburn
How dog came to live with man
How Maui obtained the magic
jawbone
Jirimpimbira
The Kamiah monster
The kindly ghost
King Hrolf and the bear's son
A kiss from the beautiful Fiorita
The magic bone
Maui nooses the sun
The nine-tailed fox
Rattle-rattle-rattle and chink-chink-
chink
She-wa-na, deity of the elements
The singing bone
Teeny-tiny
Why dog gnaws a bone
The wise owl

Bonnets. *See* Hats

Bonney, William H.
Billy the Kid

Booby birds
Green parrot's story

The book of Buddha's birth-stories. *See*
The Jatakas

The book of five headings. *See* The
Panchatantra

The book of good counsel. *See* The
Hitopadesa

The book of magic
LITTLEDALE – GHOSTS p21-25

The book of Thoth
GREEN – TALES p98-114

A book-within-a book
PERRAULT – FAMOUS p1-32

Bookoos (birds)
The bird on the roof

Books and reading
The art of reading
Bring me a light

Books and reading (*Continued*)

Doctor know-all
Doctor Lee and little Aran
Flyleaf scribblings
Kwang Hing, the book lover
The little book
The man who feared nothing
The Panchatantra
The Prince Fernando
Seven iron-souled slippers
The sorcerer's apprentice
The story in the sealed book
The wizard king
The wonder child

The boom-boom-y beast
CARPENTER – AFRICAN p13-20

The boomer fireman's fast sooner hound
ARBUTHNOT – TIME p190-192

Boone, Daniel
Adventuring: White man on the
warpath
Daniel's dear
Exploring the wilderness

Boötes
Plowman in the sky

Boots. *See* **Shoes–Boots**

Boots and his brothers
ARBUTHNOT – TIME p75-77
MY BOOK HOUSE v. 5 p156-161

Boots and the troll
HAVILAND – NORWAY p75-88
THOMPSON – ONE p62-66

The boots that never wore out
SPICER – DEVILS p33-42

Books to read; museums to visit
JAMES – MYTHS p157.

The bora of Baiame
PARKER – AUSTRALIAN p31-42

Bora rings (initiations)
The woman and the sacred bora ring

The bored tengu
PALMER – DRAGONS p30-37

Boredom
Big Matsiko
The happy cure

Born a monkey, live a monkey
SHERLOCK – WEST p135-143

Born to be rich
LOWE – LITTLE p22-26

Borneo
The adjutant-bird
The dog and the karbau
The one who said Tjik
The tiger's war against Borneo
Why there are no tigers in Borneo

Borrowed arrows
MAR – CHINESE p111-126

The borrowed donkey
DE LA IGLESIA – CAT unp.

The borrower
SERVER – LET'S p55-58

Borrowing
The man who was always borrowing
and lending

The borrowing fairies
BRIGGS – PERS. p94.

The borrowing of 100,000 arrows
WYNDHAM – CHINA p40-47

Borski, Lucia Merecka and Kate B.
Miller, tran.
A horned goat

Bostanai
BARASH – GOLDEN p30-32

The bosung pohoo. *See* The unpunctual
minister, or The bosung pohoo

Bothvar Bjarki and his brothers. *See*
King Hrolf and the bear's son

Botsford, Florence
The eagle and the owl
The little bucket

Botswana
The battle of the animals

Bottle Hill
MANNING – DWARFS p64-72

Bottles
The green grass bottle
How the ghost got in
The magic bottles

Bottles (*Continued*)
A message in a bottle
Mr. & Mrs. Vinegar
Sir Gammer Vans
Three corpses, money, and a wine-
bottle
The two bottles

Bottomley, Gordon
Atlantis

Boucher, Alan
BOUCHER – MEAD p179-180

Boundaries. *See* **Surveyors and surveying**

Boughs. *See* **Trees-Branches**

Bouki and Ti Bef
COURLANDER – PIECE p94-96

Bouki buys a burro
COURLANDER – PIECE p55-57

Bouki cuts wood
COURLANDER – PIECE p76-80

Bouki gets whee-ai
COURLANDER – PIECE p20-22

Bouki rents a horse
COURLANDER – PIECE p25-28

Bouki's glasses
COURLANDER – PIECE p89-90

Boulders. *See* **Rocks and stones**

The bow that bridges heaven
MY BOOK HOUSE v. 2 p105.

The bow, the deer, and the talking bird
BRENNER – BOY p90-94

Bowen, Vernon
The trials of Ting Ling

"Bow-wow", says the dog
MY BOOK HOUSE v. 1 p21.

Bow, wow, wow, whose dog art thou?
MY BOOK HOUSE v. 1 p23.

Bowleg Bill
GORHAM – REAL p90-95

The bowlegged god, Bes
BELTING – STARS #7

Bowling
The devil's bowling ball
The ferryman
Rip Van Winkle; the strange little
men of the mountains

Bowls
The miracle of the begging bowl
The old man of the flowers
Simpletons
The task of Prince Ishitsukuri
The three sons
The wonderful talking bowl
The wooden bowl

Bowne, John
The courageous Quaker of Flushing

Bows and arrows. *See* **Archery**

A box on the ear
MANNING – GHOSTS p9-13

The box with wings
WILSON – GREEK p90-96

Boxers
The pugilist and his wonderful helpers

Boxes
See also **Chests**
Badikan and Khan Boghu
Benizara and Kakezara
The broken box
Cherry
The cook and the house goblin
The brave little prince
The cruel uncle
The daughter of the dwarf
The golden box
The hunchback's horse
The iron box
The ivory box
The king's tower
The little black box
Petit Jean and the frog
The silver hare in a box
Snake magic
The son of the baker of Barra
The sun, the moon and the star of
morning
The three brothers
The twelve young men
The two boxes
The ungrateful children
The unseen bridegroom
Urashima
Why ants carry large bundles

Boxes (*Continued*)

, Iron
The daughter of the dwarf

Boxwood
The beardless, the lame, and the one-eyed thief

The boy Achilles
GREEN – GREEKS p16-17

A boy and a beggar
JEWETT – WHICH p47-58

The boy and his magic robe
MATSON – LONGHOUSE p29-38

The boy and Necken
KAPLAN – SWEDISH p200-208

The boy and the birds
ALMEDINGEN – RUSS. p132-146

The boy and the bull
MANNING – PETER p33-38

The boy and the cloth
COURLANDER – TIGER'S p80-82

The boy and the fox
WITHERS – I SAW p89.

The boy and the leopard
WALKER – DANCING p84-93

The boy and the monk
HACK – DANISH p72-74

The boy and the mountain-man
HACK – DANISH p90-96

The boy and the nuts
STRONG – FAVORITE p46.

The boy and the sea monsters
HARRIS – ONCE p31-58

The boy and the water-sprite
HAVILAND – SWEDEN p3-13

The boy hero of Harlem
MY BOOK HOUSE v. 4 p57-62

A boy in Russia
MY BOOK HOUSE v. 12 p191-204

A boy in the island of Bali
MY BOOK HOUSE v. 2 p176-177

The boy in the land of shadows
LITTLEDALE – GHOSTS p111-120
MacMILLAN – GLOOS. p266-273

The boy in the moon
JABLOW – MAN p21.

The boy of Newstead Abbey
MY BOOK HOUSE v. 12 p92-93

The boy of the Lake country
MY BOOK HOUSE v. 12 p42-54

The boy of the red twilight sky
MacMILLAN – GLOOS. p238-243

The boy on a broomstick
HOPE-SIMPSON – CAVAL. p78-82

A boy on the high seas
MY BOOK HOUSE v. 8 p8-17

The boy Pu-nia and the king of the sharks
COLUM – STONE p44-49

The boy Samuel
MY BOOK HOUSE v. 4 p80-81

The boy who ate too much. *See* Whale of a tale

The boy who beat the devil
BRENNER – BOY p84-89

The boy who became a reindeer
MELZACK – DAY p41-49

The boy who became king of the sharks
WHEELER – HAWAII. p125-142

The boy who became pope
O'SULLIVAN – FOLK. p133-136

The boy who could do anything
BRENNER – BOY p27-50

The boy who cried wolf
STRONG – FAVORITE p16.

The boy who crossed the great water and returned
COURLANDER – PEOPLE p63-81

The boy who cut everything to pieces
BURTON – MAGIC p53-55

The boy who drew cats
BELTING – CAT p83-89
HEARN – JAPANESE p29-35
LITTLEDALE – GHOSTS p27-33

The boy who fished for the moon
HOLDING — SKY p99-110

The boy who found fear
LANG — OLIVE p213-221

The boy who had to draw cats
CARPENTER — DOGS p195-203

The boy who kept a secret
SIDEMAN — WORLD'S p365-382

The boy who made a dream come true
MY BOOK HOUSE v. 6 p114-117

The boy who made hay
MY BOOK HOUSE v. 1 p134.

The boy who out-fibbed a princess
WITHERS — I SAW p86-88

The boy who overcame the giants
MacMILLAN — GLOOS. p184-191

The boy who played the flute
LIN — MILKY p76-86

The boy who taught the fairies tears
NYE — MARCH p62-76

The boy who told tall tales
SEKI — FOLKTALES p179-181

The boy who took care of the pigs
BRENNER — BOY p7-11

The boy who turned himself into a peanut
WITHERS — WORLD p57-58

The boy who wanted to learn witchcraft
BECHSTEIN — FAIRY p50-55

The boy who was called "thick-head"
MacMILLAN — GLOOS. p151-156

The boy who was caught by a clam
HOLDING — SKY p39-48

The boy who was lost
JAGENDORF — KING p59-64

The boy who was never afraid
HATCH — MORE p182-198
MICHAEL — PORTUGUESE
p133-138

The boy who was not afraid
BOUCHER — MEAD p31-37

The boy who was saved by thoughts
MacMILLAN — GLOOS. p157-163

The boy who would be an orator
JAGENDORF — SAND p61-66

The boy who would eat lobsters
WHEELER — HAWAII. p70-77

The boy who wouldn't give up
FEINSTEIN — FOLK p87-90

The boy who wouldn't mind his grandmother
JORDAN — BURRO p42-45

The boy with the beer keg
ASBJÖRNSEN — NORW. p131-134

The boy with the golden star
PRIDHAM — GIFT p143-156

The boy with the long hair
MATSON — LONGHOUSE p83-90

The boy with the moon on his forehead
TURNBULL — FAIRY p50-83

The boyar and the gipsy
URE — RUMANIAN p33-34

Boyars
The little brother of the sun
Luck and wit
The old man's tale of Prince Stephen
The poor man's clever daughter
Which is the greater?

The boyhood of a hero
SAWYER — DIETRICH p11-32

Boys
Among the chickens
The bad boy and the good dog
The bed
The child from the sea
The clever boy
The damned boys
The extraordinary black coat
The fly
The fox and the stork
The game board
Max and Moritz
Max and Moritz and the tailor
Momotaro
Momotaro, the peach boy
The Nuremberg store
The Oni and the three children
Stories about girls and boys

Boys (*Continued*)

The story of a good boy
A time for everything
To feed my people: The coming of
corn
The twelve young boys with golden
hair
Whale of a tale
Whistle the winds

Boys and girls, come out to play
MY BOOK HOUSE v. 1 p39.

A boy's song
MY BOOK HOUSE v. 6 p96.

The boys who met the trolls in the Hedal
woods
ASBJÖRNSEN – NORW. p9-12

Boys with golden stars
LANG – VIOLET p174-185

Bracelets
Bells on her toes
Cenerentola
The cock and the sparrow-hawk
Duke Roland's quest
Golden bracelets, golden anklets
Jackal or tiger?
The maiden who did not get her wish
My candlestick
The princess in the earth cave
Superstition: the remnants of magic
The third witch

Braggarts
The acorn and the pumpkin
Bahmoo rides the wrong frog
The battle of the firefly and the apes
Belling the cat
The big pumpkin and the big kettle
Blue legs
The boaster
The boastful gnat
The boastful tortoise
The boy who overcame the giants
The brave man of Golo
Brown owl's story
The changeling and the fond young
mother
Charlotte's web; Wilbur's boast
Chinese rival storytellers
The city mouse and the country
mouse
Clever Juan and King Tasio
The cobbler
The colonel's blanket
The dancing monkeys

The donkey and the boar
The firebird
Firefly's story
The giant and the tailor
The gingerbread man
Giuanni and the giant
The greatest boast
Green parrot's story
The hare and the tortoise
The head of the family
The Hoca and the candle
The honourable tom cat
How the Brazilian beetles got their
gorgeous coats
How the terrapin beat the rabbit
Humbug
The hunter and the tiger
John Boaster
Kantjil becomes a raksha
The lad and the fox
The lion and donkey a-hunting go
Little Black Sambo
The man who tried to catch the night
The man who would know magic
The mouse who lived under the
granary
Nasreddin Hoca and the third shot
Ol-Ambu and He-of-the-long-sleeping-
place
Old man Kurai and the one-eyed giant
Peer Gynt
Phaeton
The proud bokungu tree
The remarkable ox, rooster and dog
Salt
The tailor's bright daughter
The tale of the superman
The titmouse
Tommy was a silly boy
Well-done-Peter-Parker
The wind and the sun
The witch aunts

The bragging bat
ELLIOT – WHERE p107-113

The bragging beasts
REED – TALK. p13.

Bragi, god of poetry
AULAIRE – NORSE p64-47

Brahma and Brahmans (Brahmins)
The adder and the fox
The calm Brahman
The cat that went to heaven
The clever jackal and how he
outwitted the tiger
The dilemma of a pious man
The foolish Brahman
How the dog chose its master

Brahma and Brahmans (*Continued*)

The jackal, the barber and the
Brahmin who had seven daughters
The king and the Brahmin's child
The king who rides a tiger
The legend of the Karang
The lion-makers
The making of the earth
Nāgasvāmin and the witches
A nasty rumour
A noble Brahman's sacrifice
The origin of the bromo feast
A quarrel between thieves brings a
Brahmin relief
The ruby prince
A slip of the tongue
The story of Harisarman
A tale of two rogues
The talkative tortoise
The Thanksgiving of the Wazir
The tiger, the Brahmen, and the
jackal

The Brahman and the goat
GRAY – INDIA'S p157-158

The Brahman in the potter's shop
GAER – FABLES p110-111

The Brahmin and the villain
GAER – FABLES p43-49

The Brahmin, the tiger, and the seven
judges
BAKER – TALKING p236-241

Brahms, Johanna
The blacksmith

The brainy rabbit
GILSTRAP – SULTAN'S p61-66

Bran, son of Llyr
PICARD – HERO p60-67

Brandy
Shlemiel, the businessman

Branwen
The story of Branwen

Bratton, John W.
The teddy bears' picnic

The brave actor
BONNET – CHINESE p165-167

The brave cowman
MÜLLER – SWISS p39-43

The brave grenadier
SHEAHAN – HENRY p263-278

The brave little prince
SPELLMAN – BEAUT. p82-85

The brave little tailor
MANNING – GIANTS p90-97
SIDEMAN – WORLD'S p561-572
THOMPSON – ONE p410-418

The brave man of Golo
COURLANDER – KING'S p51-55

The grave prince
DAVIS – LION'S p93-102

Brave rabbit and bug with the golden
wings
RUDOLPH – MAGIC p42-50

The brave shepherd boy
FOSTER – STONE p22-25

The brave three hundred
BALDWIN – FAVOR. p91-94

Bravery. *See* **Courage**

The brawl between sun and moon
JABLOW – MAN p19.

Brazil
The beetle and the paca
The boy who was lost
Clever little turtle
The deer and the jaguar share a house
The elephants
The gift of manioc
The golden gourd
The grateful devil
The green sergeant
Gull taught men to use manioc for
food
The hairy man from the forest
How night was let loose and all the
animals came to be
How the Brazilian beetles got their
gorgeous coats
Jabuty, the strong
The legend of the palm tree
Mario and the yara
Milomaki
The parrot of Limo Verde
The Pleiades
So say the little monkeys
The three flutes are in the flute house
The three oranges
Why the bananas belong to the
monkey
The woman tribe

Bread
Account rendered
The beggar's prophecy
Blue water
The bride of Llyn y Fan Fach
The bun
Cast thy bread
Cattenborg
The charitable woman and the three
loaves
Clever Oonagh
East bread crusts for curly hair
Fish with the rolls
Five loaves
The forest bride
Goblin bread
Hansel and Gretel
How mankind learned to make bread
How the gypsy boy outsmarted death
Lady of the lake
The lady's loaf-field
The lake lady
The lake maiden
Leviathan and the dutiful son
Mr. Bun
Old strong charms
The old witch
One roll of bread
Owl
A prince and a dove
Prince Loaf
Prunella
Round is my bun
Salt and bread
The self-propelled carriage
The soldier and the knapsack
The spoiled daughter
The student who became a prince
The three clever brothers
The two sisters (VITTORINI – OLD)
The warm matzah
The well of D'Yeree-in-Dowan
Why the tortoise has a round back
A wise sentence
The woman of Llyn-y-fan (1) The
meeting

Bread and butter
BATCHELOR – SUPER. p113-114

Bread-free
KELSEY – ONCE p65-70

Breadfruit trees
The weary spirits of Lanai

Breadth
Long, broad and sharpsight

Break mountains
COURLANDER – PIECE p23-24

Breakfasts
Little Gustava

Breaking a mirror
BATCHELOR – SUPER. p84-86

Breastplates
Ruda, the quick thinker
The son of the King of Spain

Breathing
Magic
Puffing Potter's powerful puff
You can't hold it

Breezes. *See* **Wind**

The Bremen town musicians
BAMBERGER – FIRST p92-97
HAVILAND – GERMANY p72-85

Brer goat and brer lion
WILLIAMS – ROUND p192-194

Brer wolf's little tar men
JOHNSON – WHAT p241-243

Brian and the fox
MANNING – RED p1-9

Bricks
Sense and money

A bride for the sea god
CARPENTER – ELEPHANT'S p141-
150

The bride from the land of the spirits
BERRY – MAGIC p98-112

The bride from the sea
CARPENTER – SHIPS p277-285

The bride of Llyn y Fan Fach
SHEPPARD – WELSH p36-42

The bride-price for Olwen
PICARD – CELTIC p46-69

The bride who melted away
CARPENTER – AFRICAN p161-168

The bride who out talked the water kelpie
LEODHAS – THISTLE p82-97

The bride who would not speak
INS-SOB – FOLK p189-190

Bridegrooms
Brides, grooms and weddings

Bridegrooms (*Continued*)

Friends in life and death
If you know a story, don't keep it to
  yourself
The king who liked fairy tales
The marriage feast
The mole's bridegroom
The monkey bridegroom
Mrizala and her bridegroom
The peacock bridegroom
The prophet Elijah and the angel of
  death
The silver penny
Three bridegrooms for one bride
The toad-bridegroom
The two bridegrooms
The unseen bridegroom

Brides

Abu Zaid seeks a horse and finds a
  wife
Baboon skins
Bastianelo
Blue Beard
Bluebeard
The boy and the leopard
The clever bride of Tunisia
Clever Carmelita
A clever old bride
Dermot and Grania
The devil's bride
Donal from Donegal
The egg
The enchanted castle in the sea
The fair young bride
The forest bride
The frog
The frog bride
The giant and his royal servants
The giant's bride
The girl out of the egg
The girl who married the devil
The girl who picked strawberries
Godfather death
The honeybee bride
How Dounai won a bride for Prince
  Vladimir
Kelŏglan and the lucky exchanges
King adder
The king and his seven sons
The little mouse
The little pet Rani
The magic berries
The maiden of the mist
The maiden with the wooden helmet
Makhandu Mahlanu or The five heads
The milky way
More beautiful than the spider's web
The mouse hole
Not driving and not riding

Pecos Bill and his bouncing bride
Prince Finn the fair
The rat who made one bargain too
  many
Salakhbai and the fox
Scheherazade
The serpent's bride
Shadow-bride
The spoiled daughter
The squire's bride
The story of silly Cham-ba
Svyatogor's bride
The tale of Bonnie Baby Livingston
The tale of the Fäderäevisch
Temba wins a bride
Three bridegrooms for one bride
Three foolish brides
A trick that failed
The troll's bride
Why Eyvin won the race
The wolf-bride
The wooden bowl

Bride's brook
  TAFT – PROFILE p227-230

Brides, grooms and weddings
  BATCHELOR – SUPER. p77-83

The bridge
  MY BOOK HOUSE v. 1 p210.

The bridge of heaven
  McALPINE – JAPAN. p7-10

The bridge of St. Cloud
  U. N. – RIDE p173-177

Bridges

The badger and the magic fan
The black dog of the wild forest
Building the bridge
The devil and the railroad
The devil's bridge
The dreamer
The dutiful daughter
Fairy workmen
The fiddler of Fiddler's bridge
The fortunate shoemaker
Four tales of how the devil was
  outwitted
The frog
The giant who sucked his thumb
The goblin bridge
A happy day in the city
How strong a bridge have you?
A lucky child
Molly Whuppie
The monkey bridge
The ogre who built a bridge
Old Nick's bridge

Bridges (*Continued*)

An ossete riddle
Pappa Greatnose
The pedlar of Swaffham
The phantom bridge
Prince Mirko
Prince Murko's journey
The princess in the earth cave
The ravens build a bridge
Sam Patch's last leap
The shoemaker's dream
The speedy messenger
A story of three brothers
A swift messenger
The tengu's magic nose fan
The three billy-boats gruff
The three goats called Hurricane
Three men on the bridge
Traveling to see wonders
Why the ocean is salty
Zo, Han-Zun, who became a stone
Buddha

, **Golden**
The crystal kiosk and the diamond
ship
The snake

, **Rainbow**
Asgard and the Aesir gods
Heimdall, the watchman of Asgard
Yggdrasil, the world tree

, **Silver**
The flower of beauty

Bridles and bits
John Macdonald and the kelpie
Little John and the water horse
Pegasus and the Chimaera

Briffault, François
Father big-nose
The journey to Toulouse of the
animals that had colds

Briffault, Marie
La Ramée and the phantom
The three stags

Brigands. *See* **Bandits; Outlaws; Thieves
and thievery**

The brigands and the miller's daughter
MANNING – RED p84-92

Bring me a light
MANNING – GHOSTS p25-29

Bring the comb and play upon it!
MY BOOK HOUSE v. 1 p159.

The bringing of the light by raven. *See*
The extraordinary black coat

British Columbia. *See* **Canada–British
Columbia**

British West Indies–Granada
A shilling for a lie

Brittany. *See* **France–Brittany**

Brobdingnagians (giants)
Gulliver in the giants' country

The broken box
MARKS – SPANISH p49-69

The broken wing
SCHOOLCRAFT – FIRE p58-65

Bromo feast, the origin of the. *See* The
origin of the bromo feast

The bronze ring
SIDEMAN – WORLD'S p344-361

The brook song
MY BOOK HOUSE v. 3 p161.

Brooks
Come, little leaves
How bean got his stripe
What the children do in summer

Broome, Dora
A moon of gobbags

Brooms
The blackstairs mountain
The boy on a broomstick
A cat and a broom
Flying with witches
Journey by broomstick
There was an old woman tossed up in
a basket
The twins and the snarling witch
A witch's song

The broomstick train
HOLE – WITCHES p31.

Brother Anansi and Sir Peacock
MCNEILL – DOUBLE p30-35

Brother Breeze and the pear tree
SHERLOCK – ANANSI p13-19

Brother Rabbit's astonishing prank
ARBUTHNOT – TIME p197-198

74

Brothers

See also **Sons; Twins**
According to tradition
The aderna bird
The advantages of learning
The adventures of Silvervit and
 Lillvacker
The anger of Sande-Nyana
Anpu and Bata
The ash lad and the good helpers
Aükele'and the water-of-life
The Bakki brothers
The banishment of Diab
Bash Tchelik
The beggar in the blanket
The beginning of good conversation
The best wish
Billy Beg and the sassafras switch
The bird of the golden land
Boots and his brothers
Boots and the troll
The bow, the deer, and the talking
 bird
The boy and Necken
The boy in the land of shadows
The boy who was called "thick-head"
The castle of no return
Chien Tang
Childe Rowland and the King of
 Elfland
The children of Lir
The children of the dead woman
Christie and the growing hand
Constantes and the dragon
The coral comb
The crane's feather
The dancing horses of Acoma
Daniel the gawk
Dapplegrim
Dawn, twilight and midnight
Dear-boy
The death of the sons of Tuireann
The death of the sons of Uisne
Deidre and the sons of Usna
The devil in the steeple
Digit the midget
Doll i' the grass
The doll in the grass
The double knights
The dragon king and the lost fish-hook
The duck with red feet
The duty that was not paid
Dwarfs' caps
Eighteen rabbits
The emerald-crested phoenix
The enemy's tent
Esben and the witch
The exile of Rama
The fairy host
The fairy wife
Fate

Feedowa and Nobbin
Fereyel and Debbo Engal the witch
The first attack
The flight
Flinty
The flying ship
The fool and the birch-tree
The fountain of youth
The four brothers
Four brothers who were both wise and
 foolish
Four sworn brothers
The fox-girl and her brother
The frog
The frog princess
The frog-wife
The fruits of health
Georgic and Merlin
The ghost dog of South Mountain
The giant who had no heart in his
 body
Gisella and the goat
The golden bird
The golden castle that hung in the air
The golden chain
The golden gourd
The golden nightingale
The golden skins
The great bear
Great Head and the ten brothers
The griffon
The hair from the queen of the
 underworld
Hallabau's jealousy
The hare herd
The hare of Inaba
The hen that laid diamond eggs
Hop o' my thumb
How Maui fished up New Zealand
How men learned to sing songs
How thunder and lightning came to be
The hunger time
Hwan and Dang
Introduction (CAMPBELL – MAORI)
Iphigenia . . . The transported
 sacrifice
The jewels of the sea
Jonnikin and the flying basket
Joseph and his brethren
The juniper
The just and unjust brothers
Kakúi, bird of the night
Kashi and his wicked brothers
Keep cool
The kindly ghost
King Hrolf and the bear's son
The king of the Golden River, or the
 black brothers
King Solomon's pupils
The knight with the two swords
The lads who met the highwaymen

Brothers (*Continued*)

The lame vixon
The land of youth
Lato, the stupid one
The lion, the tiger, and the eagle
Little fool Ivan and the little
humpback horse
The little nobleman
The little orphan
The little red mannikin
Long-Neck, Fatty and Droopy
The long nose
Lucas the strong
Magic apples
The magic ball
The magic dagger
The magic mare
The magic mortar
The magic turban, the magic whip,
and the magic carpet
The man without a heart
The master and the servant
The meeting of Deirdre and Naoise
The miller's three sons
The monkey nursemaid
The mother of time and the enchanted
brothers
Myth and folktale in human actions:
The tale of the two brothers
Nastasya and the whirlwind
The nightingale Hazaran
Noodlehead and the flying horse
Nooloigah who caused his brother to
die
Old Bluebeard
The old hag of the forest
The old magician
Once in, never out again
Peregrine and the redman of
Rockingham
Pinkel
Pleiad and star of dawn
Podhu and Aruwa
The poor brother's bad luck
The poor brother's treasure
The poor man's son, the dwarfs, and
the birds
Prince Ahmed and the fairy Peribanou
Prince Daniel
The Prince of Coucy
The prince with the golden hand
The princess in the camphor tree
The princess who was dumb
The quest of the sons of Turenn
The rich landowner and his worker
The riddle of the black knight
The ring in the seashell
Rusty Jack
Salt
The salt Welsh sea

Sarita and the Duendas
The sea of Moyle
The search: who gets the chief's
daughter
The servant lass
The seven ravens
Seven Simons
The shadow boys
Shemiaka the judge
The shouts on the hill of Midkena
The silent princess
The simpleton
The singing bone
The singing flute
The singing man
The six brothers
The six companions
Sketco begins his wanderings
Sketco finds his brothers
Snake magic
The son of the hunter
Sorrow
The spring of youth
Squirrel and fox
The story of the stone lion
The story of three brothers
Strong man
Stupid Emilien
Sylvester
The tale of three brothers
The tale of the two brothers
The tale of the youngest brother
and the stupid devil
The three brothers
The three brothers and the black hen
The three brothers and the giant
The three brothers and the marvelous
things
The three brothers and the treacle
toffee
The three clever brothers
Three eels
Three fat ewes for three fine hounds
The three feathers
Three magic charms
The three ravens
Three who couldn't be parted
Three who found their hearts' desire
The three wishes
To feed my people: The coming of
corn
Tola and the sea monster
Tongue steeple
The tree that flew
The troll who hid his life
True and untrue
Tsar Boris and the devil king
Tsar Lazar anf Tsaritsa Militsa
The twelve young men
The two brothers
The two brothers and the ghost Mo'oi

Brothers (*Continued*)

The two brothers and the magistrate
Two pennies
The two wizards
The two youths whose father was
  under the sea
Volund the smith
Wakewell and his brothers
Wayland Smith
The well at the world's end
West country boy
The whispering giant
Why crocodile does not eat hen
Why the mountains are snow-covered
Why the sea is salt
The wild swans
With a wig, with a wag
The wolf in the ram's skin
The wonder ship and ship's crew
Yi Chang and the haunted house
Young John
The youth who could become an ant,
  a lion, or an eagle

Brothers and friends
SUN – LAND p106-110

The brothers of the donkey
KELSEY – ONCE p105-107

The brothers Yakschich divide their heirloom
ĆURĆIJA – HEROES p131-133

Brotherton, Alice Williams
Give praise

Brough, John, trans.
He leaves the nest
Here, forest-fires
Peaceful, the gentle deer
With tail-fans spread

Brown, John
A little story about a great man

Brown, Shirley
BROWN – AROUND p141.

The brown cow
DUDDINGTON – RUSS. p53-56

The brown man of the Muirs
BRIGGS – PERS. p164-165

Brown owl's story
SHERLOCK – IGUANA'S p43-52

The brownie o' Ferne-Den
HAVILAND – SCOTLAND p49-58

The brownie of Cranshaws
BRIGGS – PERS. p126.

The brownie of Jedburgh
BRIGGS – PERS. p122-123

The brownie of Rothiemurchus
SHEPPARD – SCOT. p75-76

Brownies
Ainsel
The black-bearded brownies of
  Boneberg
The cauld lad of Hilton
From brownie to boggart
The lairdie with the heart of gold
The little one
Mary-Ann and the cauld lad of Hylton
The Nithsdale brownie
The owl's answer to Tommy
Puddlefoot
Tops or bottoms

The brownies in the toy shop
MY BOOK HOUSE v. 3 p40-44

Browning, Elizabeth Barrett
Blessings on thee, dog of mine
Go out, children
Two children

Browning, Elizabeth Barrett
A Victorian romance

Browning, Robert
Bang-whang-whang
A cavalier tune

Browning, Robert
A Victorian romance

Browny
BUDBERG – RUSSIAN p123-128

Bruce, Margery
The half-chick

Bruce, Robert
Bannockburn

Bruce, Robert
Bannockburn
Bruce and the spider
The Holy relic of Bannockburn
Robert Bruce and the spider; how a
  king learned courage from an insect
Robert Bruce, Scotland's hero
The tale of the riddle sent to Bruce

Bruce and the spider
BALDWIN – FAVOR. p18-20

Brunettes
Blonde, brunette or redhead

Brushes, Paint
Ma Liang and his magic brush

Bryan, Brigitte
GRAHAM – BEGGAR p96.

Bryan, Ruth
The buried treasure

Bryant, Sara Cone
The gingerbread man

Bryant, William Cullen
The planting of the apple tree

Bryant, William Cullen
The father of American song

Brynhild
How Sigurd awoke Brynhild

Bubbur the giant brown-and-yellow
snake
PARKER – AUSTRALIAN p237-239

Bucca Dhu and Bucca Gwidden
MANNING – PETER p98-102

Buccaneers. *See* **Pirates**

Buck, Alan Michael
Deirdre

Buck, Pearl S.
What the children do in summer

Buckets
The girl whom the moon pitied
The little bucket

Buckeyes
Carry a horse chestnut

Buckles
The dolphins of Celebes
Volkh's journey to the East

The buckwheat
CATHON – PERHAPS p241-243

Bucky, the big, bold fawn
MY BOOK HOUSE v. 3 p85-91a

Buddha and Buddhism
See also **Bodisat; Monks, Buddhist;**
Panchatantra (fables)

Author's note
The birth years
Chu Dong Tse and the princess
The golden buffalo
The governor and the Buddhist
The hare in the moon
The horse and the eighteen bandits
Hwang and Dang
An inadvertent misunderstanding
The Jatakas
The Lake of Zangzĕ
The laughing statue
The mason's marriage
The miracle of the begging bowl
Mythical beast of the sea
Pen and four foolish ministers
The rat's bridegroom
The raven's magic gem
The snake and its benefactor
The status that sneezed
The stone monkey
That fourth leg of the dog
The wrestling match of the two
Buddhas
The young man and the priest
Zo Han-Zun, who became a stone
Buddha

Budulinek
ARBUTHNOT – TIME p132-135
FILLMORE – SHEPHERD'S p94-102

Buehr, Walter
BUEHR – SEA p92.

The buffalo and the porcupine
HEADY – TALES p90-94

Buffalo Bill
MY BOOK HOUSE v. 9 p27-38f

Buffalo Bill. *See* **Cody, Will**

The buffalo who made undue demands
BURTON – MAGIC p59-61

Buffalos
The arrows that became trees
The battle of the buffaloes
The bird that told tales
The clever jackal and how he outwitted
the tiger
The crow's pearl
The elephant's lip
The end of the world: The buffalo go
The envious buffalo
The farmer, the buffalo, and the tiger
A flower to catch a thief
The giant with the grey feathers
The girl on the rock

Buffalos (*Continued*)

The girl who used her wits
How confusion came among the
    animals
How men learned to build houses
How the world was made (1)
It happened in Kashmir
Kalulu and the leopard
Pecos Bill, the cowboy
The stupid wolf
The tiger's stripes
To feed my people: The coming of
    buffalo
To feed my people: The race between
    the buffalo and man
The tree with the difficult name
Tshiama, the snake's daughter
The victory of the buffalo
War between the crocodiles and
    Kantchil
West country boy
Why there is both day and night
A wise man on a camel
Young hunter

, **Golden**
The golden buffalo

, **Water**
The bird and the buffalo
The dilemma of a pious man
How much for a shadow?
The three brothers
The ungrateful tiger

Bugganes (fiends)
The three bugganes
Timothy and the buggane ghost

Buggies
Grandma'am Hinkel and the phanton
dog

The bugle song
    MY BOOK HOUSE v. 11 p7.

Bugles
The bugle song
The princess of Tomboro
Shawneen and the gander

Bugs. *See* **Insects**

Buh fox's number nine shoes
    COURLANDER – TERRA. p37-40

Buh mouse testifies
    See also The donkey who sinned
    COURLANDER – TERRA. p53-56

Buh rabbit and the king
    COURLANDER – TERRA. p60-64

Buh rabbit's big eat
    COURLANDER – TERRA. p33-36

Buh rabbit's graveyard
    COURLANDER – TERRA. p57-59

Buh rabbit's human weakness
    COURLANDER – TERRA. p31-32

Buh rabbit's tail
    COURLANDER – TERRA. p41-45

Buh rabbit's tight necktie
    COURLANDER – TERRA. p21-23

Builders and building
See also **Carpenters**
The clock must not stop
Eight leaves of story (3) Baglan the
    builder
The honey feast
The house that strong boy built
How men learned the build houses
How Tepozton hung the bells
The sheep and the pig that made a
    home
So say the little monkeys
The treasure thief
Why the ocean is salty

The building of Ravanitsa
    ĆURĆIJA – HEROES p33-35

The building of the fortress wall
    HOSFORD – THUNDER p21-25

Building the bridge
    MY BOOK HOUSE v. 2 p149.

Building with blocks
    MY BOOK HOUSE v. 1 p164.

Bukango and the crocodiles
    HARMAN – TALES p29-56

Bukolla
    PALMER – JOURNEY p55-67
    U. N. – RIDE p194-196

Bukolla, the wonderful cow
    BOUCHER – MEAD p8-11

Bukovina
The yellow dragon
Young happy

Bulbs
The two brothers

79

5

Bulbuls (birds)
A story of Rustem, the hero of Persia
Why the jackal howls

Bulfinch, Thomas
The battle of Roncesvalles

Bulgaria
The bag of lies
Batim the horse
The boy with the golden star
The clever billy goat
The escape of the animals
A gift from the heart
Grandmother Marta
The language of animals
The lazy one
The magic pipe
A man, a snake, and a fox
Once upon a time
The precious stone
Silian the stork
Silver leaves and golden blossoms
Simple and the princess
Sly Peter at the fair
Sly Peter's revenge
The spoiled daughter
The spring of youth
Tsar Boris and the devil king
The ungrateful bear
The uninvited guest
The unwashed pot

Bull frog knows more about rain than
the almanac
CHAPPELL – THEY p69-74

Bull of Ptah
The tale of the two brothers

The bull of Uri
MÜLLER – SWISS p33-38

Bullets, Silver
How to kill a witch
Legend of the witch of Cape Ann

Bullfighters
The poor widow bullfighter

Bullfrogs. *See* **Frogs**

Bullies
Annie Christmas
Canawlers on the E-ri-ee Canal

Bullock, Caroline Canfield
The singing geese

Bulls
Anpu and Bata
The battle of the bulls
Billy Beg and the bull
The boy and the bull
The bride who melted away
Bukolla
The cow that cried
Cuchulain, the hound of Ulster
Cuculain, the Irish hound
Diplomacy
The enchanted buck
Europa and the bull
The five friends
The flower-headed man
Grumpy Timothy Crumb
The jackal and the bear
The jackal told me
Jaco and the giant
Kari Woodencoat
Katie Woodencloak
The labors of Hercules
The lion and the bulls
The lion of hard-to-pass forest
A little bull-calf
The little bull calf
The minotaur
Moi and the red bull
The parish bull eats the grass from
the wall
A peasant sells a cow as a goat
Peder Okse
The pillow talk
The princess in the fiery tower
Rake up!
The Red Ettin
Right out in our barnyard
Santiago and the fighting bulls
The secret room
Seeley Simpkins and his bull
The sleepless dragons
The small people's cow
Smereree
The speckled bull
The steers that wouldn't draw
The story of Prince Ring and his dog
The tale of the three brothers
The traveller and the tiger
The ungrateful crocodile
When the bull bellows
The white pet
Who is the older?
The yam child

–Horns
Momus the mocker

–Noses
Why the steer has a smooth nose

, Water
The water horse and the water bull

Bulls and the color red
BATCHELOR – SUPER. p43.

Bulltop, Alfred
Old Stormalong

Bumblebee and chipmunk
JOHNSON – WHAT p236.

Bumblebees. *See* **Bees**

Bum-clocks. *See* **Beetles; Cockroaches**

The bun
ROSS – BURIED p13-18

The bunch of grapes
GREEN – BIG p58.

Bundar Bahadeer Poon
HITCHCOCK – KING p37-45

The bundle of sticks
STRONG – FAVORITE p33.

The bundle of straw and the king's son
SEKI – FOLKTALES p176-179

The bungled message
JABLOW – MAN p23.

The bungling host
MARTIN – COYOTE p19-22

Bungling Pedro
MEHDEVI – BUNGLING p17-35

Bunner, Henry C.
Casperl

Buns. *See* **Bread**

Buntings, Snow (birds)
The lost song

Bunyan, Paul
Paul Bunyan
Paul Bunyan–poem
Paul Bunyan swings his axe
Paul Bunyan's cornstalk
Sky-bright axe/Paul Bunyan
The story of big Paul Bunyan
Wintering with Paul Bunyan
Young Paul

Burgess, Gelett
The pert fire engine
The purple cow
The steamboat and the locomotive

Burgess, Thornton W.
Peter Rabbit decides to change his name

Burglars and burglary. *See* **Thieves and thievery**

Burgomasters. *See* **Lawyers**

Burgundians
The slaying of Siegfried

Burials
Butterflies
Cast they bread upon the waters
The crock of gold
Geomancer's three sons
Old Sal's curse
The son of the turtle spirit
The unmarried girl's grave

Buriats
Why there is thunder and lightning

The buried moon
JACOBS – MORE p110-117

The buried treasure
ROSS – BURIED p65-74

Burma
The bee-hunter and the oozie
The case of the calf and the colt
The cat, the dog, and the mongoose
The drunkard and the opium-eater
The elephant's bathtub
The fisherman and the king's chamberlain
The four deaf men
The four young men
The golden crow
The grateful beasts
The greedy stallkeeper and the poor traveler
The hidden treasure of Khin
How Master Thumb defeated the sun
The king who ate chaff
A kingdom lost for a drop of honey
Mister Luck and Mister Industry
The musician of Tagaung
The old man in the moon
The origin of the coconut
Partnership

Burma (*Continued*)

The tiger's minister of state
Why ants live everywhere
Why crow is black and men find
  precious stones in the earth
Why the rabbit's nose twitches
Why the tiger is so angry at the cat

—**Language**
Keys to Burmese meanings

—**Shan People**
The silver hare in a box
The trial of the stone

A burn cured
JOHNSON – WHAT p168.

Burnett, Peter (governor of California)
American family westward

Burns, Howard M. (illus.)
ROBERTSON – PHILIP. p128.

Burns
Dineivan the emu and Wahn the crows
The wood cutter's son and the two
  turtles

Burns, Robert
Bannockburn
O, Lady Mary Anne
O rattlin', roarin' Willie
The ploughman he's a bonnie lad
Tam O'Shanter
Verses
Wee Robin's Christmas song

Burns, Robert
The ploughboy poet

The burro Benedicto
JORDAN – BURRO p13-17

Burton, Virginia
Mike Mulligan and his steam shovel

Burros. *See* Donkeys

Busch, Wilhelm
Max and Moritz
Max and Moritz and the tailor
Plish and plum

Buses
Big bus, stop!
The big street in the big city
A happy day in the city
Trip to town

Bush—Fowls
Why the bush-fowl calls at dawn and
  why flies buzz

Bush—Rats
Why the bat flies at night

Bushbucks
The leopard and the bushbuck buy a
  dream
The leopard and the bushbuck go
  hunting
The leopard builds a house for the
  bushbuck

Bushes
The little nobleman
The tale of a foolish brother and of a
  wonderful bush
Why the brierbush quarreled with the
  beasts

Bushmen
The frog that swallowed the ocean

Business and business men
Luck in business
Shlemiel, the businessman

Buslayevich, Vasili
Vasili Buslayevich
Vasili Buslayevich's pilgrimage

Butcherbirds
The lost spear

Butchers
Aristotle and the three sons
The cat and the mouse
A good neighbor
The grateful goat
The greatest hoax in New York City
I'm a butcher
The pious butcher
Rub-a-dub-dub
The three butchers from Reims
The wandering apprentice
Who is strongest?

Butler, Samuel
Reaction

Butter
Antonio Canova
The fox and the wolf
The fox and the wolf and the keg of
  butter

Butter (*Continued*)
The little hen and the little cock
The ogre king of Gilgit
Shrovetide
The stupid boy

Butterball
ASBJÖRNSEN – NORW. p97-101

Buttercup
HOKE – WITCHES p32-36

Buttercups
The first buttercups
A milkweed and a buttercup

Butterflies
Dawn, twilight and midnight
Gammelyn, the dressmaker
The golden butterfly
The hermit's cabbage patch
The lost spear
Midir and Etain
The elephant and the butterfly
The nose of the Konakadet
The princess of China
The story of Maia
Sungold
The three butterflies

Butterflies
INS-SOB – FOLK p39

Butterflies, butterflies
MY BOOK HOUSE v. 1 p81

The butterfly in the granary
SUN – LAND p42-43

The butterfly's ball
MY BOOK HOUSE v. 3 p162-163

Buttermilk
The girl and the sailor

Butterworth, Mary (Peck)
Rehoboth's lady counterfeiter

Butting a sermon
JAGENDORF – SAND p163-165

Buttons
The tale of a Pakistan parrot
Old Meg, the witch

Buya marries the tortoise
BURTON – MAGIC p98-101

The buyer of oxen
BARASH – GOLDEN p82-83

Buzzards
How much you remind me of my
husband!
How rabbit stole fire from the
buzzards
How the sun came
Mr. Rabbit meets his match again
Mr. Wren borrows money of Mr.
Buzzard
Peter Rabbit decides to change his
name
Waiting on salvation
Who?
Why the buzzard eats the rooster's
children
Why the world is the way it is

–Necks
Uncle rabbit flies to heaven

Bye-lo, Bubbeli, sleep
MY BOOK HOUSE v. 1 p117

Bye-o! Bye-o!
MY BOOK HOUSE v. 1 p90

Byron, George Gordon, Lord
Solitude

Byron, George Gordon, Lord
The boy of Newstead Abbey

C

Cabala (language)
The mechanical man of Prague

El cabalo de siete colore. *See* The
horse of seven colors

Cabbages
Annie goes to the cabbage field
The big cabbage and the big kettle
The ghost in the cabbage patch
The hermit's cabbage patch
Large cabbages
The little girl and the hare
The three silver bells
Transportation problem

Cables
The cauldron of Brekkan

Cacti
Lazy lout of a plant
Near God's cactus
The plains' call
A world of beauty: The Peyote
religion

Caddis fly (worm)
The adventures of a water baby
The fairyland of science

Cadmus . . . The dragon's teeth
UNTERMEYER – FIRE. p91-94

Cadoc, Saint
The house in the valley
Saint Cadog and King Arthur
Saint Cadog and the mouse

Cadwalader and all his goats. *See* Eight
leaves of story (8) Cadwalader and all
his goats

Cadwalader and his goat
SHEPPARD – WELSH p146-148

Cadwalader's goat
NYE – MARCH p46-53

Caesar, Julius
Julius Caesar . . . The Ides of March

Cages
An emir and two thieves

The gold bird
The tiger, the Brahman, and the
jackal
The wild man

Cailleaches
The grateful old cailleach

Cakes
The black woodpecker
Donkey-skin
The fairy wife
Fin M'Coul and Cucullin
The full moon
Hansel and Gretel
The Hoca as Tamerlane's tax collector
The horned witches
Johnny-cake
The johnnycake
King Alfred and the cakes
The magician Palermo
The pancake
The poffertjes pan
The Red-Ettin
A selfish husband
The son of the baker of Barra
The stone of victory
The tinner, the dog, the Jew and the
cake
The wonderful cake

Cakrapani
The calves

The calabash children
ARNOTT – AFRICAN p112-118

Calabash of the winds
THOMPSON – HAWAII. p70-75

Calabashes
Goso the teacher
How crab got a hard back
The magic calabash
The story of Hinemoa
Tim for wealth and happiness
The time of deep darkness
Wend' Yamba

Caldera Dick
LEACH – RAINBOW

Caledonia
The tale of the lay of Amadhain Mhor
The tale of the sons of Cathmor

84

Calendars
    Ra and his children

California
    The acorn maidens
    Ants
    The beginning of the world and the
        making of California
    Coyote and the alder stump
    Early days and ways in America
    How California was made
    How coyote brought back people
        after the flood
    How man brought fire to earth
    How rattlesnake got his fangs
    How spider got his thread
    How the first rainbow was made
    Humbug
    The old woman and the bear
    Why there are shooting stars

−Clear Lake
    How coyote put fish in Clear Lake

−Columbia
    A couple of lost towns

−Cucamonga
    The lost treasure of Cucamonga

−Diablo Mountain
    How coyote got his voice

−Klamath river
    How coyote put salmon in the
        Klamath river

−Mount Shasta
    Why grizzly bears walk on all fours

−San Francisco
    Henry Crabb−a born loser

−San Joaquin valley
    The Indian shinny game
    The San Joaquin valley of California

−Sierra mountains
    The poet of the Sierras

, Southern
    Battle with the Sockdolager
    To hot to handle
    Why fly rubs his hands together

−Yosemite National Park
    Worm moon

California
    LEACH − RAINBOW p70-72

California's lost diamonds
    WILLIAMS − LOST p51-58

The Caliph stork, told by Selim Baruch,
    the stranger
    HAUFF − FAIRY p7-27

Caliphs
    Impossible tales
    The stork caliph
    The tory of Caliph stork
    The tailor's bright daughter
    The tale of Caliph stork

Callin' the dog
    LEACH − RAINBOW p189-190

Calling the Chinook
    HEADY − TALES p62-66

Calliopes
    The circus parade

The calm Brahman
    SPELLMAN − BEAUT. p33-36

The calves
    REED − TALK. p46.

Camas roots
    The legend of the star children

Cambodia
    The fish with bent noses
    How much for a shadow?
    How music began
    The seed of happiness

The camel and his neighbor
    GAER − FABLES p26-28

The camel in the lion's court
    GAER − FABLES p77-80

Camellias
    The man who bought a dream

Camels
    Ali and the camels
    The baby camel
    The circus parade
    Fareedah's carpet
    The golden lion
    How the camel got his hump
    How the camel got his proud look
    Mary and the Christ-child
    The mighty wrestlers
    The proud camel and the rude
        monkey
    A Sherlock Holmes of the steppes
    There's no telling on which side a
        camel will lie down
    The twice blessed Arab
    A wise man on a camel
    The wise old camel
    Zeus and the horse

Camlet flowers
The origin of the camlet flower

The camp on the Big Onion
ARBUTHNOT — TIME p185-187

Camphor trees
The magic listening cap
The princess in the camphor tree

Camwood powder
Why robin has a red breast

Canada
See also **Indians of North America—Tribes—Algonquin—Bella Coola—Kutchin—Loucheux—Tlingit**
The boy in the land of shadows
The boy of the red twilight sky
The boy who overcame the giants
The boy who was called "thick-head"
The boy who was saved by thoughts
The coming of the corn
The dance of death
The duck with red feet
Ermine and the hunter
The fall of the spider man
The first mosquito
The first pig and porcupine
The giant with the grey feathers
The girl who always cried
Glooskap's country
Great heart and the three tests
How Glooskap made the birds
How rabbit deceived fox
How rabbit lost his tail
How raven brought fire to the Indians
How summer came to Canada
How turtle came
The Indian Cinderella
Jean Labadie's dog
The locusts and the oats
The moon and his frog-wife
The mouse and the sun
The Northern lights
Owl with the great head and eyes
The partridge and his drum
The passing of Glooskap
Rabbit and the grain buyers
Rabbit and the Indian chief
Rabbit and the moon-man
Rainbow and the autumn leaves
The song-bird and the healing-waters
Sparrow's search for rain
Star-boy and the sun dance
A story of big Paul Bunyan
The strong boy
There was an old, old Indian
The tobacco fairy from the blue hills
Why the sun is brighter than the moon
The youth and the dog dance

, **British Columbia**
Atam and Im
Frogs in the moon
Why the sun is brighter than the moon

, **French**
The canoe in the rapids
The fairy quite contrary
The fountain of youth
The ghostly fisherman
The golden phoenix
Jacques the woodcutter
Jean Labadie's big black dog
Jean Labadie's dog
The loup-garou in the woods
The lutin in the barn
The Princess of Tomboso
Scurvyhead
Sir Goldenhair
The skunk in Tante Odette's oven
The sly thief of Valenciennes
The speckled hen's egg
The talking cat

—**New Brunswick**
Black Bartelmy
Gluskap
The piper

—**Nova Scotia**
How whale happens to smoke a pipe
Wokun

—**Quebec**
The duel
Marching to Quebec

—**Songs**
Canadian songs
I yay! I Yay! I Yay!
O if my top would only spin
Roll it, bowl it
A song of the Canadian lumberjack
There was an old, old Indian

Canada jays (birds)
The bear's head

Canadian songs
MY BOOK HOUSE v. 1 p130-131

Canals
Canawlers on the E-ri-ee canal
Wampum eater and the canal

Canaries
The cat and the starling
How the finch got his colors

Canary Islands
The most precious possession

The canary that liked apricots
KELSEY – ONCE p61-64

Canawlers on the E-ri-ee canal
JAGENDORF – UPSTATE p53-56

Candles
The broken box
The carnation youth
Death's godchild
Godfather death
The Hoca and the candle
John Gethin and the candle
Little Nancy Etticoat
The sleeping prince
The twelve silly sisters
The wager
White-bear-King Valemon
William Winter
The wood cutter's son and the two
turtles

Candlesticks
The golden candelabra
The golden candlestick
The mouse climbed up the candlestick
My candlestick
The silent princess
The weight of the cart

Candy
See also **Chocolate**
Hippety hop to the barber chop
The sugar-plum tree

Canes
The inquiring rabbit, or the strongest
thing in the world
The magic walking stick
The three brothers

Cannetella
MANNING – WIZARDS p118-127

Cannibal
MARTIN – NINE p38-42

The cannibal and his sweet singing bird
CARPENTER – AFRICAN p195-203

The cannibal frogs
JOHNSON – WHAT p169.

The cannibal who ate too fast
HOLLADAY – BANTU p24-25

The cannibal's drum
HOLLADAY – BANTU p38-41

Cannibals
See also **Amizemus**
The black-breasted magpie
Bobo, black dog, and the cannibal
woman
The dancing bird
Gheeger Gheeger the cold west wind
The giant ogre, Kloo-Teekl
Ka-Hai and the sorcerer Tama-i-wao
The love of Kenelinda
Mullian-ga the morning star
The ninwits
Onions
The rain bird
The story of the shining princess
The three sisters and the cannibals

Canniness. *See* **Cleverness; Trickery**

Cannons
The governor and the cannon
The wise men of Hebron

The canoe in the rapids
CARLSON – TALKING p54-65

Canoes
The boy in the land of shadows
A contest with skillful spirits
The drifting canoe
The fisherman who caught the sun
How Yehl, the hero, freed the beam-
ing maiden
Kela and the giant bird Halulu
The magic banana
The man who paddled to the moon's
house
The man who refused help
Mirabella
Rata and his canoe
The raven and the sharks
Sketco begins his wanderings
A song of the Canadian lumberjack
The star children dwelt in a deep cave
The story of Hine-Moa and Tutanekai
The strong boy
Ten little Indians
The three monsters of the sea
The unlucky fisherman
Waukewa's eagle

Canova, Antonio
Antonio Canova

Cantatas
Hiawatha childhood

Canterbury bells
Dainty little maiden

Canute, King
King Canute on the seashore

Cap o' rushes
See also Caporushes
HAVILAND – ENGLAND p76-88
WILLIAMS – FAIRY p117-123

The cap that mother made
MY BOOK HOUSE v. 3 p12-18

Caporushes
LINES – TALES p23-31

The capricious month
MINCIELLI – TALES p107-110

Captain Cook
ARBUTHNOT – TIME p320-321

Captain Fokke of Holland
See also The strange ship of Captain
Fokke
LAWSON – STRANGE p24-33

Captain Samuel Samuels
IVES – TALES p237-246

Captains, Sea
The beggar's prophecy
A boy on the high seas
The dancing fires of Saint Elmo
The dark cliffs of Dover
The ghost ship
A grand old skipper
Maiden Lane in the golden days
Plum pudding
The rich widow of Stavoren
The sea captain
Seán na Bánóige
The skipper and the dwarfs
Steamboat Bill and the captain's top
hat
The strange ship of Captain Fokke
Why the sea is salt

The captain's goose
JONES – SCAND. p84-88

A captive snake half dead with fright
REED – TALK. p44.

Captives, Indian
The ordeal of Hannah Dustin

Capturing the moon
JABLOW – MAN p51.

Capusas (evil spirits)
Evil rocks and the evil spirit of Peru

Carabaos. *See* Water buffalos

The caravan
HAUFF – CARAVAN p1-6
HAUFF – FAIRY p5-8
LARSON – PALACE p86-95

The caravan continues
HAUFF – CARAVAN p28-29,
50-51, 109-110, 139-143

The caravan ends
HAUFF – CARAVAN p209-220

The caravan reaches the end of the
desert
HAUFF – CARAVAN p175.

Caravans
Gideon, the warrior
The open road
The peddler's caravan
Rodents rampant on a field azure

Cardiff town
PUGH – TALES p97-104

Cardinals
How the cardinal got his red feathers
How the finch got her colors
How the redbird got his color

The cardinal's concert
BOWES – BIRD p32-39

Cards, Playing
Padre Ulivo and his guests
Peppino
Prince Finn the Fair
The soldier and the knapsack
The strange adventures of the
cowboy-sailor
The sword of light

The carefree monastery
BUDBERG – RUSSIAN p247-250

The careless master
CARPENTER – HORSES p121-123

A careless word summons the devil. *See*
The devil's bride

Carelessness
The thoughtless abbot
Three little kittens
A-tisket, a-tasket
The untidy mermaid

Carey, Henry
Of all the girls that are so smart
Pretty Sally

Caribbean Sea
Armadillo's story
Brown owl's story
Chimpanzee's story
Firefly's story
Green parrot's story
Little Capuchin monkey's story
The meeting
What is a crick crack story

Caribou
Lights of the caribou

The carl of the drab coat
PILKINGTON — SHAM. p139-149

The carlanco
HAVILAND — SPAIN p50-57

Carle, Eric
HEADY — TALES p125.

Carleton, William
A legend of Knockmany

Carlson, Natalie Savage
The lutin in the barn

The carnation youth
EELS — SPAIN p15-24

Carnations
Alas!
The golden carnation

Carnivals. See Fairs

Carnoy, Henri
The bronze ring
Six sillies

Carob trees
The great bird in the carob tree

The carp that became a dragon
VO-DINH — TOAD p51-55

Carpenter, John Alden
Krazy Kat

Carpenters
Aristotle and the three sons
The elephant and the carpenters
The greatest hoax in New York city
How the mosquitoes came to Oneata
Hwan and Dang
The king's tower
The little bird that found the pea
The little bird's rice
The ogre who built a bridge
The silent princess
The smoke horse
Spotless the lion and Trusty the
carpenter
The three golden ducats
The wonderful wooden peacock flying
machine

The carpenter's boar
REED — TALK. p64-67

Carpets
The dove maiden
Horns
I don't know where and I don't know
what
King Solomon's carpet
The magic carpet
The magic turban, the magic whip,
and the magic carpet
The Mopoke and the moon
Prince Ahmed
Prince Prigio
The Shah weaves a rug
The spotted rug
The strangest thing in the world
The three brothers and the marvelous
things
The three feathers
The youth who trusted in God

Carriages
The little girl of Griff House
The luck boy of Toy Valley
The poor boy and the princess
The self-propelled carriage
The snow-queen

Carrick, Valery
The bun
The little house
Mr. Samson cat
Snowflake

Carroll, Lewis
Jabberwocky
Mock turtle's song

Carrots
Eat your carrots
How the carrot-counter got his name

Carrots (*Continued*)

The old lady and the monkeys
Traveling to see wonders

Carry a horse chestnut
BATCHELOR – SUPER. p7-8

Carry an acorn
BATCHELOR – SUPER. p5

Carter, Isabel Gordon
Old Bluebeard

The cartman's stories
SPELLMAN – BEAUT. p59-63

Carts
A Belgian morning
The boy hero of Harlem
Christening the baby in Russia
Come, let's go to Sant Anita
David Copperfield and little Em'ly
The little toy land of the Dutch
Mary milks the cow
Necessity
The open road
The sin of a saint
The swan, the crab, and the pike
The weight of the cart
The wild ride in the tilt cart

The case of a widow before a sagacious
magistrate
HSIEH – CHINESE p51-55

The case of the calf and the colt
AUNG – KINGDOM p62-65

The case of the mouse-deer and the
crocodile's eggs
MORRIS – UPSTAIRS p9-15

Casey at the bat
MY BOOK HOUSE v. 7 p144c-144e

Casey Jones
LEACH – RAINBOW p50-53
MY BOOK HOUSE v. 5 p64-65

Casey Jones and locomotive no. 638
SHAPIRO – HEROES p7-57

Casey's comeback
MY BOOK HOUSE v. 7 p144f-144h

Casi Lampu'a Lentemue'
BELPRE – TIGER p75-82

Caskets
The devil's apprentice
Fairy caskets
The golden casket
An inadvertent misunderstanding
Pandora . . . the fateful casket
Teta the magician
The two step-sisters
Urashima

Casks
Caldera Dick
The magic belt
The money cask

Casperl
CHILD – CASTLES p227-241

Cassava (roots)
Why yams and cassava hide in the
ground

Cassiopeia, Queen
The boastful queen

Cast thy bread
BARASH – GOLDEN p18-21

Cast thy bread upon the waters
NAHMAD – PEASANT p151-155

The castle in the cornfield
PICARD – LADY p63-77

The castle in the lake
JORDAN – BURRO p72-75

The castle of no return
ALEGRIA – THREE p90-99
THOMPSON – ONE p14-19

The castle of Seoul
INS-SOB – FOLK p68-69

The castle of the three giants
SPICER – 13 p7-21

Castles
Anangarati and the men of four
castles
Ashypelt
Black Colin of Loch Awe
Casperl
The city east of the moon and south
of the sun
Damian and the dragon
East of the sun and north of the earth
East of the sun and west of the moon
The flitting of the ghosts
The flying castle

90

Castles (*Continued*)

The fruits of health
The giant of the brown beech wood
Gobborn seer
The gold-rich king
The golden apples of Loch Erne
The golden bird
The golden box
The golden castle that hung in the
  air
The heart of Princess Joan
The honey feast
The house in the valley
The invisible hands
Jack and his golden snuff-box
John the bear
King Johnny
The king of the fishes
Lancelot and Galahad
The legend of Eilean Donan castle
The little grey man
Little Lady Margaret
Longshanks, girth, and keen
Lord Peter
The lost half-hour
The magic lamp
The magic ring
Maid Lena
Menaseh's dream
Merman Rosmer
Mighty Mikko
The miller's three sons
The most precious gift
The old soldier and the mischief
The prince and the demon
Prince Finn the fair
The princess who was dumb
Puss in boots
The sea captain's wife
The sea knight
The seller of dreams
The sharpshooter
The skull
The son of the baker of Barra
The Soria-Moria-castle
The sword of light
A tale of a boy who set out to learn
  fear
The three brothers
The three musicians
The three sons of the King of Antua
Uwaine and the Lady of the fountain
The wandering cobbler
The well o' the world's end
, **Sea**
  The enchanted castle in the sea
−**Towers**
  The princess who saw everything
    in her kingdom
  The sorcerer's apprentices

A cat and a broom
  HOPE-SIMPSON − CAVAL. p133-142

Cat and dog
  SHERLOCK − WEST p93-96

The cat and mouse in partnership
  HAVILAND − GERMANY p32-40

The cat and the chanticleer
  BLOCH − UKRAIN. p11-18

The cat and the crab
  SEKI − FOLKTALES p25.

The cat and the dog
  O'SULLIVAN − FOLK. p13.
  INS-SŎB − FOLK p25-29

The cat and the fox
  BORSKI − GOOD p55-56
  BUDBERG − RUSSIAN p49-53

The cat and the hen
  DOBBS − MORE p63-65

The cat and the king's daughter
  BELTING − CAT p53-59

The cat and the mice
  HARDENDORFF − TRICKY p27-32

The cat and the mouse
  DE LA IGLESIA − CAT unp.
  REEVES − THREE unp.

The cat and the prophet
  CARPENTER − DOGS p145-153

The cat and the sea
  BELTING − CAT p79-82

The cat and the starling
  KRYLOV − 15 p13-15

The cat bride
  CARPENTER − DOGS p153-162

The cat-chalice of Vlaardingen
  LEEUW − LEGENDS p75-80

A cat for a hare
  JORDAN − BURRO p48-51

The cat inspector
  JAGENDORF − NEW p226-230

A cat is a cat is a cat
  VO-DINH − TOAD p123-128

The cat of Bubastis
  CARPENTER − DOGS p184-194

The cat on the dovrefell
  ASBJORNSEN – EAST p118-120
  JONES – SCAND. p105-107

The cat that went to heaven
  CARPENTER – DOGS p81-88

The cat, the cock and the lamb
  See also Bremen-town musicians
  COTHRAN – WITH p49-54

The cat, the dog, and death
  COURLANDER – PIECE p34-36

The cat, the dog, and the mongoose
  CARPENTER – DOGS p52-63

The cat, the mountain goat, and the fox
  BELPRE´– TIGER p113-117

The cat, the tiger, and the man
  MASEY – STORIES p84-87

The cat which lost a claw
  JOHNSON – WHAT p164.

The cat who came indoors
  TRACEY – LION p115-117

The cat with the crooked tail
  CARPENTER – DOGS p43-51

Catamarans (boats)
  How the mosquitoes came to Oneata

The cataract of Lodore
  MY BOOK HOUSE v. 7 p47.

Cataracts. *See* **Waterfalls**

Catches
  JOHNSON – WHAT p238-239

Catching hares in winter
  RANKE – GERMANY p193.

Catching the thief
  LEACH – NOODLES p20.

The caterpillar
  GREEN – BIG p44-45

Caterpillars
  The adventures of a water baby
  A fuzzy fellow without feet

The long one
The mighty warrior in hare's house
The princess's slippers
Son of the long one

Catfish and his terrible end
  HASKETT – GARINS p24-25

Cathedral of Saint James
  Pietro Bailliardo

Cathedral of Santiago de Compostella, Spain
  Pietro Bailliardo

Cathedrals. *See* **Churches and cathedrals;** names of cathedrals

Cather, Katherine Dunlap
  The duty that was not paid
  The luck boy of Toy Valley

Catherine and her fate
  PROTTER – CHILD. p88-92

Catherine and the Fates
  McNEILL – DOUBLE p73-80

Catherine, my dearie
  MY BOOK HOUSE v. 1 p124.

Catherine's tea party
  PROTTER – CHILD. p75-77

Cathmor
  The tale of the sons of Cathmor

Catholicism
  See also **Nuns; Priests;** etc.
  Guy Fawkes . . . The gunpowder plot
  The sharpshooter

A Catio Indian legend
  LEACH – RAINBOW p300-301

Cats
  A, B, C, kitty's in the snow I see!
  The adventures of Alexander Selkirk
  Ah Tcha the sleeper
  All the cats consulted
  The animal musicians
  The ape and the two cats
  Au Sung meets Kim Lee
  The audacious kitten
  Baba Yaga
  Baba Yaga and the little girl with
    the kind heart
  Bahram and the snake prince
  The barnyard

Cats *(Continued)*

Bear, fox, and man
The beckoning cat
The bed
Belling the cat
The big cat and the big rat
The bold heroes of Hungry Hill
"Bow-wow", says the dog
The boy on a broomstick
The boy who drew cats
The boy who had to draw cats
The Bremen town musicians
The bridge of St. Cloud
Bye-o! Bye-o!
Cattenborg
The Cavallino
Ceátach
Christening the baby in Russia
The city mouse and the country
  mouse
Clever Carmelita
The clever cat and the giant
The clumber pup
The cock, the cat, and the fox
The Connemara donkey
Conversation
The country of the mice
Curd ears
Dame Wiggins of Lee
The devil and the pit
Dick Whittington and his cat
Diddle, diddle on a bass fiddle
A dinar for a donkey
The dog, the cat, and the mouse
Donkeys! Dogs! Cats! Rats!
Don't run away my kitty
The duel of the cat and the mouse
The Earl of Cattenborough
The farmer in the dell
Fate of the vulture
First adventures
The first witch's cat
The five friends
The foolish dog and his reflection
The four friends
The fox and the cat
A frog he would a-wooing go
George and the field glasses
The ghost that didn't want to be a
  ghost
Giacco and his bean
Gigi and the magic ring
The glass house
Golden bracelets, golden anklets
The grateful animals and the talisman
The grateful beasts
The grateful mouse
Great A, little A, bouncing B
The greatest person in the world
The hearth-cat

The hermit cat
Hey diddle diddle
The holy cat of Tibet
The honourable tom cat
The house mouse and the country
  mouse
How Kwaku Ananse destroyed a
  kingdom
How people got the first cat
How the coconut tree was saved
How the Manx cat lost its tail
How tiger learned to hunt
The hunting cat
I love little pussy
I saw a crow a-flying cow
I stand in the pulpit and preach
If so, where is the cat?
The inquiring rabbit, or The strongest
  thing in the world
The Irish luck of Brian Hughes
Jack and his comrades
Jack and his friends
The jeweled ring
Keloǧlan the kindhearted
The king o' the cats
The king of the cats
King Solomon's cat
A kingdom lost for a drop of honey
The kingdom without a cat
Kisander
The kitten and falling leaves
The kitten and the knitting needles
Knurremurre the troll
Krazy Kat
Kuratko, the terrible
The ladle that fell from the moon
The lame cat and the potter
The lazy cat
The learned cat
The little cat and the knitting needles
The little girl and the new dress
Little Gustava
The little hen and the little cock
Little Mukra
The long-eared cat and the vulture
Lord Peter
The lost children
The mad dog
The magic amber
The magic egg
The magic ring
The man who swallowed the mouse
The marriage of Tom and the vixen
Mary covered with gold and Mary
  covered with pitch
The master cat
Meat or cat?
Mr. Korbes the fox
Mr. Samson cat
Mr. Wheeler
Mrs. Fox's wedding

Cats (*Continued*)

Mrs. Tabby Gray
Mittens the cat
The mongoose, the owl, the cat and
the mouse
Moon pearls
The mouse surrounded
The musicians of Bremen
Mysteries of the sea
Odd Olle
The old woman and the thief
The owl and the pussy-cat
Pán Kotsky
The parrot
Poor Jack and the cat
The poor miller's boy and the cat
The poor old lady
The precious stone
Prince Prigio
Puss in boots
Pussy cat, pussy cat
Pussy, kittie
Pussy, pussy, dear pussy
Pussy sits beside the fire
The rajah went to Delhi
Reen — reen — reeny — croak — frog
Ride away, ride away
The river of lantern land
Rodents rampant on a field azure
The rose is red
The secret room
Shippei Taro
Shippei Taro and the monster cat
Silver leaves and golden blossoms
The silver ship
Sing, sing! What shall I sing?
The six companions
The son of the baker of Barra
The sorcerer's apprentice(s)
Squire Per
The squirrel went out to cut the hay
The stolen jewel
A strange choice
The struggle between the wolf and the
fox
The sun, the moon and the star of
morning
The swan princess
The sweet misery
The tabby who was such a terrible
glutton
The tale of Peter Rabbit
The talking cat
The tapping ghost of Edinburg
The thirteen enchanted cats
The thirteenth floor
Thor and the giants
The three copecks
Three little kittens
The three sons of the King of Antua

The thunder cat
Tippity Witchit's Hallowe'en
The town mouse and the country
mouse
The traveller and his host
Twelve great black cats and the red
one
The twins and the snarling witch
Two children
The two foolish cats
The ugly duckling
A voyage to Brobdingnag
Wee robin's Christmas song
What happens to the envious
When the cat and the tiger lived
together
When the rooster was king of the cats
The white hound
The white pet
Whittington and his cat
Who is strongest?
Who's on the roof?
Why cat eats first
Why cats always wash after eating
Why cats always wash themselves after
eating
Why cats and dogs are enemies
Why cats and dogs fight
Why cats lie on the doorstep in the
sun
Why cats live with women
Why dogs and cats are not friends
Why dogs wag their tails
Why the bagobo like the cat
Why the cat and dog cannot live at
peace
Why the dog and the cat are enemies
Why the tiger is so angry at the cat
William Winter
Winkle, Tinkle, and Twinkle
The witch of Laggan
The wolf and the cat
The world's smartest cat
The wrestlers

, Black
Bahri of the beauty spot
Black cats
The black cat of Cotabato
The black cat of the witch-dance-
place
The enchanted black cat
How cats came to purr
Jip and the witch of Walgrave
Nangato
Seán na Bánóige
Sixpence for a breeze

, Fur
The cat, the mountain goat, and
the fox

Cats *(Continued)*
, Mountain
The cats of the mountain
The wizard earl
, Persian
The most precious possession
—Tails
The puss's tail
The tail of the cat
Why the tiger is so angry at the cat
, Tiger
The tiger cat
, Tortoise shell
Knurremurre
, White
The cat bride
The cats of the mountain
The little white cat
Mainly in moonlight
The palace of the white cat
The story of silly Cham-ba
The white cat
The white cat and the green snake
The white pet
, Wild
A kind heart

The cats
MANNING — DAMIAN p67-74

Cat's eyes
The necklace

The cats of the mountain
BELTING — CAT p73-78

The cat's tail
WITHERS — I SAW p72-74

Catskin
JACOBS — MORE p204-210
REEVES — ENGLISH p81-95

Cattenborg
KAPLAN — SWEDISH p1-16

Cattle. *See* Cows

The cattle egret
HEADY — WHEN p27-30

The cattle raid of Cooley
O'FAOLÁIN — IRISH p47-87

Caucasia
The tale of the pig

The cauld lad of Hilton
BRIGGS — PERS. p120-121
WILLIAMS — FAIR p110-113

The cauldron of Brekkan
VANSITTART — DARK p23-29

Cauldrons (pots)
See also Kettles; Teakettles
Juan Bobo and the caldron
The magic head
The miser
The story of Blathnot
Thor and the jotun Aegir

Cauliflower
The ghost in the cabbage patch

A cause of war
HAZELTINE — HERO p12-25

Caution
The fox, the wolf, and the horse
Look behind as well as before
The sick lion and the fox

A cavalier tune
MY BOOK HOUSE v. 10 p19.

Cavaliers. *See* Knights and knighthood

The cavallino
MINCIELI — TALES p35-39

The cave of Hercules
LAURITZEN — BLOOD p129-149

Cave people
A Chinese cinderella

The cave that talked
KOREL — LISTEN p60-63

Caves
Amin and the Ghul
Andrew and the mermaid
Au Sung meets Kim Lee
The bean tree
The boy Pu-nia and the king of the sharks
The boy who overcame the giants
Chucho, who's afraid?
The coyote and the two dogs
Dan-Gun, first King of Korea
The dropping-cave
Eggborn
The eel, the man, and the cave
The fifty-one thieves

Caves (*Continued*)

The first of May
The giant bones
The giant in the cave
The goat and the eagle
The golden chain
The golden lion
The golden phoenix
The golden sheep
The good sword
The Groschen hole in the Mürz Valley
The Haddam witches
The hoard
How Tammas Maciver Macmurdo
  Maclennan met his match
Ida of Toggenburg
Jack and the giant Cormoran
Jack and the giant Thunderdell
The king of the mountain
The king's true children
The lost prince
The lost spear
The magic carpet
Mirza and the ghul
Mohammed and the spider
The monkey, the tiger, and the jackal
  family
Ned Puw's farewell
Nefyn the mermaid
No man with the Cyclops
Old man moon
Omganda and the gold
Oudelette
The piper of Keil
Polyphemus, the Cyclops
The poor man's son, the dwarfs, and
  the birds
The princess in the earth cave
The princess of Mount Nam-Nhu
Rabbit and the Indian chief
The river of lantern land
Roommates
The sage in the cave
The secret commonwealth
The secret of Kaboniyan
Señor coyote and the dogs
A story of guile
The story of the tortoise and the
  monkey
The sword of the stone
The three golden hairs of the king of
  the cave giants
Tiger lily and the dragon
The valley of ten thousand waterfalls
The Welshman and the hazel staff
Where Arthur sleeps
Where the kings of Judah sleep their
  last sleep
The white hound
Why people keep dogs
The witch who lived in a cave

The wood cutter's son and the two
  turtles
Zini and the witches

Cawein, Madison
The twilight

The ceabharnach
LEODHAS — SEA p87-100

Ceátach
O'SULLIVAN — FOLK. p38-56

Cedar trees
Anpu and Bata
The bored tengu

Ceilings
Why spider lives in ceilings

Celebes (island)
The boat that would not move
The dolphins of Celebes
How Celebes got its name
How confusion came among the
  animals
Pursuit of the Hadji

Celery
MANNING — GIANNI p43-53

Celts
The adventures of Manawyddan
The bride-price for Olwen
The children of Lir
The dream of Rhonabwy
Goosey, goosey, gander
The house of the rowan trees
Midir and Etain
Oisin, son of Finn MacCool
Old King Cole
The pursuit of the hard man
The secret commonwealth
The voyage of Maeldun

—**Brythons**
The lion with the steady hand

—**Goidels**
The quest of the sons of Turenn

Cemeteries
See also **Burials**
The black stone
The drunkard and the opium-eater
The ghost of Peg-Leg Peter
The golden candlestick
The jewel of the fox's tongue
The lazy one

Cemeteries *(Continued)*

The man who walked widdershins
round the kirk
A merry tale of Rich Neck Town
The tailor and the devil
The two friends

Cenerentola
HAVILAND — ITALY p3-19

La Cenerentola
LUM — ITALIAN p91-105

Cenerentola
VITTORINI — OLD p63-68

Cenerentola or Cinderella
MINICELI — OLD p24-34

Centaurs
The blue centaur

Centaurs
JACOBSON — LEGEND. p36-37

The center of the world
LEACH — RAINBOW p283-284

The centipede girl
INS-SOB — FOLK p97-100

Centipedes
My Lord Bag-o'-Rice
My Lord Bag of Rice
Three tests for the prince

Century plants
Children of cloud

Cerberus
JACOBSON — FIRST p48-50

Cereals
The magic mare

Ceres
Proserpine

The cerval's secret name
ELLIOT — WHERE p25-33

Cervantes, Miguel de
Surprising adventures of Don
Quixote of La Mancha

Cervantes, Miguel de
A Spanish hero

Ceylon. *See* India—Ceylon

The chafers and the dove
ELLIOT — SINGING p124-137

Chaff
How the little fox went after chaff
The king who ate chaff

Chains
Billy B_____'s adventure
The eagle on a chain
Peter and the witch of the wood
The wild man

, Golden
The geese and the golden chain
The golden chain
The golden chain from heaven
The good sword
The juniper
The princess of the mountain
The youth who trusted in God

Chairs
The boastful queen
The master-smith
Padre Ulivo and his guests
The wishing chair of the Lord of
Errigal

, Golden
The girl and the golden chair
A tailor in heaven

Chalices
The crowza stones
How the clergyman retrieved the
golden chalice from the goblins of
Gotland

Chamberlains
The fisherman and the king's
chamberlain
The good sword
Many moons

Chameleon finds—
LEACH — HOW p39-40

Chameleons
The feast of plums
The goat and the eagle
How chameleon became king of the
animals
How the lizards got their markings
The hunter's child
The infallible salt bird
Lion, chameleon, and chicken
The ostrich and the crocodile

Chameleons *(Continued)*
 The race
 The ritual coming-of-age
 The secret store
 The singing chameleon
 Two friends: how they parted
 Why the chameleon shakes his head

Chamisso, Albert von
 A tragic story

Chamoud, Simone
 Little cricket

Champa flowers
 Soonimaya

The champion
 COURLANDER – TERRA. p69-73

Chandasimha, his son and their two
 wives
 GRAY – INDIA'S p223-230

The changeling
 JUDA – WISE p22-27
 WILLIAMS – FAIRY p44-48

The changeling and the fond young
 mother
 LEODHAS – THISTLE p74-81

The changelings
 SHEPPARD – WELSH p178-182

Changing luck
 LEACH – LUCK p15-18

Chanina and the angels
 BAKER – TALKING p232-235

Chanson de Geste, or Song of deeds. *See*
 The world's great epics

Chanson de Roland
 The song of Roland

Chanticleer and Partlet
 MY BOOK HOUSE v. 3 p176-180

Chanticleer . . . his strange dream
 UNTERMEYER – FIRE. p227-231

Chanticleers. *See* Chickens–Roosters

Chapels
 Lyonesse
 Saint Quien Sabe
 Sir Gawain and the green knight

Chapman, Arthur
 The plains' call

Character
 See also **Superstitions–Character;**
 names of various characteristics
 A Victorian romance
 What grown-ups can learn from
 children's books
 What is a fable?

Character
 BATCHELOR – SUPER. p60-68

Charcoal
 Flaming tales
 The turtle prince

The charcoal burner choja
 SEKI – FOLKTALES p151-155

Chariots and charioteers
 Cuchullin keeps the gap of the north
 Cuculain, the Irish hound
 The home-coming of Odysseus
 Joseph and his brethren
 Phaeton
 Phaeton, the boy who rode the chariot
 of the sun
 The spear slaughterer and the chariot
 and horses of Sigar

The charitable woman and the three
 loaves
 NAHMAD – PORTION p94-96

Charity
 Golden goodness
 The great spirit of the toad
 The happy prince
 The punishment
 The robe
 The seven years of blessing
 The shepherd's nosegay
 The story of Wang Li
 The treasure in the basket
 The wandering cobbler
 The weaver's worry

Charlemagne
 The battle of Roncesvalles
 The death of Roland
 Karl the Great and the robber
 A Roland for an Oliver
 The song of Roland
 The squires win golden spurs

Charles V, Emperor of Netherlands
 The emperor's questions

Charles Legoun and his friend
COURLANDER − PIECE p91-93

Charles Loon
FARJEON − SILVER p26-35

Charles the Bold of Burgundy
MULLER − SWISS p90-92

Charley, Barley, Buck and Rye
MY BOOK HOUSE v. 1 p94.

Charley, Bonnie Prince
Charley's neat and Charley's sweet
Over the hill to feed my sheep

Charley's neat and Charley's sweet
MY BOOK HOUSE v. 1 p94.

Charlotta's web; Wilbur's boast
MY BOOK HOUSE v. 5 p54-63

A charm against witches
GARNER − GOBLINS p115.

A charm for spring flowers
CATHON − PERHAPS p42.

Charms
See also Amulets; Superstitions; etc.
Carry a horse chestnut
Carry an acorn
The first witch's cat
Four-leaf clover
Hang up a horseshoe
Hema and the goblin-woman
King All-tusk
The monkey and the banana
Simple and the princess
The son of the hen-wife
The three lucky charms
Three magic charms

Charms
BATCHELOR − SUPER. p3-8
JOHNSON − WHAT p25-29

"Charter Oak"
The oak that helped outwit a king

Chase, Richard
Whitebear Whittington

The chase of Slieve Gallion
SUTCLIFF − HIGH p70-76

Chattees
The jackal, the barber and the Brahmin
who had seven daughters
The valiant chattee-maker

The chatterbox
BUDBERG − RUSSIAN p43-48

Chaucer, Geoffrey
The alchemist
Chanticleer and Partlet
Palamon and Arcite
A perfect knight
The tale of Chanticleer
The three young men and death

Chaucer, Geoffrey
The royal page

Cheating
The baker's daughter
The battle of the animals
The boy with the beer keg
Clever−clever−clever
A clever judge
The crab and the monkey
The devil and the bailiff
The fox and the wolf
General Moulton's boot
The hoca as Tamerlane's tax collector
A lesson for the bat
Luc, the king's woodsman
Miaden Lane in the golden days
Quinces and oranges
The silly goose
Six-and-four
Two rascals

Cheating the devil
JOHNSON − WHAT p165.

Checkers
Ra and his children

Cheerfulness
See also Laughter
At Christmas play and make good
cheer
Billy, Billy, come and play
Gudbrand of the hillside
Happy Hans
Heap on more wood
I heard the bells on Christmas day
Jog on, jog on
O I'm a jolly old cowboy
O well for the fisherman's boy
Of speckled eggs the birdie sings
Ooka and the two first sons
Over in the meadow

Cheerfulness (*Continued*)

The story of Tom Thumb
Winnie-the-Pooh

Cheese
The ash lad who had an eating match
with the troll
The cobbler
The crow and the fox
Dwarf stories
The emperor and the deaf man
The farmer and the harvesters
A fine cheese
The gipsies' church
The rabbit and the tiger
Raking for the moon
Rolling cheese gathers no moss
The three stags
Yankees

Chelm. *See* Poland—Chelm

Chemists. *See* Pharmacists

Chénier, André—Poems
Pannychis

Cherries. *See* Cherry trees—Fruit

Cherry
MANNING — PETER p85-97

Cherry of Zennor
BRIGGS — PERS. p86-91

Cherry trees
George Washington and his hatchet
Little maid of far Japan
Padre Ulivo and his guests
The princess of light
Ubazakura

—Flowers
The old man who made flowers
bloom
The old man who made trees
blossom

—Fruit
Anansi an' de cherries
The day the sky fell

Ches (god)
The magic eagle
The tree goddess

Chess
The fairy grotto

The game of chess
The game of chess in the mountains
The golden apples of Loch Erne
How Loki outwitted a giant
King Conal's horses
The man who sold magic
Prince Finn the Fair
The pursuit of Dermot and Grania
Ragnarokk, the destiny of gods
Sissa and the troublesome trifles
The wooing of Elain
The youth who became an ant, a lion
or an eagle

Chestnut trees and chestnuts
Benizara and Kakezara
Carry a horse chestnut
The crab and the monkey
The kettle and the chestnut
Saturday, Sunday, Monday

Chestnuts
LEACH — NOODLES p28-29
LEACH — RAINBOW p234-235

Chests
Aunt Karin's chest
The box with wings
The crimson purse
The fairy wife
The farmer who went to plough
The girl without hands
The great fish
How the devil married three sisters
Lars, my lad!
The little chest
Little Claus and Big Claus
Merman Rosmer
The shepherd's nosegay
The ten chests
The three chests
The tongue-cut sparrow
The woman in the chest

Chi and Yi
ALEXANDER — PEBBLES p23.

Chicadees
Why the chickadee goes crazy once
a year

Chicken Little
SIDEMAN — WORLD'S p61-64

Chickens (general, including hens)
See also stories beginning with Cock,
Hen, Rooster
The aged infant
Anansi and the old hag

100

Chickens (*Continued*)

Aniello
The animal musicians
At the wedding of Miss Jenny Wren
The barnyard
The boy who was caught by a clam
The cat and the hen
The clucking hen
Copperhead in the bin
Drakestail
The falcon and the hen
The farmer's boy
Fishing for a chicken
The five friends
Five little chicks
Four friends
The fox and the little red hen
The half-chick
The hardhearted rich man
Hark, hark! Bow-wow!
The hawk and the hen
The head of the family
Hickety, pickety, my black hen
The hill demon
How Kwaku Ananse won a kingdom
  with a grain of corn
The hunchback's horse
I stand in the pulpit and preach
It's perfectly true!
Jack and the beanstalk
The jackal and the hen
Jean Labadie's dog
The journey to Toulouse of the
  animals that had colds
Juan Bobo, the sow, and the chicks
A kind heart
The king who rides a tiger
Lion, chameleon, and chicken
Little Gustava
The little hen and the little cock
The little red hen and the grain of
  wheat
The little red hen and the wheat
The magic bird
A man, a snake, and a fox
The miser's wife
Mr. Korbes the fox
The mountain hen and the fox
The one-legged chicken
The oystercatcher, the duck and the
  hen
The pavilion of peril
The peasant and his hen
The planting party
Polenta, polenta, and more polenta
The queen and the golden egg
Rag, tag and bobtail
The ram and the pig who went into
  the woods to live by themselves
Reynard the fox

The ritual coming-of-age
The silly owls and the silly hens
Smereree
A song for Easter
The story of the smart parrot
There was a little man and his name
  was Gice
There was an old man with a beard
The three brothers and the black hen
Two children
Wend' Yamba
A white hen sitting
Why chicken lives with man
Why crocodile does not eat hen
Why lion lives in the forest
William T. Trinity
The wonderful cake

—Roosters (cocks)
The bold heroes of Hungry Hill
The Bremen town musicians
The cat and the chanticleer
The cat, the cock and the lamb
Chanticleer and Partlet
Chanticleer . . . his strange dream
The devil's gifts
The dog and the cock
Dry-bone and Anansi
The escape of the animals
The fairies and the smith
The falcon and the cock
The four-leafed shamrock and the
  cock
The fox and the cock
The frontier contest
The giant archer of the sky
Goblin bread
The golden cockerell
He leaves the nest
How rooster got his comb
How the cock got his red crown
Jack and his comrades
Jack and his friends
Keloğlan and God's greatness
Know your own strength
Krencipal and Krencipalka
Kuratko the terrible
The lady and the devil
Little capuchin monkey's story
The little gray mouse and the
  handsome cock
The little purse with two pennies
The little rooster and the little
  hen
The magic acorn
The magic egg
The March cock and the coffin
The musicians of Bremen
The nutcracker and sugardolly
The ogre and the cock
Oversmart is bad luck
Prunella

Chickens—Roosters (*Continued*)

Quarrel
The rabbit who wanted to be a man
The radiant khan
The remarkable ox, rooster and dog
The saga of Stretch Garrison
The sheep and the pig that made a home
The silly owls and the silly hens
The spiteful nany goat
The stone in the cock's head
The struggle between the wolf and the fox
The sun callers
The tale of chanticleer
The tipsy rooster
The toad is the emperor's uncle
The tufty hen
The turtle prince
The twin brothers
The village rooster and William Smith
The vixen and the rooster
When the rooster was king of the cats
Which was witch?
The white pet
Why rooster is so neat
Why the buzzard stole the rooster's chicken
Why the cock eats worms
A woman had a rooster
The woodsman's daughter and the lion

Chicory
The dark king

Chief above and chief below
TRACEY – LION p93-98

The chief astrologer
PROTTER – CHILD. p202-208

The chief of the Guernsi
COURLANDER – KING'S p13.

Chief of the night riders
RASKIN – TALES p71-77

The chief of the well
COURLANDER – PIECE p15-19

The chief with the wonderful servants.
See The queen's riddles

A chiefess and a riddle
THOMPSON – LEGENDS p54-65

The chief's knife
COURLANDER – OLODE p50-53

Chien Tang
MANNING – DRAGONS p20-24

Child, Lydia Maria
Over the river

The child and the colt
CURCIJA – YUGOSLAV p71-83

The child and the fig
MICHAEL – PORTUGUESE p9-14

The child and the mariner
LAWSON – STRANGE p14-15

The child from the sea
O'SULLIVAN – FOLK. p188.

Child, I must sweep the hut today
MY BOOK HOUSE v. 1 p147.

Child, I see thee!
MY BOOK HOUSE v. 1 p152.

A child in a Mexican garden
MY BOOK HOUSE v. 4 p103.

The child in the bamboo tree
McALPINE – JAPAN. p127-133

The child of death
SUN-LAND p117-119

Child of the sun
JABLOW – MAN p86-87

The child sold to the devil
THOMPSON – ONE p72-73

Child Study Association of America
CHILD – CASTLES p300.

Childe Roland
See also Childe Rowland
BRIGGS – PERS. p46-50

Childe Rowland
MANNING – ENGLISH p44-51
WILLIAMS – FAIRY p196-205

Childe Rowland and the King of Elfland
FINLAY – FOLK p45-53

Children
See also **Babies; Boys; Girls; Twins**
The calabash children

Children (*Continued*)

Cornelia's jewels; a mother's love and pride
The doe and the lioness
Gooloo the magpie and the waroogas
How Kwaku Ananse won a kingdom with a grain of corn
Jingling rhymes and jingling money
Johnnie and Grizzle
The kingdoms
The king's true children
The kittel-kittel car
The lost children
Maggie Tulliver goes to live with the gypsies
The old wizard and the children
The pied piper of Frenchville
The pied piper of Hamelin; a minstrel's enchanted music
The ratcatcher of Hamelin
The selfish giant
The song of the doves
Stan Bolovan
The stolen turnips
The sun and the moon
The tale about lost time
The terror of the ogres
There was an old woman who lived in a shoe
A token of friendship
Toto gets married
Unanana and the elephant
What the children do in summer
The wicked bankiva
The witch

The children and the bear
MY BOOK HOUSE v. 1 p206-207

The children and the ghost-woman
GREY – SOUTH (2) p14-18

The children in the wood
JACOBS – MORE p120-126

Children of Cloud
HAYES – INDIAN p103-111

"Children of light"
Glooskap's country

The children of Lir
GARNIER – LEGENDS p127-150
O'FAOLAIN – IRISH p27-39
PICARD – CELTIC p9-20
PILKINGTON – THREE p90-95
WILSON – IRELAND n.p.

The children of the dead woman
O'SULLIVAN – FOLK. p176-179

Children of the sun
CARPENTER – SOUTH p115-121

The children of Tuireann return to Erin
PILKINGTON – THREE p63-67

The children who could do without their elders
BURTON – MAGIC p73-74

The children who lived in a tree-house
ARNOTT – AFRICAN p140-149

The children's crusade
MY BOOK HOUSE v. 10 p30-37

Children's literature
What grown-ups can learn from children's books

The children's sea
LEEUW – INDO. p117-126

Children's songs of ancient Greece (by Theognis)
MY BOOK HOUSE v. 1 p204.

Chile
Clever Carmelita
The cowskin boat
The fox who was not so smart
The good man and the kind mouse
Lion and man
The pretty bird
The ring in the seashell
The strange adventures of Alcavilu
The toromiro of Rapa-Nui
–Caldera
Caldera Dick

Chili (plant)
Some impatient mule drivers

The chili plant
ALEGRIA – THREE p59-63

Chiltota birds
Faithful to death

Chimaera
Bellerophon . . . the winged horse
Pegasus and the Chimaera

A Chimalteco story
LEACH – RAINBOW p291-292

The chimera
JACOBSON – FIRST p51-53

Chimney sweep
MY BOOK HOUSE v. 1 p67.

Chimney sweeps
The prince and the chimney sweep

Chimneys
The boy who was not afraid
La Cenerentola
Traveling through the chimney

Chimpanzees. *See* **Monkeys**

Chimpanzee's story
SHERLOCK – IGUANA'S p53-67

Chin and Yi
BONNET – CHINESE p159-163

Chin-Chin Kobakama
HEARN – JAPANESE p9-17
PALMER – FAIRY p69-74

China
See also **Formosa; Korea**
Ah Tcha the sleeper
The ambassador from Chi
Aunt Piety
Baskets in a little cart
A beautiful young woman as the head
of the family
The big Chinese drum
The bird on the roof
The blue rose
The boastful tortoise
Borrowed arrows
The borrowing of 100,000 arrows
The boy who played the flute
The brave actor
The case of a widow before a sagacious
magistrate
The cat and the mice
Chi and Yi
Chin and Yi
Chu and the king of the underworld
A converted thief
Crabs at the doorsteps
The dark maiden from the ninth
heaven
The dinner that cooked itself
Discovery of salt
The dissatisfied good man
Do you know how the ants were
discovered
The dutiful daughter
The egg
Egg born
The eight perfect ones on the ocean
The empty city

Eterna
The fairy grotto
The fairy wife
The faithful wife
The farmer and the hoe
Fear, the greatest enemy
The five tiger general
General Chang's strategy
General Chu-Ki Liang
The giant archer of the sky
Gift of the unicorn
The girl on the green tree
The girl who used her wits
The golden boat
The golden calf
The great bell
The greatest archer
The greedy man in the moon
Growing wings
He sang himself out of prison cell
The head-hunters
Heaven and earth and man
The heavenly spinning maid
The hidden hoe
Hok Lee and the dwarfs
How marriages are made
How the camel got his proud look
How the ox came upon earth
How to weigh an elephant
The hungry serpent
In China the people say
The inn of donkeys
The journey of the Chinese honey-
seller
The king of the forest
The king's joke
Kwang Hing, the book lover
The ladle that fell from the moon
Lao Lai-Tse, the tactful
Large cabbages
The laziest man in the world
Learning magic
Legend of how ants came to earth
The legend of Tchi-Niu
The legend of the narcissus
Little Chinese tales
The little lion dog and the blue prince
The long nose
The long-nosed giant
The lucky serving maid
Ma Liang and his magic brush
The magic bell
The magic melons
Magicians of the way
The man in the mirror
The man who loved flowers
The man who nearly became fishpaste
The man who sold a ghost
The man who sold thunder
The man who stole a rope
The man who would know magic

China (*Continued*)

Mang Jen and his mother
Marking the boat to locate the sword
The marvelous pear seed
The mason's marriage
The mast of sand
Meeting in the road
The milky way
Money makes cares
Monkey
The mouse climbed up the candlestick
The mysterious path
The mystery of the scroll
The nung-guama
The old lady and the monkeys
An old story of the three sworn
  brothers
One hundred thousand arrows
The oyster and the heron
Painted skin
The pavilion of peril
The peasant-girl's captive
The polite children
The potter and the gate
The priest and the pear tree
A prince went hunting
The princess and the scarf
The princess of China
Prospect and retrospect
The quellers of the flood
The rain makers
Recruits
The red-maned horse
The remarkable ox, rooster, and dog
Revolt
The rice puller of Chaohwa
The road to China
The royal monument pavilion
The sage in the cave
A San and the Wang Liang
Self-convicted
A shiver of ghosts
Shoes don't match
Simple Wang
A simpleton of the family
A son of the turtle spirit
The spear and shield of Huantan
A springtime dream
Stealing the bell
The stolen rope
The stone monkey
The story of a fairy serpent
The story of a man in a shell
The story of Ming-Y
The story of Wang Li
A suspicious wife with an enforced
  extra husband
Sze-Ma Gwang, the quick one
Tao-K'an and his mother
The terrible-tempered dragon

The text
Three anecdotes
The three copper pieces
The three dwarfs
Three magic charms
The three precious packets
Through the eyes
Tiki-Tiki-Tembo
A tongue of gold and words of jade
Traveling to see wonders
The trial of the stone
The trials of Ting Ling
Tsai Shun, the faithful
The two brothers
The two fools
The unexpected happened
The victorious lute
The voice of the bell
A warning from the gods
The wedding of the dragon-god
Wen Yen-Poh, the thinker
Which was witch?
The white snake lady
Why frogs speak Chinese
Why the cock eats worms
Why the dog and the cat are enemies
A wife with false economy
William Winter
Winter rose
The wise judge
The wise man's pillow
A wit to outwit wit
The witless imitator
Wong Siang, the clever
Wu Meng, the thoughtful
The yellow dragon
The young head of the Cheng family

, Central
  The fox, the hare, and the toad
    have an argument
  The story of the fairy boat

—Language
  How pictures become words

, North
  The cricket fight
  The king of the mountain

, South
  The fox turns a somersault
  The little hare's clever trick
  The wishing cup

, Southeast
  How the deer lost his tail

, Southwest
  Soo Tan the tiger and the little
    green frog

, West
  A Chinese cinderella
  The fox outwits the tiger

China—West (*Continued*)

    How people got the first cat
How rooster got his comb
How the cock got his red crown
The magic pancakes at the
   Footbridge tavern
The moon and the stars

A Chinese cinderella
   HUME — FAVORITE p15-22

Chinese dragons
   JACOBSON — FIRST p13-16

Chinese magnolia
   The great bear

Chinese nursery rhymes
   MY BOOK HOUSE v. 1 p76-77

Chinese rival storytellers
   WITHERS — I SAW p128.

Chingola birds
   The legend of the chingola bird

Chink, chink, chockett
   MY BOOK HOUSE v. 1 p70.

The chipmunk who chattered too much
   CATHON — PERHAPS p66-70

Chipmunks
   How chipmunk got his stripes
One day, one night

Chirimías (musical instruments)
   The sweetest song in the woods

Chocolate
   Pennyworth

Chocorua Mountain
   TAFT — PROFILE p231-236

The choja who became a monkey
   SEKI — FOLKTALES p142-145

Chokecherries
   Itsayaya and the chokecherries

Cholera
   The three companions

The choosing of the high-king of Erin
   PILKINGTON — THREE p85-89

Chopin, Frederic
   The little dog waltz

Courilo's little comb
   ALMEDINGEN — KNIGHTS p149-
164

Chrisman, Arthur Bowie
   Ah Tcha the sleeper

Christening the baby in Russia
   MY BOOK HOUSE v. 14 p63-72

Christenings
   The feathered fiend
The light princess
Little black imp!
The magician's heart
Potok's dancing and the snakes
Prince Prigio
Prince Sneeze
The troll's invitation
We'll never be ready in time!
The worst spinster in Norfolk

The Christian bell
   PILKINGTON — THREE p114-118

Christian dancing in rural Georgia
   JOHNSON — WHAT p236-237

Christians
   The American saga
The children of Lir
The fig bough
Fridolin
The golden helmet
Ida of Toggenburg
An impossible penance
The Jewish pope
The martyrs of Thebes
Merlin
Verena and the jug
Vladimir's adventure in search of a
   fortune

Chistiansen, Reider Thorwald
   Flying with witches

Christie and the growing hand
   GREEN — LEPRECHAUN p74-84

Christmas, Annie
   Annie Christmas

Christmas
   See also **St. Nikolas Day**
At Christmas
At Christmas play and make good
   cheer

Christmas (*Continued*)

The brownies in the toy shop
The cat on the dovrefell
Charles the Bold of Burgundy
The deacon of Darkwater
Down by the River Avon
Eve of the wise men
The five friends
Gawaine and the green knight
Get up, little horsey
The glass peacock
Goblin gold
A happening on Christmas eve
Hark, the Christmas bells are ringing
The hauntings at Thorhallstead
Heap on more wood
Hildur the elf queen
The house mouse and the country
  mouse
How Ysengrin the wolf was taught to
  fish
I heard the bells on Christmas day
An impossible penance
Jingle bells, jingle bells
King Hrolf and the bear's son
The little engine that could
Little fir tree
Little Jack Horner
The luck boy of Toy Valley
The man in the moon
Mary, Mary, so contrary
Merry Christmas
The mill that grinds at the bottom of
  the sea
The night before Christmas
The nutcracker and sugardolly stories
Old Surly and the boy
A rhyme from Santo Domingo
The shepherd of Silverstead
The shoemaker and the elves
Sir Gawain and the green knight
The tale of nutcracker
Taliesin
Tall tales from the Gotham Inn
Tarn Wethelan
Tatterhood
The three magi
The two wishes
The visits of St. Peter to his people
Wakewell and his brothers
Wee Robin's Christmas song
The weefolk
Why the sea is salt
The wonderful night

−**Isle of Man**
The old Christmas

Christmas rose
The winter flower

A Christmas song at sea
MY BOOK HOUSE v. 8 p187.

Christmas trees
The glass peacock
The wonderful night

A chronicle of Kiev
MY BOOK HOUSE v. 10 p118.

Chu and the king of the underworld
BONNET − CHINESE p127-132

Chu Cuoi's trip to the moon
ROBERTSON − FAIRY p25-35

Chu Dong Tu and the princess
SUN − LAND p53-57

Chucho, who's afraid?
BRENNER − BOY p113-120

Chug-chug along the O-hi-o
JAGENDORF − UPSTATE p212-
215

Church, Alfred J.
The sack of Troy
The slaying of Hector

Churches and cathedrals
The building of Ravanitsa
Devil in church
Eight leaves of story (3) Baglan the
  builder
The enchanted cow
Fair, brown, and trembling
The fairy funeral
The gipsies' church
The golden altar of the Church of St.
  Joseph
The golden nightingale
The good woman
An impossible penance
Katie Woodencloak
The Lord said, this is my house
The mermaid in church
The miracle of Our Lady of Guadalupe
Moving the church
The nightingale Hazaran
Pietro Bailliardo
Preacher and the devil
The red shoes
The sermon
The tailor in the church
Tall Peter and short Peter
Timothy and the buggane ghost
What the preacher's talking about

−**Roofs**
The three Bugganes−I

Churches and cathedrals *(Continued)*

–Steeples
The devil in the steeple
Gianni and the ogre
How Tepozton hung the bells
The phantom painter in the steeple
Tongue steeple

Churchyards. *See* Cemeteries

Churns
The self-kicking machine
The wonder ship and ship's crew

Cicadas (insects)
Uncle Coyote's last mischief

Cid, El ("Cid Campeador")
See also The world's great epics
The cave of Hercules
Epilogue: a final word
The story of the Cid
The wedding of the Cid's daughters

The Cid . . . The will to conquer
UNTERMEYER – FIRE. p189-192

Cigarettes
The compulsive gift–a cigarette

Cilyad, King
The quest for Olwen (1) The destiny

Cincinnatus
The story of Cincinnatus

Cincinnatus: the man who would not be king
STRONG – FAVORITE p47-51

Cinder Joe becomes king
MABERGER – FIRST p117-118

Cinder-maid
JACOBS – EUROPE. p1-12

Cinderella
BAKER – TALKING p25-32
LINES – NURSERY p33-48
MY BOOK HOUSE v. 4 p12-22
PERRAULT – COMPLETE p58-70
PERRAULT – FAMOUS p167-192
SIDEMAN – WORLD'S p72-81
TUDOR – TASHA p84-91

Cinderella dressed in green
MY BOOK HOUSE v. 1 p83.

Cinderella of New Hampshire
JAGENDORF – NEW p37-45

Cinderella or The little glass slipper
ARBUTHNOT – TIME p99-102
PERRAULT – CLASSIC p77-97

"Cinderellas"
Ashputtel
Benizara and Kakezara
The blue lotus flower
Cap o'rushes
Caporushes
Cenerentola
La Cenerentola
Cenerentola or Cinderella
A Chinese Cinderella
Cinder-maid
The enchanted cow
Fair, brown, and trembling
A girl and a stepmother
The hearth-cat
The jeweled slipper
Kari Woodencoat
Katie Woodencloak
The Korean goblins
Little burnt-face
Mother Holle
The princess in the tower
The princess of the mountain
Rhodopis and her gilded sandals
Rushen Coatie
The story of Mead Moondaughter
Tam and Tessa
Tattercoats
Turkey girl
A willow-wand and a brocade slipper
Zezolla and the date-palm tree

Cindrars, Blaise
Why no one ever carries the alligator down to the water

Circe (goddess)
Odysseus and Circe

Circe the enchantress
GREEN – GREEKS p62-63

Circles
Move clockwise, and other circle superstitions

Circus
See also Clowns
The adventures of General Tom Thumb

Circus (*Continued*)

The banshee's birthday treat
Freddy, the pad dog
Go ask your mother for fifty cents
The greatest show on earth
Jumbo was an elephant

The circus man
MY BOOK HOUSE v. 8 p143-154

The circus parade
MY BOOK HOUSE v. 3 p46-47

Cities
Bang-whang-whang
Baskets in a little cart
The big street in the big city
The empty city
Go out, children
A happy day in the city
The legend of Llangorse Lake
Lines for a city child
Prince Hassak's march
Snow in the city
Sybaris . . . life of luxury

Citizenship
Your America

Citrons
The three citrons

The city east of the moon and south of
the sun
BOUCHER – MEAD p75-94

The city mouse and the country mouse
MY BOOK HOUSE v. 2 p84-86
STRONG – FAVORITE p91.

The city of the winter sleep
SHEAHAN – HENRY p165-179

City, sunken. *See* The sunken city

The city under the sea
SHEAHAN – HENRY p279-315

Civets
The feast of plums

Civilization
Lost arts

Clach Mor and the witch of Badenoch
BRIGGS – PERS. p175.

Clamshells. *See* **Shells**

Clams
The boy who was caught by a clam
The cruel uncle
The three monsters of the sea

Clancy, Mrs. Rockwell
East Indian rhymes

Clans. *See* **Scotland–Clans**

Clarinha
LOWE – LITTLE p90-94

The classic traveler's yarn: The tale of
the shipwrecked sailor
JAMES – MYTHS p120-127

Clay
The girl who could spin clay and
straw into gold

Cleanliness
Betty Stogs and the Little People
Musk and amber
The prince and the giant's daughter
Tortoise and the baboon
Why cat eats first
Why cats always wash after eating
Why cats always wash themselves after
eating

Clement, Saint
Whistle the wind

Clergymen
See also **Dervishes; Holy men; Priests**
Anansi and the crabs
Buh Rabbit's human weakness
Bungling Pedro
Butting a sermon
The charcoal burner
The damned boys
The demon wrestler
The devil and the Good Book
The devil in the barrel
The devil in the steeple
The dream
The feathered fiend
Gabriel, blow your horn!
The hodja preaches a sermon
How the clergymen retrieved the
golden chalice from the goblins of
Gotland
Is he fat?
King James and the questions
The mermaid in church
The parson and the sexton
The pastor and the sexton
The pig in the church

Clergymen (*Continued*)

Preacher and the devil
Preacher Pete and Mike Fink
The pudding that broke up the preaching
The tail of St. George's dragon
The voyage of the Lass of Glasgow
The weaver-woman's movement
What the preacher's talking about
Willie and the pig

The clever billy goat
PRIDHAM – GIFT p81-83

The clever blue tit and the fox
BAMBERGER – FIRST p155-158

The clever boy
WITHERS – WORLD p51-53

The clever bride of Tunisia
NAHMAD – PEASANT p61-68

Clever Carmelita
CARPENTER –ꞏSOUTH p83-92

The clever cat and the giant
DE REGNIERS – GIANT p79-80

The clever children and the king tailor
SPELLMAN – BEAUT. p40-43

Clever – clever – clever
HARDENDORFF – TRICKY p63-70

Clever Dick
PICARD – FAUN p75-86

The clever earthworm
VO-DINH – TOAD p41-44

(The) Clever Elsie
See also Changing luck; Clever Elsie
and her companions
ARBUTHNOT – TIME p49-51
DOBBS – ONCE p96-104
RANKE – GERMANY p184-185

Clever Elsie and her companions
THOMPSON – ONE p388-390

The clever fox
DOBBS – MORE p93-96

The clever goatherd and the greedy giant
SPICER – GIANTS p60-68

Clever Grethel
ROSS – BLUE p35-40

A clever hunter. *See* The magic calabash

The clever jackal and how he outwitted
the tiger
SIDDIQUI – TOON. p104-108

Clever Jacob Gibson
JAGENDORF – UPSTATE p235-240

Clever Juan and King Tasio
SECHRIST – ONCE p173-177

A clever judge
DEUTSCH – TALES p28-31

Clever Kadra
CARPENTER – AFRICAN p21-30

The clever lad from Skye
LEODHAS – SEA p25-50

The clever lass
JACOBS – EUROPE p188-193

The clever little jackal
ELLIOT – WHERE p16-24

The clever little tailor
PROTTER – CHILD. p57-62

Clever little turtle
JAGENDORF – KING p55-59

The clever lord
SEKI – FOLKTALES p189-190

Clever Manka
ARBUTHNOT – TIME p136-138
FILLMORE – SHEPHERD'S p144-152

Clever Mistress Murray
JAGENDORF – GHOST p37-43

A clever old bride
INS-SÖB – FOLK p190-191

Clever Oonagh
MAYNE – GIANTS p148-160
WILLIAMS – FAIRY p56-68

Clever Pat
HAMPDEN – GYPSY p57-61

The clever peasant
DOBBS – ONCE p34-37

The clever peasant girl
MAAS – MOON p116-122
NAHMAD – PORTION p89-93
THOMPSON – ONE p350-353
WILSON – GREEK p24-27

The clever question
HASKETT – GRAINS p43-46

The clever squirrel
LEEUW – INDO. p36-39

The clever thief
PROTTER – CHILD. p209-211

The clever thieves
TASHJIAN – THREE p33-35

Clever Tom and the leprechaun
WILSON – IRELAND n.p.

The clever weaver
LANG – OLIVE p115-118

Cleverer than the devil
URE – RUMANIAN p57-61

Cleverness
See also Anansi stories; Trickery
The albahaca plant
The Amharas: rulers of high Africa
Amin and the ghul
Among the chickens
The anger bargain
The art of reading
The ash lad who had an eating match
with the troll
The ass gets the better of the wolf
At the lion's cave
The beacon light
The bird and the buffalo
The bob-tailed monkey and the king's
honey
Borrowed arrows
The borrower
The borrowing of 100,000 arrows
The boy and the water-sprite
The boy who was caught by a clam
The brainy rabbit
Browny
Buh rabbit's graveyard
Buh rabbit's tight necktie
Bungling Pedro
The case of a widow before a sagacious
magistrate
The case of the calf and the colt
The cat and the crab
The chatterbox
The cock and the fox
The count and the little shepherd
Coyote rings the wrong bell
Crab
Crafty crab
The crafty farmer
The crafty servant
The crow and the pitcher
The crow in the banyan tree
The cruel uncle

Cum and Koompang
The czar's general and the clever
peasant
The deluded dragon
The devil's bridge
Digit the midget
Djamukh–son of a deer
The donkey and the lions
A dozen at a blow
Dwarf stories
The Earl of Cattenborough
Errato di Barletto
The fairy Helena
The farmer's clever daughter
The farmer's old horse
The fickleness of fortune
The field of Boliauns
Fin M'Coul and Cucullin
Fish with the rolls
The fly
Four tales of how the devil was
outwitted
Four very skillful people
The fox and the bird
The fox and the cat
The fox and the clever wren
The fox and the cock
The fox and the crow
The fox and the snail
The fox outwits the lion
The fox outwits the tiger
The fox, the hare, and the toad have
an argument
From tiger to Anansi
The giant and the dwarf
The girl who played a trick on the
devil
The girl who used her wits
Gobbleknoll
Gobborn seer
Grace at meals
The gypsy and the snake
The hairy-armed ogre of Kyoto
The hairy boggart
The handkerchief
Hantsjc and the remarkable beast
Hare makes a fool of leopard
Hatchet Kasha
The hedgehog and the rabbit
The hoca and the candle
How Abunawas was exiled
How coyote became a friend to man
How Grigori Petrovich divided the
geese
How Loki outwitted a giant
How Prince Bondhu became a boat-
man
How Suan became rich
How the donkey saved a village
How the ghost got in
How the king chose a daughter-in-law

Cleverness (*Continued*)

How the porcupine fooled the elephant
How the rabbit fooled the elephant
How the sons filled the hut
A hungry wolf
The hunter and his talking leopard
The iguana's poison bag
Ijapa and Yanrinbo swear an oath
Ilmarinen . . . how he won his bride
The ingrates
Intole the giant
It's better to be smart than strong
Iwa the crafty one
The jabuty and the jaguar
Jack and the Welsh giant
Jack who could do anything
The jackal and the fig tree
Jesper who herded the hares
Johnny Gloke
Journey in a well
Juan Bobo
Kabundi's eye
Kalulu and the leopard
Kantjil brings the elephants to heel
Kantkil's lime pit
Kashi and his wicked brothers
Keloğlan in the service of the padishah
The kid and the tiger
The king of the forest
The king of the leaves
The king's thief
Kitava the gambler
Kuzmá get-rich-quick
Lad Carl
The ladle that fell from the moon
The lazy woman
Legend of how ants came to earth
León and the lion
The leopard and the tortoise
The lion and the hare
The lion and the hare go hunting
The lion and the wily rabbit
Lion bones and the Gardula magicians
Little fish and big fish
The magic cap
A man, a snake, and a fox
The man, the serpent, and the fox
The man with the green feather
The master cat
The men and the monkeys
Mighty Mikko
The miller-king
Mirza and the ghul
Molly Whipple
The monkey and Mr. Janel Sinna
The monkey and the shark
The monkey bridegroom
The monkey's heart
The monkey's liver
The "new preacher"

The ogre courting
Oh dear!
Old Ave Henry and the smart logger man
The old man's tale of Prince Stephen
The old woman swims the sea
One hundred thousand arrows
The one-legged crane
Onsongo and the Masai cattle
Outriddling the princess
The peasant and the donkey
The perfect husband
Pig in the poke
Pinkel
Plum pudding
Poisonous persimmons
The poor man's clever daughter
Porridge with a troll
Prince Prigio
The princess on the glass mountain
The princess who saw everything in her kingdom
Rabbit and lion
Rabbit, fox, and the rail fence
Rabbit scratches buh elephant's back
Redcoat the fox
Ricky of the tuft
Ricky with a tuft
Riquet with the quiff
The royal geese
The salt at dinner
The schoolmaster and the devil
The sea king and the fox
The short horse
Shrewd Todie and Lyzer the miser
The silly goose war
The silly jelly-fish
The simple-minded bootmaker as a miraculous healer
The simpleton
The sly gypsy
The sly gypsy and the stupid devil
The smart husband and the smarter wife
Smart working man, foolish boss man
The soldier and the tsar
Some impatient mule-drivers
Soo Tan the tiger and the little green fox
The soup stone
Stavr Godinovich and his clever wife
Stone soup in Bohemia
The stone stew
A story of guile
The story of the three little pigs
The stupid fellow
The stupid hunter and the crafty bird
The stupid wolf
Sze-Ma Gwang, the quick one
The ten chests
The thief and the king's treasure

112

Cleverness (*Continued*)

The three butchers from Reims
The three clever brothers
The three cups of water
Three skillful men
Three sons of a chief
Three tales of the mouse-deer
The three year sleeping boy
The tiger and the rabbit
The tiger's war against Borneo
The tortoise and the crocodile
Tortoise triumphant
The traveller and the tiger
The trial of the stone
The troll who hid his life
The turtle outwits the lion
The turtle, the hippo, and the
  elephant
The turtle, the storks and the jackal
Two out of one
Two ways to count to ten
The ungrateful snake
The ungrateful tiger
The victory of the buffalo
War between the crocodiles and
  Kantchil
The well
The whale and the sea slug
What a clever child can do
What the lemur is saying at night
Which?
Who was most skillful?
Why Kwaku Ananse stays on the
  ceiling
Why there are no tigers in Borneo
The wild huntsman
The wise goat
The wise monkey
The wise witness
A wit to outwit wit
The woman who flummoxed the
  fairies
Wong Siang, the clever
  Yankees
The young head of the Cheng family
Young Pollard and the brawn of
  Bishop Auckland

Cliff dweller
  RUSHMORE – DANCING p109-120

Cliff dwellers and dwellings
Ko-pa-ta, the gambling god
The rain god's reprisal
She-wa-na, diety of the elements
Young hunter

Cliffs
Amin and the ghul

The battle at White Cliff house
Hema and the goblin-woman
Ka-Hai and the sorcerer Tama-i-wao
The lost sun, moon, and stars
Lovers' leaps
Sartak-Pai

Climbing
The caterpillar
Gianni and the ogre
The upper world

Cloaks. *See* **Clothes–Coats**

The clock must not stop
  JAGENDORF – GHOST p93-98

Clocks
Big clock-tick, tock!
The cuckoo and the clock
Hickory, dickory dock
The magic clock

Cloth
See also **Linen**
The crane wife
Don't make a bargain with a fox
How the miser turned into a monkey
The hunchback's horse
The lad who went to the north wind
The lucky serving maid
Ooka and the suspect statue
Petit Jean and the frog
The princess and the fisherman
Rich woman, poor woman
The three gifts
White-bear-King-Valemon

–Brocade
An inadvertent misunderstanding

, Golden
Banks with binks

Clothes
See also **Underwear**
The boy and the leopard
Catskin
The clever children and the king tailor
The cobbler and the dwarfs
The emperor's new clothes
The fog
The frog and his clothes
The gift of the hairy one
The girl who wore too much
The goblins at the bath house
Judge not the vessel
Juha at the banquest
Katie Woodencloak
King Stephen was a worthy peer

Clothes (*Continued*)

The land beyond the fire
The magic horns
The man from Paradise
The never never land
Reward drives the familiar spirits
  away
The sacred drum of Tepozteco
The stolen bairn and the Sidh
Tattercoats
The weefolk

—Aprons
  The girl and the sailor
  Little blue apron

—Coats
  See also **Clothes—Robes**
  Aruman, a hero of Java
  The brownie of Jedburgh
  The cauld lad of Hilton
  The coat remakes many a man
  The coat that taught the housewife
  The divided cloak
  The donkey lettuce
  Eat, my fine coat!
  The extraordinary black coat
  Jack the giant-killer
  The Kildare pooka
  The kind pixy
  The mountain and the rivers
  The mouse and the sun
  Pinkel
  The pooka
  The queen's necklace
  The red cloak, told by Zaleukos,
    the Greek
  The royal waistcoat
  The saddle
  Sir Walter Raleigh
  A strange guest
  The sun and the north wind
  Three magic charms
  The vanishing rice-straw coat
  The wind and the sun

—Dresses
  See also **Clothes, Wedding**
  Cinder-maid
  Donkey skin
  Fair, brown, and trembling
  Gammelyn, the dressmaker
  Hans Hansen's hired girl
  The little girl and the new dress
  The little dressmaker
  The three walnuts

—Pants
  The boy in the moon
  To be seen

—Ponchos
  The magic poncho

—Robes
  The boy and his magic robe
  The butterfly in the granary
  The invisible silk robe
  The milky way
  The robe
  Two novices who behaved like a
    pair of otters
  The white hen
  Why there is thunder and lightning
  The women who came down from
    heaven

—Shirts
  East of the sun and west of the
    moon
  Faithful John
  The happy man
  The lucky shirt
  Vasilia the beautiful

—Skirts
  Butterflies

—Smocks
  Jankyn and the witch

—Wedding
  The firebird
  The hermit's cabbage patch
  The princess's wedding garments

Clothing wrong side out
  BATCHELOR — SUPER. p121-122

The cloud
  MY BOOK HOUSE v. 7 p95.

The cloud horse
  CARPENTER — ELEPHANT'S p135-
  140

The cloud princess
  MONTROSE — WINTER p57-66

Clouds
  The bow that bridges heaven
  Children of cloud
  If I could walk
  Little shepherd's song
  The maiden and the ratcatcher
  The match-making of a mouse
  The mole's bridegroom
  A mouse in search of a wife
  Pretty, see the cloud appear!
  The princess of Mount Nam-Nhu
  The proud father
  The rat's bridegroom
  The sage and the mouse
  Segizbai and the little mouse-girl
  The shepherd of clouds
  The singing man
  Snow

Clouds (*Continued*)
The spider weaver
The stone crusher of Banjang
The strongest
The wedding of the mouse
Who is strongest?

Clouds
MY BOOK HOUSE v. 3 p48.

Clover
Four-leaf clover

Clowns
See also Trickery
Chief above and chief below
Freddy, the pad dog
John Boaster
Little Hansworst
A midsummer night's dream
Punchinello
The sultan's fool

Clubs. *See* Sticks

The clucking hen
MY BOOK HOUSE v. 1 p214.

The clumber pup
FARJEON – LITTLE p47-73

Clytie
ARBUTHNOT – TIME p215.
MY BOOK HOUSE v. 3 p151-155

Cnut, King
Cnut and Edmund

Cnut and Edmund
LEEKLY – KING p46-60

Coaches
The piskey revelers

Coal and coal-mining
The blackstairs mountain
Dwarf stories
The golden coal
The haunted mine
How bean got his stripe
Straw, bean, and coal
The straw, the coal and the bean
Young John

Coat o'clay
JACOBS – MORE p82-88

The coat remakes many a man
CHAPPELL – THEY p75-79

The coat that taught the housewife
MINCIELI – TALES p84-89

Coates, Henry T.
November's party

Coats-of-arms
The bull of Uri
The Manx coat of arms
The simple maid of Hunsingoo
The unicorn and the dwarf

Coatsworth, Elizabeth
The story of Wang Li
Summer rain
Swift things are beautiful
Witches' song

The cobbler
LUM – ITALIAN p106-115

The cobbler and the dwarfs
MANNING – DWARFS p109-111

The cobbler astrologer and the forty
thieves
HARDENDORFF – FROG'S p46-58

Cobblers. *See* Shoemakers

The cobbler's deity
SPELLMAN – BEAUT. p79-81

Cobblers do not judge above the shoe
CHAPPELL – THEY p30-35

Cobwebs. *See* Spiders–Webs

Cock and hen in the wood
BAMBERGER – FIRST p50-53

The cock and his loving wives
REED – TALK. p15.

The cock and the fox
ASBJÖRNSEN – NORW. p135-136
WILSON – SCOTTISH p91-92

The cock and the hen
MANNING – GLASS p83-85
WITHERS – I SAW p95-96

The cock and the neighbor's hen
BAMBERGER – FIRST p88-90

The cock and the sparrow-hawk
SECHRIST – ONCE p25-27

The cock at the tsar's throne
ĆURĆIJA – YUGOSLAV p7-11

The cock-crow stone
MANNING – PETER p22-25

The cock is crowing
MY BOOK HOUSE v. 1 p208.

The cock, the cat, and the fox
DUDDINGTON – RUSS. p21-24

The cock, the mouse, and the little red
hen
ARBUTHNOT – TIME p13-15
MY BOOK HOUSE v. 2 p192-199

The cock who went traveling
RANKE – GERMANY p24-27

Cockchafers (insects)
The story of Maia

The cockroach and the mouse
LOWE – LITTLE p114-122

Cockroaches
The bee, the harp, the mouse, and
the bum-clock
Mistress cockroach
Perez and Martina
The rabbit who wanted to be a man

Cocks. See Chickens–Roosters

The cock's on the housetop
MY BOOK HOUSE v. 1 p42.

The cock's stone. See The three blue
stones

Coconuts and coconut trees
The boat that would not move
The foolish, timid, little hare
How the coconut tree came to be
How the coconut tree was saved
The little lizard's sorrow
The old woman and the thief
The origin of the coconut
The three monsters of the sea
The turtle of Tamaru

Cody, Will
Buffalo Bill
He died hard
There goes a scout

Coffee
The lady who put salt in her coffee
Pancho and the Duendes

Coffee mills
How cats came to purr
The mill at the bottom of the sea

The coffin that moved itself
SPICER – GHOSTS p65-72

Coffins
The death watch
Hans and his master
Isis and Osiris
The man who helped carry the coffin
The March cock and the coffin
Merisier, stronger than the elephants
Rabbi Amram's coffin
Vania and the vampire

Coins
See also Gold; etc.
Basia, the babbler
The first of May
Flip a coin
The greedy stallkeeper and the poor
traveler
Hunting in the light
Money superstitions
The queen's care
The rain-lady and the ghost
The salmon's revenge
The three copper pieces
Toontoony pie

Cold
The beacon light
The boastful Alaskans
A curious tale
The fire on the mountain
Frozen music
The giant and the Rumanian
The gift of Father Frost
Janot cooks for the emperor
The judgement of Hailu
The king's cream
The little match-girl
The owl's punishment
Red king and green king
The son of the hunter
Why crane's feathers are brown and
otter doesn't feel the cold
Young Charlotte

The cold heart (Part 1)
HAUFF – FAIRY p111-138

The cold heart (Part 2)
HAUFF – FAIRTY p194-219

The cold May night
O'SULLIVAN – FOLK p15-18

Cold moon
BUDD – FULL p66-70

Cold, son of wind and snow
MY BOOK HOUSE v. 1 p145.

Colds (disease)
The journey to Toulouse of the
animals that had colds

Coleridge, Samuel Taylor
Answer to a child's question
A boy of the Lake country

Coleridge, Samuel Taylor
A wizard of the twilight

Coleridge, Sara
Trees

College education. *See* **Education**

Collen, Saint
Collen and the fair small folk

Collen
VANSITTART – DARK p40-47

Collen and the fair small folk
JONES – WELSH p159-163

Colombia (South America)
A Catio Indian legend
The great flood
How life and light came into the world
Mr. Toad sets out on a journey
The mysterious lake
The poor old lady
Reen-reen-reeny-croak-frog
The snake that swallowed a girl
The tree goddess
When I see a lady
When Mrs. Bird wants Mr. Bird

–Santo Domingo
The Lord said, this is my house

The colonel's blanket
JAGENDORF – SAND p101-107

Colonial life and customs
The baker's dozen
Chief of the night riders

The duel
Foreward. The witch house still stands
Giant of the Green Mountains
The goose from Flatbush
Governor Wentworth's search for a
wife
The great scare
Hanging at Wessaguscus
A happening on Christmas eve
Hearts and pirates
Jonathan Moulton and the devil
Kayuta, the drop star
The killing of Mogg Megone
The mystery of Pelham House
The oak that helped outwit a king
Old Meg, the witch
The ordeal of Hannah Dustin
The part-time prisoner
Scandalous affairs of a baronet and a
tavern maid
Stonewall Silas Clapp
The strange battle of Windham
A token of friendship
The white deer of Onota
The wreck of the Palatine

The colony of cats
SIDEMAN – WORLD'S p758-769

Colorado
–San Juan Mountains
How the people sang the mountains
up

Colorado
LEACH – RAINBOW p73-75

Colorado River
Lost arts

Colored coats
HEADY – WHEN p53-57

Colors
See also **Birds–Colors**
The boy who made a dream come true
Bulls and the color red
The chafers and the dove
How the Brazilian beetles got their
gorgeous coats
The hunting dog and the purple fish
The indigo jackal
The lady's room
Ooka and the pup's punishment
The secret room

The colts in the pumpkin
CARPENTER – HORSES p115-120

Coltsfoot (plant)
Jack and the wizard

Colum, Padraic
The dream of Ronabbway
How Ma-ui snared the sun and made
him go more slowly across the
heavens
The king of the birds
The return of Odysseus

Columbine and her playfellows of the
Italian pantomime
MY BOOK HOUSE v. 7 p119-125

Columbus, Christopher
All about Columbus
In Columbus' time

The comb, the flute and the spinning
wheel
MANNING – MERMAIDS p66-72

Combs
Baba Yaga
The bride-price for Olwen
Chourilo's little comb
The coral comb
The cruel giant
The geese and the golden chain
How the moon and the stars came
to be
My candlestick
Pleiad and star of dawn
Snow-white and the seven dwarfs

Come, let's go to Sant' Anita
MY BOOK HOUSE v. 1 p70.

Come, little leaves
MY BOOK HOUSE v. 2 p70.

Come look!
LEACH – SOUP p65-67

Comets
Davy Crockett, the yaller blossom o'
the forest

Comics. See **Clowns; Fools and foolishness**

The coming of Arthur
HAZELTINE – HERO p100-118

The coming of Asin
U.N. – RIDE p206-212

The coming of Finn
BAKER – TALKING p52-62

The coming of Fionn MacCool
PILKINGTON – SHAM. p132-138

The coming of Glam. See The hauntings
at Thorhallstead

The coming of magic
JENNINGS – BLACK p1-18

The coming of Oscar
O'SULLIVAN – FOLK. p60-74

The coming of the corn
MacMILLAN – GLOOS. p179-183

The coming of the Spaniards
SECHRIST – ONCE p107-109

The coming of the yams
COURLANDER – HAT p96-100

Commaerts, Emile
A Belgian morning

Commodore Vanderbilt's first boat
JAGENDORF – GHOST p50-58

Common sense
Basia, the babbler
Buh rabbit's tail
The czar's general and the clever
peasant
The dilemma of a pious man
Good luck and common sense
Good sense and good fortune
How Ologbon-Ori sought wisdom
The lion-makers
The scholars and the lion
Sense and money
Terrapin's pot of sense
Why are giants so stupid?

The companion
ASBJÖRNSEN – NORW. p84-96

Companions. See **Friendship**

Company
JOHNSON – WHAT p89-91

Compasses
The quivering needle

Compassion. See **Charity; Mercy**

The competition of fools
ILLYES – ONCE p186-190

118

Complaining. *See* Grumbling

The compulsive gift—a cigarette
LEACH — SOUP p90-91

Comyn, Red
The tale of the riddle sent to Bruce

Conall Yellowclaw
MANNING — GIANTS p79-84

Conan's punishment
WILSON — SCOTTISH p195-199

Conceit. *See* Pride

The conch shell of Ram
McNEILL — SUNKEN p146-148

Conchobar and Teeval
YOUNG — HOW p21-27

Conclusion
KOREL — LISTEN p119-122
MINCIELI — OLD p121-123

Condors
The fox and the mole
The great white condor
Greed in heaven, growth on earth
The king of the mountains
The little frog of the stream
The magic ball
A trick that failed

Confession
The rope

Confidence. *See* Self reliance

Confucianism
Author's note

Congo
The bad boy and the good dog
The lazy man and the water spirit
Open your beak, my little bird
The tug of war
What the squirrel saw
Why the dog is the friend of man

—Angola
Why robin has a red breast

, Belgian
The black-handed monkey
The cannibal who ate too fast
The cannibal's drum
The dwarfs of the anthill

The frog and the moon
How the bat caught friendship
with the moon
Kabundi's eye
The leopard and the antelope
The leopard's tricks
The lion, the leopard, and the
antelope
The monkey's feast
The seven-headed giant
The sloogeh dog and the stolen
aroma
Tshiama, the snake's daughter
Tshikashi Tshikulu and the
woman
The two white stones
The weasel and his mother
The worthless man of poverty

, French
Why crocodile does not eat hen

—Ituri forest
The bird with the most beautiful
song

Conjure bags
JOHNSON — WHAT p224.

Conjurers. *See* Magicians; Witches; Wizards

Conkling, Grace H.
A child in a Mexican garden

Conn, King of Ireland
The coming of Finn
The king who could not sleep
The lordship of the Fianna

Connecticut
The bee man and the boundary man
The devil and the card players
Diamond Jim and Big Bill
The giant kingfisher of Mount Riga
I'm a peddler
The oak that helped outwit a king
The smart husband and the smarter
wife
Tiny Perry

—East Haddam
The Haddam witches

—Hebron
The wise men of Hebron

—New Haven
The ghostly hitchhiker
Lady Eaton's curse

—Windham
The frogs of Windham town
The great scare
The strange battle of Windham

Connecticut
  LEACH – RAINBOW p76-77

The Connemara donkey
  FARJEON – LITTLE p184-203

Connla and the fairy maiden
  ARBUTHNOT – TIME p127-128

Connla of the golden hair
  GARNIER – LEGENDS p99-103

Consideration
  See also Courtesy; Generosity;
    Kindness; Mercy
  The good-luck teakettle
  How the finch got his colors
  Joseph and his brethren
  Old Johnny Appleseed
  Old pipes and the dryad
  Princess Nelly and the Seneca chief
  The Red Ettin
  Two birds and their nest

Constancy. *See* Loyalty

Constantes and the dragon
  HAVILAND – GREECE p3-19
  MANNING – DRAGONS p9-19

Constellations
  See also Moon; Stars; Sun; etc.
  Bears in the sky
  The boastful queen
  The bowlegged god, Bes
  The dog and the giant
  The giant archer of the sky
  Giants, dragons, and gods
  The great bear
  Gull taught men to use manioc for
    food
  He who bound the dragons of Chaos
  The heavenly spinning maid
  How the people began
  It is time for a night chant
  The kneeler's twelve tasks
  Leo the king
  Maya-mayi the seven sisters
  The men fashion the frames of their
    kayaks
  The milky way
  The moon husband
  Pleiad and star of dawn
  Pleiades
  Plowman in the sky
  The river flows full through the sky
    land

Si Jura carved a house post
The sing-bonga beheld men
The southern cross
The spindles are still
The star children dwelt in a deep cave
The star path
The sun drives copper-colored rein-
  deer
The three flutes are in the flute house
Twins in the sky
Udleqdjun in the sky
The waters beneath: The great river
  monster
Why people watch the dipper
The woman who came down from
  heaven

Contentment
  The apple of contentment
  Evening at the farm
  Four friends
  Laughing song
  Nanny and Conn
  Nurses' song
  The princess who wanted to play
    with the stars
  Pyoli
  The talisman
  The tobacco fairy from the blue hills
  What are you able to build with your
    blocks?
  The world is so full

A contest with skillful spirits
  THOMPSON – LEGENDS p28-37

Contests
  See also Races, Athletic
  Coral sea contest
  Cottontail's song
  The day of the scholars
  The devil and the seamstress
  The giant outwitted
  The jumping contest
  The queen's riddles
  A tall tale contest
  Thor and the giants
  To outleap a rabbit

Contracts
  A peasant tricks the devil
  The road to hell
  Why cats and dogs fight

Contrariness. *See* Stubbornness

The contrary wife
  U.N. – RIDE p159-162

120

The contrary woman
COURLANDER – FIRE p35-39

Convents
Beatrice . . . and the statue

Conversation. *See* Talk

Conversation
MY BOOK HOUSE v. 1 p163.

A converted thief
HSIEH – CHINESE p35-36

The cook and the house goblin
MANNING – GHOSTS p30-37

Cook Islands

–Mangaia
Why porpoise is not a fish

Cook-a-doodle-doo!
MY BOOK HOUSE v. 1 p32.

Cooke, Flora J.
Clytie
How the robin's breast became red

Cooked for fifteen
NYE – MARCH p9-15

Cookies
A baker's dozen
The baker's dozen
The bobtail monkey and the king's
honey

The cooking-spit of the women of
Fincara
PILKINGTON – THREE p68-72

Cooks and Cookery
See also names of food; Dinners;
Feasts; Food
Anansi and turtle and pigeon
The beardless, the lame, and the
one-eyed thief
Clever Grethel
The coat that taught the housewife
The dinner that cooked itself
The dwarf and the cook, the Little
People of Turkey
Dwarf long nose
Evan's problem
Fiesta for mountain men
The full moon

The gipsy and the goose
How much for a shadow?
Jacques the woodcutter
Janot cooks for the emperor
The king and Kuffie
The king's cream
The magic ring
Maria sat on the fire
Meat or cat?
Minute pudding
The most necessary thing in the world
The new way of tamin' wolves
Olaf Goddardson and the sword
Macvibin
The one-legged crane
Paul Bunyan
The pot-that-cooked-by-itself
The rival cooks
The sea of gold
Snout the dwarf
A wise sentence

The cook's big fish
SUN – LAND p104-105

Cookus, Bopple and Yeakle
JAGENDORF – UPSTATE p254-260

The Coomacka-tree
SHERLOCK – WEST p7-12

Coomaraswamy, Ananda K.
Ramayana

Cooper, George
Come, little leaves

Cooperation
The boy who made a dream come
true
The bundle of sticks
Dame Wiggins of Lee
The doll under the briar rosebush
The duty that was not paid
Groceries
Hodja and the jumbled jobs
A husband for the chief's daughter
Joseph and his brethren
Late
The lion and the mouse
The little gray pony
Little Gulliver
The little rooster and the little hen
The mouse that keeps her promise
My maid Mary
O I'll build a square with my pretty
red blocks
The owl's answer to Tommy
Robin and Richard were two pretty
men

Cooperation (*Continued*)

Row, row, a'fishing we'll go!
The sheep and the pig that made a
home
The shoemaker and the elves
Snow-white and Rose-red
The squirrel went out to cut the hay
The story of Li'l Hannibal
The story of Tom Thumb
Three old maids a-skating went
Thus I guard my mother's lambkins
The tortoise and the reedbuck run a
race
Up in the green orchard
Wilbur Wright and Orville Wright
Willie boy, Willie boy

Coopers
The witless imitator

Coots (birds)
How the world was made (1)
How to cook a coot

Copper and coppersmiths
Fishing for pots in the pond
Fording the river in a copper cauldron
Four brothers who were both wise and
foolish
The girl on the green tree
The gypsy and the snake
The summer of the big snow
The tinder box
Traveling through the chimney

The copper pan
JUDA – WISE p8-15

The copper soup-bowl
ZAGLOUL – BLACK p35-44

Copperhead in the bin
JAGENDORF – SAND p123-126

Copy-kitten
ARBUTHNOT – TIME p259.

Coral
Nicola Pesce
O sailor, come ashore

The coral comb
LAWSON – STRANGE p94-100
PICARD – FAUN p123-134

Coral Sea contest
COTHRAN – MAGIC p38-44

Coranieids (people)
The three plagues of Britain

Cord. *See* **String**

Cormac, King of Ireland
The king who could not sleep

The cormorant and the fishes
GREEN – BIG p66-67

Cormorants
The princess and the dwarf

Corn
The adventures of Manawyddan
Anansi and turtle and pigeon
The brownie of Cranshaws
The coming of the corn
The crow and the grain of corn
The emperor and the deaf man
The fox and the wolf
The friendly mouse
The great blessing of the land
The griffon
Hanging at Wessaguscus
Hare and the corn bins
Harvest moon
How Kwaku Anansi won a kingdom
with a grain of corn
How the people came from the lower
world
How the people came to the middle
place
The hundred-headed daffodil
The king and the corn
The lark and her young ones
Little Capuchin monkey's story
Malachi and Red Cap the leprechaun
The Namashepani
The origin of corn
The planting party
Pretty, see the cloud appear!
The quarrel
Rabbit and the grain buyers
Saint Cadog and the mouse
The sack of corn
Simon and his rocky acre
Spider and squirrel
The story of Mon-do-min
The thieving fairies
Tim for wealth and happiness
To feed my people: The coming of
corn
Tobacco woman and corn spirit
The war of the plants
Why crow has a right to the first corn
Why the spider has a narrow waist

Corn (*Continued*)

−Cribs
Copperhead in the bin

−Fields
The castle in the cornfield
Constantes and the dragon
The dragon and his grandmother
The hunchback and the miser

−Grinding
Cliff dweller

−Shuckings
The short horse

−Stalks
Paul Bunyan's cornstalk

The corn maiden
PICARD − FAUN p47-56

Corn moon
BUDD − FULL p40-44

Cornelia's jewels
BALDWIN − FAVOR. p69-72

Cornelia's jewels; a mother's love and
pride
STRONG − FAVORITE p93-95

Cornets
King Johnny

Cornmeal
The jackal and the bear

"Corpse candles"
Prince Alun and the "Cannwyl Corph"

The corsair of Spouting Horn
JAGENDORF − NEW p21-25

Corsica
The donkey and the lions
Golden hair

Corvetto
MINCIELI − OLD p64-72

Costa Rica
Juan in heaven
The peasant and the horseman
Sibu, the god who builds

Cotton
A girl and a stepmother
How a man became unwitched

John Henry
The nightingale and the cotton trees
Sam Patch's last leap
Simón and his rocky acre
The spider weaver
Who is responsible

Cottontail and the sun
CURRY − DOWN p48-50

Cottontail's song
CURRY − DOWN p104-110

Cottonwood trees
The arrows that became trees

"Council of the Seasons"
The twelve months

Count Alaric's lady
PICARD − FAUN p137-155

The count and the little shepherd
MEHDEVI − BUNGLING p7-16

Count Bertrand
PICARD − FAUN p209-232

Count crow and the princess
ALEGRÍA − THREE p122-128

The Count of Estremadura
MICHAEL − PORTUGUESE p146-153

Count Roger and the Fata Morgana
TOOR − GOLDEN p151-156

Counterfeiters
Rehoboth's lady counterfeiter

Counting
Ali and the camels
Anansi and five
Exactly so
The giant who counted stones
Gizo's counting trick
Gotham way of counting
The hero of Adi Nifas
How many donkeys?
How the carrot-counter got his name
How the Kadawbawa men counted
themselves
Leaving paradise
The number of spots
One against a hundred
The rabbit and the crocodile
The seven crazy fellows
The thieves and the king's treasure

Counting (*Continued*)

The thoughtless abbot
Three skillful men
The tinker and his wife
Two ways to count to ten
The white hare and the crocodiles
The wise men of Gotham

—Rhymes
Baa, baa, black sheep
Counting out rhymes
Dame Durden
Diddle, diddle, dumpling
Engine, engine number nine
Five little chicks
Here come three jolly, jolly
  sailor boys
John Brown had a little Indian
Mary milks the cow
Old King Cole
One, two, three, four
Over in the meadow
Row, row, a'fishing we'll go!
Rub-a-dub-dub
Ten little Indians
There were three duckies
There were two blackbirds
There were two little boys
Three little kittens
Three old maids a-skating went

The counting of the crocodiles
  See also Kantchil's lime pit
  COURLANDER — TIGER'S p87-89

Counting out rhymes
  JOHNSON — WHAT p107-112

Country life
The barnyard
The bloodless battle of the elm
A boy in Russia
The boy who made hay
Charlotte's web; Wilbur's boast
The city mouse and the country mouse
The clucking hen
Dame Durden
Elsa and the ten elves
Evening at the farm
The farmer in the dell
The farmer's boy
The gingerbread man
Higgledy, piggledy! See how they run!
The house mouse and the country
  mouse
I should like to plough
I stand in the pulpit and preach
The little pig
Maggie Tulliver goes to live with the
  gypsies

Minnie and Mattie
My maid Mary
O 'twas on a bright mornin' in
  summer
Over the river and through the woods
The ploughman he's a bonnie lad
The seventh father of the house
The shaking of the pear tree
A Swedish evening
There was a little boy
Turkey in the straw
The ugly duckling
When I was a baby
White fields
Willie boy, Willie boy
A young Quaker of New England

The country of the mice
  HUME — FAVORITE p102-108
  WILLIAMS — OLD p197-205

The country under the hill
  PALMER — JOURNEY p117-141

The country swain
  MEHDEVI — BUNGLING p93-98

Counts and countesses
Aucassin and Nicolette
The cold heart — Part 2
The curse
The fortunes of Said
The honey feast
Jan the eighth Van Arkel
The little horse of seven colors
The mysterious letter
Rufus

A couple of lost squadrons
  WILLIAMS — LOST p87-92

A couple of lost towns
  WILLIAMS — LOST p117-125

Courage
See also Heroes and heroines
The adventures of Florian
The adventures of Perseus
Adventuring: white man on the war-
  path
The Ailpein bird, the stolen princess,
  and the brave knight
An American miner's song
Antar the hero
The ape and the firefly
Arnold Winkelried
Aruman, a hero of Java
As you like it
The battle of Nembro Wood
The battle of the firefly and the apes

124

Courage (*Continued*)

Bomba, the brave
Beowulf . . . the fight with Grendal
The boy and the sea monsters
The boy hero of Harlem
A boy on the high seas
The boy who was never afraid
The boy who was not afraid
The boy with the golden star
Bran, son of Llyr
The brave actor
The brave cowman
The brave grenadier
The brave little prince
The brave little tailor
The brave men of Golo
The brave prince
The brave shepherd boy
The brave three hundred
Buffalo Bill
Charles the Bold of Burgundy
Chucko, who's afraid?
Cincinnatus; the man who would not
  be king
The crab that tried to swallow the
  moon
The chrochera
Cuchullin keeps the gap of the north
Cuchullin parleys with Maeve
The cuckoo's reward
Cuculain, the Irish hound
The dance of death
Daniel in the lions' den
Dante's voyage to the inferno, purga-
  tory and paradise
David, the shepherd boy
The death of Roland
The death watch
The demon with the matted hair
Djamukh-son of a deer
The empty city
Exploring the wilderness
Fearless John and the giant monster
The fight with Ferdia
Finn and the Fianna
Finn MacCool
The fire in the mountain
The fisherman who caught the sun
George Rogers Clark and the conquest
  of the Northwest
The ghostly hand of Spital house
The giant of the brown beech wood
The great fish
The hare who was afraid of nothing
The heroine of the Mohawk Valley
How beaver got his fine fur
How Beowulf delivered Heorot
How Finn won his father's place
How Jack sought the golden apples
How Sigurd awoke Brynhild

How Tammas Maciver Macmurdo
  Maclennan met his match
How three pilgrims called Ilya to the
  rescue of Kiev
The hungry old witch
Isun Boshi, the one-inch lad
Jack and the beanstalk
Jack the giant-killer
Joan of Arc
Kantjil to the rescue
The key maiden of Tegupelden
The king of the fishes
The kinh
The knights of the silver shield
The labors of Hercules
Laka and the Little-People Menehune's
  Little People
The lass that couldn't be frightened
The legend of William Tell
The lemon and his army
Little Gulliver
The little-man-as-big-as-your-thumb-
  with-mustaches-seven-miles-long
The lost spear
Malati and the prince
The man who feared nothing
Marko, the champion of Serbian
  liberty
The master of the winds
Meg o' the moors
The moon's escape
My Lord Bag of Rice
Nancy's brook
Nazar the brave
Nicola Pesca
The Nuremberg stove
Of a tailor and a bear
Old Johnny Appleseed
The one who wasn't afraid
The ordeal of Hannah Dustin
The origin of the wrekin
Pen and four foolish ministers
The piper of Keil
Podhu and Aruwa
The price of a curse
Prince Finn the Fair
Prince Murko's journey
Princess Nelly and the Seneca chief
The rabbit in the moon
The rebel
The Red Ettin
The red swan
The riddle of the black knight
Robert Bruce and the spider; how a
  king learned courage from an insect
The ruby prince
Samba the coward
The Scotty who knew too much
The secret of heather-ale
The serpent's bride
Shingebiss

Courage *(Continued)*

Siegfried ... who knew no fear
Sir Beaumains, the kitchen knight
Sir Gawain and the green knight
The sleeping beauty
Snow-white and Rose-red
The Song of Roland
A Spanish hero
The story of Regulus
A story of Rustem, the hero of
  Persia
A story of the Cid
The story of White Arab
The swallowing monster
The tale of the Rhine-gold
The terrible Olli
Thorsteinn Shiver
The three brothers
The three little eggs
The three misty women
The three teeth of the king
Three tests for the prince
Tredeschin
The trial by fire
The truth about Pecos Bill
Una and the Red Cross knight
The valiant chattee-maker
The valiant tailor
Viriato: the youth who held back the
  Roman empire
Vladimir's adventures in search of
  fortune
Wawanosh
Who hath no courage must have legs
Why cats live with women
Why dogs live with men
The wizard of Oz, the cowardly lion

Courage
  CATHON – PERHAPS p180.

The courage of Mairi
  SHEPPARD – SCOT. p93-98

The courageous Quaker of Flushing
  JAGENDORF – GHOST p25-30

Courtesy
  See also **Discourtesy**
  Billy, Billy, come and play
  The boy and the cloth
  How the Brazilian beetles got their
    gorgeous coats
  How the finch got her colors
  I took a walk one evening
  The magic mango
  The marriage of Sir Gawain
  Old Mother Hubbard
  One misty, moisty morning

The polite children
The porcupines
Pussy sits beside the fire
Quaker, Quaker, how is thee?
River child
The shepherd's nosegay
Sir Walter Raleigh
Three little kittens
Two children
The village of cream puffs
When I see a lady

The courtin'
  JOHNSON – WHAT p153-154

The courting of the bat, the spider and
  the beetle
  BURTON – MAGIC p102-104

Courts
  The cartman's stories
  The jackal's lawsuit
  Reineke fox
  The tiger in court
  Tregeagle
  The trial at Avichara-Pura
  The ungrateful snake

Courtship
  See also **Love; Suitors;** titles beginning
    with Courting
  The dinner that cooked itself
  A frog he would a-wooing go
  Froggie went a-courting
  Hiram goes courting
  How Cuchulain wooed his wife
  A husband for the chief's daughter
  The leopard and the rabbit go courting
  The winning of Gerd

The courtship of Lemminkainen
  MAYNE – HEROES p162-171

Cousins
  The man who helped carry the coffin
  Princess Scri and Prince Sedana

Coverlets
  Constantes and the dragon
  Esben and the witch
  My candlestick
  Olli and the rich troll
  The terrible Olli

The covetous minister
  NAHMAD – PEASANT p76-79

Covetousness. *See* **Jealousy**

126

The cow doesn't miss her lost tail till
  fly time
  CHAPPELL – THEY p59-63

The cow maiden
  LOWE – LITTLE p106-113

Cow or donkey?
  WALKER – WATER. p55-57

The cow that ate the piper
  O'SULLIVAN – FOLK. p247-248

The cow that cried
  BRENNER – BOY p100-105

Cowardice
  The battle of the animals
  The battle of the firefly and the apes
  The brave men of Golo
  The brave prince
  Duke Roland's quest
  Gawaine and the green knight
  The giant and the tailor
  Good advice
  The hare was afraid of nothing
  The mouse and the rat
  Nazar the brave
  Opportunity
  The rats in council
  The riddle of the black knight
  Samba the coward
  The three teeth of the king
  The travellers and the bear
  Viriato: The youth who held back the
    Roman empire
  The wizard of Oz. The cowardly lion

The cowardly lion. See The wizard of Oz

Cowboy songs
  O, I'm a jolly old cowboy
  Pecos Bill
  Pecos Bill and his bouncing bride

Cowboys
  See also Gauchos
  Battle with the Sockdolager
  Blanche's high-flying Halloween
  Bowleg Bill
  Coyote cowboy/Pecos Bill
  Ed Grant out West
  The end of the trail
  Fiest for mountain men
  The hungry trout
  Jumping the Grand Canyon
  A kind heart
  O I'm a jolly old cowboy

  Pecos Bill
  Pecos Bill and his bouncing bride
  Pecos Bill, the cowboy
  The plains' call
  Rat and the rustlers
  The rough rider
  Sourdough special
  The strange adventures of the cowboy-
    sailor
  A tale of a dog's tail
  Three bad men
  Three fingered Ike's story
  Too hot to handle
  The truth about Pecos Bill

The cowboy's life
  MY BOOK HOUSE v. 4 p192b.

The cowherd with the belt of skin
  GARNIER – LEGENDS p16-21

Cowherds
  Ero and the Kadi
  The honourable tom cat
  Kashi and his wicked brothers
  Krishna the cowherd
  Lod, the farmer's son
  The milky way
  The speckled bull
  The thousandth gift
  The twelve dancing princesses

The cowherd's son
  LEEKLY – KING p31-45

Cowitch creepers (plant)
  Anansi play with fire, Anansi get
    burned

Cows
  See also Bulls
  The adder and the fox
  Ananse and the king's cow
  The barnyard
  The bee, the harp, the mouse, and the
    bum-clock
  The bee, the mouse and the bum-clock
  Belena
  Bola Bola
  Bouki and Ti Bef
  The boy who made hay
  The brown cow
  Bukolla
  Bukolla, the wonderful cow
  Bye-lo, Bubbeli, sleep
  The calves
  The case of the calf and the colt
  The cat and the mouse
  The cattle egret
  The cowboy's life

Cows (*Continued*)

The cowskin boat
The cunning old man and the three
  rogues
The disappearance of Ifan Gruffydd's
  daughter
The dog in the manger
Edward Frank and the friendly clow
The enchanted cow
Ero and the Kadi
The fairies and the cow
The farmer's boy
The first gods and giants
The friendly cow all red and white
A German evening
A giant of the brown beech wood
Giant pear and giant cow
Giant pears and giant cows
The gingerbread man
The good crawford
Grazing on the roof
The green glass bottle
The Haddam witches
The heavenly spinning maid
Hereafterthis
A holy man and a sacred cow
The house with the front door at the
  back
How Kwaku Ananse won a kingdom
  with a grain of corn
How the cows flew across the sea
I stand in the pulpit and preach
Idy, the fox-chasing cow
I'm a butcher
Jack and the beanstalk
The jackal's lawsuit
The kind farmer
King Appolonides
Lady of the lake
Lazy Tom
The little bull-calf
The little girl named I
Little Liese comes a-running
Little maid, pretty maid
The lost cows
The love of Kenelinda
Luran and the fairies
The magic bottles
The magic cap
The magic herdboy
The maiden in the country under-
  ground
Mapandangare, the great baboon
The marvelous cow of Llyn Barfog,
  the Little People of Wales
Mary and the Christ-child
Mary milks the cow
Nidden and Didden and Donal Beg
  O'Neary
O 'twas on a bright mornin' in summer

Old Gally Mander
Old pipes and the dryad
The old witch
On being a happy cow
One-eye, two-eyes, and three-eyes
Onsongo and the Masai cattle
The owl in the moon
Peter Ox
The poor ploughman and the rich
  nobleman
Prince Finn the fair
The purple cow
Reinar was watching his cows
Rushen Coatie
The saga of Stretch Garrison
Saint Cadog and King Arthur
Sly Peter's revenge
The small people's cow
The son of the hen-wife
A song for Easter
The story of Blathnat
The story of Tom Thumb
Sun, moon, and morning star
Sungold and the remarkable cow
The tale of Dick o' the cow
The talking fish
There was a little boy
There was a little man and his name
  was Gice
There was a piper had a cow
There was an old man
They protect their seed
The three cows
To outleap a rabbit
The two bottles
Two cows
The two step-sisters
The wee, wee mannie and the big,
  big coo
The white lady of Pumphul
Why crabs are flat
Would you like to see goats dance on
  stilts?
The year of Nyangondhu's cattle

, Fairy
  The farmer and the fairy cow

, Golden
  The flower-headed man
  The golden calf
  The prince of the seven golden
    cows

—Horns
  The spotted cow

—Skins
  The golden skins

—Tails
  The cow doesn't miss her lost tail
    till fly time

128

The cowskin boat
CARPENTER – SHIPS p191-201

Cowslips
Go out, children
The green mist
A milkweed and a buttercup

Cox, Palmer
The brownies in the toy shop

Coyote and mole
CURRY – DOWN p101-103

Coyote and the alder stump
COTHRAN – WITH p65-66

Coyote and the bear
COTHRAN – WITH p44-48

Coyote and the crying song
COURLANDER – PEOPLE p82-85

The coyote and the evil witches
MATSON – LONGHOUSE p39-48

The coyote and the stump. See Coyote
and the alder stump; The coyote and
the bear

The coyote and the two dogs
HARDENDORFF – TRICKY p55-61

Coyote cowboy/Pecos Bill
STOUTENBURG – AMER. p24-36

Coyote helps decorate the night
COURLANDER – PEOPLE p25-26

Coyote rings the wrong bell
JAGENDORF – KING p187-189

Coyotes
The ant and the yellow jacket
The bears
The beginning of the world and the
making of California
The bungling host
Calling the Chinook
Cottontail's song
The end of the world
Fickle Miss Frog
The fire bringer
The fishnet and the bear
The five swallow sisters
The foolishness of Cochinito
The good luck tree
The Hopi turtle
How and why: Don't be greedy story
How and why: Why the bear waddles
when he walks

How animals brought fire to man
How coyote became a friend to man
How coyote got his voice
How coyote helped to light the world
How coyote helped put fish in Clear
Lake
How coyote put salmon in the Kla-
math river
How crane saved coyote
How death came
How the first rainbow was made
The hunger time
Itsayaya and the chokecherries
Itsayaya and the otter
Itsayaya frees the salmon
Itsayaya's revenge
The Kamiah monster
The monster
Old man moon
One day, one night
Orphan boy
Pecos Bill
Pecos Bill and his bouncing bride
Pecos Bill, the cowboy
Popo and the coyote
The rabbit who wanted to be a man
The rescue of fire
The securing of light
Señor coyote
Señor coyote and the dogs
Señor coyote settles a quarrel
The sun callers
The sun, the moon and the stars
The theft of dawn
The two-faces
Two friends, coyote and bull snake,
exchange visits
Ugly boy
Uncle Coyote's last mischief
The upper world
The weasel
West country boy
Why fly rubs his hands together
Why there are shooting stars
The young coyote's visit

–Color
Why coyote is the color of the
ground

–Tails
The coyote and the bear

Coyote's needle
COURLANDER – PEOPLE p143-144

Coyote's new hairdo
CURRY – DOWN p80-89

The crab
BORSKI – GOOD p47.
THOMPSON – ONE p418-419

The crab and the monkey
SAKADE – JAPAN. p94-96

The crab and the needlefish
GREY – SOUTH (1) p5-7

The crab that tried to swallow the moon
CARPENTER – SHIPS p131-137

The crab, the crocodile and the jackal
TURNBULL – FAIRY p27-32

Crabs
Anansi and the crabs
The Arabe duck
The battle of the frogs and the mice
The boy who wouldn't mind his
grandmother
Casi Lampu'a Lentemue
The cat and the crab
Crafty crab
The crane and the crab
The crane, the fish and the crab
The Da-Trang crabs
The four friends
The golden crab
The greedy boy and the coconut crab
A horned goat
How crab got a hard back
How the fiddler crabs came to be
The magic ruby
The monkey and the crab
The moon's escape
The pilgrim and the crab
The sand-carrier crab
The search for the magic lake
The swan, the crab, and the pike
Teaching baby crab to walk
The two crabs
Why crabs are flat
Why crab's eyes stick out
Why the crab has no head or how the
first river was made
Why the tides ebb and flow

Crabs at the doorsteps
HSIEH – CHINESE p32-34

The crackling mountain
BUCK – FAIRY p96-97

Cradles
The bird of the golden land

Crafts and craftsmen
The fortunes of Said
The inn in the forest

The king's son and the straw hat
maker
The magic banana

The craftsman's wife
NAHMAD – PORTION p97-99

Crafty crab
COTHRAN – MAGIC p73-74

The crafty farmer
MANNING – ENGLISH p52-55

The crafty servant
HARDENDORFF – TRICKY p81-85

Craik, Dinah M. Muloch
The shaking of the pear tree

Cranberries
The three cranberries

The cranberry feast
COTHRAN – MAGIC p8-12

Crane, Louise
The empty city

Crane, T. F., trans.
The clever peasant

The crane and the crab
GAER – FABLES p84-86

The crane and the fox
BLOCH – UKRAIN. p36-38

The crane, the fish and the crab
WILLIAMS – ROUND p53-56

The crane who taught the birds to dance
and make corroboree
NORLEDGE – ABORIGINAL p58.

The crane wife
PRATT – MAGIC unp.
SEKI – FOLKTALES p77-80

Cranes
Arap Sang and the cranes
The battle on the Isle of Camphor
The Brahman in the potter's shop
The crow's reward
The fox and the crane
How crane got his long beak
How crane got his long legs
How crane saved coyote
How Mr. Crane's eyes became blue
How the sun was made

Cranes (*Continued*)

King crow and Sir parrot
Lame tame crane
O my dame had a lame tame crane
The one-legged crane
Onsongo and the Masai cattle
The owl in the moon
The poor weaver and the princess
Queen crane
The snake and its benefactor
The tortoise who talked too much
Two out of the sack
The vulture's advice
Why crane's feathers are brown and
    otter doesn't feel the cold
The wolf and the crane

−**Feathers**
    The crane's feather

The crane's feather
    GINSBURG − MASTER p59-80

The crane's report
    GAER − FABLES p96-102

Cranston, Samuel
    Hearts and pirates

Crawfish. *See* **Crayfish**

Crawford, John Martin
    Wainamoinen finds the lost-words

Crayfish
    The birth of the River Emajõgi
    The end of the world
    The raccoon and the crawfish
    Who?

Cream. *See* **Milk−Cream**

Creangä, Ion
    A sketch of Ion Creangä's life

Creation
    See also **God; Man**
    The acorn maidens
    The beginning of the world and the
        making of California
    The big tree and the big bird
    Children of the sun
    Creator makes−
    Destruction and creation myths: The
        book of the divine cow
    The earth is on a fish's back
    The fall of the earth giants

The flood
Glooskap's country
Heaven and earth and man
The heavenly lovers
How life and light came into the world
How spider got his thread
How the Caribs first came to Honduras
How the earth was made to fit the sky
How the world was made (1)
How the world was made (2)
In the beginning
In the first times
Introduction (CAMPBELL − MAORI)
Legend of the first Filipinos
Magic
The making of the earth
The moon painters
Naba Zid-Wendé
Ra and his children
The revolt of the utensils
Takamagahara
Tiamat
The time of deep darkness
Wainamoinen finds the lost-words
Who?
Why crows are black
Why porpoise is not a fish
Why the world is the way it is

The creation of man
    AULAIRE − NORSE p26-30

The creation of the wolf
    MAAS − MOON p56-59

The creation of the world
    AULAIRE − NORSE p21-25

Creator makes−
    LEACH − HOW p41-43

Credit
    The dead creditor
    Sand in the bag

The creek of whale oil
    OMAN − ESKIMO p43-48

The crested curassow
    SHERLOCK − WEST p13-20

Crete
    The baby that was sold
    Europa and the bull
    The minotaur

"Crick crack" stories
    Armadillo's story
    Brown owl's story

"Crick crack stories" (*Continued*)

Chimpanzee's story
Firefly's story
Green parrot's story
Little Capuchin monkey's story
What is a crick crack story

The cricket and the ant
ARBUTHNOT – TIME p210-211

The cricket fight
HUME – FAVORITE p33-38

Crickets
The ant, the lamb, the cricket, and
the mouse
Come, little leaves
Dancing he would go
The doctor who knew everything
Little cricket
The magic ball
Over in the meadow
Tsirtsur and Peziza
The war between the lion and the
cricket
Why the possum's tail is bare

Crime and criminals
See also **Bandits; Murder; Thieves and
thievery; etc.**
Black Sam Bellamy
The Haitians in the Dominican
Republic
The honest criminal
The iniquitous Captain Lightfoot
Rehoboth's lady counterfeiter
Richard Feverel and the hay-rick
A severe punishment
The story of a gentleman
The unusual excuse

Crimea
The spring ay-petri

The crimson purse
SPICER – GOBLINS p70-78

The crimson purse and the talking raven
SPICER – KNEELING p92-106

Crippled. *See* Handicapped

Crispin, Saint
Saint Crispin and the old one

Criticism
The battle of the firefly and the apes

The Count of Estremadura
How the Brazilian beetles got their
gorgeous coats
Momus the mocker
The two crabs

The crochera
MacMANUS – BOLD p44-63

The crock of gold
DOWNING – RUSSIAN p159-163

Crockett, Davy
Davy Crockett
Davy Crockett, the yaller blossom o'
the forest
Frontier fighter/Davy Crockett

Crocodiles. *See* **Alligators and crocodiles**

The crocodile's daughter
CARPENTER – SOUTH p18-26

The crocodile's mouth
STOUTENBURG – CROC. p9-11

Crocodile's share
COURLANDER – KANT. p81-83

Crocus flowers bloom like fire
MY BOOK HOUSE v. 1 p205.

Crofters
The lads who met the highwaymen
The maid of the waves
The man who helped carry the coffin
The oyster catcher, the duck and the
hen
The tale the crofter told

Cromwell, Oliver
Hector protector

Cromwell and the friar
O'SULLIVAN – FOLK. p237-240

Crones, Old. *See* Witches

The crop division. *See* The devil's
partnership

Croppers. *See* **Share-croppers**

Crops
The fox and the bear
The hairy boggart's field
Saint Sava and the devil

132

Crops *(Continued)*
The strange feathery beast
Tops or bottoms
Why bears eat meat

Cross my heart
BATCHELOR – SUPER. p112-113

Cross your fingers
BATCHELOR – SUPER. p115-116

Crosses
"Bread and butter"
The coming of the Spaniards
Cross my heart
Cross your fingers
The father's steps
The horse that liked to play tricks
Kirsten McVurich
Lionbruno
The three golden ducats
The tiyanak
Una and the Red Cross knight

Crossing the river
COURLANDER – TERRA. p91-92

The crow and the flamingo
GREEN – BIG p116.

The crow and the fox
GREEN – BIG p195.

The crow and the grain of corn
SIDDIQUI – TOON. p124-129

The crow and the pitcher
ARBUTHNOT – TIME p207.
STRONG – FAVORITE p80.

The crow and the serpent
KOREL – LISTEN p107-108

The crow and the soap
KELSEY – ONCE p75-78

The crow and the sparrow
SIDDIQUI – TOON. p44-49
SPELLMAN – BEAUT. p12-14

The crow and the water jug
GREEN – BIG p21.

The crow and the whale
GILHAM – BEYOND p51-67

The crow in the banyan tree
GAER – FABLES p34-36

The crow in the rose-apple tree
GAER – FABLES p156-157

The crow-Peri
BUCK – FAIRY p29-34

The crowned snake
BECHSTEIN – FAIRY p7-11

The crowning of a king
SAWYER – DIETRICH p93-103

Crowns
Arap Sang and the cranes
Cinder Joe becomes king
Constantes and the dragon
The crowned snake
The frog-wife
Golden
The golden helmet
King adder
The shepherd's crown
The snake crown

Crows
See also Ravens
Anansi and the crabs
Anansi steals the palm wine
At the wedding of Miss Jenny Wren
"Bow-wow", says the dog
The boy and his magic robe
The boy and the birds
The boy who wouldn't give up
The camel in the lion's court
The cold May night
The dappled deer and the intelligent crow
The deer and its friends
Dhungura-ngarian: where the pelican danced
Do scarecrows scare crows?
Eight leaves of story (3) Baglan the builder
The firebird
A flower to catch a thief
The four friends
The fox and the crow
The friendly mouse
Gizo's counting trick
The golden butterfly
The greedy crow
The growing rock
The hair from the queen of the underworld
The hermit cat
How confusion came among the animals
The hunter's child
I don't know where and I don't know what

Crows (*Continued*)

I saw a crow a-flying low
The infallible salt bird
It won't do you any good
The jackal and the fig tree
King crow and Sir parrot
The king of the crows
Light-O-Leap and the fowler
The lion and the hare
The little crow
Little Gustava
The louse and the crow
The magic mare
The magic storm
Mr. Crow and the mussel
The mouse and his friends
The old crow teaches the young crow
Old Meg, the witch
Otto would a-riding go
Over in the meadow
The parrot and the crow
The partridge and the crow
Peter Rabbit decides to change his
  name
The plot
The poor weaver and the princess
The princess with the golden hair
The quarrel
The raven and the crow
Rusty Jack
The silver river
The snake and its benefactor
Spotless the lion and Trusty the
  carpenter
The squirrel went out to cut the hay
The story ends
There was a crow
Three princes and their beasts
The vain ox
Wahn the crow Wirinum
The white snake
Why crow has a right to the first corn
Why crow is black and men find
  precious stones in the earth
Why crows are black
Yung-Kyng-Pyung

—**Feathers**
  The dancing horses of Acoma
  Dressed in strange feathers

, **Golden**
  The golden crow

—**Language**
  The magic ear

—**Tails**
  Mr. Crow takes a wife

The crows and the owls
  KOREL — LISTEN p11-66

The crow's pearl
  VO—DINH — TOAD p115-122

The crow's reward
  GAER — FABLES p108-110

The crowza stones
  MANNING — PETER p120-124

Crucibles
  The melting pot

The cruel giant
  SHEPPARD — WELSH p85-89

The cruel rich man as the devil's horse.
  See The angry baron

The cruel stepmother
  RANKE — GERMANY p65-67

The cruel uncle
  MAHER — BLIND p53-71

Cruelty
  The black cat of Cotabato
  Blue legs
  Chameleon finds—
  The coming of Asin
  The fall of the spider man
  The girl without arms
  How Kwaku Ananse destroyed a
    kingdom
  How rattlesnake got his fangs
  How Yehl, the hero, freed the beam-
    ing maiden
  The hunter and the dove
  Kakui, bird of the night
  The knight of La Sarraz
  The legend of William Tell
  Look behind as well as before
  Mother of the forest
  The mousetower
  Patient Griselda
  Prince Wicked
  The princess in the tower
  The Red Ettin
  The sad, sorry sister
  The six brothers
  The small red feather
  The snake and the dreams
  The song of strength
  The twelve months
  The ugly duckling
  The white bird sister
  The wicked polecat

The crumb in the beard
  THOMPSON — ONE p355-359

Crusades and crusaders
Black Colin of Loch Awe
The children's crusade
The miserly miller
The ring of Hallwil

Crying. *See* **Tears**

Crying turkeys
RUSHMORE – DANCING p103-104

The crystal bowl
JOHNSON – HARPER p196-211

The crystal kiosk and the diamond ship
EKREM – TURKISH p1-12

The crystal mountain
ALMEDINGEN – RUSS. p118-131

The crystal of love
SUN – LAND p69-71

Crystals
The magic crystal
The three brothers and the marvelous
things

Cuba. *See* **West Indies–Cuba**

Cube, Helmut von
The spider

Cuchulain (Cuculain, Cuchulainn, Cuchu-
llin, Cucullin, etc.)
Clever Oonagh
How Cuchulain wooed his wife
A legend of Knockmany
The love of Cuchulainn and Finn,
and the only jealousy of Emer, his
wife

Cuchulain, the hound of Ulster
PICARD – HERO p126-141

Cuchulainn and the smith's wife
O'SULLIVAN – FOLK. p74-79

Cuchullin keeps the gap of the north
O'FAOLAIN – IRISH p52-59

Cuchullin parleys with Maeve
O'FAOLAIN – IRISH p60-66

The cuckoo
DEUTSCH – MORE p69-72
DEUTSCH – TALES p69-72

The cuckoo and the clock
MONTROSE – WINTER p126-138

The cuckoo and the donkey
MY BOOK HOUSE v. 1 p122.

Cuckoo in the hedge
JAGENDORF – MERRY p17-24

Cuckoos
The birds' St. Valentine day
"Bow-wow", says the dog
Charley, Barley, Buck and Rye
How strong, a bridge have you?
In spring the birds do sing
The master and the servant
Mirzhan and the lord of the kingdom
under the sea
The nightingale and the cotton tree
Saint Peter's horses
The two sillies
When I was a baby

The cuckoo's reward
BARLOW – LATIN p134-137

Cuculain (Cucullin)
MY BOOK HOUSE v. 10 p188-202

Cucumbers
The blue lotus flower
Golden bracelets, golden anklets
The greedy man in the moon
The man who was only three inches
tall

Cudgels. *See* **Sticks**

Culdees (Irish Christians)
North Salem's Irish? Ruins

Culhwch, Prince
The quest for Olwen (1) The destiny

Cum and Koompang
KRUEGER – SERPENT p90-97

Cummings, E. E.
All in green went my love riding

Cumulative stories. *See* **Repetitive
rhymes and stories**

Cunning. *See* **Cleverness; Trickery**

The cunning old man and the three rouges
MANNING – DAMIAN p87-93

Cunnigham, Caroline
   The little scarred one

Cupboards
   Old Mother Hubbard

Cupid and Psyche
   ARBUTHNOT – TIME p221-225

Cupid and Psyche . . . The trial of love
   UNTERMEYER – FIRE. p76-85

Cups
   The crystal of love
   The little lizard's sorrow
   The magic crystal
   The wishing cup

   , Fairy
   Horse and hattock

Curassows, Crested
   The jaguar and the crested curassow

Curd ears
   GRAY – INDIA'S p184-185

Cures. *See* **Balsam trees; Healing**

Curfew
   Wee Willie Winkie

Curosity
   Blue Beard
   The blue lake
   Cherry
   The country under the hill
   East o' the sun and west o' the moon
   George and the field glasses
   Goldilocks and the three bears
   The magic berries
   The moon and his frog-wife
   The nutcracker and sugardolly stories
   The peeping servant
   The shepherd with the curious wife
   The silver jug
   What's your name?
   Where by you going, you Devon
      maid?

Curosity punished
   BORSKI – GOOD p61.

The curious John Greye papers
   TAFT – PROFILE p30-33

A curious tale
   FELTON – WORLD'S p133-138

The curious wife
   MASEY – STORIES p46-49

The curlew flies
   FARJEON – SILVER p 147-150

Curlews (birds)
   In the mist
   Poll comes to court
   The silver curlew

Currency. *See* **Money**

The curse
   LEEUW – LEGENDS p146-151

The curse of Polyphemus
   ARBUTHNOT – TIME p235.

The curse of the Abenaki
   TAFT – PROFILE p153-162

The curse on the only son
   INS-SŎB – FOLK p51-54

Curses
   The auld cailleach's curse
   The bell of Monte Pino
   The blessing and a curse
   Blodeuedd and the slaying of Llew
   The faery flag of Dunnegan
   The flow of beauty
   The ghost ship
   The giant worm of the well
   How cats came to purr
   The kneeler's twelve tasks
   Lady Eaton's curse
   The Lambton worm
   The lame vixon
   Legend of the Witch of Cape Ann
   The light princess
   The lost cows
   Love at first sight
   The magic ear
   Melisande
   The mop servant
   Nāgasvāmin and the witches
   Old Sal's curse
   The price of a curse
   The Red Ettin
   The secret of the hidden treasure
   The serpent prince
   The silent princess
   Sirene, the mermaid
   The sleeping beauty in the wood
   The story of General Gim Dŏg-
      Nyŏng

136

Curses (*Continued*)
The story of Sigurd
The swans of Ballycastle
The tale of the ghost ship
The three banshees
Wild rose
The youth who trusted in God

Curtains
The silent princess

Curtis, Mary I.
The scarlet maple

Curupiras (hairy men)
The hairy men from the forest

Custer, George Armstrong
Yellow hair: George Armstrong
Custer

Customs (duty)
The duty that was not paid

Cut them for health
LEACH – SOUP p104-106

Cutters and cutting
Rich woman, poor woman
The ritual coming-of-age

Cuttlefish
The dragon king and the lost
fish-hook
The Kraken

Cyclones
Big winds
A Kansas cyclone
A Missouri cyclone

Cyclopes
JACOBSON – LEGEND. p3-6

Cyclops
No man with the Cyclops
Odysseus in the land of the giants
Polyphemus, the Cyclops

Cypress trees
The enchanted knife
Madschun
Pygmalion . . . The marvelous statue
The Twins

The czar's frog daughter
PROTTER – CHILD. p99-109

The czar's general and the clever peasant
PROTTER – CHILD. p97-98

Czechoslovakia
A Bohemian evening
Budulinek
The cat, the goose, and the fox
Clever Manka
The devil's gifts
The dishonest tailor
The girl who clung to the devil's back
A gullible world
Intelligence and luck
Katcha and the devil
King Svatopluk and the three sticks
Knowledge and luck
Kuratko the terrible
The little rooster and the little hen
Longshanks, girth, and keen
The magic mountain
The prince who rode through a
mousehole
Radowid
Rattle-rattle-rattle and chink-chink-
chink
The shepherd's nosegay
The shoemaker's apron
Smolicheck
The three golden hairs
The three golden hairs of grandfather
know all
The twelve months
The wood fairy

–Prague
The mechanical man of Prague

Czechoslovakian rhymes
MY BOOK HOUSE v. 1 p128-129

D

The Da-Trang crabs
  SUN – LAND p74-79

Da Vinci, Leonardo
  The wonderland of an artist's
  workshop

Daffodils
  Crocus flowers bloom like fire
  Daffy-down-dilly
  The hundred-headed daffodil
  The magic hill

Daffy-down-dilly
  MY BOOK HOUSE v. 1 p25.

Daggers (stilettos)
  The adventures of Silvervit and
  Lillvacker
  The dark king
  The magic dagger

Dagobert, King
  King Dagobert

Dahomey
  How poverty was revealed to the
  King of Adja

Dainty little maiden
  MY BOOK HOUSE v. 1 p155.

Dairying
  See also Cows
  How Urseli became a princess

Dame Durden
  MY BOOK HOUSE v. 1 p58.

Dame Wiggins of Lee
  MY BOOK HOUSE v. 2 p188-191

Damer's gold
  O'SULLIVAN – FOLK. p240-242

Damian and the dragon
  MANNING – DAMIAN p1-17

The damned boys
  RANKE – GERMANY p189.

Damocles, sword of. *See* The sword of
Damocles

Damon and Pythias
  BALDWIN – FAVOR. p82-84

Damon and Pythias; the most faithful of
  friends
  STRONG – FAVORITE p67-71

Dams
  The five swallow sisters
  Itsayaya frees the salmon
  The lost secrets of Charles Hatfield
  Why the motmot lives in a hole

Damsels, House
  The house damsel

Dan-Gun, first King of Korea
  INS-SŎB – FOLK p3-4

Dana, People of (The Dannaans)
  The chase of Slieve Gallion
  The children of Lir
  The children of Tuireann return to
  Erin
  The choosing of the high-king of Erin
  The cooking-spit of the women of
  Fincara
  The death of the sons of Tuireann
  The first three hundred years
  How the Fomorians came into Erin
  Kian and the children of Tuireann
  Lugh and his father's murderers
  Midir and Etain
  The quest of the children of Turenn
  The sea of Moyle
  The shouts on the Hill of Midkena

The dance at Hickory Creek
  JAGENDORF – SAND p141-145

Dance, little baby, dance up high!
  MY BOOK HOUSE v. 1 p18.

The dance of death
  MacMILLAN – GLOOS. p192-196

The dance of the animals
  BELPRE´– TIGER p97-103

The dance of the fishes
  KRYLOV – 15 p3-7

Dance, raven, dance
  COTHRAN – MAGIC p22-24

138

Dance to your daddie
MY BOOK HOUSE v. 1 p58.

The danced-out shoes
THOMPSON – ONE p19-21

Dancers and dancing
About Jan the Prince, Princess
Wonderface, and the flamebird
All my lambkins and all my bear
cubs
Anansi and the elephant go
hunting
Anansi's hat-shaking dance
The barrel-organ
The beetle's hairpiece
Blue legs
Bohra the kangaroo
The boy and the monk
A boy in the island of Bali
Bucca Dhee and Bucca Gwidden
The case of the mouse-deer and the
crocodile's eggs
Catskin
La Cenerentola
Christian dancing in Georgia
Cinder-maid
Cinderella or the little glass
slippers
"Cinderellas"
Columbine and her playfellows of
the Italian pantomine
Count Alaric's lady
The crane who taught the birds to
dance and make corroboree
Damian and the dragon
Davy Crockett, the yaller blossom
o' the forest
The fairy wife
The faun and the woodcutter's
daughter
The fiddler going home
The fiddler of Echternach
The fisherman and his soul
Freddy and his fiddle
The goat well
The good woman
He danced fine—o—
The heron's ball
Hop, Mother Annika!
How the groundhog lost his tail
Hwan and Dang
It's better to be smart than strong
The jinni's magic flute
Katcha and the devil
Kuiluile, the dancing girl
The lamb with the golden fleece
The little black box
The little dog waltz

The lizard's big dance
The magic fiddle
The magic pipe
The magic veil
The magical tune
The magician's revenge
Manny MacGilligan's story
The marriage feast
The miraculous flute
Monkey-dance and sparrow-dance
Morgan and the three fairies
Navahchoo
Nella's dancing shoes
The old man and the devils
Old man Elias and the dancing sheriff
The old man with the bump
The old men who had wens
The out-foxed fox
The palace in the Rath
Peekaboo, I see you!
The piskey revelers
Potak's dancing and the snakes
The pots that sang
The prince and the sky-blue filly
Prince Prigio
The princess with the golden shoes
The red shoes
Rhys at the fairy dance
The royal banquet
The ruby prince
Seven iron-souled slippers
Shizuka's dance
Sir Michael Scott
Six—and—four
Skillywidden
The sly thief of Valenciennes
Sonny-boy Sim
The spirit who danced
Star-boy and the sun dance
The swineherd who married a princess
The tale of nutcracker
Tam O'Shanter
The trials of Ting Ling
Twelve dancing princesses
Ugly boy
'Water's locked'!
The weeping lass at the dancing place
Why the possum's tail is bare
Why there are shooting stars
The wood fairy
Young Kate
The youth and the dog dance
The youth who wanted some fun

The dancing bird
PARKER – AUSTRALIAN p177-183

The dancing feather
MARRIOTT – AMER. p165-170

The dancing fires of Saint Elmo
CARPENTER – SHIPS p79-87

Dancing he would go
MINCIELI – TALES p96-100

The dancing horse of Acoma
RUSHMORE – DANCING p140-158

The dancing kettle
UCHIDA – DANCING p3-10

The dancing monkeys
MY BOOK HOUSE v. 2 p92-93

The dancing mortar of Block Island
JOHNSON – WHAT p264.

The dancing palm tree
WALKER – DANCING p15-26

The dancing princess
JOHNSON – PRINC. p50-67

The dancing stars
JABLOW – MAN p99.

The dancing teapot
MARMUR – JAPAN. p57-60

The dancing water, singing apple, and speaking bird
JACOBS – EUROPE. p51-65
THOMPSON – ONE p319-326

Dandelions
How dandelions were made
Magic

Danes
The golden helmet
The man who lost his shadow
The tale of Nornagest

Danger
The escape of the animals
God bless you
The pavilion of peril
A prince went hunting
The sword of Damocles

The dangers of sorcery
HOPE-SIMPSON – CAVAL. p224-225

Daniel in the lion's den
MY BOOK HOUSE v. 6 p180-183

Daniel O'Connell and the trickster
O'SULLIVAN – FOLK. p231-232

Daniel the gawk
CREANGĂ – FOLK p152-166

Daniels, Guy
KRYLOV – 15 p39.

Daniel's deer
LEACH – RAINBOW p36-37

Dante Alighieri
Dante's voyage to the inferno, puratory, and paradise
The divine comedy
The man who lived in the world of dreams

Dante's voyage to the inferno, puratory, and paradise
MY BOOK HOUSE v. 11 p156.

Danube River
Dunay
The warm Matzah

Daphne
Apollo and Daphne . . . The laurel wreath

The dappled deer and the intelligent crow
GAER – FABLES p74-77

Dapplegrim
MANNING – BEASTS p70-83

The daring prince
MY BOOK HOUSE v. 3 p127.

The dark and stormy night
WITHERS – I SAW p35.

The dark cliffs of Dover
FELTON – TRUE p49-56

The dark guest
GARNER – GOBLINS p76-77

The dark king
LUM – ITALIAN p43-56

The dark maiden from the ninth heaven
BONNET – CHINESE p139-144

The dark tower
VANSITTART – DARK p71-80

Darkness
Anansi plays dead
Bohra hunts the dark

Darkness (*Continued*)

Donal from Donegal
Fear of the dark
The fire dogs
How chipmunk got his stripes
How the people came to the middle
place
In a dark wood
Jack the giant-killer
The lost gift
Mancrow, bird of darkness
O gungbemi and the battle in the
bush
Prince Finn the Fair
The sun, the moon and the stars
A wit to outwit wit

Darrah, Lydia
An unsung heroine

Dasent, Sir George Webbe
Boots and his brothers
Dapplegrim
Lord Peter
The princess on the glass hill
The seven foals
The white bear

The date gatherers
MONTGOMERIE – 25 p22-23

Date palm trees. *See* **Palm trees**

Dates (fruit)
Cenerentola or Cinderella
A dish of laban
Kantjil discovers the wisdom of Allah

Dates to Cairo
WILSON – GREEK p 122-125

Datu Omar and the fairy
ROBERTSON – PHILIP. p53-62

Daugherty, James
Buffalo Bill

Daughter and stepdaughter
DUDDINGTON – RUSS. p11-15

The daughter of the dwarf
MANNING – GIANNI p108-118

Daughter of the jade emperor
SUN – LAND p37-38

The daughter of the King Ron
LEODHAS – HEATHER p81-93

Daughters
The apple of contentment
Ash sweeper and the wishing wand
The black giant of Luckless River
Cap o' rushes
Caporushes
The clever lass
The coming of Oscar
The czar's frog daughter
The demon's daughter
Diamonds and toads
The disappearance of Ifan Gruffydd's
daughter
The doll
The dutiful daughter
The fairies
The feather of Finist the falcon
The foolish father-in-law
The foolish wife and her three foolish
daughters
The goldspinners
The great fish
How death came into the world
The delicate daughter
The innkeeper's daughter
Iphigenia . . . The transported
sacrifice
The jackal, the barber and the
Brahmin who had seven daughters
King Lindom
The land beyond the fire
The little duck
Love like salt
The master of the winds
The melodius napkin
The most obedient wife
The nut branch
Peerifool
The princess in the tower
The princess who loved her father
like salt
Salt and bread
The salt at dinner
The seven mice
The smart daughter
The soldier's return
The sun, the moon and the star of
morning
The tale of the Earl of Mar's daughter
The tale of the Faderaevisch
The three chests
The three princesses in the mountain-
in-the-blue
The three traveling artisans
To the devil with the money
The troll's bride
Utzel and his daughter Poverty
The wedding of the Cid's daughters
Whitebear Whittington
The wind-demon
The woodcutter's daughter

Daughters-in-law
The cobbler's deity

David (Biblical)
Bostanai
David, the shepard boy
Enmity between man serpent
Introduction (Tales of David and
Solomon)
King David and the angel of death
Preacher and the devil
Tales of David and Solomon
The value of a boiled egg
The weeping willow

David Alroy
BARASH – GOLDEN p45-48

David and Goliath
DE REGNIERS – GIANT p39-46

David and Goliath . . . The shepherd boy
and the giant
UNTERMEYER – FIRE p109-112

David and the big drum
GREEN – LEPRECHAUN p107-117

David Copperfield and little Emily
MY BOOK HOUSE v. 7 p182-198

David, the shepherd boy
MY BOOK HOUSE v. 7 p73-83

David Wright and the fairies
SHEPPARD – SCOT. p125-127

Davies, William H.
The child and the mariner

Davis, Mary Gould
The enchanted cow

Davy Crockett
GORHAM – REAL p34-46
LEACH – RAINBOW p38-42

Davy Crockett, the yaller blossom o' the
forest
SHAPIRO – TALL p53-67

Dawlish fair
MY BOOK HOUSE v. 2 p67.

Dawn
The goblins at the bath house
The theft of dawn

Dawn, twilight and midnight
ALMEDINGEN – RUSS. p27-38

Day, John Prayer

Day. *See* **Daylight**

Day dreaming. *See* **Absentmindedness**

Day dreaming
JACOBS – EUROP. p110-114

The day of the scholars
MacMANUS – HIBERIAN p224-232

The day the sky fell
WITHERS – I SAW p81-84

The day Tuk became a hunter
MELZACK – DAY p13-20

Daylight
See also **Dawn**
The greedy rich man
How night was let loose and all the
animals came to be
How raven brought fire to the
Indians
How raven found the daylight
How the people came to the middle
place
Maui catches the sun
Raven and the sun
The time of deep darkness
Why the sun shines in the daytime
and the moon shines at night
Why there is both day and night

The days of the first monkeys
FEINSTEIN – FOLK p38-41

Days of the week
As Tommy Snooks and Bessie
Brooks
Everyday luck
Friday
Firday the thirteenth
The king and the shepherd
March and the shepherd
The moon's face
Moving day
One day, one night
Why there is a man in the moon

De la Mare, Walter
Ashputtel
Clever Grethel
The fly
The dancing princesses
I saw three witches
Old Shellover
Silver
Two poems

142

De la Mare, Walter
JOHNSON – PRINC. p308.

de Monvel, M.B., illus.
Catherine's tea party

De Morgan, Mary
JOHNSON – HARPER p319-320
JOHNSON – PRINC. p308-309

The deacon of Darkwater
BOUCHER – MEAD p63-67

Dead
The babymakers
The bride from the land of the
spirits
Hoichi the earless
Isis and Osiris
The journey to the land of the dead
The land of the dead
The lass and her good stout
blackthorn stick
Manny MacGilligan's story
Maria sat on the fire
The master thief
The milky way
The mysterious letter
Proserpine
Shall I be so?
Three corpses, money and a wine-
bottle
The Vetala's stories

The dead creditor
RANKE – GERMANY p163.

The dead man who was alive
BRENNER – BOY p96-99

A dead secret
BUCK – FAIRY p218-220
LITTLEDALE – GHOSTS p73-78

Deaf
The bell of Monte Pino
The blind man and the deaf man
The blind man, the deaf man and the
donkey
Bouki gets whee-ai
The emperor and the deaf man
The four deaf men
Four good men
"Good day, fellow!" "Axe handle!"
Justice
Old pipes and the dryad
The three deaf men
A visitor from Paradise
The wise judge

Deaf men and their answers
LEACH – NOODLES p 86-87

Dealing with ghosts
JOHNSON – WHAT p168.

Dear-boy
ILLYÉS – ONCE p93-101

Dearmaid and Grania
SUTCLIFF – HIGH p129-152

Death
See also **Burials; Cemeteries; Dead;
Funerals**
The ant in search of her leg
Aunt Misery
Beppo Pipetta and his knapsack
The big black umbrella
The birth of the islands
The boy in the land of shadows
The boy with the beer keg
The bungled message
The cat, the dog, and death
The child of death
Count Bertrand
The dance of death
Does a dog's howl mean death?
The encounter with death
The faithless apprentice
The finch with the golden voice
Fionn in search of his youth
Friends in life and death
The game of chess in the mountains
The gay goss-hawk
The giant okab
A glass of water, please
Glooskap's country
Godfather death
The homecoming of Beorhthnoth
Beohthelm's son
The hour of death
How death came into the world
How summer came to Canada
How the gypsy boy outsmarted
death
How the people began
Ivan and his knapsack
Ivan and his sack
The journey to the land of the dead
King David and the angel of death
Kralyevich Marko's death
Kuluile, the dancing girl
Leviathan and the fox
The little king on the Viking ship
The lonely house
Luc, the king's woodsman
The man who looked for death
Maui and the death goddess
Maui and the fire goddess
Mrizala and her bridegroom, death

Death (*Continued*)

Ooka and the death decree
Orpheus . . . The fabulous musician
Over the hill
Padre Ulivo and his guests
Prince Alun and the "Cannwyl
  Corph"
Princess Golden-hair and the great
  black raven
The prophet Elijah and the angel of
  death
The red king and the witch
The robber Simhavikrama
The seven dead men of the Venetian
  lagoon
The shadow boys
The slaying of Siegfried
Socrates . . . The cup of hemlock
The soldier and the knapsack
The southern cross
The spirit's drum
The story of O-Tei
The tale of the ghost ship
The tale of the gypsy and his strange
  love
Tell me, when will I die?
The thirteen enchanted cats
The three companions
The three enchanted maidens
The three young men and death
The tinker of Tamlacht
The two righteous men
The voyage below the water
The weeping lass at the dancing place
The white stone canoe

Death
JOHNSON – WHAT p73-76

Death a prisoner
MÜLLER – SWISS p52-56

Death and the old man
COURLANDER – TERRA.
  p108-111

Death and the soldier
DOWNING – RUSSIAN p97-115

The death of Balder
ARBUTHNOT – TIME p240-244
AULAIRE – NORSE p128-136
HOSFORD – THUNDER p93-99

The death of Cuchullin
O'FAOLAIN – IRISH p101-109

The death of Dearmid
SUTCLIFF – HIGH p157-169

The death of Deirdre
PILKINGTON – THREE p225-232
WILSON – SCOTTISH p 185-192

The death of Hector
GREEN – GREEKS p30-31

The death of Paris
GREEN – GREEKS p36-37

The death of Koshchei the deathless
BUCK – FAIRY p35-46

The death of Kwasind
MAYNE – HEROES p204-212

The death of Roland
WESTWOOD – MEDIEVAL
  p119-127

The death of the children of Lir
PILKINGTON – THREE p119-123

The death of the sons of Tuireann
PILKINGTON – THREE p78-81

The death of the sons of Uisne
PILKINGTON – THREE p218-224

The death of the Yugovichi's mother
ĆURCIJA – HEROES p51-54

The death of Uwaine
PICARD – STORIES p172-180

The death watch
DOWNING – RUSSIAN p168-171

Death's godchild
ALEGRÍA – THREE p52-55

The debt
See also The folk-tales of Kashmir
COURLANDER – TIGER'S p78-79

Debts
Anansi steals the palm wine
Boiled wheat for a bountiful harvest
Grasp all, lose all
The green isle
Ikkyu and the merchant's moneybags
The man who couldn't pay his debts
The tale of a debt repaid

Deceit. *See* Deception; Disloyalty;
Hypocrisy

Deception
Anpu and Bata
The bone that testified

144

Deception (*Continued*)
Datu Omar and the fairy
The deer of five colors
The devil duped
The fate of the vulture
Granny Shelock
Holding the bag
Kalulu and his money farm
The king and the barber
The man in the moon
Monkey fat
Nancy's brook
The shepherd's boy
The Siamese pepper cure
The spider and the lizard
The task of Prince Kurumamochi
The wolf in sheep's clothing

The decision
LEEUW – INDO. p65-67

Decisions
From a moral alphabet
The goldsmith, the wood carver, the
tailor, and the hermit who quarreled
over a wooden woman
Old boss and George
The potter and the gate
The stars above: Long Sash and his
people

Decrees
The barrel decree
Bostanai
The dream

Deegeenboya the soldier bird
PARKER – AUSTRALIAN p80-86

Deep insight
GREEN – BIG p234.

Deer
See also **Antelopes; Elk; etc.**
The banyan deer
The birth of Oisin
The bow, the deer, and the talking
bird
The crystal mountain
The dancing water, singing apple, and
speaking bird
The dappled deer and the intelligent
crow
The dicot tree and the deer
Different, but not better
Djamukh–son of a deer
The doe and the lioness
The eagle and the owl

The enchanted buck
The faun and the woodcutter's
daughter
The first Thanksgiving day
The foolish, timid, little hare
The four friends
The fox and the lion in partnership
The heavenly maiden and the
woodcutter
Hiawatha's fasting
The hunter of Perak
Jack the giant-killer
The labors of Hercules
Land, water and wind
The lizards and the stag
The loup-garou in the woods
The man who learned the language
of the animals
The marriage of Arthur
The mighty hunter
Mister deer's my riding horse '
The mop servant
The mother of Oisin
The mouse and his friends
Nkalimeva
Oisin, son of Finn Mac Cool
Oisin's mother
The out-foxed fox
The outwitted hunter
Peaceful, the gentle deer
The pigeon, the deer and the turtle
The quest for Oleven (4) Fulfilling
the tasks 2/ The oldest animals
Rainbow and the autumn leaves
The rescue of fire
Saint Neot
Smolicheck
Sofo's escape from the leopard
Sonny-boy Sim
The speedy messenger
The stag-hunt
The stag prince
The story of Noschoy Dalta of Ujjain
The stupid wolf
Tar-sa's luck
The three enchanted princes
The three friends
The three stags
The two youths whose father was
under the sea
Unlucky Mussah
The white deer of Onota
The wife from another world
The wild huntsman
The wizard earl

, **Golden**
The cruel stepmother
The golden deer
The golden stag

Deer (*Continued*)

— **Horns** (antlers)
Bucky, the big bold fawn
The good luck tree
How deer got his horns
How the deer got his horns
— **Skins**
The hunter and the hind

— **Tails**
How the deer lost his tail
How the raven brought the fire

— **Teeth**
Why the deer's teeth are blunt

The deer and its friends
TOOZE — WONDER. p96-99

The deer and the jaguar share a house
U.N. — RIDE p198-201

The deer and the snake
INS—SŎB — FOLK p94-95

Deer Mice. *See* **Mouse-Deer**

The deer of five colors
UCHIDA — MAGIC p65-71

The deer, the hare, and the toad
INS—SŎB — FOLK p33-34

A deer trick
JAGENDORF — SAND p50-53

The deer woman
MARRIOTT — AMER. p161-164

Defeat
The battle of the animals

The defeat of the Fomorians
PILKINGTON — THREE p25-30

Defects
The mole and the rabbits

Deirdre
The fate of the sons of Usnach

Deirdre
HAZELTINE — HERO p173-183

Deirdre and the sons of Uisne
PILKINGTON — THREE p125-232

Deirdre and the sons of Usna
GARNIER — LEGENDS p166-181
PICARD — HERO p115-124

Deities. *See* **God; Gods and goddesses;
Jesus Christ**

Dekker, Edward Douwes. *See* **Multatuli,
pseud.**

Delarue, Paul
DELARUE — FRENCH p117.

Delaware
Arnsy Maull, the conjure man
Dutch Peter and the fortunetelling
tailor
The enemy in the night
Fearless John and the giant monster
The fiddler of Fiddler's bridge
Fiery-tempered Jake
The ghost of Samuel Chew
Herman and his horse

Delaware
LEACH — RAINBOW p77-78

Delicacy
The princess on the pea
The real princess

The delicate daughter
TRACEY — LION p88-92

The deluded dragon
MANNING — RED p10-15

Demeter
Plowman in the sky

Demigods. *See* **Gods and goddesses**

The demon giant of Mount Ariake
SPICER — 13 p94-102

The demon mason
MANNING — PETER p169-177

The demon with the matted hair
JOHNSON — HARPER p40-47

The demon wrestler
See also Parson Wood and the devil
MANNING — PETER p129-138

Demons
See also names of demons
Adares, King of Arabia
The adventures of little Peachling
The blacksmith in the moon
The book of magic
The children of Lir

Demons (*Continued*)

The exploits of Hanuman
The fairy Helena
The farmer and the demon
The fiddle
The first three hundred years
The flower faces
Four tales of Rama and Sita
Gisella and the goat
The golden boat
Golden bracelets, golden anklets
The handsome apprentice
The hill demon
Ironhead
Izanagi's descent to Hades
Jack, the King of England's son, and
  the giant with three heads
Jankyn and the witch
Kate Contrary
Khrishna the cowherd
The king of the demons and the
  worm Shamir
King Solomon and Asmodeus
The king's dream
The kittel-kittel car
The little nobleman
The loss of Sīta
The lost gift
The magic belt
The magic wand
The magician and his pupil
Michael Scott and the demon
Monkey
The monkey bridge
The monkey nursemaid
The peach boy
The peppercorn oxen
The prince and the demon
The princess and the demon
The princess's slippers
Rabbi Leib and the witch Cunegunde
Rāmā's conquest of Rāvana
The Rāmāyana
The reluctant familiar
Simple and the princess
The singing bell
The soldier and the knapsack
Something wonderful
Spears of lightning
The stone owl's nest
The talking fish
The tiyanak
To the Tengu goblins
Twelve great black cats and the red
  one

, **Air**
  The children of Lir

, **Wind**
  The wind-demon

The demon's daughter
MANNING – DEVILS p15-29

Denmark
  See also **Danes**
The anger bargain
Authun and the bear
The best wish
Big, big lies!
The boy and the monk
The boy who was never afraid
The cauldron of Brekkan
The dog king in Denmark
Esben Ashblower
Fiddivaw
The fisherman's son
The fox and the stork
The fruits of health
The golden bird
Graadonner
Graylegs
The green knight
Haltefanden (the lame devil)
The hen with the golden legs
How Beowulf delivered Heorot
The jumping contest
The king and the bishop
King Find's daughter
The land of youth
The lazy boy
Lazy Hans
The little black man
Little Claus and big Claus
The little duck
The little horse
The little king on the Viking ship
The little nag
Lost and found
The louse skin
The loveliest rose
Maid Lena
Master Erik
The mill at the bottom of the sea
The most obedient wife
Olaf the mermaid's son
Peder Okse
Peter Ox
The princess with the golden shoes
The princess with the twelve pair of
  golden shoes
The rich Per Muller
A ride to hell
The seven stars
The sleigh ride
The squires win golden spurs
The stupid boy
The talisman
Three pennyworth
The three princesses
Thumbelina

Denmark (*Continued*)

To the devil with the money
The treasure
Trillevip
Tripple-trapple
The troll's daughter
The twin brothers
The ugly duckling
Who put the salt in the sea?

—Jutland
The boy and the mountain-man
Peter Ox

Dentures
Half a yard

Department stores
Lucky star of Herald Square

Dependability. *See* Loyalty;
Steadfastness

Dependence
The horse without a master

Derby ram
STOUTENBURG – CROC. p57-61

The Derbyshire ram
MANNING – BEASTS p84-85

Dermot and Grania
PICARD – HERO p142-155

The dervish and the wolf
GREEN – BIG p171.

Dervishes (clergymen)
Aram and the shepherd
The handsome Kahveci
Kabadaluk: The little Arab boy
The magic dagger
The maiden who did not get her wish
Shah Ismail and the Turkmen maiden

Desert
The absent-minded tailor
Bani Hilal; a tribe is born
The caravan
The caravan continues
The caravan ends
The caravan reaches the end of the
desert
The cat and the prophet
Children of cloud
Dates to Cairo
The evil spirits of Crooked Mountain

How crane saved coyote
How fire was brought from lightning
An inadvertent misunderstanding
The king of the dark desert
King Solomon's carpet
The legend of Crooked Mountain
Little burnt-face
Man-eagle
Navahchoo
Palace in Bagdad
The prince and the three Fates
Prince Finn the fair
The princess
Rodents rampant on a field azure
The tailor's bright daughter
Tobacco woman and corn spirit
The turquoise stones
Wampum eater and the canal
Why coyote is the color of the
ground
Why the world is the way it is

Deserters
The dragon and his grandmother

The desolation of Vatnsdal. *See* The
hauntings at Thorhallstead

Destiny. *See* Fate

The destiny. *See* The quest for Olwen
(1) The destiny

The destiny of Princess Tien Dung
GRAHAM – BEGGAR p79-89

Destruction
The boy who cut everything to pieces
Phaeton; The boy who rode the
chariot of the sun

Destruction and creation myths: The
book of the divine cow
JAMES – MYTHS p13-19

Detectives
A Sherlock Holmes of the steppes
William Winter

Detectors
The king's daughter cries for the
moon

Determination
All about Columbus
A boy on the high seas
The circus man
The hairbrained monkey

Determination (*Continued*)

John Henry, the big-steel-drivin'
  man
The little engine that could
The strong boy
The ugly duckling

The devil and our Lord
  RANKE – GERMANY p156-157

The devil and the bailiff
  ASBJÖRNSEN – NORW. p168-169

The devil and the card players
  JOHNSON – WHAT p162-163

The devil and the Good Book
  JAGENDORF – UPSTATE p10-13

The devil and the man
  RANKE – GERMANY p171-172

The devil and the pit
  DURHAM – TIT p63-66

The devil and the railroad
  BRENNER – BOY p79-83

The devil and the seamstress
  BAMBERGER – FIRST p174-175

The devil and the summoner
  WESTWOOD – MEDIEVAL
  p111-117

The devil and the tailor
  WILLIAMS – FAIRY p288-291

The devil duped
  RANKE – GERMANY p170-171

Devil in church
  COURLANDER – TERR. p95-97

The devil in red flannel
  JAGENDORF – NEW p231-235

The devil in the barrel
  JAGENDORF – NEW p84-88

The devil in the steeple
  JAGENDORF – NEW p153-157

The devil in the wheat
  JAGENDORF – MERRY p119-123

The devil to pay
  PALMER – JOURNEY p82-94

Devils
  See also names of devils e.g. **"Black
  woodsman"**
About devils
Arnsy Maull, the conjure man
The bad-tempered wife
Bendebukk
Beppo Pipetta and his knapsack
The best devil in the land
Big Hermel
The blacksmith and the devil
The blind man and the devils
The boots that never wore out
The boy who beat the devil
The boy with the beer keg
The bridge of St. Cloud
Cheating the devil
Chief of the night riders
The child sold to the devil
A Chimalteco story
Cleverer than the devil
The count and the little shepherd
Daniel the gawk
The demon mason
The demon wrestler
The demon's daughter
Duffy and the devil
Evil rocks and the evil spirit of Peru
Faust
The feathered fiend
The ferryman
Fiddler John and the devil
Fiery-tempered Jake
Finger never says 'Look here' it says
  'Look yonder'
Fish maid
Four tales of how the devil was
  outwitted
A game of dice
General Moulton's boot
The girl who clung to the devil's back
The girl who married the devil
The girl who played a trick on the
  devil
Godfather death
Grandmother's tale
The grateful devil
The grateful prince
The green-bearded king
The groschen hole in the Mürz
  Valley
The gyspy fiddle
Haddam witches
The hairs of the baron's head
Haltefanden (the lame devil)
Hantsjc and the remarkable beast
The hermit and the devil
The hired man
The hopping lights on Devil's hill
How men become enemies
How tadpoles lost their tails

Devils *(Continued)*

How the devil fetched the mayor
How the devil married three sisters
How the duyvil gave New Amsterdam
  to the English
The husband, the wife, and the devil
An impossible penance
Ivan and his knapsack
Ivan and his sack
Izanagi's descent to Hades
Jack at Hell Gate
John Gethin and the candle
Jonathan Moulton and the devil
Katcha and the devil
Khasynget's grandmother
The knight of Steenhuisheerd
Kristina and the devil
The lady and the devil
Lady Eleanore's mantle
The legend of Peter Rugg
The legend of the almond tree
Lionbruno
Little Johnny Sheepskin
Little one-inch
The little red mannikin
Lost and found
The lucky hunter
Magic in Marblehead
The man who was rescued from hell
Master and pupil
The master-smith
The merchant, Saint Michael, and the
  devil
Michael Scott and the demon
The midget and the giant
The midnight hunt
The mill at the bottom of the sea
The mill that grinds at the bottom of
  the sea
The miserly miller
Momotaro, or The story of the son of
  a peach
The nandi bear
Olaf the mermaid's son
The old man and the devils
Old Nick's bridge
An old woman sows discord
One grain more than the devil
Padre Ulivo and his guests
Pancho Villa and the devil
Parson Wood and the devil
A peasant tricks the devil
Pietro Bailliardo
Preacher and the devil
The price of eggs
The Rehepapp and Vanapagan
A ride to hell
The river that was stolen
The road to hell

The rooster, the hand mill and the
  swarm of hornets
The sacred cod and the striped
  haddock
The sailor and the devil's daughter
St. Sava and the devil
The schoolmaster and the devil
The shoemaker's apron
The sign at the smithy door
The singing bell
The sly gypsy and the stupid devil
So many countries, so many customs
The soldier and the devil
The soldier who did not wash
The soul of the Countess Kathleen
Spuyten duyvil
Stackalee
The stone owl's nest
The strange adventures of the
  cowboy-sailor
The strange feathery beast
Stumping the devil
The tailor and the devil
The tale of the three footsteps
The tale of the youngest brother and
  the stupid devil
That fellow
The three clever brothers
The three golden ducats
Three times and out
The three traveling artisans
The tinker of Tamlacht
Tom Walker and the devil
The tongue-cut sparrow
A trickster tricks the devil
Tripple-trapple
The troubadour and the devil
Tsar Boris and the devil king
Twelve great black cats and the red
  one
Verena and the jug
The voice in the jug
The white mule ghost
Why cats lie on the doorstep in the
  sun
Why dog has a fur coat and woman
  has seven tempers
Why the devil keeps out of Indiana
The witch of Berkeley
The witch's skin
The young girl and the devil

The devil's apprentice
  SPICER – DEVILS p7-18

The devil's bowling ball
  SPICER – WITCHES p67-71

The devil's bride
  DURHAM – TIT p70-74
  TAFT – PROFILE p142-143

The devil's bridge
SHEPPARD – WELSH p173-177

The devil's daughter. *See* The sailor and
the devil's daughter

The devil's gifts
FILLMORE – SHEPHERD'S
p172-184

The devil's granny
SPICER – DEVILS p101-110

The devil's partnership
DURHAM – TIT p34-36

The devil's trick
SINGER – ZLATEH p71-73

The devil's wife as godmother
RANKE – GERMANY p44-45

The devil's wood
JOHNSON – WHAT p264-265

Devotion. *See* Love

Dew
The little white cat
The white cat

Dewi Dal
SHEPPARD – WELSH p106-108

Dhungura-ngarian: Where the pelican
danced
NORLEDGE – ABORIGINAL p25.

Dialect, Negro
Buh fox's number nine shoes
Buh mouse testifies
Buh rabbit and the king
Buh rabbit's big eat
Buh rabbit's graveyard
Buh rabbit's human weakness
Buh rabbit's tail
Buh rabbit's tight necktie
The champion
Crossing the river
Death and the old man
Devil in church
The do-all ax
Hot times
The king and Kuffie
The moon's a woman
Old boss and George
Old boss, John, and the mule
Old master and okra

Preacher and the devil
Rabbit, fox, and the rail fence
Rabbit scatches buh elephant's back
Reform meeting
Sharing the crops
The skull
Slow train to Arkansas
Terrapin's pot of sense
The Texas sandstorm
Waiting on salvation
The well
What the preacher's talking about

Diamond cut diamond
LANG – OLIVE p46-55

Diamond Jim and Big Bill
JAGENDORF – NEW p212-215

Diamonds
The bird which laid diamonds
California's lost diamonds
The castle of the three giants
The hazel-nut child
The hen that laid diamond eggs
The just reward
The knockers of Ballowal
Mr. Frost
The necklace
The princess who loved her father like
salt
Sinbad and the Roc
Sinbad the sailor
The tale of a foolish brother and of a
wonderful bush

Diamonds
BATCHELOR – SUPER. p70-71

Diamonds and toads
PERRAULT – FAMOUS p149-156

Diana (goddess)
Endymion . . . The sleeping shepherd

Diaz, Ruy
The story of the Cid

Dice
A game of dice
The Tengu's magic nose fan

Dick Whittington and his cat
HAVILAND – ENGLAND p56-75
MY BOOK HOUSE v. 5 p33-44
REEVES – ENGLISH p221-234
SIDEMAN – WORLD'S p483-494

Dickens, Charles
David Copperfield and little Emily

Dickens, Charles (*Continued*)
London streets
The magic fishbone

Dickens, Charles
JOHNSON – PRINC. p309.

Dickery, dickery dare
MY BOOK HOUSE v. 1 p24.

Dickinson, Emily
A fuzzy fellow without feet
The mushroom
The sea
A thunderstorm

The dicot tree and the deer
HASKETT – GRAINS p33-34

A dictionary of American weather folk-lore
SLOANE – FOLK. p29-63

Dictionary of magic beasts
PALMER – DRAGONS p9-29

Did the tailor have a nightmare?
SERWER – LET'S p59-67

Diddle, diddle, dumpling
MY BOOK HOUSE v. 1 p37.

Diddle, diddle on a bass fiddle
MY BOOK HOUSE v. 1 p73.

Dieting
Winnie-the-Pooh
The wise doctor

Dietrich defends the snow queen
SAWYER – DIETRICH p59-85

Dietrich is knighted
SAWYER – DIETRICH p86-92

Dietrich of Berne
The boyhood of a hero
The crowning of a king
Emperor of Rome
The making of a hero

Dietrich of Bern
PICARD – GERMAN p23-34

Different, but not better
GREEN – BIG p154.

Digging
Johnny-cake
Why people keep dogs

Diggory
SHEAHAN – HENRY p337-353

Digit the midget
DAVIS – LION'S p53-61

Dijns
How the camel got his hump

Dikes
The boy hero of Harlem
The flooding of the Lower Hundred
The giant who counted stones

The dilemma of a pious man
GHOSE – FOLK p31-36

Dimples
BATCHELOR – SUPER. p65.

A dinar for a donkey
KELSEY – ONCE p54-60

Dinewan the emu and Goomble-gubbon the turkey
PARKER – AUSTRALIAN p15-19

Dinewan the emu and Wahn the crows
PARKER – AUSTRALIAN p127-128

Dinner for the monk
See also Two feasts for Anansi
COURLANDER – TIGER'S p111-114

The dinner that cooked itself
BIRCH – CHINESE p37-42

Dinner with the tota
COURLANDER – FIRE p65-71

Dinners
See also **Feasts**
Eat, my fine coat!
Pán Kotsky
The royal banquet

Diogenes the wise man
BALDWIN – FAVOR. p88-90

Diomedes
The wounded archer

Dionysius, King
Damon and Pythias
Damon and Pythias: the most faithful of friends
The sword of Damocles

152

Dionysius, King (*Continued*)

The sword of Damocles, the man who
would be king

Diplomacy
KOREL – LISTEN p98-118

Diplomats
The ambassador from Chi
The crane's report
The English nobleman, the diplomat,
and the great crested bustard
King crow and Sir parrot
Lao Lai-Tse the tactful
The tiger's minister of state

Dirr, Adolf
The fisherman's son

Dirt
Doctor know all
The golden calf
The moon raised the sky
Musk and amber
Ooka andthe cleanest case
Pappa Greatnose

The dirt boy
SEKI – FOLKTALES p43-47

Disappearance
The legend of Peter Rugg

The disappearance of Ifan Gruffydd's
daughter
SHEPPARD – WELSH p119-122

The disappearance of Rhys
SHEPPARD – WELSH p159-163

Disasters
See also names of disasters, e.g.
Earthquakes; etc.
Buh rabbit's big eat

Disbelief
HOPE-SIMPSON – CAVAL. p144-145

Discontent
See also **Grumbling**
The city mouse and the country
mouse
Clytie
The dissatisfied good man
The ghost that didn't want to be a
ghost
How the people of Ife became
scattered

Little fir tree
The little rabbit who wanted red wings
The magic mountain
The man who kept house
The mouse, the bird and the sausage
Ooka and the wonderful wishes
Other island
Peter Rabbit decides to change his
name
The poor old lady
The steamboat and the locomotive
The three wishes
The wise man's pillow

The discontented fish
ARNOTT – AFRICAN p156-159

Discord
The lion and the bulls
An old woman sows discord

Discourtesy
The blacksmith lion and the conceited
goat
The cock and the neighbor's hen
The lady of the linden tree
The proud camel and the rude monkey

Discovery
See also **Explorers and exploration**
The curious John Greye papers
Lord Sinclair and the Zeno brothers
North Salem's Irish? ruins
Tales of the ambiguous Dighton Rock

Discovery of salt
WYNDHAM – CHINA p9-13

Disguises
See also **Transformations**
The donkey in the lion-skin
The grateful prince
Griselda
Thi Kinh
The two kings

A dish of laban
HAMPDEN – GYPSY p111-112

The dish ran away with the spoon
LEACH – SOUP p46-47

Dishes
See also **Bowls; Cauldrons;** etc.
The black art
The dish ran away with the spoon
The poor people who wanted to be
rich
Why women always wash the dishes

Dishes (*Continued*)

−**Bowls**
    The copper soup-bowl
    The man who wanted to bury
        his son

−**Saucers**
    The tale of the silver saucer and
        the russet apple

The dishonest tailor
    SPICER − GOBLINS p97-105

Dishonesty
    See also **Cheating**
    Ali Sundos
    A boy of the Lake country
    The crow and the sparrow
    The debt
    A gift for a gift
    The golden bird
    The greedy tailor
    Holding the bag
    How Jack sought the golden apples
    Joseph and his brethren
    Kalevala, land of heroes
    The long nose
    Mary Colvin
    The mouse climbed up the candlestick
    The peasant and the waterman
    The pilgrim and the judge
    Richard Feverel and the hay-rick
    Straight and crooked
    Teeny-tiny
    The ten chests
    The trial by fire
    Uncle Mitya's horse

The disillusionment of the Tibetan tiger
    MORRIS − UPSTAIRS p71-78

Dislike. *See* **Enmity**

Disloyalty
    The beggar in the blanket
    Blodeuedd and the slaying of Llew
    The dragon's revenge
    Dressed in strange feathers
    A fox in hiding
    The griffon
    The merchant's wife
    An old story of the three sworn
        brothers
    The sea-king's daughter
    The werewolf

Disobedience
    The African hunter and the forbidden
        room

The beauty and the beast
The bell of Monte Pino
The boy who wouldn't mind his
    grandmother
Cherry
The dark king
Geriant and Enid
The gingerbread man
The golden bird
The green frog
The hermit with two heads
How night was let loose and all the
    animals came to be
How Sigurd awoke Brynhild
It's all the fault of Adam
Jack O'Leary's plow
King Hilary and the beggarman
Maggie Tulliver goes to live with the
    gypsies
The maiden with the wooden helmet
The monkey and the banana
More south than south, more north
    than north
The nutcracker and sugardolly stories
Old Nanny's ghost
The poor people who wanted to be
    rich
Rabbi Joseph Della Reina
The raven's magic gem
Reen-reen-reeny-croak-frog
The seven mice
Smolicheck
Star-boy and the sun dance
The tale of bat
The tale of Peter Rabbit
The tale of the two brothers
Thor's journey to Jōtun-heim
The three silver balls
Tippity Witchit's Hallowee'en
The turtle and the storks and the
    jackal
The turtle who loved a monkey
West country boy
Where to lay the blame
Why frogs croak in wet weather
Why the dog lost his wife
Why the woodpecker has a long nose
Why there is thunder and lightning
The worthless man of poverty
Yuki-Onna

The disobedient giant
    BARLOW − LATIN p97-103

Disobedient Hawa
    HASKETT − GRAINS p95-97

Disputes. *See* **Quarreling**

Dissatisfaction. *See* **Discontent**

154

The dissatisfied good man
 BONNET − CHINESE p83-87

Distaffs
 The key in the distaff
 The third witch

Distribution
 A fair distribution
 How Grigori Petrovich divided the
  geese
 The shrewd peasant
 The two brothers

Dittany (plants)
 The magic eagle

Divers and diving
 The beginning of the world and the
  making of California
 How kingfisher got his necklace
 I'll tell her
 Nicola Pesce

The divided cloak
 NAHMAD − PORTION p123.

The divine comedy
 MY BOOK HOUSE v. 12 p154-155

Divorce
 Izanagi's descent to Hades

"Dixie" (song)
 Minstrel making

Djamukh−song of a deer
 FOSTER − STONE p53-62

The do-all ax
 See also The sword that fought by
  itself
 COURLANDER − TERRA. p80-83

Do hands foretell the future?
 BATCHELOR − SUPER. p67-68

Do it yourself
 LEACH − NOODLES p19.

Do pearls bring tears?
 BATCHELOR − SUPER. p72-73

Do scarecrows scare crows?
 BATCHELOR − SUPER. p31-32

Do warts come from toads?
 BATCHELOR − SUPER. p36-38

Do you know how the ants were
 discovered?
 HSIEH − CHINESE p21-23

Dobbs, Rose
 The foolish dragon
 The happy cure
 The pine tree
 Please all−please none
 The stubborn sillies
 Why cats always wash themselves
  after eating
 The wise king and the little bee

Dobryna's embassy to Khan Amryl
 ALMEDINGEN − KNIGHTS p33-47

Dobrynia and Alyosha
 DOWNING − RUSSIAN p17-27

The doctor and his pupil
 THOMPSON − ONE p45-48

Dr. Doolittle stories
 Rarest animal of all

Doctor know-all
 RANKE − GERMANY p142-144

Doctor know-it-all
 SIDEMAN − WORLD'S p468-475

Doctor Lee and little Aran
 O'SULLIVAN − FOLK. p184-188

The doctor who knew everything
 BUDBERG − RUSSIAN p74-77

Doctors. See Healing; Physicians; Witch-
 doctors; Wizards

Dodge, Mary Mapes
 Snow
 What they say
 Who can crack nuts?

The doe and the lioness
 GREEN − BIG p71.

Does a dog's howl mean death?
 BATCHELOR − SUPER. p22.

Does food cause bad dreams?
 BATCHELOR − SUPER. p103-104

The dog and the cock
 DUDDINGTON − RUSS. p38-40

The dog and the donkey
  LEEKLEY – RIDDLE p43-47

The dog and the giant
  GRINGHUIS – GIANTS p64-68

The dog and the karbau
  COURLANDER – KANT. p107-108

The dog and the maiden
  MANNING – RED p154-158

The dog and the shadow
  ARBUTHNOT – TIME p206.

Dog couldn't be cured
  WILLIAMS – ROUND p181-185

The dog in the manger
  ARBUTHNOT – TIME p204.
  MY BOOK HOUSE v. 3 p197.

The dog king in Denmark
  JONES – SCAND. p161-164

Dog luck
  CARPENTER – DOGS p15-24

The dog that fought a duel
  CARPENTER – DOGS p119-127

The dog that learned to read
  CARPENTER – DOGS p204-212

The dog, the cat, and the mouse
  MINCIELI – TALES p65-71

Dogs
  The adventures of Little Peachling
  Anansi and fish country
  Anansi and the old hag
  The animal musicians
  The arrows that became trees
  The ass and the pet dog
  The ass that was flayed
  Au Sung meets Kim Lee
  Baba Yaga
  Baba Yaga and the little girl with the
    kind heart
  The bad boy and the good dog
  Bahram and the snake prince
  The barnyard
  Be careful what you say
  Bear, fox and man
  The bed
  A Belgian morning
  The black dog of the wild forest
  Blessings on thee, dog of mine
  The blue dog

Bobo, black dog, and the cannibal
  woman
Bola Bola
The bold heroes of Hungry Hill
"Bow-wow," Says the dog
Bow, wow, wow, whose dog art thou?
The boy hero of Harlem
The Bremen town musicians
Brothers and friends
Browny
Buttercup
The castle of no return
Cat and dog
The cat and the dog
The cat, the dog, and death
The cat, the dog, and the mongoose
Chanticleer and Partlet
The clumber pup
The coyote and the two dogs
Cuculain, the Irish hound
Dame Wiggins of Lee
The dance of the animals
The donkey and the dog
The donkey and the lap dog
Donkeys! Dogs! Cats! Rats!
Don't beat your dog
The dragon's tail
Drat the wind!
Dutch Peter and fortunetelling tailor
The dwarfs of the anthill
The envious neighbor
The faery and the kettle
The faithful dog
The farmer's boy
Finlay the hunter
Finn and the grey dog
Finn and the young hero's children
Fionn's journey to Lochlan
The fire dogs
First adventures
The first mosquito
The first witch's cat
The fisherman's son
The five friends
The foolish dog
The foolish dog and his reflection
The forest wolf and the prairie wolf
Four friends
Freddy, the pad dog
The frog
The frog bride
"General" dog and his army
The ghost dog of South Mountain
Giacco and his bean
The giant with the grey feathers
The giant worm of the well
Gigi and the magic ring
The girl who played a trick on the
  devil
Golden bracelets, golden anklets
The golden horse

156

Dogs *(Continued)*

The good dogs and the good assessor
The good sword
The grateful animals and the talisman
The grateful beasts
The grave of a faithful dog
The greedy dog
Ha! Tio rabbit is bigger
Hans, the horn, and the magic sword
Happy Boz'el (Boz'll)
Hark, hark! Bow-wow!
The hearth-cat
Hey diddle diddle
Hi-y, hi-yi, hytola
The hobyahs
Hong Do-Ryŏng, the filial tiger
How dog came to live with man
How dog outwitted shepherd
How men learned about evil
How the camel got his hump
How the little fox went after chaff
The hunter's child
I had a little dog
The ingrates
The inquiring rabbit, or the strongest
  thing in the world
Iron, steel and strongest-of-all
Jack and his comrades
Jack and his friends
Jean Labadie's dog
Jean Labadie's big, black dog
The journey to Toulouse of the
  animals that had colds
The jurga
Keloğlan the kindhearted
The king of the animals
The king of the dark desert
The king who rides a tiger
A kingdom lost for a drop of honey
Krazy Kat
The laird's lass and the gobha's son
The lame dog
The language of animals
The laughing merman
Lawkamercyme
Lion and man
The little dog waltz
The little duck
The little girl and the new dress
Little Gulliver
The little hen and the little cock
Little Lady Margaret
Little Mukra
Little Peppino
The long-nosed princess
A lucky child
The mad dog
The magic amber
The magic ring

The magnificent hounds of Finn
  MacCool
A man, a snake, and a fox
The man who always helped the
  needy
Mary covered with gold and Mary
  covered with pitch
Mboyo and the giants
The milky way
Momotaro
Momotaro: boy-of-the-peach
Momotaro, or The story of the son
  of a peach
Momotaro, the peach boy
The monkey's liver
Mysteries of the sea
Nabulela
The Northern lights
O where has my little dog gone
Okraman's medicine
The old dog and the gray wolf
The old laird and his dog
The old man and his dogs
The old man of the flowers
The old man who made flowers bloom
The old man who made trees blossom
Old Mother Hubbard
Old Plott
The one who wasn't afraid
The oni's daughter
Ooka and the pup's punishment
Ooka and the shattering solution
Orthrus
The peach boy
Plish and plum
Popo and the coyote
The prince and the Three Fates
Prince Daniel
Princess Rosette
The proud goat
Pussy sits beside the fire
The rain bird
The remarkable ox, rooster, and dog
The renowned and world-famous adventures
  of Punch and Judy
The rescue of fire
Ride away, ride away
The ridiculous donkey
Rip Van Winkle; the strange little men of
  the mountain
Rip Van Winkle's dog
Sandy MacNeil and his dog
Seerko
Señor coyote and the dogs
The shaggy dog
The shepherd who fought the March wind
Shippei Taro
Shippei Taro and the monster cat
The sloogah dog and the stolen aroma
The stolen jewel
The stone memorial to a dog

Dogs (*Continued*)

The story of Mrs. Tubbs
The story of Prince Ring and his dog
The story of Suka's dog
Sun, moon, and morning star
The sun, the moon and the star of morning
Sweet misery
Swift-as-the-wind, Hold fast and Hard-as-iron
The tale of the king's jewel
The tale of the three brothers
Tape measure
That fourth leg of the dog
There was a farmer had a dog
The three dogs
The three languages
The three who made Ku
Thus I guard my mother's lambkins
The tinder box
The tinner, the dog, the Jew and the cake
To feed my people: The coming of buffalo
Tsimbarume, the hardened bachelor
The twin brothers
The twins
The two dogs—Burrajahnee and Inneroogun
Typing up the stones
The ugly duckling
An unsolved riddle
The very obstinate man
The walk
A wanderer with a dog
The wandering apprentice
Where, O where has my little dog gone?
The white pet
White-toes and Bushy-bride
Who is responsible
Why cats and dogs are enemies
Why dog gnaws a bone
Why dogs and cats are not friends
Why dogs carry their tails over their backs
Why dogs live with men
Why goat cannot climb a tree
Why God made the dog
Why people keep dogs
Why the animals have no fire
Why the cat and dog cannot live at peace
Why the chameleon shakes his head
Why the dog and the cat are enemies
Why the dog is the friend of man
Why the dog lost his wife
Why the dogs sniff at each other
Wild worms and swooning shadows
Willie and the pig
The witch of Laggan
The wizard of Oz. The cowardly lion
The wolf and the dog
The wolf and the watch-dog
Would you like to see goats dance on stilts?
Yi Chang and the haunted house
Young happy

The youth and the dog dance

—**Deerhounds**
Finn MacCool
The sorcerer's apprentice(s)

, **Fairy**
Above the wind, with the wind, or below the wind?

—**Fur**
Why dog has a fur coat and woman has seven tempers

—**Greyhounds**
The Ailp king's children
The eight leaves of story (5) The man who killed his greyhound
Finn MacCool

—**Hounds**
The giant of the brown beech wood
The hill of the bellowing oxen
The hound Gelert
How Tammas Maciver Macmurdo Maclennan met his match
Idy, the fox-chasing cow
Inside again
King Herla
The marriage of Arthur
The musicians of Bremen
The old hag of the forest
The partridge, the fox and the hound
Prince Finn the fair
The seven enchanted pigs and the hound whelp of Iroda
Sonny-boy Sim
This hound hath loved me
Three fat ewes for three fine hounds
The three golden eggs
The three sons of the King of Antua
The white cat
The white hound

, **Hunting**
The hunting dog and the purple fish
Sikakokub and the hunting dog

—**Language**
Does a dog's howl mean death?
The story of King Frost
The three languages

, **Midget**
The boy with the long hair

—**Noses**
The dog's nose is cold
Why the dog has a cold wet nose

—**Origin**
Dog luck

158

Dogs (*Continued*)
–Pekingese
  The little lion dog and the blue
    prince
–Poodles
  About the good American witch
  Prince Sneeze
–St. Bernard's
  Grandma'am Hinkel and the
    phantom dog
–Scottish Terriers
  Little Gustava
  The Scotty who knew too much
–Tails
  Dog's hoop
  A tale of a dog's tail
  Why dogs carry their tails over
    their backs
  Why dogs wag their tails
, White
  The man who made the trees
    bloom
, Wild
  The prince and the Three Fates
  The wild dog and the king's son

Dog's hoop
  LEACH – HOW p62.

The dog's nose is cold
  SHERLOCK – WEST p34-38

The dogs of Bahloo
  PARKER – AUSTRALIAN p109-112

Dogwood
  Indian legends of shrubs in our
    gardens

Dokanoos (fruit)
  Anansi and the alligator eggs
  Kisander

Dolbier, Maurice
  The half-pint Jinni

The doll
  MANNING – GIANNI p67-75

Doll-houses
  Racketty-packetty house

Doll i' the grass
  MY BOOK HOUSE v. 4 p24-33

The doll in the grass
  BAMBERGER – FIRST p31-32

The doll under the briar rosebush
  MY BOOK HOUSE v. 3 p204-209

Dolls
  Catherine's tea party
  Fair Vasilissa and Baba Yaga
  Knowledge and luck
  My lady sea
  The Prince Fernando
  Racketty-packetty house
  Samson and the doll in green and
    brown
  San fairy Ann
  Sara Crewe
  The unseen bridegroom
  Vasilia the beautiful
  Vassilissa the beautiful
, Golden
  The golden dolls

Doll's daydream
  FARJEON – SILVER p22-25

Dolomites (mountains)
  The prince of the Dolomites and the
    princess of the moon

Dolphins
  The adventures of Perseus
  The princess and the scarf
  The three enchanted princes

The dolphins of Celebes
  COURLANDER – KANT. p43-44

Dominican Republic
  The Haitians in the Dominican
    Republic
  The king's towers
  Who rules the roost

Dominies
  The phantom painter in the steeple

Don Lopez of Spain
  WILLIAMS – OLD p45-50

Don Quixote of La Mancha, surprising
  adventures of. *See* Surprising adventures
  of Don Quixote of La Mancha

Donal from Donegal
  MacMANUS – BOLD p64-82

Donal O'Ciaran from Connaught
  MacMANUS – BOLD p120-137

Donal O'Donnell's standing army
  MacMANUS – HIBERIAN
  p240-250

The donkey and the boar
  GREEN – BIG p146-147

The donkey and the dog
  La FONTAINE – FABLES p24.

The donkey and the lap dog
  La FONTAINE – FABLES p57.
  MY BOOK HOUSE v. 2 p50-51

The donkey and the lions
  CARPENTER – HORSES p231-238

The donkey and the nightingale
  KRYLOV – 15 p10-12

The donkey driver
  COURLANDER – PRICE p81-83

The donkey in company
  GREEN – BIG p206.

The donkey in the lion-skin
  HARDENDORFF – TRICKY p109-
  110

The donkey in the lion's skin
  La FONTAINE – FABLES p54-55

The donkey lettuce
  MANNING – WITCHES p72-82

Donkey, mind your mother!
  KELSEY – ONCE p1-7

Donkey skin
  PERRAULT – CLASSIC p197-224
  PERRAULT – COMPLETE p92-99

The donkey, the ox and the farmer
  GREEN – BIG p41-42
  NAHMAD – PEASANT p132-137

The donkey, the table, and the stick
  McNEILL – SUNKEN p52-57
  REEVES – ENGLISH p195-209

A donkey transformed
  WALKER – WATER. p62-64

The donkey who sinned
  COURLANDER – FIRE p15-17

The donkey who was an ass
  KOREL – LISTEN p31-37

The donkey with sponges and the donkey
with salt
  La FONTAINE – FABLES p44-45

Donkeys
  The abahaca plant
  Afar in the desert (quagga)
  And upon the fourth bray
  The ass and the pet dog
  The ass gets the better of the wolf
  The ass in the lion's skin
  The ass in the tiger skin
  The ass that lays money
  The ass that was flayed
  The ass's promise
  The basket-maker's donkey
  The bean tree
  The bird and the buffalo
  The bird which laid diamonds
  The blind man and the deaf man
  The blind man, the deaf man and the
    donkey
  The bold heroes of Hungry Hill
  The borrowed donkey
  Bouki buys a burro
  Bouki cuts wood
  The Bremen town musicians
  The brothers of the donkey
  The burro Benedicto
  The changeling
  The circus parade
  The Connemara donkey
  Cow or donkey?
  The cuckoo and the donkey
  A dinar for a donkey
  The dog and the donkey
  The dog and the karbau
  The enormous genie
  The escape of the animals
  The foolish ass
  The foolish wolf
  The foolishness of Cochinito
  The four friends
  The gold-lined donkey
  The golden castle that hung in the air
  The grateful ass
  Hani the simple
  Happy Boz'll
  The hero in the village
  How many donkeys?
  How the donkey saved a village
  A hungry wolf
  The inn of donkeys
  Jack and his comrades
  Jack and his friends
  Juan Bobo and old tiger
  Keloğlan and the ooh-genie
  The Kildare pooka
  The king's joke
  The kneeling tree
  Know your own strength

160

Donkeys (*Continued*)

Kwaku Ananse and the donkey
The legend of the moor's legacy
The lion and donkey a-hunting go
The lion and the hare go hunting
The lion calls up his troops
Long-neck, Fatty and Droopy
Maggie Tulliver goes to live with the
gypsies
The magic pancakes at the Footbridge
tavern
The man and the boy and the donkey
Mary and the Christ-child
The merchant of Mecca and the up-
stairs donkey
A message for a donkey
The messenger donkey
A midsummer night's dream
The miller, his son, and the donkey
Mr. Toad sits out on a journey
Misuse of a name
Molla Nasreddin and his donkey
The musicians of Bremen
Musk and amber
The night of the big wind
The nine doves
Nothing-at-all
One mean trick deserves another
The peasant and the donkey
Pinocchio
Please all please none
Pomegranates for sale
Popo and the coyote
Puss in boots
(The) quartet
The ridiculous donkey
The saddle
Salvador and the coyote
Salvador and the goat
The Spanish donkey and the Indians
The struggle between the wolf and the
fox
The surprising adventures of Don
Quixote of La Mancha
The thief and the donkey
The three brothers
Tony Di-Moany
Too heavy
The transformed donkey
Una and the Red Cross knight
The ungrateful snake
What should I do, What shouldn't I
do?
The white dove
The wise old camel
The wise woodland maid
Young happy

—Ears
Why donkeys have long ears

—Language
The animal languages
The animal musicians
Brown owl's story
How the sun was made
The talking donkey

—Skin
Donkey-skin

—Tails
The donkey's tail

The donkeys ask for justice
COURLANDER – KING'S p74-77

Donkeys! Dogs! Cats! Rats!
HARDENDORFF – TRICKY p87-91

Donkey's egg(s)
HARDENDORFF – TRICKY p119-
120
WITHERS – WORLD p18.

The donkey's tail
KELSEY – ONCE p83-88

Don't beat your dog
CARPENTER – DOGS p89-94

Don't make a bargain with a fox
JAGENDORF – KING p15-18

Don't run away my kitty
MY BOOK HOUSE v. 1 p132.

Don't tease the tengu!
PRATT – MAGIC unp.

Don't throw stones from not yours to
yours
U. N. – RIDE p99-100

Doodles
Flyfear scriblings

Dookiram, the poor one
MacFARLANE – TALES p71-91

Doors
The big prescription
The blacksmith in the moon
Budulinek
The dark king
Dumb Juan and the bandits
The enchanted castle in the sea
The good old man
How the devil married three sisters
It's all the fault of Adam

Doors (*Continued*)

Jean Sot
The marvelous doors, The Little
  People of Italy
The miracle on the Jaffa Sea
Nasreddin minds the door
Ooka and Tosuke's tax
The servant and the door
Smolicheck

Dorani
LANG – OLIVE p76-84

Doré, Gustave
The thief and the donkey

Dormice
The butterfly's ball
The elf and the dormouse
A mad tea-party
Pinocchio

Double Arend of Meeden
LEEUW – LEGENDS p33-37

The double-headed snake of Newbury
PALMER – DRAGONS p75-78

The double knights
McNEILL – DOUBLE p7-15

The dough image
LEACH – RAINBOW p246-248

Douglas, Mona
Little red bird

The dove and the ant
La FONTAINE – FABLES p25.

The dove and the eagle
MARKS – SPANISH p102-117

The dove maiden
WILSON – GREEK p76-87

Doves
Anansi and five
Answer to a child's question
The black giant of Luckless River
Bola Bola
The boy who was never afraid
The chafers and the dove
Coyote and the crying song
The devil's apprentice
Earl Mar's daughter
Esben and the witch
The fisherman
The flight
The grateful ant

Heart of the west wind
How vanity made the dove sad
The hunter and the dove
The huntsman and his wife
King Shibi
The legend of the Prince Ahmed Al
  Kamel
Little Gustava
Little Rosa and Long Leda
The magic mare
The magpie's nest
The mother of time and the enchanted
  brothers
The necklace
The nine doves
Noah's ark
Pepito
The pheasant, the dove, the magpie,
  and the rat
Prince Ahmed
A prince and a dove
The raven
The restless pigeon and his wife
The ritual coming-of-age
The silver penny
The song of the doves
The story of Prince Ahmed
The three citrons
The three lemons
Whence came the birds?
The white dove
The white dove of the city of the
  swinging gate
Why ducks have flat feet

–Eggs
Juanito and the princess

, Fairy
Cenerentola

Dow, Rev. Lorenzo
Gabriel, blow your horn!

Down by the River Avon
MY BOOK HOUSE v. 12 p15-29

Down in a cottage
MY BOOK HOUSE v. 1 p59.

Down to Arabia
LARSON – PALACE p31-45

The downfall of witches
HOPE-SIMPSON – CAVAL. p224-226
226

Downing, Charles
Badikan and Khan Boghu
The beardless, the lame, and the one-
  eyed thief
Heart and mind

162

Downing, Charles (*Continued*)

Master and pupil
The nightingale Hazaran

A dozen at a blow
JACOBS – EUROPE. p81-89

A dozen is thirteen
COTHRAN – WITH p18-22

The dracae. *See* The fairy midwife

The dragon and his grandmother
MANNING – DRAGONS p79-86

The dragon and the dragoon
HARDENDORFF – FROG'S p119-130

The dragon and the stepmother
MANNING – RED p146-153

The dragon foul and fell
McHARGUE – BEASTS p13-27

The dragon king and the lost fish-hook
WILLIAMS – ROUND p16-26

Dragon kings of the East
McHARGUE – BEASTS p29-35

The dragon of Rhodes
WESTWOOD – MEDIEVAL p15-19

The dragon of the well
MANNING – DRAGONS p123-128

The dragon of Utrecht
LEEUW – LEGENDS p11-14

The dragon who lost his fire
MONTROSE – WINTER p36-46

Dragonflies
The adventures of a water baby
The brook song
The butterfly's ball

Dragons
The adventures of Perseus
Ah Tcha the sleeper
Alison Gross
All light comes from the sun
Bald pate
Bash Tchelik
Baskets in a little cart
Beowulf
Beowulf conquers Grendel
Billy Beg and his bull

The black spider
The boy who played the flute
Cadmus . . . The dragon's teeth
The carp that became a dragon
Casperl
The castle of no return
Chinese dragons
The clever goatherd and the greedy
    giant
The clever little tailor
Constantes and the dragon
The cowherd with the belt of skin
Damian and the dragon
Dawn, twilight and midnight
The deluded dragon
Dobryna's embassy to Khan Amryl
The eight-headed-dragon
The enchanted princess
Farmer Giles of Ham
The foolish dragon
The friendly frog
Georgic and Merlin
The golden apples of Loch Erne
The golden castle that hung in the air
A handful of hay
The hoard
Horns
The horsefly
How Jack sought the golden apples
Jack the giant-killer
Japanese dragons
John the true
Kempe Owyne
The king of the fishes
The Laidley worm of Spindlestone
    Heugh
The Lambton worm
The last of the dragons
The laughing statue
Lazarus and the dragons
The little bull-calf
The lost half-hour
Lunching with dragons
The magic ring
Maid Lena
Marko the rich and Vassili (Vasily)
    the luckless
Mighty Mikko
The miller's four sons
The monkey's liver
The mountain witch and the
    dragon-king
My Lord Bag of Rice
The necklace
Nikita and the dragon
Nikita and the last of the dragons
The nine doves
The nine peahens and the golden
    apples
Once in, never out again
Oraggio and Bianchinetta

Dragons (*Continued*)

Peahens and golden apples
Penteclemas and the pea
Pepito
The prince and the dragons
The prince and the sky-blue filly
The prince with the golden hand
The princess in the fiery tower
The princess of light
The quellers of the flood
Ragnar Lodbrok and his sons
Ragnarokk, the destiny of the gods
The raven
Ravenspring
St. George and the dragon
Siegfried . . . Who knew no fear
The silly jelly-fish
Simple and the princess
The sleepless dragon
The spotted cow
The spring of youth
Stan Bolovan
The story of Hime
The student who became a prince
The student who was forced to be
king
Sturdy Hans
Swift-as-the-wind, Hold fast and
Hard-as-Iron
Sylvester
The tale of the Rhine-Gold
Tangerina
The task of the chief councillor
Otomo-no-Miyuki
The terrible-tempered dragon
The thirteenth son of the King of
Erin
The three dogs
The three enchanted princes
The three plagues of Britain
Three princes and their beasts
The three suitors
Throwmount and Oakpull
Tiamat
Tristram and Isolt
The twins
The two righteous men
Una and the Red Cross knight
Urashima
A wanderer with a dog
The wedding of the dragon-god
The white hound
Why crow is black and men find
precious stones in the earth
Why the cock eats worms
Wild worms and swooning shadows
The wonderful tree
Yanni
The yellow dragon
Yggdrasil, the world tree

The young man and the priest
The young Urashima

, **Eastern**
Dragon kings of the East

, **Golden**
The trials of Ting Ling
The yellow dragon

, **Marble**
Tiger lily and the dragon

—**Scales**
The rich man and his son-in-law
The yellow dragon

, **Sea**
See also **Sea monsters**
The dragon foul and fell
The dragon king and the lost fish-
hook
The good sword
The legend of Urashima

Dragons
JACOBSON – FIRST p11-27
VO-DINH – TOAD p137-141

The dragon's revenge
PRATT – MAGIC unp.

The dragon's tail
MARKS – SPANISH p25-48

Dragoons. *See* **Soldiers**

Drak, the fairy
PALMER – FAIRY p23-30

Drake, Sir Francis
Drake's cannon ball
Of the great and famous
A song of Drake's men

Drake, Joseph Rodman
The assembling of the Fays

Drake's cannon ball
MAYNE – HEROES p62.

Drakestail
HAVILAND – FRANCE p76-92
MANNING – BEASTS p226-234

Drat the wind!
WITHERS – I SAW p22-23

The dreadful and never imagined adventure of the windmills. *See* Surprising
adventures of Don Quixote of La
Mancha

The dream
  BRASH – GOLDEN p118.
  BUDBERG – RUSSIAN p188-200
  RANKE – GERMANY p189-190

The dream of Nam Kha
  SUN – LAND p51-52

Dream behind bars
  GREEN – BIG p75-76

The dream of Macsen (Maxen) Wledig
  JONES – WELSH p141-151
  PICARD – TALES p41-50

The dream of Ronabbway (Rhonabwy)
  HAZELTINE – HERO p135-146
  JONES – WELSH p126-138
  PICARD – CELTIC p144-154

A dream of the Sphinx
  CARPENTER – AFRICAN p63-69

The dreamer
  CHILD – CASTLES p69-77

Dreamland opens here
  MY BOOK HOUSE v. 1 p91.

Dreams
  JOHNSON – WHAT p20-24
  LEACH – NOODLES p17-18

Dreams and dreaming
  Ali Sundos
  Bostanai
  Chanticleer . . . his strange dream
  Chin and Yi
  The cold heart – Part 1
  Damian and the dragon
  Dante's voyages to the inferno,
    purgatory, and paradise
  The death of Balder
  The decision
  Does food cause bad dreams?
  The dutiful daughter
  Ed Grant has a dream
  The fairies in the White Mountains
  The feathers from the bird Venus
  The fortunate shoemaker
  The giant's stairs
  The golden horse with the silver
    mane
  The golden stag
  A good neighbor
  Haku's power
  How coyote brought back people
    after the flood
  How the water lily came

Itsayaya and the chokeberries
Joseph and his brethren
Juan in heaven
The judgment of Paris
Kantjil interprets a dream
Keloğlan in the service of the
  padishah
King Orfeo
The king's dream
The king's friend
The king's true children
The litle shepherd's dream
Luck from heaven and luck from the
  earth
Maimonides and the king's dream
The man who bought a dream
The man who lived in the world of
  dreams
Menaseh's dream
The mighty hunter
Mister frog's dream
The money cask
Other island
The peace pipe
The pedlar of Swaffham
The pedlar's dream
The phoenix and the falcon
The piece of straw
A poor peasant and two nobles
Red king and green king
The Russian and the Tatar
Saint Michael and the idle husband
The secretive little boy and his little
  sword
The secret-keeping boy
The seller of dreams
The shoemaker's dream
The silver ship
The snake and the dreams
The spring
A springtime dream
The tale of chanticleer
A town in a snuff-box
The tsar's son-in-law and the winged
  old woman
The weight of the cart
Westwoods
The white stone canoe
The wise man's pillow
Wnyken, Blynken, and Nod
The young man and the priest

Dress. See **Clothes; names of dress**

Dressed in strange feathers
  GREEN – BIG p214.

Dressmakers
  See also **Sewing**
  The clever lad from Skye

Dressmakers (*Continued*)

The devil and the seamstress
Gammelyn, the dressmaker
The little dressmaker

The drifting canoe
NORLEDGE – ABORIGINAL p40-43

Drills and drilling
John Henry, the big steel-drivin' man

Drinking
See also **Alcoholism**
The bird and the buffalo
The castle of the three giants
The clever lad from Skye
Thor and the giants
The vanishing rice-straw coat
The wonder ship and ship's crew

Drivers
The big street in the big city
Mrs. Peterkin wishes to go to drive

"Drolls" (tales)
The giants of Towednack

Drones. *See* **Bees**

Drop the handkerchief
LEACH – SOUP p87-89

The dropping-cave
SHEPPARD – SCOT. p159-162

Drought
The boastful tortoise
The cattle egret
The chief of the well
The fate of the turtle
The ghost-bird
The good crawford
Good-speed and the elephant king
The great bird in the carob tree
The great scare
The hermit and the Sea of Man
Kuluile, the dancing girl
The legend of the palm tree
Lion, chameleon, and chicken
The magic bone
The meeting
Mumbele and the goats
Nansii and the eagle
Paul Bunyan's cornstalk
Prince Prigio
Rabbit at the water hole
The rainmaker Wirinun
The son of the tortoise

The strange battle of Windham
Teutli, the mountain that is alive
Tlacuache the saint
The toad is the emperor's uncle
The tortoise who talked too much
The turtle and the storks and the jackal
The well
The wise priest

Drowning
An endless story
Five drowned
The haunted lagoon
It's all in knowing how
The shadow boys
Sketco begins his wanderings
Sketco finds his brothers
Spuyten duyvil
Wokun

Drowning the eel
LEACH – NOODLES p35.

Drugs
The drunkard and the opium-eater
The lady who put salt in her coffee

Druids
See also **Hamadryads**
The Ailp king's children
The birth and boyhood of Finn
The coming of Finn
The coming of Fionn MacCool
Cuchulain, the hound of Ulster
The death of Deirdre
The defeat of the Fomorians
The foretelling
The golden apples of Loch Erne
The hill of the bellowing oxen
The king of Araby's daughter
The mother of Oisin
Oisin's mother
Saint Patrick and the Hill of Tara
The tale of Columba and the angel
The tale of the sons of Cathmor
The welcome

Drums
Bang-whang-whang
The big Chinese drum
The boy who was called "thick-head"
The cannibal's drum
David and the big drum
The dicot tree and the deer
The dragon and the dragoon
The impudent little mouse
The jackal and the hen
The jackal with the torn nose

Drums (*Continued*)

The king who ate chaff
The king's drum
Kuluile, the dancing girl
The leopard and the bushbuck buy
a drum
Little sister and the Zimwi
The louse skin drum
The magic drum
Merisier, stronger than the elephants
The orchestra
Osebo's drum
The ploughboy poet
The sacred drum of Tepozteco
The silent drum
The singing drum and the mysterious
pumpkin
The sky god's daughter
The spirit's drum
Three who found their hearts' desire
The tortoise and the magic drum
Why crab's eyes stick out

The drums call the village to dance
MY BOOK HOUSE v. 1 p147.

The drunkard and the opium-eater
AUNG – KINGDOM p74-79

Drunkards. *See* **Alcoholism**

Dryads. *See* **Hamadryads**

Dry-bone and Anansi
SHERLOCK – WEST p77-85

Du Bois, William Pene
CHILD – CASTLES p301.

Ducats, Golden
The three golden ducats

The duck and the moon
GREEN – BIG p177.

The duck with red feet
MacMILLAN – GLOOS. p146-150

The duckling's journey
BAMBERGER – FIRST·p8-9

Ducks
Anansi and five
The Arabe duck
Auntie, where are you going?
The barnyard
The battle on the Isle of Camphor

The bee, the mouse, and the bum-
clock
Biggoon and the little duck
The birds' St. Valentine's day
Boots and the troll
"Bow-wow," says the dog
The boy who was called "thick-head"
The cock's on the housetop
The crane's report
Donal O'Donnell's standing army
Drakestail
The farmer's boy
The forgotten bride
The fox and the eagle
Gaya-dari the platypus
The golden deer
Goose dance
The hen agreed to hatch the duck
egg, but she didn't agree to take the
duckling for a swim
The herdsman of Cruachan
How crab got a hard back
How the mud turtle came to live in
the water
I saw a ship a-sailing
Johnnie and Grizzle
Juan Bobo
Krencipal and Krencipalka
The lame duck
The little duck
The little rabbit who wanted red
wings
The little red hen and the grain of
wheat
Mr. Korbes the fox
The oyster catcher, the duck and the
hen
Please give me a ride on your back
The precious stone
Rabbit and the grain buyers
Rag, tag and bobtail
The rarest animal of all
Reen-reen-teeny-croak-frog
Shingebiss
The story of Mrs. Tubbs
Sungold
The talkative tortoise
There were three duckies
Thousands and thousands of ducks
Ticky-picky boom-boom
The travelling frog
The twelve wild ducks
The two beggars
The ugly duckling
Why ducks have flat feet
Would you like to see goats dance on
stilts?

—Bills
How duck got his bill

Ducks (*Continued*)

−Eggs
The giant who had no heart in his body

, Flying
The fate of the turtle

, Golden
The mysterious lake

−Mallards
The peacock's mistake

−Mandarins
Oshidori

−Sheldrakes
The duck with red feet

, Wild
Gombel and the wild ducks
Mister Frog's dream
The talkative tortoise

Duck's ditty
MY BOOK HOUSE v. 3 p62.

The duel
TAFT − PROFILE p98-102

The duel of the cat and the mouse
GUIRMA − TALES p70-84

Duels
Black Roderic
The dog that fought a duel
A game of dice
The kappa's arm
The lamentable story of Connlach, son of Cuchulain
The long-nosed princess

Duendes (Little People)
Pancho and the Duendes
Sarita and the Duendes

Duffy and the devil
MANNING − PETER p202-212

Duikers
The feast of plums

Duke Roland's quest
PICARD − FAUN p29-43

Dukes and duchesses
The Count of Estremadura
The girl who clung to the devil's back
Katcha and the devil
Kristina and the devil

Lars, my servant
Rashi and Duke Gottfried
The young lord of Lorn

Dulcimers
Sadko

Dumb. *See* Fools and foolishness

Dumb Juan and the bandits
BRENNER − BOY p14-18

Dummling
MANNING − GLASS p100-114

Dumplings (cookery)
FARJEON − SILVER p15-21

Dumplings
Mother Codling is flummoxed
The old woman who lost her dumplings

Dunay
DOWNING − RUSSIAN p11-16

Dunbar, Paul Lawrence
The knight

Duncan, King
The tale of the royal exiles

Dungeons
The three journeys of Ilya of Murom

The duped giant
RANKE −− GERMANY p35-36

Dushan, Tsar of Serbia
Tsar Dushan's wedding

Dust. *See* Dirt

Dustin, Hannah
The ordeal of Hannah Dustin

Dutch
Anthony and the Mossbunker
The enemy in the night
The ghost and Hans Van Duin
Hi-Ho, the mosquitoes of New Jersey!

Dutch-Americans
Wolfert Webber, or Golden dreams

Dutch nursery rhymes
MY BOOK HOUSE v. 1 p126-127

Dutch Peter and the fortunetelling
  tailor
  JAGENDORF – UPSTATE p141-147

"Dutchman, Flying"
  The ghost ship

The dutiful daughter
  CHILD – CASTLES p135-159
  HODGES – SEREND. p138-174

A dutiful son
  INS-SOB – FOLK p44-45

The duty that was not paid
  MY BOOK HOUSE v. 6 p159-163

The dwarf and the cook, The Little
  People of Turkey
  BELTING – ELVES p61-65

The dwarf and the goose
  HAUFF – CARAVAN p52-108

Dwarf long nose
  LANG – VIOLET p148-173

Dwarf stories
  MÜLLER – SWISS p113-134

Dwarfs
  The adventures of Billy Macdaniel
  Alberich and the dwarfs
  The birthday of the Infanta
  The black stone
  Bottle Hill
  The city east of the moon and south
    of the sun
  The cobbler and the dwarfs
  The daughter of the dwarf
  Dietrich defends the snow queen
  The field of Ragwort
  Fir cones
  Freddy and his fiddle
  Gareth and Linette
  The giant and the dwarf
  The girl who picked strawberries
  Goggle-eyes
  Griselda
  The hazel-nut child
  The hillman and the housewife
  The hoard
  Hok Lee and the dwarfs
  How Odin brought the mead to As-
    gard
  King Fergus MacLeide and the wee
    folk
  King Herla'a quest

The king of the Golden River, or The
    Black brothers
  Knurremurre
  Kuluile, the dancing girl
  Little Mukra
  The little white cat
  The lost cows
  The magic bottles
  The magic mortar
  The magic peas
  Maid Lena
  The making of a hero
  My Lord Bag-o'-Rice
  The nutcracker and sugar dolly
    stories
  The poor man's son, the dwarfs, and
    the birds
  Prince Charming, the mare's son
  The prince of the Dolomites and the
    princess of the moon
  The princess and the glass mountain
  The princess on the glass mountain
  Rattle-rattle-rattle and chink-chink-
    chink
  The shepherd and the dwarf
  The sick boy, the greedy hunters, and
    the dwarfs, The Little People of
    North America
  The silver bell
  The skipper and the dwarfs
  Snout the dwarf
  Snow-white
  Snow-white and Rose-red
  Snow-white and the seven dwarfs
  The story of Maia
  The story of Sigurd
  The swan princess
  The tale of the Rhine-gold
  Thor gains his hammer
  The three brothers and the marvelous
    things
  The three dwarfs
  The three enchanted mares
  The three little men in the wood
  The three musicians
  Thumbkin
  The tiger and the dwarf
  Timimoto
  Ting-a-ling and the five magicians
  Tolkien's magic ring
  Tom Thumb
  The two men and the two dwarfs
  Una and the Red Cross knight
  The unicorn and the dwarf
  The water dwellers
  The water of life
  Wayland Smith
  The whalers and the dwarfs, The
    Little People of the Eskimo
  The whispering giant
  The white cat

Dwarfs (*Continued*)

The wonderful plow, the Little People
of the Island of Rugen
The world of the gods

, Fairy
Little Berry

Dwarfs' caps
BECHSTEIN – FAIRY p19-28

The dwarfs of the anthill
HOLLADAY – BANTU p26-29

Dyaks of Sarawak
Si Jura carved a house post

Dyers
The impudent little mouse

Dynamite
Hungry hog

E

Each little bird that sings
CATHON – PERHAPS p165-194

Each little flower that opens
CATHON – PERHAPS p127-162

The eagle and the lark
MONTROSE – WINTER p139-143

The eagle and the owl
ROSS – BURIED p109-112
SHEPPARD – WELSH p54-58

The eagle and the wren
MONTGOMERIE – 25 p56-57

Eagle boy
MARTIN – NINE p31-37

The eagle on a chain
GREEN – BIG p150-151

Eagles
Alas!
The apples of Iduna
The bat and the eagle
The battle of the animals
The beauty and her gallant
The beginning of the world and the
making of California
The bird and the buffalo
Bird Cu
Birds' St. Valentine day
Blodeuedd and the slaying of Llew
The boy who was saved by thoughts
Cast thy bread upon the waters
Clarinha
The cold May night
The creek of whale oil
The cruel uncle
The dancing feather
The dancing horses of Acoma
The dove and the eagle
The dove maiden
Farmer Weathersky
Fly again, my proud eagle
The fox and the eagle
The friendship of the tortoise and
the eagle
The giant archer of the sky
The girl with the rose-red slippers
Golden hood
The golden oriole
The golden snuff-box
The greedy hawk
The handsome apprentice

The haunted forest
How coyote brought back people
after the flood
How coyote got his voice
Idunn's apples of youth
Itsayaya's revenge
Jack and his golden snuff-box
Joshokiklay and the eagle
King of the birds
The king of the dark desert
King Solomon's carpet
Kralyevich Marko and the eagle
Kutlee-Seek-Vik
The land of youth
The last of the thunderbirds
The lion, the tiger and the eagle
The lion with the steady hand
Lleu and the flowerface
Loki
Loki . . . The apples of youth
The magic mirror
The magician Palermo
Maid Lena
Man-eagle
Marko, the champion of Serbian
liberty
Marya Morévna
Nansii and the eagle
Near God's cactus
Nella's dancing shoes
The ostrich
The owl's punishment
Pepito
Prince Finn the Fair
The quest for Olwen (4) Fulfilling
the tasks 2/ The oldest animals
Radowid
The rescue of fire
Rhodopis and her gilded sandals
The ritual coming-of-age
Sinbad and the Roc
Snow-white and Rose-red
The spring of youth
The stone of victory
A tale of the Tontlawald
The tale of Vassilissa the wise
Tall Peter and short Peter
The theft of dawn
The three brothers and the marvelous
things
The three enchanted mares
The three princesses in the mountain-
in-the-blue
The three walnuts
Thunderbird
Tiger lily and the dragon

Eagles (*Continued*)

The two youths whose father was
  under the sea
Waukewa's eagle
The witch and the earthen jar
Yggdrasil, the world tree
The youth who could become an ant,
  a lion or an eagle

—**Feathers**
The goat and the eagle
Juanito and the princess
Yiankos

, **Golden**
The magic eagle
The melodius napkin
The prince and the vizier's son

, **Sea**
Birdling

Earl Fitzgerald in the enchanted hill
  BRIGGS – PERS. p26-28

Earl Mar's daughter
  MANNING – BEASTS p177-183

The earl of Cattenborough
  JACOBS – EUROPE. p90-97

Early days and ways in America
  JOHNSON – WHAT p272-280

Early Kansas
  JOHNSON – WHAT p276-277

Earrings
Bells on her toes
Ears and earrings
The lizard's tail
The man who sold magic
The singing sack
The wild woman of the woods

The earrings,
  BELPRE – TIGER p27-31

Ears
See also **Hearing, Sense of; Listening**
A box on the ear
Clever–clever–clever
The coyote and the two dogs
Daniel O'Connell and the trickster
Hoichi the earless
The magic ear
The tale of the little mook
Three skillful men

, **Goat**
Goat's ears
The Tsar Trajan's ears

, **Horse**
King March has horse's ears
March has horse's ears
March's ears

, **Mule**
Midas
Midas . . . The greed for gold
Pinocchio
An unhappy lord

Ears and earrings
  BATCHELOR – SUPER. p119-120

Earth
See also **Creation; Dirt**
The beginning of the world and the
  making of California
The bridge of heaven
The flood
God's own country
The golden earth
Goto, king of the land and the water
Heaven and earth and man
How the earth was made to fit the
  sky
How the earth's fire was saved
Introduction (CAMPBELL – MAORI)
The jewel of the fox's tongue
The lake maiden
Land, water and wind
Luck from heaven and luck from the
  earth
Nathlook: Susie, my name
A noble Brahman's sacrifice
The poor man's clever daughter
The proud bokungu tree
The son of the hunter
A spadeful of earth
The spider
The Warau people discover the earth
Who?
Why the sun shines in the daytime and
  the moon shines at night

The earth is on a fish's back
  BELTING – EARTH p9-10

The earthquake
  GRAY – INDIA'S p58-61

Earthquakes
Agayk and the strangest spear
The golden horse
How California was made
The sacred drum of Tepozteco
A warning from the gods

East
See also **Far East**

East *(Continued)*

The ballad of east and west
I'm going to Lady Washington's
Quaker, Quaker, how is thee?
The sea king and the fox
West country boy

East Indian rhymes
MY BOOK HOUSE v. 1 p126.

East Indies
The wise monkey

East of the sun and north of the earth
KAPLAN – SWEDISH p142-161

East o' the sun and west o' the moon
See also East of the sun and west of
the moon
ARBUTHNOT – TIME p88-93
MY BOOK HOUSE v. 7 p31-39
THOMPSON – ONE p113-122
WILLIAMS – ROUND p145-160

East of the sun and west of the moon
BAKER – TALKING p123-137
ASBJÖRNSEN – EAST p1-15
JONES – SCAND. p60-73
SIDEMAN – WORLD'S p615-630

Easter
At the pike's command
The box with wings
The magic mountain
Marko, the champion of Serbian
liberty
Max and Moritz
The ratcatcher's daughter
Saint Patrick and the Hill of Tara

Easter Island
How yams got their eyes
The toromiro of Rapi-Nui

Eat bread crusts for curly hair
BATCHELOR – SUPER. p14-15

Eat, my fine coat!
WALKER – WATER. p51-54

Eat your carrots
LEACH – SOUP p113.

Eating
See also **Appetite; Cooks and cookery;
Dinners; Food** etc.
The ash lad who had an eating match
with the troll

Porridge with a troll
Smart working man, foolish boss man
Thor and the giants
Whale of a tale
The wonder ship and ship's crew

Eaton, Lady Anne
Lady Eaton's curse

Eavesdropping. *See* **Listening**

Echo and Narcissus: the chattering
nymph and the proud youth
STRONG – FAVORITE p55-59

Echo–Dwarfs
Old pipes and the Dryad

Echoes
Echo and Narcissus; the chattering
nymph and the proud youth
The story of the tortoise and the
monkey

Eclipses
The fire dogs
The mink and the sun

The economical son
DE LA IGLESIA – CAT unp.

Economy. *See* **Thrift**

Ecuador
Faithful to death
The five eggs
The head of the Inca
The search for the magic lake

Ed Grant has a dream
FELTON – WORLD'S p145-150

Ed Grant out West
FELTON – WORLD'S p109-114

Eden, Garden of
The tree from Adam's grave

**Eden, Richard and Francesco Maria
Guazzo**
Belief

Editors
The boy who would be an orator

Edmund, King of England
Cnut and Edmund

Education
The long walk
Twist-mouth family

Edward Frank and the friendly cow
GARNER — GOBLINS p41.

The eel and the porgy
VO-DINH — TOAD p45-49

The eel, the man, and the cave
NORLEDGE — ABORIGINAL p51.

Eells, Elsie Spicer
How the Brazilian beetles got their
gorgeous coats
Why the bananas belong to the
monkey
Why the sea moans

Eels
The battle that tilted the sea
The frog that swallowed the ocean
The ghostly fisherman
King O'Toole and his goose
Little fish and big fish
Loch Ness; last laugh?
Never trust an eel
The right time to laugh
Three eels

Eerin the small gray owl
PARKER — AUSTRALIAN p240-245

Efate (islands)
The silent drum

Effigies
See also **Intaglios**
Aükelé and the water-of-life
Lost arts
Shadrack, Meshach, and Abednego . . .
The fiery furnace
The shepherd and the fairy hillock

Efts
The Lambton worm

The egg
LIN — MILKY p64-71

The egg of fortune
SPICER — LONG p92-97

Eggborn
BIRCH — CHINESE p123-137

Eggs
Amin and the ghul

Anansi and candlefly
The bird of the golden land
Boiled wheat for a bountiful harvest
The crochera
The cruel uncle
Dawn, twilight and midnight
The egg
Eggborn
The elephant's tail
The emperor and the deaf man
The fisherman's son
Five dozen eggs
The fox and the hare in winter
The girl out of the egg
Gizo's counting trick
Go Zu-Mong, King of Goguryŏ
The great fish
The hen that laid diamond eggs
Humpty Dumpty
The hyena's egg
Jack and the beanstalk
Jack and the wizard
The leprechaun in the basket
The magic egg
The old lady and the monkeys
The ostrich and the crocodile
The price of eggs
Snake story
The speckled hen's egg
The stone monkey
The story of an egg
Tema's promise to the white bird
The three brothers and the black hen
The three little eggs
The three silver balls
The tortoise and the crocodile
The troll who hid his life
The two youths whose father was
under the sea
The value of a boiled egg
Why crocodile does not eat hen
The wise witness
The youth who could become an ant,
a lion or an eagle

—Dove
The necklace

, Golden
The hen that laid the golden eggs
Jack and the beanstalk
The magic bird
The queen and the golden egg
The three golden eggs

—Omelettes
The dwarf and the goose
An expensive omelette

, Rotten
How Master Thumb defeated the
sun

Eggs, Rotten (*Continued*)

The little hen and the little cock

Egotism
The mice
Peter Rabbit decides to change his
name
The two crabs
Yes, that's the girl who struts about

Egrets
The bird and the buffalo
The boastful tortoise
The cattle egret

Egypt
Abdune and the friendly snake
The adventures of Sinuhe
Ali Sundos
Anpu and Bata
The babe Moses
Bird of the sun
The black prince
The book of Thoth
The bowlegged god, Bes
The cat of Bubastis
The classic traveler's yarn: The tale
of the shipwrecked sailor
Clever Kadra
The copper soup-bowl
Destruction and creation myths: The
book of the divine cow
Don't beat your dog
A dream of the Sphinx
The enchanted tortoise
The endless story
The faithful friend
Forty days hath Ramadan
The girl with the rose-red slippers
Gods in all-too-human situations; The
contendings of Horus and Seth
Goha the wise
The gold falcon
The golden-headed fish
The golden lotus
The grateful ass
The great Queen Hatshepsut
The greedy friend
Helen in Egypt
Historical inscription—or fiction? The
seven-year famine
History as propaganda: The Princess
of Bakhtan
Horus the avenger
Human passions in the gods: Isis
challenges Re
Introduction (JAMES – MYTHS)
Isis and (the) Osiris
Isis and the secret name of Ra

Joseph and his brethren
The judgment of Karakoush
Khalid and Aantar
Khnemu of the Nile
The king and the corn
King Setnau and the Assyrians
The lady and the devil
The land of the dead
The lost jewel
The magic crocodile
Magical elements in religious beliefs:
The wanderings of Isis and the
agony of Horus
A morality tale: Truth and falsehood
A mother's advice
Myth and folktale in human actions:
The tale of the two brothers
Osiris—martyrdom and myth: The
life and death of Osiris
The peasant and the workman
The prince and the Sphinx
The prince and the Three Fates
The princess and the demon
The princess and the thief
Principal Egyptian deities
Ra and his children
Rhodopis and her gilded sandals
The sailor and the sea serpent
Se-Osiris and the sealed letter
Sphinxes
The story of the Greek princess
The story in the sealed book
The story of the shipwrecked sailor
A story on stone: The divine birth of
Hatshepsut
The taking of Joppa
The tale of a rich king: The treasure
of Rhampinities
The tale of the two brothers
Tales of past glories: Cheops and the
magicians
Teta the magician
There's always a reason
The thief and the king's treasure
To pay through the nose
The treasure thief
The vain ox
What will people say
The wise old camel
A wise priest learns a lesson: Khaem-
wese and Tabubu
The wizard of the Nile
The wonder child

—**Alexandria**
The tailor and the prince, told by
Mulech

—**Bala Lake**
The legend of Bala Lake

—**Bibliography**
Books to read: Museums to visit

Egypt (*Continued*)

−Cairo
Ali and the camels

−Thebes
The martyrs of Thebes

The eight-headed dragon
UCHIDA − DANCING p27-33

Eight leaves of story (1) The three
staunch swineherds of Britain
JONES − WELSH p195-196

Eight leaves of story (2) The sigh of
Gwyddno Long-shank
JONES − WELSH p197-198

Eight leaves of story (3) Baglan the
builder
JONES − WELSH p199-201

Eight leaves of story (4) A harp on the
water
JONES − WELSH p202-204

Eight leaves of story (5) The man who
killed his greyhound
JONES − WELSH p205-207

Eight leaves of story (6) The sun of
Llanfabon
JONES − WELSH p208-209

Eight leaves of story (7) Red-hat otter
JONES − WELSH p210-211

Eight leaves of story (8) Cadwalader
and all his goats
JONES − WELSH p212-215

The eight perfect ones on the ocean
CARPENTER − SHIPS p203-212

Eighteen rabbits
HAMPDEN − GYPSY p119-125

The eighth child. *See* Lord Krishna or
The eighth child

Einion and the Fair family
SHEPPARD − WELSH p48-53

Einion Las and the Fair family
MORAY − FAIR p123-133

Ekrem, Selma
EKREM − TURKISH p117.

Ekun and Opolo go looking for wives
COURLANDER − OLODE p19-23

El Cid. *See* Cid, El

El Salvador
How much you remind me of my
husband!
The origin of the balsam tree
Pedro Alvarado and the Indian girl

Elands
The tree with the difficult name

Elder trees
Goat's ears
The kitten and falling-leaves
The stone king

The elders of Chelm and Genendel's key
SINGER − WHEN p45-51

Electricity
ARBUTHNOT − TIME p331-333

Elements
She-wa-na, deity of the elements
Waiting on salvation

The elephant and the butterfly
CUMMINGS − FAIRY p17-23

The elephant and the carpenters
GAER − FABLES p148-149

The elephant and the gnat
GAER − FABLES p41-43

The elephant at court
WYNDHAM − TALES p73-75

Elephant drivers
The bee-hunter and the oozie

The elephant hunters
COURLANDER − KING'S p68-70

The elephant in favor
KRYLOV − 15 p24-25

Elephantine (Island)
Khnemu of the Nile

Elephants
Afar in the desert
The age of the partridge
Anansi and the elephant exchange
knocks
Anansi and the elephant go hunting

Elephants (*Continued*)

Anansi, the oldest of animals
Arap Sang and the cranes
The bet between Matjan and Gadja
The blind men and the elephant
The cat who came indoors
The circus man
The circus parade
The clever little jackal
The foolish jackal
The foolish, timid, little hare
The frog's saddle horse
Get ready, get set, go
The giant elephant
The girl on the rock
Go ask your mother for fifty cents
Good-speed and the elephant king
The hare and the tiger
The hare in the moon
How confusion came among animals
How men learned to build houses
How the dog chose its master
How the hare learned to swim
How the rabbit fooled the elephant
How to weigh an elephant
The jackal and the elephant
Jumbo was an elephant
Kalulu and the elephant
Kalulu and the leopard
Kantjil becomes a raksba
Kantjil brings the elephants to heel
Kantchil's lime pit
The kindly ant-bear
The king's friend
The little bird's rice
The little girl named I
The long-nosed giant
Madame giraffe
The man who lost his way
Merisier, stronger than the elephants
The miracle of the begging bowl
Mister Honey Mouth
The mouse and the elephant
Nkalimeva
Old Noah
Oliphaunt
On just being yourself
Podhu and Aruwa
Rabbit, elephant and hippopotamus
Rabbit scratches buh elephant's back
The rabbit steals the elephant's dinner
The rabbit takes his revenge on the
  elephant
The race
A secret told to a stranger
Sindbad the sailor
The son of the tortoise
Thunder, elephant and Dorobo
Tortoise triumphant
Tricksy rabbit

The tug of war
The turtle, the hippo, and the elephant
Unanana and the elephant
The ungrateful snake
The vain jackal
Why elephant and whale live where
  they do
Why some animals live with man
Why the crab has no head or how the
  first river was made
A world of nonsense
The zoo in the park

−**Ears**
The elephant at court

−**Hairs**
How the porcupine fooled the
  elephant

−**Tails**
The elephant's tail

The elephants
  WITHERS − I SAW p55.

The elephant's bathtub
  CARPENTER − ELEPHANT'S p13-21

The elephant's child
  ARBUTHNOT − TIME p316-320

The elephant's lip
  CARPENTER − ELEPHANT'S p176-
  183

The elephant's tail
  COURLANDER − HAT p80-85

The elevator
  MY BOOK HOUSE v. 1 p183.

Elevator operators
The elevator

The elf and the dormouse
  MY BOOK HOUSE v. 3 p39.

The elfin knight
  VANSITTART − DARK p18.

Elidorus in fairyland
  SHEPPARD − WELSH p89-92

Elijah (Biblical)
Introduction (Tales of the prophet
  Elijah)
A portion in Paradise
The prophet Elijah and the angel
  of death
Rabbit Joseph Della Reina

Elijah (*Continued*)

    Rabbi Joshua Ben Levi and the
      prophet Elijah
    The seven-year blessing
    The seven years of blessing
    Tales of the prophet Elijah
    Torah and honor

Eliot, George
    Maggie Tulliver goes to live with the
      gypsies

Eliot, George
    The little girl of Griff House

Elizabeth I, Queen
    Sir Walter Raleigh

Elixir of life. *See* **Youth, Eternal**

Elk
    The bungling host
    The man who loved Hai Quai
    West country boy

Elliott, Geraldine
    The number of spots

Elm trees
    The bloodless battle of the elm

"Elmer and the dragon"
    Tangerina

Elmo, Saint
    The dancing fires of Saint Elmo

Elopement
    Deidre and the sons of Usna

Elsa and the ten elves
    MY BOOK HOUSE v. 4 p45-49

Elves
    Childe Roland
    Childe Rowland
    Childe Rowland and the king of
      Elfland
    The creation of the world
    The crimson purse
    Elsa and the ten elves
    An explanation of the grasshopper
    The fiddler going home
    The girl who didn't know how to
      spin, The Little People of
      Scandinavia

    Gremlins, elves and leprechauns
    Gwarwyn-a-Throt
    Hildur the elf queen
    Jip and the witch of Walgrave
    The little elf
    The seven Simons
    The shepherd of clouds
    The shoemaker and the elves
    Tam Lin
    Thomas the rhymer
    Tolkien's magic ring
    Tongue steeple
    Wild Edric
    The youth who wanted some fun

The elves and the shoemaker
    ARBUTHNOT – TIME p33-34
    HAVILAND – GERMANY p13-20

Elysium
    See also **Heaven**
    The search for the land of bliss

Embroidery
    Good advice
    The impudent little mouse

Embry, Margaret
    Blanche's high-flying Halloween

The emerald-crested phoenix
    EKREM – TURKISH p32-45

The emerald lizard
    U. N. – RIDE p250-252

Emeralds
    The city under the sea
    The necklace
    The tree goddess

Emergencies
    The Brownie o' Ferne-Den

Emerson, Ralph Waldo
    We thank thee

An emir and two thieves
    WILLIAMS – OLD p265-277

Emirs
    The wrestlers

Emma of Haarlem
    LEEUW – LEGENDS p71-74

Emmet, Dan
    Minstrel making

Emperor, Jade
    Daughter of the jade emperor
    The destiny of Princess Tien Dung
    The silver river

The emperor and the deaf man
    NAHMAD – PORTION p133-134

Emperor of Rome
    SAWYER – DIETRICH p150-169

The emperor of the province
    McALPINE – JAPAN. p171-176

Emperors
    Archery
    Discovery of salt
    The faithful wife
    The hermit and the Sea of Man
    It all comes to light
    Janet cooks for the emperor
    Karl the Great and the robber
    Ma Liang and his magic brush
    The messengers from the moon
    Noodlehead and the flying horse
    The princess of China
    A prompt settlement
    A search for the magic lake
    The story of the fairy boat
    The story of white Arab

The emperor's magic bow
    ROBERTSON – FAIRY p66-75

The emperor's new clothes
    ARBUTHNOT – TIME p348-350
    SIDEMAN – WORLD'S p401-408
    TUDOR – TASHA p34-37

The emperor's pilgrimage to Mount Fuji
    McALPINE – JAPAN. p185-187

The emperor's questions
    LEEUW – LEGENDS p15-20

The empty city
    HAZELTIME – HERO p416-427

Emus (birds)
    Deegeenboya the soldier bird
    Dinewan the emu and Goomble-
    gubbon the turkey
    How the sun was made
    The Wi-oombeens and Piggi-billa

The enchanted black cat
    CARPENTER – DOGS p222-234

The enchanted buck
    BERGER – BLACK p43-54

The enchanted castle in the sea
    EELLS – SPAIN p57-68

The enchanted cow
    HOKE – WITCHES p37-44
    SPICER – LONG p47-69

The enchanted hedgehog
    BORSKI – GOOD p13-17

The enchanted island
    MY BOOK HOUSE v. 8 p132-142

The enchanted knife
    LANG – VIOLET p129-132

The enchanted mule
    HAVILAND – SPAIN p70-87

The enchanted palace
    BARLOW – LATIN p9-17

The enchanted prince
    MANNING – PRINCES p49-56

The enchanted princess
    BECHSTEIN – FAIRY p116-121
    RANKE – GERMANY p39-40

The enchanted sky
    OMAN – ESKIMO p64-65

The enchanted tortoise
    CARPENTER – AFRICAN p205-213

The enchanted waterfall
    BROWN – AROUND p33-41

Enchantment. See Magic

The enchantment of Gearoidh Iarla
    O'FAOLAIN – IRISH p232-234

The encounter with death
    SUN – LAND p67-68

The end of Arthur
    PICARD – STORIES p283-292

The end of Odysseus
    GREEN – GREEKS p76-77

The end of the evening
    KAULA – AFRICAN p155.

The end of the golem
    NAHMAD – PORTION p169-170

The end of the trail
FELTON – NEW p159-164

The end of the world
HEADY – TALES p81-85

The end of the world: The buffalo go
MARRIOTT – AMER. p138-139

An endless story
SEKI – FOLKTALES p30.

The endless story
ZAGLOUL – BLACK p153-160

The endless tale
BALDWIN – FAVOR. p99-103

Endor, Witch of
The witch of Endor

Endurance
The mole and the rabbits
The tiny god

Endymion . . . The sleeping shepherd
UNTERMEYER – FIRE p42-43

Enemies. See **Enmity**

The enemy in the night
JAGENDORF – UPSTATE p137-140

The enemy's tent
GINSBURG – MASTER p116-121

Engagements
The beginning of good conversation

Engine, engine number nine
MY BOOK HOUSE v. 1 p85.

Engineers
Casey Jones

Engines. See **Trains–Engines**

England
Adrian and Bardus
The adventures of General Tom
Thumb
The adventures of Manawyddan
The almond bough
And I dance mine own child
Arthur, King of Britain

The baker's daughter
The barrel-organ
The basket-maker's donkey
The bear in the coach
Beowulf conquers Grendel
The big cabbage and the big kettle
The blinded giant
The boggart
A boy of the Lake country
Bran, son of Llyr
The buried moon
The butterfly's ball
Cap o' rushes
Caporushes
The castle in the cornfield
Catskin
The changeling
A charm against witches
Chicken Little
Childe Roland
The children in the wood
Cinderella
Clever Pat
The clumber pup
Coat o' clay
The cock, the mouse, and the little
red hen
The coming of Arthur
The Connemara donkey
Cuckoo in the hedge
The devil and the tailor
The devil in the wheat
Dick Whittington and his cat
The donkey, the table, and the stick
The fairy child
The false knight
Fifty red night-caps
Findings are keepings
The fish and the ring
The flower without a name
From a moral alphabet
The ghostly hand of Spital house
The giant and the mite
The giant worm of the well
The gingerbread man
The girl who kissed the peachtree
The glass peacock
The golden ball
The golden snuff-box
The goldfish
Goldilocks and the three bears
Gotham way of counting
Grazing on the roof
The Green children
Gulliver in the giants' country
Guy Fawkes . . . The gunpowder plot
Habetrot and Scantlie Mab
The hairy boggart's field
Happy Boz'el
The hare and the lord
Hasty porridge in the boiling water

England (*Continued*)

The head of brass
Hear ye!
The Hedley kow
Henny-Penny
Hereafterthis
High diddle diddle, the fool in the middle
The Hobyahs
The homecoming of Beorhtnoth Beorhthelm's son
How Beowulf delivered Heorot
How Jack sought the golden apples
How the camel got his hump
How the ghost got in
How the trivet came home
I was going along the road
I was traveling those parts
In a dark wood
In those days
The interesting history of old Mother Goose
Is he fat?
Jack and the beanstalk
Jack Hannaford
Jack the giant-killer
John the blacksmith destroys the wasps in the straw
Johnny-cake
Johnny Gloke
Kate Crackernuts
The key of the kingdom
The kind farmer
King Alfred and the cakes
The king and the corn
King Canute on the seashore
King Herla's quest
King Hilary and the beggarman
King John and the Abbot
The king of England and his three sons
The king o' the cats
The king of the cats
The king's daughter cries for the moon
The king's friend
Lady Melicent
The lady of the linden tree
The lady of the wood
The lady's room
The Lambton worm
Lawkamercyme
Leaving paradise
The lion and the unicorn
A little bull-calf
The little dressmaker
The little fish and the big fish
A little history of the Gotham folk tales
Little Jip
Little John and the tanner of Blyth

The little lady's roses
The little red hen and the grain of wheat
The lovebirds
The magician and his pupil
The magpie's nest
The man in the moon
The man who lived on an island
Meet-on-the-road
Meg o' the moors
The midnight hunt
The miller of the dee
The miracle of the poor island
Mr. & Mrs. Vinegar
Mr. Miacca
Mr. Vinegar
Mrs. Mag and her nest
Molly Whipple
Molly Whuppie
The moon in the pond
The moonrakers
My own self
The necklace
Never trust an eel
News!
Nothing-at-all
An old king and his three sons of England
Old King Cole
Old mother wiggle-waggle
Old Nanny's ghost
Old Nick's bridge
Old Sal's curse
Old Surly and the boy
The old witch
The old woman and her pig
The old woman and the Hedley kow
The one-eyed ogre of Sessay
Pannychis
The pedlar of Swaffham
The pedlar's dream
Pengersec and the witch of Fraddom
Pennyworth
The pied piper of Frenchville
The piper with the hoofs of a goat
The poor ploughman and the rich nobleman
A pottle o' brains
The princess of Canterbury
Puddock, mousie and ratton
Raking for the moon
The Red Ettin
Redcoat the fox
Robin Hood
Rolling cheese gathers no moss
The royal page
Rushen Coatie
San fairy Ann
The schoolmaster and the devil
Scrapefoot
The seventh princess

182

England (*Continued*)

The shepherd, the king, and the south-
west wind
Simpleton Peter
Sir Beaumains, the kitchen knight
Sir Walter Raleigh
A son of Adam
A spadeful of earth
The stars in the sky
The stone king
The stone stew
The story of the three bears
The story of the three little pigs
The story of Tom Thumb
The strange visitor
Stupid's cries
The tale of the two cunning servants
Tall tales from the Gotham Inn
Tarn Wethelan
Tattercoats
Teeny-tiny
This is how it began
The three cows
Three feathers
Three men on the bridge
The three sillies
The three wishes
The Tims
Titty mouse and Tatty mouse
Tom Hickathrift
Tom Thumb
Tom Tit Tot
The tournament in Ireland
The transformed donkey
The travels of a fox
The true lord of the merry men of
Gotham
The tulip bed
The two princesses
Tying up the stones
A voice speaks from the well
Wat Tyler . . . The peasant's revolt
Wayland Smith
The well of the three heads
The well of the world's end
Westwoods
When woods awake
White-faced simminy
Whittington and his cat
William of Cloudslee
The wise men of Gotham
The witch in the hill
The world's great epics
Yallery Brown
Ye merry doings of Robin Hood
Young Kate

—Cornwall
Baker's knee
Betty Stogs' baby

The boy and the bull
Bucca Dhu and Bucca Gwidden
Cherry
The cock-crow stone
The crowza stones
The demon mason
The demon wrestler
Duffy and the devil
Fairies on the gump
The feathered fiend
From the head downward
The giant Holiburn
The giant of the mount
The giants of Towednack
The giants who wanted a son
Jack and the giant Cormoran
The knockers of Ballowal
The lady of the wood
Lutey and the mermaid
Lyonesse
Madgy Figgey and the sow
The mermaid in church
Mr. Noy
Parson Wood and the devil
Peepan pee
Peter and the piskies
The piskey revelers
The piskie thresher
Saint Margery Daw
Saint Neot
Skillywidden
The small people's cow
Sneezy Snatcher and Sammy
Small
The spriggans' treasure
Tarn Wethelan
The thieving fairies
The tinner, the dog, the Jew, and
the cake
Tom and giant blunderbus
Tregeagle
The two sillies
The wish-hound
The witch of Fraddam

—Devon
Where by you going, you Devon
maid?
Why peacock looks at his tail

—Dover
The dark cliffs of Dover

—Gloucestershire
Owl

—Hertfordshire
The river god (of the River Mimram)

—History
In the days of Queen Anne

—Lincolnshire
Yallery Brown

England (*Continued*)

, North
The ji-jaller bag
Jip and the witch of Walgrave
Jonas and the boggart of Brix-
worth
The Laidley worm of Spindlestone
Heugh
Mary-Ann and the cauld lad of
Hylton
Peregrine and the redman of
Rockingham
The princess who wanted to play
with the stars
The well of the world's end
Young Pollard and the brawn of
Bishop Auckland

—Northamptonshire
Tops and bottoms
Tops or bottoms

—Northumberland
Billy B————'s adventure

—Worcestershire
The borrowing fairies

—Yorkshire
The boggart

The English nobleman, the diplomat, and
the great crested bustard
MORRIS — UPSTAIRS p91-97

English nursery rhymes
MY BOOK HOUSE v. 1 p18-57

Enmity
Different, but not better
The forest wolf and the prairie wolf
The fox and the grapes
How men become enemies
The knight of Steenhuisheerd
The mongoose, the owl, the cat and
the mouse
Three bad men
Why cats and dogs are enemies

Enmity between man and serpent
NAHMAD — PORTION p51-53

The enormous genie
TASHJIAN — THREE p23-31

Ents (tree people)
Tolkien's magic ring

The envious buffalo
GAER — FABLES p132-133

The envious neighbor
BUCK — FAIRY p281-285
LANG — VIOLET p121-128

Envy. *See* Jealousy

The epic (Slovo)
DOWNING — RUSSIAN p81-93

Epics
The fate of the children of Lir
The fate of the children of Tuireann
The homecoming of Beorhtnoth
Beorhthelm's son
Ilmarinen . . . How he won his bride
Njal the lawyer
The Rāmāyana
Tolkien's magic ring
The Vētāla's stories
The world's great epics

—England
How Beowulf delivered Heorot
Sir Beaumains, the kitchen knight
Una and the Red Cross knight

—Finland
Kalevala, land of heroes

—France
The song of Roland

—Germany
The tale of the Rhine-gold

—Greece
The home-coming of Odysseus

, Hindu
Khrishna the cowherd
Rāmayāna

—India
The exile of Rama
This hound hath loved me

—Ireland
Cuculain, the Irish hound

—Japan
The battle of Ichi-no-Tani
The fall of the Heike
The poem of the sea
The secret meeting at Shishi ga
Tani

—Norway
Frithjof, the Viking

—Persia
A story of Rustem, the hero of
Persia

—Rome
The wanderings of Aeneas

Epics *(Continued)*

–Russia
The word of Igor's armament

–Spain
The story of the Cid

Epilogue: a final word
LAURITZEN – BLOOD p150-151

Epiphany eve
The kneeling tree

Episodic stories
The sly thief of Valenciennes

Eppelin of Gailingen
PICARD – GERMAN p184-188

Equality
A boy in Russia
How the people of Ife became
scattered
The pillow talk
The two pots

Ergosai-Batyr
MASEY – STORIES p109-112

Eric-fines
The children of Tuireann return to
Erin
The cooking-spit of the women of
Fincara
The death of the sons of Tuireann
The gifted skin of the pig
The golden apples of Hisberna
Lugh and his father's murderers
The seven enchanted pigs, and the
hound whelps of Iroda
The shouts on the hill of Midkena
The spear slaughterer and the chariot
and horses of Sigar

Ericson, Leif
The American saga
The spell-song

Ericson, Thorvald
The American saga

Erie canal
Canawlers on the E-ri-ee Canal

Erin. *See* **Ireland**

Erin, men of
The battle of the bulls
Cuchullin keeps the gap of the north
Cuchullin parleys with Maeve
The death of Cuchullin
The fight with Ferdia
The pillow talk
Ulster awake

Ermine
Lox and the two ermines

Ermine and the hunter
MacMILLAN – GLOOS. p172-178

Ero and the Kadi
ČURČIJA – YUGOSLAV p84.

Ero and the tsar
ČURČIJA – YUGOSLAV p69-70

Ero from the other world
ČURČIJA – YUGOSLAV p16.

Errantry
TOLKIEN – READER (Part 4)
p24-27

Errato di Barletto
MINCIELLI – TALES p18-21

Esben and the witch
MANNING – WITCHES p46-61

Esben Ashblower
HATCH – MORE p49-56

The escape of the animals
PRIDHAM – GIFT p107-115

Escapes
The beetle and a drop of honey
The flight

The Eskimo widow . . . And her strange
son
UNTERMEYER – FIRE. p252-255

Eskimos
About Eskimos stories
Agayk and the strangest spear
The Angakok and the mother of seals
Aye-Mee and the mermaid
The bear woman
The blind boy and the loon
The boy who became a reindeer
The cranberry feast
The creek of whale oil
The cruel uncle

Eskimos *(Continued)*

The day Tuk became a hunter
The enchanted sky
The extraordinary black coat
The hardhearted rich man
How raven found the daylight
How the people began
How the raven brought light to the
  world
How thunder and lightning came to
  be
Kagssagssuk, the homeless boy who
  became a strong man
Kutlee-Seek-Vik (Where the bird skin
  was cooked)
The last of the Thunderbirds
Leealura and Maleyato
A legend of Kotzebue
The legend of Pathasos
Lights of the caribou
The lost song
The man who killed the sea monster
The man who married a snow goose
The moon husband
Nathlook: Susie, my name
Netchillik and the bear
The owl and the raven
Raven fools his grandchildren
The sea otter girl
The sea serpent
The Sedna legend
The spirit of slumber
Through the needle's eye
The two men and the two dwarfs
Udleqdjun in the sky
The very obstinate man
Whale of a tale
The Whalers and the dwarfs, The
  Little People of the Eskimos
Whistle the wind
The witch
The woman who raised a bear as a son

—Rhymes
  I yay! I yay! I yay!

Essays
  On fairy stories

Esther . . . Who saved her people
  UNTERMEYER – FIRE. p117-121

Estonia
  The birth of the River Emajõgi
  The clever peasant girl
  The cook and the house goblin
  The creation of the wolf
  The farmer's clever daughter
  The gift of Father Frost

The goblins at the bath house
The goldspinners
The grateful prince
The lord of gold
The magic mirror
The milky way
The moon painters
The northern frog
The old traveler
The Rehepapp and Vanapagan
Tall Peter and short Peter
The water dwellers
When I was a baby
Why the hare's lip is split
The wolf's food
The wood of Tontla

Esyllt. *See* Isolte

Eterna
  BIRCH – CHINESE p152-165

The eternal wanderer
  LEACH – RAINBOW p293-294

The eternal wanderer of the Pampas
  JAGENDORF – KING p18-23
  LITTLEDALE – GHOSTS p39-44

Eternity
  See also Heaven; Youth, Eternal
  The bird and the man
  The soldier and the knapsack

Ethelred, King
  The cowherd's son

Ethiopia. *See* Africa–Ethiopia

Etzel, Theodor
  The stag-hunt

Europa and the bull
  MANNING – BEASTS p38.

Europe
  See also Names of countries of Europe
  How bean got his stripe

Eurydice
  Orpheus and Eurydice
  Orpheus . . . The fabulous musician

Eurystheus, King
  The kneeler's twelve tasks

Evans, Eva Knox
  How the milky way began

186

Evans, Mary Ann. *See* Eliot, George

Evan's problem
  PUGH – TALES p129-133

Eve. *See* Adam and Eve (Biblical)

Eve of the wise men
  MY BOOK HOUSE v. 1 p224.

Evening at the farm
  MY BOOK HOUSE v. 10 p79.

Evening. *See* Night

Evergreen trees
  How Glooskap made the birds
  The singing fir-tree
  Why some trees are evergreen
  Why the evergreen trees never lose
    their leaves

The everlasting house
  MARTIN – NINE p55-60

Everyday luck
  LEACH – LUCK p79-85

Everyone's glad in our city today
  MY BOOK HOUSE v. 1 p75.

Everywhere you go
  LEACH – SOUP p109-110

Evil
  About devils
  The anger of Sande-Nyana
  The bad prince
  Bird of power
  Blodeuedd and the slaying of Llew
  Boys with golden stars
  The buried moon
  The clever squirrel
  The crackling mountain
  The creation of the wolf
  The dance of death
  The days of the first monkeys
  Death and the old man
  The deer woman
  The divided cloak
  The dream
  The eight leaves of story (4) A harp
    on the water
  The envious neighbor
  The fisherman and his soul
  Golden hair
  The golden mountain

The great flood
The grizzly and the rattlesnake men
The hairs of the baron's head
Hok Lee and the dwarfs
Horus the avenger
How men learned about evil
The hunter and the hind
Iwanich and the magic ring
The land of the dead
The legend of Llangorse Lake
The legend of Pathasos
The lion who listened to a jackal
Lord Krishna, or The eighth child
Luck from heaven and luck from the
  earth
Magic in Marblehead
The man who learned the language
  of the animals
The mechanical man of Prague
Moon pearls
Naba Zid-Wende
The old man of the flowers
Pandora . . . the fateful casket
The princess who wanted to solve
  riddles
The queen's necklace
Ra and his children
She-wa-na, deity of the elements
Smart Dai-adalla
The sorcerer's apprentice(s)
Naba Zid-Wende
The tailor in the church
The tale of bat
Thomas the rhymer
Three fat ewes for three fine hounds
Tiger woman
The tongue-cut sparrow
The tyrant who became a just ruler
The waters beneath: Fifty young men
  and a turtle
The wicked bankiva
The wicked house of Duncan Macbain
The wicked weasel
The witch and her four sons
The wolf and the stork
The world beyond

Evil rocks and the evil spirit of Peru
  JAGENDORF – KING p238-241

Evil spirits. *See* Spirits, Evil

The evil spirits of Crooked Mountain
  HAYES – INDIAN p93-101

The evil woman thrown into a pit. *See*
  The bad-tempered wife

Evseyka
  BUDBERG – RUSSIAN p116-122

Ewing, Juliana Horatia
The ogre courting
The owl's answer to Tommy

Exactly so
LEACH – SOUP p131-133

Exaggeration
See also Falsehood; Liars; "Tall Tales"
Lazarus and the dragons
Mr. Samson cat
Preacher and the devil
The spear and shield of Huantan
The story of an egg
The tail of St. George's dragon
The Texas sandstorm
Three fast men

Exchanges. See Traders and trading

Excuses
The unusual excuse

Executions
The father's steps

Exile
The banishment of Diab
The banishment of Rama
Chourilo's little comb
How Abunawas was exiled
The love of a Mexican prince and princess
The poem of the sea
The siege of joyous Gard
The tale of the royal exiles

The exile of Rāma
MY BOOK HOUSE v. 10 p175-187

An expensive omelette
MICHAEL – PORTUGUESE p118-120

Experience
The children who could do without their elders
The tiger's whisker

An explanation of the grasshopper
MY BOOK HOUSE v. 2 p77.

The exploits of Hanuman
GRAY – INDIA'S p124-132

Explorers and exploration
The American saga
The golden earth
The hazel-nut child
Other island
Pushing westward with Lewis and Clark

Exploring the wilderness
MY BOOK HOUSE v. 9 p7-26

The extraordinary black coat
COTHRAN – MAGIC p3-7

Extravagance
How the donkey saved a village
The riddle
The teacher and his pupil

Extremes
It is foolish to carry matters to extremes

Eye-glasses. See Glasses, Eye

Eyes
See also Blind
The baker's neighbor
The boy who taught the fairies tears
The boys who met the trolls in the Hedal woods
The brave little prince
The carnation youth
The coyote and the two dogs
The eel and the porgy
The fairy frog
Fairy ointment
How the redbird got his color
In the beginning
Johnny and the witch-maidens
Kabundi's eye
Left eye, right eye
Little one eye, little two eyes and little three eyes
Long, broad and sharpsight
Longshanks, girth, and keen
Manstin, the rabbit
The ogre who built a bridge
Old wall eyes
The princess and the dwarf
The singing bone
Straight and crooked
Three skillful men
Through the eyes
To your good health

–Color
The man who sold magic

–Eyelashes
Musk and amber

The eyes of owls
REED – TALK. p35.

F

The fable of the plough and the plough-share
GHOSE – FOLK p145.

Fables. *See* **Animals**; names of animals

Fables and fabulists
GAER – FABLES p3-5

The fables of India
GAER – FABLES p7-8

Fabliaux
Jacques the woodcutter

Fabre, Jean Henri
The fairyland of science

Fabrics. *See* **Cloth**

Faces
See also **Noses; Tongues;** etc.
Dimples
The flower faces
The old man and the devils
The two-faces

Fact or fancy?
JACOBSON – FIRST p63

"The Faerie queene"
Una and the Red Cross knight

The faery and the kettle
WILSON – SCOTTISH p99-102

The faery flag of Dunnegan
WILSON – SCOTTISH p66-74

Fair, brown, and trembling
PILKINGTON – SHAM. p19-29

A fair distribution
BORSKI – GOOD p1-2

The fair maiden of Astolat
PICARD – STORIES p217-234

Fair play. *See* **Judges and justice**

Fair Vasilissa and Baba Yaga
DOWNING – RUSSIA p176-184

Fair wages for all
JUDA – WISE p16-21

The fair young bride
BECHSTEIN – FAIRY p138-141

Fairies
See also **Fairyland;** names of types
of fairies; titles beginning with
Faery, Fairy
The adventures of Florian
The adventures of Nera
The aged infant
Ainsel
Alison Gross
Arawn
The assembling of the fays
The baker's daughter
A bauchan in the family
Beauty and the beast
The bell of Monte Pino
The bewitched court
The birth of Oisin
The boy who taught the fairies tears
Cardiff town
The carl of the drab coat
Cenerentola
The changeling
The changeling and the fond young
mother
The chase of Slieve Gallion
Childe Rowland
The children of the dead woman
Chin-chin Kobakama
Clever Dick
The comb, the flute and the spinning
wheel
Connla of the golden hair
Cooked for fifteen
The corn maiden
Count Alaric's lady
The country under the hill
The crystal bowl
Datu Omar and the fairy
David Wright and the fairies
Dewi Dal
Diamonds and toads
The dinner that cooked itself
The disappearance of Ifan Gruffydd's
daughter
The dog and the maiden
Donkey-skin
Dorani
Drak, the fairy
Einion and the Fair family
Einion Las and the Fair family

Fairies (*Continued*)

Ermine and the hunter
The faery flag of Dunnegan
The fall of the spider man
The fiddlers of Strathspey
Finvarra
The first buttercups
The first of May
The flight
The flower-headed man
The fountain
The friendly frog
The giant who counted stones
The gold falcon
The good crawford
Granny Shelock
The grateful beasts
The great flood
Half a yard
The hazel-nut child
The heart of Princess Joan
The hearth-cat
How Finn won his father's place
How summer came to Canada
How these tales came to be told
John Shea and the fairy treasure
John the bear
John the painter
Kahukura and the fairies
Kahukura and the fairy fisherman
Kate Mary Ellen and the fairies
Kilmeny
King Orfeo
The king who wanted a beautiful wife
Kukuile, the dancing girl
The lady's room
The lake lady
The lass that lost the laird's daughter
Leaving paradise
Left eye, right eye
The lion, the tiger, and the eagle
Lionbruno
The little fairy
Little finger
The Little People
The lord of gold
The love of Cuchulainn and Fann,
  and the only jealousy of Emer, his
  wife
Lox and the two ermines
The luck fairies
Luran and the fairies
The magic belt
The magic carpet
The magic fishbone
The magic hill
The magic wand
The magnificent hounds of Finn
  MacCool
The maiden in the tower

The maiden, the knight, and the
  waterfall
The meal mill at Eathie
Melisande
Midir and Etain
A midsummer night's dream
The mignonette fairy
The milky way
The miller and th fairies
The miraculous stag
Morgan and the three fairies
The mother of Oisin
The mud-snail fairy
My own self
Niamb of the golden hair
The night of the big wind
Nikkessen's pool
The Northern lights
The old man who said "Why"
Once upon a time
The page boy and the silver goblet
The palace in the Rath
Pearly-dew John
The Phynnodderee
The piper
The piper of Sutherland
The piper who could not play
Prince Prigio
The princess and the dwarf
The princess of Mount Nam-Nhu
Princess Rosette
The princess who knew her own mind
The pursuit of Dermot and Grania
The quest of the children of Turenn
Racketty-packetty house
The Red Etin
Riquet with the quiff
Saturday, Sunday, Monday
Seán Palmer's voyage to America
  with the fairies
The secret commonwealth
Shon Shenkin
Sir Launfal
Sir Orfeo
Skillywidden
The sleeping beauty
The sleeping beauty in the wood
The snowman
The son of the baker of Barra
The songstress and the fairies
The stolen bairn and the Sidh
The story of Prince Fairyfoot
The story of Tom Thumb
Stupid Peruonto
The sun-king's hair
The tailor and the prince, told by
  Mulech
The tale of a foolish brother and of a
  wonderful bush
The tale of the hump-backed men
Tam Lin

Fairies (*Continued*)

Thomas the rhymer
The thread of life
The three citrons
(The) three wishes
Ting-a-ling
Ting-a-ling and the five magicians
Ting-a-ling's visit to Tur-il-i-ra
The tobacco fairy from the blue hills
Tom Thumb
A toy princess
The tulip bed
The two princesses
Undine
The wee red man
Why pigs have curley tails
The widow's lazy daughter
The wild man
Will-o'-the wisp
The wishing cup
The wizard of Reay's book of magic
The wonder of Skoupa
The wonderful knapsack
The wonders of the three donals
The wooing of Etain
The young man who married a fairy
The youth who wanted some fun
Yuki-Onna
Zezolla and the date-palm tree

—Animals
    The moss-green princess

, Blue
    The place of strife

—Cups. *See* Cups, Fairy

—Dwarfs. *See* Dwarfs, Fairy

—Dictionaries
    Fairy dictionary

—Farmers
    The two millers

—Feasts
    The miser and the fairy feast

—Flags
    The faery flag of Dunnegan

—Flowers
    The fairy garden

—Forest
    Jackal or tiger?

—Gifts
    Ricky of the tuft
    Ricky with a tuft

—Gold
    The thirteenth floor

—Grottoes
    The fairy grotto

—Harps. *See* Harps and harpists, Fairy

, Heroic
    Childe Roland
    Earl Fitzgerald in the enchanted hill
    The fairies and the smith
    The green children
    Heroic poems
    The return of Oisin
    The tacksman and the ox
    Tamlane
    True Thomas
    Wild Edric

, Highland
    The farmer and the fairy hillock

, Homely
    See also Habetrot; Rumpelstiltskin
    The borrowing fairies
    Cherry of Zennor
    The fairy midwife
    Habetrot
    Habetrot and Scantlie Mab
    Homely fairies
    The Laird o'Co
    The leprechaun
    Skillywidden
    Tops and bottoms
    The woman of peace and the kettle

, Household
    The nis

—Islands. *See* Islands, Fairy

—Lizards. *See* Lizards, Fairy

—Money. *See* Money, Fairy

—Music
    The coming of Fionn MacCool
    The disappearance of Rhys
    How Finn won his father's place
    The hunchback's gift
    The piskey revelers
    Rhys at the fairy dance

—Nature
    The swraig and the three blows
    The merrow and the soul cages
    Nature fairies
    The old man of Cury
    The seal fisher and the roane
    The water horse and the water bull

—Queens
    True Thomas
    Una and the Red Cross knight

—Swords
    How Fionn found his sword
    The smith and the faeries

—Trees
    The crow in the rose-apple tree

Fairies—Trees (*Continued*)

Diggory
The fairy tree of Doolas woods

, Trooping
Betty Stogs and the Little People
The fairies and the cow
The fairy funeral
The gudewife's midnight labours
Horse and hattock
The miser and the fairy feast
Rhys at the fairy dance
The stolen lady
The thieving fairies
Trooping fairies

, Tutelary
The boggart
The brownie of Cranshaws
The brownie of Jedburgh
The cauld lad of Hilton
From brownie to boggart
The kind pixy
Nithsdale brownie
The pooka
Puddlefoot

—Wands
Ash sweeper and the wishing wand
The brave grenadier
The death of Balder
Ermine and the hunter
The giant of the brown beech wood
The magic wand
The melancholy prince and the girl
of milk and blood
The two princesses
The youth and the dog dance

—Wood
The wood fairy

Fairies
BATCHELOR – SUPER. p124-129
JACOBSON – LEGEND. p12-23
PERRAULT – CLASSIC p67-75
PERRAULT – COMPLETE p42-46

The fairies and the cow
BRIGGS – PERS. p70-72

The fairies and the smith
BRIGGS – PERS. p51-54

The fairies in the White Mountains
JAGENDORF – NEW p54-56

Fairies on the gump
MANNING – PETER p103-109

The fairies' revenge
SHEPPARD – WELSH p6-12

Fairness. *See* **Judges and justice**

Fairs
The banshee's birthday treat
Birdling
Kantjil holds a festival
The lads who met the highwaymen
Mr. and Mrs. Vinegar
The palace of the night
Prince Hat beneath the earth
Shrovetide
Sly Peter at the fair

The fairy
PROTTER – CHILD. p68-69

Fairy and child
MY BOOK HOUSE v. 3 p25.

The fairy bird
BERGER – BLACK p106-122

Fairy caskets
FARJEON – SILVER p182-187

The fairy child
WILLIAMS – FAIRY p140-145

Fairy dictionary
PALMER – FAIRY p9-19

Fairy forests
MY BOOK HOUSE v. 6 p190

The fairy frog
BERGER – BLACK p33-42
O'SULLIVAN – FOLK. p169-171

The fairy funeral
BRIGGS – PERS. p62.

The fairy garden
SHEPPARD – WELSH p129-130

Fairy gardens
HAVILAND – GREECE p61-69

The fairy grotto
BONNET – CHINESE p175-178
MÜLLER – SWISS p101-105

The fairy Helena
MANNING – GLASS p139-145

The fairy host
PILKINGTON – THREE p109-113

Fairy Ilona and Argelus
ILLYES – ONCE p84-89

The fairy midwife
See also The fairy ointment
BRIGGS – PERS. p92-93

Fairy money
O'SULLIVAN – FOLK. p174-175

Fairy mother
HAVILAND – GREECE p83-90

The fairy nurseling. *See* The fairy midwife

The fairy of Hawili Falls
ROBERTSON – PHILIP. p97-105

The fairy of the three-branched oak
ILLYES – ONCE p258-263

Fairy ointment
SHEPPARD – WELSH p142-145

The fairy quite contrary
BARBEAU – GOLDEN p46-57

Fairy rings (circles)
The disappearance of Ifan Gruffydd's
daughter
The disappearance of Rhys
John Gethin and the candle
John the painter
The lucky circle
The young man who married a fairy

The fairy shoemaker
PALMER – FAIRY p55-58

Fairy tales (general)
The king who liked fairy tales
On fairy stories
The wife who liked fairy tales

, Oldest
Elidorus in fairyland

The fairy tree of Doolas woods
BELTING – THREE p110-120

Fairy tricks
SHEPPARD – WELSH p93-97

The fairy wife
BAKER – TALKING p40-44
BONNET – CHINESE p21-28
HAVILAND – GREECE p39-51
O'SULLIVAN – FOLK. p171-174

The fairy woman's revenge
BOUCHER – MEAD p49-53

Fairy workmen
SHEPPARD – SCOT. p17-20

Fairyland
Childe Roland
Elidorus in fairyland
The fairies and the smith
The lad who returned from Faerye
Mr. Noy
A musical visit to fairyland
The tale of the land of Cockaigne
Tamlane
Thomas the rhymer

The fairyland of science
MY BOOK HOUSE v. 6 p184-190

Faith
The babe Moses
Damon and Pythias; the most faithful
of friends
Daniel in the lion's den
David, the shepherd boy
Gideon, the warrior
Ifor the scoffer
Joan of Arc
Joseph and his brethren
The martyrs of Thebes
Old Johnny Appleseed
The wizard of the Nile
The wrestling match of the two
Buddhas

The faithful dog
JAGENDORF – SAND p34-36

The faithful friend
ZAGLOUL – BLACK p65-73

Faithful John
THOMPSON – ONE p199-205

The faithful Morgiana
MOZLEY – ARABY p26-37

Faithful to death
JAGENDORF – KING p111-113

The faithful wife
BONNET – CHINESE p155-158

Faithfulness. *See* **Loyalty**

The faithless apprentice
O'FAOLAIN – IRISH p193-195

Faithlessness. *See* **Disloyalty; Hypocrisy**

Fakirs. *See* Holy men

Falasha: the mystery people
DAVIS – LION'S p167-168

The falcon and the cock
GREEN – BIG p194.

The falcon and the hen
GAER – FABLES p36-37

Falcons
The adventures of Iain Direach
The beginning of the world and the
making of California
The birds' St. Valentine's day
The fisherman's son
How Ian Direach got the blue falcon
Ian Direach
Idunn's apples of youth
The Indian shinny game
The king and the falcon
The king of the dark desert
Loki . . . the apples of youth
Marya Moréona
The midget and the giant
Phenist the bright-eyed falcon
The phoenix and the falcon
The raven
A strange reward
Thor and the Jotun Geirrod
The three enchanted princes

–Feathers
The feather of Finist the falcon

–Wings
The broken wing

Fall. *See* Autumn

The fall of Serbia
CURCIJA – HEROES p46-47

The fall of the earth giants
U. N. – RIDE p243-249

The fall of the Heike
McALPINE – JAPAN p65-77

The fall of the spider man
MacMILLAN – GLOOS. p26-34

The fall of Troy
GREEN – GREEKS p44-45

Fallico, Arturo
Italian nursery rhymes

The false fakir
TURNBULL – FAIRY p91-102

The false knight
WILLIAMS – FAIRY p88.

The false shaman
MARTIN – NINE p47-50

Falsehood
See also Liars; Tall tales
The bat and the eagle
The big, big rabbit
The bird that told tales
The blue lake
The boy who out-fibbed a princess
Catching hares in winter
Dookiram, the poor one
Fire and water, truth and falsehood
The first shlemiel
Five lies that could be true
The forty whoppers
The four young men
The great festival
The hare's kidneys
Impossible tales
Jesper who herded the hares
King Appolonides
The laughing statue
Legend of how ants came to earth
The man who sold magic
Mr. Crow and the mussel
A morality tale: truth and falsehood
The mouse and the frog
A nasty rumour
Omar's big lie
The princess and the string of lies
Pwyll and Pryderi (2) the birth of
Pryderi
The rabbit grows a crop of money
The sweet Mochi's parents
True and untrue
The would-be wizard

Falseness. *See* Dishonesty; Hypocrisy;
Treachery; Trickery

Fame
Three who found their heart's desire

The fame of the princess
McALPINE – JAPAN. p133-136

Famine
Anansi and fish country
Antelope's mother: the woman in
the moon
The battle at White Cliff house
The brainy rabbit
The dog, the cat, and the mouse
The giant with the grey feathers
Grandfather's advice

Famine (*Continued*)

Historical inscription—or fiction? The
   seven-year famine
How monkey king became a slave
How summer came to Canada
Ijapa demands corn fufu
Kabundi's eye
Kwaku Ananse and the whipping cord
Lion, chameleon, and chicken
The punishment
St. Cadog and the mouse
The sea-mammy

The famine and the fruit tree
   ELLIOT – WHERE p114-121

Fans
The badger and the magic fan
Coyote's new hairdo
Don't tease the tengu!
The girl who used her wits
Kupti and Imani
Little maid of far Japan
The search for the magic lake
The tengu's magic nose fan

—**Feather**
Bird of power

Far East
See also names of countries
The turtle and the storks and the
   jackal
The turtle outwits the lion
The turtle who loved a monkey

The far horizon
   LAWSON – STRANGE p113-129

Fareedah's carpet
   LARSON – PALACE p46-59

Farjeon, Eleanor
The giant and the mite
Nella's dancing shoes
Palamon and Arcite
The princess of China
The seventh princess
The witch! The witch!

Farjeon, Eleanor
   JOHNSON – PRINC. p309-310

The farm
   JOHNSON – WHAT p55-56

The farmer and his son
   FEINSTEIN – FOLK p51-54

The farmer and the demon
   SECHRIST – ONCE p119-125

The farmer and the fairy cow
   SHEPPARD – WELSH p115-118

The farmer and the fairy hillock
   SHEPPARD – SCOT. p9-13

The farmer and the harvesters
   MINCIELI – TALES p80-83

The farmer and the hoe
   HARDENDORFF – TRICKY p51-53

Farmer Giles of Ham
   TOLKIEN – READER (Part 3) p5-79

The farmer in the dell
   MY BOOK HOUSE v. 1 p102-103

The farmer of Babbia
   COURLANDER – FIRE p113-118

The farmer, the bear, and the fox
   BLOCH – UKRAIN. p64-67

The farmer, the buffalo, and the tiger
   ROBERTSON – FAIRY p76-80

Farmer Weathersky
   MANNING – WIZARDS p47-57

The farmer who went to plough
   BAMBERGER – FIRST. p10

Farmers
See also **Ploughmen**
The angry baron
Ashoremashika
Assipattle and the giant sea serpent
The Bakki brothers
The boggart
The boots that never wore out
The boy who made hay
The brownie O'Ferne-Den
Bukolla
The cartman's stories
The castle of Seoul
The cat and the mouse
The ceabharnach
Chief of the night riders
Cinder Joe becomes king
Clever–clever–clever
The clever lass
Clever Manka
The conch shell of ram
Cooked for fifteen
Copperhead in the bin
The corn maiden
The crafty farmer

196

Farmers (*Continued*)

The crane wife
Crocodile's share
The crow and the sparrow
Dame Durden
The dancing palm tree
David Wright and the fairies
The dead creditor
The debt
The deer of five colors
The devil in red flannel
The devil in the barrel
The devil's bride
The devil's gifts
Dewi Dal
Diggory
The disappearance of Rhys
The dwarf and the cook, the Little
  People of Turkey
Evan's problem
Evening at the farm
The fairies' revenge
The fairy woman's revenge
Febold Feboldson
The forest bride
The four deaf men
The fox turns a somersault
The fruits of health
The gift and the giver
The gingerbread man
A girl and a stepmother
Gold
Golden bracelets, golden anklets
The good crawford
Gudbrand of the hillside
Gwarwyn-a-Throt
The gwraig and the three blows
The hairy boggart
Hantsjc and the remarkable beast
The hauntings at Thorhallstead
The hen that laid the golden eggs
Hildur the elf queen
The hired man
The house with the front door at the
  back
How God's wheel turns
How Kwaku Ananse became bald
How much for a shadow?
How Urseli became a princess
I should like to plough
Idy, the fox-chasing cow
Ifor the scoffer
It's already paid
Jack Hannaford
Jackal or tiger?
James Gray and the Clashnichd
Johnnie and Grizzle
Jones and the boggart of Brixworth
Keep cool
The kind farmer

The king of the Golden River, or the
  Black brothers
The king who rides a tiger
The king's rice pudding
The lame vixon
Large cabbages
The lazy fox
Lazy Peter and his three-cornered hat
The little birch tree
Little Claus and Big Claus
The little gray pony
The little horse
The little red pig
The magic purse of the swamp maiden
Making your own
The man in the moon
The marvelous cow of Llyn Barfog, The
  Little People of Wales
Master and man
The miracle flame
A moon of Gobbags
The most obedient wife
The mouse's bride
My maid Mary
Nidden and Didden and Donal Beg
  O'Neary
Nuberu
Old Nanny's ghost
Old Stormalong
Olli and the rich troll
One grain more than the devil
The one who said Tjik
Peder Okse
Peter Ox
The piskie thresher
The planting party
The ploughman he's a bonnie lad
Plowman in the sky
Polenta, polenta, and more polenta
The poor people who wanted to be
  rich
The poor ploughman and the rich
  nobleman
The precious stone
The priest and the pear tree
The prize
The queen's care
Ride, ride a horsey
The seventh son
The shepherd of Silverstead
The silver on the hearth
Skillywidden
The sleigh ride
The smart daughter
The smiling innkeeper
The snake and the dreams
The spider weaver
Stormy swallows the anchor
The story of Cincinnatus
The story of Mrs. Tubbs
The story of Tom Thumb

Farmers *(Continued)*

The storyteller
The string of lies
The thieving fairies
The three chests
The three cows
The three cups of water
The Three Fates
The three laughs of the leipreachán
Ti-Tiriti-Ti
The tiger's tail
Tongue steeple
Tony Di-Moany
Tops and bottoms
Tops or bottoms
The treasure
The untidy mermaid
A visitor from paradise
A voyage to Brobdingnag
When I was a baby
Why the parrot speaks man's words
Willie boy, Willie boy
The wise old woman
The wishing ring
The woman of Llyn-y-fan (1) The
   meeting
The yellow dragon
The young giant
The young piper, the Little People of
   Ireland

The farmer's boy
   MY BOOK HOUSE v. 1 p108-109

The farmer's clever daughter
   McNEILL – DOUBLE p49-55
   RANKE – GERMANY p125-127

The farmer's old horse
   SIDDIQUI – TOON. p65-69

Farming by the moon
   BATCHELOR – SUPER. p17-18

The farmyard
   BLOCH – UKRAIN. p73-76

Farragut, David
   Young midshipman David Farragut

Fashion
   BATCHELOR – SUPER. p119-123

Fastitocalon
   TOLKIEN – READER (Part 4)
   p48-49

Fate
   See also Fates, Three; Fortune;
      Fortune-tellers; Luck; Prophets and
      Prophecies
   The baby that was sold
   Catherine and her fate
   The charcoal burner choja
   The destiny of Princess Tien Dung
   The fortunate maiden
   From a moral alphabet
   The hawk and the nightingale
   Kabadaluk
   Kabadaluk: the little Arab boy
   A king and destiny
   The king who tried to cheat destiny
   The pig, the goat and the sheep
   Stone patience and knife patience
   The story of O-Tei
   The story of the king who would be
      stronger than fate

Fate
   CURCIJA – YUGOSLAV p140-152

Fate and the faggot gatherer
   JEWETT – WHICH p95-103

The fate of the children of Lir
   PILKINGTON – THREE p83-123

The fate of the children of Tuireann
   PILKINGTON – THREE p9-81

Fate of the Magicos
   JORDAN – BURRO p68-71

The fate of the sons of Usnach
   O'FAOLÁIN – IRISH p88-100

The fate of the turtle
   LANG – OLIVE p99-104

The fate of the vulture
   GRAY – INDIA's p181-183

Fates, Three
   Catherine and the fates
   The prince and the Three Fates
   The Three Fates
   The three golden hairs
   The three golden hairs of Grand-
      father Know all

Father big-nose
   DELARUE – FRENCH p21-28

Father catfish
   VO-DINH – TOAD p23-27

Father fights son in the tribe of Hilal
   DAVIS – TEN p12-27

A father-in-law and his son-in-law
COURLANDER – KING'S p71-73

The father of American song
MY BOOK HOUSE v. 12 p116-117

Fathers
See also **Daughters; Sons**
The aged father
The daughter of the dwarf
The divided cloak
The fight with Wabun
The girl without arms
Grandfather's advice
The heather beer
How Finn won his father's place
Ivo Senkovich and Aga of Ribnik
Kutlee-Seek-Vik
The lamentable story of Connlach,
  son of Cuchulain
The legend of Tchi-Niu
The old father who went to school
The people who lived near a mountain
The princess who loved her father
  like salt
Sohrab and Rustum . . . the tragic
  encounter
The truest adventures of the truthful
  mountain boy

The father's steps
MÜLLER – SWISS p224-225

Fatty
LEACH – SOUP p128-130

Faultfinding. *See* **Criticism**

Faults
Reform meeting

The faun and the woodcutter's daughter
PICARD – FAUN p7-25

Faust
The song of the flea

Faust
MY BOOK HOUSE v. 12 p163-186

Fawkes, Guy
Guy Fawkes . . . The gunpowder plot

Fay, Andreas
The caterpillar

Fays
The assembling of the fays

Fear
See also **Cowardice**
The adventures of Florian
The boy who found fear
The city mouse and the country mouse
The deer and the jaguar share a house
The earthquake
The falcon and the cock
The foolish, timid, little hare
The giant okab
The hare
The horse, the lion, and the wolf
How the deer lost his tail
King Fergus and the water-horse
The mad dog
The mice in council
The mouse and the rat
The old men who had wens
Plop!
Spider and the lion
The story of the fraids
A tale of a boy who set out to learn
  fear
The tapping ghost of Edinburg
The terrible black snake's revenge
The terrible leak
The three brothers
The three companions
The ugly duckling
The wagtail and the rainbow
The wedding of the dragon-god
Why animals are afraid of fire
Why the hare's lip is split

Fear the dark
BATCHELOR – SUPER. p104-105

The fear of the lion king
KOREL – LISTEN p69-71

Fear, the greatest enemy
ALEXANDER – PEBBLES p29.

Fearless John and the giant monster
JAGENDORF – UPSTATE p148-152

Fearlessness. *See* **Courage**

The feast
COURLANDER – KING'S p56-57

Feast for the Dead ("Mange Mort")
The lizard's big dance

The feast for the fox
GAER – FABLES p18-20

The feast of plums
    ELLIOT – SINGING p138-
    153

Feasts
    See also **Fairies–Feasts**; names of
        feasts
    The butterfly in the granary
    The cranberry feast
    The daughter of the dwarf
    Deidre and the sons of Usna
    The fire on the mountain
    The girl and the crocodile
    The greedy spider
    The honey feast
    How duck got his bill
    How God helped Mammo
    How Michael Scot went to Rome
    How Pakayana the spider got his small
        waist
    How the birds came to have their
        many colors
    Juha at the banquest
    The king and his seven sons
    King Fergus MacLeide and the wee
        folk
    The king's joke
    Kutlee-Seek-Vik
    The little pet Rani
    The magic bone
    The marriage feast
    Monkey
    The monkey's feast
    Nazar the brave
    The origin of the bromo feast
    Pamudjo's feast
    Pwyll and Pryderi (1) The marriage
        of Pwyll and Rhiannon
    The raven and the crow
    The sacred drum of Tepozteco
    The story of White Arab
    A strange guest
    The stranger and the miller
    Thor and the jotun Aegir
    Thor's visit to Hymir
    Two feasts for Anansi
    Water drops
    With and without
    The year of the feast at Simbi

The feather of Finist the falcon
    LINES – TALES p31-45

The feathered friend
    See also **Parson Wood and the devil**
    MANNING – PETER p139-143

Feathers
    See also **Birds–Colors; Fans, Feather;**
        names of birds
    The adventures of Iain Direach
    Anansi and the alligator eggs
    Anansi and turtle and pigeon
    Arap Sang and the cranes
    The beautiful feathers
    The blind king and the magic bird
    Chimpanzee's story
    The crane wife
    The dancing feather
    The demon giant of Mount Ariake
    The dove maiden
    The emperor's magic bow
    Farmer Weathersky
    The firebird
    The giant of the brown beech wood
    Hantsjc and the remarkable beast
    How Cormac MacArt got his branch
    Kahukura and the fairies
    How the king of the birds was chosen
    The lame duck
    The lion and the hare go hunting
    The man with the green feather
    Musk and amber
    The nine doves
    Pepito
    The prince and giant's daughter
    The rabbit prince
    The rain-god's daughter
    The search for the magic lake
    The skillful huntsman
    The small red feather
    The spirit who danced
    The story of a good boy
    The story of Zal
    The swan maiden
    Temba wins a bride
    The three feathers
    Tropsyn
    Unlucky Mussah
    The white dove
    Why the whipporwill weeps and wails
    The woman who came down from
        heaven
    The youth and the dog dance

    –Beds
        The real princess

    –Cloaks
        Kalelea and his wish
        Why the sun is brighter than the
            moon

    , Golden
        The feathers from the bird Venus
        The gold bird
        The gold falcon
        The golden goose
        The golden horse
        The golden peacock

200

Feathers, Golden (*Continued*)
   The little nobleman
   The prince and the vizier's son
, Goose
   The man who married a snow goose
, Magic
   The goat and the eagle

Feathers and flax
   FARJEON – SILVER p90-96

The feathers from the bird Venus
   RANKE – GERMANY p71-74

Febold Feboldson
   GORHAM – REAL p73-89

Feedowa and Nobbin
   MacFarlane – TALES p71-77

Feet
   Best foot forward
   The cow that ate the piper
   The coyote and the two dogs
   Georgie goes a-sparkin'
   The girl without hands
   An inadvertent misunderstanding
   The mixed-up feet and the silly
      bridegroom
   Sleepy feet
   The story of Prince Fairyfoot
   The uglier foot
   Why ducks have flat feet

   –Bones
      The three tasks
   –Heels
      Achilles and Polyxena
      The slaying of Hector

Felton, Harold W.
   A word from the author

Felton, Harold W.
   FELTON – NEW (preface)
   FELTON – WORLD'S p151.

Fence post. *See* Deaf men and their
answers

Fencers and fencing
   The three brothers

Fences
   Mboyo the hunter
   Rabbit, fox, and the rail fence

The turtle prince
Why lizard can't sit

Fenisana
   SAVORY – ZULU p38-42

Fennel (plant)
   Goblin gold

Fereyel and Debbo Engal the witch
   ARNOTT – AFRICAN p200-201
   HOPE-SIMPSON – CAVAL. p156-
   167

Fergar, Mary, joint author
   The magic dagger
   The peasant and the donkey
   The story of the boy who couldn't
      keep anything in his head
   The three apples
   Two watermelon stories

Ferns
   Hie away, hie away
   Prince Ferdinand
   Tortoise and Barbarinsa's daughters

   –Seed
      Luc, the king's woodsman
      The wizard earl

Ferrié Madame
   The serpent and the grape-grower's
   daughter

Ferries and ferrymen
   "Good day, fellow!" "Axe handle"!
   The lady of Tylwyth Teg
   Marko the rich and Vasily the luckless
   The rich man and his son-in-law
   The three golden hairs
   The three golden hairs of Grandad Sol
   The three golden hairs of Grandfather
      Know All
   The three golden hairs of the king of
      the cave giants
   Three wonderful beggars

The ferryman
   HARDENDORFF – FROG'S p59-74

Festivals
   See also Feasts
   The boy who made a dream come true
   Francois Villon, the vagabond of Paris
   Get up little horsey
   The great festival
   Here we come, we children come
   Kantjil holds a festival

Festivals (*Continued*)

The magic horse
The melting pot
The ogre king of Gilgit
Potok's dancing and the snakes
The princess and the demon
Princess Nelly and the Seneca chief
A story for Kiem
Why owls see only at night
Young hunter

Feuds
The tale of a debt repaid

A few lost bones
  WILLIAMS – LOST p1-6

A few lost ladies
  WILLIAMS – LOST p108-116

Fiammenghi, Giolia
  SHERLOCK – IGUANA's p98.

Fianna (Fians). *See* under **Finn MacCool**

The Fians asleep in the Great Rock
  WILSON – SCOTTISH p205-207

Fickle Miss Frog
  HEADY – TALES p95-100

Fickleness
  The wooing of Lottie Moon

The fickleness of fortune
  GRAY – INDIA'S p197-201

Fiddivaw
  HATCH – MORE p138-149

The fiddle
  MANNING – GLASS p122-125

Fiddler John and the devil
  DURHAM – TIT p96-106

The fiddler going home
  MANNING – GIANNI p173-178

The fiddler of Echternach
  U. N. – RIDE p169-172

The fiddler of Fiddler's bridge
  JAGENDORF – UPSTATE p125-131

Fiddlers. *See* **Violinists**

The fiddlers of Strathspey
  SHEPPARD – SCOT. p32-37

Fidelity. *See* **Loyalty**

Field, Eugene
  Fairy and child
  The sugar-plum tree
  Wynken, Blynken, and Nod

Field, Rachel
  A charm for spring flowers
  Old Gally Mander
  Snow in the city
  Something told the wise geese

Field mouse and house mouse
  WILSON – GREEK p28-30

The field of Boliauns
  WILLIAMS – FAIRY p135-139

The field of ragwort
  MANNING – DWARFS p38-41

Fields and streams
  The barren stones
  The cock is crowing
  The cock's on the housetop
  The giant Holiburn
  Laughing song
  Little Boy Blue
  Little Peppino
  The milkman and the monkey
  A Swedish evening
  White fields
  Willie boy, Willie boy

Fiends
  See also **Bugganes; Demons; Devils;**
  etc.
  The feathered fiend
  Tregeagle

Fiery-tempered Jake
  JAGENDORF – UPSTATE p132-136

Fiesta for mountain men
  FELTON – NEW p119-126

Fiestas. *See* **Festivals**

Fifes
  Bang–whang–whang
  The magic fife

The fifty-one thieves
  SECHRIST – ONCE p189.

Fifty red night-caps
    WILLIAMS – FAIRY p9-10

The fig bough
    MICHAEL – PORTUGUESE p42-49

The fig tree
    COTHRAN – MAGIC p66-68

Fig trees and figs
    Aruman, a hero of Java
    Behold the fig tree
    The bird which laid diamonds
    The child and the fig
    The chili plant
    Dinner for the monk
    Ero and the tsar
    The flying angel
    Gizo's counting trick
    The magic bird
    The tale of the little mook
    The three figs
    A yard of nose

The fight between the octopus and the whale
    GREY – SOUTH (1) p13-14

The fight with crazy man
    DAVIS – LION'S p85-88

The fight with Ferdia
    O'FAOLAIN – IRISH p67-75

The fight with Wabun
    LEEKLEY – WORLD p100-110

The fighting rams
    CREDLE – TALL p82-88

Fights and fighting
    See also Quarreling
    Annie Christmas
    The cricket fight
    The giants of Towednack
    Mike Fink
    A story about Our Lord Jesus Christ
    The tiger who understood people

The figurehead
    LAWSON – STRANGE p132-140

Figureheads
    LAWSON – STRANGE p130-140

Fiji Islands
    The boy who was caught by a clam
    The woman who wanted to cook
        with salt water

Filibusters
    Henry Crabb – a born loser

Filipinos. See Philippine Islands

Fill, bowl! Fill!
    ARBUTHNOT – TIME p175-176

Fillan, Saint
    The Holy relic of Bannockburn

Fillmore, Parker
    Katcha and the devil

Fin. See Finn MacCool

Fin M'Coul and Cucullin
    MANNING – GIANTS p25-31

The finch with the golden voice
    ILLYES – ONCE p69-73

Finches
    How the finch got her colors

The finding of the Eleanba Wunda
    PARKER – AUSTRALIAN p45-48

Findings are keepings
    PICARD – LADY p33-40

A fine cheese
    LEACH – NOODLES p36.

The finest liar in the world
    LANG – VIOLET p17-21

Fingal. See Finn MacCool

Finger, Charles J.
    The hungry old witch
    The magic ball

Finger games
    Here's the church

Finger never says 'Look here'; it always says 'Look yonder'
    CHAPPELL – THEY p53-58

Fingernails
Cut them for health
The louse and the fingernail
Maui and the fire goddess

Fingers
Clever Oonagh
The fish with bent noses
The giant in the cave
A long one and a short one
The story of the five fingers
The ten dwarfs of Aunt Greenwater

Fink, Mike
River roarer/Mike Fink

Finland
The bear says north
The boots that never wore out
The courtship of Lemmkinkäinen
The forest bride
Ilmarinen . . . how he won his bride
Kalevala, land of heroes
Mary, Mary, so contrary!
Mighty Mikko
Olli and the rich troll
Something wonderful
The terrible Olli
The three chests
Wainamoinen finds the lost-words
Why the fish do not speak
The world's great epics

"Finlandia"
Kalevala, land of heroes

Finlay the giant killer
McNEILL – DOUBLE p95-104

Finlay the hunter
WILLIAMS – FAIRY p272-283

Finn and the Fianna
O'FAOLÁIN – IRISH p139-141
SUTCLIFF – HIGH p26-33

Finn and the grey dog
SUTCLIFF – HIGH p46-56

Finn and the young hero's children
LINES – TALES p204-209
SUTCLIFF – HIGH p34-45

Finn MacCool (including Fianna)
The battle of Gavra
The beginning of the Fians
The birth and boyhood of Finn
The birth of Oisin

The carl of the drab coat
Ceatach
The chase of Slieve Gallion
Clever Oonagh
The coming of Finn
The coming of Fionn MacCool
The coming of Oscar
Conan's punishment
Dearmid and Grania
The death of Dearmid
Dermot and Grania
The Fiana asleep in the Great Rock
Fin M'Coul and Cucullin
Finn and the Fianna
Finn and the grey dog
Finn and the young hero's children
Finn MacCool
Finn MacCool, the giants and the
    small men
Fionn in search of his youth
Fionn's journey to Lochlan
The giolla dacker and his horse
The green isle
The horses of the Fianna
The hostel of the quicken
The house of the rowan trees
How Finn became head of the Fianna
How Finn Maccumhail was in the house
    of the rowan tree without power to
    stand or leave or sit down
How Finn won his father's place
How Fionn found his sword
The king who could not sleep
A legend of Knockmany
The lordship of the Fianna
The mother of Oisin
Niamb of the golden hair
Oisin in the land of the ever young
Oisin, son of Finn MacCool
Oisin's mother
Prince Finn the fair
The pursuit of Dermot and Grania
The pursuit of the hard man
The return of Oisin
The sea captain
The tale of the lay of the smithy
The tale of the sons of Cathmor
Tales from the Episode of the Fians
The young Finn

Finn MacCool
PICARD – HERO p83-96

Finn MacCool, the giants and the small
men
O'FAOLÁIN – IRISH p235-242

Finvarra
MORAY – FAIR p177-193

Fionn in search of his youth
O'SULLIVAN – FOLK. p57-60

204

Fionn. *See* Finn MacCool

Fionn's journey to Lochlan
WILSON – SCOTTISH p178-184

Fior Usga
PILKINGTON – SHAM. p150-152

Fir cones
MANNING – DWARFS p125-128

Fir trees
Little fir tree

Firdusi (Abul Kasim Mansur)
A story of Rustem, the hero of Persia

Fire
See also **Arson**
The antelope and the spider
The bat and the turtle
A beautiful young woman as the head
of the family
The birth of the islands
Bukolla
Cat and dog
The cuckoo's reward
The dancing fires of Saint Elmo
Don't beat your dog
Fair Vasilissa and Baba Yoga
Fiddivaw
The first fire
The first mosquito
The fruits of health
The great flood
The half-chick
Here, forest-fires
How animals brought fire to man
How Cormac MacArt got his branch
How fire was brought from lightning
How frogs lost their tails
How Mackay first brought fire into
the world
How mankind learned to make bread
How men brought fire to earth
How men learned to make fire
How people got fire
How rabbit deceived fox
How rabbit stole fire from the
buzzards
How raven brought fire to the Indians
How the beaver lost the hair on his
tail
How the earth's fire was saved
How the little owl's name was changed
How the people got fire
How the raven brought the fire
How the robin's breast became red
How the village of Pivanhonkapi per-
ished

Ironhead
John the blacksmith destroys the
wasps in the straw
The judgement of Hailu
The Kamiah monster
The land beyond the fire
The lemur and the shrew
The little bird's rice
The magic ball
The magic ring
Maui and the fire goddess
Maui the fire-bringer
Maui the Great
The mistress of fire
Mullian-ga the morning star
Naba Zid-Wende'
Nananbouclou and the piece of fire
Nicola Pesce
Nooloigah and the fire
The ogre king of Gilgit
Old master and okra
The old women who were turned into
birds
The phantom fire ship
The planting party
The rescue of fire
The shepherd with the curious wife
Shlemiel, the businessman
The stone memorial to a dog
A story about Our Lord Jesus Christ
Tam Lin
The task of the Minister Abe-no-Miushi
The theft of fire
The trials of Ting Ling
The twelve months of the year
Vasilia the beautiful
When the rooster was king of the cats
Why animals are afraid of fire
Why chicken lives with man
Why fly rubs his hands together
Why the animals have no fire
The wicked house of Duncan Macbain
Wind and wave and wandering flame
The young head of the Cheng family

Fire, a story of the Alabama Indians
LEACH – RAINBOW p289.

Fire, a story of the Toba Indians
LEACH – RAINBOW p301.

Fire and the moon
JABLOW – MAN p18.

Fire and water, truth and falsehood
COURLANDER – FIRE p119-120

The fire boy
SEKI – FOLKTALES p70-77

The fire bringer . . . Prometheus
CATHON – PERHAPS p12-17

The fire dogs
INS-SOB – FOLK p11.

Fire engines
The pert fire engine

Fire goddess
The ice ship in the hot sea

Fire magic and the mud hen
CARPENTER – ELEPHANT'S p204-211

"Fire of Need"
The farmer and the fairy hillock

The fire on the mountain
See also Janot cooks for the emperor
COURLANDER – FIRE p7-13
U. N. – RIDE p106-111

The fire plume
SCHOOLCRAFT – FIRE p77-89

Fire, water, and honor
LEEUW – INDO. p58-60

Fire worshippers
Rescue from the fire worshippers

Fireballs
For love of a woman
How the raven brought light to the world

The firebird
ALMEDINGEN – RUSS. p48-69
DOWNING – RUSSIA p205-217
DUDDINGTON – RUSS. p125-133
WYNDHAM – RUSS. p70-94

The fire-bird, the horse of power, and the Princess Vasilissa
ARBUTHNOT – TIME p142-147

Firebirds
Prince Ivan and the firebird

The firebringer . . . Prometheus
UNTERMEYER – FIRE p9-12

Firecrackers. See Fireworks; Fourth of July

Firedrakes
Prince Prigio
Prince Prigio and the firedrake

Fireflies
The absent-minded king
Anansi and candlefly
The ape and the firefly
The battle of the firefly and the apes
The butterfly's ball
Hiawatha's childhood
How stars and fireflies were made
The moon-maiden
Saint Peter's horses
The three Magi
Twinkling bugs

The firefly
WITHERS – I SAW p90-91

Firefly's story
SHERLOCK – IGUANA'S p68-75

The firemakers
COTHRAN – MAGIC p45-48
PARKER – AUSTRALIAN p61-67

Firemen
Mighty Mose, the Bowery B'hoy

Firewood. See Wood–Firewood

Fireworks
See also Fourth of July
The boy who beat the devil
The flying trunk

First adventures
MY BOOK HOUSE v. 1 p160-161

The first attack
PILKINGTON – THREE p200-208

The first buttercups
CATHON – PERHAPS p141-142

The first fire
SCHEER – CHEROKEE p25-29

The first gods and giants
AULAIRE – NORSE p12-20

The first mosquito
MACMILLAN – GLOOS . p50-57

The first of May
HAVILAND – GREECE p71-81

The first pig and porcupine
MacMILLAN – GLOOS. p110-116

206

The first shlemiel
SINGER − ZLATEH p55-65

The first sorrow of story-telling.
See The quest of the children of
Turenn

The first task: a gourd full of bees. *See*
Tiger story, Anansi story

The first tears
JABLOW − MAN p10.

The first Thanksgiving day
MY BOOK HOUSE v. 5 p113-114b

The first three hundred years
PILKINGTON − THREE p96-102

The first witch's cat
LEEKLEY − RIDDLE p51-55

The first woman to say "Dim"
COURLANDER − OLODE p121-123

The first zebra
ELLIOT − WHERE p53-59

Fish
Anansi and fish country
Anansi and the alligator eggs
The Arabe duck
Are fish buffaloes?
Cast thy bread
The castle of no return
The cat and the dog
A Chinese Cinderella
The clever earthworm
The cook's big fish
The cormorant and the fishes
The crane and the crab
The crane, the fish and the crab
The dance of the fishes
The discontented fish
The double knights
The earth is on a fish's back
The faithful wife
The flood
The four fishes
The frog and the stork
From the head downward
The fruits of health
The girl and the crocodile
The girl out of the egg
The golden-headed fish
The golden nightingale

The grandmother and the crocodile
The great fish
The great fish of Maui
The groach of the Isle of Lok
Hecho the lazy
A holy man and a sacred cow
How a fish swam in the air
How coyote put fish in Clear Lake
How Maui obtained the magic jawbone
How men learned to build houses
How men learned to make fire
How the duyvil gave New Amsterdam
to the English
How to catch a fish
Is fish a brain food?
The jeweled slipper
Keloğlan the kindhearted
The king and the ring
The king of the fishes
A Kupua plays tricks
The land of youth
The length of life
Leviathan and the dutiful son
Leviathan and the fox
Lie-a-stove
The little fish and (the) big fish
The little horse
Lost and found
The magic amber
The magic mare
Mang Jen and his mother
The miller's three sons
Mr. Rabbit steals Mr. Fox's fish
Mythical beast of the sea
Nicola Pesca
The night of the big wind
Noodlehead and the flying horse
The old woman and the fish
The origin of the platypus
Over in the meadow
Peter went fishing on Sunday
The precious stone
The princess with the golden hair
Radowid
The return of the land-otter
Saint Neot
The sea of gold
Sense and money
The sky-eater
The stars in the sky
The stolen jewel
Tam and Tessa
There was a naughty boy
The Three Fates
The twin brothers
Two novices who behaved like a pair
of otters
The water-sprite and the bear
The weary spirits of Lanai
The white snake
Why porpoise is not a fish

Fish (*Continued*)

Why rabbit have short tail
Why spider has a little head and a big behind
Why the fish do not speak
The witch of Lok Island
Young John
The youth who could become an ant, a lion, or an eagle

—Bones
The magic fishbone
The songstress and the fairies
A willow wand and a brocade slipper

—Bream, Red
The dragon king and the lost fish-hook

—Bullhead
Raven and the sun

—Carp
The carp that became a dragon

—Catfish
Catfish and his terrible end
Father catfish
Illinois River tall tale
The lizard and the catfish
The pet catfish
The sad tale of Tom the catfish

—Cod
The goodoo of Wirreebilla
The sacred cod and the striped haddock
Wahn the crow Wirinun

—Devilfish
Old Stormalong
The sculpin and the fox

—Flounder
How Loki outwitted a giant
The lobster and the flounder
The white horse of Volendam
Why flounder's two eyes are on the same side of his face

, Fried
The greedy stallkeeper and the poor traveler

—Gills
The prisoner

, Golden
The peasant and his three sons
The twins

—Goldfish
Clytie
The goldfish

—Grouper
The prisoner

—Haddock
The sacred cod and the striped haddock

—Halibut
The everlasting house

—Herring
Big fox and little fox
The comb, the flute and the spinning wheel
How the herring became king of the sea
The troll's daughter

, Large
Battle with the sockdolager
Tik and Lap and the giant fish

—Mackerel
Bowleg Bill
The comb, the flute and the spinning wheel
The wiliwili trees

—Minnows
The little turtle

—Needlefish
The crab and the needlefish

—Pike
At the pike's command
Foolish Emilyan and the talking fish
Stupid Emilien
The swan, the crab, and the pike
The three princesses of Whiteland

—Porgy
The carp that became a dragon
The eel and the porgy

—Salmon
The cold May night
The eagle and the owl
The giant kingfisher of Mount Riga
The giant who had no heart in his body
The great fish
How coyote put salmon in the Klamath River
Itsayaya and the otter
Itsayaya frees the salmon
Khasynget's grandmother
The magic fishbone
The quest for Olwen (4) Fulfilling the tasks 2/ The oldest animals

, Salted
Never trust an eel

208

Fish *(Continued)*

−Scales
The story of a good boy
Unlucky Mussah

, Silver
The goldifsh
The master mariner
The seven wishes

−Snapper, Red
The jewels of the sea

−Sturgeon
The giant sturgeon
Jonas and the sturgeon
Khasynget's grandmother
Sadko
The tale of Anthony's nose

, Talking
The talking fish

−Tarpon
The sea-mammy

−Trout
The adventures of a water baby
The battle of the birds and the
fish
Diamond Jim and Big Bill
The hungry trout
Over in the meadow
The tale of a watch
The tame trout
The white trout

The fish and the ring
REEVES − ENGLISH p35-48

Fish-hawks
The girl who always cried

Fish-hooks
The dragon king and the lost fish-
hook
How Maui fished up New Zealand
The jewels of the sea
The luck of the sea and the luck of
the mountain
Maui the fire-bringer
Maui−the trickster

The fish maid
ILLYES − ONCE p180-185

Fish nets
Kahukura and the fairy fishermen

Fish story
WITHERS − WORLD p29.

The fish thief
SEKI − FOLKTALES p3-4

The fish with bent noses
CARPENTER − ELEPHANT'S
p22-30

Fish with the rolls
GREEN − BIG p24.

Fisher, Anne B.
How the first rainbow was made

Fisher, Leonard Everett (illus.)
FELTON − WORLD'S p151.

The fisherlad and the mermaid's ring
LEODHAS − THISTLE p119-135

The fisherman
COURLANDER − KING'S p22-24

The fisherman and his soul
HOKE − WITCHES p125-168

The fisherman and his wife
ARBUTHNOT − TIME p54-58

The fisherman and the genie
MOZLEY − ARABY p38-45

The fisherman and the king's chamberlain
AUNG − KINGDOM p34-38

The fisherman and the mermaid
SHEPPARD − WELSH p1-5

The fisherman and the seal maid
SHEPPARD − SCOT. p145-149

The fisherman who caught the sun
MY BOOK HOUSE v. 6 p198-200

The fisherman's son
HACK − DANISH p1-12
MANNING − BEASTS p39-44

The fishermen
COURLANDER − PIECE p64-69

Fishermen and fishing
See also Fish; Ice fishing; Whales and
whaling
The adventures of Kahukura and Te
Kanawa, the Little People of
Polynesia
Agagayk and the strangest spear
The animal wife
Basia, the babbler
The blue cap

Fishermen and fishing (*Continued*)

The boy of the red twilight sky
The boy who fished for the moon
A bride for the sea god
The butterfly in the granary
The cat and the dog
The ceabharnach
Charles Loon
The child from the sea
The city under the sea
The clever earthworm
The coral comb
The crystal of love
Disobedient Hawa
The dragon king and the lost fish-hook
Drowning the eel
The enchanted island
The fairy funeral
The fire plume
The firemakers
The flying spirits of Niihau
For love of a woman
The fountain of youth
The four abdallahs
The fox and the hare in winter
The frog and his clothes
The ghostly fisherman
Golden
The golden candelabra
The golden crab
The goldifsh
Goolay-yali the pelican
The great fish
Green parrot's story
The half-pint jinni
A holy man and a sacred cow
How Maui fished up New Zealand
How Maui fished up the island
How spider helped a fisherman
How the black turnstone came to
nest near the sea
How Ysengrin the wolf was taught to
fish
The jewels of the sea
Jonas and the sturgeon
Kahukura and the fairy fishermen
The king of the fishes
The king's true children
The Lambton worm
The lark, the wolf, and the fox
The lass and her good stout black-
thorn stick
The laughing merman
The legend of Urashima
Lionbruno
The little footprints
The little grey man
Lost in memory
MacCodrum of the seals
The magic mango

The magic veil
A man, a snake, and a fox
The man who helped carry the coffin
The man who nearly became fishpaste
The man who was always borrowing
and lending
The master mariner
Maui—the trickster
Men of the sea
The mermaids and the simpleton
The merman's revenge
Nefyn the mermaid
A new way of tamin' wolves
Nicola Pesca
O well for the fisherman's boy
The old man and his fishing line
Old man Kurai and the one-eyed giant
The old man of Cury
The old tiger and the hare
The otters and the fox
The oyster and the heron
The princess and the fisherman
The princess of Centerbury
The return of the land-otter
Reynard and the fisherman's dream
Row, row! A-fishing we'll go!
The sacred fish of Polaman
Saint Michael and the idle husband
The sea of gold
The seal fisher and the roane
The seven dead men of the Venetian
lagoon
The seven wishes
Sketco begins his wanderings
Stine Bheag o'Tarbat
Sumlee's broken stick
The sun-king's hair
The tale of a watch
Tell Barney Beal
Tepozton
That fellow
Three eels
The three fish and the fishermen
The three golden hairs
The three golden hairs of Grandad Sol
The three little men in the wood
The toad-bridegroom
The tortoise and the lion
The tortoise-wife
A toy princess
The troll's bride
Twelve great black cats and the red
one
The twins
Undine
The unlucky fisherman
Urashima
Urashima Taro
Urashima Taro and the princess of the
sea
Where to lay the blame

210

Fishermen and fishing (*Continued*)
The white horse of Volendam
Why the bear has a stumpy tail
Why the bear is stumpy-tailed
Why the bear's tail is short
Why the crocodile hates man
The year of Nyangondhu's cattle
Yiankos
Young Gim and the robbers
Young Michael and the uninvited
guest
The youth who could become an ant,
a lion, or an eagle

Fishers (birds)
The summer birds

The fishes and the wolf
DOBBS – MORE p66-67

Fishing for a chicken
MINCIELI – TALES p46-48

Fishing for pots in the pond
JAGENDORF – GYPSIES p134-145

The fishnet and the bear
HEADY – TALES p29-31

Fitzgerald, Earl
Earl Fitzgerald in the enchanted
hill

Five dozen eggs
LEACH – NOODLES p69.

Five drowned
LEACH – RAINBOW p208-209

The five eggs
U. N. – RIDE p217-219

Five fathoms tall/Stormalong
STOUTENBURG – AMER. p37-50

The five friends
BELTING – CAT p90-95

Five in a glove
BAMBERGER – FIRST p17-19

The 500 hats of Bartholomew Cubbins
ARBUTHNOT – TIME p296-302

Five lies that could be true
TOOZE – WONDER. p121-124

Five little chicks
MY BOOK HOUSE v. 1 p64.

Five loaves
CREANGǍ – FOLK p120-125

The five swallow sisters
MARTIN – COYOTE p46-49

The five tiger general
BONNET – CHINESE p49-56

(The) five wise words
LANG – OLIVE p56-65
SIDEMAN – WORLD'S p252-264

The five young men
McALPINE – JAPAN. p136-140

Fjords and mountain peaks
MY BOOK HOUSE v. 12 p187-189

Flags
The blind man and the devils
George Washington and the first
American flag
The princess who was rescued from
slavery

Flamebirds
About Jan the Prince, Princess Wonderface, and the flamebird

Flaming tales
JAGENDORF – GYPSIES p148-151

Flamingos
The crane's report
The crow and the flamingo
The crow's reward
The exile of Rama
The magic ball
The peacock bridegroom

Flash-of-the-paddle and Listener-to-the-
heavenly-voice
WHEELER – HAWAII. p49-69

Flatboats
The boatman he's a lucky man
A story about Abe Lincoln

Flattery
The adventurous winnower
Chanticleer . . . his strange dream
The crow and the fox
The crow in the rose-apple tree
The fox and the cock
The fox and the crow
The giant elephant
The hawk and the wildcat

211

Flattery (*Continued*)

King Canute on the seashore
The long-eared cat and the vulture
The raven and the crow
The raven and the fox
The tale of Chanticleer

Flax
The bride-prince for Olwen
Feathers and flax
How the queen of the sky gave gifts
to men
—Seed
The quest for Olwen (4) Fulfilling
the tasks 3/ The lame ant

The flea
HAVILAND – SPAIN p3-17
ROSS – BURIED p43-53

Fleas
Anansi and candlefly
The bedbug, the house, and the flea
The bird of the golden land
Constantes and the dragon
Coyote and mole
The frogs of yonder mountain cry
How raven brought fire to the Indians
The hunger time
The jumping contest
The little milleress
The little turtle
The mouse and the flea
The song of the flea
Tropsyn
Tsar Boris and the devil king
Why the flea hops
Why the flea jumps

Fleece, Golden. *See* **Golden fleece**

The fleeing deer
REED – TALK. p48.

Flies
See also some titles beginning with Fly
Abunuwas the wit
Baby Bye, here's a fly
Beaver moon
The brave little tailor
Donal O'Ciarin from Connaught
A dozen at a blow
The foolish lad and the flies
The fox who was not so smart
Freya's wonderful necklace
The friendly frog
The gardener and the bear
The horsefly

How Au Sung repaid Kim Lee
How the lizard lost and regained his
farm
Hyena and the oil with the flies in it
The liars' contest
The man who struck his father
Nabookin
Nazar the brave
The old lady who swallowed a fly
That is why he was always called Pooh
The three lucky charms
Tola and the sea monster
Two pieces of meat confuse the mind
of the fly
Why fly rubs his hands together
Why the bush-fowl calls at dawn and
why flies buzz

The flight
BAKER – GOLDEN p131-134
PILKINGTON – THREE p156-164

The flight of the animals
GAER – FABLES p123-126

The flight with the Wendigo
LEEKLY – WORLD p92-99

Flint
Esben and the witch

Flint bird
RUSHMORE – DANCING p7-21

Flinty
BUDBERG – RUSSIAN p201-212

Flip a coin
BATCHELOR – SUPER. p54.

The flitting of the ghosts
LEODHAS – TWELVE p51-69

The flood
LEEKLEY – WORLD p35-49
REED – TALK. p79-82

The flooding of the Lower Hundred
SHEPPARD – WELSH p131-133

Floods
The black cat of Cotabato
The cat and the sea
Count Bertrand
Dwarf stories
Eight leaves of story (2) The sigh of
Gwyddno Long-shank
The frog heralds
The giant who counted stones
The giant who rode on the ark
The gold table
The great flood
The home of the saints

212

Floods (*Continued*)

How coyote brought back people
    after the flood
How the coconut tree was saved
How turkey got his white tail
Irraweka, mischief-maker
The lost city of Ys
The magic ruby
The making of the earth
Noah's ark
The oxen and the afanc
The quellers of the flood
The rain god's reprisal
Raven and the sun
The sea-maiden who had a stone image
    for husband
The serpent prince
Spring flood
The terrible-tempered dragon
The valley of 10,000 waterfalls
The warning from the gods
The wedding of the dragon-god
The weeping lady of Llyn Glasfryn
The year of the feast at Simbi
The yellow dragon

Floors
Not to care a straw

Florian
The horse and the colt
The mole and the rabbits

Florida
The milky way
Mosquitoes
Odds and ends
To feed my people: The coming of
    corn

Florida
    LEACH — RAINBOW p79-80

Flour
Per and the north wind
The two millers

The flower faces
    HODGES — SEREND. p117-137

The flower-headed man
    ILLYES — ONCE p163-169

Flower moon
    BUDD — FULL p23-27

The flower of beauty
    EELS — SPAIN p143-157

A flower to catch a thief
    ROBERTSON — FAIRY p36-43

The flower without a name
    FARJEON — LITTLE p36-39

Flowers
Becky's garden
Blodeuedd and the slaying of Llew
A charm for spring flowers
Crocus flowers bloom like fire
The dutiful daughter
Each little flower that opens
The friendly frog
The great festival
How summer came to Canada
In those days
Jorinda and Joringel
A legend of the flowers
The legend of the mulberry tree
Little bells, pretty flowers of the
    steppes
The man who loved flowers
A milkweed and a buttercup
Mr. Noy
No flowers
Odd Olle
The old man of the flowers
Peboan and Seegwun
The poor girl who stepped out
    golden flowers
Pretty flowers of the steppes
Rosy Posy
The shepherd and the princess
The shepherd's nosegay
Spring flowers
The tale of Bat
The three butterflies
Where are my roses?
The winter flower
Young Kate
, **Artificial**
The wise king and the little bee
, **Blue**
Forget-me-not!
, **Golden**
The beauty and her gallant
The danced-out shoes
The golden bird
—**Pots**
Cenerentola
—**Sellers**
The feather of Finist the falcon
The legend of the mulberry tree
, **Silver**
The king's dream
—**Spirits**
The story of Maia

The flute made of maple-wood
ILLYES – ONCE p90-92

Flutes and flutists
Abdune and the friendly snake
About Jan the Prince,
Princess Wonderface, and the
flamebird
The black prince
The black stone
The blackbird and the pine needle
The boy who played the flute
Clever little turtle
The comb, the flute and the spinning
wheel
The coming of Fionn MacCool
The crystal of love
Damian and the dragon
The giant of the brown beech wood
Goat's ears
The golden horse
How rabbit deceived fox
The jinni's magic flute
John the painter
The lamb with the golden fleece
The land of youth
The miraculous flute
Musk and amber
Odd Olle
The orchestra
The prince and the sky-blue filly
The prince of the seven golden cows
Quinces and oranges
The ram with the golden fleece
The rescue of fire
The singing flute
The story of Hinemoa
The story of Hine-Moa and Tutanekai
The swineherd who married a
princess
The three flutes are in the flute house
The three musicians
To your good health
The witch and the swan maiden

The fly
CATHON – PERHAPS p82.
VO-DINH – TOAD p99-104

Fly again, my proud eagle
HARRIS – ONCE p113-148

The fly and the bee
BAMBERGER – FIRST p33-35

Fly catchers, Scissor-tailed
Bird of power

Flying
See also **Aviation**
Anansi and turtle and pigeon

The boy on a broomstick
The flight of the animals
Journey by broomstick
The Namashepani
The tree that flew
Why Kwaku Ananse stays on the
ceiling
Witch flights
A witch's song
The wonderful wooden peacock fly-
ing machine
The wonderland of an artist's work-
shop
The wren
The young fox and the old fox

The flying angel
MINCIELI – TALES p40-43

The flying castle
ILLYES – ONCE p42-59

"Flying Dutchman"
The ghost ship

The Flying Dutchman
LAWSON – STRANGE p17-23

The flying horse, Pegasus
CARPENTER – HORSES p64-74

The flying kettle
WITHERS – WORLD p84.

The flying ship
ALMEDINGEN – RUSS. p70-81
BUCK – FAIRY p129-137
HAVILAND – RUSSIA p66-86

The flying spirits of Niihau
THOMPSON – LEGENDS p9-13

The flying trunk
TUDOR – TASHA p43-46

The flying turtle
GREEN – BIG p196.

Flying with witches
HOPE-SIMPSON – CAVAL. p82-84

Flyleaf scribblings
JOHNSON – WHAT p196-205

Foals. *See* **Horses**

Fodder
Soonimaya

The foe in the dark
JAGENDORF – UPSTATE p80-83

Fog
Borrowed arrows
The borrowing of 100,000 arrows
The corsair of Spouting Horn
The harbor
Shingling the fog
Wampum eater and the canal

The fog
HEADY – TALES p21-24

The fog, by Carl Sandburg
MY BOOK HOUSE v. 1 p184.

The foggy stew
FELTON – TRUE p24-29

Folk songs
The Arkansas fiddler
The battle of Kossovo
The battle of Mishar
The beginning of the Serbian uprising
against the Turks
The boll weevil
The brothers Yakshich divide their
heirloom
The building of Ravanitsa
Building the bridge
The crocodile's mouth
The death of the Yugovichi's mother
Derby ram
The fall of Serbia
The gray goose
Ivan of Semberiya
Ivo Senkovich and Aga of Ribnik
The kind pasha and Mehat the shepherd
King Vukashin's wedding
Kralyevich Marko
Kralyevich Marko abolishes the
wedding-tax
Kralyevich Marko and Alil-Aga
Kralyevich Marko and Mina Of Kostur
Kralyevich Marko and Mussa
Kassedzhiya
Kralyevich Marko and the Arab
Kralyevich Marko and the eagle
Kralyevich Marko's death
Kralyevich Marko's ploughing
Kralyevich Marko's wedding
Little Radoyitsa
Maksim Tsernoyevich's wedding
Milutin, Tsar Lazar's servant
Noah's ark
Old Hiram's goat
Old Novak and the village elder,
Bogossav
Outlaw Vukossav's wife
Pa Grumble
Paul and the robber
The raggle, taggle gypsies

The rise and decline of the Serbian
kingdom
Serbian knights and outlaws
The sick Doytchin
The sow got the measles
Strawberry roan
Sultan Murat's challenge
The swapping song
Sweet Betsy from Pike
Tsar Dushan's wedding
Tsar Lazar and Tsaritsa Militsa
Tsar Lazar's supper
Urosh and his uncles
What Ivan Kossantchich saw in the
Turkish camps
When I was a baby

Folk-tales (Skazki)
DOWNING – RUSSIAN p97-229

Folks
JOHNSON – WHAT p68-69

Fomorians (people)
The defeat of the Fomorians
How the Fomorians came into Erin

Food
See also names of food
Animal crackers
Any more food?
Bouki gets whee-ai
The bungling host
The clever bride of Tunisia
A contest with skillful spirits
Does food cause bad dreams?
Donkeys! Dogs! Cats! Rats!
Eat your carrots
The fall of the spider man
The first zebra
The gun, the pot, and the hat
Hatchet Kasha
Household spirit brings food
Hwan and Dang
The king who slept
The magic egg
The magic horns
The man who paddled to the moon's
house
The man who wanted to bury his son
Minute pudding
Musakalala, the talking skull
The never never land
New Year's hats for the statues
Okraman's medicine
Old Bluebeard
The old woman and the tramp
The Pleiades
The princess who loved her father the
best

Food (*Continued*)

Rabbit and the Indian chief
The red king and the witch
St. Francis and the wolf
Salvador and the coyote
The smell of money for the smell of
    food
The stone stew
Sun, moon, and morning star
The tale of the land of Cockaigne
Tit for tat
The tsar's son-in-law and the winged
    old woman
The two misers
An unsolved riddle
Why the dog is the friend of man
The wolf

Food
    BATCHELOR – SUPER. p9-18

The fool
    MASEY – STORIES p132-139

The fool and the birch-tree
    DOWNING – RUSSIAN p172-175

The fool of God
    LEEKLEY – RIDDLE p73-91

The foolish ass
    WILSON – GREEK p88-89

The foolish Brahman
    GRAY – INDIA'S p212.

The foolish dog
    BLOCH – UKRAIN. p68-72

The foolish dog and his reflection
    STRONG – FAVORITE p92.

The foolish dragon
    DOBBS – ONCE p15-18

Foolish Emilyan and the talking bird
    WYNDHAM – RUSS. p12-30

The foolish father-in-law
    JABLOW – MAN p67-70

The foolish jackal
    GAER – FABLES p134-136

Foolish kings
    VANSITTART – DARK p19-29

The foolish lad and the flies
    LOWE – LITTLE p36-37

The foolish man
    TASHJIAN – ONCE p3-10

A foolish mourner
    INS-SÖB – FOLK p193-194

The foolish, timid, little hare
    MY BOOK HOUSE v. 3 p76-80

The foolish wife and her three foolish
daughters
    HAVILAND – GREECE p29-37

The foolish wolf
    DOBBS – MORE p75-80

The foolishness of Cochinito
    ROSS – MEXICO p35-49

Fools and foolishness
See also Clowns; Trickery
The alchemist
Are fish buffaloes?
Bardiello
Bastianelo
Big Hermel
The blacksmith's dilemma
The bobtail monkey
The boy and the cloth
The boy who was called "thick-head"
Bungling Pedro
The castle in the cornfield
Changing luck
Chestnuts
Clever Elsie and her companions
Coat o' clay
The competition of fools
The country swain
The crystal mountain
Cuckoo in the hedge
The day of the scholars
The donkey and the lap dog
The donkey who was an ass
Donkey's eggs
Don't tease the tengu!
Dumb Juan and the bandits
Dummling
The elders of Chelm and Genendel's
    key
The emperor's new clothes
Esben and the witch
A fine cheese
The flying ship
Four brothers who were both wise
    and foolish
Friar Blockhead and the Lord
The ghost of Haniesh MacDonald, the
    fool of the family
Giufà
The goat
The gold-lined donkey

Fools and foolishness (*Continued*)

The golden chain
Gotham way of counting
Grillo
Guno and Koyo
Guno's hunger
Hani the simple
The hare herd
Hare makes a fool of leopard
The harebrained monkey
High diddle diddle, the fool in the
  middle
Hodja and the jumbled jobs
The holes of Lagos
How the dotty Afghan woodman died
How the ghost got in
How the mosquitoes came to Oneata
How the sons filled the hut
How the trivet came home
How Urseli became a princess
I was wondering
The indigo jackal
Introduction (The wisdom and folly
  of women)
The invisible silk robe
Ivan the fool
Jack Hannaford
Jean Sot
The jester who fooled a king
John the blacksmith destroys the
  wasps in the straw
Juan Bobo and the caldron
Juan Bobo and the princess who
  answered riddles
Judge not the vessel
The king and the corn
King Johnny
The lame vixon
Leave well enough alone
Lightening the load
The little fish and the big fish
Little fool Ivan and the little hump-
  back horse
The little priest
The little rabbit who wanted red
  wings
The lost half-hour
The lucky man
The mad man, the dead man, and the
  devil
The magician and his pupil
The man from paradise
Many moons
The mermaid and the simpleton
Mr. Vinegar
The monkey gardeners
Morgan and the pot of brains
Moving the church
Nabookin
Nanny and Conn

Never trust an eel
The nine doves
No supper
Noodlehead and the flying horse
Odd Olle
One mean trick deserves another
Other wise men of Gotham
Otto would a-riding go
The parish bull eats the grass from
  the wall
The peasant and his three sons
Pedro de Males Artes, or clumsy Pedro
Peter Rabbit decides to change his
  name
Poor old cricket!
The poor ploughman and the rich
  nobleman
A pottle o' brains
The princess of Canterbury
The princess on the glass mountain
The princess who wanted to solve
  riddles
Riquet with the quiff
A sad tale of a silly fellow
The Scotty who knew too much
The sea of gold
The seven wishes
Shrovetide
Silly John
The silly men of Russia
Silly Saburo
Simple and the princess
The simple-minded bootmaker as a
  miraculous healer
Simple Simon met a pie-man
The simpleton
A simpleton of the family
Simpleton Peter
Simpletons
Sing something
Six sillies
Smart Sam'l Danny
Sofo's escape from the leopard
Stealing the bell
The story of silly Cham-ba
The story of the boy who couldn't
  keep anything in his head
The straight and narrow way
Stretching the bench
Stupid Emilien
The stupid fellow
Stupid Peruonto
The sultan's fool
A tale of a boy who set out to learn
  fear
The tale of a foolish brother and of a
  wonderful bush
The tale of the silver, golden, and
  diamond prince
Tall tales from the Gotham Inn
Telling the horses apart

Fools and foolishness (*Continued*)

They hide a bell
They protect their seed
This is how it began
The three feathers
Three foolish brides
Three foolish wives
Three fools
Three men on the bridge
The three sillies
Three silly schoolmasters
The tinker and his wife
Tony Di-Moany
The town of fools
The tree that flew
The troll's daughter
The true lord of the merry men of
  Gotham
The turtle who could not stop talking
The two fools
Two novices who behaved like a pair
  of otters
The two sillies
The unusual excuse
Vardiello
Waiting on salvation
The well diggers
What should I have said?
When a man is foolish
Who am I?
Who maketh the dumb to speak
The wisdom and folly of women
A wise man on a camel
The wise men of Chelm
The wolf in the ram's skin
The wonder ship and ship's crew
The wonderful tune

Fool's luck
  LEACH – LUCK p55-56

Fool's paradise
  SINGER – ZLATEH p5-16

A foot and a stick or man is the measure
  LEACH – SOUP p134-140

The foot racers of Payupki
  COURLANDER – PEOPLE p101-114

Footmen
  The little dressmaker

Footsteps
  The little footprints
  The tale of the three footsteps

For a peaceful night
  HOPE-SIMPSON – CAVAL. p210-211

For love of a woman
  TAFT – PROFILE p179-182

Force. *See* **Power; Strength**

Fording the river in a copper cauldron
  JAGENDORF – GYPSIES p170-176

Foresight. *See* **Fortune; Fortune-tellers;
  Prophets and Prophecies**

The forest bride
  FILLMORE – SHEPHERD'S p26-39

The forest wolf and the prairie wolf
  GREEN – BIG p55-56

Foresters. *See* **Woodsmen**

Forests
  The adventures of Alexander Selkirk
  Angus
  As you like it
  Baba Yaga and the little girl with the
    kind heart
  The big warm dog
  The boys who met the trolls in the
    Hedal woods
  Budulinek
  Building the bridge
  The children in the wood
  Christening the baby in Russia
  Datu Omar and the fairy
  Down by the river Avon
  The escape of the animals
  Exploring the wilderness
  Fairy forests
  The faun and the woodcutter's
    daughter
  The foolish, timid, little hare
  The giant of the brown beech wood
  The girl who met the witch of the
    woods
  Hansel and Gretel
  Hansel and Grethel
  The haunted forest
  Hiawatha's childhood
  Hiawatha's fasting
  How Dounai won a bride for Prince
    Vladimir
  How Glooskap made the birds
  How Moremi saved the town of Ife
  How rabbit lost his tail
  The inn in the forest
  Jack and his golden snuff-box
  Jankyn and the witch
  Johnnie and Grizzle
  Jorinda and Joringel
  Katie Woodencloak

Forests *(Continued)*

The King of Araby's daughter
The king of the wood
The knights of the silver shield
The lion of hard-to-pass forest
Little black Sambo
Little Red Riding Hood
Little Tom Thumb
The many children of Mr. and Mrs.
  Twelve
Menaseh's dream
A midsummer night's dream
Mirabella
Mowgli's brother
Olode the hunter becomes an oba
Old Johnny Appleseed
Peer Gynt
Peter and the witch of the wood
Porridge with a troll
The prince who made the silence
  speak
The quarrel about the woods
Red Riding Hood
Robin Hood
The sleeping beauty in the wood
The snake
Stan Bolovan
The story of big Paul Bunyan
The strong boy
The tale about last time
The three brothers
The three clever brothers
The three wishes
The twelve months
The twilight
Two brothers
Una and the Red Cross knight
Vassilissa the beautiful
When woods awake
Why lion lives in the forest
The wood cutter's son and the two
  turtles
The wood of Tontla
Written in the stars
Ye merry doinges of Robin Hood
Young Kate
The young Tamlin

A foretale to the cattle raid of Cooley.
See How Conor MacNessa became King
of Ulster

The foretelling
  PILKINGTON – THREE p127-145

Foretelling the future
  HOPE-SIMPSON – CAVAL. p53.

Foreword
  ROBERTSON – PHILIP. p9-17

Foreword. The witch house still stands
  RASKIN – TALES p7-8

Forget-me-not!
  CATHON – PERHAPS p147.

Forgetfulness. *See* **Memory**

Forgiveness
  See also **Penitence**
  Aruman, a hero of Java
  The black pool
  Cinderella
  Joseph and his brethren
  The melting pot
  The sin of a saint
  The tempest
  Three little kittens
  The winter's tale

The forgotten bride
  WILSON – GREEK p141-147

Forgotten something?
  BATCHELOR – SUPER. p98-99

Forks
  LEACH – SOUP p35-37

Formorians
  The quest of the children of Turenn
  (The first sorrow of story-telling)

Formosa
  The head-hunters

The fort of Rathangan
  GARNER – GOBLINS p35.

The fortunate maiden
  DOWNING – RUSSIA p224-226

The fortunate shoemaker
  HARDENDORFF – TRICKY p33-39

Fortune
  See also **Luck, Good; Wealth**
  The blue flame
  The fickleness of fortune
  The lovebirds
  Making your own
  Rusty Jack
  The tale of the false prince
  The three sons
  The three young maids who went to
    seek their fortunes

A fortune in a stick
  JOHNSON – WHAT p174.

The fortune of the poet's son
SIDDIQUI – TOON. p50-54

Fortunetellers
The blind man and the devils
Bouki cuts wood
Dutch Peter and the fortunetelling
tailor
The grateful devil
The king who tried to cheat des-
tiny
Ooka and the wasted wisdom
Princess Sicilia and the shepherd
The sacred amulet
A sad tale of a silly fellow
The soothsayers
Tea grounds

Fortune telling
JOHNSON – WHAT p30-35

The fortunes of Said
HAUFF – FAIRY p139-193

Forty days hath Ramadan
ZAGLOUL – BLACK p125-128

The forty whoppers
DEUTSCH – FAR p55-64
DEUTSCH – MORE p55-64

Foundlings
See also titles beginning with
Changeling
Lleu and the flowerface
Tepozton
Three wonderful beggars

The fountain
BAMBERGER – FORST p187-188

The fountain of Arethusa
TOOR – GOLDEN p122-125

The fountain of youth
BARBEAU – GOLDEN p90-108

Fountains
Baskets in a little cart
The finch with the golden voice
The pert fire-engine
The princess with the golden hair
The three golden hairs of the king of
the cave giants
Uwaine and the Lady of the fountain
The white parrot

The four abdallahs
MANNING – MERMAIDS p122-128

Four-and-twenty tailors
MY BOOK HOUSE v. 1 p39.

The four brothers
FEINSTEIN – FOLK p42-46

Four brothers who were both wise and
foolish
HAVILAND – SPAIN p18-35

The four deaf men
AUNG – KINGDOM p31-33

The four fishes
MANNING – DAMIAN p29-35

(The) four friends
KOREL – LISTEN p83-89
SIDDIQUI – TOON. p136-139

Four good men
DAVIS – LION'S p92-93

Four-leaf clover
BATCHELOR – SUPER. p3-4

The four-leafed shamrock and the cock
O'SULLIVAN – FOLK. p225-226

The four musicians
ARBUTHNOT – TIME p35-37

Four riddles
U. N. – RIDE p53-58

Four sworn brothers
INS-SOB – FOLK p162-166

Four tales of how the devil was outwitted
MÜLLER – SWISS p213-223

Four tales of Rama and Sita
WILLIAMS – OLD p206-239

Four very skillful people
WITHERS – WORLD p62-63

The four young men
U. N. – RIDE p42-45

Fourth of July
Go ask your mother for fifty cents
How Robert Fulton harnessed the
giant

The Fourth of July
MY BOOK HOUSE v. 5 p113.

The fowler, the parrot and the king
NAHMAD – PEASANT p110-113

Fowlers
Light-O-Leap and the fowler
The storyteller

Fowls. *See* names of fowls

Fox, George, joint author
Disbelief

Fox and raven steal the moon
JABLOW – MAN p39-40

The fox and the bear
UCHIDA – MAGIC p103-111

The fox and the bird
WILSON – SCOTTISH p93-94

The fox and the cat
GREEN – BIG p192-193

The fox and the clever wren
PROTTER – CHILD. p176-177

The fox and the cock
DURHAM – TIT p92.
HARDENDORFF – TRICKY p71-74

The fox and the crane
STRONG – FAVORITE p23.

The fox and the crow
ARBUTHNOT – TIME p225.
LA FONTAINE – FABLES p8-9
STRONG – FAVORITE p34.
WILSON – GREEK p126-128

The fox and the eagle
O'SULLIVAN – FOLK. p6-7

The fox and the geese
BAMBERGER – FIRST p91.

The fox and the grapes
ARBUTHNOT – TIME p207.
GREEN – BIG p15.
STRONG – FAVORITE p81.

The fox and the hare
DUDDINGTON – RUSS. p16-18

The fox and the hare in winter
RANKE – GERMANY p3-4

The fox and the hedgehog
BAMBERGER – FIRST p150-151

The fox and the heron
O'SULLIVAN – FOLK. p3-5

The fox and the lion in partnership
WILSON – GREEK p103-106

The fox and the little bannock
WILSON – SCOTTISH p88-90

The fox and the little red hen
JOHNSON – WHAT p138-139

The fox and the mole
BARLOW – LATIN p62-67

The fox and the quail
MASEY – STORIES p113-115

The fox and the snail
BAMBERGER – FIRST p149-150

The fox and the stork
BAMBERGER – FIRST p161-163
HACK – DANISH p151-163
LA FONTAINE – FABLES p52-53
MONTGOMERIE – 25 p36.

The fox and the thrush
BUDBERG – RUSSIAN p135-136

The fox and the wolf
BAKER – TALKING p71-76
RANKE – GERMANY p5.

The fox and the wolf and the keg of
butter
SHEPPARD – SCOT. p79-84

The fox and the wolf at the wedding
ILLYES – ONCE p60-62

The fox as shepherd
ASBJÖRNSEN – NORW. p106-107
BAMBERGER – FIRST p86-87

The fox-girl and her brother
INS-SOB – FOLK p171-174

A fox in hiding
GREEN – BIG p165.

The fox in Inishkea
O'SULLIVAN – FOLK. p7-8

A fox in saint's clothing
GAER – FABLES p129-132

The fox outwits the lion
WILSON – GREEK p222-223

The fox outwits the tiger
HUME – FAVORITE p67-68

The fox, the hare, and the toad have
an argument
HUME – FAVORITE p23-26

The fox, the wolf, and the horse
LA FONTAINE – FABLES p56.

The fox turns a somersault
HUME – FAVORITE p99-100

The fox who lost his tail
LA FONTAINE – FABLES p58-59

The fox who wanted to whistle
BARLOW – LATIN p18-22

The fox who was not so smart
JAGENDORF – KING p69-71

The fox who was too sly
PRATT – MAGIC unp.

Foxes
  The adder and the fox
  Amin and the ghul
  The art of reading
  Aunt Piety
  Badikan and Khan Boghu
  The battle
  The bear and the fox who made a bet
  Bear, fox, and man
  The bear says north
  Big fox and little fox
  The billy goat and the sheep
  The boy and the fox
  The boy who was called "thickhead"
  The bragging beasts
  Brian and the fix
  Budulinek
  Buh fox's number nine shoes
  Buh rabbit's tail
  The bun
  The bungling host
  The cat and the chanticleer
  The cat and the fox
  The cat, the goose, and the fox
  The cat, the mountain goat, and the
   fox
  Chanticleer and Partlet
  Chanticleer . . . his strange dream
  The clever billy goat
  The clever blue tit and the fox
  Clever–clever–clever
  The clever fox
  The cock and the fox
  The cock, the cat, and the fox
  The cock, the mouse, and the little
   red hen

The cock who went traveling
Crafty crab
The crane and the fox
The crow and the fox
The crow in the banyan tree
The dilemma of a pious man
The dog and the cock
The donkey who was an ass
Don't make a bargain with a fox
Drakestail
The escape of the animals
The fairy quite contrary
The farmer, the bear, and the fox
The fear of the lion king
The feast for the fox
The first pig and porcupine
The fish thief
Five in a glove
The friendly animals
The gingerbread man
The goat in the well
The gold bird
The golden bird
The golden nightingale
Greed in heaven, growth on earth
The hare in the moon
Henny-Penny
The herdsman of Cruachan
The hero in the village
A horned goat
How Ian Deriach got the blue falcon
How rabbit deceived fox
How the fox and the hedgehog be-
  came friends
How the foxes became red
How the little fox went after chaff
How the long-tailed bear lost his tail
How the porcupine outwitted the
  fox
How the wolf lost his tail
How Ysengrin the wolf was taught to
  fish
A hungry wolf
Idy, the fox-chasing cow
The ingrates
Inside again
Itsayaya's revenge
The jewel of the fox's tongue
Johnny and the three goats
Johnny-cake
Journey in a well
The kid and the tiger
King fox
King Kantjil's kingdom expands
The king of the forest
The king's vine
Kuzma get-rich-quick
The lad and his animals
The lad and the fox
The lame vixon

222

Foxes (*Continued*)

Lazarus and the dragons
The lazy fox
Leviathan and the fox
The lion and the fox
The lion and the goat
The lion and the hare
The little fox
The little grey goose
The little house
The magic egg
The magpie and the fox
A man, a snake, and a fox
The man, the serpent, and the fox
The marriage of Tom and the vixen
Master Erik
Mighty Mikko
The miller-king
Mirabella
Mr. Bun
Mister Deer's my riding horse
Mr. Fox learns what trouble is
Mr. Korbes the fox
Mr. Rabbit steals Mr. Fox's fish
Mr. Samson cat
Mrs. Fox's wedding
Mittens the cat
The mountain hen and the fox
The nine-tailed fox
Nothing-at-all
An old Korean story
Old man Kurai and the one-eyed
  giant
Old mother wiggle-waggle
The otters and the fox
The out-foxed fox
Oversmart is bad luck
Pán Kotsky
The partridge, the fox and the hound
Peahens and golden apples
The peasant and the sheep
The perfect husband
Peter Rabbit decides to change his
  name
Pig in the poke
The princess who saw everything in
  her kingdom
Rabbit and the grain buyers
Rabbit, fox, and the rail fence
The rabbit in the moon
The raven and the fox
Reaching an understanding
Redcoat the fox
Reineke fox
Revolt
Reynard and Bruin
Reynard and the fisherman's dream
Reynard the fox
Ruba and the stork
Salakhbai and the fox

The sculpin and the fox
The sea king and the fox
The serpent
The sick lion and the fox
The skinned goat
The song-bird and the healing waters
Soo Tan the tiger and the little green
  frog
The spiteful nanny goat
Squirrel and fox
The stars above: pursuit of the bear
A story about the little rabbits
The straw ox
The struggle between the wolf and the
  fox
The tale of chanticleer
Tar-baby
The theft of fire
Three princes and their beasts
Through the jungle
The traveller and the tiger
The traveller, the fox, and the tiger
The travels of a fox
A trick that failed
The tufty hen
The two-faces
The two foxes
Two women or twelve men
The two youths whose father was
  under the sea
The ungrateful bear
The ungrateful snake
The unlucky goat
Unlucky Mussah
The vixen and the boatmen
The vixen and the rooster
Wee robin's Christmas song
Why the bear has a stumpy tail
Why the bear's tail is short
Why the tip of fox's tail is white
Why the woodchuck comes out in
  midwinter
A wicked fox
The witch and the earthen jar
The witsduks
The wolf and the fox
The wolf, the fox, and the jug of
  honey
The wonderful tar-baby story
The woodcock and the fox
The woodman and the fox
The young fox and the old fox

—Tails
  Fish with the rolls
  The fox and the hare in winter
  The fox who lost his tail
  Why the tip of fox's tail is white

The fox's daughter
ARBUTHNOT — TIME p166-168

France, Anatole
    Catherine's tea party

France, Marie de
    A mouse in search of a wife

France
    About this book
    The adventures of General Tom
        Thumb
    The animals' paradise
    As you like it
    Aucassin and Nicolette
    Aucassin and Nicolette . . . Their
        difficult romance
    The beauty and her gallant
    Beauty and the beast
    The big, big rabbit
    Blue Beard
    The blue foal
    A book-within-a-book; The picture
        story of Perrault's famous French
        fairy tales
    The bridge of St. Cloud
    Catherine's tea party
    The child sold to the devil
    Cinderella
    Cinderella or the little glass slipper
    The cormorant and the fishes
    The crafty servant
    The crow and the fox
    The dancing fires of Saint Elmo
    Diamonds and toads
    The doctor and his pupil
    The dog that fought a duel
    The donkey's egg
    Donkey's eggs
    The dragon of Rhodes
    Drakestail
    The enchanted black cat
    The fairy
    The fairyland of science
    The fox and the grapes
    Francois Villon, the vagabond of Paris
    Georgic and Merlin
    The girl who played a trick on the
        devil
    Goblin gold
    The gold dragoon
    Gulersh and the princess of France
    Hop o' my thumb
    The horse that liked to play tricks
    The hunchback's horse
    The invisible hobgoblin
    The jewel
    Joan of Arc
    Joan of Arc . . . the warrior maid
    John the bear
    The journey to Toulouse of the
        animals that had colds

    The kingdom without a cat
    The knight and the palfrey
    The lady and the toad
    The leg of gold
    The leper's miracle
    Little cricket
    The little gardener with golden hair
    Little Johnny Sheepskin
    The little juggler . . . and the Virgin
    Little Red Riding-Hood
    The love of three oranges
    The maiden in the tower
    The man from paradise
    The master cat
    The midget and the giant
    The miller's four sons
    The miller's three sons
    The mole and the rabbits
    Pappa Greatnose
    Petit Jean and the frog
    The pig, the goat and the sheep
    The princess and the shepherd
    Puss in boots
    La Ramée and the phantom
    The rats in council
    Reynard and the fisherman's dream
    Ricky of the tuft
    Ricky with a tuft
    A Roland for an Oliver
    The self-propelled carriage
    The serpent and the grape-grower's
        daughter
    The sharpshooter
    Simple-minded Jeanne
    The sleeping beauty
    The sleeping beauty in the wood
    The song of Roland
    The strange feathery beast
    The three blue stones
    The three butchers from Reims
    The three enchanted mares
    The three hunters
    The three stags
    The three wasted wishes
    Toto gets married
    The twelve dancing princesses
    The unicorn and the dwarf
    What news? News enough!
    When the bull bellows
    Whistle the wind
    The white cat
    The wise priest
    The wolf in the ram's skin
    The world's great epics
    The young Lord of Lorn

    −Alsace-Lorraine
        The kittel-kittel car

    −Brittany
        The dream of Macsen Wledig
        The little book

France–Brittany (*Continued*)

The story of Ywenec
The werewolf
The widow and the korrigans, the
   Little People of Brittany
The witch of Lok Island

–Normandy
The two lovers

–Paris
François Villon, the vagabond of
   Paris
In Paris there is a street

–Pître
The two lovers

Francis, Saint
St. Francis and the wolf

François Villon, the vagabond of Paris
MY BOOK HOUSE v. 9 p120-128

Francolins (birds)
The hyena's medicine man

Frankenberg, Robert
SCHEER – CHEROKEE p80.

Frankincense trees
The weeping willow

Frankland, Sir Charles Henry
Scandalous affairs of a baronet and a
   tavern maid

Fraud. *See* Dishonesty

Freckles
The village of cream puffs

Freddy and his fiddle
MANNING – DWARFS p14-23

Freddy, the pad dog
MY BOOK HOUSE v. 5 p214-221

Frederick William, King of Prussia
The kingdoms

Free, J. N.
The immortal J. N.

Freedom
Androcles and the lion
Androclus and the lion

The boy of Newstead Abbey
The eagle on a chain
The escape of the animals
The horse without a master
The legend of Tchi-Niu
The messenger donkey
The nightingale and the khan
Princess September
The rebel
The victory of the buffalo
The war of the animals against the
   birds
When the iguana grows armor
The wolf and the dog
The wolf and the watch-dog

French, Allen
Grettir becomes an outlaw
Njal the lawyer

French Canadians
See also Canada, French
Canadian songs
O if my top would only spin

French language
About the good American witch

French nursery rhymes
MY BOOK HOUSE v. 1 p124-125

Frenchmen
See also France
Charley, Barley, Buck and Rye
Donal O'Ciaran from Connaught

Frey and Gerd, the jotun maiden
AULAIRE – NORSE p96-99

Freya's wonderful necklace
AULAIRE – NORSE p84-86

Friar Blockhead and the Lord
JORDAN – BURRO p80-85

The friar on Errigal
O'SULLIVAN – FOLK. p144-149

Friars
Cromwell and the friar
The story of Suka's dog
The viper and the friar's rope

Friday
LEACH – LUCK p44-47

Friday the thirteenth
BATCHELOR – SUPER. p48-49

Fridolin
    MULLER – SWISS p195-199

Friendless pavilion
    KRUEGER – SERPENT p44-49

The friendly animals
    MANNING – BEASTS p164-176

The friendly cow all red and white
    MY BOOK HOUSE v. 1 p159.

The friendly frog
    PERRAULT – COMPLETE p135-162

The friendly mouse
    MONTGOMERIE – 25 p38-40

The friendly sharks
    CARPENTER – SHIPS p139-150

Friends
    JOHNSON – WHAT p44-45

Friends in life and death
    THOMPSON – ONE p147-150

Friendship
    See also Loyalty
    The badger's gratitude
    The beggar in the blanket
    The blue jackal
    The boy and the leopard
    A boy of the Lake country
    Brothers and friends
    The canoe in the rapids
    Cardiff town
    The cat, the dog, and the mongoose
    Catfish and his terrible end
    Chin and Yi
    Cookus, Bopple and Yeakle
    Cuchulain, the hound of Ulster
    Damon and Pythias
    Damon and Pythias; the most faithful
        of friends
    The dappled deer and the intelligent
        crow
    The death of Roland
    The dog's nose is cold
    The dragon of the well
    The elephant and the butterfly
    The faithful friend
    The fight with Ferdia
    The first woman to say "Dim"
    The five friends
    (The) four friends
    The fox and the wolf
    Frithjof, the Viking

    The gardener and the bear
    The grateful mouse
    The hare in the moon
    The Harvard professor
    The hawk's friends
    How men became enemies
    How the bat caught friendship with
        the moon
    How the fox and the hedgehog
        became friends
    In the days of Queen Anne
    The inseparable friends
    The ivory box
    The jackal told me
    The journey to Lagos
    The king's friend
    Life in Concord
    Light-O-Leap and the fowler
    The lion and the mouse
    Magic and friendship
    The magic garden
    Malati and the prince
    The man who missed the Tay Bridge
        Train
    Mr. Hampden's shipwreck
    Momotaro
    Momotaro, the peach boy
    A mother's advice
    The mouse and his friends
    The musical silver goat
    Ooka and the stronger stick
    The outwitted hunter
    Pacala and Tandala
    The prince of the seven golden cows
    The prize
    A Roland for an Oliver
    The six companions
    The song of Roland
    The sparrow whose tongue was cut
        out
    A tale of two mandarins
    Test of a friendship
    The three friends
    Tiger in the forest, Anansi in the web
    The tiny god
    The tiny, tiny man
    A token of friendship
    The tree that flew
    Trust your friends
    The tug of war
    The two friends
    Two friends, coyote and bull snake,
        exchange visits
    Two friends; how they parted
    Two rascals
    The vulture's advice
    The white pet
    A wizard of the twilight

The friendship of the hare and the parrot
    TOOZE – WONDER. p103-106

The friendship of the tortoise and the eagle
BURTON – MAGIC p116-119

Friendship without envy
green - big p118.

Frigate birds
Green parrot's story

Frigg and the goddesses
AULAIRE – NORSE p80-83

The Frisian ride
MÜLLER – SWISS p47-51

Frithiof's journey to the Orkneys
HAZELTINE – HERO p305-315

Frithjof, the Viking
MY BOOK HOUSE v. 10 p130-150

Frobisher, Sir Martin
The curious John Greye papers

Fröding, Gustaf
A Swedish evening

The frog
LANG – VIOLET p186-192
LUM – ITALIAN p22-32
MANNING – BEASTS p142-147
MANNING – PRINCES p84-96
ROSS – BURIED p35-41

The frog and his clothes
EELLS – SPAIN p129-134

The frog and the moon
HOLLADAY – BANTU p83.

The frog and the ox
ARBUTHNOT – TIME p205.

The frog and the stork
TASHJIAN – THREE p41-47

The frog bride
TOOR – GOLDEN p23-27

A frog he would a wooing go
MANNING – BEASTS p138-141

The frog heralds
PARKER – AUSTRALIAN p58-60

The frog jacket
TOOZE – WONDER. p71-73

The frog jumps back in its puddle, even when seated in a golden chair
CHAPPELL – THEY p13-18

The frog-king
ARBUTHNOT – TIME p41-43
THOMPSON – ONE p128-131

The frog prince
HAVILAND – GERMANY p3-12
SIDEMAN – WORLD'S p64-71

The frog princess
DUDDINGTON – RUSS p87-94
PONSOT – RUSSIAN p43-50
THOMPSON – ONE p93-97

The frog that swallowed the ocean
CARPENTER – SHIPS p27-36

The frog, the mouse, and the hawk
JOHNSON – WHAT p243-244

The frog-wife
CURČIJA – YUGOSLAV p170-180

The frog with the golden key
RANKE – GERMANY p34.

Froggie goes a-courting
MY BOOK HOUSE v. 1 p111.

Froggie went a-courting
STOUTENBURG – CROC. p31-33

Frogs
The adventures of Nomvula
Ananse and the king's cow
Anansi and the crabs
The ant and the frog
Bahmoo and the frog
Bahmoo rides the wrong frog
The battle of the frogs and the mice
The black-handed monkey
Bullfrog knows more about rain than
the almanac
The cannibal frogs
The chief of the well
Crossing the river
The czar's frog daughter
Dancing he would go
The duckling's journey
Ekun and Opolo go looking for wives
The fairy frog
Fickle Miss Frog
Five in a glove
The friendly frog
Froggie goes a-courting
Froggie went a-courting

Frogs (*Continued*)

Glooskap's country
The golden snuff-box
The great scare
The green frog
The groach of the Isle of Lok
The hare
The hare's lip
Hei, Jim along Josey
Here we sail so fast and free
How animals brought fire to man
I-know-not-what of I-know-not-where
Jack and his golden snuff-box
Juan and the helpful frog
The king of the frogs
The legend of the star children
The length of life
The little frog of the stream
The little house
The long one
The lost spear
The man who was only three inches
  tall
May it not happen
The miserly frog
Mister frog's dream
The moon and his frog-wife
The mouse and the frog
The northern frog
Nuberu
Nyame's well
Over in the meadow
The owl in the moon
Pakpai and Boto
Petit Jean and the frog
Puddock, mousie and ratton
The puffed-up frog
The rain makers
Reen-reen-reeny-croak-frog
The right time to laugh
The self-kicking machine
Silly John
Smart Dai-adalla
The soldier's return
Son of the long one
Soo Tan the tiger and the little green
  frog
The stone frogs
The story of Harisarman
The story of Maia
The strange battle of Windham
The tale of a frog
The three golden hairs
The three languages
Toontoony pie
The travelling frog
Turkey in the straw
Twins of gold and silver
The two frogs
Vassillissa the wise

The warning of the frogs
The well
The well of the world's end
White-toes and Bushy-bride
Why frogs speak Chinese
Why lizard can't sit
Why the rabbit's nose twitches
The witch of Lok Island
Yung-Kyung-Pyung

—Language
  The cricket fight
  The three languages
  Why frogs croak in wet weather

—Tails
  How frog lost his tail
  How frogs lost their tails
  How tadpoles lost their tales

Frogs in the moon
  JABLOW — MAN p24.
  LEACH — HOW p31-33.

The frogs of Windham town
  JAGENDORF — NEW p202-205

The frogs of yonder mountain cry
  WITHERS — I SAW p130

The frog's saddle horse
  HARDENDORFF — FROG'S p15-16

Frog's wives make ndiba pudding
  COURLANDER — KING'S p58-59

From a moral alphabet
  GREEN — BIG p166-170

From a wayfarer's notebook: eighteenth
century
  IVES — TALES p45-50

From a wayfarer's notebook: nineteenth
century
  IVES — TALES p121-129

From a wayfarer's notebook: seventeenth
century
  IVES — TALES p3-5

From Brownie to boggart
  BRIGGS — PERS. p129-130

From the head downward
  MANNING — PETER p43-47

From tiger to Anansi
  SHERLOCK — ANANSI p3-12

The frontier contest
  MÜLLER — SWISS p60-62

Frontier fighter/Davy Crockett
STOUTENBURG — AMER. p64-76

Frost, Robert
The last word of a bluebird as told
to a child
One guess

Frost
The gift of Father Frost
How summer came to Canada
King Frost and the snow maiden
Master Frost
A matter of importance
The story of King Frost
Where the frost comes from

The frost, the sun, and the wind
DOWNING — RUSSIA p185-186

Frozen girl. *See* Young Charlotte

Frozen music
WITHERS — WORLD p48-49

Fruit
See also names of fruit
The beauty and the beast
The jackal, the barber and the Brah-
min who had seven daughters
The little white cat
The three brothers and the marvelous
things
The wonderful tree

The fruits of health
HATCH — MORE p105-118

Fry, Rosalie K.
The king of the hares

Fuel
See also names of fuels
The woodcutter of Gura

Fulfilling the tasks. *See* The quest for
Olwen

The full moon
LEACH — NOODLES p49.

Full moons
BUDD — FULL p8-11

Fuller, Eunice
Gulliver in the giants' country

Fulton, Robert
How Robert Fulton harnessed the
giant

Funerals
The pious butcher
The queen of the planets
The worthless man of poverty

Funny, funny
BRENNER — BOY p52-58

Fur. *See* **Animals—Fur**

Furies
Orestes and the Furies

Furnaces
Drakestail
Shadrack, Meshach, and Abednego . . .
The fiery furnace

Furniture
Deirdre and the sons of Uisne

A fuzzy fellow without feet
CATHON — PERHAPS p93.

Fyleman, Rose
Why pigs have curly tails

G

Gaberlunzie men
The tale of the Gaberlunzie man

Gabre Manfas, Saint
Saint Gabre Manfas and his animals

Gabriel, blow your horn!
IVES — TALES p131-134

Gag, Wanda, trans.
Doctor know-it-all
The frog prince
The hedgehog and the rabbit
Nothing at all
The sorcerer's apprentice

The galah and Oola the lizard
PARKER — AUSTRALIAN p138-139

Galahad, Sir
The quest of the Holy Grail

Galahad . . . The Holy Grail
UNTERMEYER — FIRE. p177-181

Galaxy
Whistle the winds

Galland, Antoine, trans.
Aladdin and the wonderful lamp
Ali Baba and the forty thieves
The magic carpet

Gallantry
Antar the hero

The Gallas: mounted warriors of high
Africa
DAVIS — LION'S p89-92

Gallows
The fiddler of Echternach
The golden ball
Reynard the fox

Galsworthy, John
April

Gamblers and gambling
Annie Christmas
The battle at White Cliff house
Dog's hoop
The greatest wealth in the world
How horses came to the Navaho
How Juan married a princess
How Sima humbugged a crocodile

The Indian shinny game
Kitava the gambler
Ko-pa-ta, the gambling god
The magician Palermo
Man-eagle
Stackalee
The tengu's magic nose fan
This hound hath loved me
The two-faces

The gambler's wife
SUN — LAND p61-66

The gambling ghosts
LEODHAS — GAELIC p39-45

A game
GARNER — GOBLINS p213-215

The game board
COURLANDER — FIRE p77-80

The game mother
AYRE — SKETCO p136-148

The game of chess
NAHMAD — PORTION p75-77

The game of chess in the mountains
SUN — LAND p120-123

A game of dice
LAWSON — STRANGE p34-42

The game of Tlachtli
WILLIAMS — ROUND p217-222

Games
JOHNSON — WHAT p235-237

Games and rhythms
A-tisket, a-tasket
Baa, baa, black sheep
Bring the comb and play upon it!
Bumblebee and chipmunk
Christian dancing in rural Georgia
Dog's hoop
Drop the handkerchief
The farmer in the dell
The ferryman
Grandmother's tale
Handy-spandy
Hippety hop to the barber shop
Hop, my horsey, leap and spring
How and why: Why the bear waddle:
   when he walks
Hully-gully
It snows and it blows
Jack, be nimble

229

Games and rhythms (*Continued*)

John Brown had a little Indian
Lazy old Mary
The little gray pony
Lucy Locket lost her pocket
Once I saw a little bird
The orchestra
Pease-porridge hot
Peekaboo, I see you!
Pippi plays tag with some policemen
Pop! Goes the weasel!
Pwyll and Pryderi (1) The marriage
  of Pwyll and Rhiannon
Pwyll and Rhiannon
Quaker, Quaker, how is thee?
Ring around a rosy
The swing
Teddy bear, teddy bear
Ten little Indians
Three little kittens
Three old maids a-skating went
The three princesses in the mountain-
  in-the-blue
The turquoise stones
The two wizards
We've come to see Miss Jenny Jones
Where are my roses?
Why dogs carry their tails over their
  backs
A zoo in the park

Gammelyn, the dressmaker
  ROSS – BLUE p81-90

Ganesha
  JACOBSON – LEGEND. p46-47

Gannett, Ruth Stiles
  Tangerina

The gardener and the bear
  GAER – FABLES p39-41

The gardener, the abbot and the king
  MEHDEVI – BUNGLING p109-117

Gardens and gardening
  Arawn
  Becky's garden
  Bostanai
  The boy with the moon on his fore-
    head
  Buh rabbit's graveyard
  A child in a Mexican garden
  Christie and the growing hand
  Dainty little maiden
  Fairy gardens
  The fountain
  How rabbit deceived fox
  How the parrots helped the women
  How the porcupine fooled the
    elephant

The ivory box
The jackal, the barber and the Brahmin
  who had seven daughters
The lazy gardener and the little red
  man
The little gardener with golden hair
The lost gift
The magic fife
The magic garden
The magician's garden
The man who bought a dream
Mary, Mary, quite contrary
A milkweed and a buttercup
The monkey gardeners
My beloved is gone down into his
  garden
The Panditji and the guavas
Pomona . . . The tree and the vine
The princess of Mount Nam-Nhu
The robe
The selfish giant
Señor Billy Goat
Sir Goldenhair
The straight and narrow way
The tale of Peter Rabbit
The three apples
The twelve dancing princesses
The white parrot
Why spiders live in dark corners
The wise old camel

Gardner, Emelyn Elizabeth
  Rusty Jack

Gardner, Gerald
  The power of thought

Gareth and Linette
  LINES – TALES p209-222
  PICARD – STORIES p101-117

Garlic
  Dan-Gun, First King of Korea
  The lemon and his army
  Onions and garlic

Garner, Alan
  How Finn Maccumhail was in the
    house of the Rowan Tree without
    power to stand or leave or sit down
  The secret commonwealth
  Wild worms and swooning shadows

Garuda
  JACOBSON – LEGEND. p23-25

Gate, Ethel May
  The magic sandals

Gate, Ethel May
  JOHNSON – HARPER p320-321

Gates
  Baba Yaga and the little girl with the
    kind heart

231

Gates *(Continued)*

Casperl
The legend of the Arabian magician
The potter and the gate
The white dove of the city of the
swinging gate

Gathering song of Donuil Dhu
MY BOOK HOUSE v. 10 p20.

Gauchos (cowboys)
The eternal wanderer of the Pampas
The little black book of magic

Gawaine and the green knight
PICARD – STORIES p53-64

Gawayne and the green knight
VANSITTART – DARK p105-119

Gay, John
The peacock, the turkey and the
goose
The shepherd's dog and the wolf
The two owls and the sparrow
The wild boar and the ram

Gay, John
Fables and fabulists

Gay go up and gay go down
MY BOOK HOUSE v. 1 p54.

The gay goss-hawk
LEODHAS – HEATHER p61-67

Gaya-dari the platypus
PARKER – AUSTRALIAN p233-236

Gazelles
The girl who lived with the gazelles
Spider and the lion
The tree with the difficult name

Geasas (obligations)
The adventures of Ciad
The golden apples of Loch Erne
The knight of the glen's steed o' bells
Prince Finn the Fair
The sword of light
The well o' the world's end

Geese
Auntie, where are you going?
The bee, the mouse, and the bum-clock
The birds' St. Valentine's day
A boy in the island of Bali
The boy who became a reindeer
The cat, the goose, and the fox
Charlotte's web; Wilbur's boast
The dwarf and the goose
Dwarf long nose
A fair distribution
The five friends
The flying turtle

The fox and the geese
The golden goose
Goose dance
Goosey, goosey, gander
The gray goose
The hardhearted rich man
How Grigori Petrovich divided the
geese
How one should carve a goose
How the sea gulls learned to fly
How the world was made (1)
The hungry time
If so where is the cat?
The journey to Toulouse of the
animals who had colds
The jumping contest
King O'Toole and his goose
The king, the saint and the goose
The lake that flew
Lazy Hans
Little Firenko
The little grey goose
Little Rosa and long Leda
The magic ball
Maximilian and the goose boy
The man who married a snow goose
The mountain that clapped to-gether
The ogre courting
Old Mother Goose
The peacock, the turkey and the goose
The ram and the pig who went into
the woods to live by themselves
Reaching an understanding
The royal geese
St. Cuddy and the gray geese
Shawneen and the gander
The sheep and the pig that made a
home
The silly goose
The singing geese
Smereree
Snout the dwarf
Something told the wise geese
Taper Tom
Tattercoats
The three goslings
Three times lucky
Tiger lily and the dragon
The turtle who could not stop talking
The ugly duckling
The white pet
The wild geese and the tortoise
The wrong song

, Golden
Taper-Tom who made the princess
laugh

The geese
GREEN – BIG p221.

The geese and the golden chain
MANNING – MERMAIDS p98-107

The geese and the swans
BUDBERG – RUSSIAN p177-181

Gems. *See* Jewels; names of jewels, e.g.
Amber

Gems
BATCHELOR – SUPER. p69-73

General Chang's strategy
MAR – CHINESE p43-52

General Chu-Ki Liang
BONNET – CHINESE p105-107

"General" dog and his army
CARPENTER – DOGS p245-255

General Moulton's boot
TAFT – PROFILE p137-141

General Pumpkin
INS-SŎB – FOLK p66-68

Generals
The czar's general and the clever
peasant
Fear, the greatest enemy
The feathers from the bird Venus
The five tiger general
A swift messenger
The tale of the pig
Three times and out
The tiger priest

Generosity
See also Consideration; Kindness
The almond bough
Baa, baa, black sheep
Balder, the god of light
The beautiful weaver and the golden
shell
The best wish
The butterfly in the granary
Cinderella
The cook and the house goblin
A dozen is thirteen
The duty that was not paid
Finn and the Fianna
Freddy and his fiddle
How Beowulf delivered Heorot
How coyote put fish in Clear Lake
The hurt sparrow
Joan of Arc
The knockers of Ballowal
Koi and the kola nuts
The lady's loaf-field
The lairdie with the heart of gold
Life in Concord
Little Freddie with his fiddle
Little girl, little girl
The little rooster and the little hen
The little Sawah

The magic garden
The maiden, the knight, and the
waterfall
The man from Kailasa
The messenger
The miller and the fairies
Mr. Lucky Straw
The most useful tree in the world
The necklace
One good turn deserves another
Pen and four foolish ministers
The plain princess
The puss's tail
Robin Hood
Row, row, a'fishing we'll go!
The royal monument pavilion
The sin of a saint
The snake and the dreams
The soul of the Countess Kathleen
The sparrow whose tongue was cut out
The star florins
A story of three brothers
The story of Wali Dâd the simple-
hearted
There was a little boy
The three brothers and the black hen
The tinner, the dog, the Jew and the
cake
Vladimir's adventures in search of
fortune
Wali Dâd the simple-hearted
The witch
The wonderful knapsack

Genies
Bahram and the snake prince
The banishment of Diab
The enormous genie
The fisherman and the genie
The grateful animals and the talisman
The half-pint jinni
The jeweled slipper
The jinni's magic flute
Keloğlan and the ooh-genie
Keloğlan the kindhearted
The Little People
The magic carpet
The mosquitoes
The Prince Fernando
The princess
The sand-carrier crab
The slave of the lamp

The genii of the hearth
GRAHAM – BEGGAR p33-43

Genius
The long-nosed giant
The magic turban, the magic whip,
and the magic carpet

Gentleness
  Cinderella
  The cobbler astrologer and the forty
    thieves
  I love little pussy
  Patient Griselda
  The sun and the north wind
  The wind and the sun

Gentlin' the ram
  JAGENDORF — SAND p92-96

Geography. *See* **Mountains; Sea; etc.**

The geomancer's three sons
  INS-SŎB — FOLK p48-51

Geordie and ten-shilling Jock
  EDMONDS — TRICKSTER p30-35

George, Saint
  Saint George and the dragon

George and the field glasses
  GREEN — LEPRECHAUN p42-52

George Rogers Clark and the conquest
  of the Northwest
  MY BOOK HOUSE v. 9 p66-71

George Washington and his hatchet
  BALDWIN — FAVOR. p39-40

George Washington and the first American
flag
  MY BOOK HOUSE v. 5 p116-126

Georgia
  Buh fox's number nine shoes
  Bye-o! Bye-o!
  Christian dancing in rural Georgia
  Go to sleepy, little baby
  Many, many stars are in the skies

Georgia (Russia)
  The giant and the dwarf

Georgia
  LEACH — RAINBOW p81-83

Georgic and Merlin
  DELARUE — FRENCH p71-84

Georgie goes a-sparkin'
  JAGENDORF — SAND p88-91

Geraint and Enid
  PICARD — STORIES p137-152

Geraint and the knight of the sparrow-
hawk
  PICARD — STORIES p126-136

A German evening
  MY BOOK HOUSE v. 2 p140.

German nursery rhymes
  MY BOOK HOUSE v. 1 p120-123

Germany
  The animal languages
  The baron's haughty daughter
  Bear, fox, and man
  Big Hermel
  The black woodpecker
  The blacksmith in the moon
  The brave little tailor
  The caravan
  The caravan continues
  The caravan ends
  The caravan reaches the end of the
    desert
  The cat and mouse in partnership
  Catching hares in winter
  The clever Elsie
  The cock who went traveling
  The cruel stepmother
  The damned boys
  The day the sky fell
  The dead creditor
  The devil and our Lord
  The devil and the man
  The devil duped
  The devil's wife as godmother
  Dietrich of Bern
  Different, but not better
  Doctor know-all
  The donkey in company
  The dream
  Dream behind bars
  The duped giant
  The dwarf, and the goose
  The eagle on a chain
  The enchanted princess
  Eppelin of Gailingen
  Faithful John
  The farmer's clever daughter
  The feathers from the bird Venus
  Fish with the rolls
  The fox and the clever wren
  The fox and the hare in winter
  The fox and the wolf
  The frog prince
  The frog with the golden key
  Frozen music
  The ghost ship
  The giant's stone
  The giant's toy
  The girl out of the egg
  The girl who married the devil
  The girl without hands
  The gold bird
  The gold-rich king
  The golden bird
  The goose-girl
  Grace at meals
  The grateful ant
  The greatest boast
  The green-skinned princess
  Gudrun
  The hairs of the baron's head

Germany (*Continued*)

Hans Hansen's hired girl
Hansel and Gretel
The hare herd
The hedgehog and the hare
Helping to lie
The hermit and the devil
The house damsel
Household spirit brings food
The household spirit in Rotenbach
How the devil fetched the mayor
The innkeeper of Moscow
Journey in a well
The juniper
Karl the Great and the robber
The king's thief
The knight of Staufenberg
The lad who went to the north wind
The lazy woman
The lion and the bulls
The little grey man
The little hen and the little cock
The little round pot
The magic lamp
The magic swan
The man in the moon
Max and Moritz
Max and Moritz and the tailor
A meeting of two servants
Mr. Korbes the fox
Mother Holle
The mountain hen and the fox
The mouse and the frog
The mouse and the snail
The mousetower
Moving the church
Mrizala and her bridegroom, death
An old woman sows discord
One-eye, two-eyes, and three-eyes
The origin of the Lake of Vitte
The ox as mayor
The parish bull eats the grass from the wall
The peasant and his three sons
The peasant pewit
A peasant sells a cow as a goat
A peasant tricks the devil
The pig in the church
The poor and the rich
The poor brother's treasure
The poor people who wanted to be rich
The porcupines
Prince Ferdinand
The pugilist and his wonderful helpers
The quarrel about the woods
Rapunzel
Reaching an understanding
The red cloak
Reineke fox

The rescue of Fatima
Reward drives the familiar spirits away
The road to hell
The robber baron . . . and the bat
Rumpelstiltskin
The seven mice
The shepherd and the dwarf
The shepherd and the kings' daughters
The shoemaker and the elves
Siegfried
The six brothers
The six swans
The skinned goat
The slaying of Siegfried
Snow-white and Rose-red
Snow-white and the seven dwarfs
The spider
The stag-hunt
The starling of Segringen
A story about Our Lord Jesus Christ
The strange adventure of Baron Munchausen
Straw, bean, and coal
Stretching the bench
The struggle between the wolf and the fox
The swineherd who married a princess
The tailor and the prince
A tailor in heaven
A tale of a boy who set out to learn fear
The tale of frost and his neighbors
The tale of the Fäderäevisch
The tale of the little sausage and the little mouse
The tale of the silver, golden, and diamond prince
The tale of the youngest brother and the stupid devil
The thing on the hedge
The three brothers
The three butterflies
The three golden hairs of the king of the cave giants
The three spinners
The three traveling artisans
Till Eulenspiegel
Tom Thumb
The twelve dancing princesses
Two children
Tyl's task
The vengeance of Kriemhild
Walther of Aquitaine
The water of life
The water-sprite and the bear
The werewolf
Why the bear is stumpy-tailed
Why the dogs sniff at each other
The wild huntsman
The wishing ring

Germany (*Continued*)

The wolf and the lamb
The wolf and the seven kids
The wolf and the seven little kids
The woman in the chest
The wood nymphs
The wren
The wren and the bear
The young giant
A young prince named Siegfried
Zeus and the horse

—**Black forest**
Casperl
The cold heart—Part 1; Part 2
Haensel and Gretel
Hansel and Grettel
The tailor's apprentice . . . And
the bear
—**Bremen**
The Bremen town musicians
The musicians of Bremen
—**Coblenz**
There was an old man of Coblenz—
limerick
—**Cologne**
The Heinzelmännchen
Rabbi Amram's coffin
Richmuth of Cologne
—**Hamelin**
The pied piper of Hamelin; A min-
strel's enchanted music
The ratcatcher of Hamelin
—**Nuremberg**
The Nuremberg stove
—**Palatinate**
The wreck of the Palatine
—**Rhine River**
The Loreley . . . The siren's song
The seven proud sisters
—**Saxony**
A gift for a gift
—**Schwarzenborn**
They dig a well
They hide a bell
They measure the depth of the well
They protect their seed
—**Worms**
Rashi and Duke Gottfried
—**Würtemberg**
The golden chain
The iron box

Gessar Khan
Yoro reveals himself as Gessar Khan

"**Gesta Romanorum**"
The dog and the donkey

The first witch's cat
The fool of God
Lunching with dragons
On being a happy cow
On just being yourself
The race with Rosamond
The riddle of the black knight
The ridiculous donkey
Strike there!
The talking nightingale
The ten chests
The three gifts

Get out of the way
MY BOOK HOUSE v. 1 p93.

Get ready, get set, go
REED – TALK. p28-29

Get up, little horsey
MY BOOK HOUSE v. 1 p65.

Getting out of bed right
BATCHELOR – SUPER. p102.

Getting the moon back into the sky
JABLOW – MAN p50.

Gettysburg address
Lincoln's Gettysburg address

Ghana. See **Africa—Ghana**

Gheeger Gheeger the cold west wind
PARKER – AUSTRALIAN p118-121

The ghost and Hans Vãn Duin
IVES – TALES p29-37

A ghost at the door
LITTLEDALE – GHOSTS p153-156

The ghost-bird
U. N. – RIDE p112-115

The ghost dog of South Mountain
CARPENTER – DOGS p163-172

The ghost goblins' gold
SPICER – GHOSTS p120-128

The ghost of Hamish MacDonald, the fool
of the family
LEODHAS – TWELVE p27-39

The ghost in the cabbage patch
MINCIELI – TALES p50-53

The ghost of Peg-leg Peter
JAGENDORF – GHOST p19-24

The ghost of Samuel Chew
JAGENDORF – UPSTATE p153-158

Ghost of the Lane of Monkey's leap
JORDAN – BURRO p60-63

The ghost ship
CARPENTER – SHIPS p111-119
HAUFF – CARAVAN p30-49

A ghost story
JOHNSON – WHAT p178-179

The ghost that didn't want to be a ghost
LEODHAS – GHOSTS p79-90

Ghost towns
A couple of lost towns

The ghostly fisherman
CARLSON – TALKING p66-76

The ghostly hand of Spital house
SPICER – GHOSTS p16-23

The ghostly hitchhiker
LEACH – RAINBOW p195-198

Ghosts
About ghosts
Ashypelt
The beauty and her gallant
The big black umbrella
Big ghost, little ghost–Who's scared
of a ghost?
Blanche's high-flying Halloween
The blue flame
The bogles from the howff
A box on the ear
The boy who was never afraid
The boy who was not afraid
The brave cowman
Bring me a light
The buried moon
The children of the dead woman
The children and the ghost-woman
The coffin that moved itself
The deacon of Darkwater
A dead secret
Dealing with ghosts
The demon mason
The drowned bells of the abbey
The drunkard and the opium-eater
Five drowned
The flitting of the ghosts

The Frisian ride
General Moulton's boot
The golden chain
Golden hair
The good woman
Grandma'am Hinkel and the phantom
dog
The grateful old cailleach
The green mist
The gypsy in the ghost house
Hans and his master
The haunted boat
The haunted house
The hauntings at Thorhallstead
The headless horseman
Hoichi the earless
The honest ghost
Hoodoo bags and ghosts in Tennessee
The hopping lights on Devil's hill
The house that lacked a bogle
How Tammas Maciver Macmurdo
Maclennan met his match
How the ghost got in
In a dark wood
Introduction (LEODHAS – TWELVE)
The invisible hands
Jack O'Leary's plow
The key maiden of Tegerfelden
The kindly ghost
The lads who met the highwaymen
Lady Morris in her mansion
The Lady's loaf-field
The leg of gold
The legend of the virgin Arang
The lonely house
The maiden Suvarna
The man o' the clan
The man who didn't believe in ghosts
The man who helped carry the coffin
The man who sold a ghost
The man who walked widdershins
round the kirk
Miss Jenny Jones
Monsters and ghosts
The mystery of Pelham House
The naughty girl and the ghost-giant
Never
Never mind them watermelons
The old man with the bump
Old Nanny's ghost
Old Sal's curse
The old soldier and the mischief
The phantom ship
Pirate Yan Yost of Communipaw
The princess who was rescued from
slavery
The rain-lady and the ghost
La Ramée and the phantom
The return of the land-otter
The revenge of the serpent
The ring

Ghosts (*Continued*)

The sea captain's wife
A shiver of ghosts
The skull
The spider specter of the pool
The story of Ming-Y
The strange adventure of Paddy
  O'Toole
The tailor in the church
The tale the crofter told
The tale of the ghost ship
The tapping ghost of Edinburg
The thing on the hedge
Thorsteinn Shiver
Tim Felt's ghost
Timothy and the buggane ghost
Tregeagle
The two brothers and the ghost Mo'oi
Vania and the vampire
The walking boundary stone
The weeping lady of Llyn Glasfryn
The weeping lass at the dancing place
The white lady of Pumphul
The wicked house of Duncan Macbain
The wild ride in the tilt cart
Witches and ghosts
Yallery Brown
Yi Chang and the haunted house
The young Irish lad from the hiring
  fair

, **Air**
  The magic lamp

—**Dogs**
  The blue dog
  The old laird and his dogs
  Sandy MacNeil and his dog

—**Giants**
  The giant bones

, **Mountain**
  The magic lamp

—**Mules**
  The white mule ghost

Ghuls (demons)
  Amin and the ghul
  Mirza and the ghul

Giacco and his bean
  HARDENDORFF — TRICKY p75-80

Gianni and the ogre
  MANNING — GIANNI p7-12

The giant and his royal servants
  PILKINGTON — SHAM. p1-9

The giant and the dwarf
  MANNING — GIANTS p18-24

The giant and the mite
  FARJEON — LITTLE p120-124
  MAYNE — GIANTS p211-215

The giant and the Rumanian
  URE — RUMANIAN p24-25

The giant and the tailor
  BAMBERGER — FIRST p113-117

The giant archer of the sky
  SPICER — 13 p109-117

The giant beanstalk
  DURHAM — TIT p56-62

The giant bones
  LEODHAS — GAELIC p30-38
  MAYNE — GIANTS p195-203

The giant elephant
  GAER — FABLES p71-74

The giant Holiburn
  MANNING — PETER p125-128

The giant in the cave
  MANNING — GIANTS p85-89

The giant kingfisher of Mount Riga
  JAGENDORF — NEW p183-189

The giant-nonsense verse
  DE REGNIERS — GIANT p127-130

The giant of the brown beech wood
  MacMANUS — BOLD p138-157
  MAYNE — GIANTS p119-137

Giant of the Green Mountains
  TAFT — PROFILE p108-117

The giant of the hills
  JAGENDORF — NEW p62-66

The giant of the mount
  MANNING — PETER p77-81

The giant ogre, Kloo-Teekl
  HARRIS — ONCE p87-111

The giant okab
  MEHDEVI — PERSIAN p62-68

The giant outwitted
  PALMER — JOURNEY p106-116

Giant, pear and giant cow
  MÜLLER — SWISS p181.

Giant pears and giant cows
  DE REGNIERS — GIANT p174-175

Giant skeeters in the brass pot
JAGENDORF – SAND p154-158

The giant sturgeon
LEEKLEY – WORLD p79-91

The giant who counted stones
STOUTENBURG – FEE p37-54

The giant who had no heart in his body
ASBJÖRNSEN – EAST p42-52
DE REGNIERS – GIANT p81-93
JONES – SCAND. p16-26
MANNING – GIANTS p98-106
MAYNE – GIANTS p108-118
THOMPSON – ONE p8-14

The giant who loved adventure
STOUTENBURG – FEE p105-126

The giant who played with pygmies
STOUTENBURG – FEE p91-104

The giant who rode on the ark
DE REGNIERS – GIANT p131-134
STOUTENBURG – FEE p7-21

The giant who stole a river
MAYNE – GIANTS p27-34

The giant who sucked his thumb
STOUTENBURG – FEE p22-36

The giant who took a long time to grow
STOUTENBURG – FEE p55-74

The giant with the grey feathers
MacMILLAN – GLOOS. p231-237

The giant worm of the well
SPICER – 13 p40-50

Giants
See also names of giants, e.g. **Carls**
The adventures of Ciad
The adventures of Iain Direach
The adventures of Pengo
Angus
The apples of Iduna
Badikan and Khan Boghu
Bash Tchelik
Beowulf fights a battle with the sea
Billy Beg and his bull
The black giant of Luckless River
The blinded giant
The boy who overcame the giants
Bran, son of Llyr
The brave little tailor

Brian and the fox
The bride-price for Olwen
Bukolla
The carl of the drab coat
The castle of the three giants
The clever cat and the giant
The clever goatherd and the greedy
giant
The clever little tailor
Clever Oonagh
The cobbler
Conall Yellowclaw
The cowherd with the belt of skin
The crochera
The cruel giant
Cúchúlainn and the smith's wife
Cyclopes
David and Goliath
David and Goliath . . . The shepherd
boy and the giant
David, the shepherd boy
Dearmid and Grania
The demon giant of Mount Ariake
Dermot and Grania
Dietrich defends the snow queen
Dietrich of Bern
The disobedient giant
Djamukh-son of a deer
The dog and the giant
Donal from Donegal
The donkey lettuce
The dove maiden
A dozen at a blow
The duped giant
Edward Frank and the friendly cow
The fairy frog
The fairy tree of Doolas Woods
The faithless apprentice
Fin M'Coul and Cucullin
Finlay the giant killer
Finlay the hunter
Finn and the young hero's children
Finn MacCool
Finn MacCool, the giants and the
small men
The first gods and giants
The first pig and porcupine
The flight with the Wendigo
The flower of beauty
The fountain of youth
The friendly frog
The frog
Geraint and Enid
Giuanni and the giant
Gog and Magog
The golden ball
The gouty giant
The greedy giant and the Palau
Islands
Gulliver in the giants' country
Gulliver's travels to Lilliput

Giants (*Continued*)

The hairy-armed ogre of Kyoto
Halde Hat and Dulde Hat
A handful of hay
Hans, the horn, and the magic sword
He who laughs last
The herdsman of Cruachan
Hereward
The holy mountain
Horses of the thunder
How Glooskap made the birds
How grasshopper came to be and men
  obtained tobacco
How Ian Direach got the blue falcon
How Loki outwitted a giant
How summer came to Canada
How Tepozton killed the giant
How the bee got his bumble
How the giant Finn made the Isle of
  Man
How to shake hands with a giant
The hungry giant
Ian Direach
In the beginning
Intole the giant
Jack and the beanstalk
Jack and the giant Cormoran
Jack and the giant Tantarem
Jack and the giant Thunderdell
Jack and the Welsh giant
Jack, the giant Galligantua, and the
  enchanter
Jack the giant-killer
Jack, the King of England's son, and
  the giant with three heads
Jaco and the giant
James Gray and the Clashnichd
John the bear
Johnny Gloke
Jonas and the boggart of Brixworth
Juanito and the princess
King Johnny
King Kantjil's kingdom expands
The knights of the silver shield
The labors of Hercules
Lad, the farmer's son
The last of the giants
A legend of Knockmany
The legend of Pathasos
The little bull calf
The little white cat
Loki . . . The apples of youth
Loppa and Ion Loppa-Fosterling
The lovesick giant
Lucas the strong
Lyonesse
The magica music
Maria Marina
The master-maid
Mboyo and the giants

The midget and the giant
Miska and the man-with-the-iron-head
Moi and the red bull
Molly Whuppie (Whipple)
Monsters, witches and giants
A moon of gobbags
The mop servant
More south than south, more north
  than north
Mornin', mighty Mose
The mountain and the rivers
The naughty girl and the ghost-giant
Nazar the brave
The nine-headed giant
No man with the Cyclops
The Northern lights
Odysseus in the land of the giants
The ogre courting
The ogre king of Gilgit
Ojji Ben Onogh
Oisin in the land of the ever young
Olaf the mermaid's son
The old hag of the forest
Old man knowall
Old man Kurai and the one-eyed
  giant
Old man moon
Old Stormalong
The one-eyed giant
The one-eyed ogre of Sessay
The origin of the Lake of Vitte
The origin of the wrekin
Paul Bunyan
Paul Bunyan—poem
Paul Bunyan swings his axe
Peerifool
Pidicino
The poor man's son, the dwarfs, and
  the birds
The prince and the giant's daughter
The prince and the sky-blue filly
Prince Loaf
The princess with the golden hair
The pursuit of Dermot and Grania
The pursuit of the hard man
The quest for Olwen (3) In search of
  Olwen
The quest for Olwen (4) Fulfilling the
  tasks
The quest for Olwen (5) The Culhwch
  marries Olwen
Rabbit and the Indian chief
Rhitta of the beards
Salt
Sartak-Pai
The sea captain
The selfish giant
The seven-headed giant
The sharpshooter
The Shee an Gannon and the Gruagach
  Gaire

Giants *(Continued)*

The shepherd's nosegay
Sigiris Sinno, the mighty one
Sindbad the sailor
Sir Gammer Vance
Sir Gammer Vans
Smereree
Sneezy Snatcher and Sammy Small
The snowman
A spadeful of earth
The spirit of the stone
Squirrel and fox
The stone of victory
The story of Bensurdatu
The story of Prince Ring and his dog
The strong boy
The tale of the lay of the Amadhain Mhor
The tale of the lay of the smithy
The tale of the Rhine-gold
The tale of the superman
Tarn Wethelan
Tavadan and the fire giant
There was an old man of Coblenz—limerick
Thor and the giants
Thor and the jotun Geirrod
Thor and the jotun Rungnir
Thor and the jotun Utgardsloki
Thor gains his hammer
Thor's combat with Rungnir
Thor's hammer is stolen
Thor's journey to jotun-heim
Thor's unlucky journey
Thor's visit to Hymir
The three brothers
The three brothers and the giant
The three bugganes
Three fat ewes for three fine hounds
The three giants
The three golden apples
The three golden hairs of the king of the cave giants
The three-legged jumping giant
The three lemons
The three plagues of Britain
The three sons of the King of Antua
Three tales of the mouse-deer
The three teeth of the king
The thunder man
Thunderbird
Ting-a-ling
Ting-a-ling's visit to Tur-il-i-ra
Tom and giant blunderbus
Tom Hickathrift
The trade that no one knows
The trials of Ting Ling
The troll who hid his life
Una and the Red Cross knight
Unyany

The valiant tailor
A voyage to Brobdingnag
The whispering giant
The white cat
The white sword of light
Why are giants so stupid?
Why the ocean is salty
The wild woman of the woods
The witch in the stone boat
The world of the gods
The young giant
Young hunter
The young man and the giant
The young shepherd

—History
History of the giants

Giants
   JACOBSON — LEGEND. p3-11

The giant's bride
   WILLIAMS — OLD p322-328

The giant's causeway
   GARNIER — LEGENDS p104-111

Giants, dragons, and gods
   GRINGHUIS — GIANTS p15-20

The giants of Towednack
   MAYNE — GIANTS p138-147
   WILLIAMS — FAIRY p216-248

The giant's stairs
   PALMER — FAIRY p78-84

The giant's stone
   RANKE — GERMANY p36.

The giant's toy
   RANKE — GERMANY p35.

The giants who wanted a son
   STOUTENBURG — FEE p75-90

Gib Morgan
   GORHAM — REAL p136-147
   LEACH — RAINBOW p58-59

Gideon, the warrior
   MY BOOK HOUSE v. 9 p134-139

The gift and the giver
   DAVIS — LION'S p172-177

A gift for a gift
   PROTTER — CHILD. p178-180

Gift for the lazy
   DAVIS — LION'S p130-132

A gift from the heart
  PRIDHAM – GIFT p11-15

The gift of Father Frost
  MAAS – MOON p17-25

The gift of gold
  TASHJIAN – THREE p63-77

The gift of manioc
  CARPENTER – SOUTH p57-63

The gift of Saint Nicholas
  ARBUTHNOT – TIME p169-172

The gift of the hairy one
  THOMPSON – HAWAII. p53-59

The gift of the holy man
  SIDDIQUI – TOON. p70-81

The gift of the moon goddess
  BARLOW – LATIN p38-42

Gift of the unicorn
  WYNDHAM – CHINA p34-37

The gift to the hummingbird
  BOWES – BIRD p72-77

The gifted skin of the pig
  PILKINGTON – THREE p43-48

Gifts
  The adventures of Silvervit and
    Lillvacker
  The ass that lays money
  Authun and the bear
  Bungling Pedro
  La Cenerentola
  Chanina and the angels
  A converted thief
  The devil's gifts
  The fairy
  The frog and the moon
  The good luck tree
  The hare in the moon
  How one should carve a goose
  The hunchback's gift
  An inadvertant misunderstanding
  The ivory box
  The leopard and the antelope
  The lost gift
  The mermaid and the simpleton
  The mountain and the rivers
  My Lord Bag-o'-Rice
  Nasradin Hodja returns a gift
  Ooka and the terrible-tempered
    tradesman
  Pamudjo's feast
  The passing of Glooskap
  Phenist the bright-eyed falcon
  The seventh princess
  Swan white and fox tail
  The tale of Nornagest
  Thor gains his hammer
  The thousandth gift
  The three gifts
  The three golden hairs
  The three sons
  The two caddies of tea
  Two novices who behaved like a pair
    of otters
  Wali Dâd the simple-hearted
  The white spider's gift
  With and without

Gigi and the magic ring
  MY BOOK HOUSE v. 7 p199-209

Gilbert, W. S.
  The bad baronets

Giles, H. A.
  The stone monkey

Gillham, Charles E.
  How the foxes became red

Gingerbread
  Dawlish fair
  Haensel and Gretel
  Hansel and Grettel
  The sugar-plum tree

The gingerbread boy
  ARBUTHNOT – TIME p168-169

The gingerbread man
  MY BOOK HOUSE v. 2 p58-66
  SIDEMAN – WORLD'S p573-579

Ginseng (plant)
  A dutiful son
  The nine-headed giant
  A white-eared tiger

The giolla dacker and his horse
  SUTCLIFF – HIGH p77-95

Giotto's Tower
  The rose of midwinter, The Little
    People of Italy

Gipsies. See Gypsies

The gipsies' church
  URE – RUMANIAN p99-100

The gipsy and the goose
URE – RUMANIAN p16-18

The giraffe hunters
COURLANDER – KING'S p90-94

Giraffes
Madame giraffe
Ol-Ambu and He-of-the-long-sleeping-place
Old Noah

Girdles (armor)
Gawaine and the green knight
The prince and the vizier's son
Rake up!
Saint George and the dragon
Sir Gawain and the green knight

, Golden
The golden horse

A girl and a stepmother
TOOZE – WONDER. p50-54

The girl and her water buckets
JABLOW – MAN p19.

The girl and the crocodile
TRACEY – LION p99-102

The girl and the golden chair
SHEPPARD – WELSH p98-100

The girl and the puma
JAGENDORF – KING p23-27

The girl and the sailor
O'SULLIVAN – FOLK. p223-224

The girl in the moon
DEUTSCH – MORE p79-84

The girl on the green tree
BONNET – CHINESE p15-20

The girl on the hill
TRACEY – LION p83-87

The girl on the rock
TRACEY – LION p66-73

The girl out of the egg
RANKE – GERMANY p59-61

The girl who always cried
MacMILLAN – GLOOS. p244-250

The girl who clung to the devil's back
SPICER – DEVILS p117-127

The girl who could spin clay and straw
into gold
KAPLAN – SWEDISH p58-70

The girl who didn't know how to spin,
The Little People of Scandinavia
BELTING – ELVES p70-76

The girl who forgot her hoe
TRACEY – LION p55-60

The girl who kissed the peach-tree
FARJEON – LITTLE p83-90

The girl who lived with the gazelles
CARPENTER – AFRICAN p77-85

The girl who married the devil
RANKE – GERMANY p42-44

The girl who met the witch of the woods
NYBLOM – WITCH p35-65

The girl who overpowered the moon
JABLOW – MAN p30-34

The girl who picked strawberries
MANNING – DWARFS p49-52

The girl who played a trick on the devil
COOPER – FIVE p7-25

The girl who used her wits
MY BOOK HOUSE v. 4 p137-141

The girl who weaves by night
KRUEGER – SERPENT p136-143

The girl who wore too much
KRUEGER – SERPENT p106-111

The girl whom the moon pitied
JABLOW – MAN p21.

The girl with the rose-red slippers
GREEN – TALES p210-214

The girl without arms
SEKI – FOLKTALES p98-104

The girl without hands
RANKE – GERMANY p84-89

Girls
Catherine's tea party
The earrings
Kayuta, the drop star
The little girl named I

Girls (*Continued*)
Poor little girl, rich little girl
Stories about girls and boys

Gisella and the goat
MANNING – GLASS p174-181

Giuanni and the giant
DE REGNIERS – GIANT p60-68

Giufà
LUM – ITALIAN p183-194

Giuseppi, the cobbler
MY BOOK HOUSE v. 1 p63.

Give praise
MY BOOK HOUSE v. 5 p115.

Giving away secrets
MORRIS – UPSTAIRS p105-113

Gizo's counting trick
AARDEMA – TALES p31-40

Glascony
The blacksmith and the devil

Glass
Day dreaming
The master-maid
The princess on the glass hill

The glass house
WYATT – GOLDEN p45-49

The glass man and the golden bird
MANNING – GLASS p115-121

Glass mountain, The princess and the.
See The princess and the glass mountain

A glass of water, please
MARRIOTT – AMER. p201-204

The glass peacock
FARJEON – LITTLE p263-271

Glassblowing
The crystal bowl

Glasses, Eye
Bouki's glasses
Look through glass
The monkey and the spectacles

Globes
The goldfish

Glooskap (spirit)
The fall of the spider man
The first mosquito
How Glooskap made the birds
How rabbit deceived fox
How rabbit lost his tail
How summer came to Canada
How turtle came
The moon and his frog-wife
Owl with the great head and eyes
The partridge and his drum
The passing of Glooskap
Rabbit and the grain buyers

Glooskap
GARNER – GOBLINS p210-212

Glooskap, the whale, and the sorcerer
WILLIAMS – ROUND p208-216

Glooskap's country
MacMILLAN – GLOOS. p1-9

Gloves
Five in a glove

Gloves
LEACH – SOUP p92-95

Glowworms. *See* Fireflies

Gluskap
LEACH – RAINBOW p287-288

The gluttonous wife
BELPRE – TIGER p85-86

Gluttony
The blue lake
The cannibal who ate too fast
The crow and the whale
General Pumpkin
The sky-eater
The tabby who was such a terrible
glutton
The three gluttons and the hunter
Three times and out
The wolf and the fox
The woodman and the fox

The gnat and the lion
GREEN – BIG p43.

Gnats
The boastful gnat
The elephant and the gnat
The stag-hunt

Gnomes
The creation of the world

Gnomes (*Continued*)
Griselda
The lost cows
The rat-catcher's daughter
The royal waistcoat
Sif's golden hair

Gnus
From a moral alphabet

Good luck. *See* **Luck, good**

Go ask your mother for fifty cents
MY BOOK HOUSE v. 1 p104.

Go out, children
MY BOOK HOUSE v. 1 p185.

Go to sleepy, little baby
MY BOOK HOUSE v. 1 p90.

Go Zu-Mong, King of Goguryŏ
INS-SŎB – FOLK p4-7

Goannas (lizards)
How the black snake got its fangs

The goat
BULATKIN – EURASIAN p90-94

The goat and her three kids
CREANGĂ – FOLK p126-134

The goat and the eagle
ELLIOT – SINGING p18-31

The goat and the wolf
MONTGOMERIE – 25 p32-33

The goat in the well
GREEN – BIG p52-53

A goat one day was feeling fine
MY BOOK HOUSE v. 1 p106.

The goat that flagged the train
LEACH – RAINBOW p243-244

The goat that went to school
CREDLE – TALL p133-144

The goat well
COURLANDER – FIRE p57-63

The goat who couldn't sneeze
JORDAN – BURRO p33-38

The goatherd who won a princess. *See*
The finest liar in the world (variant)

Goatherds
The clever goatherd and the greedy
giant
The fairy wife
The girl who clung to the devil's back
The herdsman
The wild man
The wishing star

Goats
The adventures of Alexander Selkirk
Anansi and the old hag
The animal musicians
The billy goat and the king
The billy goat and the sheep
The bird and the buffalo
The blacksmith lion and the conceited
goat
The boy and the sea monsters
The Brahman and the goat
Brer goat and brer lion
Cadwalader and his goat
Cadwalader's goat
The carlanco
The cat, the mountain goat, and the
fox
The cave that talked
The clever billy goat
The dance of the animals
Dry-bone and Anansi
Dwarf stories
Eight leaves of story (8) Cadwalader
and all his goats
The fisherman's son
The fool and the birch-tree
The giant in the cave
Gisella and the goat
The golden-haired children
The grateful goat
The greedy tailor
Hear ye!
Heidi in the Alpine pasture
A horned goat
How crab got a hard back
The jackal's lawsuit
Johnny and the three goats
Johnny and the witch-maidens
Justice
Kantjil interprets a dream
The kid and the tiger
The king of the mountain
The king who rides a tiger
The leopard's wine
The lion and the goat
Little one eye, little two eyes and
little three eyes
The magic egg
The man who sold a ghost
A message in a bottle
Miss goat

Goats (*Continued*)

The mountain goats
Mumbele and the goats
The musical silver goat
Oeyvind and Marit, a story of Norway
Old Hiram's goat
Old Mother Hubbard
Old pipes and the dryad
One mean trick deserves another
Per and the north wind
The pig, the goat and the sheep
Pinkel
The princess's slippers
The proud goat
(The) quartet
The ram and the goat
Saint Martin and the honest man
Saint Sava and the devil
Salvador and the goat
The scholar, the monkey, and the goat
Señor Billy Goat
Shlemiel the businessman
Simpletons
Sister Alionushka, brother Ivanushka
The skinned goat
Smereree
The spiteful nanny goat
A story of guile
The struggle between the wolf and the fox
The stupid wolf
The tabby who was such a terrible glutton
The tale of the Balaton
Tatterhood
Tecle's goat
The thief's goat
Thor and the giants
Thor's journey to jotun-heim
(The) three billy goats gruff
The three deaf men
The three goats called Hurricane
Ticky-picky boom-boom
The tiger and the goats
Transportation problem
The two goats
The unlucky goat
Who is strongest?
Who is the older?
Why goat cannot climb a tree
Why the spider has a narrow waist
The wise goat
The wolf and the seven kids
The wolf, the goat, and the kid
The wood fairy
Would you like to see the goats dance on stilts?
Zlateh the goat

, **Silver**
The musical silver goat

–**Skin**
The crock of gold
Why the sun is brighter than the moon

–**Tails**
It's better to be smart than strong

Goat's ears
LANG – VIOLET p46-49

The goats who killed the leopard
COURLANDER – FIRE p25-26

Gobbleknoll
GARNER – GOBLINS p1-2

Gobborn seer
JACOBS – MORE p60-64
PILKINGTON – SHAM. p104-106

Goblets
The borrower
The danced-out shoes
How Cormac MacArt got his branch
The page boy and the silver goblet
The pooka of the mill

Goblin bread
SPICER – WITCHES p43-48

The goblin bridge
INS-SÖB – FOLK p126-128

Goblin gold
SPICER – GOBLINS p9-19

The goblin-spider
HEARN – JAPANESE p18-20
GARNER – GOBLINS p78-81

Goblins
About goblins
The adventures of Nera
All in green went my love riding
Baldur the bright
Bash Tchelik
The beast
Bucca Dhu and Bucca Gwidden
The changelings
A charm against witches
The cook and the house goblin
The crimson purse
The dark guest
The dishonest tailor
Edward Frank and the friendly cow
The fiddler going home
Findings are keepings
The fort of Rothangan
A game
The ghost goblins' gold

Goblins (*Continued*)

Glooskap
Gobbleknoll
The golden ax
The golden ball
Great Head and the ten brothers
The green mist
The green-skinned princess
The hairy boggart's field
Hallowe'en
Hema and the goblin-woman
Hoichi the earless
How Finn became head of the Fianna
How foolish men are!
How the clergyman retrieved the golden chalice from the goblins of Gotland
In the strange isle
The invisible baby
The invisible hobgoblin
John Connu Rider
The Korean goblins
Krencipal and Krencipalka
The lady of the wood
The lass that couldn't be frightened
The leprechaun in the basket
A letter
The little black man
Little Jip
The Little People
Loki
The long-nosed goblins
The lucky circle
The magic cap
The magic peas
The mallet of wealth
The man with the green feather
Meeting in the road
Moowis
Overheard on a salt marsh
Pappa Greatnose
The piper of Shacklow
The place of strife
The pooka of the mill
Prayer
Ramayana
The river god (of the River Mimram)
The secret commonwealth
The smoker
The snow man
Tarn Wethelan
The Tengu's magic nose fan
The term
The three sons
Three who found their hearts' desire
The three dwarfs
The three silver balls
Three tales of the goblins who lived on the sea-bottom
To the Tengu goblins
Tops or bottoms

The trade that no one knows
A voice speaks from the well
The voyage of Maelduin
Vukub-Cakix
Water drops
Wild worms and swooning shadows
Willow
Yallery Brown

The goblins at the bath house
MANNING – GHOSTS p14-20

God

All things beautiful
The angel
The ant and the tower to God
The ant in search of her leg
Atam and Im
The babe Moses
The barren stones
The buyer of oxen
The cat, the dog, and death
Charles Legoun and his friend
Creator makes—
Daniel in the lions' den
David, the shepherd boy
The devil's partnership
The foolish man
Godfather death
Ha! Tío rabbit is bigger
La Hormiguita
How God helped Mammo
How God's wheel turns
How Kwaku Ananse won a kingdom with a grain of corn
How stars and fireflies were made
How the people of Ife became scattered
Ivan and his sack
Joseph and his brethren
Keloglan and God's greatness
The king and the ring
King Canute on the seashore
The lazy hornet
The lizard's big dance
The marriage of the mouse
Men of different colors
Noah's ark
The poor wolf
Rabbi Joseph Della Reina
Rabbit Joshua Ben Levi and the prophet Elijah
The rich man's dinner party
The sheep is the cousin of the ox
The tale of the wrath of God
The shepherd's crown
The terror of the ogres
The three wishes
The tinker of Tamlacht
The true lord of the merry men of Gotham

247

God (*Continued*)
The visits of St. Peter to his people
Who is strongest?
Why the cat and dog cannot live at peace
The youth who trusted in God

God bless you
LEACH – SOUP p120-121

God hath made me to laugh
MY BOOK HOUSE v. 1 p217.

Goddess of mercy
A willow wand and a brocade slipper

Goddess of the trees
The tree goddess

Godfather death
BECHSTEIN – FAIRY p186-192
THOMPSON – ONE p73-76

Godfathers
The little gardener with golden hair

Godmothers
Death's godchild
The devil's wife as godmother
The maiden in the tower
Two out of the sack

Gods and goddesses
See also names of gods and goddesses
The adventures of Magboloto
The anger of Sande-Nyana
The apples of Iduna
Attila the conqueror
Baldur the bright
Balder, the god of light
The battle at White Cliff house
Bears in the sky
The beef tongue of Orula
Blue water
The boastful queen
The bowlegged, god, Bes
Bragi, god of poetry
Brian and the fox
A bride for the sea god
The building of the fortress wall
The cat and the sea
The cat of Bubastis
Chameleon finds –
The choja who became a monkey
Collen
The cuckoo's reward
The death of Balder
The dog and the giant
The eight-headed dragon

Europa and the bull
The fairy grotto
The fall of the earth giants
Fatty
The first gods and giants
Friendless pavilion
Frigg and the goddesses
The game of Tlachtli
The gift of the moon goddess
Gluskap
The golden axe
Golden flower and the three warriors
The golden helmet
The great bird in the carob tree
The great blessing of the land
The great Queen Hatshepsut
The great white condor
The greatest person in the world
The hermit and the Sea of Man
Horus the avenger
How locusts came to be
How Loki outwitted a giant
How Odin brought the mead to Asgard
How the earth was made to fit the sky
How the queen of the sky gave gifts to men
The hundred-headed daffodil
The beginning
Introduction (CAMPBELL – MAORI)
Isis and Osiris
Isis and the secret name of Ra
Khrishna the cowherd
Khnemu of the Nile
The king and his seven sons
The kneeler's twelve tasks
Ko-pa-ta, the gambling god
The legend of Tchi-Niu
The lost gift
Maui and the death goddess
Maui and the fire goddess
Maui, the demi-god
Merlin
Monkey
The monster Mo-o
Mother's day
Nāgasvāmin and the witches
Nala and Damayanti
Nananbouclou and the piece of fire
The new day
Njord, Frey and Freya
A noble Brahman's sacrifice
Nuberu
Palamon and Arcite
The peacock and the puhuy
Phaeton; the boy who rode the chariot of the sun
Plowman in the sky
The prince and the Sphinx
The princess and the demon
Princess Scri and Prince Sedana
The punishment of Loki
Ra and his children

Gods and goddesses (*Continued*)

The rabbit and the crocodile
The rabbit in the moon
Ragnarokk, the destiny of the gods
The rain-god's daughter
The rain god's reprisal
The rainbow
Ramayana
The return of the spring
Revenge of the tin god
The rice cake that rolled away
Riches or happiness?
The river god
The sacred dream of Tepozteco
The sea serpent
The Sedna legend
The seventh son
She-wa-na, deity of the elements
Sibu the god-who-builds
Simón and his rocky acre
Skade, the ski-goddess
The sky people
The soul in the mountain rice
Spider boy and the sun god's twins
The tale of the two brothers
Tepozton
There's no deity there
Thor gains his hammer
Thor, the thunder-god
Thor's combat with Rungnir
Thor's hammer is stolen
Thor's unlucky journey
Thor's visit to Hymir
The thunder cat
The tiny god
Tithonus, the grasshopper
The toad is the Emperor's uncle
A tongue of gold and words of jade
The tree goddess
The tubmaker who flew to the sky
The twins of the god Mars
A warning from the gods
The wedding of the dragon-god
The well of immortality
Why the moon wanes
Why the mountains are snow-covered
Why the ocean is salty
The winning of Gerd
The world of the gods
Yama and the poor man
Yoro reveals himself as Gessar Khan

–Egypt
The classic traveler's yarn: The
tale of the shipwrecked sailor
Destruction and creation myths:
The book of the divine cow
Gods in all-too-human situations:
The contendings of Horus and
Seth
Historical inscription–or fiction?:
The seven-year famine
History as propaganda: The Prin-
cess of Bakhtan
Human passions in the gods: Isis
challenges Re
Magical elements in religious be-
liefs: The wanderings of Isis and
the agony of Horus
A morality tale: truth and false-
hood
Myth and folktale in human
actions: The tale of the two
brothers
Osiris–martyrdom and myth: The
life and death of Osiris
Principal Egyptian deities
A story on stone: The divine
birth of Hatshepsut
The tale of a rich king: The
treasure of Rhampinitus
Tales of past glories: Cheeps and
the magicians
A wise priest learns a lesson:
Khaemwese and Tabubu

–Greece
Achilles and Polyxena
The adventures of Perseus
The anger of Achilles
The apple of discord
Atalanta . . . The fleet-footed
runner
Baucis and Philemon . . . The re-
ward hof hospitality
Bellerophon . . . The winged horse
The boy Achilles
A cause of war
Cerberus
The Chimera
Circe the enchantress
The death of Hector
The death of Paris
The end of Odysseus
The firebringer . . . Prometheus
The flying horse, Pegasus
The golden fleece
Helen in Egypt
Helen of Sparta
The home-coming of Odysseus
The horses of Rhesus
How Agamemnon came home
How Odysseus came home
Iphigenia at Aulis
Iphigenia in Tauris
The judgment of Paris
The labors of Hercules
The luck of Troy
The madness of Odysseus
The Nemean lion
The night of doom

Gods and goddesses—Greece *(Continued)*
  Odysseus and the lotus eaters
  Odysseus and the nymph
  The one-eyed giant
  Orestes and the Furies
  Orthrus
  Penelope and her suitors
  Phaethon . . . The chariot of the
    sun
  Phaeton
  The Princess Nausicaa
  The return of the heroes
  The revenge (Tennyson)
  Scylla and Charybdis
  The slaying of Hector
  The slaying of the suitors
  The story of Protesilaus
  The story of Telephus
  Tales of Troy
  Twins in the sky
  Una and the Red Cross knight
  The unhappy island
  Winds and ogres
  The wooden horse
  The wounded archer

—Hawaii
  A battle nobody won
  Spears of lightning
  A strange sled race
  The time of deep darkness

—India
  Lord Krishna or the eighth child
  Pyoli
  The Rameyana

, Indian
  The man who loved Hai Quai

—Ireland
  The children of Lir
  Midir and Etain

—Japan
  The birth of the islands
  The bridge of heaven
  Izanagi and Izanami
  Izanagi's descent to Hades
  The luck of the sea and the luck of
    the mountain
  The rabbit in the moon

, Mountain
  Koichi and the mountain god

—Norway
  Frithjof, the Viking
  Loki
  Loki . . . The apples of youth
  Odin . . . The price of wisdom
  The stealing of Iduna
  The tale of the Rhine-gold
  Thor

  Thor . . . How the thunderer was
    tricked
  Thor's journey to Jotun-Heim

, Roman
  The adventures of Perseus
  The home-coming of Odysseus
  The labors of Hercules
  Phaeton
  The wanderings of Aeneas

, Russia
  A chronicle of Kiev

, Water
  The snail Choja

Gods in all-too-human situations: The
  contendings of Horus and Seth
  JAMES — MYTHS p46-60

God's own country
  JAGENDORF — SAND p108-109

God's well
  JAGENDORF — UPSTATE p270-273

Godsons
  The imposter
  The servant who took the place of
    his master

Godwin
  The cowherd's son

Goethe, Johann Wolfgang von
  The story of Faust

Goethe, Johann Wolfgang von
  Faust

Gofes (evil spirits)
  The beginning of spirit societies

Gog and Magog
  JACOBSON — LEGEND. p7-9

Goggle-eyes
  HAMPDEN — GYPSY p133-138

Goha the wise
  ZAGLOUL — BLACK p59-64

Gold
  Alberich and the dwarfs
  Alchemy: the magic science
  Alexander of Macedon at the gates
    of paradise
  Ali Sundos
  Allah will provide

Gold (*Continued*)

The anger of Sande-Nyana
Ashypelt
Bardiello
Basia, the babbler
The beggar's prophecy
The birch twig
The bird which laid diamonds
The black-bearded Brownies of
  Boneburg
Black Sam Bellamy
The boy who was never afraid
Bring me a light
The cartman's stories
The castle of the three giants
The child in the bamboo tree
A clever judge
The clever thief
The cock and the hen
The cock and the neighbour's hen
The crock of gold
Damer's gold
The dark king
The days of the first monkeys
The devil's gifts
The doll
The donkey lettuce
The dreamer
The drunkard and the opium-eater
Dwarf stories
The enchanted castle in the sea
The enchanted knife
The enormous genie
Faithful John
Feedowa and Nobbin
The ferryman
The field of Ragwort
Findings are keepings
The first buttercups
The flea
The fool
The fool and the birch-tree
The foolish man
General Moulton's boot
The ghost goblins' gold
The giant in the cave
The gift of gold
The gift of the holy man
The girl who could spin clay and
  straw into gold
Giving away secrets
The glass house
Goblin gold
The goose from Flatbush
Grandmother Marta
The grateful devil
Grazing on the roof
The greedy friend
The gypsy in the ghost house
The hairs of the baron's head

The handsome apprentice
Hans and his master
Hantsjc and the remarkable beast
The heavenly lovers
Heimdall, the watchman of Asgard
The hex and the oxen
How the devil fetched the mayor
The hypocrite and the merchant's
  pledge
The insatiable beggar
The invisible hands
Ivan of Semberiya
Jack and the beanstalk
Jack and the wizard
Jaco and the giant
The jeweled ring
The ji-jaller bag
Katie Woodencloak
Keloğlan and God's greatness
Keloğlan and the ooh-genie
The king and his friend
The king and the corn
The king of the Golden River, or The
  black brothers
King Solomon's carpet
The lad who returned from Faerye
The lady who put salt in her coffee
The lass and her good stout blackhorn
  stick
The legend of the mason
The lreprechaun
The leprechaun and the wheelbarrow
The little milleress
The little red bogie-man
The little round pot
The little Sawah
The lord of gold
The lost gold bars of Juan Blanco
Luck
Luck and wit
The magic bird
The magic garden
The magic grocery store
The magic mountain
The magic purse of the swamp maiden
The magic turban, the magic whip, and
  the magic carpet
The magician and the bandits
The man who bought a dream
The man who stayed too long
Mary covered with gold and Mary
  covered with pitch
Midas
Midas . . . The greed for gold
The miller and the fairies
The miller-king
The mop servant
Mother Holle
The night of four times
Old Gally Mander
The old man of the flowers

Gold *(Continued)*

The old man who made flowers bloom
The old man who made trees blossom
Old Nanny's ghost
Omganda and the gold
One more child
One roll of bread
Patrick O'Donnell and the leprechaun
The pedlar of Swaffham
Per and the north wind
Peter and the witch of the wood
Piboon's golden mountain
The pot of gold
Prince Loaf
The princess of light
Punchinello
Quinces and oranges
The rat-catcher's daughter
Rattle-rattle-rattle and chink-chink-
  chink
The rich man and the poor man
The robe
The sea of gold
The seven-year blessing
The shepherd and the dwarf
The shoemaker's dream
The sly thief of Valenciennes
The small man and the weaver
The snow-wife
The soldier and the devil
The son of strength
The son of the baker of Barra
The Spanish donkey and the Indians
Squirrel and fox
Stan Bolovan
The star florins
The story of the haunted jars
The story of the stone lion
The swamp Nushi's messenger
The tailor and the devil
The tale of a foolish brother and of
  a wonderful bush
The tale of a proverb
The tale of the Rhine-gold
The terrible black snake's revenge
The text
Thor gains his hammer
The thousand pieces of gold
The three precepts
Three times and out
The three words of advice
The three young men and death
The tinderbox
The Tiyanak
Tom Walker and the devil
The tortoise-wife
The treasure
Tsali of the Cherokees
The twelve months of the year
The two beggars

The two caddies of tea
Vardiello
The wandering cobbler
The weaver's worry
The wee red man
The Welshman and the hazel staff
Where to lay the blame
White squash boy
White-toes and Bushy-bride
The white witch of Espeloo
Why ants have small waists
Why Eyvin won the race
The wonderful knapsack
The wonderful talking bowl
The wood fairy
The would-be wizard
The wrestling match of the two
  Buddhas
Zap

Gold
  MANNING – WIZARDS p40-46

The gold bird
  THOMPSON – ONE p231-237

The gold dragoon
  MANNING – JONNIKIN p1-11

The gold dust that turned to sand
  MONTGOMERIE – 25 p58-59

The gold falcon
  ZAGLOUL – BLACK p129-141

The gold-lined donkey
  DAVIS – LION'S p45-53

Gold mines and mining
  California's lost diamonds
  Humbug
  The man who started it all and the
    man who couldn't forget
  Of gold and men
  Queen of the Comstock

The gold-rich king
  RANKE – GERMANY p74-79

The gold table
  JAGENDORF – KING p176-180

Golden
  BECHSTEIN – FAIRY p133-137

The golden altar of the church of St.
Joseph
  U. N. – RIDE p231-233

The golden apples of Hisberna
  PILKINGTON – THREE p38-42

The golden apples of Loch Erne
    MacMANUS – BOLD p179-192

The golden ax(e)
    SPICER – GOBLINS p28-34
    UCHIDA – MAGIC p73-81

The golden ball
    JACOBS – MORE p12-15
    MANNING – GHOSTS p62-67

The golden bird
    ASBJÖRNSEN – NORW. p49-55
    HATCH – MORE p214-237
    MY BOOK HOUSE v. 7 p134-143

The golden boat
    ROSS – BURIED p139-146

The golden box
    HAMPDEN – GYPSY p24-33

Golden bracelets, golden anklets
    TOOZE – WONDER. p83-87

The golden buffalo
    VO-DINH – TOAD p129-135

The golden butterfly
    LEEUW – INDO. p14-20

The golden calf
    LIN – MILKY p72-75

The golden candelabra
    MEHDEVI – PERSIAN p69-80

The golden candlestick
    BARASH – GOLDEN p92-94

The golden carnation
    TOOR – GOLDEN p14-21

The golden casket
    MANNING – DAMIAN p146-154

The golden castle that hung in the air
    ASBJÖRNSEN – NORW. p139-149

The golden chain
    PROTTER – CHILD. p185-192

The golden chain from heaven
    SEKI – FOLKTALES p54-57

The golden coal
    MÜLLER – SWISS p135-137

The golden cockerell
    ALMEDINGEN – RUSS. p147-163

The golden crab
    MANNING – BEASTS p106-113

The golden crow
    AUNG – KINGDOM p57-61

The golden deer
    BECHSTEIN – FAIRY p111-115
    REED – TALK. p52-57

The golden dolls
    BULATKIN – EURASIAN p71-74

The golden earth
    COURLANDER – FIRE p127-129

The golden eggplant
    SEKI – FOLKTALES p173-175

Golden fleece
    Jason . . . The golden fleece
    The lamb with the golden fleece
    The ram with the golden fleece
    The sleepless dragon

The golden fleece
    HOPE-SIMPSON – CAVAL. p38-51
    McNEILL – SUNKEN p114-121

Golden flower and the three warriors
    CARPENTER – SOUTH p123-128

Golden goodness
    JAGENDORF – KING p135-138

The golden goose
    GAER – FABLES p164-166
    LINES – NURSERY p49-56
    SIDEMAN – WORLD'S p100-108

The golden gourd
    CARPENTER – SOUTH p64-70

Golden hair
    MANNING – GHOSTS p21-24

The golden-haired children
    BUCK – FAIRY p237-250

The golden-headed fish
    LANG – OLIVE p66-75
    SIDEMAN – WORLD'S p537-548

The golden helmet
    LEEUW – LEGENDS p52-56

Golden hood
    COLUM – STONE p97-107

The golden horse
    WILSON – GREEK p169-179

The golden horse with the silver
mane
JAGENDORF – NEW p126-132

The golden lamb
LARSON – PALACE p60-69

The golden lion
HAVILAND – ITALY p79-90
HODGES – SEREND. p38-60

The golden lotus
GREEN – TALES p85-90

The golden lynx
BAKER – GOLDEN p123-130

The golden mountain
WYNDHAM – TALES p22-32

The golden nightingale
WILSON – GREEK p129-140

The golden oriole
TOOZE – WONDER. p115-117

The golden peacock
TOOZE – WONDER. p36-42

The golden phoenix
BARBEAU – GOLDEN p7-25

The golden pitcher
BULATKIN – EURASIAN p22-26

The golden prince of the conch shell
WILLIAMS – OLD p136-164

The golden sheep
BECHSTEIN – FAIRY p40-49

Golden shoes
SERVER – LET'S p74-79

The golden skins
SPELLMAN – BEAUT. p86-89

The golden slipper, the magic ring, and
the twigs
MASEY – STORIES p122-131

The golden snuff-box
REEVES – ENGLISH p157-175

The golden stag
WYATT – GOLDEN p1-5

The golden tortoise
SUN – LAND p80-82

The golden touch
ARBUTHNOT – TIME p229.
MY BOOK HOUSE v. 7 p210-224

The golden touch; the king who worshipped gold
STRONG – FAVORITE p8-11

The golden twins
SPICER – LONG p29-46

The goldenrod
CATHON – PERHAPS p153.

The goldfinch
MY BOOK HOUSE v. 2 p45.

Goldfinches
The enchantment of Gearoidh Iarla

Goldfinches
CATHON – PERHAPS p183.

Goldfish. See Fish–Goldfish

The goldfish
FARJEON – LITTLE p40-46
THOMPSON – ONE p241-244

Goldilocks
The story of the three bears
The three bears

Goldilocks and the three bears
MY BOOK HOUSE v. 3 p20-24

Gold-rushes. See Gold mines and mining

Goldsmith, Oliver
The mad dog

Goldsmith, Oliver
Old Noll

The goldsmith, the wood carver, the
tailor, and the hermit who quarreled
over a wooden woman
NAHMAD – PEASANT p90-95

Goldsmiths
The Brahmin and the villain
The cold heart–(Part 2)
The fortunes of Said
The golden tortoise
The inn in the forest
The king of the Golden River, or
The Black brothers
The servant and the door

Goldsmiths (*Continued*)

The three princesses in the mountain-
in-the-blue
The wishing ring

The goldspinners
MAAS – MOON p86-98

The golem
NAHMAD – PORTION p155-170

The golem and the bridal pair
NAHMAD – PORTION p163-166

The Golem of Rabbi Judah Löw
NAHMAD – PORTION p159-162

Golems
The end of the Golem
Introduction (The Golem)
The mechanical man of Prague
Why the scroll of the law fell to the
ground

Goliath (Biblical)
David and Goliath

Gombel and the wild ducks
UCHIDA – SEA p91-98

Gonae
JAGENDORF – GYPSIES p180-181

Gondolas
Errantry

Gongs
The bobtail monkey

Good advice
DURHAM – TIT p107-114
GREEN – BIG p34.

Good advice, a guinea a piece
URE – RUMANIAN p69-71

The good crawford
SHEPPARD – SCOT. p128-130

"Good day, fellow!" "Axe handle!"
ASBJÖRNSEN – NORW. p158-160

The good dogs and the good assessor
JAGENDORF – SAND p146-149

The good fortune kettle
HAVILAND – JAPAN p23-29
SEKI – FOLKTALES p107-111

Good Friday
The magic mountain

The good housewife and her night helpers
WILSON – SCOTTISH p115-120

The good housewife and her night labors
HAVILAND – SCOTLAND p59-70

The good judge
BUDBERG – RUSSIAN p65-69

Good luck. *See* Luck, good

Good luck and bad luck
DURHAM – TIT p81-84

Good luck and common sense
WILSON – GREEK p21-23

Good luck and great riches
LOWE – LITTLE p67-71

The good-luck teakettle
ROSS – BURIED p161-172

The good luck tree
HEADY – TALES p86-89

The good man and the kind mouse
See also The miller-king
JAGENDORF – KING p72-78

Good morning, Peter
MY BOOK HOUSE v. 1 p165-167

Good morrow, 'tis St. Valentine's day
MY BOOK HOUSE v. 1 p209.

A good neighbor
BARASH – GOLDEN p84-87

The good old man
WILLIAMS – FAIRY p76-81

Good or bad?
WITHERS – I SAW p32.

Good sense and good fortune
BORSKI – GOOD p3-12

The good son
GINSBURG – MASTER p152-158

Good-speed and the elephant king
GAER – FABLES p86-89

The good sword
CHILD – CASTLES p181-195

The good witch-doctor in the mountains
JAGENDORF – UPSTATE p207-211

The good woman
MANNING – GHOSTS p119-123

Goodnaturedness. *See* **Cheerfulness**

Goodness
See also **Generosity; Kindness**
Ashoremashika
Ask a foolish question
Beauty and the beast
Cinder Joe becomes king
The clever squirrel
The crackling mountain
The crow-Peri
The dove and the eagle
The forest bride
The golden boat
Golden goodness
The golden touch; the king who worshipped gold
The grateful ant
The great flood
The greatest wealth in the world
The happy prince
Hok Lee and the dwarfs
Kindai and the ape
The king on trial
The kinh
Kralyevich Marko and the eagle
The land of the dead
The little bucket
The little lion dog and the blue prince
The little mermaid
Luck from heaven and luck from the earth
The milky way
Mr. Miacca
The mother of time and the enchanted brothers
Mother Sunday
Patient Griselda
Poor little girl, rich little girl
The Prince of Coucy
The princess and the fisherman
The princess who wanted to solve riddles
The robber Simhavikrama
The snake who bit a girl
The soul of the Countess Kathleen
The story of a good boy
The story of Ailill and Etaine
Suppāraka the mariner
Tale of the good, gay lady
The two kings
The two righteous men

The weight of the cart
The world beyond

The goodoo of Wirreebilla
PARKER – AUSTRALIAN p43-44

Goola-willeels the topknot pigeons
PARKER – AUSTRALIAN p219-220

Goolay-yali the pelican
PARKER – AUSTRALIAN p129-132

Gooloo the magpie and the waroogas
PARKER – AUSTRALIAN p201-204

Goose dance
LEEKLEY – WORLD p50-54

The goose from Flatbush
RASKIN – TALES p51-55

The goose-girl
ARBUTHNOT – TIME p64-66
SIDEMAN – WORLD'S p264-275
THOMPSON – ONE p221-226

Goose girls. *See* **Gooseherds**

Goose Matt
ILLYES – ONCE p193-198

Gooseherds
See also **Geese**
The prince and the goose girl
The sleeping prince
Tattercoats
The three golden eggs

Goosey, Goosey, Gander
MY BOOK HOUSE v. 1 p22.

Gordian knot
A horse afraid of his shadow

The Gordian knot; the destiny of Alexander
STRONG – FAVORITE p12-14

Gordon, George, Lord Byron
Solitude

Gorgons
Medusa

Goso the teacher
WITHERS – I SAW p144-146

256

Goss-hawks
The gay goss-hawk

Gossip
Buh rabbit's human weakness
The buried treasure
The chatterbox
Giving away secrets
How a fish swam in the air
The hunchback's gift
The iron box
It's perfectly true!
The magic peas
A nasty rumour
The silly goose war
The treasure

Gotham
Cuckoo in the hedge
The devil in the wheat
Drowning the eel
A fine cheese
Gotham way of counting
Grazing on the roof
The hare and the lord
Hasty porridge in the boiling water
Hear ye!
High diddle, diddle, the fool in the middle
How the trivet came home
John the blacksmith destroys the wasps in the straw
The little fish and the big fish
A little history of the Gotham folk tales
Never trust an eel
Other wise men of Gotham
The poor ploughman and the rich nobleman
Raking for the moon
Rolling cheese gathers no moss
Tall tales from the Gotham Inn
This is how it began
Three men on the bridge
The true lord of the merry men of Gotham

Gotham way of counting
JAGENDORF – MERRY p124-130

Gotland
How the clergyman retrieved the golden chalice from the goblins of Gotland

Goto, king of the land and the water
ARNOTT – AFRICAN p167-178

Gouillon, Louis
Georgic and Merlin

Gourds
Bouki rents a horse
Bundar Bahadeer Poon
The calabash children
Hwan and Dang
The man who had no wife
Pemba and the python and the friendly rat
The story of Hine-Moa and Tutanekai
Tiger story, Anansi story

, Golden
The golden gourd

The gouty giant
MAYNE – GIANTS p63-70

Governesses
Cenerentola

The governor and the Buddhist
INS-SOB – FOLK p71-73

The governor and the cannon
JAGENDORF – SAND p159-162

Governor Wentworth's search for a wife
TAFT – PROFILE p88-97

Governors
Cinderella of New Hampshire
The ghost of Peg-Leg Peter
The governor and the cannon
Governor Wentworth's search for a wife
Hearts and pirates
Juha at the banquet
The legend of the governor and the veteran
A lie for a lie
An old story of the three sworn brothers
The penitent governor
Puffing Potter's powerful puff

Gowdie, Isobel
A witch's confession

Gower, John
Adrian and Bardus

Graadonner
HACK – DANISH p13-23

Grace at meals
GREEN – BIG p132-133

Grackles
How the finch got her colors

Graham, Gail B.
GRAHAM – BEGGAR p96.

Grahame, Kenneth
Duck's ditty
The open road

Grain
The charcoal burner Choja
The endless story
The impostor
Rabbit and the grain buyers
The sea of pearls
The white snake
−**Merchants**
The wonderful bed

A grain of millet
INS-SÖB – FOLK p196-197

Granaries
The butterfly in the granary
The mouse who lived under the
granary

Grand Canyon
Catches
Jumping the Grand Canyon
Paul Bunyan's cornstalk

A grand old skipper
FELTON – TRUE p57-64

Le grand sultan. *See* The golden phoenix

Grandchildren
Chin and Yi
Raven fools his grandchildren

Grandfather tells some tales
ARNOTT – TALES p78.

Grandfathers
A ghost at the door
Lazy Tom keeps house
The thread of life
The two sisters
What a clever child can do
The wooden bowl

Grandfather's advice
DEUTSCH – TALES p63-68

Grandma'am Hinkel and the phantom
dog
LEACH – RAINBOW p244-245

The grandmother and the crocodile
TRACEY – LION p51-54

Grandmother Marta
PRIDHAM – GIFT p100-106

Grandmothers
And I dance mine own child
The black stone
The blind boy and the loon
The boy who wouldn't mind his
grandmother
Budulinek
The dragon and his grandmother
The fairy frog
The flight with the Wendigo
The girl who met the witch of the
woods
Granny Shelock
How Maui obtained the magic jawbone
Khasynget's grandmother
Little Red Riding Hood
Red Riding Hood
A story for Kiem
Sven and Lilli
The theft of fire
The three golden hairs of the king
of the cave giants
To feed my people: The coming of
corn
The yellow dragon
Young hunter

Grandmother's tale
SINGER – ZLATEH p21-23

Granny Shelock
MEHDEVI – BUNGLING p37-43

Granny's blackie
ARBUTHNOT – TIME p148-149

Grant, Ed
Meet Ed Grant

Grapes and grape-vines
The best wish
The daughter of the dwarf
The fox and the grapes
The king's vine
Why the deer's teeth are blunt

Graphology
How pictures become words
The soothsayers

Grasp all, lose all
LANG – OLIVE p90-98

Grass
Anansi's hat-shaking dance
The barren stones
The bird which laid diamonds
The judgment of the wind
The parish bull eats the grass from
the wall
A secret told to a stranger
The sparrow and the stalk of grass
Who is strongest?

Grasscutters
Wali Dad the simple-hearted

The grasshopper and the ant
ARBUTHNOT – TIME p211.

Grasshopper green
MY BOOK HOUSE v. 2 p76.

Grasshoppers
The butterfly's ball
The devil in the wheat
An explanation of the grasshopper
How coyote put fish in Clear Lake
How grasshopper came to be and men
obtained tobacco
The jumping contest
Laughing song
The message from the moon
Mogo, Popo, and Wogo
The princess who knew her own mind
Tithonus, the grasshopper
Why grasshopper spits tobacco juice

The grateful animals and the talisman
THOMPSON – ONE p244-248

The grateful ant
GREEN – BIG p73.

The grateful ass
SPICER – KNEELING p58-73

The grateful beasts
CARPENTER – ELEPHANT'S p114-
124

The grateful devil
SPICER – DEVILS p71-82

The grateful goat
MANNING – BEASTS p86-90

The grateful lion
GREEN – BIG p11-14

The grateful monkey's secret
UCHIDA – SEA p22-32

The grateful mouse
GAER – FABLES p149-152

The grateful old cailleach
LEODHAS – GAELIC p46-57

The grateful prince
LANG – VIOLET p73-95
MAAS – MOON p60-81

The grateful snake
BAMBERGER – FIRST p122-125

The grateful statues
SAKADE – JAPAN. p106-111

The grateful stork
UCHIDA – MAGIC p133-144

The grateful weasel
O'SULLIVAN – FOLK. p10-12

Gratitude
See also **Ingratitude**
The bow that bridges heaven
Browny
The cap that mother made
The clever jackal and how he outwitted
the tiger
Dwarf stories
Evening at the farm
The first Thanksgiving Day
The fisherman and the mermaid
The good man and the kind mouse
The governor and the Buddhist
Harvest moon
Heidi in the Alpine pasture
The injured lion
The Laird O 'Co
The lion and the fox
The lion and the mouse
Little Gulliver
The lost spear
The maiden, the knight and the water-
fall
The Nuremberg stove
Old pipes and the dryad
Providence
Ruddy-my-beard
The shoemaker and the elves
The Thanksgiving of the Wazir
The tiger's grave
Vladimir's adventures in search of
fortune
We thank thee
The wolf's reward
The wonderland of an artist's work-
shop

Grave diggers
The king o' the cats
The king of the cats
The meat hungry man and the grave
digger

The grave of a faithful dog
INS-SOB – FOLK p92-93

Graveyards. *See* **Cemeteries**

Gravity
The light princess

The gray goose
STOUTENBURG – CROC. p19-21

Graylegs
HATCH – MORE p3-21

Grazing on the roof
JAGENDORF – MERRY p77-86

Grease (fat)
The bride who melted away
The gluttonous wife
Tavadan and the fire giant

Great A, little A, bouncing B
MY BOOK HOUSE v. 1 p52.

The great-aunt
HOPE-SIMPSON – CAVAL. p212-223

The great bear
JABLOW – MAN p105-112
LEACH – HOW p133-134

The great bell
BUCK – FAIRY p264-268

The great bird in the carob tree
CARPENTER – SOUTH p11-17

The great blessing of the land
JAGENDORF – KING p122-126

Great Britain
See also **England;** names of individual
countries
Alison Gross
Beowulf
The cauldron of Brekkan
Clever Jacob Gibson
Collen
The dark tower
The dream of Maxen Wledig

The elfin knight
Farmer Giles of Ham
Foolish kings
Gawayne and the green knight
Gog and Magog
Hereward
Hereward the wake
King Herla
King Herla, The Little People of the
British Isles
King John and the Abbot of Canter-
bury
The king of the cats
The lion with the steady hand
The magic head
The marriage of Sir Gawain
Merlin
The pedlar of Swaffham
The quest of the sons of Turenn
Ragnar Lodbrok and his sons
The rose
Saxons
The secret commonwealth
Sir Bevis of Hampton
Tam Lin
The three little pigs
The three plagues of Britain
The three ravens
An unhappy lord
The unicorn and the dwarf
Wild worms and swooning shadows
William of Cloudslee

The great festival
FEINSTEIN – FOLK p21-24

The great fish
GREEN – BIG p235-240
MICHAEL – PORTUGUESE p92-104

The great fish of Maui
CAMPBELL – MAORI p15-19

The great flood
INS-SOB – FOLK p16-18
JAGENDORF – KING p81-83
SECHRIST – ONCE p8-10

Great Head and the ten brothers
GARNER – GOBLINS p101-104

Great heart and the three tests
MacMILLAN – GLOOS. p164-171

Great hunting!
WITHERS – WORLD p85-86

Great Lakes
The devil's wood
Legends

The great liar
O'SULLIVAN – FOLK. p249-252

The great lizard of Nimple
COURLANDER – TIGER'S p140-141

The great medicine horse
CARPENTER – HORSES p222-230

The great Queen Hatshepsut
GREEN – TALES p59-65

The great sacrifice
JAGENDORF – UPSTATE p216-221

The great scare
RASKIN – TALES p37-42

"Great spirit." See "Spirit, Great"

The great spirit of the toad
PRATT – MAGIC unp.

The great white condor
BARLOW – LATIN p50-56

The greater sinner
THOMPSON – ONE p343-344

The greatest archer
BIRCH – CHINESE p9-19

The greatest boast
WITHERS – WORLD p33.

The greatest hoax in New York City
JAGENDORF – GHOST p72-78

The greatest person in the world
BELTING – CAT p16-20

The greatest show on earth
MY BOOK HOUSE v. 8 p154a-154b

The greatest wealth in the world
JAGENDORF – KING p233-236

Greatness
    See also Power; Strength
How the dog chose its master
The king and the ring
Luck and wit
The mole's bridegroom
The mouse and the elephant
The penalty of greatness
A song for the new chief
The wedding of the mouse
Which is the greater?

Grebes
Goose dance

Greece
    See also Gods and goddesses–Greece
The adventures of Perseus
Alas!
The animal wife
The ass gets the better of the wolf
Atalanta's race; a contest for love or
    death
The battle of the frogs and the mice
The bay-tree maiden
The beardless one
Big Matsiko
The boastful gnat
The box with wings
The brave three hundred
The cats
A cause of war
The clever peasant girl
The clever thief
Constantes and the dragon
The cunning old man and the three
    rogues
Cyclopes
Damian and the dragon
Dates to Cairo
Diogenes the wise man
The dove maiden
Fairy gardens
Fairy mother
The fairy wife
Field mouse and house mouse
The first of May
The flying horse, Pegasus
The foolish ass
The foolish wife and her three foolish
    daughters
The forgotten bride
The four fishes
The fox and the crow
The fox and the lion in partnership
The fox outwits the lion
Goblin bread
The golden casket
The golden crab
The golden horse
The golden nightingale
Good luck and common sense
The grateful animals and the talisman
The greater sinner
The greedy dog
The hair from the queen of the under-
    world
Here we come, we children come
The imposter
The labors of Hercules
The laurel maiden
Lazarus and the dragons

Greece (*Continued*)

The learned young professor
The lion and the mouse
The lion, the tiger, and the eagle
Luck
The magic bird
Medusa
The melodius napkin
The mouse keeps her promise
Musk and amber
My candlestick
My lady sea
No man with the Cyclops
Oh and Alas
Pelops and Poseidon
Penteclemas and the pea
Pleiad and star of dawn
Polyphemus, the Cyclops
The prince and the vizier's son
The princess who loved her father like
  salt
The quarrel
Quinces and oranges
The red cloak
The return of Odysseus
The servant who took the place of
  his master
The silent princess
The silly slave
Sirens
The six companions
The slaying of Hector
The sleeping prince
The sleepless dragon
The son of the hunter
The sun-child
The sun, the moon and the star of
  morning
The sword of Damocles; the man who
  would be king
Sybaris . . . Life of luxury
The Three Fates
The three golden apples
The three precepts
The three walnuts
The three words of advice
The tortoise and the hare
The tortoise-wife
The twelve months of the year
The twins
Twins in the sky
The ungrateful snake
The unlucky goat
The unlucky man
Where are my roses?
The wild man
The wise ant
The wolf wears a sheepskin
The wonder of Skoupa
The world's great epics
Yiankos

—Songs
Children's songs of ancient
  Greece (by Theognis)

Greed
See also **Misers**
Aldar-Kos and the greedy rich man
Anansi plays dead
The anger of Sande-Nyana
The baby camel
The blind boy and the loon
The boy and the nuts
The buffalo who made undue de-
  mands
A Chinese cinderella
The clever goatherd and the greedy
  giant
The crow and the whale
The dancing monkeys
The devil's gifts
The eternal wanderer
The farmer and the fairy cow
Feedowa and Nobbin
Fiddler John and the devil
The first zebra
The foolish dog and his reflection
The forest wolf and the prairie wolf
A gift for a gift
The giraffe hunters
The golden axe
The golden crow
The golden goose
The golden mountain
The golden touch
The golden touch; the king who wor-
  shipped gold
The goldfish
Gombel and the wild ducks
Grasp all, lose all
A handful of peas
Hansel and Grethel
Hare and the hyena
The hen that laid the golden eggs
The hex and the oxen
Holding the bag
How and why: Don't be greedy story
How foolish men are!
How grasshopper came to be and men
  obtained tobacco
How locusts came to be
How much for a shadow?
How Pakayana the spider got his
  small waist
How spider got a bald head
How spider got a thin waist
How spider helped a fisherman
How the milky way began
How the travelers shared their meal
How Ysengrin the wolf was taught to
  fish
The hunger time

Greed (*Continued*)

The hurt sparrow
Ijapa cries for his horse
Ijapa demands corn fufu
The insatiable beggar
Jonathan Moulton and the devil
The just reward
The key maiden of Tegerfelden
King Appolonides
Kwaku Ananse and the greedy lion
Kwaku Ananse and the whipping cord
The Lake of Zangzě
The lady's loaf--field
Lazy Peter and the king
The legend of the Moor's legacy
A lie for a lie
The little rooster and the little hen
The magic berries
The man who had plenty of good
  peanuts
The man who loved Hai Quai
Mary covered with gold and Mary
  covered with pitch
Master and man
Nidelgret
The nutcracker and sugardolly stories
The old man of the flowers
The old man who cut bamboo
The old man with the bump
Piboon's golden mountain
Poor little girl, rich little girl
The price of greed
The prize
Rake up!
The rat-catcher's daughter
Reen-reen-reeny-croak-frog
The rice cake that rolled away
Rich woman, poor woman
The rooster and the sultan
St. Cuddy and the gray geese
The sick boy, the greedy hunters, and
  the dwarfs, The Little People of
  North America
The simpleton
The small red feather
The story of the five toes
The story of the haunted jars
The story of the stone lion
The sun and the moon
The sunken city
The tale of the Rhine-gold
A tale of two rogues
Three bridegrooms for one bride
The three brothers
The three figs
The three wishes
Tom Walker and the devil
The tongue-cut sparrow
The twelve months
The two brothers

Two feasts for Anansi
The two friends
The two wishes
The ungrateful children
A voice from heaven
White squash boy
Why spiders live in dark corners
Why the sea is salt
Why the spider has a narrow waist
The witch tree of the North country
Wolfert Webber, or golden dreams

Greed in heaven, growth on earth
  JAGENDORF – KING p43-48

Greedy and speedy
  GAER – FABLES p14-18

The greedy boy and the coconut crab
  GREY – SOUTH (1) p9-11

The greedy crow
  GAER – FABLES p168-171

The greedy dog
  WILSON – GREEK p120-121

The greedy friend
  EDMONDS – TRICKSTER p120-128

The greedy giant and the Palau Islands
  GREY – SOUTH (2) p27-31

The greedy hawk
  SEKI – FOLKTALES p22-23

The greedy hyena
  HEADY – JAMBO p91-93

The greedy man in the moon
  JABLOW – MAN p7-13

The greedy old fat man
  WITHERS – I SAW p24-26

The greedy rich man
  DEUTSCH – MORE p73-78

The greedy spider
  ELLIOT – WHERE p34-40

The greedy stallkeeper and the poor
  traveler
  AUNG – KINGDOM p15-17

The greedy tailor
  PROTTER – CHILD. p153-156

Greek mythology. *See* **Gods and
goddesses–Greece**

The green-bearded king
ILLYES – ONCE p63-68

The Green children
BRIGGS – PERS. p38-39

The green frog
INS-SOB – FOLK p34-35

The green glass bottle
WILSON – IRELAND n.p.

The green isle
WILSON – SCOTTISH p200-204

The green knight
LANG – VIOLET p203-218

The green mist
GARNER – GOBLINS p216-221

Green Mountain boys
Giant of the Green Mountains

Green Mountain hero
JAGENDORF – NEW p89-94

Green Mountains, kingdom of. See The
kingdom of the Green Mountains

Green parrot's story
SHERLOCK – IGUANA'S p11-28

Green people
The Green children

The green sergeant
BAKER – TALKING p184-190

The green-skinned princess
SPICER – GOBLINS p106-117

Green willow
HEARN – JAPANESE p89-100

Greenaway, Kate
Higgledy, piggledy! see how they run!
School is over
Tommy was a silly boy
Yes, that's the girl that struts about

Greenland
The American saga
How the people began

Greenwood trees
Under the greenwood tree

Gregory, Lady
Oisin's mother

Gremlins
The Little People

Gremlins, elves and leprechauns
BATCHELOR – SUPER. p124-126

Grettir becomes an outlaw
HAZELTINE – HERO p278-295

Grettir the strong. See The hauntings at
Thorhallstead

Greye, John–Papers
The curious John Greye papers

Greyman
BOUCHER – MEAD p55-62

Grief
The birth of the islands
How death came into the world
The little lizard's sorrow
The red king and the witch
The rooster and the wind
Sorrow
The three apples
The voyage below the water
The weeping lass at the dancing place

Griffins
The flower faces
The golden apples of Hisberna
Guardians of hidden treasure
The man without a heart
Winged wonders
Yet gentle will the griffin be

–Feathers
The griffon
The singing bone

The griffon
LUM – ITALIAN p150-160

Grillo
MANNING – GIANNI p145-160

Grillparzer, Franz
Momus the mocker

Grim and the merman
JONES – SCAND. p138-139

Grimm, Jacob and Wilhelm
Clever Elsie
The fly and the bee
Doctor know-it-all

Grimm, Jacob and Wilhelm (*Continued*)

The fox and the geese
The frog prince
The giant and the tailor
The golden goose
The goose-girl
Hansel and Gretel
The hedgehog and the rabbit
Jorinda and Joringel
The little girl and the hare
Little one eye, little two eyes and little
three eyes
Mrs. Fox's wedding
The mouse, the bird and the sausage
The poor miller's boy and the cat
Porridge
Rag, tag and bobtail
Rapunzel
Red Riding Hood
Rumpelstiltzkin
The seven ravens
Sleeping beauty
Snow-white and Rose-red
Snow-white and the seven dwarfs
The snow-wife
The sorcerer's apprentice
The star florins
The straw, the coal and the bean
The three feathers
The valiant tailor
The water-sprite
The wee folk
Wild rose
The wolf and the fox
The wolf and the seven kids
The wren
The wren and the bear

Grimm, Jakob and Wilhelm
SIDEMAN – WORLD'S p829-830

Grimsey (Island)
Grim and the merman

Grinnell, George Bird
Scarface

Griselda
MARKS – SPANISH p70-83

The grizzly and the rattlesnake men
MATSON – LONGHOUSE p96-99

The groach of the Isle of Lok
MANNING – MERMAIDS p86-97

Groceries
MY BOOK HOUSE v. 1 p182.

Grocers
The magic grocery store
Sly Peter's revenge

Gronro's stone
Lleu and the flowerface

The groschen hole in the Murz Valley
MÜLLER – SWISS p163-165

Grottoes
See also **Fairies–Grottoes**
The dream at Nam Kha
The shell grotto of Nienoort

Grouchiness. *See* **Grumbling**

The groundhog family
SCHOOLCRAFT – FIRE p39-40

Groundhogs. *See* **Woodchucks**

Grouse
The bear says north
Hie away, hie away
Khasynget's grandmother
The stone of victory

Growing pains
LEACH – NOODLES p80.

The growing rock
CURRY – DOWN p121-128

Growing wings
LIN – MILKY p41-46

Growth
Melisande

Grumbling
The cock, the mouse, and the little
red hen
Grumpy Timothy Crumb
The man who kept house
The peasant and the baron
Three wishes

Grumpy Timothy Crumb
JAGENDORF – NEW p248-255

Guadalupe, Lady of
Our Lady of Guadalupe

Guardian of the house
LEACH – SOUP p56-57

Guardians of hidden treasure
JACOBSON – FIRST p35-36

Guatemala
A Chimalteco story
The emerald lizard
Golden goodness
The great blessing of the land
The little, little fellow with the big, big hat
The sacred amulet
The sweetest amulet
The sweetest song in the woods
Vukub-Cakix

Guavas
The Panditji and the guavas

Guazzo, Francesco-Maria, jt. auth.
Belief
Italy

Gudbrand of the hillside
ASBJÖRNSEN – NORW. p178-181
ARBUTHNOT – TIME p82-84
THOMPSON – ONE p384-388

The gudewife's midnight labours.
See also The horned women
BRIGGS – PERS. p73-76

Gudrun
PICARD – GERMAN p3-22

Guenevere, Queen
The end of Arthur
How Guenevere went a-maying
Lancelot and Elaine
Lancelot and Guenever
Lancelot of the lake
The marriage of Arthur
The poisoned apple
The siege of joyous Gard
Sir Launfal

Guesses
The last three guesses
Nine guesses

The guest from Heaven
DURHAM – TIT p75-80

Guests
The boy with the golden star
Clever Grethel
A strange guest
The uninvited guest
Young Michael and the uninvited guest

Guides, hunting and fishing
An adventure with a bear
A curious tale
Ed Grant has a dream
Ed Grant out West
The hideless bear
How rabbit lost his tail
A long shot
Maine's best boatman
Meet Ed Grant
Minute pudding
A most peculiar bear hide
Mount Kennebago
The new camp stove
The new camp stove burns again
Some punkins
The tale of a watch
The tame trout
Uncle Ed is chased by a bear
Uncle Ed tracks a rabbit
Uncle Ed's unusual bear hide
Who is boss?
A word from the author
The world's most truthful man

Guile. See Cleverness

Guilt
Ashoremashika
Self-convicted

Guiana(s). See West Indies–Guiana

Guinea fowls
Anansi and the elephant exchange knocks
Anansi, the oldest of animals
The fox in saint's clothing
Ijapa goes to the Osanyin shrine
The wedding of the hawk

Guinea pigs
Dry-bone and Anansi
Dwarf long nose
The princess who saw everything in her kingdom

The guinea pig's tail
CATHON – PERHAPS p71-76

Guinivere, Queen. See Guenevere, Queen

Guitars
See also Kantele(s)
The horse of seven colors
The owl and the pussy-cat
The twins
Uncle rabbit flies to heaven

Gulam . . . The jar of rice
UNTERMEYER – FIRE. p153-155

Gulersh and the princess of France
WILLIAMS – OLD p13-29

Gulf Coast
Mister Deer's my riding horse

The gull
DEUTSCH – TALES p36-43

Gull taught men to use manioc for food
BELTING – STARS #13

A gullible world
FILLMORE – SHEPHERD'S p153-159

Gulliver in the giants' country
DE REGNIERS – GIANT p136-158

Gulliver's travels to Lilliput
MY BOOK HOUSE v. 8 p38-81

Gulls. *See* **Sea gulls**

The gun, the pot, and the hat
COURLANDER – PIECE p39-49

Guno and Koyo
COURLANDER – KANT. p59-62

Guno and Koyo and the Kirs
COURLANDER – TIGER'S p118-121

Guno's hunger
COURLANDER – KANT. p73-74

Guns and gunnery
The beardless one
The devil and the man
Freddy and his fiddle
Lion and man
Little Freddie with his fiddle
A long shot
The silly men of Russia
Tiny Perry
Yankees

The gunsmith and the maiden
JAGENDORF – UPSTATE p97-100

The Guragies: workmen of high Africa
DAVIS – LION'S p126-127

Gurgle, water, gurgle
MY BOOK HOUSE v. 1 p72.

Gurus (monks, holy ones)
How much for a shadow?

Guy Fawkes . . . The gunpowder plot
UNTERMEYER – FIRE. p236-238

Gwai-nee-bu the redbreast
PARKER – AUSTRALIAN p221-225

Gwarwyn-a-Throt
SHEPPARD – WELSH p13-18

The Gwraig and the three blows
See also Swan maidens
BRIGGS – PERS. p160-163

Gypsies
See also stories beginning with Gipsies
About the gypsies
Ashypelt
Bald pate
Baldpate
The basket-maker's donkey
Batim the horse
The black dog of the wild forest
Blanche's high-flying Halloween
The boyar and the gipsy
Brian and the fox
The brigands and the miller's daughter
The changeling
The chief astrologer
Clever Pat
The deluded dragon
A dish of laban
The dog and the maiden
The dragon and the stepmother
Eighteen rabbits
Evan's problem
The fiddle
Fishing for pots in the pond
Flaming tales
The flower faces
Fording the river in a copper cauldron
The girl out of the egg
Goggle-eyes
The golden box
Gonae
Happy Boz'll
How the cows flew across the sea
How the gipsy sold his horse
How the gypsy boy outsmarted death
The husband, the wife, and the devil
I was going along the road
I was traveling those parts
Introduction (HAMPDEN – GYPSY)
It all comes to light
Jack at Hell Gate
Jack and his golden snuff-box
Jankyn and the witch
A little bull-calf

Gypsies (*Continued*)

The little fox
The little nobleman
The little snake
The lovebirds
Maggie Tulliver goes to live with the gypsies
Magic apples
Meg Merrilies
Noodlehead and the flying horse
The old gypsy woman and the Good Lord
An old king and his three sons of England
The old soldier and the mischief
The peasant's strong wife
Prop for the tree
The raggle, taggle gypsies
The red king and the witch
The riddle
Saint Peter and his trombone
The seventh princess
The silly fellow who sold his beard
The silly men of Russia
Sinko's luck
The sly gypsy
The sly gypsy and the stupid devil
Small white stones
The snake
Squirrel and fox

The stolen bairn and the Sidh
The summer of the big snow
The sun-king's hair
Sylvester
Taikon, Johan Dimitri
The tale of a foolish brother and of a wonderful bush
The tale of the gypsy and his strange love
The three princesses and the unclean spirit
The Tims
The tinker and his wife
A tramp of the Middle West
Traveling through the chimney
Tropsyn
A wanderer with a dog
A wicked fox
The yellow dragon
Young happy

The gypsies' fiddle
   JAGENDORF – GYPSIES p102-110

The gypsy and the snake
   JAGENDORF – GYPSIES p24-34

The gypsy fiddle
   HAMPDEN – GYPSY p155-157

The gypsy in the ghost house
   JAGENDORF – GYPSIES p111-117

H

Ha! Tio rabbit is bigger
JAGENDORF – KING p211-218

The Habasha and the king of kings
DAVIS – LION'S p13-23

Habetrot
See also The idle girl with the three
aunts; The three spinners
BRIGGS – PERS. p101-150

Habetrot and Scantlie Mab
JACOBS – MORE p195-200

Habit
Who can break a bad habit?

Hackett, Walter
The swans of Ballycastle

Hactins (the holy ones)
How the people sang the mountains
up

The haddam witches
HOKE – WITCHES p187-191
JAGENDORF – NEW p206-211

Hades. *See* **Hell**

Hadji (holy men)
Pursuit of the Hadji

Haensel and Gretel
THOMPSON – ONE p55-61

Hags. *See* **Witches**

Hai Quai. *See* **Shells**

Hail
The legend of the hail
The rabbit prince

Hair
The bird of the golden land
Blonde, brunette or redhead
The dark king
Eat bread crusts for curly hair
The hair from the queen of the
underworld
The hairs of the baron's head

Keloglan and the magic hairs
The little milleress
Petrosinella or Parsley
Rapunzel
The seventh princess
The tale of the two brothers
Tyl's task

–Color
The man who sold magic

, Golden
Connla of the golden hair
Dorani
Fairy gardens
The golden-haired children
The imposter
Melisande
Princess Golden-hair and the great
black raven
The princess with the golden hair
Rapunzel
Sif's golden hair
The stone horseman
The sun-king's hair
The swineherd who married a
princess
The three golden hairs
The three golden hairs of Grandad
Sol

, Long
The boy with the long hair

, Red
Prince Llewellyn and the red-haired man

–Tufts
Ricky of (with) the tuft

, White
The story of Zal

, Yellow
The yellow-haired witch

The hair from the queen of the underworld
BAMBERGER – FIRST p204-206

The hairs of the baron's head
MORRIS – UPSTAIRS p79-86

The hairy-armed ogre of Kyoto
SPICER – 13 p32-39

The hairy boggart
WILLIAMS – FAIRY p82-87

The hairy boggart's field
SPICER – GOBLINS p35-44

The hairy man from the forest
CARPENTER – SOUTH p93-99

Hairy men. *See* Curupiras

Haiti
The blacksmiths
Bouki and Ti Bef
Bouki buys a burro
Bouki cuts wood
Bouki gets whee-ai
Bouki rents a horse
Bouki's glasses
Break mountains
The cat, the dog, and death
Charles Legoun and his friend
The chief of the well
The donkey driver
The gun, the pot, and the hat
The Haitians in the Dominican
  Republic
Janot cooks for the emperor
Jean Britisse, the champion
The king of the animals
The lizard's big dance
Merisier, stronger than the
  elephants
Nananbouclou, and the piece of fire
Pierre Jean's tortoise
Sweet misery
Ticoumba and the president
Uncle Bouki rents a horse
Uncle Bouqui and little malice
The voyage below the water
Waiting for a turkey
Who is older?
Why goat cannot clim a tree

The Haitians in the Dominican Republic
JAGENDORF – KING p106-110

Haku's power
McNEILL – DOUBLE p36-40

Halde Hat and Dulde Hat
DE REGNIERS – GIANT p106-108

Hale, Lucretia
The lady who put salt in her coffee
Mrs. Peterkin wishes to go to drive

Half a yard
NYE – MARCH p16-22

Half-breeds
The lost remains of Mr. Quejo

The half-chick
ARBUTHNOT – TIME p120-122
DOBBS – ONCE p8-14
HAVILAND – SPAIN p36-49
SIDEMAN – WORLD'S p657-644

The half-pint jinni
CHILD – CASTLES p1-27

Hali becomes a poet
JONES – SCAND. p135-137

Hallabau's jealousy
ARNOTT – AFRICAN p160-166

Hallowe'en
The adventures of Nera
Alison Gross
The beekeeper and the bewitched
  hare
Blanche's high-flying Halloween
The coming of Fionn MacCool
Holiday luck
Peepan pee
The secret commonwealth
Tam Lin
Tamlane
Twelve great black cats and the red
  one
The twelve silly sisters
The young Tamlin

Hallowe'en (Halloween)
GARNER – GOBLINS p100.
MY BOOK HOUSE v. 4 p142.

Hallowell, Priscilla
The long-nosed princess

Hallowell, Priscilla
JOHNSON – PRINC. p310-311

Haltefanden (The lame devil)
HACK – DANISH p24-29

Hamadryads
Bears in the sky
The scarlet maple

Hammerman/John Henry
STOUTENBURG – AMER. p88-100

Hammers
The bird of the golden land
Fairy workmen
Hammerman/John Henry
John Henry

Hammers (*Continued*)

John Henry and double-jointed steam
 drill
Little one-inch
The magic sandals
One-inch fellow
The partridge and his drum
Sif's golden hair
The spider specter of the pool
Stinginess
The theft of Thor's hammer
Thor and the jotun Aegir
Thor gains his hammer
Thor's hammer is stolen
Wind and wave and wandering flame

Hams

The mill that grinds at the bottom of
the sea

The hand of glory
HOPE-SIMPSON – CAVAL.
p187-195

A handful of hay
MANNING – GLASS p71-82

A handful of peas
REED – TALK. p68-69

Handicapped

Four good men
The girl without arms
The good judge
How three pilgrims called Ilya to the
rescue of Kiev
The pious butcher
Samson and the doll in green and
brown

The handkerchief
GILSTRAP – SULTAN'S p51-60

Handkerchiefs

Alberto and the monsters
Dobryna's embassy to Khan Amryl
Drop the handkerchief
The enchanted castle in the sea
The fairy wife
The giant beanstalk
The gift of the holy man
How Jack sought the golden apples
A little bull-calf
The shepherd's nosegay
The tale of the foolish brother and of
a wonderful bush
The tiger priest

Handmills. *See* **Mills, Hand**

Hands

The ghostly hand of Spital house
The girl without hands
The hand of glory
The holy relic of Bannockburn
The invisible hands

–**Clapping**

Pease-porridge hot

–**Fingers**

Cross your fingers

–**Shaking**

Here is my hand on it
How to shake hands with a giant

–**Thumbs**

Thumbs up, thumbs down

The handsome apprentice
MANNING – JONNIKIN p54-67

The handsome Kahveci
EKREM – TURKISH p13-19

Handwriting. *See* **Graphology**

Handy-spandy
MY BOOK HOUSE v. 1 p33.

Hang up a horseshoe
BATCHEROR – SUPER. p6-7

Hanging at Wessaguscus
TAFT – PROFILE p37-43

Hangings

The adventures of Manawyddan
The golden ball
Seven sons

Hani the simple
NAHMAD – PEASANT p83-90

Hans and his master
MANNING – GHOSTS p55-61

Hans Clodhopper. *See* The finest liar in
the world

Hans Hansen's hired girl
WITHERS – WORLD p43-44

Hans, the horn, and the magic sword
MANNING – GIANTS p36-43

Hans the tailor and the talking animals
BECHSTEIN – FAIRY p84-96

Hansel and Gretel
   See also Haensel and Gretel; Hansel
     and Grethel
   ARBUTHNOT – TIME p43-46
   HAVILAND – GERMANY p51-71
   MANNING – WITCHES p83-93
   SIDEMAN – WORLD'S p549-560

Hansel and Gretel stories
   The witch

Hansel and Grethel
   MY BOOK HOUSE v. 4 p73-79

Hantsje and the remarkable beast
   SPICER – DEVILS p25-32

Hanukkah
   The devil's trick
   The first shlemiel
   Grandmother's tale
   Zlateh the goat

A happening on Christmas eve
   RASKIN – TALES p57-62

Happiness
   See also **Cheerfulness**
   Are fat people happy?
   Bang-whang-whang
   The bee man and the boundary man
   The blue cat
   The boy who made hay
   Catherine and the fates
   Everyone's glad in our city today
   Faust
   The Fourth of July
   The frogs of Windham town
   The gift of gold
   Go out, children
   God hath made me to laugh
   Good luck and common sense
   Good luck and great riches
   A good neighbor
   Grasshopper green
   The grateful devil
   Hark, the Christmas bells are ringing
   Hear ye!
   Heidi in the Alpine pasture
   I-yay! I-yay! I-yay!
   Laughing song
   Little fir tree
   Little Gustava
   The long-nosed princess
   The man who looked for death
   A merry tale of Merrymount
   The miller of the dee

   Money makes cares
   Nanny and Conn
   Nurse's song
   On being a happy cow
   Pannychis
   Park play
   The piece of straw
   Providence
   Radowid
   Reinar was watching his cows
   Riches or happiness?
   The seed of happiness
   The shoemaker
   Songs of joy from the Bible
   The story of Zoulvisia
   The talisman
   The thoughtless abbot
   The three gifts
   The three wishes
   Tim for wealth and happiness
   Wee Robin's Christmas song
   What are you able to build with your
     blocks?
   The wonderful tune
   The wooden bowl
   The world is so full
   Young happy

Happy Boz'll
   MANNING – RED p174-175
   WILLIAMS – FAIRY p32-33

The happy cure
   DOBBS – ONCE p27-33

A happy day in the city
   MY BOOK HOUSE v. 3 p181-195

Happy Hans
   NYBLOM – WITCH p20-34

The happy man
   GILSTRAP – SULTAN'S p26-31

The happy milkmaid
   BRENNER – BOY p12-13

The happy prince
   JOHNSON – HARPER p250-267

The happy years
   PILKINGTON – THREE p165-171

The harbor
   MY BOOK HOUSE v. 1 p184.

Harbors
   The fog
   The lady of Stavoren
   Look, see the boat!

The hardhearted rich man
MAHER – BLIND p115-131

Hardy Hardback
WILLIAMS – FAIRY p124-131

The hare
BORSKI – GOOD p60.

Hare and the corn bins
ARNOTT – AFRICAN p101-104

Hare and the hyena
ARNOTT – AFRICAN p108-111

The hare and the lord
JAGENDORF – MERRY p105-112

The hare and the tiger
BULATKIN – EURASIAN p80-81
VO-DINH – TOAD p57-64

The hare and the tortoise
ARBUTHNOT – TIME p208.
LA FONTAINE – FABLES p50-51
MY BOOK HOUSE v. 2 p106-107

The hare, badger, monkey, and otter
SEKI – FOLKTALES p4-6

The hare herd
RANKE – GERMANY p107-112

The hare in the moon
CATHON – PERHAPS p250-252
GRAY – INDIA'S p186-187
TURNBULL – FAIRY p151-157
WYATT – GOLDEN p112-117

Hare makes a fool of leopard
HASKETT – GRAINS p51-54

The hare of Inaba
HEARN – JAPANESE p42-46

The hare that ran away
ARBUTHNOT – TIME p148.

The hare who had been married
ASBJÖRNSEN – NORW. p115.

The hare who was afraid of nothing
BUDBERG – RUSSIAN p70-73

The hare with many friends
ARBUTHNOT – TIME p202.

Harebells
The king of the hares

The hairbrained monkey
GAER – FABLES p153-154

Harelips
Prospect and retrospect

Hares. *See* **Rabbits**

The hare's kidneys
TASHJIAN – THREE p49-61

The hare's lip
CATHON – PERHAPS p62-63

Hark, hark! Bow-wow!
MY BOOK HOUSE v. 1 p149.

Hark, the Christmas bells are ringing
MY BOOK HOUSE v. 1 p133.

Harlequin
Columbine and her playfellows of the
Italian pantomine

Harmachis
Horus the avenger
The prince and the Sphinx
The tale of two brothers

A harp on the water. *See* The eight leaves
of story (4) A harp on the water

Harpischords
A kiss from the beautiful Fiorita

Harps and harpists
Aliosha's visit to the bald mountain
Aucassin and Nicolette
The bee, the mouse, and the bum-
clock
Boots and the troll
The ceabharnach
The disappearance of Rhys
The duty that was not paid
The eight leaves of story (4) A harp
on the water
Finn MacCool
The flooding of the Lower Hundred
The foretelling
How Finn won his father's place
How Tristram fought against the
knight from Ireland
Jack and the beanstalk
King Orfeo
The legend of Bala Lake
The little-man-as-big-as-your-thumb-
with mustaches-seven-miles-long
The Lochmaben harper

Harps and harpists *(Continued)*
The musician of Taguang
Orpheus and Eurydice
The princess and the dwarf
The royal musician
Sir Orfeo
The stolen bairn and the Sïdh
The stone of victory
The sword of light
The tale of the Lochmaben harper
The young Tamlin

, **Fairy**
Morgan and the three fairies

, **Golden**
Jack and the beanstalk

Harris, Joel Chandler
A story about the little rabbits

Harris, Joel Chandler
'Way down South in Dixie

Hart, Johan
The hare's lip
Jan and Jaantje
The magic cap

Hartland, E.S.
How the ghost got in

Harts. *See* **Deer**

Harvard College
The power of fancy

The Harvard professor
MY BOOK HOUSE v. 12 p135-137

Harvest and harvesters
The farmer and the harvesters
Maid Lena

Harvest moon
BUDD – FULL p50-56

Haskett, Edythe Rance
HASKETT – GRAINS p120.

Hastings–Nursery songs
The bees

Hasty corners
TAFT – PROFILE p243-248

Hasty porridge in the boiling water
JAGENDORF – MERRY p64-68

The hat in the moon
JAGENDORF – SAND p97-100

Hatch, Alice
Frithiof's journey to the Orkneys

Hatch, Mary C.
The wonderful knapsack

Hatchet Kasha
WYNDHAM – TALES p38-42

Hatchets
Ergosai-Batyr
George Washington and his hatchet

Hatfield, Charles
The lost secrets of Charles Hatfield

Hathor, The lady of love (goddess)
Ra and his children

Hatred
See also **Enmity**
The black pool
Donkeys! Dogs! Cats! Rats!
The smoking mountain

Hats
The bear in the black hat
The companion
The density of Princess Tien Dung
The gun, the pot, and the hat
Halde Hat and Dulde Hat
Holding down the hat
Johnny shall have a new bonnet
The king and his seven sons
Lazy Peter and his three-cornered hat
The little, little fellow with the big,
big hat
Maid Lena
The monkeys and the little red hats
New Year's hats for the statues
O'Connell wears his hat in Parliament
Seven iron-souled slippers
Sima who wore the big hat
Test of a friendship
The three-cornered hat
Three magic charms
Tsar Peter the Great and the peasant
Water drops
The wonderful talking bowl

–**Caps**
The apple of contentment
Bendebukk
The blue cap
The cap that mother made
Fifty red night-caps
The firefly

276

Hawaiian Islands (*Continued*)

The shark in the milky way
Spears of lightning
The spirit who danced
A strange sled race
Three tales of the goblins who lived
   on the sea-bottom
The time of deep darkness
The Wiliwili trees
The woman in moon

−**Kaüai**
Kawelo the little-brother-to-the-
   rats
The little menehunes
The weary spirits of Lanai

−**Oahu**
The boy who became king of the
   sharks
Kaleleä and his wish

The hawk and the hen
DEUTSCH − TALES p1-6

The hawk and the nightingale
GREEN − BIG p70.

The hawk and the wildcat
SECHRIST − ONCE p54-56

The hawk fledgling
SEKI − FOLKTALES p190.

Hawkes, Jacquetta
The great fish
Land, water and wind
Other island

Hawks
Ani, the mother who was too proud
The birds' St. Valentine Day
The bungling host
Chimpanzee's story
The cock and the sparrow-hawk
The devil's apprentice
Dry-bone and Anansi
The elephant's tail
The fox and the bird
The frog, the mouse, and the hawk
The golden apple of Hisberna
The greedy hawk
The herdsman of Cruachan
How the little black wren got its red
   feathers
Jirimpimbira
The kindly ghost
King Shibi
The lion, the tiger, and the eagle
The little hen and the little cock

The man who always helped the
   needy
The old hag of the forest
Prince Finn the Fair
The red swan
The three golden eggs
To feed my people; The race between
   the buffalo and man
The troll who hid his life
The twin brothers
Waiting on salvation
The wedding of the hawk
Wee robin's Christmas song
Why the crab has no head or how the
   first river was made

The hawk's friends
GRAY − INDIA'S p62-67

Hawthorne, Nathaniel
The golden touch
The minotaur
The three golden apples

Hawthorne, Nathaniel
The lonely boy

Hawthorne-haws
The old man and his bush

Hay and haymakers
The boy who made hay
David Wright and the fairies
The dragon and the stepmother
The goblins at the bath house
A handful of hay
The moonrakers
Richard Feverel and the hay-rick
The tale of the silver, golden and
   diamond prince
Willie boy, Willie boy
Zlateh the goat

Hayman, Robert
Of the great and famous

The hazel-nut child
MANNING − DWARFS p84-88

Hazel trees
Ashputtel
Cinder-maid
Welshman and the hazel staff

−**Nuts**
Nut-cracker

−**Rods**
The giant of the brown beech
   wood

He calls the king's wife a liar. *See* Ol'
  guinea man

He danced fine-o
  HASKETT – GRAINS p84-86

He died hard
  IVES – TALES p277-281

He leaves the nest
  REED – TALK. p42.

He sang himself out of prison cell
  HSIEH – CHINESE p46.

He washed the monkey's face
  COBBLE – WEMBI p90-91

He who bound the dragons of Chaos
  BELTING – STARS #6

He who is feared by all
  BURTON – MAGIC p47-51

He who laughs last
  MAYNE – GIANTS p71-82

He who lives in a mountain
  NORLEDGE – ABORIGINAL p18.

He wins who waits
  LANG – OLIVE p119-130

The head-hunters
  MAR – CHINA p127-146

The head of brass
  WILLIAMS – FAIRY p186-195

The head of the family
  KELSEY – ONCE p38-44

The head of the Inca
  JAGENDORF – KING p113-116

Headaches
  Monkey
  Thor and the jotun Rungnir

Headaches
  LEACH – SOUP p126-127

Headland, Isaac T. trans.
  Chinese nursery rhymes

The headless horseman
  MANNING – GHOSTS p80-86

Heads
  Bran, son of Llyr
  The house with the heads
  Miska and the man-with-the-iron-head
  The origin of the coconut
  Pancho Villa's lost head
  The well of the three heads
  The yellow ribbon

Heady, Eleanor B.
  HEADY – TALES p125.

Healing (cures)
  See also **Herbs; Medicine; Remedies**
  The almond bough
  Ashoremashika
  The boy and the leopard
  The boy who was never afraid
  A burn cured
  The carnation youth
  Chourilo's little comb
  Chu Cuoi's trip to the moon
  Doctor Lee and little Aran
  Dog couldn't be cured
  The fire boy
  The fowler, the parrot and the king
  The frog
  Godfather death
  The golden bird
  The good son
  The gouty giant
  The grateful weasel
  The griffon
  Grillo
  Hans the tailor and the talking
    animals
  The hare herd
  The hare's kidneys
  The healing of Urre
  How Tristram fought against the
    knight from Ireland
  The just and unjust brothers
  Kate Crackernuts
  King Bean
  Kupti and Imani
  The lake lady
  The lamb with the golden fleece
  The legend of the hail
  The magic berries
  The magic carpet
  The magic ear
  The magic listening cap
  The man who was only three inches
    tall
  Medicinal
  The melodius napkin
  Nyangara, the python
  An old king and his three sons of
    England
  The palace in the Rath

278

Healing (*Continued*)

The powers of plants and trees to
protect against witches
The prince of Coucy
Protection against witches
The ram with the golden fleece
Sam Dan and the government doctor
The search for the magic lake
The simple-minded bootmaker as a
miraculous healer
The singing bone
Some white witchcraft
The son of the hen-wife
The song-bird and the healing waters
The spring
Squirrel and fox
The story of Ailill and Etaine
The story of Noschoy Datta of Ujjain
The strangest thing in the world
The tale of a Pakistan parrot
The three-legged jumping giant
The three sons of the King of Antua
To cure a sudden stitch
The two bridegrooms
Vania and the vampire
Wahconah
The wee red man
The well at the world's end
The white lady of Pumphul
Who maketh the dumb to speak
The wishing chair of the lord of
Errigal
The wishing star
Wong Siang, the clever
The wood cutter's son and the two
turtles
A world of beauty: The Peyote
religion
A yard of nose

The healing of Urre
PICARD – STORIES p242-250

Health
The fruits of health
The land of youth
To your good health

–Ointment
The adventures of Ciad
The tinker of Tamlacht

Heap on more wood
MY BOOK HOUSE v. 2 p217.

Hear how the birds
MY BOOK HOUSE v. 1 p208.

Hear ye!
JAGENDORF – MERRY p3-5

Hearing, Sense of
See also Deaf
Great heart and the three tests
Prince Ferdinand
The robber baron . . . And the bat
The wonder ship and ship's crew

Hearn, Lafcadio
The boy who drew cats
A dead secret
The woman of the snow

Heart and mind
NAHMAD – PEASANT p155-159

The heart of Princess Joan
JOHNSON – HARPER p128-165

Heart of the west wind
PICARD – MERMAID p155-170

The heart with seven heads. *See*
Father big nose

The hearth-cat
THOMPSON – ONE p173-176

Hearths
Beside the fire

–Spirits
The genii of the hearth
The spirits of the hearth
Young Bekie

Hearts
See also Livers; names of animals,
subdivision Hearts
Cross my heart
The donkey lettuce
The fisherman and his soul
The foolish dragon
The giant who had no heart in his
body
A gift from the heart
Gobbleknoll
The golden tortoise
Great heart and the three tests
Heart and mind
The heart of Princess Joan
The man without a heart
The mistress of fire
The monkey and the crocodile
The monkey's heart
Painted skin
She-wa-na, deity of the elements
The thousandth gift
Why the mole lives underground

Hearts and pirates
TAFT – PROFILE p76-84

Heat
   Cottontail and the sun
   The giant and the Rumanian
   The gift of Father Frost
   The Hoca and the candle
   Hot times
   The ogre king of Gilgit
   Phaeton; the boy who rode the
      chariot of the sun
   A trickster tricks the devil
   The wager
   Why there are four seasons in the
      year

The heather beer
   O'SULLIVAN — FOLK. p234-235

Heaven
   Beppo Pipetta and his knapsack
   The boy in the land of shadows
   The cat that went to heaven
   Death and the soldier
   Ed Grant has a dream
   The fire dogs
   The golden chain from heaven
   A good neighbor
   Heart of the west wind
   High Eden
   How King Yudhishthira came to the
      gates of heaven with his dog
   Ivan and his knapsack
   Izanagi and Izanami
   Juan in heaven
   Luck from heaven and luck from the
      earth
   The man who lived in the world of
      dreams
   The master-smith
   The never never land
   Over the hill
   The princess of light
   The robber Simhavikrama
   The smart husband and the smarter
      wife
   The smoke horse
   The spider
   A tailor in heaven
   Takamagahara
   The tale of the land of Cockaigne
   The Tengu's magic nose fan
   This hound hath loved me
   The tinker of Tamlacht
   The tower that reached from earth to
      heaven
   The upper world
   The weight of the cart
   Why there is thunder and lightning
   The woman who came down from
      heaven

The young coyote's visit
The young Urashima

, Text of
   Eggborn
   The text

Heaven and earth and man
   BIRCH — CHINESE p3-8

The heavenly lovers
   CARPENTER — ELEPHANT'S
   p212-219

The heavenly maiden and the woodcutter
   INS-SŎB — FOLK p21-25

The heavenly spinning maid
   BONNET — CHINESE p89-96

Hebel, Johann Peter
   The starling of Sebringen

Hebrews. *See* Jews

Hebrides, Scottish
   The faery and the kettle
   Finlay the giant killer
   Kilmeny
   MacCodrum of the seals
   The three teeth of the king

—Arran
   The lass that lost the laird's
      daughter

—Barra
   The son of the baker of Barra

—Benbecula
   The water-bull of Benbecula

—Eilean-H-Oige
   The sea captain

—Islay
   The ceabharnach

—Jura
   The white sword of light

—Muck
   A bauchan in the family

—Mull
   Three fat ewes for three fine
      hounds

—Skye
   The clever lad from Skye

Hecho the lazy
   FOSTER — STONE p63-70

Hector of Troy
The death of Hector
The slaying of Hector

Hector protector
MY BOOK HOUSE v. 1 p45.

The hedgehog and the hare
RANKE — GERMANY p23.

The hedgehog and the rabbit
SIDEMAN — WORLD'S p182-188

The hedgehog who became a prince
BAKER — GOLDEN p119-122

Hedgehogs
About the hedgehog who became
prince
The enchanted hedgehog
The fox and the hedgehog
How the fox and the hedgehog
became friends

—**Legs**
The hedgehog and the rabbit

Hedges
Cuckoo in the hedge
The maiden in the country under-
ground
The thing on the hedge
The two step-sisters

The hedley kow
JACOBS — MORE p55-59
MANNING — BEASTS p3-7
PALMER — DRAGONS p63-67

"Hedley kows" (magical animals)
The old woman and the Hedley kow

Heels. *See* **Feet–Heels**

Hei, Jim along Josey
MY BOOK HOUSE v. 1 p117.

Heidi in the Alpine pasture
MY BOOK HOUSE v. 5 p147-155

Height
Growing pains
Longshanks, girth, and keen

Heike (clan)
The battle of Ichi-no-Tani
The fall of the Heike

The poem of the sea
The secret meeting at Shishiga Tani

Heimdall, the watchman of Asgard
AULAIRE — NORSE p56-57

Heine, Heinrich
Two children

Heinlein, Robert A.
Space ship Bifrost

The Heinzelmannchen
PICARD — GERMAN p120-125

The heir of Linne
MANNING — ENGLISH p82-92

Heirs and Heiresses
See also **Inheritance**
The righteous heir
The tale of the heir of Linne

Helen in Egypt
GREEN — GREEKS p54-55

Helen of Sparta
GREEN — GREEKS p12-13

Helen of Troy
A cause of war
Helen in Egypt
The story of the Greek princess

Hell
Beppo Pipetta and his knapsack
Dante's voyage to the inferno,
purgatory, and paradise
The devil's wife as godmother
Fiddler John and the devil
Haltefanden (The lame devil)
How the devil married three sisters
Izanagi's descent to Hades
The man who lived in the world of
dreams
The man who was rescued from hell
Orpheus and Eurydice
Padre Ulivo and his guests
The rich Per Muller
A ride to hell
The road to hell
The tinker of Tamlacht

Helmets
The maiden with the wooden helmet
Surprising adventures of Don Quixote
of La Mancha

Help in need and Abe in deed
JAGENDORF – SAND p181-184

Helpfulness
See also Cooperation; Kindness
Casperl
The donkey and the dog
The giant who rode on the ark
The lion calls up his troops
Lion, chameleon, and chicken
The unwashed pot
The wolf and the crane
The wolf's reward

Helping to lie
RANKE – GERMANY p193-194

Hema and the goblin-woman
WHEELER – HAWAII. p171-189

Hemlock trees
Bucky, the big, bold fawn

The hemp smoker and the hemp grower
COURLANDER – KING'S p101-105

The hen agreed to hatch the duck egg,
but she didn't agree to take the
duckling for a swim
CHAPPELL – THEY p8-12

The hen that laid diamond eggs
MANNING – RED p16-22

The hen that laid the golden eggs
LA FONTAINE – FABLES p42.

The hen with the golden legs
HACK – DANISH p177-181

Hen-wives
The son of the hen-wife

HennyPenny
ARBUTHNOT – TIME p12-13
MONTGOMERIE – 25 p24-25

Henry V, King of England
The King of France went up the hill

Henry, John
Hammerman/John Henry
John Henry
John Henry and double-jointed steam
drill

Henry Crabb–a born loser
WILLIAMS – LOST p59-69

Hens. *See* Chickens

The hen's house
COBBLE – WEMBI p87-88

Hera (goddess)
Bears in the sky
The kneeler's twelve tasks

Heraldry
See also Coats-of-arms
Mythical beasts in heraldry

Herb-women
The king of the wood

Herbs
The black cat of the witch-dance-
place
The dwarf and the goose
Dwarf long nose
Godfather death
The lady who put salt in her coffee
Magic and medicine
Not to care a straw
Odysseus and Circe
The prince and the Three Fates
Snout the drawf
The two lovers
'Water's locked'!

Hercules
The giant who played with pygmies
The kneeler's twelve tasks
The labors of Hercules
Leo the king
The Nemean lion
Orthrus
The three golden apples

Hercules and the waggoner
ARBUTHNOT – TIME p204.

Herda, H.
The swan princess

Herder, Johann Gottfried
The lion and the bulls

The herdsman
DE LA IGLESIA – CAT unp.

The herdsman of Cruachan
SHEPPARD – SCOT. p167-172

282

Herdsmen
See also Cowherds; Goatherds;
Shepherds & Shepherdesses
The Alp that disappeared
The brave cowman
Fair, broun, and trembling
The forty whoppers
The four deaf men
The lost spear
The magic herdboy
The poor herdsman and his sons, The
Little People of Africa
The Shee an Gannon and the
Gruagach Gaire

Here am I, little jumping Joan
MY BOOK HOUSE v.1 p32.

Here come three jolly, jolly sailor boys
MY BOOK HOUSE v.1 p96.

Here, forest-fires
REED – TALK. p45.

Here is my hand on it
LEACH – SOUP p149-150

Here is the key
MY BOOK HOUSE v. 1 p127.

Here we come, we children come
MY BOOK HOUSE v. 1 p204.

Here we sail so fast and free
MY BOOK HOUSE v. 1 p96.

Hereafterthis
JACOBS – MORE p7-11

Here's the church
MY BOOK HOUSE v. 1 p83.

Hereward
VANSITTART – DARK p121-133

Hereward the wake
PICARD – TALES p89-109

Herford, Oliver
The audacious kitten
The elf and the dormouse

Herjulfson, Bjarni
The American saga

Herla, King of the Celts
King Herla, The Little People of the
British Isles
King Herla's quest

Herman and his horse
JAGENDORF – UPSTATE p121-124

Hermes (god)
Odysseus and Circe

The hermit and the devil
RANKE – GERMANY p155-156

The hermit and the mouse
GAER – FABLES p56-57

The hermit and the Sea of Man
KOREL – LISTEN p71-76

The hermit cat
KOREL – LISTEN p21-27

The hermit with two heads
HOLDING – SKY p61-74

The hermit's cabbage patch
GREEN – LEPRECHAUN p118-127

Hermits
The black prince
The boy who beat the devil
The carpenter's boar
The dancing water, (the) singing apple,
and (the) speaking bird
The destiny of Princess Tien Dung
The dream at Nam Kha
The goldsmith, the wood carver, the
tailor and the hermit who quarreled
over a wooden woman
How men become enemies
King All-tusk
King Bean
King Johnny
Lancelot and Galahad
Miss goat
The nightingale Hazaran
An old Sumatran legend
The prince and the sky-blue filly
Prince Finn the Fair
Prince Wicked
The proud king
The rajah who flew away
The Ramayana
The road to hell
The saga of the Waru Wanggi
The sage and the servant
Sindhu
The story of the king who would be
stronger than fate
The sun, the moon and the star of
morning
The tiger's whisker
The valley of ten thousand waterfalls
Why the motmot lives in a hole

The hero in the village
JAGENDORF – KING p49-51

The hero of Adi Nifas
COURLANDER – FIRE p45-49

Herodotus, History, book II
The treasure chamber of
Rhampsinitus

Heroes and heroines
See also **Indians of North America–**
Heroes & heroines; names of heroes
Abrahan Lincoln, 1809-1865
Abu Zaid the Hilali
Adam Bell, Clym of the Clough, and
William of Cloudesley
The adventures of Perseus
Antar the hero
Arnold Winkelried
Arthur, King of Britain
Arumuman, a hero of Java
Ask a foolish question
Attila the conqueror
The battle of Roncesvalles
Beautiful doll
The beginning of the Fians
Beowulf
Beowulf conquers Grendel
Beowulf fights a battle with the sea
The bold heroes of Hungry Hill
The boy hero of Harlem
A boy on the high seas
The boyhood of a hero
Bran, son of Llyr
The brave three hundred
Casey Jones and locomotive no. 638
A cause of war
The Cid . . . The will to conquer
The coming of Arthur
The courtship of Lemminkainen
The crochera
Cuchulain, the hound of Ulster
Cuculain, the Irish hound
Daniel in the lions' den
David, the shepherd boy
Davy Crockett
Dearmid and Grania
The death of Cuchullin
The death of Dearmid
The death of Diarmaid
The death of Kwasind
Deirdre
Deidre and the sons of Usna
Dermot and Grania
Dietrich of Bern
Donal from Donegal
Donal O'Ciaran from Connaught

A dozen at a blow
Drake's cannon ball
The dream of Maxen Wledig
The dream of Ronabbway
Esther . . . who saved her people
Dunay
The empty city
Farmer Giles of Ham
Finn and the young hero's children
Finn MacCool
Frithiof's journey to the Orkneys
Frithjof, the Viking
The frontier contest
George Washington and the first
American flag
The giant of the brown beech wood
Gideon, the warrior
The green isle
Grettir becomes an outlaw
Gudrun
Hereward
Hereward the Wake
Heroic poems (Byliny)
The home-coming of Odysseus
The homecoming of Beorhtnoth
Horatius
How Beowulf delivered Heorot
How Cuchulain wooed his wife
How Finn Maccumhail was in the
House of the Rowan Tree without
power to stand or leave or sit down
How Ma-ui snared the sun and made
him go more slowly across the
heavens
How Moremi saved the town of Ife
How Peary reached the North Pole
How Sigurd awoke Brynhild
How Yehl, the hero, freed the
beaming maiden
Hynd Horn
Ian Direach
Ilya of Murom and nightingale the
robber
Ilya of Murom and Svyatogor
Joan of Arc
Joan of Arc . . . The warrior maid
Joe Magerack, the steel-mill man
John Paul Jones, the first American
naval hero
Kâgssagssuk, the homeless boy who
became a strong man
Kalevala, land of heroes
Kian and the children of Tuireann
The King of Araby's daughter
The knight
Kralyevich Marko and Mussa
Kessedzhiya
Kralyevich Marko's death
The labors of Hercules
The legend of Marshal Gang
Gam-Czan

Heroes and heroines (*Continued*)

The legend of William Tell
Lincoln's Gettysburg address
The lion with the steady hand
Little John and the tanner of Blyth
The making of a hero
Manawyddan son of the Boundless
Manny MacGilligan's story
Marko, the champion of Serbian
  liberty
Maui the Great
Mighty Michael . . . Who could do
  anything
The minotaur
New heroes
Njal the lawyer
Of the great and famous
The old Navy
Paul Jones
Prince Finn the Fair
Prince Marko and a Moorish chieftain
Princess Nelly and the Seneca chief
Pwyll and Rhiannon
Pwyll, Pryderie and Gawl
The quest of the sons of Turenn
Ragnar Lodbrok and his sons
Rāma . . . The bow that could not be
  bent
The return of Odysseus
The return of the heroes
The revenge (Tennyson)
Robert Bruce, Scotland's hero
Robert E. Lee, a hero in war and
  peace
Robin Hood
A Roland for an Oliver
Rustem and his rose-colored steed
The sack of Troy
Scarface
Sea heroes
The search for Sita
The "Shanon" and the "Chesapeake"
Shizuka's dance
Siegfried
Since when there have been no more
  heroes in holy Russia
Sir Beaumains, the kitchen knight
Sir Bevis of Hampton
Sir Perceval
The slaying of Hector
The slaying of Siegfried
The sleepless dragon
The song of Roland
A Spanish hero
The squires win golden spurs
Stavr Godinovich and his clever wife
A story about Abe Lincoln
The story of big Paul Bunyan
A story of Rustem, the hero of Persia
The story of the Cid

Svyatogor's bride
Takero
Tales from the Episode of the Fians
Taliesin
Tam Lin
Tavadan
Tavadan and the fire giant
Te Houtaewa
The theft of fire
This hound hath loved me
Thomas Berennikov
The three journeys of Ilya of Murom
The three suitors
The tournament in Ireland
The troubles at Kawaiki
Tsali of the Cherokees
An unsung heroine
The Valkyries and Valhalla
Vasili Buslayevich
Vasili Buslayevich's pilgrimage
The vengeance of Kriemhild
Volga
Volund the smith
Wainamoinen finds the lost-words
Walther of Aquitaine
The wandering of Aeneas
The wedding of the Cid's daughters
The white hen
William of Cloudslee
The wishing chair of the Lord of
  Errigal
The wonder ship and ship's crew
The word of Igor's armament
The world of the gods
Ye merry doinges of Robin Hood
Yoro reveals himself as Gessar Khan
Young midshipman David Farragut
A young prince named Siegfried

Heroes of the sea
  LAWSON − STRANGE p43-55

Heroic poems (Byliny)
  DOWNING − RUSSIAN p3-78

The heroine of the Mohawk Valley
  IVES − TALES p81-88

The heron
  REED − TALK. p39.

Herons
  The boy who was lost
  Deep insight
  The fox and the heron
  The honest woodman
  The oyster and the heron
  The three monsters of the sea
  Tiger story, Anansi story
  The troll who hid his life

The heron's ball
WITHERS — I SAW p53-54

Herrick, Robert
There's not a budding boy

Hesiod
The hawk and the nightingale

Hesperides
The three golden apples

The hex and the oxen
JAGENDORF — UPSTATE p181-185

Hexes
See also **Curses; Witchcraft; Witches**
The wolf-bride

Hey diddle diddle
MY BOOK HOUSE v. 1 p22.

"Heyo, house!"
ARBUTHNOT — TIME p196-197

Hi-ho, the mosquitoes of New Jersey!
JAGENDORF — UPSTATE p69-71

Hi-y, hi-y, hytola
MY BOOK HOUSE v. 1 p144.

Hiaqua (shells)
The treasure of Tacoma

Hiawatha (meter)
The death of Kwasind
Wainamoinen finds the lost-words

Hiawatha childhood
MY BOOK HOUSE v. 5 p222-224

Hiawatha's fasting
MY BOOK HOUSE v. 9 p89-97

Hibernation
A long night's sleep
One day, one night
Roommates
Why bear sleeps all winter
Why the bear sleeps all winter

Hiccoughing
The goat
Hiccups

Hiccoughing
BATCHELOR — SUPER. p26-27

Hiccups
LEACH — SOUP p122-125

Hickey, pickety, my black hen
MY BOOK HOUSE v. 1 p24.

Hickory, dickory dock!
MY BOOK HOUSE v. 1 p22.

Hid-folk
The magic scythe, The Little People
of Iceland

The hidden hoe
WITHERS — WORLD p73-74

Hidden laiva or the golden ship
ARBUTHNOT — TIME p128-132

Hidden treasure
SECHRIST — ONCE p125-128

The hidden treasure of Khin
COURLANDER — TIGER'S p29-32

The hideless bear
FELTON — WORLD'S p27-30

Hiding
How Loki outwitted a giant
The wizard king

Hiding in the well
KELSEY — ONCE p100-104

Hie away, hie away
MY BOOK HOUSE v. 6 p70.

Higgledy, piggledy! see how they run!
MY BOOK HOUSE v. 1 p51.

The high adventure of the helmet of
Mambrino. *See* Surprising adventures of
Don Quixote of La Mancha

High diddle diddle, the fool in the
middle
JAGENDORF — MERRY p40-44

High Eden
JONES — WELSH p223-228

High John the conqueror
GORHAM — REAL p118-127

Highlands
The fairies and the smith

Highlands (*Continued*)

The seal fisher and the roane
The stolen lady
The tacksman and the ox
The water horse and the water bull

Highwaymen. *See* **Bandits**

Hilderbrand the Wise
The boyhood of a hero
Dietrich defends the snow queen

Hildur the elf queen
BOUCHER – MEAD p148-156

The hill demon
MANNING – DEVILS p117-126

The hill of the bellowing oxen
PILKINGTON – SHAM. p153-160

The hillman and the housewife
PILKINGTON – SHAM. p16-18

Hills
The farmer and the fairy hillock
The girl on the hill
Gobbleknoll
The hopping lights on Devil's hill
The laughing merman
The magic hill
Over the hill
The shepherd and the fairy hillock
The witch in the hill

, **Glass**
The princess on the glass hill

, **People of**
The hillman and the housewife
Midir and Etain

Himalayas (Mountains)
The long-eared cat and the vulture
The talkative tortoise
Why the mountains are snow-covered

Hina, the woman in the moon
COLUM – STONE p117-119

Hind horn
MANNING – ENGLISH p17-23

Hindus and hinduism
The flood
Garuda
The mouse and the wizard
The mouse's bride
Mythical beast of the sea
The origin of the bromo feast
Prahlada
What is a fable?
Why the moon wanes

Hindustan
Diamond cut diamond
Dorani
Jackal and tiger?
The Thanksgiving of the Wazir

Hippety hop to the barber shop
MY BOOK HOUSE v. 1 -28.

Hippodracs (monsters)
The brave grenadier

Hippogriffs (mythical animals)
Atlantes and the hippogriff
Winged wonders

Hippopotami
The bride who melted away
Horus the avenger
Old Noah
Rabbit, elephant and hippopotamus
Tortoise triumphant
The tug of war
The turtle, the hippo, and the
elephant

Hiram goes courting
MARGOLIS – IDY p57-64

The hired man
BOUCHER – MEAD p1-7
DOWNING – RUSSIAN p218-223

Historical inscription–or fiction? The
seven-year famine
JAMES – MYTHS p96-103

History
See also under names of countries
The learned young professor

History as propaganda: The Princess of
Bakhtan
JAMES – MYTHS p138-148

History of the giants
DE REGNIERS – GIANTS p16-17

Hitchhikers
The ghostly hitchhiker

Hitopadesa (India fables)
The fables of India

Hitopadesa (*Continued*)

The monkey gardeners
The silly goose

The Hitopadesa (The book of good
counsel)
GAER – FABLES p53-116

Hjuki and Bil
LEACH – HOW p33-34

The hoard
TOLKIEN – READER (Part 4)
p53-56

Hoarding. *See* Greed; Misers

Hoaxes
The greatest hoax in New York City
The Irish luck of Brian Hughes
Jean Britisse, the champion

Hobbits
Tolkien's magic ring

Hobgoblins
See also Boggarts; Brownies
The phantom painter in the steeple
The snow-queen
Stupid head
The witch of Lok Island

The hobyahs
JACOBS – MORE p127-133

Hoca, Nasreddin
Boiled wheat for a bountiful harvest
Cow or donkey?
A donkey transformed
Eat, my fine coat!
How long will it take?
I know what I'll do
It won't do you any good
It's all in knowing how
Nasreddin Hoca and the third shot
Shoes for a journey
The sounds is yours
Tell me, when will I die?
Watermelons, walnuts and the
wisdom of Allah

The Hoca and Allah's son-in-law
WALKER – WATER. p45.

The Hoca and the candle
WALKER – WATER. p37-41

The Hoca as Tamerlane's tax collector
WALKER – WATER. p29-33

The Hoca solves a problem
WALKER – WATER. p42-43

Hodja and the jumbled jobs
EDMONDS – TRICKSTER p36-44

The Hodja preaches a sermon
U. N. – RIDE p82-84

Hodja stories
Account rendered
Among the chickens
And upon the fourth bray
Archery
The changeling
The copper pan
Fair wages for all
If so where is the cat?
Introduction (JUDA – WISE)
Ishallah
A prompt settlement
Pumpkin trees and walnut vines
Rabbit soup
The sermon
A strange guest
The three questions
To the rescue
The turban
The wager
The wisdom of Allah

Hoes
Cenerentola
The farmer and the hoe
The girl who forgot her hoe
The hidden hoe
The porcupine's hoe

Hoffmann, Heinrich
Johnny head-in-air
The story of flying Robert

Hog child plays tricks
THOMPSON – LEGENDS p49-53

Hogg, James
A boy's song

Hogmanay. *See* New Year's

Hogs
See also Pig-stys
As I went to Bonner
The barnyard
The bed
Birds of a feather
The boy who took care of the pigs

Hogs (*Continued*)

Charlotte's web; Wilbur's boast
Chin and Yi
The dancing princesses
The decision
Dickery, dickery dare
Eight leaves of story (1) The three
  staunch swineherds of Britain
Eight leaves of story (3) Baglan the
  builder
The envious buffalo
The farmer's boy
The first pig and porcupine
The foolish wolf
The foolishness of Cochinito
From a moral alphabet
Giacco and his bean
Hereafterthis
Horus the avenger
How animals brought fire to man
Hungry hog
I had a little dog
Jack and the Purr Mooar
Juan Bobo
Juan Bobo, the sow, and the chicks
A kiss from the beautiful Fiorita
Krencipal and Krencipalka
A Kupua plays tricks
The labors of Hercules
Lazy Hans
The little girl named I
The little pig
The little red hen and the grain of
  wheat
The little red pig
Madgy Figgey and the sow
The man who refused help
A merry tale of Rich Neck Town
Minnie and Mattie
Misuse of a name
Mr. Samson cat
Monkey
Odysseus and Circe
Old man Edmonds and the ninety-
  nine pigs
The old woman and her pig
The owl and the pussy-cat
The pancake
The pavilion of peril
Peer Gynt
The pig in the church
Pig in the poke
The pig, the goat and the sheep
Precocious Piggy
The quest for Olwen (4) Fulfilling
  the tasks 7/ The hunting of the
  otherworld boar
The quest of the children of Turenn
The ram and the pig who went into the
  woods to live by themselves

The seven enchanted pigs, and the
  houndwhelps of Iroda
The sheep and the pig that made a
  home
The sow and her banbh
The sow got the measles
The story of Mrs. Tubbs
The story of the pig
The story of the thick fat pancake
The story of the three little pigs
The swineherd who married a princess
The tale of the pig
Tall hog
There was an old pig
This little pig went to market
The three little pigs
To market, to market
Tom, Tom, the piper's son
The tower that reached from earth
  to heaven
Why crab's eyes stick out
Why pigs root
Willie and the pig
The wonderful tree
The young girl and the devil

—Skins
  The gifted skin of the pig
  The quest of the sons of Turenn

—Boars, Wild
  Anansi steals the palm wine
  The boy who was lost
  The brave little tailor
  The bride-price for Olwen
  The carpenter's boar
  The donkey and the boar
  Esben and the witch
  The greedy hawk
  Hog child plays tricks
  How the wild boars came to be
  Kantchil's lime pit
  King Hrolf and the bear's son
  The long-howling jackal
  The man without a heart
  Mittens the cat
  The quarrel
  The quest for Olwen (4) Ful-
    filling the tasks 6/ The task of
    Ysgithyrwyn
  Rojin Rojal
  Sif's golden hair
  The struggle between the wolf and
    the fox
  Three princes and their beasts
  The tiger who understood people
  To your good health
  The wild boar and the ram
  Young Pollard and the brawn of
    Bishop Auckland

—Snouts
  How the pig got his snout

Hogs (*Continued*)
–Tails
Why pigs have curly tails

Hoichi the earless
GARNER – GOBLINS p128-132

Hok Lee and the dwarfs
BUCK – FAIRY p232-236

Holbrook, Florence
Why the evergreen trees never lose
their leaves

Holding down the hat
LEACH – NOODLES p66-68

Holding the bag
JAGENDORF – NEW p57-61
LEACH – SOUP p143.

Holes
See also **Pits; Wells**
Adrian and Bardus
The astrologer
The big mudhole
Budulinek
The coffin that moved itself
Do it yourself
Pooh goes visiting and gets into a
tight place
The road to China
The spirit's drum
The straight and narrow way
The Tsar Trajan's ears
The ungrateful tiger
The Warau people discover the earth
The white lady of Pumphul
Why the motmot lives in a hole

The holes of Lagos
JAGENDORF – KING p193-198

Holiday luck
LEACH – LUCK p49-54

Holidays
See also names of holidays
Leave well enough alone
The magic fiddle
Reward drives the familiar spirits
away

Holinshed, Raphael
The weird sisters (1)

Holland. *See* **Netherlands**

Holmes, Oliver Wendell
The broomstick train

The holy cat of Tibet
CARPENTER – DOGS p111-118

Holy Grail
Galahad . . . The Holy Grail
How Galahad came to Arthur's court
Lancelot and Galahad
Lohengrin
The quest of the Holy Grail

A holy man and a sacred cow
REED – TALK. p18-21

Holy men
See also **Gurus; Hactins; Hadji**
The false fakir
The gift of the holy man
The hermit and the Sea of Man
The king's true children
Kupti and Imani
Madschun
The miser's wife
The valley of ten, thousand waterfalls

The holy mountain
LEEUW – INDO. p45-50

The holy relic of Bannockburn
LEODHAS – GAELIC p76-80

Holy Virgin. *See* **Mary, Virgin**

Holy water
Collen
The enchanted cow
The king of the Golden River, or
The Black brothers

The homecoming of Beorhtnoth
Beorhthelm's son
TOLKIEN – READER (Part 1) p3-24

The home-coming of Odysseus
MY BOOK HOUSE v. 10 p217-227

The home of the saints
FEINSTEIN – FOLK p34-37

Homely fairies
BRIGGS – PERS. p83-85

Homer–Odyssey
The home-coming of Odysseus

Hominy
The old woman and her hominy pot

Honduras
  The eternal wanderer
  The fall of the earth giants
  How the Caribs first came to Honduras
  How the porcupine outwitted the fox
  The virgin of Honduras
  When Boquerón spoke

The honest criminal
  DE LA IGLESIA – CAT unp.

The honest ghost
  LEODHAS – TWELVE p13-25

The honest woodman
  MY BOOK HOUSE v. 3 p114-115

Honesty
  See also **Truth**
  The crow and the sparrow
  The golden boat
  The laughing merman
  The man with no nose
  Marko, the champion of Serbian
    liberty
  Martin, the honest thief
  Ooka and the honest thief
  The part-time prisoner
  The raven and his young
  The shoemaker and the elves
  The spring
  Straight and crooked
  The true scales
  The truthful peasant
  The two caddies of tea
  The wandering cobbler

Honey
  The baboon and the hare
  The beardless one
  The bee tree
  The beetle and a drop of honey
  The beginning of the Narran Lake
  The bob-tailed monkey and the king's
    honey
  The clever little jackal
  The honeybee bride
  The imposter
  The journey of the Chinese honey-
    sellers
  The king of the leaves
  A kingdom lost for a drop of honey
  Lovers' moon
  Narahdarn the bat
  An old Korean story
  A promise made should be kept
  Rabbit and lion
  The sad, sorry sister
  The secret store
  The ungrateful bear
  Why the rabbit's nose twitches

  Why the sun stopped shining
  The wolf, the fox, and the jug of
    honey

Honey badgers
  Lion and honey badger

The honey feast
  PALMER – FAIRY p59-68

The honey gatherer's three sons
  BURTON – MAGIC p39-41

Honey-guides (birds)
  The bird that would not stay dead
  Grandfather tells some tales
  The two brothers

The honeybee bride
  CARPENTER – SOUTH p175-181

Hong Do-Ryŏng, the filial tiger
  INS-SOB – FOLK p84-86

Honor
  The king and the monkey
  Torah and honor

The honourable tom cat
  MacFARLANE – TALES p46-54

Honwyma and the bear
  COURLANDER – PEOPLE p86-96

Hood, Thomas
  Precocious piggy

Hoodoo bags and ghosts in Tennessee
  JOHNSON – WHAT p219-221

Hooker and the witches
  JOHNSON – WHAT p161-162

Hoopoe birds
  The golden lion

The Hoosier poet
  MY BOOK HOUSE v. 12 p141-142

Hop, Mother Annika!
  MY BOOK HOUSE v. 1 p74.

Hop, my horsey, leap and spring
  MY BOOK HOUSE v. 1 p123.

Hop o' my thumb
  BECKSTEIN – FAIRY p154-159
  PERRAULT – FAMOUS p93-110

Hope
    The hope tree of Harlem
    Pandora . . . The fateful casket

The hope tree of Harlem
    JAGENDORF – GHOST p99-104

Hope-Simpson, Jacynth
    Revenge (Theocritus)

The Hopi turtle
    WILLIAMS – ROUND p231-232

The hopping lights on Devil's hill
    SPICER – GHOSTS p45-52

Horatius
    MAYNE – HEROES p181-194

La Hormiguita
    BELPRE´– TIGER p57-61

Hornbills
    The hyena's medicine man
    Warthog and hornbill

A horned goat
    SIDEMAN – WORLD'S p579-590

The horned witches
    PALMER – JOURNEY p7-17

The horned woman
    BAKER – TALKING p48-51
    HOKE – WITCHES p1-4

The horned women
    LITTLEDALE – GHOSTS p61-66

Hornets
    All stories are Anansi's
    A big head has a big headache
    The butterfly's ball
    Coyote rings the wrong bell
    The crab and the monkey
    Grumpy Timothy Crumb
    The lazy hornet

The hornets and the honeybees
    LA FONTAINE – FABLES p33.

Horns
    The death of Roland
    Gabriel, blow your horn!
    Heimdall, the watchman of Asgard
    The horned woman
    How to catch a unicorn
    Jack and the Lord high mayor
    The magic apples
    The magic bird

Onsongo and the Masai cattle
    The orchestra
    Squirrel and fox
    Three magic charms
    The three plagues of Britain
    The three soldiers
    Why the cock eats worms
    The wishing chair of the Lord of
        Errigal

, Drinking
    A lesson for the bat

, Golden
    The giant of the brown beech
        wood

Horns
    THOMPSON – ONE p254-256

The horny-goloch
    MANNING – BEASTS p69.

A horse afraid of his shadow
    CARPENTER – HORSES p75-82

Horse and hattock
    BRIGGS – PERS. p65.

The horse and the colt
    GREEN – BIG p230-233

The horse and the eighteen bandits
    VO-DINH – TOAD p105-113

The horse of seven colors
    COTHRAN – MAGIC p60-65

Horse-races
    Khalid and Aantar
    The three misty women
    Yama and the poor man

The horse that liked to play tricks
    CARPENTER – HORSES p156-163

The horse, the lion, and the wolf
    CARPENTER – HORSES p83-89

The horse with his head where his tail
    ought to be
    LEACH – NOODLES p70-71

The horse without a master
    CARPENTER – HORSES p20-24
    U. N. – RIDE p95-98

The horsefly
    TASHJIAN – THREE p37-39

Horsemen and horsemanship
    The blacksmith and the horseman

Horsemen and horsemanship (*Continued*)

Golden hair
The good sword
The headless horseman
Keloğlan and the magic hairs
The laughing statue
The peasant and the horseman
The sea knight
The stone horseman
The sun and the north wind
A test of skill
Three sons of a chief

Horses

About Jan the prince, Princess Won-
derface, and the flamebird
Abu Zaid seeks a horse and finds a
wife
Alexander and Bucephalus
The adventures of Iain Direach
The angry baron
The animals' paradise
Arawn
Asmund, Authun, and Odd
Atam and Im
Bation the horse
Battle with the sockdolager
The bell of Atri
The bird of the golden land
The blue foal
Bouki rents a horse
The boy with the golden star
Bran, son of Llyr
Cannetella
The careless master
The case of the calf and the colt
The castle of the three giants
The Cavallino
The child and the colt
Christening the baby in Russia
The circus parade
The city of the winter sleep
Clever Dick
The clever lad from Skye
The cloud horse
The colts in the pumpkin
Conall Yellowclaw
Constantes and the dragon
Corvetto
The cowboy's life
Damian and the dragon
The dance at Hickory Creek
Dapplegrim
David Copperfield and little Em'ly
Dear-boy
The demon's daughter
The devil's apprentice
Don Lopez of Spain
Donal from Donegal
Dookiram, the poor one

The enchanted knife
Eppelin of Gailingen
Faithful John
Farmer Weathersky
The farmer's boy
The farmer's old horse
The firebird
The fox, the wolf, and the horse
The frog's saddle horse
Get up, little horsey
Giacco and his bean
The giant of the brown beech wood
The giant who took a long time to
grow
The gift and the giver
The gingerbread man
The giolla dacker and his horse
The golden apples of Loch Erne
The golden horse with the silver mane
The good judge
The good woman
Graadonner
The great medicine horse
The green sergeant
He died hard
The headless horseman
High diddle diddle, the fool in the
middle
The horned women
How horses came to the Navaho
How Michael Scot went to Rome
How the camel got his hump
How the first horse was made
How the gipsy sold his horse
The hunchback's horse
I was wondering
Ian Direach
Ijapa cries for his horse
I'm Captain Jinks
The ingrates
Inside again
Ironhead
Jack the giant-killer
Jingle bells, jingle bells
Joan of Arc
John Macdonald and the kelpie
Jumping the Grand Canyon
The kind caliph and the horse thief
King Conal's horses
King Kojata
The king who was a gentleman
The knight
The knight and the palfrey
The knight of the glen's steed o' bells
Krencipal and Krencipalka
The lady of the lake
Lion and man
The lion who listened to a jackal
Little Claus and Big Claus
Little fool Ivan and the little hump-
back horse

Horses (*Continued*)

The little horse
The little horse of seven colors
Little John and the water horse
The little nag
The Lochmaben harper
The lutin in the barn
The magic head
The magic horse
The magic mare
The magician Palermo
Mainly in moonlight
A man, a snake, and a fox
The mare at the wedding
Mary milks the cow
Marya Morevna
Mrs. Peterkin wishes to go to drive
Moti
The nine peahens and the golden
  apples
Noodlehead and the flying horse
O I'm a jolly old cowboy
Odin's eight-legged steed
Old Gally Mander
The old hag of the forest
One grain more than the devil
Ooka and the halved horse
Oraggio and Bianchinetta
The ordeal of Leyden
Ossian is the land of eternal youth
Over the river and through the woods
Pancho Villa and the devil
Peahens and golden apples
Pecos Bill
Pecos Bill and his bouncing bride
Pecos Bill, the cowboy
Pegasus and the Chimaera
The plains' call
The poor brother's treasure
The popcorn frost
The prince and the sky-blue filly
Prince Charming, the mare's son
Prince Finn the Fair
Prince Mirko
The prince's foal
The princess and the dwarf
The princess on the glass hill
The pursuit of the hard man
A quick-running squash
Rashi and Duke Gottfried
The raven
The red-maned horse
The return of Diab
The return of Oisin
Richmuth of Cologne
Rocking-horse land
Saint Peter's horses
Scurvyhead
Secret tockens prove ownership
The seven foals

The short horse
Smereree
The snow-queen
The son of the King of Spain
Son of the south wind
Soria Moria castle
The spear slaughterer and the chariot
  and horses of Sigar
The squire's bride
The stars in the sky
The story of Prince Ahmed
A story of Rustem, the hero of Persia
A story of three brothers
The story of Tom Thumb
The strange adventure of Baron
  Munchausen
Strawberry roan
The stupid wolf
The surprising adventures of Don
  Quixote of La Mancha
The swamp Nushi's messenger
The sword of light
The tale of the Lochmaben harper
The tale of the silver, golden, and
  diamond prince
The tale of the youngest brother and
  the stupid devil
Tam Lin
Telling the horses apart
The terrible Olli
There was a horse
The thoroughbred
The three brothers
The three enchanted mares
The three giants
The three princesses and the unclean
  spirit
The three tasks
Tiger lily and the dragon
Too hot to handle
The trials of Conneda
Tropsyn
The twice-blessed Arab
The twins
The two wizards
Una and the Red Cross knight
Uncle Bouki rents a horse
Uncle Mitya's horse
The ungrateful snake
Vanya's leap
Viriato: The youth who help back the
  Roman empire
The well o' the world's end
Wend' Yamba
The white horse of Volendam
Why Eyvin won the race
The widow's son
The witch's shoes
The wonderful mare Khadra
Yama and the poor man
Yoro reveals himself as Gessar Khan

Horses (*Continued*)
You must pay for the horse, Aga
The young witch-horse
Zeus and the horse

, **Golden**
    The gold bird
    The golden bird
    The golden horse
    Jacob Heard and the golden horse
    The wonderful tree

, **Mechanical**
    The magic horse
    The story of Ticho
    The wooden horse

—**Ponies**
    Buffalo Bill
    The dancing horses of Acoma
    The little gray pony
    Santiago and the fighting bulls

—**Tails**
    Flaming tales

, **Water**
    Arawn
    Morag and the water horse
    The princess and the dwarf
    The water-bull of Benbecula
    The water horse and the water bull

, **White**
    Is a white horse lucky?

, **Winged**
    Bellerophon . . . The winged horse
    The boastful queen
    The flying horse, Pegasus
    The gold dragon
    The golden nightingale
    King Florimonde and the winged
      horse
    Saint Martin and the honest man
    The sun, the moon and the Star of
      morning
    The tale of a Pakistan parrot

The horses of Rhesus
    GREEN – GREEKS p28-29

The horses of the Fianna
    SUTCLIFF – HIGH p96-104

Horses of the thunder
    CARPENTER – HORSES p25-34

Horseshoes
    The witch's shoes
    The wizard earl

Horus the avenger
    GREEN – TALES p37-50

Hosford, Dorothy
    How Sigurd awoke Brynhild

Hospitality
    Baucis and Philemon . . . The reward
      of hospitality
    The cranberry feast
    David Copperfield and little Em'ly
    Down by the River Avon
    The fate of the vulture
    Little Gustava
    The magic horse
    Meat or cat?
    A most generous host
    The old gypsy woman and the Good
      Lord
    The tale of a debt repaid
    Tao K'an and his mother
    Ye merry doinges of Robin Hood

Hospodars
    The maiden, the knight, and the
      waterfall

The hostel of the quicken
    SUTCLIFF – HIGH p105-128

Hostnig, Hildegard, illus.
    The clever little tailor
    A gift for a gift
    The golden chain
    The iron box
    The magic storm
    Peter ox
    The truthful peasant

Hot times
    COURLANDER – TERRA. p67-68

Hough, Charlotte
    Angus

The hound Gelert
    SHEPPARD – WELSH p134-136

The hour of death
    O'SULLIVAN – FOLK. p165.

House, Everlasting. *See* The everlasting
house

The house damsel
    RANKE – GERMANY p31.

The house in the valley
    LEEKLEY – KING p68-76

The house in the woods
SECHRIST – ONCE p128-131

The house mouse and the country mouse
ASBJORNSEN – NORW. p116-119

The house of the rowan trees
PICARD – CELTIC p85-110

The house that ate mosquito pie
CUMMINGS – FAIRY p24-31

The house that Jack built
JAGENDORF – SAND p15-17

The house that lacked a bogle
LEODHAS – GAELIC p100-110

The house that strong boy built
JAGENDORF – KING p34-39

The house with the front door at the back
SHEPPARD – WELSH p156-158

The house with the heads
LEEUW – LEGENDS p114-118

The house without eyes or ears
LEACH – NOODLES p55.

Household spirit brings food
RANKE – GERMANY p32.

The household spirit in Rötenbach
RANKE – GERMANY p31-32

Housekeepers
The feathers from the bird Venus
Hildur the elf queen
Snow-white and the seven dwarfs

Houses
See also Doors etc.
The deer and the jaguar share a house
The disillusionment of the Tibetan tiger
The haunted house
How men learned to build houses
How the sons filled the hut
Hwann and Dang
A leak in an old house
Misfortune comes to the house
Palace in Bagdad
The ram and the leopard
So say the little monkeys
Those who quarreled
The three little pigs

–Glass
The glass house

, Golden
Friendless pavilion

, Witch
Foreward. The witch house still stands

Housewives
Child, I must sweep the hut today
The coat that taught the housewife
The good housewife and her night helpers
The good housewife and her night labors
The hillman and the housewife
Knitting still
Mix a pancake
Polly, put the kettle on
Thus I guard my mother's lambkins
We've come to see Miss Jenny Jones

Housing, Hildegard
The bell of Monte Pino

Housman, Laurence
Ali Baba and the forty thieves
The rat-catcher's daughter
Rocking-horse land

Housman, Laurence
JOHNSON – HARPER p321-322

How a bird turned the world upside down
CATHON – PERHAPS p166-168

How a boy got a baboon
WITHERS – I SAW p135-138

How a fish swam in the air
LANG – VIOLET p114-120

How a man became unwitched
HASKETT – GRAINS p17-20

How a peasant outwitted two merchants
BORSKI – GOOD p26-28

How a Wunni ate nine evil spirits
HASKETT – GRAINS p75-79

How a young man became a chief
WITHERS – I SAW p139-140

How Abunawas was exiled
COURLANDER – FIRE p81-87

How Agamemnon came home
GREEN – GREEKS p48-49

How and why; Don't be greedy story
MARRIOTT – AMER. p131-132

How and why: The painted turtle
MARRIOTT – AMER. p124-127

How and why: Why the bear waddles
when he walks
MARRIOTT – AMER. p128-130

How animals brought fire to man
FISHER – STORIES p46-53

How animals got their beautiful coats
KAULA – AFRICAN p84-90

How Arthur gained Excalibur
PICARD – STORIES p9-15

How Au Sung repaid Kim Lee
ANDERSON – BOY p77-93

How baboons came into the world
LEACH – HOW p58.

How baby wart hog saved his father's
life
BURTON – MAGIC p68-71

How bat won the ball game
LEACH – HOW p70.

How bean got his stripe
LEACH – HOW p127-128

How beaver got his fine fur
BELTING – LONG p79-84

How Beowulf delivered Heorot
MY BOOK HOUSE v. 10 p80-88

How brer rabbit met brer tar-baby
MY BOOK HOUSE v. 4 p130-135

How California was made
FISHER – STORIES p10-15

How cats came to purr
HARDENDORFF – FROG'S p108-
118

How Celebes got its name
COURLANDER – KANT. p41.

How chameleon became king of the
animals. A story from the Baganda
people
KAULA – AFRICAN p65-70

How chipmunk got his stripes
LEACH – HOW p75-76

How confusion came among the animals
COURLANDER – KANT. p53-56

How Conor MacNessa became King of
Ulster
O'FAOLÁIN – IRISH p43-46

How Cormac MacArt got his branch
LINES – TALES p223-230
PILKINGTON – SHAM. p120-131

How coyote became a friend to man
FISHER – STORIES p74-79

How coyote brought back people after
the flood
BELTING – EARTH p67-69

How coyote got his voice
FISHER – STORIES p36-45

How coyote helped to light the world
FISHER – STORIES p16-23

How coyote put fish in Clear Lake
FISHER – STORIES p80-87

How coyote put salmon in the Klamath
River
FISHER – STORIES p96-103

How crab got a hard back
SHERLOCK – WEST p86-92

How crane got his long beak
LEACH – HOW p101.

How crane got his long legs
BELTING – LONG p67-70

How cranes saved coyote
HAYES – INDIAN p41-46

How Cuchulain wooed his wife
HAZELTINE – HERO p160-170

How death came
HEADY – TALES p109-118

How death came into the world (1)
MARRIOTT – AMER. p187-189

How death came into the world (2)
MARRIOTT – AMER. p190.

How deer got his horns
BELTING – LONG p57-59

How dog came to live with man
HASKETT – GRAINS p101-102

How dog outwitted shepherd
AARDEMA – STORY p49-53

How Don Quixote fought two armies of
sheep. *See* Surprising adventures of Don
Quixote of La Mancha

How doth the little busy bee
MY BOOK HOUSE v. 1 p143.

How Dounai won a bride for Prince
Vladimir
ALMEDINGEN – KNIGHTS p87-103

How duck got his bill
BELTING – LONG p74-75

How Fenris Wolf was bound
HOSFORD – THUNDER p73-78

How Finn became head of the Fianna
O'FAOLAÍN – IRISH p134-138

How Finn Maccumhail was in the house
of the rowan tree without power to
stand or leave or sit down
MAYNE – HEROES p24-31

How Finn won his father's place
SUTCLIFF – HIGH p18-25

How Fionn found his sword
WILSON – SCOTTISH p193-194

How fire was brought from lightning
HAYES – INDIAN p57-64

How Flint-face lost his name
BRENNER – BOY p71-75

How foolish men are!
INS-SOB – FOLK p149-152

How frog lost his tail. A story from the
Sukuma people
KAULA – AFRICAN p60-64

How frogs lost their tails
BELTING – LONG p34-36

How Galahad came to Arthur's court
PICARD – STORIES p164-171

How Glooskap made the birds
MacMILLAN – GLOOS. p18-25

How God helped Mammo
DAVIS – LION'S p153-158

How God's wheel turns
O'SULLIVAN – FOLK. p149-151

How grasshopper came to be and men
obtained tobacco
BELTING – EARTH p25-27

How Grigori Petrovich divided the geese
WYNDHAM – TALES p16-21

How Guenevere went a-maying
PICARD – STORIES p235-241

How hare asked for wisdom
HASKETT – GRAINS p40-42

How he stole the moon and the sun
AYRE – SKETCO p16-29

How horses came to the Navaho
MARRIOTT – AMER. p133-137

How I found these tales
JORDAN – BURRO p86-90

How Ian Direach got the blue falcon
LINES – TALES p45-55

How Ijapa, who was short, became long
COURLANDER – OLODE p37-39

How it came about that there is a sun
and a moon
BELTING – EARTH p28-30

How Jack sought the golden apples
MY BOOK HOUSE v. 5 p76-89

How Joan lost the sight of her eye. *See*
The fairy midwife

How Juan married a princess
SECHRIST – ONCE p135-140

How King Yudhishthira came to the
gates of heaven with his dog
TURNBULL – FAIRY p168-170

How kingfisher got his necklace
LEACH – HOW p96

How Kwaku Ananse became bald
APPIAH – ANANSE p95-104

298

How Kwaku Ananse destroyed a
kingdom
APPIAH – ANANSE p105-111

How Kwaku Ananse won a kingdom
with a grain of corn
APPIAH – ANANSE p1-26

How life and light came into the world
U. N. – RIDE p224-225

How little stork lost his tail
CATHON – PERHAPS p189-194

How locusts came to be
SECHRIST – ONCE p34-37

How Loki outwitted a giant
MAYNE – GIANTS p35-41

How long will it take?
WALKER – WATER. p60-61

How loon learned his call
LEACH – HOW p97.

How Mackay first brought fire into the
world
SHEPPARD – SCOT. p67-68

How mankind learned to make bread
LEACH – HOW p53-54

How many days has my baby to play?
MY BOOK HOUSE v. 1 p19.

How many donkeys?
DOBBS – ONCE p91-95

How many miles to Babylon?
MY BOOK HOUSE v. 1 p55.

How maple sugar came
CATHON – PERHAPS p198-200

How marriages are made
BIRCH – CHINESE p43-47

How Master Thumb defeated the sun
AUNG – KINGDOM p46-52

How Maui fished up New Zealand
WILLIAMS – ROUND p242-252

How Maui fished up the island
BERRY – MAGIC p81-88

How Maui obtained the magic jawbone
CAMPBELL – MAORI p6-10

How Ma-ui snared the sun and made him
go more slowly across the heavens
CATHON – PERHAPS p103-109

How men become enemies
URE – RUMANIAN p126-130

How men brought fire to earth
BELTING – EARTH p20-21

How men learned about evil
BELTING – EARTH p87-91

How men learned to build houses
BELTING – EARTH p12-15

How men learned to make fire
LEACH – HOW p52.

How men learned to sing songs
BELTING – EARTH p82-86

How Michael Scot went to Rome
WILSON – SCOTTISH p38-40

How Mr. Crane's eyes became blue
GILHAM – BEYOND p76-85

How Mr. Rabbit was too sharp for Mr.
Fox
ARBUTHNOT – TIME p193-194

How Molo stole the lovely Rose Red
BAKER – TALKING p251-255

How monkey king became a slave
HASKETT – GRAINS p80-81

How Moremi saved the town of Ife
COURLANDER – OLODE p113-117

How much for a shadow?
CARPENTER – ELEPHANT'S p100-
107

How much you remind me of my
husband!
JAGENDORF – KING p117-119

How music began
TOOZE – MONKEY p7-27

How mussels were brought to the creeks
PARKER – AUSTRALIAN p124-126

How night was let loose and all the
animals came to be
BELTING – EARTH p37-39

How Odin brought the mead to Asgard
HOSFORD – THUNDER p49-56

How Odysseus came home
    GREEN – GREEKS p72-73

How old Stormalong captured Mocha
Dick
    SHAPIRO – HEROES p58-104

How Ologbon-Ori sought wisdom
    COURLANDER – OLODE p65-68

How one should carve a goose
    PROTTER – CHILD. p130-131

How pa learned to grow hot peppers
    CREDLE – TALL p67-81

How Papantla got its patron saint
    ROSS – MEXICO p150-161

How Pakayana the spider got his small
waist
    U. N. – RIDE p116-118

How Peary reached the North Pole
    MY BOOK HOUSE v. 9 p128a-128b

How people became different
    HASKETT – GRAINS p89-94

How people got fire
    NORLEDGE – ABORIGINAL p55-57

How people got the first cat
    LEACH – HOW p63-64

How Percival came to Arthur's court
    PICARD – STORIES p153-163

How pictures become words
    MAR – CHINESE p147-160

How possum got his tail
    BELTING –LONG p46-50

How poverty was revealed to the King
of Adja
    COURLANDER – KING'S p45-49

How Prince Bondhu became a boatman
    GHOSE – FOLK p37-47

How rabbit deceived fox
    MacMILLAN – GLOOS. p64-71

How rabbit lost his tail
    MacMILLAN – GLOOS. p58-63

How rabbit stole fire from the buzzards
    LEACH – HOW p47-48

How rattlesnake got his fangs
    LEACH – HOW p112.

How raven brought fire to the Indians
    MacMILLAN – GLOOS. p251-258

How raven found the daylight
    MAHER – BLIND p39-51

How Robert Fulton harnessed the giant
    MY BOOK HOUSE v. 5 p48-53

How rooster got his comb
    LEACH – HOW p92-93

How she kept her geese warm
    ARBUTHNOT – TIME p272-273

How she made the baby elephant happy
    ARBUTHNOT – TIME p273-275

How Sigurd awoke Brynhild
    HAZELTINE – HERO p269-277

How Sima humbugged a crocodile
    HASKETT – GRAINS p21-23

How Sketco tricked the grizzly
    AYRE – SKETCO p173-183

How spider got a bald head
    ARKHURST – SPIDER p21-31

How spider got a thin waist
    ARKHURST – SPIDER p1-11

How spider got his thread
    LEACH – HOW p84.

How spider helped a fisherman
    ARKHURST – SPIDER p32-38

How spider taught women to weave
    BELTING – EARTH p16-19

How stars and fireflies were made
    CATHON – PERHAPS p23-27

How strong a bridge have you?
    MY BOOK HOUSE v. 1 p129.

How Suan became rich
    SECHRIST – ONCE p177-184

How summer came to Canada
    MacMILLAN – GLOOS. p10-17

How tadpoles lost their tails
    LEACH – HOW p113-114

How Tammas Maciver Macmurdo
Maclennan met his match
LEODHAS – GHOST p103-112

How Tepozton hung the bells
BRENNER – BOY p38-43

How Tepozton killed the giant
BRENNER – BOY p34-37

How Terrapin's shell was cracked
BELTING – LONG p54-56

How the animals made wings for bat and
flying squirrel
BELTING – LONG p16-22

How the bat caught friendship with the
moon
HOLLADAY – BANTU p87-88

How the beaver came to build their homes
in the water
BELTING – LONG p42-45

How the beaver lost the hair on his tail
CATHON – PERHAPS p58-61

How the bee got his bumble
DEUTSCH – TALES p15-17

How the birds came to have their many
colors
BELTING – LONG p37-38

How the black snake got its fangs
NORLEDGE – ABORIGINAL p54.

How the black turnstone came to nest
near the sea
GILHAM – BEYOND p128-134

How the Brazilian beetles got their
gorgeous coats
CATHON – PERHAPS p28-32
MY BOOK HOUSE v. 3 p172-175

How the camel got his hump
GREEN – BIG p181-185

How the camel got his proud look
ROSS – BURIED p135-138

How the cardinal got his red feathers
BELTING – LONG p62-66

How the Caribs first came to Honduras
JAGENDORF – KING p162-163

How the carrot-counter got his name
PROTTER – CHILD. p145.

How the clergyman retrieved the golden
chalice from the goblins of Gotland
MORRIS – UPSTAIRS p43-49

How the cock got his red crown
HUME – FAVORITE p27-32

How the coconut tree came to be
BELTING – THREE p121-124

How the coconut tree was saved
LEACH – HOW p126.

How the cows flew across the sea
JAGENDORF – GYPSIES p164-169

How the deer got his horns
SCHEER – CHEROKEE p55-57

How the deer lost his tail
HUME – FAVORITE p109-114

How the devil fetched the mayor
RANKE – GERMANY p161-162

How the devil married three sisters
THOMPSON – ONE p24-26

How the dog chose its master
CARPENTER – ELEPHANT'S p75-81

How the donkey saved a village
FOSTER – STONE p71-75

How the dotty Afghan woodman died
MORRIS – UPSTAIRS p115-118

How the duyvil gave New Amsterdam to
the English
JAGENDORF – GHOST p31-36

How the earth was made to fit the sky
LEACH – HOW p17.

How the earth's fire was saved
LEACH – HOW p22.

How the fiddler crabs came to be
SECHRIST – ONCE p31-34

How the finch got her colors
MY BOOK HOUSE v. 2 p143-144

How the first horse was made
LEACH – HOW p66.

How the first rainbow was made
CATHON – PERHAPS p113-125
FISHER – STORIES p60-73

How the Fomorians came into Erin
PILKINGTON – THREE p11-16

How the fox and the hedgehog became friends
RUDOLPH – MAGIC p62-71

How the foxes became red
CATHON – PERHAPS p48-52
GILHAM – BEYOND p99-105

How the ghost got in
LITTLEDALE – GHOSTS p79-82

How the giant Finn made the Isle of Man
YOUNG – HOW p1-6

How the gipsy sold his horse
ĆURČIJA – YUGOSLAV p99.

How the goddess of spring came to Scoring
MY BOOK HOUSE v. 9 p176.

How the great rocks grew
FISHER – STORIES p88-95

How the groundhog lost his tail
SCHEER – CHEROKEE p31-32

How the gypsy boy outsmarted death
JAGENDORF – GYPSIES p129-133

How the half boys came to be
MARRIOTT – AMER. p78-89

How the hare learned to swim
HEADY – JAMBO p40-45

How the herring became king of the sea
YOUNG – HOW p37-44

How the Kadawbawa men counted themselves
TOOZE – WONDER. p125-126

How the kakok bird came to be
SECHRIST – ONCE p22-24

How the king chose a daughter-in-law
URE – RUMANIAN p19-21

How the king of the birds was chosen
BOWES – BIRD p7-14

How the kuhreihen began
MÜLLER – SWISS p23-28

How the letter X got into the alphabet
DOBBS – ONCE p70-73

How the lion rewarded the mouse's kindness
APPIAH – ANANSE p89-93

How the little black wren got its red feathers
NORLEDGE – ABORIGINAL p14.

How the little fox went after chaff
BLOCH – UKRAIN. p49-59

How the little owl's name was changed
GILHAM – BEYOND p44-50

How the lizard lost and regained his farm
COURLANDER – HAT p70-76

How the lizards got their markings
SECHRIST – ONCE p49-51

How the long-tailed bear lost his tail
BELTING – LONG p13-15

How the Manx cat lost its tail
YOUNG – HOW p29-36

How the milky way began
DOBBS – ONCE p51-53

How the miser turned into a monkey
LIN – MILKY p33-40

How the monkey came to be
SECHRIST – ONCE p37-38

How the moon and (the) stars came to be
CATHON – PERHAPS p110-111
SECHRIST – ONCE p12-13

How the mosquitoes came to Oneata
WILLIAMS – ROUND p233-241

How the mud turtle came to live in the water
JOHNSON – WHAT p244-245

How the ox came upon earth
BONNET – CHINESE p103-104

How the parrots helped the women
COBBLE – WEMBI p69-71

How the peasants bought wisdom
CURCIJA – YUGOSLAV p137-139

How the people began
LEACH – HOW p37-38

How the people came from the lower world
COURLANDER – PEOPLE p10-24

How the people came to the middle
place
MARRIOTT – AMER. p65-72

How the people got fire
LEACH – HOW p49-51

How the people of Ife became scattered
COURLANDER – OLODE p110-112

How the people sang the mountains up
LEACH – HOW p23-24

How the pig got his snout
APPIAH – ANANSE p39-45

How the porcupine fooled the elephant
COBBLE – WEMBI p77-79

How the porcupine outwitted the fox
BARLOW – LATIN p113-118

How the ptarmigans learned to fly
GILHAM – BEYOND p86-98

How the queen of the sky gave gifts to
men
CATHON – PERHAPS p246-249

How the rabbit fooled the elephant
JABLOW – MAN p27-29

How the rabbit made enemies by trying
to be too friendly
BURTON – MAGIC p94-95

How the rabbit stole the otter's coat
SCHEER – CHEROKEE p69-74

How the rajah got rich
WILLIAMS – OLD p165-179

How the raja's son won the Princess Labam
LINES – TALES p56-66

How the raven brought light to the world
MELZACK – DAY p57-58

How the raven brought the fire
AYRE – SKETCO p112-123

How the raven stole the stars
AYRE – SKETCO p1-15

How the redbird got his color
SCHEER – CHEROKEE p62-64

How the robin's breast became red
CATHON – PERHAPS p181-182

How the sea gulls learned to fly
GILHAM – BEYOND p17-30

How the sons filled the hut
WYNDHAM – TALES p13-15

How the spider was made
CATHON – PERHAPS p94-99

How the sun came
MARRIOTT – AMER. p30-32

How the sun was made
LEACH – HOW p18-19
PARKER – AUSTRALIAN p21-23

How the terrapin beat the rabbit
SCHEER – CHEROKEE p37-42

How the Tewas came to first mesa
COURLANDER – PEOPLE p145-155

How the travelers shared their meal
HITCHCOCK – KING p33-36

How the trivet came home
JAGENDORF – MERRY p51-63

How the turkey got his beard
SCHEER – CHEROKEE p43-46

How the turtle fooled the leopard
COBBLE – WEMBI p112-113

How the village of Pivanhonkapi
perished
COURLANDER – PEOPLE p119-125

How the water lily came
CATHON – PERHAPS p150-152

How the whales reached the sea
BELTING – LONG p60-61

How the wild boars came to be
LOWE – LITTLE p38-40

How the wildcat got his spots
BELTING – LONG p71-73

How the wolf lost his tail
MONTGOMERIE – 25 p30-31

How the world got wisdom
ARKHURST – SPIDER p50-58

How the world was made (1)
MARRIOTT – AMER. p21-26

How the world was made (2)
MARRIOTT – AMER. p27-29

How these tales came to be told
MINCIELI – OLD p3-13

How they bring back the village of cream
puffs when the wind blows it away
ARBUTHNOT – TIME p379-381

How Thor found his hammer
ARBUTHNOT – TIME p238-240

How three pilgrims called Ilya to the
rescue of Kiev
ALMEDINGEN – KNIGHTS p15-32

How thunder and lightning came to be
MAHER – BLIND p99-105

How thunder got back into the sky
JABLOW – MAN p97-98

How thunder makes the lightning
JABLOW – MAN p93-96

How tiger learned to hunt
LEACH – HOW p78.

How to catch a fish
REED – TALK. p62-63

How to catch a unicorn
JACOBSON – FIRST p30-31

How to catch unicorns
PALMER – DRAGONS p43-45

How to cook a coot
LEACH – NOODLES p79.

How to kill a witch
JOHNSON – WHAT p164-165

How to shake hands with a giant
DE REGNIERS – GIANT p176.

How to sleep well
BATCHELOR – SUPER. p100-102

How to tell stories to children
BROWN – AROUND p v.-x.

How to weigh an elephant
ALEXANDER – PEBBLES p11.

How Tristram fought against the knight
from Ireland
PICARD – STORIES p82-88

How Trystan won Esyllt
JONES – WELSH p115-118

How turkey got his white tail
BELTING – LONG p89-92

How turtle came
MacMILLAN – GLOOS. p35-40

How turtle keeps from getting wet
LEACH – HOW p116.

How Urseli became a princess
WILLIAMS – OLD p313-321

How vanity made the dove sad
BOWES – BIRD p58-64

How whale happens to smoke a pipe
LEACH – HOW p79.

How wisdom came to man
LEACH – HOW p45-46

How wisdom was spread throughout the
world
APPIAH – ANANSE p147-152

How yams got their eyes
LEACH – HOW p129.

How Yehl, the hero, freed the beaming
maiden
MY BOOK HOUSE v. 6 p102-107

How Ysengrin the wolf was taught to
fish
WESTWOOD – MEDIEVAL p57-61

Howard, Joan
Mrs. Wallaby Jones
The thirteenth floor

Howell, D. M. G.
The gouty giant

Howitt, Mary
The sea gull
The squirrel

Htin Aung, Maung. See Aung, Maung Htin

Hudson River legends: Captain Kidd;
Buried treasure
JOHNSON –WHAT p259-263

Hull, Eleanor
How Cuchulain wooed his wife

Hully-gully
JOHNSON – WHAT p236.

Human passions in the gods: Isis
challenges Re
JAMES – MYTHS p21-27

304

Human stupidity
CREANGA – FOLK p61-66

Humbug
LEACH – RAINBOW p226.

Humility. *See* Meekness

The hummingbird and the carabao
SECHRIST – ONCE p43-46

Hummingbirds
Coyote's needle
The gift to the hummingbird
The legend of Pitch Lake
Why the birds are different colors

Humor
The empty city
The hare and the lord
Hear ye!
Icebergs
Introduction (Tales of wit and wisdom)
Luck and wit
The reluctant familiar
Tales of wit and wisdom
The talking-match

Humpbacks. *See* Hunchbacks

Humperdinck, Engelbert
Hansel and Grettel

Humpty Dumpty
The interesting history of old Mother
Goose

Humpty Dumpty
MY BOOK HOUSE v. 1 p46.

The hunchback and the miser
SPICER – OWL'S p86-105

Hunchbacks
Kwaku Ananse and the rain maker
The old humpback
The old man and his fishing line
The palace in the Rath
Prospect and retrospect
Saturday, Sunday, Monday
The tale of the hump-backed men

The hunchback's gift
THOMPSON – ONE p166-170

The hunchback's horse
CARPENTER – HORSES p205-215

The hundred-headed daffodil
CATHON – PERHAPS p230-235

Hungarian rhymes
MY BOOK HOUSE v. 1 p136.

Hungary. *See also* **Magyars**
The adventures of Pengo
Attila the conqueror
Bendebukk
The caterpillar
The cock and the hen
The competition of fools
Dear-boy
Dummling
The fairy Helena
Fairy Ilona and Argelus
The fairy of the three-branched oak
The fiddle
The finch with the golden voice
The fish maid
The flower-headed man
The flute made of maple-wood
The flying castle
The fox and the wolf at the wedding
Gisella and the goat
The glass man and the golden bird
Goose Matt
The green-bearded king
The gypsy fiddle
A handful of hay
Hans and his master
The healing of Urre
Jack at Hell Gate
Joe Magerack, the steel-mill man
Kalamona and the winds
Kate Contrary
King Matthias and the old man
The lamb with the golden fleece
The lazy cat
Little Berry
Little Firenko
Little Kathy free-as-the-wind
Long-Neck, Fatty and Droopy
The lost children
Martin, the honest thief
The miraculous stag
Miska and the man-with-the-iron-head
The musical silver goat
The nine peahens and the golden
apples
Oh dear!
Pearly-dew John
The peppercorn oxen
The poor girl who stepped out golden
flowers
Prince Mirko
Prince Murko's journey
The ram with the golden fleece
Ravenspring
The rooster and the hen

Hungary (*Continued*)

The rooster and the sultan
The secret-keeping boy
The secretive little boy and his little
 sword
The seven ravens
Seven Simons
The shepherd who understood the
 language of the animals
The simple-minded bootmaker as a
 miraculous healer
The spotted cow
The tudent who became a prince
The student who was forced to be
 king
The tale of the Balaton
The three lemons
The three wishes
Tree-root, iron-strong, and hill-roller
The truest adventures of the truthful
 mountain boy
The two girls and the iron-nose witch
Uletka
The vain king
Victor
What grown-ups can learn from
 children's books
What happens to the envious
The witch and the swan maiden
The wonderful tree
Wooden Peter

 —**Transylvania**
 The demon's daughter
 The Pied Piper of Hamelin

Hunger
 See also **Famine**
 Anansi and the plantains
 The camel in the lion's court
 The dervish and the wolf
 The fall of the spider man
 Gentlin' the ram
 The giant kingfisher of Mount Riga
 Guno's hunger
 How thunder and lightning came to be
 The lion's threats
 The meat hungry man and the grave
  digger
 Raven and the sun
 The scholar and the thieves
 The six companions
 The son of the hunter

Hunger moon
 BUDD — FULL p75-79

The hunger time
 MARTIN — COYOTE p23-30

The hungry giant
 MEHDEVI — BUNGLING p85-91

Hungry hog
 LEACH — NOODLES p82.

The hungry old witch
 HOKE — WITCHES p90-100

The hungry rider
 DE LA IGLESIA — CAT unp.

The hungry serpent
 BONNET — CHINESE p117-121

Hungry servant reproaches stingy master.
 See The three cups of water

The hungry trout
 FELTON — NEW p87-102

A hungry wolf
 HUME — FAVORITE p55-61

Huns
 Attila the conqueror
 The miraculous stag
 Walther of Aquitaine

Hunt, Wolf Robe, illus.
 RUSHMORE — DANCING p164.

The hunter
 PILKINGTON — THREE p137-145

The hunter and his talking leopard
 COURLANDER — KING'S p64-66

The hunter and the dove
 KOREL — LISTEN p49-53

The hunter and the hind
 WALKER — DANCING p27-34

The hunter and the tiger
 GINSBURG — MASTER p145-151

The hunter of Perak
 COURLANDER — KANT. p29-32

The hunter on the moon
 JABLOW — MAN p22.

Hunters and Hunting
 Adventuring; White man on the
  warpath
 The African hunter and the forbidden
  room
 Agayk and the strangest spear
 Anansi hunts with tiger

306

Hunters and Hunting (*Continued*)

Anansi steals the palm wine
The antelope and the spider
The antelope skin
Bear, fox, and man
The biggest crocodile in the world
The blind boy and the loon
The boom-boomy-y beast
The boy and his magic robe
The boy with the long hair
The brave men of Golo
The cat and the fox
The ceabharnach
The chief's knife
The cold heart—Part 2
Count Bertrand
The cranberry feast
The crane's feather
Curse of the Abenaki
The Da-Trang crabs
The dancing bird
Davy Crockett
Davy Crockett, the yaller blossom o'
  the forest
The day Tuk became a hunter
The devil and the man
The dicot tree and the deer
The donkey lettuce
The dragon king and the lost fish-hook
The duck with red feet
The dwarfs of the anthill
The elephant hunters
Ermine and the hunter
Finlay the hunter
The fortunes of Saïd
The fountain of Arethusa
The four friends
A fox in hiding
Frontier fighter/Davy Crockett
The giraffe hunters
The golden fleece
The golden stag
Goola-willeels the topknot pigeons
The great bear
Great hunting!
The hairy man from the forest
Helping to lie
The honourable tom cat
How the dog chose its master
How tiger learned to hunt
I don't know where and I don't know
  what
Idy, the fox-chasing cow
The jewels of the sea
King Herla
The legend of Pathasos
The leopard and the bushbuck buy a
  dream
The leopard and the bushbuck go
  hunting

The leopard and the tortoise
The lion and donkey a-hunting go
The lion's threats
The little scarred one
The long-howling jackal
A long night's sleep
The loup-garou in the woods
The lucky hunter
The magic calabash
The magic ruby
The man who had no wife
The man who loved Hai Quai
The man who refused help
The man with a lion head in a can
The man with the chair on his head
Mboyo and the giants
Mboyo the hunter
The men and the monkeys
The mighty hunter
The miller and the water sprite
The miller's four sons
The miraculous stag
Mountains of Manitou
Navahchoo
Netchillik and the bear
Olode the hunter becomes an oba
The one-horned mountain goat
The one who wasn't afraid
The outwitted hunter
The pigeon, the deer and the turtle
Princess Maring, the huntress
The princess on the glass mountain
Queen crane
Rabbit and the grain buyers
The rabbit who wanted to be a man
Rojin Rojal
Roommates
The sand-carrier crab
A secret told to a stranger
The seven-headed giant
The shipwrecked prince
The sick boy, the greedy hunters, and
  the dwarfs, The Little People of
  North America
The silly men of Russia
Sindhu
The six brothers
The six companions
The skillful huntsman
The sky beings: thunder and his
  helpers
The sky people
Snow-white and the seven dwarfs
The son of the hunter
The stars above: pursuit of the bear
A strange reward
The stupid hunter and the crafty bird
The summer birds
The swan princess
The tale of Vassilissa the wise
The talking nightingale

Hunters and Hunting (*Continued*)

The three gluttons and the hunter
The three hunters
Three jovials huntsmen
Tiny Perry
The tiny, tiny man
Two hunters
The two men and the two dwarfs
Ugly boy
The vain ox
The waters beneath: fifty young men
  and a turtle
The waters beneath: The great river
  monster
The waters beneath: The underwater
  village
What the squirrel saw
The wheel of fate
Who should get the neck ring?
Why no one ever carries the alligator
  down to the water
Why the crab has no head or how the
  first river was made
Wikki, the weaver
The wild huntsman
The wise bird and the hunter; an old
  Hebrew fable
The wise woodland maid
The witch of Laggan
The woodpecker and the jade stone
Written in the stars
Young hunter
The young hunter and the Juju man

The hunters and the antelope
  WITHERS — I SAW p143.

The hunter's child
  ELLIOT — SINGING p111-123

Hunters' moon
  BUDD — FULL p57-60

The hunters of Kentucky
  JOHNSON — WHAT p155-156

The hunting cat
  CARPENTER — DOGS p74-80

The hunting dog and the purple fish
  CARPENTER — SHIPS p247-253

Hunting in the light
  KELSEY — ONCE p119-121

The huntsman and his wife
  DUDDINGTON — RUSS. p107-115

Hurry up, engine
  MY BOOK HOUSE v. 1 p92.

The hurt sparrow
  BUCK — FAIRY p181-183

A husband for the chief's daughter
  BURTON — MAGIC p107-109

The husband of the rat's daughter
  MANNING — BEASTS p160-163

The husband, the wife, and the devil
  JAGENDORF — GYPSIES p152-163

The husband who was to mind the house
  ARBUTHNOT — TIME p84-85
  ASBJÖRNSEN — EAST p19-23

Husbands
  The castle of no return
  The death of Koshchei the deathless
  The first woman to say "Dim"
  The five eggs
  A fortune in a stick
  The haughty princess
  Lion and the woman
  The mad man, the dead man, and the
    devil
  The magic storm
  Male and female created he them: The
    river of separation
  The man who kept house
  The miller's three sons
  The moon husband
  Now would I laugh, were I not dead
  An old woman sows discord
  The perfect husband
  A selfish husband
  The smart husband and the smarter
    wife
  Stubborn husband, stubborn wife
  A suspicious wife with an enforced
    extra husband
  Two unfaithful husbands
  Who is boss?

The hut in the forest
  ARBUTHNOT — TIME p38-41

Hutchinson, Veronica S.
  Billy Beg and his bull
  Three billy goats gruff

Huts. *See* **Houses**

Hwan and Dang
  WILLIAMS — ROUND p1-15

Hyde, Mark Powell
  The squires win golden spurs

Hydra
A school of sea monsters

The hyena and the moon
JABLOW – MAN p48-49

Hyena and the oil with the flies in it
AARDEMA – TALES p41-51

The hyena man
DAVIS – LION'S p3-7

Hyenas
The adventures of Nomvula
The battle between the birds and the
beasts
The bean pot
The bob-tailed monkey and the king's
honey
The brave prince
The donkey who sinned
The donkeys ask for justice
The goat and the eagle
Grandfather tells some tales
The greedy hyena
Hare and the hyena
How animals got their beautiful coats
The infallible salt bird
The jackal's lawsuit
The light in the house
The lion's share
Live alone; die alone
The lizard's lost meat
The man who turned into a hyena
Mister Honey Mouth
To outleap a rabbit
Why the lion, the vulture, and the
hyena do not live together
The wrestlers

The hyena's egg
ARNOTT – TALES p9-19

The hyena's medicine man
HARMAN – TALES p144-152

Hymns, Homeric
Tithonus, the grasshopper

Hynd horn
MAYNE – HEROES p32-36

Hypocrisy
The baboon and the hare
The battle of the frogs and the mice
The crane and the crab
The dappled deer and the intelligent
crow
The friendship of the tortoise and the
eagle
The giant elephant
Gigi and the magic ring
How Jack sought the golden apples
The race
The shepherd's dog and the wolf
The snake and the dreams
The tailless jackal
The tale of chanticleer
The tiger's tail
The trial by fire
Una and the Red Cross knight

The hypocrite and the merchant's pledge
NAHMAD – PORTION p147-149

Hyraxes (animals)
Why the hyrax has no tail

I

I am not Sarajevo
   ĆURČIJA – YUGOSLAV p42.

I don't know where and I don't know what
   BUDBERG – RUSSIAN p1-23

I had a little dog
   MY BOOK HOUSE v. 1 p106.

I had a little husband
   MY BOOK HOUSE v. 1 p27.

I had a little husband no bigger than my
thumb. *See* The interesting history of
old Mother Goose

I had a little mule
   MY BOOK HOUSE v. 1 p106.

I had a little nut tree
   MY BOOK HOUSE v. 1 p37.

I had a piece of pie
   MY BOOK HOUSE v. 1 p98.

I heard the bells on Christmas day
   MY BOOK HOUSE v. 2 p217.

I-know-not-what of I-know-not-where
   DOWNING – RUSSIAN p116-137

I know what I'll do
   WALKER – WATER. p49-50

I love little pussy
   MY BOOK HOUSE v. 1 p143.

I saw a crow a-flying low
   MY BOOK HOUSE v. 1 p107.

I saw a ship a-sailing
   MY BOOK HOUSE v. 1 p35.

I saw three witches
   HOPE-SIMPSON – CAVAL. p35-36

I should like to plough
   MY BOOK HOUSE v. 1 p136.

I stand in the pulpit and preach
   MY BOOK HOUSE v. 1 p117.

I took a walk one evening
   MY BOOK HOUSE v. 1 p75.

I was going along the road
   HAMPDEN – GYPSY p63-65

I was traveling those parts
   HAMPDEN – GYPSY p101-104

I was wondering
   LEACH – NOODLES p38.

I went to the animal fair
   MY BOOK HOUSE v. 1 p104.

I yay! I yay! I yay!
   MY BOOK HOUSE v. 1 p131.

Ian Direach
   PICARD – HERO p97-106

Ibn Ezra, Abraham
   Any more food?
   The barrel decree
   Judge not the vessel
   The talking talisman

Ibsen, Henrik
   Peer Gynt

Icarus and Daedalus
   ARBUTHNOT – TIME p220-221

Ice
   Five drowned
   The fox and the hare in winter
   How the wolf lost his tail
   Hunger moon
   The inquiring rabbit, or the strongest
      thing in the world
   The ogre king of Gilgit
   Papa Greatnose
   The Prince of Coucy
   The strongest
   The water dwellers

Ice-cold lemonade
   MY BOOK HOUSE v. 1 p88.

Ice cream
   The king's cream

Ice fishing
   The coyote and the bear
   The old tiger and the hare
   Why the bear's tail is short

The ice ship in the hot sea
CARPENTER — SHIPS p101-109

Ice skating
Three old maids a-skating went

Icebergs
LEACH — RAINBOW p188.

Iceland
The American saga
Asmund, Authun, and Odd
Authun and the bear
The Bakki brothers
The boy who was not afraid
Bukolla
Buolla, the wonderful cow
The city east of the moon and south
of the sun
The deacon of Darkwater
The fairy woman's revenge
Frithiof's journey to the Orkneys
Grettir becomes an outlaw
Greyman
Grim and the merman
Hali becomes a poet
The haunted boat
The hauntings at Thorhallstead
Hildur the elf queen
The hired man
The laughing merman
Loppa and Jon Loppa-Fosterling
The magic scythe, the Little People
of Iceland
The money cask
Njal the lawyer
Now would I laugh, were I not dead
The ogres in the stone boat
Old man knowall
Poor Jack and the cat
The poor man's son, the dwarfs, and
the birds
Prince Sigurd and his sister
Saemunel the Learned
The shepherd of Silverstead
The spell-song
The story of Mead Moondaughter
The story of Prince Ring and his dog
Thorsteinn Shiver
Tongue steeple
The troll's bride
Wakewell and his brothers

Ida of Toggenburg
MÜLLER — SWISS p200-204

Idaho
The ant and the yellow jacket
The bears
The buffalo and the porcupine
Calling the chinook
The end of the world
Fickle Miss Frog
The fishnet and the bear
The fog
The good luck tree
How death came
Itsayaya and the chokecherries
Itsayaya and the otter
Itsayaya frees the salmon
Itsayaya's revenge
One day, one night
The rope
The sun, the moon, and the stars
The upper world
The weasel
Why an Illinoian wouldn't buy Idaho
land
The young coyote's visit

—Coeur D'Alene
Why the animals have no fire

Idaho
LEACH — RAINBOW p83-84

Ideas
Caravan

Identity
Who am I?

"Ides of March"
Julius Caesar . . . The Ides of March

The idle boy
MANNING — WIZARDS p58-60

Idleness. See Laziness

Idols. See Gods and goddesses; Statues

Idunn's apples of youth
AULAIRE — NORSE p87-90

Idy, the fox-chasing cow
MARGOLIS — IDY p36-44

Iei trees
Sungold and the remarkable cow

If I could work
MY BOOK HOUSE v. 1 p62.

If my shoe is narrow, what matter if
the world is wide
CHAPPELL — THEY p64-68

If so where is the cat?
JUDA – WISE p60-65

If you know a story, don't keep it to
yourself
MASEY – STORIES p104-108

Ifor the scoffer
PUGH – TALES p83-96

Igor, Grand Prince of Kiev
The word of Igor's armament

The iguana and the black snake
PARKER – AUSTRALIAN p69-74

Iguanas
The meeting
When the iguana grows armor
–Tails
Armadillo's story

The iguana's poison bag
U. N. – RIDE p20-24

Ihi! Ihi! Ihi!
MY BOOK HOUSE v. 1 p80.

Ijapa and the hot-water test
COURLANDER – OLODE p90-95

Ijapa and the oba repair a roof
COURLANDER – OLODE p58-60

Ijapa and Yanrinbo swear an oath
COURLANDER – OLODE p69-71

Ijapa cries for his horse
COURLANDER – OLODE p40-44

Ijapa demands corn fufu
COURLANDER – OLODE p104-106

Ijapa goes to the Osanyin shrine
COURLANDER – OLODE p86-89

Ikkyu and the merchant's moneybags
EDMONDS – TRICKSTER p14-20

Ikpoom
AARDEMA – TALES p51-58

Iliad (Homer)
See also The world's great epics
The battle of the frogs and the mice

I'll tell her
LEACH – NOODLES p85.

Illinois
Butting a sermon
The dance at Hickory Creek
Giant skeeters in the brass pot
The good dogs and the good assessor
The governor and the cannon
Harvest moon
Help in need and Abe in deed
The miller and the blue jay
Old Johnny Appleseed
Preacher Peter and Mike Fink

–Albion
The white mule from the other
world

–Cairo
Sand in the bag

–Chicago
All's well that ends well

–Springfield
Springfield got it

Illinois
LEACH – RAINBOW p84-85

Illinois River tall tale
JAGENDORF – SAND p138-140

Illiteracy
Bouki's glasses

Illtud, Saint
Eight leaves of story (3) Baglan the
builder

Illusion
Dream behind bars
Left eye, right eye

Illustrators
The Norwegian folk tales and their
illustrators

Ilmarinen . . . how he won his bride
UNTERMEYER – FIRE. p160-163

Ilya of Murom
The three journeys of Ilya of Murom

Ilya of Murom and nightingale the robber
DOWNING – RUSSIAN p36-42

Ilya of Murom and Svyatogor
  DOWNING – RUSSIAN p28-35

I'm a butcher
  MY BOOK HOUSE v. 1 p128.

I'm a little Indian
  MY BOOK HOUSE v. 1 p71.

I'm a peddler
  MY BOOK HOUSE v. 1 p94.

I'm Captain Jinks
  MY BOOK HOUSE v. 1 p93.

I'm going to Lady Washington's
  MY BOOK HOUSE v. 1 p82.

Images. *See* Effigies; Statues

Imagination
  The assembling of the fays
  The bow that bridges heaven
  Clouds
  Clytie
  Daffy-down-dilly
  Dream behind bars
  The elf and the dormouse
  An explanation of the grasshopper
  The fairyland of science
  The fog
  Grasshopper green
  I saw a ship a-sailing
  Jack Frost
  Jean Labadie's big black dog
  The knight
  Little Diamond and the north wind
  Mary, Mary, quite contrary
  A musical visit to fairyland
  My lady wind
  The night before Christmas
  Ooka and the willow witness
  Paper boats
  The planting of the apple tree
  The power of fancy
  Pretty, see the cloud appear!
  Snow
  The star
  The sugar-plum tree
  The surprising adventures of Don
    Quixote of La Mancha
  The tale of nutcracker
  The twilight
  The village of cream puffs
  Wynken, Blynken, and Nod

Imhotep (architect)
  Khnemu of the Nile

Imitation
  The peddler and his monkeys
  The wolf turned shepherd

Immigrants
  The melting pot
  The movie show

The immortal J. N.
  JAGENDORF – SAND p57-60

Immortality
  Isis and Osiris
  Isis and the secret name of Ra
  The portrait of the Tien
  The well of immortality
  Why crows are black

"Immortals"
  The dissatisfied good man
  The long nose
  The man who loved flowers

Impatience
  The babbling reed-warbler
  East o' the sun and west o' the moon
  Lohengrin
  Lox and the two ermines
  The magpie's nest
  The rice puller of Chaohwa

Impersonations
  See also Magic; Witchcraft; titles
    beginning with Changeling
  The aged infant
  As you like it
  King John and the abbot
  Nails

Impertinence. *See* Discourtesy

An impossible penance
  VITTORINI – OLD p96-101

Impossible tales
  U . N . – RIDE p77-81

Impossibility
  Arawn
  The blacksmith's dilemma
  The fox and the grapes
  The jackal and the elephant
  The stone lute

The imposter
  WILSON – GREEK p200-211

Imposters
  Conclusion
  The holy cat of Tibet
  How these tales came to be told
  The learned men
  The tale of the false prince
  The wild dog and the king's son

Imprisonment. *See* **Prisons and prisoners**

Improbable tales from Africa
  WITHERS – WORLD p59-66

Imps
  The last three guesses
  Little black imp!
  Lost and found
  "Nimmy-nimmy not!"
  Nine guesses
  Poll and Doll
  Ruddy-my-beard
  The strong boy
  Tsirtsur and Peziza
  The witching wood

Impudence
  Arachne . . . The eternal spinner
  The ambassador from Chi
  Misuse of a name
  Shizuka's dance
  Toontoony pie
  Zeus and the horse

The impudent little mouse
  SPELLMAN – BEAUT. p64-68

In a dark wood
  WITHERS – I SAW p67.

In China the people say
  WYNDHAM – CHINA p84-85

In Columbus' time
  MY BOOK HOUSE v. 5 p112.

In Coney Island by the sea
  JAGENDORF – UPSTATE p24-27

In Paris there is a street
  WITHERS – I SAW p75.

In Russia the people say
  WYNDHAM – TALES p88-89

In Spring the birds do sing
  MY BOOK HOUSE v. 1 p57.

In the beginning
  HOSFORD – THUNDER p7-12

In the days of Queen Anne
  MY BOOK HOUSE v. 12 p32-35

In the first times
  SECHRIST – ONCE p11-12

In the mist
  FARJEON – SILVER p119-124

In the paddy field
  REED – TALK. p35.

In the Springtime
  MY BOOK HOUSE v. 1 p148.

In the strange isle
  GARNER – GOBLINS p174.

In those days
  FARJEON – LITTLE p179-183

In unity is strength
  KAULA – AFRICAN p96-100

An inadvertent misunderstanding
  GHOSE – FOLK p56-64

The Inchcape rock
  BALDWIN – FAVOR. p114-118

Indecision
  The man and the mango trees
  Pamudjo's feast
  Two pieces of meat confuse the mind
    of the fly

Indepedence. *See* **Freedom**

India
  The adder and the fox
  The advantages of learning
  The age of the partridge
  Anangarati and the man of four castes
  The ass in the lion's skin
  The ass that was flayed
  The ass's promise
  The ballard of east and west
  The banishment of Rāma
  The banyan deer
  The bat's choice
  The battle on the Isle of Camphor
  The beautiful blue jay
  The beetle and a drop of honey
  Black clouds at midnight
  The blind man and the deaf man
  The blind man, the deaf man and the
    donkey
  The blue jackal
  The bold little bowman

India (*Continued*)

The boy with the moon on his forehead
The bragging beasts
The Brahman and the goat
The Brahman in the potter's shop
The Brahmin and the villain
The Brahmin, the tiger, and the seven judges
The brave little prince
The calm Brahman
The calves
The camel and his neighbor
The camel in the lion's court
A captive snake half dead with fright
The carpenter's boar
The cartman's stories
The cat bride
The cat that went to heaven
The cave that talked
Chandasimha, his son and their two wives
The clever children and the king tailor
The cobbler's deity
The cock and his loving wives
The conch shell of Ram
The crab, the crocodile and the jackal
The crane and the crab
The crane, the fish and the crab
The crane's report
The crow and the serpent
The crow and the sparrow
The crow in the banyan tree
The crow in the rose-apple tree
The crows and the owls
The crow's reward
Curd ears
The dappled deer and the intelligent crow
The demon with the matted hair
The dilemma of a pious man
Diplomacy
The dog that learned to read
The donkey in the lion-skin
The donkey who was an ass
Dookiram, the poor one
The earthquake
The elephant and the carpenters
The elephant and the gnat
The envious buffalo
The exile of Rama
The exploits of Hanuman
The eyes of owls
The fable of the plough and the ploughshare
The fables of India
The falcon and the hen
The false fakir
The fate of the vulture
The fear of the lion king

The feast for the fox
The fickleness of fortune
The fleeing deer
The flight of the animals
The flood
The flying turtle
The foolish Brahman
The foolish jackal
The foolish, timid, little hare
The four friends
Four tales of Rama and Sita
The fox in saint's clothing
Ganesha
The gardener and the bear
Garuda
Get ready, get set, go
The giant elephant
The glass house
The golden deer
The golden goose
The golden skins
The golden stag
Good-speed and the elephant king
The grateful goat
The grateful mouse
Greedy and speedy
The greedy crow
Gulam . . . The jar of rice
A handful of peas
The hare in the moon
The harebrained monkey
The hawk's friends
He leaves the nest
Here, forest-fires
The hermit and the mouse
The hermit and the Sea of Man
The hermit cat
The heron
The Hitopadesa (The book of good counsel)
A holy man and a sacred cow
How King Yudhishthira came to the gates of heaven with his dog
How Prince Bondhu became a boatman
How the dog chose its master
How the rabbit fooled the elephant
How the raja's son won the Princess Labam
How to catch a fish
The hunter and the dove
The impudent little mouse
In the paddy field
An inadvertent misunderstanding
An Indian love story
The indigo jackal
It happened in Kashmir
The jackal and the crocodile
The jackal and the hen
The jackal, the barber, and the Brahmin who had seven daughters

India (*Continued*)

The jackal told me
The judgement of the shepherd
Khrishna the cowherd
The kid and the tiger
King All-tusk
The king and his seven sons
The king and the monkey
The king and the shoemaker
The king and the wrestler
King crow and Sir parrot
King Great Virtue
King Shibi
The king's friend
The king's remorse
The king's true children
Kitava the gambler
The lame cat and the potter
The lazy gardener and the little red man
The length of life
Light-O-Leap and the fowler
The lion and the goat
The lion and the hare
The lion and the wily rabbit
The lion of hard-to-pass forest
The lion who listened to a jackal
The lion-wolf
The little bird that found the pea
The little bird's rice
Little Black Sambo
The little pet Rani
The lizard's tail
The long-eared cat and the vulture
The long-howling jackal
Look here!
Lord Krishna, or The eighth child
The loss of Sītā
The louse and the crow
Love at first sight
The magic bottles
The maiden and the ratcatcher
The man from Kailasa
The mighty wrestlers
The milkman and the monkey
The miracle of the begging bowl
Miss goat
The mongoose, the owl, the cat and the mouse
The monkey and the crocodile
Monkey fat
The monkey gardeners
The monkey king's bridge
Monkey-lord and crocodile
The monkey nursemaid
The monkey's heart
The monkey's search for Sītā
The moon princess
The monsoon season
Mother's day

The mouse and his friends
The mouse and the wizard
The mouse surrounded
The mouse's bride
Mousey the merchant
Mowgli's brothers
Nāgasvāmin and the witches
Nala and Damayanti
A nasty rumour
A noble Brahman's sacrifice
One more child
Other legendary beings
The otters and the fox
The outwitted hunter
The Panchatantra
The Panditji and the guavas
Paper boats
Peaceful, the gentle deer
The peacock bridegroom
The peacock's mistake
The peddler and his monkeys
The pilgrim and the crab
The plot
Prahlada
The price of greed
The prince and the demon
The prince of the six weapons
Prince sun and Princess moon
Prince Wicked
The prince's revenge
The princess of the mountain
Proverbs and sayings
Pyoli
The quarrel
A quarrel between thieves brings a Brahmin relief
The rajah who flew away
Rāma . . . The bow that could not be bent
Rāma's conquest of Ravana
The Ramayana
Ranjit and the tigers
The restless pigeon and his wife
The rich man and the tailor
Riches or happiness?
The robber Simhavikrama
Rodents rampart on a field of azure
The sage and the mouse
The sage and the servant
The scholars and the lion
A school for crocodiles
The search for Sita
Seeing a brace of rabbits
Selections from Rabindranath Tagore
The servant and the door
The shipwrecked prince
The silly goose
Sindhu
Sing something
Sissa and the troublesome trifles
A slip of the tongue

316

India (*Continued*)

The sneeze that won a wife
So many countries, so many customers
The speech of beasts
Spotless the lion and Trusty the
  carpenter
The stone monkey
The story ends
The story of Harisarman
The story of Ir, Bir, Dau, and I
The story of Noschoy Datta of Ujjain
The story of Suka's dog
The story of the hunted jars
The story of the king who would be
  stronger than fate
The story of Wali Dâd the simple-
  hearted
The story without an end
The straight and narrow way
Suppāraka the mariner
A tale of two rogues
The talkative king
The talkative tortoise
Teton
There's no telling on which side a
  camel will lie down
The thief's goat
This hound hath loved me
The three friends
The three suitors
The tiger and the goats
The tiger cat
The tiger, the Brahman, and the jackal
The tiny bird and the king
The tortoise and the two swans
The tortoise who talked too much
The traveller and the tiger
The turtle who could not stop talking
The twin parrots
The two brothers
The two foxes
Two novices who behaved like a pair
  of otters
The two sisters
The ugly king
The ungrateful lion
The unsolved riddle
Upa and her admirers
The valiant chattee-maker
The valiant potter
The vetala's stories
The vulture's advice
The wheel of fate
When the cat and the tiger lived to-
  gether
While other birds at will may go
Why?
Why the moon has scars on her face
Why the moon wanes
The wild geese and the tortoise

A wise man on a camel
With tail-fans spread
The wonderful bed
A world of nonsense
The world's great epics

—Assamese
  Feedowa and Nobbin
  The honourable tom cat
  The king and the Brahmin's child
  The unpunctual minister, or the
    Bosung pohoo

—Benares
  The king and the Nagas
  The monkey bridge

—Bombay
  The potted princess

—Buguns
  How the earth was made to fit the
    sky

—Calcutta
  The nightingale and the cotton
    tree

—Ceylon
  The blue lotus flower
  A bride for the sea god
  The cloud horse
  The deer and its friends
  Five lies that could be true
  The friendship of the hare and the
    parrot
  The frog jacket
  A girl and a stepmother
  Golden bracelets, golden anklets
  The golden oriole
  The golden peacock
  The greatest person in the world
  How the Kadawbawa men counted
    themselves
  The invisible silk robe
  The jeweled ring
  The king's drum
  The leopard and the mouse deer
  The magic lute player
  The making of the earth
  The mouseling
  The parrot and the crow
  The pearl necklace
  The Ramayana
  Sigiris Sinno, the mighty one
  The trials at Avichára—Pura
  The turtle prince
  The turtle, the storks and the
    jackal
  The vain jackal
  Who is responsible

India—Ceylon (*Continued*)

The wonderful wooden peacock
flying machine

—Gilgit
The ogre king of Gilgit

—Khasis
How thunder makes the lightning
The tree that shadowed the world

—Khowas
How the earth was made to fit
the sky

, Middle
How man learned to sing songs

, Northeast
How men learned to build houses
Why the mountains are snow-
covered

—Orissa—Konds
How the first horse was made

—West
The magic muntr

Indian children
MY BOOK HOUSE v. 3 p93.

The Indian Cinderella
MacMILLAN — GLOOS. p142-145

Indian legends of shrubs in our gardens
CATHON — PERHAPS p154-160

An Indian love story
GRAY — INDIA'S p36-37

Indian pipes (flower)
The origin of Indian pipes

The Indian shinny game
COTHRAN — WITH p56-64

Indiana
Abe Lincoln in Indiana
The colonel's blanket
Copperhead in the bin
Georgie goes a-sparkin'
Old Johnny Appleseed
Old man Edmonds and the ninety-nine
pigs

—Adams co.
God's own country

—Grand co.
The sad tale of Tom the catfish

—Hindostan
The miracle flame

—Lake co.
Gentlin' the ram

—North Manchester
Why the devil keeps out of Indiana

—Richmond
The hat in the moon

—Vincennes
Shiny tales of Vincennes

—Wabash co.
The little prairie hen and the big
Indiana
Why the devil keeps out of Indiana

—Wayne co.
The hat in the moon

Indiana
LEACH — RAINBOW p86.

Indians of Africa
—Fjort
Why crocodile does not eat hen

Indiana of Guiana
Bahmoo and the frog

Indians of Latin America
Clever little turtle
The coming of Asin
The deer and the jaguar share a house
The gift of manioc
The girl and the puma
The great bird in the carob tree
Gull taught man to use manioc for
food
The hero in the village
The honeybee bride
How much you remind me of my
husband
I'm a little Indian
The legend of Pitch Lake
The legend of the palm tree
The miracle of Our Lady of
Guadalupe
The origin of the balsam tree
Our Lady of Guadalupe
The peasant and the horseman
Pedro Alvarado and the Indian girl
The Pleiades
A promise made should be kept
The sea serpent
The snake that swallowed a girl
The Spanish donkey and the Indians
The three flutes are in the flute house
When Boquerón spoke

Indians of Latin America—Tribes

—Andean
A trick that failed

318

Indians of Latin America (*Continued*)

—Araucanian
  The ring in the seashell
  The strange adventures of Alcavilu

—Aymaran
  The great white condor

—Aztec
  Near God's cactus

—Carib
  The crocodile's daughter

—Catío
  A Catío Indian legend

—Chaco
  How spider taught women to
  weave

—Chimalteco
  A Chimalteco story

—Cuna
  The disobedient giant

—Esmerelda
  The tree goddess

—Guarani
  The gift of the moon goddess
  The white spider's gift

—Inca
  Children of the sun
  The head of the Inca
  The magic poncho
  The magic sandals of Hualachi
  The search for the magic lake
  The youth who made friends with
  the beasts and the birds

—Jibaro
  The man who fled a nagging wife

—Lien
  Tavadan

—Maya
  Ani, the mother who was too
  proud
  Bech, the ambitious quail
  The cardinal's concert
  The compulsive gift—a cigarette
  The cuckoo's reward
  The fall of the earth giants
  The gift to the hummingbird
  How the king of the birds was
  chosen
  How the porcupine outwitted the
  fox
  How vanity made the dove sad
  The revolt of the utensils
  The story of Cozumel, the lazy
  swallow
  The sweetest song in the woods

Why owls see only at night
Why the motmot lives in a hole
Why the whippoorwill weeps and
  wails
The woodpecker and the jade
  stone

—Miskito
  The eternal wanderer

—Mundurucu
  How night was let loose and all
  the animals came to be

—Nicarao
  Mister frog's dream

—Ona
  Sun and moon

—Quiche
  The sacred amulet

—Sapalla
  The great white condor

—Taulipang
  The armadillos

—Tehuelche
  The enchanted palace

—Timotean
  The magic eagle

—Toba
  Fire, a story of the Toba Indians
  How men learned to make fire
  How thunder got back into the sky

—Warrau
  The pot-that-cooked by itself

—Yahuna
  Milomaki

Indians of North America
  Adventuring: white man on the war-
  path
  The ambitious maiden
  The ass in the tiger skin
  Autumn
  The bear woman
  Beautiful doll
  The boy in the land of shadows
  The boy of the red twilight sky
  The boy who overcame the giants
  The boy who was called "thick-head"
  The boy who was saved by thoughts
  Buffalo Bill
  The bungling host
  Cannibal
  Children of Cloud
  The chipmunk who chattered too
  much
  The coming of the corn
  Cottontail and the sun

Indians of North America (*Continued*)

Cottontail's song
Coyote and mole
Coyote's new hairdo
The dance of death
The date gatherers
The duck with red feet
Eagle boy
The emerald lizard
Ermine and the hunter
The everlasting house
Exploring the wilderness
The fall of the spider man
The false shaman
The first mosquito
The first pig and porcupine
The first Thanksgiving day
The five swallow sisters
The forest wolf and the prairie wolf
The friendly mouse
Full moons
George Rogers Clarke and the conquest of the Northwest
The giant who loved adventure
The girl who always cried
Glooskap's country
Great heart and the three tests
The great medicine horse
The growing rock
The Haddam witches
Hanging at Wessaguscus
Hiawatha childhood
Hiawatha's fasting
Hi-Ho, the mosquitoes of New Jersey!
How a bird turned the world upside down
How crane saved coyote
How fire was brought from lightning
How Glooskap made the birds
How maple sugar came
How rabbit deceived fox
How rabbit lost his tail
How raven brought fire to the Indians
How summer came to Canada
How the people came from the lower world
How the water lily came
How turtle came
How Yehl, the hero, freed the beaming maiden
The hunger time
Indian legends of shrubs in our gardens
Introduction: Four world corners
John Brown had a little Indian
Kayuta, the drop star
The killing of Mogg Megone
The legend of Crooked Mountain
Legend of the arbutus
Little bear
Little burnt-face

Little good baby
The little scarred one
Love story
Lovers' leaps
Lox and the two ermines
Man-eagle
The man who lost his way
The man who loved Hai Quai
The man who rode the bear
The moon and his frog-wife
The mountain goats
Mountains of Manitou
The mouse and the magician
The mouse and the sun
Navahchoo
The Northern lights
The nose of the Konakadet
Old man moon
The origin of Indian pipes
Orphan boy
The out-foxed fox
Owl with the great head and eyes
The partridge and his drum
The passing of Glooskap
The peace pipe
Pecos Bill, the cowboy
Pocohontas
A pound of tobacco
Princess Nelly and the Seneca chief
Pushing westward with Lewis and Clark
Rabbit and the grain buyers
Rabbit and the Indian chief
Rabbit and the moon-man
Rainbow and the autumn leaves
Raven and the sun
A red berry and two hills of snow
The rescue of fire
The sea serpent
The securing of light
The sick boy, the greedy hunters, and the dwarfs. The Little People of North America
The song-bird and the healing waters
Sparrow's search for rain
Spring
Stealing the springtime
The story of a princess
The strong boy
Strong man
Summer
The tale of bat
The tale of the three footsteps
Ten little Indians
The theft of dawn
The theft of fire
There was an old, old Indian
The three fish and the fishermen
Thunderbird
The tobacco fairy from the blue hills
Tobacco woman and corn spirit

Indians of North America (*Continued*)

The treasure of Tacoma
The turquoise stones
The two-faces
Ugly boy
The unlucky fisherman
The upper world
Waukewa's eagle
West country boy
The whale that smoked a pipe
The white deer of Onota
Why coyote is the color of the ground
Why the animals have no fire
Why the tip of fox's tail is white
Why the woodchuck comes out in
  midwinter
Why the world is the way it is
Winter
Worm moon
The Witsduks
The youth and the dog dance

—Alabama
  Fire, a story of the Alabama
    Indians

—California
  The beginning of the world and
    the making of California
  How animals brought fire to man
  How California was made
  How coyote became a friend to
    man
  How coyote got his voice
  How coyote put fish in Clear Lake
  How coyote put salmon in the
    Klamath River
  How the first rainbow was made
  How the great rocks grew
  What happened to six wives who
    ate onions
  Why grizzly bears walk on all
    fours
  Why women talk more than men
, Captives of
  Princess Nelly and the Seneca chief
  A red berry and two hills of snow
—Heroes and heroines
  The game mother
  How he stole the moon and the
    sun
  How Sketco tricked the grizzly
  How the raven brought the fire
  How the raven stole the stars
  The lonely house
  The man who sat on the tide
  The raven and the grizzly bear
  The raven and the sharks
  The raven paints the birds for war
  The shadow boys
  Sketco begins his wanderings

Sketco finds his brothers
The thunder man
—Origin
  The monster
—Songs
  See also **Lullabies, Indian**
  American Indian songs
  Butterflies, butterflies
  Ihi! Ihi! Ihi!
  Little good baby
  Pretty, see the cloud appear!
—Terms
  SCHOOLCRAFT – FIRE p90.
—Tribes
  —Abenaki
    Curse of the Abenaki
  —Achomawi
    How the first rainbow was made
    Why mole's front paws are bent
  —Acoma
    The battle at White Cliff house
    Blue legs
    Blue water
    Cliff dweller
    Crying turkeys
    The dancing horses of Acoma
    Flint bird
    Ko-pa-ta, the gambling god
    A note about the Acomas
    The rain god's reprisal
    She-wa-na, deity of the elements
    Spider boy and the sun god's
      twins
    Young hunter
  —Algonquin
    The broken wing
    The fire plume
    Glooskap
    Moowis
    Peboan and Seegwun
    The red swan
    Sheem
    Tcakabesh snares the sun
    Wahconah
    Wawanosh
    The white stone canoe
  —Apache
    Dog's hoop
    The evil spirits of Crooked Moun-
      tain
    How the people sang the mountains
      up
    To feed my people: The coming
      of buffalo
    Why dogs carry their tails over
      their backs

Indians of North America—Tribes (*Continued*)

—Arapaho
Over the hill
Yellow hair: George Armstrong
Custer

—Assiniboin
Why Crane's feathers are brown
and otter doesn't feel the cold

—Bella Bella
How the whales reached the sea

—Bella Coola
Child of the sun

—Blackfoot
The giant with the grey feathers
The Kamiah monster
Scarface
Star-boy and the sun dance

—Catawba
How rabbit stole fire from the
buzzards

—Cherokee (Tsali)
About the Cherokee
The first fire
How deer got his horns
How the animals made wings for
bat and flying squirrel
How the cardinal got his red
feathers
How the groundhog lost his tail
How the people got fire
How the rabbit stole the otter's
coat
How the redbird got his color
How the sun came
How the terrapin beat the rabbit
How the turkey got his beard
Pleiades
The rabbit and the possum seek a
wife
The rabbit and the tar wolf
Tsali of the Cherokees
Why groundhog's tail is short
Why some trees are evergreen
Why the deer's teeth are blunt
Why the mole lives underground
Why the possum's tail is bare
Why the terrapin's shell is scarred

—Cheyenne
See also **Lullabies, Indian—Cheyenne**
How the world was made (1)
To feed my people: The coming of
corn
To feed my people: The race between the buffalo and man

The waters beneath: Fifty young
men and a turtle
The waters beneath: The great
river monster
Yellow hair: George Armstrong
Custer

—Chikasaw
Nanih Waya: The sacred bluff

—Chippewa
The bear's head
The fight with Wabun
The flight with the Wendigo
The flood
The giant sturgeon
Goose dance
The groundhog family
How kingfisher got his necklace
Manabozho's nephew
Partridge and rock tripe
The raccoon and the crawfish
The raccoon and the old man
Shingebiss
Sleepy feet
The summer birds
The theft of fire
The three cranberries
The walk around the island
Why there are four seasons in the
year
Wolf wisdom

—Choctaw
Nanih Waya: The sacred bluff

—Chukchansi. *See* **Indians of North
America—Tribes—Yokut**

—Comanche
How and why: Don't be greedy
story
How and why: Why the bear
waddles when he walks
The owl in the moon
A world of beauty: The Peyote
religion

—Cowlitz
The songs of the animals

—Cree
Bears in the sky
How beaver got his fine fur
How crane got his long legs

—Creek
See also **Indians of North America—
Tribes—Yuchi**
The arrows that became trees
How bat won the ball game
How possum got his tail
How terrapin's shell was cracked
How the animals made wings for
bat and flying squirrel

Indians of North America—Tribes (*Continued*)
  —Creole
    See also Lullabies, Indian-Creole
    Jean Sot
    Why goat cannot climb a tree
  —Crow
    The great medicine horse
  —Cucamonga
    The lost treasure of Cucamonga
  —Diegueño
    Ants
  —Duck
    The legend of Pathasos
  —Duwamish
    The grizzly and the rattlesnake men
  —Flathead. *See* Indians of North
    America—Tribes—Salish

Indians of North America—Tribes
  —Gabrielino
    How California was made
  —Hopi
    The beetle's hairpiece
    The boy who crossed the great
      water and returned
    Coyote and the crying song
    Coyote helps decorate the night
    Coyote's needle
    The foot racers of Payupki
    Honwyma and the bear
    The Hopi turtle
    How the people came from the
      lower world
    How the Tewas came to the first
      mesa
    How the village of Pivanhonkapi
      perished
    Joshokiklay and the eagle
    The journey to the land of the
      dead
    The land of the Hopis
    Mockingbird gives out the calls
    Notes on Hopi oral literature
    Sikakokuh and the hunting dog
    Sleep, sleep, sleep!
    The sun callers
    Two friends, coyote and bull
      snake, exchange visits
    Why the salt is far away
    The womb of the earth
    The world beyond
  —Intertribal
    Bird of power
    The dancing feather

  —Inuit
    Kunïkdjuaq, a bear story of the
      Inuit
  —Iroquois
    Great Head and the ten brothers
    How chipmunk got his stripes
    The old woman and her hominy
      pot
    The sky beings: thunder and his
      helpers
    The smoker
    Why crow has a right to the first
      corn
  —Jicarilla. *See* Indians of North
    America—Tribes—Apache
  —Juni. *See* Indians of North America
    —Tribes—Zuni
  —Karok
    The acorn maidens
    How animals brought fire to man
    How coyote became a friend to
      man
    How coyote put salmon in the
      Klamath river
    Why animals are afraid of fire
  —Kikiallu
    The boy and his magic robe
  —Kiowa
    The end of the world: The buffalo
      go
    How death came into the world
    How the half boys came to be
    Saynday and smallpox: The white
      man's gift
    The waters beneath: The under-
      water village
    A world of beauty: The Peyote
      religion
  —Kutchin
    Fox and raven steal the moon
  —Kutenai
    How it came about that there is a
      sun and a moon
  —Lillolet
    Frogs in the moon
    Why the sun is brighter than the
      moon

Indians of North America—Tribes—Lipan.
See Indians of North America—Tribes—
Apache
  —Loucheux
    The boy in the moon
    How the long-tailed bear lost his
      tail

Indians of North America—Tribes (*Continued*)

—Luiseño
How rattlesnake got his fangs
Why fly rubs his hands together

—Mandan
Planters' moon

—Micmac
Glooskap, the whale, and the
sorcerer
Gluskap
The great bear
Wokun

—Miwok
How coyote brought back people
after the flood
How the great rocks grew

—Modoc
How death came into the world
How the world was made (2)
Why bat flies alone

—Mohawk
The heroine of the Mohawk Valley
Wahconah

—Mono
What happened to six wives who
ate onions

—Musquakie
The stars above: pursuit of the
bear

—Narraganset
Hunters' moon
The serpent of Carbuncle Hill

—Natchez
How turtle keeps from getting wet

—Navaho
How horses came to the Navaho
It is time for a night chant
Male and female created he them:
The river of separation

—Nez Perce (Nimipoo)
The ant and the yellow jacket
The bears
The buffalo and the porcupine
Calling the Chinook
The end of the world
Fickle Miss Frog
The fishnet and the bear
The fog
The good luck tree
How death came
Itsayaya and the chokecherries
Itsayaya and the otter
Itsayaya frees the salmon
Itsayaya's revenge

The monster
One day, one night
The rope
The sun, the moon, and the stars
The weasel
The young coyote's visit

—Nootka. *See* **Lullabies, Indian—
Nootka**

—Numipu
The Kamiah monster

—Ojibwa
Hiawatha's childhood
How grasshopper came to be and
men obtained tobacco
Lovers' moon
The origin of corn
Why there is both day and night

—Okanagon
Moon of blood

—Oneida
A token of friendship

—Ottawa
Sturgeon moon

—Paiute. *See* **Indians of North
America—Tribes—Snake**

—Passamaquoddy
Glooskap, the whale, and the
sorcerer
How loon learned his call
How whale happens to smoke a
pipe
Hunger moon
Wolf moon

—Pawnee
How the beaver came to build
their homes in the water

—Pawtuxet
The serpent of Carbuncle Hill

—Penobscot
Cold moon
Why grasshopper spits tobacco
juice

—Peyote
Bird of power

—Pomo
How coyote helped to light the
world
How coyote put fish in Clear Lake

—Ponca
The deer woman

—Pueblo (Tewa)
Butterflies, butterflies
The compulsive gift—a cigarette
The coyote and the bear

Indians of North America—Tribes (*Continued*)

—Sahaptian
   How duck got his bill
—Salish
   Flower moon
   The Kamiah monster
   The songs of the animals
—Samish
   The maiden of Deception Pass
—San Nicolas
   The lost woman of San Nicolas
—Sauk (Sac and Fox)
   A glass of water, please
   Harvest moon
   How and why: The painted turtle
—Seminole (Mikasuki)
   The milky way
   To feed my people: The coming
      or corn
—Seneca
   Beaver Moon
   The kettle and the chestnut
   Princess Nelly and the Seneca chief
—Shasta
   Why women talk more than men
—Shawnee
   How the wildcat got his spots
—Sioux
   Gobbleknoll
   The Kamiah monster
—Skagit
   The coyote and the evil witches
   The legend of the star children
—Snake (Paiute)
   How men brought fire to earth
—Sokokis
   Chocorua Mountain
—Swinomish
   The boy with the long hair
   The legend of Pathasos
   The legend of the hail
   The legend of the star children
   The mink and the sun
   The mink and the weasel
   The raven and the crow
   Sam Dan and the government
      doctor
   The witch and her four sons
—Tahltan
   How the birds came to have their
      many colors
   Why people watch the dipper
   Why the animals live where they do

Why the tides ebb and flo
—Talamancan
   Sibu, the god-who-builds
—Tewa (Pueblo)
   How the people came to the
      middle place
   How the Tewas came to first mesa
   How turkey got his white tail
   The stars above: Long Sash and
      his people
   Turkey girl
—Thompson
   Atam and Im
—Tlingit
   The arrow chain
   The Lincoln totem pole
   The return of the land-otter
—Wampanoag
   The story of Mon-do-min
—Wintu
   How frogs lost their tails
—Wiyot (Wishosk)
   How spider got his thread
—Yokut (Chukchansi)
   How coyote got his voice
   Why ducks have flat feet
—Yuchi (Creek)
   The stars are silver reindeer
   Who?

Indians of North America—Tribes—Zuñi
(Juñi)
   Bears in the sky
   The center of the world
   Corn moon
   Pretty, see the cloud appear!
   To feed my people: The coming of
      corn
   Why there are shooting stars

Indians of the North Pacific
   The boy and the sea monsters
   Fly again, my proud eagle
   The giant ogre, Kloo-Teekl
   The one-horned mountain goat
   The wild woman of the woods

The indigo jackal
   GRAY — INDIA'S p159-160

Indonesia
   Bajan Budiman, the sharpshooter
   The battle of the buffaloes
   The bet between Matjan and Gadja
   The blue cat

Indonesia (*Continued*)

The boat that would not move
The children's sea
The clever squirrel
Crocodile's share
The decision
The dog and the karbau
The dolphins of Celebes
Fire, water, and honor
The golden butterfly
Guno and Koyo
Guno and Koyo and the Kris
Guno's hunger
The Holy mountain
How Celebes got its name
How confusion came among the
  animals
The hunter of Perak
Kantchil's lime pit
The Kris of Adja Saka
The learned men
The legend of Pasopati
The legend of the Karang
The little Sawah
The magic oysters
The messenger
The mighty hunter
Mohammed and the spider
An old Sumatran legend
The one who said Tjik
The origin of the bromo feast
The origin of the water jars
Pamudjo's feast
Pursuit of the Hadji
The sacred fish of Polaman
The saga of the Waru Wanggi
The soul in the mountain rice
The stone crusher of Banjang
The three companions
Three tales of the mouse-deer
The tiger's tail
The tiger's war against Borneo
Two out of one
War between the crocodiles and
  Kantchill
The well diggers
Why crows are black
Why the waringen tree is holy
Why there are no tigers in Borneo
The wonder-tree
The wood carver of Ruteng

  –**History**
    The victory of the buffalo

  –**Kendang Mountains**
    The legend of the Karang

Industry
  Biting Marion
  Building the bridge

The circus man
The city mouse and the country
  mouse
The cock, the mouse, and the little
  red hen
Dick Whittington and his cat
The honest woodman
How doth the little busy bee
Jamie Watt and the giant in the tea-
  kettle
John Henry, the big steel-drivin' man
The little red hen and the grain of
  wheat
The luck boy of Toy Valley
Miska and the man-with-the-iron head
Mister Luck and Mister Industry
This little ant worked with might and
  main
The wise ant

The infallible salt bird
  ELLIOT – SINGING p96-110

Infidelity
  The knight of Staufenberg
  The mosquitoes
  Nooloigah who caused his brother to
    die
  The people who lived near a mountain
  Two unfaithful husbands

Ingalls, Daniel H. H.
  The calves
  The eyes of owls
  The heron
  In the paddy field
  The monsoon season
  Seeing a brace of rabbits
  The silly goose

The ingrates
  THOMPSON – ONE p2-3

Ingratitude
  The adder and the fox
  Adrian and Bardus
  The Alp that disappeared
  The falcon and the cock
  The falcon and the hen
  The golden deer
  How locusts came to be
  How the village of Pivanhonkapi
    perished
  The ingrates
  Inside again
  The judgment of the wind
  The Kildare pooka
  A lie for a lie
  The man, the serpent, and the fox
  The man who loved Hai Quai

326

Ingratitude (*Continued*)
The nutcracker and sugardolly stories
The old father who went to school
Pigling and her proud sister
The silent drum
The snake and its benefactor
Snow-white and Rose-red
The spotted rug
The twelve months
The ungrateful bear
The ungrateful children
The ungrateful lion
The ungrateful snake
The ungrateful tiger
Why no one ever carries the alligator down to the water

Ingratitude is the way of the world
BECHSTEIN – FAIRY p97-102

Inheritance
See also **Heirs**
The coming of the yams
Fly again, my proud eagle
Fridolin
The ghost dog of South Mountain
The old laird and his dog
The princess of Tomboso
The three gifts

The iniquitous Captain Lightfoot
TAFT – PROFILE p214-223

Initiative
The boy who made a dream come true
Exploring the wilderness
How Robert Fulton harnessed the giant
Jamie Watt and the giant in the teakettle
The little red hen and the grain of wheat
The luck boy of Toy Valley
The sheep and the pig that made a home
Shingebiss

The injured lion
KAULA – AFRICAN p91-95

Injustice
The foolish man
Grettir becomes an outlaw
Journey in a well
Judgment of Karakoush
The just and unjust brothers
The tale of a proverb
Tortoise and the lizard
The trial at Avichára-Pura

The inn in the forest
HAUFF – FAIRY p101-110

The inn of donkeys
BIRCH – CHINESE p89-94

The innkeeper of Moscow
RANKE – GERMANY p90-94

The innkeeper's daughter
MICHAEL – PORTUGUESE p121-129

Inns and Innkeepers
The ass that lays money
The bell of Monte Pino
The bean tree
The black spider
The buried treasure
The ghostly hand of Spital house
The gold bird
The grateful devil
The immortal J. N.
Ingratitude is the way of the world
The inn in the forest
The innkeeper of Moscow
The innkeeper's daughter
It's already paid
The luck fairies
The magic pancakes at the Footbridge tavern
Per and the north wind
Rag, tag and bobtail
Shlemiel, the businessman
Sly Peter at the fair
Sly Peter's revenge
The smiling innkeeper
The tale of Tom Corwin
The three brothers
To pay through the nose
The twelve young men
The wandering apprentice
Why Eyvin won the race
The wicked house of Duncan Macbain

Innocence
Anansi borrows money
The father's steps
The legend of Llangorse Lake
Summer snow

The inquiring rabbit, or the strongest thing in the world
MINCIELI – TALES p72-75

Inquisitiveness. *See* **Curiosity**

Insanity
The dance of death

The insatiable beggar
DURHAM – TIT p93-95

Insects
See also names of insects
Brave rabbit and bug with the golden
wings
Cannibal
The cats
The fairyland of science
Flint bird
How night was let loose and all the
animals came to be
One guess
Over in the meadow
A secret told to a stranger
The three plagues of Britain
Twinkling bugs
The war between the lion and the
cricket
Why the woodpecker has a long nose

Insects and other critters
JOHNSON – WHAT p100-106

Insecurity. *See* Security

The separable friends
BURTON – MAGIC p112-116

Inside again
JACOBS – EUROPE. p165-169

Insults. *See* Impudence

Intaglios (effigies)
Lost arts

Intelligence
Bear, fox, and man
The farmer, the buffalo, and the tiger
The fox and the cat
The fox and the lion in partnership
Is fish a brain food?
Ricky of the tuft
Ricky with a tuft
Simpleton Peter
The smart daughter
Stories about Kampen
The tailor's bright daughter
The tiger's stripes
Waiting on salvation
The world's smartest cat

Intelligence and luck
THOMPSON – ONE p363-365

The interesting history of old Mother
Goose
MY BOOK HOUSE v. 12 p213-220

Interference
The battle of the firefly and the apes
Goldilocks and the three bears
The nutcracker and sugar dolly stories

Intole the giant
COBBLE – WEMBI p118-119

Intolerance. *See* Tolerance

Introduction
CAMPBELL – MAORI p4-5
DUDDINGTON – RUSS. p7-9
GINSBURG – MASTER p11-17
HAMPDEN – GYPSY p9-16
JAMES – MYTHS p5-10
JUDA – WISE p1-4
LEODHAS – TWELVE p xi-xiii
MANNING – ENGLISH p1-4
WALKER – DANCING p11-13

Introduction: Early Spain
LAURITZEN – BLOOD p3-5

Introduction: Four world corners
MARRIOTT – AMER. p1-17

Introduction: From sun-spirit to spider-
man
SHERLOCK – WEST p1-6

Introduction (The Golem)
NAHMAD – PORTION p157-158

Introduction (The righteous and the pious)
NAHMAD – PORTION p109-110

Introduction (Tales of David and Solomon)
NAHMAD – PORTION p41-43

Introduction (Tales of the prophet Elijah)
NAHMAD – PORTION p23-26

Introduction (Tales of wit and wisdom)
NAHMAD – PORTION p131-132

Introduction (The wisdom and folly of
women)
NAHMAD – PORTION p87-88

Introductory
JOHNSON – WHAT p3-8

Introductory note
TOLKIEN – READER (Part 2) p2.

328

Inventions
  The boy who made a dream come true
  How Robert Fulton harnessed the
    giant
  Jamie Watt and the giant in the tea-
    kettle
  The luck boy of Toy Valley
  Maui the fire bringer
  The self-kicking machine
  Wilbur Wright and Orville Wright
  The wonderland of an artist's work-
    shop

Invincibility
  The sage and the mouse

Invisibility
  The butterfly in the granary
  The dancing princesses
  The enchanted palace
  The farmer and the demon
  Halde Hat and Dulde Hat
  The Indian Cinderella
  Little Burnt-face
  The little scarred one
  The magic cap
  Prince Ferdinand
  Prince Loaf
  Punchinello
  A San and the Wang Liang
  The story of Noschoy Datta of Ujjain
  The twelve dancing princesses
  Winter rose

The invisible baby
  SHEAHAN – HENRY p180-196

The invisible hands
  MICHAEL – PORTUGUESE p20-27

The invisible hobgoblin
  SPICER – GOBLINS p45-53

The invisible silk robe
  TOOZE – WONDER. p26-31

The invisible thief
  MASEY – STORIES p88-103

Iowa
  LEACH – RAINBOW p87.

Iphigenia at Aulis
  GREEN – GREEKS p20-21

Iphigenia in Tauris
  GREEN – GREEKS p52-53

Iphigenia . . . the transported sacrifice
  UNTERMEYER – FIRE. p48-52

Iran (Persia)
  The just judgment
  Mirza and the ghul
  Nabookin
  The quivering needle
  Rustem and his rose-colored steed

Iraq
  See also Bagdad
  The crimson purse and the talking
    raven
  The stork caliph
  The tailor's bright daughter
  The unlucky shoes of Ali Abou

Ireland
  The adventures of Ciad
  Aristotle and the three sons
  Art, King of Leinster
  The battle of Gavra
  The bee, the harp, the mouse and the
    bum-clock
  The bee, the mouse and the bum-clock
  Beside the fire
  The big cat and the big rat
  Billy Beg and the bull
  The bird of the golden land
  The birth and boyhood of Finn
  The birth of Oisin
  The black art
  The blacksmith and the horseman
  The bold heroes of Hungry Hill
  Bottle Hill
  The boy Pu-nia and the king of sharks
  The boy who became Pope
  Bran, son of Llyr
  The carl of the drab coat
  The cat and the dog
  The ceabharnach
  Ceatach
  The chase of Slieve Gallion
  The child from the sea
  The children of Lir
  The children of the dead woman
  The children of Tuireann return to
    Erin
  The choosing of the high-king of Erin
  The Christian bell
  Clever Oonagh
  Clever Top and the Ireprechaun
  The cold May night
  The coming of Finn
  The coming of Fionn MacCool
  The coming of Oscar
  Conall Yellowclaw
  Conchobar and Teeval
  The Connemara donkey
  Connla of the golden hair
  The cooking-spit of the women of
    Fincara

Ireland (*Continued*)

The cow that ate the piper
The cowherd with the belt of skin
The crochera
Cromwell and the friar
Cuchulain, the hound of Ulster
Cuchulainn and the smith's wife
Cuculain, the Irish hound
Damer's gold
Daniel O'Connell and the trickster
The day of the scholars
Dearmid and Grania
The death of Cuchullin
The death of Dearmid
The death of Deirdre
The death of the children of Lir
The death of the sons of Tuireann
The death of the sons of Uisne
The defeat of the Fomorians
Deirdre
Deidre and the sons of Usine
Deidre and the sons of Usna
Dermot and Grania
Doctor Lee and little Aran
Donal from Donegal
Donal O'Ciaran from Connaught
Donal O'Donnell's standing army
Earl Fitzgerald in the enchanted hill
The enchantment of Gearoidh Iarla
Fair, brown, and trembling
The fairy frog
The fairy host
Fairy money
The fairy tree of Doolas woods
The fairy wife
The fate of the children of Lir
The fate of the children of Tuireann
The fate of the sons of Usnach
The field of Boliauns
Fin M'Coul and Cucullin
Finn and the Fianna
Finn and the grey dog
Finn and the young hero's children
Finn MacCool
Finn MacCool, the giants and the small
  men
Finvarra
Fionn in search of his youth
Fior Usga
The first attack
The first three hundred years
The flight
The foretelling
The fort of Rothangan
The four-leafed shamrock and the
  cock
The fox and the eagle
The fox and the heron
The fox in Irishkea
The friar on Errigal

The giant and his royal servants
The giant in the cave
The giant of the brown beech wood
The giant who sucked his thumb
The giant's causeway
The giant's stairs
The gifted skin of the pig
The giolla dacker and his horse
The girl and the sailor
Gobborn seer
The golden apples of Hisberna
The golden apples of Loch Erne
Golden hood
The good woman
The grateful weasel
The great liar
The green glass bottle
Gulersh and the princess of France
The happy years
The headless horseman
Hina, the woman in the moon
The horned woman
The horses of the Fianna
The hostel of the quicken
The hour of death
The house of the rowan trees
How Cormac MacArt got his branch
How Cuchulain wooed his wife
How Finn became head of the Fianna
How Finn won his father's place
How God's wheel turns
How the Fomorians came into Erin
How Tristram fought against the
  knight from Ireland
The hunchback's gift
The hunter
Ian Direach
Jack and his comrades
Jack and his friends
Jack and the lord high mayor
Jack O'Leary's plow
John Shea and the fairy treasure
Kate Mary Ellen and the fairies
Kian and the children of Tuireann
Kilcolman castle
The Kildare pooka
King Conal's horses
King Fergus and the water-horse
King Fergus MacLeide and the wee
  folk
King O'Toole and his goose
The King of Araby's daughter
The king of the dark desert
The king, the saint and the goose
The king who could not sleep
The king who was a gentleman
The knight of the glen's steed o'bells
The lamentable story of Connlach, son
  of Cuchulain

Ireland (*Continued*)

The land ship
The last battle
A legend of Knockmany
The leprechaun and the wheelbarrow
The leprechaun in the basket
The little bull calf
A long time to Monday
The lordship of the Fianna
The lost city of Ys
The love of Cuchulainn and Fann, and
the only jealousy of Emer, his wife
Lugh and his father's murderers
The mad man, the dead man, and the
devil
The magic head
The magical tune
The magnificent hounds of Finn Mac-
Cool
The magpie and the fox
The maiden in the country under-
ground
The man who had no story
The man who lost his shadow
The man who struck his father
The man who swallowed the mouse
The man who was rescued from hell
The man with the bag
Manny MacGilligan's story
The March cock and the coffin
The meeting of Deidre and Naoise
The Merrow and the soul cages
The messenger
Midir and Etain
The mop servant
The mother of Oisin
Nanny and Conn
Niamb of the golden hair
Nidden and Didden and Donal Beg
O'Neary
The night of the big wind
O'Connell wears his hat in Parliament
Oisin in the land of the ever young
Oisin, son of Finn MacCool
Oisin's mother
The old crow teaches the young crow
The old hag of the forest
The old hag's long leather bag
Ossian in the land of eternal youth
Paddy and the leprechaun
The palace in the Rath
Patou MacDaniel
Patrick O'Donnell and the leprechaun
The piper who could not play
The pooka of the mill
Prince Finn the Fair
The princess and the dwarf
The princess and the vagabone
The proud princess
The pursuit of Dermot and Grania
The pursuit of the hard man

Queen o' the tinkers
The queen of the planets
The quest of the children of Turenn
The Red Etin
The return
The return of Oisin
The sailor and the rat
Saint Martin and the honest man
Saint Patrick and the Hill of Tara
The Sea of Moyle
Seán na Bánóige
Seán na Scuab
Seán Palmer's voyage to America with
the fairies
Secret tokens prove ownership
The seven enchanted pigs, and the
houndwhelps of Iroda
The shadow
Shawneen and the gander
The Shee an Gannon and the Gruagach
Gaire
The shouts on the hill of Midkena
The smell of money for the smell of
food
The soldier's billet
The son of strength
Song of the leprechaun or fairy shoe-
maker
The soul of the Countess Kathleen
The sow and her Banbh
The spear slaughterer and the chariot
and horses of Sigar
The speckled bull
The stone of victory
The story of Ailill and Etaine
The story of Iubdan, King of the lepre
and the lepracaun
The strange adventure of Paddy
O'Toole
The swans of Ballycastle
The sword of light
The tale of Columba and the angel
The tale of Liban the siren
Terence the tailor's jacket
The thirteenth son of the King of Erin
The three golden eggs
The three laughs of the leipreachan
The three most famous tales
The three sons of the King of Antua
The three tasks
The tinker of Tamlacht
The tournament in Ireland
The trials of Conneda
The twelve silly sisters
The two bottles
Two women or twelve men
The two youths whose father was
under the sea
The uglier foot
The voyage of Maelduin (Maeldun)
The wee red man
The welcome
The well at the world's end

Ireland (*Continued*)

The well o' the world's end
The well of D'yeree-in-Dowan
The white cat
White fields
White hen
The white trout
The widow's daughter
The widow's lazy daughter
The will of the wise man
Wind and wave and wandering flame
The wishing chair of the Lord of Errigal
The wizard earl
The wonder ship and ship's crew
The wonderful cake
The wonders of the three donals
The wooing of Etain
The world's great epics
Young Conall of Howth
The young Finn
The young piper, the Little People of Ireland

–History
The story of Branwen

–Lough Neagh
How the giant Finn made the Isle of Man

, North
King John and the Abbot of Canterbury

–Ulster
The battle of the bulls
Cuchullin keeps the gap of the north
Cuchullin parleys with Maeve
The fight with Ferdia
How Conor MacNessa became King of Ulster
The pillow talk
Ulster awake

Irish
Clever Pat
North Salem's Irish? Ruins
Tim Felt's ghost
The young Irish lad from the hiring fair

The Irish luck of Brian Hughes
JAGENDORF – GHOST p85-92

Iron
The blacksmith's dilemma
The fairies and the smith
The fairy wife
The lake lady

The lake maiden
Miska and the man-with-the-iron-head
Victor
The young man who married a fairy

The iron box
PROTTER – CHILD. p181-185

"Iron men"
Aileel and Ailinda

Iron, steel and strongest-of-all
TOOR – GOLDEN p91-103

Ironhead
MANNING – DEVILS p56-68

Irraweka, mischief-maker
SHERLOCK – WEST p21-26

Irresponsibility
Elsa and the ten elves
The girl who used her wits
Old Noll
The owl's answer to Tommy
The youth who wanted some fun

Irving, Washington
Prince Ahmed
Wolfert Webber, or golden dreams

Irving, Washington
JOHNSON – HARPER p322-323

A rover in the Catskills

Is a white horse lucky?
BATCHELOR – SUPER. p41-42

Is fish a brain food?
BATCHELOR – SUPER. p16.

Is he fat?
THOMPSON – ONE p429-430

Is the opal unlucky?
BATCHELOR – SUPER. p69-70

Isaiah (Biblical)
The dangers of sorcery

Ishallah
JUDA – WISE p105-112

Isis
Horus the avenger

Isis and Osiris
GREEN – TALES p21-36
MOZLEY – EGYPT p28-37

Isis and the secret name of Ra
    MOZLEY — EGYPT p24-37

The island
    ARBUTHNOT — TIME p276-277

Islands
    The adventures of Alexander Selkirk
    The adventures of Ciad
    A bauchan in the family
    Becky's garden
    The birth of the islands
    The boy in the land of shadows
    The boy of the red twilight sky
    The boy who played the flute
    The cloud horse
    The crane wife
    The dancing princesses
    The enchanted island
    The fairy garden
    The far horizon
    The ferryman
    The first fire
    Flash-of-the-paddle and Listener-to-
        the-heavenly voice
    The flight with the Wendigo
    The giant who stole a river
    The golden-headed fish
    The great lizard of Nimple
    The green isle
    The home of the saints
    Horus the avenger
    How the mosquitoes came to Oneata
    The hungry serpent
    In the strange isle
    The kappa's arm
    The kingdom of ocean
    Lie-A-Stove
    The little white cat
    The lost half-hour
    The man who lived on an island
    Maui the Great
    The miracle of the Poor Island
    Momotaro
    Momotaro: boy-of-the-peach
    Momotaro, the peach boy
    Odysseus and Circe
    Other island
    The princess and the dwarf
    The princess Nausicaa
    The rabbit and the crocodile
    The sailor and the sea serpent
    The sea captain
    The serpent prince
    Sindbad the sailor
    The story of Prince Ring and his dog
    The story of the shipwrecked sailor
    The swans of Ballycastle
    Tangerina

    The tempest
    Tom Walker and the devil
    The unhappy island
    The voyage of Maeldun (Maeldun)
    The walk around the island
    A warning from the gods
    The white cat
    The witch of Lok Island

Isle of Man
    Billy Beg and the sassafras switch
    Conchobar and Teeval
    How the giant Finn made the Isle of
        Man
    How the herring became king of the
        sea
    How the Manx cat lost its tail
    Jack and the Purr Mooar
    The little footprints
    The Manx coat of arms
    A moon of Gobbays
    Nikkessen's pool
    Olaf Goddardson and the sword
        Macabuin
    The old Christmas
    The Phynnodderee
    Smereree
    The story of Blathnot
    Tehi Tegi
    The three bugganes
    The three-legged jumping giant
    Timothy and the buggane ghost

Isolte
    How Tristram fought against the knight
        from Ireland
    How Trystan won Esyllt
    Tristram and Isolt

Israel
    The crimson purse
    David and Goliath
    David and Goliath . . . The shepherd
        boy and the giant
    Don't throw stones from not yours to
        yours
    King Solomon and the Queen of Sheba
    Rabbit Joseph Della Reina
    The seven-year blessing

    —Ascalon
        The witches of Ascalon

Issoumbochi, The story of. *See* The story
    of Issoumbochi

Isun Boshi, the one-inch lad
    UCHIDA — DANCING p159-169

It
    MY BOOK HOUSE v. 6 p161.

It all comes to light
   MANNING — RED p66-71

It happened in Kashmir
   GHOSE — FOLK p116-117

It is foolish to carry matters to extremes
   LEACH — SOUP p147-148

It is God that hath made us
   MY BOOK HOUSE v. 1 p216.

It is time for a night chant
   BELTING — STARS # 12

It snows and it blows
   MY BOOK HOUSE v. 1 p87.

It won't do you any good
   WALKER — WATER. p67.

Italian nursery rhymes
   MY BOOK HOUSE v. 1 p62-63

Italy
   The adventures of Bona and Nello
   The adventurous winnower
   Antonio Canova
   The art of reading
   The ass that lays money
   The bell of Monte Pino
   Bastianelo
   The beacon light
   Beppo Pipetta and his knapsack
   The boy who made a dream come true
   The capricious month
   Catherine and the fates
   The cavallino
   Cenerentola
   Cenerentola or Cinderella
   Clever Elsie and her companions
   The clever peasant
   The coat that taught the housewife
   The cobbler
   The colony of cats
   Columbine and her playfellows of the
      Italian pantomime
   Conclusion
   Corvetto
   Count Roger and the Fata Morgana
   Crab
   The crumb in the beard
   Dancing he would go
   The dancing water, the singing apple,
      and (the) speaking bird
   The dark king
   The divine comedy
   The dog, the cat, and the mouse
   Donkeys! Dogs! Cats! Rats!

The eagle and the owl
Errato di Barletto
The farmer and the harvesters
The firefly
Fishing for a chicken
The flying angel
The fountain of Arethusa
The frog
The frog bride
The ghost in the cabbage patch
Gigi and the magic ring
Giuanni and the giant
Giufà
The golden carnation
The golden lion
The griffon
How the devil married three sisters
How these tales came to be told
An impossible penance
The ingrates
The inquiring rabbit, or the strongest
   thing in the world
Iron, steel and strongest-of-all
King Bean
The king who wanted a beautiful wife
A kiss from the beautiful Fiorita
Lionbruno
The little bucket
A long one and a short one
The magic mare
The man, the serpent, and the fox
The man who lived in the world of
   dreams
March and the shepherd
The marvelous doors, the Little People
   of Italy
Mece and the shoemaker's daughters
The melancholy prince and the girl of
   milk and blood
The merchant, Saint Michael, and the
   devil
A message for a donkey
The mother of time and the enchanted
   brothers
The mysterious letter
Nella's dancing shoes
Nicola Pesca (Pesce)
The one-legged crane
Oraggio and Bianchinetta
Padre Ulivo and his guests
The parrot
Petrosinella or parsley
Pidicino
Pietro Bailliardo
Pinocchio
Pintosmalto
Plenta, polenta, and more polenta
The pot of gold
Preziosa, the she-bear
The prince of the Dolomites and the
   princess of the moon

Italy *(Continued)*

Princess Sicilia and the shepherd
Punchinello
Rags-and-tatters
The raven
The return of spring
The rose of midwinter, The Little
People of Italy
Saint Crispin and the old one
St. Francis and the wolf
Saturday, Sunday, Monday
The serpent
The shepherd's pipe
The ship that sailed on water and on
land
The singing-bone
The songstress and the fairies
The spindle, the shuttle and the
needle
The stone in the cock's head
The story of Bensurdatee
A strange reward
Stupid Peruonto
The talking tree
The thoughtless abbot
The thread of life
The three brothers
The three citrons
The three enchanted princes
Three fools
The three goslings
The three languages
The three rings
The three silver balls
The three sisters and the old witch
Ti-Tiriti-Ti
The twelve young men
Two different interpretations of the
same pact
The two sisters
The tyrant and the miller
Vardiello
The visits of St. Peter to his people
A wise sentence
The wise woodland maid
The wonderful night
The wooden bowl
Written in the stars
A yard of nose
The youth who could become an ant,
a lion, or an eagle
Zezolla and the date-palm tree

−Atri
The bell of Atri

−Campania
Little Peppino

−15th century
The wonderland of an artist's
workshop

−Florence
La Cenerentola
The Divine comedy
The enchanted cow
The marvelous doors, The Little
People of Italy
The most precious possession
The red cloak, told by Zaleukos,
the Greek
The rose of midwinter, The Little
People of Italy
The wise judge

−Lombardy
If I could work

−Palermo
The beautiful weaver and the
golden shell

−Rome
Aeneas . . . His wanderings
The twins of the god Mars
The wanderings of Aeneas

−Tuscany
The cats of the mountain
Giuseppi, the cobbler
Why dog gnaws a bone
Why the fleas jump

−Venice
Dwarf stories
How the peasants brought wisdom
Lord Sinclair and the Zeno brothers
The seven dead men of the Venetian
lagoon

Italy
HOPE-SIMPSON − CAVAL. p196-197

Itching
Anansi play with fire, Anansi gets
burned

It's a pleasure
LEACH − NOODLES p72.

It's all in knowing how
WALKER − WATER. p65-66

It's all the fault of Adam
WALKER − DANCING p65-71

It's already paid
PROTTER − CHILD. p193-198

It's been well used
SEKI − FOLKTALES p192-193

It's better to be smart than strong
JAGENDORF − KING p244-248

It's perfectly true
SIDEMAN – WORLD'S p33-37

It's raining
MY BOOK HOUSE v. 1 p67.

It's Spring
MY BOOK HOUSE v. 1 p208.

Itsayaya and the chokecherries
HEADY – TALES p41-44

Itsayaya and the otter
HEADY – TALES p57-61

Itsayaya frees the salmon
HEADY – TALES p45-49

Itsayaya's revenge
HEADY – TALES p50-56

Ivan and his knapsack
PROTTER – CHILD. p115-123

Ivan and his sack
CREANGĂ – FOLK p136-151

Ivan of Semberiya
ĆURČIJA – HEROES p155-160

Ivan the fool
BUDBERG – RUSSIAN p182-187

Ivashko and the witch
WYNDHAM – RUSS. p32-41

Iversen, Pat Shaw
The Norwegian folk tales and their
illustrators

Ives, Burl
IVES – TALES p305.

Ivo Senkovich and Aga of Ribnik
ĆURČIJA – HEROES p136-142

Ivory
The son of the hunter
Sylvester

The ivory box
PICARD – MERMAID p109-129

Ivy
Queen of the Comstock

Iwa the crafty one
THOMPSON – LEGENDS p80-85

Iwanich and the magic ring
BUCK – FAIRY p172-180

Izanagi and Izanami
McALPINE – JAPAN. p4-6

Izanagi's descent to Hades
McALPINE – JAPAN. p16-22

J

"J. B."
The strange white beast

Jaberoos (birds)
The old women who were turned
into birds

Jabberwocky
MANNING – BEASTS p103-105

The jabuty and the jaguar
CARPENTER – SOUTH p43-49

Jabuty, the strong
CARPENTER – SOUTH p36-42

Jack and his comrades
MANNING – BEASTS p199-208

Jack and his friends
PILKINGTON – SHAM. p46-51

Jack and his golden snuff-box
MANNING – RED p72-83

Jack and Jill
Hjuki and Bil

Jack and Jill
MY BOOK HOUSE v. 1 p40.

Jack and the beanstalk
DE REGNIERS – GIANT p18-30
JOHNSON – WHAT p139-141
LINES – NURSERY p5-22
HAVILAND – ENGLAND p3-21
MANNING – GIANTS p9-17
MAYNE – GIANTS p98-107
MY BOOK HOUSE v. 5 p20-32
REEVES – ENGLISH p127-146
SIDEMAN – WORLD'S p131-146
TUDOR – TASHA p65-71
WILLIAMS – FAIRY p155-168

Jack and the giant Cormoran
MANNING – GIANTS p44-47

Jack and the giant Tantarem
MANNING – GIANTS p47-50

Jack and the giant Thunderdell
MANNING – GIANTS p57-60

Jack and the lord high mayor
MacMANUS – HIBERIAN p126-140

Jack and the Purr Mooar
YOUNG – HOW p91-93

Jack and the robbers
ARBUTHNOT – TIME p172-174

Jack and the Welsh giant
MANNING – GIANTS p50-53

Jack and the wizard
MANNING – WIZARDS p78-85

Jack at Hell Gate
MANNING – DEVILS p39-50

Jack, be nimble
MY BOOK HOUSE v. 1 p39.

Jack Frost
MY BOOK HOUSE v. 2 p186-187

Jack Hannaford
REEVES – ENGLISH p1-9

Jack in the giants's new ground. *See*
Stan Bolovan

Jack O'Leary's plow
SPICER – GHOSTS p36-44

Jack, the giant Galligantua, and the enchanter
MANNING – GIANTS p60-66

Jack the giant-killer
See also Jack, the giant Galligantua,
and the enchanter; Jack, the King
of England's son, and the giant with
three heads
DE REGNIERS – GIANT p3-15
MAYNE – GIANTS p83-97
MY BOOK HOUSE v. 6 p140-158
SIDEMAN – WORLD'S p715-723

Jack, the King of England's son, and the
giant with three heads
MANNING – GIANTS p53-57

Jack who could do anything
JAGENDORF – KING p28-30

The jackal and the bear
HITCHCOCK – KING p47-52

The jackal and the crocodile
SIDDIQUI – TOON. p55-60
SPELLMAN – BEAUT. p37-39

The jackal and the elephant
GREEN – BIG p153.

The jackal and the fig tree
ELLIOT – SINGING p84-95

The jackal and the hen
GAER – FABLES p37-38

Jackal or tiger?
LANG – OLIVE p150-164

The jackal, the barber and the Brahmin
who had seven daughters
BAKER – GOLDEN p58-77

The jackal told me
WYATT – GOLDEN p107-111

The jackal who tried to copy the lion
GREEN – BIG p61.

The jackal with the torn nose
SIDDIQUI – TOON. p130-135

Jackals
The battle of the animals
The blue jackal
The brainy rabbit
The camel and his neighbor
The camel in the lion's court
The clever jackal and how he out-
witted the tiger
The clever little jackal
The crab, the crocodile and the jackal
The crow in the rose-apple tree
The dappled deer and the intelligent
crow
The deer and its friends
The farmer's old horse
The foolish jackal
The giant elephant
The girl who forgot her hoe
The hare in the moon
How the travelers shared their meal
How to catch a fish
The indigo jackal
King All-tusk
The leopard and the mouse deer
The lion of hard-to-pass forest
The lion who listened to a jackal
The lion's share
The lizard's tail
The long-howling jackal
The monkey, the tiger, and the jackal
family
Mowgli's brothers
The muula tree
The ostrich and the crocodile

Pakpai and Boto
Partnership
The poor weaver and the princess
A school for crocodiles
The son of the tortoise
Spotless the lion and Trusty the car-
penter
Through the jungle
The tiger in the palanquin
The tiger, the Brahman, and the jackal
To outleap a rabbit
The turtle and the storks and the jackal
The turtle, the storks and the jackal
Two novices who behaved like a pair
of otters
The ungrateful snake
The ungrateful tiger
The vain jackal
What should I do, what shouldn't I do?
Why the dog is the friend of man
Why the jackal howls
The wise goat

–Noses
The jackal with the torn nose

–Tails
The tailless jackal

The jackals and the tiger
HUME – FAVORITE p93-98

The jackal's lawsuit
COURLANDER – FIRE p29-33

Jaco and the giant
SPICER – 13 p86-93

Jacob, Dorothy
The powers of plants and trees to
protect against witches

Jacob Heard and the golden horse
IVES – TALES p51-57

Jacobs, Joseph
The demon with the matted hair
The hedley kow
Jack and his comrades
Jack and the beanstalk
Jack the giant-killer
The king o' the cats
Master of all masters
The old witch
The three little pigs
The three sillies
Tom Thumb
The well o' (of) the world's end

Jacobs, Joseph
JOHNSON – HARPER p323-324

Jacques the woodcutter
BARBEAU – GOLDEN p109-
120

Jade
A flower to catch a thief
Gift of the unicorn
The woodpecker and the jade stone
The young head of the Cheng family

Jade emperor
The carp that became a dragon
The ravens build a bridge
The toad is the emperor's uncle

Jaegers
How the ptarmigans learned to fly

Jagendorf, M. A.
The eternal wanderer of the Pampas
The Haddam witches

The jaguar and the crested curassow
SHERLOCK – WEST p27-33

Jaguars
The deer and the jaguar share a house
The jabuty and the jaguar
A story of guile
Who's strong?

Jails. *See* Prisons & prisoners

Jakfruit
The golden oriole

Jamaica. *See* West Indies–Jamaica

James V, King
King James and the questions
The stranger and the miller
The tale of the Gaberlunzie man

James VI, King
The tale of the king's jewel
The tale of the Laird of Logie
To kill a king, from "News from
Scotland"

James, Grace
Reflections
The tea-kettle

James, Jesse
Jesse James

James Gray and the Clashnichd
SHEPPARD – SCOT. p163-166

Jamie Watt and the giant in the teakettle
MY BOOK HOUSE v. 5 p45-47

Jammes, Francis
The animals' paradise

Jan, King
The jester who fooled a king

Jan and Jaantje
ROSS – BURIED p121-126

Jan the eighth Van Arkel
LEEUW – LEGENDS p101-103

Janey's shoes
CREDLE – TALL p145-156

Jankyn and the witch
MANNING – RED p31-41

Janot cooks for the emperor
COURLANDER – PIECE p101-104

Japan
About the magic animals
The accomplished and strange tea-
kettle
The adventures of little Peachling
The advice that cost a thousand ryo
The August moon
The badger and the boatmen
The badger and the magic fan
The badger's gratitude
The battle of Ichi-no-Tani
The beckoning cat
Bedding in one's ear
Benizara and Kakezara
The birth of the islands
The bored tengu
The boy who drew cats
The boy who told tall tales
The bridge of heaven
The bundles of straw and the king's
son
The cat and the crab
The charcoal burner Choja
The child in the bamboo tree
Chin-Chin Kobakama
The choja who became a monkey
The clever lord
The counting of the crocodiles
The crab and the monkey
The crackling mountain
The crane wife
The dancing kettle
The dancing teapot

340

Japan (*Continued*)

A dead secret
The deer of five colors
The demon giant of Mount Ariake
The dirt boy
Don't tease the tengu!
The dragon king and the lost fish-hook
The dragon's revenge
The eight-headed dragon
The emperor of the province
The enchanted waterfall
An endless story
The envious neighbor
The fall of the Heike
The fire boy
The fish thief
The five young men
The foolish lad and the flies
The fox and the bear
A fox who was too sly
The frogs of yonder mountain cry
The girl without arms
The goblin-spider
The golden axe
The golden chain from heaven
The golden eggplant
Gombel and the wild ducks
The good fortune kettle
The good-luck teakettle
The ungrateful monkey's secret
The grateful statues
The grateful stork
The great spirit of the toad
The greedy hawk
Green willow
Haku's power
The hare, badger, monkey and otter
The hare of Inaba
The hawk fledgling
The hurt sparrow
The husband of the rat's daughter
The ice ship in the hot sea
Isun Boshi, the one-inch lad
It's been well used
Izanagi and Izanami
Izanagi's descent to Hades
The jewels of the sea
Kachi Kachi mountain
Koichi and the mountain god
A leak in an old house
The legend of Urashima
Little maid of far Japan
Little one-inch
Little pictures from far Japan
The long-nosed goblins
Luck from heaven and luck from the earth
The luck of the sea and the luck of the mountain
The lucky tea-kettle

The magic ear
The magic kettle
The magic listening cap
The magic mortar
The magic purse of the swamp maiden
The magic teakettle
The magic veil
The maiden with the wooden helmet
The man who bought a dream
The man who made the trees bloom
The match-making of a mouse
The matsuyama mirror
The messenger from the moon
Mr. Lucky Straw
The mole's bridegroom
Momotaro
Momotaro: boy-of-the-peach
Momotaro: or The story of the son of a peach
Momotaro, the peach boy
The monkey and the crab
The monkey and the pheasant
The monkey bridegroom
Monkey-dance and sparrow-dance
The monkeys' jizo-sama
The monkey's liver
The moon-maiden
The mountain where old people were abandoned
The mountain witch and the peddler
My lord Bag-o' Rice
New Year's hats for the statues
The nun as judge
The ogre and the cock
The ogre who built a bridge
The old man and his dog
The old man and the devils
The old man of the flowers
The old man who cut bamboo
The old man who made flowers bloom
The old man who made trees blossom
The old man with the bump
The old men who had wens
The old woman who lost her dumplings
One-inch fellow
The oni and the three children
The oni's daughter
Ooka and the barbered beast
Ooka and the cleanest case
Ooka and the death decree
Ooka and the halved horse
Ooka and the honest thief
Ooka and the marble monster
Ooka and the pup's punishment
Ooka and the shattering solution
Ooka and the stolen smell
Ooka and the stronger stick
Ooka and the suspect statue
Ooka and the telltale tale
Ooka and the terrible-tempered tradesman

ANTME

Japan (*Continued*)

Ooka and the two first sons
Ooka and the wasted wisdom
Ooka and the willow witness
Ooka and the wonderful wishes
Ooka and Tosuke's tax
Oshidori
The peach boy
The piece of straw
The pillow
The poem of the sea
The princess and the fishermen
The princess of light
The quail and the badger
The rabbit and the bear
The rabbit and the crocodile
The rabbit in the moon
The rabbit who crossed the sea
The rain leak in an old house
Reflections
The rice cake that rolled away
The salt-grinding millstones
The sea of gold
The secret meeting at Shishi ga Tani
Shippei Taro
Shippei Taro and the monster cat
Shizuka's dance
The silly jelly-fish
Silly Saburo
Sima who wore the big hat
The skeleton's song
Sleep my baby! Sleep my baby!
The snail Choja
The sparrow whose tongue was cut out
The spell of the mermaid
The spider specter of the pool
The spider weaver
Star catching
Stinginess
The story of Aoyagi
The story of Hime
The story of Issoumbochi
The swamp Nushi's messenger
The sweet Mochi's parents
Takamagahara
Takero
A tall tale contest
Tape measure
The task of Prince Ishitsukuri
The task of Prince Kurumamochi
The task of the chief councillor Otomo-no-Miyuki
The task of the deputy chief councillor Iso-no-Kamimaro
The task of the minister Abe-no-Miushi
The tea-kettle
The tengu's magic nose fan
The terrible black snake's revenge
The terrible leak

There's no deity there
The three lucky charms
Three tests for the prince
The three year sleeping boy
Tiki-Tiki-Tembo
Timimoto
The tiny god
To the tengu goblins
The tongue-cut sparrow
The toothpick warriors
The tubmaker who flew to the sky
The two foolish cats
Ubazakura
Urashima
Urashima Taro
Urashima Taro and the princess of the sea
The vanishing rice-straw coat
The way of the master
The wedding of the mouse
The whale and the sea slug
The white bird sister
The white hare and the crocodiles
Why jellyfish has no shell
Why the jellyfish has no bones
The wicked polecat
The wife's portrait
Willow
The wise old woman
The wolf's reward
The woman of the snow
The woman who came down from heaven
The wonderful talking bowl
The wooden bowl
The wrestler of Kyushu
The wrestling match of the two Buddhas
The young Urashima
Yuki-Onna

−**Kyoto**
The hairy-armed ogre of Kyoto
One-inch fellow
Reflections
The two frogs

−**Kyushu**
The kappa's arm

−**Lullabies.** *See* **Lullabies−Japan**

−**Mt. Fujiyama**
The emperor's pilgrimage to Mount Fuji
The magic veil

−**Nagasaki**
The rats of Nagasaki

−**Osaka**
The two frogs

Japan current
The ice ship in the hot sea

Japanese dragons
  JACOBSON – FIRST p16.

A Japanese lullaby
  MY BOOK HOUSE v. 1 p78.

Jars
  See also Jugs
  Ali Sundos
  The little house
  A man, a snake, and a fox
  The story of the haunted jars
  Through the jungle
  The ungrateful bear
  The white parrot
  The witch and the earthen jar
  Zohair and the witch

Jars
  LEACH – SOUP p52-55

Jason
  The golden fleece

Jason . . . The golden fleece
  UNTERMEYER – FIRE. p29-37

Jataka tales
  The carpenter's boar
  The fables of India
  The golden deer
  A handful of peas
  How to catch a fish
  The monkey king's bridge

The Jatakas
  GAER – FABLES p119-171

Jauss, Anne Marie
  LOWE – LITTLE p124.

Java
  Aruman, a hero of Java
  The bet between Matjan and Gadja
  Crocodile's share
  The hunter of Perak
  The Kris of Adji Saka
  The legend of Pasopati
  The little Sawah
  Pamudjo's feast
  Princess Scri and Prince Sedana
  The tiger's war against Borneo

Jays (birds)
  See also Blue jays
  Partridge and rock tripe

Jealousy
  Ashoremashika
  Bad luck put into the bag
  The bald old man
  The blue lotus flower
  The brave little prince
  The carnation youth
  The children of Lir
  Christie and the growing hand
  Cupid and Psyche . . . The trial of love
  The dancing water, (the) singing apple, and (the) speaking bird
  Daniel in the lion's den
  David, the shepherd boy
  The donkey and the lap dog
  The elephant's bathtub
  The envious buffalo
  The envious neighbor
  The exile of Rama
  The fairy frog
  The first of May
  Friendship without envy
  The golden lion
  Goto, king of the land and the water
  Hallabau's jealousy
  The haunted lagoon
  How men learned about evil
  How men learned to sing songs
  The innkeeper's daughter
  It all comes to light
  Joseph and his brethren
  Kashi and his wicked brothers
  The kindly ghost
  King John and the abbot I. The three questions
  The king's black curtain
  The king's true children
  Lancelot and Elaine
  The little black men and the honey-bees
  The little rabbit who wanted red wings
  The long-nosed goblins
  The love of Cuchulainn and Fann, and the only jealousy of Emer, his wife
  The mad dog
  Maggie Tulliver goes to live with the gypsies
  Midir and Etain
  Nabulela
  Ooka and the halved horse
  Ooka and the wonderful wishes
  The partridge and the crow
  The peacock, the turkey and the goose
  The peasant and the waterman
  Phenist the bright-eyed falcon
  The reward of treachery
  The ring in the porridge bowl
  The royal musician
  Silver leaves and golden blossoms
  The six swans
  Snow-white and the seven dwarfs

Jealousy (*Continued*)

The stag prince
The stone horseman
The story of Hine-Moa and Tutanekai
The story of the talking bird
Sun and moon and the pretty girl
The sword of Damocles; the man who
    would be king
The tale of the hump-backed men
Tam and Tessa
The thoughtless abbot
The three figs
Three times and out
The three wishes
The trial by fire
The twins
What happened to the envious
Why the rabbit's nose twitches
Why the spider has a narrow waist
The winter's tale
The young wife of Nam Xuong

Jean Britisse, the champion
    COURLANDER – PIECE p105-110

Jean Labadie's big black dog
    CARLSON – TALKING p30-42

Jean Labadie's dog
    U. N. – RIDE p272-278

Jean Sot
    LEACH – LUCK p57-59
    LEACH – RAINBOW p235-237

Jellyfish
The monkey's liver
The silly jelly-fish
Why jellyfish has no shell
Why the jellyfish has no bones

The jellyfish's journey
    ROBERTSON – PHILIP. p43-52

Jeremiah
    WITHERS – I SAW p44.

Jerome, Saint
The affable lion

Jerusalem
Cast they bread upon the waters
King Solomon's pupils
Rashi and Duke Gottfried
The robe

Jester who herded the hares
    LANG – VIOLET p133-147

Jesse James
    LEACH – RAINBOW p177-180

The jester who fooled a king
    HAVILAND – POLAND p82-90

Jesters. *See* **Clowns; Fools and foolishness**
Jokesters

Jesus Christ
Behold the fig tree
Wind bloweth where it listeth

Jesus Christ
The bitter withy
The black woodpecker
A Chimalteco story
The devil and our Lord
Friar Blockhead and the Lord
Get up, little horsey
How and why: The painted turtle
How the wild boars came to be
Ilya of Murom and Svyatogor
Ivan and his knapsack
Lazy lout of a plant
The Lord said, This is my house
A lyke-wake dirge
The master-smith
The miraculous flute
The old gypsy woman and the good
    Lord
Owl
The oystercatcher, the duck and the
    hen
Padre Ulivo and his guests
The poor and the rich
The sacred cod and the striped haddock
Saint Peter and his trombone
The shoemaker's apron
A story about Our Lord Jesus Christ
A story of three brothers

–Birth
The shepherd's pipe
The wonderful night

The jewel
    BARASH – GOLDEN p62-63

The jewel of the fox's tongue
    INS-SOB – FOLK p18-20

The jeweled ring
    TOOZE – WONDER. p88-93

The jeweled slipper
    GRAHAM – BEGGAR p45-56

Jewelry
See also Bracelets; Necklaces; Rings
Bells on her toes

−Brooches
The little white cat

−Lockets
The plain princess
Rabbi Leib and the witch
Cunegunde
The servant who took the place
of his master

Jewels
Andrew and the mermaid
Bahri of the beauty spot
The Brahmin and the villain
The city under the sea
The cold heart−Part 2
Cornelia's jewels
Diamond cut diamond
Diamonds and toads
The donkey lettuce
The dove maiden
The dragon king and the lost fish-hook
Dwarf stories
The emerald-crested phoenix
The fairies
The fortunes of Saïd
The four abdallahs
General Moulton's boot
A handful of hay
Hansel and Gretel
How and why: The painted turtle
Jackal or tiger
The jackal, the barber and the
Brahmin who had seven daughters
Kabadaluk
Kahukura and the fairies
Keloğlan and God's greatness
King Solomon's carpet
The lost jewel
The luck of the sea and the luck of
the mountain
Magic and medicine
The man in the mirror
The miller-king
Pepito
The Prince Fernando
The princess
The raven's magic gem
Sadko
The shell grotto of Nienoort
The son of the hen-wife
The Spanish donkey and the Indians
The stolen jewel
The task of the chief councillor
Otomo-no-Miyuki
Superstition: the remnants of magic

The Vetāla's stories
Why crow is black and men find
precious stones in the earth
The would-be wizard

The jewels of the sea
UCHIDA − DANCING p61-72

Jewett, Eleanore M.
Tiger woman
Which was witch?
Yi Chang and the haunted house

The Jewish pope
BARASH − GOLDEN p36-42

Jews
See also Rabbis
Adares, King of Arabia
Akiba and the daughter of Kalba
Sabbu'a
Alexander of Macedon at the gates of
Paradise
Any more food?
Ask a foolish question
The barrel decree
The bone that testified
The borrower
Bostanai
The buyer of oxen
Cast thy bread
Cast thy bread upon the waters
Chanina and the angels
The charitable woman and the three
loaves
A Chimalteco story
The clever peasant girl
The covetous minister
The craftsman's wife
David Alroy
The devil's trick
Did the tailor have a nightmare?
The divided cloak
The donkey, the ox, and the farmer
The dove maiden
The dream
The elders of Chelm and Genendel's
key
The emperor and the deaf man
The end of the Golem
Enmity between man and serpent
Falasha: the mystery people
The first shlemiel
Fool's paradise
The fortunate maiden
The game of chess
The giant who rode on the ark
The golden candlestick
Golden shoes

Jews (*Continued*)

The Golem
The Golem and the bridal pair
The Golem of Rabbi Judah Löw
A good neighbor
Grandmother's tale
The hypocrite and the merchant's
 pledge
Introduction (The Golem)
Introduction (The righteous and the
 pious)
Introduction (Tales of David and
 Solomon)
Introduction (Tales of the prophet
 Elijah)
Introduction (Tales of wit and wisdom)
Introduction (The wisdom and folly
 of woman)
The jewel
Joshua and the princess
Judge not the vessel
A king and destiny
King David and the angel of death
The king of the demons and the worm
Shamir
King Solomon and Asmodeus
King Solomon and the Queen of
 Sheba
King Solomon's carpet
King Solomon's pupils
The learned young professor
Let's steal the moon
Leviathan and the dutiful son
Leviathan and the fox
The lion and the sage
The magic bird
Maimonides and the bottle of poison
Maimonides and the king's dream
The mechanical man of Prague
A meeting of scholars
The melting pot
Menaseh's dream
The merchant with nothing to sell
The merchant's son and the slave
The merchant's wife
The mixed-up feet and the silly
 bridegroom
Modesty and wisdom
The movie show
Other legendary beings
The pasha's sword
The penitent governor
The pious butcher
The pious washerwoman
The pomegranate seed
A portion in Paradise
The prince of Coucy
The princess and Rabbit Joshuah
The prophet Elijah and the angel of
 death

Rabbi Amram's coffin
Rabbi Joseph Della Reina
Rabbi Joshua ben Levi and the prophet
 Elijah
Rabbi Leib and the witch Cunegunde
Rashi and Duke Gottfried
The red slippers of Honiem
The righteous and the pious
The righteous heir
The righteous is delivered out of
 trouble and the wicked comes in his
 stead
The robe
The royal banquet
Saadia the potmender
The sack of corn
The saving of a soul
The seven years of blessing
Shiny tales of Vincennes
Shlemiel, the businessman
Shrewd Todie and Lyzer the miser
The snow in Chelm
The sin of a saint
Solomon and his pride
Solomon and the four winds
The spring
The stolen ring
The story of Mordecai and Esther
The stupid hunter and the crafty
 bird
Tales of David and Solomon
Tales of the prophet Elijah
Tales of wit and wisdom
The talking talisman
The task of the serpent
The test
The three litigants
The three rings
The tinner, the dog, the Jew and the
 cake
Torah and honor
The treasure
The true scales
Tsirtsur and Peziza
The two bridegrooms
The two righteous men
Utzel and his daughter Poverty
The value of a boiled egg
A voice from heaven
The warm matzah
The weight of the cart
When Shlemiel went to Warsaw
Where the kings of Judah sleep their
 last sleep
Who am I?
Who maketh the dumb to speak
Why the scroll of the law fell to the
 ground
Why the steer has a smooth nose
The wind and the ant
The wisdom and folly of women

Jews (*Continued*)

The wise bird and the hunter: an old
Hebrew fable
The wise men of Chelm
The witches of Ascalon
Zlateh the goat

The ji-jaller bag
FINLAY — FOLK p76-85

Jingle bells, jingle bells
MY BOOK HOUSE v. 1 p87.

Jingles. *See* **Nursery rhymes; Repetitive
rhymes and stories**

Jingling rhymes and jingling money
JAGENDORF — NEW p133-138

Jinnis. *See* **Genies**

The jinni's magic flute
CARPENTER — AFRICAN p145-152

Jip and the witch of Walgrave
FINLAY — FOLK p9-19

Jirimpimbira
ARNOTT — TALES p52-64

Jizo
The grateful statues
New Year's hats for the statues

Joan of Arc
MY BOOK HOUSE v. 10 p98-107

Joan of Arc . . . the warrior maid
UNTERMEYER — FIRE. p193-197

Joe Magarac
GORHAM — REAL p148-158
LEACH — RAINBOW p54-57

Joe Magarac and his U.S.A. citizen papers
SHAPIRO — HEROES p199-256

Joe Magarac the steel man
SHAPIRO — TALL p111-124

Joe Magerack, the steel-mill man
JAGENDORF — UPSTATE p167-171

Jog on, jog on
MY BOOK HOUSE v. 1 p148.

John Connu Rider
GARNER — GOBLINS p3.

John, King
Humpty Dumpty
King John and the abbot I. The three
questions
King John and the abbot II. The three
answers
King John and the Abbot of Canter-
bury
This is how it began

John, Lord of the Isles
The tale of the wrath of God

John Boaster
BAMBERGER — FIRST p183-186

John Brown had a little Indian
MY BOOK HOUSE v. 1 p100.

John Gethin and the candle
SHEPPARD — WELSH p29-31

John Henry
GORHAM — REAL p106-117
LEACH — RAINBOW p33-35
SHAPIRO — TALL p97-109

John Henry and double-jointed steam
drill
SHAPIRO — HEROES p105-154

John Henry, the big steel-drivin' man
MY BOOK HOUSE v. 5 p135-139

John Macdonald and the kelpie
SHEPPARD — SCOT. p38-42

John Paul Jones. the first American naval
hero
MY BOOK HOUSE v. 8 p90a-90b

John Reid and the mermaid
SHEPPARD — SCOT. p155-158

John Shea and the fairy treasure
McNEILL — DOUBLE p87-94

John Tabor, whaler
IVES — TALES p179-189

John the bear
THOMPSON — ONE p3-8

John the blacksmith destroys the wasps
in the straw
JAGENDORF — MERRY p87-92

John the painter
SHEPPARD — WELSH p123-128

John the true
JACOBS – EUROPE. p170-179

Johnnie and Grizzle
JACOBS – EUROPE. p180-187

Johnny and the three goats
MY BOOK HOUSE v. 2 p47-49

Johnny and the witch-maidens
MANNING – WITCHES p115-122

Johnny and Tommy and the bear
JOHNSON – WHAT p250.

Johnny Appleseed
GORHAM – REAL p159-165
LEACH – RAINBOW p28-32
SHAPIRO – TALL p45-51

Johnny-cake
HAVILAND – ENGLAND p22-29
WILLIAMS – FAIRY p34-38
WITHERS – I SAW p27-31

Johnny Gloke
JACOBS – MORE p78-81
REEVES – ENGLISH p23-34

Johnny head-in-air
PROTTER – CHILD. p166-167

Johnny McGorry and the red stocking
WITHERS – I SAW p45.

Johnny shall have a new bonnet
MY BOOK HOUSE v. 1 p20.

Johnson, A. E., trans.
Puss in boots

Johnson, Edward
Hanging at Wessaguscus

Johnson, John E.
WITHERS – WORLD p118.

Jokeli
MY BOOK HOUSE v. 1 p66.

The jokes of Single-Toe
ARBUTHNOT – TIME p122-124

Jokesters. *See* **Clowns; Trickery**

The jolly tailor who became king
HAVILAND – POLAND p13-27

Jonas and the boggart of Brixworth
FINLAY – FOLK p119-127

Jonas and the sturgeon
JAGENDORF – UPSTATE p75-79

Jonathan Moulton and the devil
RASKIN – TALES p29-35

Jones, Casey
Casey Jones
Casey Jones and locomotive no. 638

Jones, Gwyn
Beowulf and Grendel
The birth of Pryderi

Jones, John Paul
John Paul Jones, the first American
naval hero
Of sea-going snakes
Paul Jones

Jonnikin and the flying basket
MANNING – JONNIKIN p12-18

Jordan
The affable lion

Jorinda and Joringel
SIDEMAN – WORLD'S p388-393

Joseph and his brethren
LINES – TALES p231-250
MY BOOK HOUSE v. 10 p48-53

Joshokiklay and the eagle
COURLANDER – PEOPLE p50-59

Joshua (Biblical)
Why the steer has a smooth nose

Joshua and the princess
DOBBS – MORE p34-38

Joshua trees
The absent-minded tailor

Jotuns
Bragi, god of poetry
The creation of the world
The first gods and giants
Frey and Gerd, the jotun maiden
Idunn's apples of youth
Loki, the god of the jotun race
Odin, the all-father
Odin's eight-legged steed
The theft of Thor's hammer

Jotuns *(Continued)*

Thor and the jotun Aegir
Thor and the jotun Geirrod
Thor and the jotun Rungnir
Thor and the jotun Utgardsloki

Journey by broomstick
PALMER – JOURNEY p142-160

Journey in a well
GREEN – BIG p155-156

The journey of the Chinese honeyseller
MORRIS – UPSTAIRS p87-89

The journey to Lagos
COURLANDER – OLODE p82-85

The journey to the land of the dead
COURLANDER – PEOPLE p129-142

The journey to Toulouse of the animals
that had colds
DELARUE – FRENCH p67-70

Joy. *See* **Happiness; Laughter**

Juan and the helpful frog
SECHRIST – ONCE p150-156

Juan Bobo
BELPRE – TIGER p49-54

Juan Bobo and old tiger
JAGENDORF – KING p269-273

Juan Bobo and the caldron
ALEGRÍA – THREE p74-75

Juan Bobo and the princess who answered
riddles
ALEGRÍA – THREE p115-121

Juan Bobo, the sow, and the chicks
ALEGRÍA – THREE p31-33

Juan Cigarron
HAVILAND – SPAIN p58-69

Juan in heaven
JAGENDORF – KING p89-93

Juanito and the princess
ALEGRÍA – THREE p100-106

Judas
Kirsten McVurich

Judd, Mary Catherine
How the water lily came
Legend of the arbutus

Judge not the vessel
BARASH – GOLDEN p73-76

The judge of Bellinzona
MÜLLER – SWISS p142-144

The judgement of Hailu
McNEILL – DOUBLE p62-66

The judgement of the shepherd
TURNBULL – FAIRY p117-126

The judgements of a magistrate
INS-SÖB – FOLK p187-188

Judges and justice
See also titles beginning with Judge-
ment, Judgment, Just
The adder and the fox
The adventures of Perseus
Ali Sundos
Aruman, a hero of Java
The baker's neighbor
Balder, the god of light
The bee-hunter and the oozie
The bees and the drones
The bell of Atri
Boiled wheat for a bountiful harvest
The bone that testified
The Brahmin, the tiger, and the
seven judges
The case of a widow before a sagacious
magistrate
The case of the calf and the colt
The case of the mouse-deer and the
crocodile's eggs
Charles the Great and the snake
The clever jackal and how he outwitted
the tiger
A clever judge
The colts in the pumpkin
The covetous minister
Daniel in the lions' den
The dilemma of a pious man
The dishonest tailor
The dog that learned to read
Doll i' the grass
Enmity between man and serpent
An expensive omelette
Fair wages for all
The farmer's clever daughter
Finn and the Fianna
The fire on the mountain
Five loaves
The fly
François Villon, the vagabond of
Paris

Judges and justice (*Continued*)

Geordie and ten-shilling Jock
The ghost of Samuel Chew
The goat and the eagle
The golden bird
The good judge
The greedy friend
The greedy stallkeeper and the poor
    traveler
Heart and mind
The hermit cat
The honest woodman
The hornets and the honeybees
How Jack sought the golden apples
How much for a shadow?
How the Brazilian beetles got their
    gorgeous coats
How the finch got her colors
How the lizard lost and regained his
    farm
The infallible salt bird
The ingrates
Inside again
The judgements of a magistrate
Juha and the dispute over a goat
The just judgment
Justice
The kind caliph and the horse thief
The king and the falcon
King Firdy the Just
King Hilary and the beggarman
The knights of the silver shield
The land of the dead
Large cabbages
The legend of William Tell
The little red mannikin
Lohengrin
The lonely lioness and the ostrich
    chicks
The lost spear
The magic bell
A man, a snake, and a fox
The man, the serpent and the fox
The marvelous pear seed
The miraculous flute
Nabookin
The nun as judge
Old Pipes and the dryad
The one who said Tjik
The onion and the rose
Ooka and the barbered beast
Ooka and the cleanest case
Ooka and the death decree
Ooka and the halved horse
Ooka and the honest thief
Ooka and the marble monster
Ooka and the pup's punishment
Ooka and the shattering solution
Ooka and the stolen smell
Ooka and the stronger stick

Ooka and the suspect statue
Ooka and the telltale tale
Ooka and the terrible-tempered trades-
    man
Ooka and the two first sons
Ooka and the wasted wisdom
Ooka and the willow witness
Ooka and the wonderful wishes
Ooka and Tosuke's tax
The otters and the fox
Pacala the lawyer
Partnership
The peasant and the donkey
The peasant and the sheep
The peasant and the workman
The pert fire engine
Phaeton
Pigling and her proud sister
The pilgrim and the judge
The poor man's clever daughter
The price of eggs
The righteous heir
The rough rider
The secret royal insector, Bag Mun-Su
Self-convicted
Shemiaka the judge
Shoes don't match
Shrewd Todie and Lyzer the miser
The six swans
The sloogeh dog and the stolen aroma
The smart daughter
The snake who bit a girl
Snow-white and Rose-red
The song of Roland
Souchmant's trial and triumph
The sound is yours
The story of the talking bird
The strong boy
Summer snow
Tell a tale of Ara Spence
The test
The thousand pieces of gold
The tiger, the Brahmen, and the jackal
To pay through the nose
A token of friendship
Tortoise and the lizard
The traveller and the tiger
The trial of the stone
The twelve months
The two brothers and the magistrate
Two different interpretations of the
    same pact
Two watermelon stories
The tyrant who became a just ruler
The ungrateful tiger
The value of a boiled egg
Vassily and Curly Head the brigand
Vladimir's adventures in search of for-
    tune
War between the crocodiles and
    Kantchil

Judges and justice *(Continued)*

The war of the animals against the birds
What will people say
Who is responsible
Why the bagobo like the cat
The will of the wise man
The wise judge
The wise old camel
A wise sentence
The woodcutter's daughter
Ye merry doings of Robin Hood
Yiankos
You are right!

The judgment of Karakoush
U. N. – RIDE p101-104

The judgment of Paris
GREEN – GREEKS p10-11

The judgment of the wind
COURLANDER – FIRE p51-56

Juggling
The baron's haughty daughter
The ceabharnach
Hwan and Dang
The little juggler . . . And the virgin
The trials of Ting Ling

Jugs
See also **Milk-Jugs**
The crow and the water jug
Jars
The potted princess
Trim Tram Turvey
Verena and the jug
The voice in the jug

Juha and the dispute over a goat
NAHMAD – PEASANT p137-141

Juha at the banquet
NAHMAD – PEASANT p140-141

Julius Caesar . . . The Ides of March
UNTERMEYER – FIRE. p105-108

Jumbo was an elephant
MY BOOK HOUSE v. 1 p105.

Jumping
See also **Leaping**
Here am I, little jumping Joan
How grasshopper came to be and men obtained tobacco
Jeremiah
Sam Patch

Sam Patch, the jumpin' man
Sam Patch's last leap
The son of the hunter
The three-legged jumping giant
Why the flea jumps

The jumping contest
GREEN – BIG p134-136

Jumping the Grand Canyon
FELTON – NEW p21-32

Jungle
The case of the mouse-deer and the crocodile's eggs
The cat who came indoors
How Papantla got its patron saint
Mowgli's brothers
The mysterious path
Pyoli
The story of Wali Dâd the simple-hearted
Through the jungle
Wembi, the singer of stories

The juniper
THOMPSON – ONE p334-341

Junkmen
The dancing kettle
The good fortune kettle
The magic teakettle

Jupiter
Phaethon . . . The chariot of the sun
Phaeton; the boy who rode the chariot of the sun
The ridiculous wishes
The three wasted wishes

The jurga
BELPRE – TIGER p37-41

The just and unjust brothers
SPICER – LONG p130-144

Just his luck
LEACH – LUCK p22-23

The just judgment
EDMONDS – TRICKSTER p51-60

The just reward
THOMPSON – ONE p409-410
WYNDHAM – TALES p57-61

Justice. *See* **Judges and justice**

Justice
COURLANDER – FIRE p73-76

Jutland
Hans, the horn and the magic sword
The skipper and the dwarfs

K

Ka, the god of the sea
  The sailor and the sea serpent

Ka-Hai and the sorcerer Tama-i-wao
  WHEELER – HAWAII. p190-212

Kabadaluk
  MANNING – GIANNI p13-23

Kabadaluk: the little Arab boy
  ĆURĆIJA – YUGOSLAV p20-36

Kabundi's eye
  HOLLADAY – BANTU p80-82

Kachi Kachi mountain
  SEKI – FOLKTALES p6-9

Kaffirs
  The bird that would not stay dead
  The cannibal and his sweet singing
    bird

Kâgssagssuk, the homeless boy who became a strong man
  MAYNE – HEROES p37-44

Kahukura and the fairy fishermen
  CAMPBELL – MAORI p43-45

Kahukura and the fairies
  CAMPBELL – MAORI p39-42

Kakui, bird of the night
  U. N. – RIDE p202-205

Kakuys (owls)
  The sad, sorry sister

Kalahari Desert
  The battle of the animals

Kalamona and the winds
  ILLYES – ONCE p269-284

Kaldersha band
  The gypsy and the snake

Kaleleä and his wish
  WHEELER – HAWAII. p143-163

Kalevala (epic)
  See also The world's great epics

The courtship of Lemminkäinen
The death of Kwasind
Why the bear cannot play the kantele

Kalevala, land of heroes
  MY BOOK HOUSE v. 10 p151-164

Kalidasa
  The fleeing deer

Kalmuks
  Two rascals

Kalulu and his money farm
  KAULA – AFRICAN p32-42

Kalulu and the elephant
  ELLIOT – WHERE p72-78

Kalulu and the leopard
  ELLIOT – WHERE p1-9

"Kalwala"
  Ilmarinen . . . how he won his bride

Kambara (Island)
  How the mosquitoes came to Oneata

The Kamiah monster
  MARTIN – COYOTE p53-60

Kamiyo of the river
  TRACEY – LION p22-25

Kanchils. See Mouse-deer

Kangaroo rats
  The Southern cross

Kangaroos
  Bohra the kangaroo
  Gwai-nee-bu the redbreast
  The kaola bear and the tribal laws
  Mrs. Wallaby Jones
  Old Noah
  Please give me a ride on your back
  The right time to laugh
  The spirit of the waterhole
  The two dogs-Burrajahnee and
    Inneroogun
  The young man and the kangaroo
  The zoo in the park

Kansas
Early days and ways in America
Early Kansas
A tramp of the Middle West

Kansas
LEACH – RAINBOW p88-91

A Kansas cyclone
JOHNSON – WHAT p226.

Kanteles (guitars)
Why the bear cannot play the kantele

Kantjil and the monkey business
BRO – HOW p79-87

Kantjil becomes a raksha
BRO – HOW p29-38

Kantjil brings the elephants to heel
BRO – HOW p88-95

Kantjil discovers the wisdom of Allah
BRO – HOW p49-54

Kantjil grows strong at the welling-well
BRO – HOW p13-21

Kantjil holds a festival
BRO – HOW p107-117

Kantjil interprets a dream
BRO – HOW p55-71

Kantjil to the rescue
BRO – HOW p96-106

Kantchil's lime pit
COURLANDER – KANT. p7-10
U. N. – RIDE p28-31

The kaola bear and the tribal laws
NORLEDGE – ABORIGINAL p59.

Kapingamarangi (island)
Why flounder's two eyes are on the
same side of his face

Kapoi and the owl-king
WHEELER – HAWAII. p164-167

Kapok birds
How the kapok bird came to be

Kappas (water sprites)
The kappa's arm

The kappa's arm
PRATT – MAGIC unp.

Karang, legend of the. *See* The legend of
the Karang

Karbaus (animals)
The dog and the karbau
The victory of the buffalo

Karelia (country)
The gull
Why the bear cannot play the kantele

Kari Woodencoat
BAKER – GOLDEN p19-33

Karl the Great and the robber
PICARD – GERMAN p89-102

Kashi and his wicked brothers
SIDDIQUI – TOON. p37-43

Kashmir
The boy and the cloth
The debt
It happened in Kashmir
The traveler and the nut tree

Katcha and the devil
FILLMORE – SHEPHERD'S p160-171
ROSS – BLUE p110-122

Kate Contrary
MANNING – GLASS p182-186

Kate Crackernuts
WILLIAMS – FAIRY p49-55

Kate Mary Ellen and the fairies
COLUM – STONE p68-75

Katie Woodencloak
THOMPSON – ONE p177-187

Katydids
Fairy and child

Kaula, Edna Mason
KAULA – AFRICAN p157.

Kavin, Saint
King O'Toole and his goose
The king, the saint and the goose

Kawelo the little-brother-to-the-rats
WHEELER – HAWAII. p78-93

Kayacan, Feyyaz and Mary Fergar
The magic dagger
The peasant and the donkey

Kayacan, Feyyaz and Mary Fergar
(*Continued*)
The story of the boy who couldn't
keep anything in his head
The three apples
Two watermelon stories

Kayaks (boats)
The man who killed the sea monster
The men fashion the frame of their
kayaks

Kayuta, the drop star
RASKIN – TALES p91-96

Kazakh SSR
Aldar-Kos and the greedy rich man
The animals' quarrel
The baby camel
The cat, the tiger, and the man
The curious wife
Ergosai-Batyr
The fool
The fox and the quail
The forty whoppers
The golden slipper, the magic ring,
and the twigs
If you know a story, don't keep it to
yourself
The invisible thief
The magic garden
Mirzhan and the lord of the kingdom
under the sea
Old man Kurai and the one-eyed giant
Salakhbai and the fox
Segizbai and the little mouse-girl
A Sherlock Holmes of the steppes
The stupid wolf
Three bridegrooms for one bride
The woodcutter's daughter

Keats, John
Child, I see thee!
Dawlish fair
Meg Merrilies
There was a naughty boy
Verses
Where be you going, you Devon maid?

Keats, John
Sweet peas and Grecian urns

Keble, John
All things beautiful

Keelboats
A trail of tall tales

Keel-Wee, a Korean Rip Van Winkle
JEWETT – WHICH p74-81

Keep cool
JACOBS – EUROPE. p115-120

Keightley, Thomas
The boggart

Kela and the giant bird Halulu
WHEELER – HAWAII. p94-111

Kelea, the surf princess
CARPENTER – SHIPS p121-130

Kelly, F. Beverly
Freddy, the pad dog

Keloğlan and God's greatness
WALKER – ONCE p80-101

Keloğlan and the lucky exchanges
WALKER – ONCE p104-113

Keloğlan and the magic hairs
WALKER – ONCE p44-55

Keloğlan and the magician
WALKER – ONCE p26-41

Keloğlan and the ooh-genie
WALKER – ONCE p8-23

Keloğlan in the service of the padishah
WALKER – ONCE p116-128

Keloğlan the kindhearted
WALKER – ONCE p58-77

The kelpie
MORAY – FAIR p70-90

Kelpies. *See* Water spirits

Kelsey, Alice Geer
How many donkeys?
Pumpkin trees and walnut vines

Kemoc the hermit
The Christian bell
The death of the children of Lir

Kempe Owyne
MANNING – BEASTS p196-198

Kennedy, Patrick
The enchantment of Gearoidh Iarla
The haughty princess
The Kildare pooka
The palace in the Rath

Kentucky
The barnyard

Kentucky *(Continued)*

Daniel's dear
Davy Crockett
Davy Crockett, the yaller blossom o'
the forest
Exploring the wilderness
Hully-gully
The hunters of Kentucky
Jumbo was an elephant
Over the hill to feed my sheep

—**Mountains**
Charley's neat and Charley's sweet
Froggie goes a-courting
I saw a crow a-flying low

Kentucky
LEACH — RAINBOW p91-92

Kenya
The mighty warrior in hare's house

—**Kamba**
Sun and moon and the pretty girl

—**Masai**
The moon's face

Kerchiefs. *See* **Handkerchiefs; Scarves**

Kernel
MICHAEL — PORTUGUESE p112-117

The kettle and the chestnut
BELTING — THREE p94-101

Kettles
See also **Teakettles**
Bergamot
The big cabbage and the big kettle
The big pumpkin and the big kettle
The faery and the kettle
The flying kettle
Luran and the fairies
The magic kettle
Polly, put the kettle on
The woman of peace and the kettle

The key in the distaff
ASBJÖRNSEN — NORW. p128-130

The key maiden of Tegerfelden
MÜLLER — SWISS p70-89

The key of the kingdom
WITHERS — I SAW p70.

The key to Bibbley-Babbley-town
MY BOOK HOUSE v. 1 p127.

Keys
Blue Beard
Bluebeard
Cherry
Damian and the dragon
The devil's apprentice
Donal from Donegal
The elders of Chelm and Genendel's
key
The enchanted princess
The flower of beauty
The giant of the brown beech wood
Guardian of the house
The heir of Linne
Here is the key
Jack and the wizard
The secret room
The trade that no one knows

, **Golden**
The adventures of Florian
The frog with the golden key

Keys to Burmese meanings
AUNG — KINGDOM p81-95

Khalid and Aantar
ZAGLOUL — BLACK p143-151

Khasynget's grandmother
GINSBURG — MASTER p27-33

Khnemu of the Nile
GREEN — TALES p51-58

Khonsu
The princess and the demon

Khrishna the cowherd
COURLANDER — TIGER'S p63-71

Ki-Lin
The untamable unicorn

Kian and the children of Tuireann
PILKINGTON — THREE p17-24

Kicking
The ass gets the better of the wolf
The wee, wee mannie and the big,
big coo

The kid and the tiger
SPELLMAN — BEAUT. p75-78

Kidd, Captain
The goose from Flatbush
Hudson River legends: Captain Kidd
Buried treasure

Kidnapping
  The earrings
  Fenisana
  Pwyll and Rhiannon

"Kiev Cycle"
  Aliosha's visit to the bald mountain
  Chourilo's little comb
  Dobrynia and Alyosha
  Dobryna's embassy to Khan Amryl
  Dunay
  The fortunate maiden
  How Dounai won a bride for Prince
    Vladimir
  How three pilgrims call Ilya to the
    rescue of Kiev
  Ilya of Murom and nightingale the
    robber
  Nikita and the last of the dragons
  Potok's dancing and the snakes
  Samson and the doll in green and
    brown
  Souchmant's trial and triumph
  Stavr Godinovich and his clever wife
  Vassily and Curly Head the brigand
  Volkh's journey to the East
  Young Michael and the uninvited
    guest

Kigbo and the bush spirits
  COURLANDER – OLODE p45-49

Kihuru (birds)
  The greedy hyena

Kilcolman castle
  MY BOOK HOUSE v. 12 p30-31

The Kildare pooka
  PALMER – DRAGONS p38-42
  PILKINGTON – SHAM. p52-54

Killing. See **Murder**

The killing of Mogg Megone
  TAFT – PROFILE p50-58

Kilmeny
  MORAY – FAIR p58-69

Kilns
  The dark maiden from the ninth
    heaven

Kim, Yong Hwan
  ANDERSON – BOY p94.

Kimonas
  Benizara and Kakezara

  The princess of light
  The woman who came down from
    heaven

The kind caliph and the horse thief
  CARPENTER – HORSES p58-63

The kind farmer
  FARJEON – LITTLE p272-288

A kind heart
  FELTON – NEW p34-49

The kind pasha and Mehat the shepherd
  ĆURČIJA – HEROES p143-145

The kind pixy
  BRIGGS – PERS. p136.

Kindai and the ape
  AARDEMA – TALES p77-85

The kindly ant-bear
  ELLIOT – WHERE p101.

The kindly ghost
  MANNING – GHOSTS p103-110

Kindness
  See also **Generosity**
  Angus
  Arap Sang and the cranes
  Are there such women?
  Baba Yaga
  Baba Yaga and the little girl with the
    kind heart
  The babe Moses
  The bachelors and the python
  A baker's dozen
  Balder, the god of light
  Beauty and the beast
  The birch twig
  The bold heroes of Hungry Hill
  Cast thy bread upon the waters
  Catherine and her fate
  The Choja who became a monkey
  Cinder Joe becomes king
  A converted thief
  Dame Wiggins of Lee
  The daughter of the King Ron
  Diamonds and toads
  The dove and the ant
  Eighteen rabbits
  The elephant and the carpenters
  The enchanted waterfall
  The fairies
  The flying ship
  The fruits of health
  The game of chess in the mountains
  The giant who had no heart in his
    body

Kindness (*Continued*)

The good-luck teakettle
The good old man
The grateful beasts
The grateful devil
The grateful goat
The grateful statues
The greedy man in the moon
He danced five-o
How the black turnstone came to
  nest near the sea
How the lion rewarded the mouse's
  kindness
The hungry giant
Hwan and Dang
The injured lion
Isun Boshi, the one-inch lad
Jester who herded the hares
Kantjil to the rescue
Keloğlan the kindhearted
The Kildare pooka
The king and the shoemaker
The kitten and the knitting needles
The legend of Urashima
The lion and the mouse
The little cat and the knitting needles
The little duck
Little Gulliver
Lucky Rose Tuttle
The magic fiddle
Magic in Marblehead
The magic melons
The magic wand
The maiden in the country
  underground
The man who always helped the
  needy
Morgan and the three fairies
Mother Holle
Mother's girl and father's girl
Musk and amber
The old hag's long leather bag
The old amn who made flowers
  bloom
The old man who made trees blossom
The old witch
Pemba and the python and the
  friendly rat
The Phynnodderee
The prince who rode through a
  mousehole
The princess and the fisherman
The princess with the golden hair
The queen's care
The queen's necklace
Rattle-rattle-rattle and chink-chink-
  chink
The sand-carrier crab
The seven stars of the north
Snow-white and Rose-red

The spring of youth
A story about Abe Lincoln
The strange adventures of Alcavilu
Sven and Lilli
The tale of nutcracker
The talking fish
The three wishes
The tinker of Tamlacht
The two sisters
The two wishes
The ungrateful tiger
Vladimir's adventures in search of
  fortune
The wee red man
Wend' Yamba
The white unicorn
Why pigs have curly tails
Why the evergreen trees never lose
  their leaves
The wind and the sun
A wizard of the twilight
The wooden bowl
Young John
The young Urashima
The youth who made friends with the
  beasts and the birds

Kindness to animals
Heidi in the Alpine pasture
I love little pussy
Little Gustava
Mrs. Tabby Gray
The rarest animal of all

King Adder
  BAMBERGER – FIRST p55-57

King Alfred and the cakes
  BALDWIN – FAVOR. p3-6

King All-tusk
  WYATT – GOLDEN p6-12

A king and destiny
  NAHMAD – PORTION p152-153

The king and his friend
  DE LA IGLESIA – CAT unp.

The king and his seven sons
  MacFARLANE – TALES p55-70

The king and Kuffie
  See also The beef tongue of Orula
  COURLANDER – TERRA. p84-86

The king and Robin Hood
  MANNING – ENGLISH p138-148

The king and the barber
  MICHAEL – PORTUGUESE
  p139-145

The king and the bishop
THOMPSON – ONE p362.

The king and the Brahmin's child
MacFARLANE – TALES p113-122

The king and the corn
FARJEON – LITTLE p1-6

The king and the falcon
GREEN – BIG p14.

The king and the merman
LEEKLEY – KING p13-30

The king and the monkey
GAER – FABLES p143-146

The king and the Nagas
PALMER – DRAGONS p89-95

The king and the peasant
U.N. – RIDE p142-144

The king and the ring
WALKER – DANCING p43-50

The king and the shepherd
TASHJIAN – THREE p9-15

The king and the shoemaker
SPELLMAN – BEAUT. p8-11

The king and the two owls
NAHMAD – PEASANT p95-97

The king and the wise man
DE LA IGLESIA – CAT unp.

The king and the wrestler
WITHERS – WORLD p76-77

King Appolonides
LEEKLEY – KING p61-67

King Arthur . . . The shield and the hammer
UNTERMEYER – FIRE. p167-171

King Bean
THOMPSON – ONE p122-126

King Canute on the seashore
BALDWIN – FAVOR. p7-10

King Conal's horses
O'FAOLÁIN – IRISH p181-185

King crow and Sir parrot
GAER – FABLES p102-104

King Dagobert
MY BOOK HOUSE v. 1 p124.

King David and the angel of death
NAHMAD – PORTION p47-48

King Estmere
MANNING – ENGLISH p62-69

King Fergus and the water-horse
COLUM – STONE p85-89

King Fergus MacLeide and the wee folk
O'FAOLÁIN – IRISH p110-122

King Find's daughter
HACK – DANISH p97-105

King Firdy the Just
DAVIS – LION'S p112-115

King Florimonde and the winged horse
PICARD – MERMAID p187-203

King fox
MANNING – GIANNI p76-102

King Frost and the snow maiden
ALMEDINGEN – RUSS. p82-94

King Great Virtue
GRAY – INDIA'S p1-7

King Herla
VANSITTART – DARK p9-17

King Herla, The Little People of the British Isles
BELTING – ELVES p41-46

King Herla's quest
LEEKLEY – KING p77-96

King Hilary and the beggarman
MY BOOK HOUSE v. 3 p70-75

King Hrolf and the bear's son
JONES – SCAND. p183-222

King James and the questions
SHEPPARD – SCOT. p122-124

King John and the abbot
BALDWIN – FAVOR. p11-17

King John and the Abbot of Canterbury
JACOBS – MORE p159-162
U. N. – RIDE p189-193

King Johnny
MANNING – GIANTS p67-78

358

King Kantjil's kingdom expands
BRO – HOW p72-78

King Jojata
BUCK – FAIRY p141-153

King Laurin goes awooing
SAWYER – DIETRICH p112-128

King Lindorm
THOMPSON – ONE p127-128

King March has horse's ears
MORRIS – UPSTAIRS p51-58

King Matthias and the old man
ILLYES – ONCE p191-192

King Nollekens of Norfolk
FARJEON – SILVER p36-46

The king o' the cats
JACOBS – MORE p169-171
LITTLEDALE – GHOSTS p121-124
See also King of the cats

King O'Toole and his goose
ARBUTHNOT – TIME p125-127

The King of Araby's daughter
MacMANUS – BOLD p83-100

The King of England and his three sons
JACOBS – MORE p142-158

The King of France went up the hill
MY BOOK HOUSE v. 1 p41.

The King of Sedo
COURLANDER – KING'S p19-21

The king of the animals
COURLANDER – PIECE p97-100

The king of the birds
CATHON – PERHAPS p174-179
SHEPPARD – WELSH p59-62

The king of the cats
BAMBERGER – FIRST p209-212
WILLIAMS – FAIRY p106-109

The king of the crows
MANNING – JONNIKIN p23-34

The king of the dark desert
GARNIER – LEGENDS p31-41

The king of the demons and the worm
Shamir
SERWER – LET'S p9-17

"The king of the fish". See Father big-
nose

The king of the fishes
JACOBS – EUROPE. p19-30

The king of the forest
COURLANDER – TIGER'S p46-48

The king of the frogs
HARMON – TALES p57-63

The king of the Golden River, or the
Black brothers
ARBUTHNOT – TIME p367-379

The king of the hares
CHILD – CASTLES p29-39

The king of the leaves
JAGENDORF – KING p218-221

The king of the mountain
HUME – FAVORITE p85-92

The king of the mountains
JAGENDORF – KING p40-43

King of the restless sea
THOMPSON – LEGENDS p23-27

King of the serpents
JACOBSON – FIRST p40-41

The king of the wood
SHEAHAN – HENRY p317-336

The king on trial
DURHAM – TIT p67-69

King Orfeo
MANNING – ENGLISH p97-104

King Setnau and the Assyrians
MOZLEY – EGYPT p38-43

King Shibi
GRAY – INDIA'S p32-33

King Solomon and Asmodeus
NAHMAD – PORTION p61-66

King Solomon and the Queen of Sheba
DAVIS – LION'S p168-172
NAHMAD – PORTION p56-60

King Solomon's carpet
BAKER – TALKING p218-231

King Solomon's cat
BELTING – CAT p28-30

King Solomon's pupils
BARASH – GOLDEN p13-17

King Stephen was a worthy peer
MY BOOK HOUSE v. 1 p149.

King Svatopluk and the three sticks
U. N. – RIDE p128-130

The king, the saint and the goose
WILLIAMS – FAIRY p24-29

King Vukashin's wedding
ĆURČIJA – HEROES p19-23

The king who ate chaff
COURLANDER – TIGER'S p33-34

The king who could not sleep
O'SULLIVAN – FOLK. p21-37

The king who lived fairy tales
BUDBERG – RUSSIAN p38-42

The king who rides a tiger
HITCHCOCK – KING p80-95

The king who slept
EELLS – SPAIN p79-92

The king who tried to cheat destiny
NAHMAD – PEASANT p53-59

The king who wanted a beautiful wife
THOMPSON – ONE p353-355

The king who was a gentleman
MacMANUS – HIBERIAN p36-47

A kingdom lost for a drop of honey
AUNG – KINGDOM p28-30

The kingdom of ocean
MANNING – MERMAID p41-45

The kingdom of the Green Mountains
SHEPPARD – SCOT. p1-8

The kingdom without a cat
CARPENTER – DOGS p25-34

The kingdoms
BALDWIN – FAVOR. p95-98

Kingfishers (birds)
The giant kingfisher of Mount Riga
How kingfisher got his necklace

, Australian
How the sun was made

Kings (birds)
The eagle and the wren

Kings and Queens
About the hedgehog who became prince
The absent-minded king
Adam Bell, Clym of the Clough, and William of Cloudesly
The adventures of Bona and Nello
The adventurous winnower
The Albahaca plant
The animal wife
The apple of contentment
Arawn
As many as – – –
The ash lad and the good helpers
Authun and the bear
Baboon skins
Beowulf
Beppo Pipetta and his knapsack
The bewitched court
The billy goat and the king
Bird language
The bird of the golden land
The bird which laid diamonds
The blackbird's song
The blind king and the magic bird
The blue cat
The blue parrot
Bostanai
The boy who found fear
The boy with the moon on his fore-head
The Brahmin and the villain
Bran, son of Llyr
The brave little prince
Bukango and the crocodiles
The bundles of straw and the king's son
The calm Brahman
The captain's goose
The cat with the crooked tail
Cenerentola
Chandasimha, his son and their two wives
The chief of the Guernsi
The choosing of the high-king of Erin
Cinder Joe becomes king
The city east of the moon and south of the sun
The city under the sea
The clever lass

Kings and Queens (*Continued*)

The clever peasant girl
The clever weaver
Cobblers do not judge above the shoe
Corvetto
The country of the mice
The cuckoo and the clock
Damian and the dragon
The dancing water, (the) singing apple,
 and (the) speaking bird
The dark king
The date gatherers
The day of the scholars
The decision
Doctor know all
The dog king in Denmark
Donal O'Ciaran from Connaught
Donkey skin
Dookiram, the poor one
Double Arend of Meedan
Down to Arabia
Drakestail
The dream
The dutiful daughter
The eight leaves of story (4) A harp
 on the water
The elephant's bathtub
The endless tale
Esther . . . who saved her people
The faithful friend
The farmer's clever daughter
The feathers from the bird Venus
The fickleness of fortune
Fior Usga
Five lies that could be true
The flea
The flower-headed man
The fool of God
Foolish kings
The fortune of the poet's son
The fowler, the parrot and the king
The friendly frog
The full moon
The geese and the golden chain
Giacco and his bean
The gift and the giver
A gift for a gift
The gift of gold
The gift of the holy man
The girl without hands
Go Zu-Mong, King of Goguryo
Gobborn seer
The goblin bridge
The gold-rich king
The golden bird
The golden chain
The golden cockerell
The golden deer
The golden-headed fish
The golden peacock

The golden prince of the conch shell
The golden stag
The golden touch; the king who wor-
 shipped gold
Goto, king of the land and the water
Granny Shelock
The grateful animals and the talisman
Greedy and speedy
The green-bearded king
The green sergeant
Greyman
The griffon
Gudrun
The happy cure
The hare's kidneys
The haughty princess
The hazel-nut child
The hoard
The horse of seven colors
The house without eyes or ears
How Conor MacNessa became King of
 Ulster
How people became different
How poverty was revealed to the
 King of Adja
How the king chose a daughter-in-law
I don't know where and I don't know
 what
The impudent little mouse
In those days
Intelligence and luck
The invisible baby
The invisible silk robe
Iron, steel and strongest-of-all
It is foolish to carry matters to
 extremes
It's all the fault of Adam
The jackal and the elephant
The jellyfish's journey
Jester who herded the hares
John the true
Jonnikin and the flying basket
Karl the Great and the robber
The knight of the glen's steed o' bells
Kojata
The land of youth
The land ship
Lars, my lad!
The laughing statue
Lazy Peter and the king
The little bird's rice
The little dressmaker
The little fairy
Little Kathy free-as-the-wind
The little king on the Viking ship
The little shepherd's dream
Lord Kirshna or The eighth child
The lucky shirt
The lute player
The magic calabash
The magic mare

Kings and Queens (*Continued*)

The magic mirror
The magic mortar
The maiden Suvarna
The man who was only three inches tall
March's ears
The master cat
The messenger
A midsummer night's dream
Mighty Mikko
The miller-king
The miller of the dee
The miracle of the begging bowl
The miracle of the Poor Island
Molly Whuppie
The monkey king's bridge
Nala and Damayanti
Nicola Pesce
The nightingale Hazaran
An old king and his three sons of England
Other wise men of Gotham
Pappa Greatnose
The parson and the sexton
The pastor and the sexton
The peasant and his three sons
Petit Jean and the frog
The philosophers of King Darius
The pillow talk
Pinkel
Pintosmalto
The Prince Fernando
Prince Mirko
Prince Wicked
The prince's revenge
The princess and the glass mountain
The princess and the vagabone
Princess Rosette
The princess who loved her father like salt
The princess who was dumb
The proud king
Puss in boots
The queen and the golden egg
Queen o' the tinkers
The Queen of Underland
The queen's care
The queen's necklace
Ramiro II, the monk
The raven
Red king and green king
The red king and the witch
Rhitta of the beards
Robert of Sicily . . . The proudest king
Robin Hood
The royal banquet
The royal waistcoat
Rumpelstiltzkin
Rustem and his rose-colored steed

Saint Patrick and the Hill of Tara
Salt and bread
The salt at dinner
Scurvyhead
The secret-keeping boy
The secretive little boy and his little sword
The self-propelled carriage
Seven Simons
Seven sons
Shah Abbas and the cobbler
The shepherd of clouds
The sheriff complains to the king
The shipwrecked prince
The silver jug
The silver penny
The silver ship
The singing flute
Sir Orfeo
Sister Alionushka, brother Ivanushka
The slaying of Siegfried
The sleeping beauty in the wood
The sly thief of Valenciennes
The smart daughter
The snake in the bottle
Snow white and the seven dwarfs
The son of the hunter
The song of Gimmile
The speckled bull
The speech of beasts
The spider and the lizard
The stolen jewel
The stone in the cock's head
The stone of victory
The story of Branwen
The story of Cincinnatus
The story of Iubdan, King of lepra and the lepracaun
The story of the king who would be stronger than fate
The storyteller
The student who was forced to be king
The stupid boy
The stupid fellow
Stupid Peruonto
The sun-king's hair
The sun, the moon and the star of morning
Sungold and the remarkable cow
Swift-as-the-wind, Hold fast, and Hard-as-iron
A swift messenger
The sword of Damocles; the man who would be king
The sword of light
The sword of the stone
The tale of a Pakistan parrot
The tale of a proverb
The tale of a rich king: The treasure of Rhampinitis
The tale of Columba and the angel

Kings and Queens (*Continued*)

The tale of Nornagest
The tale of the Balaton
The tale of the Gaberlunzie men
The tale of the Laird of Logie
The tale of the little mook
The talkative king
The talkative tortoise
The talking tree
Tam and Tessa
Tatterhood
Tavadan and the fire giant
The tempest
The Thanksgiving of the Wazir
There is only one pretty child in the
  world and every mother has it
The third witch
The thirteenth son of the King of
  Erin
Thorsteinn Shiver
The thoughtless abbot
The three apples
The Three Fates
The three golden eggs
The three golden hairs
The three golden hairs of Grandad Sol
The three little men in the wood
The three plagues of Britain
The three princesses of Whiteland
The three ravens
The three teeth of the king
The three traveling artisans
The thunder cat
Ti-Tiriti-Ti
The tiny bird and the king
The tipsy rooster
Tom Thumb
Tom Tit Tot
Toontoony pie
The tortoise-wife
The treasure chamber of Rhampsinitus
Tredeschin
Tricky Peik
The truthful peasant
Tsar Boris and the devil king
The twelve young boys with golden
  hair
The twin brothers
The two kings
The two wizards
The tyrant who became a just ruler
The tyrannical king
The ugly king
Uncle Bouqui and little malice
The unpunctual minister, or The Bo-
  sung pohoo
The vain king
The valiant tailor
The vengeance of Kriemhild
The Vetāla's stories

Volund the smith
The water of life
The welcome
The well o' the world's end
The well of D'yeree-in-Dowan
The werewolf
Westwoods
Where Arthur sleeps
The white bride and the black bride
Why ants have small waists
The will of the wise man
The winter's tale
The witch and the swan maiden
The witch of Wandaland
With and without
The wonderful bed
The woodman and the fox
Written in the stars
You have a napkin
Young Conall of Howth

The king's black curtain
  DAVIS – LION'S p26-28

The king's cream
  MY BOOK HOUSE v. 6 p209-221

The king's daughter cries for the moon
  FARJEON – LITTLE p7-31

The king's dream
  TOOZE – WONDER. p43-49

The king's drum
  COURLANDER – KING'S p32-35

The king's friend
  PICARD – LADY p111-138
  WYATT – GOLDEN p93-97

The king's hares
  BAKER – GOLDEN p9-18
  THOMPSON – ONE p258-265

The king's haughtiness punished. *See*
  The king on trial

The king's jewels
  LEACH – SOUP p45.

The king's joke
  MAR – CHINESE p21-27

The king's rabbits
  PROTTER – CHILD. p31-40

The king's remorse
  GRAY – INDIA'S p26-31

The king's rice pudding
  LEEUW – LEGENDS p57-59

The king's son and the straw hat maker
URE – RUMANIAN p117-125

The king's thief
McNEILL – DOUBLE p122-128

The king's tower
U. N. – RIDE p265-267

The king's true children
SPELLMAN – BEAUT. p49-55

The king's vine
ĆURĆIJA – YUGOSLAV p100-109

Kingsley, Charles
Adventures of a water baby
The golden fleece
How the goddess of spring came to
Scoring

Kinsella, Hazel Gertrude
The first buttercups

Kipling, Rudyard
The ballad of east and west
How the camel got his hump
Mowgli's brothers
The potted princess

Kipling, Rudyard
JOHNSON – PRINC. p311-312

Kirkyards. See Cemeteries

Kirsten McVurich
LAWSON – STRANGE p69-80

Kisander
SHERLOCK – ANANSI p35-40

A kiss from the beautiful Fiorita
TOOR – GOLDEN p81-90

Kisses
The forgotten bride
Margrette
The swineherd

Kitava the gambler
GRAY – INDIA'S p172-180

Kites
The boy who wouldn't give up
Calabash of the winds

Kites (birds)
The cock who went traveling
The dilemma of a pious man
The hawk fledgling
Legend of the first Filipinos

The kittel-kittel car
MANNING – DEVILS p87-97

Kittelsen, Theodor
The Norwegian folk tales and their
illustrators

The kitten and falling leaves
MY BOOK HOUSE v. 3 p133.

The kitten and the knitting needles
BAMBERGER – FIRST p110-111

Kletke, H.
The magic swan

The kling kling bird
SHERLOCK – ANANSI p41-46

Knapsacks
Beppo Pipetta and his knapsack
The old soldier and the mischief
The soldier and the knapsack
The wonderful knapsack

Kneading-troughs
Boots and the troll

The kneeler's twelve tasks
GRINGHUIS – GIANTS p39-45

The kneeling tree
SPICER – KNEELING p15-28

Knees
Barker's knee

The knife
MÜLLER – SWISS p138-141

The knight
MY BOOK HOUSE v. 4 p129.
KRYLOV – 15 p21-23

The knight and the naiad of the lake
PICARD – FAUN p181-189

The knight and the palfrey
CARPENTER – HORSES p172-182

The knight of La Sarraz
MÜLLER – SWISS p97-100

364

The knight of Staufenberg
PICARD – GERMAN p161-166

The knight of Steenhuisheerd
LEEUW – LEGENDS p104-108

The knight of the almond blossom
WILLIAMS – OLD p51-59

The knight of the glen's steed o' bells
McMANUS – HIBERIAN p74-84

The knight with the two swords
WESTWOOD – MEDIEVAL p31-39

Knights and knighthood
See also **Arthur, King**
The Ailpein bird, the stolen princess,
and the brave knight
Aliosha's visit to the bald mountain
Arthur, King of Britain
Atlantes and the hippogriff
The baron's haughty daughter
The bashful prince
Beaumains . . . The knightly kitchen-
boy
Bernardo and the red knight
The black spider
A cavalier tune
Chourilo's little comb
The death of Uwaine
Dietrich is knighted
Dobryna's embassy to Khan Amryl
The double knights
The dragon of Rhodes
The elfin knight
Emma of Haarlem
Eppelin of Gailingen
The false knight
The fig bough
Gareth and Linette
Gawaine and the green knight
Geraint and Enid
Geraint and the knight of the sparrow-
hawk
The green knight
The hairy-armed ogre of Kyoto
He who laughs last
How Arthur gained Excalibur
How Dounai won a bride for Prince
Vladimir
How Galahad came to Arthur's court
How Guenevere went a-maying
How Percival came to Arthur's court
How three pilgrims called Ilya to the
rescue of Kiev
How Tristram fought against the
knight from Ireland

Kalamona and the winds
Karl the great and the robber
King Arthur . . . The shield and the
hammer
The lad and his animals
The lady of the linden tree
Lancelot and Elaine
Lancelot and Gawaine
Lancelot of the lake
Lancelot . . . The lady of Shalott
Little one eye, little two eyes, and
little three eyes
The loathly lady
Lohengrin
The magic fife
The marriage of Arthur
The marriage of Gawaine
The marriage of Sir Gawain
Nikita and the last of the dragons
The one-eyed ogre of Sessay
Opportunity
The palace of the white cat
A perfect knight
Potok's dancing and the snakes
Prince Ahmed
The princess and the dwarf
The princess and the glass mountain
The princess on the Glass Hill
The princess on the glass mountain
The riddle of the black knight
Robin Hood
Robin Hood and Sir Richard at the
lee
A Roland for an Oliver
St. George and the dragon
Samson and the doll in green and
brown
The sea knight
Serbian knights and outlaws
The simple maid of Hunsingoo
Sir Beaumains, the kitchen knight
Sir Bevis of Hampton
Sir Gawain and the green knight
Sir Goldenhair
Sir Launfal
Sir Perceval
Sir Walter Raleigh
Souchmant's trial and triumph
The story of Bensurdatu
The story of Prince Ahmed
The story of Ywenec
Stretch, Puff, and Blazer
Surprising adventures of Don Quixote
of La Mancha
The sword in the stone
The tale of the knight and the shepherd
lass
Tam Lin
Tarn Wethelan
The tournament in Ireland
The treachery of Morgan LeFay

Knights and Knighthood (*Continued*)

Tristram and Isolt
Una and the Red Cross knight
Uwaine and the lady of the fountain
Vassily and Curly Head the brigand
Volkh's journey to the east
Why a lady sits next to a knight at
table
Winkle, Tinkle, and Twinkle
Young Bekie
Young Michael and the uninvited
guest
The Young Tamlin

The knights of the silver shield
MY BOOK HOUSE v. 7 p173-181

Knitting
The kitten and the knitting needles
The shepherd who fought the March
wind
The widow's lazy daughter

—Needles
The little cat and the knitting
needle

Knitting still
MY BOOK HOUSE v. 1 p128.

Knives
Bendebukk
The chief's knife
The enchanted knife
The four brothers
The groach of the Isle of Lok
Guno and Koyo and the Kris
How Celebes got its name
How the rajah got rich
The Kamiah monster
The Kris of Adji Saka
The luck boy of Toy Valley
Maid Lena
The old woman and the thief
The sleeping prince
Stone patience and knife patience
A stork is not always a stork
A strange choice
A tale of a dog's tail
To your good health
Why a lady sits next to a knight at
table
The witch of Lok Island
Wokun

Knobs, bed
The magic bed-knob

Knock on wood
BATCHELOR — SUPER. p111-112

"Knockers"
Barker's knee

The knockers of Ballowal
MANNING — PETER p64-71

Knots, Gordian
The Gordian knot; the destiny of
Alexander
A horse afraid of his shadow

Know your own strength
DAVIS — LION'S p80-84

Knowledge
See also **Wisdom**
The birth and boyhood of Finn
Bragi, god of poetry
The demon with the matted hair
Doctor know-all
The doctor who knew everything
Good sense and good fortune
The man who feared nothing
The merchant with nothing to sell
One grain more than the devil
The prince of the six weapons
Prince Prigio
The two brothers and the magistrate

Knowledge and luck
BULATKIN — EURASIAN p114-119

Knurremurre
MANNING — DWARFS p9-13

Knurremurre the troll
BELTING — CAT p21-27

Ko-pa-ta, the gambling god
RUSHMORE — DANCING p88-102

Kobolds (fairies)
The honey feast

Kodiak Island
The man who killed the sea monster
The man who married a snow goose

Koi and the kola nuts
AARDEMA — STORY p54-61

Koichi and the mountain god
UCHIDA — SEA p121-132

Kojata
MANNING — WIZARDS p95-108

Kola nuts
Koi and the kola nuts

Konkadet (sea monsters)
The false shaman
The nose of the konkadet

Kookooburras (birds)
The frog that swallowed the ocean

Korea
The aged father
The ants and the hare
Au Sung meets Kim Lee
The bald old man
The bedbug, the house, and the flea
The blind man and the devils
A boy and a beggar
The bride who would not speak
Butterflies
The cat and the dog
A clever old bride
The curse on the only son
Dan-Gun, first King of Korea
The deer and the snake
The deer, the hare, and the toad
The dutiful daughter
A dutiful son
Fate and the faggot gatherer
The fire dogs
A foolish mourner
Four sworn brothers
The fox-girl and her brother
General Pumpkin
The geomancer's three sons
Go Zu-Mong, King of Goguryŏ
The goblin bridge
The governor and the Buddhist
A grain of millet
The grave of a faithful dog
The great flood
The green frog
The heavenly maiden and the wood-
cutter
Hong Do-Ryŏng, the filial tiger
How Au Sung repaid Kim Lee
How foolish men are!
Hwan and Dang
The jewel of the fox's tongue
The judgements of a magistrate
Kahukura and the fairies
Keel-Wee, a Korean Rip Van Winkle
The Lake of Zanazĕ
Lazybones
The legend of Marshal Gang Gam-Czan
The legend of Zŏn U-Czi
The legend of the virgin Arang
The locust, the ant, and the kingfisher
The magic amber
The magic cap
The mallet of wealth
The man who feared nothing
The man who wanted to bury his son

The mast of sand
Mother tells a story
The mountain and the rivers
The mountain witch and the dragon-
king
The mud-snail fairy
Nails
The nine-headed giant
The nine-tailed fox
An old Korean story
The old tiger and the hare
The onion and the rose
Onions
The pheasant, the dove, the magpie
and the rat
The pheasants and the bell
Pigling and her proud sister
Poisonous persimmons
The rat's bridegroom
The revenge of the serpent
Rival magicians
The scholar of Kosei
The secret royal inspector, Bag Mun-Su
A selfish husband
The seven stars of the north
The sheep is the cousin of the ox
The statue that sneezed
The stone memorial to a dog
The story of a gentleman
The story of Admiral Yi
The story of General Gim Dŏg-Nyŏng
The story of Hong Gil-Dong
The story of Zibong
The story-spirits
The sun and the moon
Sweet dung, the cake-tree, and the
bugle of life
A talkative old woman
Three corpses, money, and a wine-
bottle
Three foolish brides
Three foolish wives
The three sons
The three stars
The three unmarried ministers
Three who found their heart's desire
The three wishes
The tiger and the dwarf
The tiger and the persimmon
The tiger-girl
The tiger priest
Tiger woman
The tiger's grave
The tiger's whisker
The toad-bridegroom
The traveller, the fox, and the tiger
The two brothers and the magistrate
Two lies
The two sisters, Rose and Lotus
Two unfaithful husbands
The ungrateful tiger

Korea (*Continued*)
The unmarried girl's grave
The valley of 10,000 waterfalls
Which was witch?
The white-eared tiger
Why frogs croak in wet weather
The wife from another world
The wife from heaven
Yi Chang and the haunted house
Yoni and her stepmother
The young gentleman and the tiger
Young Gim and the robbers
The young man and the priest
The young widow
Zo Han-Zun, who became a stone
Buddha
−Diamond Mountains
The valley of ten thousand water-
falls
−Seoul
The castle of Seoul
The centipede girl
The police marshal

The Korean goblins
ANDERSON − BOY p59-76

Korean map of tales
INS-SÖB − FOLK p2.

Korrigans (Little People)
Goblin gold
The widow and the Korrigans, The
Little People of Brittany

The Kraken
BUEHR − SEA p35-47
MANNING − BEASTS p224-225

Krakens (sea monsters)
A school of sea monsters

Kralyevich and the Vila
ĆURČIJA − HEROES p58-60

Kralyevich Marko
ĆURČIJA − HEROES p55-108

Kralyevich Marko abolishes the wedding-
tax
ĆURČIJA − HEROES p95-99

Kralyevich Marko and Ali-Aga
ĆURČIJA − HEROES p77-79

Kralyevich Marko and Mina of Kostur
ĆURČIJA − HEROES p80-86

Kralyevich Marko and Mussa Kessedzhiya
ĆURČIJA − HEROES p100-108

Kralyevich Marko and the Arab
ĆURČIJA − HEROES p87-94

Kralyevich Marko and the eagle
ĆURČIJA − HEROES p61-62

Kralyevich Marko drinks wine during the
Ramadhan
ĆURČIJA − HEROES p68-70

Kralyevich Marko recognizes his father's
sabre
ĆURČIJA − HEROES p63-66

Kralyevich Marko's death
ĆURČIJA − HEROES p105-108

Kralyevich Marko's ploughing
ĆURČIJA − HEROES p67.

Kralyevich Marko's wedding
ĆURČIJA − HEROES p71-76

Krazy Kat
MY BOOK HOUSE v. 2 p172-175

Krencipal and Krencipalka
BAKER − TALKING p204-209
HAVILAND − POLAND p28-37

The Kris of Adji Saka
COURLANDER − KANT. p85-87

Krises. *See* **Knives**

Krishna (god)
Khrishna the cowherd
Why the moon wanes

Kristina and the devil
PROTTER − CHILD. p124-129

Krueger, Kermit
KRUEGER − SERPENT p159.

Krylov, Ivan Andreevich
The elephant at court
The geese
The little chest
Misuse of a name
The quartet
Three fables
The wolf and the cat

Krylov, Ivan Andreevich
KRYLOV − 15 p38-39

Kuhreihen
How the Kuhreihen began

Kuluile, the dancing girl
GUIRMA – TALES p16-28

Kuna (Island)
The monster mo-o

Kunikdjuaq, a bear story of the
Inuit
LEACH – RAINBOW p275-276

Kupti and Imani
LANG – OLIVE p176-187

A Kupua plays tricks
THOMPSON – HAWAII. p45-52

Kupuas
The gift of the hairy one
Hog child plays tricks

Kuratko the terrible
HAVILAND – CZECH. p21-33
FILLMORE – SHEPHERD'S p82-86

Kutlee-Seek-Vik
OMAN – ESKIMO p33-36

Kuzenko sudden-wealthy
WYNDHAM – RUSS. p44-59

Kuzma'get-rich-quick
DUDDINGTON – RUSS. p31-37

Kwaku Ananse and the donkey
APPIAH – ANANSE p71-87

Kwaku Ananse and the greedy lion
APPIAH – ANANSE p27-37

Kwaku Ananse and the rain maker
APPIAH – ANANSE p113-121

Kwaku Ananse and the whipping cord
APPIAH – ANANSE p57-69

Kwang Hing, the book lover
ALEXANDER – PEBBLES p20.

L

La Fontaine, Jean de
The acorn and the pumpkin
The cormorant and the fishes
The crow and the fox
The fox and the crow
The fox and the grapes
The honest woodman
The pig, the goat and the sheep
The rats in council
The raven and the fox
The thief and the donkey
The wolf turned shepherd

La Fontaine, Jean de
Fables and fabulists

La Vieja y Su Cabra. *See* The fig tree

Laban (drink)
A dish of laban

Labor. *See* **Work**

The labors of Hercules
MY BOOK HOUSE v. 9 p151-163

Lace
More beautiful than the spider's web
Snow-White and the seven dwarfs
The white spider's gift

The lad and his animals
MANNING – GIANNI p76-86

The lad and the fox
HAVILAND – NORWAY p30-32

The lad and the north wind
HAVILAND – NORWAY p67-74

Lad Carl
JONES – SCAND. p77-83

The lad who returned from Faerye
JONES – WELSH p164-168

The lad who went to the north wind
ARBUTHNOT – TIME p74-75
ASBJÖRNSEN – EAST p23-27
BROWN – AROUND p69-79
LINES – TALES p66-69

Ladders
Drakestail
Walking under ladders

The ladle that fell from the moon
HSIEH – CHINESE p24-27

Ladles
The three petitions

The lads who met the highwaymen
LEODHAS – GHOSTS p91-102

The lady and the devil
HASKETT – GRAINS p68-70

The lady and the toad
McNEILL – SUNKEN p58-64

Ladybirds
Fairy forests
To the lady-bird

"Lady Day" (holiday)
The field of Boliauns

Lady Eaton's curse
TAFT – PROFILE p121-130

Lady Eleanore's mantle
TAFT – PROFILE p144-148

Lady Melicent
PICARD – LADY p181-203

Lady Morris in her mansion
JAGENDORF – UPSTATE p57-59

The lady of Stavoren
U. N. – RIDE p178-185

Lady of the lake
The bride of Llyn y Fan Fach
How Arthur gained Excalibur
The knight with the two swords

Lady of the lake
NYE – MARCH p32-45

The lady of the linden tree
PICARD – LADY p1-13

The lady of the wood
GARNER – GOBLINS p56-61

The lady of Tylwyth Teg
PALMER – FAIRY p50-54

Lafitte, Jean
The privateer turned patriot

Lagoons
The haunted lagoon
The seven dead men of the Venetian
lagoon

The Laidley worm of Spindlestone Heugh
FINLAY – FOLK p66-75
WILLIAMS – FAIRY p306-311

The Laird o'Co
See also The farmer of Deunant; Sir
Godfrey Macullock
BRIGGS – PERS. p97-98

The Laird of Abbotsford
MY BOOK HOUSE v. 12 p108-109

The lairdie with the heart of gold
LEODHAS – HEATHER p45-59

Lairds
The lass that lost the laird's daughter
The tale of the Laird of Logie

The laird's lass and the gobha's son
LEODHAS – THISTLE p17-38

Laka and the Little-People
WHEELER – HAWAII. p213-232

The lake lady
WILLIAMS – FAIRY p255-262

The lake maiden
MANNING – MERMAIDS p114-121

The Lake of Zangzĕ
INS-SŎB – FOLK p45-46

Lake people
The princess and the scarf

The lake that flew
CREDLE – TALL p96-99

Lakes
See also Names of countries, sub-
division name of lake
The beginning of the Narran Lake
Belena
The blue lake
The boy and Necken
A boy of the lake country
The castle in the lake
Chien Tang
The children of Lir

Cliff dweller
The cock is crowing
The destiny of Princess Tien Dung
The fairy garden
The forgotten bride
The frog-wife
The golden ax
The golden lotus
Hiawatha's fasting
The honest woodman
How the giant Finn made the Isle of
Man
How the rabbit fooled the elephant
The hungry old witch
Itsayaya and the chokecherries
Itsayaya and the otter
Jankyn and the witch
King Fergus and the water-horse
The King of Araby's daughter
The knight and the Naiad of the lake
The light princess
The magic lake
The mysterious lake
Naba Zid-Wendé
Near God's cactus
The origin of the Lake of Vitte
The sacred fish of Palamon
The search for the magic lake
Shingebiss
The spirit's drum
The tale of the Balaton
The waters beneath: Fifty young men
and a turtle
The waters beneath: The underwater
village
The weeping lady of Llyn Glasfryn
The witch of Lok Island

Lamas
The ogre king of Gilgit

Lamb, Charles and Mary
The winter's tale

The lamb with the golden fleece
THOMPSON – ONE p265-267

Lambs. *See* **Sheep**

The Lambton worm
BRIGGS – PERS. p179-183
JACOBS – MORE p215-221
WILLIAMS – OLD p1-12

The lame cat and the potter
WYATT – GOLDEN p101-106

The lame dog
BAKER – TALKING p77-87

The lame duck
  DUDDINGTON – RUSS. p25-27
  TUDOR – TASHA p75-78

Lame tame crane
  MY BOOK HOUSE v. 1 p95.

The lame vixon
  MANNING – BEASTS p209-223

The lamentable story of Connlach, son of Cuchulain
  GARNIER – LEGENDS p151-156

Lamps
  See also Lanterns
  Aladdin and his wonderful lamp
  Aladdin and the wonderful lamp
  The baby that was sold
  Bendebukk
  Esben and the witch
  The girl who overpowered the moon
  How dandelions were made
  The magic lamp
  The magician returns
  New lamps for old
  The princess
  The slave of the lamp
  The slave of the ring
  The underground palace

  –Wicks
  Pinocchio

Lancashire –––?
  HOPE-SIMPSON – CAVAL. p201-202

Lancashire–fiction
  HOPE-SIMPSON – CAVAL. p198-201

Lancelot, Sir
  The end of Arthur
  The fair maid of Astolat
  The healing of Urre
  The poisoned apple

Lancelot and Elaine
  PICARD – STORIES p75-81

Lancelot and Galahad
  PICARD – STORIES p181-193

Lancelot and Gawaine
  PICARD – STORIES p274-282

Lancelot and Guenever
  PICARD – STORIES p251-262

Lancelot of the lake
  PICARD – STORIES p65-74

Lancelot . . . The lady of Shalott
  UNTERMEYER – FIRE. p172-176

The land beyond the fire
  PICARD – MERMAID p205-218

Land. See Earth

"Land of Bliss"
  The search for the land of bliss

The land of the dead
  GREEN – TALES p126-134

The land of the Hopis
  COURLANDER – PEOPLE p7-9

Land of wonders
  JAGENDORF – UPSTATE p186-188

The land of youth
  HACK – DANISH p75-89

The land ship
  McNEILL – SUNKEN p12-23

Land, water and wind
  GREEN – BIG p27-30

The land where there were no old men
  URE – RUMANIAN p169-171

Landlords
  The ass that lays money
  The donkey, the table, and the stick
  A fair distribution
  The giant who took a long time to grow
  The gift of the holy man
  The green grass bottle
  How one should carve a goose
  The king who rides a tiger
  The lad and the north wind
  The lad who went to the north wind
  The magician's revenge
  Sinko's luck
  The story of silly Cham-ba
  The string of lies
  Tregeagle
  The wonderful knapsack

The lady who put salt in her coffee
  ARBUTHNOT – TIMEp356-358

The lady's loaf-field
  LEODHAS – GAELIC p68-74

The lady's quest
GRAY – MAINLY p125-141

The lady's room
FARJEON – LITTLE p138-141

Landowners
The rich landowner and his worker
The tale of frost and his neighbors

Lang, Andrew
On fairy stories
Prince Prigio
Prince Prigio and the firedrake
The spell-song
The story of Sigurd
The witch in the stone boat

Lang, Andrew
JOHNSON – HARPER p324-325
SIDEMAN – WORLD'S p831.

Lang, Mrs. Andrew
The return of the land-otter

Langer, Susanne K.
The crystal bowl

Langer, Susanne K.
JOHNSON – HARPER p325-326

Landobards
Frigg and the goddesses

Language
See also **Animals–Language; Birds–Language;** etc.
The boy and the cloth
The Haitians in the Dominican Republic
How pictures became words
How the people came from the lower world

The language of animals
JACOBS – EUROPE. p66-71
THOMPSON – ONE p303-306

The language of the birds
GILSTRAP – SULTAN'S p88-95

Lanka (Island). *See* **Sinbala (Island)**

Lanterns
Fish story
The girl who used her wits

The honest ghost
Pinkel
The river of lantern land
A story for Kiem

Lao Lai-Tse, the tactful
ALEXANDER – PEBBLES p21.

Laos
The beggar and the rice
Dinner for the monk
The elephant's lip

Lapland
Dog luck
The giant outwitted
The giant's bride
The lazy men who married the sun's daughter
The lovesick giant
The mermaid and the boy
The old woman swims the sea
The troll who hid his life
Volund the smith
Why the bear's tail is short

Large cabbages
HSIEH – CHINESE p13-15

The lark and her young ones
GREEN – BIG p38-39

The lark, the wolf, and the fox
HAVILAND – POLAND p39-54

Larks (skylarks)
Answer to a child's question
The eagle and the lark
The giant archer of the sky
Saint Patrick and the Hill of Tara
The singing chameleon
There was an old man with a beard

Lars, my lad!
HAVILAND – SWEDEN p60-92

Lars, my servant
PROTTER – CHILD. p9-20

The lass and her good stout blackthorn stick
LEODHAS – TWELVE p147-160

The lass that couldn't be frighted
LEODHAS – HEATHER p69-79

The lass that lost the laird's daughter
LEODHAS – SEA p53-71

The lass who went out at the cry of
dawn
  LEODHAS – THISTLE p62-73

Lassoing
  Pecos Bill
  Pecos Bill and his bouncing bride

The last battle
  PILKINGTON – THREE p209-217

The last of the dragons
  MANNING – BEASTS p14-25

The last of the giants
  SHEPPARD – SCOT. p85-88

The last of the thunderbirds
  MELZACK – DAY p85-92

The last ship
  TOLKIEN – READER (Part 4) p61-
  64

The last three guessses
  FARJEON – SILVER p174-179

The last treachery
  SAWYER – DIETRICH p170-190

The last word of a bluebird as told to a
child
  CATHON – PERHAPS p169.

Late
  MY BOOK HOUSE v. 2 p153.

Lato, the stupid one
  HITCHCOCK – KING p101-110

Latvia
  The angry baron
  The bad-tempered wife
  The bird and the man
  The devil and the pit
  The devil's bride
  The devil's partnership
  Fiddler John and the devil
  The fox and the cock
  The giant beanstalk
  Good advice
  Good luck and bad luck
  The guest from Heaven
  The hunting cat
  The insatiable beggar
  The king on trial
  Mother luck
  One-eye, two-eyes, and three-eyes
  The poor brother's bad luck

The princess on the glass mountain
The silly goose war
The three cups of water
Tit for tat
Why dogs and cats are not friends
The wolf and the ram

"Laughing Jackasses." *See* Kingfishers,
Australian

The laughing merman
  McNEILL – SUNKEN p36-39

Laughing song
  MY BOOK HOUSE v. 2 p75.

The laughing statue
  HODGES – SEREND. p97-116

Laughter
  The animal languages
  The bee, the harp, the mouse, and
  the bum-clock
  The bee, the mouse and the bum-
  clock
  Big Matsiko
  The billy goat and the king
  The frog that swallowed the ocean
  God hath made me to laugh
  The hare's lip
  It is God that made us
  The kling kling bird
  The lamb with the golden fleece
  The light princess
  Little Hansworst
  The magic swan
  Maui and the death goddess
  Pacala and Tandala
  The ram with the golden fleece
  The right time to laugh
  Skade, the ski-goddess
  The sleigh ride
  Songs of joy from the Bible
  The tale of Godfrey Malbone
  Taper Tom
  Taper-Tom who made the princess
  laugh
  The three laughs of the leipreachan
  Two friends: how they parted
  The unsmiling princess
  Why the hare's lip is split

Launfal, Sir
  Sir Launfal

Laurel
  Apollo and Daphne . . . The laurel
  wreath
  The great flood

Laurel (*Continued*)

Indian legends of shrubs in our gardens
The twelve dancing princesses

The laurel maiden
BELTING – THREE p47-53

Laurin (dwarf king)
Emperor of Rome
King Laurin goes awooing

Lavender's blue
MY BOOK HOUSE v. 1 p56.

Law
See also **Judges and justice; Lawyers**
Ero and the Kadi
The fire on the mountain
The jackal's lawsuit
The kaola bear and the tribal laws
Njal the lawyer
Upa and her admirers
Why the scroll of the law fell to the ground

Lawkamercyme
JACOBS – MORE p65-66

Lawson, Marie A.
The strange ship of Captain Fokke

Lawson, Robert
Willie's bad night

Lawyers
Clever Manka
The legend of the governor and the lawyer
The merchant, Saint Michael, and the devil
Pacala the lawyer
The ring in the porridge bowl
The three butchers from Reims

The lay of Prince Igor
DOWNING – RUSSIAN p81-93

Lazarus, Emma
The new colossus

Lazarus and the dragons
McNEILL – SUNKEN p108-113

The laziest man in the world
LIN – MILKY p47-50

Laziness
See also **Procrastination**
Alas!
All change
Allah will provide
The ass that was flayed
The beggar and the rice
Betty Stogs' baby
Chin-Chin Kobakama
The cock and the neighbour's hen
The cock, the mouse, and the little red hen
The devil and the pit
Dobryna's embassy to Khan Amryl
Elsa and the ten elves
Fareedah's carpet
Fiddivaw
The first shlemiel
Fool's paradise
Gift for the lazy
The girl who could spin clay and straw into gold
Gulam . . . The jar of rice
Hani the simple
Hans Hansen's hired girl
Hecho the lazy
The home of the saints
How baboons came into the world
How Brer Rabbit met Brer tar-baby
How God helped Mammo
How the camel got his hump
How the monkey came to be
The idle boy
The jackal and the bear
The just judgment
The Kildare pooka
The king's drum
The laughing statue
Legend of the first Filipinos
Lie-a-stove
The little black book of magic
Little Boy Blue
Little Johnny Sheepskin
The little nenehunes
The loafer
The louse and the fingernail
The luck fairies
Madschun
The miser's wife
Mr. Frost
Nazar the brave
The never never land
The owl's answer to Tommy
Peter and the witch of the wood
Pinocchio
Porridge with a troll
Quinces and oranges
Rabbit and the grain buyers
The rabbit and the tar wolf
The rubber man
Ruddy-my-beard

Laziness (*Continued*)

A rupee earned
Saint Michael and the idle husband
Shaydoola
The sigakok bird
Silian the stork
The snow-wife
The spoiled daughter
The story of a lazy man
The story of Cozumel, the lazy
   swallow
The story of Li'l Hannibal
Stupid Peruonto
The tale of the silver saucer and the
   russet apple
The ten dwarfs of Aunt Greenwater
The thirteen flies
The thoughtless abbot
The three bugganes
Tim for wealth and happiness
The tufty hen
The two brothers and the ghost Mo'oi
Utzel and his daughter Poverty
The well of immortality
Why the hyrax has no tail
The widow's daughter
The widow's lazy daughter
The woman in moon
The would-be wizard

The lazy boy
   THOMPSON – ONE p308-309

The lazy cat
   BELTING – CAT p67-72

The lazy fox
   BARLOW – LATIN p23-27

The lazy gardener and the little red man
   SPELLMAN – BEAUT. p15-18

Lazy Hans
   HACK – DANISH p129-133
   MANNING – WITCHES p27-37

The lazy hornet
   CATHON – PERHAPS p86-88

Lazy lout of a plant
   JORDAN – BURRO p39-41

The lazy maiden
   BORSKI – GOOD p20-25

The lazy man
   TASHJIAN – THREE p3-6

The lazy man and the water spirit
   BURTON – MAGIC p24-29

The lazy man who married the sun's
   daughter
   JABLOW – MAN p81-82

Lazy old Mary
   MY BOOK HOUSE v. 1 p98.

The lazy one
   PRIDHAM – GIFT p138-142

Lazy Peter and his three-cornered hat
   ALEGRÍA – THREE p66-78

Lazy Peter and the king
   ALEGRÍA – THREE p111-114

Lazy Tom
   MARGOLIS – IDY p22-26

Lazy Tom keeps house
   MARGOLIS – IDY p27-35

The lazy woman
   RANKE – GERMANY p134.

Lazybones
   INS-SÖB – FOLK p189.

Le Fevre, Felicite
   The cock, the mouse, and the little
   red hen

Leach, Maria
   LEACH – LUCK p112.
   LEACH – RAINBOW p319.

Lead mines and mining
   Born to be rich
   I was traveling those parts

Leadership
   A boy on the high seas
   Buffalo Bill
   Exploring the wilderness
   How Beowulf delivered Heorot
   Joan of Arc
   Joseph and his brethren
   The knight
   The knights of the silver shield
   Marko, the champion of Serbian
      liberty
   Robert Bruce, Scotland's hero
   The wanderings of Aeneas
   The word of Igor's armament
   Ye merry doinges of Robin Hood
   Young midshipman David Farragut

Leaf by Niggle
   TOLKIEN – READER (Part 2)
   p85-112

A leak in an old house
PRATT – MAGIC unp.

Leaks
The boy hero of Harlem
The terrible leak

Leander, Richard
The wishing ring

Leaping
The six companions
The wild man

Lear, Edward
Nonsense rhymes
The owl and the pussy-cat
Please give me a ride on your back
There was an old man of Coblenz –
limerick
There was an old man with a beard

The learned cat
WYNDHAM – TALES p7.

Learning magic
WILLIAMS – OLD p131-135

The learned men
, COURLANDER – TIGER'S
p122-126

The learned young professor
DOBBS – MORE p39-42

Learning. See Knowledge; Scholarship;
Wisdom

Leather
Saint Martin and the honest man

Leave well enough alone
DOBBS – MORE p15-17

Leaves
Ah Tcha the sleeper
The boy and the leopard
Come, little leaves
The king of the leaves
Lazy Hans
Prince Hat beneath the earth
Rainbow and the autumn leaves
Tortoise and Babarinsa's daughters

, Copper
Katie Woodencloak

, Silver
Katie Woodencloak
The white parrot

Leaving paradise
FARJEON – LITTLE p149-173

Lebanon
The tail of St. George's dragon

Ledoux, Charles
Little Johnny Sheepskin

Lee, Robert E.
Robert E. Lee, a hero in war and
peace

Leealura and Maleyato
MELZACK – DAY p69-75

Leeds devil
The best devil in the land

Leeuw, Adele
The rain-lady and the ghost

Left eye, right eye
NYE – MARCH p54-61

A leg for the lion
ARNOTT – TALES p36-43

The leg of gold
MANNING – GHOSTS p124-127

The legend of Bala Lake
SHEPPARD – WELSH p78-81

The legend of Crooked Mountain
HAYES – INDIAN p17-29

The legend of Eilean Donan castle
WILSON – SCOTTISH p49-55

Legend of how ants came to earth
WYNDHAM – CHINA p55-62

A legend of Knockmany
DE REGNIERS – GIANT p109-124

A legend of Kotzebue
OMAN – ESKIMO p37-39

The legend of Llangorse Lake
SHEPPARD – WELSH p82-84

The legend of Marshal Gang Gam-Czan
INS-SOB – FOLK p56-58

The legend of Pasopati
LEEUW – INDO. p9-13

The legend of Pathasos
MATSON – LONGHOUSE p103-111

The legend of Peter Rugg
TAFT – PROFILE p169-174

The legend of Pitch Lake
JAGENDORF – KING p249-251

A legend of Saint Nicholas
LEEUW – LEGENDS p66-70

A legend of Tchi-Niu
BUCK – FAIRY p154-161

The legend of the almond tree
LOWE – LITTLE p50-51

The legend of the Arabian magician
IRVING – TALES p13-27

Legend of the arbutus
CATHON – PERHAPS p130-132

The legend of the chingola bird
U. N. – RIDE p213-214

Legend of the first Filipinos
SECHRIST – ONCE p3-7

A legend of the flowers
PARKER – AUSTRALIAN p113-117

The legend of the governor and the
lawyer
IRVING – TALES p113-121

The legend of the governor and the
veteran
IRVING – TALES p125-137

The legend of the hail
MATSON – LONGHOUSE p100-102

The legend of the Karang
LEEUW – INDO. p104-108

The legend of the magic lute
IRVING – TALES p99-109

The legend of the mason
IRVING – TALES p67-72

The legend of the Mayon volcano
ROBERTSON – PHILIP. p107-115

The legend of the Moor's legacy
IRVING – TALES p31-43

The legend of the mulberry tree
MONTROSE – WINTER p47-56

The legend of the narcissus
CATHON – PERHAPS p143-146

The legend of the palm tree
HARDENDORF – FROG'S p25-28

The legend of the Prince Ahmed Al Kamel
IRVING – TALES p75-96

The legend of the star children
MATSON – LONGHOUSE p61-74

The legend of the three beautiful
princesses
IRVING – TALES p47-64

The legend of the two discreet statues
IRVING – TALES p141-152

The legend of the virgin Arang
INS-SÖB – FOLK p121-123

Legend of the witch of Cape Ann
TAFT – PROFILE p149-152

The legend of Urashima
MARMUR – JAPAN. p17-24

The legend of William Tell
MY BOOK HOUSE v. 10 p44-47

The legend of Zon U-Czi
INS-SÖB – FOLK p224-234

A legendary land
TOOR – GOLDEN p121-190

Legends
JOHNSON – WHAT p259-265

Legs
The Hoca solves a problem
Skade, the ski-goddess
Snout the dwarf

, Golden
The leg of gold

, Three
The three-legged jumping giant

Leif the Lucky
The spell-song

Leif the Lucky . . . What he discovered
UNTERMEYER – FIRE. p164-166

The lemon and his army
CURCIJA – YUGOSLAV p112-119

Lemons and lemon trees
The three lemons

The lemur and the shrew
ELLIOTT – WHERE p79-86

Lemurs
What the lemur is saying at night

Length
How Ijapa, who was short, became
long
Long, broad and sharpsight

The length of life
SPELLMAN – BEAUT. p56-58

Lent
How Michael Scot went to Rome
Shrovetide

Leo the king
GRINGHUIS – GIANTS p46-49

Leodhas, Sorche Nic
The giant bones
Sandy Macneil and his dog

Leodhas, Sorche Nic
LEODHAS – TWELVE p167-173

Leon and the lion
LEACH – RAINBOW p295-297

Leonardson (Leonard, Lenorson), Samuel
The ordeal of Hannah Dustin

Leonidas
The brave three hundred

The leopard and the antelope
HOLLADAY – BANTU p63-65

The leopard and the bushbuck buy a drum
BURTON – MAGIC p41-43

The leopard and the bushbuck go hunting
BURTON – MAGIC p43-47

The leopard and the mouse deer
TOOZE – WONDER. p111-114

The leopard and the rabbit go courting
BURTON – MAGIC p89-94

The leopard and the tortoise
COBBLE – WEMBI p55-61

The leopard builds a house for the
bushbuck
BURTON – MAGIC p121-124

Leopards
All stories are Anansi's
Anansi and candlefly
Anansi hunts with tiger
Anansi's old riding-horse
The boy and the leopard
The cat who came indoors
Dinner with the tota
The donkey who sinned
The feast for the fox
The girl who forgot her hoe
The goats who killed the leopard
Hare makes a fool of leopard
How confusion came among the
animals
How dog came to live with man
How dog outwitted shepherd
How hare asked for wisdom
How Kwaku Ananse destroyed a
kingdom
How the turtle fooled the leopard
The hunter and his talking leopard
Kalulu and the leopard
The lion, the leopard, and the antelope
The man who refused help
The peace between the leopard and
the antelope
The ram and the leopard
The stone lute
The three who made Ku
Tiger in the forest, Anansi in the web
Tiger story, Anansi story
The tiger who understood people
The tortoise and the lion
Tshiama, the snake's daughter
What the lemur is saying at night
Why some animals live with man
Why spider lives in ceilings
Why women won't listen
Work-let-me-see

–Spots
Grandfather tells some tales
The number of spots
Osebo's drum

–Tails
All about the tail of the leopard

The leopard's tricks
HOLLADAY – BANTU p68-69

The leopard's wine
  HOLLADAY – BANTU p66-67

Lepchas
  The tower that reached from earth
  to heaven

Lepers
  The man who always helped the
  needy
  The two bridegrooms

The leper's miracle
  LEEKLEY – KING p119-127

The leprechaun
  BRIGGS – PERS. p109-111

The leprechaun and the wheelbarrow
  GREEN – LEPRECHAUN p9-20

The leprechaun in the basket
  SPICER – GOBLINS p20-27

Leprechauns
  The banshee's birthday treat
  Christie and the growing hand
  Clever Tom and the leprechaun
  David and the big drum
  The field of Boliauns
  George and the field glasses
  The good housewife and her night
  labors
  The green grass bottle
  Gremlins, elves and leprechauns
  The hermit's cabbage patch
  King Fergus MacLeide and the wee
  folk
  The Little People
  Malachi and Red Cap the leprechaun
  Paddy and the leprechaun
  Patrick O'Donnell and the leprechaun
  The piper who could not play
  The salmon's revenge
  Shawneen and the gander
  Terence the tailor's jacket
  The three brothers and the treacle
  toffee
  The three laughs of the leipreachan
  The young piper, the Little People
  of Ireland

Lerbs, Karl
  Reaching an understanding

Lerch, Marilyn
  SIDDIQUI – TOON. p159.

Lessing, Gotthold Ephraim
  The bunch of grapes
  Different, but not better
  The donkey in company
  Dressed in strange feathers
  Friendship without envy
  The ostrich
  Zeus and the horse

A lesson for the bat
  WALKER – DANCING p59-64

Let's steal the moon
  SERWER – LET'S p80-85

A letter
  GARNER – GOBLINS p98-99

A letter to my love
  GRAY – MAINLY p57-72

Letters
  The clumber pup
  The flying Dutchman
  The mysterious letter
  Se-Osiris and the sealed letter
  The turban
  Why Eyvin won the race
  Why the dogs sniff at each other

Lettish (people)
  Grandfather's advice

Lettuce
  The donkey lettuce

Leviathan and the dutiful son
  NAHMAD – PORTION p125-127

Leviathan and the fox
  NAHMAD – PORTION p143-146

Leviathans (sea monsters)
  A school of sea monsters

Lewis, C. S.
  The queen of Underland

Lewis, Clara M.
  Chicken Little

Lewis and Clark expedition
  Pushing westward with Lewis and
  Clark

Leyssac, Paul, trans.
  It's perfectly true!
  Little Claus and Big Claus
  The little match-girl

Leyssac, Paul, trans. (*Continued*)
The little mermaid
The red shoes
The ugly duckling

Liars
See also **Tall tales**
The adventurous winnower
The ash lad who made the princess
say, "You're a liar"
The bag of lies
Big, big lies!
The boy who cried wolf
The cook's big fish
The dragon's tail
The finest liar in the world
The gold falcon
The great liar
Helping to lie
Kalulu and his money farm
The king who was a gentleman
Lies for a wager
A long-bow story
The man with the book of spells
Pacala saves Tandala
Peer Gynt
Real stuff
The shepherd's boy
The shipwrecked prince
The string of lies
Two lies
The vain king
The well of D'Yeree-in-Dowan
The wise liar
Zab

The liars' contest
COURLANDER – HAT p25-29

Liberia. *See* **Africa–Liberia**

Liberia–land of promise
HASKETT – GRAINS p11-14

Liberian proverbs
HASKETT – GRAINS p113.

Liberty. *See* **Freedom**

Lice
The bedbug, the louse, and the flea
The louse and the crow
The louse and the fingernail
The louse skin
The louse skin drum
Mr. Louse and Mrs. Louse
Why the flea hops

Lichen
Partridge and rock tripe

Licorice
Magic

Lie a-bed
MY BOOK HOUSE v. 1 p157.

Lie-a-stove
BAKER – TALKING p210-217

A lie for a lie
NAHMAD – PEASANT p43-45

Lies. *See* **Falsehood; Liars; Tall tales**

Lies for a wager
ČURČIJA – YUGOSLAV p37-41

Lieutenants
The dragon and the dragoon

Life
See also **Immortality**
Bash Tchelik
The game of chess in the mountains
God bless you
How life and light came into the world
The journey to the land of the dead
Kuluile, the dancing girl
The thread of life
The troll who hid his life

, **Eternal**
The cat, the dog, and death
The search: who gets the chief's
daughter?
The well of immortality

Life in Concord
MY BOOK HOUSE v. 12 p122-134

Life in the heights
GREEN – BIG p72.

Lifting
Thor and the giants

Light
All light comes from the sun
Balder, the god of light
The beacon light
The boy in the land of shadows
Bring me a light
The extraordinary black coat
Fair Vasilissa and Baba Yaga
The girl who overpowered the moon

Light (*Continued*)

The hopping lights on Devil's hill
How chipmunk got his stripes
How life and light came into the world
How the people began
How the people came to the middle
  place
How the raven brought light to the
  world
How the sons filled the hut
How the sun came
Ian Direach
The king's dream
O gunghemi and the battle in the bush
The princess of light
The securing of light
The sun, the moon, and the stars
The sword of light
The twist-mouth family
The white sword of light
Who?
Why the sun is brighter than the moon
Why the sun stopped shining
Why there is both day and night

The light in the house
  KAULA – AFRICAN p133-138

Light-O-Leap and the fowler
  GAER – FABLES p91-96

The light princess
  JOHNSON – PRINC. p190-233
  ROSS – BLUE p162-185

Lightening the load
  LEACH – NOODLES p37.

Lighthouses
  Little Gulliver

Lightning
  The armadillos
  The battle at White Cliff house
  The buckwheat
  How fire was brought from lightning
  How thunder and lightning came to be
  How thunder makes the lightning
  Mighty Michael . . . Who could do
    anything
  Mother of the forest
  The passing of Glooskap
  The shepherd of clouds
  Spears of lightning
  Sun, thunder, lightning and the stars
  Swen-Naba; king of the warlocks
  The tale of Anthony's nose
  Thor and the jotun Rungnir
  Thunder and lightning
  The thunder man

Thunderbird
Who is strongest?
Who's strong?
Why there is thunder and lightning
Yanni

Lights of the caribou
  OMAN –ESKIMO p49-57

Lilies
  Dainty little maiden
  The lily and the bear
  My beloved is going down into his
    garden

Lilliputians
  Gulliver's travels to Lilliput

The lily and the bear
  EELLS– SPAIN p109-116

Lime
  Kantchil's lime pit
  The righteous is delivered out of
    trouble and the wicked come in his
    stead

Lime trees
  Little Rosa and Long Leda

Lincoln, Abraham
  Abraham Lincoln, 1809-1865
  Abe Lincoln in Indiana
  Help in need and Abe in deed
  A story about Abe Lincoln

The Lincoln totem pole
  LEACH – RAINBOW p232-233

Lincoln's Gettysburg address
  MY BOOK HOUSE v. 11 p170d-171

Linden trees
  Baucis and Philemon . . . The reward
    of hospitality
  The golden bird
  The lady of the linden tree
  The little rooster and the little hen
  Summer snow

Linderman, Frank B.
  Stealing the springtime

Lindgren, Astrid
  Pippi plays tag with some policemen

Lindsay, Maud
  The little gray pony
  Mrs. Tabby Gray

Lindsay, (Nicholas) Vachel
An explanation of the grasshopper
The little turtle
Yet gentle will the griffin be

Lindsay, (Nicholas) Vachel
A tramp of the Middle West

Lineage
Fly again, my proud eagle

Linen
The magic sandals
The talisman
Vasilia the beautiful

Lines for a city child
MY BOOK HOUSE v. 1 p185.

Lines written in dejection
HOPE-SIMPSON – CAVAL. p226.

Linnets
The three golden eggs

Linseed
The enchanted princess

The lion and donkey a-hunting go
LA FONTAINE – FABLES p34-35

Lion and honey badger
KAULA – AFRICAN p43-48

Lion and man
JAGENDORF – KING p65-69

The lion and the bulls
GREEN – BIG p198-199

The lion and the fox
FEINSTEIN – FOLK p16-20

The lion and the goat
KOREL – LISTEN p115-118

The lion and the hare
KOREL – LISTEN p108-114
MONTGOMERIE – 25 p50-52

The lion and the hare go hunting
COURLANDER – FIRE p105-110

The lion and the mouse
ARBUTHNOT – TIME p203.
BROWN – AROUND p91-96
LA FONTAINE – FABLES p14-15

MY BOOK HOUSE v. 2 p108-109
STRONG – FAVORITE p60.

The lion and the sage
BARASH – GOLDEN p49-50

The lion and the unicorn
JACOBSON – FIRST p32.
MANNING – BEASTS p121.

The lion and the wily rabbit
GAER – FABLES p82-84

Lion and the woman
KAUL – AFRICAN p139-145

The lion and the woodcutter
DOBBS – MORE p81-85

Lion bones and the Gardula magicians
DAVIS – LION'S p70-72

The lion calls up his troops
LA FONTAINE – FABLES p22-23

Lion, chameleon, and chicken. A story
from the Gogo people
KAULA – AFRICAN p49-54

The lion-makers
DOBBS – ONCE p24-26

The lion of hard-to-pass forest
GAER – FABLES p60-69

The lion on the path
TRACEY – LION p1-5

The lion, the leopard, and the antelope
HOLLADAY – BANTU p70-75

The lion, the tiger, and the eagle
MANNING – DAMIAN p139-145

The lion who listened to a jackal
GAER – FABLES p141-143

The lion with the steady hand
PICARD – TALES p25-39

The lion-wolf
KOREL – LISTEN p44-48

Lionbruno
LUM – ITALIAN p135-149

Lions
According to tradition
The affable lion
Antar the hero
At the lion's cave

Lions (*Continued*)

The bee tree
The blacksmith lion and the conceited
  goat
The blue belt
The boastful gnat
The bragging beasts
The brave prince
Brer goat and brer lion
Bucky, the big, bold fawn
The buffalo who made undue demands
Buh rabbit's graveyard
The camel in the lion's court
Cast they bread
The cat who came indoors
The cave that talked
The circus parade
Curd ears
The dance of the animals
The dance of the fishes
Daniel in the lions' den
Diplomacy
The doe and the lioness
The donkey and the lions
The donkey in company
The donkey in the lion's skin
The donkey who sinned
The donkey who was an ass
The enchanted castle in the sea
The farmer's old horse
The fear of the lion king
The fisherman's son
The flight of the animals
The flower of beauty
The foolish jackal
The foolish, timid, little hare
The fox and the lion in partnership
The fox outwits the lion
The friendly frog
The girl on the rock
The girl who forgot her hoe
The gnat and the lion
The goat and the eagle
The golden lion
The grateful lion
The hawk's friends
The horse, the lion, and the wolf
How baby wart hog saved his father's
  life
How chameleon became king of the
  animals
How the dog chose its master
How the lion rewarded the mouse's
  kindness
Hyena and the oil with the flies in it
In Coney Island by the sea
In unity is strength
The Indian shinny game
The infallible salt bird
The injured lion

It's better to be smart than strong
The jackal told me
The jackal who tried to copy the lion
Kalulu and his money farm
The king who slept
Know your own strength
Kwaku Ananse and the greedy lion
The labors of Hercules
The lame dog
A leg for the lion
Leo the king
León and the lion
The little lion dog and the blue prince
The lonely lioness and the ostrich
  chicks
Madame giraffe
The magic bone
The magic carpet
The marriage of Tom and the vixen
The mermaid and the boy
The mouse keeps her promise
Musk and amber
The Nemean lion
On just being yourself
One good turn deserves another
The ostrich chicks
Prince Finn the fair
The princess who was dumb
The quarrel
Rabbit and lion
Reineke fox
Reynard the fox
The scholars and the lion
A shilling for a lie
The sick lion and the fox
Spider and the lion
Spotless the lion and Trusty the
  carpenter
The story of the Cid
The story of the stone lion
The talking house
Three princes and their beasts
The tortoise and the lion
The trap
The tree with the difficult name
The turtle outwits the lion
The vain jackal
The war between the lion and the
  cricket
What should I do, what shouldn't
  I do?
The white parrot
Who hath no courage must have legs
Why ants live everywhere
Why lion lives in the forest
Why the bagobo like the cat
Why the lion, the vulture, and the
  hyena do not live together
The wind-demon
The wizard of Oz. The cowardly lion
The woodsman's daughter and the
  lion

Lions (*Continued*)

The youth who could become an ant,
a lion or an eagle
—Hair
The beardless one
Juanito and the princess
Lion and the woman
Yiankos
—Heads
The man with a lion head in a can
—Mountain
Three bad men
, Stone
Ooka and the marble monster
—Whiskers
The lion's whiskers

The lion's share
COURLANDER — KING'S p78-79
DAVIS — LION'S p77-80

The lion's threats
HEADY — JAMBO p24-26

The lion's whiskers
DAVIS — LION'S p7-12

Listening
The six companions
The son of the hunter
The spider and the lizard

The listening king
LOWE — LITTLE p95-96

Lithuania
The czar's general and the clever
peasant
Fiddler John and the devil
The foolish father-in-law
A ghost at the door
The haunted forest
Three princes and their beasts
Why the sun shines in the daytime and
the moon shines at night
The wolf

Litters. *See* Palanquins

Little Annie and the whaler captain
JAGENDORF — NEW p261-266

Little bear
COTHRAN — WITH p84-89

Little bells, pretty flowers of the steppes
MY BOOK HOUSE v. 1 p133.

Little Beppo Pippo
MY BOOK HOUSE v. 1 p63.

Little Berry
ILLYÉS — ONCE p27-33

The little birch tree
PICARD — MERMAID p61-76

A little bird sits in the willow
MY BOOK HOUSE v. 1 p73.

The little bird that found the pea
WITHERS — I SAW p102-107

A little bird told me
BATCHELOR — SUPER. p28-29

The little bird's rice
SPELLMAN — BEAUT. p44-48

The little black book of magic
CARPENTER — SOUTH p71-82

The little black box
MONTROSE — WINTER p114-125

Little black imp!
FARJEON — SILVER p169-173

The little black man
HACK — DANISH p36-43

The little black men and the honeybees
CARPENTER — AFRICAN p53-62

Little Black Sambo
MY BOOK HOUSE v. 2 p118-123

Little blue apron
MY BOOK HOUSE v. 3 p210.

Little Bo-Peep
MY BOOK HOUSE v. 1 p32.

The little book
LAWSON — STRANGE p143-154

Little Boy Blue
MY BOOK HOUSE v. 1 p33.

"Little brother and big sister". *See* The
three stags

The little brother of the sun
URE — RUMANIAN p87-89

The little bucket
ROSS — BURIED p103-108

A (The) little bull-calf
  HAMPDEN – GYPSY p17-23
  JACOBS – MORE p186-191
  MANNING – RED p93-97
  PILKINGTON – SHAM. p10-15

Little burnt-face
  ARBUTHNOT – TIME p177-179

Little Capuchin monkey's story
  SHERLOCK – IGUANA'S p29-42

The little cat and the knitting needles
  BECHSTEIN – FAIRY p184-185

The little chest
  WYNDHAM – TALES p71-73

Little Chinese tales
  WITHERS – WORLD p73-75

Little Claus and Big Claus
  SIDEMAN – WORLD'S p739-757
  THOMPSON – ONE p397-407

A little cock sparrow
  MY BOOK HOUSE v. 1 p52.

The little creature
  HOPE-SIMPSON – CAVAL. p37.

Little cricket
  ROSS – BURIED p113-120

The little crow
  HEADY – WHEN p47-51

Little diamond and the north wind
  MY BOOK HOUSE v. 4 p119-128

The little dog waltz, a story of the
  musician, Chopin
  MY BOOK HOUSE v. 2 p150-151

The little dressmaker
  FARJEON – LITTLE p125-137

The little duck
  HATCH – MORE p33-48

The little elf
  PALMER – FAIRY p92.

The little engine that could
  MY BOOK HOUSE v. 2 p200-207

The little fairy
  ĆURČIJA – YUGOSLAV p55-60

Little finger
  MANNING – GIANNI p127-140

Little fire tree
  SIDEMAN – WORLD'S p331-344

Little Firenko
  MANNING – GLASS p41-49

The little fish and (the) big fish
  JAGENDORF – MERRY p69-76
  WILLIAMS – OLD p84-95

Little Folk. See Little People

Little fool Ivan and the little humpback
  horse
  LINES – TALES p70-85

The little footprints
  YOUNG – HOW p63-67

The little fox
  MANNING – RED p98-104

Little Freddie with his fiddle
  ASBJÖRNSEN – NORW. p61-66
  ARBUTHNOT – TIME p85-88

The little frog of the stream
  BARLOW – LATIN p57-61

The little gardener with golden hair
  THOMPSON – ONE p30-35

The little girl and the hare
  MY BOOK HOUSE v. 3 p111-113

The little girl and the new dress
  MY BOOK HOUSE v. 1 p168-169

Little girl, little girl
  MY BOOK HOUSE v. 1 p56.

The little girl named I
  CUMMINGS – FAIRY p32-39

The little girl of Griff House
  MY BOOK HOUSE v. 12 p97-101

Little good baby
  MY BOOK HOUSE v. 1 p80.

The little gray mouse and the handsome
  cock
  EKREM – TURKISH p61-65

The little gray pony
  MY BOOK HOUSE v. 2 p17-22

The little grey goose
MONTGOMERIE – 25 p20-21

The little grey man
McNEILL – SUNKEN p149-154

Little Gulliver
MY BOOK HOUSE v. 5 p103-110

Little Gustava
MY BOOK HOUSE v. 2 p30-32

Little Hansworst
MY BOOK HOUSE v. 2 p164-171

The little hare's clever trick
HUME – FAVORITE p115-119

The little hen and the little cock
RANKE – GERMANY p5-8

A little history of the Gotham folk tales
JAGENDORF – MERRY p137-150

The little horse
HATCH – MORE p150-166

The little horse of seven colors
LOWE – LITTLE p17-21

The little house
ROSS – BURIED p31-34

Little Jack Horner
MY BOOK HOUSE v. 1 p48.

Little Jip
MANNING – GHOSTS p74-79

Little John and the Sheriff of Nottingham
MANNING – ENGLISH p119-126

Little John and the tanner of Blyth
ARBUTHNOT – TIME p244-249

Little John and the water horse
CARPENTER – HORSES p148-155

Little Johnny
BAMBERGER – FIRST p214-220

Little Johnny Sheepskin
DELARUE – FRENCH p96-103

The little juggler . . . And the virgin
UNTERMEYER – FIRE. p207-210

Little Kathy free-as-the-wind
ILLYES – ONCE p199-202

Little King Boggin
MY BOOK HOUSE v. 1 p40.

The little king on the Viking ship
CARPENTER – SHIPS p173-182

Little Lady Margaret
PICARD – MERMAID p77-89

The little lady's roses
FARJEON – LITTLE p174-178

Little Liese comes a-running
MY BOOK HOUSE v. 1 p121.

The little lion dog and the blue prince
CARPENTER – DOGS p173-183

The little, little fellow with the big, big hat
JAGENDORF – KING p126-131

The little lizard's sorrow
VO-DINH – TOAD p81-87

Little maid of far Japan
MY BOOK HOUSE v. 3 p164.

Little maid, pretty paid
MY BOOK HOUSE v. 1 p56.

The little-man-as-big-as-your-thumb-with-mustaches-seven-miles-long
MY BOOK HOUSE v. 7 p112-118

The little match-girl
SIDEMAN – WORLD'S p610-615

The little menehunes
BERRY – MAGIC p22-29

The little mermaid
LINES – TALES p85-106
SIDEMAN – WORLD'S p218-251

The little milleress
MANNING – JONNIKIN p40-46

Little Miss Muffet
MY BOOK HOUSE v. 1 p40.

The little mouse
KAPLAN – SWEDISH p209-229

The little mouse with the long tail
JOHNSON – WHAT p141-142

Little Mukra
MANNING – DWARFS p53-63

The little nag
HACK – DANISH p30-35

Little Nanny Etticoat
  MY BOOK HOUSE v. 1 p41.

The little nobleman
  MANNING – RED p118-126

Little numskull stories of the moon
  JABLOW – MAN p50-55

The little one
  SHEPPARD – SCOT. p72-74

Little one eye, little two eyes and little
three eyes
  SIDEMAN – WORLD'S p424-434

Little one-inch
  SAKADE – JAPAN. p66-71
  SEKI – FOLKTALES p90-92

The little orphan
  EKREM – TURKISH p46-51

Little People
  See also names of Little People e.g.
  Leprechauns
  The adventures of Kahukura and Te
    Kanawa, The Little People of
    Polynesia
  Betty Stogs and the Little People
  The boy who was saved by thoughts
  The castle in the cornfield
  The cold heart–Part 1
  Collen and the fair small folk
  Donal O'Donnell's standing army
  The dwarf and the cook, The Little
    People of Turkey
  Eight leaves of story (7) Red-hat otter
  The girl who didn't know how to spin,
    The Little People of Scandinavia
  The good housewife and her night
    helpers
  The Heinzelmannchen
  The house with the front door at the
    back
  The hunchback and the miser
  King Herla, The Little People of the
    British Islands
  The lad who returned from Faerye
  The lazy gardener and the little red man
  The little footprints
  Little John and the tanner of Blyth
  The little menehunes
  The magic scythe, The Little People
    of Iceland
  The man who lived on an island
  The marvelous cow of Llyn Barfog,
    The Little People of Wales

The marvelous doors, The Little
  People of Italy
The Namashepani
Patou MacDaniel
Peregrine and the redman of Rocking-
  ham
The piper of Keil
The police marshal
Rip Van Winkle; the strange men of the
  mountain
The seven wishes
The sick boy, the greedy huntesr, and
  the dwarfs, The Little People of North
  America
The small men and the weaver
The small people's cow
The smith and the faeries
Throwmount and Oakpull
The tiny, tiny man
The tobacco fairy from the blue hills
The tune of Iolo ap Hugh, The Little
  People of Wales
The wee folk
The whalers and the dwarfs, The Little
  People of the Eskimo
Whippety stourie
The white cat and the green snake
The white wolf
The widow and the Korrigans, The
  Little People of Brittany
The wonder ship and ship's crew
The wonderful plow, The Little
  People of the Island of Rugen
The young piper, the Little People of
  Ireland

The Little People
  JENNINGS – BLACK p130-143

Little Peppino
  MY BOOK HOUSE v. 1 p62.

The little pet rani
  WILLIAMS – ROUND p57-66

Little pictures from far Japan
  MY BOOK HOUSE v. 6 p196-197

The little pig
  MY BOOK HOUSE v. 1 p198-199

The little prairie hen and the big Indiana
  JAGENDORF – SAND p84-87

The little priest
  KRUEGER – SERPENT p50-55

The little purse with two pennies
  CREANGĂ – FOLK p86-92

The little rabbit who wanted red wings
  MY BOOK HOUSE v. 2 p87-91

Little Radoyitsa
ĆURČIJA – HEROES p151-154

Little red bird
MANNING – BEASTS p240-241

The little red bogie-man
SHEPPARD – WELSH p167-172

The little red hen and the grain of wheat
MY BOOK HOUSE v. 2 p13-16

The little red mannikin
MANNING – DEVILS p110-116

The little red pig
MARGOLIS – IDY p11-21

Little Red Riding Hood
BAMBERGER – FIRST p125-130
LINES – NURSERY p57-66
PERRAULT – CLASSIC p33-37
PERRAULT – COMPLETE p71-77
PERRAULT – FAMOUS p137-146
THOMPSON – ONE p76-78

Little robin redbreast
MY BOOK HOUSE v. 1 p23.

The little rooster and the little hen
MY BOOK HOUSE v. 2 p71-74

Little Rosa and long Leda
KAPLAN – SWEDISH p17-34

The little round pot
BAMBERGER – FIRST p20-23

The little Sawah
LEEUW – INDO. p30-35

The little scarred one
CHILD – CASTLES p59-67

Little shell
SECHRIST – ONCE p93-97

The little shepherd's dream
BECHSTEIN – FAIRY p12-18

Little shepherd's song
MY BOOK HOUSE v. 6 p173.

Little sister and the Zimwi
AARDEMA – TALES p86-94

The little snake
HAMPDEN – GYPSY p79-83

The little sticky rice basket
KRUEGER – SERPENT p56-61

Little stories about the moon
JABLOW – MAN p19-24

Little Stormy
FELTON – TRUE p5-12

A little story about a great man
JAGENDORF – SAND p47-49

Little tall tales
WITHERS – WORLD p82-87

Little Tom Thumb
BUDBERG – RUSSIAN p150-153
PERRAULT – COMPLETE p26-41

Little Tommy Tucker
MY BOOK HOUSE v. 1 p42.

The little toy land of the Dutch
MY BOOK HOUSE v. 4 p56.

The little turtle
MY BOOK HOUSE v. 1 p162.

The little white cat
HARDENDORFF – FROG'S p83-107

"Little women"
The witch's curse

Littledale, Freya
LITTLEDALE – GHOSTS p167.

Live alone; die alone
DAVIS – LION'S p127-130

Livers
See also names of animals, subdivision
–Livers
Cottontail and the sun
It won't do you any good
The little priest
The magic bird
Why jellyfish has no shell

The lizard and the catfish
HASKETT – GRAINS p82-83

The lizard-hand
LEACH – HOW p44.

Lizards
The adventures of a water baby
The chief of the well
The children's sea
The emerald lizard
The galah and Oola the lizard
How the lizard lost and regained
  his farm
How the lizards got their markings
A letter to my love
The little lizard's sorrow
The lost spear
The one who said Tjik
Over in the meadow
The precious stone
Pursuit of the Hadji
The rescue of fire
The sky god's daughter
Spears of lightning
The spider and the lizard
The sword of the stone
Tortoise and the lizard
Wayamba the turtle
The wedding of the hawk
Why ducks have flat feet
Why lizard can't sit

, **Fairy**
Little Berry

, **Golden**
Golden goodness

—Necks
Why the lizard stretches his neck

, **Sea**
The great lizard of Nimple

—Tails
The lizard's tail

, **Wood**
The babymakers

The lizards and the stag
GREEN — BIG p82.

The lizard's big dance
COURLANDER — PIECE p50-54

The lizard's lost meat
COURLANDER — OLODE p24-28

The lizard's tail
TURNBULL — FAIRY p84-90

Llamas
The holy cat of Tibet

Lleu and the flowerface
JONES — WELSH p53-67

Lludd, King
The three plagues of Britain

The loafer
DE LA IGLESIA — CAT unp.

Loafing. *See* **Laziness**

Loans
Anansi borrows money
The king and his friend
Treasure in the basket

The loathly lady
WESTWOOD — MEDIEVAL p25-30

The lobster and the flounder
GREY — SOUTH (1) p7-9

Lobsters
Adventures of a water baby
The boy Pu-nia and the king of the
  sharks
The boy who would eat lobsters
King of the restless sea
Krencipal and Krencipalka
The mock turtle's song
Why flounder's two eyes are on the
  same side of his face

Loch Ness: last laugh?
McHARGUE — BEASTS p99-107

The Loch Ness monster
BUEHR — SEA p72-83

The Lochmaben harper
MANNING — ENGLISH p93-96

Locks
Prince Ferdinand

The locust, the ant, and the kingfisher
INS-SOB — FOLK p35.

Locusts
The endless tale
The fairyland of science
How locusts came to be
The princess in the camphor tree
The would-be wizard

The locusts and the oats
WITHERS — I SAW p48.

Lod, the farmer's son
WILSON — SCOTTISH p18-
27

Lofting, Hugh
    The rarest animal of all
    The story of Mrs. Tubbs

Loggers. *See* **Lumbermen**

Lohengrin
    MY BOOK HOUSE v. 10 p89-97

Loki
    The apples of Iduna
    The building of the fortress wall
    The death of Balder
    How Ferris Wolf was bound
    The punishment of Loki
    Thor gains his hammer
    Thor's unlucky journey

Loki
    GARNER – GOBLINS p188-200

Loki . . . The apples of youth
    UNTERMEYER – FIRE. p131-135

Loki, the god of the jotun race
    AULAIRE – NORSE p42-43

Loki's monstrous brood
    AULAIRE – NORSE p50-53

Loki's punishment
    AULAIRE – NORSE p137-139

Lokman
    The doe and the lioness

London (England)
    Dick Whittington and his cat
    The pedlar of Swaffham
    See-saw, Sacaradown
    Whittington and his cat

London bridge
    The pedlar's dream

London streets
    MY BOOK HOUSE v. 12 p102-103

Loneliness
    Angus
    The cranberry feast
    The dark king
    Here am I, little jumping Joan
    How coyote brought back people
      after the flood
    How coyote got his voice
    Oh, deary me

The lonely boy
    MY BOOK HOUSE v. 12 p120-121

The lonely house
    AYRE – SKETCO p72-85

The lonely lioness and the ostrich chicks
    AARDEMA – TALES p70-76

A long-bow story
    LANG – OLIVE p25-29

Long, broad and sharpsight
    MANNING – WIZARDS p26-39

The long-eared cat and the vulture
    GAER – FABLES p57-60

The long-howling jackal
    GAER – FABLES p90-91

Long John and the mermaid
    MANNING – MERMAIDS p54-58

Long memories
    WITHERS – WORLD p59.

Long-neck, Fatty and Droopy
    ILLYES – ONCE p42-44

A long night's sleep
    GINSBURG – MASTER p55-58

The long nose
    BONNET – CHINESE p33-42

The long-nosed giant
    MAR – CHINESE p11-19

The long-nosed goblins
    SAKADE – JAPAN. p29-34

The long-nosed princess
    JOHNSON – PRINC. p254-306

The long one
    AARDEMA – TALES p19-30

A long one and a short one
    WITHERS – I SAW p92.

A long shot
    FELTON – WORLD'S p51-56

A long time to Monday
    BROWN – AROUND p1-6

The long walk
    DAVIS – LION'S p116-125

Longevity. *See* **Old age**

Longfellow, Henry Wadsworth
    The death of Kwasind
    Hiawatha's childhood
    Hiawatha's fasting
    I heard the bells on Christmas
        day
    Thor

Longfellow, Henry Wadsworth
    The Harvard professor

Longshanks, girth, and keen
    FILLMORE – SHEPHERD'S p103-118

Longspurs (birds)
    Mrs. Longspur's second marriage

Look behind as well as before
    BURTON – MAGIC p126-127

Look here!
    JABLOW – MAN p52.

Look, see the boat!
    MY BOOK HOUSE v. 1 p184.

Look through glass
    LEACH – SOUP p73-77

Looking glasses. *See* **Mirrors**

Loons
    The blind boy and the loon
    How loon learned his call
    The passing of Glooskap
    The Sedna legend

Loppa and Jon Loppa-Fosterling
    BOUCHER – MEAD p107-109

Lord, The. *See* **God; Jesus Christ**

Lord Krishna or The eighth child
    MacFARLANE – TALES p92-101

The lord of gold
    McNEILL – SUNKEN p127-131

The lord of Massachusetts
    JAGENDORF – NEW p147-152

Lord Peter
    MANNING – BEASTS p29-37
    THOMPSON – ONE p226-230

The Lord said, this is my house
    JAGENDORF – KING p79-80

Lord Sinclair and the Zeno brothers
    TAFT – PROFILE p18-23

Lords
    Adrian and Bardus
    The clever lord
    The golden eggplant
    The hare and the lord
    The hawk fledgling
    The heir of Linne
    An unhappy lord

Lords of the Isles
    The tale of the wrath of God

The lordship of the Fianna
    HAZELTINE – HERO p184-202

The Loreley . . . The siren's song
    UNTERMEYER – FIRE. p223-226

Lorenzini, Carlo
    Pinocchio

Lories (birds)
    The fairy bird

Lorikeets
    Why the parrot repeats man's words

Losers
    Henry Crabb–a born loser

The loss of Sītā
    GRAY – INDIA'S p107-116

Lost
    The boy who was lost
    Haensel and Gretel
    Hansel and Gretel
    Little Tom Thumb

Lost and found
    HATCH – MORE p119-137

Lost arts
    WILLIAMS – LOST p100-107

The lost children
    MANNING – GLASS p187-194

A lost chord in Tijuana brass
    WILLIAMS – LOST p70-86

The lost city of Ys
    COLUM – STONE p30-35

The lost cows
  MULLER – SWISS p57-59

The lost gift
  HODGES – SEREND. p61-96

The lost gold bars of Juan Blanco
  WILLIAMS – LOST p185-192

The lost half-hour
  CHILD – CASTLES p41-57
  SHEAHAN – HENRY p147-164

Lost in lava
  WILLIAMS – LOST p157-164

Lost in memory
  FARJEON – SILVER p114-118

The lost jewel
  MOZLEY – EGYPT p14-19

The lost lover of Pearl Hart
  WILLIAMS – LOST p29-35

The lost payroll at Wickenburg
  WILLIAMS – LOST p36-50

The lost prince
  MANNING – MERMAIDS p15-24

The lost remains of Mr. Quejo
  WILLIAMS – LOST p19-28

The lost saints
  WILLIAMS – LOST p137-146

The lost secrets of Charles Hatfield
  WILLIAMS – LOST p147-156

A lost ship of the desert
  WILLIAMS – LOST p177-184

The lost song
  GINSBURG – MASTER p139-144

The lost spear
  MY BOOK HOUSE v. 6 p132-139

The lost sun, moon, and stars
  THOMPSON – HAWAII. p33-39

The lost treasure of Cucamonga
  WILLIAMS – LOST p132-136

The lost woman of San Nicolas
  WILLIAMS – LOST p93-99

A lot of silence makes a great noise.
  A story from the Swahili people
  KAULA – AFRICAN p126-132

Lotus
  The beautiful blue jay
  The blue lotus flower
  The making of the earth
  That fourth leg of the dog
  , Golden
    The golden lotus
  , Silver
    Malati and the prince

Lotus eaters
  Odysseus and the lotus eaters

Loudness. See Noise

Louis and Theobald
  LEEKLEY – KING p97-118

Louis Le Gros
  Louis and Theobald

Louisiana
  Dreamland opens here
  Jean Sot
  Mister Honey Mouth

  –New Orleans
    The privateer turned patriot

Louisiana
  LEACH – RAINBOW p93-95

The Loup-Garow in the woods
  CARLSON – TALKING p77-87

The louse and the crow
  WITHERS – I SAW p108-111

The louse and the fingernail
  COBBLE – WEMBI p22-26

The louse skin
  THOMPSON – ONE p283-286

The louse skin drum
  WITHERS – WORLD p67-68

Love
  See also Courtship; Lovers
  Adventure in plaindealing
  Andrew Moir and the seal-people
  Atalanta's race; a contest for love
    or death
  The banishment of Diah

Love (*Continued*)

The beautiful weaver and the golden shell
The beggar in the blanket
The beginning of good conversation
Belena
The best wish
The black pool
A bride for the sea god
The bride from the land of the spirits
Chu Dong Tu and the princess
Clever Kadra
The cock and his loving wives
Count Alaric's lady
The courage of Mairi
The crystal of love
Cupid and Psyche . . . The trial of love
Damon and Pythias; the most faithful
  of friends
The days of the first monkeys
The death of Diarmaid
Dermot and Grania
The dragon of the well
Einion (Las) and the fair family
The elephant and the carpenters
Emma of Haarlem
The fair maid of Astolat
The fairy of Hawili Falls
Finvarra
The fisherlad and the mermaid's ring
The fisherman and his soul
For love of a woman
Friendless pavilion
Frithjof, the Viking
Frithiof's journey to the Orkneys
The genii of the hearth
Geraint and Enid
The giant okab
The handsome Kahveci
The happy prince
Heart of the west wind
The house in the valley
The hunter and the hind
An Indian love story
Iwanich and the magic
Jack and the wizard
John Reid and the mermaid
The Kelpie
Kilmeny
The king of the mountain
Kunikdjuaq, a bear story of the Inuit
The laird's lass and the gobba's son
Lancelot of the lake
Lancelot . . . The lady of Shalott
The legend of Tchi-Niu
Lion and the woman
The lion with the steady hand
Lionbruno
The little birch tree
The little gray mouse and the hand-
  some cock

The man who didn't believe in ghosts
The man who lived in the world of
  dreams
The marriage of Sir Gawain
The musical silver goat
Nala and Damayānti
Nancy's brook
Narcissus and Echo . . . Their hopeless
  love
Nguyen Ky and the singer
Niamb of the golden hair
The nightingale
Palamon and Arcite
Patient Griselda
Popo and the princess
The portrait of the Tien
Prince Ahmed
The prince who rode through a mouse-
  hole
The princess who loved her father
  like salt
The pumpkin child
Pygmalion . . . The marvelous statue
Queen o' the tinkers
Ricky of the ruft
Riquet with the quiff
The river
Rodents rampant on a field azure
The rose is red
Salt and bread
The salt at dinner
A salty tale
Scandalous affairs of a baronet and a
  tavern maid
The sea captain's wife
The sea-king's daughter
The selfish giant
Sir Orfeo
The stone memorial to a dog
The story of a fairy serpent
The story of Iubdan, King of the lepra
  and the lepracaun
The story of Ming-Y
The story of Mordecai and Ester
The story of Noschoy Datta of Ujjain
The story of Prince Ahmed
The story of Ywenec
The tale of Lang Johnnie Mor
The tale of the gypsy and his strange
  love
The three unmarried ministers
Three who found their hearts' desire
The three wishes
Tiger woman
Tristram and Isolt
True love in the Blue Mountains
The tsarina's greatest treasure
Twins in the sky
Why the mole lives underground
Willow

Love (*Continued*)

The wishing chair of the Lord of Erri-
gal
The wooing of Etain
Wu Meng, the thoughtful
The young Tamlin

, **Mother**
The babe Moses
The changeling and the fond
young mother
Cornelia's jewels
Mrs. Tabby Gray
Old mother wind
Only a sparrow
A Roumanian lullaby
Sleep, sleep, my little one!
Sleep, sleep, sleep!
The stolen bairn and the sidh
Tippity Witchit's Hallowe'en
When I was a baby

—**Potions**
A midsummer night's dream
The tiger's whisker

, **Tests**
Cap o'rushes
Caporushes

Love and lovers
BATCHELOR — SUPER. p74-76

Love and sentiment
JOHNSON — WHAT p82-88

Love and war
IVES — TALES p89-95

Love at first sight
GRAY — INDIA'S p206-211

Love like salt
LEACH — SOUP p118-119

Love luck
LEACH — LUCK p32-36

The love of a Mexican prince and
princess
JAGENDORF — KING p181-186

The love of Cuchulainn and Fann, and
the only jealousy of Emer, his wife
MORAY — FAIR p17-27

The love of Kenelinda
SAVORY — ZULU p42-46

The love of three oranges
DELARUE — FRENCH p57-66

Love story
IVES — TALES p7-11

The lovebirds
FARJEON — LITTLE p244-247

The loveliest rose
HACK — DANISH p145-150

Lovers
Aucassin and Nicolette
Aucassin and Nicolette . . . Their
difficult romance
Deidre and the sons of Usna
The dutiful daughter
The fountain of Arethusa
The legend of the Mayon volcano
The legend of the three beautiful
princesses
The lost lover of Pearl Hart
Love and lovers
The maiden in the tower
Mr. Noy
Pyramus and Thisbe . . . The mul-
berry tree
Rojin Rojal
The silver river
The story of Hinemoa
The tale of the Laird of Logie
The tempest
The two lovers
The weeping lass at the dancing place

Lovers' leaps
LEACH — RAINBOW p223-225

Lovers' moon
BUDD — FULL p28-34

The lovesick giant
PALMER — JOURNEY p95-105

Lowe, Patricia Tracy
LOWE — LITTLE p124.

Lowell, Amy
The sea shell

Lowrimore, Burton
The old woman and the bear

Lox and the two ermines
WILLIAMS — ROUND p223-230

Loyalty
Benito the faithful
The cat with the crooked tail
The chief of the Guernsi
The craftsman's wife

Loyalty (*Continued*)

Damon and Pythias; the most faithful
    of friends
David, the shepherd boy
The dog that fought a duel
East o' the sun and west o' the moon
The exile of Rama
The faithful dog
The faithful friend
Faithful John
The faithful Morgiana
Faithful to death
The faithful wife
The five wise words
The gambler's wife
The home-coming of Odysseus
The house that Jack built
The house with the heads
How men learned about evil
John the true
The knights of the Silver Shield
The laughing merman
The lion and the bulls
Little Gulliver
Malati and the prince
The man who lived in the world of
    dreams
Oshidori
Patient Griselda
The price of a curse
The return of Odysseus
Sir Beaumains, the kitchen knight
Sir Orfeo
The snow-queen
The stone memorial to a dog
The story of the Cid
The story-spirits
A suspicious wife with an enforced
    extra husband
This hound hath loved me
A token of friendship
The trial by fire
Two birds and their nest
Una and the Red Cross knight
The wanderings of Aeneas
Your America

Loyalty oaths
Mr. X and the loyalty oath

Luc, the king's woodsman
    PUGH – TALES p21-28

Lucas, Mrs. Edgar, trans.
    The wild swans

Lucas the strong
    SECHRIST – ONCE p196-204

Lucifer. *See* Devil(s)

Luck
See also Charms; Rings; Superstitions
Be careful!
Birthday luck
Bottle Hill
Changing luck
The egg of fortune
Everyday luck
Fool's luck
The foolish man
Friday
Good luck and bad luck
The half-pint Jinni
Holiday luck
The insatiable beggar
Intelligence and luck
Jean Sot
Just his luck
Knowledge and luck
Love luck
Make a wish
Making your own
The man who learned the language of
    the animals
Mister Luck and Mister Industry
Money luck
Mother luck
Nazar the brave
Nothing to lose
Old man Elias and the dancing sheriff
The poor and the rich
Poor old cricket!
Rodents rampant on a field azure
School luck
Sinko's luck
Street luck
Sumlee's broken stick
Tar-sa's luck
Thirteen
What is luck?
Which?

, Bad
    Bad luck put into the bag
    The copper soup-bowl
    The fox who lost his tail
    How God's wheel turns
    The poor brother's bad luck
    The rich widow of Stavoren
    Ruddy-my-beard
    The unlucky fisherman
    The unlucky man
    The unlucky shoes of Ali Abou

, Good
    At the pike's command
    The bold heroes of Hungry Hill
    Chinese dragons
    The cobbler's deity
    The crowned snake

Luck, Good (*Continued*)

Dates to Cairo
The dreamer
Fate
The fortunate maiden
Good luck and common sense
Good luck and great riches
The good luck tree
Good sense and good fortune
The great bird in the carob tree
The Hedley kow
The hope tree of Harlem
How a man became unwitched
The hunchback and the miser
The Irish luck of Brian Hughes
Isun Boshe, the one-inch lad
The magic kettle
The magic teakettle
The midnight hunt
Misfortune comes to the house
Mr. Lucky Straw
The pooka of the mill
The piece of straw
The sacred amulet
The simple-minded bootmaker as a
    miraculous healer
Three times lucky
The turquoise stones
The white deer of Onota
Yiankos

Luck
    BATCHELOR – SUPER. p111-118
    JOHNSON – WHAT p57-61
    MANNING – DAMIAN p189-190

Luck and blessing contest. *See* Good luck
and bad luck

Luck and wit
    URE – RUMANIAN p90-98

The luck boy of Toy Valley
    MY BOOK HOUSE v. 6 p108-113

The luck fairies
    EELLS – SPAIN p37-43

Luck from heaven and luck from the
earth
    SEKI – FOLKTALES p155-157

Luck in business
    BATCHELOR – SUPER. p56-57

The luck of the sea and the luck of the
mountain
    McALPINE – JAPAN. p23-34

The luck of Troy
    GREEN – GREEKS p38-39

Luckier and luckier
    LEACH – LUCK p71-75

The lucky beggar
    LEACH – LUCK p30-31

Lucky break
    BATCHELOR – SUPER. p116-117

A lucky child
    DUDDINGTON – RUSS. p79-82

The lucky circle
    SPICER – GOBLINS p62-69

The lucky hunter
    BORSKI – GOOD p72-75

The lucky man
    LEACH – LUCK p62-65

Lucky Rose Tuttle
    JAGENDORF – NEW p79-83

The lucky serving maid
    BONNET – CHINESE p179-182

The lucky shirt
    LEACH – LUCK p86-87

Lucky star of Herald Square
    JAGENDORF – GHOST p79-84

The lucky tea-kettle
    McALPINE – JAPAN. p202-210

Lucy Locket lost her pocket
    MY BOOK HOUSE v. 1 p26.

Luggage
    Monkey

Lugh and his father's murderers
    PILKINGTON – THREE p31-37

Lullabies
    American Indian songs
    Bye-lo, Bubbeli, sleep
    Bye-o! Bye-o!
    Fairy and child
    Go to sleepy, little baby
    Lie-a-bed
    Little red bird
    A midsummer night's dream
    Old mother wind
    Rock-a-bye, baby
    Sleep, baby, sleep

Lullabies (*Continued*)

The sleepy song
Sweet and low
Wynken, Blynken, and Nod

—Africa
Sleep, sleep, my little one

, Indian
Sleep, sleep, sleep!

—Cheyenne
Little good baby

—Creole
Dreamland opens here

—Nootka
Ihi! Ihi! Ihi!

—Japan
A Japanese lullaby
Sleep my baby! Sleep my baby!

—Rumania
A Roumanian lullaby
Sleep, my baby! Sleep an hour

Lullabies
MY BOOK HOUSE v. 1 p118-119

Lumbermen
Adirondack skeeters
The honest woodman
Old Abe Henry and the smart logger
man
Paul Bunyan
Paul Bunyan swings his axe
Paul Bunyan's cornstalk
Sky-bright axe/Paul Bunyan
A song of the Canadian lumberjack
The story of big Paul Bunyan
Why the devil keeps out of Indiana
Wintering with Paul Bunyan

Lummis, Charles F.
The coyote and the bear

Lunching with dragons
LEEKLEY — RIDDLE p62-65

Lundbergh, Holger
NYBLOM — WITCH p211.

Lungs
It won't do you any good

Luran and the fairies
SHEPPARD — SCOT. p64-66

The lute player
LANG — VIOLET p65-72

Lutes
Columbine and her playfellows of the
Italian pantomime
Dorani
Hoichi the earless
The legend of the magic lute
The magic lute
The magic lute player
Nguyen Ky and the singer
Orpheus . . . The fabulous musician
The piper with the hoofs of a goat
The princess who hid her slippers
The stone lute
The story of Noschoy Datta of Ujjain
The victorious lute

Lutey and the mermaid
MANNING — PETER p11-16

Luther, Martin
The magpie and the raven
The mouse and the frog
The wolf and the lamb

The lutin in the barn
LITTLEDALE — GHOSTS p101-110

Luxembourg
The fiddler of Echternach
Turnip thief!

Luzon. *See* **Philippine Islands**

Luxury
Four friends
Sybaris . . . Life of luxury

Luz, the story-teller
BRENNER — BOY p6.

A lyke-wake dirge
VANSITTART — DARK p103-104

Lynx of the forest
DUDDINGTON — RUSS. p19-20

Lynxes
The flood
The golden lynx
How thunder makes the lightning
Manabozho's nephew

Lyonesse
MANNING — PETER p26-32

Lyrebirds
The right time to laugh

Lyres
The coming of Fionn MacCool
Fairy mother

M

Ma Liang and his magic brush
   WYNDHAM – CHINA p73-83

Mabie, Hamilton Wright
   Thor and the giants

Mabinogian (book)
   The birth of Pryderi
   The dream of Ronabbway
   Manawyddan son of the Boundless

Macaroni
   The cobbler
   The three goslings

Macaulay, Lord
   Horatius

MacCodrum of the seals
   WILSON – SCOTTISH p1-7

MacDonald, George
   The light princess
   Little Diamond and the north wind

MacDonald, George
   JOHNSON – PRINC. p312-313

Macdonell, Ann
   Gigi and the magic ring

MacDowell, Edward
   Of a tailor and a bear

Mace, Joseph
   Simple-minded Jeanne

Macedonia
   A horse afraid of his shadow

Maces
   The terror of the ogres

McGinley, Phyllis
   The plain princess

MacGregor, Rob Roy
   Black Roderic

The Machimoodus noise
   TAFT – PROFILE p166-168

MacLean, Lady Elizabeth
   The tale of the lady of the rock

Macleod, Fiona
   The moon-child

Macler, Frédéric
   The golden-headed fish

Macmanus, Seumas
   The giant of the brown beech wood
   The old hag of the forest

Macmillan, Cyrus
   The boy in the land of shadows

McNeer, May
   Shizuka's dance

McNeill, Janet
   He who laughs last

Macy, Rowland Hussey
   Lucky star of Herlad Square

The mad dog
   MY BOOK HOUSE v. 3 p63-69

The mad man, the dead man, and the
devil
   McMANUS – HIBERIAN p174-184

A mad tea-party
   ARBUTHNOT – TIME p381-384

Madagascar (Island)
   Strange men with tails
   Two two rascals

Madame giraffe
   AARDEMA – STORY p32-37

Madgy Figgey and the sow
   MANNING – PETER p144-149

Madness. *See* **Insanity**

The madness of Odysseus
   GREEN – GREEKS p14-15

Madoc ap Maredudd
   The dream of Rhonabwy

Madonnas
   The boy who made a dream come true

Madschun
LANG – OLIVE p1-9

Maeve, Queen of Connacht
Cuchullin keeps the gap of the north
Cuchullin parleys with Maeve
The death of Cuchullin
The pillow talk
Ulster awake

Magarac, Joe
Joe Magarac
Joe Magarac and his U. S. A. citizen papers
Joe Magarac the steel man
Steelmaker/Joe Magarac

Magellan, Ferdinand
The coming of the Spaniards

Magellan Straits
Mr. Hampden's shipwreck

Maggie Tulliver goes to live with the gypsies
MY BOOK HOUSE v. 8 p189-224

Magi, Three
The three Magi

Magic
See also **Magicians; Witches; Wizards;** etc./titles beginning with Enchant . . .
About witches, enchantments and spells
The adventures of Florian
The adventures of Manawyddan
The Ailp king's children
Alchemy: the magic science
Aliosha's visit to the bald mountain
Alison Gross
. . . and the magic they made
The ass that lays money
The beauty and the beast
Bendebukk
The bird of the valley
The black cat of the witch-dance-place
The blue parrot
The book of Thoth
Brian and the fox
The Caliph Stork, told by Selim Baruch, the stranger
The carnation youth
Casperl
The castle of no return
The centipede girl

The changeling
The child and the fig
The children of Lir
Christie and the growing hand
Circe the enchantress
The coming of Fionn MacCool
The cow maiden
The cow that cried
The crane's feather
The cruel giant
The dancing bird
The dark king
The dead man who was alive
The do-all ax
The doctor and his pupil
The dog and the maiden
The donkey, the table, and the stick(s)
Dorani
Down to Arabia
Dry-bone and Anansi
The dutiful daughter
East of the sun and west of the moon
The fairy frog
The feather of Finist the falcon
Fickle Miss Frog
The flower of beauty
Foolish Emilyan and the talking fish
The forest bride
The frog
The frog and his clothes
The frog jacket
The frog prince
The frog with the golden key
The giant of the brown beech wood
The girl out of the egg
Gisella and the goat
The glass man and the golden bird
Glooskap, the whale, and the sorcerer
The goblin bridge
The gold bird
The golden crab
The golden lotus
The good luck tree
The great fish
The great flood
The green-bearded king
The gypsies' fiddle
The head of brass
The heart of Princess Joan
The hearth-cat
The horned-woman
The house of the rowan trees
How Cormac MacArt got his branch
How Maui fished up New Zealand
How Maui fished up the island
How Maui obtained the magic jawbone
How raven found the daylight
How Tepozton killed the giant
How Urseli became a princess
I now-not-what of I-know-not-where

Magic (*Continued*)

The invisible baby
The invisible hobgoblin
The ivory box
John Shea and the fairy treasure
Jorinda and Joringel
The kindly ghost
King Herla's quest
The king of the dark desert
The king of the Golden River, or the
  Black brothers
The king of the hares
The king who slept
The king's rabbits
Kupti and Imani
The lad who went to the north wind
The lady and the toad
The lady's quest
The land of the dead
Lars, my servant
Learning magic
The legend of Zon U-Czi
A letter to my love
The lily and the bear
The little black book of magic
The little crow
The little horse
The little people
The little pet Rani
Little Rosa and long Leda
Little shell
Lord Peter
The lucky hunter
MacCodrum of the seals
Maid Lena
Makhandu Mahlanu or The five heads
Malintzin
The man who sold magic
The man who stayed too long
The man who turned into a hyena
The man who would know magic
Maria Marina
Maria sat in the fire
The marriage of Gawaine
The marriage of Sir Gawain
Maui catches the sun
Maui nooses the sun
Maui—the trickster
The monster
Monsters and ghosts
More south than south, more north
  than north
A mouse from the Mabinogian
My candlestick
The mysterious lake
Odysseus and Circe
Oh and Alas
Oh dear!
Oisin, son of Finn MacCool
The old hag of the forest

One grain more than the devil
The peasant and his three sons
Pengersac and the witch of Fraddom
Petit Jean and the frog
The pied piper of Hamelin; a minstrel's
  enchanted music
The plain princess
The poor widow bullfighter
The Prince Fernando
Prince Lindworm
Prince rabbit
The princess and the shepherd
The princess who was dumb
The princess with the golden shoes
The quest of the sons of Turenn
Radowid
Rags and tatters
The rajah who flew away
Saemunel the learned
The sage and the mouse
St. Cadog and King Arthur
The salmon's revenge
Se-Osiris and the sealed letter
Seán na Bánóige
A secret told to a stranger
The serpent and the grape-grower's
  daughter
The serpent's bride
The seven foals
Seven iron-souled slippers
The seven ravens
The she-bear
Sinko's luck
The sleeping beauty in the wood
The snake chief
Snout the dwarf
The snowman
The song of the doves
The soothsayers
The spindle, the shuttle and the
  needle
The story of a fairy serpent
The strange adventures of Alcavilu
Stupid Emilien
Stupid Peruonto
The supernatural crossbow
Superstition: the remnants of magic
The swan maiden
The sword in the stone
A tale of a boy who set out to learn
  fear
The tale of the silver, golden, and
  diamond prince
The tale of the two brothers
Tales of enchantment
Tales of magic, black and white
Tam Lin
The three brothers
The three gifts
The three little eggs
The three oranges

Magic (*Continued*)

The three plagues of Britain
The three sons of Gorla
The three sons of the King of Antua
The three teeth of the king
The tikgi birds
Tim for wealth and happiness
A time of witches
The trade that no one knows
The treachery of Morgan LeFay
The trials of Dyfed
The troll's daughter
The twelve young men
Water drops
The weasel
The wee red man
The white cat and the green snake
The white dove of the city of the
  swinging gate
The white hound
The white trout
Whitebear Whittington
Wild rose
The wild swans
The witch and her four sons
The witch of Lok Island
The wizard king
The wizard of Reay's book of magic
The woodsman's daughter and the
  lion
The young coyote's visit
Young Gim and the robbers
—History
  The coming of magic

Magic
  LEACH – SOUP p9-16

The magic acorn
  WYNDHAM – RUSS. p62-67

The magic amber
  JEWETT – WHICH p82-94

Magic and friendship
  GUIRMA – TALES p45-56

Magic and medicine
  JENNINGS – BLACK p67-80

The magic apples
  BAKER – TALKING p118-122
  HAMPDEN – GYPSY p69-78

The magic baby shoes
  ROSS – MEXICO p104-120

The magic ball
  HOKE – WITCHES p56-64

The magic banana
  BERRY – MAGIC p13-21

The magic bed-knob
  ARBUTHNOT – TIME p306-309

The magic bell
  MAR – CHINESE p29-41

The magic belt
  MANNING – PRINCESS p57-65

The magic berries
  DOWNING – RUSSIAN p190-204

The magic bird
  THOMPSON – ONE p256-258
  WILLIAMS – OLD p60-73

The magic bone
  ELLIOT – SINING p154-167

The magic bottles
  SPELLMAN – BEAUT. p22-25

The magic calabash
  COTHRAN – MAGIC p27-30

The magic cap
  INS-SÓB – FOLK p152-154
  ROSS – BURIED p127-133

The magic carpet
  SIDEMAN – WORLD'S p673-714

The magic clock
  MONTROSE – WINTER p81-87

The magic crocodile
  MOZLEY – EGYPT p8-24

The magic crystal
  GRAHAM – BEGGAR p57-69

The magic dagger
  NAHMAD – PEASANT p141-147

The magic drum
  ARNOTT – AFRICAN p124-132
  BURTON – MAGIC p19-24

The magic eagle
  BARLOW – LATIN p89-96

The magic ear
  SEKI – FOLKTALES p139-142

The magic egg
  RUDOLPH – MAGIC p3-13

The magic fiddle
  DOBBS – MORE p49-62

The magic fife
  McNEILL – SUNKEN p65-78

The magic fishbone
  JOHNSON – PRINC. p76-97

The magic garden
  MASEY – STORIES p50-61

The magic grocery store
  BRENNER – BOY p44-47

The magic head
  VANSITTART – DARK p54-67

The magic herdboy
  TRACEY – LION p78-82

The magic hill
  JOHNSON – PRINC. p132-136

The magic horns
  ARNOTT – AFRICAN p78-84

The magic horse
  BAMBERGER – FIRST p79-82
  MY BOOK HOUSE v. 8 p92-107

Magic in Marblehead
  JAGENDORF – NEW p139-146

The magic kettle
  SIDEMAN – WORLD'S p382-387

The magic lake
  MANNING – MERMAIDS p73-78

The magic lamp
  RANKE – GERMANY p98-104

The magic listening cap
  UCHIDA – MAGIC p3-10

The magic lute
  MARKS – SPANISH p118-132

The magic lute player
  TOOZE – WONDER. p74-76

The magic mango
  CARPENTER – ELEPHANT'S
  p166-175

The magic mare
  TOOR – GOLDEN p65-66

The magic melons
  HSIEH – CHINESE p16-17

The magic mirror
  MAAS – MOON p104-115
  MICHAEL – PORTUGUESE p28-34

The magic mortar
  UCHIDA – MAGIC p33-41

The magic mountain
  SPICER – WITCHES p18-23

The magic muntr
  HODGES – SEREND. p5-23

The magic oysters
  LEEUW – INDO. p127-134

The magic pancakes at the Footridge
tavern
  HUME – FAVORITE p79-84

The magic peas
  SPICER – GOBLINS p89-96

The magic pipe
  PRIDHAM – GIFT p16-20

The magic poncho
  CARPENTER – SOUTH p129-136

The magic purse of the swamp maiden
  UCHIDA – SEA p42-54

The magic ring
  ALMEDINGEN – RUSS. p180-192
  BUDBERG – RUSSIAN p217-235
  CURCIJA – YUGOSLAV p123-136
  McNEILL – SUNKEN p24-35

The magic ruby
  ROBERTSON – FAIRY p81-88

The magic sandals
  JOHNSON – HARPER p108-127

The magic sandals of Hualachi
  U. N. – RIDE p220-223

The magic scythe, The Little People of
Iceland
  BELTING – ELVES p84-90

The magic storm
  PROTTER – CHILD. p41-45

The magic swan
  MANNING – BEASTS p114-120

The magic tabo
  SECHRIST – ONCE p184-188

The magic teakettle
SAKADE – JAPAN. p17-24

The magic turban, the magic whip, and
the magic carpet
BUCK – FAIRY p257-263

The magic veil
MARMUR – JAPAN. p47-50

The magic walking stick
PROTTER – CHILD. p156-160

The magic wand
MANNING – JONNIKIN p136-144

Magical elements in religious beliefs: The
wanderings of Isis and the agony of
Horus
JAMES – MYTHS p36-45

The magical music
STOCKTON – TING p73-140

The magical tune
MANNING – MERMAIDS p59-65

The magical wooden head
CAMPBELL – MAORI p46-50

The magician and his pupil
WILLIAMS – FAIRY p181-185

The magician and the bandits
FEINSTEIN – FOLK p59-63

The magician Palermo
EELLS – SPAIN p159-173

The magician returns
MOZLEY – ARABY p18-20

Magicians
See also **Witches; Wizards;** etc.
The adventures of learning
Aladdin and his wonderful lamp
Aladdin and the wonderful lamp
Art, King of Leinster
Atlantes and the hippogriff
The book of Thoth
Ceátach
The child and the fig
The crystal bowl
The dishonest tailor
Don Lopez of Spain
Fate of the mágicos
The fish and the ring
The greedy tailor
Hema and the goblin-woman

How the carrot-counter got his name
Iwanich and the magic ring
Ka-Hai and the sorcerer Tama-i-Wao
Keloğlan and the magician
King Kojata
Laka and the Little-People; Menehue's
Little-people
The legend of the Arabian magician
Lelu and the flowerface
Lion bones and the Gardula magicians
Longshanks, girth, and keen
The lost jewel
Madschun
Master and pupil
The master of magic and spells
The masters of magic
Maui, the demi-god
Merlin
The mink and the weasel
The most precious gift
The mouse and the magician
The old magician
The partridge and his drum
The potted princess
The princess and the pigeons
The red swan
Rival magicians
Six-and-four
The sorcerer's apprentice
The stone in the cock's head
The story in the sealed book
The story of Blathnat
The story of Caliph stork
The story of Harisarman
The story of Tom Thumb
The tale about lost time
The tale of Caliph stork
Tales of past glories: Cheops and the
magicians
Taliesin
Teta the magician
The three brothers and the black hen
The three monsters of the sea
The three suitors
Ting-a-ling and the five magicians
Tom Thumb
The two princesses
Una and the Red Cross knight
Wainamoinen finds the lost-words
The wandering apprentice
The whale and the sorcerer
Where to lay the blame
Why the world is the way it is
A wisp of straw
The wonder child
The yellow dragon

The magician's garden
PICARD – MERMAID p219-241

The magician's heart
JOHNSON – HARPER p86-107

The magician's revenge
  NYE – MARCH p77-83

Magicians of the way
  BIRCH – CHINESE p80-88

Magistrates. *See* **Judges and justice**

The magnificent hounds of Finn MacCool
  CARPENTER – DOGS p64-73

The magpie and the fox
  O'SULLIVAN – FOLK. p8-9

The magpie and the raven
  GREEN – BIG p191.

Magpies
  The dutiful daughter
  How the donkey saved a village
  Mrs. Mag and her nest
  Nidden and Didden and Donal Beg
    O'Neary
  The pheasant, the dove, the magpie,
    and the rat
  The princess who always had to have
    the last word
  The weasel
  –**Eggs**
    The prince and the giant's daughter

The magpie's nest
  MY BOOK HOUSE v. 2 p42-44

Magyars
  The boy who kept a secret
  The miraculous stag

Mahabkarata (India epic)
  See also The World's great epics
  This hound hath loved me

Mahogany trees
  The virgin of Honduras

Maid Lena
  THOMPSON – ONE p78-88

The maid of the waves
  McNEILL – SUNKEN p155-160

The maiden and the moon
  GINSBURG – MASTER p122-128

The maiden and the ratcatcher
  KOREL – LISTEN p53-60

The maiden in the country underground
  PILKINGTON – SHAM. p94-101

The maiden in the tower
  THOMPSON – ONE p21-23

Maiden Lane in the golden days
  JAGENDORF – UPSTATE p48-52

The maiden of Deception Pass
  MATSON – LONGHOUSE p17-27

The maiden of Kossovo
  CURCIJA – HEROES p48-50

The maiden of the mist
  BERRY – MAGIC p45-49

The maiden Suvarna
  MANNING – GHOSTS p95-100

The maiden, the knight, and the waterfall
  MY BOOK HOUSE v. 7 p40-47

The maiden who did not get her wish
  EKREM – TURKISH p21-31

The maiden with the wooden helmst
  BUCK – FAIRY p47-50

Maids-in-waiting
  The three aunts

Mail-carriers. *See* **Postmen**

Maimonides
  A meeting of scholars

Maimonides and the bottle of poison
  NAHMAD – PEASANT p60-61

Maimonides and the king's dream
  NAHMAD – PORTION p137-138

Maine
  An adventure with a bear
  Charley, barley, buck and rye
  Cold moon
  The corsair of Spouting Horn
  A curious tale
  Ed Grant out West
  For love of a woman
  The hideless bear
  How loon learned his call
  How whale happens to smoke a pipe
  The killing of Mogg Megone
  A long shot
  Meet Ed Grant
  Minute pudding
  A most peculiar bear hide

Maine (*Continued*)
The new camp stove
The new camp stove burns again
Paul Bunyan swings his axe
The skipper and the witch
The smart woman of Kennebunkport
Some punkins
The stubbornest man in Maine
The tale of a watch
The tame trout
Tell Barney Beal
Uncle Ed is chased by a bear
Uncle Ed tracks a rabbit
Uncle Ed's unusual bear hide
Who is boss?
Why grasshopper spits tobacco juice
Wolf moon
A word from the author
The world's most truthful man
Young Paul

—Mt. Kennebago
Mount Kennebago

Maine
LEACH – RAINBOW p96-98

Maine's best boatman
FELTON – WORLD'S p101-107

Mainly in moonlight
GRAY – MAINLY p39-55

Maize. *See* Corn

Majorca (island)
About Majorcan tales
Augustine the thief
A box on the ear
Bungling Pedro
The count and the little shepherd
The country swain
The gardener, the abbot and the king
Granny Shelock
The hungry giant
The man who couldn't pay his debts
The princess with the golden hair
Tony Di-Moany

Make a wish
BATCHELOR – SUPER. p106-109
LEACH – LUCK p88-92

The maker of maps
LAWSON – STRANGE p115-129

Makhandu Mahlanu or The five heads
SAVORY – ZULU p29-33

The making of a hero
SAWYER – DIETRICH p33-58

The making of the earth
TOOZE – WONDER. p32-35

Making your own
LEACH – LUCK p69-70

Maksim Tsernoyevich's wedding
CURCIJA – HEROES p111-125

Malachi and Red Cap the leprechaun
GREEN – LEPRECHAUN p85-95

Malati and the prince
PICARD – FAUN p59-72

Malaya
The bet between Matjan and Gadja
The case of the mouse-deer and the
crocodile's eggs
The hunter of Perak
The hunter on the moon
The old humpback
The old man and his fishing line
The princess in the camphor tree
Two out of one
The war of the plants
Why the tides ebb and flow

Malcolm III, King
The tale of the royal exiles

Male and female created he them; The
river of separation
MARRIOTT – AMER. p90-95

Malintzin
BRENNER – BOY p125-128

The mallet of wealth
INS-SÖB – FOLK p143-145

Mallorca. *See* Majorca

Malory, Sir Thomas
The coming of Arthur

Malt
Esben and the witch

Man
See also Creation; Women
The acorn maidens
Bear, fox, and man
The Brahmin, the tiger, and the seven
judges
Chameleon finds

Man (*Continued*)

The creation of man
Creator makes – – –
The crocodile's daughter
Different, but not better
The dilemma of a pious man
The disillusionment of the Tibetan
tiger
The dog's nose is cold
Donal O'Donnell's standing army
The escape of the animals
Folks
The giant and the mite
The giant's toy
The horsefly
How confusion came among the
animals
How coyote brought back people after
the flood
How death came
How dog came to live with man
How mankind learned to make bread
How men learned to make fire
How rabbit stole fire from the buzzards
How the camel got his hump
How the dog chose its master
How the people began
How the people got fire
How the world was made (1)
How wisdom came to man
The ingrates
Lion and man
Male and female created he them: The
river of separation
A new world
The one who wasn't afraid
The philosophers of King Darius
The snake who bit a girl
The strongest
The three who made Ku
The tiger who understood people
The tiger's stripes
The time of deep darkness
To feed my people: The race between
the buffalo and man
Why bears eat meat
Why chicken lives with man
Why dogs live with men
Why porpoise is not a fish
Why some animals live with man
Why the bagobo like the cat
Why the world is the way it is
The wolf's food

A man, a snake, and a fox
PRIDHAM – GIFT p55-62

The man and the boy and the donkey
STRONG – FAVORITE p52-54

The man and the mango trees
HOLLADAY – BANTU p30-32

Man-eagle
HAYES – INDIAN p77-86

The man from Kailasa
See also Kantchil's lime pit
COURLANDER – TIGER'S p58-62

The man from paradise
THOMPSON – ONE p408-409

The man in the mirror
WITHERS – WORLD p75.

The man in the moon
BAMBERGER – FIRST p206
JABLOW – MAN (preface)
LEEUW – LEGENDS p112-113
RANKE – GERMANY p157.

The man in the moon came down too
soon
TOLKIEN – READER (Part 4) p34-38

The man in the moon stayed up too late
TOLKIEN – READER (Part 4) p31-33

The man o' the clan
LEODHAS – GAELIC p81-90

The man, the serpent, and the fox
VITTORINI – OLD p34-37

The man who always helped the needy
burton - magic p29-35

The man who became a chimpanzee
COBBLE – WEMBI p34-36

The man who bought a dream
SEKI – FOLKTALES p157-160
UCHIDA – MAGIC p93-100

The man who climbed down a moonbeam
JABLOW – MAN p53-55

The man who could see everything
NORLEDGE – ABORIGINAL p62.

The man who couldn't pay his debts
MEHDEVI – BUNGLING p99-107

The man who didn't believe in ghosts
LEODHAS – GHOSTS p24-34

The man who entertained the bear. *See*
The cranberry feast

The man who feared nothing
JEWETT – WHICH p65-73

The man who fled a nagging wife
JABLOW – MAN p19.

The man who had no story
O'SULLIVAN – FOLK p182-184

The man who had no wife
COBBLE – WEMBI p93-97

The man who has plenty of good peanuts
MY BOOK HOUSE v. 1 p95.

The man who helped carry the coffin
LEODHAS – GHOSTS p65-77

The man who hung his powder horn on
the moon
JABLOW – MAN p46-47

The man who kept house
BAMBERGER – FIRST p71-74

The man who kicked aside riches. *See*
Good luck and bad luck

The man who killed his greyhound. *See*
The eight leaves of story (5) The man
who killed his greyhound

The man who killed the sea monster
MAHER – BLIND p31-38

The man who learned the language of
the animals
ARNOTT – AFRICAN p5-12

The man who lived in the world of dreams
MY BOOK HOUSE v. 11 p152-170

The man who lived on an island
PICARD – LADY p100-110

The man who looked for death
COURLANDER – OLODE p15-18

The man who lost his shadow
O'SULLIVAN – FOLK. p235-236

The man who lost his way
MONTGOMERIE – 25 p46-47

The man who loved flowers
BONNET – CHINESE p9-14

The man who loved Hai Quai
MY BOOK HOUSE v. 6 p127-130

The man who made the trees bloom
MARMUR – JAPAN. p61-66

The man who married a snow goose
MAHER – BLIND p79-98

The man who missed the Tay Bridge
train
LEODHAS – TWELVE p127-145

The man who nearly became fishpaste
BIRCH – CHINESE p55-61

The man who paddled to the moon's
house
JABLOW – MAN p41-43

The man who refused help
COBBLE – WEMBI p72-74

The man who rode the bear
CREDLE – TALL p100-114

The man who sat on the tide
AYRE – SKETCO p124-135

The man who sold a ghost
WYNDHAM – CHINA p48-51

The man who sold magic
GRAY – MAINLY p143-164

The man who sold thunder
BONNET – CHINESE p77-82

The man who started it all and the man
who couldn't forget
IVES – TALES p223-227

The man who stayed too long
BRENNER – BOY p48-50

The man who stole a rope
WYNDHAM – CHINA p38-39

The man who struck his father
O'SULLIVAN – FOLK. p136-143

The man who swallowed the mouse
O'SULLIVAN – FOLK. p12.

The man who tried to catch the night
BURTON – MAGIC p61-63

The man who turned into a hyena
TRACEY – LION p46-50

The man who walked widdershins round
the kirk
LEODHAS – GHOSTS p35-42

The man who wanted to bury his son
INS-SŎB – FOLK p43-44

The man who was always borrowing
and lending
 BURTON – MAGIC p35-39

The man who was only three inches
tall
 SIDDIQUI – TOON. p91-97

The man who was rescued from hell
 O'SULLIVAN – FOLK. p151-164

The man who would know magic
 WYNDHAM – CHINA p67-72

The man with a lion head in a can
 DAVIS – LION'S p184-188

The man with no nose
 FEINSTEIN – FOLK p47-51

The man with the bag
 COLUM – STONE p76-84

The man with the book of spells
 URE – RUMANIAN p26-32

The man with the chair on his head
 LEACH – NOODLES p15-16

The man with the green feather
 SPICER – GOBLINS p54-61

The man with a heart
 BECHSTEIN – FAIRY p125-132

Manabozho
 The fight with Wabun
 The flight with the Wendigo
 The flood
 The giant sturgeon
 Goose dance
 Sleepy feet
 The theft of fire
 The walk around the island
 Wolf wisdom

Manabozho's nephew
 LEEKLEY – WORLD p27-34

Manannan MacLir, King
 The Manx coat of arms

Manawyddan son of the Boundless
 HAZELTINE – HERO p147-159

Mancrow, bird of darkness
 SHERLOCK – WEST p65-70

Mandarins
 The beginning of good conversation
 Daughter of the jade emperor
 The tailor and the mandarin
 A tale of two mandarins
 Tiger lily and the dragon
 The two caddies of tea
 You are right!

Mang Jen and his mother
 ALEXANDER – PEBBLES p20.

Mangaia (island)
 The turtle of Tamaru

Mango mountain
 KRUEGER – SERPENT p70-74

Mango trees and mangoes
 The blue lotus flower
 Bundar Bahadeer Poon
 The dilemma of a pious man
 The four brothers
 How the Brazilian beetles got their
  gorgeous coats
 The king and the monkey
 The magic mango
 The man and the mango trees
 The monkey king's bridge
 Monkey–lord and crocodile
 The wonderful bed

 , Golden
  Malati and the prince

 –Seeds
  Dookiram, the poor one

Manikins
 The laird's lass and the gobha's son

Manioc (plants, roots)
 The gift of manioc

Manitous
 The fight with Wabun
 The flight with the Wendigo
 The flood
 The giant sturgeon
 Goose dance
 How grasshopper came to be and men
  obtained tobacco
 Manabozho's nephew
 Sleepy feet
 The theft of fire
 The walk around the island
 Wolf wisdom

Manners. *See* **Courtesy**

Mannikins
The little red mannikin

Manning-Sanders, Ruth
Zini and the witches

Manny MacGilligan's story
MacMANUS — BOLD p158-168

Manono (island)
The ticklish thief

Manstin, the rabbit
PALMER — DRAGONS p68-74

Mantis
The wedding of the hawk

Mantles
The coming of Fionn MacCool
Lady Eleanore's mantle
The white spider's gift

Manx
How the Manx cat lost its tail

The Manx coat of arms
YOUNG — HOW p7-10

The many children of Mr. and Mrs.
Twelve
KRUEGER — SERPENT p27-36

Many, many stars are in the skies
MY BOOK HOUSE v. 1 p86.

Many moons
JOHNSON — PRINC. p234-249

Maoris
The great fish of Maui
How Maui obtained the magic jaw-
bone
Introduction (CAMPBELL — MAORI)
Kahukura and the fairies
Kahukura and the fairy fisherman
The magical wooden head
Maui and the death goddess
Maui and the fire goddess
Maui nooses the sun
Maui the fire-bringer
Rata and his canoe
The story of Hinemoa
The story of Hine-Moa and Tutanekai
Te Houtaewa and the Kumaras
Tinirau and his pet whale
The trial by fire
The troubles at Hawaiki

Map, Walter
The cowherd's son
The king and the merman

Map-making
The maker of maps

Mapandangare, the great baboon
TRACEY — LION p39-45

Maple sugar
Glooskap

Maple trees
The flute made of maple-wood
The scarlet maple
The shepherd and the king's daughters

Mapou trees
Merisier, stronger than the elephants

Marble
Chanina and the angels

Marbles
A shilling for a lie

March and the shepherd
VITTORINI — OLD p3-6

The March cock and the coffin
O'SULLIVAN — FOLK. p191-192

March has horse's ears
NYE — MARCH p3-8

Marches
Armadillo's story
Brown owl's story
Chimpanzee's story
Firefly's story
Green parrot's story
Little Capuchin monkey's story

Marching to Quebec
JOHNSON — WHAT p158.

March's ears
SHEPPARD — WELSH p69-71

Mare, de la, Walter
The ride-by-nights

The mare at the wedding
CARPENTER — HORSES p183-192

Marelles, Charles
The pied Piper of Hamelin

Margaret, Queen of Scotland
The tale of the royal exiles

Margery, Saint
Saint Margery Daw

Margrette
MANNING – MERMAIDS p46-53

Maria, the Jewess (c.100 A.D.)
Alchemy; the magic science

Maria Marina
PONSOT – RUSSIAN p51-64

Maria sat on the fire
BRENNER – BOY p121-124

Maribous
Deep insight

Mariners. See Sailors

Marines
The Connemara donkey

Mario and the yara
CARPENTER – SOUTH p137-143

Mario, Marietta, and Vanno
MY BOOK HOUSE v. 1 p63.

Marionettes. See Puppets

Markets
To market, to market

Marking the boat to locate the sword
WYNDHAM – CHINA p66.

Marko, the champion of Serbian liberty
MY BOOK HOUSE v. 11 p29-48

Marko the rich and Vassili (Vasily) the
luckless
DUDDINGTON – RUSS. p57-65
WILLIAMS – ROUND p90-101

Marmosets (monkeys)
The little lion dog and the blue prince

Marmots
Dance, raven, dance

Marriage
Bride's brook
The chief of the Guernsi

The double-headed snake of Newbury
The hemp smoker and the hemp grower
How marriages are made
Ironhead
Love and sentiment
The mason's marriage
The talisman
The youth who trusted in God

The marriage feast
SAVORY – ZULU p56-60

The marriage of Arthur
PICARD – STORIES p16-26

The marriage of Gawaine
PICARD – STORIES p118-125

The marriage of Pwyll and Phiannon.
See Pwyll and Pryderi (1)

The marriage of Rama and Sita
GRAY – INDIA'S p89-95

The marriage of Sir Gawain
PICARD – TALES p149-158

The marriage of the mouse
COURLANDER – FIRE p89-92

The marriage of the robin and the wren
MONTGOMERIE – 25 p44-45

The marriage of Tom and the vixen
BELTING – CAT p37-44

Marryat, Captain Charles
The old Navy

Mars, W. T.
ROBERTSON – FAIRY p95.

Mars
The twins of the god Mars

Marshall, Archibald
The princess

Marshall, Archibald
JOHNSON – PRINC. p313.

Marshall, James W.
The man who started it all and the
man who couldn't forget

Marshes
Damian and the dragon
Overheard on a salt marsh

Martin, Jeanne
The sharpshooter

Martin, Saint
Saint Martin and the honest
man

Martin, Stefan
LITTLEDALE – GHOSTS p167.

Martin Grogan and the merrow
LAWSON – STRANGE p83-93

Martin, the honest thief
ILLYÉS – ONCE p125-129

Martyrs
See also **Saints**; names of Saints
Osiris–martyrdom and myth: The
life and death of Osiris
Verena and the jug

The martyrs of Thebes
MÜLLER – SWISS p185-187

The marvelous cow of Llyn Barfog, The
Little People of Wales
BELTING – ELVES p53-54

The marvelous doors, The Little People
of Italy
BELTING – ELVES p11-14

The marvelous pear seed
WYNDHAM – CHINA p20-24

Mary, Virgin
Beatrice . . . And the statue
The cruel stepmother
The little juggler . . . And the Virgin
The virgin of Honduras

Mary and the Christ-child
MY BOOK HOUSE v. 1 p218-223

Mary-Ann and the cauld lad of Hylton
FINLAY – FOLK p96-108

Mary covered with gold and Mary
covered with pitch
BECHSTEIN – FAIRY p179-183

Mary had a little lamb
MY BOOK HOUSE v. 1 p88.

Mary, Mary, quite contrary
MY BOOK HOUSE v. 1 p25.

Mary, Mary, so contrary!
FILLMORE – SHEPHERD'S p64-68

Mary milks the cow
MY BOOK HOUSE v. 1 p135.

Mary of Trefriw, Saint
Prince Llewellyn and the red-haired
man

Marya Morevna
BUDBERG – RUSSIAN p154-172
DUDDINGTON – RUSS. p95-106

Maryland
Adventure in plaindealing
All the cats consulted
The blue dog
Clever Jacob Gibson
Cookus, Bopple and Yeakle
God's well
Here come three jolly, jolly sailor
boys
Here we sail so fast and free
Lazy old Mary
A merry tale of Rich Neck Town
O my dame had a lame tame crane
One, two, three, four
Ring around a rosy
Romance at Tulip Hill
The singing geese
The spider in the wall
Tell a tale of Ara Spence
There was a farmer had a dog
Three little tales of Washington
Ting-a-ling-ling
What's your name?
The white mule ghost
William T. Trinity

Maryland
LEACH – RAINBOW p99-101

Masefield, John
The boy on a broomstick
Mr. Hampden's shipwreck
Sea fever
A wanderer's song

Mason, Arthur
The night of the big wind

Masons
See also **Stonemasons**
The building of the fortress wall
The demon mason
The legend of the mason
Odin's eight-legged steed

The mason's marriage
LIN – MILKY p16-23

Masoy and the ape
SECHRIST – ONCE p110-118

Masquerades
The theft of Thor's hammer

Massachusetts
Chief of the night riders
The devil in the steeple
The golden horse with the silver mane
Jingling rhymes and jingling money
The lord of Massachusetts
A merry tale of Merrymount
The sacred cod and the striped
haddock
The strange adventures of the cowboy-
sailor
The Wilbur witches
–Berkshires
The rival cooks
–Boston
Never
–Cape Ann
Legend of the witch of Cape Ann
–Charlestown
Tom Walker and the devil
–Concord
Life in Concord
–Dighton Rock
North Salem's Irish? Ruins
Tales of the ambiguous Dighton
Rock
–Gloucester
Old Meg, the witch
–Great Barrington
The phantom bridge
–Holyoke
Tim Felt's ghost
–Marblehead
Magic in Marblehead
Scandulous affairs of a baronet
and a tavern maid
–Merrimack Valley
The ordeal of Hannah Dustin
–Newbury
The double-headed snake of
Newbury
–Pelham
The mystery of Pelham House

–Pigeon Cove
Foreward, The witch house still
stands
–Rehoboth
Rehoboth's lady counterfeiter
–Salisbury
The devil's bride
–Springfield
Hooker and the witches
–Watertown
The haunted houses of Watertown
–Weymouth
Hanging at Wessaguscus

Massachusetts
LEACH – RAINBOW p101-105

Massage
The story of Noschoy Datta of Ujjain

Masson, Elsie
The witch of Lok Island

The mast of sand
INS-SOB – FOLK p77-78

Master and man
DEUTSCH – MORE p45-54

Master and pupil
NAHMAD – PEASANT p104-110

The master and the servant
TASHJIAN – ONCE p29-38

The master cat
ARBUTHNOT – TIME p102-105

Master Erik
HACK – DANISH p182-194

Master Frost
DUDDINGTON – RUSS. p41-45

The master-maid
JACOBS – EUROPE. p142-158

The master mariner
SHEAHAN – HENRY p23-42

Master of all masters
ARBUTHNOT – TIME p17.
MY BOOK HOUSE v. 3 p148-149

The master of magic and spells
LOWE – LITTLE p75-80

The master of the winds
GINSBURG – MASTER p34-47

The master-smith
THOMPSON – ONE p66-72

The master thief
JACOBS – EUROPE. p121-128
THOMPSON – ONE p391-395

The masters of magic
JENNINGS – BLACK p19-37

The match-making of a mouse
BULATKIN – EURASIAN p82-84

Matches
The little match-girl

Mathematicians
Many moons

Mathematics
See also Mutiplication
Problems

Mats
The old lady and the monkeys

The matsuyama mirror
HEARN – JAPANESE p102-108

A matter of importance
DOBBS – MORE p43-44

Mattresses
Musk and amber
The real princess

Maugham, W. Somerset
Princess September

Maugham, W. Somerset
JOHNSON – PRINC. p314.

Maui and the death goddess
CAMPBELL – MAORI p25-29

Maui and the fire goddess
BERRY – MAGIC p89-97
CAMPBELL – MAORI p20-24

Maui catches the sun
BERRY – MAGIC p74-80

Maui nooses the sun
CAMPBELL – MAORI p11-14

Maui, the demi-god
BERRY – MAGIC p65-73

Maui the fire-bringer
U. N. – RIDE p14-19

Maui the Great
See also Ride with the sun
COURLANDER – TIGER'S p132-139

Maui-the-trickster
THOMPSON – LEGENDS p66-71

Maui traps sun
THOMPSON – HAWAII. p60-64

Mauritus
The martyrs of Thebes

Max and Moritz
PROTTER – CHILD. p168-170

Max and Moritz and the tailor
PROTTER – CHILD. p171-175

Maxen Wledig, Emperor of Rome
The dream of Maxen Wledig

Maximianus, Emperor
The martyrs of Thebes

Maximilian and the goose boy
BALDWIN – FAVOR. p107-113

May Colvin
MANNING – ENGLISH p24-29

May Day
As it fell upon a day
Catherine, my dearie
The cuckoo and the donkey
Down by the river Avon
The first of May
Little bells, pretty flowers of the
steppes
A merry tale of Merrymount
Song on May morning
There are twelve months
There's not a budding boy
Ye merry doinges of Robin Hood

May it not happen
COURLANDER – FIRE p111-112

Maya–mayi the seven sisters
PARKER – AUSTRALIAN p148-154

Mayas. See Indians of Latin America–
Maya

Mayne, William
  Adam Bell, Clym of the Clough, and
    William of Cloudesley
  The courtship of Lemminkainen
  Prince Marko and a Moorish chief-
    tain
  Pwyll, Pryderi, and Gawl
  Sir Perceval
  The troubles at Hawaiki

Mayors
  The broken box
  How the devil fetched the mayor
  The ox as mayor
  The quarrel about the woods
  Sean na Scuab

Mazimuzimus (cannibals)
  The adventures of Nomvula
  The wicked Mazimuzimu

Mboyo and the giants
  COBBLE – WEMBI p120-123

Mboyo the hunter
  COBBLE – WEMBI p115-116

Mead (drink)
  The Ailp king's children
  Bragi, god of poetry
  How Odin brought the mead to Asgard

Meadows
  I took a walk one evening
  Over in the meadow
  The princess on the Glass Hill
  The shepherd's crown
  Young Kate

The meal mill at Eathie
  SHEPPARD – SCOT. p139-144

Meanness
  See also Cruelty; Evil; etc.
  The bad-tempered wife
  The eternal wanderer of the Pampas
  The hillman and the housewife
  How Flint-face lost his name
  Katcha and the devil
  Knurremurre
  A lie for a lie
  The little scarred one
  Malachi and Red Cap the leprechaun
  Mango mountain
  The old man who made flowers
    bloom
  The old man who made trees blossom
  Old Plott

Princess Janina and the troll Bradalba
Rattle-rattle-rattle and chink-chink-
  chink
The smart husband and the smarter
  wife
Smart working man, foolish boss man
There's always a reason
Two out of the sack
The two sisters
Wend' Yamba
The year of Nyangondhu's cattle

Measles
  The son got the measles

Measure twice, cut once
  CHAPPELL – THEY p36-41

Measures and measurement
  The cat and the dog
  Exactly so
  A foot and a stick or man is the
    measure
  The piskey revelers
  Tape measure
  They measure the depth of the well
  The true scales

Meat
  How people got fire
  The parrot and the crow
  The stupid boy
  The three who made Ku

The meat hungry man and the grave
digger
  COBBLE – WEMBI p82-84

Meat or cat?
  KELSEY – ONCE p8-14

Mecca
  The merchant of Mecca and the up-
    stairs donkey

Mece and his merry pranks. Fishing for
  a chicken; The flying angel; The
  ghost in the cabbage patch; Mece and the
  shoemaker's daughter; Polenta, polenta,
  and more polenta
  MINCIELI – TALES p40-53

Mece and the shoemaker's daughters
  MINCIELI – TALES p43-46

The mechanical man of Prague
  SERWER – LET'S p39-54

Meddlesomeness. See Interference

416

Medea
The golden fleece

Medicinal
JOHNSON – WHAT p48-54, 214-218

Medicine
See also Drugs; Healing
The bride of Llyn y Fan Fach
The frog heralds
The kappa's arm
The king and his seven sons
Magic and medicine
River child
The tiger's grave

Medicine men
Agayk and the strangest spear
The Angakok and the mother of seals
The black swans
Gheeger Gheeger the cold west wind
The grizzly and the rattlesnake men
Honwyma and the bear
How maple sugar came
The hyena's medicine man
The Kamiah monster
The lady and the devil
The legend of Pathasos
A legend of the flowers
The monkey and the banana
The peace pipe
The rainmaker Wirinun
Sam Dan and the government doctor
The stone frogs
The wonders seen by Wurrunna

Medieval legends. See Middle Ages

Medusa
The adventures of Perseus
Perseus . . . The head of Medusa

Medusa
JACOBSON – LEGEND. p28-30

Meekness
Buh mouse testifies
The golden crow
Joshua and the princess
The king on trial
The proud king
The stone monkey

Meet Ed Grant
FELTON – WORLD'S p15-19

Meet-on-the-road
WITHERS – I SAW p68-69

The meeting
See also The woman of Llyn-y-fan
(1) The meeting
SHERLOCK – IGUANA'S p5-10

Meeting in the road
GARNER – GOBLINS p133.

The meeting of Deirdre and Naoise
PILKINGTON – THREE p146-155

A meeting of scholars
BARASH – GOLDEN p88-91

A meeting of two servants
WITHERS – I SAW p85.

Meg Merrilies
MY BOOK HOUSE v. 8 p188.

Meg o' the moors
SPICER – WITCHES p32-37

Megerle, Ulrich. See Sancta Clara,
Abraham a

Mehdevi, Alexander
MEHDEVI – BUNGLING p119.

Meinrad and the ravens
MULLER – SWISS p205-209

Meissner, August Gottlieb
The mouse and the snail
Pride goes before a fall

Melancholy. See Grief; Sadness

The melancholy prince and the girl of
milk and blood
TOOR – GOLDEN p47-53

Meleager
Crocus flowers bloom like fire

Melisande
JOHNSON – PRINC. p138-163

Mellitot and Iolanda
PICARD – MERMAID p243-254

The melodius napkin
MANNING – DAMIAN p117-128

Melons
The jackal, the barber and the
Brahmin who had seven daughters
The magic melons
Why frogs speak Chinese
The woman who came down from
heaven

The melting pot
MY BOOK HOUSE v. 11 p173-216

Memorials
The little sticky rice basket

Memory
See also **Absent-mindedness;**
Superstitions–Memory
Bees in the bonnets in New Jersey
Forgotten something?
How the letter X got into the alphabet
Long memories
The Northern lights
The scholar of Kosei
Stupid's cries

Memory
BATCHELOR – SUPER. p96-99
HOPE-SIMPSON – CAVAL. p153-
156

The men and the monkeys
FEINSTEIN – FOLK p64-67

The men fashion the frames of their
kayaks
BELTING – STARS #10

Men of different colors
HEADY – WHEN p91-94

Men of Erin. *See* **Erin, Men of**

Men of the sea
BATCHELOR – SUPER. p57-59

Menaseh's dream
SINGER – WHEN p83-96

Mendelssohn, Felix
A musical visit to fairyland

Menehunes
The adventures of Kahukura and Te
Kanawa, the Little People of
Polynesia
Laka and the Little People
The little menehunes

Menelaus, King of Sparta
The anger of Achilles
A cause of war
Helen in Egypt
The story of the Greek princess

The merchant of Mecca and the upstairs
donkey
MORRIS – UPSTAIRS p121-127

The merchant, Saint Michael, and the
devil
MINCIELI – TALES p60-64

The merchant with nothing to sell
SERWER – LET'S p19-21

Merchants
Ali Sundos
The armless maiden
The beardless, the lame, and the
one-eyed thief
Beauty and the beast
The bob-tailed monkey and the king's
honey
The bone that testified
The boy and the birds
The caravan
The caravan continues
The caravan ends
The caravan reaches the end of the
desert
The cartman's stories
Cast thy bread upon the waters
Catherine and her fate
La Cenerentola
The city under the sea
The comb, the flute and the spinning
wheel
The covetous minister
The debt
Diamond cut diamond
The dog and the donkey
Dookiram, the poor one
The dutiful daughter
The economical son
Fair Vasilissa and Baba Yaga
The fear of the lion king
The feather of Finist the falcon
The flower faces
The fortunate maiden
The gift and the giver
The gift of the holy man
The gold-lined donkey
The golden carnation
The golden lion
The golden mountain
He wins who waits
The head of the family
The hired man
How a peasant outwitted two mer-
chants
The hypocrite and the merchant's
pledge
If my shoe is narrow, what matter if
the world is wide
Ikkyu and the merchant's moneybags
The ivory box
The judgement of Hailu
The kind caliph and the horse thief
The king and his seven sons

418

Merchants (*Continued*)

King Firdy the Just
The king who rides a tiger
The land beyond the fire
The lily and the bear
The little gray pony
A long-bow story
The lord of Massachusetts
The lovesick giant
Lucky star of Herald Square
The man who bought a dream
Marko the rich and Vassili (Vasily) the luckless
A message for a donkey
The messenger
The mice and the previous seeds
The most precious possession
The mountain of gold
Mousey the merchant
Nawasi goes to war
The nut branch
Ooka and the terrible-tempered tradesman
The parrot
A peasant sells a cow as a goat
Peder Okse
The pedlar of Swaffham
Pepito
The phoenix and the falcon
Pintosmalto
A portion in Paradise
Quinces and oranges
Rabbit and the grain buyers
The red cloak
The rich man and his son-in-law
The righteous heir
Rodents rampart on a field azure
Shiny tales of Vincennes
The silly fellow who sold his beard
The stone in the cock's head
The story of Wali Dad the simple-hearted
The tale of Godfrey Malbone
The thousand pieces of gold
The three litigants
The three ravens
Three silly schoolmasters
Three wonderful beggars
Tiny Perry
The true scales
Two different interpretations of the same pact
Vasilia the beautiful
Wali Dad the simple hearted
The wise merchant

The merchant's son and the slave
NAHMAD – PEASANT p40-42

The merchant's wife
NAHMAD – PORTION p102-106

Mercury (god)
Strike there!

Mercy
The babe Moses
The hunter and the dove
Joseph and his brethren
A story about Abe Lincoln
Vladimir's adventures in search of fortune

Meredith, George
Richard Feverel and the hay

Merisier, stronger than the elephants
COURLANDER – PIECE p9-14

Merkel, Karl, illus.
The Soria-Maria-castle

Merlin
The dark tower
Saxons

Merlin
VANSITTART – DARK p81-89

The mermaid and the boy
LANG – VIOLET p219-233

The mermaid and the simpleton
PICARD – MERMAID p11-27

The mermaid in church
MANNING – PETER p178-182

The mermaid of Zug
MULLER – SWISS p93-96

Mermaids
See also **Mermen**
Andrew and the mermaid
Aye-Mee and the mermaid
Basia, the babbler
The blue lake
The bride from the sea
The comb, the flute and the spinning wheel
Conchobar and Teeval
The fisherlad and the mermaid's ring
The fisherman and his soul
The fisherman and the mermaid
The fisherman and the seal maid
The fisherman's son
The geese and the golden chain
The groach of the Isle of Lok
John Reid and the mermaid
The kingdom of ocean
The lake maiden
The little mermaid

Mermaids (*Continued*)

Long John and the mermaid
The lost prince
Lutey and the mermaid
The magic lake
The magical tune
The maid of the waves
Margrette
Nefyn the mermaid
The old man of Cury
Rake up!
Sirene, the mermaid
The spell of the mermaid
Sven and Lilli
Swan white and fox tail
The three mermaids
The untidy mermaid
Urashima
The wiliwili trees
The woman of Llyn-y-fan (1) The meeting
The woman of Llyn-y-fan (2) The parting
The woman of Llyn-y-fan (3) The sequel

Mermaids
JACOBSON – LEGEN. p31-32

The merman
MY BOOK HOUSE v. 6 p178-179

Merman Rosmer
MANNING – MERMAIDS p108-113

The merman's revenge
LEEUW – LEGENDS p28-32

Mermen
The blue men of the Minch
The four abdallahs
The geese and the golden chain
Grim and the merman
The king and the merman
The laughing merman
Margrette
Olaf the mermaid's son
The seal catcher and the merman
The seal fisher and the roane
The twin brothers

Mermen
JACOBSON – LEGEND. p32-33

Merriment. *See* **Laughter**

The merrow and the soul cages
BRIGGS – PERS. p142-148

Merrows
Martin Grogan and the merrow

Merry Christmas
MY BOOK HOUSE v. 2 p217.

Merry-go-rounds
The story of Ticho

A merry tale of Merrymount
JAGENDORF – NEW p158-162

A merry tale of Rich Neck Town
JAGENDORF – UPSTATE p241-247

A message for a donkey
MINCIELI – TALES p54-56

A message from the moon
COURLANDER – KING'S p106-108

A message in a bottle
GRAY – MAINLY p73-90

The messenger
COURLANDER – KANT. p65-70
PILKINGTON – THREE p172-181

The messenger donkey
COURLANDER – FIRE p41-43

Messengers
The armless maiden
The bungled message
An inadvertent misunderstanding
The Kris of Adji Saka
Little Mukra
The magic sandals of Hualachi

The messengers from the moon
McALPINE – JAPAN. p179-185

A meteoric loss
WILLIAMS – LOST p126-131

Metzger, Berta
The banyan deer
The golden boat
How the camel got his proud look
The talkative king
Why ants have small waists

The mewlips
TOLKIEN – READER (Part 4) p45-46

Mexican rhymes
MY BOOK HOUSE v. 1 p70-71

Mexico
The ant, the lamb, the cricket and the mouse
Bird Cu
The bow, the deer, and the talking bird
The boy who beat the devil
The boy who could do anything
The boy who took care of the pigs
The boy who wouldn't mind his grandmother
The burro Benedicto
The castle in the lake
A cat for a hare
A child in a Mexican garden
Chucho, who's afraid?
The cow that cried
The coyote and the two dogs
Coyote rings the wrong bell
The dead man who was alive
The devil and the railroad
Dumb Juan and the bandits
Fate of the Magicos
The foolishness of Cochinito
Friar Blockhead and the Lord
Funny, funny
Ghost of the lane of Monkey's leap
The goat who couldn't sneeze
The happy milkmaid
Henry Crabb—a born loser
The holes of Lagos
How Flint-face lost his name
How horses came to the Navaho
How I found these tales
How Papantla got its patron saint
How Tepozton hung the bells
How Tepozton killed the giant
Lazy lout of a plant
Leon and the lion
The lost saints
The love of a Mexican prince and princess
Luz, the story-teller
The magic baby shoes
The magic grocery store
Malintzin
The man who stayed too long
Maria sat on the fire
The million-dollar somersaults
The miracle of Our Lady of Guadalupe
Mogo, Popo, and Wogo
One roll of bread
Our Lady of Guadalupe
Pancho and the Duendes
Pancho Villa and the devil
Pancho Villa's lost head
The peacock and the puhuy
The poor widow bullfighter
Popo and the coyote
Popo and the princess

Preface: Story time in Mexico
The princess and Jose
The rabbit in the moon
The rabbit who wanted to be a man
Revenge of the tin god
The river that was stolen
The sacred drum of Tepozteco
Saint Quien Sabe
Salvador and the coyote
Salvador and the goat
Santiago and the fighting bulls
Sarita and the Duendes
Senor coyote
Senor coyote and the dogs
Senor coyote settles a quarrel
Simon and his rocky acre
The smoking mountain
Some impatient mule-drivers
The story of Ticho
Story-telling in Milpa Alta
Tales of magic, black and white
Tepozton
Teutli, the mountain that is alive
Things that happened long ago
Tlacuache the saint
The war between the lion and the cricket
What makes moonshine on water
When the iguana grows armor
The woman of rock

—**Mexico City**
Near God's cactus

—**Tecate**
The lost gold bars of Juan-Blanco

—**Tijuana**
A lost chord in Tijuana brass

—**Veracruz—Popolucas**
How tiger learned to hunt

—**Yucatan**
The cockoo's reward

Meyer, Kuno, trans.
The fort of Rathangan

Micah Rood's apple tree
TAFT — PROFILE p175-178

Mice
See also **Dormice**; titles beginning with **Mouse**
The adventures of Manawyddan
All the cats consulted
Aniello
The animals' quarrel
The ant, the lamb, the cricket, and the mouse
Baba Yaga and the little girl with the kind heart

Mice (*Continued*)

The battle of the frogs and the mice
The bed
The bee, the harp, the mouse, and the bum-clock
The bee, the mouse and the bum-clock
Belling the cat
Birds of a feather
Buh mouse testifies
The bungling host
A captive snake half dead with fright
The cat and mouse in partnership
The cat and the mice
The cat and the mouse
The child sold to the devil
The city mouse and the country mouse
The clever cat and the giant
The cock, the mouse, and the little red hen
The cockroach and the mouse
Conversation
The country of the mice
Curd ears
Daughter and stepdaughter
Dick Whittington and his cat
Diggory
Dog couldn't be cured
The dog, the cat, and the mouse
The dragon who lost his fire
The duel of the cat and the mouse
Ergosai-Batyr
Field mouse and house mouse
The flea
The flood
The forest bride
The four friends
The friendly mouse
A frog he would a-wooing go
The frog, the mouse, and the hawk
Froggie goes a-courting
The geese and the swans
Gigi and the magic ring
The glass house
The goblins at the bath house
The golden snuff-box
The good man and the kind mouse
The grateful mouse
The hermit and the mouse
Hickory, dickery dock!
The holy cat of Tibet
The house mouse and the country mouse
How the foxes became red
How the lion rewarded the mouse's kindness
How the peasants brought wisdom
I saw a ship a-sailing
The impudent little mouse
The inquiring rabbit, or the strongest thing in the world

It's all the fault of Adam
Jack and his golden snuff-box
King Setnau and the Assyrians
King Solomon's cat
The kingdom without a cat
Kisander
Krazy Kat
The lass that couldn't be frighted
Light-O-Leap and the fowler
The lion and the mouse
The little bird's rice
Little fir tree
The little gray mouse and the handsome cock
The little house
The little mouse
The little mouse with the long tail
The little red hen and the grain of wheat
The louse skin drum
The magic egg
The magic ring
The man who swallowed the mouse
The marriage of the mouse
The match-making of a mouse
Mr. Korbes the fox
Mistress cockroach
The mongoose, the owl, the cat and the mouse
The mother of time and the enchanted brothers
Nangato
Ole shut-eyes, the sandman
Perez and Martina
The piper who could not play
The poor people who wanted to be rich
Puddock, mousie and ratton
Puss in boots
The rabbit prince
Reen-reen-reeny-croak-frog
The rescue of fire
Rodents rampart on a field azure
The sage and the mouse
St. Cadog and the mouse
Segizbai and the little mouse-girl
Senor coyote
The seven mice
The silver jug
The six companions
The stone in the cock's head
The story of Maia
The story of Tom Thumb
The tale of Nutcracker
The tale of the little sausage and the little mouse
Tcakabesh snares the sun
Three tests for the prince
Thumbelina
Titty mouse and Tatty mouse
The town mouse and the country mouse

Mice (*Continued*)

A tramp of the Middle West
The trials of Dyfed
The twins and the snarling witch
The unsmiling princess
The wedding of the mouse
Who is strongest?
Why cat eats first
Why cats and dogs fight
Why cats lie on the doorstep in the sun
Why dogs and cats are not friends
Why the dog and the cat are enemies
Why the tip of fox's tail is white
The wicked weasel
Willie's bad night
Winkle, Tinkle, and Twinkle
The wolf and the mouse
The woman and the mouse
The world's smartest cat

The mice
    MY BOOK HOUSE v. 6 p131.

The mice and the precious seeds
    DE LA IGLESIA – CAT (unp.)

The mice in council
    LA FONTAINE – FABLES p18-19

Michael, Saint
    Saint Michael and the idle husband

Michael Scott and the demon
    LEODHAS – THISTLE p136-143

Michelet, S. C., illus.
    Toto gets married

Michigan
    Old boss and George

Michigan
    LEACH – RAINBOW p105-108

Micronesia
    Animal and bird stories
    Sirene, the mermaid
    Stories about girls and boys

Midas, King
    The golden touch
    The golden touch; the king who worshipped gold

Midas
    ARBUTHNOT – TIME p228-229

Midas . . . The greed for gold
    UNTERMEYER – FIRE. p72-75

Middle Ages
    The alchemist
    Aucassin and Nicolette
    Cnut and Edmund
    The cowherd's son
    The death of Roland
    The devil and the summoner
    The dragon of Rhodes
    The house in the valley
    How Ysengrin the wolf was taught to fish
    The king and the merman
    King Appolonides
    King Herla's guest
    The knight with the two swords
    The leper's miracle
    The loathly lady
    Louis and Theobald
    The man who climbed down a moonbeam
    The nightingale
    St. Cuddy and the gray geese
    Sir Gawain and the green knight
    Sir Launfal
    Sir Orfeo
    The tale of chanticleer
    The three plagues of Britain
    The three young men and death
    The two lovers

Middlewest
    Engine, engine number nine
    Old Johnny Appleseed
    A tramp of the Middle West
    The village of cream puffs

The midget and the giant
    COOPER – FIVE p76-87

Midgets
    Digit the midget
    The duck with red feet
    The half-pint jinni
    The hazel-nut child
    Hop o' my thumb
    How Master Thumb defeated the sun
    I had a little husband
    Isun Boshi, the one-inch lad
    Kernel
    Little finger
    The little-man-as-big-as-your-thumb-with-mustaches-seven-miles-long
    Little one-inch
    Little shell
    Little Tom Thumb
    The man who was only three inches tall

Midgets (*Continued*)
One-inch fellow
Pidicino
The princess of China
The story of Tom Thumb
The tale of the little mook
Thumbelina
Thumbkin
Timimoto
Tiny Perry

Midir and Etain
O'FAOLAIN – IRISH p23-26

Midir and Etain
PICARD – CELTIC p36-45

Midnight
'Twas midnight

The midnight hunt
WILLIAMS – FAIRY p302-305

Midsummer eve
Maid Lena

A midsummer night's dream
MY BOOK HOUSE v. 6 p38-58

The midwife. *See* The fairy midwife

Midwives
The brownie of Jedburgh
The fairy child
The fairy midwife
Left eye, right eye
The Nithsdale brownie

The mighty hunter
LEEUW – INDO. p109-112

Mighty Michael . . . Who could do
anything
UNTERMEYER – FIRE. p239-242

Mighty Mikko
See also The miller-king
FILLMORE – SHEPHERD'S p11-25

Mighty Mose, the Bowery b'hoy
JAGENDORF – UPSTATE p3-9

The mighty warrior in hare's house
KAULA – AFRICAN p118-125

The mighty wrestlers
WITHERS – WORLD p2-6

The mignonette fairy
CATHON – PERHAPS p148-149

Migrations
How the people came from the lower
world

Mike Fink
GORHAM – REAL p47-62
LEACH – RAINBOW p43-47

Mike Mulligan and his steam shovel
ARBUTHNOT – TIME p265-267

Milesians
The children of Lir

Military strategy (tactics)
General Chang's strategy
The victorious lute

Milk
The crow and the whale
The girl who met the witch of the
woods
The man who turned into a hyena
Mary milks the cow
The milkmaid and her pail
Noodlehead and the flying horse
Puss in boots
Pyoli
The test
Yiankos
Zohair and the witch

–**Cream**
Ainsel
Bewitched cream
The elders of Chelm and Genendel's
key
The king's cream
Nidelgret

–**Jugs**
The castle in the cornfield

The milkmaid and her pail
ARBUTHNOT – TIME p207.
STRONG – FAVORITE p15.

Milkmaids and milkmen
A Belgian morning
The big street in the big city
The devil's bride
Good morning, Peter
The happy milkmaid
Little maid, pretty maid
Mary milks the cow
O 'twas on a bright mornin' in summer
Where be you going, you Devon maid?

The milkman and the monkey
SPELLMAN – BEAUT. p28-30

A milkweed and a buttercup
MY BOOK HOUSE v. 4 p118.

Milky way (constellations)
The badger and the magic fan
How the milky way began
The Indian Cinderella
Little Burnt-face
The mink and the sun
The star path

The milky way
JABLOW – MAN p102-104
LEACH – RAINBOW p290.
LIN – MILKY p24-32

The mill at the bottom of the sea
BAKER – TALKING p104-112

The mill that grinds at the bottom of the
sea
ASBJÖRNSEN – NORW. p108-114

Miller, (Cincinnatus Heine) Joaquin
The poet of the Sierras

Miller, Kate B., joint trans.
A horned goat

Miller, Olive Beaupre
The airplane
Big bus, stop!
A boy on the high seas
The bridge
Bucky, the big bold fawn
The circus parade
Exploring the wilderness
The first Thanksgiving day
The Fourth of July
Francois Villon, the vagabond of Paris
The greatest show on earth
Hallowe'en
A happy day in the city
The little toy land of the Dutch
Look, see the boat!
The mad dog
Mary and the Christ-child
Mister postman
New Year's day
O I'll build a square with my pretty
red blocks
Policeman Joe
The road to China
A song for Easter
Thunder and lightning

Tippity Witchit's Hallowe'en
The Yankee peddler

The miller and the blue jay
JAGENDORF – SAND p178-180

The miller and the fairies
SHEPPARD – WELSH p101-105

The miller and the water sprite
BECHSTEIN – FAIRY p174-178

The miller, his son, and the donkey
LA FONTAINE – FABLES p30-32

The miller-king
TASHJIAN – ONCE p13-26

The miller of the dee
BALDWIN – FAVOR. p36-38

Millers
Blow, wind, blow, and go, mill, go!
The brigands and the miller's daughter
Dwarfs' caps
The Earl of Cattenborough
Ero from the other world
The finest liar in the world
The fisherman and the seal maid
The golden coal
King James and the questions
The little gray pony
The little milleress
The miserly miller
The pooka of the mill
The poor miller's boy and the cat
The rich man and his son-in-law
Rumpelstiltzkin
Silver leaves and golden blossoms
The skipper and the dwarfs
The stranger and the miller
The talking donkey
The three golden hairs of the king of
the cave giants
The two millers
The tyrant and the miller
The water-sprite and the bear
The young giant

The miller's four sons
THOMPSON – ONE p292-296

The miller's three sons
DELARUE – FRENCH p29-44

Millet
The fool
A grain of millet
The great flood
The snake
Three fast men

425

The millet seed
BAMBERGER – FIRST p118-122

Millinery. *See* Hats

The million-dollar somersaults
ROSS – MEXICO p50-61

A million stories
WITHERS – I SAW p47.

Mills
See also Coffee mills; Watermills
The blinded giant
Blow, wind, blow and go, mill, go!
The goose from Flatbush
Lies for a wager
The mead mill at Eathie
Mother Codling and her family
The one-eyed ogre of Sessay

, Hand
The enormous genie
The magic acorn
The mill that grinds at the bottom
of the sea
The rooster, the hand mill and the
swarm of hornets
The salt Welsh sea
The three sons
Three who found their hearts'
desire
Who put the salt in the sea?
Why the sea is salt

Millstones
The black bodach
The enchanted castle in the sea
Mr. Korbes the fox
The prince and the demon
The self-propelled carriage

Milne, A. A.
King Hilary and the beggarman
The magic hill
Pooh goes visiting and gets into a tight
place
Prince rabbit
That is why he was always called Pooh
Winnie-the-Pooh

Milne, A. A.
JOHNSON – HARPER p326.
JOHNSON – PRINC. p314-315

Milomaki
LEACH – RAINBOW p302.

Milton, John
Song on May morning

Milutin, Tsar Lazar's servant
ČURČIJA – HEROES p44-45

Minarets
The legend of the mason
Up and down the minaret
The voice from the minaret

Mind
The giant and the mite
Heart and mind

Minden, Gerhard von
Different, but not better

Mineral springs
The song-bird and the healing waters

Mines and mining
See also types of mining
An American miner's song
Barker's knee
Ghost of the lane of Monkey's leap
A gift for a gift
The haunted mine
The little gray pony
The poet of the Sierras
The secret of the hidden treasure

Ministers. *See* Clergymen

Ministers (political)
The covetous minister
Diplomacy
Dookiram, the poor one
Pen and four foolish ministers
The rajah who flew away
The royal banquet
Siengmieng, the minister
A strange reward
The task of the minister Abe-no-miushi
Teton
The Thanksgiving of the Wazir
The three unmarried ministers
The troubadour and the devil
The unpunctual minister, or the bo-
sung pohoo
Westwoods
The witch of Wandaland

Mink
Child of the sun
How the sea gulls learned to fly

The mink and the sun
MATSON – LONGHOUSE p123-127

The mink and the weasel
MATSON – LONGHOUSE p113-121

Minnesota
LEACH – RAINBOW p108-109

Minnie and Mattie
MY BOOK HOUSE v. 1 p156.

Minoan maze and Minoans
Lost arts

Minor monsters
McHARGUE – BEASTS p53-59

The minotaur
JACOBSON – LEGEND. p40-42
MAYNE – HEROES p92-126

Minstrel making
IVES – TALES p283-303

Minstrels
Aucassin and Nicolette
Aucassin and Nicolette . . . their difficult romance
The birth of Robin Hood
The golden twins
Kalevala, land of heroes
The King of Sedo
King Orfeo
The pied piper of Hamelin; a minstrel's enchanted music
The piper with the hoofs of a goat
The princess and the vagabone
Rufus
Sadko the minstrel
The seven proud sisters
A song for the new chief
The song of Gimmile
The thunder cat
The wonderful tune

Minute pudding
FELTON – WORLD'S p71-77

Mirabella
MICHAEL – PORTUGUESE p35-41

The miracle flame
JAGENDORF – SAND p118-122

The miracle of Our Lady of Guadalupe
JAGENDORF – KING p198-202

The miracle of the begging bowl
CARPENTER – ELEPHANT'S p108-113

The miracle of the Poor Island
FARJEON – LITTLE p74-82

The miracle on the Jaffa Sea
CARPENTER – SHIPS p237-245

Miracles
The man who made the trees bloom
Padre Ulivo and his guests
The penitent governor
The pious washerwoman
Saint Michael and the idle husband

The miraculous flute
LOWE – LITTLE p44-46

The miraculous stag
BAKER – TALKING p199-203

Mirages
Beereeun the miragemaker

Mirror
LEACH – SOUP p68-72

Mirrors
The basilisk, king serpent
Bergamot
Breaking a mirror
Come look!
The cruel giant
The dragon of Utrecht
Evan's problem
The greedy dog
Hiding in the well
The Jewish pope
Leon and lion
The lutin in the barn
The magic calabash
The magic mirror
The man in the mirror
The matsuyama mirror
The monkey and the mirror
The nun as judge
Reflections
Simple Wang
The snow-queen
Snow-white
Snow White and the seven dwarfs
Sven and Lilli
The tale of the two cunning servants
The untidy mermaid

Mirza and the ghul
SPICER – KNEELING p29-44

Mirzhan and the lord of the kingdom
under the sea
MASEY – STORIES p38-45

Mischief and mischief-makers
See also **Trickery**
The boy who would eat lobsters
The dancing palm tree
Irraweka, mischief-maker
The kappa's arm
Max and Moritz
Max and Moritz and the tailor
The old soldier and the mischief
The origin of the coconut
The origin of the coconuts
Uncle Coyote's last mischief
Vukub-Cakix

The miser
DOBBS – MORE p22-25

The miser and the fairy feast
BRIGGS – PERS. p66-69

The miserly frog
DEUTSCH – TALES p32-35

The miserly miller
LEEUW – LEGENDS p92-96

Misers
The bell of Atri
The borrower
Fairies on the gump
The first buttercups
The great scare
The Groschen hole in the Murz
Valley
How he stole the moon and the sun
How the miser turned into a monkey
How the raven stole the stars
The hunchback and the miser
Hwan and Dang
The jurga
Malachi and Red Cap the leprechaun
The man who made the trees bloom
Marko the rich and Vasily the luckless
Ooka and Tosuke's tax
The peasant and the workman
The rain-lady and the ghost
The ride in the night
Shrewd Todie and Lyzer the miser
The three cups of water
The treasure of Altamira
The two misers
The tyrant and the miller

The miser's wife
GILSTRAP – SULTAN'S p67-74

Misfortune comes to the house
SECHRIST – ONCE p82-85

Miska and the man-with-the-iron-head
MY BOOK HOUSE v. 7 p11-19

Miss goat
WYATT – GOLDEN p81-84

Miss Jenny Jones
LEACH – RAINBOW p214-216

The missing fog bell
CARPENTER – SHIPS p255-264

Missionaries
Fridolin
The tale of Columba and the angel
Tsali of the Cherokees

Missions
The lost saints

Mississippi
Callin' the dog
Catches
Johnny and Tommy and the bear
Mr. Fox learns what trouble is
Mr. Wren borrows money of Mr.
Buzzard
Mosquitoes
Nanih Waya: The sacred bluff
A negro couple talks of witchcraft
Negro folktales from Mississippi
The story of the fraids
When Uncle Henry was a little tiny
boy

Mississippi
LEACH – RAINBOW p109-111

Mississippi River
Annie Christmas
River roarer/Mike Fink
A trail of tall tales
The waters beneath: The great river
monster

Missouri
Jesse James

Missouri
LEACH – RAINBOW p112-113

A Missouri cyclone
JOHNSON – WHAT p225-226

Missouri River
River roarer/Mike Fink

Mr. and Mrs. Vinegar
  WILLIAMS — FAIRY p96-102

Mr. Bun
  TUDOR — TASHA p72-74

Mr. Crow and the mussel
  GILHAM — BEYOND p121-126

Mr. Crow takes a wife
  GILLHAM — BEYOND p31-43

Mister deer's my riding horse
  COTHRAN — WITH p40-43

Mr. fox learns what trouble is
  JOHNSON — WHAT p248-249

Mister frog's dream
  BARLOW — LATIN p104-112

Mr. Frost
  BUDBERG — RUSSIAN p54-64

Mr. Hampden's shipwreck
  MY BOOK HOUSE v. 8 p172-187

Mister Honey Mouth
  COTHRAN — WITH p34-39

Mr. Korbes the fox
  WILLIAMS — ROUND p166-171

Mr. Louse and Mrs. Louse
  WITHERS — I SAW p79-80

Mister Luck and Mister Industry
  AUNG — KINGDOM p18-23

Mr. Lucky Straw
  SAKADE — JAPAN. p78-81

Mr. Miacca
  WILLIAMS — FAIRY p146-148

Mr. Noy
  MANNING — PETER p183-190

Mister Postman
  MY BOOK HOUSE v. 1 p182.

Mister rabbit meets his match again
  ARBUTHNOT — TIME p199.

Mr. rabbit steals Mr. fox's fish
  JOHNSON — WHAT p247-248

Mr. Samson cat
  ROSS — BURIED p19-25
  TUDOR — TASHA p21-24

Mr. Toad sets out on a journey
  MY BOOK HOUSE v. 1 p68.

Mr. Vinegar
  ARBUTHNOT — TIME p17-19

Mr. Wheeler
  SHERLOCK — WEST p144-151

Mr. wren borrows money of Mr. Buzzard
  JOHNSON — WHAT p249-250

Mr. X and the loyalty oath
  IVES — TALES p71-74

Mistletoe
  The death of Balder

Mistress Cockroach
  MEHDEVI — PERSIAN p81-92

The mistress of fire
  GINSBURG — MASTER p48-54

Mrs. Fox's wedding
  BAMBERGER — FIRST p160-161

Mrs. Longspur's second marriage
  GILLHAM — BEYOND p106-116

Mrs. Mag and her nest
  WILLIAMS — FAIRY p179-180

Mrs. Peterkin wishes to go to drive
  ARBUTHNOT — TIME p359-360

Mrs. Stowe's oranges
  JOHNSON — WHAT p176-177

Mrs. Tabby Gray
  MY BOOK HOUSE v. 3 p129-132

Mrs. Wallaby Jones
  ARBUTHNOT — TIME p328-331

Mists
  In the mist
  The maiden of the mist

Misunderstanding
  The four deaf men
  An inadvertent misunderstanding
  It's been well used
  The pillow
  A time for everything

Misuse of a name
  GREEN — BIG p81.

Mitchell, Lucy Sprague
The big street in the big city
Biting Marion
The three trucks

Mites
The giant and the mite

Mitsuhashi, Yoko
KRUEGER – SERPENT p159.

Mittens the cat
BAMBERGER – FIRST p44-47

Mix a pancake
MY BOOK HOUSE v. 1 p157.

The mixed-up feet and the silly bridegroom
SINGER – ZLATEH p39-50

The mock turtle's song
MY BOOK HOUSE v. 3 p170-171

Mockery
The bird that told tales

Mockingbird gives out the calls
COURLANDER – PEOPLE p60-62

Mockingbirds
The cardinal's concert
How the people came from the lower
world
Weedah the mockingbird

Moderation
The grateful monkey's secret
The horse and the colt

The "modern" sea monster
BUEHR – SEA p48-71

Modesty
Becky's garden
The cobbler astrologer and the forty
thieves

Modesty and wisdom
NAHMAD – PORTION p124.

Moe, Jorgen Engerbretsen
The ash lad who had an eating match
with the troll
The doll under the briar rosebush
East of the sun and west of the moon
The giant who had no heart in his body
Gudbrand of the hillside
The mill that grinds at the bottom of
the sea
The Norwegian folk tales and their
illustrators
The parson and the sexton
The princess on the glass hill
Squire Per
Taper-Tom who made the princess
laugh
Three billy goats gruff
The three princesses in the mountain-
in-the-blue
Why the sea is salt

Moe, Jorgen Engerbretsen
ASBJÖRNSEN – EAST p137.
SIDEMAN – WORLD'S p830.

Moe, Moltke
The princess who always had to have
the last word

Mogo, Popo and Wogo
JORDAN – BURRO p64-67

The Moha Moha
BUEHR – SEA p84-87

Mohammed
A blessing and a curse
The cat and the prophet

Mohammed and the spider
LEEUW – INDO. p90-93

Moi and the red bull
HARMAN – TALES p153-162

The mole and the rabbits
GREEN – BIG p64-65

Moles
Coyote and mole
The fox and the mole
How raven brought fire to the Indians
How the people came to the middle
place
The kettle and the chestnut
The lark, the wolf, and the fox
The open road
The secret store
The securing of light
The story of Maia
The theft of fire
Thumbelina
Why the mole lives underground
Willie's bad night

Moles (*Continued*)

, **Duck-billed**
The right time to laugh

—**Paws**
Why mole's front paws are bent

The mole's bridegroom
SEKI — FOLKTALES p29-30

Molin, Charles
Tavadan
Tavadan and the fire giant

Moll, Ernest George
The dark guest

Molla Nasreddin and his donkey
BULATKIN — EURASIAN p64-68

Mollusks (shell-fish)
The hunting dog and the purple fish

Molly Whuppie (or Whipple)
BROWN — AROUND p7-21
HAVILAND — ENGLAND p44-45
REEVES — ENGLISH p183-194

Momotaro
See also following and variant titles
HEARN — JAPANESE p126-132
LINES — TALES p107-117

Momotaro: boy-of-the-peach
ARBUTHNOT — TIMES p159-162
UCHIDA — DANCING p97-106

Momotaro, or The story of the son of a peach
HAVILAND — JAPAN p47-71

Momotaro, the peach boy
SEKI — FOLKTALES p40-43

Momus the mocker
GREEN — BIG p207.

Monasteries
The ancient land of Tigre
The carefree monastery
Fridolin
The little book
The tale of Liban the siren
Thi Kinh

—**Einsiedln**
Meinrad and the ravens

—**Iona**
The tale of Columba and the angel

Money
See also types of money; **Superstitions** —**Money**
The ass that lays money
The boy and the water-sprite
The chief of the Guernsi
The dead creditor
The deluded dragon
The devil duped
Fiddler John and the devil
A gift from the heart
Hereafterthis
How Juan married a princess
How the pig got his snout
Kernel
The milkman and the monkey
The musical silver goat
The old witch
Pamudjo's feast
The rabbit grows a crop of money
Sense and money
The smell of money for the smell of food
The sticky-sticky pine
Story of a nickel and a dime
The terrible Olli
There was a little boy
Three corpses, money, and a wine-bottle
To the devil with money!
The treasure of Tacoma
Two dollar curse
Upa and her admirers
With a wig, with a wag

, **Fairy**
Fairy money

—**Trees**
Kalulu and his money farm

Money
BATCHELOR — SUPER. p52-55
JOHNSON — WHAT p70-72

The money cask
BOUCHER — MEAD p136-138

Money-lenders
The conch shell of ram
The fly

Money luck
LEACH — LUCK p66-68

Money makes cares
BONNET — CHINESE p149-153

Money superstitions
BATCHELOR — SUPER. p52-54

Mongolia
The golden dolls
The golden pitcher
The smoke horse

The mongoose, the owl, the cat and the mouse
GRAY – INDIA'S p55-57

Mongooses
The cat, the dog, and the mongoose
The king who rides a tiger
The lonely lioness and the ostrich chicks
The ostrich chicks
The tree with the difficult name

The monk and the bird. *See* The bird and the man

Monkey
WILLIAMS – ROUND p27-42

The monkey and Mr. Janel Sinna
TOOZE – MONKEY p53-69

The monkey and the banana
COBBLE – WEMBI p12-19

The monkey and the crab
SEKI – FOLKTALES p15-16

The monkey and the crocodile
KOREL – LISTEN p14-20
SECHRIST – ONCE p60-63

The monkey and the mirror
KRYLOV – 15 p27.

The monkey and the pheasant
SEKI – FOLKTALES p16-20

The monkey and the shark
MONTGOMERIE – 25 p26-27

The monkey and the spectacles
KRYLOV – 15 p17.

The monkey bridegroom
SEKI – FOLKTALES p167-170

The monkey bridge
CARPENTER – SHIPS p213-225

Monkey-dance and sparrow-dance
SAKADE – JAPAN. p25-28

Monkey fat
WYATT – GOLDEN p13-21

The monkey gardeners
GAER – FABLES p120-122

The monkey gardeners
GREEN – BIG p18-20

The monkey king's bridge
REED – TALK. p58-61

Monkey-lord and crocodile
WYATT – GOLDEN p98-100

The monkey nursemaid
MANNING – DEVILS p51-55

The monkey prince and the witch
ROBERTSON – PHILIP. p23-32

The monkey, the tiger, and the jackal family
SIDDIQUI – TOON. p109-112

Monkeys
See also **Baboons**
The adjutant bird
The adventures of Little Peachling
The age of the partridge
All about the tail of the leopards
All around the cobbler's bench
Anansi steals the palm wine
The barrel of water
The bet between Matjan and Gadja
The black-handed monkey
The bobtail monkey
Born a monkey, live a monkey
The Brahmin and the villain
Bundar Bahadeer Poon
The choja who became a monkey
Chucho, who's afraid?
The circus parade
The crab and the monkey
The dancing monkeys
The days of the first monkeys
The decision
The exploits of Hanuman
The foolish dragon
The foolish, timid little hare
Four tales of Rama and Sita
Ghost of the Lane of Monkey's leap
The grateful monkey's secret
Greedy and speedy
Ha! Tio rabbit is bigger
A handful of peas
The hare and the tiger
The hare, badge, monkey and otter
The hare in the moon
The harebrained monkey
He washed the monkey's face
The house that strong boy built
How monkey king became a slave
How music began
How the miser turned into a monkey
How the monkey came to be
Kantjil and the monkey business

432

Monkeys (*Continued*)

The king and his seven sons
The king and the monkey
The king's drum
The legend of the Karang
The light in the house
The little pet rani
Lunching with dragons
The magic belt
The magic bone
Malati and the prince
The many children of Mr. and Mrs.
  Twelve
The men and the monkeys
The milkman and the monkey
Mister Luck and Mister Industry
Momotaro
Momotaro: boy-of-the-peach
Momotaro, or The story of the son
  of a peach
Momotaro, the peach boy
The night of the full moon
Nkalimeva
The old lady and the monkeys
Old Noah
Peach boy
The pearl necklace
The peddler and his monkeys
Pop! goes the weasel!
The prince who wanted the moon
The proud camel and the rude monkey
The quarrel
The quartet
The rabbit in the moon
The rain leak in an old house
Rama's conquest of Ravana
The Ramayana
The rarest animal of all
The scholar, the monkey, and the goat
The search for Sita
The smart woman of Kennebunkport
So say the little monkeys
The stone monkey
The story of the tortoise and the monkey
Temba's monkey friends
The terrible leak
There was a monkey
Tiger in the forest, Anansi in the web
The tortoise and the monkey
The turtle and the monkey share a tree
The turtle who loved a monkey
The two foolish cats
Two friends: how they parted
The ungrateful tiger
Who can break a bad habit?
Why jellyfish has no shell
Why the bananas belong to the monkey
Why the jellyfish has no bones
The wise old camel
Work-let-me-see

The year of the monkeys of Ramogi
The zoo in the park
—Apes
  Adrian and Bardus
  The ape and the firefly
  The ape and the two cats
  The battle of the firefly and the apes
  How confusion came among the
    animals
  Kindai and the ape
  Masoy and the ape
, Bob-tailed
  The bob-tailed monkey and the king's
    honey
, Capuchin
  Little capuchin monkey's story
—Chimpanzees
  Chimpanzee's story
  The man who became a chimpanzee
  The queen's care
—Gibbons
  The ungrateful crocodile
—Hearts
  A lot of silence makes a great noise
  The monkey's heart
  The wise monkey
—Livers
  The jellyfish's journey
  The monkey's liver
  The silly jelly-fish
  Why the jellyfish has no bones

Monkeys
  MY BOOK HOUSE v. 1 p142.

The monkeys and the little red hats
  CARPENTER — AFRICAN p71-75

The monkeys' feast
  HOLLADY — BANTU p76-77

The monkey's heart
  ARNOTT — AFRICAN p135-139
  GAER — FABLE p126-129

Monkeys in the sausage tree
  AARDEMA — STORY p38-43

The monkeys' jizo-sama
  SEKI — FOLKTALES p128-130

The monkey's liver
  PRATT — MAGIC unp.
  SEKI — FOLKTALES p25-27

The monkey's pomegranate
  LOWE — LITTLE p97-102

The monkey's search for Sita
GRAY – INDIA'S p116-124

Monks
See also **Gurus**
The archbishop's mule
The best wish
The boy and the monk
The boy who taught the fairies
tears
The carefree monastery
Dietrich is knighted
Dinner for the monk
The drowned bells of the abbey
Elidorus in fairyland
The farmer of Babbia
The four brothers
The girl on the green tree
The golden buffalo
The horse and the eighteen bandits
Hwan and Dang
The legend of the mason
Marko the rich and Vasily the luckless
Meinrad and the ravens
The miracle of the begging bowl
North Salem's Irish? Ruins
Old Nick's bridge
The prince's revenge
Ramiro II, the monk
The ring of Hallwil
Robin Hood
Robin Hood and the monk
The Siamese pepper cure
The story of General Gim Dog-Nyong
The tale of Columba and the angel
That fourth leg of the dog
The three stars
The three wishes
The tiger's tail
A tongue of gold and words of jade
Two two brothers and the magistrate
The ungrateful tiger
The wild man

Monro, Harold
Overheard on a salt marsh

The monsoon season
REED – TALK. p49.

Monsoons
Why the monsoon comes each year

The monster
HEADY – TALES p101-108

The monster mo-o
THOMPSON – HAWAII. p65-69

The monster of Loch Ness
JACOBSON – FIRST p60-61

Monsters
See also **Sea monsters;** names of
monsters
Alberto and the monsters
Bahri of the beauty spot
The basilisk, king serpent
Beauty and the beast
Bellerophon . . . The winged horse
Beowulf conquers Grendel
Beowulf . . . The fight with Grendel
The grave cowman
Bundar Bahadeer Poon
The cat and the king's daughter
Centaurs
Cerberus
The chimera
The dragon foul and fell
Dragons kings of the East
The emerald-crested phoenix
The fairy bird
Fifty red night-caps
The finding of the Eleanba Wunda
Finn MacCool
How Beowulf delivered Heorot
Iwanich and the magic ring
Kalamona and the winds
The Kamiah monster
King Hrolf and the bear's son
Kuluile, the dancing girl
The Lambton worm
Loki's monstrous brood
Manstin, the rabbit
Minor monsters
Nabulela
The Nemean lion
The northern frog
Oisin in the land of the ever young
One-inch fellow
Orthrus
Pegasus and the chimaera
Polyphemus, the Cyclops
Prince Murko's journey
The prince of the six weapons
Prince Prigio and the firedrake
The Red Etin
The ruby prince
The search for Sita
Shah Ismail and the Turkmen maiden
The swallowing monster
The terrible family
Una and the Red Cross knight

Monsters and ghosts
JENNINGS – BLACK p113-129

Monsters of prehistoric times
BUEHR – SEA p19-25

Monsters of the Middle Ages
  BUEHR – SEA p26-34

Monsters, witches and giants
  BRIGGS – PERS. p169-171

Montana
  Ed Grant out West

Montana
  LEACH – RAINBOW p114-116

Montanus, Martinus
  Grace at meals

Montassier, Nicolas
  The love of three oranges

Montgomerie, Norah and William
  Finn and the young hero's children

Months of the year
  See also **Seasons**
  The capricious month
  Courage
  Forty days hath Ramadan
  Grandmother Marta
  Jan and Jaantje
  Julius Ceasar . . . The Ides of March
  March and the shepherd
  November's party
  Princess September
  The quarrel between the months
  Song on May morning
  There are twelve months
  The twelve months
  Th twelve months of the year
  The twelve young men

Monuments. *See* **Statues**

Moon
  Anansi's rescue from the river
  Animals, people and the moon
  Antelope's mother: the woman in the
    moon
  Ants
  The arrow chain
  The August moon
  Autumn
  The babymakers
  Beaver moon
  The blacksmith in the moon
  A boy in the Island of Bali
  The boy in the moon
  The boy who fished for the moon
  Boys and girls, come out to play

The brawl between sun and moon
The brothers Yakshich divide their
  heirloom
The bungled message
The buried moon
Cadwaladr's goat
Capturing the moon
Chu Cuoi's trip to the moon
Cold moon
The Coomacka-tree
Corn moon
The crab that tried to swallow the
  moon
The daring prince
The dogs of Bahloo
The duck and the moon
Eight leaves of story (6) The sun of
  Llanfabon
Farming by the moon
A fine cheese
Fire and the moon
The first tears
The fire dogs
Flower moon
The foolish father-in-law
Fox and raven steal the moon
The fox and the mole
The frog and the moon
The frog that swallowed the ocean
Frogs in the moon
A full moon
Full moons
Getting the moon back into the sky
The giant-nonsense verse
The girl and her water buckets
The girl in the moon
The girl who overpowered the moon
The girl whom the moon pitied
The goldfish
Good-speed and the elephant king
The great flood
The greedy man in the moon
Hare and the corn bins
The hare in the moon
Harvest moon
The hat in the moon
The heavenly lovers
Hey diddle diddle
Hina, the woman in the moon
Hjuki and Bil
How cyote helped to light the world
How crane got his long legs
How dandelions were made
How he stole the moon and the sun
How it came about that there is a sun
  and a moon
How life and light came into the world
How men brought fire to earth
How men learned about evil
How the bat caught friendship with
  the moon

Moon (*Continued*)

How the moon and (the) stars came
  to be
How the people sang the mountains up
How the rabbit fooled the elephant
Hunger moon
The hunter on the moon
Hunters' moon
The hyena and the moon
The king's daughter cries for the moon
The king's tower
Krazy Kat
The legend of the star children
Let's steal the moon
The little brother of the sun
Little Johnny
Little numskull stories of the moon
Little stories about the moon
Look here!
The lost sun, moon, and stars
Lovers' moon
The maiden and the moon
The man in the moon
The man in the moon came down too
  soon
The man in the moon stayed up too
  late
The man who climbed down a moon-
  beam
The man who fled a nagging wife
The man who hung his powder horn
  on the moon
The man who paddled to the moon's
  house
Many moons
The message from the moon
The messengers from the moon
The mopoke and the moon
The night of the full moon
The old humpback
The old man and his bush
The old man and his fishing line
The old man in the moon
Old man moon
The old man who said "Why"
Old Shellover
The old woman and her hominy pot
The owl and the pussy-cat
The owl in the moon
The owl's answer to Tommy
Planters' moon
The prince of the Dolomites and the
  princess of the moon
Prince sun and princess moon
Ra and his children
Rabbit and the moon-man
The rabbit in the moon
Raking for the moon
Rescuing the moon
The river of lantern land

The securing of light
The silver hare in a box
The sky-eater
The snow in Chelm
Spears of lightning
Spring
Star-boy and the sun dance
Star catching
Stars in the water
Sturgeon moon
Summer
Sun and moon
Sun and moon and the pretty girl
The sun and the moon
Sun, moon, and stars: Little numskull
  stories
The sun, the moon and the star of
  morning
The sun, the moon, and the stars
Sweet and low
There was an old woman tossed up in
  a basket
Three jovial huntsmen
To the rescue
Turnip thief!
Twins of gold and silver
The very obstinate man
What makes moonshine on water
Which is better, the sun or the moon?
Who?
Why people watch the dipper
Why sun and moon live in the sky
Why the moon has scars on her face
Why the moon wanes
Why the sun and moon live in the sky
Why the sun and the moon live in the
  sky
Why the sun is brighter than the moon
Why the sun shines in the daytime and
  the moon shines at night
Why there are shadows on the moon
Why there is a man in the moon
Winter
The witches of Ascalon
Wolf moon
The woman in moon
Worm moon
Wynken, Blynken, and Nod
Yet gentle will the griffin be

—Festivals
  The golden boat

—Goddess
  The gift of the moon goddess
  The old man in the moon

—People
  The lost spear
  The messengers from the moon
  The moon-maiden

Moon (*Continued*)

—Queen
  The story of Hime

The moon
  JOHNSON – WHAT p96-99

The moon and his frog-wife
  MacMILLAN – GLOOS. p106-109

The moon and other sky beings
  JABLOW – MAN p59-76

The moon and the stars
  JABLOW – MAN p75.

The moon-child
  LAWSON – STRANGE p54-55

The moon husband
  MAHER – BLIND p139-158

The moon in the pond
  MONTGOMERIE – 25 p14-15

The moon-maiden
  MY BOOK HOUSE v. 6 p222-224

Moon of blood
  BUDD – FULL p35-39

A moon of gobbags
  MAYNE – GIANTS p170-176

The moon painters
  MAAS – MOON p7-16

Moon pearls
  LARSON – PALACE p25-30

The moon princess
  SPELLMAN – BEAUT. p94-98

The moon raised the sky
  JABLOW – MAN p22-23

Moon, so round and yellow
  MY BOOK HOUSE v. 2 p40.

The moon's a woman
  COURLANDER – TERRA. p112-113

The moon's escape
  SECHRIST – ONCE p75-78

The moon's face
  JABLOW – MAN p3-24
  LEACH – HOW p34.

Moonlight
  According to tradition
  Fox and raven steal the moon
  Mainly in moonlight
  The man who climbed down a moon-
    beam

The moonrakers
  JABLOW – MAN p51.

Moonstones
  The necklace

Moorachug and Meenachug
  FINLAY – FOLK p20-27

Moore, Clement
  The night before Christmas

Moors
  The broken box
  The fig bough
  The invisible hands
  The knight of the almond blossom
  The legend of the Moor's legacy
  The little horse of seven colors
  Prince Marko and a Moorish chieftain
  The princess who knew her own mind
  Samba the coward
  The subterranean passage

Mo-os (dragons)
  The monster mo-o
  Spears of lightning

Moose
  Beaver moon
  Why the animals live where they do

Moowis
  GARNER – GOBLINS p52-54

The mop servant
  PILKINGTON – SHAM. p61-70

The mopoke and the moon
  PARKER – AUSTRALIAN p56-57

Morag and the water horse
  WILSON – SCOTTISH p103-106

A morality tale: Truth and falsehood
  JAMES – MYTHS p76-83

Morals. *See* Character

Moravia
  King Svatopluk and the three sticks

Moray, Ann
MORAY – FAIR p207.

Mordaunt, Elinor
The prince and the goose girl

Mordaunt, Elinor
JOHNSON – HARPER p327.

More, P. E., trans.
A captive snake half dead with fright
Selections from Rabindranath Tagore
While other birds at will may go

More beautiful than the spider's web
JAGENDORF – KING p226-229

More south than south, more north than
north
PROTTER – CHILD. p20-31

Morelles, Charles
Drakestail

Morgan, Mary de
The heart of Princess Joan
A toy princess

Morgan and the pot of brains
PUGH – TALES p29-36

Morgan and the three fairies
SHEPPARD – WELSH p25-28

Morley, Christopher
Animal crackers

Mornin', mighty Mose
JAGENDORF – GHOST p59-63

The morning and the sunset that
lighteth up the sky
CATHON – PERHAPS p101-125

Mornings
A Belgian morning
The brothers Yakshich divide their
heirloom
Good morning, Peter

Morocco
The girl who lived with the gazelles
The handkerchief
The story of Prince Ahmed

Morons
Chestnuts

Morris, Governor
Lady Morris in her mansion

Morris, Kenneth
Manawyddan son of the Boundless

Morrow, Barbara
SPICER – KNEELING p125.

Mortars
Baba Yaga
The crab and the monkey
The dancing mortar of Block Island
The magic mortar

Moser, Friedrich Karl von
The eagle on a chain

Moses (Biblical)
The babe Moses
Maimonides and the bottle of poison

Moslems
Once there was and once there was not
Pursuit of the Hadji
Warthog and hornbill

Mosques
The baby mosque

Mosquito
LEACH – SOUP p144-146

Mosquito nets
The old lady and the monkeys

Mosquitoes
Adirondack skeeters
The battle of the firefly and the apes
Big mosquitoes
Blood on his forehead
Firefly's story
The first mosquito
The flying kettle
The giant ogre, Kloo-Teekl
Giant skeeters in the brass pot
Hi-ho, the mosquitoes of New Jersey!
The house that ate mosquito pie
How the mosquitoes came to Oneata
It is foolish to carry matters to ex-
tremes
The liars' contest
The little turtle
Moon of blood
Old man Kurai and the one-eyed giant
Seeing far and hearing far
The tyrannical king
Wu Meng, the thoughtful

Mosquitoes
LEACH – RAINBOW p189.

438

The mosquitoes
SUN – LAND p113-116

Moss
How Master Thumb defeated the sun

The moss-green princess
BERGER – BLACK p3-14

Mossi (people)
Kuluile, the dancing girl
Magic and friendship
Naba Zid-Wende

A most generous host
DAVIS – LION'S p102-107

The most necessary thing in the world
BECHSTEIN – FAIRY p106-110

The most obedient wife
ARBUTHNOT – TIME p93-96

A most peculiar bear hide
FENTON – WORLD'S p121-125

The most precious gift
PUGH – TALES p135-143

The most precious possession
VITTORINI – OLD p28-33

The most useful tree in the world
BURTON – MAGIC p56-59

Mother Codling and her family
FARJEON – SILVER p11-14

Mother Coddling is flummoxed
FARJEON – SILVER p47-63

Mother Goose
As I went to Bonner
As Tommy Snooks and Bessie Brooks
Baa, baa, black sheep
Bat, bat, come under my hat
Billy, Billy, come and play
Birds of a feather
Blow, wind, blow, and go, mill, go!
Bobby Shafto's gone to sea
"Bow-wow", says the dog
Bow, wow, wow, whose dog art thou?
Boys and girls, come out to play
The cock's in the housetop
Daffy-down-dilly
Dance, little baby, dance up high!
Dickery, dickery dare

Diddle, diddle, dumpling
Four-and-twenty tailors
Gay go up and gay go down
Goosey, goosey, gander
Great A, little A, bouncing B
Handy-spandy
Hector protector
Here am I, little Jumping Joan
Hey diddle diddle
Hickety, pickety, my black hen
Hickory, dickory dock!
Hippety hop to the barber shop
How many days has my baby to play?
How many miles to Babylon?
I had a little husband
I had a little nut tree
I saw a ship a-sailing
Jack and Jill
Jack, be nimble
Jingling rhymes and jingling money
Johnny shall have a new bonnet
The King of France went up the hill
Lavender's blue
Little Bo-Peep
Little Boy Blue
A little cock sparrow
Little girl, little girl
Little Jack Horner
Little King Boggin
Little maid, pretty maid
Little Miss Muffet
Little Nancy Etticoat
Little robin redbreast
Little Tommy Tucker
Lucy Locket lost her pocket
Mary, Mary, quite contrary
My lady wind
Oh, here's a leg for a stocking
Old King Cole
Old Mother Goose
Old Mother Hubbard
Once I saw a little bird
One misty moisty morning
Pat-a-cake, pat-a-cake, baker's man!
Pease-porridge hot
A pie sat on a pear-tree
Polly, put the kettle on
Pussy cat, pussy cat
Pussy sits beside the fire
Ride a cock-horse to Banbury Cross
Ride away, ride away
A robin and a robin's son
Robin and Richard were two pretty men
Rock-a-bye, baby
Rub-a-dub-dub
See-saw, Margery Daw
Simple Simon
Sing a song of sixpence
Sing, sing! – What shall I sing?
Sleep, baby, sleep

Mother Goose (*Continued*)

Smiling girls, rosy boys
There was a crow
There was a horse
There was a monkey
There was a piper had a cow
There was an old man
There was an old woman
There was an old woman of Harrow
There was an old woman tossed up in
  a basket
There was an old woman who lived
  in a shoe
There was an owl
There were two blackbirds
This little pig went to market
To market, to market
Tom, Tom, the piper's son
Up in the green orchard
Wee Willie Winkie
What's the news of the day
Willie boy, Willie boy

−**History**
  The interesting history of old
  Mother Goose

Mother Holle
  ARBUTHNOT − TIME p37-38

Mother Luck
  DURHAM − TIT p17-23

Mother, may I go out to swim. *See* The
  interesting history of old Mother Goose

The mother of Oisin
  O'FAOLAIN − IRISH p142-147

Mother of the forest
  BURTON − MAGIC p63-68

The mother of time and the enchanted
  brothers
  TOOR − GOLDEN p105-119

Mother Sunday
  MANNING − GIANNI p24-30

Mother tells a story
  ANDERSON − BOY p51-58

Mothers
  See also **Love, Mother; Step-mothers**
  Abe Lincoln in Indiana
  Antelope's mother: the woman in the
    moon
  The cuckoo
  The death of the Yugovichi's mother
  Dobryna's embassy to Khan Amryl

A dutiful son
Fairy mother
The golden horse
The golden nightingale
The grave of a faithful dog
The green frog
The little sticky rice basket
The man who wanted to bury his son
Mang Jen and his mother
The matsuyama mirror
More south and south, more north
  than north
The mystery of the scroll
Nastasya and the whirlwind
Ooka and the wasted wisdom
Peter and the witch of the wood
Sakunaka, the handsome young man
Seven sons
The seven stars of the north
The singing man
The six brothers
The town of fools
Tsai Shun, the faithful
The weasel and his mother
The wise old woman

A mother's advice
  ZAGLOUL − BLACK p103-107

Mother's Day
  The adventures of Perseus
  The babe Moses
  The cap that mother made
  Chink, chink, chocket
  The exile of Rama
  Life in Concord
  Mrs. Tabby Gray
  Over in the meadow
  Princess Nelly and the Seneca chief
  A Roumanian lullaby
  The strong boy
  Thus I guard my mother's lambkins

Mother's day
  SPELLMAN − BEAUT. p26-27

Mother's girl and father's girl
  CREANGA − FOLK p93-101

Mothers-in-law
  The girl on the green tree
  Pleiad and star of dawn

Moths
  The butterfly's ball
  The liars' contest

Moti
  LANG − OLIVE p165-175

Motorcycles
The big street in the big city

Motmots (birds)
Why the motmot lives in a hole

Mould
The quellers of the flood

Mounds
Pwyll and Pryderi (1) The marriage
of Pwyll and Rhiannon
The trials of Dyfed

Mount Kennebago
FELTON – WORLD'S p41-44

The mountain and the rivers
INS-SŎB – FOLK p14-15

The mountain goats
MARTIN – NINE p43-47

The mountain hen and the fox
RANKE – GERMANY p17.

Mountain lords
The greedy tailor
How the carrot-counter got his name

Mountain-men
The boy and the mountain-man
The fox and the stork
The hen with the golden legs

The mountain of gold
DOWNING – RUSSIAN p145-150

The mountain of hope
SUN – LAND p58-60

Mountain songs
The barnyard

The mountain where old people were
abandoned
SEKI – FOLKTALES p183-186

The mountain witch and the dragon-king
INS-SŎB – FOLK p169-171

The mountain witch and the peddler
UCHIDA – MAGIC p83-90

Mountains
See also names of mountains
The adventures of Ciad
Aliosha's visit to the bald mountain

The Alp that disappeared
The beginning of the world and the
making of California
The blackstairs mountain
Bukolla
Casperl
The crimson purse
Crocus flowers bloom like fire
The donkey lettuce
The dream at Nam Kha
The enchanted palace
The fall of the earth giants
The fire on the mountain
Fjords and mountain peaks
The gold bird
The golden peacock
The good sword
The great flood
Halde Hat and Dulde Hat
The hardhearted rich man
He who lives in a mountain
Heidi in the Alpine pasture
The holy mountain
How God helped Mammo
How little stork lost his tail
How the people came to the middle
place
How the people sang the mountains
up
If I could work
The inquiring rabbit, or The strongest
thing in the world
Jack, the giant Galligantua, and the
enchanter
A Japanese lullaby
Kachi Kachi mountain
The king and the wrestler
The king of the mountain
The legend of Crooked Mountain
The legend of the Karang
The legend of the star children
Life in the heights
The little engine that could
Longshanks, girth, and keen
The love of a Mexican prince and
princess
The luck of the sea and the luck of
the mountain
The Machimoodus noise
The magic grocery store
The magic mountain
The maiden and the ratcatcher
The maiden, the knight, and the
waterfall
Malintzin
The man who loved Hai Quai
The man who stayed too long
Mango mountain
The marriage of the mouse
The monkeys' jizo-sama
The moon-maiden

Mountains (*Continued*)

No flowers
The oba asks for a mountain
Old Pipes and the dryad
Once upon a time
The people who lived near a mountain
Pepito
The Phynnodderee
The pied piper of Hamelin; a minstrel's enchanted music
The poet of the Sierras
The poor herdsman and his sons, the Little People of Africa
Popo and the princess
Pride goes before a fall
Prince Finn the Fair
The prince with the golden hand
Princess Janina and the troll Bradalba
The princess of the mountain
The proud father
The rabbit and the bear
Rip Van Winkle; the strange little men of the mountain
A rover in the Catskills
The silent princess
The smoking mountain
The spring ay-petri
The stone-crusher of Banjang
The story of Zoulvisia
The strongest
The swamp Nushi's messenger
A tale of two mandarins
Teutli, the mountain that is alive
The three brothers
The thunder cat
Tiger woman
The truest adventures of the truthful mountain boy
The turtle prince
The turtles and the mountain tunnel
The two lovers
Why the mountains are snow-covered
The wonder of Skoupa
The yellow-haired witch

, **Crystal**
The crystal mountain

, **Glass**
The frog
The princess and the glass mountain
The princess on the glass mountain
The swan princess
The three lemons

, **Golden**
The golden mountain

, **Marble**
The lion, the tiger, and the eagle

—**Spirits**
Why the monsoon comes each year

, **White**
The prince of the Dolomites and the princess of the moon

Mountains of Manitou
TAFT – PROFILE p264-267

The mountains that clapped to-gether
GILLHAM – BEYOND p1-16

Mourners
The brothers of the donkey
How Prince Bondhu became a boatman
Hwan and Dang

The mouse and his friends
GRAY – INDIA'S p49-54

The mouse and the elephant
LA FONTAINE – FABLES p10-11

The mouse and the flea
GILHAM – BEYOND p68-75

The mouse and the frog
GREEN – BIG p74.

The mouse and the magician
MONTGOMERIE – 25 p54-55

The mouse and the rat
KRYLOV – 15 p7.

The mouse and the sausage
HARDENDORFF – FROG'S p155-157

The mouse and the snail
GREEN – BIG p46.

The mouse and the sun
MacMILLAN – GLOOS. p225-230

The mouse and the wizard
TURNBULL – FAIRY p127-135

Mouse bride. *See* A prince and a dove

The mouse climbed up the candlestick
MY BOOK HOUSE v. 1 p77.

Mouse-deer
The bet between Matjan and Gadja
The case of the mouse-deer and the crocodile's eggs
The friendship of the hare and the parrot
Kantchil and the monkey business
Kantchil becomes a raksha
Kantchil brings the elephants to heel

Mouse-deer (*Continued*)

Kantchil discovers the wisdom of
Allah
Kantchil's lime pit
Kantil grows strong at the welling-
well
Kantjil holds a festival
Kantjil interprets a dream
Kantjil to the rescue
Kantchil's lime pit
King Kantjil's kingdom expands
The leopard and the mouse deer
One against a hundred
The securing of light
Three tales of the mouse-deer
The tiger's war against Borneo
Two out of one
The ungrateful crocodile
War between the crocodiles and
Kantchil
Why there are no tigers in Borneo

A mouse from the Mabinogian
WILLIAMS – FAIRY p312-328

The mouse hole
WILLIAMS – OLD p285-312

A mouse in search of a wife
GREEN – BIG p88-89

The mouse keeps her promise
WILSON – GREEK p148-150

The mouse surrounded
REED – TALK. p25-27

The mouse, the bird and the sausage
BAMBERGER – FIRST p53-55

The mouse who lived under the granary
GREEN – BIG p54.

The mouseling
TOOZE – WONDER. p59-63

The mouse's bride
TURNBULL – FAIRY p103-109

The mousetower
PICARD – GERMAN p103-105

Mousey the merchant
GRAY – INDIA'S p38-39

Mouths
Muskalala, the talking skull
Twist-mouth family

Move clockwise, and other circle superstitions
BATCHELOR – SUPER. p86-88

The movie show
LEACH – RAINBOW p255-256

Moving
The boggart
The leprechaun and the wheelbarrow
Mrs. Longspur's second marriage
The pooka

Moving day
BATCHELOR – SUPER. p93-94

Moving the church
RANKE – GERMANY p179.

Mowgli's brothers
MY BOOK HOUSE v. 5 p182-213

Mowing
Donal O'Cairan from Connaught

Moyers, William
FELTON – NEW (Preface)

Mrizala and her bridegroom, death
RANKE – GERMANY p45-50

Mud
The bear went over the mountain

The mud-snail fairy
INS-SOB – FOLK p29-31

Mudhens
The beginning of the world and the
making of California
Fire magic and the mud hen
The firemakers

Mugwort
Dan-Gun, first King of Korea

Mukerji, Dhan Copal
The search for Sita

Mulberry trees
The fire boy
The gift of the hairy one
The ingrates
The legend of the mulberry tree
Pyramus and Thisbe . . . The mul-
berry tree

Mule-drivers
The advantages of learning
Some impatient mule-drivers

Mules
The archbishop's mule
The art of reading
Buffalo Bill
The clever thieves
The enchanted mule
The house that Jack built
I had a little mule
Kernel
The little gardener with golden hair
Old boss, John, and the mule
Old Plott
The popcorn patch
The talking mule
Tell me, when will I die?
The white mule from the other world
The white mule ghost

The mullah's oven
KELSEY – ONCE p20-23

Mullian-ga the morning star
PARKER – AUSTRALIAN p87-90

Multatuli, pseud (Edward Douwes Dekker)
Fables

Multiplication
Two of everything

Mumbele and the goats
HEADY – WHEN p15-20

Mummies
Teen-ager

Munchausen, Baron
The strange adventure of Baron Munchausen

Muntrs (magic words)
The magic muntr

Murder
Ashoremashika
Blue Beard
Bluebeard
The brown man of the Muirs
The clever lord
The coffin that moved itself
The flute made of maple-wood
The fool and the birch-tree
For love of a woman

The greater sinner
The haunted house of Watertown
The killing of Mogg Melone
The king's remorse
The legend of the virgin Arang
The little sticky rice basket
The lost remains of Mr. Quejo
Meinrad and the ravens
Micah Rood's apple tree
Nooloigah who caused his brother to die
The red cloak
Self-convicted
Sketco begins his wanderings
The tree that walked

Murray, Mrs. Robert
Clever Mistress Murray

Musakalala, the talking skull
LITTLEDALE – GHOSTS p67-72

Museums
Books to read; museums to visit
The invisible baby
The Irish luck of Brian Hughes

The mushroom
CATHON – PERHAPS p18.

Mushrooms
Allah will provide
The lame duck
The princess on the glass mountain

Music
The bird of the valley
The delicate daughter
Ergosai-Batyr
Frozen music
The girl and the crocodile
The girl on the hill
The girl on the rock
The girl who forgot her hoe
How the Kuhreihen began
How the miser turned into a monkey
Kamiyo of the river
The lion on the path
The magic herdboy
The magic lute player
The magical music
The magical tune
The man who turned into a hyena
Mapandangare, the great baboon
Midas
Ned Puw's farewell
Nyangara, the python
Of a tailor and a bear
The palace in the Rath
Rabbit and tortoise

Music (*Continued*)

Sadko
Sakunaka, the handsome young man
The singing chameleon
Some songs of old New York
The three sisters and the cannibals
A town in a snuff-box
Tsimbarume, the hardened bachelor
The victorious lute
The water sprite

—Boxes
  The poor boy and the princess
  The swineherd

—Melodies
  The piper with the hoofs of a goat
  The wonderful tune

—Teachers
  The neck

Musical instruments
See also names of instruments
How music began
What they say

The musical silver goat
  ILLYÉS — ONCE p74-77

A musical visit to fairyland
  MY BOOK HOUSE v. 6 p59-61

The musician of Tagaung
  See also The hero of Adi Nifas
  COURLANDER — TIGER'S p35-37

Musicians
See also names of musicians; types of
  musicians
The Bremen town musicians
Gisella and the goat
Hwan and Dang
The neck
Orpheus . . . The fabulous musician
The pied piper of Frenchville
The royal musician
The three musicians
The musicians
  KRYLOV — 15 p18-20

The musicians of Bremen
  See also The journey to Toulouse of
  the animals that had colds
  SIDEMAN — WORLD'S p631-636

Musk and amber
  WILSON — GREEK p107-119

Muskets. *See* **Guns & gunnery**

Muskrats
The flood
Over in the meadow
Peter Rabbit decides to change his
  name

Mussels
How mussels were brought to the
  Creeks
Mr. Crow and the mussel

Mustard seeds
The seed of happiness

Mutes
The bride who out talked the water
  kelpie
Brother Anansi and Sir Peacock
Gulersh and the princess of France
Prince Ivan and the sun princess

Mutiny
Captain Samuel Samuels

The muula tree
  ELLIOT — WHERE p95-100

My beloved is gone down into his garden
  MY BOOK HOUSE v. 2 p78.

My boat
  MY BOOK HOUSE v. 1 p163.

My candlestick
  MANNING — DAMIAN p106-116

My lady sea
  MANNING — DAMIAN p18-28

My lady wind
  MY BOOK HOUSE v. 1 p46.

My Lord Bag-o'(of)-Rice
  HEARN — JAPANESE p47-52
  MANNING — DRAGONS p38-42

My maid Mary
  MY BOOK HOUSE v. 1 p51.

My own self
  JACOBS — MORE p16-19

Myna(h) birds
The bird that told tales
Captain Fokke of Holland
The strange ship of Captain Fokke

Myrrh
Rabbi Joseph Della Reina

The mystery of Pelham House
RASKIN – TALES p79-83

Mysteries
California's lost diamonds
Lost arts
The lost gold bars of Juan Blanco
Lost in lava
The lost secrets of Charles Hatfield
The lost treasure of Cucamongo
A meteoric loss
A trio of lost monsters
The yellow ribbon

Mysteries of the sea
JAGENDORF – NEW p236-239

The mysterious lake
JAGENDORF – KING p83-88

The mysterious letter
LUM – ITALIAN p14-21

The mysterious path
LITTLEDALE – GHOSTS p83-86

The mystery of Pelham House
RASKIN – TALES p79-83

The mystery of the scroll
MAR – CHINESE p87-96

Myth and folktale in human actions: The
tale of the two brothers
JAMES – MYTHS p61-75

Mythical beast of the sea
JACOBSON – FIRST p46-47

Mythical beasts in heraldry
JACOBSON – FIRST p66-67

Mythology
See also Gods and goddesses
The flood
Prahlada
Why the moon wanes

N

Naake, John T.
   The book of magic

Naba Zid-Wende
   GUIRMA – TALES p1-15

Nabookin
   BULATKIN – EURASIAN p103-105

Nabulela
   SAVORY – ZULA p47-52

Nagas (Naginis)
   The king and the Nagas

Nagasvamin and the witches
   GRAY – INDIA'S p202-205

Nagging
   The language of the birds
   Mango mountain
   The wood carver of Ruteng

Nahmad, H. M.
   The ape and the two cats
   Cast thy bread upon the waters
   The covetous minister
   The donkey, the ox and the farmer
   The fowler, the parrot and the king
   The goldsmith, the wood carver, the
      tailor, and the hermit who quarreled
      over a wooden woman
   Hani the simple
   Juha and the dispute over a goat
   Juha at the banquet
   The king and the two owls
   The king who tried to cheat destiny
   A lie for a lie
   Maimonides and the bottle of poison
   The merchant's son and the slave
   The pilgrim and the judge
   The red slippers of Honum
   Shah Abbas and the cobbler
   The stupid hunter and the crafty bird
   The teacher and his pupil
   Three times lucky
   Zohair and the witch

Nahuals (magic people)
   Funny, funny

Nahuaques (Little People)
   Malintzin

Naiads
   The knight and the naiad of the lake

Nail Soup
   CURČIJA – YUGOSLAV p153-154

Nails
   The old woman and the tramp
   The white dove of the city of the
      swinging gate

Nails
   INS-SÖB – FOLK p37-38

Nala and Damayanti
   GRAY – INDIA'S p68-88

The Namashepani
   HEADY – WHEN p21-26

Names
   The birth of Pryderi
   Casi Lampu'a Lentemue
   A cat is a cat is a cat
   The cerval's secret name
   The curlew flies
   Duffy and the devil
   The fairy wife
   The farmer of Babbia
   The flower without a name
   Forget-me-not!
   From a moral alphabet
   From tiger to Anansi
   Gwarwyn-a-Throt
   How crab got a hard back
   How the carrot-counter got his name
   The hungry rider
   Isis and Osiris
   Isis and the secret name of Ra
   The last three guesses
   Master of all masters
   "Nimmy-nimmy-not!"
   Nine guesses
   The ogre who built a bridge
   Peter Rabbit decides to change his
      name
   Princess September
   Puddlefoot
   Rabbit Joseph Della Reina
   Rumpelstiltzkin
   The seven Simeons Simeonovich
   Shah Meram and Sade Sultan
   Six sillies
   The sky god's daughter
   Tiki-Tiki-Tembo

Names (*Continued*)

Tom Tit Tot
Tortoise and Babarinsa's daughters
The tree with the difficult name
Trillevip
Water's locked!
The white hen
Whitebear Whittington
Why the lizard stretches his neck
The witching wood
The young man who married a fairy
Your name
Yung-Kyung-Pyung

, Place
  Bride's brook
  Chocorua mountain
  Hasty Corners
  How Celebes got its name
  Nancy's brook

Names
  CATHON — PERHAPS p129.

Naming the baby
  FARJEON — SILVER p82-89

Nanai (Asiatic tribe)
  The strongest

Nananbouclou and the piece of fire
  COURLANDER — PIECE p62-63

Nancy's brook
  TAFT — PROFILE p237-242

The nandi bear
  JACOBSON — FIRST p58-59

Nangato
  BELPRE — TIGER p21-25

Nanih Waya: The sacred bluff
  MARRIOTT — AMER. p73-77

Nanny and Conn
  McMANUS — HIBERIAN p48-59

Nansii and the eagle
  AARDEMA — STORY p44-48

Napkins
  Donal O'Donnell's standing army
  Dummling
  The melodius napkin
  You have a napkin

Napoleon, Emperor
  Did the tailor have a nightmare?

Narahdarn the bat
  PARKER — AUSTRALIAN p226-229

Narcissus (flowers)
  Crocus flowers bloom like fire
  Echo and Narcissus: the chattering
    nymph and the proud youth
  The legend of the Narcissus
  Narcissus and Echo . . . Their hopeless
    love
  The two brothers

Narcissus and Echo . . . Their hopeless
  love
  UNTERMEYER — FIRE. p44-47

Nasradin Hodja returns a gift
  ĆURĆIJA — YUGOSLAV p18-19

Nasreddin Hoca and the third shot
  WALKER — WATER. p46-48

Nasreddin minds the door
  WALKER — WATER. p58-59

Nastasya and the whirlwind
  WILLIAMS — OLD p240-255

A nasty rumour
  GRAY — INDIA'S p34-35

Nathlook: Susie, my name
  OMAN — ESKIMO p1-23

Native American Church
  Bird of power
  A world of beauty: The Peyote
    religion

Nats (tree spirits)
  The ungrateful tiger

Nature
  See also names of forms of nature
  A boy of the Lake country
  The fairyland of science
  The father of American song
  Names
  The princess who wanted to play with
    the stars

Nature fairies
  BRIGGS — PERS. p139-141

The naughty girl and the ghost-giant
  GREY — SOUTH (2) p22-26

Nausicaa
  The Princess Nausicaa

Navahchoo
HAYES – INDIAN p31-40

Nawasi goes to war
COURLANDER – KING'S p80-86

Nazar the brave
TASHJIAN – ONCE p71-84

Near God's cactus
JORDAN – BURRO p18-21

Neatness
Engine, engine, number nine
The little girl and the new dress
The little toy land of the Dutch
A story about the little rabbits
When Mrs. Bird wants Mr. Bird
Why rooster is so neat

Nebraska
Febold Feboldson

Nebraska
LEACH – RAINBOW p116-117

Nebuchadnezzar
Shadrack, Meshach, and Abednego
. . . The fiery furnace

Necessity
The crow and the pitcher
The most necessary thing in the world

Necessity
URE – RUMANIAN p62-64

The neck
LAWSON – STRANGE p101-112

"**Neck riddles**"
A riddle is a wonderful thing

The necklace
PICARD – LADY p78-99

Necklaces
Annie Christmas
The bears
Bells on her toes
The covetous minister
Freya's wonderful necklace
The grateful beasts
The hawk and the hen
How the moon and (the) stars came
to be
Jackal or tiger?

The lion and the hare
The man who sold magic
Moon pearls
The pearl necklace
The price of a curse
The price of greed
The princess of the mountain
The queen's necklace
Ruda, the quick thinker
The search for Sita
The snake prince

, **Jade**
The jeweled slipper

Ned Puw's farewell
BAKER – TALKING p45-47

Needles
Krencipal and Krencipalka
Leealura and Maleyato
Old Mother Twitchett
One-inch fellow
The quivering needle
Rag, tag and bobtail
The spindle, the shuttle and the
needle
The tufty hen

, **Golden**
The princess with the golden shoes

Needlework
See also names of types of needlework
Little Lady Margaret

Needy. *See* **Poverty**

Neferu–Ra
The princess and the demon

Neff, Mary
The ordeal of Hannah Dustin

Nefyn the mermaid
SHEPPARD – WELSH p109-114

Neglect
The bee-hunter and the oozie
The eternal wanderer of the Pampas
The harebrained monkey
The weeping lady of Llyn Glasfryn
The wren

A negro couple talks of witchcraft
JOHNSON – WHAT p221-223

Negro folktales from Mississippi
JOHNSON – WHAT p246-252

450

Negroes
See also **Africa; Haiti**
The big black umbrella
Brer wolf's little tar men
Conjure bags
The Count of Estremadura
The enchanted castle in the sea
The fiddler of Fiddler's bridge
The frog, the mouse, and the hawk
Hammerman/John Henry
High John the conqueror
The hope tree of Harlem
How brer rabbit met brer tar-baby
How tadpoles lost their tails
John Henry
John Henry and double-jointed steam
  drill
John Henry, the big steel-drivin' man
Johnny and Tommy and the bear
The king who slept
Little Black Sambo
Little Gulliver
The little rabbit who wanted red wings
Mister Deer's my riding horse
Mr. Fox learns what trouble is
Mr. Rabbit steals Mr. Fox's fish
Mr. Wren borrows money of Mr.
  Buzzard
The one-legged chicken
Railroad Bill
The sad tale of three slavers
A squirrel
Stackalee
A story about the little rabbits
The story of Li'l Hannibal
The story of the fraids
The talking mule
Tar-baby
A tar burner's brer rabbit stories
The three oranges
The white dove of the city of the
  swinging gate
The white mule ghost
Why bear sleeps all winter
Why cat eats first
Why elephant and whale live where
  they do
Why rabbit has a short tail
Why sheep does not come in out of the
  rain
Why the birds are different colors
The wood cutter's son and the two
  turtles

—**Rhymes**
A goat one day was feeling fine
I had a little dog
I had a little mule

Neighbors
The envious neighbor

A good neighbor
The old man and his dog
The ram and the pig who went into
  the woods to live by themselves
The ride in the night
Stinginess

Nella's dancing shoes
ROSS – BLUE p73-80

Nemcova, B.
Radowid

The Nemean lion
JACOBSON – FIRST p56-57

Nenetz (Samoyeds) (people)
The cuckoo

Neot, Saint
Saint Neot

Nepal
Bundar Bahadeer Poon
How the travelers shared their meal
The jackal and the bear
The king who rides a tiger
Lato, the stupid one
The perfect husband
The proud father
The soldier's return
Soonimaya
The stolen jewel
Why the flea hops
Why the jackal howls

Nephews
The kettle and the chestnut
The spirit of the waterhole
The ti-trees
The unlucky fisherman

Neptune, King
The goldfish

Nereids
The boastful queen
My candlestick

Nesbit, Edith
The last of the dragons
The magician's heart
Melisande

Nesbit, Edith
JOHNSON – HARPER p328-329
JOHNSON – PRINC. p315-316

Ness, Loch
   Loch Ness; last laugh?
   The Loch Ness monster
   The monster of Loch Ness

Netchillik and the bear
   MELZACK — DAY p35-40

Netherlands
   The black-bearded brownies of
      Boneberg
   The boy hero of Harlem
   Captain Fokke of Holland
   The castle of the three giants
   The coffin that moved itself
   The courageous Quaker of Flushing
   The curse
   The devil's bowling ball
   Double Arend of Meeden
   Dutch nursery rhymes
   Emma of Haarlem
   The emperor's questions
   The ghost ship
   The golden helmet
   Hantsjc and the remarkable beast
   The haunted house
   The hopping lights on Devil's hill
   The house with the heads
   Jan and Jaantje
   Jan the eighth Van Arkel
   The king's rice pudding
   The knight of Steenhuisheerd
   Knurremurre the troll
   The lady of Stavoren
   A legend of Saint Nicholas
   Life in the heights
   Little Hansworst
   The little toy land of the Dutch
   The magic cap
   The man in the moon
   The merman's revenge
   The miserly miller
   The peeping servant
   The phantom ship
   The poffertjis pan
   The punishment
   The rain-lady and the ghost
   Reynard the fox
   The rich widow of Stavoren
   The shell grotto of Nienoort
   The shoemaker's dream
   The simple maid of Hunsingoo
   Stories about Kampen
   The strange ship of Captain Fokke
   Summer snow
   The sunken city
   The three clever brothers
   The three misty women
   The two wishes
   The whispering giant
   The white lady of Pumphul

   The white witch of Espeloo
   Why bears eat meat
   Why cats always wash after eating
   Why pigs root
   A wisp of straw

   —Amsterdam
      The fortunate shoemaker

   —Freisland
      The beggar's prophecy
      The hunchback and the miser
      The ring in the porridge bowl
      The seven wishes
      The singing bell
      The stone owl's nest
      The three golden ducats

   —Harlem
      The boy hero of Harlem

   —Leyden
      The ordeal of Leyden

   —Utrecht
      The dragon of Utrecht

   —Volendam
      The white horse of Volendam

Nets
   The friendly mouse
   The little bird's rice
   The witch of Lok Island

Nevada
   The lost remains of Mr. Quejo
   Of silver and men
   Queen of the Comstock

   —Virginia City
      A few lost ladies

Nevada
   LEACH — RAINBOW p118-119

Never
   LEACH — RAINBOW p205-207

Never mind them watermelons
   LEACH — RAINBOW p241-242

The never never land
   BAMBERGER — FIRST p48-50

Never trust an eel
   JAGENDORF — MERRY p99-104

The new camp stove
   FELTON — WORLD'S p63-70

The new camp stove burns again
   FELTON — WORLD'S p85-92

452

The new colossus
MY BOOK HOUSE v. 11 p172.

The new day
HOSFORD – THUNDER p107-
110

New England
The American saga
The ballad of Lord Lovell
The battle of the Nile
Bewitched cream
Billy boy
Black Sam Bellamy
Bride's brook
Bumblebee and chipmunk
A burn cured
The cannibal frogs
The cat which lost a claw
Charms
Cheating the devil
Chocorua Mountain
Company
Conjure bags
Counting out rhymes
The courtin'
The curious John Greye papers
Curse of the Abenaki
The dancing mortar of Black Island
Dealing with ghosts
Death
The devil and the card players
The devil's bride
Dreams
The duel
The farm
Flyleaf scribblings
Folks
For love of a woman
A fortune in a stick
Fortune telling
The fox and the little red hen
Friends
Games
General Moulton's boot
A ghost story
Giant of the Green Mountains
The gingerbread man
Governor Wentworth's search for a
  wife
Hanging at Wessaguscus
Hasty Corners
The haunted house of Watertown
Hearts and pirates
Here comes three jolly, jolly sailor
  boys
Hooker and the witches
How to kill a witch
The hunters of Kentucky

I'm a peddler
The iniquitous Captain Lightfoot
Insects and other critters
Introductory
Jack and the beanstalk
A Kansas cyclone
The killing of Mogg Megone
Lady Eaton's curse
Lady Eleanore's mantle
The legend of Peter Rugg
Legend of the witch of Cape Ann
The little mouse with the long tail
The little red hen and the wheat
Lord Sinclair and the Zeno brothers
Love and sentiment
Luck
The Machimoodus noise
The man who has plenty of good
  peanuts
Marching to Quebec
Medicinal
Micah Rood's apple tree
Mrs. Stowe's oranges
Money
The moon
Mountains of Manitou
Nancy's brook
North Salem's Irish? Ruins
Nursery tales
Odds
Odds and ends
Old Noah
Old songs
Old stories
The old woman and her pig
The ordeal of Hannah Dustin
The phantom bridge
The power of fancy
Problems
Raising the wind
Rehoboth's lady counterfeiter
Religious
Rhymes and jingles
The rival cooks
Scandalous affairs of a baronet and
  a tavern maid
The serpent of Carbuncle Hill
A severe punishment
Signs and sayings
Snakes
Some New England superstitions
Sometime
The song of the Darby ram
Spelling
Spring flood
The steers that wouldn't draw
Stonewall Silas Clapp
The story of Mon-do-min
The strange battle of Windham
Stumping the devil
Tales of the ambiguous Dighton Rock

New England (*Continued*)

Tea grounds
Those young men
The three young maids who went to
  seek their fortunes
Tim Felt's ghost
Tom Walker and the devil
The traveler
The travels of a fox
Tricks and catches
The twist-mouth family
The village rooster and William Smith
Wahconah
The warning of the frogs
Warts
The weather
The whale that smoked a pipe
The Wilbur witches
Wishes
Witches and ghosts
With a wig, with a wag
The wreck of the Palatine
A young Quaker of New England

New Guinea
The dancing stars
Fire and the moon
The man who paddled to the moon's
  house

New Hampshire
The big warm dog
Cinderella of New Hampshire
The giant of the hills
Governor Wentworth's search for a
  wife
Old Ave Henry and the smart logger
  man

−**Exeter**
Holding the bag

−**Hampton**
General Moulton's boot
Jonathan Moulton and the devil

−**North Salem**
North Salem's Irish? Ruins

−**White Mountains**
Becky's garden
The fairies in the White Mountains
Nancy's brook
Three times and out

New Hampshire
LEACH − RAINBOW p120-121

New heroes
MY BOOK HOUSE v. 7 p144.

New Jersey
Bees in the bonnets in New Jersey
The best devil in the land
The foe in the dark
The gunsmith and the maiden
Hi-Ho, the mosquitoes of New Jersey!
Jonas and the sturgeon
Mosquitoes
Pirate Yan Yost of Communipaw
The saga of Stretch Garrison
Sam Patch's last leap
The seven sisters
The strange trial
The treasure under the tree
The young witch-horse

New Jersey
LEACH − RAINBOW p121-123

New lamps for old
MANNING − WIZARDS p70-73

New Mexico
The battle at White Cliff house
Blue legs
Blue water
The cat, the cock and the lamb
The center of the world
Cliff dweller
The coyote and the bear
Crying turkeys

The dancing horses of Acoma
Flint bird
Ko-pa-ta, the gambling god
Lost in lava
A note about the Acomas
Pecos Bill, the cowboy
The rain god's reprisal
She-wa-na, deity of the elements
Spider boy and the sun god's twins
To feed my people: The coming of
  buffalo
To feet my people: The coming of
  corn
Turkey girl
Young hunter

New Mexico
LEACH − RAINBOW p124-125

The "new preacher"
 DOBBS – MORE p31-33

A new way of tamin' wolves
 JAGENDORF – UPSTATE p60-63

A new way to cure old witch-hunting
 JAGENDORF – NEW p244-247

A new world
 AULAIRE – NORSE p151-155

New Year, Lunar (Tet)
 The spirits of the hearth

New Year's
 The crane wife
 The dark maiden from the ninth
  heaven
 Gawaine and the green knight
 Goblin gold
 The grateful statues
 Holiday luck
 Ikkyu and the merchant's moneybags
 The little match-girl
 The magic horse
 The magic mortar
 The man who missed the Tay Bridge
  train
 The man who stayed too long
 The marriage of Gawaine
 Old Surly and the boy
 Sir Gawain and the green knight
 Tongue steeple
 Young Charlotte

New Year's day
 MY BOOK HOUSE v. 3 p45.

New Year's hats for the statues
 UCHIDA – SEA p84-90

New York
 Clever Mistress Murray

The clock must not stop
Commodore Vanderbilt's first boat
The devil and the Good Book
A dozen is thirteen
The ghost of Peg-Leg Peter
The ghostly hitchhiker
The Irish luck of Brian Hughes
Kayuta, the drop star
Lady Morris in her mansion
Lucky star of Herald Square
Maiden Lane in the golden days
Mighty Mose, the Bowery b'boy
Mornin', mighty Mose
The phantom fire ship
The phantom painter in the steeple
Pig in the poke
Sam Patch, the jumpin' man
Some songs of old New York
A token of friendship
Why crow has a right to the first corn
The witch tree of the North country
Young Charlotte

−**Adirondack Mountains**
 Adirondack skeeters
 The tale of Anthony's nose

−**Albany**
 The baker's dozen

−**Catskills**
 A rover in the Catskills

−**Coney Island**
 In Coney Island by the sea

−**Erie Canal**
 Canawlers on the E-ri-ee Canal

−**Flushing**
 The courageous Quaker of Flushing

−**Fort Schuyler**
 The tale of the three footsteps

−**Fort Ticonderoga**
 Giant of the Green Mountains

−**Genesee Falls**
 Sam Patch, the jumpin' man
 Sam Patch's last leap

−**History**
 Anthony and the Mossbunker
 Wolfert Webber, or golden dreams

−**Hudson River**
 Hudson River legends: Captain
  Kidd; Buried treasure
 Legends
 The phantom ship of the Hudson

New York (*Continued*)

Rip Van Winkle: the strange little
men of the mountain
Rip Van Winkle's dog

–**Mohawk Valley**
The heroine of the Mohawk Valley

–**New York City**
The bloodless battle of the elm
Mighty Mose, the Bowery b'hoy
The movie show

–**Harlem**
The hope tree of Harlem

–**Long Island**
The tale of the three footsteps

–**Manhattan Island**
The greatest hoax in New York
City
How the duvyil gave New Am-
sterdam to the English
Spuyten duyvil

–**Niagara Falls**
Sam Patch, the jumpin' man
Sam Patch's last leap

–**Saratoga Springs**
A new way of tamin' wolves

–**Schoharie Hills**
Rusty Jack

–**Sheepshead Bay**
The devil and the Good Book

–**Westchester**
The tale of the three footsteps

New York
LEACH – RAINBOW p126-129

New Zealand
How Maui fished up New Zealand
How Maui fished up the island
Kahukura and the fairy fishermen
Maui the fire-bringer
The story of Hine-Moa and Tutanekai
Te Houtaewa and the Kumaras
The trial by fire
The troubles at Hawaiki

–**North Island**
The great fish of Maui

–**Rotorua**
The story of Hinemoa

Newell, Peter
A milkweed and a buttercup

Newfoundland
Five drowned
How loon learned his call
Lord Sinclair and the Zeno brothers
That fellow

News!
JACOBS – MORE p182-183

"News from Scotland"
To kill a king, from "News from
Scotland"

Newsome, Effie Lee
Bats

Nguyen Ky and the singer
SUN – LAND p83-88

Niamb of the golden hair
SUTCLIFF – HIGH p153-156

Niassa and the ogre
MANNING – PRINCES p9-13

Nicaragua
The eternal wanderer
Ha! Tio rabbit is bigger
The king of the leaves
Mister frog's dream
Uncle coyote's last mischief
Uncle rabbit flies to heaven

–**Managua**
A sacred pledge should not be
broken

Nicholas, Saint
A baker's dozen
A legend of Saint Nicholas
The wonder of Skoupa

Nicola Pesce (Pesca)
LUM – ITALIAN p57-68
TOOR – GOLDEN p157-165

Nidden and Didden and Donal Beg
O'Neary
McMANUS – HIBERIAN p141-147

Nidelgret
MÜLLER – SWISS p44-46

Nigeria
The antelope skin
Antelope's mother: the woman in
the moon
Ashoremashika
The boy and the leopard
The chief's knife

Nigeria (*Continued*)

The dancing palm tree
Ekun and Opolo go looking for wives
The first woman to say "Dim"
How Ijapa, who was short, became
  long
How Moremi saved the town of Ife
How Ologbon-Ori sought wisdom
How the people of Ife became
  scattered
The hunter and the hind
Ijapa and the hot-water-test
Ijapa and the Oba repair a roof
Ijapa and Yanrinbo swear an oath
Ijapa cries for his horse
Ijapa demands corn fufu
Ijapa goes to the Osanyin shrine
Introduction (WALKER – DANCING)
It's all the fault of Adam
The journey to Lagos
Kigbo and the bush spirits
The king and the ring
A lesson for the bat
The lizard's lost meat
The man who looked for death
O gungbemi and the battle in the bush
The oba asks for a mountain
Olode the hunter becomes an oba
Olomu's bush rat
The quarrel between Ile and Orun
The reward of treachery
A secret told to a stranger
Sofo's escape from the leopard
The staff of Oranmiyan
Test of a friendship
Tortoise and Babarinsa's daughters
The tortoise and the magic drum
Warthog and hornbill
Why no one lends his beauty
Why the lion, the vulture, and the
  hyena do not live together
The wrestlers
Yoruba proverb

–Efiks
Why sun and (the) moon live in
  the sky

–Ibido
Why the sun and (the) moon live
  in the sky

Night
See also **Darkness**
A Bohemian evening
The dark and stormy night
The extraordinary black coat
For a peaceful night
A German evening
The gold dragoon

How chipmunk got his stripes
How night was let loose and all the
  animals came to be
The king's daughter cries for the moon
A lyke-wake dirge
The man who paddled to the moon's
  house
The man who tried to catch the night
Maui and the death goddess
One day, one night
A quiet night
The six brothers
The swan princess
A Swedish evening
The tale of the gypsy and his strange
  love
Tavadan and the fire giant
The time of deep darkness
Why the sun shines in the daytime
  and the moon shines at night
Why there is both day and night

The night before Christmas
  MY BOOK HOUSE v. 2 p213.

The night of doom
  GREEN – GREEKS p42-43

The night of four times
  MANNING – JONNIKIN p35-39

The night of the big wind
  ARBUTHNOT – TIME p360.

The night of the full moon
  FEINSTEIN – FOLK p79-82

The nightingale
  SIDEMAN – WORLD'S p47-60
  WESTWOOD – MEDIEVAL p21-23

The nightingale and the cotton tree
  BELTING – THREE p142-145

The nightingale and the Khan
  BULATKIN – EURASIAN p85-89

The nightingale Hazaran
  NAHMAD – PEASANT p9-15

Nightingales
At the wedding of Miss Jenny Wren
Bird language
The boy and the birds
The donkey and the nightingale
Friendship without envy
The giant archer of the sky
The hawk and the nightingale
Jorinda and Joringel
Koichi and the mountain god
Little Rosa and long Leda

Nightingales (*Continued*)

Mirzhan and the Lord of the kingdom
  under the sea
The princess with the golden hair
The silent princess
The swineherd
The talking nightingale

—**Golden**
The golden nightingale

Nightmares
Did the tailor have a nightmare?

Nikita and the dragon
  BUDBERG – RUSSIAN p213-216

Nikita and the last of the dragons
  ALMEDINGEN – KNIGHTS p179-190

Nikkessen's pool
  YOUNG – HOW p45-48

"Nimmy-nimmy-not!"
  FARJEON – SILVER p180-181

The nine doves
  MANNING – DRAGONS p43-54

Nine guesses
  FARJEON – SILVER p97-102

The nine-headed giant
  DE REGNIERS – GIANT p31-38
  INS-SŎB – FOLK p166-169

The nine peahens and the golden apples
  MANNING – GLASS p27-40

The nine-tailed fox
  INS-SŎB – FOLK p38.

The nine white sheep
  MANNING – JONNIKIN p145-152

The ninwits
  GINSBURG – MASTER p129-138

The Nis
  JACOBSON – LEGEND. p17-19

Nisses
The girl who didn't know how to spin,
The Little People of Scandinavia

Nithsdale brownie
  BRIGGS – PERS. p124-125

Nitokris, Queen
Rhodopis and her gilded sandals

Nixies
The knight of Staufenberg

Njal the lawyer
  HAZELTINE – HERO p296-304

Njord, Frey and Freya
  AULAIRE – NORSE p58-63

Nkalimeva
  SAVORY – ZULU p34-38

No flowers
  WILLIAMS – ROUND p253-258

No man with the Cyclops
  WILSON – GREEK p97-102

No supper
  LOWE – LITTLE p58-61

Noah's ark
The flood
The giant who rode on the ark
The home of the saints
How the Manx cat lost its tail
Old Noah
Why cats lie on the doorstep in the
  sun
Why the birds are different colors
Why the dog has a cold wet nose

Noah's ark
  MY BOOK HOUSE v. 2 p101-104
  STOUTENBURG – CROC. p41-43

Nobility
See also names of nobility, e.g.
  **Kings and queens; Princes and
  princesses** etc.
Benizara and Kakezara
The danced-out shoes
The donkey and the boar
The English nobleman, the diplomat,
  and the great crested bustard
The golden tortoise
A poor peasant and two nobles
The quail and the badger

A noble Brahman's sacrifice
  GRAY – INDIA'S p165-171

Noise
The brownie of Rothiemurchus
The fox and the wolf
The great scare
Jingling rhymes and jingling money
The machimoodus noise
Plop!
The prince and the demon

458

Noise *(Continued)*
The strange battle of Windham
The tyranical king
The wise men of Hebron

Nomads
The laughing statue

Nonsense
The age of the animals
Air castles
All change
Are fish buffaloes?
Big, big lies!
The big Chinese drum
Big mosquitoes
The big pumpkin and the big kettle
The boastful Alaskans
The boy who turned himself into a
  peanut
The clever boy
The donkey's egg
Fish story
The flying kettle
Four very skillful people
Frozen music
The giant-nonsense verse
Great hunting!
The greatest boast
Hans Hansen's hired girl
The hidden hoe
Improbable tales from Africa
The king and the wrestler
The light princess
Little Chinese tales
Little tall tales
Long memories
The louse skin drum
The man in the mirror
The mighty wrestlers
Old wall eyes
The pet catfish
The popcorn frost
The pugilist and his wonderful helpers
The remarkable ox, rooster, and dog
Rival story tellers
Seeing far and hearing far
The shadow
A shilling for a lie
Shingling the fog
The ship that sailed on water and on
  land
Sing something
Snake story
The stolen rope
The story without an end
The three brothers
The three gluttons and the hunter
There was an old man with a beard

Three skillful men
The transformed donkey
Traveling to see wonders
A trip to the sky
Two speedy people
Tying up the stones
What news? News enough!
Who am I?
A world of nonsense

Nonsense rhymes
MY BOOK HOUSE v. 2 p154.

Noodlehead and the flying horse
JAGENDORF – GYPSIES p52-92

"Noodles"
Catching the thief
Chestnuts
Do it yourself
Dreams
Drowning the eel
A fine cheese
I was wondering
Lightening the load
The man with the chair on his head
Rescuing the moon
Sense and money
Shoes don't match
Silly John
Telling the horses apart
Trip to town
The wise men of Gotham
The wrong man

Nooloigah and the fire
NORLEDGE – ABORIGINAL p15-17

Nooloigah who caused his brother to die
NORLEDGE – ABORIGINAL p20-
  22

Normans
Gudrun

Norns
Yggdrasil, the world tree

Norse Myths
Asgard and the Aesir gods
Balder, the god of light
The battle of Nembro Wood
Bragi, god of poetry
The creation of man
The creation of the world
The death of Balder
The first gods and giants
Frey and Gerd, the jotun maiden
Freya's wonderful necklace

Norse Myths (*Continued*)

Frigg and the goddesses
Heimdall, the watchman of Asgard
Idunn's apples of youth
Loki, the god of the jotun race
Loki's monstrous brood
Loki's punishment
A new world
Njord, Frey and Freya
Odin, the all-father
Odin's eight-legged steed
Ragnarokk, the destiny of the gods
Sif's golden hair
Skade, the ski-goddess
The stealing of Iduna
The theft of Thor's hammer
Thor
Thor and the jotun Aegir
Thor and the jotun Geirrod
Thor and the jotun Rungnir
Thor and the jotun Utgard-sloki
Thor, the thunder-god
Thor's journey to Jotun-heim
The Valkyries and Valhalla
Yggdrasil, the world tree

Norse nursery rhymes
MY BOOK HOUSE v. 1 p60-61

North America
See also names of North American
countries; **Indians of North America**
Scarface
The sick boy, the greedy hunters, and
the dwarfs, The Little People of
North America

North Carolina
The bear and the wildcat
The bear in the black hat
The big mudhole
The blizzard of '98
Exploring the wilderness
The fighting rams
Get out of the way
The goat that went to school
How pa learned to grow hot peppers
How tadpoles lost their tails
Janey's shoes
The lake that flew
The man who rode the bear
Old Bluebeard
Old Dan Tucker
Old Plott
The perambulatin' pumpkin
The popcorn patch
The pudding that broke up the
preaching
Saved by a turkey

The self-kicking machine
The short horse
A tall turnip
Why bear sleeps all winter
Why sheep does not come in out of
the rain
Why the birds are different colors

North Carolina
LEACH − RAINBOW p130-131

North Dakota
Early days and ways in America
Paul Bunyan swings his axe
Planters' moon

North Dakota
LEACH − RAINBOW p132-133

A North Dakota sod house
JOHNSON − WHAT p277-278

North Pole
Gluskap
How Peary reached the North Pole

North Salem's Irish? Ruins
TAFT − PROFILE p13-17

North star
How rattlesnake got his fangs

The northern frog
MAAS − MOON p128-141

Northern lights. *See* **Aurora borealis**

The Northern lights
MACMILLAN − GLOOS. p202-210

Northwest
The ant and the yellow jacket
The bears
The buffalo and the porcupine
Callin the chinook
The end of the world
Fickle Miss Frog
The fishnet and the bear
The fog
George Rogers Clark and the conquest
of the Northwest
The good luck tree
How death came
Itsayaya and the chokecherries
Itsayaya and the otter
Itsayaya frees the salmon
Itsayaya's revenge
The monster
One day, one night

Northwest (*Continued*)

The rope
Stealing the springtime
The sun, the moon, and the stars
The weasel
The young coyote's visit

Norton, Mary
The magic bed knob
The student-witch

Norway
See also **Norse myths**
The adventures of Ciad
The apples of Iduna
The ash lad and the good helpers
The ash lad who had an eating match
  with the troll
The ash lad who made the princess
  say, "You're a liar"
The bear and the fox who made a bet
The blue belt
Boots and his brothers
Boots and the troll
The boy who out-fibbed a princess
The boy with the beer keg
The boys who met the trolls in the
  Hedal woods
The building of the fortress wall
Butterball
The charcoal burner
Cock and hen in the wood
The cock and the fox
The companion
The contrary wife
Dapplegrim
The death of Balder
The devil and the bailiff
Doll i' the grass
The doll in the grass
East o' the sun and west o' the moon
East of the sun and west of the moon
Fjords and mountain peaks
The fox as shepherd
Friends in life and death
The giant who had no heart in his
  body
The giant who stole a river
The golden bird
The golden castle that hung in the air
"Good day, fellow!" "Axe handle"
Gudbrand of the hillside
The hare who had been married
Hjuki and Bil
The house mouse and the country
  mouse
How Odin brought the mead to
  Asgard
In the beginning
Jesper who herded the hares

Johnny and the three goats
Kari Woodencoat
Katie Woodencloak
The key in the distaff
The king's hares
The king's rabbits
The lad and the north wind
The lad who went to the north wind
Little Freddie with his fiddle
Lord Peter
The magic apples
The magic storm
The man who kept house
The mare at the wedding
The master-smith
"You're a liar"
The mill that grinds at the bottom
  of the sea
More south than south, more north
  than north
The new day
Not driving and not riding
Oeyvind and Marit, a story of Norway
Olaf Goddardson and the sword
  Macabuin
The old woman against the stream
The pancake
The parson and the sexton
The pastor and the sexton
Peer Gynt
The princess on the glass hill
The princess who always had to have
  the last word
The punishment of Loki
The ram and the pig who went into
  the woods to live by themselves
The seven foals
The seventh father of the house
The sheep and the pig that made a
  home
The Soria-Moria castle
Squire Per
The squire's bride
The story of the thick fat pancake
The swan maiden
The tabby who was such a terrible
  glutton
The tale of Nornagest
Taper Tom
Taper-Tom who made the princess
  laugh
Thor and the giants
Thor gains his hammer
Thor's combat with Rungnir
Thor's hammer is stolen
Thor's unlucky journey
Thor's visit to Hymic
Thorsteinn Shiver
The three aunts
The three billy goats gruff
The three goats called Hurricane

Norway (*Continued*)

The three princesses in the mountain-
in-the-blue
The three princesses of Whiteland
True and untrue
The twelve wild ducks
The two step-sisters
Wayland Smith
The white bear
White-bear-King-Valemon
Why the bear is stumpy-tailed
Why the sea is salt
The winning of Gerd
The world of the gods

—**Sagas**
Frithjof, the Viking

The Norwegian folk tales and their illustrators
ASBJÖRNSEN — NORW. p5-8

Norwegians
The American saga

The nose of the konakadet
MARTIN — NINE p27-31

Noses
The badger and the magic fan
Cardiff town
The crow's pearl
Don't tease the tengu!
The drunkard and the opium-eater
Dwarf long nose
Fairy tricks
Father big-nose
A flower to catch a thief
Half a yard
How turtle came
The long nose
The long-nosed princess
The man with no nose
The old woman and the fish
The princess of Tomboso
A quarrel between thieves brings a
Brahmin relief
The ridiculous wishes
Snout the dwarf
The tale of Anthony's nose
The tengu's magic nose fan
The three wasted wishes
Toontonny pie
The wishing cup
A yard of nose

Not driving and not riding
ASBJÖRNSEN — NORW. p137.

Not to care a straw
LEACH — SOUP p28-30

A note about the Acomas
RUSHMORE — DANCING p159-163

Notes on Hopi oral literature
COURLANDER — PEOPLE p156-164

Nothing at all
ARBUTHNOT — TIME p259-262
MONTGOMERIE — 25 p37.

Nothing to lose
LEACH — LUCK p76-78

Nova Scotia. *See* **Canada—Nova Scotia**

November's party
CATHON — PERHAPS p208-209

Now would I laugh, were I not dead
BOUCHER — MEAD p95-97

Noyes, Alfred
A Christmas song at sea
Fairy forests
A song of Drake's men

Ntunjambili
SAVORY — ZULU p9-14

Nu-Kua
Heaven and earth and man

Nuberu
MARKS — SPANISH p133-146

The number of spots
DOBBS — ONCE p77-85

Numbers
See also **Superstitions—Numbers**
Alchemy: the magic science
The baker's dozen
Superstition
Thirteen
The thirteenth floor

Numbers
BATCHELOR — SUPER. p44-51

"Numbskull stories." *See* **Simple-minded
Jeanne**

Numbskulls. *See* **Fools**

Numismatics
The thirteenth floor

The nun as judge
SEKI – FOLKTALES p188-189

The nung-guama
BONNET – CHINESE p97-102

Nuns
   Beatrice . . . And the statue
   Kirsten McVurich
   The melodious napkin
   The voyage of the Lass of Glasgow

Nun's priest tale. *See* Chanticleer and
Partlet

Nunus (underworld Little People)
Ntunjambili

The Nuremberg stove
MY BOOK HOUSE v. 5 p162-181

Nursery rhymes
   The airplane
   All the cats consulted
   Animal crackers
   The bees
   Big bus, stop!
   Building with blocks
   Butterflies, butterflies
   The cock's on the housetop
   Conversation
   How doth the little busy bee
   I love little pussy
   I'm Captain Jinks
   Little good baby
   The little turtle
   The mouse climbed up the candlestick
   My boat
   O I'll build a square with my pretty
     red blocks
   Of all the girls that are so smart
   Park play
   Policeman Joe
   Tommy was a silly boy
   What are you able to build with your
     blocks?
   What makes moonshine on water
   When Uncle Henry was a little tiny
     boy
   Where, O where has my little dog
     gone?
   The world is so full

  –America
    A-tisket, a-tasket
    The boatman he's a lucky man!
    Bye-o! Bye-o!
    Charley, Barley, Buck and Rye

    Charley's neat and Charley's sweet
    Cinderella dressed in green
    Dreamland opens here
    Engine, engine number nine
    The farmer in the dell
    Get out of the way
    Go ask your mother for fifty cents
    Go to sleepy, little baby
    Here come three jolly, jolly sailor
     boys
    Here we sail so fast and free
    Here's the church
    Hurry up, engine
    I had a piece of pie
    I saw a crow a-flying low
    I went to the animal fair
    Ice-cold lemonade
    I'm a peddler
    I'm going to Lady Washington's
    It snows and it blows
    Jingle bells, jingle bells
    Lazy old Mary
    The man who has plenty of good
     peanuts
    Many, many stars are in the skies
    Mary had a little lamb
    O my dame had a lame tame crane
    One, two, three, four
    Over the hill to feed my sheep
    Over the river
    Pinny, pinny, poppy show!
    Quaker, Quaker, how is thee?
    Ring around a rosy
    The rose is red
    Star light, star bright
    Teddy bear, teddy bear
    There was a farmer had a dog
    There was an old pig
    Ting-a-ling-ling
    Wake up, Jacob
    We've come to see Miss Jenny
     Jones
    What's your name?
    When I go a-courting
    William T. Trinity

  –Indians
    American Indian songs
    Ihi! Ihi! Ihi!

  –China
    Chinese nursery rhymes
    Old mother wind
    There was an old woman
    There was a little boy

  –Czechoslovakia
    Annie goes to the cabbage field
    Auntie, where are you going?
    A Bohemian evening
    Czechoslovakian rhymes
    How strong a bridge have you?

Nursery Rhymes–Czechoslovakia
(Continued)
   I'm a butcher
   Knitting still
–**England**
   See also **Mother Goose**
   As I went to Bonner
   As Tommy Snooks and Bessie
    Brooks
   Baa, baa, black sheep
   Bat, bat, come under my bat
   Billy, Billy, come and play
   Birds of a feather
   Blow, wind, blow, and go, mill go!
   Bobby Shafto's gone to sea
   "Bow-wow", says the dog
   Bow, wow, wow, whose dog art
    thou?
   Boys and girls, come out to play
   The butterfly's ball
   Daffy-down-dilly
   Dance, little baby, dance up high!
   Dickery, dickery dare
   Diddle, diddle, dumpling
   English nursery rhymes
   Four-and-twenty tailors
   Gay go up and gay go down
   Goosey, goosey, gander
   Great A, little A, bouncing B
   Handy-spandy
   Hector protector
   Here am I, little jumping Joan
   Hey diddle diddle
   Hickety, pickety, my black hen
   Hickory, dickory dock!
   Hippety hop to the barber shop
   How many days has my baby to
    play?
   How many miles to Babylon?
   Humpty Dumpty
   I had a little husband
   I had a little nut tree
   I saw a ship a-sailing
   Jack and Jill
   Jack, be nimble
   Johnny shall have a new bonnet
   The King of France went up the
    hill
   Lavender's blue
   Little Bo-peep
   Little Boy Blue
   A little cock sparrow
   Little girl, little girl
   Little Jack Horner
   Little King Boggin
   Little maid, pretty maid
   Little Miss Muffet
   Little Nanny Etticoat
   Little robin redbreast
   Little Tommy Tucker
   Lucy Locket lost her pocket

Mary, Mary, quite contrary
My Lady wind
My maid Mary
Oh, here's leg for a stocking
Old King Cole
Old Mother Goose
Old Mother Hubbard
Once I saw a little bird
One misty moisty morning
Pat-a-cake, pat-a-cake, baker's man!
Pease-porridge hot
Peter, Peter, pumpkin eater
A pie sat on a pear tree
Polly put the kettle on
Pussy cat, pussy cat
Pussy sits beside the fire
Ride a cock-horse to Banbury
  Cross
Ride away, ride away
A robin and a robin's son
Robin and Richard were too pretty
  men
Rock-a-bye, baby
Rub-a-dub-dub
See-saw, Margery Daw
See-saw, Sacaradown
Sing, sing!–What shall I sing?
Sleep, baby, sleep
Smiling girls, rosy boys
There was a crow
There was a horse
There was a little boy
There was a monkey
There was a piper had a cow
There was an old man
There was an old woman
There was an old woman of
  Harrow
There was an old woman tossed
  up in a basket
There was an old woman who
  lived in a shoe
There was an owl
There were two blackbirds
This little pig went to market
Three little kittens
To market, to market
Up in the green orchard
Wee Willie Winkie
What's the news of the day
When woods awake
Willie boy, Willie boy

 –**11th Century**
   In spring the birds do sing
   There are twelve months
 –**16th Century**
   Simple Simon
   Sing a song of sixpence
–**Finland**
   Hi-y, hi-yi, hytola

Nursery Rhymes–Finland (*Continued*)

Rhymes of Finland
Thus I guard my mother's lambkin

–France
At the wedding of Miss Jenny Wren
Catherine, my dearie
French nursery rhymes
King Dagobert
There was an old dame called
   Tartine

–Germany
A, B, C, Kitty's in the snow I see!
The cockoo and the donkey
German nursery rhymes
Hop, my horsey, leap and spring
Little Liese comes a-running
O where has my little dog gone
Sum-m, sum-m, sum-m!
Would you like to see goats dance
   on stilts

–Hungary
Hungarian rhymes
I should like to plough
Round is my bun

–India, East
East Indian rhymes
The rajah went to Delhi
Through the jungle

–Indians of North America
Sleep, sleep, sleep!

–Ireland
Down in a cottage
O 'twas on a bright mornin' in
   summer

–Italy
Giuseppi, the cobbler
If I could work
Italian nursery rhymes
Little Beppo Pippo
Little Peppino

–Japan
A Japanese lullaby

–Mexico
Chink, chink chockett
Come, let's go to Sant' Anita
I'm a little Indian
This little ant worked with might
   and main
This one stole an egg

–Netherlands
Dutch nursery rhymes
Here is the key
The key to Bibbley-Babbley town
There was a little man and his
   name was Gice
There were three duckies

–Norway
The boy who made hay
Mary milks the cow
Norse nursery rhymes
Reinar was watching his cows
Row, row, a fishing we'll go!
The squirrel went out to cut the
   hay

–Poland
Big clock–tick, tock!
Diddle, diddle on a bass fiddle
Gurgle, water, gurgle
A little bird sits in the willow
Polish rhymes
Pussy, pussy, dear pussy
A woman had a rooster

–Russia
Don't run away my kitty
Hark, the Christmas bells are ring-
   ing
Little bells, pretty flowers of the
   Steppes
Russian rhymes

–Scotland
Dance to your daddle
Tom, Tom, the piper's son
Welsh and Scotch rhymes

–South America
South American rhymes
When I see a lady
When Mrs. Bird wants Mr. Bird

–Columbia
Right out in our barnyard
The toads in the lake

–Spain
Five little chicks
Get up, little horsey
Pussy, kittie
Spanish nursery rhymes
Who's on the roof?

–Sweden
Everyone's glad in our city today
Hop, Mother Annika!
I took a walk one evening
Otto would a-riding go
Peekaboo, I see you!
Swedish rhymes
There were two little boys

–Switzerland
Chimney sweep
It's raining
Jokeli
O will you shoe our pony, pray?
The roosters at the old crown inn
Swiss nursery rhymes

Nursery Rhymes—Wales (*Continued*)

—Wales
Dame Durden
Welsh and Scotch rhymes

Nursery tales
JOHNSON — WHAT p135-144; 191-195

Nurses and nursing
The hunter
The ogres in the stone boat
The sneeze that won a wife
The tale of the heir of Linne
Tree-root, iron-strong and hill-roller
Ubazakura

Nurse's song
MY BOOK HOUSE v. 2 p152.

Nursing a fairy. *See* The fairy midwife

The nut branch
BECHSTEIN — FAIRY p168-173

Nut-cracker
BAMBERGER — FIRST p146-149

The nutcracker and sugardolly stories
MY BOOK HOUSE v. 4 p83-102

Nutcrackers
The tale of nutcracker

Nutmeg
I had a little nut tree

Nuts and nut trees
The boy and the nuts
He who is feared by all
How night was let loose and all the
animals came to be
How these tales came to be told
I had a little nut tree
Ironhead

Is he fat?
Kate Crackernuts
The melancholy prince and the girl
of milk and blood
Miska and the man-with-the-iron-head
The rubber man
The shepherd and the princess
The traveler and the nut tree
Who can crack nuts?

, Golden
The white parrot

—Shells
Cock and hen in the wood

Nyame (Nyami)
Osebo's drum
The sword that fought by itself

Nyame's well
COURLANDER — HAT p93-95

Nyangara, the python
TRACEY — LION p10-14

Nymphs
Apollo and Daphne . . . The laurel
wreath
Bears in the sky
The death of Paris
Echo and Narcissus; the chattering
nymph and the proud youth
The fountain of Arethusa
The Little People
The magic veil
Narcissus and Echo . . . Their hopeless
love
Nella's dancing shoes
Odysseus and the nymph

, Tree
Dookiram, the poor one
The king and his seven sons

O

O gungbemi and the battle in the bush
COURLANDER – OLODE p96-99

O if my top would only spin
MY BOOK HOUSE v. 1 p130.

O I'll build a square with my pretty red
blocks
MY BOOK HOUSE v. 1 p164.

O, I'm a jolly old cowboy
MY BOOK HOUSE v. 1 p100.

O, Lady Mary Ann
MY BOOK HOUSE v. 1 p153.

O my dame had a lame tame crane
MY BOOK HOUSE v. 1 p95.

O rattlin', roarin' Willie
MY BOOK HOUSE v. 1 p153.

O sailor, come ashore
MY BOOK HOUSE v. 1 p157.

O 'twas on a bright mornin' in summer
MY BOOK HOUSE v. 1 p59.

O well for the fisherman's boy
MY BOOK HOUSE v. 1 p154.

O where has my little dog gone
MY BOOK HOUSE v. 1 p107.

O will you shoe our pony, pray?
MY BOOK HOUSE v. 1 p66.

The oak and the reed
LA FONTAINE – FABLES p16.
MONTGOMERIE – 25 p60.

The oak that helped outwit a king
RASKIN – TALES p21-27

Oak trees
See also Acorns
The acorn and the pumpkin
Baucis and Philemon . . . The reward
of hospitality
Boots and his brothers
Bundar Bahadeer Poon
The clever jackal and how he
outwitted the tiger
A clever jedge
Dummling
The frog with the golden key
Haltefandon (The lame devil)

Marko the rich and Vasily the luckless
The mother of time and the enchanted
brothers
Old pipes and the dryad
The pedlar of Swaffham
The son of strength
Straight and crooked
Three wonderful beggars
Through the eyes
The tree that flew

–Branches
The fairy of the three-branched
oak

Oaths
Ijapa and Yanrinbo swear an oath
The quarrel about the woods

Oatmeal
Hasty porridge in the boiling water

Oats
The locusts and the oats

The oba asks for a mountain
COURLANDER – OLODE p77-81

Obedience
Ainsel
The big street in the big city
Biting Marion
Come, little leaves
The dragon of Rhodes
The dutiful daughter
The end of the golem
How Jack sought the golden apples
Joan of Arc
The little black man
The little pig
The most obedient wife
Noah's ark
Over in the meadow
Patient Griselda
Policeman Joe
Sir Beaumains, the kitchen knight
A story about the little rabbits
Stubborn husband, stubborn wife
What does little birdie say?

Obesity
Are fat people happy?
Fatty

Obligations. *See* Geasas

Observation
    Boots and his brothers
    The boy who made a dream come true
    Hiawatha's childhood
    Jamie Watt and the giant teakettle

Obstinacy. *See* Stubbornness

Occupations
    See also Trades; names of occupations
    Augustine the thief
    The fisherman
    The miller's four sons
    The seven stars

Ocean
    See also Sea; etc.
    The Da-Trang crabs
    The eight perfect ones on the ocean
    The frog that swallowed the ocean
    The kingdom of ocean
    The mill at the bottom of the sea
    The seven seas
    The titmouse
    Why the ocean is salty

Ochre
    The fairy frog

O'Connell wears his hat in Parliament
    O'SULLIVAN – FOLK. p232-233

O'Connor, Captain W. F.
    The story of the stone lion

Octopus
    The battle that tilted the sea
    The fight between the octopus and
       the whale
    Old Stormalong
    The three monsters of the sea
    Why the jellyfish has no bones

Odd Olle
    NYBLOM – WITCH p132-159

Odds
    JOHNSON – WHAT p36-43

Odds and ends
    JOHNSON – WHAT p266-271

Odin
    The apples of Iduna
    Frigg and the goddesses
    How Odin brought the mead to
       Asgard
    In the beginning

Loki, the god of the jotun race
    The Valkyries and Valhalla
    The world of the gods
    Yggdrasil, the world tree

Odin, the all-father
    AULAIRE – NORSE p38-39

Odin . . . The price of wisdom
    UNTERMEYER – FIRE. p122-124

Odin's eight-legged steed
    AULAIRE – NORSE p68-71

Odors
    The baker's neighbor
    The fire on the mountain
    The greedy stallkeeper and the poor
       traveler
    How much for a shadow?
    Magic
    Ooka and the stolen smell

Odysseus
    The boy Achilles
    Circe the enchantress
    Cyclopes
    The end of Odysseus
    The home-coming of Odysseus
    How Odysseus came home
    The luck of Troy
    The madness of Odysseus
    The one-eyed giant
    Penelope and her suitors
    The princess Nausicaa
    The return of Odysseus
    Scylla and Charybdis
    The slaying of the suitors
    Winds and ogres
    The wounded archer

Odysseus and Circe
    WILLIAMS – ROUND p102-108

Odysseus and the lotus eaters
    GREEN – GREEKS p56-57

Odysseus and the nymph
    GREEN – GREEKS p66-67

Odysseus in the land of the giants
    DE REGNIERS – GIANT p70-78

Odyssey. *See* The World's great epics

Oedipus
    The riddle of the Sphinx

Oeyvind and Marit, a story of Norway
    MY BOOK HOUSE v. 3 p137-145

Of a tailor and a bear
    MY BOOK HOUSE v. 3 p134-135

Of all the beasts that roam the woods
    MY BOOK HOUSE v. 1 p106.

Of all the girls that are so smart
    MY BOOK HOUSE v. 1 p169.

Of gold and men
    IVES – TALES p229-236

Of sea-going snakes
    IVES – TALES p115.

Of silver and men
    IVES – TALES p247-254

Of speckled eggs the birdie sings
    MY BOOK HOUSE v. 1 p158.

Of the great and famous
    MAYNE – HEROES p61.

Ofermod. *See* The homecoming of Beorhtnoth Beorhthelm's son

Off we'll go. *See* Little pictures from far Japan

Ogier, the Dane
    The squires win golden spurs

The ogre and the cock
    SAKADE – JAPAN . p94-101

The ogre courting
    MAYNE – GIANTS p161-169

The ogre king of Gilgit
    SPICER – GIANTS p76-84

The ogre who built a bridge
    UCHIDA – SEA p72-83

Ogres
    The adventures of Little Peachling
    Alas!
    Bation the horse
    The beauty and the beast
    The carlanco
    Corvetto
    The dirt boy
    The dove maiden
    The Earl of Cattenborough
    The enchanted buck
    Gianni and the ogre
    The giant ogre, Kloo-Teekl
    The golden chain from heaven

The golden deer
The golden horse
The golden nightingale
The hairy-armed ogre of Kyoto
Hop o' my thumb
How Master Thumb defeated the sun
The imposter
Isun Boshi, the one-inch lad
Jack and the beanstalk
Little Tom Thumb
The master cat
Momotaro
Momotaro: boy-of-the-peach
Momotaro, the peach boy
The mother of time and the enchanted brothers
Musk and amber
Niassa and the ogre
The old men who had wens
The one-eyed ogre of Sessay
The oni and the three children
The oni's laughter
Peach boy
Peppino
Petrosinella or parsley
Prince Charming, the mare's son
Prince Daniel
Puss in boots
The rice cake that rolled away
Shippei Taro
The singing drum and the mysterious pumpkin
The sleeping beauty in the wood
The son of the King of Spain
The story of Issoumbochi
The story of Prince Ring and his dog
The sun, the moon and the star of morning
The swamp nushi's messenger
Temba's magic boat
The terror of the ogres
The three citrons
The three little eggs
The three lucky charms
The three walnuts
Timimoto
The tiny, tiny man
The wild woman of the woods
Winds and ogres

The ogress in the stone boat
    BOUCHER – MEAD p99-105

Oh and alas
    WILSON – GREEK p1-8

Oh dear!
    ILLYÉS – ONCE p203-212

Oh, deary me
    LEACH – RAINBOW p213-214

Oh, here's a leg for a stocking
  MY BOOK HOUSE v. 1 p20.

Ohio
  Hiram goes courting
  Idy, the fox-chasing cow
  The immortal J. N.
  Johnny Appleseed
  Lazy Tom
  Lazy Tom keeps house
  The little red pig
  A little story about a great man
  Old Johnny Appleseed
  Old stories
  The pot of gold
  Rainbow-walker/Johnny Appleseed
  The tale of Tom Corwin
  The witch of Ohio
  The world's smartest cat

  —Bellaire
    The house that Jack built

  —Belmont Co.
    The house that Jack built

  —Bloomfield
    The sad tale of three slavers

  —Chillicothe
    The sky-foogle of Chillicothe

  —Cincinnati
    A deer trick

  —Crawford Co.
    Smart Sam'l Danny

  —Edinburg
    The tapping ghost of Edinburgh

  —Knox Co.
    Seeley Simpkins and his bull

  —Mt. Vernon
    Seeley Simpkins and his bull

  —Oxford
    The wooing of Lottie Moon

  —Piquay Co.
    A deer trick

  —Portage Co.
    The faithful dog

  —Xenia
    The boy who would be an orator

Ohio
  LEACH — RAINBOW p134-135

Ohio River
  The boatman he's a lucky man!
  A trail of tall tales

Oil
  How these tales came to be told
  The owl and the raven

  , Palm
    Hyena and the oil with the flies
    on it

  , Sacred
    The story of the shipwrecked sailor

Oil-workers
  Gib Morgan
  Real stuff

Ointment
  Cherry
  The fairy child
  Fairy ointment
  The gold-rich king
  Peepan pee

Oisin
  The return of Oisin

Oisin in the land of the ever young
  O'FAOLAIN — IRISH p163-174

Oisin, son of Finn MacCool
  PICARD — CELTIC p111-126

Oisin's mother
  LINES — TALES p251-256

Ojje Ben Onogh
  COURLANDER — FIRE p103-104

Oki (island)
  The white hare and the crocodiles

Okinawa
  —Naha
    The bundles of straw and the
    king's son

Oklahoma
  About the Cherokee

Oklahoma
  LEACH — RAINBOW p136-137

Okra
  Ikpoom

Okraman's medicine
  COURLANDER — HAT p49-54

Ol-Ambu and He-of-the-long-sleeping-place
  AARDEMA – TALES p59-69

Ol' guinea man
  COTHRAN – MAGIC p71-72

Olaf Goddarson and the sword Macabuin
  YOUNG – HOW p11-16

Olaf the mermaid's son
  McNEILL – SUNKEN p87-95

Olcott, Frances Jenkins
  The black cat of the witch-dance-
    place
  Forget-me-not!
  The hundred-headed daffodils
  Surprising adventures of Don Quixote
    of La Mancha
  The witch's shoes

Old age
  The age of the animals
  The aged father
  The auld cailleach's curse
  The Bremen town musicians
  Catherine and her fate
  Cleverer than the devil
  Death and the old man
  The deer, the hare, and the toad
  The eagle and the owl
  The golden pitcher
  Grandfather's advice
  The king and the shoemaker
  The land where there were no old men
  Lao Lai-Tse, the tactful
  The man who wanted to bury his son
  Mother of the forest
  The mountain where old people were
    abandoned
  Naba Zid-Wende
  Ojje Ben Onogh
  The old man who said "Why"
  The old man's tale of Prince Stephen
  The old woman and the bear
  The old woman and the thief
  The old woman swims the sea
  The poor old lady
  The raven and his young
  The red king and the witch
  Santiago and the fighting bulls
  The sign at the smithy door
  The spell of the mermaid
  The stone in the garden
  The story of Mrs. Tubbs
  The tale about lost time
  The ungrateful children
  Who is the older?
  The wise old woman
  The year Nyangondhu's cattle

The year of the feast at Simbi
The year of the monkeys of Ramogi
You must pay for the horse, Aga
The young fox and the old fox

Old Ave Henry and the smart logger man
  JAGENDORF – NEW p72-75

The old bear in the tree
  GREEN – BIG p31.

Old Bluebeard
  COTHRAN – WITH p26-33
  WILLIAMS – FAIRY p209-215

Old boss and George
  COURLANDER – TERRA. p93-94

Old boss, John, and the mule
  COURLANDER – TERRA. p87-90

Old chapbook. *See* Jack the giant killer

The old Christmas
  YOUNG – HOW p105-109

The old crow teaches the young crow
  O'SULLIVAN – FOLK. p14-15

Old Dan Tucker
  MY BOOK HOUSE v. 1 p93.

The old dog and the gray wolf
  CARPENTER – DOGS p213-221

The old father who went to school
  U. N. – RIDE p137-141

Old Gally Mander
  HOKE – WITCHES p15-18

The old gypsy woman and the Good Lord
  JAGENDORF – GYPSIES p107-110

The old hag of the forest
  HOKE – WITCHES p65-79

The old hag's long leather bag
  HAVILAND – IRELAND p26-38

Old Hiram's ghost
  STOUTENBURG – CROC. p46-47

The old humpback
  LEACH – HOW p31.

Old Johnny Appleseed
  MY BOOK HOUSE v. 4 p213-217

An old king and his three sons of England
  MANNING – RED p159-168

Old King Cole
MY BOOK HOUSE v. 1 p44.

An old Korean story
ANDERSON – BOY p37-50

The old lady and the monkeys
LIN – MILKY p87-92

The old lady who swallowed a fly
WITHERS – I SAW p39-41

The old laird and his dogs
LEODHAS – GAELIC p91-99

The old magician
BECHSTEIN – FAIRY p122-124

The old man and his bush
LEACH – HOW p30-31

The old man and his dog
CARPENTER – DOGS p136-144

The old man and his fishing line
JABLOW – MAN p21-22

The old man and his sons
LA FONTAINE – FABLES p60.

The old man and the devils
HEARN – JAPANESE p53-56

Old man Edmonds and the ninety-nine pigs
JAGENDORF – SAND p80-83

Old man Elias and the dancing sheriff
JAGENDORF – NEW p240-243

The old man in the moon
AUNG – KINGDOM p71-73

Old man knowall
BOUCHER – MEAD p110-119

Old man Kurai and the one-eyed giant
MASEY – STORIES p1-11

Old man moon
MARTIN – COYOTE p31-38

The old man of Cury
BRIGGS – PERS. p149-151

The old man of the flowers
UCHIDA – DANCING p147-156

"Old Man of the Sea"
Sindbad the sailor
The three golden apples

The old man who cut bamboo
SEKI – FOLKTALES p118-120

The old man who made flowers bloom
See also The old man who made the trees bloom; etc.
SEKI – FOLKTALES p120-125

The old man who made the trees bloom
McALPINE – JAPAN. p95-105

The old man who made trees blossom
SAKADE – JAPAN. p87-93

The old man who said "Why"
CUMMINGS – FAIRY p7-15

The old man with the bump
UCHIDA – DANCING p37-45

The old man's tale of Prince Stephen
URE – RUMANIAN p147-152

Old master and okra
COURLANDER – TERRA. p76-79

Old Meg, the witch
RASKIN – TALES p43-49

The old men who had wens
SEKI – FOLKTALES p126-128

Old Mother Goose
MY BOOK HOUSE v. 1 p23.

Old Mother Hubbard
MY BOOK HOUSE v. 1 p38.

Old Mother Twitchett
LEACH – SOUP p58-61

Old mother wiggle-waggle
JACOBS – MORE p201-203

Old mother wind
MY BOOK HOUSE v. 1 p76.

Old Nanny's ghost
SPICER – GHOSTS p73-82

The old Navy
MAYNE – HEROES p73-74

Old Nick's bridge
SPICER – DEVILS p19-24

Old Noah
MY BOOK HOUSE v. 1 p112.

Old Noll
MY BOOK HOUSE v. 12 p36-41

Old Novak and the village elder, Bogossav
ĆURČIJA – HEROES p134-135

Old Pipes and the dryad
MY BOOK HOUSE v. 6 p18-37

Old Plott
CREDLE – TALL p43-52

Old Sal's curse
SPICER – WITCHES p49-53

Old Shellover
MY BOOK HOUSE v. 2 p185.

The old soldier and the mischief
MANNING – RED p55-61

Old songs
JOHNSON – WHAT p152-160

Old stories
JOHNSON – WHAT p161-179;
253-258

Old Stormalong
LEACH – RAINBOW p23-24
MY BOOK HOUSE v. 4 p183-192
SHAPIRO – TALL p31-43

An old story of the three sworn brothers
HSIEH – CHINESE p41-42

The old storyteller
FOSTER – STONE p1-4

Old strong charms
LEACH – SOUP p111-112

An old Sumatran legend
LEEUW – INDO. p40-44

Old Surly and the boy
FARJEON – LITTLE p289-292

The old tiger and the hare
INS-SOB – FOLK p157-160

The old traveler
MAAS – MOON p26-30

Old wall eyes
WITHERS – WORLD p25-27

The old witch
HOKE – WITCHES p80-84
JACOBS – MORE p101-106
MANNING – WITCHES p11-17

The old wizard and the children
BAMBERGER – FIRST p136-138

The old woman against the stream
ASBJÖRNSEN – NORW. p112-114

The old woman and her hominy pot
JABLOW – MAN p14.

The old woman and her pig
ARBUTHNOT – TIME p7-8
JOHNSON – WHAT p135-138

The old woman and the bear
COTHRAN – WITH p55.

The old woman and the fish
HAVILAND – SWEDEN p50-59

The old woman and the Hedley kow
BRIGGS – PERS. p176-178

The old woman and the thief
SIDDIQUI – TOON. p140-143

The old woman and the tramp
HAVILAND – SWEDEN p15-29

An old woman sows discord
RANKE – GERMANY p163-164

The old woman swims the sea
CARPENTER – SHIPS p151-160

The old woman who lost her dumplings
HEARN – JAPANESE p21-28

The old women who were turned into
birds
NORLEDGE – ABORIGINAL p27-28

The oldest animals. *See* The quest for
Olwen (4) Fulfilling the tasks

Ole shut-eyes, the sandman
MY BOOK HOUSE v. 2 p26-29

Oliphaunt
TOLKIEN – READER (Part 4) p47.

Olive trees and olives
Ali Sundos
The horse of seven colors
The singing flute
The thousand pieces of gold

474

Olli and the rich troll
McNEILL – DOUBLE p115-121

Olode the hunter becomes an oba
COURLANDER – OLODE p32-36

Olomu's bush rat
COURLANDER – OLODE p11-14

Olympic games
Pelops and Poseidon

Omar's big lie
CARPENTER – AFRICAN p129-135

Omens
The lost gift
Yoro reveals himself as Gessar Khan

Omganda and the gold
HARMAN – TALES p163-185

On being a happy cow
LEEKLEY – RIDDLE p66-72

On fairy stories
TOLKIEN – READER (Part 2) p3-84

On just being yourself
LEEKLEY – RIDDLE p56-61

Once I saw a little bird
MY BOOK HOUSE v. 1 p25.

Once in, never out again
HOPE-SIMPSON – CAVAL. p95-105

Once there was and once there was not
WYNDHAM – TALES p62-67

Once upon a time
PRIDHAM – GIFT p7-9

One against a hundred
BRO – HOW p22-28

One day, one night
HEADY – TALES p25-28

One-eye, two-eyes, and three-eyes
ARBUTHNOT – TIME p60-64
DURHAM – TIT p24-29
THOMPSON – ONE p188-194

The one-eyed giant
GREEN – GREEKS p58-59

One-eyed Likho
DOWNING – RUSSIAN p164-167

The one-eyed ogre of Sessay
SPICER – GIANTS p103-108

One good turn deserves another
GREEN – BIG p223.

One grain more than the devil
HARDENDORFF – FROG'S p131-140

One guess
CATHON – PERHAPS p82.

The one-horned mountain goat
HARRIS – ONCE p3-30

One hundred thousand arrows
ALEXANDER – PEBBLES p28.

One-inch fellow
HAVILAND – JAPAN p3-21

The one-legged chicken
MICHAEL – PORTUGUESE p130-132

The one-legged crane
VITTORINI – OLD p7-13

One mean trick deserves another
CARPENTER – ELEPHANT'S p82-90

One misty moisty morning
MY BOOK HOUSE v. 1 p42.

One more child
SPELLMAN – BEAUT. p31-32

One roll of bread
BRENNER – BOY p76-78

One! Two! Three!
KELSEY – ONCE p113-118

One, two, three, four
MY BOOK HOUSE v. 1 p99.

The one who said Tjik
COURLANDER – KANT. p103-104

The one who wasn't afraid
DEUTSCH – TALES p7-16

Oneata (island)
How the mosquitoes came to Oneata

O'Neill, "Giant"
An American miner's song

The oni and the three children
SEKI – FOLKTALES p51-54

The onion and the rose
EDMONDS – TRICKSTER p138-143

Onions
The farmer and the harvesters
What happened to six wives who ate
onions

Onions
INS-SŎB – FOLK p20-21

Onions and garlic
BATCHELOR – SUPER. p13-14

Onis (ogres)
The three lucky charms

The oni's laughter
SEKI – FOLKTALES p36-40

Only a sparrow
GREEN – BIG p172-173

The only people
DAVIS – LION'S p73-77

Onokoro (Japanese island)
The bridge of Heaven

Onsongo and the Masai cattle
HARMAN – TALES p118-143

Ooka and the barbered beast
EDMONDS – OOKA p70-74

Ooka and the cleanest case
EDMONDS – OOKA p87-91

Ooka and the death decree
EDMONDS – OOKA p92-96

Ooka and the halved horse
EDMONDS – OOKA p81-86

Ooka and the honest thief
EDMONDS – OOKA p27-32

Ooka and the marble monster
EDMONDS – OOKA p22-26

Ooka and the pup's punishment
EDMONDS – OOKA p12.

Ooka and the shattering solution
EDMONDS – OOKA p17-21

Ooka and the stolen smell
EDMONDS – OOKA p7-11

Ooka and the stronger stick
EDMONDS – OOKA p75-80

Ooka and the suspect statue
EDMONDS – OOKA p61-64

Ooka and the telltale tale
EDMONDS – TRICKSTER p61-67

Ooka and the terrible-tempered tradesman
EDMONDS – OOKA p33-38

Ooka and the two first sons
EDMONDS – OOKA p65-69

Ooka and the wasted wisdom
EDMONDS – OOKA p57-60

Ooka and the willow witness
EDMONDS – OOKA p45-50

Ooka and the wonderful wishes
EDMONDS – OOKA p51-56

Ooka and Tosuke's tax
EDMONDS – OOKA p39-44

Opals
Is the opal unlucky?

The open road
ARBUTHNOT – TIME p351-356

Open your break, my little bird
MY BOOK HOUSE v. 1 p146.

Operas
The bad baronets
Hansel and Grettel
Lohengrin
The sky at night
The tale of the Rhine-Gold

Opium-eaters
The drunkard and the opium-eater

Opossums
How brer rabbit met brer tar-baby
How possum got his tail
How the sun came
The possums, the man, and the tree
The rabbit and the possum seek a wife

Opossums (*Continued*)

The story of Li'l Hannibal
Why the terrapin's shell is scarred
Why the possum's tail is bare

Opportunity
MY BOOK HOUSE v. 10 p18.

Optimism
The hare who had been married
The twelve young men

Oracles
The Gordian knot, the destiny of
Alexander

Oraggio and Bianchinetta
LUM – ITALIAN p171-182

Oranges
The love of three oranges
Mrs. Stowe's oranges
Pleiad and star of dawn
Quinces and oranges
Seven iron-souled slippers
The three oranges

Orators. *See* Speakers

Orchards. *See* Trees

The orchestra
MY BOOK HOUSE v. 1 p187.

Orchestras
The quartet
The wonderful tune
Yung-Kyung-Pyung

Orchis root
Prince Ferdinand

The ordeal of Hannah Dustin
TAFT – PROFILE p44-49

The ordeal of Leyden
LEEUW – LEGENDS p38-45

Ordeals
The fire on the mountain

Oregon
A meteoric loss
Why bat flies alone

–Grant's Pass
Uncle Ed tracks a rabbit

Oregon
LEACH – RAINBOW p138.

Orestes
Iphigenia in Tauris

Orestes and the Furies
GREEN – GREEKS p50-51

Organ-grinders
The barrel-organ
Budulinek
The glass peacock
Of speckled eggs the birdie sings

Orient. *See* names of Oriental countries

The origin of corn
BELTING – EARTH p22-24

The origin of fire. *See* The firemakers

The origin of Indian pipes
CATHON – PERHAPS p133-134

The origin of the balsam tree
U. N. – RIDE p241-242

The origin of the bromo feast
LEEUW – INDO. p26-29

The origin of the camlet flower
U. N. – RIDE p215-216

The origin of the coconut
HTIN – KINGDOM p43-45

The origin of the Lake of Vitte
RANKE – GERMANY p35.

The origin of the platypus
NORLEDGE – ABORIGINAL p60-61

The origin of the water jars
LEEUW – INDO. p51-55

The origin of the winds. *See* Whistle the winds

The origin of the wrekin
BRIGGS – PERS. p184-185

Orioles
The golden oriole

Orion
The dog and the giant

Orkney Islands
Frithiof's journey to the
Orkneys
Sixpence for a breeze

Ornaments
Bells on her toes

Orphan boy
MARTIN – COYOTE p49-53

Orphans
Ah Tcha the sleeper
Aileel and Ailinda
Celery
The first tears
The girl in the moon
Hans and his master
Johnny and the witch-maidens
The jurga
Kuzenko sudden-wealthy
The legend of the chingola bird
Little Berry
The little orphan
Mary-Ann and the cauld lad of Hylton
Menaseh's dream
An old story of the three sworn
brothers
Old Surly and the boy
Oudelette
The skull
The stolen jewel
The story of Mordecai and Esther
Wend' Yamba
Westwoods
The wooden bowl

Orpheus and Eurydice
ARBUTHNOT – TIME p217-218

Orpheus . . . The fabulous musician
UNTERMEYER – FIRE. p69-71

Orthrus
JACOBSON – FIRST p51-57

Osebo's drum
COURLANDER – HAT p32-37

Oshidori
BUCK – FAIRY p223-224

Osiris
Isis and Osiris
The land of the dead

Osiris – martyrdom and myth: The life
and death of Osiris
JAMES – MYTHS p28-35

Osman the Great
The eagle on a chain

Ospreys
The hawk's friends
The tortoise and the osprey

An ossete riddle
FOSTER – STONE p34-37

Ossetes (people)
The thoroughbred

Ossian in the land of eternal youth
GARNIER – LEGENDS p49-57

The ostrich
GREEN – BIG p80.

The ostrich and the crocodile
ELLIOT – SINGING p44-55

The ostrich chicks
HEADY – JAMBO p85-90

Ostriches
Afar in the desert
Lonely lioness and the ostrich chicks
The magic ball

Other island
GREEN – BIG p121-126

Other legendary beings
JACOBSON – LEGEND. p47-51

Other people's beds
LEACH – SOUP p42-44

Other wise men of Gotham
BALDWIN – FAVOR. p21-27

Otters
Adventures of a water baby
Eight leaves of story (7) Red-hat otter
The end of the world
The handsome apprentice
The hare, badger, monkey, and otter
The hare in the moon
The herdsman of Cruachan
How death came
How the rabbit stole the otter's coat
How to catch a fish
Itsayaya and the otter
Partnership
Prince Finn the fair
The singing chameleon
Trust your friends

Otters (*Continued*)

Two notices who behaved like a pair
of otters
The unlucky fisherman
Why crane's feathers are brown and
otter doesn't feel the cold

The otters and the fox
GAER – FABLES p139-141

Otto would a-riding go
MY BOOK HOUSE v. 1 p75.

Oudelette
MANNING – GIANNI p103-107

Our Lady of Guadalupe
The miracle of Our Lady of
Guadalupe

Our Lady of Guadalupe
JORDAN – BURRO p27-29

The out-foxed fox
CURRY – DOWN p111-120

Outlaw Vukossav's wife
ĆURČIJA – HEROES p146-150

Outlaws
See also **Bandits**
Billy the Kid
The brigands and the miller's daughter
Grettir becomes an outlaw
Jesse James
The kind Pasha and Mehat the
shepherd
Little Radoyitsa
Old Novak and the village elder,
Bogossav
Robin Hood
Serbian knights and outlaws

Outriddling the princess
LEACH – NOODLES p50-53

The outwitted hunter
GAER – FABLES p136-139

Ovens
The geese and the swans
Hansel and Gretel
The old witch
Olli and the rich troll
The skunk in Tante Odette's oven

Over in the meadow
MY BOOK HOUSE v. 1 p138-141

Over the hill
MARRIOTT – AMER. p194-195

Over the hill to feed my sheep
MY BOOK HOUSE v. 1 p99.

Over the river
MY BOOK HOUSE v. 1 p87.

Overheard on a salt marsh
PALMER – FAIRY p75-77

Oversmart is bad luck
JAGENDORF – KING p256-259

Overweight. *See* **Obesity**

Owen, Ruth Bryan
The good sword
The people of Mols

Owl
LEACH – HOW p98.

The owl
MY BOOK HOUSE v. 3 p28.

The owl and the pussy-cat
MY BOOK HOUSE v. 2 p180.

The owl and the raven
MELZACK – DAY p21-25

The owl and the wolf
LOWE – LITTLE p103-105

The owl in the moon
JABLOW – MAN p15-17

The owl with the great head and eyes
MacMILLAN – GLOOS. p80-88

Owls
The baker's daughter
Bird Cu
Blodeuedd and the slaying of Llew
The broken wing
Brown owl's story
The Caliph stork
The crows and the owls
The eagle and the owl
Eerin the small gray owl
The first fire
The girl who always cried
A glass of water, please
The hermit cat
Hiawatha's childhood
How and why: Don't be greedy story
How and why: Why the bear waddles
when he walks

Owls (*Continued*)

How the little owl's name was changed
How the people got fire
How the raven brought the fire
It's perfectly true
Itsayaya's revenge
Kantjil to the rescue
Kapoi and the owl king
The king and the two owls
King of the birds
Ko-pa-ta, the gambling god
Laka and the Little-People
The legend of the Prince Ahmed Al
  Kamel
Little capuchin monkey's story
Lleu and the flowerface
The magic bell
The magpie's nest
The mongoose, the owl, the cat and
  the mouse
Old Mother Goose
The one who said Tjik
Orphan boy
Paul Bunyan
The plot
The pot of gold
Prince Ahmed
The quarrel
The quest for Olwen (4) Fulfilling the
  the tasks 2/ The oldest animals
The silly owls and the silly hens
The son of the King of Spain
A song of the railroad men
The story ends
The story of Caliph stork
The story of Prince Ahmed
The tale of Caliph stork
There was an old man with a beard
There was an owl
A tramp of the Middle West
The twilight
Why owls see only at night
Why there are four seasons in the
  year
Why there is both day and night
The wise owl
The wren

−**Eyes**
  The eyes of owls

−**Feathers**
  The plumage of the owl

−**Nests**
  The stone owl's nest

The owl's answer to Tommy
  MY BOOK HOUSE v. 3 p29-38

The owl's punishment
  DEUTSCH − TALES p52-55

Owzels
  The quest for Olwen (4) Fulfilling the
    tasks 2/The oldest animals

The ox as mayor
  RANKE − GERMANY p185-186

Oxen
  The animal languages
  Badikan and Khan Boghu
  The big Chinese drum
  The buyer of oxen
  Come, let's go to Sant' Anita
  The donkey, the ox, and the farmer
  Enmity between man and serpent
  The hex and the oxen
  How the camel got his hump
  How the ox came upon earth
  I should like to plough
  Keloglan and the lucky exchanges
  The kid and the tiger
  Krencipal and Krencipalka
  Lad Carl
  Lion and man
  The man without a heart
  Midir and Etain
  Onions
  Ooka and the barbered beast
  Paul Bunyan
  Paul Bunyan swings his axe
  Paul Bunyan's cornstalk
  The peppercorn oxen
  Peter ox
  The quarrel about the woods
  The remarkable ox, rooster and dog
  Saint Neot
  The sheep is the cousin of the ox
  The story of big Paul Bunyan
  The straw ox
  The tacksman and the ox
  Three princes and their beasts
  Trim Tram Turvey
  The vain ox
  A wicked fox
  Wooden Peter

, **Fairy**
  The story of the shining princess

−**Hides**
  The enchanted buck
  The thoughtless abbot

−**Horns**
  The magic horns

The oxen and the afanc
  SHEPPARD − WELSH p43-47

The oyster and the heron
  HARDENDORFF − TRICKY p41-43

480

The oystercatcher, the duck and the hen
  SHEPPARD – SCOT. p77-78

Oysters
  How the letter X got into the alphabet
  The magic oysters

Ozarks. *See* **Arkansas–Ozarks**

P

Pa Grumble
STOUTENBURG – CROC. p22-25

Pacala and Tandala
URE – RUMANIAN p9-15

Pacala saves Tandala
URE – RUMANIAN p22-23

Pacala the lawyer
URE – RUMANIAN p38-41

Pacas (animals)
The beetle and the paca

Pacific Islands
See also names of islands
Fire magic and the mud hen

Pacific Ocean
Pushing westward with Lewis and
Clark

Paddle wheel scows
How Robert Fulton harnessed the
giant

Paddy. *See* Rice

Paddy and the leprechaun
PILKINGTON – SHAM. p71-73

Padishahs
Keloglan and God's greatness
Keloglan and the magic hairs
Keloglan and the magician
Keloglan in the service of the padishah
Keloglan the kindhearted

Padre Ulivo and his guests
LUM – ITALIAN p161-170

Pagans
The sword of the stone
The word of Igor's armament

The page boy and the silver goblet
HAVILAND – SCOTLAND p3-12

Page boys
The adventures of Florian
The beautiful princess
Count Bertrand

The princess with the golden hair
The queen's necklace
The royal page
Rufus
The three brothers and the giant

Pagodas
The horse and the eighteen bandits
The little sticky rice basket
Pen and four foolish ministers

Pails
The old woman and the fish

Painted skin
WILLIAMS – OLD p123-130

Painters and paintings
The dark maiden from the ninth
heaven
Dragons
The flower of beauty
John the painter
The Lord said, this is my house
Ma Liang and his magic brush
The phantom painter in the steeple
The smoke horse
The spider in the wall
The wife's portrait

Pakistan
The clever jackal and how he out-
witted the tiger
The crow and the grain of corn
The crow and the sparrow
The farmer's old horse
The fortune of the poet's son
Four friends
Four riddles
The gift of the holy man
The jackal and the crocodile
The jackal with the torn nose
Kashi and his wicked brothers
The man who was only three inches
tall
The monkey, the tiger, and the
jackal family
The old woman and the thief
The poor weaver and the princess
The rat who made one bargain too
many
The ruby prince
The storyteller
The tale of a Pakistan parrot

Pakistan (*Continued*)

The tiger in the palenquin
Toontoony and the barber
Toontoony pie
The two misers
The weaver's worry

Pakpai and Boto
HASKETT − GRAINS p64-67

Palace in Bagdad
LARSON − PALACE p11-24

The palace in the Rath
O'FAOLÁIN − IRISH p200-204

The palace of the night
SHEAHAN − HENRY p197-213

The palace of the white cat
MICHAEL − PORTUGUESE p164-171

Palaces
Aladdin and the princess
Beauty and the beast
Clarinha
Corvetto
East of the sun and north of the earth
The enchanted palace
The enchanted prince
Faithful John
The flower of beauty
How the king chose a daughter-in-law
Keloglan the kindhearted
King Kojata
The king who rides a tiger
The king who slept
Kojata
Lars, my lad!
The magic carpet
The magician Palermo
Oudelette
The precious stone
The prince and the birds
The prince with the golden hand
The son of the hunter
The stolen jewel
Sylvester
Where to lay the blame
The white cat and the green snake
Why the ocean is salty
The wood cutter's son and the two turtles
, **Crystal**
The crystal kiosk and the diamond ship
, **Ivory**
The six companions

, **Sea**
The jewels of the sea
Sadko
Urashima Taro
Urashima Taro and the princess of the sea
, **Silver**
The little nobleman
, **Underground**
The dark king
Dawn, twilight and midnight
The underground palace

Palamon and Arcite
LINES − TALES p256-276

Palanquins (litters)
The tiger in the palanquin

Palatines
The wreck of the Palatine

Palestine
The miracle on the Jaffa Sea
The tree from Adam's grave
−**Bethlehem**
Get up, little horsey
Mary and the Christ-child
−**Joppa**
The taking of Joppa

Palm trees
Cenerentola
The dancing palm tree
The foolish, timid, little hare
The legend of the palm tree
Zezolla and the date-palm tree
, **Blue**
The blue palm tree
−**Leaves**
The man who became a chimpanzee
−**Nuts**
Kwaku Ananse and the whipping cord
The man who became a chimpanzee

Palmer, William R.
How the beaver lost the hair on his tail

Palmistry
The soothsayers

Palungs
Why crow is black and men find
precious stones in the earth

Pamudjo's feast
COURLANDER – KANT. p35-38

Pan
Midas
Midas . . . The greed for gold

Pan Kotsky
BLOCH – UKRAIN. p24-27

P'an Ku
Heaven and earth and man

Panama
The disobedient giant
The golden altar of the church of St.
Joseph
The Spanish donkey and the Indians

The pancake
ARBUTHNOT – TIME p71-72
THOMPSON – ONE p430-433

Pancakes
Little Firenko
The magic pancakes at the Foot-
bridge tavern
Mix a pancake
The pancake
The story of the thick fat pancake
Why pigs root
The witch in the hill

The Panchatantra
The blue jackal
The crow and the flamingo
The fables of India
The lion-makers

The Panchatantra
GAER – FABLES p11-49

Pancho and the Duendes
ROSS – MEXICO p191-205

Pancho Villa and the devil
JAGENDORF – KING p202-204

Pancho Villa's lost head
WILLIAMS – LOST p7-18

The Panditji and the guavas
SPELLMAN – BEAUT. p90-93

Pandora . . . The fateful casket
UNTERMEYER – FIRE. p13-16

Pannychis
FARJEON – LITTLE p293-302

The panther in the pit
GREEN – BIG p141-142

Panthers
Davy Crockett, the yaller blossom o'
the forest
Kantjil becomes a raksha
The lion and the sage
Mowgli's brothers
The skinned goat
A wicked fox

Pantomimes
Krazy Kat
The rose and the ring

, Italian
Columbine and her playfellows
of the Italian pantomime

Paper
Donkeys! Dogs! Cats! Rats!
Lars, my servant
Pleiad and star of dawn

Paper boats
MY BOOK HOUSE v. 2 p139.

Pappa Greatnose
MANNING – GHOSTS p47-54

Papua. *See* **New Guinea**

Papyrus of Imhotep
Teta the magician

Paradise
See also **Heaven**
Alexander of Macedon at the gates of
Paradise
The animals' paradise
Beppo Pipetta and his knapsack
Fool's paradise
Leaving paradise
A new world
A portion in Paradise
The selfish giant

Paraguay
The blue virgin
The gift of the moon goddess
The legend of the chingola bird

Paraguay (*Continued*)

More beautiful than the spider's web
The white spider's gift

Parchment
The broken box

Parents
See also **Fathers; Mothers**
The children who could do without
their elders

Paris of Troy
A cause of war
The death of Paris
Helen of Sparta
The judgment of Paris
The story of the Greek princess

The parish bull eats the grass from the
wall
RANKE – GERMANY p178-179

Park play
MY BOOK HOUSE v. 1 p189.

Parodies
The circus parade

The parrot
DE LA IGLESIA – CAT (unp.)
LUM – ITALIAN p125-134

The parrot and the crow
TOOZE – WONDER. p100-102

The parrot of Limo Verde
BAKER– TALKING p179-183

Parrots
Anansi, the oldest of animals
The beetle and the paca
The bird and the buffalo
The bird that told tales
The blue parrot
The crane's report
The fowler, the parrot and the king
The fox and the mole
The friendship of the hare and the
parrot
The gold duet that turned to sand
Golden bracelets, golden anklets
Greed in heaven, growth on earth
Green parrot's story
How the Brazilian beetles got their
gorgeous coats
How the finch got her colors
How the parrots helped the women

Jackal or tiger?
The jeweled ring
King crow and Sir parrot
The legend of the Prince Ahmed Al
Kamel
The magic muntr
The maiden in the tower
The nine white sheep
Prince Ahmed
Prince Wicked
The rajah who flew away
The story of the smart parrot
The tale of a Pakistan parrot
A trick that failed
The twin parrots
The white parrot
Why the parrot repeats man's words

Parsley
Petrosinella or Parsley
Where are my roses?

The parson and the sexton
ASBJORNSEN – NORW. p15-16

Parson Wood and the devil
MANNING – PETER p129-149

Parsons. *See* **Clergymen**

Part animal, part human
JACOBSON – LEGEND. p23-47

The part-time prisoner
RASKIN – TALES p63-69

Parties
Chimpanzee's story
Games
The girl who wore too much
Little capuchin monkey's story
The woman of Llyn-y-fan (2) the
parting

Partners
The cat and mouse in partnership
The fishermen

Partnership
AUNG – KINGDOM p39-41

The partridge and his drum
MacMILLAN – GLOOS. p41-49

Partridge and rock tripe
LEEKLEY – WORLD p64-68

The partridge and the crow
ARBUTHNOT – TIME p209.

The partridge, the fox and the hound
RUDOLPH – MAGIC p51-61

Partridges
The age of the partridge
The fox who wanted to whistle
The hermit cat
A long shot
The wheel of fate

Pascal, David
KRYLOV – 15 p39.

The pasha's sword
NAHMAD – PORTION p54-55

Pasopati, legend of. *See* The legend of
Pasopati

A passel of real lies
GORHAM – REAL p174-186

The passing of Glooskap
MacMILLAN – GLOOS. p131-141

Passover, Feast of
The barrel decree

Passwords
Temba's monkey friends

The past and the future
COURLANDER – KING'S p67.

The pastor and the sexton
PROTTER – CHILD. p7-8

Pat-a-cake, pat-a-cake, baker's man!
MY BOOK HOUSE v. 1 p19.

Patch, Sam
Sam Patch's last leap

Patience
As a foolish question
The baby mosque
The boy hero of Harlem
The capricious month
Cinderella
The crow and the water jug
From a moral alphabet
He wins who waits
How the finch got her colors
The hyena man
Kupti and Imani
Lion and the woman

The lion's whiskers
The miser's wife
The necklace
The prince who rode through a
mousehole
Sir Beaumains, the kitchen knight
The sleeping prince
The stone of patience
Wend' Yamba

Patient Griselda
PERRAULT – CLASSIC p147-185
PERRAULT – COMPLETE p100-
114

Patios
The white parrot

Patou MacDaniel
GARNIER – LEGENDS p112-120

Patrick, Saint
The children of Lir
Oisin, son of Finn MacCool
Saint Patrick and the Hill of Tara
The three-legged jumping giant

Patrick O'Donnell and the leprechaun
HAVILAND – IRELAND p85-91

Patriotism
See also Heroes and heroines
The Fourth of July
George Rogers Clark and the conquest
of the Northwest
George Washington and the first
American flag
The melting pot
The privateer turned patriot
Yankee Doodle
Young Midshipman David Farragut
Your America

Patten, Brian
The beast

The pattern on tortoise's back
KAULA – AFRICAN p77-83

Paul and the robber
STOUTENBURG – CROC. p49-51

Paul Bunyan
GORHAM – REAL p14-33
JACOBSON – LEGEND. p10-11
LEACH – RAINBOW p19-22
SHAPIRO – TALL p81-95

Paul Bunyan–poem
DE REGNIERS – GIANT p171-173

Paul Bunyan swings his axe
DE REGNIERS – GIANT p159-170

Paul Bunyan's cornstalk
U. N. – RIDE p268-271

Paul Jones
MAYNE – HEROES p69-70

The pavilion of peril
BIRCH – CHINESE p95-100

Pavilions
The royal monument pavilion

, Golden
Friendless pavilion

Payment
The magic clock
Steam—how much
The three precepts

Pawnbrokers
The three copper pieces

Peabody, Josephine Preston
Late

Peace
Cadmus . . . The dragon's teeth
The city mouse and the country mouse
The courageous Quaker of Flushing
Field mouse and house mouse
Kantjil holds a festival
The king of the mountain
Pen and four foolish ministers
Phoenix, bird of the sun
The pursuit of Dermot and Grania
Pyoli
Ramiro II, the monk
The snake and the dreams
The spirit of the stone
The vulture's advice
Yellow hair; George Armstrong Custer

The peace between the leopard and the antelope
DAVIS – LION'S p140-143

Peace, people of. See People of peace

The peace pipe
CHAFETZ – THUNDER. p27-41

Peaceful, the gentle deer
REED – TALK. p44.

The peach boy
See also The adventures of Little Peachling; titles beginning with Momotaro
ROSS – BURIED p147-160
SAKADE – JAPAN. p9-16
McALPINE – JAPAN. p81-94

Peach trees and peaches
The adventures of Little Peachling
The girl who kissed the peach-tree
Momotaro
Momotaro: boy-of-the-peach
Momotaro, or The story of the son of a peach
Momotaro, the peach boy
Monkey
Old Gally Mander
The peach boy
The princess of Mount Nam-Nhu

The peacock and the puhuy
BARLOW – LATIN p119-125

The peacock bridegroom
GHOSE – FOLK p65-66

The peacock, the turkey and the goose
GREEN – BIG p86-87

Peacocks
The battle on the Isle of Camphor
The bragging beasts
The Brahman in the potter's shop
Brother Anansi and Sir Peacock
The crane's report
Dressed in strange feathers
The exile of Rama
Friendship without envy
How crab got a hard back
King crow and Sir parrot
King Hilary and the beggarman
The nine peahens and the golden apples
Peahens and golden apples
Princess Rosette
The vulture's advice
With tail-fans spread

, Golden
The golden peacock

—Tails
Why peacock looks at his tail

The peacock's mistake
GAER – FABLES p146-147

Peahens and golden apples
LANG – VIOLET p50-64

Peanuts
The boy who turned himself into a
peanut
The man who has plenty of good
peanuts
Tim for wealth and happiness

–Leaves
One against a hundred

Pear trees and pears
Aunt Misery
The best wish
Brother Breeze and the pear tree
The devil to pay
Giant pears and giant cows
The greatest boast
I had a little nut tree
The marvelous pear seed
The master-smith
A pie sat on a pear-tree
The prest and the pear tree
The shaking of the pear tree
The shoemaker's apron
The statue that sneezed
Tam and Tessa
The three wishes

The pearl necklace
TOOZE – MONKEY p29-51

Pearls
The calm Brahman
The child and the fig
The crow's pearl
The Da-Trang crabs
Do pearls bring tears?
The geese and the golden chain
The giant who counted stones
The grateful beasts
The hawk and the hen
The machimoodus noise
Mirza and the ghul
Modesty and wisdom
My candlestick
The princess of light
The queen's necklace
The rooster and the pearl
The sand-carrier crab
The sea of pearls
Sense and money
The supernatural crossbow

Pearly-dew John
ILLYES – ONCE p228-238

Peary, Robert
How Peary reached the North Pole

Peas
Ashputtel
Dwarf stories
Esben and the witch
A handful of peas
The Heinzelmannchen
How the dotty Afghan woodman died
The little bird that found the pea
The magic peas
The man with the bag
Penteclemas and the pea
The princess and the pea
The princess on the pea
The real princess
A trip to the sky

The peasant and his hen
BORSKI – GOOD p62-65

The peasant and his three sons
RANKE – GERMANY p112-115

The peasant and the baron
BULATKIN – EURASIAN p95-97

The peasant and the donkey
NAHMAD – PEASANT p34-40

The peasant and the horseman
U. N. – RIDE p238-240

The peasant and the sheep
KRYLOV – 15 p31-32

The peasant and the tsar
BULATKIN – EURASIAN p75-79

The peasant and the waterman
PROTTER – CHILD. p113-114

The peasant and the workman
GREEN – TALES p170-176

The peasant-girl's captive
HSIEH – CHINESE p28-29

The peasant of Larcara. See Changing
luck

The peasant pewit
RANKE – GERMANY p134-136

A peasant sells a cow as a goat
RANKE – GERMANY p139-141

A peasant tricks the devil
RANKE – GERMANY p172-174

488

Peasants
  Adrian and Bardus
  The angry baron
  The animal languages
  The astrologer and the physician
  Bernardo and the red knight
  A boy in Russia
  The brigands and the miller's daughter
  Bukolla
  The child of death
  The clever bride of Tunisia
  The clever Elsie
  The clever peasant
  The clever peasant girl
  The clever thieves
  The competition of fools
  The coral comb
  Crab
  The crafty servant
  The czar's general and the clever
    peasant
  The dance of the fishes
  The destiny of Princess Tien Dung
  The devil duped
  A fair distribution
  The five eggs
  The fly
  The flying ship
  The frog
  The geese
  The gift of Father Frost
  The girl who kissed the peach-tree
  Golden hair
  Good luck and common sense
  Grandfather's advice
  Greyman
  Hatchet Kasha
  How a peasant outwitted two mer-
    chants
  How Grigori Petrovich divided the
    geese
  How Loki outwitted a giant
  How one should carve a goose
  How the peasants bought wisdom
  The husband, the wife, and the devil
  An impossible penance
  The iron box
  Iron, steel and strongest-of-all
  The just reward
  Kernel
  The king and the peasant
  The king who liked fairy tales
  The king who tried to cheat destiny
  The lord of gold
  The magic bottles
  Nasradin Hodja returns a gift
  Once upon a time
  Our Lady of Guadalupe
  A poor peasant and two nobles
  The princess's wedding garments
  The proper way to lay the table

  The road to hell
  The rooster, the hand mill and the
    swarm of hornets
  The serpent and the peasant
  The seven Simons
  Shemiaka the judge
  The shrewd peasant
  The silly men of Russia
  Snegourka, the snow maiden
  Sorrow
  The sound is yours
  A story about Our Lord Jesus Christ
  The story of Aoyagi
  Straight and crooked
  A strange reward
  Sungold and the remarkable cow
  The tale of a foolish brother and of a
    wonderful bush
  The tale of frost and his neighbors
  The tale of the Faderaevisch
  The tale of the silver, golden, and
    diamond prince
  The tale of the silver saucer and the
    russet apple
  The thing on the hedge
  Thomas Berennikov
  The Three Fates
  The three figs
  Three fools
  The three wishes
  Thumbkin
  Ti-Tiriti-Ti
  The treasure
  The truthful peasant
  Tsar Peter the Great and the peasant
  The ungrateful snake
  The uninvited guest
  Vania and the vampire
  Wat Tyler . . . The peasant's revolt
  The winter flower
  The wise wife
  The woman who wanted to cook with
    salt water
  The wood of Tontla
  You are right!

The peasant's strong wife
  JAGENDORF – GYPSIES p39-46

Pease-porridge hot
  MY BOOK HOUSE v. 1 p47.

Peat
  The three banshees

Peboan and Seegwun
  SCHOOLCRAFT – FIRE p5-10

Pecos Bill
  GORHAM – REAL p63-72

LEACH – RAINBOW p25-27
SHAPIRO – TALL p7-21

Pecos Bill and his bouncing bride
ARBUTHNOT – TIME p187-190

Pecos Bill, the cowboy
MY BOOK HOUSE v. 4 p193-211

The peddler and his monkeys
BULATKIN – EURASIAN p69-70

Peddlers
See also titles beginning with Pedlar
The blue dog
The golden casket
The hare, badger, monkey and otter
The haunted house of Watertown
If my shoe is narrow, what matter if
the world is wide
I'm a peddler
Jacques the woodcutter
The kneeling tree
Lady Melicent
Lawkamercyme
The magic carpet
The magician returns
The man who sold magic
Micah Rood's apple tree
The mountain witch and the peddler
The nutcracker and sugar dolly stories
Ooka and the suspect statue
Tell me, when will I die?
The three golden hairs of Grandad Sol
Vania and the vampire
A wife with false economy
The wonders of the three donals
The Yankee peddler

The peddler's caravan
MY BOOK HOUSE v. 4 p11.

The peddler's song
MY BOOK HOUSE v. 7 p145.

Peder Okse
HACK – DANISH p169-176

The pedlar of Swaffham
JACOBS – MORE p98-100
WILLIAMS – ROUND p161-165

The pedlar's dream
REEVES – ENGLISH p71-79

Pedro Alvarado and the Indian girl
JAGENDORF – KING p119-121

Pedro de Males Artes, or clumsy Pedro
LOWE – LITTLE p84-89

Peekaboo, I see you!
MY BOOK HOUSE v. 1 p74.

Peele, George
A voice speaks from the well

Peepan pee
MANNING – PETER p194-201

The peeping servant
SPICER – WITCHES p54-59

Peer Gynt
MY BOOK HOUSE v. 9 p98-119

Peerie folk
Peerifool

Peerifool
HAVILAND – SCOTLAND p25-48

Pegasus
The flying horse, Pegasus

Pegasus and the Chimaera
ARBUTHNOT – TIME p227-228

Pegs, wooden
Pepelea's peg

Pele (goddess)
A battle nobody won

Pelicans
Dhungura-ngarian: where the pelican
danced
Goolay-jali the pelican
A handful of hay

–**Beaks**
Green parrot's story

Pelops and Poseidon
CARPENTER – SHIPS p47-57

Pemba and the python and the friendly
rat
CARPENTER – AFRICAN p113-119

Pen and four foolish ministers
KRUEGER – SERPENT p62-69

The penalty of greatness
CATHON – PERHAPS p34-35

Penance. *See* **Penitence; Punishment**

Penelope
  The return of Odysseus
  The slaying of the suitors

Penelope and her suitors
  GREEN – GREEKS p70-71

Pengersec and the witch of Fraddom
  WILLIAMS – FAIRY p170-178

Pengo and the giants. *See* The adventures of Pengo

Pengo and the span high man. *See* The adventures of Pengo

Penguins
  Troubles with a penguin

Penitence
  The birth of Pryderi
  An impossible penance
  Pietro Bailliardo

The penitent governor
  BARASH – GOLDEN p51-54

Pennies
  The boy and the bull
  Dancing he would go
  Freddy and his fiddle
  Little Freddie with his fiddle
  The little purse with two pennies
  Pennyworth
  The rooster and the sultan
  The skillful huntsman
  Three pennyworth
  The wonderful knapsack

  , Silver
  The silver penny

Pennsylvania
  Cinderella dressed in green
  The dough image
  Early days and ways in America
  Exploring the wilderness
  The ghost dog of South Mountain
  Grandma'am Hinkel and the phantom
    dog
  The great sacrifice
  The haunted mine
  The hex and the oxen
  Joe Magarac
  Joe Magarac the steel man
  Joe Magerack, the steel-mill man
  Pioneer days in Pennsylvania
  A trickster tricks the devil

–Blue Mountains
  The good witch-doctor in the
    mountains
  True love in the Blue Mountains
–Bucks County
  Land of wonders
–Monongahela River
  Along the Monongahela
–Ohio River
  Chug-chug along the O-hi-o
–Oil City
  Gib Morgan
–Philadelphia
  Big ghost, little ghost–Who's
    scared of a ghost?
  Quaker, Quaker, how is thee?
–Pittsburgh
  Johnny Appleseed
  Steelmaker/Joe Magarac
–South Mountains
  The wolf-bride
–Susquehanna River
  Young John

Pennsylvania
  LEACH – RAINBOW p140-142

Pennsylvania Dutch rhymes
  MY BOOK HOUSE v. 1 p116-117

Pennyworth
  FARJEON – LITTLE p208-215

Penteclemas and the pea
  MANNING – DAMIAN p36-40

Peonies
  The search for the land of bliss

People. *See* Man

The people from Schwarzenborn
  RANKE – GERMANY p177-178

People of Dana. *See* Dana, People of

The people of Mols
  ROSS – BURIED p55-63

The people of peace (fairies)
  The fairies and the smith
  The son of the baker of Barra
  The woman of peace and the kettle

The people who lived near a mountain
NORLEDGE – ABORIGINAL
p35-37

Pepelea's peg
URE – RUMANIAN p42-44

Pepito
MANNING – DRAGONS p62-75

Pepper and peppers
How pa learned to grow hot peppers
The monkey and the crocodile
The Siamese pepper cure

The peppercorn oxen
MANNING – DEVILS p69-75

Peppino
MANNING – GIANNI p179-192

Per and the north wind
HARDENDORFF – TRICKY p111-118

Perak
The hunter of Perak

The perambulatin' pumpkin
CREDLE – TALL p16-20

Perambulators. *See* Baby carriages

Percy, William Alexander
Little shepherd's song

Peregrine and the redman of Rockingham
FINLAY – FOLK p54-65

Perez and Martina
ALEGRIA – THREE p56-58

The perfect husband
HITCHCOCK – KING p23-32

A perfect knight
MY BOOK HOUSE v. 10 p7.

Perfection
The great bell

Perfume
Magic
The story of the shipwrecked sailor
The tale of the two brothers

Peril. *See* Danger

Peris (angels)
Wali Dad the simple-hearted

Perrault, Charles
Blue Beard
Cinderella
The fairy
Puss in boots

Perrault, Charles
SIDEMAN – WORLD'S p831.
About this book

Perry-the-Winkle
TOLKIEN – READER (Part 4)
p41-44

Persea trees
The tale of the two brothers

Perseus
The adventures of Perseus
The boastful queen

Perseus . . . The head of Medusa
UNTERMEYER – FIRE. p86-90

Perseverance
The boy who made a dream come true
Bruce and the spider
The circus man
Down by the river Avon
The hare and the tortoise
The home-coming of Odysseus
The Hoosier poet
How Robert Fulton harnessed the
giant
Jamie Watt and the giant in the tea-
kettle
King Great Virtue
Kitava the gambler
The labors of Hercules
The little engine that could
The little man-as-big-as-your-thumb-
with-mustaches-seven-miles-long
The little rooster and the little hen
The luck boy of Toy Valley
The prince who rode through a
mousehole
The princess on the glass hill
Rhodopis and her gilded sandals
Robert Bruce, Scotland's hero
The rooster and the sultan
Shingebiss
Sir Beaumains, the kitchen knight
The six swans
A Spanish hero
Wee robin's Christmas song
Wilbur Wright and Orville Wright

492

Persia

Amin and the ghul
The baby mosque
Bahram and the snake prince
Bostanai
Bread-free
The brothers of the donkey
The canary that liked apricots
The crow and the soap
A dinar for a donkey
Donkey, mind your mother!
The donkey's tail
Down to Arabia
Fareedah's carpet
The flower faces
The fowler, the parrot and the king
The giant okab
The golden candelabra
The goldsmith, the wood carver, the
  tailor, and the hermit who quarreled
  over a wooden woman
The head of the family
Hiding in the well
How the milky way began
Hunting in the light
A lie for a lie
The magic horse
Meat or cat?
The miser
Mistress Cockroach
Molla Nasreddin and his donkey
One! Two! Three!
The philosophers of King Darius
Pomegranates for sale
Prince Ahmed and the fairy Peribanou
The pumpkin child
The queen's care
The quilt
The quivering needle
The reluctant familiar
Ruba and the stork
The saddle
Shah Abbas and the cobbler
The Shah weaves a rug
Simpletons
Sohrab and Rustum . . . The tragic
  encounter
The specialist
Steam—how much
The stone in the garden
The story of Rustem, the hero of
  Persia
The story of Zal
Stubborn husband, stubborn wife
The tailless jackal
Too heavy
Treasure in the basket
Two cows
Up and down the minaret
The voice from the minaret
What should I do, what shouldn't I
  do?

What the rose did to the cypress
Who am I?
The world's great epics
Zab

Persimmons

The crab and the monkey
The monkey and the crab
Poisonous persimmons
The tiger and the persimmon
The tiger's grave
Why the terrapin's shell is scarred

Persiphone

The return of the Spring

Persistence. *See* **Perseverance**

The pert fire-engine
MY BOOK HOUSE v. 4 p218-224

Peru

Children of the sun
Evil rocks and the evil spirit of Peru
The fox and the mole
The game of Tlachtli
The little frog of the stream
The magic poncho
The magic sandals of Hualachi
Teen-ager
A trick that failed
The youth who made friends with
  the beasts and the birds

—Andes Mountains
  Golden flower and the three
  warriors

—Cuzco
  The greatest wealth in the world

—Lima
  The baker's neighbor
  Tale of the good, gay lady

Perversity. *See* **Stubbornness**

Pestalozzi, Johann Heinrich
The old bear in the tree

The pet catfish
WITHERS – WORLD p87.

Peter the Great

Tsar Peter the Great and the peasant

Peter, Saint

The bean tree
Beppo Pipetta and his knapsack
Ed Grant has a dream

Peter, Saint (*Continued*)

How the wild boars came to be
Ivan and his knapsack
Ivan and his sack
The master-smith
The miraculous flute
Saint Peter and his trombone
Saint Peter's horses
A story about Our Lord Jesus Christ
A story of three brothers
A tailor in heaven
The terror of the ogres
The two wishes
The visits of St. Peter to his people
Why the dogs sniff at each other

Peter and the piskies
MANNING – PETER p1-6

Peter and the witch of the wood
HOKE – WITCHES p112-124

Peter ox
HATCH – MORE p167-181
PROTTER – CHILD. p1-6
THOMPSON – ONE p423-427

Peter, Peter, pumpkin eater
MY BOOK HOUSE v. 1 p36.

Peter Rabbit decides to change his name
MY BOOK HOUSE v. 3 p49-58

Peter went fishing on Sunday
WITHERS – I SAW p34.

Petit Jean and the frog
DELARUE – FRENCH p3-14

Petrash, Rosalie
TOOZE – MONKEY p72.

Petroglyphs
North Salem's Irish? Ruins
Tales of the ambiguous Dighton Rock

Petrosinella or parsley
MINCIELI – OLD p35-41

Petrovitch, W. M.
The friendly animals

Pets. *See* Types of pets, Dogs, Cats, etc.

Phaedrus
The bees and the drones
Fables and fabulists

Phaethon . . . The chariot of the sun
UNTERMEYER – FIRE. p21-24

Phaeton
MY BOOK HOUSE v. 7 p90-95

Phaeton; the boy who rode the chariot
of the sun
STRONG – FAVORITE p17-22

The phantom bridge
TAFT – PROFILE p163-165

The phantom fire ship
JAGENDORF – GHOST p44-49

The phantom painter in the steeple
JAGENDORF – UPSTATE p18-23

The phantom ship
SPICER – GHOSTS p7-15

The phantom ship of the Hudson
LEACH – RAINBOW p229.

Phantom ships
LAWSON – STRANGE p17-42

Phantoms. *See* **Ghosts**

Pharaohs
Anpu and Bata
The babe Moses
Horus the avenger
Isis and Osiris
Khnemu of the Nile
The prince and the Sphinx
Ra and his children
Se-Osiris and the sealed letter
The tale of the two brothers

Pharmacists
The big prescription
The lady who put salt in her coffee
The magic walking stick
The wood cutter's son and the two
turtles

The pheasant, the dove, the magpie, and
the rat
INS-SOB – FOLK p32.

Pheasants
The adventures of little Peachling
The bride who would not speak
The demon giant of Mount Ariake
Momotaro
Momotaro: boy-of-the-peach
Momotaro, or The story of the son of
a peach
Momotaro, the peach boy
The monkey and the pheasant

Pheasants (*Continued*)
The peach boy
The revenge of the serpent

The pheasants and the bell
INS-SÖB – FOLK p96-97

Phenist the bright-eyed falcon
DUDDINGTON – RUSS. p134-144

Philemon
Baucis and Philemon . . . The reward
of hospitality

Philip V
The legend of the magic lute

Philip of Valois, King of France
A strange reward

Philippe, Gobillot
Petit Jean and the frog

Philippine Islands
The absent-minded king
The battle of the firefly and the apes
The bird and the buffalo
The black cat of Cotabato
The coming of the Spaniards
The crab that tried to swallow the
moon
Datu Omar and the fairy
The dolphins of Celebes
The fairy of Hawili Falls
Foreword
The hawk and the wildcat
How the coconut tree came to be
The jellyfish's journey
Legend of the first Filipinos
The legend of the Mayon volcano
The monkey and the crocodile
The monkey prince and the witch
The moon's escape
Princess Maring, the huntress
The tiyanak
The turtle and the monkey share a
tree
Two out of one
The tyrannical king
White squash boy
Why dogs wag their tails
Why the carabao's hoof is split
Why the ocean is salty
Why the sky is high
Why women always wash the dishes
The wicked bankiva

—Tribes—Apayao
How the coconut tree was saved

—Tribes—Bagabo
How the lizards got their mark-
ings
Why the bagabo like the cat

—Tribes—Bicol
How Juan married a princess

—Tribes—Bukidnon
How the moon and stars came
to be

—Tribes—Igorot
The great flood

—Tribes—Ilocanos
Why the ocean is salty

—Tribes—Lubanum
The spirit of the stone

—Tribes—Luzon
The seven crazy fellows

—Tribes— Panpangan
The farmer and the demon

—Tribes—Sigakok
The sigakok bird

—Tribes—Tagalog
The aderna bird
Alberto and the monsters
Benito the faithful
Clever Juan and King Tasio
The cock and the sparrow-hawk
The fifty-one thieves
The house in the woods
How Suan became rich
The hummingbird and the carabao
Lucas the strong
The magic tabo
The rich man and the poor man

—Tribes—Tinguian
How the earth's fire was saved
How the kakok bird came to be
How the monkey came to be
In the first times
Misfortune comes to the house
The secret of Kaboniyan
Those who quarreled
The tikgi birds
Whence came the birds?
Why there are shadows on the
moon

—Tribes—Visayan
The adventures of Magboloto
The ape and the firefly
The artificial earthquake
Hidden treasure
How the fiddler crabs came to be
Juan and the helpful frog
Little shell
Masoy and the ape
The poor boy and the princess

Philippine Islands (*Continued*)

—Tribes—Zambal
How locusts came to be

Philistines
David and Goliath

Philoctetes
The wounded archer

Philosopher's stone
Alchemy: the magic science

Philosophers
The advantages of learning
The magic muntr
Maimonides and the bottle of poison
Socrates . . . The cup of hemlock
Solomon-the-wise and the golden
plough

The philosophers of King Darius
COURLANDER — TIGER'S p106-
110

Philosophy
The learned young professor
The past and the future

Phoenicians
North Salem's Irish? Ruins
Tales of the ambiguous Dighton Rock

The phoenix and the falcon
ALMEDINGEN — RUSS. p164-179

Phoenix, bird of the sun
McHARGUE — BEASTS p37-43

Phoenixes
Bird of the sun
Discovery of salt
East of the sun and north of the earth
The emerald-crested phoenix
The golden phoenix
The sorcerer's apprentice(s)

—Feathers
The phoenix and the falcon

Phosphorus
Is fish a brain food?

Photograph upside down
BATCHELOR — SUPER. p92-93

Phrenology
The soothsayers

Phrygia
The golden touch; the king who wor-
shipped gold
The Gordian knot; the destiny of
Alexander

The Phynnodderee
YOUNG — HOW p69-72

Physicians
The astrologer and the physician
The bride of Llyn y Fan Fach
The doctor and his pupil
Fool's paradise
Godfather death
The gouty giant
The hare's kidneys
Help in need and Abe in deed
The lake maiden
Luc, the king's woodsman
The red cloak
The spotted rug
The treasure of Altamira
The wise doctor
The woman of Llyn-y-fan (3) The
sequel

Pianos
The little dog waltz
A musical visit to fairyland

Piboon's golden mountain
KRUEGER — SERPENT p127-135

Picard, Barbara Leonie
How Loki outwitted a giant
The three wishes
Volund the smith
The werewolf

Piccolo players
David and the big drum

Pickles
Ooka and the cleanest case

Picnics
The teddy bears' picnic

Pictographs
How pictures become words

Picts
Saxons

Picts (*Continued*)

The secret of heather-ale

Pictures
How pictures become words

Pidicino
MINCIELI – TALES p11-17

A pie sat on a pear-tree
MY BOOK HOUSE v. 1 p27.

The piece of straw
UCHIDA – DANCING p109-119

The Pied Piper of Frenchville
JACOBS – MORE p1-6

The Pied Piper of Hamelin
SIDEMAN – WORLD'S p13-22

The Pied Piper of Hamelin; a minstrel's
enchanted music
STRONG – FAVORITE p82-90

Pierre Jean's tortoise
COURLANDER – PIECE p29-33

Pierrot
Columbine and her playfellows of the
Italian pantomime

Pies
A new way to cure old witch-hunting
The perambulatin' pumpkin
Simple Simon
There was an old woman
Tom Tit Tot

Pietro Bailliardo
LUM – ITALIAN p69-78

Piety
The dilemma of a pious man
Introduction (The righteous and the
pious)
The pious butcher
The righteous and the pious
Thomas the rhymer

The pig in the church
RANKE – GERMANY p190.

Pig in the poke
JAGENDORF – UPSTATE p34-36

Pig-skins. *See* **Hogs–Skins**

Pig-stys
Katie Woodencloak

The pig, the goat and the sheep
GREEN – BIG p127-128

The pigeon, the deer and the turtle
FEINSTEIN – FOLK p25-29

Pigeons
Alas!
Anansi and turtle and pigeon
The boy who found fear
Clever Pat
The friendly mouse
Goola-willeels the topknot pigeons
The greedy crow
How Maui fished up New Zealand
How Tepozton hung the bells
Kamiyo of the river
Light-O-Leap and the fowler
The melodius napkin
The princess and the pigeons
The restless pigeon and his wife
The three sons of the King of Antua
Tiger lily and the dragon

, **Golden**
The peasant and his three sons

Piggi-billa the porcupine
PARKER – AUSTRALIAN p189-191

Pigling and her proud sister
MY BOOK HOUSE v. 6 p191-195

Pig-men
A Kupua plays tricks

Pigs. *See* **Hogs**

Pigtails
A tragic story

Pigwidgeons
Prince Hassak's march

The pilgrim and the crab
KOREL – LISTEN p81-83

The pilgrim and the judge
NAHMAD – PEASANT p19-22

Pilgrims and pilgrimages
Aunt Misery
The blue palm tree
The first Thanksgiving day
Four tales of Rama and Sita

Pilgrims and pilgrimages (*Continued*)

How three pilgrims called Ilya to the rescue of Kiev
The king's true children
The magic purse of the swamps maiden
A merry tale of Merrymount
Monkey
The mother of time and the enchanted brothers
Padre Ulivo and his guests
Pietro Bailliardo
The ten chests
Two different interpretations of the same pact
Volkh's journey to the east

Pilkington, F. M.
How Cormac MacArt got his branch

Pillars
Nicola Pesce
The silent princess

, Golden
Soonimaya

The pillow
SEKI – FOLKTALES p193-194

The pillow talk
O'FAOLAIN – IRISH p47-51

Pillows
The wise man's pillow

Pills
The man who sold thunder

Pilots
Annie Christmas

Pinching
The prince and the demon

Pincushions
The prince with the golden hand

Pine, pitch
The Kamiah monster

The pine tree
DOBBS – ONCE p3-7

Pine trees
Building the bridge
Christening the baby in Russia

The death of Deirdre
The fairies in the White Mountains
The first mosquito
Hiawatha's childhood
Maya-mayi the seven sisters
The old man of the flowers
The sticky-sticky pine
The terrible-tempered dragon
The wife's portrait
The wonder of Skoupa

–Cones
Fir cones

–Needles
The blackbird and the pine needle
The girl on the green tree
The pine tree

Pinkel
HAVILAND – SWEDEN p33-49

Pinocchio
ARBUTHNOT – TIME p346-348

Pinny, pinny, poppy show!
MY BOOK HOUSE v. 1 p88.

Pinon nuts
Spider boy and the sun god's twins

Pins
Are pins lucky?
The bird of the golden land
See a pin

Pintosmalto
MINCIELI – OLD p98-107

Pioneer days in Pennsylvania
JOHNSON – WHAT p275-276

Pioneers, American
Buffalo Bill
Early days and ways in America
Early Kansas
Exploring the wilderness
The first Thanksgiving day
George Rogers Clark and the conquest of the Northwest
George Washington and the first American flag
The miracle flame
A North Dakota sod house
Old Johnny Appleseed
Primitive times in West Virginia
Princess Nelly and the Seneca chief
Pushing westward with Lewis and Clark
The San Joaquin Valley of California

Pioneers, American (*Continued*)

The witch of Ohio
The Yankee peddler

—**Western**
American family westward

The pious butcher
NAHMAD — PORTION p117-119

The pious washerwoman
NAHMAD — PORTION p100-101

The piper
LEACH — RAINBOW p267-268

The piper of Keil
WILSON — SCOTTISH p28-32

The piper of Shacklow
GARNER — GOBLINS p91.

The Piper of Sutherland
SHEPPARD — SCOT. p26-31

The piper who could not play
GREEN — LEPRECHAUN p31-41

The piper with the hoofs of a goat
PICARD — LADY p165-180

Pipers
The cow that ate the piper
The judgements of a magistrate
King March has horse's ears
The magical tune
March's ears
Old Pipes and the dryad
The Pied Piper of Frenchville
The Pied Piper of Hamelin
The Pied Piper of Hamelin; a minstrel's
enchanted music
The ratcatcher of Hamelin
The silver chanter of the
MacCrimmons
There was a piper had a cow
Tom, Tom, the piper's son
The young piper, the Little People of
Ireland

Pipes (musical)
I don't know where and I don't know
what
The magic pipe
March has horse's ears
The piper
The princess and the shepherd
The shepherd and the king's daughters
The shepherd's nosegay

The shepherd's pipe
The tale of the silver saucer and the
russet apple
Tattercoats
An unhappy lord

Pipes (smoking)
The blacksmith in the moon
How whale happens to smoke a pipe
The origin of Indian pipes
The smoker
The whale that smoked a pipe
You are right!

, **Peace**
The peace pipe

Pippi Longstocking
Pippi plays tag with some policemen

Pippi plays tag with some policemen
ARBUTHNOT — TIME p279-281

The pira game
LOWE — LITTLE p62-63

Pirate Yan Yost of Communipaw
JAGENDORF — UPSTATE p101-104

Pirates
Black Bartelmy
Black Sam Bellamy
A boy on the high seas
The Corsair of Spouting Horn
The drowned bells of the abbey
The gold table
The golden altar of the church of St.
Joseph
Hearts and pirates
The Inchcape rock
The magic belt
The master mariner
The phantom fire ship
The phantom ship
Pirate Yan Yost of Communipaw
The privateer turned patriot
The rescue of Fatima
Samson and the doll in green and
brown
The singing bell
A Spanish hero
The story of Mordecai and Esther
The treasure under the tree
The unwilling pirate
The voyage of Maelduin
Wolfert Webber, or golden dreams

The piskey revelers
PALMER — FAIRY p31-44

The piskie thresher
MANNING – PETER p56-58

Piskies Pisgies). *See* Pixies

Pistols. *See* Guns and gunnery

Pitch
The fight with Wabun
Mary covered with gold and Mary
covered with pitch
Mother Holle
The sun, the moon, and the stars
The three tasks

Pitchers
The bird of seven colors
The silent princess
Trim Tram Turvey

, Golden
The golden pitcher

Pits
The bad-tempered wife
The devil and the pit
The dutiful daughter
The fairy frog
How the lion rewarded the mouse's
kindness
Kwaku Ananse and the greedy lion
The panther in the pit

, Lime
Kantchil's lime pit

Pity. *See* Mercy

The pixie laborer. *See* The Fairy midwife

Pixies
Betty Stogs' baby
The cock-crow stone
The kind pixy
Peter and the piskies
The piskey revelers
The piskie thresher
Saint Margery Daw
The three cows
Water's locked!

Place names. *See* Names, Place

The place of strife
SPICER – GOBLINS p79-88

The place of the death adders
NORLEDGE – ABORIGINAL p33.

Plagues
The buyer of oxen
The farmer and the fairy hillock
The song-bird and the healing waters
The three plagues of Britain

The plain princess
ARBUTHNOT – TIME p283-291

The plains' call
MY BOOK HOUSE v. 4 p211.

Planck, Willy, illus.
The greedy tailor
How the carrot-counter got his name
The magic walking stick

Plantains
Anansi and the plantains

Planters' moon
BUDD – FULL p17-22

The planting of the apple tree
MY BOOK HOUSE v. 4 p212.

The planting party
COURLANDER – HAT p46-48

Plants and planting
See also Gardens and Gardening;
names of plants
Farming by the moon
The legend of the chingola bird
The mushroom
The powers of plants and trees to
protect against witches
The war of the plants

–Leaves
The albahaca plant

Platypus
Biggoon and the little duck
Gaya-dari the platypus
The origin of the platypus

Playgrounds
The arrow chain

Playwrights
Down by the River Avon

Please all–please none
DOBBS – ONCE p38-41

Please give me a ride on your back
MY BOOK HOUSE v. 2 p154.

Pleiad and star of dawn
WILSON – GREEK p11-20

(The) Pleiades
JABLOW – MAN p100-101
LEACH – HOW p136-137

Plesiosaurus
Loch Ness: last laugh?

Plish and plum
PROTTER – CHILD. p161-164

Plop!
WITHERS – I SAW p123-125

The plot
KOREL – LISTEN p42-63

The ploughboy poet
MY BOOK HOUSE v. 12 p110-112

The ploughman he's a bonnie lad
MY BOOK HOUSE v. 1 p153.

Ploughs and ploughing
The anger bargain
Cincinnatus; the man who would not
be king
The crimson purse and the talking
raven
The fable of the plough and the
ploughshare
The farmer, the buffalo, and the tiger
The farmer who went to plough
How the clergymen retrieved the
golden chalice from the goblins of
Gotland
I should like to plough
Jack O'Leary's plow
Kralyevich Marko's ploughing
Nikita and the dragon
The old man's tale of Prince Stephen
The Sing-Bonga beheld men
The skillful huntsman
The wonderful plow, The Little People
of the Island of Rugen
, Golden
Solomon-the-wise and the golden
plough

Plowman in the sky
GRINGHUIS – GIANTS p59-63

Plum pudding
DOBBS – MORE p18-21

The plumage of the owl
ALEGRIA – THREE p64-65

Plumes, fire
The fire plume

Plums
The feast of plums
Good luck and bad luck
Prunella

Pluto
Proserpine
The return of the Spring

Poachers
Richard Feverel and the hay-rick
The salmon's revenge

Pocahontas
The story of a princess

Pocahontas
BALDWIN – FAVOR. p28-29

Pocci
Nut-cracker

Pockets
The little milleress
Lucy Locket lost her pocket

Podhu and Aruwa
HARMAN – TALES p64-88

Poe, Edgar Allan
The bells

The poem of the sea
McALPINE – JAPAN. p45-53

Poems by Alfred Tennyson
MY BOOK HOUSE v. 1 p154-155

Poems by Christina Rossetti
MY BOOK HOUSE v. 1 p156-157

Poems by Robert Louis Stevenson
MY BOOK HOUSE v. 1 p158.

The poet of the Sierras
MY BOOK HOUSE v. 12 p143-146

Poetical

See also **Nonsense rhymes;
Nursery rhymes; Repetition rhymes
and stories; etc.**
Abraham Lincoln, 1809-1865
The acorn and the pumpkin
Adam Bell, Clyn of the Clough, and
  William of Cloudesley
The adventures of Tom Bombadil, and
  other verses from the Red Book
Afar in the desert
Alison Gross
All about Columbus
All in green went my love riding
All things beautiful
Answer to a child's question
April
The assembling of the fays
At Christmas play and make good cheer
The audacious kitten
Awake, O north wind
The bad baronets
The ballad of east and west
The ballad of Lord Lovell
Bannockburn
The battle of the Nile
The beast
Behold the fig tree
A Belgian morning
The bells
Beside the fire
Billy boy
The birds' convention
The bitter withy
Black clouds at midnight
The blackbird
The boaster
A Bohemian evening
Bombadil goes boating
The bow that bridges heaven
The bowlegged god, Bes
A boy in the island of Bali
A boy's song
The brook song
The broomstick train
The bugle song
The butterfly's ball
The calves
A captive snake half dead with fright
Casey at the bat
Casey Jones
Cat
The cat and the starling
A cavalier tune
A charm against witches
A charm for spring flowers
Chief above and chief below
A child in a Mexican garden
The children in the wood
A chronicle of Kiev
A Christmas song at sea

The cloud
Clouds
Come, little leaves
The cormorant and the fishes
Courage
The courtin'
The cowboy's life
The crow and the fox
The dance of the fishes
The daring prince
The dark guest
Dawlish fair
The death of Kwasind
The dog in the manger
The donkey and the nightingale
The double-headed snake of Newbury
Ducks' ditty
Earl Mar's daughter
The earth is on a fish's back
The elephant in favor
The elf and the dormouse
The elfin knight
The epic (Slovo)
Errantry
Europa and the bull
Evening at the farm
An explanation of the grasshopper
The eyes of owls
The fable of the plough and the
  ploughshare
Fairy and child
Fairy forests
The fairy shoemaker
The false knight
The farmyard
Fastitocalon
The fleeing deer
The fly
For a peaceful night
The fort of Rathangan
The Fourth of July
The fox and the grapes
From a moral alphabet
A fuzzy fellow without feet
A game
Gathering song of Donuil Dhu
A German evening
A ghost story
Give praise
The goldenrod
The goldfinch
Goldfinches
Grasshopper green
The greatest show on earth
Gull taught men to use manioc for
  food
Hallowe'en
The hand of glory
The hawk and the nightingale
He leaves the nest
He who bound the dragons of Chaos

502

Poetical (*Continued*)

Heap on more wood
Here, forest-fires
The heron
Hiawatha's childhood
Hiawatha's fasting
Hie away, hie away
The hoard
The homecoming of Beorhtnoth
  Beorhthelm's son
Horatius
How the goddess of Spring came to
  Scoring
How to catch unicorns
The hunters of Kentucky
Hynd Horn
I heard the bells on Christmas day
I saw three witches
In the paddy field
In the strange isle
Indian children
It
It is time for a night chant
Jabberwocky
Jack Frost
John Connu Rider
Johnny head-in-air
Kalevala, land of heroes
Kempe Owyne
King Hilary and the beggarman
The kitten and falling leaves
The knight
The Kraken
The last ship
The last word of a bluebird as told to
  a child
Late
Laughing song
The lay of Prince Igor
The learned cat
Little blue apron
The little creature
The little elf
Little Gustava
Little maid of far Japan
Little pictures from far Japan
Little red bird
Litrle shepherd's song
The little toy land of the Dutch
A lyke-wake dirge
The man in the moon
The man in the moon came down
  too soon
The man in the moon stayed up too
  late
Marching to Quebec
Max and Moritz
Max and Moritz and the tailor
Meeting in the road
Meg Merrilies

The men fashion the frames of their
  kyaks
The merman
Merry Christmas
The mewlips
Mexican rhymes
The mice
A milkweed and a buttercup
Miss Jenny Jones
The monkey and the mirror
The monkey and the spectacles
The monsoon season
Moon, so round and yellow
The mouse and the rat
The mushroom
The musicians
My beloved is gone down into his
  garden
The new colossus
New heroes
New Year's day
The night before Christmas
Nonsense rhymes
November's party
Of the great and famous
The old Navy
Old Shellover
Old songs
Oliphaunt
Opportunity
Overheard on a salt marsh
The owl
The owl and the pussy-cat
Paper boats
Paul Bunyan—poem
Paul Jones
Peaceful, the gentle deer
The peacock, the turkey and the
  goose
The peasant and the sheep
The peddler's caravan
The peddler's song
The penalty of greatness
A perfect knight
Perry-the-Winkle
The pig, the goat and the sheep
The piper of Shacklow
The plains' call
The planting of the apple tree
Plish and plum
The poor old lady
Prayer
Princess Mee
Protection against witches
Providence
The pumpkin
The purple cow
Quartet
The raggle, taggle gypsies
The rain, wind, and snow
The rats in council

Poetical (*Continued*)

The raven and the fox
Reaction
Recollections of the Arabian Nights
Revenge
The revenge
The ride-by-nights
The river flows full through the sky
  land
The road to China
The rose
Rosy Posy
Salute to the trees
School is over
The sea
The sea-bell
The sea gull
The sea shell
Seeing a brace of rabbits
Selections from Rabindranath Tagore
Shadow-bride
The shaking of the pear tree
The "Shannon" and the "Chesapeake"
The shepherd's dog and the wolf
Si Jura carved a house post
Sibu, the god-who-builds
Silver
The Sing-Bonga beheld men
The snake
Snow
Snow in the city
The snow man
Solitude
Something told the wise geese
A song for Easter
A song of Drake's men
The song of Solomon
The song of the bee
The song of the Darby ram
The song of the flea
Song of the leprechaun or fairy shoe-
  maker
Song on May morning
The spindles are still
Spring flowers
The squirrel
The star
The star children dwelt in a deep
  cave
The stars are silver reindeer
The stone troll
The story of flying Robert
The strange visitor
The strange white beast
The sugar-plum tree
Summer rain
The sun drives copper-colored rein-
  deer
Suppose you met a witch
The swan, the crab, and the pike

A Swedish evening
Swift things are beautiful
The swing
Tam Lin
Tam O'Shanter
The term
There goes a scout
Thor
Those young men
The three flutes are in the flute house
Three jovial huntsmen
The three most famous tales
The three ravens
A thunderstorm
The titmouse
To Llewelyn (who inquired concern-
  ing wyverns)
To the lady-bird
The tragic story
The traveler
Trees
A tropical morning at sea
The troubles at Hawaiki
The twilight
Twinkling bugs
Two birds and their nest
Two children
The two owls and the sparrow
Two poems
Under the greenwood tree
A voice speaks from the well
Wainamoinen finds the lost-words
A wanderer's song
We thank thee
Westwoods
Where go the boats?
While other birds at will may go
Whisky frisky
Who can crack nuts?
Why?
Wilbur Wright and Orville Wright
The wild boar and the ram
Will-o'-the-wisp
The wind and the sun
Wind bloweth were it listeth
The witch! The witch!
The witches' reel
Witches' song
With tail-fans spread
The wolf and the cat
The wolf and the mouse
The wolf turned shepherd
The wonderful world
Wynken, Blynken, and Nod
The Yankee peddler
Yes, that's the girl that struts about
Yet gentle will the griffin be

Poets and poetry (subjects)
Atlantis
A boy of the lake country

Poetical (*Continued*)

Bragi, god of poetry
The child and the mariner
The curse on the only son
The divine comedy
The fortune of the poet's son
Hali becomes a poet
The house of the rowan trees
How Odin brought the meal to Asgard
Kilcolman castle
Kilmeny
King Fergus MacLeide and the wee
  folk
A lie for a lie
The moon child
The mother of Oisin
Oisin in the land of the ever young
The portrait of the Tien
The pursuit of the hard man
The royal page
The story of Iubdan, King of the
  Lepra and the lepracaun
Taliesin
Thomas the rhymer
Tiger lily and the dragon
A young Quaker of New England

, **American**
  The father of American song
  The Harvard professor
  The Hoosier poet
  The poet of the Sierras
  A tramp of the Middle West

, **English**
  The rebel
  The rector's son
  Sweet peas and Grecian urns
  A Victorian romance
  A wizard of the twilight

, **Scottish**
  The ploughboy poet

The poffertjes pan
  LEEUW – LEGENDS p97.

Poison
  The bean trees that are sacred to the
    witches
  How the black snake got its fangs
  The iguana and the black snake
  The iguana's poison bag
  Loki's punishment
  Maimonides and the bottle of poison
  Snow White and the seven dwarfs
  Socrates . . . The cup of hemlock
  The three young men and death

The poisoned apple
  PICARD – STORIES p209-217

Poisonous persimmons
  INS-SŎB – FOLK p188-189

Poland
  About Jan the prince, Princess Won-
    derface, and the flamebird
  About the hedgehog who became a
    prince
  Are there such women?
  The astrologer and the physicians
  Basia, the babbler
  Capturing the moon
  The cat and the fox
  The crab
  Curiosity punished
  The enchanted hedgehog
  A fair distribution
  The flight
  Giving away secrets
  The golden lynx
  Good sense and good fortune
  The hare
  The hedgehog who became a prince
  A horned goat
  How a peasant outwitted two mer-
    chants
  The jester who fooled a king
  The jolly tailor who became king
  The king and the peasant
  Krencipal and Krencipalka
  The lark, the wolf, and the fox
  The lazy maiden
  Lie-a-stove
  The lucky hunter
  The magic fife
  The peasant and his hen
  The proud king
  The quarrel between the months
  The rooster and the wind
  Sense and money
  Sinko's luck
  The sly gypsy
  The stolen ring
  Throwmount and Oakpull
  The treasure
  The wandering cobbler
  Why the sun stopped shining
  The wise witness

–**Chelm**
  Golden shoes
  The mixed-up feet and the silly
    bridegroom
  The snow in Chelm
  Who am I?
  The wise men of Chelm

–**Danzig**
  The beggar's prophecy

Polecats. *See* Skunks

Polenta, polenta, and more polenta
MINCIELI – TALES p48-50

The police marshal
INS-SOB – FOLK p129-136

Policeman Joe
MY BOOK HOUSE v. 1 p173.

Policemen
Pippi plays tag with some policemen

Polish rhymes
MY BOOK HOUSE v. 1 p72-73

The polite children
ALEXANDER – PEBBLES p12.

Politeness. *See* Courtesy

Poll and doll
FARJEON – SILVER p103-108

Poll comes to court
FARJEON – SILVER p72-81

Polly, put the kettle on
MY BOOK HOUSE v. 1 p31.

Pollywogs. *See* Frogs

Polo, the snake-girl
CARPENTER – AFRICAN p121-127

Polynesia
See also names of Polynesian countries
The adventures of Kahukura and Te Kanawa, The Little People of Polynesia
The bride from the land of the spirits
The cat and the king's daughter
How Maui fished up the island
The little menehunes
The magic banana
The maiden of the mist
Maui and the fire goddess
Maui catches the sun
Maui, the demi-god
Maui the Great
The star children dwelt in a deep cave
The story of Hine-Moa and Tutanekai
The three monsters of the sea
The whale and the sorcerer
Why flounder's two eyes are on the same side of his face
Why porpoise is not a fish

The woman who wanted to cook with salt water

Polyphemus
The one-eyed giant

Polyphemus, the Cyclops
THOMPSON – ONE p377-384

Polyps
The little mermaid

Polyxena
Achilles and Polyxena

Pombo, Rafael
The poor old lady
Reen-reen-reeny-croak-frog

The pomegranate seed
NAHMAD – PORTION p139-140

Pomegranates
The dragon of the well
He wins who waits
Keloglan and God's greatness
The melancholy prince and the girl of milk and blood
The monkey's pomegranate
Moti
One grain more than the devil
The princess who loved her father like salt
The return of the Spring

Pomegranates for sale
KELSEY – ONCE p15-19

Pomona . . . The tree and the vine
UNTERMEYER – FIRE. p99-101

Ponchos
The eternal wanderer of the Pampas

Ponds. *See* Pools

Ponies
The little gray pony
Moti
The trials of Conneda

Pony express
Buffalo Bill

Pooh goes visiting and gets into a tight place
ARBUTHNOT – TIME p304-306

The pooka
BRIGGS – PERS. p133-135

The booka of the mill
SPICER – GOBLINS p118-127

Pookas (imaginary animals)
The Kildare pooka
The twelve silly sisters

Pools
Bani Hilal; A tribe is born
The black pool
The crane and the crab
The girl who weaves by night
The golden slipper, the magic ring,
and the twigs
The grateful monkeys' secret
The little hare's clever trick
The moon in the pond
Nikkessen's pool
Pappa Greatnose
San fairy Ann
Shah Meram and Sade Sultan
The spider specter of the pool

Poor. See Poverty

The poor and the rich
RANKE – GERMANY p149-150
THOMPSON – ONE p342-343

The poor boy and the princess
SECHRIST – ONCE p168-173

The poor brother's bad luck
DURHAM – TIT p30-33

The poor brother's treasure
RANKE – GERMANY p89-90

The poor girl who stepped out golden
flowers
ILLYÉS – ONCE p78-83

The poor herdsman and his sons, The
Little People of Africa
BELTING – ELVES p15-21

Poor Jack and the cat
BAMBERGER – FIRST p144-146

Poor little girl, rich little girl
JAGENDORF – KING p260-264

The poor man's clever daughter
URE – RUMANIAN p131-143

A poor man's servant
URE – RUMANIAN p65-68

The poor man's son, the dwarfs, and the
birds
BOUCHER – MEAD p141-147

The poor miller's boy and the cat
BAMBERGER – FIRST p130-135

Poor old cricket!
LEACH – LUCK p60-61

The poor old lady
MY BOOK HOUSE v. 2 p68-69

A poor peasant and two nobles
BULATKIN – EURASIAN p123-124

The poor people who wanted to be rich
RANKE – GERMANY p183-184

The poor ploughman and the rich nobleman
JAGENDORF – MERRY p31-39

The poor weaver and the princess
SIDDIQUI – TOON. p82-90

The poor widow bullfighter
BRENNER – BOY p106-112

The poor wolf
BLOCH – UKRAIN. p28-35

Poorhouses
Odd Olle

Pop! goes the weasel!
MY BOOK HOUSE v. 1 p107.

Popcorn
Paul Bunyan swings his axe

The popcorn frost
WITHERS – WORLD p83.

The popcorn patch
CREDLE – TALL p53-54

Pope, Alexander
Hear how the birds

Popes
The boy who became pope
How Michael Scot went to Rome
The Jewish pope
Robert of Sicily . . . The proudest
king
The three languages

Poplar trees
The legend of Eilean Donan castle
Little shepherd's song

Popo and the coyote
ROSS — MEXICO p134-149

Popo and the princess
JORDAN — BURRO p22-25

Poppies
The prince with the golden hand

The porcupine and the dog
GREEN — BIG p186-188

Porcupines
Anansi and the elephant exchange
knocks
The buffalo and the porcupine
The first pig and porcupine
A horned goat
How death came into the world
How the porcupine fooled the
elephant
How the porcupine outwitted the fox
How turtle came
Juanito and the princess
The little rabbit who wanted red wings
Mboyo and the giants
The monkey and the banana
Piggi-billa the porcupine
The Scotty who knew too much
The serpents and the porcupine
The tiger's war against Borneo
The tug of war
Why the dog lost his wife
Why there are no tigers in Borneo
The Wi-oombeens and Piggi-billa

The porcupines
GREEN — BIG p213.

The porcupine's hoe
COURLANDER — HAT p86-87

Pork
Jan and Jaantje
Warthog and hornbill

Porpoises
See also **Dolphins**
Adventures of a water baby
The mock turtle's song
The sea king and the fox
Why porpoise is not a fish

Porridge
The ring in the porridge bowl
The snake who bit a girl

Porridge
BAMBERGER — FIRST p23-25

Porridge with a troll
JONES — SCAND. p98-101

Porters
Keloglan and God's greatness
Sindbad the sailor

A portion in Paradise
NAHMAD — PORTION p27-29

The portrait of the Tien
SUN — LAND p100-103

Portraits
The blackbird's song
Faithful John
The flower faces
Oraggio and Bianchinetta

Portugal
The archbishop's mule
Aunt Misery
The bashful prince
The beautiful princess
The black spider
The blind kind and the magic bird
Bola Bola
Born to be rich
The boy who was never afraid
The cat's tail
The child and the fig
Clarinha
The clever boy
The cockroach and the mouse
The Count of Estremadura
The cow maiden
An expensive omelette
The fig bough
The foolish lad and the flies
Good luck and great riches
The great fish
The hearth-cat
How the wild boars came to be
The innkeeper's daughter
The invisible hands
Kernel
The king and the barber
The legend of the almond tree
The listening king
The little horse of seven colors
The magic mirror
The master of magic and spells
Mirabella

Portugal (*Continued*)

The miraculous flute
The monkey's pomegranate
No supper
The one-legged chicken
The owl and the wolf
The palace of the white cat
Pedro do Males Artes, or clumsy
 Pedro
The pira game
The price of eggs
A prince and a dove
The princess and the pigeons
The princess in the tower
The puss's tail
The river
Seven iron-souled slippers
The shoemaker
Snow in the mountains
The string of lies
The subterranean passage
The tail of the cat
The ten dwarfs of Aunt Greenwater
The tipsy rooster
The viper and the friar's rope

Portuguese
Mario and the yara
Tales of the ambiguous Dighton Rock

Poseidon (Greek god of the sea)
Pelops and Poseidon

Possessions
Emma of Haarlem
The wise wife

Possums. *See* **Opossums**

The possums, the man, and the tree
 NORLEDGE – ABORIGINAL p47-48

Postmen
Anansi and snake the postman
Cookus, Bopple and Yeakle
Haltefanden (The lame devil)
Mister postman

The pot of gold
 MARGOLIS – IDY p51-56
 MINCIELI – TALES p27-31

The pot-that-cooked-by-itself
 CARPENTER – SOUTH p167-174

Potatoes
The devil's partnership

Friar Blockhead and the Lord
The great white condor
The leprechaun in the basket
Old boss and George
Sir Walter Raleigh

Potmenders
Saadia the potmender

Potok's dancing and the snakes
 ALMEDINGEN – KNIGHTS p49-58

Pots and pans
See also **Cauldrons; Kettles**
The beauty and the beast
Brother Breeze and the pear tree
The copper pan
The crow and the sparrow
The dish ran away with the spoon
The eternal wanderer
The fall of the spider man
Fishing for pots in the pond
Fording the river in a copper cauldron
Giant skeeters in the brass pot
The gun, the pot, and the hat
The hillman and the housewife
How the world got wisdom
How wisdom came to man
How wisdom was spread
The king's jewels
Kwaku Ananse and the whipping cord
The little round pot
The lord of Massachusetts
Porridge
The potted princess
The revolt of the utensils
The shoemaker's dream
Simple and the princess
The tortoise-wife
Tripple-trapple
Two of everything
The two pots
The unwashed pot
Work-let-me-see
A world of nonsense

The pots that sang
 HEADY – WHEN p36-41

The potted princess
 JOHNSON – PRINC. p118-131

Potter, Beatrix
The tale of Peter Rabbit

The potter and the gate
 WYNDHAM – CHINA p64-65

Potters and pottery
The Brahman in the potter's shop

Potters and pottery (*Continued*)

The elephant's bathtub
The lame cat and the potter
Ooka and the shattering solution
The origin of the water jars
The pots that sang
Tell me, when will I die?
The valiant potter

A pottle o' brains
JACOBS – MORE p134-141

Potts, Thomas
Lancashire – – –?

Pouches
The untidy mermaid

Poultry
See also names of poultry
The farmyard
Henny-Penny
Krencipal and Krencipalka

A pound of tobacco
LAWSON – STRANGE p162-163

Poverty
And I dance mine own child
Bahri of the beauty spot
Baucis and Philemon . . . The reward
of hospitality
Beauty and the beast
Bedding in one's ear
The beggar's prophecy
The best wish
The blue palm tree
The cartman's stories
Doctor know-all
Donal O'Donnell's standing army
Dookiram, the poor one
The earrings
The foolish man
Four good men
The gift of gold
The gift of the holy man
The goldfish
The greedy rich man
How poverty was revealed to the king
of Adja
Hwan and Dang
It's all the fault of Adam
The jester who fooled a king
Johnnie and Grizzle
The kind farmer
A king and destiny
The lady's loaf-field
The little round pot
Little Tom Thumb

Ma Liang and his magic brush
The man who always helped the
needy
The man who looked for death
Master and man
Mr. Vinegar
The mysterious letter
No supper
The old gypsy woman and the good
lord
The old traveler
The poor and the rich
The poor brother's bad luck
The poor brother's treasure
The poor herdsman and his sons, The
Little People of Africa
Poor little girl, rich little girl
The poor man's clever daughter
A poor man's servant
The poor people who wanted to be
rich
The poor wolf
Rags-and-tatters
Raindrops can't tell broadcloth from
jeans
The rich lady and the ring in the sea
Robin Hood
Sadko
Shemiaka the judge
The shoemaker
A slip of the tongue
The small red feather
The snake prince
The spindle, the shuttle and the
needle
The tale of the heir of Linne
The talking fish
Tao K'an and his mother
The three precepts
The three wishes
Tripple-trapple
Two pennies
A voice from heaven
The worthless man of poverty
Yama and the poor man

Powder horns
The man who hung his powder horn
on the moon

Power, Rhoda
How dandelions were made
How stars and fireflies were made
How the spider was made

Power
The ambitious maiden
Caravan
The gnat and the lion
La Hormiguita

Power (*Continued*)

Jamie Watt and the giant in the tea-
kettle
King Canute on the seashore
The lost sun, moon, and stars
The maiden and the ratcatcher
The match-making of a mouse
The mouse and the magician
A mouse in search of a wife
The philosophers of King Darius
The power of witches
The proud father
The rat's bridegroom
The shepherd with the curious wife
The stone crusher of Banjang
The sun and the north wind
The tale of the two cunning servants
Who is the mightiest
The wise man's pillow
A witch's confession

The power of fancy
JOHNSON – WHAT p178.

The power of thought
HOPE-SIMPSON – CAVAL. p172-173

The power of witches
HOPE-SIMPSON – CAVAL. p107-113

Powers, Mabel
How a bird turned the world upside
down
Why the woodchuck comes out in
midwinter

The powers of plants and trees to protect
against witches
HOPE-SIMPSON – CAVAL. p125-127

Praetorius, J.
How the carrot-counter got his name

Prahlada
REED – TALK. p89-94

Prairies and plains
A boy in Russia
Buffalo Bill
The plains call
A song of the railroad men
The village of cream puffs

Praise
The elephant at court
The elephant in favor
A song for the new chief

Pranksters. *See* **Clowns; Trickery**

Prayer
The boy with the beer keg
The devil and the Good Book
The fox and the geese
Gift for the lazy
Grace at meals
How Percival came to Arthur's court
The miser's wife
The mountain hen and the fox
The mysterious letter
The night of the full moon
The saddle
The silver on the hearth
The true scales
Up and down the minaret
Vanya's leap
The weight of the cart
The wise merchant
The wise priest

Prayer
GARNER – GOBLINS p v.

Praying mantis
The planting party

Preacher and the devil
See also Ojje Ben Onogh
COURLANDER – TERRA. p98-101

Preacher Peter and Mike Fink
JAGENDORF – SAND p150-153

Preachers. *See* **Clergymen**

Preble, Edward
Of sea-going snakes

Precaution
The wolf and the fox
The wolf, the goat, and the kid

Precepts. *See* **Sayings**

The precious stone
PRIDHAM – GIFT p130-137

Precocious piggy
MY BOOK HOUSE v. 1 p196-197

Preface: Story time in Mexico
JORDAN – BURRO p8-10

Prejudice. *See* **Tolerance**

Preparedness. *See* **Precaution**

Presents. *See* **Gifts**

The president wants no more of
Anansi. *See* Ticoumba and the president

Presidents
The blacksmiths
Ticoumba and the president

Pretense
See also **Imitation**
The blue jackal
The doctor who knew everything
The donkey in the lion's skin
The donkey, the ox and the farmer
Jaco and the giant
The man who couldn't pay his debts
The rabbit and the possum seek a
wife
The story of Harisarman
Toto gets married
The would-be wizard

The pretty bird
WITHERS – I SAW p56.

Pretty flowers of the Steppes
MY BOOK HOUSE v. 1 p133.

Pretty Sally
MY BOOK HOUSE v. 1 p169.

Pretty, see the cloud appear!
MY BOOK HOUSE v. 1 p81.

Preziosa, the she-bear
MINCIELI – OLD p54-63

The price of a curse
DAVIS – TEN p48-61

The price of eggs
LOWE – LITTLE p32-35

The price of greed
GRAY – INDIA'S p155-156

Pride
See also **Braggarts**
Ani, the mother who was too proud
The baron's haughty daughter
Bellerophon . . . The winged horse
The blacksmith lion and the con-
ceited goat
Blue legs
The buckwheat
Clever Kadra
The clever thief
The coyote and the evil witches
The crumb in the beard

Deep insight
The fountain
The fox and the crow
Graylegs
The haughty princess
How frog lost his tail
How the camel got his proud look
the key maiden of Tegerfelden
The king on trial
The little nag
The loathly lady
Ooka and the shattering solution
The parson and the sexton
The pastor and the sexton
The pearl necklace
The prince and the goose girl
The princess and the vagabone
The proper way to lay the table
The proud camel and the rude mon-
key
The proud goat
The proud king
The proud princess
The rabbit takes his revenge on the
elephant
The radiant khan
Robert of Sicily . . . The proudest
king
The seven proud sisters
Solomon and his pride
The story of Wang Li
The tiny bird and the king
Torah and honor
Tortoise and Babarinsa's daughter
The two goats
The ugly king
The vain ox
Vukub-Cakix
Wawanosh

Pride goes before a fall
GREEN – BIG p130.

The priest and the pear tree
U. N. – RIDE p38-41

Priests
The alchemist
The angel
The badger's gratitude
Baskets in a little cart
Bedding in one's ear
The bee on the cap
The boy who became pope
Chucko, who's afraid?
The coffin that moved itself
The cow that cried
The crock of gold
The dancing kettle
A dead secret
The demon's daughter

Priests (*Continued*)

The devil's bowling ball
Eggborn
The emerald lizard
The fisherman and his soul
The foolish wife and her three foolish
  daughters
The friar on Errigal
The goblin-spider
Golden goodness
The good fortune kettle
The greater sinner
Gulersh and the princess of France
Hoichi the earless
How the clergyman retrieved the
  golden chalice from the goblins of
  Gotland
Ikkyu and the merchant's moneybags
Iphigenia . . . The transported sacrifice
Katie Woodencloak
King Appolonides
The king who rides a tiger
The knight of Steenhuisheerd
Lazy Peter and the king
Learning magic
The little book
The little priest
The lost gift
The lucky tea-kettle
The magic pancakes at the Footbride
  tavern
The magic teakettle
The man who struck his father
The man who would know magic
Monkey
The one-legged chicken
The oni's laughter
Padre Ulivo and his guests
Painted skin
Red king and green king
The reward of treachery
Saint Sava and the devil
Sly Peter's revenge
The sweet Mochi's parents
Tale of the good, gay lady
A tale of two rogues
The tea-kettle
The text
There's no deity there
The three lucky charms
The three questions
The tiger priest
The tubmaker who flew to the sky
Twelve great black cats and the red
  one
When Boqueron spoke
The white snake lady
The wise priest
A wise priest learns a lesson:
  Khaemwese and Tabubu

The woman in the chest
The woodcutter of Gura
The young man and the priest
Zolo Dumah and the priest

, Moslem
  The baby mosque
  Bread-free
  The brothers of the donkey
  The canary that liked apricots
  The crow and the soap
  A dinar for a donkey
  Donkey, mind your mother!
  The donkey's tail
  The head of the family
  Hiding in the well
  Hunting in the light
  Meat or cat?
  One! Two! Three!
  Pomegranates for sale
  The quilt
  The quivering needle
  The saddle
  The specialist
  Steam—how much
  The stone in the garden
  Too heavy
  Treasure in the basket
  Two cows
  Up and down the minaret
  The voice from the minaret

Prime ministers. *See* **Ministers** (political)

Primitive times in West Virginia
  JOHNSON — WHAT p273-275

Prince Ahmed
  JOHNSON — HARPER p48-85

Prince Ahmed and the fairy Peribanou
  BUCK — FAIRY p98-124

Prince Alun and the "Cannwyl Corph"
  PUGH — TALES p37-45

A prince and a dove
  LANG — VIOLET p193-202

The prince and the birds
  MARKS — SPANISH p3-24

The prince and the chimney sweep
  NYBLOM — WITCH p66-82

The prince and the demon
  SPELLMAN — BEAUT. p19-21

The prince and the dragons
  MANNING — PRINCES p66-75

The prince and the firedrake. *See*
Prince Prigio and the firedrake

The prince and the giant's daughter
WILSON – SCOTTISH p156-172

The prince and the goose girl
JOHNSON – HARPER p226-249

The prince and the remore. *See* Prince
Prigio and the firedrake

The prince and the sky-blue filly
MANNING – PRINCES p14-27

The prince and the Sphinx
GREEN – TALES p66-72

The prince and the Three Fates
BUCK – FAIRY p286-296
LANG – OLIVE p201-212

The prince and the vizier's son
MANNING – DAMIAN p54-60

Prince Andrea and Princess Meseria
KAPLAN – SWEDISH p71-107

Prince Charming, the mare's son
CREANGA – FOLK p67-81

Prince Daniel
DUDDINGTON – RUSS. p72.

Prince Ferdinand
RANKE – GERMANY p129-134

The Prince Fernando
EELLS – SPAIN p93-107

Prince Finn the fair
MacMANUS – BOLD p19-43
MacMANUS – HIBERIAN p108-125

Prince Hassak's march
JOHNSON – HARPER p166-195

Prince Hat beneath the earth
KAPLAN – SWEDISH p162-199

The prince is puzzled. *See* Prince Prigio
and the firedrake

Prince Ivan and the firebird
PONSOT – RUSSIAN p11-20

Prince Ivan and the sun princess
ALMEDINGEN – RUSS. p105-117

Prince Lindworm
JONES – SCAND. p3-15

Prince Llewellyn and the red-haired man
SHEPPARD – WELSH p137-141

Prince Loaf
MANNING – GIANTS p118-125

Prince Marko and a Moorish chieftain
MAYNE – HEROES p172-180

Prince Mirko
MANNING – GLASS p126-138

Prince Murko's journey
CARPENTER – HORSES p90-100

The Prince of Coucy
BARASH – GOLDEN p95-101

The prince of the Dolomites and the
princess of the moon
TOOR – GOLDEN p177-190

The prince of the seven golden cows
MANNING – JONNIKIN p106-114

The prince of the six weapons
COURLANDER – TIGER'S p52-57

Prince Prigio
JOHNSON – HARPER p268-318

Prince Prigio and the firedrake
MANNING – BEASTS p91-102

Prince rabbit
JOHNSON – HARPER p18-39

Prince Sigurd and his sister
BOUCHER – MEAD p12-18

Prince Sneeze
SHEAHAN – HENRY p64-77

Prince sun and Princess moon
WYATT – GOLDEN p34-45

A prince went hunting
WITHERS – I SAW p126-127

The prince who made the silence speak
NYBLOM – WITCH p197-209

The prince who rode through a mousehole
MY BOOK HOUSE v. 7 p97-101

The prince who wanted the moon
AARDEMA – STORY p62-66

514

Prince Wicked
  GRAY – INDIA'S p8-12

The prince with the golden hand
  MANNING – DRAGONS p103-
  113

Princes and princesses
  About Jan the prince, Princess
    Wonderface, and the flamebird
  According to tradition
  The adventures of Florian
  The adventures of Iain Direach
  The adventures of Pengo
  The Ailpeinbird, the stolen princess
    and the brave knight
  Aladdin and the princess
  Alberto and the monsters
  All my lambkins and all my bear cubs
  Angus
  Arawn
  The ash lad who made the princess
    say, "You're a liar"
  Ash sweeper and the wishing wand
  Ashputtel
  Assipattle and the giant sea serpent
  Aucassin and Nicolette
  The baby that was sold
  The bad prince
  Bahram and the snake prince
  Bald pate
  Bash Tchelik
  The bashful prince
  Batim the horse
  The battle
  The bay-tree maiden
  The beacon light
  The beautiful blue jay
  The beautiful princess
  Beauty and the beast
  The bee, the harp, the mouse, and the
    bumclock
  The bee, the mouse and the bum-clock
  The best wish
  Big Matsiko
  The birthday of the Infanta
  The black dog of the wild forest
  The black prince
  The blackbird's song
  The blue belt
  The blue centaur
  The blue foal
  The box with wings
  The boy and the birds
  The boy and the leopard
  The boy who out-fibbed a princess
  The brave little prince
  The brave little tailor
  A bride for the sea god
  Cannetella

Casperl
The castle of no return
The castle of the three giants
The cat and the king's daughter
The cat bride
Cattenborg
The cauldron of Brekkan
The cavallino
Celery
La Cenerentola
Chien Tang
The child in the bamboo tree
The children of Lir
Chourilo's little comb
Chu Cuoi's trip to the moon
Chu Dong Tu and the princess
Cinder-maid
Cinderella
Cinderella or The little glass slipper
The city of the winter sleep
Clarinha
The clever bride of Tunisia
The clever peasant girl
The cloud horse
The cloud princess
The clumber pup
The coat remakes many a man
The comb, the flute and the spinning
  wheel
Conclusion
The coral comb
Count Crow and the princess
The Count of Estremadura
The cow maiden
The crab that tried to swallow the
  moon
The crumb in the beard
The crystal bowl
The crystal mountain
The danced-out shoes
The dancing princesses
Dapplegrim
The daughter of the King Ron
Dawn, twilight and midnight
The death of Koshchei the deathless
Death's godchild
The demon with the matted hair
The demon's daughter
The destiny of Princess Tien Dung
A dish of laban
Donkey-skin
Dorani
The dragon king and the lost fish-hook
The dragon of the well
East of the sun and north of the earth
East of the sun and west of the moon
The enchanted castle in the sea
The enchanted cow
The enchanted hedgehog
The enchanted princess
The endless story

Princes and princesses (*Continued*)

Esben Ashblower
Europa and the bull
Fair, brown, and trembling
The fairy frog
The fairy quite contrary
The false fakir
The fame of the princess
Farmer Weathersky
The finch with the golden voice
The firebird
The fish with bent noses
The fisherman's son
The five young men
The flight
The flower of beauty
The flying trunk
The fountain of youth
Four brothers who were both wise and foolish
The friendly frog
The frog
The frog jacket
The frog jumps back in its puddle, even when seated in a golden chair
The frog prince
The frog-princess
The fruits of health
Gammelyn, the dressmaker
The giant and his royal servants
The giant of the Brown Beech Wood
The giant who had no heart in his body
A girl and a stepmother
The gold bird
The gold-rich king
The golden bird
The golden butterfly
The golden candelabra
The golden carnation
The golden casket
The golden crab
The golden fleece
The golden-headed fish
The golden horse
The golden lion
The golden lynx
The golden nightingale
The golden phoenix
The golden prince of the conch shell
The goldspinners
Good luck and bad luck
The good sword
The grateful beasts
The grateful devil
The grateful prince
Graylegs
The green knight
The green sergeant
The green-skinned princess

Griselda
Gulersh and the princess of France
Hans, the horn, and the magic sword
The happy prince
The hare of Inaba
The haughty princess
He wins who waits
The heart of Princess Joan
Heart of the west wind
The hedgehog who became a prince
The hen that laid diamond eggs
Hereward
History as propaganda: The Princess of Bakhtan
Horns
The hound Gelert
How Ian Direach got the blue falcon
How Jack sought the golden apples
How Juan married a princess
How music began
How Prince Bondhu became a boatman
How the raja's son won the Princess Labam
How these tales came to be told
How Urseli became a princess
The hunchback's horse
The imposter
Isun Boshi, the one-inch lad
Jack at Hell Gate
Jac, the King of England's son, and the giant with three heads
The jeweled ring
The jewels of the sea
John the bear
Juan Bobo and the princess who answered riddles
Juanito and the princess
Kabadaluk
Kari Woodencoat
Kate Crackernuts
Katie Woodencloak
Kelea, the surf princess
Kempe Owyne
King Find's daughter
King March has horse's ears
The king of England and his three sons
The king of the dark desert
The king who slept
The king's daughter cries for the moon
The king's dream
The king's vine
A kiss from the beautiful Fiorita
Kojata
Kuluile, the dancing girl
Kupti and Imani
Kuzenko sudden-wealthy
The lame dog
The land of youth

516

Princes and princesses (*Continued*)

Lars, my lad!
The last of the dragons
The lazy boy
Leaving paradise
The legend of Bala Lake
The legend of the Prince Ahmed Al
Kamel
The legend of the three beautiful
princesses
Lie-a-stove
The light princess
The lily and the bear
Little Berry
The little black box
The little bull calf
Little finger
The little fox
The little gardener with golden hair
The little horse
The little horse of seven colors
The little lion dog and the blue prince
The little mermaid
The little mouse
The little nag
Little one-inch
The little pet vani
Little Rosa and long Leda
The little snake
The little white cat
Long, broad and sharpsight
The long-nosed princess
Longshanks, girth, and keen
Lord Peter
Lost and found
The lost gift
The lost half-hour
The lost prince
The louse skin
Love like salt
The love of a Mexican prince and
princess
The love of three oranges
The loveliest rose
The magic apples
The magic belt
The magic berries
The magic carpet
The magic fife
The magic fishbone
The magic hill
The magic horse
The magic lute player
The magic mango
The magic mirror
The magic sandals
The magical music
The magician Palermo
The magician's garden
The magician's heart

The maiden of Deception Pass
Malati and the prince
Many moons
Maria Marina
Mary Morevna
The master cat
The master-maid
The master mariner
The melancholy prince and the girl
of milk and blood
Melisande
The melodius napkin
The mermaid and the boy
A message in a bottle
The miller's four sons
The monkey prince and the witch
The moon princess
The moon's escape
More south than south, more north
than north
The moss-green princess
The most necessary thing in the
world
The mouseling
Mrizala and her bridegroom, death
The musical silver goat
My candlestick
My lady Sea
The mysterious lake
Nastasya and the whirlwind
The necklace
Niassa and the ogre
The nine doves
The nine peahens and the golden
apples
The old man's tale of Prince Stephen
Once in, never out again
One-eye, two-eyes, and three-eyes
One grain more than the devil
One-inch fellow
Oraggio and Bianchinetta
Outriddling the princess
The palace of the night
The parrot of Limo Verde
Patient Griselda
Peahens and golden apples
Peerifool
Peppino
Petrosinella or parsley
The piper with the hoofs of a goat
The plain princess
Pleiad and star of dawn
The poor boy and the princess
The poor girl who stepped out golden
flowers
The poor man's son, the dwarfs, and
the birds
The poor miller's boy and the cat
The poor weaver and the princess
Popo and the princess
The potted princess

Princes and princesses (*Continued*)

The proud princess
Queen crane
The question none could answer
The rabbit prince
Rags and tatters
The ram with the golden fleece
Rapunzel
The rat-catcher's daughter
The raven
Ravenspring
The real princess
The Red-Etin
The reluctant familiar
The rich man and his son-in-law
Ricky of the tuft
The riddle
A ride to hell
Riquet with the quiff
The river of lantern land
Rocking-horse land
The rose and the ring
The royal waistcoat
The ruby prince
Rushen Coatie
Salt
Samba the coward
The sea-king's daughter
The serpent
The serpent prince
The serpent's bride
The seven foals
Seven iron-souled slippers
The seven Simons
The seven stars
The seventh princess
The she-bear
The shepherd and the princess
The shepherd's crown
The shepherd's nosegay
The shipwrecked prince
Siengmieng, the minister
The silent princess
The silver ship
Sima who wore the big hat
Simple and the princess
Sir Goldenhair
Six-and-four
The six horsemen
The slave of the ring
The sleeping beauty
The sleeping beauty in the wood
The sleeping prince
The sleigh ride
The snake
Snake magic
The snake prince
The sneeze that won a wife
Snow-white
Snow-white and Rose-red

Snow White and the seven dwarfs
So many countries, so many customs
The soldier and the devil
The soldier's return
Something wonderful
The son of the baker of Barra
The son of the King of Spain
The songstress and the fairies
Soonimaya
The sorcerer's apprentice(s)
Soria Moria castle
The speedy messenger
The spider
The spider specter of the pool
The spindle, the shuttle and the needle
The spring of youth
The stolen jewel
The story of a princess
The story of Bensurdatu
The story of Prince Ahmed
The story of Prince Ring and his dog
The story of the pig
The story of the shining princess
The story of the talking bird
The story of Zal
The strangest thing in the world
Stretch, Puff and Blazer
The student who became a prince
Stupid Emilien
Stupid head
Stupid Peruonto
Sturdy Hans
Sun, moon, and morning star
The supernatural crossbow
The swineherd
The swineherd who married a princess
The tailor and the prince, told by Mulech
The tale of a foolish brother and of a wonderful bush
The tale of the pig
The tale of the silver, golden, and diamond prince
The tale of the two cunning servants
The talisman
Taper Tom
Taper-Tom who made the princess laugh
The task of Prince Ishitsukuri
The task of Prince Kurumamochi
Tattercoats
Tatterhood
The terrible-tempered dragon
The thirteenth son of the King of Erin
The thousandth gift
The three brothers
The three brothers and the marvelous things
The three dogs
The three enchanted mares

Princes and princesses (*Continued*)

The Three Fates
The three golden eggs
The three golden hairs of the king of
 the cave giants
The three languages
The three lemons
The three mermaids
Three princes and their beasts
The three princesses
The three princesses and the unclean
 spirit
The three princesses in the mountain-
 in-the-blue
The three princesses of Whiteland
The three soldiers
Three tests for the prince
The three walnuts
The three wishes
The tiger-girl
The tinderbox
Ting-a-ling
Ting-a-ling and the five magicians
The tiny god
The toothpick warriors
A toy princess
The trade that no one knows
The trial by fire
The trials of Ting Ling
Trim Tram Turvey
The turtle prince
Twelve dancing princesses
The two princesses
Unlucky Mussah
The unsmiling princess
Urashima Taro
Urashima Taro and the princess of
 the sea
Vanya's leap
Wakewell and his brothers
The well at the world's end
The well o'(of) the world's end
Westwoods
What the rose did to the cypress
The white cat
The white cat and the green snake
The white dove
The white hare and the crocodiles
The white hound
The white sword of light
The white unicorn
The white wolf
Why the sea moans
The widow's son
The wild dog and the king's son
The wild man
The wild swans
The wise liar
The wise woodland maid
The wishing star

The witch and the earthen jar
The wizard king
The wonder ship and ship's crew
The wonderful tree
The wonderful wooden peacock fly-
 ing machine
The wood cutter's son and the two
 turtles
The woodsman's daughter and the
 lion
The yellow-haired witch
Yiankos
A young prince named Siegfried
The young shepherd
The youth who could become an ant,
 a lion or an eagle
The youth who trusted in God

The prince's foal
 CARPENTER – HORSES p35-46

The prince's revenge
 GRAY – INDIA'S p19-25

The princess
 JOHNSON – PRINC. p184-189
 MANNING – WIZARDS p66-70

The princess and Jose
 BRENNER – BOY p59-64

The princess and Rabbi Joshuah
 JOHNSON – PRINC. p250-253

The princess and the demon
 GREEN – TALES p73-81

The princess and the dwarf
 PILKINGTON – SHAM. p107-119

The princess and the fisherman
 UCHIDA – DANCING p135-144

The princess and the glass mountain
 BAKER – TALKING p88-103

The princess and the pea
 BAMBERGER – FIRST p212-214
 SIDEMAN – WORLD'S p82-84

The princess and the pigeons
 MICHAEL – PORTUGUESE p50-61

The princess and the scarf
 WILLIAMS – ROUND p43-52

Princess and the shepherd
 McNEILL – DOUBLE p81-86

The princess and the string of lies
 WILLIAMS – ROUND p117-119

The princess and the thief
MOZLEY – EGYPT p64-67

The princess and the vagabone
JOHNSON – PRINC. p164-183
ROSS – BLUE p91-109

Princess Felicity
MANNING – PRINCESS p97-107

Princess Golden-hair and the great black raven
ROSS – BLUE p20-33

The princess in the camphor tree
CARPENTER – ELEPHANT'S p40-48

The princess in the earth cave
THOMPSON – ONE p347-350

The princess in the fiery tower
BAMBERGER – FIRST p102-106

The princess in the tower
MICHAEL – PORTUGUESE p62-73

Princess Janina and the troll Bradalba
NYBLOM – WITCH p177-196

Princess Maring, the huntress
ROBERTSON – PHILIP. p33-41

Princess Mee
TOLKIEN – READER (Part 4) p28-30

The Princess Nausicaa
GREEN – GREEKS p68-69

Princess Nelly and the Seneca chief
MY BOOK HOUSE v. 9 p78-88

The princess of Canterbury
JACOBS – MORE p229-232

The princess of China
JOHNSON – PRINC. p68-75

The princess of light
UCHIDA – DANCING p75-85

The princess of Mount Nam-Nhu
ROBERTSON – FAIRY p44-59

The princess of the mountain
TURNBULL – FAIRY p12-26

The Princess of Tomboso
BARBEAU – GOLDEN p26-45

The princess on the glass hill
See also The princess and the glass mountain; The princess on the glass mountain
ARBUTHNOT – TIME p78-82
ASBJÖRNSEN – EAST p28-41
HAVILAND – NORWAY p3-29
MY BOOK HOUSE v. 6 p80-91
SIDEMAN – WORLD'S p644-657
THOMPSON – ONE p205-214

The princess on the glass mountain
KAPLAN – SWEDISH p35-57
DURHAM – TIT p48-55

The princess on the pea
JOHNSON – PRINC. p2-7

Princess Rosette
PERRAULT – COMPLETE p163-184

Princess Scri and Prince Sedana
WILLIAMS – ROUND p265-273

Princess September
JOHNSON – PRINC. p32-49

Princess Sicilia and the shepherd
TOOR – GOLDEN p135-142

The princess who always had to have the last word
ASBJÖRNSEN – NORW. p77-80

The princess who hid her slippers
NYBLOM – WITCH p3-19

The princess who knew her own mind
MARKS – SPANISH p163-181

The princess who loved her father like salt
HAVILAND – GREECE p21-27

The princess who saw everything in her kingdom
BAMBERGER – FIRST p97-102

The princess who wanted to play with the stars
FINLAY – FOLK p29-36

The princess who wanted to solve riddles
THOMPSON – ONE p345-347

The princess who was dumb
EELLS – SPAIN p69-77

The princess who was rescued from slavery
THOMPSON – ONE p170-173

The princess whom nobody could
silence
See also The finest liar in the world
DOBBS – ONCE p110-117

The princess with the golden hair
MEHDEVI – BUNGLING p45-55

The princess with the golden shoes
HATCH – MORE p88-104

The princess with the twelve pair of
golden shoes
BAKER – GOLDEN p34-40

The princess's slippers
MANNING – PRINCES p28-39

The princess's wedding garments
PICARD – MERMAI D p131-140

Principal Egyptian deities
JAMES – MYTHS p10-12

Pringle, Thomas
Afar in the desert

Printing. *See* **Writing**

Printers
The sky-foogle of Chillicothe

The prisoner
HOLDING – SKY p75-86

Prisons and Prisoners
Dream behind bars
The golden dolls
A happening on Christmas eve
He sang himself out of prison cell
Herman and his horse
The legend of the governor and the
lawyer
The legend of the governor and the
veteran
The little girl and the hare
Little Radoyitsa
The lost lover of Pearl Hart
The lute player
Old man Elias and the dancing sheriff
The piper with the hoofs of a goat
Prince Hassak's march
The quest for Olwen (4) Fulfilling the
tasks 2/ The oldest animals
The sand-carrier crab
The shah weaves a rug
The sorcerer's apprentice(s)
The tale of the rescue of Kinmont
Wullie

The Thanksgiving of the Wazir
Vladimir's adventures in search of
fortune
The white cat

The privateer turned patriot
IVES – TALES p135-154

Privateers. *See* **Pirates**

The prize
DAVIS – LION'S p158-161

Problems
See also **Worry**
The carefree monastery

Problems
JOHNSON – WHAT p149-151

Processions
The magic swan
The quail and the badger
A story for Kiem

Proclamations. *See* **Decrees**

Procrastination
The hen's house
So say the little monkeys
Sometime

Professors
The learned young professor

Prometheus
The firebringer . . . Prometheus

A promise made should be kept
JAGENDORF – KING p148-151

Promises
The ass's promise
The camel in the lion's court
The cavallino
The clever goatherd and the greedy
giant
The fly
The golden slipper, the magic ring,
and the twigs
Here is my hand on it
Ironhead
John Boaster
Madschun
The magic sandals
The man who had no wife
The mouse keeps her promise

Promises (*Continued*)

Orpheus and Eurydice
The Pied Piper of Hamelin; a minstrel's enchanted music
Prince Andrea and Princess Meseria
The Prince Fernando
A sacred pledge should not be broken
Tema's promise to the white bird
The three sons of the King of Antua
The woman of rock
Yankos

A prompt settlement
JUDA – WISE p81-86

Prop for the tree
JAGENDORF – GYPSIES p146-147

Propaganda
History as propaganda: The Princess of Bakhtan

The proper way to lay the table
URE – RUMANIAN p144.

The prophet Elijah and the angel of death
NAHMAD – PORTION p33-34

Prophets and prophecies
Aeneas . . . His wonderings
And upon the fourth bray
Art, King of Leinster
The beggar's prophecy
The birth and boyhood of Finn
The blind king and the magic bird
The boy and the birds
The death of Deirdre
Deirdre
Deirdre and the sons of Uisne
The faery flag of Dunnegan
The foretelling
Foretelling the future
The geomancer's three sons
The ghost ship, told by Achmet
The Gordian knot; the destiny of Alexander
Grim and the merman
Iphigenia at Aulis
The Lambton worm
The legend of Eilean Donan castle
The legend of Marshal Gang Gam-Czan
The man who married a snow goose
The new day
Ooka and the wasted wisdom
The police marshal
Prince Ahmed
The prince and the Three Fates
Princess Rosette

The Ramayana
Rashi and Duke Gottfried
The rich man and his son-in-law
The soothsayers
Stone patience and knife patience
The sun-king's hair
Taliesin
Thomas the rhymer
The three golden hairs of Grandad Sol
True Thomas
Urosh and his uncles
A warning from the gods
The welcome
The young man and the priest

Proserpine
ARBUTHNOT – TIME p218-220

Prospect and retrospect
HSIEH – CHINESE p48-50

Prosperity
Chinese dragons

Protection
Ishallah
The mice in council
The restless pigeon and his wife
To cure a sudden stitch

Protection against witches
HOPE-SIMPSON – CAVAL. p124-127

Protesilaus
The story of Protesilaus

The proud bokungu tree
COBBLE – WEMBI p48-49

The proud camel and the rude monkey
CARPENTER – AFRICAN p153-159

The proud father
HITCHCOCK – KING p53-59

The proud goat
RUDOLPH – MAGIC p30-41

The proud king
BORSKI – GOOD p48-50

The proud princess
GARNIER – LEGENDS p121-126

Proverbs
A big head has a big headache
Bull frog knows more about rain than the almanac

Proverbs (*Continued*)

The coat remakes many a man
Cobblers do not judge above the shoe
The cow doesn't miss her lost tail
  till fly time
Finger never says "Look here'; it
  says 'Look yonder'
The frog jumps back in its puddle,
  even when seated in a golden chair
Grasp all, lose all
The hen agreed to hatch the duck egg,
  but she didn't agree to take the
  duckling for a swim
If my shoe is narrow, what matter if
  the world is wide
In China the people say
In Russia the people say
Liberian proverbs
Measure twice, cut once
Raindrops can't tell broadcloth from
  jeans
Salt
The story of Wang Li
The tale of a proverb
There is only one pretty child in the
  world and every mother has it
There's no telling on which side a
  camel will lie down
Two pieces of meat confuse the mind
  of the fly
What is a fable?
Who hath no courage must have legs
A wise man on a camel
Yoruba proverb

Proverbs and sayings
  REED – TALK p70-75

Providence
The boy with the beer keg

Providence
  MY BOOK HOUSE v. 6 p79.

Proxies
Hanging at Wessaguscus

Prunella
  MANNING – WITCHES p62-71

Ptarmigans
How the ptarmigans learned to fly

Pucas. *See* Pookas (imaginary animals)

Puck
A midsummer night's dream

Puddin' Tame
  MY BOOK HOUSE v. 1 p95.

The pudding that broke up the preaching
  CREDLE – TALL p21-26

Puddings
Plum pudding
Sneezy Snatcher and Sammy Small
The sun and the moon
The three wishes

Puddlefoot
  BRIGGS – PERS. p127-128

Puddock, mousie and ratton
  JACOBS – MORE p184-185

Puerto Rico
The albahaca plant
The animal musicians
The ant in search of her leg
The bed
The bird of seven colors
Casi Lampu'a Lentemue
The castle of no return
The cat, the mountain goat, and the
  fox
The chili plant
Count Crow and the princess
The dance of the animals
Death's godchild
The earrings
The fig tree
The gluttonous wife
La Hormiguita
The horse of seven colors
It's better to be smart than strong
Juan Bobo
Juan Bobo and the caldron
Juan Bobo and the princess who
  answered riddles
Juan Bobo, the sow, and the chicks
Juanito and the princess
The jurga
Lazy Peter and his three-cornered hat
Lazy Peter and the king
The louse skin drum
Nangato
Perez and Martina
The plumage of the owl
The rabbit and the tiger
Senor Billy Goat
The shepherd and the princess
The singing sack
Story of a nickel and a dime
The story of the smart parrot
Thousands and thousands of ducks
The three brothers and the marvelous
  things

Puerto Rico (*Continued*)

The three-cornered hat
The three figs
The three Magi
The three petitions
The three wishes
The tiger and the rabbit
The troubadour and the devil
The witch's skin
The wolf, the fox, and the jug of
  honey
The woodsman's daughter and the
  lion
The young girl and the devil

Puffballs
A letter to my love

The puffed-up frog
  GREEN – BIG p200.

Puffing Potter's powerful puff
  JAGENDORF – NEW p219-222

Puffins
Lost in memory
The man who married a snow goose

The pugilist and his wonderful helpers
  WITHERS – WORLD p35-42

Puhuys (birds)
The peacock and the puhuy

Pumas
The fox who wanted to whistle
The girl and the puma

Pumice stones
The hermit with two heads

The pumpkin
  MY BOOK HOUSE v. 4 p23.

The pumpkin child
  MEHDEVI – PERSIAN p112-117

Pumpkin trees and walnut vines
  CATHON – PERHAPS p201-204

Pumpkins
The acorn and the pumpkin
The big pumpkin and the big kettle
The colts in the pumpkin
The coming of the corn
The donkey's egg
Donkey's eggs

The faithful wife
Fearless John and the giant monster
General Pumpkin
God's own country
Kantjil discovers the wisdom of Allah
Little sister and the Zimwi
The perambulatin' pumpkin
Peter, Peter, pumpkin eater
The singing drum and the mysterious
  pumpkin
Snake magic
Some punkins
Tobacco woman and corn spirit
The traveler and the nut tree
Who am I?
The wisdom of Allah

–Vines
Paul Bunyan's cornstalk

Punch (drink)
The adventures of Billy Macdaniel

Punch and Judy
The renowned and world-famous adventures of Punch and Judy

Punchinello
  BROWN – AROUND p133-140

Punctuality. *See* **Time**

Punishment
Blue legs
The boy and his magic robe
Conan's punishment
The dancing palm tree
The fall of the spider man
The finding of the Eleanba Wunda
The first pig and porcupine
The fisherman and the king's cham-
  berlain
The friendship of the hare and the
  parrot
Frithjof, the Viking
The golden eggplant
The golden mountain
The great festival
How Kwanku Ananse became bald
How locusts came to be
How night was let loose and all the
  animals came to be
The just reward
The Kildare pooka
The knight of La Sarraz
Kwaku Ananse and the rain maker
Kwaku Ananse and the whipping cord
The lazy maiden
The legend of Pitch Lake
The little orphan

Punishment (*Continued*)

A little story about a great man
Loki's punishment
The man who stole a rope
Ooka and the death decree
The origin of the platypus
Other wise men of Gotham
Pwyll and Rhiannon
The reward of treachery
The serpent and the grape-grower's
  daughter
A severe punishment
Shinga-mamba
The soldier's billet
The story of a gentleman
A strange reward
The sunken city
The tortoise and the monkey
The waters beneath: Fifty young men and
  a turtle
The wedding of the dragon-god
The weeping lady of Llyn Glasfryn
Why the sky is high
The wicked polecat

The punishment
  LEEUW – LEGENDS p119-126

The punishment of Loki
  HOSFORD – THUNDER p101-105

Punjab
  Five wise words
  The lion and the hare

Puppets
  See also Punch and Judy
  Aruman, a hero of Java
  How Prince Bondhu became a boatman
  Little Hansworst
  Pinocchio

Puritans
  Bride's brook
  Jacob Heard and the golden horse

Purity
  The riddle of the black knight

Purnell, Idella, and Weatherwax, John M.
  The lazy hornet
  Why the tortoise has a round back
  Why the woodpecker has a long nose

The purple cow
  MY BOOK HOUSE v. 2 p163.

Purrs (wild hogs). *See* Hogs

Purses
  Beppo Pipetta and his knapsack
  The bird which laid diamonds
  The blacksmith and the devil
  The crimson purse
  The crimson purse and the talking raven
  The devil to pay
  Good advice
  Luc, the king's woodsman
  The magic purse of the swamp maiden
  The master-smith
  Molly Whipple
  Old Gally Mander
  The Princess of Tomboso
  The shepherd's nosegay
  The skillful huntsman
  The story of Bensurdatu
  The tale of frost and his neighbors
  The task of the serpent
  The three soldiers
  The tipsy rooster

The pursuit of Dermot and Grania
  O'FAOLAIN – IRISH p147-162

Pursuit of the Hadji
  COURLANDER – KANT. p77-79

The pursuit of the hard man
  PICARD – CELTIC p70-84

Pushing westward with Lewis and Clark
  MY BOOK HOUSE v. 9 p39-40

Pushkin, Alexander S.
  The learned cat

Puss in boots
  HAVILAND – FRANCE p26-37
  LINES – NURSERY p93-106
  PERRAULT – CLASSIC p53-65
  PERRAULT – COMPLETE p16-25
  PERRAULT – FAMOUS p55-70
  SIDEMAN – WORLD'S p393-401
  TUDOR – TASHA p47-51
  WILLIAMS – ROUND p172-180

"Puss in boots" stories
  Lord Peter
  The master cat
  The monkey and Mr. Janel Sinna

The puss's tail
  MICHAEL – PORTUGUESE p15-19

Pussy cat, pussy cat
  MY BOOK HOUSE v. 1 p44.

Pussy, kittie
  MY BOOK HOUSE v. 1 p64.

Pussy, pussy, dear pussy
MY BOOK HOUSE v. 1 p72.

Pussy sits beside the fire
MY BOOK HOUSE v. 1 p36.

Puzzles. *See* **Mathematics; Riddles**

Pwyll and Pryderi (1.) The marriage of
Pwyll and Rhiannon
JONES – WELSH p3-12

Pwyll and Pryderi (2.) The birth of
Pryderi
JONES – WELSH p13-19

Pwyll and Rhiannon
PICARD – HERO p51-59

Pwyll, Pryderie, and Gawl
MAYNE – HEROES p1-23

Pygmalion . . . The marvelous statue
UNTERMEYER – FIRE. p41.

Pygmies. *See* **Africa–Tribes–Pygmy**

Pyle, Howard
The apple of contentment

The enchanted island
Princess Golden-hair and the great
black raven
The skillful huntsman
The tournament in Ireland
Where to lay the blame

Pyle, Katherine
The dreamer
The dutiful daughter

Pyoli
MacFARLANE – TALES p11-18

Pyramids
Khnemu of the Nile
Teta the magician
The treasure thief

Pyramus and Thisbe . . . The mulberry
tree
UNTERMEYER – FIRE. p102-104

Pythias
Damon and Pythias
Damon and Pythias; the most faithful
of friends

Pythons. *See* **Snakes**

Q

Quail
  Bech, the ambitious quail
  The fox and the quail

The quail and the badger
  SEKI – FOLKTALES p14-15

Quaker, Quaker, how is thee?
  MY BOOK HOUSE v. 1 p82.

Quakers
  Clever Mistress Murray
  The courageous Quaker of Flushing
  The hat in the moon
  Lucky star of Herald Square
  Romance at Tulip Hill
  A young Quaker of New England

The quarrel
  KOREL – LISTEN p13-41
  SHERLOCK – ANANSI p105-112
  WILSON – GREEK p198-199

The quarrel about the woods
  RANKE – GERMANY p121.

The quarrel between Ile and Orun
  COURLANDER – OLODE p100-103

The quarrel between the months
  BORSKI – GOOD p18-19

A quarrel between thieves brings a Brahmin relief
  GHOSE – FOLK p48-50

Quarreling
  The ant and the yellow jacket
  The bee-hunter and the oozie
  The brawl between sun and moon
  The duel of the cat and the mouse
  The goldsmith, the wood carver, the tailor, and the hermit who quarreled over a wooden woman
  How California was made
  How the people came to the middle place
  How to catch a fish
  Jackal or tiger?
  The lion-wolf
  The most obedient wife
  Ooka and the stronger stick
  The origin of Indian pipes
  The otters and the fox
  The place of strife
  The quilt

The serpents and the porcupine
  Snake story
  Stubborn husband, stubborn wife
  Those who quarreled
  Three men on the bridge
  The three wishes
  Two novices who behaved like a pair of otters
  The wolf and the lamb
  The wonderful tune

Quarries
  The leprechaun and the wheelbarrow

(The) quartet
  GREEN – BIG p77-79
  KRYLOV – 15 p1-2

Quebec. See Canada–Nova Scotia

The queen and the golden egg
  MINCIELI – TALES p57-59

The queen bee
  BAMBERGER – FIRST p106-110

Queen crane
  BAKER – GOLDEN p46-53

Queen o' the tinkers
  MacMANUS – HIBERIAN p99-107

Queen of the Comstock
  IVES – TALES p255-260

The queen of the planets
  O'SULLIVAN – FOLK. p205-209

The queen of Underland
  HOPE-SIMPSON – CAVAL. p174-186

Queens. See Kings and queens

The queen's care
  HODGES – SEREND. p24-37

The queen's necklace
  NYBLOM – WITCH p83-102

The queen's riddles
  COTHRAN – MAGIC p31-37

The quellers of the flood
  BIRCH – CHINESE p20-33

The quest for Olwen (1) The destiny
JONES – WELSH p71-74

The quest for Olwen (2) At Arthur's
court
JONES – WELSH p75-81

The quest for Olwen (3) In search of
Olwen
JONES – WELSH p82-92

The quest for Olwen (4) Fulfilling the
tasks. 1/ The sword of Wrnach the giant
JONES – WELSH p93-95

The quest for Olwen (4) Fulfilling the
tasks. 2/ The oldest animals
JONES – WELSH p96-100

The quest for Olwen (4) Fulfilling the
tasks. 3/ The lame ant
JONES – WELSH p100-101

The quest for Olwen (4) Fulfilling the
tasks. 4/ The beard of Dillus the
bearded
JONES – WELSH p101-103

The quest for Olwen (4) Fulfilling the
tasks. 5/ The everlasting battle
JONES – WELSH p103-104

The quest for Olwen (4) Fulfilling the
tasks. 6/ The tusk of Ysgithyrwyn
JONES – WELSH p104-105

The quest for Olwen (4) Fulfilling the
tasks. 7/ The hunting of the otherworld
boar
JONES – WELSH p105-111

The quest for Olwen (4) Fulfilling the
tasks. 8/ The blood of the black witch
JONES – WELSH p111-112

The quest for Olwen (5) Culhwch
marries Olwen
JONES – WELSH p113-114

The quest of the children of Turenn
(The first sorrow of story-telling)
O'FAOLAIN – IRISH p3-22

The quest of the Holy Grail
PICARD – STORIES p194-208

The quest of the sons of Turenn
PICARD – TALES p9-24

The question none could answer
MONTROSE – WINTER p22-35

Questions
    See also Riddles
    Ask a foolish question
    The billy goat and the king
    The bird of seven colors
    The clever lass
    The clever question
    The dog king in Denmark
    The farmer's clever daughter
    The gardener, the abbot and the king
    How God's wheel turns
    Keloglan in the service of the padi-
        shah
    The king and the bishop
    The king and the peasant
    The king and the shepherd
    King James and the questions
    King John and the abbot
    King John and the Abbot of Canter-
        bury
    The little black man
    The marriage of Gawaine
    The "new preacher"
    The old man who said "Why"
    The old man's tale of Prince Stephen
    The parson and the sexton
    The pastor and the sexton
    The peasant and his hen
    The poor man's clever daughter
    The princess of Canterbury
    The skillful huntsman
    The talking fish
    Teasing questions
    The three golden hairs
    The three precepts
    The three questions
    Tiny teasing tales
    The tsarino's greatest treasure
    The tyrant and the miller
    What's a silly question?

Quetzel birds
    How the king of the birds was chosen
    The sacred amulet

A quick-running squash
    MY BOOK HOUSE v. 3 p104-109

Quicksand
    Black Bartelmy
    The white mule ghost

Quiet
    Sybaris . . . Life of luxury
    The valley of ten thousand waterfalls

A quiet night
    HOPE-SIMPSON – CAVAL. p210-
    211

The quilt
KELSEY – ONCE p45-47

Quilts
Boots and the troll
Did the tailor have a nightmare?

Quinces and oranges
WILSON – GREEK p68-75

Quinn, Vernon
Indian legends of shrubs in our
gardens

Quirinus
The twins of the god Mars

The quivering needle
KELSEY – ONCE p79-82

R

Ra (Amen-Ra)
The great Queen Hatshepsut
Isis and Osiris
Isis and the secret name of Ra
The king and the corn

Ra and his children
GREEN – TALES p15-20

Rabbi Amram's coffin
BARASH – GOLDEN p43-44

Rabbi Joseph Della Reina
BARASH – GOLDEN p102-110

Rabbi Joshua ben Levi and the prophet
Elijah
NAHMAD– PORTION p35-38

Rabbi Leib and the witch Cunegunde
SINGER – WHEN p29-42

Rabbis
Akiba and the daughter of Kabba
Sabbu'a
The dream
The golem of Rabbi Judah Low
The jewel
The Jewish pope
The lion and the sage
A meeting of scholars
The penitent governor
The princess and Rabbi Joshuah
The robe
The royal banquet
Shrewd Todie and Lyzer the miser
The sin of a saint
The story of Mordecai and Esther
The task of the serpent
Torah and honor
The true scales
The warm matzah
The weight of the cart
The witches of Ascalon

Rabbit and lion
TRACEY – LION p30-33

The rabbit and the bear
SEKI – FOLKTALES p9-14

The rabbit and the crocodile
UCHIDA – DANCING p49-57

Rabbit and the grain buyers
MacMILLAN – GLOOS p72-79

Rabbit and the Indian chief
MacMILLAN – GLOOS p94-105

Rabbit and the moon-man
MacMILLAN – GLOOS p89-93

The rabbit and the possum seek a wife
SCHEER – CHEROKEE p33-36

The rabbit and the tar wolf
SCHEER – CHEROKEE p47-50

The rabbit and the tiger
ALEGRIA – THREE p44-51

Rabbit and tortoise
TRACEY – LION p74-77

Rabbit at the water hole
TRACEY – LION p110-114

Rabbit, elephant and hippopotamus
TRACEY – LION p26-29

Rabbit, fox, and the rail fence
COURLANDER – TERRA. p18-20

The rabbit grows a crop of money
BURTON – MAGIC p84-89

The rabbit in the moon
JORDAN – BURRO p31-32
PRATT – MAGIC unp.
SAKADE – JAPAN. p35-37

The rabbit prince
BERGER – BLACK p91-105

Rabbit scratches buh elephant's back
See also The bet between Matjan and
Gadja
COURLANDER – TERRA. p50-52

Rabbit soup
JUDA – WISE p28-33

The rabbit steals the elephant's dinner
BURTON – MAGIC p78-81

The rabbit takes his revenge on the
elephant
BURTON – MAGIC p81-84

The rabbit who crossed the sea
SAKADE – JAPAN. p103-105

531

532

The rabbit who wanted to be a
man
BRENNER – BOY p65-70

Rabbits
Anansi and five
Anansi and snake the postman
Anansi and the elephant exchange
knocks
The ants and the hare
The baboon and the hare
The bean pot
The bee tree
The beekeeper and the bewitched hare
Bergamot
The big, big rabbit
The birds' St. Valentine day
The boy and the water-sprite
The boy who became a reindeer
The brainy rabbit
Brave rabbit and bug with the golden
wings
Brer wolf's little tar men
Buh fox's number nine shoes
Buh rabbit's big eat
Buh rabbit's graveyard
Buh rabbit's human weakness
Buh rabbit's tight necktie
The bun
The bungled message
The case of the calf and the colt
The cat and the fox
A cat for a hare
Catching hares in winter
The cerval's secret name
Cottontail and the sun
Cottontail's song
The counting of the crocodiles
Coyote rings the wrong bell
The crackling mountain
The cunning old man and the three
rogues
The deer, the hare, and the toad
Dog couldn't be cured
The donkey's egg
Dry-bone and Anansi
The earthquake
Eighteen rabbits
The fairy grotto
The first pig and porcupine
Fish with the rolls
Five in a glove
The flight of the animals
The foolish, timid, little hare
The fox and the hare
The fox and the hare in winter
The fox, the hare, and the toad have
an argument
The friendship of the hare and the
parrot

The girl on the rock
Gobbleknoll
The golden horse
Good-speed and the elephant king
Greedy and speedy
The greedy hyena
The guinea pig's tail
The hare
Hare and the corn bins
Hare and the hyena
The hare and the lord
The hare and the tiger
The hare and the tortoise
The hare, badger, monkey and otter
The hare herd
The hare in the moon
Hare makes a fool of leopard
The hare of Inaba
The hare who had been married
The hare who was afraid of nothing
The hedgehog and the hare
The hedgehog and the rabbit
Helping to lie
The hermit cat
Hiawatha's childhood
A horned goat
How a fish swam in the air
How brer rabbit met brer tar-baby
How hare asked for wisdom
How rabbit stole fire from the
buzzards
How the deer got his horns
How the hare learned to swim
How the rabbit fooled the elephant
How the rabbit made enemies by try-
ing to be too friendly
How the wildcat got his spots
A hungry wolf
The hunting cat
The infallible salt bird
The inquiring rabbit, or The strongest
thing in the world
Jack and the Lord High Mayor
Johnny and the three goats
Kalulu and his money farm
Kalulu and the elephant
Kalulu and the leopard
The king of the hares
The king of the leaves
The king's hares
The king's rabbits
Kwaku Ananse and the greedy lion
A leg for the lion
The leopard and the rabbit go court-
ing
Lion and honey badger
The lion and the hare
The lion and the hare go hunting
The lion and the wily rabbit
The lion calls up his troops
The lion on the path

Rabbits (*Continued*)

The lion's threats
The little girl and the hare
The little hare's clever trick
The little house
The little rabbit who wanted red wings
The long one
A mad tea-party
Manstin, the rabbit
The marriage of Tom and the vixen
The mighty warrior in hare's house
Mister deer's My riding horse
Mr. fox learns what trouble is
Mister honey mouth
Mr. rabbit meets his match again
Mr. rabbit steals Mr. fox's fish
The mole and the rabbits
Nansii and the eagle
Nasradin in Hodja returns a gift
The night of the full moon
The old hag of the forest
An old Korean story
The old man in the moon
The old tiger and the hare
One mean trick deserves another
The ostrich chicks
Owl with the great head and eyes
Partnership
Peter Rabbit decides to change his name
Pooh goes visiting and gets into a tight place
The prince and the dragons
Prince rabbit
The ram and the pig who went into the woods to live by themselves
Reynard the fox
The scarecrow
Seeing a brace of rabbits
Senor coyote settles a quarrel
The sheep and the pig that made a home
The silver hare in a box
The silver penny
Slow train to Arkansas
Sly Peter's revenge
Son of the long one
A song for Easter
Spider's web
A story about the little rabbits
A story of Li'l Hannibal
The straw ox
The sun-child
The tale of Peter Rabbit
The talking house
Tar-baby
A tar-burner's brer rabbit stories
The theft of fire
The three hunters
The tiger and the rabbit
The tiger's minister of state

To outleap a rabbit
The tortoise and the hare
The tree with the difficult name
Tricksy rabbit
The troll's daughter
Trust your friends
The tug of war
The two youths whose father was under the sea
Uletka
Uncle coyote's last mischief
Uncle Ed tracks a rabbit
Uncle rabbit flies to heaven
The ungrateful tiger
Wanja's choice
The well
The white hare and the crocodiles
Who can break a bad habit?
Who is strongest?
Why elephant and whale live where they do
Why the deer's teeth are blunt
Why the possum's tail is bare
Why there are four seasons in the year
Why there is both day and night
The wicked polecat
Winnie-the-Pooh
The wonderful tar baby story
The wonderful tree

—**Ears**
Ha! Tio rabbit is bigger

—**Feet**
Rabbit's foot
The wishing chair of the Lord of Errigal

, **Golden**
The peasant and his three sons

—**Kidneys**
The hare's kidneys

—**Legs**
Who hath no courage must have legs

—**Lips**
The hare's lip
Why the hare's lip is split

—**Noses**
Message from the moon
Why the rabbit's nose twitches

—**Tails**
Buh rabbit's tail
How rabbit lost his tail
How the rabbit stole the otter's coat
The rabbit and the bear
Rabbit, elephant and hippopotamus
Why rabbit has a short tail
Why rabbit have short tail

Rabbit's foot
  BATCHELOR – SUPER. p38-40

The raccoon and the crawfish
  SCHOOLCRAFT – FIRE p42-46

The raccoon and the old men
  LEEKLEY – WORLD p69-75

Raccoons
  Buh rabbit's graveyard
  Davy Crockett, the yaller blossom o'
    the forest
  The hare and the tortoise
  How possum got his tail
  How the cardinal got his red feathers
  How the redbird got his color
  Itsayaya's revenge
  Peter Rabbit decides to change his
    name
  Sonny-boy Sim
  Tiny Perry
  Why there is both day and night

The race
  See also Crafty crab
  GREEN – BIG p16.

The race with Rosamond
  LEEKLEY – RIDDLE p92-114

Races, Athletic
  Atalanta's race; a contest for love or
    death
  Atalanta . . . The fleet-footed runner
  Bandalee
  The beetle and the paca
  The boy and the water-sprite
  Brown owl's story
  The carl of the drab coat
  The castle of the three giants
  The cat and the crab
  The cat and the dog
  The crab and the needlefish
  Crafty crab
  The fox and the snail
  The fox who was not so smart
  The hare and the tortoise
  The headless horseman
  The hedgehog and the hare
  The hedgehog and the rabbit
  How chameleon became king of the
    animals
  How deer got his horns
  How the Brazilian beetles got their
    gorgeous coats
  How the terrapin beat the rabbit
  John Henry

Prince rabbit
The queen's riddles
Slow train to Arkansas
The story of little Mukra
The tale of the youngest brother and
  the stupid devil
Thor and the giants
The three enchanted mares
The tortoise and the hare
The tortoise and the reedbuck run a
  race
The turtle outwits the lion
The two boxes
Ugly boy
The whale and the sea slug
Why Eyvin won the race
Why the carabao's hoof is split

Races of man
  The firebringer . . . Prometheus
  Men of different colors
  Naba Zid-Wende

Racketty-packetty house
  BURNETT – RACKETTY p13-57

The radiant khan
  FOSTER – STONE p83-87

Radishes
  The nine-headed giant

Radowid
  PROTTER – CHILD. p132-144

Rafts
  Bull frog knows more about rain than
    the almanac
  The flood
  The marriage feast
  Mister Luck and Mister Industry

Rag, tag and bobtail
  BAMBERGER – FIRST p39-43

The raggle, taggle gypsies
  MY BOOK HOUSE v. 7 p172.

Ragnar Lodbrok and his sons
  PICARD – TALES p73-88

Ragnarokk, the destiny of the gods
  AULAIRE – NORSE p140-150

Rags. *See* Clothes–Rags

Rags and tatters
  BAKER – GOLDEN p11-118
  MANNING – PRINCES p118-124

Ragwort (plant)
The field of ragwort

Railroad Bill
LEACH – RAINBOW p175-176

Railroad men
Casey Jones
Casey Jones and locomotive
John Henry, the big steel-drivin' man
Railroad Bill

Railroad songs
A song of the railroad men

Railroads
The devil and the railroad
Old Ave Henry and the smart logger man

Rain
See also **Floods**
April
The battle at White Cliff house
The big umbrella and the little rubbers
Blue water
Brer goat and brer lion
Bull frog knows more about rain than the almanac
Frey and Gerd, the jotun maiden
How fire was brought from lightning
How Master Thumb defeated the sun
How the first rainbow was made
How turtle keeps from getting wet
Ishallah
It is God that hath made us
It's raining
The jolly tailor who became king
A leak in an old house
The legend of Crooked Mountain
Little burnt-face
The magic bone
The magic herdboy
Noah's ark
Pretty, see the cloud appear!
The quarrel between Ile and Orun
The ravens build a bridge
Saadia the potmender
The silver river
Sparrow's search for rain
The story of flying Robert
Summer rain
This little ant worked with might and main
Thunder and lightning
Ticky-picky boom-boom
Tlacuache the saint
The toad is the emperor's uncle
The toads in the lake

Tobacco woman and corn spirit
The true scales
The turtle of Tamaru
The Warau people discover the earth
When that I was but a little tiny boy
Why animals are afraid of fire
Why frogs croak in wet weather
Why sheep does not come in out of the rain
Why spider lives in ceilings
The wise priest
The witches of Ascalon
The yellow dragon

Rain
MY BOOK HOUSE v. 1 p191.

The rain bird
PARKER – AUSTRALIAN p100-103

The rain-god's daughter
WILLIAMS – OLD p74-83

The rain god's reprisal
RUSHMORE – DANCING p51-60

The rain-lady and the ghost
LITTLEDALE – GHOSTS p87-96

The rain leak in an old house
SEKI – FOLKTALES p27-29

The rain makers
KAULA – AFRICAN p55-58

The rain, wind, and snow "Rhyme and reason"
CATHON – PERHAPS p228-229

The rainbow
HEADY – WHEN p77-80

Rainbow and the autumn leaves
MacMILLAN – GLOOS. p124-130

Rainbow-walker/Johnny Appleseed
STOUTENBURG – AMER. p77-87

Rainbows
The bow that bridges heaven
The bridge of heaven
The chafers and the dove
The giant who rode on the ark
How the first rainbow was made
The Indian Cinderella
Izanagi and Izanami
Kalevala, land of heroes
The labors of Hercules
Little Burnt-face
The night of the big wind
Noah's ark

Rainbows (*Continued*)

Sturgeon moon
Swen-Naba; king of the warlocks
The wagtail and the rainbow
Why the birds are different colors
Wind and wave and wandering flame
The woman in moon

Raindrops can't tell broadcloth from jeans
CHAPPELL – THEY p25-29

The rainmaker Wirinun
PARKER – AUSTRALIAN p104-108

Rainmakers
Kwaku Ananse and the rain maker
The lost secrets of Charles Hatfield

The rainmakers
BIRCH – CHINESE p101-110

Raising the wind
JOHNSON – WHAT p163-164

The rajah went to Delhi
MY BOOK HOUSE v. 1 p79.

The rajah who flew away
REED – TALK. p30-33

Rajahs
The ant and the frog
Bajan Budiman, the sharpshooter
How the rajah got rich
The little pet rani
The stone crusher of Banjang

Rake up!
MANNING – MERMAIDS p36-40

Raking for the moon
JAGENDORF – MERRY p45-50

Rakshas (demons, ogres)
The blind man and the deaf man
The blind man, the deaf man and the
donkey
The cloud horse
Kantjil becomes a raksha
The magic muntr
Malati and the prince

Raleigh, Sir Walter
Sir Walter Raleigh

Ram, god of Fortune
The conch shell of Ram

The ram and the goat
DUDDINGTON – RUSS. p28-30

The ram and the leopard
ELLIOT – WHERE p41-52

The ram and the pig who went into the
woods to live by themselves
ASBJORNSEN – NORW. p102-105

The ram with the golden fleece
MANNING – GLASS p22-26

Rama and the Ramayana
The banishment of Rama
The exile of Rama
The exploits of Hanuman
Four tales of Rama and Sita
The loss of Sita
The monkey's search for Sita
The search for Sita

Rama . . . The bow that could not be bent
UNTERMEYER – FIRE. p148-152

Rama's conquest of Ravana
GRAY – INDIA'S p133-154

The Ramayana
See also The world's great epics
GARNER – GOBLINS p134-173
GRAY – INDIA'S p89-154
MacFARLANE – TALES p19-45

Ramee, Louise de la
The Nuremberg stove

La Ramee and the phantom
DELARUE – FRENCH p91-95

Rameses III, Pharoah
The story of the Greek princess
The treasure thief

Ramiro II, the monk
LAURITZEN – BLOOD p52-63

Rampion (plants)
Rapunzel

Randolph, Vance
Blood on his forehead

Rands, William Brighty
The peddler's caravan
The wonderful world

Ranjit and the tigers
BROWN – AROUND p81-90

Ransetsu
  Snow

Ransom
  The gold bird
  King Fergus MacLeide and the wee
  folk

Ransome, Arthur
  Baba Yaga and the little girl with the
  kind heart
  Christening the baby in Russia
  The great-aunt

Rape (plant)
  Yoni and her stepmother

Rapunzel
  HAVILAND – GERMANY p21-31
  HOKE – WITCHES p85-89
  HOPE-SIMPSON – CAVAL. p203-209
  MANNING – WITCHES p18-26
  SIDEMAN – WORLD'S p495-502
  TUDOR – TASHA p38-42

Raratonga (island)
  The prisoner

The rarest animal of all
  MY BOOK HOUSE v. 4 p113-118

Rarities
  The magic carpet

Rascals
  The bear and the two rascals
  The bold heroes of Hungry Hill
  The Brahmin and the villain
  Brother Anansi and Sir Peacock
  The cunning old man and the three
  rogues
  Holding the bag
  Juan Cigarron
  Leave well enough alone
  Peter ox
  So many countries, so many customs
  A tale of two rogues
  The three-cornered hat
  Three unscrupulous men
  Two novices who behaved like a pair
  of otters
  Two rascals
  Upa and her admirers

Rashi and Duke Gottfried
  BARASH – GOLDEN p64-66

Raspi, Rudolph Eric
  The strange adventure of Baron
  Munchausen

Rat and the rustlers
  FELTON – NEW p141-158

The rat who made one bargain too many
  SIDDIQUI – TOON. p23-31

Rata and his canoe
  CAMPBELL – MAORI p35-38

The ratcatcher of Hamelin
  PICARD – GERMAN p126-129

Ratcatchers
  The maiden and the ratcatcher

The ratcatcher's daughter
  ROSS – BLUE p41-52

Rats
  See also **Mice**
  Ah Tcha the sleeper
  Anansi and the crabs
  Anansi and the plantains
  The big cat and the big rat
  Bilba and Mayra
  Birds of a feather
  The blind man and the devils
  "Bow-wow", says the dog
  The boy who drew cats
  The boy who had to draw cats
  Bundar Bahadeer Poon
  Charlotte's web; Wilbur's boast
  Cinderella
  The Coomacka-tree
  Dame Wiggins of Lee
  Dick Whittington and his cat
  Donkeys! Dogs! Cats! Rats!
  An endless story
  A frog he would a-wooing go
  The grateful weasel
  Hare makes a fool of leopard
  How Kwaku Ananse destroyed a
  kingdom
  How people got the first cat
  How the Brazilian beetles got their
  gorgeous coats
  The husband of the rat's daughter
  The jeweled ring
  Jirimpimbira
  Kawelo the little-brother-to-the-rats
  The kindly ghost
  The laughing statue
  Little capuchin monkey's story
  Little fir tree
  The magic amber
  The maiden and the ratcatcher

538

Rats *(Continued)*
The man who always helped the
needy
The mouse and the rat
Nails
The old humpback
The old man and his fishing line
The open road
The panther in the pit
Pemba and the python and the
friendly rat
The pheasant, the dove, the magpie,
and the rat
The Pied Piper of Frenchville
The Pied Piper of Hamelin
The Pied Piper of Hamelin; a min-
strel's enchanted music
Poor Jack and the cat
The proud father
The pumpkin
The rat who made one bargain too
many
The ratcatcher of Hamelin
The sailor and the rat
The seven-headed giant
The son of the baker of Barra
The stolen jewel
The three copecks
A voyage to Brobdingnag
Why cats and dogs are enemies
Why the sendji rat has no tail
The wonderful cake
Yung-Kyung-Pyung

, **Bush**
Olomu's bush rat
The quarrel between Ile and Orun

—**Skins**
The task of the Minister Abe-no-
Miushi

—**Tails**
Why the sendji rat has no tail

, **Water**
Biggoon and the little duck
Gaya-dari the platypus
Prince Wicked
The story of Mrs. Tubbs

The rat's bridegroom
INS-SOB — FOLK p184-186

The rats in council
GREEN — BIG p148-149

The rats of Nagasaki
WITHERS — I SAW p129.

Rattle-rattle-rattle and chink-chink-chink
FILLMORE — SHEPHERD'S p134-
143

Rattlesnakes. *See* **Snakes—Rattlesnakes**

The raven
MINCIELI — OLD p84-97

The raven and his young
GREEN — BIG p92-93

The raven and the crow
MATSON — LONGHOUSE p75-82

The raven and the fox
PROTTER — CHILD. p73.

The raven and the grizzly bear
AYRE — SKETCO p149-159

The raven and the marmot. *See* Dance,
raven, dance

The raven and the sharks
AYRE — SKETCO p43-52

Raven and the sun
MARTIN — NINE p7-18

Raven fools his grandchildren
MAHER — BLIND p133-137

The raven paints the birds for war
AYRE — SKETCO p160-172

Ravens
The beginning of the world and the
making of California
The crimson purse and the talking
raven
The Da-Trang crabs
Dance, raven, dance
The dream of Rhonabwy
The exile of Rama
The extraordinary black coat
Faithful John
First fire
Fox and raven steal the moon
The fruits of health
The giant of the brown beech wood
The giant who had no heart in his
body
The giant with the grey feathers
Hiawatha's fasting
How raven brought fire to the Indians
How raven found the daylight
How the birds came to have their
many colors
How the people got fire
How the raven brought light to the
world
Ida of Toggenburg
John the true

Ravens (*Continued*)

The legend of the Prince Ahmed Al
  Kamel
Legend of the witch of Cape Ann
Leviathan and the dutiful son
The lost song
The magic ruby
The magpie and the raven
Marya Morevna
Meinrad and the ravens
Milutin, Tsar Lazar's servant
Noah's ark
The owl and the raven
Pride goes before a fall
Prince Ahmed
Princess Golden-hair and the great
  black raven
The princess who saw everything in
  her kingdom
The seven ravens
The shepherd with the curious wife
The three ravens
To feed my people: The coming of
  buffalo
The troll's daughter
Why the tides ebb and flow
The wild woman of the woods
—**Beaks**
  The nose of the konakadet
—**Feathers**
  The thunder man
  The unseen bridegroom

—**Heroes**
  Cannibal
  The cranberry feast
  Eagle boy
  The everlasting house
  The false shaman
  The game mother
  How he stole the moon and the
    sun
  How Sketco tricked the grizzly
  How the raven brought the fire
  How the raven stole the stars
  How Yehl, the hero, freed the
    beaming maiden
  The lonely house
  The man who sat on the tide
  The mountain goats
  The nose of the konakadet
  The shadow boys
  Sketco begins his wanderings
  Sketco finds his brothers
  Strong man
  The thunder man
  The unlucky fisherman
—**Skulls**
  The legend of Eilean Donan castle

The ravens build a bridge
  VO-DINH — TOAD p35-39

The raven's magic gem
  SUN — LAND p131-135

Ravenspring
  ILLYES — ONCE p215-224

Razors
  The bobtail monkey
  The cruel giant
  The dwarfs of the anthill

Reaching an understanding
  GREEN — BIG p190.

Reaction
  HOPE-SIMPSON — CAVAL. p152-
  153

The real princess
  ARBUTHNOT — TIME p282-283

Real stuff
  GORHAM — REAL p7-13

Reapers and reaping
  See also **Thrashers and thrashing**
  Kantjil to the rescue

Reason. *See* **Common sense; Wisdom**

The rebel
  MY BOOK HOUSE v. 12 p74-91

Rebirth. *See* **Reincarnation**

Recollections of the Arabian Nights
  MY BOOK HOUSE v. 8 p108.

Recruits
  BIRCH — CHINESE p166-175

The rector's son
  MY BOOK HOUSE v. 12 p64-65

Red-berries
  The devil's bride

A red berry and two hills of snow
  IVES — TALES p171-178

The red cloak
  HAUFF — CARAVAN p111-138

The Red-Etin (Ettin)
  BAKER — GOLDEN p135-147
  LINES — TALES p118-125

MY BOOK HOUSE v. 5 p90-95
PILKINGTON – SHAM. p55-60
WILLIAMS – FAIRY p292-301

Red-hat otter. *See* Eight leaves of story
(7) Red-hat otter

Red king and green king
URE – RUMANIAN p45-56

The red king and the witch
MANNING – RED p49-54

The red-maned horse
BONNET – CHINESE p183-191

Red Riding Hood
SIDEMAN – WORLD'S p212-217
TUDOR – TASHA p79-83

The red shoes
SIDEMAN – WORLD'S p436-445

The red slippers of Honiem
NAHMAD – PEASANT p22-28

The red swan
SCHOOLCRAFT – FIRE p11-28

Redbirds. *See* **Cardinals**

Redcoat the fox
PICARD – LADY p204-214

Redeemers
David Alroy

Redheads
Blonde, brunette or redhead

Reedbucks
The tortoise and the reedbuck run a
race

Reeds
The fairy grotto
The happy prince
King March has horse's ears
Midas
Midas . . . The greed for gold
The oak and the reed
Ugly boy

Reefs
The boy who was caught by a clam

Reen-reen-reeny-croak-frog
MY BOOK HOUSE v. 2 p37-39

Referees
Two novices who behaved like a pair
of otters

Reflections
HEARN – JAPANESE p110-125
ROSS – BLUE p149-161

Reflexes
BATCHELOR – SUPER. p23-27

Reform meeting
COURLANDER – TERRA. p15-17

Refrigerators
Troubles with a penguin

Regret
See also **Penitence**
The adventures of Alexander Selkirk
As you like it
Bostani
Frithjof, the Viking
The king's remorse
The maiden, the knight, and the
waterfall
Prince Prigio
The red king and the witch
Richard Feverel and the hay-rick
The selfish giant
Zeus and the horse

Regulus
The story of Regulus

The Rehepapp and Vanapagan
MAAS – MOON p82-85

Rehoboth's lady counterfeiter
TAFT – PROFILE p195-200

Reid, Whitlaw
The boy who would be an orator

Reinar was watching his cows
MY BOOK HOUSE v. 1 p61.

Reincarnation
The babymakers
The bungled message
Five lies that could be true
The grave of a faithful dog
The story of O-Tei

Reindeer
The boy who became a reindeer
The girl who overpowered the
moon

Reindeer (*Continued*)

Hiawatha's childhood
How the sea gulls learned to fly
Kalevala, land of heroes
The lazy man who married the sun's
daughter
The maiden and the moon
The night before Christmas
The ostrich
Peer Gynt
The snow-queen

Reineke fox
PICARD – GERMAN p171-183

Relics
Pietro Bailliardo

Religion
The Holy relic of Bannockburn
The lost saints
The three rings
A world of beauty: The Peote religion

Religious
JOHNSON – WHAT p92-95

The reluctant familiar
GRAY – MAINLY p25-37

The remarkable ox, rooster, and dog
WITHERS – WORLD p70-72

Remedies
Fatty
Headaches
Hiccups
Maimonides and the bottle of poison

Remembered
IVES – TALES p59-63

Remorse. *See* **Penitence; Regret**

The renowned and world-famous adventures of Punch and Judy
MY BOOK HOUSE v. 7 p160-170

Repentance. *See* **Penitence; Regret**

Repetitive rhymes and stories
See also **Games and rythms**
The barnyard
The bee, the mouse, and the bum-
clock
The boy who wouldn't give up
The cat and the mouse

Cock and hen in the wood
The cock, the mouse, and the little
red hen
The crow and the grain of corn
The farmer in the dell
The farmer's boy
First adventures
The fly and the bee
The gingerbread man
A grain of millet
Here is the key
The jackal with the torn nose
Johnny and the three goats
The little engine that could
The little gray pony
The little pig
The little red hen and the grain of
wheat
The little rooster and the little hen
The magpie's nest
The millet seed
Old Mother Hubbard
Old Noah
The old woman and her pig
The orchestra
Over in the meadow
The pancake
Polly, put the kettle on
Precocious piggy
The rooster and the hen
The rooster and the sultan
Rosy pony
The sheep and the pig that made a
home
Teddy bear, teddy bear
Temba becomes a warrior
Ten little Indians
There was a little man and his name
was Gice
There were three duckies
Three jovial huntsmen
Three old maids a-skating went
The three trucks
To market, to market
Toontoony and the barber
The wee, wee mannie
The wee, wee mannie and the big, big
coo
Where are my roses?
The young gentleman and the tiger
The zoo in the park

Reptiles. *See* **Alligators and crocodiles;
Lizards; Snakes; etc.**

Reputation
The lost half-hour
The two owls and the sparrow

542

Rescue from the fire worshippers
DAVIS – TEN p62-80

The rescue of Fatima
HAUFF – CARAVAN p144-174

The rescue of fire
CURRY – DOWN p68-79

Rescues
Anansi's rescue from the river
The bee-hunter and the oozie
The giant's causeway
Hearts and pirates
The man who feared nothing
Mr. Hampden's shipwreck
The origin of the camlet flower
The three suitors
The wreck of the Palatine

Rescuing the moon
LEACH – NOODLES p39.

Resistance
The gnat and the lion
The oak and the reed

Resourcefulness
See also Inventions
The adventures of Alexander Selkirk
A boy on the high seas
The boy who made a dream come true
The cock, the mouse, and the little
red hen
The exile of Rama
Exploring the wilderness
Jack the giant-killer
Johnny and the three goats
The king's cream
The little-man-as-big-as-your-thumb-
with-mustaches-seven-miles-long
The magic horse
Mr. Hampden's shipwreck
The Nuremburg stove
Of a tailor and a bear
Robert Bruce, Scotland's hero
Shingebiss
Young Midshipman David Farragut

Respect
Why the lion, the vulture, and the
hyena do not live together

Respectability
The fox, the hare, and the toad have
an argument

The restless pigeon and his wife
GAER – FABLES p23-26

Restrepo, Don Antonio Jose
Mr. Toad sets out on a journey
Right out in our barnyard
South American rhymes
The toads in the lake
When I see a lady
When Mrs. Bird wants Mr. Bird

Resurrection
The scholars and the lion

Retaliation. See Revenge

Retirement
The language of the birds

Retribution. See Punishment

The return
PILKINGTON – THREE p182-190

The return of Diab
DAVIS – TEN p128-146

The return of Odysseus
HAZELTINE – HERO p51-67

The return of Oisin
See also Fisherman and the mermaids
BRIGGS – PERS. p32-35
SUTCLIFF – HIGH p179-189

The return of the heroes
GREEN – GREEKS p46-47

The return of the land-otter
LITTLEDALE – GHOSTS p13-20

The return of the spring
TOOR – GOLDEN p127-133

Revenge
The artificial earthquake
The blind man and the devils
The crumb in the beard
David Wright and the fairies
Deidre and the sons of Usna
Dermot and Grania
The dragon's revenge
Drak, the fairy
The eight leaves of story (4) A harp
on the water
The elephant and the gnat
The fairies' revenge
The fairy woman's revenge

Revenge (*Continued*)

The goat and her three kids
The goats who killed the leopard
Goose Matt
How frog lost his tail
Kagssakssuk, the homeless boy who
  became a strong man
Kigbo and the bush spirits
The legend of Bala Lake
The legend of the virgin Arange
The leopard and the bushbuck go
  hunting
Lugh and his father's murderess
The magical wooden head
The magician's revenge
The monkey and the pheasant
The monkey's feast
The prince's revenge
Rabbit and the Indian chief
Sly Peter's revenge
The stag-hunt
The story of General Gim Dog-Nyong
The story of spirits
The terrible black snake's revenge
Tinirau and his pet whale
The tiny bird and the king
Tortoise and the baboon
Tortoise and the lizard
The two men and the two dwarfs
Volund the smith
The voyage of Maeldun
The whale and the sorcerer
Why the spider has a narrow waist
The wild boar and the ram
The wren

Revenge (Theocritus)
  HOPE-SIMPSON – CAVAL. p85-87

The revenge (Tennyson)
  MAYNE – HEROES p63-69

The revenge of the serpent
  JEWETT – WHICH p59-64

Revenge of the tin god
  JORDAN – BURRO p53-55

Reverence
  The first Thanksgiving day
  Mary and The Christ-child
  Providence
  The sky at night
  Songs of joy from the Bible
  We thank Thee

Revolt
  BIRCH – CHINESE p176-200

The revolt of the utensils
  LEACH – SOUP p48-51

Revolutionary War. *See* **United States–
History–Revolutionary war**

Reward drives the familiar spirits away
  RANKE – GERMANY p32-33

The reward of treachery
  WALKER – DANCING p94-97

Rewards
  The cuckoo's reward
  The czar's general and the clever
    peasant
  Dick Whittington and his cat
  The fisherman and the king's cham-
    berlain
  The greedy man in the moon
  The just reward
  Katcha and the devil
  The Kildare pooka
  The magic fiddle
  Mr. Frost
  Mother Sunday
  One good turn deserves another
  The Pied Piper of Hamelin; a min-
    strel's enchanted music
  The pooka
  Poor Jack and the cat
  Sissa and the troublesome trifles
  A strange reward
  The wolf and the crane
  The wolf and the stork

Reynard and Bruin
  JACOBS – EUROPE. p42-50

Reynard and the fisherman's dream
  EDMONDS – TRICKSTER p99-102

Reynard the fox
  GREEN – BIG p97-115

Rhesus
  The horses of Rhesus

Rhine-gold
  The tale of the Rhine-gold

Rhinoceros
  Afar in the desert
  Greedy and speedy

Rhitta of the beards
  JONES – WELSH p119-125

Rhode Island
    The cat inspector
    The devil in red flannel
    Grumpy Timothy Crumb
    Hunter's moon
    Mysteries of the sea
    A new way to cure old witch-hunting
    Old man Elias and the dancing sheriff
    Puffing Potter's powerful puff
    The rich lady and the ring in the sea
    Stonewall Silas Clapp
    The weaver-woman's movement

    —Block Island
        The dancing mortar of Block
        Island

    —Coventry
        The serpent of Carbuncle Hill

    —Newport
        Hearts and pirates
        Little Annie and the whaler cap-
        tain
        The tale of Godfrey Malbone

    —Pawtucket
        Sam Patch
        Sam Patch's last leap

    —Scituate
        Hasty Corners

Rhode Island
    LEACH — RAINBOW p143-145

Rhodes (island)
    The dragon of Rhodes

Rhododendron
    Indian legends of shrubs in our gar-
    dens

Rhodopis and her gilded sandals
    MY BOOK HOUSE v. 7 p84-89

Rhyme and reason. *See* The rain, wind,
and snow

A rhyme from Santo Domingo
    MY BOOK HOUSE v. 1 p224.

Rhymes
    See also **Nonsense rhymes; Nursery
    rhymes; Repetitive rhymes and
    stories**
    The Arkansas fiddler
    Around the corner
    As it fell upon a day
    Bang-whang-whang
    Bats
    The bear went over the mountain

Blessings on thee, dog of mine
The boll weevil
The bridge
Bring the comb and play upon it!
Child, I see thee!
The clucking hen
The cock is crowing
The crocodile's mouth
Dainty little maiden
Derby ram
The Derbyshire ram
The elevator
The firefly
The fog
The friendly cow all red and white
A frog he would a-wooing go
The frogs of yonder mountain cry
Go out, children
God hath made me to laugh
Good morrow, 'tis St. Valentine's
    day
The gray goose
Groceries
The harbor
Hark, hark! Bow-wow!
Hear how the birds
The horny-goloch
In a dark wood
In Columbus' time
In Paris there is a street
In the Springtime
The interesting history of old
    Mother Goose
It is God that hath made us
It's Spring
Jeremiah
Jingling rhymes and jingling money
Jog on, jog on
Johnny McGorry and the red stocking
The key of the kingdom
King Stephen was a worthy peer
Lawkamercyme
Lines for a city child
The lion and the unicorn
Look, see the boat!
Mary and the Christ-child
Meet-on-the-road
Minnie and Mattie
Mister postman
Mix a pancake
Monkeys
Noah's ark
O, Lady Mary Ann
O rattlin', roarin' Willie
O sailor, come ashore
Of speckled eggs the birdie sings
Old Hiram's goat
The old lady who swallowed a fly
Old mother wiggle-waggle
One guess
The orchestra

Rhymes (*Continued*)

Over in the meadow
Pa Grumble
Paul and the robber
The peasant-girl's captive
Please give me a ride on your back
Ploughman he's a bonnie lad
Poems by Alfred Tennyson
Poems by Christina Rossetti
Poems by Robert Louis Stevenson
Precocious piggy
Pretty Sally
Puddock, mousie and ratton
Rain
St. Valentine's Day
A sea-song from the shore
Shall I be so?
The sow got the measles
Story of a nickel and a dime
Strange houses
Strange story
Strawberry roan
The swapping song
Sweet Betsy from Pike
The tale of a frog
Teasing questions
Ten little Indians
There was a naughty boy
There was an old man of Coblenz—
  limerick
There was an old man with a beard
There's not a budding boy
The thief and the donkey
Thunder and lightning
Turkey in the straw
'Twas midnight
The unexpected happened
Verses, by John Keats
What does little birdie say?
What they say
When I was down beside the sea
When that I was but a little boy
When the bull bellows
A white hen sitting
Who has seen the wind?
A winky-tooden song
A zoo in the park

—Africa
  African child rhymes
  Child, I must sweep the hut today
  The drums call the village to dance
  Open your beak, my little bird
  Sleep, sleep, my little ones

—America
  All the cats consulted
  American rhymes
  The barnyard
  The farmer's boy
  Froggie goes a-courting

I had a little dog
I had a little mule
John Brown had a little Indian
Umbo was an elephant
Lame tame crane
O, I'm a jolly old cowboy
Of all the beasts that roam the
  woods
Old Dan Tucker
Puddin' Tame
Three jolly sailor boys
Three old maids a-skating went

—England
  Higgledy, piggledy! see how they
  run!
  Where be you going, you Devon
  maid?

—Finland
  Cold, son of wind and snow

—Greece
  Crocus flowers bloom like fire

—Ireland
  Weaver John

, Negro
  Of all the beasts that roam the
  woods
  A squirrel

—Norway
  Ride, ride away

—Pennsylvania
  Bye-lo, Bubbeli, sleep

—Pennsylvania (Dutch)
  I stand in the pulpit and preach
  Pennsylvania Dutch rhymes
  Ride ride a horsey

—Russia
  Pretty flowers of the steppes
  Snail, snail

—Santo Domingo
  Eve of the wise man
  A rhyme from Santo Domingo

Rhymes and jingles
  JOHNSON — WHAT p118-134

Rhymes from Ireland
  MY BOOK HOUSE v. 1 p59.

Rhymes from Shakespeare
  MY BOOK HOUSE v. 1 p148-149

Rhymes of Finland
  MY BOOK HOUSE v. 1 p144-145

Rhys at the fairy dance
  BRIGGS — PERS. p77-97

Rhythms. *See* Games and rhythms;
  Repetitive rhymes and stories

Ribbons
  The partridge and his drum
  Pleiad and star of dawn
  The yellow ribbon

Rice
  The ants and the hare
  The beggar and the rice
  The bird on the roof
  Bundar Bahadeer Poon
  The butterfly in the granary
  The clever goatherd and the greedy
    giant
  The dutiful daughter
  The fish with bent noses
  A girl and a stepmother
  Gulam . . . The jar of rice
  Hidden treasure
  The hidden treasure of Khin
  How much for a shadow?
  How the kapok bird came to be
  How the monkey came to be
  In the paddy field
  The jeweled ring
  Joe Magerack, the steel-mill man
  Light-O-Leap and the fowler
  The little bird's rice
  The little Sawah
  The little sticky rice basket
  The magic oysters
  The monkey and the pheasant
  The mouseling
  My Lord Bag-o'-(of) Rice
  The old man in the moon
  The old man of the flowers
  An old Sumatran legend
  The old woman who lost her dump-
    lings
  Ooka and the honest thief
  The princess in the camphor tree
  The rice puller of Chaohwa
  Shrovetide
  Si Jura carved a house post
  Sissa and the troublesome trifles
  The soul in the mountain rice
  The tikgi birds
  The turtle prince
  Why the mountains are snow-covered
  The wonder-tree

Rice birds
  Catfish and his terrible end
  Jack who could do anything

The rice cake that rolled away
  UCHIDA – MAGIC p123-131

Rice-cakes
  The crab and the monkey
  The grateful statues
  The mountain witch and the peddler
  The old man who made trees blossom
  The two foolish cats

Rice pudding
  The king's rice pudding

The rice puller of Chaohwa
  COURLANDER – TIGER'S p38-39

Rich. *See* Wealth

The rich lady and the ring in the sea
  JAGENDORF – NEW p223-225

The rich landowner and his worker
  BULATKIN – EURASIAN p57-63

The rich man and his son-in-law
  THOMPSON – ONE p137-142

The rich man and the poor man
  SECHRIST – ONCE p143-149

The rich man and the tailor
  SPELLMAN – BEAUT. p69-70

The rich man's dinner party
  URE – RUMANIAN p72-73

The rich Per Muller
  HACK – DANISH p106-116

The rich widow of Stavoren
  DELEEUW – LEGENDS p133-138

Rich woman, poor woman
  MANNING – WIZARDS p109-117

Richard Feverel and the hay-rick
  MY BOOK HOUSE v. 10 p54-78

Richards, Laura E.
  Rosy Posy
  Will-o'-the-wisp

Riches or happiness?
  GRAY – INDIA'S p40-44

Richmuth of Cologne
  PICARD – GERMAN p150-155

Richter, Ludwig, illus.
  The bell of Monte Pino
  Catherine and her fate
  The chief astrologer
  The clever thief

547

Richter, Ludwig, illus. (*Continued*)

How one should carve a goose
It's already paid
The king's rabbits
Lars, my servant
More south and south, more north
than north
The pastor and the sexton
The peasant and the waterman
Peter Ox
The wishing ring

Ricky of the tuft (Ricky with a tuft)
PERRAULT – COMPLETE p47-57
PERRAULT – FAMOUS p113-134

The riddle
MANNING – RED p62-65

A riddle is a wonderful thing
LEACH – NOODLES p43-44

The riddle of the black knight
LEEKLEY – RIDDLE p3-24

The riddle of the Sphinx
LEACH – NOODLES p45-46

Riddler on the hill
THOMPSON – LEGENDS p43-48

Riddles
Abe Lincoln in Indiana
As many as – –
A beautiful young woman as the head
of the family
The blihd man and the elephant
A chiefess and a riddle
The clever lass
Clever Manka
The clever peasant
The clever peasant girl
The count and the little shepherd
The dragon and his grandmother
The emperor and the deaf man
The emperor's questions
Everywhere you go
The farmer's clever daughter
The flea
Four riddles
The full moon
Hantsjc and the remarkable beast
The hidden treasure of Khin
The house of the rowan trees
The house without eyes or ears
Introduction (WALKER – DANCING)
Juan Bobo and the princess who
answered riddles
King Solomon and the Queen of Sheba
The loathly lady

The long-nosed giant
The moon's a woman
Morgan and the pot of brains
Old Mother Twitchett
An ossete riddle
Outriddling the princess
Prince rabbit
The prince with the golden hand
The princess and Jose
The princess who wanted to solve
riddles
Problems
The queen's riddles
The Red Etin
The Red Ettin
Salt
The search: who get's the chief's
daughter?
Seven sons
Simpleton Peter
Snow in the muntains
Sphinxes
Strike there!
The tale of the riddle sent to Bruce
Three sons of a chief
Transportation problem
An unsolved riddle
What the rose did to the cypress
With and without
The witless imitator
Wordplay riddles
The young head of the Cheng family

The riddling chief of Puna
THOMPSON – LEGENDS p72-79

The riddling youngster
THOMPSON – LEGENDS p86-99

Ride a cock-horse to Banbury Cross
MY BOOK HOUSE v. 1 p28.

Ride away, ride away
MY BOOK HOUSE v. 1 p24.

The ride-by-nights
HOKE – WITCHES p205.

The ride in the night
JAGENDORF – NEW p95-99

Ride ride a horsey
MY BOOK HOUSE v. 1 p116.

Ride, ride away
MY BOOK HOUSE v. 1 p60.

A ride to hell
MANNING – DEVILS p98-109

Ridicule
The brave men of Golo
The duck and the moon
The jackal and the crocodile
The seven proud sisters
The ugly king

The ridiculous donkey
GREEN – BIG p84-85

The ridiculous wishes
PERRAULT – CLASSIC p186-195
PERRAULT – COMPLETE p89-91

Right
See also **Piety**
Introduction (The righteous and the
  pious)
The righteous and the pious
The righteous is delivered out of
  trouble and the wicked comes in his
  stead
The righteous heir
The two crabs

Right out in our barnyard
MY BOOK HOUSE v. 1 p69.

The right time to laugh
MY BOOK HOUSE v. 3 p81-84

The righteous and the pious
NAHMAD – PORTION p107-127

The righteous heir
NAHMAD – PORTION p114-116

The righteous is delivered out of trouble
and the wicked comes in his stead
NAHMAD – PORTION p111-113

Riley, James Whitcomb
The brook song
The daring prince
It
Monkeys
A sea-song from the shore
A winky-tooden song

Riley, James Whitcomb
The Hoosier poet

The ring
MANNING – GHOSTS p87-89

Ring around a rosy
MY BOOK HOUSE v. 1 p84.

The ring in the porridge bowl
SPICER – OWL'S p106-124

The ring in the seashell
CARPENTER – SOUTH p151-159

The ring of Hallwil
MÜLLER – SWISS p106-109

Rings
The absent-minded king
According to tradition
Alberich and the dwarfs
Atlantes and the hippogriff
Bahram and the snake prince
Beauty and the beast
Bells on her toes
The box with wings
The cat, the dog, and the mongoose
The charcoal burner
The chief astrologer
The city under the sea
The clumber pup
Constantes and the dragon
The dancing water, the singing apple,
  and the speaking bird
Dates to Cairo
Doctor know-all
The doctor who knew everything
Donkey-skin
The enchanted island
The fairy quite contrary
Farmer Weathersky
The fish and the ring
The rish with bent noses
The fisherlad and the mermaid's ring
The fruits of health
The giant in the cave
Gigi and the magic ring
Goggle-eyes
The golden candelabra
The golden carnation
The golden slipper, the magic ring,
  and the twigs
Goto, king of the land and the water
The grateful animals and the talisman
The grateful beasts
The grateful prince
Hildur the elf queen
Hind horn
Ida of Toggenburg
The innkeeper of Moscow
The invisible hands
Iwanich and the magic ring
Jack and the wizard
The jeweled ring
Juan Bobo and the princess who
  answered riddles
The just reward
Keloglan the kindhearted
The king and the ring
The king who rides a tiger
The knight and the naiad of the lake
A little bull-calf

Rings (*Continued*)

The little gardener with golden hair
The little horse
Longshanks, girth, and keen
Lost and found
Luck
The magic lake
The magic mare
The magic ring
The magician Palermo
Maid Lena
The man who always helped the needy
The man who sold magic
The mermaid and the boy
Molly Whipple
The most obedient wife
Noodlehead and the flying horse
The northern frog
One grain more than the devil
A prince and a dove
Prince Daniel
Prince Ferdinand
Princess Felicity
The princess with the golden hair
The pumpkin child
The reluctant familiar
The rich lady and the ring in the sea
The rich man and the poor man
The rich widow of Stavoren
Richmuth of Cologne
Robin Ddu
The shepherd's nosegay
The silver penny
The slave of the ring
Snake magic
Soria Moria castle
The spring of youth
The stolen ring
The stone in the cock's head
The story of Noschoy Datta of Ujjain
Swan White and fox tail
Sylvester
The tale of a foolish brother and of a
   wonderful bush
The tale of the Rhine-gold
The tale of the two cunning servants
The three enchanted princes
The Three Fates
The three feathers
The three gifts
The three golden ducats
The three princesses of Whiteland
The three rings
Three times lucky
Tolkien's magic ring
The twins
The underground palace
Volund the smith
The wedding of the hawk
The well o' the world's end

The white snake
Why dogs wag their tales
Why the dog and the cat are enemies
The wild man
The wishing ring
The would-be wizard
Young Bekie

, Arm
   Sif's golden hair

, Neck
   Who should get the neck ring?

Rio Grande River
   How horses came to the Navaho

Rip Van Winkle; the strange little men
   of the mountain
   STRONG – FAVORITE p24-32

Rip Van Winkle stories
   The bird and the man
   Keel-Wee, a Korean Rip Van Winkle
   The wood carver of Ruteng

Rip Van Winkle's dog
   JOHNSON – WHAT p263.

Riquet with the quiff
   PERRAULT – CLASSIC p99-117

The rise and decline of the Serbian kingdom
   ĆURČIJA – HEROES p1-28

Ritchie, Alice
   Two of everything

The ritual coming-of-age
   ELLIOT – SINGING p72-83

The rival cooks
   JOHNSON – WHAT p170.

Rival magicians
   INS-SOB – FOLK p70-71

Rival storytellers
   WITHERS – WORLD p28-32

Rivalry
   Gods in all-too-human situations: The
      contendings of Horus and Seth
   The lion and the unicorn
   Riddler on the hill

The river
   MICHAEL – PORTUGUESE p154-163

River child
 JACOBSON – FIRST p42-45

The river flows full through the sky
 land
 BELTING – STARS #8

The river god (of the River Mimram)
 GARNER – GOBLINS p178-179

The river maiden
 SAVORY – ZULU p60-63

River monsters. *See* **Sea monsters**

The river of lantern land
 SHEAHAN – HENRY p78-95

River roarer Mike Fink
 STOUTENBURG – AMER. p51-63

River spirits
 The son of the tortoise

The river that was stolen
 ROSS – MEXICO p162-174

Rivers
 Baba Yaga and the little girl with the
  kind heart
 The birth of the River Emajogi
 Blue water
 The boatman he's a lucky man
 A boy of the lake country
 Bukolla
 The canoe in the rapids
 A chronicle of Kiev
 The contrary woman
 Crossing the river
 Drakestail
 Duck's ditty
 The giant who stole a river
 The gingerbread man
 The great blessing of the land
 The Hopi turtle
 How Robert Fulton harnessed the
  giant
 The judgment of the wind
 The king of the Golden River, or the
  Black brothers
 The king's true children
 Little shepherd's song
 The magic mirror
 Mike Fink
 The mole's bridegroom
 The mountain and the rivers
 The ogre who built a bridge
 The open road
 The pilgrim and the crab

Pushing westward with Lewis and
 Clark
Recollections of the Arabian nights
Sadko
The serpents and the porcupine
The serpent's bride
The silver river
The snow-queen
A song of the Canadian lumberjack
Straw, bean and coal
The strong boy
Too hot to handle
The waters beneath: the great river
 monster
Where go the boats?
Why the crab has no head or how the
 the first river was made
Why the terrapin's shell is scarred
Young Kate

Road runners (birds)
 How fire was brought from lightning
 How the king of the birds was chosen

The road to China
 MY BOOK HOUSE v. 3 p19.

The road to hell
 RANKE – GERMANY p150-154

Roads
 The clever jackal and how he out-
  witted the tiger
 The gold falcon
 The open road
 Thomas the rhymer
 The three journeys of Ilya of Murom
 The traveller and the tiger

Roanes
 The seal fisher and the roane

The robber baron . . . and the bat
 UNTERMEYER – FIRE. p220-222

The robber Simhavikrama
 GRAY – INDIA'S p161-164

Robbers. *See* **Bandits; Outlaws; Thieves
and thievery**

The robe
 BARASH – GOLDEN p5-8

Robert Bruce and the spider; how a king
 learned courage from an insect
 STRONG – FAVORITE p43-45

Robert Bruce, Scotland's hero
MY BOOK HOUSE v. 10 p21-28

Robert E. Lee, a hero in war and peace
MY BOOK HOUSE v. 11 p170a-
170c

Robert of Sicily . . . the proudest king
UNTERMEYER – FIRE p211-215

Roberts, Michael
In the strange isle

Robertson, Dorothy Lewis
ROBERTSON – FAIRY p95.
ROBERTSON – PHILIP. p128.

Robes. *See* **Clothes–Robes**

A robin and a robin's son
MY BOOK HOUSE v. 1 p36.

Robin and Richard were too pretty men
MY BOOK HOUSE v. 1 p26.

The robin and the wren
MONTGOMERIE – 25 p16-17

Robin Ddu
SHEPPARD – WELSH p32-35

Robin Hood
The birth of Robin Hood
The king and Robin Hood
Little John and the Sheriff of Notting-
ham
Little John and the tanner of Blyth
The sheriff complains to the king
The sheriff's shooting match
Sir Richard at the lee and the abbot
A story of Robin Hood
A tale of Robin Hood
Ye merry doinges of Robin Hood

Robin Hood
PICARD – HERO p31-47

Robin Hood and Sir Richard at the lee
MANNING – ENGLISH p110-115

Robin Hood and the monk
MANNING – ENGLISH p126-131

Robins
Courage
How raven brought fire to the Indians
How the robin's breast became red
Little robin redbreast

The marriage of the robin and the
wren
Pooh goes visiting and gets into a
tight place
Sometime
A story about Abe Lincoln
Wee robin's Christmas song
Why robin has a red breast

Robinson, Bill
The hope tree of Harlem

"Robinson Crusoe"
The adventures of Alexander Selkirk

Rock-a-bye, baby
MY BOOK HOUSE v. 1 p18.

Rocking-horse land
JOHNSON – HARPER p212-225

Rocks and stones
See also **Statues**
The aderna bird
Aniello
The ant and the yellow jacket
Au Sung meets Kim Lee
Bald pate
The barren stones
The beginning of good conversation
The black stone
The blue belt
The brave shepherd boy
The carnation youth
Clach Mor and the witch of Badenoch
Clarinha
Clever Tom and the leprechaun
The cock-crow stone
The crowza stones
The crystal of love
Curiosity punished
David and Goliath . . . The shepherd
boy and the giant
Donal O'Ciaran from Connaught
Don't throw stones from not yours
to yours
The duckling's journey
Evil rocks and the evil spirit of Peru
The fairy garden
The farmer and the demon
Father big-nose
The fians asleep in the Great Rock
Fickle Miss Frog
Flinty
The frog heralds
From the head downward
The giant who counted stones
The giant's stone
The giants who wanted a son
The girl on the rock

Rocks and stones (*Continued*)

Goblin gold
The growing rock
Haku's power
The holy mountain
How the great rocks grew
The hungry old witch
The Inchcape rock
Inside again
Itsayaya and the otter
The king of the demons and the worm
  Shamir
The king of the Golden River, or the
  Black brothers
The king who slept
The legend of Crooked Mountain
The little menehunes
Longshanks, girth, and keen
The magic ball
The magic mountain
Maid Lena
The man without a heart
The missing fog bell
The mountain of hope
Nidelgret
North Salem's Irish? Ruins
Ntunjambili
The old hag of the forest
Piboon's golden mountain
The precious stone
The Prince Fernando
Prince Sigurd and his sister
The punishment
Rabbit and lion
The Red Etin
Ruddy-by-beard
St. Cuddy and the gray geese
Sartak-Pai
Segizbai and the little mouse-girl
Senor coyote
Small white stones
The son of the hunter
The soup stone
The spirit of the stone
The spotted cow
The stone frogs
The stone horseman
The stone in the garden
The stone king
The stone monkey
The stone of victory
The stone owl's nest
Stone patience and knife patience
Stone soup in Bohemia
The stone stew
The story of Prince Ahmed
The stupid fellow
The sword in the stone
The sword of the stone
The tale of the lady of the rock

Tavadan and the fire giant
Temba's magic boat
The text
The three blue stones
The three-legged jumping giant
The three little eggs
The three tasks
Three who couldn't be parted
The treasure of Altamira
The trial of the stone
The two boys and the sacred carpet
  snake
Two brothers
The two dogs—Burrajahnee and
  Inneroogun
The two white stones
Tying up the stones
The walking boundary stone
The weeping lady of Llyn Glasfryn
The white parrot
The wise men of Chelm
The witch
The woman of rock
Yallery Brown
The young head of the Cheng family

, Lucky
  The woman tribe

—Pebbles
  Johnnie and Grizzle
  Kabadaluk

Rocky Mountains
  O, I'm a jolly old cowboy

Rocs (birds)
  Sinbad and the roc
  Sindbad the sailor

Rodents rampart on a field azure
  GHOSE — FOLK p123-143

Rodeos
  Pecos Bill
  Pecos Bill and his bouncing bride

Rods. *See* **Sticks**

Roegge, W., illus.
  The archer, William Tell

Rogozin, Zenuid A.
  Beowulf conquers Grendel

Rogues. *See* **Rascals**

Rojin Rojal
  LAURITZEN — BLOOD p109-128

Roland, Childe
  Childe Roland
  The death of Roland

A Roland for an Oliver
  HAZELTINE – HERO p219-234

Roland, Song of. *See* Song of Roland

Roll it, bowl it
  MY BOOK HOUSE v. 1 p130.

Rolling
  The bun
  Mr. Bun
  The pancake

Rolling cheese gathers no moss
  JAGENDORF – MERRY p93-98

Romance
  See also Love
  Aucassin and Nicolette
  Brides, grooms and weddings
  The dragon of Rhodes
  Love and lovers
  Sir Orfeo

Romance
  BATCHELOR – SUPER. p74-83

Romance at Tulip Hill
  JAGENDORF – UPSTATE p248-253

Rome, Ancient
  Androcles and the lion
  Cincinnatus: the man who would not
    be king
  Cornelia's jewels
  Cornelia's jewels; a mother's love and
    pride
  The dream of Macsen Wledig
  Horatius
  The sack of Troy
  The sharpshooter
  The story of Cincinnatus
  The story of Regulus
  Viriato: The youth who held back the
    Roman empire
  The wanderings of Aeneas

Romulus and Remus
  The twins of the god Mars

Roofs
  The battle of the buffaloes
  Grazing on the roof
  Ijapa and the oba repair a roof
  Shingling the fog
  Timothy and the buggane ghost

Rooks
  The lucky circle

Roommates
  LEACH – RAINBOW p238.

Rooms
  Bluebeard
  The lady's room
  The secret room
  The three chests
  The three silver balls

Roosevelt, Theodore
  George Rogers Clark and the conquest
    of the Northwest

Roosevelt, Theodore
  The rough rider

The rooster and the hen
  ILLYÉS – ONCE p13-14

The rooster and the pearl
  LA FONTAINE – FABLES p43.

The rooster and the sultan
  MY BOOK HOUSE v. 2 p52-56

The rooster and the sun
  JABLOW – MAN p88-90

The rooster and the wind
  BORSKI – GOOD p46.

The rooster, the hand mill and the swarm
  of hornets
  BAKER – GOLDEN p54-57

Roosters. *See* Chickens–Roosters

The roosters at the old crown inn
  MY BOOK HOUSE v. 1 p67.

Roots
  The Indian shinny game
  The shepherd and the dwarf

The rope
  HEADY – TALES p119-124

Rope and roping
  The bird of the golden land
  The boy and Necken
  The boy and the water-sprite
  How Pakayana the spider got his
    small waist
  Jack and the giant tantorem
  The man who stole a rope

Rope and roping (*Continued*)

Maui nooses the sun
One! Two! Three!
Pecos Bill
The prince and the demon
Rabbit, elephant and hippopotamus
The stolen rope
The turquoise stones
The viper and the friar's rope
The wizard of Reay's book of magic

Rosamond, Princess
The race with Rosamond

Rosaries
The mysterious lake

The rose
VANSITTART – DARK p120.

The rose and the ring
MY BOOK HOUSE v. 9 p177-224

Rose-apple trees
The crow in the rose-apple tree

The rose garden
SAWYER – DIETRICH p129-149

The rose is red
MY BOOK HOUSE v. 1 p86.

The rose of midwinter, The Little People
of Italy
BELTING – ELVES p91-94

Rosemary
The glass man and the golden bird

Roses
Arawn
Beauty and the beast
The boy with the golden star
The child and the fig
The crow's pearl
Dainty little maiden
Diamonds and toads
The fairies
The king of the fishes
A kiss from the beautiful Fiorita
Little girl, little girl
The little lady's roses
The loveliest rose
The miracle of Our Lady of Guadalupe
The miracle of the Poor Island
Our Lady of Guadalupe
Prince Lindworm

The princess who hid her slippers
Rags and tatters
The snow-queen
The swineherd
Tam Lin
Where are my roses?
Why Eyvin won the race
Why the brierbrush quarreled with the
beasts
Winter rose
The young Tamlin

, **Blue**
The blue rose

, **Golden**
Wind and wave and wandering
flame

–**Hips**
Grandmother Marta

, **Red**
Mrizala and her bridegroom, death
Snow-white
Swan White and fox tail

, **White**
Whitebear Whittington

, **Yellow**
The child and the fig

Ross, Betsy
George Washington and the first
American flag

Rossetti, Christina G.
The bow that bridges heaven
Lie a-bed
Minnie and Mattie
Mix a pancake
O sailor, come ashore
Poems
A white hen sitting
Who has seen the wind?

Rosy Posy
MY BOOK HOUSE v. 3 p128.

The rough rider
MY BOOK HOUSE v. 9 p72-77

Roumania. *See* **Rumania**

A Roumanian lullaby
MY BOOK HOUSE v. 1 p137.

Round is my bun
MY BOOK HOUSE v. 1 p136.

"Round Table"
The loathly lady

"Round Table" (*Continued*)
The marriage of Arthur
Sir Beaumains, the kitchen knight
Sir Gawain and the green knight

Roue, W. H. D.
The grateful goat

A rover in the Catskills
MY BOOK HOUSE v. 12 p113-115

Row, row, a fishing we'll go!
MY BOOK HOUSE v. 1 p61.

Rowan trees and berries
Dermot and Grania
The golden apples of Lord Erne
The hairy boggart's field
How Finn Maccumhail was in the
House of the rowan tree without
power to stand or leave or sit down
Left eye, right eye
The powers of plants and trees to
protect against witches
The pursuit of Dermot and Grania
The smith and the faeries

Rowboats
Mr. Hampden's shipwreck
Row, row! A-fishing we'll go!

Royal, Anne
Three little tales of Washington

The royal banquet
BARASH — GOLDEN p122-127

The royal geese
LARSON — PALACE p70-85

The royal monument pavilion
BONNET — CHINESE p63-68

The royal musician
FEINSTEIN — FOLK p11-15

The royal page
MY BOOK HOUSE v. 12 p11-14

The royal waistcoat
MONTROSE — WINTER p89-98

Rub-a-dub-dub
MY BOOK HOUSE v. 1 p48.

Ruba and the stork
MEHDEVI — PERSIAN p44-50

Rubber, Liquid
King Kantjil's kingdom expands

The rubber man
ARNOTT — AFRICAN p16-21

Rubbers
The big umbrella and the little
rubbers

Rubbish
Lazy Hans

Rubies
The fish with bent noses
The golden crow
Grasp all, lose all
The happy prince
He wins who waits
Lionbruno
The magic ruby
The necklace
Once there was and once there was
not
The ruby prince

The ruby prince
SIDDIQUI — TOON. p144-154

Ruda, the quick thinker
COURLANDER — KING'S p87-89

Ruddy-my-beard
PUGH — TALES p117-128

Rudeness. *See* Discourtesy

Rue (plant)
King of the serpents

Rufus
PICARD — MERMAID p171-186

The rug maker
HEADY — WHEN p31-35

Rugen, Island of
The wonderful plow, the Little People
of the island of Rugen

Rugs. *See* Carpets

Ruins
North Salem's Irish? Ruins

Rulers. *See* Kings and queens; etc.

Rum
Why rabbit have short tail

Rumania
See also **Lullabies–Rumania**
The boyar and the gipsy
Boys with golden stars
Brave rabbit and bug with the golden wings
Cleverer than the devil
Daniel the gawk
Five loaves
The giant and the Rumanian
The gipsies' church
The gipsy and the goose
The goat and her three kids
Good advice, a guinea a piece
The horse, the lion, and the wolf
How men become enemies
How stars and fireflies were made
How the fox and the hedgehog became friends
How the king chose a daughter-in-law
Human stupidity
Ivan and his knapsack
Ivan and his sack
The king's son and the straw hat maker
The land where there were no older men
The little brother of the sun
The little purse with two pennies
The little snake
Luck and wit
The magic egg
The maiden, the knight, and the waterfall
The man with the book of spells
The marriage of Tom and the vixen
Mother's girl and father's girl
Necessity
The old man's tale of Prince Stephen
Pacala and Tandala
Pacala saves Tandala
Pacala the lawyer
The partridge, the fox and the hound
Pepelea's peg
The poor man's clever daughter
A poor man's servant
Prince Charming, the mare's son
Prince Loaf
The proper way to lay the table
The proud goat
Red king and green king
The rich man's dinner party
Saint Peter's horses
The salt at dinner
A sketch of Ion Creanga's life
Sleep, my baby! Sleep an hour
Solomon-the-wise and the golden plough
Stan Bolovan
The story of a lazy man
The story of an egg
The story of the pig
A story of three brothers
The story of White Arab
The terror of the ogres
The three deaf men
The tufty hen
The twelve young boys with golden hair
What a clever child can do
Which is the greater?
Why cats and dogs fight
Why cats lie on the doorstep in the sun
Why God made the dog
Why people tell stories
Why wagtail wags her tail
You must pay for the horse, Aga

–**Transylvania**
The sun-king's hair

Rumpelstiltskin (Rumpelstiltzkin)
ARBUTHNOT – TIME p58.
BAMBERGER – FIRST p193-198
BROWN – AROUND p23-31
HAVILAND – GERMANY p41-50
SIDEMAN – WORLD'S p531-537
TUDOR – TASHA p16-20

"Rumpelstiltskin" stories
Duffy and the devil
"Nimmy-nimmy-not!"
Nine guesses
Peerifool
Tom Tit Tot

Runaways. *See* **Runners and running**

Runes (Runic alphabet)
Frey and Gerd, the jotun maiden
Yggdrasil, the world tree

Runners and running
See also **Races, Athletic**
Atalanta's race; a contest for love or death
Don't run away my kitty
The foot racers of Payupki
The gingerbread man
The golden casket
Great heart and the three tests
Johnny-cake
Life in Concord
Maggie Tulliver goes to live with the gypsies

Runners and running (*Continued*)

The nutcraker and the sugardolly
  stories
The ostrich
The pancake
A quick-running squash
Reen-reen-reeny-croak frog
The rescue of fire
The story of Li'l Hannibal
The tale of Peter Rabbit
The theft of fire
Tippity Witchit's Hallowe'en
The wonderful cake

A rupee earned
  BULATKIN – EURASIAN p39-43

Rural life. *See* **Country life**

Rushen Coatie
  JACOBS – MORE p163-168

Rushes
  Not to care a straw

Rushes, Cap o'. *See* Cap o'rushes

Rushmore, Helen
  RUSHMORE – DANCING p164.

Ruskin, John
  Dame Wiggins of Lee
  The king of the Golden River, or the
    Black brothers

Russia
  See also **"Kiev Cycle"; Siberia**
  Air castles
  The angel
  The armless maiden
  At the pike's command
  Baba Yaga
  Baba Yaga and the little girl with the
    kind heart
  Bird language
  The book of magic
  The boy and the birds
  A boy in Russia
  The brown cow
  Browny
  Building the bridge
  The bun
  The carefree monastery
  The cat and the fox
  The chatterbox
  Christening the baby in Russia
  The cock and the hen
  The cock, the cat, and the fox

The crock of gold
The crystal mountain
The czar's frog daughter
The danced-out shoes
Daughter and stepdaughter
Dawn, twilight and midnight
Death and the soldier
The death of Koshchei the deathless
The death watch
Did the tailor have a nightmare?
Dobrynia and Alyosha
The doctor who knew everything
The dog and the cock
Donal O'Ciaran from Connaught
The dream
The duck and the moon
Dunay
The elephant at court
The epic (Slovo)
Erseyka
Fair Vasilissa and Baba Yaga
The falcon and the cock
The feather of Finist the falcon
The firebird
Five in a glove
Flinty
The flying ship
Folk-tales (Skazki)
The fool and the birch-tree
Foolish Emilyan and the talking fish
The fortunate maiden
The fox and the hare
The fox and the thrush
The frog princess
The frog-princess
The frost, the sun, and the wind
The geese and the swans
The gnat and the lion
The golden ax
The golden cockerell
The golden mountain
The goldfish
The good judge
The greedy rich man
The hare who was afraid of nothing
Hatchet Kasha
Heroic poems (Byliny)
The hired man
Horns
How Grigori Petrovich divided the
  geese
How one should carve a goose
How the sons filled the hut
The huntsman and his wife
I don't know where and I don't know
  what
I-know-not-what of I know-not-where
Ilya of Murom and nightingale the
  robber
Ilya of Murom and Svatogor
In Russia the people say

558

Russia (*Continued*)

Introduction (DUDDINGTON –
RUSS.)
Ivan the fool
Ivashko and the witch
Iwanich and the magic ring
The jackal and the elephant
The just reward
The king and the falcon
King Frost and the snow maiden
King Kojata
The king who lived fairy tales
Kuzenko sudden-wealthy
Kuzma get-rich-quick
The lame duck
The lay of Prince Igor
The learned cat
The little chest
Little fool Ivan and the little hump-
back horse
The little house
Little-man-as-big-as-your-thumb-with-
mustaches-seven-miles long
Little Tom Thumb
A lucky child
The lute player
Lynx of the forest
The magic acorn
The magic berries
The magic ring
Maria Marina
Marko the rich and Vassili the luck-
less
Marya Morevna
Master Frost
The melting pot
Mr. Bun
Mr. Frost
Mr. Samson cat
The mountain of gold
The mouse who lived under the
granary
Nastasya and the whirlwind
The old dog and the gray wolf
The old woman swims the sea
Once there was and once there was
not
One-eyed Likho
Only a sparrow
The peasant and the baron
The peasant and the tsar
The peasant and the waterman
Phenist the bright-eyed falcon
The phoenix and the falcon
Prince Daniel
Prince Ivan and the firebird
Prince Ivan and the sun princess
The princess who wanted to solve
riddles
The quartet

The ram and the goat
The raven and his young
Sadko
Sadko the minstrel
Salt
The seven Simeons Simeonovich
Shemiaka the judge
The shrewd peasant
The sign at the Smithy door
The silly men of Russia
Since when there have been no more
heroes in holy Russia
Sister Alionushka, brother Ivanushka
The sly gypsy and the stupid devil
The snake and the dreams
Snegourka, the snow maiden
Snowflake
The soldier and the tsar
The soldier who did not wash
Sorrow
The speedy messenger
Stavr Godinovich and his clever wife
The stolen turnips
The story of King Frost
Straight and crooked
The straw ox
Stretch, Puff, and Blazer
Stupid Emilien
Svyatogor's bride
A swift messenger
The tale about lost time
The tale of the silver saucer and the
russet apple
The tale of Vassilissa the wise
Thomas Berennikov
The three copecks
Three fables
The three golden hairs of Grandad Sol
The three journeys of Ilya of Murom
A time for everything
To your good health
A town in a snuff-box
The town of fools
The travelling frog
The tree that flew
A trip to the sky
Tsar Peter the Great and the peasant
The turnip
The twelve months
Two brothers
The two friends
Two out of the sack
The ungrateful children
The unsmiling princess
Vania and the vampire
Vanya's leap
Vasili Buslayevich
Vasili Buslayevich's pilgrimage
Vasilia the beautiful
Vassilissa the beautiful
Vassilissa the fair and Baba Yaga

Russia (*Continued*)

Vassillissa the wise
The visit
Volga
What should I have said?
Why the cat and dog cannot live at
  peace
The wife who liked fairy tales
The wise doctor
The wise wife
The witch
The wolf and the cat
The wolf and the old woman
The woodcock and the fox
The woodman and the fox
The word of Igor's armament

−Caucasus Mountains
  The brave shepherd boy
  Djamukh−son of a deer
  Hecho the lazy
  How the donkey saved a village
  The old storyteller
  An ossete riddle
  The radiant khan
  The stone horseman
  A strange choice
  The stupid wolf
  The thoroughbred
  Unlucky Mussah
  Who is strongest?
  The wise liar
  The young storyteller

−Georgia
  Master and pupil

−Kiev
  See also **"Kiev Cycle"**
  Aliosha's visit to the bald moun-
    tain
  Chourilo's little comb
  A chronicle of Kiev
  Dobryna's embassy to Khan Amryl
  How Dounai won a bride for
    Prince Vladimir
  How three pilgrims called Ilya to
    the rescue of Kiev
  Nikita and the dragon
  Nikita and the last of the dragons
  Potok's dancing and the snakes
  Samson and the doll in green
    and brown
  Souchmont's trial and triumph
  Vassily and Curly Head the brigand
  Volkh's journey to the East
  The word of Igor's armament
  Young Michael and the uninvited
    guest

−Moscow
  The innkeeper of Moscow

The silly men of Russia
The soldier and the devil

−Steppes
  Aldar-Kos and the greedy rich man
  The animals' quarrel
  The baby camel
  The cat, the tiger, and the man
  The curious wife
  Ergosai-Batyr
  The fool
  The fox and the quail
  The golden slipper, the magic ring,
    and the twigs
  If you know a story, don't keep it
    to yourself
  The invisible thief
  The magic garden
  Mirzhan and the Lord of the king-
    dom under the sea
  Old man Kurai and the one-eyed
    giant
  Salakhbai and the fox
  Segizbai and the little mouse-girl
  A Sherlock Holmes of the Steppes
  The stupid wolf
  Three bridegrooms for one bride
  The woodcutter's daughter

−Ukrainia
  The billy goat and the sheep
  The cat and the chanticleer
  The crane and the fox
  The farmer, the bear, and the fox
  The farmyard
  The foolish dog
  The hawk and the hen
  How the little fox went after chaff
  The magic ring
  The old father who went to school
  Pan Kotsky
  The poor wolf
  Seerko
  The sparrow and the stalk of grass
  The spiteful nanny goat
  Why the cat and dog cannot live
    at peace

−Ural Mountains
  The greedy rich man

−Votyak People
  The girl whom the moon pitied

The Russian and the Tatar
  DOWNING − RUSSIAN p151-153

Russian rhymes
  MY BOOK HOUSE v. 1 p132-133

Rust, Doris
  The giant who stole a river

S

Saadia the potmender
  BARASH – GOLDEN p165-167

Sabbats
  Witches' sabbats

  —England
    Lancashire——?
    Lancashire—fiction

  —Italy
    Italy

  —Sweden
    Sweden

Sabres. *See* Swords

The sack of corn
  NAHMAD – PORTION p141-142

The sack of Troy
  HAZELTINE – HERO p37-50

Sacks
  Bad luck put into the bag
  Buttercup
  The cats
  Dry-bone and Anansi
  The gift of Father Frost
  The golden buffalo
  The golden skins
  Holding the bag
  Ivan and his sack
  King Johnny
  The lazy maiden
  Lazy Peter and the king
  Long-neck, Fatty and Droopy
  The man with the bag
  Niassa and the ogre
  Nidden and Didden and Donal Beg
    O'Neary
  Pwyll and Rhiannon
  The singing sack
  The stolen turnips
  The story spirits
  The tale of frost and his neighbors
  The three traveling artisans
  The travels of a fox
  Two out of the sack
  Why the woodpecker has a long nose
  A woman had a rooster

The sacred amulet
  BARLOW – LATIN p126-133

The sacred cod and the striped haddock
  JAGENDORF – NEW p163-165

The sacred drum of Tepozteco
  JAGENDORF – KING p190-193

The sacred fish of Polaman
  LEEUW – INDO. p140-150

A sacred pledge should not be broken
  JAGENDORF – KING p208-211

Sacrifice
  The banyan deer
  The barrel decree
  The boy and the leopard
  The Brahman and the goat
  The children's sea
  The days of the first monkeys
  The dutiful daughter
  A dutiful son
  The faithful wife
  The giant okab
  The great bell
  The great sacrifice
  The head-hunters
  The hermit and the Sea of Man
  How Papantla got its patron saint
  Iphigenia . . . The transported sacrifice
  The magic oysters
  The martyrs of Thebes
  Mellitot and Iolanda
  The miracle on the Jaffa Sea
  The mistress of fire
  A noble Brahman's sacrifice
  The rabbit in the moon
  The river that was stolen
  Saint Gabre Manfas and his animals
  The son of the tortoise
  Tavadan and the fire giant
  The voice of the bell
  The woodsman's daughter and the
    lion

The sad, sorry sister
  CARPENTER – SOUTH p160-166

A sad tale of a silly fellow
  JAGENDORF – KING p252-256

The sad tale of three slavers
  JAGENDORF – SAND p40-46

The sad tale of Tom the catfish
  JAGENDORF – SAND p115-117

561

The saddle
  KELSEY – ONCE p48-53

Saddlebags
  I know what I'll do

Saddles and saddlers
  The adventures of Manawyddan
  The gold bird
  The little nobleman
  The trials of Dyfed

Sadko
  ARBUTHNOT – TIME p138-142

Sadko the minstrel
  DOWNING – RUSSIAN p55-63

Sadness
  See also Grief
  The first tears
  Four friends
  He who laughs last
  How these tales came to be told
  The melancholy prince and the girl
    of milk and blood
  Rufus
  Stan Bolovan
  The swans of Bally castle
  The sweetest song in the woods
  An unhappy lord

Saemunel the Learned
  BOUCHER – MEAD p39-41

Safety
  See also Security
  The lizards and the stag
  What the squirrel saw
  The wolf, the goat, and the kid

The saga of Stretch Garrison
  JAGENDORF – UPSTATE p105-111

The saga of the waru Wanggi
  LEEUW – INDO. p61-64

Sagas. *See* Epics; Storytellers and story-
telling

The sage and the mouse
  GHOSE – FOLK p120-122

The sage and the servant
  KOREL – LISTEN p103-107

The sage in the cave
  ALEXANDER – PEBBLES p25.

Sages. *See* Scholars; Wisemen

Sailing and sailing vessels
  The adventures of Alexander Selkirk
  The audacious kitten
  A boy on the high seas
  Frithjof, the Viking
  The golden lotus
  Gulliver's travels to Lilliput
  Here we sail so fast and free
  How Beowulf delivered Heorot
  O well for the fisherman's boy
  Old Stormalong
  The owl and the pussy-cat
  A song of Drake's men
  The tempest
  Vladimir's adventures in search of
    fortune
  A wanderer's song
  Young midshipman David Farragut

The sailor and the devil's daughter
  COTHRAN – MAGIC p75-82

The sailor and the rat
  O'SULLIVAN – FOLK. p223.

The sailor and the sea serpent
  CARPENTER – SHIPS p15-25

Sailors
  About Sinbad's other wonderful
    journeys
  The Blue Men of the Minch
  A boy on the high seas
  The child and the mariner
  The city under the sea
  The classic traveler's yarn: The tale
    of the shipwrecked sailor
  The dark cliffs of Dover
  Five fathons tall/Stormalong
  The foggy stew
  The girl and the sailor
  The goose from Flatbush
  A grand old skipper
  Gulliver's travels to Lilliput
  Here come three jolly, jolly sailor
    boys
  How old Stormalong captured Mocha
    Dick
  John Paul Jones, the first American
    naval hero
  The king and the merman
  The kingdom of ocean
  Little Beppo Pippo
  Little Stormy

563

Sailors (*Continued*)

Love story
The master mariner
Men of the sea
My boat
No man with the Cyclops
O sailor, come ashore
O well for the fisherman's boy
Of speckled eggs the birdie sings
The old Navy
Old Stormalong
Sam Patch's last leap
The sea captain's wife
Sea-fever
The sea knight
A sea-song from the shore
Sinbad and the roc
Sinbad the sailor
The sleigh ride
Stormalong
Stormy lifts anchor
Stormy swallows the anchor
Stormy sets sail
The story of the shipwrecked sailor
The strange adventures of the
  cowboy-sailor
Supparaka the mariner
Three jolly sailor boys

—Cabin boys
  The magic storm

Saint Cadog and King Arthur
  SHEPPARD – WELSH p152-155

Saint Cadog and the mouse
  SHEPPARD – WELSH p149-151

Saint Crispin and the old one
  MINCIELI – TALES p125-128

Saint Cuddy and the gray geese
  LEODHAS – THISTLE p39-45

Saint Elmo's fire
  Twins in the sky

Saint Francis and the wolf
  VITTORINI – OLD p102-105

Saint Gabre Manfas and his animals
  DAVIS – LION'S p162-166

Saint George and the dragon
  JACOBSON – FIRST p23-26
  WILLIAMS – OLD p256-264

Saint John's day
  The king who slept
  The princess on the glass hill

Saint Lawrence Island
  The sea otter girl

Saint Leger-Gordon, Ruth E.
  Some white witchcraft

Saint Margery Daw
  MANNING – PETER p39-42

Saint Martin and the honest man
  COLUM – STONE p36-43

Saint Michael and the idle husband
  NAHMAD – PEASANT p28-33

Saint Neot
  MANNING – PETER p59-63

Saint Nicholas. *See* **Nicholas, Saint**

The saint of children
  SUN – LAND p97-99

Saint Patrick and the Hill of Tara
  COLUM – STONE p90-96

Saint Peter and his trombone
  JAGENDORF – GYPSIES p47-51

Saint Peter's horses
  CARPENTER – HORSES p109-114

Saint Quien Sabe
  ROSS – MEXICO p75-86

Saint Sava and the devil
  ČURČIJA – YUGOSLAV. p165-169
  SPICER – DEVILS p110-117

Saint Valentine's day
  MY BOOK HOUSE v. 1 p209.

Saints
  See also names of saints
  The beginning of the Serbian uprising
    against the Turks
  The boy who became pope
  The burro Benedicto
  The crowza stones
  The great festival
  The home of the saints
  How Papantla got its patron saint
  Joan of Arc
  The lizard's big dance
  The lost saints
  Our Lady of Guadalupe
  Tlacuache the saint
  The virgin of Honduras

—Hairs
  Pietro Bailliardo

Sakunaka, the handsome young
man
    TRACEY – LION p122-127

Salakhbai and the fox
    MASEY – STORIES p28-37

Salamanders
    The fairyland of science

Salesmen and salesmenship
    Sean na Scuab

Saliva
    The man who sold a ghost

Salkey, Andrew
    John Connu Rider

Sally's blue ball
    MY BOOK HOUSE v. 1 p188-189

Salmon
    The adventures of a water baby
    The five swallow sisters
    The giant who had no heart in his
        body
    Loki's punishment
    The lonely house
    The silver penny
    The tinker of Tamlacht
    The young Finn

The salmon's revenge
    GREEN – LEPRECHAUN p53-62

Salt
    Amin and the ghul
    Caporushes
    Discovery of salt
    The donkey with sponges and the
        donkey with salt
    The dragon of the well
    Esben and the witch
    The fountain of youth
    The infallible salt bird
    The lady who put salt in her coffee
    Love like salt
    The magic mortar
    The mill at the bottom of the sea
    The mill that grinds at the bottom of
        the sea
    The most necessary thing in the world
    The most precious gift
    Old strong charms
    The princess who loved her father
        like salt
    The pudding that broke up the preach-
        ing
    Some impatient mule-drivers
    Temba's bag of salt
    Tortoise and the lizard
    Who put the salt in the sea?
    Why the ocean is salty
    Why the salt is far away
    Why the sea is salt

Salt
    BATCHELOR – SUPER. p9-12
    LEACH – SOUP p114-117
    THOMPSON – ONE p420-423

Salt and bread
    U. N. – RIDE p163-165

The salt at dinner
    URE – RUMANIAN p74-83

Salt birds
    The infallible salt bird

The salt-grinding millstones
    SEKI – FOLKTALES p134-138

The salt Welsh sea
    JONES – WELSH p216-222

A salty tale
    EDMONDS – TRICKSTER p91-98

Salute to the trees
    CATHON – PERHAPS p197.

Salutes
    Three silly schoolmasters

Salvador and the coyote
    ROSS – MEXICO p15-34

Salvador and the goat
    ROSS – MEXICO p3-14

Sam Dan and the government doctor
    MATSON – LONGHOUSE p93-95

Sam Patch
    GORHAM – REAL p128-135

Sam Patch, the jumpin' man
    JAGENDORF – UPSTATE p40-47

Sam Patch's last leap
    SHAPIRO – TALL p69-79

Samba the coward
    LANG – OLIVE p36-45

Samoa
   The sky-eater

Samoyeds (people). *See* Nenetz (people)

Samson and the doll in green and brown
   ALMEDINGEN – KNIGHTS p165-
   178

Samuel (Biblical)
   The boy Samuel

Samurai
   The goblin-spider

A San and the Wang Liang
   BONNET – CHINESE p133-138

San fairy Ann
   FARJEON – LITTLE p248-262

The San Joaquin Valley of California
   JOHNSON – WHAT p278-280

San Nicolas (islands)
   The lost woman of San Nicolas

Sancta Clara, Abraham A. (Ulrich
   Megerle)
   The young fox and the old fox

Sand
   Dates to Cairo
   The gold dust that turned to sand
   The holy mountain
   The laughing statue
   The mast of sand
   The merman's revenge
   Michael Scott and the demon
   Ole shut-eyes, the sandman
   The rich widow of Stavoren
   The stubbornest man in Maine
   The Texas sandstorm
   Why there are shadows on the moon
   The wizard of Reay's book of magic

The sand-carrier crab
   VO-DINH – TOAD p89-97

Sand in the bag
   JAGENDORF – SAND p135-137

Sandals. *See* Shoes-Sandals

Sandburg, Carl
   The fog
   How the letter X got into the
   alphabet
   The village of cream puffs

Sandpipers
   Adventures of a water baby
   Coral sea contest
   The theft of fire
   The whale and the sandpiper
   The wise owl

Sandstorms. *See* Sand

Sandy MacNeil and his dog
   LEODHAS – GAELIC p17-29
   LITTLEDALE – GHOSTS p139-152

Santiago and the fighting bulls
   McNEILL – DOUBLE p23-29

Santo Domingo de Guzman
   A sacred pledge should not be broken

Sao birds
   The bird that told tales

Sapphires
   The dutiful daughter
   The happy prince

Sapsuckers
   Coyote's new hairdo

Sara Crewe
   BURNETT – RACKETTY p59-138

Saracens
   The battle of Roncesvalles

Sardinia
   Cenerentola
   Zezolla and the date-palm tree

Sarita and the Duendes
   ROSS – MEXICO p175-190

Sartak-Pai
   DEUTSCH – TALES p17-27

Sasquatches
   A trio of lost monsters

Sassafras
   Billy Beg and the sassafras switch

Satan. *See* Devil(s)

Satin bird
   NORLEDGE – ABORIGINAL p34.

Satires
  The real princess
  The swineherd

Saturday, Sunday, Monday
  WILLIAMS – ROUND p109-116

Satyrs
  King Herla

Satyrs
  JACOBSON – LEGEND. p39-40

Saudi Arabia
  Abunwas, the wit

Saul
  The witch of Endor

Sausages
  A box on the ear
  The mouse and the sausage
  The mouse, the bird and the sausage
  The ridiculous wishes
  The tale of the little sausage and the
    little mouse
  The three wasted wishes
  The three wishes

Sava, Saint
  Saint Sava and the devil

Saved by a turkey
  CREDLE – TALL p34-39

The saving of a soul
  BARASH – GOLDEN p114-117

Sawmills
  The three clever brothers

Sawyer, Ruth
  The flea
  The frog
  The princess and the vagabone

Sawyer, Ruth
  JOHNSON – PRINC. p316.

Saxons
  VANSITTART – DARK p90-102

Sayings
  See also Proverbs
  Charms
  Company
  Death
  The farm
  Folks
  Fortune telling
  Friends
  In china the people say
  In Russia the people say
  Insects and other critters
  King Solomon's pupils
  Love and sentiment
  Luck
  Medicinal
  Money
  The moon
  Odds
  Proverbs and sayings
  Religious
  Signs and sayings
  Snakes
  Some New England superstitions
  The stupid hunter and the crafty bird
  The three precepts
  Wishes

Saynday and smallpox: the white man's
gift
  MARRIOTT – AMER. p143-146

Scabbards
  How Arthur gained Excalibur
  The secret-keeping boy
  The treachery of Morgan Le Fay

Scales
  Catherine and the Fates
  Melisande

Scalps
  The red swan

Scandalous affairs of a baronet and a
tavern maid
  TAFT – PROFILE p67-75

Scandinavia
  See also names of Scandinavian
    countries
  Asmund, Authun, and Odd
  Authun and the bear
  The buried treasure
  The captain's goose
  The cat on the dovrefell
  The dog king in Denmark
  East of the sun and west of the moon
  The fox and the cock
  The giant who had no heart in his
    body
  The girl who didn't know how to spin,
    The Little People of Scandinavia
  Grim and the merman

Scandinavia (*Continued*)

Hali becomes a poet
The hauntings at Thorhallstead
How Sigurd awoke Brynhild
Jesper who herded the hares
King Hrolf and the bear's son
The Kraken
Lad Carl
Lord Peter
The neck
The Nis
The pancake
The people of Mols
Per and the north wind
Porridge with a troll
Prince Lindworm
The seven foals
A stork is not always a stork
The stupid fellow
Sungold and the remarkable cow
The tale of Nornagest
Thorsteinn Shiver
The three billy-goats gruff
The town mouse and the country
mouse
Tricky Peik
True and untrue
Volund the smith
White-toes and Bushy-bride
Why the bear has a stumpy tail
Why the sea is salt
The wild swans

—Gotland
The troll's invitation

The scarecrow
HEADY — JAMBO p13.

Scarecrows
Do scarecrows scare crows?
The jolly tailor who became king
Teeny-tiny
Terence the tailor's jacket

Scarface
HAZELTINE — HERO p447-459

The scarlet maple
CATHON — PERHAPS p210-213

Scars
The little scarred one
Scarface
Star-boy and the sun dance

Scarves (scarfs)
The beautiful blue jay
Musk and amber
My candlestick

Paddy and the leprechaun
The princess and the scarf

Scavengers
The jackal who tried to copy the lion

Scharrelmann, Wilhelm
Deep insight
Dream behind bars

Scheer, George F.
SCHEER — CHEROKEE p80.

Scheherazade
MOZLEY — ARABY p8-11

Schiller, Johann
The legend of William Tell

Schiller, Wilhelm
A German evening

Schmidt, Bernhard
The golden crab

Schmidt, Rosalie Petrash (illus.)
TOOZE — THREE p64.

The scholar and the thieves
SUN — LAND p124-125

The scholar of Kosei
COURLANDER — TIGER'S p11-15

The scholar, the monkey, and the goat
DOBBS — MORE p90-92

Scholars
Akiba and the daughter of Kalba
Sabbu'a
Ask a foolish question
The curse on the only son
David Alroy
The day of the scholars
The encounter with death
Goha the wise
A good neighbor
How God's wheel turns
Kwang Heng, the book lover
The legend of Zon U-Czi
The lion and the sage
The lion-makers
A meeting of scholars
Monkey fat
The mysterious path
Nails
Nguyen Ky and the singer
Pietro Bailliardo
A portion in Paradise

Scholars (*Continued*)
The princess and the scarf
Rabbit Joseph Della Reina
The royal monument pavilion
The sage and the mouse
The sage in the cave
The story of Mordecai and Esther
The talking talisman
Torah and honor
The transformed donkey
The treasure
Which was witch?
The wise man's pillow
The witless imitator

The scholars and the lion
COURLANDER — TIGER'S p72-75

Scholarship
The advantages of learning
Judge not the vessel

A school for crocodiles
TURNBULL — FAIRY p110-116

School is over
MY BOOK HOUSE v. 3 p27.

School luck
LEACH — LUCK p19-21

A school of sea monsters
McHARGUE — BEASTS p85-97

The schoolmaster and the devil
SPICER — DEVILS p63-71

Schoolmasters. *See* Teachers

Schools
The goat that went to school
Oeyvind and Marit, a story of Norway
The old father who went to school
Sara Crewe
Stormy lifts anchor

Schopenbauer, Arthur
The porcupines

Science
See also names of sciences
The fairyland of science
The learned young professor

Scissors
The best wish
The bride-price for Olwen
The companion

The magic mirror
The white bear
White-bear-King-Valemon

Scissors
JACOBS — EUROPE. p31-33

Scissors grinders
Ting-a-ling-ling

Scoffing
Ifor the scoffer

Scollard, Elizabeth
Goldfinches

Scorn. *See* Ridicule

Scorpions
Horus the avenger
The pavilion of peril

Scot, Reginald
Disbelief

Scotland
See also Hebrides, Scottish
The adventures of Iain Direach
The Ailp king's children
Ainsel
Andrew and the mermaid
Assipattle and the giant sea serpent
The auld cailleach's curse
The beginning of the Fians
Big fox and little fox
The black bodach
Black Colin of Loch Awe
Black Roderic
The blue cap
The Blue men of the Minch
The bride from the sea
The bride who out talked the water
  kelpie
The brownie o' Ferne-Den
The brownie of Jedburgh
The brownie of Rothiemurchus
Bruce and the spider
The cock and the fox
Conan's punishment
The courage of Mairi
David Wright and the fairies
The death of Diarmaid
The dropping-cave
The crowned bells of the abbey
The eagle and the wren
The faery flag of Dunnegan
Fairy workmen
The farmer and the fairy hillock
The fate of the sons of Usnach

Scotland (*Continued*)

The Fians asleep in the Great Rock
The fiddlers of Strathspey
Finlay the hunter
Finn and the young hero's children
Finn MacCool
Fionn's journey to Lochlan
The fisherlad and the mermaid's ring
The fisherman and the seal maid
The five friends
The flitting of the ghosts
The fox and the bird
The fox and the little bannock
The fox and the wolf
The fox and the wolf and the keg of butter
The gambling ghosts
Gathering song of Donuil Dhu
Geordie and the ten-shilling Jock
The ghost that didn't want to be a ghost
The giant bones
The giant who took a long time to grow
The good crawford
The good housewife and her night helpers
The good housewife and her night labors
The grateful old cailleach
The green isle
The gudewife's midnight labours
The herdsmen of Cruachan
Hind horn
The honest ghost
The house that lacked a bogle
How Fionn found his sword
How Ian Direach got the blue falcon
How Mackay first brought fire into the world
How Michael Scot went to Rome
How Tammas Maciver Macmurdo-Maclennan met his match
How the wolf lost his tail
Ian Direach
Introduction (LEODHAS – TWELVE)
James Gray and the Clashnichd
Jamie Watt and the giant in the tea-kettle
John Macdonald and the kelpie
John Reid and the mermaid
King James and the questions
The kingdom of the green mountains
The lads who met the highwaymen
The lady's loaf-field
The Laird o' Co
The Laird of Abbotsford
The lass and her good stout black-thorn stick
The last of the giants

The legend of Eilean Donan castle
The lion and the unicorn
The little grey goose
The little one
Loch Ness: last laugh?
The Loch Ness monster
Lod, the farmer's son
Luran and the fairies
The maid of the waves
The man who didn't believe in ghosts
The man who helped carry the coffin
The man who walked widdershins round the kirk
The marriage of the robin and the wren
The master thief
The meal mill at Eathie
The missing fog bell
The monster of Loch Ness
Morag and the water horse
The old laird and his dogs
The oyster catcher, the duck and the hen
The page boy and the silver goblet
Peerifool
The piper of Keil
The piper of Sutherland
The ploughboy poet
The prince and the giant's daughter
The Red Ettin
Robert Bruce, Scotland's hero
The robin and the wren
Sandy MacNeil and his dog
The sea captain's wife
The seal catcher and the merman
The secret of heather-ale
The shepherd and the fairy hillock
The shepherd who fought the march wind
The silver chanter of the MacCrim-mons
Sir Michael Scott
The smith and the faeries
The son of the hen-wife
Stine Bheag o' Tarbat
The stolen bairn and the Sidh
The stranger and the miller
The tail
The tailor and the devil
The tailor in the church
The tale of a debt repaid
The tale of Bonnie Baby Livingston
The tale of Columba and the angel
The tale of Dick o' the cow
The tale of Lang Johnnie Mor
The tale of the Earl of Mar's daughter
The tale of the famous flower of Servingmen
The tale of the Gaberlunzie man
The tale of the heir of Linne
The tale of the hump-backed men

Scotland (*Continued*)

The tale of the king's jewel
The tale of the knight and the
shepherd lass
The tale of the lady of the rock
The tale of the Laird of Logie
The tale of the lay of the Amadhain
Mhor
The tale of the lay of the smithy
The tale of the Lochmaben harper
The tale of the rescue of Kinmont
Wullie
The tale of the riddle sent to Bruce
The tale of the royal exiles
The tale of the sons of Cathmor
The tale of the three brothers
The tale of the wrath of God
The tale of the crofter told
Tales from the episode of the Fians
Tam Lin
Tamlane
Thomas the rhymer
The three banshees
The three sons of Gorla
The tree that walked
True Thomas
Twelve great black cats and the red
one
The voyage of the Lass of Glasgow
The walking boundary stone
The wee bannock
Wee robin's Christmas song
The wee, wee mannie
The wee, wee mannie and the big, big
coo
The weeping lass at the dancing place
Whippety stourie
The white pet
The wicked house of Duncan Mac-
bain
The wild ride in the tilt cart
Willie and the pig
The Witch of Laggan
The witches' reel
The Wizard of Reay's book of magic
The young Irish lad from the hiring
fair
The young Lord of Lorn
The young Tamlin

—**Battles**
The man o' the clan

—**Clans**

—**Campbell**
Black Colin of Loch Awe

—**Grant**
The lairdie with the heart of
gold

—**MacAlpine**
The Ailpein bird, the stolen
princess, and the brave knight

—**MacCrimmon**
The silver chanter of the
MacCrimmons

—**MacDonald**
A bauchan in the family
The daughter of the King Ron
The ghost of Haniesh
MacDonald, the fool of the
family
The man o' the clan
The man who missed the Tay
Bridge Train

—**MacIntosh**
A bauchan in the family

—**MacKay**
How MacKay first brought fire
into the world

—**MacLeod**
A bauchan in the family
The clever lad from Skye
The faery flag of Dunnegan
The ghost of Haniesh
MacDonald, the fool of the
family

—**Highlands**
The Ailpein bird, the stolen prin-
cess, and the brave knight
The beekeeper and the bewitched
hare
The bogles from the howff
The daughter of The King Ron
The gay goss-hawk
The lairdie with the heart of gold
the laird's lass and the gobhas's son
the lass that couldn't be frighted
Little John and the water horse
Spin, weave, wear
The woman who flummoxed the
fairies

—**History**
Bannockburn
The holy relic of Bannockburn
The man o' the clan

—**Lowlands**
The changeling and the fond young
mother
The lass who went out at the cry
of dawn
Michael Scott and the demon
Saint Cuddy and the gray geese

, **North**
Childe Rowland and the King of
Elfland

Scotland–North (*Continued*)
Moorachug and Meenachug
The white pet
–Perthshire
Clach Mor and the witch of Badennoch

Scott, Sir Walter
Gathering song of Donuil Dhu
Heap on more wood
Hie away, hie away
The Laird of Abbotsford

The Scotty who knew too much
GREEN – BIG p210-211

Scouts
Buffalo Bill
How rabbit lost his tail

Scrapefoot
JACOBS – MORE p94-97

"Screams"
Miss Jenny Jones
Oh, deary me
Shall I be so?
You'd scream too

Scrolls
The mystery of the scroll

The sculpin and the fox
GILHAM – BEYOND p117-120

Sculptors and sculpture
Antonio Canova
The golden lion
Goola-willeels the topknot pigeons
The marvelous doors, The Little
People of Italy
Pygmalion . . . The marvelous statue
Strike there!
The text

Scurvyhead
BARBEAU – GOLDEN p58-72

Scylla and Charybdis
GREEN – GREEKS p64-65
JACOBSON – LEGEND. p34-35

Scythes
Jonas and the boggart of Brixworth
The magic scythe, The Little People
of Iceland

Scythia
Guardians of hidden treasure

Se-Osiris and the sealed letter
GREEN – TALES p115-125

Sea
See also **Boats; Ocean; Ships and ship-
building;** etc.
The adventures of a water baby
All about Columbus
The angakok and the mother of seals
Ants
Atlantis
Beowulf fights a battle with the sea
The bird of seven colors
The boat that would not move
Bobby Shafto's gone to sea
A boy on the high seas
The boy who crossed the great water
and returned
A bride for the sea god
The bride from the sea
Captain Fokke of Holland
The child and the Mariner
A Christmas song at sea
Clytie
The coral comb
The cowskin boat
The crab that tried to swallow the
moon
The dancing fires of Saint Elmo
David Copperfield and little Em'ly
The eight perfect ones on the ocean
The far horizon
The figurehead
Figureheads
The flying Dutchman
The friendly sharks
The frog that swallowed the ocean
A game of dice
The ghost ship
Gulliver's travels to Lilliput
Here we sail so fast and free
Heroes of the sea
How the cows flew across the sea
How the fiddler crabs came to be
The hunting dog and the purple fish
I saw a ship a-sailing
The ice ship in the hot sea
The jewels of the sea
Kelea, the surf princess
The kelpie
Kirsten McVurich
Little blue apron
The little book
Little Gulliver
The little king on the Viking ship
Look, see the boat!
The lost city of Ys

Sea (*Continued*)

The luck of the sea and the luck of
  the mountain
Lyonesse
The magic mortar
The maiden of Deception Pass
The maker of maps
Martin Grogan and the merrow
The merman
The mill that grinds at the bottom of
  the sea
The miracle on the Jaffa Sea
The missing fog bell
Mr. Hampden's shipwreck
The monkey bridge
The moon-child
My boat
Mythical beast of the sea
The neck
Nicola Pesca
O sailor, come ashore
Of speckled eggs that birdie sings
Oh and alas
Old Stormalong
The old woman swims the sea
Pelops and Poseidon
Phantom ships
A pound of tobacco
Prince Finn the fair
The rabbit who crossed the sea
Rub-a-dub-dub
The sailor and the sea serpent
The seals
The seven seas
Sindbad the sailor
Sixpence for a breeze
Solitude
A song of Drake's men
Strange folk of the sea
The strange ship of Captain Fokke
Sweet and low
Terrors of the sea
The three waves
A tropical morning at sea
The two crabs
The two youths whose father was
  under the sea
Unlucky passengers
The voyage of Maeldiun
The voyage of the Lass of Glasgow
A wnaderer's song
The whale that smoked a pipe
What makes moonshine on water
When I was down beside the sea
Whistle the wind
The white horse of Volendam
Who put the salt in the sea?
Why the sea is salt
Why the sea moans
Why the tides ebb and flow

The wife of Bjorn Bryn
Wind and tempest
The wonderful horse
Wurrunna's trip to the sea
Yiankos
Young Paul

—**Kings and Queens**
  How the herring became king of
    the sea
  Noodlehead and the flying horse
  Sadko
  The speedy messenger

—**Mysteries**
  Mysteries of the sea

The sea
  MY BOOK HOUSE v. 3 p155.

The sea-bell
  TOLKIEN – READER (Part 4)
  p57-60

The sea captain
  LEODHAS – SEA p161-177

The sea captain's wife
  LEODHAS – TWELVE p107-125

Sea-cows
  The laughing merman

Sea fever
  MY BOOK HOUSE v. 8 p37a.

Sea folk
  See also names of sea folk
  Andrew Moir and the seal-people
  The fisherman and his soul
  Hema and the goblin-woman
  Ka-Hai and the sorcerer Tama-i-wao
  Mermaids
  Mermen
  My lady sea
  The prince and the vizier's son
  The sea-maiden who had a stone image
    for husband
  Strange folk of the sea
  Three tales of the goblins who lived
    on the sea-bottom
  The three waves
  Why the monsoon comes each year
  The wiliwili trees

The sea gull
  MY BOOK HOUSE v. 5 p111.

Sea gulls
  The first pig and porcupine
  The fisherman

Sea gulls (*Continued*)

The gull
How mussels were brought to the
Creeks
How raven brought fire to the Indians
How the sea gulls learned to fly
Little Gulliver
The lonely house
A sea-song from the shore

Sea heroes
MAYNE – HEROES p61-74

Sea horses
Old Stormalong
The sea shell
A sea-song from the shore
The wonderful horse

The sea king and the fox
CARPENTER – SHIPS p89-99

The sea-king's daughter
PICARD – MERMAID p141-153

The sea knight
WILLIAMS – OLD p329-332

Sea lions
Strong man

The sea-maiden who had a stone image
for husband
WHEELER – HAWAII. p112-124

The sea-mammy
SHERLOCK – WEST p130-134

Sea monsters
See also names of sea monsters;
Serpents
Assipattle and the giant sea serpent
Beowulf fights a battle with the sea
The boy and the sea monsters
The eight perfect ones on the ocean
Four brothers who were both wise
and foolish
The giant who took a long time to
grow
The golden-headed fish
The hungry serpent
Iron, steel and strongest-of-all
King Fergus MacLeide and the wee
folk
The kraken
Loch Ness: last laugh?
The Loch Ness monster
Loki's monstrous brood
The man who killed the sea monster

The "modern" sea monster
The moha moha
The monster of Loch Ness
Monsters of prehistoric times
Monsters of the Middle Ages
The moss-green princess
Of sea-going snakes
Old Stormalong
The oxen and the afanc
The sailor and the sea serpent
A school of sea monsters
Scylla and Charybdis
The sea serpent
The strange adventures of the
cowboy-sailor
Terrors of the sea
Thor and the jotun Aegir
Thor's visit to Hymir
The three-legged jumping giant
The three monsters of the sea
Tola and the sea monster
A trio of lost monsters
The waters beneath: The great river
monster
Why the sea moans
The wild woman of the woods

Sea-nymphs. *See* **Sea-folk;** names of sea
nymphs

The sea of gold
UCHIDA – SEA p11-21

The Sea of Moyle
PILKINGTON – THREE p103-108

The sea of pearls
EKREM – TURKISH p85-91

The sea otter girl
MAHER – BLIND p73-78

The sea, poem of. *See* The poem of the
sea

The sea serpent
LAWSON – STRANGE p180-192
OMAN – ESKIMO p24-26

Sea serpents. *See* **Sea monsters; Snakes**

The sea shell
MY BOOK HOUSE v. 3 p150.

Sea-shells
The sea-bell

A sea-song from the shore
MY BOOK HOUSE p202-203

Sea songs
  A Christmas song at sea
  A song of Drake's men
  A wanderer's song

Sea-trows. *See* **Sea-folk**

Sea-witches. *See* **Sea-folk**

The seal catcher and the merman
  BAKER – TALKING p63-70

The seal fisher and the roane
  BRIGGS – PERS. p152-156

Seal people
  Andrew Moir and the seal-people
  The fisherman and the seal maid
  Kirsten McVurich
  The seal fisher and the roane
  The wife of Bjorn Bryn

Seals
  The adventures of Alexander Selkirk
  The angakok and the mother of seals
  The bride from the sea
  The daughter of the King Ron
  The Eskimo widow . . . And her
    strange son
  Freya's wonderful necklace
  The great fish
  Kirsten McVurich
  MacCodrum of the seals
  The night of the full moon
  The Sedna legend
  The wife of Bjorn Bryn

The seals
  LAWSON – STRANGE p56-80

Seamstresses. *See* **Dressmakers**

Sean na Banoige
  O'SULLIVAN – FOLK. p192-204

Sean na Scuab
  O'SULLIVAN – FOLK. p248-249

Sean Palmer's voyage to America with
  the fairies
  O'SULLIVAN – FOLK. p209-220

The search for Sita
  HAZELTINE – HERO p381-399

The search for the land of bliss
  SUN – LAND p44-50

The search for the magic lake
  BARLOW – LATIN p68-81

The search: who gets the chief's daughter?
  COURLANDER – KING'S p28-31

The seashell sings
  FARJEON – SILVER p188-192

Seashells. *See* **Shells**

Seashore. *See* **Beaches**

Seasons
  See also names of seasons
  The fairy grotto
  Full moons
  The king and the shepherd
  Stealing the springtime
  The twelve months
  Urashima Taro
  Urashima Taro and the princess of
    the sea
  Why there are four seasons in the year
  The young Urashima

Seaweed
  Through the needle's eye

Sechrist, Elizabeth Hough
  How the moon and the stars came to
  be

The second sorrow of story-telling. *See*
  The children of Lir

The second task: Mr. Snake. *See* Tiger
  story, Anansi story

The secret commonwealth
  GARNER – GOBLINS p83-90

The secret-keeping boy
  MANNING – GLASS p50-62

The secret meeting at Shishi ga Tani
  McALPINE – JAPAN. p35-45

The secret of heather-ale
  WILSON – SCOTTISH p46-48

The secret of Kaboniyan
  SECHRIST – ONCE p78-80

The secret of the hidden treasure
  JAGENDORF – KING p265-269

The secret room
  WILLIAMS – FAIRY p149-152

The secret royal inspector, Bag Mun-
Su
  INS-SÖB – FOLK p54-55

The secret store
  ELLIOT – SINGING p56-71

Secret tokens prove ownership
  O'SULLIVAN – FOLK. p245-247

A secret told to a stranger
  WALKER – DANCING p51-57

The secretive little boy and his little
sword
  ILLYES – ONCE p102-112

Secrets
  The boy with the golden star
  The cartman's stories
  The crystal mountain
  A dead secret
  The farmer who went to plough
  Father big-nose
  Giving away secrets
  The heather beer
  Keloglan and the ooh-genie
  King March has horse's ears
  King Solomon's pupils
  The lost gift
  The lucky circle
  March has horse's ears
  March's ears
  Midas . . . The greed for gold
  The miller and the fairies
  Pappa Greatnose
  The snake prince
  Tar-sa's luck
  The Tsar Trajan's ears
  The wood cutter's son and the two
    turtles
  The young man who married a fairy

The securing of light
  CURRY – DOWN p22-37

Security
  Daniel in the lions' den
  The forest wolf and the prairie wolf
  The mouse and the snail
  Old Johnny Appleseed

Sedna (mother of seals)
  The angakok and the mother of seals

The Sedna legend
  MELZACK – DAY p27-34

See a pin
  LEACH – SOUP p62-64

See-saw, Margery Daw
  MY BOOK HOUSE v. 1 p51.

See-saw, Sacaradown
  MY BOOK HOUSE v. 1 p18.

The seed of happiness
  EDMONDS – TRICKSTER p86-90

Seeds
  The cuckoo's reward
  Diggory
  How one should carve a goose
  The lazy gardener and the little red
    man
  The magic garden
  Planters' moon

Seeing a brace of rabbits
  REED – TALK. p40.

Seeing far and hearing far
  WITHERS – WORLD p28.

Seeley Simpkins and his bull
  JAGENDORF – SAND p18-21

Seerko
  BLOCH – UKRAIN. p44-48

Segizbai and the little mouse-girl
  MASEY – STORIES p62-64

Selassie, Haile
  The Habasha and the King of kings

Selections from Rabindranath Tagore
  REED – TALK. p37-38

Self-confidence. *See* **Egotism; Self
reliance**

Self-convicted
  HSIEH – CHINESE p44-45

The self-kicking machine
  CREDLE – TALL p89-95

The self-propelled carriage
  THOMPSON – ONE p194-199

Self reliance
  Boots and his brothers
  The boy and the sea monsters
  A boy on the high seas
  Jack the giant-killer

Self-reliance (*Continued*)

The lark and her young ones
The little engine that could
The-little-men-as-big-as-your-thumb-
with-mustaches-seven-miles-long
The little red hen and the grain of
wheat
The necklace
Precocious piggy
The rough rider
Shingebiss
Sir Beaumains, the kitchen knight
The talkative tortoise
The ugly duckling

The selfish giant
MAYNE – GIANTS p204-210
MY BOOK HOUSE v. 4 p50-55

A selfish husband
INS-SÖB – FOLK p191.

Selfishness
Big fox and little fox
The castle in the lake
Chi and Yi
The dog in the manger
The golden gourd
The half-chick
The honey gatherer's three sons
How Yehl, the hero, freed the beam-
ing maiden
Kakui, bird of the night
The little rooster and the little hen
The mallet of wealth
The man who has plenty of good
peanuts
Mother's girl and father's girl
The nightingale and the cotton tree
Ooka and the two first sons
The peasant and the horsemen
Peer Gynt
Pigling and her proud sister
The pot of gold
The queen's necklace
The Red Ettin
The selfish giant
The silver ship
The skipper and the witch
There's always a reason
The three brothers and the black hen
The three goslings
Treasure in the basket
The twelve months
The two sisters

Selkirk, Alexander
The adventures of Alexander Selkirk

Sellar, May, trans.
The golden goose
The goose-girl
Hansel and Gretel
Jorinda and Joringel
Little one, little two eyes and little
three eyes
Rapunzel
Rumpelstilzkin
Snow-white and Rose Red
Snow-white and the seven dwarfs

The seller of dreams
SHEAHAN – HENRY p96-108

Senachie stories
The Ailpein bird, the stolen princess,
and the brave knight
The bogles from the houff
The duaghter of the King Ron
The gay goss-hawk
The lairdie with the heart of gold
The lass that couldn't be frighted
The lass who went out at the cry of
dawn
Spin, weave, wear
The woman who flummoxed the
fairies

Senators
Georgie goes a-sparkin'

Senefru (pharaoh)
The golden lotus

Senmurv (imaginary animal)
Winged wonders

Senor Billy Goat
BELPRE – TIGER p69-72

Senor coyote
EDMONDS – TRICKSTER p77-85

Senor coyote and the dogs
U. N. – RIDE p253-256

Senor coyote settles a quarrel
ROSS – BURIED p89-94

Sense. *See* **Common sense; Knowledge;
Wisdom**

Sense and money
BORSKI – GOOD p51-54

Senses
See also names of senses
The head of brass

Sensitivity
The princess and the pea

Sentiment. *See* **Love**

The sequel. *See* The woman of Llyn-y-fan (3) The sequel

Sequins, Gold
The cats

Serbia
See also **Yugoslavia**
The barren stones
The battle of Kossovo
The battle of Mishar
The beginning of the Serbian uprising against the Turks
The black giant of Luckless River
The brothers Yakshich divide their heirloom
The building of Ravanitsa
The death of the Yugovichi's mother
The devil's apprentice
The egg of fortune
The enchanted cow
The enchanted knife
The fall of Serbia
The finest liar in the world
The friendly animals
Goat's ears
The golden fleece
The golden twins
Ivan of Semberiya
Ivo Senkovich and Aga of Ribnik
The just and unjust brothers
The kind pasha and Mehat the shepherd
King Vukashin's wedding
Kralyevich Marko
Kralyevich Marko abolishes the wedding-tax
Kralyevich Marko and Alil-Aga
Kralyevich Marko and Mina of Kostur
Kralyevich Marko and Mussa Kessedzhiya
Kralyevich Marko and the Arab
Kralyevich Marko and the eagle
Kralyevich Marko drinks wine during the Ramadhan
Kralyevich Marko recognizes his brother's sabre
Kralyevich Marko's death
Kralyevich Marko's ploughing
Kralyevich Marko's wedding

The lame vixon
Little Radoyitsa
The maiden of Kossovo
Maksim Tsernoyevich's wedding
Marko, the champion of Serbian liberty
Milutin, Tsar Lazar's servant
Old Novak and the village elder Bogossav
Outlaw Vukossav's wife
Peahens and golden apples
Prince Marko and a Moorish chieftain
Saint Sava and the devil
The shepherd with the curious wife
The shelpherd's crown
The sick Doytchin
Sultan Murat's challenge
The three wishes
Three wonderful beggars
Tsar Dushan's wedding
Tsar Lazar and Tsaritsa Militsa
Tsar Lazar's supper
The Tsarino's greatest treasure
Urosh and his uncles
Vladimir's adventures in search of fortune
What is "long ago"?
What Ivan Kossantchich saw in the Turkish camp
The yellow-haired witch
The youth who trusted in God

−**History**
The rise and decline of the Serbian kingdom

Serbian knights and outlaws
CURCIJA − HEROES p109-173

Seredy, Kate
Attila the conqueror

The sermon
JUDA − WISE p71-75

Sermons
Any more food?
Butting a sermon
The Hodja preaches a sermon

The serpent
MINCIELI − OLD p42-53

The serpent and the grape-grower's daughter
DELARUE − FRENCH p104-109

The serpent and the peasant
MANNING − BEASTS p65-68

578

The serpent of Carbuncle Hill
TAFT – PROFILE p254-255

The serpent prince
KRUEGER – SERPENT p112-119

Serpents. *See* Sea monsters; Snakes

The serpents and the porcupine
KRUEGER – SERPENT p13-17

The serpent's bride
BERGER – BLACK p15-32

Serraillier, Ian
Suppose you met a witch

The servant and the door
HARDENDORFF – TRICKY p97-99

The servant lass
BAMBERGER – FIRST p60-61

The servant who took the place of his
master
THOMPSON – ONE p215-220

Servants
Ash sweeper and the wishing wand
Baba Yaga
Baba Yaga and the little girl with the
king heart
The blue flame
The bone that testified
The careless master
The carnation youth
Cherry
Cherry of Zennor
Cinderella of New Hampshire
The crafty servant
The crowned snake
Curd ears
The date gatherers
The doctor and his pupil
The dwarf and the cook, The Little
People of Turkey
Faithful John
The giant and his royal servants
The golden-headed fish
Governor Wentworth's search for a
wife
Grandmother Marta
Gwarwyn-a-Throt
Hans and his master
The house damsel
The house with the heads
Hwan and Dang
The innkeeper of Moscow

John the true
Keloglan in the service of the padishah
The Kildare pooka
The king who ate chaff
Lars, my servant
The lass that lost the laird's daughter
The learned men
Left eye, right eye
Mary-Ann and the cauld lad of Hylton
The master and the servant
The master-maid
Master of all masters
A meeting of two servants
Milutin, Tsar Lazar's servant
Mother Sunday
The onion and the rose
The peasant-girl's captive
The peeping servant
The pooka
A poor man's servant
The proud princess
Redcoat the fox
The righteous heir
The sage and the servant
The swan princess
The shepherd's nosegay
Sima who wore the big hat
The sly gypsy and the stupid devil
The stolen ring
The story of Bensurdatu
The story of Zibong
The story of spirits
Strong Gottlieb
The tale of the two cunning servants
The thoughtless abbot
The three citrons
The three golden billy-goats
Tsar Lazar and Tsaritsa Militsa
The Tsar's son and the swan-girl
The two friends
Upa and her admirers
White-faced simminy
The white snake
Willie and the pig
The wise merchant
The wolf and the watch-dog
The wrestling match of the two
Buddhas
Young Kate

Service
The King of Sedo

Sesame seed
Ali Baba and the forty thieves

Set
Horus the avenger
Isis and Osiris

Setna
  The book of Thoth
  Se-Osiris and the sealed letter

Seton, Ernest Thompson
  Why the chickadee goes crazy once
  a year

Setoun, Gabriel
  Jack Frost

Settlers. *See* **Pioneers**

The seven crazy fellows
  SECHRIST − ONCE p141-143

The seven dead men of the Venetian
lagoon
  MORRIS − UPSTAIRS p59-62

The seven enchanted pigs, and the
houndwhelp of Iroda
  PILKINGTON − THREE p56-62

The seven foals
  JONES − SCAND. p52-59
  MANNING − BEASTS p148-157

The seven-headed giant
  HOLLADAY − BANTU p42-46

Seven iron-souled slippers
  McNEILL − DOUBLE p16-22

The seven mice
  PICARD − GERMAN p167-170

The seven proud sisters
  PICARD − GERMAN p115-119

The seven ravens
  BAMBERGER − FIRST p179-182
  ILLYES − ONCE p264-268

The seven seas
  LAWSON − STRANGE p11-13

The seven Simeons Simeonovich
  McNEILL − DOUBLE p41-48

(The) seven Simons
  MANNING − GLASS p10-21
  SIDEMAN − WORLD'S p591-609

The seven sisters
  JAGENDORF − UPSTATE p93-96

Seven sons
  LEACH − NOODLES p47-48

The seven stars
  HATCH − MORE p79-87

The seven stars of the north
  INS-SOB − FOLK p12.

The seven wishes
  SPICER − OWL'S p29-40

The seven-year blessing
  SPICER − KNEELING p45-57

The seven years of blessing
  NAHMAD − PORTION p30-32

The seventh father of the house
  ASBJØRNSEN − NORW. p13-14

The seventh princess
  FARJEON − LITTLE p142-148
  ROSS − BLUE p11-19

"Seventh son"
  Where Arthur sleeps

The seventh son
  SPICER − KNEELING p74-91

A severe punishment
  JOHNSON − WHAT p169-170

Seward Peninsula
  Whale of a tale

Sewing
  The devil and the seamstress
  The frog
  The horned witches
  Leealura and Maleyato
  Spin, weave, wear
  Vassilissa the beautiful
  The widow's daughter
  The witch aunts

Sextons
  Dutch Peter and the fortunetelling
    tailor
  The ghost of Peg-leg Peter
  Is he fat?
  The king o' the cats
  The parson and the sexton

Sgeulachdans
  The beekeeper and the bewitched hare

  , Christening
    The stolen bairn and the sidh

Sgevlachdans *(Continued)*

, Wedding
The bride who out talked the water
kelpie
The fisherlad and the mermaid's
ring
The laird's lass and the gobha's son

Sha-ks
Land, water and wind

The shadow
WITHERS – WORLD p69.

The shadow boys
AYRE – SKETCO p102-111

Shadow-bride
TOLKIEN – READER (Part 4) p52.

The shadow on the wall
GRAHAM – BEGGAR p71-77

Shadow people
The lonely house
The shadow boys

Shadows
The boy in the land of shadows
Everywhere you go
The greedy stallkeeper and the poor
traveler
A horse afraid of his shadow
Kahukura and the fairies
The little black box
The man who lost his shadow
Sly Peter at the fair
The time of deep darkness
Why the woodchuck comes out in
midwinter
The young wife of Nam Xuong

Shadrack, Meshach, and Abednego . . .
The fiery furnace
UNTERMEYER – FIRE. p113-116

The shaggy dog
LEACH – RAINBOW p190-191
WITHERS – I SAW p36.

Shah Abbas and the cobbler
NAHMAD – PEASANT p15-19

Shah Ismail and the Turkmen maiden
EKREM – TURKISH p66-84

Shah Meram and Sade Sultan
EKRAM – TURKISH p92-102

The Shah-Nameh (Book of Kings). *See*
The story of Rustum, the hero of
Persia; The world's great epics

The Shah weaves a rug
CARPENTER – ELEPHANT'S p31-
39

Shakespeare, William
As it fell upon a day
As you like it
At Christmas
Good morrow, 'tis St. Valentine's
day
Hark, hark! Bow-wow!
In the Springtime
Jog on, jog on
King Stephen was a worthy peer
A midsummer night's dream
The peddler's song
Rhymes from Shakespeare
St. Valentine's day
The tempest
Under the greenwood tree
When that I was but a little tiny boy
The winter's tale

Shakespeare, William
Down by the River Avon

–Macbeth
The tale of the royal exiles
The witch! The witch!

Shaking
Alas!

The shaking of the pear tree
MY BOOK HOUSE v. 3 p146-147

Shall I be so?
LEACH – RAINBOW p217-218

Shame
The hemp smoker and the hemp
grower

Shamrocks
The four-leafed shamrock and the
cock
Kate Mary Ellen and the fairies

Sha-Nameh. *See* The world's great epics

The Shankilla
DAVIS – LION'S p136-137

Shannon, Monica
The absent-minded tailor

The "Shannon" and the "Chesapeake"
MAYNE – HEROES p71-73

Share-croppers
  Sharing the crops

Sharing. *See* **Charity: Generosity**

Sharing the crops
  COURLANDER –TERRA. p104-107

The shark in the milky way
  THOMPSON – HAWAII. p40-44

Sharks
  The adventures of Bona and Nello
  The battle that tilted the sea
  The boy Pu-nia and the king of sharks
  The boy who became king of the sharks
  The boy who would eat lobsters
  The friendly sharks
  King of the restless sea
  A lot of silence makes a great noise
  The monkey and the shark
  The monkey's heart
  The rabbit who crossed the sea
  The raven and the sharks
  The saga of Stretch Garrison
  Spears of lightning
  The thunder man

Sharpe, Mary E.
  Dame Wiggins of Lee

Sharpness
  Jack the giant-killer
  The thirteenth son of the king of Erin

The sharpshooter
  DELARUE – FRENCH p45-49

Shaving
  The bride-price for Olwen
  Kuluile, the dancing girl
  Ooka and the barbered beast

Shawls
  The weeping lass at the dancing place

Shawneen and the gander
  ARBUTHNOT – TIME p310-316

Shaydoola
  BULATKIN – EURASIAN p106-110

The she-bear
  MANNING – PRINCES p76-83

She-wa-na, deity of the elements
  RUSHMORE – DANCING p121-125

Shears. *See* **Scissors**

Sheba, Queen of
  King Solomon and the Queen of Sheba
  The tree from Adam's grave
  The wise king and the little bee

Shedlock, Marie, L.
  The blue rose

Shee (faries)
  The lass that lost the laird's daughter

The Shee an Gannon and the Gruagach Gaire
  PILKINGTON – SHAM. p161-168

Sheehogues (Little People)
  Gulersh and the princess of France

Sheem
  SCHOOLCRAFT – FIRE p66-76

Sheep
  The adventures of Bona and Nello
  Aiming too high
  All my lambkins and all my bear cubs
  The ant, the lamb, the cricket, and the mouse
  Augustine the thief
  Baa, baa, black sheep
  The bag of lies
  The best wish
  Billy Beg and the sassafras switch
  The billy goat and the sheep
  A Bohemian evening
  The castle of the three giants
  The cat, the cock and the lamb
  Charlotte's web; Wilbur's boast
  Clouds
  The companion
  Dame Wiggins of Lee
  Damian and the dragon
  David, the shepherd boy
  Derby ram
  The Derbyshire ram
  The devil in red flannel
  Eight leaves of story (8) Cadwalader and all his goats
  The escape of the animals
  The farmer's boy
  The fighting rams

Sheep (*Continued*)

Fionn in search of youth
The five friends
The foolish wolf
Gentlin' the ram
A German evening
The giant of the mount
The hill of the bellowing oxen
How Kwaku Ananse won a kingdom
  with a grain of corn
The hungry giant
The imposter
Is he fat?
The journey to Toulouse of the
  animals who had colds
The lad and the north wind
The lad who went to the north wind
The lady of the lake
The lamb with the golden fleece
A lesson for the bat
Little Bo-Peep
Little Boy Blue
Little Peppino
The magic pipe
Magicians of the way
The maiden in the country under-
  ground
Mary and the Christ-child
Mary had a little lamb
Minnie and Mattie
The nine white sheep
No man with the Cyclops
Old pipes and the dryad
The out-foxed fox
Over the hill to feed my sheep
The peasant and the sheep
The pig, the goat and the sheep
Pleiad and star of dawn
Polyphemus, the Cyclops
Popo and the coyote
The ram and the leopard
The ram and the pig who went into
  the woods to live by themselves
The ram with the golden fleece
The Red Etin
Reynard the fox
Salakhbai and the fox
The shepherd's nosegay
The shepherd's pipe
The silver bell
Silver leaves and golden blossoms
The simpleton
Sinko's luck
Sleep, baby, sleep
The sleepy song
Sly Peter's revenge
A song for Easter
The song of the Darby ram
A story of three brothers
The stupid wolf

Surprising adventures of Don Quixote
  of La Mancha
The tailless jackal
A tall turnip
There was a little man and his name
  was Gice
Three fat ewes for three fine hounds
The three walnuts
Thunder and lightning
Thus I guard my mother's lambkins
The two step-sisters
Uncle Bouqui and little malice
The white pet
Who is strongest?
Why God made the dog
Why sheep does not come in out of
  the rain
Why the hare's lip is split
The wild boar and the ram
The wolf
The wolf and the lamb
The wolf and the ram
The wolf plays shepherd
The wolf's food
The young shepherd
The youth who wanted some fun

—Eyes
  The poor girl who stepped out
    golden flowers

, Golden
  The golden lamb
  The golden sheep

, Mountain
  West country boy

—Skins
  Little Johnny Sheepskins
  The wolf in the ram's skin
  The wolf wears a sheepskin

—Tails
  The tail

—Wool
  How spider taught women to
    weave

The sheep and the pig that made a home
  MY BOOK HOUSE v. 2 p145-148

The sheep is the cousin of the ox
  INS-SOB — FOLK p31-32

The shell grotto of Nienoort
  LEEUW — LEGENDS p139-145

Shelley, Percy Bysshe
  The cloud

Shelley, Percy Bysshe
  The rebel

Shellfish
How the mosquitoes came to Oneata
Mr. Crow and the mussel

Shells
The boy of the red twilight sky
The conch shell of Ram
Little sister and the Zimwi
Longshanks, girth, and keen
The man who loved Hai Quai
The mermaid and the simpleton
The princess and the fisherman
The ring in the seashell
The sea shell
The seashell sings
The shell grotto of Nienoort
The singing drum and the mysterious
 pumpkin
The story of a man in a shell
The wild woman of the woods

, **Conch**
The golden prince of the conch
 shell

, **Cowry**
The task of the deputy chief
Iso-no-Kamimaro

, **Golden**
The beautiful weaver and the
golden shell

Shelves
The golden casket

Shemiaka the judge
THOMPSON – ONE p395-397

Shepard, Odell
The goldfinch

The shepherd and the dwarf
BAMBERGER – FIRST p82-83

The shepherd and the fairy hillock
SHEPPARD – SCOT. p14-16

The shepherd and the king's daughters
BELTING – THREE p105-109

The shepherd and the princess
BELPRE – TIGER p63-66

The shepherd of clouds
SHEAHAN – HENRY p3-22

The shepherd of Silverstead
BOUCHER – MEAD p43-48

The shepherd, the king, and the southwest wind
PICARD – LADY p14-32

The shepherd who fought the March wind
LEODHAS – TWELVE p89-105

The shepherd who understood the
language of the animals
ILLYES – ONCE p15-16

The shepherd with the curious wife
SPICER – LONG p11-28

Shepherds and shepherdesses
See also **Sheep**
Akiba and the daughter of Kalba
 Sabbu'a
Aram and the shepherd
The beacon light
The boy who cried wolf
The brave shepherd boy
The bull of Uri
The capricious month
The castle of the three giants
The children's crusade
Clever Manka
The coffin that moved itself
The comb, the flute and the spinning
 wheel
The count and the little shepherd
The country swain
David and Goliath . . . The shepherd
 boy and the giant
David, the shepherd boy
Djamukh–son of a deer
Einion and the Fair family
The emperor's questions
The enchanted palace
Endymion . . . The sleeping shepherd
Fairy gardens
The first of May
The flea
The fox as shepherd
Golden
The golden lamb
The good sword
The grateful lion
The griffon
Hali becomes a poet
The hauntings at Thorhallstead
Hildur the elf queen
How stars and fireflies were made
How the queen of the sky gave gifts
 to men
The hungry giant
The imposter
The jinni's magic flute
The judgement of the shepherd
Katcha and the devil
The kind pasha and Mehat the shep-
 herd
The king and the bishop

584

Shepherds and shepherdesses (*Continued*)

The king and the shepherd
King John and the abbot
King John and the Abbot of Canterbury
The king who slept
Kristina and the devil
The lady and the toad
The lake maiden
The lamb with the golden fleece
The language of animals
Lazy Peter and the king
A letter to my love
Little Bo-Peep
Little Boy Blue
The little frog of the stream
Little Peppino
The little shepherd's dream
Little shepherd's song
Little Tom Thumb
Luck and wit
The magic mirror
The magic pipe
The magic poncho
March and the shepherds
Mary and the Christ-child
Mellitot and Iolanda
The miller and the water sprite
Old Surly and the boy
Over the hill to feed my sheep
Patient Griselda
The peasant pewit
The place of strife
Prince Loaf
The princess and the shepherd
The princess on the glass mountain
Princess Sicilia and the shepherd
The princess who wanted to play with
the stars
Queen crane
The silver bell
The silver river
Sly Peter's revenge
The soldier's return
The sword of the stone
The tale of the Balaton
The tale of the knight and the shepherd lass
The tale of the silver saucer and the russet apple
Thus I guard my mother's lambkins
To your good health
Torah and honor
The tune of Iolo ap Hugh, The Little People of Wales
The winter's tale
The wolf plays shepherd
The wolf turned shepherd
The wolf wears a sheepskin
The wonder of Skoupa

The young Lord of Lorn
The young shepherd
The youth who wanted some fun

The shepherd's boy
ARBUTHNOT – TIME p205.

The shepherd's crown
SPICER – LONG p116-129

The shepherd's dog and the wolf
GREEN – BIG p22-23

The shepherd's nosegay
FILLMORE – SHEPHERD'S p72-81
HAVILAND – CZECH. p49-66

The shepherd's pipe
MINCIELI – TALES p76-79

The sheriff complains to the king
MANNING – ENGLISH p135-138

Sheriffs
See also **Bailiffs**
Freddy and his fiddle
Little Freddie with his fiddle
Little John and the Sheriff of
Nottingham
Old man Elias and the dancing sheriff
Sir Richard at the lee and the abbot

The sheriff's shooting match
MANNING – ENGLISH p131-135

A Sherlock Holmes of the Steppes
DEUTSCH – MORE p65-68

Sherlock, Philip Manderson
SHERLOCK – IGUANA'S p98.

Sherman, Frank Dempster
The goldenrod

Sherwood, Merriam
The wedding of the Cid's daughter

Shetland Isles
Andrew Moir and the seal-people
Black Roderic
The bride from the sea
The kelpie

Shields and shield-makers
The adventures of Manawyddan
King Arthur . . . The shield and the
hammer
The knights of the silver shield

Shields and shield-makers (*Continued*)
The spear and shield of Huantan
The trials of Dyfed

A shilling for a lie
WITHERS – WORLD p32.

Shinga-mamba
BURTON – MAGIC p105-107

Shingebiss
MY BOOK HOUSE v. 2 p96-100

Shingling the fog
WITHERS – WORLD p85.

Shinny games
The Indian shinny game

Shiny tales of Vincennes
JAGENDORF – SAND p127-131

Ship models
The three waves

The ship that sailed on water and on land
WITHERS – WORLD p9-17

Shippei Taro
SEKI – FOLKTALES p33-36

Shippei Taro and the monster cat
CARPENTER – DOGS p128-135

Ships and shipbuilding
See also **Boats; Sailing and sailing vessels;** etc.
The adventures of Ciad
The ash lad and the good helpers
Baldpate
The black art
The cat-chalice of Vlaardingen
La Cenerentola
Dick Whittington and his cat
The dutiful daughter
The flying ship
The ghost ship
The golden horse
The golden lion
The goldfish
Hardy Hardback
How the peasants bought wisdom
I saw a ship a-sailing
Lady Eaton's curse
The land ship
The lily and the bear
Look, see the boat!
Merman Rosmer
The palace of the night
The pursuit of the hard man

Salt
The seven Simons
The "Shannon" and the "Chesapeake"
Sif's golden hair
The son of the baker of Barra
The tale of the ghost ship
The three clever brothers
The three sons of the King of Antua
The three teeth of the king
The wonder ship and ship's crew
The wreck of the Palatine

, Diamond
The crystal kiosk and the diamond ship

, Flying
The flying ship

–"Palatine"
Mysteries of the sea

–Passengers
Unlucky passengers

, Phantom
The Flying Dutchman
The ghost ship
The phantom fire ship
The phantom ship
The phantom ship of the Hudson
Phantom ships

–"Seabirds"
Mysteries of the sea

, Silver
The silver ship

, Viking
The little king on the Viking ship

The shipwrecked prince
CARPENTER – ELEPHANT'S p184-194

Shipwrecks
Black Bartelmy
The classic traveler's yarn: The tale of the shipwrecked sailor
The kingdom of ocean
The little mermaid
Mr. Hampden's shipwreck
No man with the Cyclops
The palace of the night
The piper
The Prince of Coucy
The princess and the scarf
The sailor and the sea serpent
Sindbad the sailor
The story of the shipwrecked sailor
The tempest
The voyage of the lass of Glasgow
The wreck of the Palatine

A shiver of ghosts
   BIRCH – CHINESE p62-79

Shizuka's dance
   HAZELTINE – HERO p428-446

Shlemiel, the businessman
   SINGER – WHEN p55-69

Shlemiels
   The first shlemiel

The shoemaker
   LOWE – LITTLE p47-49

The shoemaker and the elves
   MY BOOK HOUSE v. 3 p95-98
   SIDEMAN – WORLD'S p464-468

Shoemakers
   The adventures of Manawyddan
   The banshee's birthday treat
   The blacksmith in the moon
   Born to be rich
   The chief astrologer
   Clever Tom and the leprechaun
   The cobbler
   The cobbler and the dwarfs
   The cobbler astrologer and the forty thieves
   The cobbler's deity
   Cobblers do not judge above the shoe
   The demon mason
   The devil's gifts
   Doctor know-all
   The doctor who knew everything
   The dwarf and the goose
   Dwarf long nose
   The fairy shoemaker
   The field of ragwort
   The fortunate shoemaker
   Guiseppi, the cobbler
   Hanging at Wessaguscus
   Hans the tailor and the talking animals
   Jack Hannaford
   The king and the shoemaker
   Lazarus and the dragons
   The leprechaun and the wheelbarrow
   The little black man
   Lleu and the flowerface
   Mirza and the ghul
   My lady sea
   Old Nick's bridge
   The origin of the wrekin
   The poffertjes pan
   The red slippers of Honiem
   Saint Crispin and the old one

   Scissors
   Shah Abbas and the cobbler
   The Siamese pepper cure
   The simple-minded bootmaker as a miraculous healer
   A spadeful of earth
   Snout the dwarf
   The three brothers and the treacle toffee
   The three laughs of the leipreachan
   The three traveling artisans
   The trials of Dyfed
   The wandering cobbler
   The wee folk
   The wild man
   The young piper, The Little People of Ireland

   –Apprentices
      Mece and the shoemaker's daughters

   , Fairy
      Song of the leprechaun or fairy shoemaker

The shoemaker's apron
   FILLMORE – SHEPHERD'S p185-192

The shoemaker's dream
   LEEUW – LEGENDS p21-27

Shoe-shine boys
   Happy Hans

Shoes
   Aruman, a hero of Java
   Billy Beg and the bull
   Buh fox's number nine shoes
   The cobbler and the dwarfs
   The covetous minister
   The cowherd with the belt of skin
   The danced-out shoes
   The donkey's tail
   Fair, brown, and trembling
   A ghost at the door
   The girl who played a trick on the devil
   Golden shoes
   If my shoe is narrow, what matter if the world is wide
   Janey's shoes
   Juan Bobo and the princess who answered riddles
   Kari Woodencoat
   The king and the shoemaker
   Lars, my lad!
   Leaving paradise
   The little bull calf
   The little one
   Nella's dancing shoes

Shoes (*Continued*)

Simple and the princess
There was an old woman who lived
    in a shoe
Twelve dancing princesses
Ugly boy
The unlucky shoes of Ali Abou
Utzel and his daughter Poverty
Water drops
A woman had a rooster

, **Baby**
The magic baby shoes

—**Boots**
Alberto and the monsters
The banshee's birthday treat
The boots that never wore out
The cow that ate the piper
The demon mason
The devil duped
General Moulton's boot
Jonathan Moulton and the devil
Lost and found
Maid Lena
The oni and the three children
Saint Martin and the honest man
Seven iron-souled slippers
Soria Moria castle
The thirteenth son of the king of
    Erin
Three times and out
The wonderful tree

, **Golden**
Golden shoes
The princess with the golden
    shoes
The princess with the twelve pair
    of golden shoes
The story of Mead Moondaughter

, **Iron**
The king who slept
Lionbruno
The woodsman's daughter and the
    lion

, **Magic**
The flying ship
King Fergus and the water-horse
The lost half-hour
Throwmount and Oakpull

—**Sandals**
The king and his seven sons
The magic sandals
The magic sandals of Hualachi
Old Nick's bridge
Rhodopis and her gilded sandals

—**Slippers**
Cenerentola
La Cenerentola

Cenerentola or Cinderella
Cinder-maid
Cinderella
Cinderella or The little glass slipper
The dancing princesses
The girl with the red-rose slippers
The golden slipper, the magic ring,
    and the twigs
The innkeeper's daughter
The jeweled slipper
Katie Woodencloak
The king of the leaves
Little Mukra
The princess of the mountain
The princess who hid her slippers
The princess's slippers
The red slippers of Honiem
Rushen Coatie
Seven iron-souled slippers
The story of little Mukra
Tam and Tessa
A willow wand and a brocade
    slipper
Zezolla and the date-palm tree

Shoes
LEACH — SOUP p96-100

Shoes don't match
LEACH — NOODLES p22.

Shoes for a journey
WALKER — WATER. p24-25

Shon Shenkin
SHEPPARD — WELSH p164-166

Shopkeepers. *See* **Merchants**

The short horse
CREDLE — TALL p64-66

Shoulder-straps
The Indian Cinderella
The little scarred one

The shouts on the Hill of Midkena
PILKINGTON — THREE p73-77

Shovels
Biting Marion
The proper way to lay the table

Showmen. *See* **Circus**

The shrewd peasant
BULATKIN — EURASIAN p125-128

Shrewd Todie and Lyzer the miser
SINGER — WHEN p3-13

Shrewdness. *See* **Cheating; Cleverness; Trickery**

Shrews
Five in a glove
The lemur and the shrew

Shrines
The anger of Sande-Nyana
The bridge of heaven
The demon giant of Mount Ariake
Ijapa goes to the Osanyin shrine
The piece of straw
The prince and the Sphinx
The shepherd's crown
The snail Choja

Shrove-tide
How Michael Scot went to Rome

Shrovetide
TASHJIAN – ONCE p51-55

Shrubs
Indian legends of shrubs in our gardens

Shuttles
Graylegs
Mother Holle
The spindle, the shuttle, and the needle

Si Jura carved a house post
BELTING – STARS #5

Siam
See also **Thailand**
The bad prince
The boy who wouldn't give up
The cat with the crooked tail
The days of the first monkeys
The farmer and his son
The four brothers
The great festival
The home of the saints
The lion and the fox
The magician and the bandits
The man with no nose
The men and the monkeys
The night of the full moon
The pigeon, the deer and the turtle
Princess September
The royal musician
The two friends
The two kings
The wicked weasel
The wise merchant

The Siamese pepper cure
MORRIS – UPSTAIRS p27-41

Sian-Tek, Lim
The legend of the Narcissus
Why crabs are flat

Siberia
The girl in the moon
How the bee got his bumble
Introduction (GINSBURG – MASTER)
The lost song
The maiden Suvarna
The one who wasn't afraid
The owl's punishment
Why dog has a fur coat and woman has seven tempers
Why there is thunder and lightning

—**Altai Tatars** (people)
The old man and his bush

—**Cheremis** (people)
Who is strongest?

—**Chukchees** (people)
Creator makes ––
The girl who overpowered the moon
The maiden and the moon
The sun drives copper-colored reindeer

—**Diomedes** (islands)
A legend of Kotzebue

—**Dolgan** (people)
The singing man

—**Evenk** (people)
Unyany

—**Ket** (people)
A long night's sleep

—**Khanty** (people)
Khasynget's grandmother

—**Koryak** (people)
The ninwits

—**Mansi** (people)
The wise owl

—**Nanay** (people)
The good son

—**Nenets** (people)
The master of the winds

—**Nivkh** (people)
The hunter and the tiger

—**Selkup** (people)
The mistress of fire

Siberia–Yakut (people) (*Continued*)

−**Yakut** (people)
The crane's feather

−**Yakurs** (people)
The girl and her water buckets

−**Yukagir** (people)
The enemy's tent

Sibu, the god-who-builds
BELTING − STARS #14

Sicily
Catherine and her fate
Count Roger and the Fata Morgana
The fountain of Arethusa
The girl who kissed the peach-tree
Nicola Pesce (Pesca)
Princess Sicilia and the shepherd
The return of the Spring
Robert of Sicily . . . the proudest king
Scylla and Charybdis
The truthful peasant
The winter's tale

−**Syracuse**
Damon and Pythias; the most
faithful of friends

The sick boy, the greedy hunters, and
the dwarfs, The Little People of North
America
BELTING − ELVES p27-34

The sick Doytchin
CURČIJA − HEROES p126-130

The sick lion and the fox
LA FONTAINE − FABLES p46-47

Sidamo (country)
The gold-lined donkey

Siddiqui, Ashraf
SIDDIQUI − TOON. p159.

Sidhe (Sidhean)
See also **Shee**
Midir and Etain
The stolen bairn and the sidh
Tam Lin

Siebenburgen
The clever blue tit and the fox
Cinder Joe becomes king
The cock and the neighbour's hen
The duckling's journey
The farmer who went to plough
The fox and the hedgehog

The fox and the snail
The millet seed
Mittens the cat
The princess in the fiery tower
The princess who saw everything in
her kingdom
The story of the five fingers

The siege of joyous Gard
PICARD − STORIES p263-273

Siegfried
PICARD − GERMAN p42-85

Siegfried . . . who knew no fear
UNTERMEYER − FIRE. p136-143

Siengmieng, the minister
KRUEGER − SERPENT p144-150

Sierra Leone–Temme (people)
How a boy got a baboon

Sieves
The well of the world's end

Sif's golden hair
AULAIRE − NORSE p44-49

The sigakok bird
SECHRIST − ONCE p24-25

The sigh of Gwyddno. *See* Eight leaves
of story (2) The sigh of Gwyddno Long-
shank

Sigiris Sinno, the mighty one
TOOZE − WONDER. p55-58

The sign at the smithy door
SPICER − DEVILS p91-101

Signs (folklore)
Charms
Company
Death
The farm
Folks
Fortune telling
Friends
Insects and other critters
Love and sentiment
Luck
Money
The moon
Odds
Religious
Snakes
Some New England superstitions
Warts

590

Signs (folklore) (*Continued*)

The weather
Wishes

Signs and sayings
JOHNSON – WHAT p209-213

Sigourd
How Sigurd awoke Brynhild

Sikakokubh and the hunting dog
COURLANDER – PEOPLE p27-45

Silence
The bride who would not speak
Fairy mother
Intelligence and luck
Knowledge and luck
A lot of silence makes a great noise
Meinrad and the ravens
The Poffertjes pan
The pot of gold
The prince who made the silence speak
The princess who was dumb
The secret of the hidden treasure
The silent maiden
The silent princess
The six swans
Sudden silence
Thomas the rhymer
The three ravens
Trim Tram Turvey
The turtle who loved a monkey
The unwashed pot
Why women always wash the dishes

The silent drum
HOLDING – SKY p87-98

The silent maiden
HEADY – WHEN p72-76

The silent princess
LANG – OLIVE p131-149
WILSON – GREEK p58-64

Silesia. *See* **Bohemia**

Silian the stork
PRIDHAM – GIFT p67-80

Silk
Catherine and her fate
The laughing statue
The legend of the mulberry tree

, **Golden**
Grayleg

Silkworms
The legend of the mulberry tree
Tape measure

Sill, Edward Rowland
Opportunity
A tropical morning at sea

Silliness. *See* **Fools and Foolishness**

The silly fellow who sold his beard
JAGENDORF – GYPSIES p17-23

The silly goose
REED – TALK. p36.

The silly goose war
DURHAM – TIT p37-40

The silly jelly-fish
HEARN – JAPANESE p36-41

Silly John
LEACH – NOODLES p26-27

The silly men of Russia
JAGENDORF – GYPSIES p122-128

The silly owls and the silly hens
JAGENDORF – KING p94-101

Silly Saburo
SAKADE – JAPAN. p45-48

The silly slave
EDMONDS – TRICKSTER p68-76

Silver
CATHON – PERHAPS p112.

Silver and silver mines
See also **Silverware**
The alchemist
The boy who took care of the pigs
The castle in the cornfield
The castle of the three giants
The cock and the neighbour's hen
Dwarf stories
The enchanted castle in the sea
Fir cones
The grateful ass
The handsome apprentice
The heavenly lovers
John Shea and the fairy treasure
Katie Woodencloak
The lady of Tylwyth Teg
The magician Palermo
Mr. Frost
The mop servant
Of silver and men

Silver and silver mines (*Continued*)

Old Gally Mander
Old Nanny's ghost

Silver and silver mines
The tale of a Pakistan parrot
The tinderbox
The tiny bird and the king
The treasure chamber of Rhampsinitus
The two fools
The witch tree of the North country

The silver bell
MANNING – DWARFS p89-94

The silver chanter of the MacCrimmons
SHEPPARD – SCOT. p69-71

The silver curlew
FARJEON – SILVER p109-113

The silver hare in a box
JABLOW – MAN p23.

The silver jug
LEACH – NOODLES p73-75

Silver leaves and golden blossoms
PRIDHAM – GIFT p116-123

The silver on the hearth
U. N. – RIDE p60-62

The silver penny
MANNING – WIZARDS p86-94

The silver river
GRAHAM – BEGGAR p91-95
SUN – LAND p39-41

The silver ship
GRAY – MAINLY p109-123

Silversmiths
The bird which laid diamonds
The borrower

Silverware
See also **Spoons** etc.
Buttercup

Sima who wore the big hat
MARMUR – JAPAN. p25-30

Simon and his rocky acre
JORDAN – BURRO p76-79

Simont, Marc
LEACH – RAINBOW p318.

Simple and the princess
PRIDHAM – GIFT p21-29

The simple maid of Hunsingoo
LEEUW – LEGENDS p127-132

The simple-minded bootmaker as a miraculous healer
ILLYES – ONCE p34-41

Simple-minded Jeanne
DELARUE – FRENCH p85-90

"Simple Simon"
The interesting history of old Mother Goose

Simple Simon met a pieman
MY BOOK HOUSE v. 1 p50.

Simple Wang
BONNET – CHINESE p123-126

The simpleton
PUGH – TALES p13-19

A simpleton of the family
HSIEH – CHINESE p47.

Simpleton Peter
REEVES – ENGLISH p103-113

Simpletons. *See* **Fools and foolishness; Stupidity**

Simpletons
MEHDEVI – PERSIAN p33-43

Simpson, Agnes
To kill a king, from "News from Scotland"

Simurgh (Sinmurv)
The story of Zal

Sin
Buh mouse testifies
The coffin that moved itself
The companion
The donkey who sinned
The friar on Errigal
The greater sinner
The hermit and the devil
The magic bird
The man in the moon
The man who struck his father
The peace between the leopard and the antelope

592

The sin of a saint
BRASH – GOLDEN p128-135

Sinbad and the roc
MOZLEY – ARABY p49-55

Sinbad the sailor
See also Sindbad the sailor
MOZLEY – ARABY p46-55

Sinbala (island)
The cloud horse
The invisible silk robe
The king's dream
The wonderful wooden peacock
flying machine

Since when there have been no more
heroes in holy Russia
DOWNING – RUSSIAN p75-78

Sincerity
A mother's advice

Sinclair, George
Sweden

Sinclair, Henry of Roslyn, Earl of the
Orkneys
Lord Sinclair and the Zeno brothers

Sindbad the sailor
SIDEMAN – WORLD'S p769-828

Sindhu
TURNBULL – FAIRY p158-167

"Sing a song of sixpence"
The interesting history of old Mother
Goose

Sing a song of sixpence
MY BOOK HOUSE v. 1 p49.

Sing before breakfast
BATCHELOR – SUPER. p19-20

The Sing-Bonga beheld men
BELTING – STARS #4

Sing, sing!–What shall I sing?
MY BOOK HOUSE v. 1 p31.

Sing something
WITHERS – WORLD p89.

Singers and singing
Anansi and turtle and pigeon
And I dance mine own child
The ass's promise
The beautiful blue jay
Benizara and Kakezara
Brer goat and brer lion
Brother Anansi and Sir Peacock
Bucca Dhee and Bucca Gwidden
The cannibal and his sweet singing
bird
Cardiff town
The children of Lir
The clever children and the king
tailor
Connla of the golden hair
Cottontail's song
The crumb in the beard
The dancing water, singing apple, and
speaking bird
The delicate daughter
Dorani
The earrings
The enemy's tent
The fisherman and his soul
The girl and the crocodile
The girl on the hill
The girl on the rock
The girl who forgot her hoe
The gull
How coyote brought back people
after the flood
How men learned to sing songs
How the groundhog lost his tail
Hwan and Dang
Kalevala, land of heroes
Kamiyo of the river
The king who slept
Little sister and the Zimwi
The Loreley . . . The siren's song
The lost song
The magic herdboy
The magician's revenge
The maiden in the tower
The man who turned into a hyena
Mapandangare, the great baboon
Mario and the yara
The musicians
Navahchoo
Nguyen Ky and the singer
Niassa and the ogre
Nyangara, the python
Of speckled eggs the birdie sings
Orpheus and Eurydice
The peasant and the baron
Pierre Jean's tortoise
The pots that sang
The pretty bird
The princess who hid her slippers
Rabbit and tortoise
Rapunzel

Singers and singing (*Continued*)

The raven and the crow
Sadko
Sakunaka, the handsome young man
Saturday, Sunday, Monday
The shah weaves a rug
The shepherd, the king, and the south-
west wind
Six-and-four
Skillywidden
A song for the new chief
The song of Gimmile
The songstress and the fairies
The sweetest song in the woods
The three sisters and the cannibals
The troubadour and the devil
Tsimbarume, the hardened bachelor
The water sprite
Why groundhog's tail is short
Why spider has a little head and a big
behind
The woman and the mouse
The wrong song
Yiankos
Young Kate

The singing bell
SPICER – OWL'S p41-55

The singing bone
THOMPSON – ONE p344-345

The singing chameleon
ELLIOT – SINGING p1-17

The singing drum and the mysterious
pumpkin
ARNOTT – AFRICAN p179-185

The singing fir-tree
MÜLLER – SWISS p210-212

The singing man
GINSBURG – MASTER p81-103

The singing flute
U. N. – RIDE p226-230

The singing geese
COTHRAN – WITH p23-25

The singing man
GINSBURG – MASTER p81-103

The singing sack
ALEGRIA – THREE p107-110

Sinko's luck
HAMPDEN – GYPSY p113-118

Sinuhe
The adventures of Sinuhe

Sir Beaumains, the kitchen knight
MY BOOK HOUSE v. 10 p8-18

Sir Bevis of Hampton
PICARD – TALES p111-129

Sir Gammer Vance
See also Sir Gammer Vans
REEVES – THREE unp.

Sir Gammer Vans
JACOBS – MORE p43-45
WILLIAMS – FAIRY p206-208

Sir Gawain and the green knight
WESTWOOD – MEDIEVAL p63-79

Sir Goldenhair
BARBEAU – GOLDEN p73-89

Sir Launfal
WESTWOOD – MEDIEVAL p41-49

Sir Michael Scott
SHEPPARD – SCOT. p109-112

Sir Orfeo
WESTWOOD – MEDIEVAL p129-
137

Sir Perceval
MAYNE – HEROES p75-91

Sir Richard at the lee and the abbot
MANNING – ENGLISH p116-119

Sir Walter Raleigh
BALDWIN – FAVOR. p30-35

Sirene, the mermaid
GREY – SOUTH (1) p28-31

Sirens
The Loreley . . . The siren's song
Scylla and Charybdis
The tale of Liban the siren

Sirens
JACOBSON – LEGEND. p26-27

Sirius
The dog and the giant

Sissa and the troublesome trifles
EDMONDS – TRICKSTER p5-13

594

The six companions
  WILSON – GREEK p42-52

The six horsemen
  CARPENTER – AFRICAN p187-194

Six sillies
  SIDEMAN – WORLD'S p177-181

The six swans
  MY BOOK HOUSE v. 7 p126-131
  SIDEMAN – WORLD'S p475-483
  THOMPSON – ONE p135-136

Sixpence for a breeze
  LAWSON – STRANGE p156-161

Size
  Errato di Barletto
  Get ready, get set, go
  The giant and the mite
  Giant pear and giant cow
  Ha! Tio rabbit is bigger

Sjaelland, Denmark (island)
  Frigg and the goddesses

Skade, the ski-goddess
  AULAIRE – NORSE p91-95

Skaters and skating
  A curious tale

Skeletons
  See also Bones; Skulls
  How coyote brought back people after the flood
  The smoker

The skeleton's song
  SEKI – FOLKTALES p145-148

A sketch of Ion Creanga's life
  CREANGA – FOLK p167-170

Sketco begins his wanderings
  AYRE – SKETCO p30-42

Sketco finds his brothers
  AYRE – SKETCO p86-101

Skiing
  Skade, the ski-goddess

Skill. *See* Cleverness

The skillful huntsman
  ARBUTHNOT – TIME p364-367

Skillywidden
  BRIGGS – PERS. p95-96
  MANNING – PETER p7-10

The skinned goat
  RANKE – GERMANY p22-23

The skipper and the dwarfs
  MANNING – DWARFS p73-77

The skipper and the witch
  JAGENDORF – NEW p8-12

Skippers, Sea. *See* Captains, Sea

The skull
  COURLANDER – TERRA. p74-75
  MANNING – GHOSTS p38-42

Skulls
  The courage of Mairi
  Vasilia the beautiful

The skunk in Tante Odette's oven
  CARLSON – TALKING p3-16

Skunks
  Fickle Miss Frog
  How the beaver came to build their homes in the water
  Peter Rabbit decides to change his name
  The rescue of fire
  The Scotty who knew too much
  The wicked polecat

Sky
  The enchanted sky
  Henny-Penny
  How the earth was made to fit the sky
  How the moon and stars came to be
  Introduction (CAMPBELL – MAORI)
  The jolly tailor who became king
  The mole's bridegroom
  The moon raised the sky
  The morning and the sunset that lighteth up the sky
  Rainbow and the autumn leaves
  The sky-eater
  Spider's web
  A trip to the sky
  The tubmaker who flew to the sky
  Why sun and moon live in the sky
  Why the sky is high

  , Red
    The boy of the red twilight sky

596

The sky at night
    MY BOOK HOUSE v. 7 p72.

The sky beings: thunder and his
helpers
    MARRIOTT – AMER. p33-40

Sky-bright axe/Paul Bunyan
    STOUTENBURG – AMER. p11-23

The sky-eater
    HOLDING – SKY p11-23

The sky-foogle of Chillicothe
    JAGENDORF – SAND p54-56

The sky god's daughter
    COURLANDER – KING'S p36-40

The sky people
    HEADY – WHEN p62-67

Slander. *See* Gossip

The slave of the lamp
    MANNING – WIZARDS p65-66

The slave of the ring
    MANNING – WIZARDS p73-77

Slaves and slavery
    Androcles and the lion
    The dolphins of Celebes
    High John the conqueror
    How monkey king became a slave
    How the miser turned into a monkey
    How the parrots helped the women
    Ivan of Semberiya
    King Johnny
    The king who slept
    The knight of the almond blossom
    The legend of Tchi-Nice
    Maimonides and the king's dream
    Malati and the prince
    The merchant's son and the slave
    Old master and okra
    The princess who was rescued from
      slavery
    The riddle
    The sad tale of three slavers
    The silly slave
    The stag prince
    The stone of patience
    Stone patience and knife patience
    Who put the salt in the sea?

The slaying of Hector
    HAZELTINE – HERO p26-34

The slaying of Siegfried
    PICARD – GERMAN p42-58

The slaying of the suitors
    GREEN – GREEKS p74-75

Sleds and sled races
    The sleigh ride
    A strange sled race

Sleep
    See also Hibernation; Superstitions–
      Sleep
    Ah Tcha the sleeper
    The city of the winter sleep
    Down to Arabia
    Endymion . . . The sleeping shepherd
    The journey to the land of the dead
    The king who could not sleep
    The kingdom of the Green Mountains
    Late
    Little Johnny
    Longshanks, girth, and keen
    Magicians of the way
    The never never land
    Old boss, John, and the mule
    Rip Van Winkle; the strange little men
      of the mountain
    The spirit of slumber
    Sybaris . . . Life of luxury
    Tavadan and the fire giant
    The three golden eggs
    The three plagues of Britain
    The three year sleeping boy
    The treasure of Tacoma
    Why some trees are evergreen

Sleep
    BATCHELOR – SUPER. p100-105

Sleep, baby, sleep
    MY BOOK HOUSE v. 1 p20.

Sleep, my baby! Sleep an hour
    MY BOOK HOUSE v. 1 p137.

Sleep my baby! Sleep my baby!
    MY BOOK HOUSE v. 1 p78.

Sleep, sleep my little one!
    MY BOOK HOUSE v. 1 p146.

Sleep, sleep, sleep!
    MY BOOK HOUSE v. 1 p80.

(The) sleeping beauty
    LINES – NURSERY p67-78
    MY BOOK HOUSE v. 6 p11-16
    PERRAULT – CLASSIC p9-31

(The) sleeping beauty (*Continued*)
    PERRAULT – FAMOUS p35-52
    SIDEMAN – WORLD'S p664-673
    THOMPSON – ONE p111-112
    TUDOR – TASHA p11-15

The sleeping beauty in the wood
    ARBUTHNOT – TIME p97-99
    HAVILAND – FRANCE p60-75
    PERRAULT – COMPLETE p1-15

"Sleeping beauty" stories
    Wild rose

The sleeping prince
    MANNING – DAMIAN p165-171

The sleepless dragon
    JACOBSON – FIRST p17-22

Sleepy feet
    LEELEY – WORLD p55-57

The sleepy song
    MY BOOK HOUSE v. 1 p119.

Sleigh, Barbara
    A cat and a broom

The sleigh ride
    FELTON – TRUE p30-39
    HATCH – MORE p199-213

Sleighs
    The gull
    Kalevala, land of heroes
    Over the river
    The snow-queen
    The water dwellers
    –Bells
        The bells
        Jingle bells, jingle bells

Slingshots
    David and Goliath

A slip of the tongue
    GRAY – INDIA'S p45-48

Slippers. *See* Shoes–Slippers

Sloes
    The twins and the snarling witch

The sloogeh dog and the stolen aroma
    AARDEMA – STORY p24-31

Slovakia
    Joe Magarac
    Joe Magarac the steel man
    King Svatopluk and the three sticks
    A wanderer with a dog

Slovenia
    The three lemons

Slow train to Arkansas
    COURLANDER – TERRA. p28-30

Slowness. *See* Tardiness

The sly gypsy
    BORSKI – GOOD p66-67

The sly gypsy and the stupid devil
    SPICER – DEVILS p43-52

Sly Peter at the fair
    PRIDHAM – GIFT p63-66

Sly Peter's revenge
    PRIDHAM – GIFT p84-94

The sly thief of Valenciennes
    BARBEAU – GOLDEN p121-138

Slyness. *See* Trickery

Small folk. *See* Little People; etc.

The small men and the weaver
    MANNING – JONNIKIN p68-73

The small people's cow
    MANNING – PETER p156-165

The small red feather
    BURTON – MAGIC p109-111

Small white stones
    HAMPDEN – GYPSY p127-131

Smallpox
    Lady Eleanor's mantle
    Saynday and smallpox: The white
        man's gift
    The waters beneath: The underwater
        village

Smart Dai-adalla
    JAGENDORF – KING p144-148

The smart daughter
    PUGH – TALES p105-115

The smart husband and the smarter
wife
JAGENDORF − NEW p175-182

Smart Sam'l Danny
JAGENDORF − SAND p37-39

The smart woman of Kennebunkport
JAGENDORF − NEW p26-29

Smart working man, foolish boss man
JAGENDORF − KING p31-33

Smell, sense of
Do you know how the ants were dis-
covered?
Legend of how ants came to earth
To pay through the nose

The smell of money for the smell of food
O'SULLIVAN − FOLK. p233-234

Smereree
YOUNG − HOW p95-100

Smiles
See also **Laughter**
How Yehl, the hero, freed the beam-
ing maiden
The language of animals
The wind and the sun

Smiling girls, rosy boys
MY BOOK HOUSE v. 1 p30.

The smiling innkeeper
DAVIS − LION'S p68-69

Smith, Albert William
The giant-nonsense verse

Smith, John
Pocahontas
The story of a princess

Smith, Stevie
The river god (of the River Mimram)

The smith and the faeries
WILSON − SCOTTISH p107-114

Smiths. *See* **Blacksmiths**

Smoke
The first mosquito
Prince Loaf
The stone lute

The smoke horse
CARPENTER − HORSES p164-171

The smoker
GARNER − GOBLINS p175-177

Smoking
See also **Tobacco**
How grasshopper came to be and men
obtained tobacco
How whale happens to smoke a pipe
A pound of tobacco

The smoking mountain
ROSS − MEXICO p62-74

Smolicheck
FILLMORE − SHEPHERD'S p87-93

Smolligosters, etc.
GORHAM − REAL p166-173

The snail Choja
SEKI − FOLKTALES p82-90

Snail, snail
MY BOOK HOUSE v. 1 p132.

Snails
The adventures of a water baby
The butterfly's ball
The dinner that cooked itself
Four-and-twenty-tailors
The fox and the snail
From a moral alphabet
Kantjil holds a festival
The mock turtle's song
The mouse and the snail
The mud-snail fairy
Old Shellover
Snail, snail

The snake
KRYLOV − 15 p33-35
MANNING − RED p127-131

The snake and its benefactor
VO-DINH − TOAD p29-34

The snake and the dreams
U. N. − RIDE p154-158

The snake and the toad
COBBLE − WEMBI p38-40

The snake chief
ARNOTT − AFRICAN p186-194

The snake crown
MULLER − SWISS p147-153

The snake in the bottle
DAVIS – LION'S p23-26

The snake king
ARNOTT – TALES p94-106

Snake magic
ARNOTT – AFRICAN p85-100

The snake monster
MANNING – JONNIKIN p91-94

Snake-pits
The little duck
The twelve wild ducks

The snake prince
LANG – OLIVE p105-114

Snake story
WITHERS – WORLD p82.

The snake that swallowed a girl
CARPENTER – SOUTH p144-150

The snake who bit a girl
TRACEY – LION p6-9

Snakes
See also **Sea monsters**; titles beginning
with Serpent
Abdune and the friendly snake
Adrian and Bardus
All stories are Anansi's
Allah will provide
Anansi and snake the postman
Anansi borrows money
The ancient land of Tigre
Ashoremashika
The bachelors and the python
The bad prince
Bahram and the snake prince
The basilisk, king serpent
Bears in the sky
The bell of Monte Pino
The boy who played the flute
The Brahmin and the villain
Bubber the giant brown-and-yellow-
snake
Buh Rabbit's tight necktie
Buya marries the tortoise
A captive snake half dead with fright
The castle of no return
The cat and the prophet
A Catio Indian legend
The cats
The centipede girl
Charles the Great and the snake

The clever squirrel
The crested curassow
The crow and the serpent
The crow in the banyan tree
The crowned snake
The Da-Trang crabs
The deer and the snake
Diamonds and toads
The dogs of Bahloo
The double-headed snake of Newbury
The dutiful daughter
The enchanted castle in the sea
Enmity between man and serpent
The fairies
Fate of the Magicos
The first fire
Flinty
Frogs in the moon
From tiger to Anansi
The golden crow
The good son
The grateful animals and the talisman
The green knight
The groach of the Isle of Lok
The gypsy and the snake
The handsome apprentice
The heart of Princess Joan
How hare asked for wisdom
How men learned to build houses
How night was let loose and all the
animals came to be
How the little black wren got its red
feathers
How the people got fire
The iguana and the black snake
The ingrates
The inseparable friends
Inside again
Isis and the secret name of Ra
Jack who could do anything
The jeweled ring
The judgment of the wind
The Kamiah monster
Keloglan the kindhearted
The king and the Nagas
King Lindorm
King of the serpents
The king who rides a tiger
The king's dream
Koi and the kola nuts
Kuzma get-rich-quick
The labors of Hercules
The language of animals
A letter to my love
The little bird's rice
Little sister and the Zimwi
The little snake
Loki's punishment
The magic ear
The magic ring
The magic ruby

600

Snakes (*Continued*)

Makhandu Mahlanu or The five heads
A man, a snake, and a fox
The man, the serpent, and the fox
The man who always helped the needy
Marko the rich and Vasily the luckless
The melodius napkin
A midsummer night's dream
Mirzhan and the lord of the kingdom under the sea
The "modern" sea monster
My Lord Bag-o'-Rice
Nala and Damayanti
Near God's cactus
Of sea-going snakes
Omganda and the gold
Orpheus and Eurydice
Pecos Bill, the cowboy
Pemba and the python and the friendly rat
Perseus . . . The head of Medusa
The pheasants and the bell
The planting party
Potok's dancing and the snakes
Prince Alun and the "Cannwyl Corph"
The prince and the Three Fates
Prince Lindworm
Prince Wicked
The princess who knew her own mind
The punishment of Loki
Quinces and oranges
Ragnar Lodbrok and his sons
The rain bird
The revenge of the serpent
The river maiden
The ruby prince
The saga of the waru Wanggi
The sage and the servant
The sand-carrier crab
The search for the magic lake
Senor coyote
Senor coyote settles a quarrel
The shepherd who understood the language of the animals
The shepherd with the curious wife
The silver on the hearth
Sindbad the sailor
The singing chameleon
A song of the railroad men
Soonimaya
The spider weaver
The spring of youth
The stolen jewel
The story of a fairy serpent
The story of the shipwrecked sailor
The sun, the moon and the star of morning
The task of the serpent
The terrible black snake's revenge

The three blue stones
The three brothers and the marvelous things
The three golden hairs
The three monsters of the sea
Three tests for the prince
The three walnuts
Three wonderful beggars
Tiger story, Anansi story
Tshiama, the snake's daughter
The twelve months of the year
The ungrateful snake
The waters beneath: The underwater village
We kill the snake god
The wedding of the hawk
What the squirrel saw
The white cat and the green snake
The white parrot
The white snake
The white snake lady
The wrestler of Kyushu

—**Adders**
The adder and the fox
King Adder
The place of the death adders

—**Anaconda**
The snake that swallowed a girl

, **Black**
The iguana's poison bag

—**Boa constrictors**
How Ijapa, who was short, became long
Lucas the strong

, **Bull**
Two friends, coyote and bull snake, exchange visits

, **Carpet**
The two boys and the sacred carpet snake

—**Cobras**
The judgement of the shepherd
Cum and Koompang
Makhandu Mahlanu or The five heads

—**Cockatrices** (imaginary)
King of the serpents

—**Fangs**
How the black snake got its fangs

—**Pythons**
The boy who turned himself into a peanut
Nyangara, the python

—**Rattlesnakes**
The end of the trail

Snakes—Rattlesnakes (*Continued*)

The grizzly and the rattlesnake men
How rattlesnake got his fangs
Lucky Rose Tuttle
Pecos Bill
Rat and the rustlers

—**Skins**
Polo, the snake-girl

—**Tongues**
Sun, moon, and morning star

—**Voices**
The snake

Snakes
JOHNSON — WHAT p62-67
JOHNSON — WHAT p233-234

Snares
See also **Traps and trapping**
The boy and the water-sprite
The boy who overcame the giants
The man who had no wife
Mighty Mikko
The mouse and the sun
Rabbit and the moon-man
The starling

The sneeze that won a wife
WYATT — GOLDEN p27-33

Sneezing
A-tishoo!
The adventures of Billy Macdaniel
The devil's bride
The doll
The goat who couldn't sneeze
God bless you
Greedy and speedy
Kantchil's lime pit
Krazy kat
The old traveler
Patou MacDaniel
Prince Sneeze
The sleeping prince
The statue that sneezed
To your good health

Sneezing
BATCHELOR — SUPER. p24-26

Sneezy Snatcher and Sammy Small
MANNING — GIANTS p32-35

Snegourka, the snow maiden
HAVILAND — RUSSIA p43-52
SIDEMAN — WORLD'S p453-459

"Snipe-hunts"
Holding the bag

Snout the dwarf
HAUFF — FAIRY p71-100

Snow
See also **Blizzards; Ice**
A.B.C. kitty's in the snow I see!
Calling the chinook
The city of the winter sleep
Flaming tales
La Hormiguita
It snows and it blows
Little pictures from far Japan
The ogre king of Gilgit
Over the river
Paul Bunyan swings his axe
Paul Bunyan's cornstalk
The rain, wind, and snow "Rhyme and reason"
The strange adventure of Baron Munchausen
A strange sled race
The summer of the big snow
There were two little boys
The three princesses in the mountain-in-the-blue
Traveling through the chimney
White fields
Why the mountains are snow-covered
The wise men of Chelm
The woman of the snow
The wonder of Skoupa
Zlateh the goat

Snow
MY BOOK HOUSE v. 2 p208.

Snow in the city
CATHON — PERHAPS p240.

Snow-birds
The mouse and the sun

The snow in Chelm
SINGER — ZLATEH p29-34

Snow in the mountains
LOWE — LITTLE p52-54

Snow-maidens
Snegourka, the snow maiden

The snow man
See also The snowman
MY BOOK HOUSE v. 1 p192.
GARNER — GOBLINS p55.

602

The snow-queen (snow queen)
MY BOOK HOUSE v. 7 p48-70
SIDEMAN – WORLD'S p150-177

Snowwhite (Snow-white)
See also Snow-white and Rose-red;
Snow-white and the seven
dwarfs
JACOBS – EUROPE. p201-211
THOMPSON – ONE p326-333

Snow-white and Rose-red
See also The twelve wild ducks
ARBUTHNOT – TIME p47-49
MY BOOK HOUSE v. 4 p34-44
SIDEMAN – WORLD'S p22-32

Snow-white and the seven dwarfs
ARBUTHNOT – TIME p51-54
MANNING – DWARFS p25-37
SIDEMAN – WORLD'S p305-319

The snow-wife
BAMBERGER – FIRST p188-193
SEKI – FOLKTALES p81-82

Snowdrops
The twelve months

Snowflake
ROSS – BURIED p27-30

The snowman
SHEAHAN – HENRY p246-262

Snuff
The stork caliph

Snuffboxes
The devil and the pit
The golden snuff-box
Jack and his golden snuff-box
A town in a snuff-box
The wandering apprentice

So many countries, so many customs
GHOSE – FOLK p89-115

So say the little monkeys
JAGENDORF – KING p52-55

Soap
The crow and the soap

Social reformers
The rebel

Socrates . . . The cup of Hemlock
UNTERMEYER – FIRE. p63-65

Sofia (illus.)
SPICER – WITCHES p95.

Sofo's escape from the leopard
COURLANDER – OLODE p61-64

Sohrab and Rustum . . . The tragic
encounter
UNTERMEYER – FIRE. p156-159

The soldier
DE LA IGLESIA – CAT unp.

The soldier and the devil
PALMER – JOURNEY p18-30

The soldier and the knapsack
U. N. – RIDE p145-153

The soldier and the tsar
BUDBERG – RUSSIAN p24-26

The soldier who did not wash
DOWNING – RUSSIAN p154-158

Soldiers
See also names of officers e.g. **Generals**
Archery
Beppo Pipetta and his knapsack
Bergamot
Blood on his forehead
The book of magic
The grave grenadier
The bride who out talked the water
kelpie
The carefree monastery
The changeling
Clever Mistress Murray
The dancing princesses
Death and the soldier
The dragon and his grandmother
The empty city
The enchanted princess
The fairy Helena
The feathers from the bird Venus
Green Mountain hero
Hatchet Kasha
Hwan and Dang
Ivan and his knapsack
Jack Hannaford
The just reward
King Matthias and the old man
The kingdom of the green mountains
The legend of the governor and the
veteran
Legend of the Witch of Cape Ann
The little black man

Soldiers (*Continued*)

The louse and the crow
The magic berries
The musical silver goat
Nail Soup
The old soldier and the mischief
The princess and Jose
The proper way to lay the table
La Ramee and the phantom
The shadow on the wall
The silver penny
The soup stone
A Spanish hero
The speedy messenger
Stone soup in Bohemia
A swift messenger
Taper Tom
Three pennyworth
The three princesses in the mountain-in-the-blue
The three soldiers
The tinderbox
The Welshman and the hazel staff
The white trout
The wonderful knapsack
The young wife of Nam Xuong

, **Female**
The innkeeper of Moscow

, **Tin**
The steadfast tin soldier

The soldier's billet
WILSON — IRELAND unp.

The soldier's return
HITCHCOCK — KING p111-121

Solitude
Asmund, Authun, and Odd
Menriad and the ravens

Solitude
MY BOOK HOUSE v. 9 p65.

Solomon, King
The birth and boyhood of Finn
The charitable woman and the three loaves
The craftsman's wife
The debt
The donkey, the ox, and the farmer
Enmity between man and serpent
The game of chess
Introduction (Tales of David and Solomon)
The king of the demons and the worm Shamir
King Solomon and Asmodeus

King Solomon and the Queen of Sheba
King Solomon's carpet
King Solomon's cat
King Solomon's pupils
The northern frog
Tales of David and Solomon
The three litigants
The tree from Adam's grave
The value of a boiled egg
The war of the plants
The wind and the ant
The wise king and the little bee

Solomon and his pride
NAHMAD — PORTION p71-74

Solomon and the four winds
NAHMAD — PORTION p67-70

Solomon, Song of. *See* Song of Solomon

Solomon Islands
—Simba
The boy who fished for the moon

Solomon-the-wise and the golden plough
URE — RUMANIAN p158-159

Solomon's temple
The miracle on the Jaffa Sea

Solvent, Universal
Alchemy: the magic science

Somalia
Nawasi goes to war

The Somalis: wizards of lion country
DAVIS — LION'S p178-179

Somaprabha and the three suitors
GRAY — INDIA'S p216-220

El Sombrero Maravilloso. *See* The three-cornered hat

Some impatient mule-drivers
BRENNER — BOY p21-22

Some mythical beasts of today
JACOBSON — FIRST p58-69

Some namesakes of the dragon
JACOBSON — FIRST p26-27

Some New England superstitions
JOHNSON — WHAT p183-190

Some punkins
FELTON – WORLD'S p127-132

Some songs of old New York
JAGENDORF – GHOST p115-125

Some white witchcraft
HOPE-SIMPSON – CAVAL. p88-90

Somersaults
The million-dollar somersaults

Something told the wise geese
CATHON – PERHAPS p239.

Something wonderful
MANNING – DEVILS p30-38

Sometime
JOHNSON – WHAT p176.

A son of Adam
JACOBS – MORE p118-119

The son of strength
McMANUS – HIBERIAN p1-9

The son of the baker of Barra
LEODHAS – SEA p3-23

The son of the hen-wife
SHEPPARD – SCOT. p176-180

The son of the hunter
U. N. – RIDE p120-127

The son of the King of Spain
MANNING – JONNIKIN p128-135

Son of the long one
HEADY – JAMBO p60-65

Son of the south wind
CARPENTER – HORSES p12-19

The son of the tortoise
SAVORY – ZULU p24-28

The son of turtle spirit
BONNET – CHINESE p69-75

The song-bird and the healing waters
MacMILLAN – GLOOS. p197-201

A song for Easter
MY BOOK HOUSE v. 2 p80-81

A song for the new chief
COURLANDER – KING'S p25-27

Song of deeds. *See* The world's great epics

A song of Drake's men
MY BOOK HOUSE v. 8 p7.

The song of Gimmile
COURLANDER – KING'S p9-12

The song of Roland
MY BOOK HOUSE v. 10 p38-43

The song of Solomon
MY BOOK HOUSE v. 3 p136.

"Song of Solomon"
Awake, O north wind
My beloved is gone down into his garden

The song of the bee
MY BOOK HOUSE v. 2 p163.

A song of the Canadian lumberjack
MY BOOK HOUSE v. 4 p180-182

The song of the Darby ram
JOHNSON – WHAT p156-157

The song of the doves
SAVORY – ZULU p52-56

The song of the flea
MY BOOK HOUSE v. 2 p185.

Song of the leprechaun or fairy shoe-maker
MY BOOK HOUSE v. 3 p94.

A song of the railroad men
MY BOOK HOUSE v. 1 p181.

Song on May morning
MY BOOK HOUSE v. 7 p171.

Songs
See also **Singing;** types of songs e.g. **Battle songs; Boatmen's songs; Lullabies; Parodies;** etc. names of countries etc., subdivision **Songs**
A-tisket, a-tasket
The ballad of Lord Lovell
The battle of the Nile
Billy Boy
"Bow-wow," says the dog
The courtin'
The cuckoo and the donkey
Froggie goes a-courting
God hath made me to laugh
Here we come, we children come
The hunchback and the miser

Songs (*Continued*)

The hunters of Kentucky
It is God that hath made us
John Brown had a little Indian
Lazy old Mary
The magic crystal
Marching to Quebec
Mock turtle's song
O. I'm a jolly old cowboy
Old songs
The orchestra
Some songs of old New York
The song of the Darby ram
The spell-song
Those young men
The traveler
A winky-tooden song
The witches' reel
A witch's song

, **American**
Yankee Doodle

, **Biblical**
Songs of joy from the Bible
Spring songs from the Bible

, **Country**
All around the cobbler's bench
Turkey in the straw

, **English**
Song on May morning

—**Indians of North America.** *See*
Indians of North America—Songs;
Lullabies, Indian

, **Railroad**
Casey Jones

, **Yankee**
The man who has plenty of good
peanuts

Songs of joy from the Bible
MY BOOK HOUSE v. 1 p216-217

The songs of the animals
LEACH — RAINBOW p277.

The songstress and the fairies
MINCIELI — TALES p22-26

Sonny-boy Sim
ARBUTHNOT — TIME p263-265

Sons
About Jan the prince, Princess
Wonderface, and the flamebird
The anger bargain
The archer, William Tell
Aristotle and the three sons
The black giant of Luckless River

The blind king and the magic bird
The bone that testified
Caravan
The cavallino
Cinder Joe becomes king
The city under the sea
The clever question
Conall Yellowclaw
The cow maiden
The curse on the only son
Day dreaming
The death of the Yugovichi's mother
Deirdre and the sons of Uisne
The divided cloak
A dutiful son
The enchanted princess
The farmer and his son
Father fights son in the tribe of Hilal
The forest bride
The frog
The geomancer's three sons
The giant who had no heart in his
body
The giants who wanted a son
Gift of the unicorn
The gold bird
The gold falcon
The golden lion
A handful of hay
The honey gatherer's three sons
Hong Do-Ryong, the filial tiger
The horse of seven colors
How Jack sought the golden apples
How the gypsy boy outsmarted death
How the sons filled the hut
The hunchback's horse
Ivo Senkovich and Aga of Ribnik
The jewel
The king and his seven sons
King Conal's horses
King Johnny
King Svatopluk and the three sticks
The knight of the glen's steed o' bells
The lamentable story of Connlach,
son of Cuchulain
The legend of Tchi-Niu
The little pet rani
Lord Peter
The magic bird
The man who struck his father
The man who wanted to bury his son
The master of magic and spells
Merman Rosmer
The miller, his son, and the donkey
The miller's four sons
My own self
The old father who went to school
An old king and his three sons of
England
The old man and his sons
Ooka and the two first sons

Sons (*Continued*)

The people who lived near a mountain
Prince Murko's journey
The prince who rode through a mousehole
The princess on the glass mountain
Pwyll and Pryderi (2) The birth of Pryderi
The quest of the sons of Turenn
Ragnar Lodbrok and his sons
The Ramayana
The Red-Etin
The red king and the witch
The self-propelled carriage
The seven foals
The seven Simeons Simeonovich
The seven stars
The seven stars of the north
The seventh son
Shah Meram and Sade Sultan
The sleigh ride
Sohrab and Rustum . . . The tragic encounter
The story of Hong Gil-Dong
The thirteenth of the King of Erin
The three sons
The three sons of Gorla
The three sons of the King of Antua
The tiger's grave
The ungrateful children
Vanya's leap
Vassillissa the wise
The water of life
The will of the wise man
The wise merchant
The woman of Llyn-y-fan (3) The Sequel
The youth who trusted in God

Sons-in-law
A father-in-law and his son-in-law

The sons of Hilal: fact and legend
DAVIS – TEN pxi-xiv

Sons of Turenn. *See* **Turenn, Sons of**

Soo Tan the tiger and the little green frog
HUME – FAVORITE p9-14

Soonimaya
HITCHCOCK – KING p11-22

Soothsayers. *See* **Fortune-tellers, etc.**

The soothsayers
JENNINGS – BLACK p81-93

The sorcerer's apprentice(s)
CHILD – CASTLES p127-133
GRAY – MAINLY p3-23
SIDEMAN – WORLD'S p205-212

Sorcery. *See* **Magicians; Witchcraft; Witches; Wizards**

Soria Moria castle
ASBJÖRNSEN – EAST p81-95
ASBJÖRNSEN – NORW. p67-76
LINES – TALES p126-136
PROTTER – CHILD. p46-56

Sorrow
The children of Lir
Deidre and the sons of Uisne
The eight leaves of story (5) The man who killed his greyhound
The fate of the sons of Usnach
The quest of the children of Turenn

Sorrow
DOWNING – RUSSIAN p138-144

Souchmant's trial and triumph
ALMEDINGEN – KNIGHTS p121-132

The soul in the mountain rice
LEEUW – INDO. p21-25

The soul of the Countess Kathleen
GARNIER – LEGENDS p22-26

Souls
Badikan and Khan Boghu
The black giant of Luckless River
The black prince
The bridge of St. Cloud
The crochera
Death and the soldier
The demon mason
The demon's daughter
The fiddle
The fisherman and his soul
A game of dice
General Moulton's boot
The gypsy fiddle
High Eden
How the people began
The land of the dead
Lights of the caribou
The little mermaid
The lucky hunter
The merrow and the soul cages
The ogre king of Gilgit
Padre Ulivo and his guests
Pietro Bailliardo

Souls (*Continued*)

The princess of the mountain
The rajah who flew away
The saving of a soul
The soldier who did not wash
The story of Aoyagi
The tale of the two brothers
The three silver balls
Tom Walker and the devil
The troll who hid his life
A Victorian romance
The white stone canoe
The witch of Fraddam

The sound is yours
WALKER — WATER. p35-36

Sounds

How much for a shadow?
The robber baron . . . and the bat
Steam-how much
What they say

Sounds
BATCHELOR — SUPER. p19-22

Soup

The green knight
Kabundi's eye
Kachi Kachi mountain
Mr. Louse and Mrs. Louse
Nail soup
Nansii and the eagle
The old woman and the tramp
Polenta, polenta, and more polenta
Rabbit soup
The soup stone
Stone soup in Bohemia
The tale of the little sausage and the little mouse
Why the bat flies at night

The soup stone
LEACH — SOUP p17-20
U. N. — RIDE p186-188

Sourdough special
FELTON — NEW p103-118

South

Brer wolf's little tar men
Christian dancing in rural Georgia
Conjure bags
The frog, the mouse, and the hawk
Games
Hammerman/John Henry
High John the conqueror
How the mud turtle came to live on the water

Hully-gully
Hurry up, engine
John Henry
Odds and ends
Old stories
Waiting on salvation
When I go a-courting

South American rhymes
MY BOOK HOUSE v. 1 p68-69

South Carolina

How rabbit stole fire from the buzzards
The talking mule
A tar burner's brer rabbit stories
Why cat eats first

South Carolina
LEACH — RAINBOW p146-147

South Dakota

—**Black Hills**
Wind in the Black Hills

South Dakota
LEACH — RAINBOW p148-149

South from hell-fer-sartin. *See*
Changing luck

South Pacific Islands

See also names of islands
The adventures of Kahukura and Te Kanawa, The Little People of Polynesia
The battle of the birds and the fish
The battle that tilted the sea
The boy who fished for the moon
The boy who was caught by a clam
The cat and the sea
The children and the ghost-woman
The children's sea
The crab and the needlefish
The fight between the octopus and the whale
The greedy boy and the coconut crab
The greedy giant and the Palau Islands
The hermit with two heads
The lobster and the flounder
The magic oysters
The naughty girl and the ghost-giant
The prisoner
The silent drum
Sirene, the mermaid
The sky-eater
The story of a good boy
The ticklish thief
Tik and Lap and the giant fish

South Pacific Islands (*Continued*)

The turtle of Tamaru
The turtles and the mountain tunnel
The two brothers and the ghost Mo'oi
The whale and the sandpiper

Southeast (United States)
The stars are silver reindeer

The Southern cross
PARKER – AUSTRALIAN p24-25

Southey, Carolyn Bowles
To the lady-bird

Southey, Robert
The cataract of Lodore
The three bears

Southwest (United States)
The beetle's hairpiece
Billy the Kid
The bow who crossed the great water
and returned
Coyote and the crying song
Coyote helps decorate the night
Coyote's needle
The foot racers of Payupki
Honwyma and the bear
How the people came from the lower
world
How the people came to the middle
place
How the Tewas came to first mesa
How the village of Pivanhonkapi
perished
Josh Kiklay and the eagle
The journey to the land of the dead
The land of the Hopis
Lost arts
Lost in lava
Notes on Hopi oral literature
Sikahokuh and the hunting dog
The sun callers
Two friends, coyote and bull snake,
exchange visits
Why the salt is far away

The sow and her Banbh
O'SULLIVAN – FOLK . p14.

The sow got the measles
STOUTENBURG – CROC. p12-13

Space ship Bifrost
ARBUTHNOT – TIME p389-392

A spadeful of earth
WILLIAMS – FAIRY p114-116

Spades
Boots and his brothers
The crow and the sparrow

Spain
The Arabe duck
The astrologer
The battle of Nembro wood
The battle of Roncesvalles
Bernardo and the red knight
The bird which laid diamonds
The birthday of the Infanta
The black stone
The blue lake
Bring me a light
The carlanco
The carnation youth
The castle of no return
The cat and the mouse
The cave of Hercules
The Cid . . . The will to conquer
Clever–clever–clever
Don Lopez of Spain
The double knights
The dove and the eagle
The dragon's tail
The economical son
The enchanted castle in the sea
The enchanted mule
Epilogue: a final word
The flea
The flower of beauty
Four brothers who were both wise
and foolish
The frog
The frog and his clothes
Griselda
The half-chick
The herdsman
The honest criminal
The hungry rider
Juan Cigarron
The king and his friend
The king and the wise man
King Estmere
The king who slept
The knight of the almond blossom
The legend of the Arabian magician
The legend of the governor and the
lawyer
The legend of the governor and the
veteran
The legend of the magic lute
The legend of the mason
The legend of the Moor's legacy
The legend of the Prince Ahmed Al
Kamel
The legend of the three beautiful
princesses
The legend of the two discreet statues
The lily and the bear

Spain (*Continued*)

The little shepherd's dream
The loafer
The luck fairies
The magician Palermo
Maimonides and the bottle of poison
The mice and the precious seeds
Nuberu
The parrot
The Prince Fernando
The princess who knew her own mind
The princess who was dumb
Ramiro II, the monk
The ring
Rojin Rojal
A salty tale
The soldier
The son of the King of Spain
The song of Roland
A Spanish hero
The stolen wine
The story of the Cid
The strangest thing in the world
The surprising adventures of Don
  Quixote of La Mancha
The three wishes
The treasure of Altamira
Viriato: The youth who held back the
  Roman empire
The vixen and the boatmen
The vixen and the rooster
The wedding of the Cid's daughters
The white dove of the city of the
  swinging gate
The white parrot
The wood cutter's son and the two
  turtles
The world's great epics

−Cordoba
  The covetous minister

−Granada
  The broken box
  The magic lute
  The prince and the birds

  −"Alhambra"
    The legend of the Arabian
      magician
    The legend of the governor and
      the lawyer
    The legend of the magic lute
    The legend of the mason
    The legend of the Moor's leg-
      acy
    The legend of the Prince
      Ahmed Al Kamel
    The legend of the three
      beautiful princesses
    The legend of the two discreet
      statues

−History
  Introduction: Early Spain

−Madrid
  The half-chick
  Sun, moon, and morning star

−Toledo
  Prince Ahmed

Spaniards
  A Catio Indian legend
  The coming of the Spaniards
  The girl and the puma
  The greatest wealth in the world
  The head of the Inca
  The ordeal of Leyden
  Pedro Alvarado and the Indian girl
  The Spanish donkey and the Indians
  When Boqueron spoke

The Spanish donkey and the Indians
  JAGENDORF − KING p222-225

A Spanish hero
  MY BOOK HOUSE v. 12 p156-162

Spanish nursery rhymes
  MY BOOK HOUSE v. 1 p64-65

Spankings
  Smolicheck

The sparrow and the stalk of grass
  BLOCH − UKRAIN. p60-63

Sparrow-hawks
  Benito the faithful

The sparrow whose tongue was cut out
  MARMUR − JAPAN. p41-46

Sparrows
  Aiming too high
  Answer to a child's question
  Badikan and Khan Boghu
  The black giant of Luckless River
  "Bow-wow", says the dog
  The bunch of grapes
  Cooked for fifteen
  The crow and the sparrow
  Dewi Dal
  The elephant and the gnat
  How Au Sung repaid Kim Lee
  The hurt sparrow
  The legend of Eilean Donan castle
  A little cock sparrow
  Little Gustava
  The magpie's nest
  The maiden in the country under-
    ground

610

Sparrows (*Continued*)

Monkey-dance and sparrow-dance
Only a sparrow
The prince and the dragons
The search for the magic lake
The silent princess
The swan princess
The tale of Peter Rabbit
Why cat always wash after eating

—**Language**
The magic ear

—**Tongues**
The tongue-cut sparrow

Sparrow's search for rain
MacMILLAN – GLOOS. p117-123

Speakers
The boy who would be an orator
He sang himself out of prison cell

The spear and shield of Huan-tan
COURLANDER – TIGER'S p40-42

The spear slaughterer and the chariot and
horses of Sigar
PILKINGTON – THREE p49-55

Spearmint
The donkey's tail

Spears
Agayk and the strangest spear
The bridge of heaven
The coming of Fionn MacCool
How crane got his long beak
How the turtle fooled the leopard
Izanagi and Izanami
The lordship of the Fianna
The lost spear
Podhu and Aruwa
The princess and the dwarf
Sif's golden hair
The slaying of Siegfried
The tsar's son-in-law and the
winged old woman
Why the sky is high

Spears of lightning
THOMPSON – HAWAII. p20-27

The specialist
KELSEY – ONCE p128-131

The speckled bull
GARNIER – LEGENDS p12-15
O'SULLIVAN – FOLK. p117-130

The speckled hen's egg
CARLSON – TALKING p43.

Spectacles. *See* **Glasses, Eye**

Speech
See also **Speakers; Talk**
The golden casket
Ol' guinea man
The peasant and the workman
The prince who made the silence
speak
Who maketh the dumb to speak
Why the fish do not speak

The speech of beasts
WYATT – GOLDEN p50-58

Speed
The adventures of Ciad
Clever Manka
Donal from Donegal
How Michael Scot went to Rome
Jack the giant-killer
Little Mukra
The little nobleman
The magic sandals of Hualachi
The mouse and the snail
Oraggio and Bianchinetta
Pietro Bailliardo
The poor man's clever daughter
Red king and green king
The rice puller of Chaohwa
The sword of light
Three fast men
Three fat ewes for three fine hounds
Two speedy people
Who hath no courage must have legs

The speedy messenger
THOMPSON – ONE p297-303

The spell of the mermaid
PRATT – MAGIC unp.

The spell-song
HOPE-SIMPSON – CAVAL. p53-56

Spelling
JOHNSON – WHAT p145-148

Spells. *See* **Magic; Witchcraft; Witches**

Spenser, Edmund
For a peaceful night

Una and the Red Cross knight

Spenser, Edmund
Kilcolman castle

Spheres, Golden
The adventures of Florian

Sphinx
A dream of the Sphinx
Horus the avenger
The prince and the Sphinx
The riddle of the Sphinx

Sphinxes
JACOBSON – LEGEND. p43-45

Spicer, Dorothy Gladys
About ghosts

Spicer, Dorothy Gladys
SPICER – DEVILS p128.
SPICER – GHOSTS Preface
SPICER – GOBLINS p127.
SPICER – KNEELING p123.
SPICER – LONG p159.
SPICER – OWL'S p125.
SPICER – WITCHES p95.

Spices
The lass that lost the laird's daughter
The lemon and his army
Rabbi Joseph Della Reina

The spider
MANNING – GIANNI p62-66
GREEN – BIG p174.

Spider and squirrel
ARNOTT – AFRICAN p64-67

Spider and the lion
ARNOTT – AFRICAN p25-31

The spider and the lizard
ELLIOT – WHERE p60-65

Spider boy and the sun god's twins
RUSHMORE – DANCING p22-34

The spider in the wall
JAGENDORF – UPSTATE p280-285

The spider specter of the pool
SPICER – GHOSTS p24-35

The spider weaver
SAKADE – JAPAN. p59-65

Spiders
See also **Anansi stories**

The antelope and the spider
Arachne . . . The eternal spinner
Bandalee
The black spider
Brother Breeze and the pear tree
The center of the world
The courting of the bat, the spider
and the beetle
The fairyland of science
The fall of the spider man
The first fire
Flint bird
The foot racers of Payupki
The frog and the moon
Gizo's counting trick
The gnat and the lion
The goblin-spider
Grasshopper green
The greedy spider
How Kwaku Ananse became bald
How Pakayana the spider got his
small waist
How spider got a bald head
How spider got a thin waist
How spider helped a fisherman
How spider taught women to weave
How the fair rainbow was made
How the half boys came to be
How the lion rewarded the mouse's
kindness
How the people came from the lower
world
How the people came to the middle
place
How the people got fire
How the pig got his snout
How the spider was made
How the sun came
How the village of Pivanhonkapi
perished
How the world got wisdom
How wisdom was spread throughout
the world
Joshokiklay and the eagle
The journey to the land of the dead
Kisander
The kling kling bird
Kuluilé, the dancing girl
Little Miss Muffet
The magic bone
Mohammed and the spider
Nansii and the eagle
Nkalimeva
Over in the meadow
The panther in the pit
The quarrel
Robert Bruce, Scotland's hero
The rubber man
Sikakokuh and the hunting dog
Star-boy and the sun dance
Ticky-picky boom-boom

Spiders (*Continued*)

The upper world
The white spider's gift
Why rabbit have short tail
Why spider has a little head and a big
   behind
Why spider lives in ceilings
Why spiders live in dark corners
Why the lizard stretches his neck
Why the salt is far away
Wikki, the weaver
The womb of the earth
The young coyote's visit
Yung-Kyung-Pyung

—Webs
   The boastful gnat
   Bruce and the spider
   Charlotte's web; Wilbur's boast
   Fairies on the gump
   How spider got his thread
   More beautiful than the spider's
      web
   Pursuit of the Hadji
   The quarrel
   Robert Bruce and the spider; how
      a king learned courage from an
      insect
   The spider
   Spider's web
   There was an old woman tossed
      up in a basket

Spider's web
   ARNOTT — AFRICAN p74-77

Spies
   King Crow and Sir parrot
   Samson and the doll in green and
      brown

Spigots
   The best wish

Spin, weave, wear
   LEODHAS — HEATHER p95-111

Spinach
   The grandmother and the crocodile

The spindle-imp
   FARJEON — SILVER p64-71

The spindle, the shuttle, and the needle
   VITTORINI — OLD p69-73

Spindles
   The frog-princess

The sleeping beauty
The sleeping beauty in the wood

, **Golden**
   A girl and a stepmother
   Graylegs

The spindles are still
   BELTING — STARS #9

Spinning
   Arachne . . . The eternal spinner
   Daughter and stepdaughter
   Frigg and the goddesses
   The girl who could spin clay and
      straw into gold
   The girl who didn't know how to spin,
      The Little People of Scandinavia
   The goldspinners
   The good housekeepers and her
      night helpers
   The good housewife and her night
      labors
   Gwarwyn-a-Throt
   Habetrot
   Habetrot and Scantlie Mab
   The heavenly spinning maid
   The horned woman
   The horned women
   How spider taught women to weave
   How the king chose a daughter-in-law
   The key in the distaff
   The king who wanted a beautiful wife
   Kupti and Imani
   The lame duck
   The lazy woman
   Left eye, right eye
   The luck fairies
   The man in the moon
   The man with the bag
   The milky way
   Musk and amber
   The old Christmas
   One-eye, two-eyes, and three-eyes
   Peerifool
   Poll and doll
   Rumpelstiltzkin
   Silver leaves and golden blossoms
   The silver river
   The sleeping beauty in the wood
   The Soria-Moria castle
   The spindles are still
   The strange visitor
   The sun, the moon and the star of
      morning
   The third witch
   The three aunts
   The three brothers
   The three spinners
   Tom Tit Tot
   Trillevip

Spinning (*Continued*)

The twins and the snarling witch
The two step-sisters
Vassilissa the beautiful
Whippety stourie
The white lady of Pumphul
The widow's daughter
The widow's lazy daughter
Wild rose
The wild swans
The witch aunts
The wood fairy

Spinning-wheels
The blackstairs mountain
The comb, the flute and the spinning
wheel
Graadonner
Prince Hat beneath the earth

, **Golden**
East of the sun and west of the
moon
A girl and a stepmother

The spinning women by the spring. *See*
Mother luck

Spinsters
Three old maids a-skating went

"Spirit, Great"
The peace pipe
The tale of bat
Thunderbird

The spirit of slumber
OMAN – ESKIMO p40-42

The spirit of the stone
SECHRIST – ONCE p98-104

The spirit of the waterhole
NORLEDGE – ABORIGINAL p12-
13

The spirit who danced
THOMPSON – LEGENDS p38-42

Spirits
See also **Ghosts;** names of spirits
The Bora of Baiame
A boy and a beggar
The fire plume
The fish maid
The flying spirits of Nuhau
The golden ax
The golden chain
The haunted lagoon

He who lives in a mountain
The horned witches
How death came
If you know a story, don't keep it to
yourself
The journey to the land of the dead
Kigbo and the bush spirits
Maui, the demi-god
O gungbemi and the battle in the bush
Reward drives the familiar spirits
away
The son of the turtle spirit
The three princesses and the unclean
spirit
The wife from another world
The wise owl
The woman of the snow
The yellow dragon

, **Evil**
A contest with skillful spirits
The evil spirits of Crooked
Mountain
How a Wuuni ate nine evil spirits
The weary spirits of Lanai

, **Forest**
A trick that failed

, **Hearth**
The spirits of the hearth

, **Household**
Household spirit brings food
The household spirit in Rotenbach

, **Land**
The bride from the land of the
spirits
Maui, the demi-god

, **Mountain**
The talking donkey
True love in the Blue Mountains

–**Societies**
The beginning of spirit societies

The spirit's drum
KRUEGER – SERPENT p120-126

The spirits of the hearth
SUN – LAND p28-30

Spite. *See* **Revenge**

The spiteful nanny goat
BLOCH – UKRAIN. p39-43

The spoiled daughter
PRIDHAM – GIFT p48-54

Sponges
   The donkey with sponges and the
      donkey with salt
   Some impatient mule-drivers

Spoons
   The swan princess
   , Silver
      The wild swans

Sports. *See* **Athletes and athletics;**
   names of sports

Spotless the lion and Trusty the carpenter
   GAER – FABLES p20-23

Spots
   The tortoise and the lion

The spotted cow
   MANNING – GLASS p86-93

The spotted rug
   COURLANDER – TIGER'S p100-
   105

Spriggans (Little People)
   Fairies on the gump
   The miser and the fairy feast

The spriggans' treasure
   MANNING – PETER p82-84

Spring
   April
   Behold the fig tree
   The birds' St. Valentine's day
   Children's songs of ancient Greece
      (by Theognis)
   The cock is crowing
   Crocus flowers bloom like fire
   Flower moon
   God hath made me to laugh
   The green mist
   The groundhog family
   Hear how the birds
   Here we come, we children come
   How the goddess of Spring came to
      Scoring
   In Spring the birds do sing
   In the Springtime
   It's Spring
   Legend of the arbutus
   Little Gustava
   Mary and the Christ-child
   Peboan and Seegwun
   Planters' moon

The planting of the apple tree
Proserpine
The return of the Spring
The search for the land of bliss
The selfish giant
A song for Easter
The song of Solomon
Song on May morning
The stealing of Iduna
Stealing the Springtime
There's not a budding boy
A winky-tooden song
Worm moon

Spring, Goddess of
   How the goddess of Spring came to
      Scoring
   The stealing of Iduna

(The) Spring
   BUDD – FULL p13-27
   BARASH – GOLDEN p140-143

The spring ay-petri
   BULATKIN – EURASIAN p120-122

Spring flood
   LEACH – RAINBOW p187.

Spring flowers
   CATHON – PERHAPS p236-237

The spring of youth
   PRIDHAM – GIFT p35-44

Spring songs from the Bible
   MY BOOK HOUSE v. 2 p78-79

Springfield got it
   JAGENDORF – SAND p166-169

Springs (water)
   The fairy wife
   Santiago and the fighting bulls
   The song-bird and the healing waters
   Stan Bolovan
   The three golden hairs of Grandfather
      Know All
   The three-legged jumping giant

A springtime dream
   BONNET – CHINESE p145-148

Sprites, Water
   The miller and the water sprites
   The water-sprite

Spuyten duyvil
   LEACH – RAINBOW p227-228

Spyri, Johanna
　Heidi in the Alpine pasture

Squash
　A quick-running squash
　White squash boy

Squid
　The kraken
　The sand-carrier crab

Squire Per
　ASBJORNSEN – NORW. p122-127

The squire's bride
　ASBJÖRNSEN – NORW. p56-60
　MY BOOK HOUSE v. 6 p98-101

The squires win golden spurs
　HAZELTINE – HERO p203-218

The squirrel
　CATHON – PERHAPS p64-65
　MY BOOK HOUSE v. 1 p106.

Squirrel and fox
　HAMPDEN – GYPSY p139-146

The squirrel went out to cut the hay
　MY BOOK HOUSE v. 1 p60.

Squirrels
　See also Chipmunks
　The boy and the water-sprite
　Bucky, the big, bold fawn
　The clever squirrel
　Dwarf long nose
　Firefly's story
　The giant sturgeon
　The greedy old fat man
　He who is feared by all
　Hiawatha's childhood
　The little rabbit who wanted red
　　wings
　The nutcracker and sugardolly
　　stories
　Of all the beasts that roam the woods
　The serpent prince
　The snake and the toad
　Spider and squirrel
　The twins and the snarling witch
　What the squirrel saw
　Whisky frisky
　The wicked weasel
　The woodman and the fox
　Zini and the witches

, Flying
　How the animals made wings for
　　bat and flying squirrel

, Ground
　The theft of dawn

, Rock
　The witsduks

Stables and stablemen
　Cannetella
　Esben and the witch
　The little nag
　The three tasks

Stackalee
　LEACH – RAINBOW p181-183

The staff of Oranmiyan
　COURLANDER – OLODE p118-120

Staffs. See Sticks

The stag-hunt
　GREEN – BIG p222.

The stag prince
　BUCK – FAIRY p81-88

Stag, The miraculous. See The miraculous stag

Stags. See Deer

Stairways
　The ogre and the cock

Stan Bolovan
　LANG – VIOLET p96-110
　MANNING – DRAGONS p25-37

The star
　MY BOOK HOUSE v. 2 p83.

Star-boy and the sun dance
　MacMILLAN – GLOOS. p217-224

Star catching
　JABLOW – MAN p76.

The star children dwelt in a deep cave
　BELTING – STARS #2

The star florins
　BAMBERGER – FIRST p16-17

Star light, star bright
　MY BOOK HOUSE v. 1 p86.

616

The star path
GRINGHUIS – GIANTS p69-73

Star people
The fall of the spider man
The legend of the star children
The lost spear
Lox and the two ermines

Starch
The tongue-cut sparrow

Starfish
The adventures of a water baby
David Copperfield and little Em'ly
The two crabs

The starling of Segringen
GREEN – BIG p94-96

Starlings
The cat and the starling
Jackal or tiger?

Stars
See also **Constellations**
Bani Hilal: a tribe is born
Boys with golden stars
The brothers Yakshich divide their
heirloom
Coyote helps decorate the night
The dancing stars
The end of the evening
The great bear
The heart of Princess Joan
The heavenly lovers
How dandelions were made
How stars and fireflies were made
How the moon and stars came to be
How the ox came upon earth
How the people began
How the raven stole the stars
How the water lily came
It is God that hath made us
The legend of the Karang
The legend of the star children
The little frog of the stream
The lost sun, moon, and stars
Lucky star of Herald Square
Many, many stars are in the skies
Mary and the Christ-child
The milky way
The moon and the stars
Mullian-ga the morning star
Nananbouclou and the piece of fire
The necklace

The old man who said "why"
Pleiad and star of dawn
The Pleiades
The princess who wanted to play
with the stars
Raven and the sun
The river of lantern land
The securing of light
The seven stars
The seven stars of the north
The sky at night
The summer birds
Sun, moon, and stars: Little numskull
stories
The sun, the moon and the star of
morning
The sun, the moon, and the stars
Sun, thunder, lightning and the stars
The thoughtless abbot
The three Magi
The three stars
Thunderbird
Tyl's task
What happened to six wives who ate
onions
Who?
Why there are shooting stars
The wishing star
Written in the stars
Wynken, Blynken, and Nod

, **Golden**
The boy with the golden star

, **Shooting**
The fall of the spider man

The stars above: Long Sash and his people
MARRIOTT – AMER. p59-62

The stars above: pursuit of the bear
MARRIOTT – AMER. p56-58

The stars are silver reindeer
BELTING – STARS #1

The stars in the sky
JACOBS – MORE p177-181
REEVES – ENGLISH p177-181

Stars in the water
JABLOW – MAN p76.

States' rights
Robert E. Lee, a hero in war and
peace

Statue of Liberty
The new colossus

The statue that sneezed
    JEWETT – WHICH p41-46

Statues
    The barrel decree
    Beatrice . . . And the statue
    Beauty and the beast
    The blue virgin
    The dancing palm tree
    Errato di Barletto
    Father big-nose
    The giant who had no heart in his
        body
    The giant who played with
        pygmies
    The golden lion
    The goldsmith, the wood carver,
        the tailor, and the hermit who
        quarreled over a wooden woman
    The grateful devil
    The grateful statues
    The happy prince
    The horse and the eighteen bandits
    How Papantla got its patron saint
    John the true
    The king of the fishes
    The kingdom of ocean
    The lass who went out at the cry of
        dawn
    The laughing statue
    The legend of the two discreet
        statues
    The lost saints
    Madschun
    The merchant, Saint Michael, and the
        devil
    New Year's hats for the statues
    The nine white sheep
    The oni's daughter
    Ooka and the cleanest case
    Ooka and the suspect statue
    Pappa Greatnose
    Pygmalion . . . The marvelous statue
    The raven
    Saint Quien Sabe
    The singing fir-tree
    The virgin of Honduras
    The youth who could become an ant,
        a lion or an eagle
    Zo Han-Zun, who became a stone
        Buddha

    , Gold
        When Boqueron spoke

    , Marble
        The flower of beauty

Stavr Godinovich and his clever wife
    DOWNING – RUSSIAN p47-54

The steadfast tin soldier
    ARBUTHNOT – TIME p333-335
    SIDEMAN – WORLD'S p446-453

Steadfastness
    The hare and the tortoise
    The knight and the naiad of the lake
    The tortoise and the hare

Stealing. See Thieves and thievery

The stealing of Iduna
    MY BOOK HOUSE v. 9 p172-176

Stealing the bell
    WYNDHAM – CHINA p63.

Stealing the Springtime
    COTHRAN – WITH p76-83

Steam
    Sly Peter at the fair
    A wise sentence

Steam engines
    Jamie Watt and the giant in the tea-
        kettle

Steam–how much
    KELSEY – ONCE p122-127

Steam shovel operators
    Biting Marion
    Mike Mulligan and his steam shovel

The steamboat and the locomotive
    MY BOOK HOUSE v. 5 p96-102

Steamboat Bill and the captain's top hat
    SHAPIRO – HEROES p155-198

Steamboats (Steamships)
    A happy day in the city
    How Robert Fulton harnessed the
        giant
    The melting pot
    Mr. Hampden's shipwreck
    When Uncle Henry was a little tiny
        boy

Steel-workers
    Hammerman/John Henry
    Joe Magarac
    Joe Magarac and his U.S.A. citizen
        papers
    Joe Magarac the steel man
    Joe Magerack, the steel-mill man
    John Henry

Steel-workers *(Continued)*

John Henry and double-jointed
stream drill

Steele, Sir Richard
In the days of Queen Anne

Steelmaker/Joe Magarac
STOUTENBURG — AMER. p101-112

The steers that wouldn't draw
JOHNSON — WHAT p177-178

Steinhowel, Heinrich
The grateful ant

Stepdaughters
The giant beanstalk
The little black box
Mother Luck
One-eye, two-eyes, and three-eyes
Tam and Tessa
Three princes and their beasts
The two princesses
The two step-sisters
The well of the three heads

Stepfathers
The little bull-calf

Stephens, James
White fields

Stepmothers
The adventures of Bona and Nello
The adventures of Iain Direach
Ashputtel
Baba Yaga
Baba Yaga and the little girl with the
kind heart
Baskets in a little cart
Benizara and Kakezara
The bride-price for Olwen
Cenerentola or Cinderella
The child and the colt
The child and the fig
The children of Lir
The chili plant
A Chinese cinderella
Cinder-maid
Cinderella
Cinderella or The little glass slipper
The cruel stepmother
Daughter and stepdaughter
The dragon and the stepmother
The enchanted black cat
Fair Vasilissa and Baba Yaga
The fire boy

The first three hundred years
The gay goss-hawk
A girl and a stepmother
The girl whom the moon pitied
The girl without arms
The girl without hands
The golden apples of Loch Erne
Hansel and Gretel
The haunted forest
The hearth-cat
It all comes to light
The juniper
Katie Woodencloak
King Conal's horses
The knight of the glen's steed o' bells
The Korean goblins
The lion's whiskers
The little duck
Little Rosa and long Leda
The lost children
Lynx of the forest
MacCodrum of the seals
Mary covered with gold and Mary
covered with pitch
Master Frost
Mother Holle
Mother Sunday
Mother's girl and father's girl
The mouse hole
The piper
Pleiad and star of dawn
The prince and the sky-blue filly
Prince Finn the fair
Prince Sigurd and his sister
Rattle-rattle-rattle and chink-chink-
chink
Rushen Coatie
Saturday, Sunday, Monday
Snow-white
Snow White and the seven dwarfs
The snow-wife
The soldier's return
Soonimaya
The speckled bull
The story of King Frost
The story of Mead Moondaughter
The story of Prince Ring and his dog
The swans of Ballycastle
A tale of the Tontlawald
Three fat ewes for three fine hounds
The three giants
The three golden eggs
The three little men in the wood
The three mermaids
The three stags
The twelve months
The twins and the snarling witch
The two sisters, Rose and Lotus
Vasilia the beautiful
Vassilissa the beautiful
Vassilissa the fair and Baba Yaga

Stepmothers (*Continued*)

The well of the world's end
The white bird sister
The white bride and the black bride
White-toes and Bushy-bride
The wild swans
A willow wand and a brocade slipper
The witch
The witch of Wandaland
Yoni and her stepmother
Zezolla and the date-palm tree

Steppes. *See* **Russia-Steppes**

Stepsons
The youth who made friends with
the beasts and the birds

Sterrett, Frances R.
The king's cream

Stevens, Wallace
The snow man

Stevenson, Robert Louis
Bring the comb and play upon it!
Building with blocks
The friendly cow all red and white
Of speckled eggs the birdie sings
Poems
Rain
The swing
What are you able to build with your
blocks?
When I was down beside the sea
Where go the boats?
The world is so full

Stevenson, Robert Louis
Bring the comb and play upon it!
The friendly cow all red and white

Stewards
The ass that lays money
The cook and the house goblin
Sir Orfeo
Tregeagle
The young Lord of Lorn

Stew
The foggy stew
Tiger in the forest, Anansi in the web

Stick-to-itiveness. *See* **Perseverance**

Sticks
The ass that lays money

Brother Breeze and the pear tree
The bundle of sticks
The devil's gifts
The donkey, the table, and the stick
Dummling
The enormous genie
Esben and the witch
A fortune in a stick
The giant of the brown beech wood
The giant with the grey feathers
The gift of the holy men
The green grass bottle
The groach of the Isle of Lok
I don't know where and I don't
know what
Jack and the Purr Mooar
Keloglan and the ooh-genie
King Svatopluk and the three sticks
The lad and the north wind
The lad who went to the north wind
The lass and her good stout black-
thorn stick
Lazy Hans
The little bird's rice
Long-Neck, Fatty and Droopy
The long nose
The magic wand
The moss-green princess
One mean trick deserves another
Per and the north wind
The planting party
Saturday, Sunday, Monday
The silver bell
The singing man
Sinko's luck
Stan Bolovan
Sumlee's broken stick
The wandering staff
Water drops
The weasel
Why frogs speak Chinese
Why there is a man in the moon
The witch of Lok Island
The wonder ship and ship's crew
The wrestling match of the two
Buddhas

The sticky-sticky pine
SAKADE – JAPAN. p55-58

Stilettos. *See* **Daggers**

Stilts
Would you like to see goats dance on
stilts

Stine Bheag o' Tarbat
SHEPPARD – SCOT. p131-138

Stinginess
See also **Greed; Misers**
The black woodpecker
Dinner for the monk
The farmer and the harvesters
The hillman and the housewife
The man from Kailasa
Old Gally Mander
Old Plott
The skunk in Tante Odette's oven

Stinginess
SEKI – FOLKTALES p192.

"Stingy innkeeper cured of serving weak bear". *See* The three cups of water

Stoats. *See* **Ermine**

Stockings
The man who had no story

Stockton, Frank B.
Old Pipes and the dryad
Prince Hassak's march

Stockton, Frank R.
JOHNSON – HARPER p329.

Stokes, Whitley
The voyage of Maelduin

The stolen bairn and the sidh
LEODHAS – THISTLE p46-61

The stolen jewel
HITCHCOCK – KING p53-75

The stolen lady
BRIGGS – PERS. p80-82

The stolen ring
BARASH – GOLDEN p155-161

The stolen rope
WITHERS – WORLD p73.

The stolen turnips
BUDBERG – RUSSIAN p251-272

The stolen wine
DE LA IGLESIA – CAT unp.

The stone crusher of Banjang
COURLANDER – KANT. p97-100

The stone frogs
PARKER – AUSTRALIAN p143-147

The stone horseman
FOSTER – STONE p5-16

The stone in the cock's head
HAVILAND – ITALY p43-53

The stone in the garden
KELSEY – ONCE p89-94

The stone king
SPICER – WITCHES p60-66

The stone lute
COURLANDER – KING'S p95-97

The stone memorial to a dog
INS-SŎB – FOLK p93-94

The stone monkey
MANNING – BEASTS p45-48
TURNBULL – FAIRY p1-11

The stone of patience
EKREM – TURKISH p103-111

The stone of victory
COLUM – STONE p13-29

The stone owl's nest
SPICER – OWL'S p115-28

Stone patience and knife patience
BUCK – FAIRY p225-231

Stone quarries
About the good American witch

Stone soup in Bohemia
MORRIS – UPSTAIRS p17-25

The stone stew
EDMONDS – TRICKSTER p113-119

The stone troll
TOLKIEN – READER p39-40 part 4

Stonemasons
The bee man and the boundary man
The grateful mouse
Haku's power
Saint Quien Sabe
The sly thief of Valenciennes
The stone crusher of Banjang

Stone crushers. *See* **Stonemasons**

Stones. *See* **Rocks and stones**

Stonewall Silas Clapp
TAFT – PROFILE p103-107

Stools
Bomba, the brave
The yam child

Store-keepers. *See* Merchants

Stories about girls and boys
GREY – SOUTH (1) p28.

Stories about Kampen
LEEUW – LEGENDS p46-51

The stork caliph
U. N. – RIDE p66-76

A stork is not always a stork
JONES – SCAND. p110-111

Storks
The caliph stork, told by Selim
Baruch, the stranger
The fox and the stork
The frog and the stork
Golden bracelets, golden anklets
The grateful stork
The hazel-nut child
How little stork lost his tail
Krazy Kat
The little toy land of the Dutch
Ruba and the stork
Silian the stork
The story of Caliph stork
Sungold
The tale of Caliph stork
The tale of the Earl of Mar's daughter
The turtle and the storks and the
jackal
The turtle, the storks and the jackal
The wise old camel
The wolf and the stork

Storks and babies
BATCHELOR – SUPER. p30.

Storm, Dan
Senor coyote settles a quarrel
The war between the lion and the
cricket

Storm, Theodor
Little Johnny

Stormalong
GORHAM – REAL p96-105

Storms
See also Blizzards; Cyclones; Lightning;
Rain; Snow; Thunder
Big winds
The black stone
The boy of the red twilight sky
The bragging bat
Count Bertrand
The farmer and the demon
The first of May
The fisherman and the mermaid
The flower faces
How Urseli became a princess
The legend of Crooked Mountain
The legend of Peter Rugg
The lost gift
The magic storm
The man who helped carry the coffin
The man who missed the Tay Bridge
train
Marya Morevna
The master mariner
Never
Nuberu
The old man with the bump
The ordeal of Leyden
The phantom bridge
Prince Finn the fair
The princess and the pea
The return
The sea knight
The sea of Moyle
The shepherd of clouds
The tale of the wrath of God
The tempest
Thunder and lightning
The thunder cat
A thunderstorm
Tsai Shun, the faithful
Why the motmot lives in a hole
Wind and tempest
The yellow dragon

Stormy lifts anchor
FELTON – TRUE p13-17

Stormy sets sail
FELTON – TRUE p18-23

Stormy swallows the anchor
FELTON – TRUE p40.

A story about Abe Lincoln
MY BOOK HOUSE v. 5 p129-134

A story about Our Lord Jesus Christ
RANKE – GERMANY p154-155

A story about the little rabbits
MY BOOK HOUSE v. 3 p123-126

The story ends
KOREL – LISTEN p64-67

A story for Kiem
ROBERTSON – FAIRY p17-24

The story in the sealed book
MOZLEY – EGYPT p49-57

The story of a fairy serpent
HSIEH – CHINESE p72-74

The story of a gentleman
INS-SOB – FOLK p123-126

The story of a good boy
GREY – SOUTH (2) p7-9

The story of a lazy man
CREANGA – FOLK p82-85

The story of a man in a shell
HSIEH – CHINESE p56-57

Story of a nickel and a dime
WITHERS – I SAW p49-51

The story of a princess
IVES – TALES p13-28

The story of Admiral Yi
INS-SOB – FOLK p77.

The story of Ailill and Etaine
GARNIER – LEGENDS p157-165

The story of an egg
URE – RUMANIAN p153-157

The story of Aoyagi
BUCK – FAIRY p297-305

The story of Bensurdatu
HAVILAND – ITALY p20-41

The story of big Paul Bunyan
MY BOOK HOUSE v. 4 p161-179

The story of Blathnat
YOUNG – HOW p17-20

The story of Branwen
JONES – WELSH p20-35

"Story of Burnt Njal" (book)
Njal the lawyer

The story of Caliph stork
BUCK – FAIRY p269-280

The story of Cincinnatus
BALDWIN – FAVOR. p58-64

The story of Cozumel, the lazy swallow
BOWES – BIRD p51.

The story of flying Robert
PROTTER – CHILD. p165.

The story of General Gim Dog-Nyong
INS-SOB – FOLK p58-59

A story of guile
HARDENDORFF – FROG'S p75-82

The story of Harisarman
WILLIAMS – ROUND p67-72

The story of Hime
MARMUR – JAPAN. p31-40

The story of Hinemoa
CAMPBELL – MAORI p52-56

The story of Hine-Moa and Tutanekai
BERRY – MAGIC p56-64

The story of Hong Gil-Dong
INS-SOB – FOLK p207-223

The story of Ir, Bir, Dau, and I
WITHERS – I SAW p112-114

The story of Issoumbochi
MARMUR – JAPAN. p11-16

The story of Iubdan, King of the lepra
and the lepracaun
MORAY – FAIR p28-44

The story of King Frost
BUCK – FAIRY p64-67

The story of Li'l Hannibal
MY BOOK HOUSE v. 3 p116-122

The story of little Mukra
MOZLEY – ARABY p59-69

The story of Maia
MANNING – DWARFS p112-124

The story of Mead Moondaughter
BOUCHER – MEAD p162-169

The story of Ming-Y
BUCK – FAIRY p51-63

The story of Mrs. Tubbs
ARBUTHNOT – TIME p267-272

The story of Mon-do-min
  TAFT – PROFILE p251-253

The story of Mordecai and Esther
  BARASH – GOLDEN p147-154

The story of Noschoy Datta of Ujjain
  GHOSE – FOLK p13-27

The story of O-Tei
  BUCK – FAIRY p125-128

The story of Prince Ahmed
  WILLIAMS – OLD p30-44

The story of Prince Fairyfoot
  BURNETT – RACKETTY p141-190

The story of Prince Ring and his dog
  BOUCHER – MEAD p123-135

The story of Protesilaus
  GREEN – GREEKS p24-25

The story of Regulus
  BALDWIN – FAVOR. p65-68

A story of Robin Hood
  BALDWIN – FAVOR. p127-133

A story of Rustem, the hero of Persia
  MY BOOK HOUSE v. 10 p228-240

The story of Sigurd
  LINES – TALES p276-284

The story of silly Cham-ba
  WILLIAMS – OLD p180-196

The story of Suka's dog
  GHOSE – FOLK p85-88

The story of Telephus
  GREEN – GREEKS p18-19

The story of the boy who couldn't keep anything in his head
  NAHMAD – PEASANT p123-130

The story of the Cid
  MY BOOK HOUSE v. 10 p108-117

The story of the fairy boat
  HUME – FAVORITE p69-73

The story of the five fingers
  BAMBERGER – FIRST p36-39

The story of the five toes
  BAMBERGER – FIRST p9.

The story of the fraids
  JOHNSON – WHAT p251-252

The story of the Greek princess
  GREEN – TALES p185-201

The story of the haunted jars
  GHOSE – FOLK p118-119

The story of the king who would be stronger than fate
  BUCK – FAIRY p68-80

The story of the pig
  CREANGA – FOLK p102-119

The story of the shining princess
  BERGER – BLACK p68-78

The story of the shipwrecked sailor
  GREEN – TALES p151-158

The story of the smart parrot
  JAGENDORF – KING p242-244

The story of the stone lion
  MANNING – BEASTS p122-129

The story of the talking bird
  MY BOOK HOUSE v. 8 p109-131

The story of the thick fat pancake
  BAMBERGER – FIRST p26-30

The story of the three bears
  ARBUTHNOT – TIME p8-9
  LINES – NURSERY p23-32

The story of the three little pigs
  ARBUTHNOT – TIME p10-11
  LINES – NURSERY p117-127

The story of the tortoise and the monkey
  HUME – FAVORITE p39-46

A story of the wind
  MY BOOK HOUSE v. 1 p200.

The story of three brothers
  URE – RUMANIAN p160-166

The story of Ticho
  ROSS – MEXICO p87-103

The story of Tom Thumb
  MY BOOK HOUSE v. 5 p11-19
  REEVES – ENGLISH p63-70

The story of Wali Dad the simple-hearted
  BUCK – FAIRY p19-28

624

The story of Wang Li
  CHILD − CASTLES p211-225

The story of white Arab
  CREANGĂ − FOLK p1-60

The story of William Tell
  BALDWIN − FAVOR. p41-44

The story of Ywenec
  MORAY − FAIR p153-173

The story of Zal
  PALMER − DRAGONS p79-86

The story of Zibong
  INS-SŎB − FOLK p103-105

The story of Zoulvisia
  LANG − OLIVE p222-236

A story on stone: The divine birth of
Hatshepsut
  JAMES − MYTHS p84-95

The story-spirits
  INS-SŎB − FOLK p154-157
  WILLIAMS − ROUND p279-288

The story without an end
  WITHERS − WORLD p101-103

The storyteller
  COURLANDER − FIRE p99-102
  SIDDIQUI − TOON. p155-157

Storytellers and storytelling
  About Eskimo stories
  All stories are Anansi's
  And I dance mine own child
  Au Sung meets Kim Lee
  The bored tengu
  Buh Rabbit's big eat
  The caravan
  The caravan continues
  The caravan reaches the end of the
    desert
  The cartman's stories
  The children of Lir
  Chinese rival storytellers
  The clever boy
  The crimson purse
  The dark and stormy night
  The dog that learned to read
  The end of the evening
  The endless story
  The endless tale
  The faithless apprentice
  The fate of the sons of Usnach
  Five lies that could be true

  The flying trunk
  The forty whoppers
  The four young men
  From tiger to Anansi
  Goblin bread
  The golden casket
  The golden lamb
  Gonae
  Grandfather tells some tales
  How Au Sung repaid Kim Lee
  How I found these tales
  How these tales came to be told
  How to tell stories to children
  If you know a story, don't keep it to
    yourself
  Impossible tales
  Intelligence and luck
  Introduction (WALKER− DANCING)
  Johnny McGorry and the red stocking
  The king who liked fairy tales
  The king's rabbits
  The Korean goblins
  The laughing statue
  The liars' contest
  The little king on the Viking ship
  The loup-garou in the woods
  Luz, the story-teller
  Manning MacGilligan's story
  A million stories
  Mother tells a story
  An old Korean story
  Old stories
  The old storyteller
  Once there was and once there was
    not
  Ooka and the telltale tale
  The parrot
  The peasant and the tsar
  Preface: Story time in Mexico
  The quest of the children of Turenn
  Scheherazade
  The silent princess
  The silly slave
  The story-spirits
  Taikon, Johan Dimitri
  Tall tales from the Gotham Inn
  The thirteen enchanted cats
  The three enchanted maidens
  The three giants
  The three most famous tales
  Three silly schoolmasters
  Uwaine and the lady of the fountain
  The Vetala's stories
  Wembi, the singer of stories
  What is a crick crack story
  Why people tell stories
  The wife who liked fairy tales
  The woman in moon
  The wonders of the three donals
  The woodcutter's daughter
  The young storyteller

Story-telling in Milpa Alta
  BRENNER – BOY p5-26

Stoves
  Foolish Emilyan and the talking fish
  Keloglan and the lucky exchanges
  Lie-a-stove
  The new camp stove
  The new camp stove burns again
  The Nuremberg stove

Stow, Harriet Beecher
  Mrs. Stowe's oranges

Straight and crooked
  DUDDINGTON – RUSS. p66-71

The straight and narrow way
  REED – TALK. p22-27

The strange adventure of Baron Munchausen
  MY BOOK HOUSE v. 2 p182-184

The strange adventure of Paddy O'Toole
  MANNING – GHOSTS p68-73

The strange adventures of Alcavilu
  BARLOW – LATIN p28-37

The strange adventures of the cowboy-
  sailor
  JAGENDORF – NEW p117-125

The strange battle of Windham
  TAFT – PROFILE p85-87

A strange choice
  FOSTER – STONE p26-33

The strange feathery beast
  COOPER – FIVE p58-75

Strange folk of the sea
  LAWSON – STRANGE p81-100

A strange guest
  JUDA – WISE p94-99

Strange houses
  WITHERS – I SAW p38.

The strange journey of Tuflongbo
  REEVES – THREE unp.

Strange men with tails
  CARPENTER – AFRICAN p93-101

A strange reward
  VITTORINI – OLD p38-44

The strange ship of Captain Fokke
  LITTLEDALE – GHOSTS p125-134

A strange sled race
  THOMPSON – HAWAII. p28-32

Strange story
  WITHERS – I SAW p17.

The strange trial
  JAGENDORF – UPSTATE p72-74

The strange visitor
  WILLIAMS – FAIRY p132-134

The strange white beast
  MANNING – BEASTS p158-159

The stranger and the miller
  SHEPPARD – SCOT. p117-121

Strangers
  The blue jackal
  The caravan
  Little Red Riding Hood
  Red Riding Hood
  A severe punishment
  The wandering staff
  The werewolf

The strangest thing in the world
  PROTTER – CHILD. p77-81

Straw
  Bedding in one's ear
  The borrowing of 100,000 arrows
  The bundles of straw and the king's
    son
  The girl who could spin clay and
    straw into gold
  The girl who picked strawberries
  How bean got his stripe
  How the milky way began
  Mr. Lucky Straw
  Not to care a straw
  The piece of straw
  A wisp of straw

Straw, bean and coal
  RANKE – GERMANY p27.

The straw ox
  HAVILAND – RUSSIA p53-65
  MANNING – BEASTS p8-13

The straw, the coal and the bean
  BAMBERGER – FIRST p58-59

626

Strawberries
The first strawberries
The flute made of maple-wood
The girl who picked strawberries
The little rooster and the little hen
Mother Luck
The princess who hid her slippers
The three little men in the wood
The twelve months
What the children do in summer

Strawberry roan

STOUTENBURG – CROC. p14-17

Streams. *See* **Fields and streams**

Street luck
LEACH – LUCK p24-29

Strength
See also **Giants**
Annie Christmas
The ant in search of her leg
Aunt Karin's chest
Bas Celik
The blacksmith and the horseman
The blue belt
The blue foal
The boy with the golden star
Break mountains
The bundle of sticks
The champion
The clever goatherd and the greedy
giant
The clever little tailor
The cobbler
The dirt boy
The dog and the karbau
Donal from Donegal
The donkey and the lions
Double Arend of Meeden
Fin M'Coul and Cucullin
Fionn in search of his youth
Four sworn brothers
The fox, the hare, and the toad have
an argument
The giant and the mite
The giant outwitted
The giant who sucked his thumb
The giant who took a long time to
grow
Grettir becomes an outlaw
Hammerman/John Henry
The hauntings at Thorhallstead
Horns
How Cuchulain wooed his wife
Ilya of Murom and Svyatogor
In unity is strength
The inquiring rabbit or the strongest
thing in the world

Jabuty, the strong
Jaco and the giant
Jan the eighth Van Arkel
Joe Magarac
Joe Magarac the steel man
Joe Magerack, the steel-mill man
John Henry
John the bear
Kagssagssuk, the homeless boy who
became a strong man
Kantjil brings the elephants to heel
Kantjil grows strong at the welling-
well
Khrishna the cowherd
Know your own strength
Laka and the Little-People
Lazarus and the dragons
The little bull calf
The little nobleman
Lod, the farmer's son
Loki's monstrous brood
Lucas the strong
The man who feared nothing
Merisler, stronger than the elephants
The midget and the giant
Mighty Michael . . . Who could do
anything
Mighty Mose, the Bowery b'hoy
Mirza and the ghul
Mister honey mouth
A mouse in search of a wife
Nikita and the dragon
The nine-headed giant
The Northern lights
The old man and his sons
Paul Bunyan
The peasant's strong wife
Pride goes before a fall
The prince and the dragons
The proud father
The sage and the mouse
A secret told to a stranger
Segizbai and the little mouse-girl
The shark in the milky way
Sigiris Sinno, the mighty one
The six companions
Sky-bright axe/Paul Bunyan
The slaying of Siegfried
The son of strength
Soria Moria castle
The speckled bull
Stan Bolovan
The stone crusher of Banjang
The stone in the garden
The story of Zoulvisia
The strong boy
Strong Gottlieb
Strong man
The strongest
Sturdy Hans
Takero

Strength (*Continued*)

The tale of the superman
Thor and the giants
Thor's journey to Jotun-Heim
Three fat ewes for three fine hounds
The three-legged jumping giant
Three princes and their beasts
Tom Hickathrift
Tortoise triumphant
Tree-root, iron-strong and hill-roller
The tug of war
The turnip
The turtle, the hippo, and the elephant
The two lovers
The unicorn and the dwarf
Vukub–Cakix
Waiting on salvation
The war of the animals against the
  birds
Who is strongest?
Who's strong?
Why cats live with women
Why dogs live with men
The wrestler of Kyushu
The young giant
Young Paul

Stretch, Puff and Blazer
  BULATKIN – EURASIAN p44-56

Stretching the bench
  RANKE – GERMANY p179.

Strike there!
  LEEKLEY – RIDDLE p115-138

String
  Dawn, twilight and midnight
  The midget and the giant

The string of lies
  LOWE – LITTLE p72-74

String on your finger
  BATCHELOR – SUPER. p96-98

The strong boy
  MY BOOK HOUSE v. 6 p118-126

Strong Gottlieb
  BECHSTEIN – FAIRY p62-71

Strong man
  MARTIN – NINE p51-54

The strongest
  DEUTSCH – MORE p39-43

The struggle between the wolf and the
  fox
  RANKE – GERMANY p8-17

Stubborn husband, stubborn wife
  MEHDEVI – PERSIAN p93-103

The stubborn sillies
  DOBBS – ONCE p105-109

Stubbornness
  The contrary wife
  The contrary woman
  The country under the hill
  Kate Contrary
  Kigbo and the bush spirits
  The man who walked widdershins
    round the kirk
  Mary, Mary, so contrary!
  The most obedient wife
  The old woman against the stream
  The pert fire-engine
  Phaeton
  The right time to laugh
  Scissors
  The very obstinate man
  The wee, wee mannie and the big, big
    coo
  Why women won't listen

The stubbornest man in Maine
  JAGENDORF – NEW p13-20

The student from Paradise. *See* The guest
  from Heaven

The student who became a prince
  McNEILL – DOUBLE p67-72

The student who was forced to be king
  ILLYES – ONCE p23-26

The student-witch
  HOPE-SIMPSON – CAVAL. p1-15

Students
  See also **Scholars**
  The dream at Nam Kha
  The pira game
  Six-and-four
  The terrible-tempered dragon

Stumbling
  Tripping and stumbling

Stumping the devil
  JOHNSON – WHAT p177.

The stupid boy
  HACK – DANISH p164-168

Stupid Emilien
   PONSOT – RUSSIAN p31-42

The stupid fellow
   HARDENDORFF – TRICKY p101-
   108

Stupid head
   MANNING – PRINCES p125-128

The stupid hunter and the crafty bird
   NAHMAD – PEASANT p97-99

Stupid Peruonto
   LUM – ITALIAN p79-90

The stupid wolf
   FOSTER – STONE p17-21
   MASEY – STORIES p116-117

Stupidity
   See also **Fools and foolishness**
   Buh rabbit's tight necktie
   The case of the calf and the colt
   The clever billy goat
   The counting of the crocodiles
   A foolish mourner
   How Ologbon-Ori sought wisdom
   How the rabbit fooled the elephant
   Human stupidity
   The hunter and his talking leopard
   It's already paid
   The jackal and the bear
   Jan and Jaantje
   Lars, my lad!
   Lato, the stupid one
   The magic cap
   The magician's heart
   The man from Kailasa
   The man who lost his way
   Mary, Mary, so contrary!
   Nazar the brave
   Now would I laugh, were I knot dead
   The people of Mols
   Pierre Jean's tortoise
   Pride goes before a fall
   The quivering needle
   Ricky of the tuft
   Senor coyote and the dogs
   Shaydoola
   The silent maiden
   Simple-minded Jeanne
   A slip of the tongue
   The sly gypsy and the stupid devil
   Stories about Kampen
   The tale of the youngest brother and
   the stupid devil
   A talkative old woman
   The two foolish cats
   Why are giants so stupid?

The would-be wizard

Stupid's cries
   JACOBS – MORE p211-124

Sturdy Hans
   MÜLLER – SWISS p171-176

Sturgeon moon
   BUDD – FULL p45-49

Stuyvesant, Peter
   Anthony and the Mossbunker
   The courageous Quaker of Flushing
   The ghost of Peg-leg Peter

Submarines
   The story of Admiral Yi

The subterranean passage
   MICHAEL – PORTUGUESE p74-83

Success
   The musician of Tagaung

Sudden silence
   BATCHELOR – SUPER. p49-51

Sugar cane
   The camel and his neighbor
   Nkalimeva
   The tiger in the palanquin

The sugar-plum tree
   MY BOOK HOUSE v. 2 p223-224

Sugarbirds
   The lost spear

"Sugardolly"
   The nutcracker and sugardolly stories

Sugimoto, Chiyono
   The good-luck teakettle
   The peach boy
   Urashima

Suicide
   The hairs of the baron's head
   Ifor the scoffer

Suitors
   See also **Courtship**
   Anangarati and the men of four
   castes
   The artifical earthquake

Suitors (*Continued*)

Bahmoo and the frog
Bas Celik
The beauty and her gallant
The beginning of good conversation
The blue rose
Count crow and the princess
The crumb in the beard
Drak, the fairy
Ekun and Opolo go looking for wives
The five young men
For love of a woman
The fountain
Georgie goes a-sparkin'
The girl on the hill
The girl who married the devil
Great heart and the three tests
How Prince Bondhu became a boat-
man
How the Raja's son won the Princess
Laban
Intelligence and luck
Kabadaluk
The king who liked fairy tales
The louse skin
Madschun
The magician's garden
The marriage feast
The mason's marriage
The most obedient wife
Pen and four foolish ministers
Penelope and her suitors
Pomona . . . The tree and the vine
The princess and the shepherd
The princess and the string of lies
The princess and the vagabone
Pwyll and Rhiannon
The red-maned horse
The sea otter girl
The seven proud sisters
The shepherd's nosegay
The slaying of the suitors
The swineherd who married a princess
Three bridegrooms for one bride
The three misty women
The three suitors
The three tasks
Three tests for the prince
The three traveling artisans
Tortoise and Babarinsa's daughters
Tsar Boris and the devil king
The two bridegrooms
The white hound
The white spider's gift
Why the monsoon comes each year
The wizard king
The wooing of Lottie Moon

Sultan Murat's challenge
CURCIJA – HEROES p36.

Sultans
Caravan
The chief astrologer
The handkerchief
The happy man
The invisible thief
Kralyevich Marko and Mussa
Kessedzhiya
Kralyevich Marko drinks wine during
the Ramadhan
Madschun
The magic carpet
The rooster and the sultan
Scheherazade
The unusual excuse

The sultan's fool
GILSTRAP – SULTAN'S p32-39

Sumatra
Bajan Budiman, the sharpshooter
The battle of the buffaloes
The bet between Matjan and Gadja
Crocodile's share
Guno and Koyo
Guno's hunger
The hunter of Perak
An old Sumatran legend
The stone crusher of Banjang
The tiger's tail
The wood carver of Ruteng

, **West**
The victory of the buffalo

Sumlee's broken stick
KRUEGER – SERPENT p151-158

Sum-m, sum-m, sum-m!
MY BOOK HOUSE v. 1 p122.

Summer
Corn moon
Grasshopper green
How summer came to Canada
Ice-cold lemonade
Little Burnt-face
Lovers' moon
A midsummer night's dream
Moon of blood
O 'twas on a bright mornin' in summer
Old pipes and the dryad
Proserpine
The return of the Spring
The shaking of the pear tree
Sturgeon moon
What the children do in summer
When I was a baby
Why there are four seasons in the
year
A winky-tooden song
The wise ant

630

Summer
  BUDD – FULL p28-50

The summer birds
  LEEKLEY – WORLD p76-78

The summer of the big snow
  JAGENDORF – GYPSIES p35-38

Summer rain
  CATHON – PERHAPS p238.

Summer snow
  LEEUW – LEGENDS p60-65

Sun
  All light comes from the sun
  Ants
  Bird of the sun
  The brawl between sun and moon
  Child of the sun
  Children of the sun
  Clytie
  Cottontail and the sun
  The extraordinary black coat
  The fire dogs
  The fisherman who caught the sun
  The foolish father-in-law
  Frey and Gerd, the jotun maiden
  The frost, the sun, and the wind
  The giant archer of the sky
  The girl in the moon
  Golden flower and the three warriors
  The golden peacock
  The greatest wealth in the world
  The greedy rich man
  The heavenly lovers
  The heron's ball
  How and why: Why the bear waddles
    when he walks
  How beaver got his fine fur
  How chipmunk got his stripes
  How coyote helped to light the world
  How dandelions were made
  How fire was brought from lightning
  How he stole the moon and the sun
  How it came about that there is a
    sun and a moon
  How Ma-ui snared the sun and made
    him go more slowly across the
    heavens
  How master Thumb defeated the sun
  How men learned about evil
  How rooster got his comb
  How the bat caught friendship with
    the moon
  How the cock got his red crown
  How the half boys came to be
  How the people sang the mountains
    up
  How the sun came

How the sun was made
How Yehl, the hero, freed the beam-
  ing maiden
The inquiring rabbit, or the strongest
  thing in the world
The king of the mountains
The lazy man who married the sun's
  daughter
The legend of the star children
The lost sun, moon, and stars
The maiden and the ratcatcher
The man in the moon
The man who paddled to the moon's
  house
The match-making of a mouse
A matter of importance
Maui catches the sun
Maui nooses the sun
Maui the fire-bringer
Maui the Great
The mink and the sun
The mole's bridegroom
The moon and his frog-wife
The moon's a woman
The moon's face
The mouse and the sun
A mouse in search of a wife
The palace of the night
The peasant and his hen
Phaethon . . . The chariot of the sun
Phaeton
Phaeton; the boy who rode the chariot
  of the sun
Phoenix, bird of the sun
The planting party
Prince Ivan and the sun princess
Prince sun and Princess moon
The proud father
Quinces and oranges
The rat's bridegroom
Raven and the sun
Rhodopis and her gilded sandals
The river of lantern land
The rooster and the sun
The sage and the mouse
Scarface
The securing of light
Segizbai and the little mouse-girl
The six brothers
Spider boy and the sun god's twins
The spider weaver
Star-boy and the sun dance
The stone crusher of Banjang
The strongest
Tavadan
Tcakabesh snares the sun
The terrible Olli
A tropical morning at sea
Twins of gold and silver
Uletka
The wedding of the mouse

Sun (*Continued*)

Which is better, the sun or the moon?
The white dove of the city of the
  swinging gate
Who?
Why crow is black and men find prec-
  ious stones in the earth
Why mole's front paws are bent
Why sun and moon live in the sky
Why the bush-bowl calls at dawn and
  why flies buzz
Why the buzzard eats the rooster's
  children
Why the sun and moon live in the sky
Why the sun is brighter than the
  moon
Why the sun shines in the daytime
  and the moon shines at night
Why the sun stopped shining
Why there are shadows on the moon
The wind and the sun

Sun and moon
  LEACH – RAINBOW p303-304

Sun and moon and the pretty girl
  JABLOW – MAN p64-66

The sun and the moon
  INS-SOB – FOLK p7-10

The sun and the north wind
  LA FONTAINE – FABLES p17.

The sun callers
  COURLANDER – PEOPLE p126-128

The sun-child
  BAMBERGER – FIRST p164-170

The sun drives copper-colored reindeer
  BELTING – STARS #11

The sun-king's hair
  HAMPDEN – GYPSY p35-43

Sun, moon, and morning star
  EELLS – SPAIN p117-128

Sun, moon and stars: Little numskull
  stories
  JABLOW – MAN p75-76

The sun of Llanfobon. *See* Eight leaves
of story (6) The sun of Llanfobon

The sun, the moon, and the star of
morning
  WILSON – GREEK p182-197

The sun, the moon, and the stars
  HEADY – TALES p15-20

Sun, thunder, lightning, and the stars
  JABLOW – MAN p79-117

Sunday
  The mountain hen and the fox
  Why there is a man in the moon

Sunfish
  The adventures of a water baby

Sunflowers
  Clytie

Sung-ling, P'u
  The mysterious path

Sungold
  BAMBERGER – FIRST p198-203

Sungold and the remarkable cow
  BELTING – THREE p17-24

The sunken city
  McNEILL – SUNKEN p7-11

Sunrises
  How the sun was made

Sunsets
  The morning and the sunset that
  lighteth up the sky

Superiority
  The speckled hen's egg

Supermen
  The tale of the superman

The supernatural crossbow
  SUN – LAND p21-27

Supernatural legends
  See also Ghosts
  Curse of the Abenaki
  The devil's bride
  For love of a woman
  General Moulton's boot
  The haunted house of Watertown
  Lady Eaton's curse
  Lady Eleanore's mantle
  The legend of Eilean Donan castle
  The legend of Peter Rugg
  Legend of the witch of Cape Ann
  The Machimoodus noise

632

Supernatural legends (*Continued*)

    Micah Rood's apple tree
    The phantom bridge
    Tom Walker and the devil
    Wild worms and swooning shadows

Superstition: the remnants of magic
    JENNINGS – BLACK p144-160

Superstitions
    Action
    Animals
    Bells on her toes
    Brides, grooms and weddings
    Carry an acorn
    Character
    Charms
    Company
    Conjure bags
    Death
    The devil's wood
    Dreams
    Drop the handkerchief
    Everywhere you go
    The farm
    Fashion
    The figurehead
    Flip a coin
    Folks
    Food
    Forks
    Fortune telling
    Four-leaf clover
    Friends
    Gems
    Gloves
    God bless you
    Guardian of the house
    Hang up a horseshoe
    Insects and other critters
    Love and sentiment
    Luck
    The man who walked widdershins
      round the kirk
    Medicinal
    Memory
    Money
    The moon
    Numbers
    Odds
    Religious
    Romance
    Salt
    Shoes
    Sixpence for a breeze
    Snakes
    Some New England superstitions
    Sounds
    The spider in the wall
    Unlucky passengers

    The victorious lute
    The voyage of the Lass of Glasgow
    Warts
    The wedding of the dragon-god
    The wind's eye
    Wishes

  −Action
    Best foot forward
    Breaking a mirror
    Move clockwise, and other circle
      superstitions
    Moving day
    Photograph upside down
    Thumbs up, thumbs down
    Tripping and stumbling

  −Animals
    Black cat
    Bulls and the color red
    Do warts come from toads?
    Is a white horse lucky?
    Rabbit's foot

  −Birds
    Birds
    Do scarecrows scare crows?
    A little bird told me
    Storks and babies
    Swans

  −Character
    Are fat people happy?
    Blonde, brunette or redhead
    Dimples
    Your name

  −Fairies
    Gremlins, elves and leprechauns
    Witches and witchcraft

  −Fashion
    Clothing wrong side out
    Ears and earrings
    Umbrellas

  −Food
    An apple a day
    Eat bread crusts for curly hair
    Farming by the moon
    Is fish a brain food?
    Onions and garlic
    Salt

  −Gems
    Diamonds
    Do pearls bring tears?
    Is the opal unlucky?

  −Luck
    Are pins lucky?
    Bread and butter
    Cross my heart
    Cross your fingers
    Knock on wood
    Lucky break

Superstitions *(Continued)*

—Memory
Forgotten something?
String on your finger

—Money
Money superstitions
Two dollar curse

—Numbers
Friday the thirteenth
Sudden silence
"Thirteen" superstitions
"Three" superstitions

—Reflexes
Hiccoughing
Reflexes
Sneezing
Yawning

—Romance
Love and lovers

—Sleep
Does food cause bad dreams?
Fear of the dark
Getting out of bed right
How to sleep well

—Sounds
Better not whistle!
Does a dog's howl mean death?
Sing before breakfast

—Wishes
Make a wish
Wishbone

—Work
Luck in business
Men of the sea
Work

Superstitions
LAWSON — STRANGE p141-154

Supparaka the mariner
GRAY — INDIA'S p13-18

Suppose you met a witch
HOPE-SIMPSON — CAVAL. p16-22

Surfing
The bride from the land of the spirits
Kelea, the surf princess

Surinam
The crocodile's daughter

Surprise for the black bull
CREDLE — TALL p115-121

"Surprises and answers"
Deaf men and their answers
Growing pains
How to cook a coot
Hungry hog
I'll tell her
Through the needle's eye

Surprising adventures of Don Quixote of La Mancha
MY BOOK HOUSE v. 11 p90-106

Surriage, Agnes
Scandalous affairs of a baronet and a tavern maid

Surveyors and surveying
The bee man and the boundary man
Bride's brook
George Rogers Clark and the conquest of the Northwest
Help in need and Abe in deed
The wicked house of Duncan Macbain

Suspicion
A meeting of scholars

A suspicious wife with an enforced extra husband
HSIEH — CHINESE p63-66

Sutter, John August
The man who started it all, the man who couldn't forget

Sven and Lilli
MANNING — MERMAIDS p9-14

Svyatogor's bride
DOWNING — RUSSIAN p8-10

The swallowing monster
ARNOTT — TALES p65-69

Swallows
At the wedding of Miss Jenny Wren
Children's songs of ancient Greece (by Theognis)
The five swallow sisters
The greedy man in the moon
The happy prince
Here we come, we children come
The imposter
Itsaysya frees the slamon
Mirzhan and the lord of the kingdom under the sea
The secret store
The story of Maia
The story of Mrs. Tubbs

Swallows (*Continued*)

The task of the deputy chief councillor Iso-no-Kamimaro
Thumbelina

—Nests
    The story of Cozumel, the lazy swallow

The swamp Nushi's messenger
    SEKI — FOLKTALES p57-60

Swamps
    The jackal and the elephant
    The magic purse of the swamp maiden
    Tom Walker and the devil
    Why rabbit has a short tail

The swan maiden(s)
    BAMBERGER — FIRST p111-113
    JACOBS — EUROPE. p98-105

The swan princess
    HOKE — WITCHES p176-186

The swan, the crab, and the pike
    KRYLOV — 15 p36-37

Swan white and fox tail
    McNEILL — DOUBLE p105-114

Swans
    The black swans
    The blue parrot
    The children of Lir
    The Christian bell
    The city east of the moon and south of the sun
    The death of the children of Lir
    The fairy host
    The first three hundred years
    The geese and the swans
    The golden apples of Hisberna
    The golden slipper, the magic ring, and the twigs
    How Jack sought the golden apples
    How Loki outwitted a giant
    Ivashko and the witch
    Little Firenko
    Lohengrin
    The lost prince
    The magic swan
    Maid Lena
    Midir and Etain
    Prince Finn the fair
    The red Swan
    The sea of Moyle
    The six swans
    Souchmant's trial and triumph
    The three sons of the king of Antua
    The tortoise and the two swans
    The tsar's son and the swan-girl
    The ugly duckling
    Volund the smith
    The weeping lady of Llyn Glasfryn
    The wild swans
    The witch and the swan maiden

Swans
    BATCHELOR — SUPER. p32-33

The swans of Ballycastle
    CHILD — CASTLES p259-289

Swapping. *See* **Traders and trading**

The swapping song
    STOUTENBURG — CROC. p44-45

Swearing
    See also **Curses**
    Preacher Peter and Mike Fink

Sweden
    The adventures of Silvervit and Lillvacker
    All my lambkins and all my bear cubs
    Aunt Karin's chest
    Beowulf fights a battle with the sea
    The boy and Necken
    The boy and the fox
    The boy and the water-sprite
    The cap that mother made
    Cattenborg
    East of the sun and north of the earth
    Elsa and the ten elves
    The girl who could spin clay and straw into gold
    The girl who met the witch of the woods
    Godfather death
    Halde Hat and Dulde Hat
    Happy Hans
    King Lindorm
    The lad and the fox
    The lame dog
    Lars, my lad!
    Lars, my servant
    The little mouse
    Little Rosa and long Leda
    Odd Olle
    The old woman and the fish
    The old woman and the tramp
    Peter and the witch of the wood
    Pinkel
    The prince and the chimney sweep
    Prince Andrea and Princess Meseria
    Prince Hat beneath the earth
    The prince who made the silence speak
    The princess and the glass mountain
    The princess and the string of lies

Sweden (*Continued*)

The princess in the earth cave
Princess Janina and the troll Bradalba
The princess on the glass mountain
The princess who hid her slippers
The princess who was rescued from
   slavery
Queen Crane
The queen's necklace
The rich man and his son-in-law
The rooster, the hand mill and the
   swarm of hornets
Salt and bread
The six swans
Sleeping beauty
The spindles are still
Swan white and fox tail
A tale of the Tontlawald
The three wishes
The white bride and the black bride
Why Eyvin won the race

Sweden
   HOPE-SIMPSON − CAVAL. p197-198

Swedes
The enemy in the night
The hauntings at Thorhallstead
Hi-ho, the mosquitoes of New
   Jersey!

A Swedish evening
   MY BOOK HOUSE v. 2 p141.

Swedish rhymes
   MY BOOK HOUSE v. 1 p74-75

Sweet and low
   MY BOOK HOUSE v. 1 p118.

Sweet Betsy from Pike
   STOUTENBURG − CROC. p53-55

Sweet dung, the cake-tree, and the bugle
   of life
   INS-SŎB − FOLK p178-180

Sweet misery
   COURLANDER − PIECE p37-38

The sweet Mochi's parents
   SEKI − FOLKTALES p195-197

Sweet peas and Grecian urns
   MY BOOK HOUSE v. 12 p66-73

The sweetest song in the woods
   JAGENDORF − KING p132-135

Sweetness
   Clever Manka

Swen-Naba; king of the warlocks
   GUIRMA − TALES p85-99

Swift, Jonathan
   Gulliver in the giants' country
   Gulliver's travels to Lilliput
   A voyage to Brobdingnag

Swift-as-the-wind, Hold fast and Hard-as-
   iron
   BAMBERGER − FIRST p175-178

A swift messenger
   DUDDINGTON − RUSS. p46-52

Swift things are beautiful
   CATHON − PERHAPS p11.

Swiftness. *See* **Speed**

Swimmers and swimming
The hermit with two heads
The carp that became a dragon
The Hoca solves a problem
How tadpoles lost their tales
How the hare learned to swim
I'll tell her
Jean Britisse, the champion
The king on trial
The learned young professor
The light princess
Nicola Pesce
The son of the turtle spirit
The turtle outwits the lion
The whale and the sea slug

Swindlers
Henry Crabb−a born loser
Shlemiel, the businessman

The swineherd
   ARBUTHNOT − TIME p343-346

The swineherd who married a princess
   RANKE − GERMANY p121-124

Swineherds
Eight leaves of story (1) The three
   staunch swineherds of Britain
The wild man

The swing
   MY BOOK HOUSE v. 3 p92.

Swiss nursery rhymes
   MY BOOK HOUSE v. 1 p66-67

Switzerland
  The Alp that disappeared
  The archer, William Tell
  Arnold Winkelried
  The brave cowman
  Charles the Bold of Burgundy
  The clever little tailor
  Death a prisoner
  Dwarf stories
  The fairy grotto
  The father's steps
  The fountain
  Four tales of how the devil was out-
    witted
  Fridolin
  The Frisian ride
  Giant pear and giant cow
  Giant pears and giant cows
  The golden coal
  The groschen hole in the Murz Valley
  How the Kuhreihen began
  Ida of Toggenburg
  John Boaster
  The judge of Bellinzona
  The key maiden of Tegerfelden
  The knife
  The knight of La Sarraz
  The legend of William Tell
  The lost cows
  The magic peas
  The man with the green feather
  The martyrs of Thebes
  Meinrad and the ravens
  Nidelgret
  The old bear in the tree
  The ring of Hallwil
  The singing fir-tree
  The snake crown
  The story of William Tell
  Sturdy Hans
  The three languages
  The three ravens
  Tredeschin
  Verena and the jug
  —History
    William Tell and the founding of
      the Swiss Confederation
  —Mountains
    Heidi in the Alpine pasture
  —Uri
    The bull of Uri
    The frontier contest
  —Zug
    The mermaid of Zug
  —Zurich
    Charles the Great and the snake

The sword in the stone
  PICARD — STORIES p1-8

The sword of Damocles
  BALDWIN — FAVOR. p78-81

The sword of Damocles; the man who
  would be king
  STRONG — FAVORITE p64-66

The sword of light
  McMANUS — HIBERIAN p148-159

The sword of the stone
  MANNING — JONNIKIN p115-127

The sword of Urnach. *See* The quest for
  Olwen (4) Fulfilling the tasks

The sword that fought by itself
  COURLANDER — HAT p88-92

Swords
  The adventures of Ciad
  The adventures of Iain Direach
  The blue belt
  The boy with the golden star
  Brian and the fox
  The bride-price for Olwen
  The castle of no return
  Chandasimha, his son and their two
    wives
  Chin-Chin Kobakama
  The companion
  The cowherd with the belt of skin
  The Crochera
  Donal from Donegal
  The dove maiden
  The dragon and the stepmother
  The eight-headed dragon
  The giant of the brown beech wood
  The good sword
  Hans, the horn, and the magic sword
  How Arthur gained Excalibur
  How thunder makes the lightning
  How Tristram fought against the
    knight from Ireland
  Ian Direach
  Jack and the giant Thunderdell
  Jack and the giant-killer
  King Arthur . . . The shield and the
    hammer
  King Hrolf and the bear's son
  The knight with the two swords
  Little one-inch
  The little white cat
  The magic berries
  The maiden, the knight, and the water-
    fall
  Marking the boat to locate the sword
    Macabuin
  Molly Whipple
  The mop servant

Swords (*Continued*)

The nine-headed giant
Olaf Goddardson and the sword
Oraggio and Bianchinetta
The pasha's sword
The proper way to lay the table
The quest for Olwen (4) Fulfilling the tasks
The secretive little boy and his little sword
Shah Abbas and the cobbler
Siegfried . . . who knew no fear
The sneeze that won a prize
The soldier and the tsar
Something wonderful
Soria Moria castle
The story of General Gim Dog-Nyong
The story of Zoulvisia
Sylvester
The tale of the lay of the smithy
The thirteenth son of the King of Erin
The three brothers and the giant
The three gifts
The toothpick warriors
The treachery of Morgan Le Fay
The twins
The well of D'yeree-in-Dowan
The white cat
The white hound
The white sword of light
A young prince named Siegfried

Swordsmen
Black Roderic
The kappa's arm

Sybaris . . . Life of luxury
UNTERMEYER – FIRE. p60-62

Sycamore trees
The first fire

Sylvester
MANNING – RED p42-48

Symbols
. . . and the magic they made
Heaven and earth and man
How pictures become words
Old strong charms

Symington, Inez
The cat, the cock and the lamb

Syria
A dish of laban
Eighteen rabbits
Good advice

Impossible tales
The kneeling tree
The red slippers of Honiem
A wicked fox

Sze-Ma Gwang, the quick one
ALEXANDER – PEBBLES p16.

T

The tabby who was such a terrible
glutton
  ASBJORNSEN – NORW. p161-167

Tablecloths
  The ass that lays money
  The best wish
  Brother Breeze and the pear tree
  The devil's gifts
  Horns
  The lad and the north wind
  Per and the north wind
  Sinko's luck
  The stolen turnips
  The three brothers
  The three soldiers
  You have a napkin

Tables
  Banks with binks
  The bean tree
  The donkey, the table, and the stick
  The enormous genie
  The gold table
  Long-Neck, Fatty and Droopy

Tableware
  Forks
  Shrewd Todie and Lyzer the miser
  Why a lady sits next to a knight at
  table

Taboos
  The magic tabo
  The worthless man of poverty

The tacksman and the ox
  BRIGGS – PERS. p36-37

Tadpoles. *See* **Frogs**

Tagore, Rabinranath
  Paper boats
  Selections
  While other birds at will may go

Taikon, Johan Dimitri
  JAGENDORF – GYPSIES p179-181

The tail
  WITHERS – I SAW p71.

The tail of St. George's dragon
  U. N. – RIDE p92-94

The tail of the cat
  LOWE – LITTLE p81-83

The tailless jackal
  MEHDEVI – PERSIAN p22-32

The tailor and the devil
  SHEPPARD – SCOT. p89-92

The tailor and the mandarin
  SUN – LAND p89-90

The tailor and the prince, told by Mulech
  HAUFF – CARAVAN p176-208

A tailor in heaven
  RANKE – GERMANY p155.

The tailor in the church
  MANNING – GHOSTS p43-46

Tailorbirds
  The tiny bird and the king

Tailors
  The absent-minded tailor
  The blind king and the magic bird
  The grave little tailor
  The clever children and the king
  tailor
  The clever little tailor
  Damer's gold
  The devil and the tailor
  Did the tailor have a nightmare?
  The dishonest tailor
  A dozen at a blow
  The dreamer
  Four-and-twenty tailors
  The giant and the tailor
  The goldsmith, the wood carver, the
  tailor, and the hermit who quarreled
  over a wooden woman
  The greedy tailor
  Hans the tailor and the talking animals
  The Heinzelmannchen
  A horned goat
  The horse that liked to play tricks
  The hunchback and the miser
  The impudent little mouse
  Johnny Gloke
  The jolly tailor who became king
  King Stephen was a worthy peer
  The little black man
  The master-smith
  Max and Moritz and the tailor
  Measure twice, cut once
  The miller's four sons
  Of a tailor and a bear

640

Tailors (*Continued*)

One-eyed Likho
The rich man and the tailor
The royal waistcoat
The silent princess
Soonimaya
The stolen jewel
Straw, bean and coal
Sylvester
The tale of the false prince
Terence the tailor's jacket
The three bugganes, I
The tree traveling artisans
The three walnuts
Timothy and the buggane ghost
The tiny, tiny man

The tailor's apprentice . . . And the bear
UNTERMEYER – FIRE. p216-219

The tailor's bright daughter
CARPENTER – ELEPHANT'S p195-203

Tails
See also names of animals, subdivision
Tails
Clever–clever–clever
The coyote and the two dogs
Strange men with tails

Takamagahara
McALPINE – JAPAN. p3-4

Takero
BROWN – AROUND p111-121

Takgabbies (goblins)
Three who found their hearts' desire

The taking of Joppa
GREEN – TALES p177-184

The tale about lost time
BUDBERG – RUSSIAN p85-94

A tale of a boy who set out to learn fear
THOMPSON – ONE p48-55

The tale of a debt repaid
LEODHAS – CLAYMORE p33-35; p99-107

A tale of a dog's tail
FELTON – NEW p3-19

The tale of a foolish brother and of a wonderful bush
MANNING – RED p132-138

The tale of a frog
WITHERS – I SAW p120-121

The tale of a Pakistan parrot
SIDDIQUI – TOON. p114-123

The tale of a proverb
NAHMAD – PEASANT p130-132

The tale of a rich king: The treasure of Rhampinitus
JAMES – MYTHS p128-137

The tale of a watch
FELTON – WORLD'S p45-49

The tale of Anthony's nose
JAGENDORF – UPSTATE p14-17

The tale of bat
CHAFETZ – THUNDER. p15-26

The tale of Bonnie Baby Livingston
LEODHAS – BY p69-80

The tale of Caliph stork
See also The story of Caliph stork
HAUFF – FAIRY p9-20

The tale of chanticleer
GREEN – BIG p158-164
WESTWOOD – MEDIEVAL p7-13

The tale of Columba and the angel
LEODHAS – CLAYMORE p14-21; p64-72

The tale of Dick o' the cow
LEODHAS – BY p53-67

The tale of frost and his neighbors
RANKE – GERMANY p104-106

The tale of Godfrey Malbone
JAGENDORF – NEW p267-272

The tale of Lang Johnnie Mor
LEODHAS – BY p81-91

The tale of Liban the siren
GARNIER – LEGENDS p42-48

The tale of Nornagest
JONES – SCAND. p165-172

The tale of nutcracker
MY BOOK HOUSE v. 2 p218-222

The tale of Peter Rabbit
MY BOOK HOUSE v. 2 p112-117

The tale of Princess Kaguya. I The child in the bamboo tree; II the fame of the princess; III The five young men; IV The task of Prince Kurumamochi; V The task of the minister Abe-no-Mishi; VI The task of the chief councillor Otomo-no-Miyuki; VII The task of Prince Ishitsukuri; VIII The task of the deputy chief councillor Iso-no-Kamimaro; IX The emperor of the province; X The August moon; XI The messengers from the moon; XII The emperor's pilgrimage to Mount Fuji
McALPINE − JAPAN. p127-187

A tale of Robin Hood
MANNING − ENGLISH p105-148

The tale of the Balaton
BAKER − TALKING p191-198

The tale of the Earl of Mar's daughter
LEODHAS − BY p43-52

The tale of the Faderaevisch
RANKE − GERMANY p40-42

The tale of the false prince
HAUFF − FAIRY p53-69

The tale of the famous flower of Serving-men
LEODHAS − BY p93-103

The tale of the Gaberlunzie man
LEODHAS − CLAYMORE p37-42; p116-128

The tale of the ghost ship
HAUFF − FAIRY p21-32

Tale of the good, gay lady
JAGENDORF − KING p236-238

The tale of the gypsy and his strange love
JAGENDORF − GYPSIES p93-101

The tale of the heir of Linne
LEODHAS − BY p105-117

The tale of the hump-backed men
SHEPPARD − SCOT. p21-25

The tale of the king's jewel
LEODHAS − CLAYMORE p42-48; p150-157

The tale of the knight and the shepherd lass
LEODHAS − BY p119-130

The tale of the lady of the rock
LEODHAS − CLAYMORE p35-37; p108-115

The tale of the Laird of Logie
LEODHAS − CLAYMORE p42-48; p129-139

The tale of the land of Cockaigne
BECHSTEIN − FAIRY p141-144

The tale of the lay of the Amadhain Mhor
LEODHAS − BY p15-29

The tale of the lay of the smithy
LEODHAS − BY p1-14

The tale of the little mook
HAUFF − FAIRY p33-52

The tale of the little sausage and the little mouse
RANKE − GERMANY p18-19

The tale of the Lochmaben harper
LEODHAS − BY p31-42

Tale of the old man who made the dead trees blossom. See The old man and his dog

The tale of the pig
PROTTER − CHILD. p110-112

The tale of the rescue of Kinmont Wullie
LEODHAS − CLAYMORE p42-48; p140-149

The tale of the Rhine-gold
MY BOOK HOUSE v. 11 p73-89

The tale of the riddle sent to Bruce
LEODHAS − CLAYMORE p24-29; p81-90

The tale of the royal exiles
LEODHAS − CLAYMORE p21-24; p73-80

The tale of the silver, golden, and diamond prince
RANKE − GERMANY p79-84

The tale of the silver saucer and the russet apple
BUDBERG − RUSSIAN p78-84

The tale of the sons of Cathmor
LEODHAS − CLAYMORE p14-18; p49-63

The tale of the superman
  ARNOTT – AFRICAN p43-55

The tale of the tail of a bear
  JAGENDORF – NEW p100-105

The tale of the three brothers
  SHEPPARD – SCOT. p50-55

The tale of the three footsteps
  JAGENDORF – GHOST p15-18

A tale of the Tontlawald
  LANG – VIOLET p1-16

The tale of the two brothers
  GREEN – TALES p135-148

The tale of the two cunning servants
  PICARD – LADY p139-164

The tale of the wrath of God
  LEODHAS – CLAYMORE p29-33;
  p91-98

The tale of the youngest brother and the
  stupid devil
  RANKE – GERMANY p167-170

The tale of Tom Corwin
  JAGENDORF – SAND p30-33

A tale of two mandarins
  MONTROSE – WINTER p109-113

A tale of two rogues
  GRAY – INDIA'S p188-196

The tale of Vassilissa the wise
  BUDBERG – RUSSIAN p95-115

The tale the crofter told
  LEODHAS – GHOSTS p43-53

Tales from the Episode of the Fians
  WILSON – SCOTTISH p175-207

Tales of David and Solomon
  NAHMAD – PORTION p39-83

Tales of enchantment
  TOOR – GOLDEN p13-119

Tales of magic, black and white
  BRENNER – BOY p95-128

Tales of past glories: Cheops and the
  magicians
  JAMES – MYTHS p104-119

Tales of the ambiguous Dighton Rock
  TAFT – PROFILE p24-29

Tales of the Heike
  McALPINE – JAPAN. p35-77

Tales of the prophet Elijah
  NAHMAD – PORTION p21-38

Tales of Troy
  GREEN – GREEKS p6-7

Tales of wit and wisdom
  NAHMAD – PORTION p129-153

Taliesin
  PICARD – HERO p68-79

The talisman
  U. N. – RIDE p166-168

Talismans
  Black Colin of Loch Awe
  The craftsman's wife
  The Golem of Rabbi Judah Low
  The hill of the bellowing oxen
  The talking talisman

Talk
  Basia, the babbler
  The beginning of good conversation
  Belling the cat
  The bride who out talked the water
    kelpie
  The chatterbox
  The chipmunk who chattered too
    much
  Echo and Narcissus: the chattering
    nymph and the proud youth
  Esben Ashblower
  Hidden treasure
  Intelligence and luck
  The magpie and the raven
  March has horse's ears
  Musakalala, the talking skull
  The princess who always had to have
    the last word
  The princess whom nobody could
    silence
  The skull
  Tecle's goat
  The tortoise who talked too much
  The turtle who could not stop
    talking
  Why women talk more than men

The talkative king
  ROSS – BURIED p75-80

A talkative old woman
INS-SOB – FOLK p192.

The talkative tortoise
GAER – FABLES p162-164
GHOSE – FOLK p28-30

The talkative turtle
DAVIS – LION'S p189-191

The talkative wife and the discovered
treasure. *See* The silly goose war

Talkativeness. *See* **Talk**

The talking cat
CARLSON – TALKING p17-29

The talking donkey
BECHSTEIN – FAIRY p72-78

The talking fish
TASHJIAN – ONCE p41-49

The talking house
HEADY – JAMBO p72-76

The talking-match
LEACH – RAINBOW p188.

The talking mule
LEACH – RAINBOW p239-240

The talking nightingale
LEEKLEY – RIDDLE p48-50

The talking talisman
BARASH – GOLDEN p67-69

The talking tree
BAKER – TALKING p9-17

Tall hog
LEACH – NOODLES p65.

Tall Peter and short Peter
MAAS – MOON p47-55

A tall tale contest
SEKI – FOLKTALES p181-183

Tall tales
An adventure with a bear
Anthony and the Mossbunker
Battle with the Sockdolager
The bear and the wildcat
The bear in the black hat
Big mosquitoes
The big mudhole
The blizzard of '98

Bowleg Bill
The boy who told tall tales
Callin' the dog
Coyote cowboy/Becos Bill
A curious tale
Davy Crockett
Ed Grant has a dream
Ed Grant out West
The end of the trail
Febold Feboldson
Fiesta for mountain men
The fighting rams
Five fathoms tall/Stormalong
The flying kettle
Frontier fighter/Davy Crockett
Gib Morgan
The goat that went to school
Great hunting!
Hammerman/John Henry
The hideless bear
High John the conqueror
How pa learned to grow hot peppers
The hungry trout
I was going along the road
Ikpoom
Illinois River tall tales
Janey's shoes
Joe Magarac
Joe Magarac the steel man
John Henry
Johnny Appleseed
Jumping the Grand Canyon
A kind heart
The lake that flew
Little tall tales
A long shot
Maine's best boatman
The man who rode the bear
Meet Ed Grant
Mike Fink
Minute pudding
A most peculiar bear hide
Mount Kennebago
The new camp stove
The new camp stove burns again
Old Plott
Old Stormalong
Once there was and once there was
not
A passel of real lies
Paul Bunyan
Pecos Bill
Pecos Bill and his bouncing bride
The perambulatin' pumpkin
The pet catfish
The popcorn frost
The popcorn patch
The pudding that broke up the
preaching
Rainbow-walker/Johnny Appleseed
Rat and the rustlers

Tall tales (*Continued*)
Real stuff
River roarer/Mike Fink
Sam Patch
Sam Patch's last leap
Saved by a turkey
The self-kicking machine
Shingling the fog
The short horse
Sky-bright axe/Paul Bunyan
Smolligosters, etc.
Snake story
Some punkins
Sourdough special
Steelmaker/Joe Magarac
Stormalong
Surprise for the black bull
A tale of a dog's tail
The tale of a watch
A tall turnip
The tame trout
Three bad men
Three-fingered Ike's story
Too hot to handle
A trail of tall tales
The truth about Pecos Bill
Uncle Ed is chased by a bear
Uncle Ed tracks a rabbit
Uncle Ed's unusual bear hide
The voice in the jug
Who is boss?
A word from the author
The world's most truthful man
The wrestler of Kyushu

Tall tales
JOHNSON – WHAT p228-232

Tall tales from the Gotham Inn
JAGENDORF – MERRY p113-118

The tall trees in the greenwood
CATHON – PERHAPS p195-214

A tall turnip
CREDLE – TALL p30-33

Talmud, The
The fishes and the wolf
The princess and Rabbi Joshuah

The Talmud
JOHNSON – PRINC. p317.

Tam and Tessa
MANNING – JONNIKIN p74-90

Tam Lin
MANNING – ENGLISH p56-61
PICARD – HERO p107-112

VANSITTART – DARK p48-53
WILSON – SCOTTISH p41-45

Tam O' Shanter
HOPE-SIMPSON – CAVAL. p146-151

Tamarisk (tamarind) trees
The golden crow
Isis and Osiris

Tambourines
The flea

The tame trout
FELTON – WORLD'S p31-39

Tamlane
BRIGGS – PERS. p43-45
JACOBS – MORE p172-176
WILLIAMS – FAIRY p263-271

Tangerina
ARBUTHNOT – TIME p275-276

Tanners
Little John and the tanner of Blyth
Nikita and the dragon

Tanukis (animals)
The magic kettle

Tao K'an and his mother
ALEXANDER – PEBBLES p12.

Taoism
Author's note
The man who would know magic

Tapa cloth
The gift of the hairy one
Hina, the woman in the moon
The monster mo-o

Tapas. *See* Hermits

Tape measure
LEACH – SOUP p141-142

Taper Tom
HAVILAND – NORWAY p50-64

Taper-Tom who made the princess laugh
ASBJÖRNSEN – NORW. p20-24

Tapestries
Corvetto
Little Lady Margaret

Tapirs
    Jabuty, the strong

The tapping ghost of Edinburg
    JAGENDORF – SAND p26-29

Tar
    The moon painters
    The straw ox
    The terrible black snake's revenge

Tar-baby
    WILLIAMS – OLD p118-122

A tar burner's brer rabbit stories
    JOHNSON – WHAT p240-245

Tar-sa's luck
    KRUEGER – SERPENT p18-26

Tara, Hill of
    The coming of Fionn MacCool
    How Finn became head of the Fianna
    How Finn won his father's place
    The lordship of the Fianna
    Saint Patrick and the Hill of Tara

Tarbooshes. See Hats—Tarbooshes

Tardiness
    The crab
    How terrapin's shell was cracked
    The tale about lost time

Tarn Wethelan
    GARNER – GOBLINS p116-125

Taro (plants)
    A contest with skillful spirits
    Fire magic and the mud hen
    The little menehunes
    The weary spirits of Lanai

Tars (musical instruments)
    The specialist

Tartars
    The nightingale and the Khan
    A poor peasant and two nobles
    Souchmant's trial and triumph

Tartary
    The blue centaur
    Samson and the doll in green and
        brown

The task of Prince Ishitsukuri
    McALPINE – JAPAN. p159-163

The task of Prince Kurumamochi
    McALPINE – JAPAN. p140-148

The task of the chief councillor Otomo-
    no-Miyuki
    McALPINE – JAPAN. p152-159

The task of the deputy chief councillor
    Iso-no-Kamimaro
    McALPINE – JAPAN. p163-171

The task of the minister Abe-no-Miushi
    McALPINE – JAPAN. p148-152

The task of the serpent
    BARASH – GOLDEN p9-12

Tasks. See Tests; Work

Tatooing
    Why the moon has scars on her face

Tattercoats
    ARBUTHNOT – TIME p19-21
    JACOBS – MORE p67-72
    REEVES – ENGLISH p11-22

Tatterhood
    MANNING – WITCHES p94-103

Tavadan
    MAYNE – HEROES p213-222

Tavadan and the fire giant
    MAYNE – GIANTS p42-54

Taxation
    Account rendered
    The bat
    Double arend of Meeden
    The good dogs and the good assessor
    The Hoca as Tamerlane's tax collector
    It's all in knowing how
    Kralyevich Marko abolishes the
        wedding-tax
    The legend of the two discreet statues
    Ooka and Tosuke's tax
    A prompt settlement
    The quest of the children of Turenn
    Surprise for the black bull

Taxis
    The big street in the big city

Taylor, Jane
    I love little pussy
    The star

Tcakabesh snares the sun
  JABLOW – MAN p79-80

Tchaikowsky, Peter
  The tale of nutcracker

Te Houtaewa and the Kumaras
  CAMPBELL – MAORI p57-60

Tea
  Ah Tcha the sleeper
  Fiery-tempered Jake
  The gift of the moon goddess
  Knurremurre the troll
  The little girl named I
  Polly, put the kettle on
  The two caddies of tea
  William Winter

Tea grounds
  JOHNSON – WHAT p19.

The tea-kettle
  HEARN – JAPANESE p69-79
  MANNING – BEASTS p130-137

Tea-kettles. *See* Teakettles

The teacher and his pupil
  NAHMAD – PEASANT p33-34

Teachers
  The almond bough
  And upon the fourth bray
  The five wise words
  Gift of the unicorn
  Goso the teacher
  The king of the mountain
  The king's black curtain
  The prince and the vizier's son
  The scholar and the thieves
  The schoolmaster and the devil
  The silly slave
  Stormy lifts anchor
  The swans of Ballycastle
  The talking talisman
  Taper Tom
  Tell me, when will I die?
  Three silly schoolmasters
  The twin parrots
  Two cows
  The way of the master
  Why the tiger is so angry at the cat
  The woman in the chest

Teaching baby crab to walk
  BURTON – MAGIC p71.

Teakettles
  The accomplished and strange tea-
    kettle
  The dancing kettle
  The good fortune kettle
  The good-luck teakettle
  Jamie Watt and the giant in the tea-
    kettle
  The lucky tea-kettle

Teals (birds)
  The owl's punishment

Tears
  Bastianelo
  The boy who taught the fairies tears
  The carnation youth
  The death of Balder
  Damian and the dragon
  Do pearls bring tears?
  The dragon and the stepmother
  The dutiful daughter
  Elsa and the ten elves
  The first of May
  The first tears
  The giant Holiburn
  The girl who always cried
  The girl who used her wits
  How crab got a hard back
  Johnny and the three goats
  The light princess
  Little Rosa and long Leda
  Malintzin
  The mouse climbed up the candlestick
  The necklace
  The queen's necklace
  Stan Bolovan
  The three sillies
  The weeping lady of Llyn Glasfryn
  The weeping lass at the dancing place

Teasing
  The accomplished and strange
    teakettle

Teasing questions
  WITHERS – I SAW p47.

Tecle's goat
  COURLANDER – FIRE p93-97

Teddy bear, teddy bear
  MY BOOK HOUSE v. 1 p91.

Teddy bears. *See* Toys and toy shows

The teddy bears' picnic
  MY BOOK HOUSE v. 2 p57.

Teen-ager
    LEACH – SOUP p86.

Teeny-tiny
    MY BOOK HOUSE v. 4 p143-144
    WILLIAMS – FAIRY p30-31
    WITHERS – I SAW p59-61

Teeth
    See also **Dentures**
    The stone horseman
    The stone of victory
    The Texas sandstorm
    The three teeth of the king

Tehi Tegi
    YOUNG – HOW p101-104

"Tein eigin"
    The farmer and the fairy hillock

Telephus
    The story of Telephus

Telescopes
    The magic carpet
    The strangest thing in the world

Tell, William
    The archer, William Tell
    The legend of William Tell
    The story of William Tell
    William Tell and the founding of the
        Swiss Confederation

Tell a tale of Ara Spence
    JAGENDORF – UPSTATE p274-279

Tell Barney Beal
    JAGENDORF – NEW p30-34

Tell me, when will I die?
    WALKER – WATER. p13-23

Telling the horses apart
    LEACH – NOODLES p21.

Tema's promise to the white bird
    HASKETT – GRAINS p59-63

Temba becomes a warrior
    ARNOTT – TALES p116-123

Temba wins a bride
    ARNOTT – TALES p124-144

Temba's bag of salt
    ARNOTT – TALES p107-115

Temba's magic boat
    ARNOTT – TALES p44.

Temba's monkey friends
    ARNOTT – TALES p70-77

Temper
    The adventures of Alexander Selkirk
    The anger bargain
    Ask a foolish question
    A baker's dozen
    The boots that never wore out
    Cadwalader and his goat
    Damian and the dragon
    Fiery-tempered Jake
    The girl who clung to the devil's back
    How pa learned to grow hot peppers
    The jurga
    Katcha and the devil
    Keep cool
    Kristina and the devil
    The lost half-hour
    Master and man
    The master and the servant
    Never
    Ooka and the terrible-tempered
        tradesman
    The prince and the goose girl
    The princess and the vagabone
    Snow-white and Rose-red
    The terrible-tempered dragon
    The twelve months

The tempest
    MY BOOK HOUSE v. 8 p18-35

Temples
    Bedding in one's ear
    The boy who drew cats
    The boy who had to draw cats
    The demon giant of Mount Ariake
    The horse and the eighteen bandits
    Khnemu of the Nile
    The king of the demons and the worm
        Shamir
    Kitava the gambler
    Koichi and the mountain god
    The miracle of the begging bowl
    The monkey's jizo-sama
    The piece of straw
    The spirit's drum
    The sweet Mochi's parents
    Willow

    –**Mortuary temple of Hatshepsut**
        The great Queen Hatshepsut

    –**Thoth**
        Teta the magician

Temptation
    The blue palm tree
    A son of Adam

The ten chests
    LEEKLEY – RIDDLE p25-40

Ten Commandments
    The king of the demons and the worm
        Shamir

The ten dwarfs of Aunt Greenwater
    LOWE – LITTLE p27-29

Ten little Indians
    MY BOOK HOUSE v. 2 p94-95

Tengus (goblins)
    The badger and the magic fan
    The bored tengu
    Don't tease the tengu!
    The vanishing rice-straw coat

The tengu's magic nose fan
    UCHIDA – SEA p33-41

Tennessee
    The barnyard
    Davy Crockett
    Davy Crockett, the yaller blossom o'
        the forest
    Froggie goes a-courting
    Frontier fighter/Davy Crockett
    Hoodoo bags and ghosts in Tennessee
    Old stories
    Who?

Tennessee
    LEACH – RAINBOW p150-151

Tennyson, Alfred
    The bugle song
    Dainty little maiden
    The kraken
    The merman
    O well for the fisherman's boy
    The owl
    Poems
    Recollections of the Arabian Nights
    The revenge
    Sweet and low
    What does little birdie say?

Tennyson, Alfred
    The rector's son

Tents
    The enemy's tent

Tepozton
    BRENNER – BOY p28-33

Terence the tailor's jacket
    GREEN – LEPRECHAUN p21-30

The term
    GARNER – GOBLINS p40.

Termites
    The planting party
    The proud bokungu tree

Terrapin's pot sense
    See also Anansi stories
    COURLANDER – TERRA. p24-27

Terrapins
    How terrapin's shell was cracked
    How the terrapin beat the rabbit
    Slow train to Arkansas
    Why the terrapin's shell is scarred

The terrible black snake's revenge
    UCHIDA – SEA p112-120

The terrible family
    JACOBSON – FIRST p48-57

The terrible leak
    UCHIDA – MAGIC p13-21

The terrible Olli
    FILLMORE – SHEPHERD'S p53-63

The terrible-tempered dragon
    PALMER – DRAGONS p46-54

Terror. See Fear

The terror of the ogres
    URE – RUMANIAN p101-113

Terrors of the sea
    LAWSON – STRANGE p178-192

The test
    NAHMAD – PORTION p135-136

Test of a friendship
    WALKER – DANCING p80-83

A test of skill
    ARNOTT – AFRICAN p40-42

Tests
    See also Work
    The bride-price for Olwen
    The clever bride of Tunisia

Tests (*Continued*)

Cliff dweller
The five young men
Flint bird
The giant and his royal servants
Great heart and the three tests
Ilmarinen . . . how he won his bride
Jankyn and the witch
The king of Araby's daughter
The king's rabbits
The kneeler's twelve tasks
The prince and the giant's daughter
Prince sun and princess moon
The princess and the shepherd
The servant who took the place of
  his master
The son of the King of Spain
The three clever brothers
The three sons of Gorla
The three tasks
Three tests for the prince
The unseen bridegroom
The worthless man of poverty

Teta the magician
  GREEN – TALES p91-97

Teton
  MacFARLANE – TALES p123-136

Teutli, the mountain that is alive
  BRENNER – BOY p23-26

Texas
Bigfoot Wallace
Coyote cowboy/Pecos Bill
Davy Crockett, the yaller blossom o'
  the forest
Fiesta for mountain men
I had a piece of pie
A kind heart
Mosquitoes
O. I'm a jolly old cowboy
Pecos Bill
Pecos Bill and his bouncing bride
Pecos Bill, the cowboy
Sourdough special
Strawberry roan
A tale of a dog's tail
Three bad men
The truth about Pecos Bill
Wake up, Jacob

Texas
  LEACH – RAINBOW p152-154

The Texas sandstorm
  COURLANDER – TERRA. p65-66

The text
  BIRCH – CHINESE p138-151

"Text of Heaven". *See* "Heaven, Text of"

Thackeray, William Makepeace
  The rose and the ring
  A tragic story

Thackeray, William Makepeace
  Watching Vanity Fair go by

Thailand
The biggest crocodile in the world
The bird that told tales
The black pool
Cum and Koompang
Friendless pavilion
The girl who weaves by night
The girl who wore too much
The golden prince of the conch shell
The heavenly lovers
The little priest
Mango mountain
The many children of Mr. & Mrs.
  Twelve
Piboon's golden mountain
The serpent prince
The serpents and the porcupine
Siengmieng, the minister
The spirit's drum
Sumlee's broken stick
Tar-sa's luck
Why the parrot repeats man's words
Yama and the poor man

"Thank yous". *See* **Gratitude**

Thanksgiving day
The courtin'
The first Thanksgiving day
Give praise
Over the river and through the woods
Providence
The pudding that broke up the preach-
  ing
The sky at night
Songs of joy from the Bible
We thank thee

The thanksgiving of the wazir
  LANG – OLVIE p30-35

That fellow
  LEACH – RAINBOW p261-262

That fourth leg of the dog
  VO-DINH – TOAD p75-80

That is why he was always called Pooh
ARBUTHNOT — TIME p302-304

Thaxter, Celia
Little Gustava

Thayer, Ernest Lawrence
Casey at the bat

Theaters
Down by the River Avon
The Prince Fernando

The theft of dawn
CURRY — DOWN p38-47

The theft of fire
CURRY — DOWN p51-79
LEEKLEY — WORLD p11-19

The theft of Thor's hammer
AULAIRE — NORSE p100-103

Theobald, Count
Louis and Theobald

Theocritis
Revenge

Theodoric the great, Emperor of Rome
Emperor of Rome

Theognis
Children's songs of ancient Greece
Here we come, we children come

There are twelve months
MY BOOK HOUSE v. 1 p57.

There goes a scout
MY BOOK HOUSE v. 4 p192a

There is only one pretty child in the
world and every mother has it
CHAPPELL — THEY p3-7

There was a crow
MY BOOK HOUSE v. 1 p54.

There was a farmer had a dog
MY BOOK HOUSE v. 1 p85.

There was a horse
MY BOOK HOUSE v. 1 p54.

There was a little boy (1)
MY BOOK HOUSE v. 1 p77.

There was a little boy (2)
MY BOOK HOUSE v. 1 p199.

There was a little man and his name was
Gice
MY BOOK HOUSE v. 1 p126.

There was a monkey
MY BOOK HOUSE v. 1 p52.

There was a naughty boy
MY BOOK HOUSE v. 1 p152.

There was a piper had a cow
MY BOOK HOUSE v. 1 p29.

There was an old dame called Tartine
MY BOOK HOUSE v. 1 p124.

There was an old man
MY BOOK HOUSE v. 1 p30.

There was an old man of Coblenz—
limerick
DE REGNIERS — GIANT p135.

There was an old man with a beard
MY BOOK HOUSE v. 2 p154.

There was an old, old Indian
MY BOOK HOUSE v. 1 p131.

There was an old pig
MY BOOK HOUSE v. 1 p107.

There was an old woman
MY BOOK HOUSE v. 1 p27; p76.

There was an old woman of Harrow
MY BOOK HOUSE v. 1 p26.

There was an old woman tossed up in a
basket
MY BOOK HOUSE v. 1 p41.

There was an old woman who lived in a
shoe
MY BOOK HOUSE v. 1 p43.

There was an owl
MY BOOK HOUSE v. 1 p50.

There were three duckies
MY BOOK HOUSE v. 1 p127.

There were two blackbirds
MY BOOK HOUSE v. 1 p51.

There were two little boys
MY BOOK HOUSE v. 1 p74.

There's always a reason
ZAGLOUL — BLACK p75-79

There's bigger fools than Tildy. *See*
Changing luck

There's no deity there
SEKI – FOLKTALES p194-195

There's no telling on which side a camel
will lie down
REED – TALK p78.

There's not a budding boy
MY BOOK HOUSE v. 1 p208.

Thet, Paw OO
AUNG – KINGDOM p96.

They just go round
LEACH – RAINBOW p188.

They dig a well
RANKE – GERMANY p178.

They hide a bell
RANKE – GERMANY p177.

They measure the depth of the well
RANKE – GERMANY p178.

They protect their seed
RANKE – GERMANY p177.

"They say" stories
CHAPPELL – THEY p3-79

They sow salt
RANKE – GERMANY p177.

Thi Kinh, Saint
The saint of children

Thi Kinh
GRAHAM – BEGGAR p23-31

The thief and the donkey
PROTTER – CHILD. p74.

The thief and the king's treasure
MOZLEY – EGYPT p58-67

The thief's goat
KOREL – LISTEN p27-31

Thieves and thievery
See also **Bandits**
The adventures of Manawyddan
Ali Baba and the forty thieves
The animal musicians
The ass that was flayed
Augustine the thief
The bee on the cap

The black bodach
The bob-tailed monkey and the king's
honey
Boiled wheat for a bountiful harvest
The boy who taught the fairies tears
The Bremen town musicians
A cat for a hare
Catching the thief
The charcoal burner
The chief astrologer
Chucko, who afraid?
The city of the winter sleep
The clever thief
The clever thieves
The cobbler astrologer and the forty
thieves
Conall Yellow Claw
A converted thief
The covetous minister
Crab
The crafty farmer
Deegeenboya the soldier bird
The devil's bride
Diamond cut diamond
Dog couldn't be cured
The donkey, the table, and the stick
The donkey's tail
An emir and two thieves
The enormous genie
The fair young bride
The faithful Morgiana
The faithless apprentice
The farmer and the hoe
The feast of plums
The fifty-one thieves
The first buttercups
The fish with bent noses
The five friends
A flower to catch a thief
Four friends
The ghostly hand of Spital house
The giant of the mount
The giant with the grey feathers
The grateful beasts
The great spirit of the toad
The greedy boy and the coconut crab
The guest from Heaven
Guno and Koyo
Halde Hat and Dulde Hat
Haltefanden (The lame devil)
The hand of glory
Hanging at Wessaguscus
Hereafterthis
The house with the heads
How Kwaku Ananse became bald
How rabbit deceived fox
How the deer lost his tail
How the devil fetched the mayor
How the milky way began
Ijapa and the hot-water test
Ijapa and Yanrinbo swear an oath

Thieves and thievery (*Continued*)

Ijapa goes to the Osanyin shrine
The infallible salt bird
The iniquitous Captain Lightfoot
The inn in the forest
The invisible baby
The invisible thief
Iwa the crafty one
Jack and his comrades
Jack and his friends
Jack Hannaford
Jean Labadie's big black dog
Jean Labadie's dog
Jean Sot
The kind caliph and the horse thief
King Conal's horses
King Firdy the Just
The king's thief
The knight of the glen's steed o' bells
Lad Carl
Lato, the stupid one
A leak in an old house
The little shepherd's dream
Magic and friendship
The magic bell
The magic cap
The man from Kailasa
The man who climbed down a moon-
  beam
The man who couldn't pay his debts
The man who sold magic
The man who stole a rope
The man who was only three inches
  tall
The man with the book of spells
Martin, the honest thief
The marvelous pear seed
The master thief
The messenger
The miller's four sons
The miser and the fairy feast
Molla Nasreddin and his donkey
Mother tells a story
Moti
The musicians of Bremen
The Namashepani
A new way to cure old witch-hunting
Okraman's medicine
The old hag's long leather bag
The old woman and the thief
Olomu's bush rat
Ooka and the cleanest case
Ooka and the honest thief
Ooka and the suspect statue
Ooka and the telltale tale
Ooka and the willow witness
The origin of the coconut
Pacala and Tandala
The Panditji and the guavas
Paul and the robber

The peasant and his three sons
The pomegranate seed
Poor old cricket!
Prince Ferdinand
The princess and the thief
Pwyll and Pryderi (2) The birth of
  Pryderi
A quarrel between thieves brings a
  Brahmin relief
Rabbit and the grain buyers
The rabbit and the tar wolf
The rabbit steals the elephant's
  dinner
The racoon and the old men
The road to hell
The robber Simhavikrama
Robin Ddu
The royal banquet
The rubber man
The saddle
The sage and the servant
Saint Peter's horses
The scarecrow
The scholar and the thieves
Secret tokens prove ownership
A selfish husband
Seven Simons
The shah weaves a rug
Shawneen and the gander
The Siamese pepper cure
The sly thief of Valenciennes
The snake in the bottle
Son of the long one
The sow and her Banbh
Stealing the bell
The stolen ring
The stolen rope
The stolen wine
The story of Harisarman
Stubborn husband, stubborn wife
The stubborn sillies
The task of the serpent
Tecle's goat
The terrible leak
Teton
The thirteen enchanted cats
Thor's hammer is stolen
Three corpses, money, and a wine-
  bottle
The three enchanted maidens
The three giants
The three litigants
Three princes and their beasts
The three walnuts
The ticklish thief
The tiger and the persimmon
Tiger lily and the dragon
The treasure
The treasure chamber of Rhampsinitus
The treasure thief
The trial of the stone

Thieves and thievery (*Continued*)

Turnip thief
Two pennies
Two watermelon stories
Uncle Bouqui and little malice
Uncle Mitya's horse
The unexpected happened
A visitor from paradise
The wandering apprentice
The weaver's worry
The white pet
The white trout
William Winter
The wise judge
With a wig, with a wag
The woman in the chest
The wonderful talking bowl
The would-be wizard
Young Gim and the robbers
Zab

The thieving fairies
BRIGGS – PERS. p63-64

Thimbles
The King of Araby's daughter
The princess with the golden shoes

The thing on the hedge
RANKE – GERMANY p34.

Things that happened long ago
BRENNER – BOY p51-94

Think in four wives
HASKETT – GRAINS p35-39

The third sorrow of story-telling. *See*
The fate of the sons of Usnach

The third witch
PICARD – FAUN p89-108

Thirst
Beereeun the miragemaker
The crow and the pitcher
The dilemma of a pious man
Great heart and the three tests
Red king and green king
Saint Gabre Manfas and his animals
Sister Alionushka, brother Ivanushka
The six companions
The son of the hunter

Thirsty. *See* Deaf men and their answers

Thirteen
LEACH – LUCK p95-100

The thirteen enchanted cats
O'FAOLAIN – IRISH p189-192

The thirteen flies
MANNING – JONNIKIN p47-53

"Thirteen" superstitions
BATCHELOR – SUPER. p46-48

The thirteenth floor
ARBUTHNOT – TIME p323-327

The thirteenth son of the King of Erin
MANNING – DRAGONS p87-94

This hound hath loved me
HAZELTINE – HERO p362-380

This little ant worked with might and main
MY BOOK HOUSE v. 1 p71.

This is how it began
JAGENDORF – MERRY p6-16

This little pig went to market
MY BOOK HOUSE v. 1 p19.

This one stole an egg
MY BOOK HOUSE v. 1 p71.

Thistledown
A moon of gobbags
The twelve wild ducks
The wild swans

Thistles
Musk and amber
My candlestick

Thomas Berennikov
MAYNE – HEROES p223-230

Thomas the rhymer
BAKER – GOLDEN p148-160
MANNING – ENGLISH p82-85
WILSON – SCOTTISH p8-17

Thompson, Ernest Seton
Why the brierbrush quarreled with the beasts

Thor
The theft of Thor's hammer
The world of the gods

Thor
MY BOOK HOUSE v. 9 p171.

Thor and the giants
DE REGNIERS – GIANT p94-105

Thor and the jotun Aegir
AULAIRE – NORSE p120-127

Thor and the jotun Geirrod
AULAIRE – NORSE p104-107

Thor and the jotun Rungnir
AULAIRE – NORSE p117-119

Thor and the jotun Utgardsloki
AULAIRE – NORSE p108-116

Thor gains his hammer
HOSFORD – THUNDER p13-19

Thor . . . How the thunderer was tricked
UNTERMEYER – FIRE. p125-130

Thor, the thunder-god
AULAIRE – NORSE p40-41

Thornbushes
Christie and the growing hand
Malachi and Red Cap the leprechaun
Turnip thief!

Thorne-Thomson, Gudrun
Why the sea is salt

Thorns
The bobtail monkey
The golden helmet
The grateful lion
The injured lion
The jackal with the torn nose
Keloglan and the lucky exchanges
Kindai and the ape
Toontoony and the barger
Why the brierbrush quarreled with
the beasts

The thoroughbred
DEUTSCH – TALES p44-51

Thor's combat with Rungnir
HOSFORD – THUNDER p79-84

Thor's hammer is stolen
HOSFORD – THUNDER p57-63

Thor's journey to Jotun-Heim
MY BOOK HOUSE v. 9 p164-171

Thor's unlucky journey
HOSFORD – THUNDER p27-40

Thor's visit to Hymir
HOSFORD – THUNDER p41-47

Thorsteinn Shiver
JONES – SCAND. p153-158

Thorvald, Freydis
The American saga

Those who quarreled
SECHRIST – ONCE p80-82

Those young men
JOHNSON – WHAT p157-158

Thoth (mes), King of Egypt
The book of Thoth
A dream of the Sphinx
Ra and his children

Thought
The boy who was saved by thoughts
The poor man's clever daughter
The power of thought

The thoughtless abbot
LUM – ITALIAN p33-42

The thousand and one nights. *See* Aiming
too high; The donkey, the ox and the
farmer

The thousand pieces of gold
GILSTRAP – SULTAN'S p40-50

Thousand and thousands of ducks
WITHERS – I SAW p52.

The thousandth gift
PICARD – MERMAID p49-60

Thrashers and thrashing
The clever blue tit and the fox
Donal O'Ciaran from Connaught
Happy Box'll
The kind pixy
The piskie thresher
The Rehepapp and Vanapagan
A story about Our Lord Jesus Christ

Thread
Bahram and the snake prince
Fairies on the gump
The tale of the youngest brother and
the stupid devil
Why ants have small waists

The thread of life
VITTORINI – OLD p79-85

Three anecdotes
WYNDHAM – CHINA p63-66

The three apples
NAHMAD – PEASANT p99-104

The three aunts
McNEILL – SUNKEN p138-145
THOMPSON – ONE p162-166

The three autos. *See* The three trucks

Three bad men
FELTON – NEW p51-58

The three banshees
SHEPPARD – SCOT. p104-108

The three bears
SIDEMAN – WORLD'S p525-531

The three billy goats gruff
ARBUTHNOT – TIME p70-72
ASBJORNSEN – EAST p16-18
HAVILAND – NORWAY p45-49
JONES – SCAND. p102-104
SIDEMAN – WORLD'S p361-364
THOMPSON – ONE p1-2

The three blue stones
DELARUE – FRENCH p50-56

Three bridegrooms for one bride
MASEY – STORIES p16-27

The three brothers
MINCIELI – TALES p90-95
NORLEDGE – ABORIGINAL p26.
RANKE – GERMANY p53-59
WITHERS – WORLD p55-56
ZAGLOUL – BLACK p45-58

The three brothers and the black hen
PICARD – FAUN p111-120

The three brothers and the giant
DE REGNIERS – GIANT p49-59

The three brothers and the marvelous
things
ALEGRIA – THREE p15-24

The three brothers and the treacle toffee
GREEN – LEPRECHAUN p63-73

The three bugganes
YOUNG – HOW p73-89

The three butchers from Reims
COOPER – FIVE p26-40

The three butterflies
BAMBERGER – FIRST p35-36

The three chests
FILLMORE – SHEPHERD'S p40-52

Three Chippewa fables
SCHOOLCRAFT – FIRE p39-46

The three citrons
MINCIELI – OLD p108-120
THOMPSON – ONE p103-111

The three clever brothers
SPICER – DEVILS p82-91

The three companions
LEEUW – INDO. p56-57

The three copecks
BELTING – CAT p45-52

The three copper pieces
BONNET – CHINESE p29-32

The three-cornered hat
COTHRAN – MAGIC p55-59

Three corpses, money, and a wine-bottle
INS-SOB – FOLK p186.

The three cows
JACOBS – MORE p89-91

The three cranberries
SCHOOLCRAFT – FIRE p41-42

The three cups of water
DURHAM – TIT p41-45

The three deaf men
URE – RUMANIAN p145-146

The three dogs
MANNING – DRAGONS p114-122

Three dreams. *See* Dreams

The three dwarfs
BONNET – CHINESE p57-61

Three eels
ČURČIJA – YUGOSLAV. p62-68

The three enchanted maidens
O'FAOLÁIN – IRISH p186-188

The three enchanted mares
CARPENTER – HORSES p126-135

The three enchanted princes
MINCIELI – OLD p73-83

Three fables
WYNDHAM – TALES p68-75

Three fast men
COURLANDER – KING'S p17-18

Three fat ewes for three fine hounds
LEODHAS – SEA p73-85

The Three Fates
WILSON – GREEK p214-221

(The) three feathers
BAMBERGER – FIRST p139-143
JACOBS – MORE p37-42

The three figs
BELPRE – TIGER p123-127

Three-fingered Ike's story
FELTON – NEW p127-139

The three fish and the fisherman
MONTGOMERIE – 25 p18-19

The three flutes are in the flute house
BELTING – STARS #3

Three foolish brides
INS-SOB – FOLK p194.

Three foolish wives
INS-SOB – FOLK p194-195

Three fools
VITTORINI – OLD p55-62

The three friends
WYATT – GOLDEN p22-26

The three giants
O'FAOLAIN – IRISH p196-199

The three gifts
LEEKLEY – RIDDLE p139-176

The three gluttons and the hunter
WITHERS – WORLD p65-66

The three goats called Hurricane
BAMBERGER – FIRST p84-86

The three golden apples
MAYNE – GIANTS p1-26

The three golden billy-goats
ILLYES – ONCE p239-257

The three golden ducats
SPICER – OWL'S p74-85

The three golden eggs
MacMANUS – HIBERIAN p25-35

The three golden hairs
FILLMORE – SHEPHERD'S p119-133
McNEILL – SUNKEN p40-51

The three golden hairs of Grandad Sol
BULATKIN – EURASIAN p9-21

The three golden hairs of Grandfather Know All
HAVILAND – CZECH. p67-90

The three golden hairs of the king of the cave giants
MANNING – GIANTS p107-117

The three goslings
HAVILAND – ITALY p67-77

The three hunters
HARDENDORFF – TRICKY p23-25
WITHERS – I SAW p77.

Three jolly sailor boys
MY BOOK HOUSE v. 1 p96.

The three journeys of Ilya of Murom
DOWNING – RUSSIAN p43-46

Three jovial huntsmen
MY BOOK HOUSE v. 3 p110.

The three languages
MÜLLER – SWISS p177-180
THOMPSON – ONE p306-308

The three laughs of the leipreachan
O'SULLIVAN – FOLK. p179-181

The three-legged jumping giant
SPICER – GIANTS p69-75

"Three legs"
The Manx coat of arms

The three lemons
See also The love of three oranges
BELTING – THREE p75-93
MANNING – GLASS p146-158

The three litigants
NAHMAD – PORTION p81-83

The three little eggs
BERGER – BLACK p79-90

Three little kittens
MY BOOK HOUSE v. 1 p53.

The three little men in the wood
MANNING – DWARFS p78-83

The three little pigs
BAMBERGER – FIRST p11-15

The three little pigs
SIDEMAN – WORLD'S p459-464
WILLIAMS – FAIRY p39-43

Three little tales of Washington
JAGENDORF – UPSTATE p229-234

The three lucky charms
SEKI – FOLKTALES p47-51

The three Magi
BELPRE´– TIGER p105-111

Three magic charms
HSIEH – CHINESE p67-71

Three men on the bridge
JAGENDORF – MERRY p25-30

The three mermaids
MANNING – MERMAIDS p25-35

The three misty women
SPICER – WITCHES p80-87

The three monsters of the sea
BERRY – MAGIC p30-44

The three most famous tales
O'FAOLÁIN – IRISH p1.

The three musicians
BECHSTEIN – FAIRY p160-167

Three old maids a-skating went
MY BOOK HOUSE v. 1 p110.

The three oranges
WILLIAMS – OLD p106-112

Three pennyworth
HACK – DANISH p134-144

The three petitions
BELPRE´– TIGER p119-121

The three plagues of Britain
JONES – WELSH p152-158
WESTWOOD – MEDIEVAL p93-97

The three precepts
MANNING – DAMIAN p172-178

The three precious packets
BIRCH – CHINESE p48-54

Three princes and their beasts
LANG – VIOLET p34-45

The three princesses
HACK – DANISH p117-128

The three princesses and the unclean
spirit
MANNING – RED p169-173

The three princesses in the blue mountain
ASBJÖRNSEN – EAST p72-80
THOMPSON – ONE p88-93

The three questions
JUDA – WISE p43-48

The three ravens
MÜLLER – SWISS p166-170
MANNING – GIANNI p54-61
VANSITTART – DARK p134-135

The three rings
VITTORINI – OLD p92-95

(The) three sillies
MY BOOK HOUSE v. 6 p174-177
WILLIAMS – FAIRY p249-254

Three silly schoolmasters
CARPENTER – ELEPHANT'S p125-134

The three silver balls
MANNING – GHOSTS p111-118

The three sisters and the cannibals
TRACEY – LION p103-109

The three sisters and the old witch
MINCIELI – TALES p121-124

Three skillful men
WITHERS – WORLD p60.

The three soldiers
JACOBS – EUROPE. p72-80

The three sons
INS-SÖB – FOLK p146-149

Three sons of a chief
COURLANDER – KING'S p50.

The three sons of Gorla
WILSON – SCOTTISH p137-147

The three sons of the King of Antua
O'FAOLAIN – IRISH p205-214

The three sorrows of storytelling
See also The children of Lir
Deidre and the sons of Uisne
The fate of the children of Lir
The fate of the children of Tuireann

The three spinners
RANKE – GERMANY p97-98

The three stags
DELARUE – FRENCH p15-20

The three stars
INS-SÖB – FOLK p13-14

The three staunch swineherds of Britain.
See Eight leaves of story (1) The three
staunch swineherds of Britain

The three suitors
DAVIS – LION'S p179-184
McNEILL – DOUBLE p56-61

"Three" superstitions
BATCHELOR – SUPER. p44-46

Three tales of the goblins who lived on
the sea-bottom
WHEELER – HAWAII. p171-232

Three tales of the mouse-deer
LEEUW – INDO. p68-80

The three tasks
MacMANUS – HIBERIAN p202-211

The three teeth of the king
LEODHAS – SEA p139-159

Three tests for the prince
UCHIDA – MAGIC p53-62

Three times and out
JAGENDORF – NEW p46-53

Three times lucky
NAHMAD – PEASANT p113-123

The three traveling artisans
RANKE – GERMANY p50-52

The three trucks
MY BOOK HOUSE v. 1 p177-178

The three unmarried ministers
INS-SÖB – FOLK p106-110

Three unscrupulous men
BURTON – MAGIC p104-105

The three walnuts
WILSON – GREEK p157-165

The three wanderers
ILLYES – ONCE p177-179

The three wasted wishes
PERRAULT – FAMOUS p159-164

The three waves
CARPENTER – SHIPS p265-275

Three who couldn't be parted
ROBERTSON – FAIRY p89-93

Three who found their hearts' desire
JEWETT – WHICH p136-157

The three who made Ku
HASKETT – GRAINS p107-112

(The) three wishes
ALEGRIA – THREE p76-79
CHILD – CASTLES p161-179
DOBBS – ONCE p86-90
ILLYES – ONCE p156-157
JACOBS – MORE p107-109
JEWETT – WHICH p104-108
McNEILL – SUNKEN p122-126
MY BOOK HOUSE v. 6 p92-95
PICARD – MERMAID p91-108
SPICER – LONG p98-115

Three wonderful beggars
LANG – VIOLET p22-33

The three words of advice
THOMPSON – ONE p359-361

The three year sleeping boy
SEKI – FOLKTALES p186-188

The three young maids who went to seek
their fortunes
JOHNSON – WHAT p175-176

The three young men and death
WESTWOOD – MEDIEVAL p51-55

Threshers and threshing. *See* **Thrashers
and thrashing**

Thrift
The economical son
Geordie and ten-shilling Jock
The good housewife and her night
labors
Mousey the merchant
The teacher and his pupil
A wife with false economy

Through the eyes
LIN – MILKY p51-56

Through the jungle
MY BOOK HOUSE v. 1 p79.

Through the needle's eye
LEACH – NOODLES p83-84

Thrownmount and Oakpull
BORSKI – GOOD p29-33

Thrushes
Answer to a child's question
The eagle and the owl
The fox and the thrush
The magpie's nest
Of speckled eggs the birdie sings
Old Shellover

Thumb, Tom. *See* **Tom Thumb**

Thumbelina
SIDEMAN – WORLD'S p189-205
TUDOR – TASHA p52-57

Thumbkin
JACOBS – EUROPE. p194-200
MANNING – DWARFS p42-48

Thumbs
See also **Tom Thumb**
The birth and boyhood of Finn
Th giant who sucked his thumb

Thumbs up, thumbs down
BATCHELOR – SUPER. p94-95

Thunder
Horses of the thunder
How thunder and lightning came to
be
How thunder got back into the sky
How thunder makes the lightning
How Yehl, the hero, freed the
beaming maiden
In the first times
The man who sold thunder
The rainbow
The rescue of fire

Rip Van Winkle; the strange little
men of the mountain
The shepherd of clouds
The singing man
The sky beings: thunder and his
helpers
Swen-Naba; king of the warlocks
The tale of the superman
The theft of Thor's hammer
Thor and the jotun Rungnir
Thor, the thunder-god
Thor's journey to Jotun-Heim
Why the sun shines in the daytime
and the moon shines at night
Why there is thunder and lightning
Yanni

Thunder and lightning
ARNOTT – AFRICAN p32-34
MY BOOK HOUSE v. 1 p195.

The thunder cat
GRAY – MAINLY p165-181

Thunder, elephant and Dorobo
HARMAN – TALES p19-28

The thunder man
AYRE – SKETCO p53-71

Thunderbird
CHAFETZ – THUNDER. p3-13

A thunderstorm
CATHON – PERHAPS p244-245

Thurber, James
Many moons
The Scotty who knew too much
The tiger who understood people

Thurber, James
JOHNSON – PRINC. p317-318

Thus I guard my mother's lambkins
MY BOOK HOUSE v. 1 p144.

Thutmose
The prince and the sphinx

Thyme
The frog and his clothes

Ti-Tiriti-Ti
BAKER – GOLDEN p89-100

The Ti-trees
NORLEDGE – ABORIGINAL p29-31

Tiamat
  JACOBSON – FIRST p11-13

Tibet
  The age of the animals
  The country of the mice
  The disillusionment of the Tibetan
    tiger
  The gold dust that turned to sand
  The holy cat of Tibet
  A hungry wolf
  The jackals and the tiger
  Plop!
  The story of silly Cham-ba
  The story of the stone lion
  The story of the tortoise and the
    monkey
  Yoro reveals himself as Gessar Khan

  –Himalayas. *See* "Abominable
    snowmen"

  –Sekkim
    The tower that reached from
      earth to heaven

Tickbirds
  The ghost-bird
  The sky people

The ticklish thief
  HOLDING – SKY p111-124

Ticks, Bull
  West country boy

Ticky-picky boom-boom
  SHERLOCK – ANANSI p76-83

Ticoumba and the president
  COURLANDER – PIECE p58-61

Tides
  The bird and the buffalo
  The boy who was caught by a clam
  The dragon king and the lost fish-
    hook
  The fisherman
  The frog that swallowed the ocean
  The giant of the mount
  The hummingbird and the carabao
  The luck of the sea and the luck of
    the mountain
  The man who sat on the tide
  Thor's unlucky journey
  Why the tides ebb and flow
  The woman who wanted to cook with
    salt water

Tidiness. *See* **Neatness**

Tientjens, Eunice
  Antar the hero

Tierra del Fuego
  Sun and moon

The tiger and the dwarf
  INS-SŎB – FOLK p78-81

The tiger and the goats
  GAER – FABLES p154-155

The tiger and the persimmon
  INS-SŎB – FOLK p184.

The tiger and the rabbit
  BELPRE´– TIGER p11-18

The tiger cat
  BELTING – CAT p60-62

The tiger-girl
  INS-SŎB – FOLK p88-89

The tiger in court
  HUME – FAVORITE p74-78

Tiger in the forest, Anansi in the web
  SHERLOCK – WEST p59-64

The tiger in the palanquin
  SIDDIQUI – TOON. p32-36

Tiger-lilies
  Tiger story, Anansi story

Tiger lily and the dragon
  PICARD – FAUN p159-178

The tiger priest
  INS-SŎB – FOLK p90-92

Tiger story, Anansi story
  SHERLOCK – WEST p45-58

The tiger, the Brahmen, and the jackal
  ARBUTHNOT – TIME p149-151
  BUCK – FAIRY p168-171

The tiger who understood people
  GREEN – BIG p35-36

Tiger woman
  CHILD – CASTLES p243-257
  JEWETT – WHICH p29-40

Tigers
  Anansi and candlefly
  Anansi and the old hag

Tigers (*Continued*)

Anansi and turtle and pigeon
Anansi hunts with tiger
Anansi play with fire, Anansi get
  burned
Armadillo's story
The ass in the tiger skin
The bet tetween Matjan and Gadja
Bouki and Ti Bef
The Brahmin and the villain
The Brahmin, the tiger, and the
  seven judges
The camel in the lion's court
The carpenter's boar
The cat, the tiger, and the man
Chu Cuoi's trip to the moon
The circus parade
The clever jackal and how he out-
  witted the tiger
The coral comb
Crocodile's share
The curse of the only son
Dan-Gun, first King of Korea
The dilemma of a pious man
The disillusionment of the
  Tibetan tiger
The farmer, the buffalo and the tiger
The five tiger general
The foolish, timid, little hare
Four sworn brothers
The fox outwits the tiger
The fox, the hare, and the toad have
  an argument
From tiger to Anansi
General Pumpkin
George and the field glasses
The gift of the moon goddess
Ha! Tio rabbit is bigger
The hare and the tiger
Hong Do-Ryong, the filial tiger
The honourable tom cat
How confusion came among the
  animals
How people got the first cat
How the deer lost his tail
How the raja's son won the Princess
  Labam
How tiger learned to hunt
The hunter and the tiger
Jackal or tiger?
The jackals and the tiger
Juan Bobo and old tiger
Kantjil grows strong at the welling-
  well
Kantjil interprets a dream
Kantchil's lime pit
The kid and the tiger
The king of the forest
The king of the mountain
The king who rides a tiger

The kling kling bird
A leak in an old house
The lion, the tiger, and the eagle
Little Black Sambo
Malati and the prince
The monkey, the tiger, and the
  jackal family
Moti
The mouse and the wizard
Mowgli's brothers
Nazar the brave
On just being yourself
The perfect husband
The polite children
The price of greed
The quarrel
The rabbit and the tiger
The rain leak in an old house
Ranjit and the tigers
Soo Tan the tiger and the little green
  frog
Soonimaya
The story of General Gim Dog-Nyong
The sun and the moon
The terrible leak
Three tales of the mouse-deer
Three who found their hearts' desire
Ticky-picky boom-boom
The toad is the emperor's uncle
The traveller and the tiger
The traveller, the fox, and the tiger
The tree that shadowed the world
Two out of one
The ungrateful tiger
The valiant chattee-maker
The valiant potter
When the cat and the tiger lived
  together
The white-eared tiger
Why the tiger is so angry at the cat
Why there are no tigers in Borneo
Why women won't listen
The wind-demon
The young gentleman and the tiger
The young man and the priest
The youth who could become an ant,
  a lion or an eagle

—**Tails**
    Miss goat
    The old tiger and the hare
    The tiger's tail

The tiger's grave
    INS-SOB – FOLK p82-84

The tiger's minister of state
    COURLANDER – TIGER'S p20-23

The tiger's stripes
    VO-DINH – TOAD p65-73

662

The tiger's tail
COURLANDER – KANT. p19-21

The tiger's war against Borneo
COURLANDER – KANT. p23-27

The tiger's whisker
COURLANDER – TIGER'S p16-19

Tigre (country)
The ancient land of Tigre
How God helped Mammo
Saint Gabre Manfas and his animals

Tik and Lap and the giant fish
GREY – SOUTH (2) p9-13

The tikgi birds
SECHRIST – ONCE p86-90

Tiki-Tiki-Tembo
BROWN – AROUND p43-50
HARDENDORFF – FROG'S p40-45

Tiles
Not to care a straw
The three golden ducats

Till Eulenspiegel
PICARD – GERMAN p130-149
STRONG – FAVORITE p35-42

Tim Felt's ghost
JOHNSON – WHAT p171-173

Tim for wealth and happiness
GUIRMA – TALES p100-113

Time
See also **Clocks; Procrastination**
Buh Fox's number nine shoes
The head of brass
The king and the shepherd
The lost half-hour
The mother of time and the
enchanted brothers
The past and the future
Sudden silence
The sun, the moon, and the stars
The swans of Ballycastle
The tale about lost time
The thread of life
A time for everything
The wood carver of Ruteng

A time for everything
DEUTSCH – MORE p85-93

The time of deep darkness
THOMPSON – HAWAII. p11-14

A time of witches
JENNINGS – BLACK p94-112

Timimoto
MANNING – DWARFS p104-108

Timothy and the buggane ghost
SPICER – GHOSTS p112-119

The Tims
FARJEON – LITTLE p204-207

Tin and tinsmiths
The knockers of Ballowal
Revenge of the tin god
The three words of advice
The tinner, the dog, the jew, and the
cake

The tinder box
MANNING – BEASTS p49-60
SIDEMAN – WORLD'S p320-331
TUDOR – TASHA p58-64

Tinder-boxes
Dwarf stories
The fisherman's son

Ting-a-ling
STOCKTON – TING p3-37

Ting-a-ling-ling
MY BOOK HOUSE v. 1 p84.

Ting-a-ling and the five magicians
STOCKTON – TING p39-72

Ting-a-ling's visit to Tur-il-i-ra
STOCKTON – TING p141-161

Ting-ting birds. *See* **Blackbirds**

Tinirau and his pet whale
CAMPBELL – MAORI p30-34

The tinker and his wife
MANNING – RED p112-117

The tinker of Tamlacht
MacMANUS – HIBERIAN p10-24

Tinkers
See also **Peddlers**
The accomplished and strange
teakettle
The lass who went out at the cry
of dawn
The lucky tea-kettle
Queen o' the tinkers

Tinkers (*Continued*)

The question none could answer
The tea-kettle

The tinner, the dog, the Jew, and the cake
MANNING — PETER p150-155

Tinni (plant)
The sword that fought by itself

The tiny bird and the king
SPELLMAN — BEAUT. p71-74

The tiny god
UCHIDA — MAGIC p113-121

Tiny Perry
JAGENDORF — NEW p169-174

Tiny teasing tales
WITHERS — I SAW p46.

The tiny, tiny man
BECHSTEIN — FAIRY p56-61

Tipis
Bird of power

Tippett, James S.
Groceries
Park play

Tippity Witchit's Hallowe'en
MY BOOK HOUSE v. 4 p145-158

The tipsy rooster
LOWE — LITTLE p55-57

Tit for tat
DURHAM — TIT p46-47

Tithonus, the grasshopper
CATHON — PERHAPS p83-84

Titian (artist)
The boy who made a dream come true

Titmice
The titmouse

The titmouse
KRYLOV — 15 p8-9

Titty mouse and Tatty mouse
WITHERS — I SAW p62-66

The tiyanak
ROBERTSON — PHILIP. p117-127

Tlacuache the saint
ROSS — MEXICO p121-133

To be seen
LEACH — SOUP p101-103

To cure a sudden stitch
HOPE-SIMPSON — CAVAL. p124-125

To feed my people: The coming of buffalo
MARRIOTT — AMER. p112-119

To feed my people: The coming of corn
MARRIOTT — AMER. p96-99;
100-104; 105-111

To feed my people: The race between the buffalo and man
MARRIOTT — AMER. p120-123

To kill a king, from "News from Scotland"
HOPE-SIMPSON — CAVAL.
p109-113

To Llewelyn, (who inquired concerning wyverns)
PALMER — DRAGONS p87.

To market, to market
MY BOOK HOUSE v. 1 p33.

To outleap a rabbit
DAVIS — LION'S p61-67

To pay through the nose
ZAGLOUL — BLACK p91-95

To the devil with the money!
BAKER — TALKING p113-117

To the lady-bird
CATHON — PERHAPS p89.

To the rescue
JUDA — WISE p76-80

To the tengu goblins
GARNER — GOBLINS p82.

To your good health
HAVILAND — RUSSIA p3-19

The toad-bridegroom
INS-SŎB — FOLK p175-178

The toad is the emperor's uncle
VO-DINH – TOAD p15-22

Toads
The boy who wanted to learn
witchcraft
The bragging bat
The bragging beasts
Brown owl's story
The deer, the hare, and the toad
Diamonds and toads
Do warts come from toads?
The eagle and the owl
The fairies
Fate of the Magicos
Father catfish
The fox, the hare, and the toad have
an argument
The great spirit of the toad
How turtle came
An impossible penance
The knight of La Sarraz
The lady and the toad
The lazy boy
Mr. Toad sets out on a journey
The open road
Over in the meadow
The prince who rode through a
mousehole
The snake and the toad
The three feathers
Thumbelina
Turkey in the straw
The ungrateful tiger

The toads in the lake
MY BOOK HOUSE v. 1 p68.

Toadstools
The elf and the dormouse

Toasts
Tsar Lazar's supper

Tobacco
The blacksmith in the moon
The centipede girl
The compulsive gift–a cigarette
Daniel O'Connell and the trickster
The fire plume
How grasshopper came to be and men
obtained tobacco
Hwan and Dang
Owl with the great head and eyes
Partridge and rock tripe
A pound of tobacco
Sean Palmer's voyage to America
with the fairies

Sir Walter Raleigh
Why grasshopper spits tobacco juice

–Pouches
The hunter of Perak

The tobacco fairy from the blue hills
MacMILLAN – GLOOS. p211-216

Tobacco woman and corn spirit
HAYES – INDIAN p65-76

Toe-counting
The story of the five toes
This little pig went to market
This one stole an egg

Toenails
The witch and her four sons

Toffee
The three brothers and the treacle
toffee

Toggenburg, Ida of
Ida of Toggenburg

A token of friendship
RASKIN – TALES p15-20

Tokens
Black Colin of Loch Awe
Secret tokens prove ownership

Tokgabbins (goblins)
The Korean goblins

Tola and the sea monster
HASKETT – GRAINS p26-32

Tolerance
The ballad of East and West
I took a walk one evening
Joan of Arc
Lion and the woman
The mad dog
The melting pot
The new Colossus
Reaching an understanding
The rebel
The sheep and the pig that made a
home
The village of cream puffs

Tolkien, J. R. R.
Introductory note

Tolkien's magic ring
TOLKIEN − READER p ix-xvi

Tolstoy, Leo
The duck and the moon
The falcon and the cock
The gnat and the lion
The Jackal and the elephant
The king and the falcon
The mouse who lived under the
granary
The raven and his young
Uncle Mitya's horse
The wolf and the old woman

Tolstoy, Leo N.
A boy in Russia
How one should carve a goose
The peasant and the waterman

Tom and giant blunderbus
MANNING − PETER p110-119

Tom and old giant Denbros. See The
giants of Towednack

Tom Hickathrift
JACOBS − MORE p46-54

Tom Thumb
The adventures of General Tom
Thumb
I had a little husband
Little one inch
Little Tom Thumb
The story of Issaumbochi
The story of Tom Thumb
The young giant

Tom Thumb
HAVILAND − ENGLAND p30-43
LINES − NURSERY p107-116
PERRAULT − CLASSIC p119-145
SIDEMAN − WORLD'S p38-46
THOMPSON − ONE p310-314

Tom Tit Tot
ARBUTHNOT − TIME p21-23
BAKER − TALKING p33-39
LINES − NURSERY p79-92
REEVES − ENGLISH p147-155
THOMPSON − ONE p158-162
WILLIAMS − FAIRY p11-19

Tom, Tom, the piper's son
MY BOOK HOUSE v. 1 p34.

Tom Walker and the devil
TAFT − PROFILE p131-136

Tomatoes
The rabbit who wanted to be a man

Tombs
See also Temples
The book of Thoth
The legend of Tchi-Niu
The pasha's sword
The pious washerwomen
The tale of Liban the siren
Where the kings of Judah sleep their
last sleep

Tommy was a silly boy
MY BOOK HOUSE v. 1 p150.

Tongas Island (Alaska)
The Lincoln totem pole

Tongatabu (islands)
The hermit with two heads

Tongs
The prince and the demon

Tongue, Ruth L.
Drake's cannon ball

The tongue-cut sparrow
HAVILAND − JAPAN p31-46
HEARN − JAPANESE p57-59
McALPINE − JAPAN. p188-201
MY BOOK HOUSE v. 3 p165-169
SAKADE − JAPAN. p38-44
SEKI − FOLKTALES p115-118
UCHIDA − DANCING p123-131

A tongue of gold and words of jade
BONNET − CHINESE p109-110

Tongue steeple
BOUCHER − MEAD p25-30

Tongues
The beef tongue of Orula
How the bee got his bumble
The king and Kuffie
The mallet of wealth
The three sisters and the old witch

Tontlawald, A tale of the. See A tale of
the Tontlawald

Tony Di-Moany
MEHDEVI − BUNGLING p57-67

Too heavy
KELSEY − ONCE p132-134

Too hot to handle
FELTON — NEW p77-85

Tools
See also names of tools
Forks
Why some animals live with man

Toontoony and the barber
SIDDIQUI — TOON. p98-103

Toontoony pie
SIDDIQUI — TOON. p15-22

Toor, Frances
Mexican rhymes

The toothpick warriors
SAKADE — JAPAN. p49-54

Toothpicks
Chin-chin Kobakama

Tooze, Ruth
TOOZE — MONKEY p72.
TOOZE — THREE p64.

Topknots
The prince and the demon

Tops
O if my top would only spin

Tops and bottoms
BRIGGS — PERS. p99-100

Tops or bottoms
GARNER — GOBLINS p11-12

Torah
The story of Mordecai and Esther
The warm matzah

Torah and honor
BARASH — GOLDEN p111-113

The toromiro of Rapa-Nui
U. N. — RIDE p279-282

Tortoise and Babarinsa's daughters
WALKER — DANCING p73-79

Tortoise and the baboon
ARNOTT — AFRICAN p22-24

The tortoise and the crocodile
COBBLE — WEMBI p28-31

The tortoise and the hare
WILSON — GREEK p166-168

The tortoise and the lion
ELLIOT — SINGING p32-43

Tortoise and the lizard
ARNOTT — AFRICAN p13-15

The tortoise and the magic drum
CARPENTER — AFRICAN p31-39

The tortoise and the monkey
ELLIOT — WHERE p87-94

The tortoise and the osprey
ELLIOT — WHERE p66-71

The tortoise and the reedbuck run a race
BURTON — MAGIC p95-98

The tortoise and the two swans
MONTGOMERIE — 25 p48-49

Tortoise triumphant
ELLIOT — WHERE p128-134

The tortoise who talked too much
KOREL — LISTEN p76-81

The tortoise-wife
WILSON — GREEK p31-39

Tortoises (turtles)
The adjutant bird
The bee tree
The boastful tortoise
Buya marries the tortoise
The dancing palm tree
The enchanted tortoise
The friendship of the tortoise and
the eagle
The girl who forgot her hoe
Grandfather tells some tales
The hare and the tortoise
The hawk's friends
How animals got their beautiful coats
How Ijapa, who was short, became
long
Ijapa cries for his horse
Ijapa goes to the Osanyin shrine
The infallible salt bird
The jabuty and the jaguar
Jabuty, the strong
Kalulu and his money farm
The length of life
The leopard and the bushbuck go
hunting
The leopard and the tortoise
A lesson for the bat
The magic drum

Tortoises (*Continued*)

The mouse and his friends
The outwitted hunter
Pierre Jean's tortoise
Rabbit and tortoise
Rabbit at the water hole
The son of the tortoise
The story of the tortoise,and the
   monkey
The talkative king
The talkative tortoise
Urashima Taro
Urashima Taro and the princess of
   the sea
Why the tortoise has a round back
The wild geese and the tortoise
The wonderful tree

, Golden
   The golden tortoise
   The supernatural crossbow

−Shells
   The animal wife
   Antelope's mother: the woman
      in the moon
   Chimpanzee's story
   The pattern on tortoise's back
   The tortoise and the osprey

"Tota"
   Dinner with the tota

Totems
   The boy and the sea monsters
   Fly again, my proud eagle
   The giant ogre, Kloo-Teekl
   The Lincoln totem pole
   The mountain goats
   The one-horned mountain goat
   Strong man
   The wild woman of the woods

Toto gets married
   PROTTER − CHILD. p70-72

Touch
   The baker's neighbor

The tournament in Ireland
   HAZELTINE − HERO p119-134

Tournaments
   Lionbruno
   Prince Ahmed
   The story of Prince Ahmed

Towels
   Baba Yaga
   You have a napkin

Tower of Babel. *See* Babel, Tower of

The tower that reached from earth to
heaven
   HUME − FAVORITE p62-66

Towers
   The beetle and a drop of honey
   The dark tower
   The golden horse
   The legend of the governor and the
      lawyer
   The legend of the Prince Ahmed Al
      Kamel
   The legend of the three beautiful
      princesses
   Longshanks, girth, and keen
   The maiden in the tower
   The merman's revenge
   A mouse in search of a wife
   The mousetower
   The prince who wanted the moon
   The princess in the fiery tower
   The princess in the tower

A town in a snuff-box
   BUDBERG − RUSSIAN p139-149

The town mouse and the country mouse
   ARBUTHNOT − TIME p205.
   SIDEMAN − WORLD'S p300-305

The town of fools
   BUDBERG − RUSSIAN p173-176

A toy princess
   JOHNSON − PRINC. p8-31

Toys and toy shops
   See also Dolls
   The brownies in the toy shop
   The children and the bear
   Don't run away my kitty
   Go to sleepy, little baby
   Good morning, Peter
   A happy day in the city
   Hark, the Christmas bells are ringing
   Hop, my horsey, leap and spring
   Jack Frost
   A Japanese lullaby
   Jokeli
   Little Beppo Pippo
   The little engine that could
   Little Hansworst
   The luck boy of Toy Valley
   My boat

Toys and toy shops (*Continued*)

O if my top would only spin
O I'll build a square with my pretty
  red blocks
O lady Mary Ann
O will you shoe our pony, pray?
Paper boats
A rhyme from Santo Domingo
Ride a cock-horse to Banbury Cross
Ride, ride away
Rocking-horse land
Roll it, bowl it
Sally's blue ball
Smiling girls, rosy boys
The steadfast tin soldier
The sugar-plum tree
The tale of nutcracker
Teddy bear, teddy bear
The teddy bear's picnic
A toy princess
What are you able to build with your
  blocks?
What they say
When I was down beside the sea
Where go the boats?
The witch

The trade that no one knows
  GARNER – GOBLINS p105-114

Traders and Trading
Ananse and the king's cow
Are there such women?
The ass in the lion's skin
The bundles of straw and the king's
  son
The flower faces
Gudbrand of the hillside
The jeweled ring
The lion and the hare go hunting
Luckier and luckier
Mr. and Mrs. Vinegar
The monkey and the crab
Rabbit and the grain buyers
Ruda, the quick thinker
The story of silly Cham-ba
The swapping song
The tail of the cat
Temba becomes a warrior

Trades
The adventures of Manawyddan
The devil's apprentice
The king's son and the straw hat
  maker
The miller's four sons
The rug maker
The seven Simons
The three brothers

Trager, Helen G.
  AUNG – KINGDOM p96.

A tragic story
  MY BOOK HOUSE v. 4 p136.

A trail of tall tales
  IVES – TALES p155-169

Trains
Casey Jones
The goat that flagged the train
John Henry, the big steel-drivin' man
The man who missed the Tay Bridge
  train
Pecos Bill, the cowboy
Pennyworth
A song of the railroad men
When I go a-courting

  –Engines
    The big engine
    Engine, engine number nine
    Hurry up, engine
    The little engine that could
    The steamboat and the locomotive

Traitors
  See also **Betrayal; Disloyalty**
Bech, the ambitious quail
Elidorus in fairyland
The indigo jackal
Karl the Great and the robber
The singing bone

A tramp of the Middle West
  MY BOOK HOUSE v. 12 p147-153

Tramps
The broken box
Jan and Jaantje
The leprechaun and the wheelbarrow
The old traveler
The old woman and the tramp
The stone stew
A visitor from paradise

Trang Tu (Taoist scholar)
The encounter with death

Transformations
  See also names of animals and birds;
  Magic
Beauty and the beast
The blue centaur
East o' the sun and west o' the moon
Eggborn
The fox turns a somersault
The frog princess

Transformations (*Continued*)

The hermit and the mouse
Hong Do-Ryong, the filial tiger
Keloglan and the magician
The six swans
Tiger woman

The transformed donkey
WITHERS – WORLD p45-46

Transporation. *See* names of types

Transportation problem
LEACH – NOODLES p59.

The trap
HEADY – WHEN p81-84

Trappers and trapping
The blind boy and the loon
The canoe in the rapids
The clever jackal and how he
outwitted the tiger
Jack and the giant Cormoran
Khasynget's grandmother
A leg for the lion
A legend of Kotzebue
The pigeon, the deer and the turtle
Tcakabesh snares the sun
The tiger in the palanquin

The traveler
JOHNSON – WHAT p153.

Traveling through the chimney
JAGENDORF – GYPSIES p118-121

Traveling to see wonders
WITHERS – WORLD p31.

The traveler and the nut tree
See also in Folk-tales of Kashmir
COURLANDER – TIGER'S p76-77

The traveller and his host
ĆURČIJA – YUGOSLAV. p181-183

The traveller and the tiger
KOREL – LISTEN p89-97

The traveller, the fox, and the tiger
INS-SOB – FOLK p174-175

Travellers
Aeneas . . . His wanderings
Bald pate
The barrel-organ
The bold heroes of Hungry Hill
Changing luck

The cock who went traveling
The dragon and the dragoon
The eternal wanderer of the Pampas
The four young men
The golden lion
Goose Matt
The greedy stallkeeper and the poor
traveler
Hans, the horn, and the magic sword
How much for a shadow?
How the travelers shared their meal
I was going along the road
The journey to Lagos
The journey to Toulouse of the
animals that had colds
Just his luck
Khalid and Aantar
Lars, my lad!
Leaf by Niggle
The little lizard's sorrow
Magical elements in religious beliefs:
The wanderings of Isis and the agony
of Horus
The old traveler
The Phynnodderee
A prince and a dove
The pugilist and his wonderful helpers
The return of Odysseus
The seventh father of the house
Sindbad the sailor
A stork is not always a stork
The story of the shipwrecked sailor
The strange journey of Tuflongbo
The three journeys of Ilya of Nurom
The three wanderers
Three who found their hearts' desire
Thumbkin
The tiger priest
The tiny, tiny man
The twelve young men
The two frogs
The ungrateful tiger
The voyage of Maelduin (Maeldun)
A wanderer with a dog
When Shlemiel went to Warsaw
Why people tell stories
The wonders seen by Wurrunna

The travellers and the bear
MONTGOMERIE – 25 p53.

The travelling frog
BUDBERG – RUSSIAN p129-154

The travels of a fox
ARBUTHNOT – TIME p15-17
JOHNSON – WHAT p191-194
WITHERS – I SAW p18-21

Treachery
The deer and the snake

670

Treachery (*Continued*)

The five wise words
The golden twins
The grateful prince
Guy Fawkes . . . The gunpowder plot
It all comes to light
Kashi and his wicked brothers
The king and the ring
Lancelot and Guenevei
Lancelot of the lake
The mouse and the frog
The mousetower
Nangato
The nightingale Hazaran
The ostrich chicks
The part-time prisoner
The poisoned apple
The Rajah who flew away
The reward of treachery
The taking of Joppa
The tale of the two brothers

The treachery of Morgan LeFay
  PICARD — STORIES p27-36

Treasure

The adventures of Little Peachling
Ali Baba and the forty thieves
The bad-tempered wife
The beggar's prophecy
The bird of seven colors
The black bodach
The blue dog
The brave cowman
The bride-price for Olwen
The broken box
The buried treasure
Cast thy bread
Charles the Bold of Burgundy
The chatterbox
The companion
The crimson purse and the talking
  raven
Crying turkeys
The deer and the snake
Discovery of salt
The egg
The enchanted palace
The envious neighbor
The field of Boliauns
Finlay the giant killer
The ghost and Hans Van Duin
The giants of Towednack
The good sword
Grillo
Guardians of hidden treasure
Hantsjc and the remarkable beast
The haunted house
Hidden treasure
The hidden treasure of Khin

The hoard
Holding the bag
How a fish swam in the air
Hudson River legends; Captain Kidd;
  buried treasure
Jack and the giant Cormoran
John Gethin and the candle
King Solomon's carpet
The lady of Stavoren
The legend of the Moor's legacy
The legend of the two discreet statues
The little grey man
The lost treasure of Cucamonga
The magic melons
The magic wand
Maid Lena
Momotaro, or The story of the son
  of a peach
The most precious gift
One grain more than the devil
The peach boy
The pedlar of Swaffham
The pedlar's dream
The poor brother's treasure
The quest of the children of Turenn
The red king and the witch
The robe
The sage and the servant
The sea captain's wife
The secret of the hidden treasure
The shell grotto of Nienoort
The silly goose war
Sindbad the sailor
The smart daughter
The snow in Chelm
Snow-white
Snow-white and Rose-red
The spider in the wall
The spriggans' treasure
The story of Iubdan, King of the
  Lepra and the lepracaun
The stupid fellow
The tale of a rich king: The treasure
  of Rhampinitus
The thief and the king's treasure
Three pennyworth
Timimoto
The tongue-cut sparrow
The tsarino's greatest treasure
Victor

The treasure
  BARASH — GOLDEN p162-164
  HATCH — MORE p22-32

The treasure chamber of Rhampsinitus
  THOMPSON — ONE p366-368

Treasure in the basket
  KELSEY — ONCE p32-37

The treasure of Altamira
MARKS — SPANISH p84-101

The treasure of Tacoma
COTHRAN — WITH p67-75

The treasure thief
GREEN — TALES p202-209

The treasure under the tree
JAGENDORF — UPSTATE p88-92

Treaties
About the Cherokee

Tredeschin
MÜLLER — SWISS p154-162

Tree and leaf
TOLKIEN — READER (part 2)
p3-112

Tree-climbing
Shoes for a journey
Why goat cannot climb a tree
The young coyote's visit

The tree from Adam's grave
BELTING — THREE p69-74

The tree goddess
BARLOW — LATIN p82-88

Tree-houses
The children who lived in a tree-house

Tree of life
The tree from Adam's grave

Tree-root, iron-strong and hill-roller
ILLYES — ONCE p130-155

The tree that flew
BELTING — THREE p25-38

The tree that shadowed the world
BELTING — THREE p39-46

The tree that walked
BELTING — THREE p64-68

The tree with the difficult name
WILLIAMS — ROUND p186-191

Trees
See also Fairies—Trees; names of trees
The adder and the fox
The barren stones

The bear and the fox who made a bet
The beginning of good conversation
The big tree and the big bird
Casperl
The Coomacka-tree
The devil's wood
The duped giant
Eight leaves of story (3) Baglan the
builder
The flight with the Wendigo
The foolish man
The fruits of health
The giant sturgeon
The gift of the moon goddess
The girl on the green tree
Golden hood
The golden twins
The good luck tree
Grasp all, lose all
The hope tree of Harlem
The hostel of the quicken
How frogs lost their tails
The judgment of the wind
Kamiyo of the river
The kindly ghost
The king of the wood
The king who ate chaff
The little nobleman
The magic baby shoes
The maiden in the country under-
ground
The man who made the trees bloom
The monkey gardeners
The most useful tree in the world
The mountain hen and the fox
The oak that helped outwit a king
The old man and his dog
Old Pipes and the dryad
Pappa Greatnose
Porridge with a troll
The possums, the man, and the tree
The powers of plants and trees to
protect against witches
The proud father
The saga of the waru Wanggi
Salute to the trees
A secret told to a stranger
Silver leaves and golden blossoms
Sing something
The stag prince
The strongest
The tale of the three brothers
The talking tree
The tall trees in the greenwood
The terror of the ogres
The thirteen enchanted cats
The tinderbox
The traveler and the nut tree
Up in the green orchard
The weasel and his mother
The white parrot

672

Trees (*Continued*)

Why the waringen tree is holy
The wiliwili trees
Willow
The wonder-tree
The wonderful tree
The wood cutter's son and the two
  turtles
The wood nymphs
The woodcutter of Gura

—**Bark**
Binewan the emu, and Wahn the
  crows

, **Beans**
The bean tree

—**Branches**
The enchanted prince
The golden slipper, the magic
  ring, and the twigs
The magic walking stick
The princess with the golden shoes
The sun, the moon and the stars
  of morning

, **Fruit**
The famine and the fruit tree
The girl who kissed the peach-tree

, **Golden**
The king's dream
The task of Prince Kurumanochi

, **Kneeling**
The kneeling tree

—**Leaves**
How Glooskap made the birds
How Trystan won Esyllt
Khalid and Aantar
Leaf by Niggle
November's party

, **Sacred**
The golden helmet
Rata and his canoe

, **Singing**
The story of the talking bird

—**Spirits**
See also **Nats**
Tar-sa's luck

—**Stumps**
Coyote and the alder stump

, **World**
Ragnarokk, the destiny of the gods
Yggdrasil, the world tree

Trees
CATHON — PERHAPS p214.

Trefoil (plant)
Goblin gold

Tregeagle
MANNING — PETER p48-55

The trial at Avichara-Pura
See also The judgement of Karakoush
COURLANDER — TIGER'S p49-51

The trial by fire
MY BOOK HOUSE v. 7 p26-30

The trial of the stone
COURLANDER — TIGER'S p24-28
MAR — CHINESE p71-85

The trials of Conneda
GARNIER — LEGENDS p182-190

The trials of Dyfed
JONES — WELSH p36-52

The trials of Ting Ling
CHILD — CASTLES p79-95

Tribes. *See* **Africa—Tribes; Indians of
North America—Tribes**

A trick that failed
CARPENTER — SOUTH p50-56

Trickery
See also **Anansi stories**
Abunuwas the trickster
Agayk and the strangest spear
The alchemist
Aristotle and the three sons
The badger and the boatmen
The badger and the magic fan
The bag of lies
Bandalee
The bean pot
The bear and the fox who made a
  bet
The beautiful princess
Big Matsiko
Bouki and Ti Bef
The boy Pu-nia and the king of the
  sharks
The Brahman and the goat
Bread-free
Buh fox's number nine shoes
Canawlers on the E-ri-ee Canal
A cat for a hare
Catches
The champion
Chanticleer and Partlet
Chestnuts

Trickery (*Continued*)

Chu and the king of the underworld
Clever Grethel
The cormorant and the fishes
The covetous minister
The coyote and the bear
The crackling mountain
The crane, the fish and the crab
The crock of gold
The cunning old man and the three
  rogues
The damned boys
Daniel O'Connell and the trickster
A deer trick
The devil to pay
Diamond cut diamond
The dilemma of a pious man
A dinar for a donkey
Dinewan the emu and Goomble-
  Gubbon the turkey
Donkey, mond your mother!
The donkey, the ox, and the farmer
A donkey transformed
Don't make a bargain with a fox
Don't tease the tengu!
Fairy tricks
The fish thief
The fishermen
Five dozen eggs
The fox and the bear
The fox and the crane
The fox and the eagle
The fox and the hare in winter
The fox and the heron
The fox and the stork
The fox and the wolf and the keg of
  butter
The fox and the wolf at the wedding
A fox in hiding
The fox in Inishkea
The fox who was not so smart
A fox who was too sly
The game of chess
Geordie and ten-shilling Jock
The ghost in the cabbage patch
The giant outwitted
The gift of the holy man
The giraffe hunters
Gizo's counting trick
The goat in the well
The gold-lined donkey
The golden skins
Gooloo the magpie and the waroogas
The greatest hoax in New York City
The greedy friend
The gun, the pot, and the hat
Hare and the corn bins
The hare and the tiger
The hawk and the wildcat
Hodja and the jumbled jobs

Hog child plays tricks
Holding down the hat
The horse that liked to play tricks
Holding the bag
The horse with his head where his tail
  ought to be
How a peasant outwitted two mer-
  chants
How and why: Don't be greedy story
How chameleon became king of the
  animals
How confusion came among the
  animals
How death came into the world
How dog outwitted shepherd
How rabbit deceived fox
How raven found the daylight
How Sketco tricked the grizzly
How spider helped a fisherman
How the deer got his horns
How the hare learned to swim
How the mosquitoes came to Oneata
How the terrapin beat the rabbit
How wisdom came to man
How Ysengrin the wolf was taught to
  fish
The hunger time
Hyena and the oil with the flies in it
I know what I'll do
The iguana and the black snake
Ijapa and the hot-water test
Ikkyu and the merchant's money bags
The Irish luck of Brian Hughes
It's already paid
Itsayaya's revenge
Jack and the lord high mayor
The jackal and the bear
The jackal and the crocodile
Jaco and the giant
Jean Britisse, the champion
The just judgment
Kalulu and the elephant
The Kamiah monster
Kantjil and the monkey business
Kantjil becomes a raksha
Kantjil discovers the wisdom of Allah
Kantjil grows strong at the welling-
  well
Kantjil holds a festival
Kantjil interprets a dream
Kantjil to the rescue
Khasynget's grandmother
King Kantjil's kingdom expands
The king's drum
The king's joke
The lazy fox
A leg for the lion
A legend of Knockmany
The leopard's tricks
Little Claus and Big Claus
The little hare's clever trick

674

Trickery (Continued)

Little Kathy free-as-the-wind
The little, little fellow with the big, big hat
Little Red Riding Hood
Loki, the god of the jotun race
The long one
The lord of Massachusetts
The louse and the fingernail
Maiden Lane in the golden days
The man who sold a ghost
The man who sold magic
The mare at the wedding
Martin, the honest thief
Maui and the fire goddess
Maui the Great
Maui—the trickster
Mece and the shoemaker's daughters
A message for a donkey
The mighty warrior in hare's house
Mister deer's my riding horse
Mister honey mouth
The monkey and the crocodile
Nidden and Didden and Donal Beg O'Neary
Now would I laugh, were I not dead
The ogre and the cock
An old Korean story
One against a hundred
One mean trick deserves another
The onion and the rose
Ooka and the telltale tale
Ooka and the willow witness
The out-foxed fox
Oversmart is bad luck
Owl with the great head and eyes
Paddy and the leprechaun
Pakpai and Boto
Pancho and the Duendes
The peasant pewit
A peasant tricks the devil
Peter ox
The pilgrim and the judge
The pira game
Polenta, polenta, and more polenta
Punchinello
The rabbit and the crocodile
The rabbit and the tiger
Rabbit, elephant and hippopotamus
The rabbit who crossed the sea
Rag, tag, and bobtail
The rat who made one bargain too many
Red Riding Hood
Reynard and Bruin
Reynard and the fisherman's dream
Reynard the fox
The ride in the night
A salty tale
Sarita and the Duendes

Sayndy and smallpox: The white man's gift
The seed of happiness
Senor coyote
Senor coyote and the dogs
The servant lass
The shepherd's boy
The silly slave
The silver jug
Sissa and the troublesome trifles
Sly Peter at the fair
Sly Peter's revenge
The smart woman of Kennebunkport
The smiling innkeeper
The smoke horse
The soldier's billet
Spider and squirrel
Spider and the lion
The spider specter of the pool
Spider's web
The story of Zibong
Sweet dung, the cake-tree, and the bugle of life
The tale of Tom Corwin
Tall hog
Tar-baby
Temba's bag of salt
The tengu's magic nose fan
The theft of fire
Thor and the jotun Utgardsloki
Thor . . . How the thunderer was tricked
Thor's journey to jotun-heim
Thor's unlucky journey
The three brothers and the giant
Ticoumba and the president
The tiger in the palanquin
Till Eulenspiegel
Trust your friends
(The) tug of war
Tyl's task
The ungrateful crocodile
The uninvited guest
The vanishing rice-straw coat
Wahn the crow Wirinun
The way of the master
The weary spirits of Lanai
The weaver's worry
Well-done-Peter-Parker
The well of D'yeree-in-Dowan
The white hare and the crocodiles
Why bears eat meat
Why the bat flies at night
Why the bear's tail is short
Why the carabao's hoof is split
Why the deer's teeth are blunt
Why the dog and the cat are enemies
Why the jellyfish has no bones
Why the possum's tail is bare
Why the spider has a narrow waist
Why the tiger is so angry at the cat

Trickery (*Continued*)

Willie and the pig
The wolf in the ram's skin
The wolf wears a sheepskin
The woodcock and the fox

Tricks
Catches

Tricks and catches
JOHNSON – WHAT p113-117

A trickster tricks the devil
JAGENDORF – UPSTATE p193-195

Tricksy rabbit
AARDEMA – STORY p9-17

Tricky Peik
HARDENDORFF – TRICKY p11-22

Trillevip
BAKER – GOLDEN p41-45

Trim Tram Turvey
MANNING – GIANNI p161-172

Trinidad
Brer goat and brer lion
Brother Anansi and Sir Peacock

–**Pitch Lake**
The legend of Pitch Lake

A trio of lost monsters
WILLIAMS – LOST p165-176

A trip to the sky
WITHERS – WORLD p19-22

Trip to town
LEACH – NOODLES p24.

Tripping and stumbling
BATCHELOR – SUPER. p91.

Tripple-trapple
MANNING – DEVILS p9-14

Tristram, Sir
How Tristram fought against the
knight from Ireland
How Trystan won Esyllt
The tournament in Ireland

Tristram and Isolt
PICARD – STORIES p89-100

Trivets
How the trivet came home

The troll who hid his life
SPICER – 13 p22-31

Trolls
The adventures of Silvervit and
Lillvacker
The ash lad who had an eating
match with the troll
Beowulf and Grendel
The blue belt
Boots and the troll
The boy who was never afraid
The boys who met the trolls in the
Hedal woods
Bukolla, the wonderful cow
Butterball
The cat on the dovrefell
Cattenborg
The companion
The creation of the world
East of the sun and north of the
earth
East of the sun and west of the moon
The first gods and giants
The fisherman's son
The girl who didn't know how to spin,
The Little People of Scandinavia
The golden bird
The golden castle that hung in the air
The good sword
Kari Woodencoat
Katie Woodencloak
Knurremurre the troll
The little horse
Loppa and Jon Loppa-Fosterling
Lord Peter
Master Erik
Olli and the rich troll
Perry-the-Winkle
Porridge with a troll
Princess Janina and the troll
Bradalba
The princess with the golden shoes
The princess with the twelve pair
of golden shoes
Ragnar Lodbrok and his sons
The seven foals
The seven stars
The shepherd of Silverstead
Sir Gawain and the green knight
(The) Soria-Moria-castle
Square Per
The stone troll
The story of Mead Moondaughter
The terrible Olli
Thor and the jotun Aegir
The three billy goats gruff

Trolls (*Continued*)

Three pennyworth
The three princesses
The three princesses in the mountain-
in-the-blue
The three princesses of Whiteland
To the devil with the money
The twelve wild ducks
Wakewell and his brothers
White-bear-King-Valemon
White-toes and Bushy-bride
The widow's son
The wild swans
The witch in the stone boat
The wonderful knapsack

The troll's bride
BOUCHER – MEAD p157-161

The troll's daughter
HATCH – MORE p59-78

The troll's invitation
PALMER – FAIRY p85-91

Trombones
Saint Peter and his trombone

Trooping fairies
BRIGGS – PERS. p55-59

A tropical morning at sea
MY BOOK HOUSE v. 6 p201.

Tropsyn
MANNING – RED p105-111

The troubadour and the devil
ALEGRIA – THREE p84-85

Troubadours. *See* Minstrels

The troubles at Hawaiki
MAYNE – HEROES p195-203

Troubles with a penguin
ARBUTHNOT – TIME p321-322

Trowbridge, John Townsend
Evening at the farm

Troy
A cause of war
The luck of Troy
The night of doom
The sack of Troy
The slaying of Hector
Tales of Troy
The wooden horse

Trucks
The big street in the big city
Good morning, Peter
The three trucks

True and untrue
JONES – SCAND. p89-97
THOMPSON – ONE p278-283

The true lord of the merry men of
Gotham
JAGENDORF – MERRY p131-136

True love in the Blue Mountains
JAGENDORF – UPSTATE p172-177

The true scales
BARASH – GOLDEN p144-146

True Thomas
See also The return of Oisin
BRIGGS – PERS. p29-31

The truest adventures of the truthful
mountain boy
ILLYES – ONCE p158-162

Trumpets
Anthony and the Mossbunker
How the duyvil gave New Amsterdam
to the English
John Henry
The renowned and world-famous
adventures of Punch and Judy
Shlemiel, the businessman
Spuyten duyvil
The three musicians

Trunks
The flying trunk
Mrs. Tabby Gray
The three laughs of the leipreachan

Trust. *See* Faith; Loyalty

Trust your friends
HEADY – JAMBO p66-70

Truth
The adventurous winnower
The boy who taught the fairies tears
The cartman's stories
The elephant hunters
Fire and water, truth and falsehood
The good judge
The honest woodman
An inadvertent misunderstanding
The Indian Cinderella
The just and unjust brothers

Truth (*Continued*)

A morality tale: Truth and falsehood
Naba Zid-Wende
The philosophers of King Darius
Richard Feverel and the hay-rick
Socrates . . . The cup of hemlock
Sturgeon moon
Thomas the rhymer
The world's most truthful man

The truth about Pecos Bill
FELTON – NEW p xi-xvi

The truthful peasant
PROTTER – CHILD. p93-96

Trystan. *See* **Tristram, Sir**

Tsai Shun, the faithful
ALEXANDER – PEBBLES p17.

Tsali of the Cherokees
MARRIOTT – AMER. p147-154

Tsar Boris and the devil king
SPICER – DEVILS p53-63

Tsar Dushan's wedding
ĆURČIJA – HEROES p5-17

Tsar Lazar and Tsaritsa Militsa
ĆURČIJA – HEROES p39-41

Tsar Lazar's supper
ĆURČIJA – HEROES p42-43

Tsar Peter the Great and the peasant
WYNDHAM – TALES p33-37

The tsar saltan. *See* The boy with the
golden star

The Tsar Trajan's ears
ĆURČIJA – YUGOSLAV. p12-17

The tsarino's greatest treasure
SPICER – LONG p145-158

Tsars
The child and the colt
The cock at the tsar's throne
Ero and the tsar
The frog-wife
Kabadaluk: the little Arab boy
Little fool Ivan and the little
humpback horse
The magic ring
The peasant and the tsar
The soldier and the tsar

To your good health
The wise wife

The tsar's son and the swan-girl
ĆURČIJA – YUGOSLAV p155-164

The tsar's son-in-law and the winged old
woman
ĆURČIJA – YUGOSLAV p85-98

Tshiama, the snake's daughter
HOLLADAY – BANTU p55-62

Tshikashi Tshikulu and the woman
HOLLADAY – BANTU p33-37

Tsimbarume, the hardened bachelor
TRACEY – LION p15-21

Tsirtsur and Peziza
SINGER – WHEN p17-26

Tuatha de Danaan (people). *See*
Dana, People of

Tubes, Lead
The curious John Greye papers

The tubmaker who flew to the sky
UCHIDA – MAGIC p43-50

Tubs
Rub-a-dub-dub

Tudor, Tasha
TUDOR – TASHA p92.

The tufty hen
RUDOLPH – MAGIC p14-29

(The) tug of war
ARNOTT – AFRICAN p153-155
HEADY – JAMBO p18-22
KAULA – AFRICAN p71-76

Tuhan (god)
Kantchil's lime pit

Tula Lake
How the world was made (2)

The tulip bed
REEVES – ENGLISH p97-102

The tune of Iolo ap Hugh, The Little
People of Wales
BELTING – ELVES p22-26

Tunnels
The flower faces
John Henry, the big steel-drivin' man
The snake monster
The turtles and the mountain tunnel

The turban
JUDA – WISE p5-7

Turenn, Sons of
The quest of the children of Turenn

Turgenev, Ivan
Only a sparrow

Turkey
See also **Turks**
Account rendered
Among the chickens
And upon the fourth bray
Archery
Bahri of the beauty spot
Baldpate
The blackbird and the pine needle
Boiled wheat for a bountiful harvest
The boy who found fear
The changeling
The chief astrologer
The copper pan
Cow or donkey?
The crow-Peri
The crystal kiosk and the diamond
   ship
The dervish and the wolf
A donkey transformed
The dwarf and the cook, The Little
   People of Turkey
Eat, my fine coat!
The emerald-crested phoenix
Fair wages for all
The flying trunk
Getting the moon back into the sky
The golden-haired children
The handsome Kahveci
The Hoca and Allah's son-in-law
The Hoca and the candle
The Hoca as Tamerlane's tax collector
The Hoca solves a problem
Hodja and the jumbled jobs
The Hodja preaches a sermon
How long will it take?
How many donkeys?
I know what I'll do
If so where is the cat?
Introduction (JUDA – WISE)
Ishallah
It won't do you any good
It's all in knowing how
Keloglan and God's greatness
Keloglan and the lucky exchanges

Keloglan and the magic hairs
Keloglan and the magician
Keloglan and the ooh-genie
Keloglan in the service of the padishah
Keloglan the kindhearted
The kind caliph and the horse thief
The little gray mouse and the hand-
   some cock
The little orphan
The magic dagger
The magic turban, the magic whip,
   and the magic carpet
The maiden who did not get her wish
Marko, the champion of Serbian
   liberty
Nasreddin Hoca and the third shot
Nasreddin minds the door
The peasant and the donkey
The prince's foal
A prompt settlement
Rabbit soup
The sea of pearls
The sermon
The seventh son
Shah Ismail and the Turkmen maiden
Shah Meram and Sade Sultan
Shoes for a journey
The silent princess
The sin of a saint
The sound is yours
The stag prince
The stone of patience
Stone patience and knife patience
The story of the boy who couldn't
   keep anything in his head
A strange guest
Tell me, when will I die?
The three apples
The three questions
To the rescue
The turban
Two watermelon stories
Volga
The wager
Watermelons, walnuts and the wisdom
   of Allah
The wind-demon
The wisdom of Allah

–Constantinople
   Kabadaluk: the little Arab boy

Turkey girl
LEACH – RAINBOW p284-286

Turkey in the straw
MY BOOK HOUSE v. 1 p113.

Turkeys
Anansi and the old hag
Cliff dweller

Turkeys (*Continued*)

Crab
Crying turkeys
Dinewan the emu and Goomble-
gubbon the turkey
Drakestail
The farmer's boy
The first Thanksgiving Day
The magic ball
The owl and the pussy-cat
The peacock, the turkey and the
goose
Saved by a turkey
The story of Li'l Hannibal
The ugly duckling
Waiting for a rooster
Wayamba the turtle and Woggoon
the turkey
The woman had a turkey

—**Beards**
How the turkey got his beard

—**Tails**
How turkey got his white tail

, **Wild**
Bech, the ambitious quail
The miller and the blue jay
Why the whippoorwill weeps
and wails

Turks
The bag of lies
The beginning of the Serbian uprising
against the Turks
Ero from the other world
The fall of Serbia
Kralyevich Marko and Alil-Aga
Kralyevich Marko and Mina of Kostur
Old Novak and the village elder,
Bogossav
What Ivan Kossantchich saw in the
Turkish camp
You must pay for the horse, Aga

The turnip
BAMBERGER — FIRST p7-8
WITHERS — I SAW p98-99

Turnip thief!
JABLOW — MAN p6.

Turnips
God's own country
The rabbit who wanted to be a man
Star-boy and the sun dance
The stolen turnips
A tall turnip

Turnstones (birds)
How the black turnstone came to nest
near the sea

The turquoise stones
HAYES — INDIAN p47-56

The turtle and the monkey share a tree
U. N. — RIDE p25-27

The turtle (and) the storks and the jackal
TOOZE — THREE p7-21
TOOZE — WONDER p107-110

The turtle of Tamaru
HOLDING — SKY p49-60

The turtle outwits the lion
TOOZE — THREE p45-61

The turtle prince
TOOZE — WONDER. p64-70

The turtle, the hippo, and the elephant
COBBLE — WEMBI p104-107

The turtle, the storks and the jackal. *See*
The turtle (and) the storks and the
jackal

The turtle who could not stop talking
MY BOOK HOUSE v. 2 p178-179

The turtle who loved a monkey
TOOZE — THREE p23-43

Turtles
See also **Tortoises**
Ananse and his visitor, turtle
Anansi and turtle and pigeon
Armadillo's story
Bandalee
The bat and the eagle
The bat and the turtle
The battle that tilted the sea
The blue lotus flower
Clever little turtle
Clytie
The deer and its friends
Drat the wind!
Fastitocalon
The fate of the turtle
Father catfish
The flying turtle
The four friends
The hare and the tortoise
The Hopi turtle
How and why: The painted turtle
How California was made
How the mud turtle came to live in
the water

Turtles (*Continued*)

How the turtle fooled the leopard
How the world was made (1)
How turtle came
How turtle keeps from getting wet
Intole the giant
The king and the Nagas
The legend of Urashima
The little turtle
Mock turtle's song
The monkey's liver
The mountain witch and the dragon-king
Pakpai and Boto
The pigeon, the deer and the turtle
The pilgrim and the crab
Rainbow and the autumn leaves
The snake and its benefactor
The son of the turtle spirit
The talkative turtle
Tam and Tessa
The three friends
Tiger story, Anansi story
The tufty hen
Urashima
The waters beneath: fifty young men
and a turtle
Wayamba the turtle
Wayamba the turtle and Woggoon the
turkey
Why the carabao's hoof is split
The wood cutter's son and the two
turtles
The young Urashima

, **Golden**
The emperor's magic bow

, **Sea**
Flash-of-the-paddle and Listener-
to-the-heavenly voice

—**Shells**
Osebo's drum
The turtle, (and) the storks and the
jackal

The turtles and the mountain tunnel
GREY — SOUTH (1) p14-17

Tusser, Thomas
At Christmas play and make good
cheer

Tutors. *See* **Teachers**

Tutu bird
WILLIAMS — OLD p96-98

Twas midnight
WITHERS — I SAW p37.

(The) twelve dancing princesses
HAVILAND — FRANCE p3-25
MY BOOK HOUSE v. 4 p28-33
SIDEMAN — WORLD'S p723-738

Twelve great black cats and the red one
LEODHAS — TWELVE p3-11

The twelve months
BUDBERG — RUSSIAN p27-37
HAVILAND — CZECH. p3-20
McNEILL — SUNKEN p79-86
MY BOOK HOUSE v. 6 p71-79

The twelve months of the year
WILSON — GREEK p224-229

The twelve silly sisters
COLUM — STONE p50-57

The twelve wild ducks
ASBJÖRNSEN — NORW. p182-189

The twelve young boys with golden hair
URE — RUMANIAN p114-116

The twelve young men
LUM — ITALIAN p116-124

The twice-blessed Arab
MOZLEY — ARABY p56-58

The twilight
MY BOOK HOUSE v. 2 p41.

The twin brothers
HACK — DANISH p44-71

The twin parrots
GAER — FABLES p28-30

Twinkling bugs
CATHON — PERHAPS p22.
MY BOOK HOUSE v. 3 p61.

Twins
Baldur the bright
Boys with golden stars
The cat and the mice
The changelings
Cold moon
The double knights
The game of Tlachtli
The golden twins
The house in the woods
It all comes to light
The legend of the star children
The little, little fellow with the big,
big hat
Nanih Waya: The sacred bluff
Ntunjambili

Twins (*Continued*)

Ooka and the two first sons
The place of strife
The sick boy, the greedy hunters,
  and the dwarfs, The Little People
  of North America
Spider boy and the sun god's twins
Swen-Naba; king of the warlocks
Throwmount and Oakpull
Tricky Peik
True and untrue
Vukub – Cakix
Why the salt is far away

The twins
  MANNING – DAMIAN p179-188

The twins and the snarling witch
  MANNING – WITCHES p38-45

Twins in the sky
  GRINGHUIS – GIANTS p21-26

Twins of gold and silver
  JABLOW – MAN p71-74

The twins of the god Mars
  TOOR – GOLDEN p167-176

(The) twist-mouth family
  JOHNSON – WHAT p194-195
  LEACH – RAINBOW p249-252

The two beggars
  DOBBS – MORE p26-30

Two birds and their nest
  MY BOOK HOUSE v. 2 p45.

The two bottles
  PILKINGTON – SHAM. p89-93

The two boxes
  BURTON – MAGIC p72.

The two boys and the sacred carpet snake
  NORLEDGE – ABORIGINAL p44.

The two bridegrooms
  BARASH – GOLDEN p77-81

(The) two brothers
  ARNOTT – AFRICAN p195-199
  BONNET – CHINESE p169-173
  BUDBERG – RUSSIAN p243-246
  KOREL – LISTEN p37-41

The two brothers and the ghost Mo'oi
  GREY – SOUTH (2) p18-21

The two brothers and the magistrate
  INS-SOB – FOLK p101-103

The two caddies of tea
  SUN – LAND p72-73

Two children
  MY BOOK HOUSE v. 2 p138.

Two cows
  KELSEY – ONCE p108-112

The two crabs
  MY BOOK HOUSE v. 2 p33-34

Two different interpretations of the
  same pact
  VITTORINI – OLD p50-54

The two dogs–Burrajahnee and Inneroogun
  NORLEDGE – ABORIGINAL p52-53

Two dollar curse
  BATCHELOR – SUPER. p55.

The two-faces
  ARBUTHNOT – TIME p179-185

Two feasts for Anansi
  COURLANDER – HAT p18-19

The two foolish cats
  UCHIDA – SEA p55-60

The two fools
  BONNET – CHINESE p115-116

The two foxes
  KOREL – LISTEN p67-122

The two friends
  FEINSTEIN – FOLK p83-86
  LITTLEDALE – GHOSTS p97-100

Two friends, coyote and bull snake,
  exchange visits
  COURLANDER – PEOPLE p97-100

Two friends: how they parted
  COURLANDER – KING'S p60-63

(The) two frogs
  LANG – VIOLET p111-113
  SIDEMAN – WORLD'S p146-149

The two girls and the iron-nose witch
  ILLYES – ONCE p225-227

The two goats
  LA FONTAINE – FABLES p28-29

Two hunters
BURTON – MAGIC p119-121

The two kings
FEINSTEIN – FOLK p30-33

Two lies
INS-SOB – FOLK p195.

The two lovers
WESTWOOD – MEDIEVAL p87-91

The two men and the two dwarfs
MAHER – BLIND p107-114

The two millers
SHEAHAN – HENRY p229-245

The two misers
SIDDIQUI – TOON. p61-64

Two novices who behaved like a pair of
otters
GHOSE – FOLK p67-70

Two of everything
CHILD – CASTLES p291-299

Two out of one
COURLANDER – KANT. p119-121

Two out of the sack
THOMPSON – ONE p251-254

The two owls and the sparrow
GREEN – BIG p175-176

Two pennies
ĆURĆIJA – YUGOSLAV p43-54

Two pieces of meat confuse the mind of
the fly
CHAPPELL – THEY p42-46

Two poems
HOPE-SIMPSON – CAVAL. p35-37

The two pots
LA FONTAINE – FABLES p40-41

The two princesses
REEVES – ENGLISH p49-62

(The) two rascals
BULATKIN – EURASIAN p98-102
CARPENTER – AFRICAN p103-112

The two righteous men
BARASH – GOLDEN p26-29

The two sillies
MANNING – PETER p213-215

The two sisters
TURNBULL – FAIRY p33-44
VITTORINI – OLD p75-78

The two sisters, Rose and Lotus
INS-SOB – FOLK p201-207

Two speedy people
WITHERS – WORLD p61.

The two step-sisters
THOMPSON – ONE p150-157

Two unfaithful husbands
INS-SOB – FOLK p197.

Two watermelon stories
NAHMAD – PEASANT p79-83

Two ways to count to ten
CARPENTER – AFRICAN p47-52

The two white stones
HOLLADAY – BANTU p47-54

The two wishes
LEEUW – LEGENDS p152-157

The two wizards
MANNING – WIZARDS p22-25

Two women or twelve men
O'SULLIVAN – FOLK. p10.

The two youths whose father was under
the sea
COLUM – STONE p58-67

Tying up the stones
WITHERS – WORLD p47.

Tyler, Wat
Wat Tyler . . . The peasant's revolt

Tyl's task
EDMONDS – TRICKSTER p45-50

Tylwyth Teg (fairies)
The lady of Tylwyth Teg

The tyrant and the miller
VITTORINI – OLD p45-49

The tyrant who became a just ruler
ARBUTHNOT – TIME p209.

Tyrants
The sword of Damocles

The tyrannical king
WITHERS – I SAW p131-132

Tyre
The hunting dog and the purple fish

U

Ubazakura
    BUCK – FAIRY p221-223

Udleqdjun in the sky
    LEACH – HOW p138-139

The uglier foot
    O'SULLIVAN – FOLK. p252-253

Ugliness
    The bashful prince
    Beauty and the beast
    The birthday of the Infanta
    Joshua and the princess
    The magician's heart
    The man who was only three inches
        tall
    The marriage of Gawaine
    Mellitot and Iolanda
    Riquet with the quiff
    The singing chameleon
    Stupid Peruonto
    The tale of Godfrey Malbone

Ugly boy
    MARTIN – COYOTE p39-45

The ugly duckling
    ARBUTHNOT – TIME p291-295
    MY BOOK HOUSE v. 2 p131-137;
        v. 12 p205-212
    SIDEMAN – WORLD'S p116-130

The ugly king
    WYATT – GOLDEN p59-80

Ukrainia. *See* **Russia–Ukrainia**

Uletka
    MANNING – GLASS p94-99

Ulster awake
    O'FAOLAIN – IRISH p76-83

Ulysses. *See* **Odysseus**

Umbrellas
    The big black umbrella
    The big umbrella and the little rubbers
    The elf and the dormouse
    Hiram goes courting
    Ranjit and the tigers
    The story of flying Robert

Umbrellas
    BATCHELOR – SUPER. p122-123

Una and the Red Cross knight
    MY BOOK HOUSE v. 11 p8-28

Unanana and the elephant
    ARNOTT – AFRICAN p68-73

Uncle Bouki rents a horse
    U. N. – RIDE p259-264

Uncle Bouqui and little malice
    JAGENDORF – KING p155-161

Uncle coyote's last mischief
    U. N. – RIDE p234-237

Uncle Ed is chased by a bear
    FELTON – WORLD'S p57-62

Uncle Ed tracks a rabbit
    FELTON – WORLD'S p139-143

Uncle Ed's unusual bear hide
    FELTON – WORLD'S p21-26

Uncle Mitya's horse
    MY BOOK HOUSE v. 2 p46.

Uncle rabbit flies to heaven
    JAGENDORF – KING p205-208

Uncles
    The ass that lays money
    Bundar Bahadeer Poon
    The children in the wood
    The cruel uncle
    The grateful ass
    Great Head and the ten brothers
    The half-pint jinni
    The raven and the grizzly bear
    The raven and the sharks
    A salty tale
    Sketco begins his wanderings
    Urosh and his uncles
    The youth who trusted in God

Under the greenwood tree
    MY BOOK HOUSE v. 11 p72.

Underground
    See also **Underworld**
    The danced-out shoes
    The golden sheep

Underground (*Continued*)

How Maui fished up New Zealand
I was traveling those parts
The queen of underland
The soldier and the knapsack
The subterranean passage
Why the mole lives underground

The underground palace
MANNING – WIZARDS p61-65

Underseas (Underwater)
The city under the sea
The cooking-spit of the women of
Fincara
The devil's apprentice
Evseyka
Mirzhan and the lord of the kingdom
under the sea
Prince Andrea and Princess Meseria
The pursuit of the hard man
Sadko the minstrel
Tola and the sea monster
The water dwellers
The waters beneath: The underwater
village

Understanding. *See* **Tolerance**

Underwear
The nine white sheep
To be seen

Underworld
See also **Hell**
The bewitched court
The black stone
Chief above and chief below
Chin and Yi
Chu and the king of the underworld
The game of Tlachtli
The giant who counted stones
The hair from the queen of the
underworld
How marriages are made
How the carrot-counter got his name
How the people came from the lower
world
How the people came to the middle
place
Maui, the demi-god
Orpheus . . . The fabulous musician
Prince Daniel
Proserpine
The three precious packets
The treasure of Altamira
Tsimbarume, the hardened bachelor
The unseen bridegroom

Urashima

Undine
JACOBSON – LEGEND. p13-17

Undset, Sigrid
Buttercup

The unexpected happened
HSIEH – CHINESE p37-38

Unforgiveness
How frog lost his tail

The ungrateful bear
PRIDHAM – GIFT p95-99

The ungrateful children
WYNDHAM – TALES p47-56

The ungrateful crocodile
BRO – HOW p39-48

The ungrateful lion
GAER – FABLES p166-168

The ungrateful snake
DAVIS – LION'S p143-149
WILSON – GREEK p53-57

The ungrateful tiger
CARPENTER – ELEPHANT'S p151-
158
INS-SŎB – FOLK p183.

Ungratefulness. *See* **Ingratitude**

Unhappiness. *See* **Grief; Sadness**

The unhappy island
GREEN – GREEKS p22-23

An unhappy lord
VANSITTART – DARK p33-39

The unicorn and the dwarf
CARPENTER – HORSES p216-221

Unicorns
The beast with a single horn
The boy with the golden star
The brave little tailor
Clever Dick
Gift of the unicorn
How to catch a unicorn
How to catch unicorns
The lion and the unicorn
Pride goes before a fall
The strange white beast

Unicorns (*Continued*)

The untamable unicorn
The white unicorn

The uninvited guest
PRIDHAM — GIFT p45-47

Union of South Africa. *See* **Africa, South**

Union of Sovet Socialist Republics. *See* **Russia**

United States
See also names of states; **Eskimos; Indians of North America; Negroes; Tall tales;** etc.
Around the corner
The bear went over the mountain
The dark and stormy night
Drat the wind!
Good or bad?
The great medicine horse
The greedy old fat man
Jeremiah
Johnny McGorry and the red stocking
The johnny-cake
The man who hung his powder horn
  on the moon
A million stories
The old lady who swallowed a fly
The old woman and her hominy pot
The owl in the moon
Paul Bunyan's cornstalk
Peter went fishing on Sunday
The shaggy dog
Strange houses
Strange story
Teasing questions
Tiny teasing tales
The travels of a fox
'Twas midnight
The walk
What's a silly question?
Why rooster is so neat
Why there is a man in the moon

—History—17th century
From a wayfarer's notebook:
  seventeenth century

—History—18th century
From a wayfarer's notebook:
  eighteenth century

—History—1770's
A boy on the high seas
George Rogers Clark and the
  conquest of the Northwest

—History—Revolutionary war
The foe in the dark
The gunsmith and the maiden
Love and war
Of sea-going snakes
An unsung heroine

—History—19th century
From a wayfarer's notebook:
  nineteenth century

—History—War of 1812
Young midshipman David Farragut

—History—1857-1870
Buffalo Bill

—History—Civil war
Lincoln's Gettysburg address
Robert E. Lee, a hero in war and
  peace

—Navy
Of sea-going snakes

Unity
In unity is strength
King Svatopluk and the three sticks
The old man and his sons
The pigeon, the deer and the turtle

Unkindness. *See* **Meanness**

The unlucky fisherman
MARTIN — NINE p19-25

The unlucky goat
WILSON — GREEK p65-67

The unlucky man
WILSON — GREEK p151-156

Unlucky Mussah
FOSTER — STONE p38-47

Unlucky passengers
LAWSON — STRANGE p164-177

The unlucky shoes of Ali Abou
CARPENTER — ELEPHANT'S p66-74

The unmarried girl's grave
INS-SOB — FOLK p39-40

The unpunctual minister, or the Bosung
pohoo
MacFARLANE — TALES p102-112

The unseen bridegroom
JACOBS — EUROPE. p129-141

Unselfishness. *See* **Generosity; Kindness**

The unsmiling princess
BUDBERG – RUSSIAN p236-240

An unsolved riddle
GHOSE – FOLK p51-53

An unsung heroine
IVES – TALES p75-80

The untamable unicorn
McHARGUE – BEASTS p61-73

Untidiness. *See* **Carelessness**

The untidy mermaid
MANNING – MERMAIDS p79-85

Untruth. *See* **Falsehood; Liars; Tall tales**

The unusual excuse
GILSTRAP – SULTAN'S p75-80

The unwashed pot
PRIDHAM – GIFT p30-34

The unwilling pirate
IVES – TALES p39-44

Unyany
GINSBURG – MASTER p104-115

Up and down the minaret
KELSEY – ONCE p24-31

Up in the green orchard
MY BOOK HOUSE v. 1 p30.

Upa and her admirers
GHOSE – FOLK p71-84

The upper world
MARTIN – COYOTE p7-11

The Uppsala ride. *See* King Hrolf and
the bear's son

Urashima
See also The legend of Urashima
HEARN – JAPANESE p80-88
ROSS – BURIED p173-187

Urashima Taro
SEKI – FOLKTALES p111-114

Urashima Taro and the princess of the
sea
ARBUTHNOT – TIMES p162-166
UCHIDA – DANCING p13-23

Urosh and his uncles
CURCIJA – HEROES p24-28

Uruguay
The hungry old witch
The origin of the camlet flower
Oversmart is bad luck
A sad tale of a silly fellow

Usefulness
The lion calls up his troops
The rooster and the pearl
The sheep is the cousin of the ox

Utah
LEACH – RAINBOW p155-156

Utensils. *See* **Pots and pans**

Utopias
The far horizon

Utzel and his daughter Poverty
SINGER – WHEN p73-80

Uwaine and the lady of the fountain
PICARD – STORIES p37-52

Uzbecks
Once there was and once there was
not

V

Vagabones. *See* Minstrels

The vain jackal
    TOOZE – WONDER. p94-95

The vain king
    ILLYES – ONCE p113-114

The vain ox
    ZAGLOUL – BLACK p81-89

Valentine day
    Birds' St. Valentine day
    Good morrow, 'tis Saint Valentine's
        day
    The rose is red
    St. Valentine's day

Valet, Vincent
    The three blue stones

Valets
    The leg of gold
    The prince of the seven golden cows

Valhalla
    The Valkyries and Valhalla

The valiant chattee-maker
    BAKER – TALKING p242-250

The valiant potter
    U. N. – RIDE p46-52

The valiant tailor
    TUDOR – TASHA p25-33

The Valkyries and Valhalla
    AULAIRE – NORSE p72-79

The valley of ten thousand waterfalls
    JEWETT – WHICH p124-135

Valleys
    The king of the Golden River, or the
        Black brothers
    Uwaine and the Lady of the fountain

The value of a boiled egg
    NAHMAD – PORTION p44-46

Vampires
    Vania and vampire

The youth who trusted in God

Van Alstine, Nancy
    The heroine of the Mohawk Valley

Van Dyke, Henry
    Salute to the trees

Vanderbilt, Cornelius, Jr.
    Commodore Vanderbilt's first boat

Vanderdecken, Captain Cornelius
    The flying Dutchman

Vania and the vampire
    SPICER – GHOSTS p92-100

Vanir (gods)
    Njord, Frey and Freya

The vanishing rice-straw coat
    McALPINE – JAPAN p121-126

Vanity
    Echo and Narcissus; the chattering
        nymph and the proud youth
    The eternal wanderer of the Pampas
    The fox who wanted to whistle
    How vanity made the dove sad
    The jackal and the crocodile
    King Solomon's carpet
    The lady of the linden tree
    The peacock and the puhuy
    The peacock's mistake
    The story of Cozumel, the lazy
        swallow
    The vain jackal
    Watching Vanity Fair go by

Vanya's leap
    CARPENTER – HORSES p101-108

Vapor
    The money cask

Vardiello
    BAKER – TALKING p18-24
    MINCIELI – OLD p14-23

Vases
    Fairy gardens

687

Vasili Buslayevich
DOWNING – RUSSIAN p64-68

Vasili Buslayevich's pilgrimage
DOWNING – RUSSIAN p69-74

Vasilia the beautiful
See also Vassilissa the beautiful (and
variant titles)

Vassilissa the beautiful
ALMEDINGEN – RUSS. p9-26
PONSOT – RUSSIAN p21-30

Vassilissa the fair and Baba Yaga
DUDDINGTON – RUSS. p116-124

Vassillissa the wise
LINES – TALES p137-150

Vassily and Curly Head the brigand
ALMEDINGEN – KNIGHT p105-119

Vegetables
See also names of vegetables
The ghost in the cabbage patch
The ogre and the cock
Stone soup in Bohemia
Too heavy
The war of the planets

Veils
The magic mare
The magic veil
Maid Lena

Venezuela
Juan Bobo and old tiger
The magic eagle
Poor little girl, rich little girl
The secret of the hidden treasure
The singing flute

Vengeance. See **Revenge**
The vengeance of Kriemhild
PICARD – GERMAN p58-85

Ventriloquists
The talking cat

Venus
Atalanta's race; a contest for love or
death
Cupid and Psyche . . . The trial of love

Verena and the jug
MÜLLER – SWISS p189-194

Vermont
The devil in the barrel
Green Mountain hero

Lucky Rose Tuttle
The ride in the night
The tale of the tail of a bear
Well-done-Peter-Parker

–Swanton
The curious John Greye papers

Vermont
LEACH – RAINBOW p157-158

Verses, by John Keats
MY BOOK HOUSE v. 1 p152.

The very obstinate man
JABLOW – MAN p44-45

Vestal Virgins
The twins of the god Mars

Vetala's stories
Anangariti and the men of four castes
Chandasimha, his son and their two
wives

The Vetala's stories
GRAY – INDIA'S p213-230

Veterans
The legend of the governor and the
veteran

Viceroys
The parrot

Victor
ILLYÉS – ONCE p170-176

A Victorian romance
MY BOOK HOUSE v. 12 p94-96

The victorious lute
MAR – CHINESE p97-110

Victory, Stone of
The stone of victory

The victory of the buffalo
COURLANDER – KANT. p13-16

Vietnam
Author's note
The beggar in the blanket
The beginning of good conversation
Brothers and friends
The butterfly in the granary
The carp that became a dragon
A cat is a cat is a cat
The child of death

Violinists and violins (*Continued*)
Brer goat and brer lion
Davy Crockett, the yaller blossom o' the forest
Diddle, diddle on a bass fiddle
The fiddle
The fiddler going home
Fiddler John and the devil
The fiddler of Echternach
The fiddler of Fiddler's bridge
The fiddlers of Slathspey
Freddy and his fiddle
The gypsy fiddle
The gypsies' fiddle
Hey diddle diddle
How men learned to sing songs
Little Freddie with his fiddle
The magic fiddle
The melting pot
The mermaid and the boy
The miracle flame
A musical visit to fairyland
Musk and amber
Ned Puw's farewell
A new way of tamin' wolves
Of a tailor and a bear
Old King Cole
The orchestra
The piper who could not play
The puss's tail
Sonny-boy Sim
The tailor's apprentice . . . And the bear
The three musicians
The tune of Iolo ap Hugh, The Little People of Wales

The viper and the friar's rope
LOWE – LITTLE p30-31

Virgil
Dante's voyage to the inferno, purgatory, and paradise
The wanderings of Aeneas

Virgin, Holy. *See* **Mary, Virgin**

Virgin Islands
Crafty crab
Ol' Guinea man
The sailor and the devil's daughter

The virgin of Honduras
JAGENDORF – KING p164-167

Virginia
Legends
Old stories

–Jamestown
The story of a princess

Virginia
LEACH – RAINBOW p159-160

Virgins
See also **Mary, Virgin**
The great bell
The legend of the virgin Arang

Viriato: The youth who held back the Roman empire
LAURITZEN – BLOOD p6-51

Virtues
See also **Character;** names of virtues
The craftsman's wife
How men learned about evil
King Great Virtue
Patient Griselda

Viscachas (rodents)
Don't make a bargain with a fox

Vishnu (god)
The flood
The making of the earth
Prahlada
Why the moon wanes

Visions
The saving of a soul

The visit
WITHERS – I SAW p97.

A visitor from paradise
JACOBS – EUROPE p159-164

The visits of St. Peter to his people
VITTORINI – OLD p106-110

The vixen and the boatmen
DE LA IGLESIA – CAT unp.

The vixen and the rooster
DE LA IGLESIA – CAT unp.

Vixens. *See* **Foxes**

Vladimir, Prince
Aliosha's visit to the bald mountain
Chourilo's little comb
A chronicle of Kiev
Dobryna's embassy to Khan Amryl
Dobrynia and Alyosha

Vladimir, Prince (*Continued*)

Dunay
How Dounai won a bride for Prince
Vladimir
How three pilgrims called Ilya to the
rescue of Kiev
Ilya of Murom and nightingale the
robber
Nikita and the last of the dragons
Potok's dancing and the snakes
Samson and the doll in green and
brown
Souchmant's trial and triumph
Stavr Godinovich and his clever wife
Vassily and Curly Head the brigand
Volkh's journey to the East
Young Michael and the uninvited
guest

Vladimir's adventures in search of fortune
MY BOOK HOUSE v. 7 p102-111

Vo-Dinh
VO-DINH p143.

A voice from heaven
BARASH – GOLDEN p22-25

The voice from the minaret
KELSEY – ONCE p71-74

The voice in the jug
CREDLE – TALL p122-132

The voice of the bell
McNEILL – SUNKEN p132-137

A voice speaks from the well
GARNER – GOBLINS p62.

Voices
The horsefly
The listening king
The peacock and the puhuy
The unseen bridegroom
Why women won't listen

Volcanoes
A battle nobody won
The girl who kissed the peach-tree
The head of the Inca
The ice ship of the hot sea
Ko-pa-ta, the gambling god
The legend of the Mayon volcano
Lost in lava
The strange adventures of Alcavilu
Tavadan and the fire giant
The trial by fire
When Boqueron spoke

–**Lava**
A strange sled race

Volga
DOWNING – RUSSIAN p3-7

Volkh's journey to the East
ALMEDINGEN – KNIGHTS p133-147

Volsunga saga
The story of Sigurd
The world's great epics

Volund the smith
JONES – SCAND. p173-182
MAYNE – HEROES p144-161

The voyage below the water
COURLANDER – PIECE p71-75

The voyage of Maelduin (Maeldun)
GARNER – GOBLINS p13-34
GARNIER – LEGENDS p58-98
PICARD – CELTIC p127-143

The voyage of the Lass of Glasgow
LAWSON – STRANGE p165-177

A voyage to Brobdingnag
MAYNE – GIANTS p177-194

Vroman, Tom
ASBJÖRNSEN – EAST p139.

Vukashin, King of Serbia
King Vukashin's wedding

Vukub-Cakix
GARNER – GOBLINS p4-10

Vultures
Arap Sang and the cranes
The Brahman in the potter's shop
Cast thy bread
The crane's report
The crow's reward
The fate of the vulture
The golden nightingale
The long-eared cat and the vulture
The quarrel
The search for Sita
Soonimaya
The ungrateful tiger

–**Baldness**
The quarrel between Ile and Orun
Why the lion, the vulture, and the
hyena do not live together

The vulture's advice
GAER – FABLES p112-116

W

Waddell, Helen
  Joseph and his brethren

Wadsworth, Olive A.
  Over in the meadow

Wadsworth, William
  A boy of the lake country

The wager
  JUDA – WISE p100-104

Wagers (bets)
  The bear and the fox who made a bet
  The clever lad from Skye
  Gudbrand of the hillside
  The innkeeper of Moscow
  The Irish luck of Brian Hughes
  The judgement of Hailu
  Lies for a wager
  Ooka and the halved horse
  Sadko the minstrel
  The tailor and the devil
  The tale of the Lochmaben harper
  Thor gains his hammer
  Thor's unlucky journey
  The truthful peasant
  The uglier foot
  The wager

Wages
  Fair wages for all
  The poor man's son, the dwarfs, and
    the birds

Wagner, Richard
  Lohengrin
  The tale of the Rhine-gold

Wagner, Richard–"The ring of the Nibelungs"
  Alberich and the dwarfs

Wagons
  Buffalo Bill
  The king's cream
  The little gray pony
  Pecos Bill, the cowboy
  The story of big Paul Bunyan
  A tramp of the Middle West
  The tufty hen
  Way down south in Dixie

–Yokes
  The Gordian knot; the destiny of
    Alexander

The wagtail and the rainbow
  PARKER – AUSTRALIAN p140-142

Wagtails
  Why wagtail wags her tail

Wahconah
  TAFT – PROFILE p256-263

Wahlenberg, Anna
  Peter and the witch of the wood

Wahn the crow Wirinun
  PARKER – AUSTRALIAN p91-99

Wainamoinen finds the lost-words
  HAZELTINE – HERO p316-331

Waiting for a turkey
  COURLANDER – PIECE p111-112

Waiting on salvation
  COURLANDER – TERRA. p11-14

Wake up, Jacob
  MY BOOK HOUSE v. 1 p84.

Wakes
  An unsolved riddle

Wakewell and his brothers
  BOUCHER – MEAD p21-24

Wales
  See also **Welshmen**
  The adventures of Manawyddan
  The aged infant
  Arawn
  Ashypelt
  Belena
  The bewitched court
  Blodeuedd and the slaying of Llew
  Bran, son of Llyr
  The bride of Llyn y Fan Fach
  The bride-price for Olwen
  Cadwalader and his goat
  Cardiff town
  The changelings
  Collen and the fair small folk
  The cruel giant
  The devil's bridge

Wales (*Continued*)

Dewi Dal
The disappearance of Ifan Gruffydd's daughter
The disappearance of Rhys
The dream of Macsen Wledig
The dream of Ronabbway
The dream of Rhonabwy
The eagle and the owl
Edward Frank and the friendly cow
Eight leaves of story (1) The three staunch swineherds of Britain
Eight leaves of story (2) The sigh of Gwyddno Long-shank
Eight leaves of story (3) Baglan the builder
The eight leaves of story (4) A harp on the water
The eight leaves of story (5) The man who killed his greyhound
Eight leaves of story (6) The sun of Llanfabon
Eight leaves of story (7) Red-hat otter
Eight leaves of story (8) Cadwalader and all his goats
Eighteen rabbits
Einion and the Fair family
Einion Las and the Fair family
Elidorus in fairyland
Evan's problem
The fairies' revenge
The fairy garden
Fairy ointment
Fairy tricks
The fairy wife
The farmer and the fairy cow
The fisherman and the mermaid
The flooding of the Lower Hundred
Foolish kings
The ghost goblin's gold
The girl and the golden chair
Goggle-eyes
The golden box
The good old man
Gwarwyn-a-Throt
The gwraig and the three blows
High Eden
The hound Gelert
The house with the front door at the back
How Trystan won Esyllt
Ifor the scoffer
Jack and the giant tantarem
Jack and the Welsh giant
Jack, the King of England's son, and the giant with three heads
John Gethin and the candle
John the painter
Kempe Owyne
King March has horse's ears

King of the birds
The lad who returned from Faerye
The lady of Tylwyth Teg
The lake lady
The legend of Bala Lake
The legend of Llangorse Lake
The little red bogie-man
Lleu and the flowerface
Luc, the king's woodsman
The lucky circle
Magic apples
Manawyddan son of the Boundless
March's ears
The marvelous cow of Llyn Barfog, The Little People of Wales
Merlin
The miller and the fairies
Morgan and the pot of brains
Morgan and the three fairies
The most precious gift
A mouse from the Mabinogian
Ned Puw's farewell
Nefyn the mermaid
The oxen and the afanc
The place of strife
Prince Alun and the "Cannwyl Corph"
Prince Llewellyn and the red-haired man
Pwyll and Pryderi (1) The marriage of Pwyll and Rhiannon
Pwyll and Pryderi (2) The birth of Pryderi
Pwyll and Rhiannon
Pwyll, Pryderie, and Gawl
The quest for Olwen (1) The destiny
The quest for Olwen (2) At Arthur's court (4) Fulfilling the tasks 4/ The beard of Dillus the bearded
The quest for Olwen (3) In search of Olwen
The quest for Olwen (4) Fulfilling the tasks 1/ The sword of Wrynach 2/ The oldest animals
The quest for Olwen (4) Fulfilling the tasks 3/ The lame ant
The quest for Olwen (4) Fulfilling the tasks 5/ The everlasting battle
The quest for Olwen (4) Fulfilling the tasks 6/ The tusk of Ysgithyrwyn
The quest for Olwen (4) Fulfilling the tasks 7/ The hunting of the otherworld boar
The quest for Olwen (4) Fulfilling the tasks 8/ The blood of the black witch
The quest for Olwen (5) Culhwch marries Olwen
Rhitta of the beards
Robin Ddu
Ruddy-my-beard
St. Cadog and King Arthur
St. Cadog and the mouse

Wales (*Continued*)

The salt Welsh Sea
Shon Shenkin
The simpleton
Six-and-four
Small white stones
The smart daughter
A spadeful of earth
Squirrel and fox
The story of Branwen
Taliesin
The three brothers and the treacle
  toffee
Three jovial huntsmen
The three plagues of Britain
The tune of Iolo ap Hugh, The Little
  People of Wales
The weeping lady of Llyn Glasfryn
The Welshman and the hazel staff
Where Arthur sleeps
The woman of Llyn-y-fan (1) The
  meeting
The woman of Llyn-y-fan (2) The
  parting
The woman of Llyn-y-fan (3) The
  sequel
The young man who married a fairy
The youth who wanted some fun

—**Cardiff**
  Cardiff town

—**Dyfed**
  The trials of Dyfed

—**Shrewsbury**
  The origin of the wrekin

—**Shropshire**
  The origin of the wrekin
  Wild Edric

Waley, Arthur
  Meeting in the road

Wali Dad the simple-hearted
  LANG – OLIVE p188-200

The walk
  WITHERS – I SAW p33.

The walk around the island
  LEEKLEY – WORLD p111-117

Walker, Marian
  Sally's blue ball

Walking
  Bread and butter
  First adventures
  How long will it take?
  The mink and the weasel

Teaching baby crab to walk
The two crabs
Why grizzly bears walk on all fours

The walking boundary stone
  LEODHAS – GAELIC p58-67

Walking-sticks
  The destiny of Princess Tien Dung
  The magic walking-stick
  Three who found their hearts' desire

Walking under ladders
  BATCHELOR – SUPER. p89-90

Wallabies. *See* **Kangaroos**

Wallets. *See* **Purses**

Walls
  The building of the fortress wall
  The emperor's magic bow
  The golden cockerell
  The heart of Princess Joan
  The lost city of Ys
  The match-making of a mouse
  Odin's eight-legged steed
  The sword of light
  The tale of the sons of Cathmor
  The wedding of the mouse

  , **Chinese**
    The faithful wife

  , **Stone**
    Stonewall Silas Clapp

Wallu-barl the bark lizard
  PARKER – AUSTRALIAN p230-
  231

Walnut trees and walnuts
  Boots and his brothers
  The cavallino
  A gift from the heart
  The mallet of wealth
  Pumpkin trees and walnut vines
  Strange houses
  The three walnuts
  Watermelons, walnuts and the wisdom
    of Allah
  The wisdom of Allah

Walruses
  Dream behind bars

Walther of Aquitaine
  PICARD – GERMAN p35-41

Waltzes. *See* Dancers and dancing

Wampum eater and the canal
  HAYES – INDIAN p87-92

A wanderer with a dog
  HAMPDEN – GYPSY p85-87

Wanderers. *See* Travellers

A wanderer's song
  MY BOOK HOUSE v. 8 p91.

The wandering apprentice
  BECHSTEIN – FAIRY p29-39

The wandering cobbler
  BORSKI – GOOD p34-40

The wandering staff
  BECHSTEIN – FAIRY p193-202

The wanderings of Aeneas
  MY BOOK HOUSE v. 10 p203-216

Wands. *See* Fairies–Wands

Wanja's choice
  HEADY – JAMBO p78-82

The war between the cranes and the
peacocks
  1. The crane's report; 2. King Crow
  and Sir Parrot; 3. The battle on the
  Isle of Camphor; 4. The betrayal;
  5. The crow's reward; 6. The
  Brahman in the potter's shop; 7.
  The vulture's advice
  GAER – FABLES p96-116

War between the crocodiles and Kantchil
  COURLANDER – KANT. p89-94

The war between the lion and the cricket
  ROSS – BURIED p95-102

The war of the animals against the birds
  GUIRMA – TALES p29-44

The war of the plants
  COURLANDER – TIGER'S p127-
  131

The Warau people discover the earth
  SHERLOCK – WEST p39-44

Warblers, Reed
  The babbling reed-warbler

Ward, Lynd
  Shizuka's dance

Wardrop, Margery
  The serpent and the peasant

The warm matzah
  BARASH – GOLDEN p58-61

Warmth
  Why the dog is the friend of man
  The wind and the sun

A warning from the gods
  WYNDHAM – CHINA p52-54

The warming of the frogs
  JOHNSON – WHAT p170-171

Warnings
  The clever earthworm
  The woman of Llyn-y-fan (1) The
  meeting

Warriors
  Antar the hero
  Art, King of Leinster
  Beowulf . . . The fight with Grendel
  The brave prince
  Cadmus . . . The dragon's teeth
  Ceatach
  Chin-Chin Kobakama
  The coming of Asin
  The coming of Fionn MacCool
  The coming of Oscar
  Dietrich of Bern
  Down to Arabia
  The fight with crazy man
  Golden flower and the three warriors
  Gudrun
  Hereward the wake
  The lion with the steady hand
  The maiden of Kossovo
  Moowis
  The mountain witch and the dragon-
  king
  My Lord Bag-o'-Rice
  Nawasi goes to war
  Oisin, son of Finn MacCool
  The pursuit of the hard man
  The slaying of Siegfried
  Sohrab and Rustum . . . The tragic
  encounter
  The stars above: Long Sash and his
  people
  Temba becomes a warrior
  The toothpick warriors
  Vukub-Cakix
  Walther of Aquitaine
  Young Conall of Howth

The young Finn

, Female
Faithful to death

Wars
The blue virgin
A cause of war
The journey of the Chinese honey-
seller
More beautiful than the spider's
web
Nawasi goes to war
The oba asks for a mountain
The peace pipe
The rabbit and the possum seek
a wife
Samba the coward
Sissa and the troublesome trifles
The story of Branwen
The struggle between the wolf and
the fox
Viriato: The youth who held back
the Roman empire

Warthog and hornbill
KAULA – AFRICAN p19-24

Warthogs
How baby wart hog saved his
father's life
Kalulu and his money farm
The kindly ant-bear
The trap
Warthog and Hornbill

Warts
Do warts come from toads?
Some white witchcraft

Warts
JOHNSON – WHAT p77-81

Waru Wanggi, The saga of the. See The
saga of the Waru Wanggi

Washing and washerwomen
The ass that was flayed
The carnation youth
The count and the little shepherd
The crow and the soap
East of the sun and west of the moon
The elephant's bathtub
The invisible hobgoblin
The magic sandals of Hualachi
Musk and amber
The pious washerwomen

Washington, George
George Washington and his hatchet
George Washington and the first
American flag
The great sacrifice
A happening on Christmas eve
I'm going to Lady Washington's
Remembered

Washington (state)
Moon of blood
The songs of the animals

–Puget Sound
The boy and his magic robe
The boy with the long hair
The coyote and the evil witches
The grizzly and the rattlesnake
men
The legend of Pathasos
The legend of the hail
The legend of the star children
The maiden of Deception Pass
The mink and the sun
The mink and the weasel
The raven and the crow
Sam Dan and the government
doctor
The witch and her four sons

–Tacoma
The treasure of Tacoma

Washington
LEACH – RAINBOW p160-162

Washington, D. C.
Three little tales of Washington

Wasps
The bear and the fox who made a bet
The bees and the drones
The butterfly's ball
The carlanco
The cock and the hen
Drakestail
The golden gourd
The hornets and the honeybees
John the blacksmith destroys the
wasps in the straw
The sick boy, the greedy hunters, and
the dwarfs, The Little People of
North America
The story of Cozumel, the lazy swallow
The story of Mrs. Tubbs
The toad is the emperor's uncle

Waste
Maria sat on the fire

Wat Tyler . . . The peasants' revolt
  UNTERMEYER – FIRE. p232-235

Watches
  The borrower
  The child and the colt
  How Jack sought the golden apples

Watching Vanity Fair go by
  MY BOOK HOUSE v. 12 p104-107

Watchmen
  Eight leaves of story (2) The sigh of
  Gwyddno Long-shank
  Heimdall, the watchman of Asgard

Water
  See also **Waterfalls**
  The adventures of Silvervit and
  Lillvacker
  Anansi and the crabs
  Aukele and the water-of-life
  The barrel of water
  Baskets in a little cart
  The beginning of the world and the
  making of California
  Benito the faithful
  The bird and the buffalo
  The blackstairs mountain
  The boy who wouldn't mind his
  grandmother
  The brave shepherd boy
  The bundles of straw and the king's
  son
  The carnation youth
  The cattle egret
  Cliff dweller
  The crow and the sparrow
  The dancing water, singing apple and
  speaking bird
  The dragon and the stepmother
  The faithful friend
  The feast
  Fior Usga
  Fir cones
  Fire and water, truth and falsehood
  Fire, water, and honor
  The fish with bent noses
  The five wise words
  The giant who stole a river
  A glass of water, please
  God's well
  Goto, king of the land and the water
  Gurgle, water, gurgle
  The half-chick
  How mankind learned to make bread
  How the earth's fire was saved
  How the people got fire
  The hummingbird and the carabao

An inadvertent misunderstanding
The inquiring rabbit, or The strongest
  thing in the world
The just and unjust brothers
The king and the falcon
Land, water and wind
The magic carpet
The mast of sand
The miller and the fairies
Mister Luck and Mister Industry
Netchillik and the bear
The nine-headed giant
The ninwits
The planting party
The prince with the golden hand
The prince's foal
Prunella
The rabbit and the tar wolf
Rabbit at the water hole
Raven and the sun
The right time to laugh
The search for the magic lake
The shepherd and the princess
The shepherd's crown
The soldier's return
Soonimaya
Stan Bolovan
Stars in the water
The tale of Vassilissa the wise
Teutli, the mountain that is alive
The three cups of water
The three oranges
The ticklish thief
Tortoise and Babarinsa's daughters
The trials of Ting Ling
True and untrue
Warthog and hornbill
Water's locked!
The well at the world's end
The well o' the world's end
The well of D'Yeree-in-Dowan
Who is strongest?
Why the sun and moon live in the sky

  , **Dancing**
    The dancing water, the singing
    apple, and the speaking bird

  , **Golden**
    The story of the talking bird

  , **Salt**
    The woman who wanted to cook
    with salt water
    Wurrunna's trip to the sea

  , **Silver**
    The white parrot

Water babies
  The adventures of a water baby

Water buffaloes
  The farmer and his son
  The hummingbird and the carabao
  Kantjil becomes a raksha
  The little priest
  The milky way
  Why the carabao's hoof is split

The water-bull of Benbecula
  LEODHAS — SEA p121-137

Water-carriers
  The girl and her water buckets
  The legend of the Moor's legacy
  Rags and tatters

Water drops
  MANNING — GHOSTS p90-94

The water dwellers
  MAAS — MOON p123-127

The water horse and the water bull
  BRIGGS — PERS. p157-159

Water-horses. *See* **Horses, Water**

Water jars, The origin of. *See* The origin
  of the water jars

Water-lilies
  The farmer and the fairy cow
  How the water lily came
  The man with no nose

Water nymphs
  Clytie
  The partridge and his drum

Water of life
  The three golden hairs

The water of life
  ARBUTHNOT — TIME p67-70

Water rats. *See* **Rats, Water**

Water spirits (sprites)
  See also **Kappas; Water babies;**
    Water nymphs
  The bachelors and the python
  Biggoon and the little duck
  The boy and the water-sprite
  The bride who out talked the water
    kelpie
  The dutiful daughter
  John Macdonald the kelpie
  The lazy man and the water spirit

Mario and the yara
The princess who loved her father
  like salt
The strong boy
Swan white and fox tail
Undine
Why spider has a little head and a big
  behind

The water-sprite
  BAMBERGER — FIRST p163-164
  TRACEY — LION p61-65

The water-sprite and the bear
  PICARD — GERMAN p106-114

Water sprites. *See* **Water spirits**

Water tanks
  The hermit and the Sea of Man
  The unlucky goat

Waterbeetles
  From a moral alphabet

Waterbucks
  In unity is strength

Waterfalls
  The bugle song
  The cataract of Lodore
  The enchanted waterfall
  The fairy of Hawili Falls
  The great fish
  The king of the Golden River, or The
    Black brothers
  The maiden, the knight, and the
    waterfall
  The valley of ten thousand waterfalls
  Waukewa's eagle

Watering
  The monkey gardeners

Watermelons
  Buh rabbit's graveyard
  Never mind them watermelons
  The ride in the night
  Strange houses
  Two watermelon stories
  Uncle coyote's last mischief

Watermelons, walnuts and the wisdom of
Allah
  WALKER — WATER. p27-28

Watermen (sea people)
The peasant and the watermen

Watermills
The prince and the dragons

The waters beneath: Fifty young men
and a turtle
MARRIOTT – AMER. p41-46

The waters beneath: The great river
monster
MARRIOTT – AMER. p51-58

The waters beneath: The underwater
village
MARRIOTT – AMER. p46-50

Water's locked!
WILLIAMS – FAIRY p284-287

Watkins, Hope Brister
How little stork lost his tail

Watt, James
Jamie Watt and the giant in the
teakettle

Watts, Isaac
How doth the little busy bee

Waukewa's eagle
HARDENDORFF – FROG'S p17-24

Waves
Wind and wave and wandering flame

Wawanosh
SCHOOLCRAFT – FIRE p47-57

Wax
The boy who was never afraid
Why the bananas belong to the
monkey

'Way down south in Dixie
MY BOOK HOUSE v. 12 p138-140

The way of the master
EDMONDS – TRICKSTER p129-137

Wayamba the turtle
PARKER – AUSTRALIAN p210-213

Wayamba the turtle and Woggoon the
turkey
PARKER – AUSTRALIAN p214-218

Wayland Smith
WILLIAMS – OLD p333-344

We kill the snake god
DAVIS – LION'S p137-139

We thank thee
MY BOOK HOUSE v. 5 p115.

Weakness
Buh rabbit's human weakness
The dog and the karbau
The king of the animals
The lion and the mouse
The one who said Tjik
The slaying of Hector
The war of the animals against the
birds
What is a fable?

Wealth
See also **Coins; Money; Treasure;** etc.
The adventures of Ciad
Ah Tcha the sleeper
The anger bargain
The beggar's prophecy
The best wish
The blue palm tree
Born to be rich
Bottle Hill
The buyer of oxen
Catherine and her fate
The ceabharnach
The choja who became a monkey
Clever Manka
The clever thief
Cornelia's jewels; a mother's love and
pride
Dates to Cairo
The devil's gifts
Dick Whittington and his cat
The dissatisfied good man
Donal from Donegal
Donal O'Ciaran from Connaught
Don't throw stones from not yours to yours
The fly
The fortunate shoemaker
The ghost dog of South mountain
The gift of gold
The gift of the holy man
The golden touch
The golden touch; the king who
worshipped gold
Good advice
Good advice, a guinea a piece
Good luck and common sense
Good luck and great riches
The greatest wealth in the world
The greedy man in the moon
The greedy rich man

Wealth (*Continued*)

Happy Hans
The hardhearted rich man
How flint-face lost his name
How raven found the daylight
How Suan became rich
How the rajah got rich
Lady Morris in her mansion
The lady of Stavoren
The Lake of Zangze
The little lizard's sorrow
Little Tom Thumb
The magic horns
The magic tabo
The maiden Suvarna
The mallet of wealth
The man who looked for death
Marko the rich and Vasily the luckless
Marko the rich and Vassili the luckless
Mister Luck and Mister Industry
The mysterious letter
The old traveler
One more child
Palace in Bagdad
The philosophers of King Darius
The piece of straw
The poor and the rich
The poor brother's treasure
Poor Jack and the cat
Poor little girl, rich little girl
The poor man's clever daughter
The poor old lady
The poor people who wanted to be rich
The poor weaver and the princess Radowid
Raindrops can't tell broadcloth from jeans
The raven's magic gem
The rich lady and the ring in the sea
The rich landowner and his worker
The rich man and the tailor
The rich man's dinner party
The rich Per Muller
The rich widow of Stavoren
Riches or happiness
Salakhbai and the fox
The seven years of blessing
Shemiaka the judge
The shoemaker
The silver bell
Sir Launfal
The skipper and the dwarfs
The spindle, the shuttle and the needle
The spring
The sunken city
Supparaka the mariner
The tale of the false prince
The thief and the king's treasure

The thoughtless abbot
Three bridegrooms for one bride
Three who found their hearts' desire
Tim for wealth and happiness
Tripple-trapple
The twelve young men
Two of everything
Vardiello
Vladimir's adventures in search of fortune
Wend' Yamba
What a clever child can do
Where Arthur sleeps
Which is the greater?
The wise merchant
The wishing chair of the Lord of Errigal

Weapons
See also names of weapons, e.g.,
Spears; Swords
The black swans
Conchobar and Teeval
How Maui obtained the magic jawbone
The legend of Pascpoti
The magic banana
Maui nooses the sun
The Mopoke and the moon
Nawasi goes to war
The prince of the six weapons
The saga of the Waru Wanggi
The spear and shield of Huantan

The weary spirits of Lanai
  THOMPSON — LEGENDS p14-22

The weasel
  HEADY — TALES p75-80

The weasel and his mother
  HOLLADAY — BANTU p89-93

Weasels
All around the cobbler's bench
The grateful beasts
The grateful weasel
King of the serpents
The mink and the weasel
Pop! goes the weasel!
The theft of fire
Tshiama, the snake's daughter
The weasel
The wicked weasel

Weather
See also names of seasons; **Rain; Seasons; Snow; Storms**; etc.
The beginning

Weather (*Continued*)
The beginning
Belief
The boy of the red twilight sky
Bull frog knows more about rain than
  the almanac
The capricious month
Disbelief
Grandmother Marta
March and the shepherd
The rain, wind, and snow "Rhyme
  and reason"
The shepherd of clouds
Tell Barney Beal
The twelve months
The winning of Gerd
Winkle, Tinkle, and twinkle
The wise priest

—**Almanack, American**
The almanacks

—**Bureaus**
The thirteenth floor

, **Dictionaries**
A dictionary of American weather
  folklore
The weather
JOHNSON — WHAT p9-18

Weather instruments
SLOANE — FOLK. p20-28

Weather witches: Two points of view
HOPE-SIMPSON — CAVAL. p143-145

Weatherwax, John M., jt. author
The lazy hornet
Why the tortoise has a round back
Why the woodpecker has a long nose

Weaver, John
MY BOOK HOUSE v. 1 p59.

The weaver-woman's monument
JAGENDORF — NEW p256-260

Weavers and weaving
Arachne . . . The eternal spinner
Baba Yaga
Baba Yaga and the little girl with
  the kind heart
The beautiful weaver and the golden
  shell
The clever weaver
The crane wife
The dog that learned to read
Down in a cottage
The emperor's new clothes
The eternal wanderer of the Pampas
Fareedah's carpet

The forest bride
Frithjof, the Viking
The frog
The frog bride
The geese and the swans
The ghost goblin's gold
The girl who didn't know how to spin,
  The Little People of Scandinavia
The girl who weaves by night
The handkerchief
The home-coming of Odysseus
How spider taught women to weave
How the spider taught women to
  weave
How the spider was made
The invisible silk robe
The luck fairies
The magic baby shoes
Musk and amber
The old woman and her hominy pot
Peerifool
The poor weaver and the princess
The princess and the fisherman
The rug maker
The shah weaves a rug
The silver river
The small men and the weaver
The spider weaver
Spin, weave, wear
The thirteen flies
The three aunts
The three blue stones
The twins and the snarling witch
Vasilia the beautiful
The white hen
The widow's daughter
The widow's lazy daughter
Wikki, the weaver
The wild swans
The witch aunts

—**Looms**
Prince Hat beneath the earth

The weaver's worry
EDMONDS — TRICKSTER p104-112

"**Wedding march**"
A musical visit to fairyland

The wedding of the Cid's daughters
HAZELTINE — HERO p235-251

The wedding of the dragon-god
MAR — CHINESE p55-70

The wedding of the hawk
COURLANDER — KING'S p41-44

The wedding of the mouse
UCHIDA — DANCING p89-94

Weddings
A battle and a wedding
Bees in the bonnets in New Jersey
Brides, grooms and weddings
The devil's bride
Earl Mar's daughter
The fox and the wolf at the wedding
Hasty Corners
How rabbit lost his tail
King Herla
King Vukashin's wedding
Kralyevich Marko abolishes the
wedding-tax
Kralyevich Marko's wedding
Love and sentiment
The mare at the wedding
A merry tale of Merrymount
Mrs. Fox's wedding
Nazar the brave
Patient Griselda
Pwyll and Pryderi (1) The marriage
of Pwyll and Rhiannon
Saint Peter and his trombone
A story of Robin Hood
The story spirits
Sylvester
The tale of the Earl of Mar's daughter
Toto gets married
The truest adventures of the truthful
mountain boy
Tsar Dushan's wedding
The two friends

The wee bannock
HAVILAND – SCOTLAND p13-24
JACOBS – MORE p73-77

Wee folk. *See* names of wee folk. e.g.,
Leprechauns; Little people; Midgets, etc.

The wee folk
BAMBERGER – FIRST p158-160

The wee red man
MacMANUS – HIBERIAN p85-98

Wee robin's Christmas song
MY BOOK HOUSE v. 2 p209-212

The wee, wee mannie
JACOBS – MORE p192-194
WILLIAMS – FAIRY p20-23

The wee, wee mannie and the big, big coo
MY BOOK HOUSE v. 3 p99-103

Wee Willie Winkie
MY BOOK HOUSE v. 1 p28.

Weedah the mockingbird
PARKER – AUSTRALIAN p75-79

Weeds
The great blessing of the land
How tadpoles lost their tails

The weeping lady of Llyn Glasfryn
SPICER – GHOSTS p53-64

The weeping lass at the dancing place
LEODHAS – TWELVE p41-49

The weeping willow
BELTING – THREE p102-104

Weevils, Boll
The boll weevil

Weight
Are fat people happy?
How to weigh an elephant
The long-nosed giant
Why the steer has a smooth nose

The weight of the cart
BARASH – GOLDEN p136-139

Weightlessness. *See* **Gravity**

Weights and measures. *See* **Measures and
measurement**

The weird-sisters (1, 2)
HOPE–SIMPSON – CAVAL. p57-58;
58-61

The welcome
PILKINGTON – THREE p191-199

We'll never be ready in time!
FARJEON – SILVER p151-158

The well
See also "Nyame's well"
COURLANDER – TERRA. p46-49

The well at the world's end
See also The well of the world's end
THOMPSON – ONE p237-240

The well diggers
COURLANDER – TIGER'S p115-117

Well-done-Peter-Parker
JAGENDORF – NEW p106-114

The well of D'Yeree-in-Dowan
PILKINGTON – SHAM. p74.

The well of immortality
SUN – LAND p19-20

The well of the three heads
REEVES – ENGLISH p115-126

The well (o') of the world's end
FINLAY – FOLK p109-118
MacMANUS – HIBERIAN p251-263
MANNING – BEASTS p235-239
REEVES – ENGLISH p211-220
WILLIAMS – FAIRY p69-75

"Well of wisdom"
Odin, the all-father

Wells
The auld cailleach's curse
Bani Hilal: A tribe is born
Baskets in a little cart
The Brahmin and the villain
The chief of the well
Chien Tang
The clever billy goat
The clever fox
Diamonds and toads
The doll under the briar rosebush
The dragon of the well
Drakestail
The emerald-crested phoenix
The fairy
The five wise words
The frog prince
Getting the moon back into the sky
The goat in the well
The goat well
God's well
The gold bird
The golden cockerell
The hare and the tiger
He wins who waits
Hiding in the well
The horned witches
How Cormac MacArt got his branch
The imposter
In the beginning
Journey in a well
Just his luck
Kantjil gorws strong at the welling-well
Keloglan and God's greatness
Kojata
The lame vixon
The lion and the hare
The lion and the wily rabbit
The little milleress
The maiden in the country under-
ground
Mainly in moonlight
Mother Holle
The nightingale Hazaran
Nyame's well
The Panditji and the guavas
Peppino

The Prince Fernando
The prince with the golden hand
The rabbit and the tar wolf
Tam Lin
The terror of the ogres
They dig a well
They measure the depth of the well
The three golden hairs
The three-legged jumping giant
The three stags
The three walnuts
Tiki-Tiki-Tembo
To the rescue
To your good health
The water-sprite
The weeping lady of Llyn Glasfryn
The wolf and the fox

Welsh and Scotch rhymes
MY BOOK HOUSE v. 1 p58.

The Welshman and the hazel staff
SHEPPARD – WELSH p19-24

Welshmen
Three jovial huntsmen

Wembi, the singer of stories
COBBLE – WEMBI p9-12, 20-21,
27-28, 32-34, 37-38, 41-43, 46-47,
50-51, 54-55, 62-64, 68-69, 72,
75-76, 80-82, 85-87, 89-90,
92-93, 98-99, 102-103, 108, 112,
114-115, 117, 120, 124

Wen Yen-Poh, the thinker
ALEXANDER – PEBBLES p14.

Wend' Yamba
GUIRMA – TALES p57-69

Wendigo
The flight with the Wendigo

Wentworth, Benning
Governor Wentworth's search for a
wife

Werenskiold, Erik
The Norwegian folk tales and their
illustrators

The werewolf
PALMER – DRAGONS p55-62
PICARD – GERMAN p156-160

Werewolves
A poor man's servant
The strange feathery beast

West
  The ballad of East and West
  The boy in the land of shadows
  Buffalo Bill
  California's lost diamonds
  A couple of lost squadrons
  A couple of lost towns
  A few lost bones
  Henry Crabb—a born loser
  How it came about that there is
    a sun and a moon
  Lost arts
  A lost chord in Tijuana brass
  The lost gold bars of Juan
    Blanco
  Lost in lava
  The lost lover of Pearl Hart
  The lost payroll at Wickenburg
  The lost remains of Mr. Quejo
  The lost secrets of Charles
    Hatfield
  The lost treasure of Cucamonga
  The lost woman of San Nicolas
  A meteoric loss
  Pancho Villa's lost head
  Pecos Bill, the cowboy
  The plains' call
  The poet of the Sierras
  Pushing westward with Lewis and
    Clark
  A trio of lost monsters

West country boy
  MARTIN – COYOTE p11-19

West Indies
  See also names of islands; Anansi
    stories
  Born a monkey, live a monkey
  Cat and dog
  The dog's nose is cold
  Dry-bone and Anansi
  How crab got a hard back
  The lord of Massachusetts
  Mancrow, bird of darkness
  Mr. Wheeler
  The sea-mammy
  Tiger in the forest, Anansi in the web
  Tiger story, Anansi story
  Why women won't listen
  Work-let-me-see
  —Arawaks (people)
    Introduction. From sun-spirit to
      spider-man
  —Caribs (people)
    The Coomacka-tree
    Introduction: From sun-spirit to
      spider-man
    Irraweka, mischief maker

    The jaguar and the crested
      curassow
  —Cuba
    The beef tongue of Orula
    The heron's ball
    The silly owls and the silly hens
  —Guiana
    The armadillos
    Bahmoo and the frog
    Bahmoo rides the wrong frog
    The crested curassow
    The honeybee bride
    The jabuty and the jaguar
    The pot-that-cooked by itself
    A promise that should be kept
    Smart Dai-adalla
    When a man is foolish
    Who's strong?
  —Jamaica
    See also Anansi stories
    The gold table
    John Connu Rider
    Kisander
  —Waraus (people)
    The Warau people discover the
      earth

West Virginia
  Early days and ways in America
  Primitive times in West Virginia

West Virginia
  LEACH – RAINBOW p162-163

Western Islands. See Hebrides, Scottish

Westwoods
  FARJEON – LITTLE p91-115

Wetzel, Lewis
  Adventuring: white man on the
    warpath

We've come to see Miss Jenny Jones
  MY BOOK HOUSE v. 1 p89.

The whale and the sandpiper
  See also Coral Sea contest
  GREY – SOUTH (1) p23-27

The whale and the sea slug
  SEKI – FOLKTALES p23-24

The whale and the sorcerer
  BERRY – MAGIC p113-121

Whale of a tale
  COTHRAN – MAGIC p18-21

The whale that smoked a pipe
CARPENTER – SHIPS p161-171

The whalers and the dwarfs, The Little
People of the Eskimo
BELTING – ELVES p47-52

Whales and whaling
The blind boy and the loon
Caldera Dick
Cast thy bread
Coral Sea contest
The crow and the whale
The cruel uncle
Fair, brown, and trembling
The fight between the octopus and
the whale
The first mosquito
Five fathoms tall/Stormalong
Glooskap, the whale, and the sorcerer
Glooskap's country
How summer came to Canada
How the whales reached the sea
How whale happens to smoke a pipe
Jabuty, the strong
John Tabor, whaler
The land of youth
Little Annie and the whaler captain
Long John and the mermaid
The lost prince
The man who killed the sea monster
Marko the rich and Vasily the
luckless
Mister honey mouth
The mother of time and the
enchanted brothers
Old Stormalong
Saint Michael and the idle husband
The Sedna legend
Sinbad and the sailor
The sleigh ride
The strange adventures of the cowboy-
sailor
Sven and Lilli
The three monsters of the sea
Three wonderful beggars
Tinirau and his pet whale
Why elephant and whale live where
they do
–Oil
The creek of whale oil

A whaling adventure
MY BOOK HOUSE v. 8 p142a-142b

What a clever child can do
URE – RUMANIAN p35-37

What are you able to build with your
blocks?
MY BOOK HOUSE v. 1 p164.

What does little birdie say?
MY BOOK HOUSE v. 1 p154.

What grown-ups can learn from children's
books
ILLYES – ONCE p7-12

What happened to six wives who ate
onions
FISHER – STORIES p54-59

What happens to the envious
ILLYES – ONCE p213-214

What is a crick crack story
SHERLOCK – IGUANA'S p1-4

What is a fable?
GAER – FABLES p5-7

What is "long ago"?
SPICER – LONG p9-10

What is luck?
LEACH – LUCK p7-13

What Ivan Kossantchich saw in the
Turkish camp
CURCIJA – HEROES p37-38

What makes moonshine on water
LEACH – HOW p13.

What news? News enough!
WITHERS – WORLD p7-8

What should I do, what shouldn't I do?
MEHDEVI – PERSIAN p104-111

What should I have said?
THOMPSON – ONE p428-429

What the children do in summer
MY BOOK HOUSE v. 1 p212-213

What the lemur is saying at night
COBBLE – WEMBI p64-67

What the preacher's talking about
COURLANDER – TERRA. p102-103

What the rose did to the cypress
BUCK – FAIRY p185-217

What the squirrel saw
ARNOTT – AFRICAN p105-107

What they say
MY BOOK HOUSE v. 1 p207.

What will people say
ZAGLOUL – BLACK p29-33

What's a silly question?
WITHERS – I SAW p35.

What's the news of the day
MY BOOK HOUSE v. 1 p37.

What's your name?
MY BOOK HOUSE v. 1 p95.

Wheat
The beggar's prophecy
Boiled wheat for a bountiful harvest
The devil in the wheat
The devil's partnership
How Loki outwitted a giant
The lady of Stavoren
The lady's loaf-field
The little red hen and the wheat
A long-bow story
The rich widow of Stavoren
The storyteller
The sunken city

The wheel of fate
REED – TALK. p16.

Wheelbarrows
The leprechaun and the wheelbarrow
There was an old woman of Harrow
Trip to town
The wonder ship and ship's crew

Wheels
How God's wheel turns
The spindles are still

When a man is foolish
JAGENDORF – KING p151-154

When Boqueron spoke
JAGENDORF – KING p167-170

When I go a-courting
MY BOOK HOUSE v. 1 p92.

When I see a lady
MY BOOK HOUSE v. 1 p69.

When I was a baby
MY BOOK HOUSE v. 1 p145.

When I was down beside the sea
MY BOOK HOUSE v. 1 p159.

When Mrs. Bird wants Mr. Bird
MY BOOK HOUSE v. 1 p68.

When Shlemiel went to Warsaw
SINGER – WHEN p99-116

When that I was but a little tiny boy
MY BOOK HOUSE v. 1 p149.

When the bull bellows
WITHERS – I SAW p78.

When the cat and the tiger lived together
BELTING – CAT p63-66

When the iguana grows armor
JORDAN – BURRO p57-59

When the rooster was king of the cats
BELTING – CAT p11-15

When Uncle Henry was a little tiny boy
MY BOOK HOUSE v. 1 p97.

When woods awake
MY BOOK HOUSE v. 1 p57.

Whence came the birds?
SECHRIST – ONCE p20-22

Where are my roses?
MY BOOK HOUSE v. 1 p205.

Where Arthur sleeps
WALES – WELSH p169-174

Where be you going, you Devon maid?
MY BOOK HOUSE v. 1 p152.

Where go the boats?
MY BOOK HOUSE v. 3 p91b.

Where, O where has my little dog gone?
MY BOOK HOUSE v. 1 p107.

Where the frost comes from
PARKER – AUSTRALIAN
p174-176

Where the kings of Judah sleep their last
sleep
NAHMAD – PORTION p49-50

Where to lay the blame
CHILD – CASTLES p197-209
HARDENDORFF – FROG'S
p142-154

Whetstones
The sleeping prince

Which?
 LEACH – LUCK p48.

Which is better, the sun or the moon?
 JABLOW – MAN p75.

Which is the greater?
 URE – RUMANIAN p84-86

Which was a witch?
 HOKE – WITCHES p172-175
 JEWETT – WHICH p11-15

While other birds at will may go
 REED – TALK. p38.

Whining. *See* Grumbling

Whippety stourie
 WILSON – SCOTTISH p75-80

Whippoorwills
 Why the whippoorwill weeps and
 wails

Whips and whippings
 The czar's general and the clever
 peasant
 The dragon and his grandmother
 Kwaku Ananse and the whipping cord
 The magic turban, the magic whip,
 and the magic carpet
 Mrs. Peterkin wishes to go to drive
 The shepherd's nosegay
 The twelve young men
 What they say
 Work-let-me-see

Whirlpools
 The cauldron of Brekkan
 Hasty porridge in the boiling water

Whirlwinds
 The dancing bird
 The giant of the Brown Beech Wood
 The little-man-as-big-as-your-thumb-
 with mustaches-seven-miles-long
 The magic grocery store
 Nastasya and the whirlwind
 Sparrow's search for rain

Whisky frisky
 MY BOOK HOUSE v. 2 p82.

Whiskey jacks (birds)
 The bear's head
 Partridge and rock tripe

The whispering giant
 SPICER – GIANTS p51-59

Whistle the wind(s)
 CARPENTER – SHIPS p69-78
 COTHRAN – MAGIC p13-17

Whistles and whistling
 Better not whistle!
 Clever Dick
 The fox who wanted to whistle
 The griffon
 Jack and the lord high mayor
 Jesper who herded the hares
 The king's hares
 The king's rabbits
 The princess on the glass mountain
 The princess who hid her slippers
 Something wonderful
 The three princesses in the mountain-
 in-the-blue
 The three soldiers
 The young Irish lad from the hiring fair
 Young Michael and the uninvited guest

 , Golden
 The King of Araby's daughter

White, E. B.
 Charlotte's web; Wilbur's boast

The white bear
 MANNING – BEASTS p184-195

White-bear-King-Valemon
 ASBJÖRNSEN – NORW. p150-157

The white bird sister
 SEKI – FOLKTALES p92-98

The white bride and the black bride
 THOMPSON – ONE p97-102

The white cat
 See also A prince and a dove
 ARBUTHNOT – TIME p113-120
 PILKINGTON – SHAM. p30-45
 THOMPSON – ONE p26-30

The white cat and the green snake
 MANNING – PRINCES p108-117

The white deer of Onota
 RASKIN – TALES p85-90

The white dove
 MANNING – WITCHES p104-114

The white dove of the city of the swinging
 gate
 EELLS – SPAIN p135-142

The white-eared tiger
INS-SŎB – FOLK p86-88

White-faced simminy
WILLIAMS – FAIRY p153-154

White fields
MY BOOK HOUSE v. 1 p193.

White gum trees
The southern cross

The white hare and the crocodiles
HAVILAND – JAPAN p73-89

The white hen
MacMANUS – BOLD p169-178

A white hen sitting
MY BOOK HOUSE v. 1 p156.

The white horse of Volendam
CARPENTER – HORSES p136-140

The white hound
PICARD – FAUN p235-255

The white lady of Pumphul
SPICER – GHOSTS p83-91

White mountains
Mountains of Manitou

The white mule from the other world
JAGENDORF – SAND p170-172

The white mule ghost
JAGENDORF – UPSTATE p261-269

The white parrot
EELLS – SPAIN p3-13

The white pet
FINLAY – FOLK p37-44
WILSON – SCOTTISH p81-87

The white snake
TASHJIAN – ONCE p57-68

The white snake lady
BONNET – CHINES p43-47

The white spider's gift
BARLOW – LATIN p43-49

White squash boy
ROBERTSON – PHILIP. p63-69

The white stone canoe
SCHOOLCRAFT – FIRE p29-38

The white sword of light
LEODHAS – SEA p103-119

White-toes and Bushy-bride
JONES – SCAND. p41-51

The white trout
GARNIER – LEGENDS p9-11

The white unicorn
MONTROSE – WINTER p99-108

The white witch of Espeloo
SPICER – WITCHES p24-31

The white wolf
BECHSTEIN – FAIRY p79-83

Whitebear Whittington
ROSS – BLUE p123-137

Whiting (fish)
The mock turtle's song

Whitman, Walt
Two birds and their nest

Whitney, Annie Weston
The singing geese

Whitsunday
Gareth and Linette
How Galahad came to Arthur's court

Whittier, John Greenleaf
The double-headed snake of Newbury
The pumpkin

Whittier, John Greenleaf
The young Quaker of New England

Whittington, Dick
Whittington and his cat

Whittington and his cat
ARBUTHNOT – TIME p27-31
BALDWIN – FAVOR. p134-150

Who?
LEACH – HOW p15-16

Who am I?
SERWER – LET'S p68-73
WITHERS – WORLD p80.

Who can break a bad habit?
CARPENTER – AFRICAN p41-45

Who can crack nuts?
MY BOOK HOUSE v. 4 p82.

Who has seen the wind?
   MY BOOK HOUSE v. 1 p201.

Who hath no courage must have legs
   CHAPPELL – THEY p47-52

Who is boss?
   FELTON – WORLD'S p79-84

Who is responsible
   TOOZE – WONDER. p118-120

Who is strongest?
   FOSTER – STONE p48-52
   WITHERS – I SAW p100-101

Who is the mightiest?
   WITHERS – I SAW p122.

Who is the oldest?
   COURLANDER – PIECE p70.

Who maketh the dumb to speak
   BARASH – GOLDEN p55-57

Who put the salt in the sea?
   CARPENTER – SHIPS p59-68

Who rules the roost
   JAGENDORF – KING p102-106

Who should get the neck ring?
   COBBLE – WEMBI p125-128

Who the man in the moon is. *See* Frogs
in the moon; Hjuki and Bil; The moon's
face; The old humpback

Who was Anansi?
   SHERLOCK – ANANSI p1-2

Who was most skillful?
   WITHERS – I SAW p143.

Whopping cough
   Stumping the devil

Who's on the roof?
   MY BOOK HOUSE v. 1 p64.

Who's strong?
   JAGENDORF – KING p142-144

Why?
   REED – TALK. p50.

Why a lady sits next to a knight at table
   LEACH – SOUP p33-34

Why an Illinoian wouldn't buy Idaho land
   JOHNSON – WHAT p227.

Why animals are afraid of fire
   BELTING – LONG p76-78

Why ants carry large bundles
   LEACH – HOW p107.

Why ants have small waists
   CATHON – PERHAPS p90-92

Why ants live everywhere
   LEACH – HOW p105-106

Why are giants so stupid?
   DE REGNIERS – GIANT p69.

Why bat flies alone
   LEACH – HOW p71-72

Why bear sleeps all winter
   LEACH – HOW p73-74

Why bears eat meat
   LEEUW – LEGENDS p109-111

Why cat eats first
   LEACH – HOW p65.

Why cats always wash after eating
   HARDENDORFF – TRICKY
   p121-122

Why cats always wash themselves after
eating
   DOBBS – ONCE p67-69

Why cats and dogs are enemies
   DOBBS – MORE p83-85

What cats and dogs fight
   BELTING – CAT p34-36

Why cats lie on the doorstep in the sun
   BELTING – CAT p31-33

Why cats live with women
   HEADY – WHEN p85-89

Why chicken lives with man
   LEACH – HOW p91.

Why coyote is the color of the ground
   HAYES – INDIAN p9-16

Why crabs are flat
   CATHON – PERHAPS p77.

Why crab's eyes stick out
   LEACH – HOW p121-122

Why crane's feathers are brown and otter
doesn't feel the cold
BELTING – LONG p23-25

Why crocodile does not eat hen
LEACH – HOW p111.

Why crow has a right to the first corn
LEACH – HOW p100.

Why crow is black and men find precious
stones in the earth
BELTING – EARTH p77-81

Why crows are black
LEEUW – INDO. p113-116

Why dog gnaws a bone
LEACH – HOW p86.

Why dog has a fur coat and woman has
seven tempers
BELTING – EARTH p75-76

Why dogs and cats are not friends
CARPENTER – DOGS p35-42

Why dogs carry their tails over their backs
BELTING – LONG p26-28

Why dogs live with men
HEADY – WHEN p42-46

Why dogs wag their tails
SECHRIST – ONCE p38-42

Why donkeys have long ears
DOBBS – MORE p86-89

Why ducks have flat feet
BELTING – LONG p39-41

Why elephant and whale live where they
do
LEACH – HOW p80-81

Why Eyvin won the race
NYBLOM – WITCH p103-120

Why flounder's two eyes are on the same
side of his face
LEACH – HOW p117.

Why fly rubs his hands together
LEACH – HOW p108.

Why frogs croak in wet weather
LEACH – HOW p115.

Why frogs speak Chinese
ALEXANDER – PEBBLES p15.

Why goat cannot climb a tree
LEACH – HOW p67.

Why God made the dog
LEACH – HOW p59.

Why grasshopper spits tobacco juice
LEACH – HOW p109-110

Why grizzly bears walk on all fours
FISHER – STORIES p24-35

Why groundhog's tail is short
BELTING – LONG p29-33

Why jellyfish has no shell
LEACH – HOW p118-120

Why Kwaku Ananse stays on the ceiling
APPIAH – ANANSE p139-145

Why lion lives in the forest
LEACH – HOW p77.

Why lizard can't sit
LEACH – RAINBOW p241.

Why mole's front paws are bent
BELTING – LONG p51-53

Why no one ever carries the alligator
down to the water
DOBBS – ONCE p54-59

Why on one lends his beauty
COURLANDER – OLODE p124-126

Why owls see only at night
BOWES – BIRD p45-50

Why peacock looks at his tail
LEACH – HOW p102.

Why people keep dogs
LEACH – HOW p60-61

Why people tell stories
URE – RUMANIAN p172-177

Why people watch the dipper
LEACH – HOW p135.

Why pigs have curly tails
DOBBS – ONCE p45-50

Why pigs root
LEEUW – LEGENDS p89-91

Why porpoise is not a fish
LEACH – HOW p85.

Why rabbit has (have a) short tail
LEACH – HOW p69.
WILLIAMS – ROUND
p195-196

Why robin has a red breast
LEACH – HOW p95.

Why rooster is so neat
LEACH – HOW p94.

Why sheep does not come in out of the rain
LEACH – HOW p68.

Why some animals live with man
BELTING – EARTH p70-73

Why some trees are evergreen
LEACH – HOW p125.

Why spider has a little head and a big behind
LEACH – HOW p82-83

Why spider lives in ceilings
ARKHURST – SPIDER p12-20

Why spiders live in dark corners
ARKHURST – SPIDER p40-49

Why sun and moon live in the sky
LEACH – HOW p20-21

Why the animals have no fire
LEACH – HOW p57.

Why the animals live where they do
BELTING – LONG p85-88

Why the bagobo like the cat
SECHRIST – ONCE p46-49

Why the bananas belong to the monkey
DOBBS – ONCE p60-66

Why the bat flies at night
ARNOTT – AFRICAN p150-152

Why the bear cannot play the kantele
DEUTSCH – MORE p31-37

Why the bear has a stumpy tail
See also Why the bear is stumpy-tailed
BAMBERGER – FIRST p43-44
JONES – SCAND. p108-109

Why the bear is stumpy-tailed
ARBUTHNOT – TIME p73-74
HAVILAND – NORWAY p65-66

Why the bear sleeps all winter
CATHON – PERHAPS p45-47

Why the bear's tail is short
DEUTSCH – MORE p11-14

Why the birds are different colors
LEACH – HOW p89-90

Why the brierbrush quarreled with the beasts
CATHON – PERHAPS p33.

Why the bush-fowl calls at dawn and why flies buzz
ARNOTT – AFRICAN p56-63

Why the buzzard eats the rooster's children
JABLOW – MAN p91-92

Why the carabao's hoof is split
SECHRIST – ONCE p56-60

Why the cat and dog cannot live at peace
DEUTSCH – MORE p25-29

Why the chameleon shakes his head
COURLANDER – KING'S p98-100

Why the chickadee goes crazy once a year
CATHON – PERHAPS p170-173

Why the cock eats worms
BONNET – CHINESE p111-114

Why the crab has no head or how the first river was made
ARNOTT – AFRICAN p35-39

Why the crocodile hates man
LEEUW – INDO. p94-98

Why the deer's teeth are blunt
SCHEER – CHEROKEE p58-60

Why the devil keeps out of Indiana
JAGENDORF – SAND p111-114

Why the dog and the cat are enemies
GREEN – BIG p32-33

Why the dog has a cold wet nose
DOBBS – MORE p68-71

Why the dog is the friend of man
ARNOTT – AFRICAN p1-4

Why the dog lost his wife
COBBLE – WEMBI p99-101

Why the dogs sniff at each other
RANKE – GERMANY p21.

Why the evergreen trees never lose their
leaves
CATHON – PERHAPS p205-207

Why the fish do not speak
DEUTSCH – MORE p1-5

Why the flea hops
HITCHCOCK – KING p76-79

Why the flea jumps
LEACH – HOW p103.

Why the hare's lip is split
DEUTSCH – TALES p19-23

Why the hyrax has no tail
HEADY – WHEN p68-71

Why the jackal howls
HITCHCOCK – KING p97-100

Why the jellyfish has no bones
SAKADE – JAPAN. p83-86

Why the lion, the vulture, and the hyena
do not live together
COURLANDER – OLODEp54-57

Why the lizard stretches his neck
APPIAH – ANANSE p47-56

Why the mole lives underground
SCHEER – CHEROKEE p51-54

Why the monsoon comes each year
ROBERTSON – FAIRY p60-65

Why the moon has scars on her face
BELTING – EARTH p62-65

Why the moon wanes
REED – TALK. p83-88

Why the motmot lives in a hole
BOWES – BIRD p65-71

Why the mountains are snow-covered
BELTING – EARTH p58-61

Why the ocean is salty
BELTING – EARTH p55-57
SECHRIST – ONCE p17-19

Why the parrot repeats man's words
U. N. – RIDE p34-37

Why the possum's tail is bare
SCHEER – CHEROKEE p75-79

Why the rabbit's nose twitches
AUNG – KINGDOM p24-27

Why the salt is far away
COURLANDER – PEOPLE p115-118

Why the scroll of the law fell to the
ground
NAHMAD – PORTION p167-168

Why the sea is salt
HAVILAND – NORWAY p30-44
LEACH – HOW p28-29
SIDEMAN – WORLD'S p108-115
WILLIAMS – ROUND p130-144

Why the sea moans
CATHON – PERHAPS p217-227

Why the sendji rat has no tail
BURTON – MAGIC p101-102

Why the sky is high
SECHRIST – ONCE p15-16

Why the spider has a narrow waist
APPIAH – ANANSE p123-137

Why the steer has a smooth nose
DOBBS – MORE p72-74

Why the sun and (the) moon live in the
sky
ARNOTT – AFRICAN p133-134
JABLOW – MAN p59-61

Why the sun is brighter than the moon
BELTING – EARTH p32-33

Why the sun shines in the daytime and
the moon shines at night
JABLOW – MAN p62-63

Why the sun stopped shining
BORSKI – GOOD p57-59

Why the terrapin's shell is scarred
SCHEER – CHEROKEE p65-68

Why the tides ebb and flow
LEACH – HOW p25-27

Why the tiger is so angry at the cat
AUNG – KINGDOM p53-55

Why the tip of fox's tail is white
BELTING – LONG p93-94

Why the tortoise has a round back
CATHON – PERHAPS p78-81

Why the waringen tree is holy
LEEUW – INDO. p81-89

Why the whippoorwill weeps and wails
BOWES – BIRD p15-18

Why the woodchuck comes out in
midwinter
CATHON – PERHAPS p53-57

Why the woodpecker has a long nose
CATHON – PERHAPS p184-187

Why the world is the way it is
HAYES – INDIAN p3-8

Why there are four seasons in the year
BELTING – EARTH p49-53

Why there are no tigers in Borneo
LEEUW – INDO. p99-103

Why there are shadows on the moon
SECHRIST – ONCE p14.

Why there are shooting stars
BELTING – EARTH p46-48

Why there is a man in the moon
JABLOW – MAN p3-5

Why there is both day and night
BELTING – EARTH p34-36

Why there is thunder and lightning
BELTING – EARTH p41-45

Why wagtail wags her tail
LEACH – HOW p99.

Why wisdom is found everywhere
COURLANDER – HAT p30-31

Why women always wash the dishes
ROBERTSON – PHILIP. p71-80

Why women talk more than men
FISHER – STORIES p104-110

Why women won't listen
SHERLOCK – WEST p112-117

Why yams and cassava hide in the
ground
HASKETT – GRAINS p47-49

The wicked bankiva
SECHRIST – ONCE p28-31

A wicked fox
HAMPDEN – GYPSY p105-109

The wicked house of Duncan Macbain
LEODHAS – GHOSTS p13-23

The wicked Mazimuzimu
SAVORY – ZULU p19-23

The wicked polecat
MARMUR – JAPAN. p51-56

The wicked weasel
FEINSTEIN – FOLK p55-58

Wickedness. See Cruelty; Evil

Widmann, Willy, illus.
The czar's frog daughter
Ivan and his knapsack
Kristina and the devil
Radowid

The widow and the Korrigans, The
Little People of Brittany
BELTING – ELVES p77-83

Widows
Adventure in plaindealing
Bring me a light
Butterflies
The case of a widow before a
sagacious magistrate
The cats of the mountain
Chanticleer . . . his strange dream
The devil and the summoner
The doll
The Eskimo widow . . . And her
strange son
The fairy woman's revenge
The hill demon
How much you remind me of my
husband!
The lady of Stavoren
The legend of the narcissus
The little red pig
The man who was rescued from hell
My own self
The nung-guama
Oh and alas
Pedro de Males Artes or clumsy Pedro
The poor widow bullfighter
The Red-Etin
The rich widow of Stavoren
The serpent prince
The smart woman of Kennebunkport
Summer snow
A talkative old woman
The young widow

The widow's daughter
MacMANUS – HIBERIAN p233-239

The widow's lazy daughter
    HAVILAND — IRELAND p61-84

The widow's son
    ASBJORNSEN — EAST p121-132

Width
    Longshanks, girth, and keen

The wife from another world
    JEWETT — WHICH p109-123

The wife from heaven
    INS-SOB — FOLK p136-139

The wife of Bjorn Bryn
    LAWSON — STRANGE p57-68

The wife who liked fairy tales
    DOWNING — RUSSIAN p227-229

A wife with false economy
    HSIEH — CHINESE p30-31

The wife's portrait
    SEKI — FOLKTALES p170-173

Wigs
    Scurvyhead
    Sir Goldenhair
    The widow's son

Wikki, the weaver
    AARDEMA — STORY p18-23

The Wilbur witches
    JOHNSON — WHAT p165-168

Wilbur Wright and Orville Wright
    MY BOOK HOUSE v. 5 p66-67

The wild boar and the ram
    GREEN — BIG p62-63

The wild dog and the king's son
    CARPENTER — DOGS p235-244

Wild Edric
    BRIGGS — PERS. p40-42

The wild geese and the tortoise
    TURNBULL — FAIRY p45-49

The wild huntsman
    CARPENTER — HORSES p141-147

The wild man
    MANNING — DAMIAN p94-105

The wild ride in the tilt cart
    LEODHAS — GHOSTS p54-64

Wild rose
    BAMBERGER — FIRST p61-66

The wild swans
    ARBUTHNOT — TIME p335-343
    BAMBERGER — FIRST p207-209
    JONES — SCAN. p27-40
    LINES — TALES p150-170
    ROSS — BLUE p53-72

The wild woman of the woods
    HARRIS — ONCE p59-85

Wild worms and swooning shadows
    GARNER — GOBLINS p180-187

Wildcats
    The bear and the wildcat
    The hawk and the wildcat
    How the wildcat got his spots
    The hungry giant

Wilde, Lady
    The horned women

Wilde, Oscar
    The birthday of the Infanta
    The fisherman and his soul
    The happy prince
    The selfish giant

Wilde, Oscar
    JOHNSON — HARPER p330.
    JOHNSON — PRINC. p318.

The wiliwili trees
    COTHRAN — MAGIC p49-52

The wiliwili trees of Paula. *See* The wiliwili trees

Will-o'-the-wisp
    PALMER — FAIRY p21-22

The will of the wise man
    MacMANUS — HIBERIAN p160-173

William, King of Sicily
    The king and the merman

William of Cloudslee
    PICARD — TALES p131-147

William of Malmesbury
    The witch of Berkeley

William T. Trinity
  MY BOOK HOUSE v. 1 p98.

William Tell and the founding of the
  Swiss Confederation
  MULLER – SWISS p3-19

William Winter
  NYE – MARCH p23-31

Williams, William Carlos
  The term

Williams-Ellis, Amabel
  Clever Oonagh
  The giants of Towednack

Willie and the pig
  SHEPPARD – SCOT. p113-116

Willie boy, Willie boy
  MY BOOK HOUSE v. 1 p45.

Willie's bad night
  ARBUTHNOT – TIME p277-279

Willingness
  Dick Whittington and his cat
  Knitting still
  The little red hen and the grain of
  wheat
  My maid Mary
  The sheep and the pig that made
  a home
  Williston, Teresa Pierce
    The tongue-cut sparrow

Willow
  GARNER – GOBLINS p36-39

Willow Trees
  Green willow
  A little bird sits in the willow
  A message in a bottle
  The most obedient wife
  Ooka and the willow witness
  The prince and the dragons
  The story of Aoyagi
  The weeping willow
  The white witch of Espeloo

A willow wand and a brocade slipper
  SUN – LAND p126-130

Willows in the snow. *See* Little pictures
  from far Japan

Wills (legal)
  The broken box

The case of a widow before a sagacious
  magistrate

Wilmot-Buxton, E. M.
  How the queen of the sky gave gifts
  to men

Wilson, James
  Casey's comeback

Wilson, T. Woodrow
  Your America

Wind
  Above the wind, with the wind, or
  below the wind?
  Adares, King of Arabia
  The bear says north
  A beautiful young woman as the
  head of the family
  Big winds
  Bilba and Mayra
  Blow, wind, and go, mill, go!
  Brother Breeze and the pear tree
  Calabash of the winds
  Calling the chinook
  Children of cloud
  The cloud princess
  Cold, son of wind and snow
  Come, little leaves
  East of the sun and west of the moon
  The fight with Wabun
  The foolish father-in-law
  The frost, the sun, and the wind
  The giant of the brown beech wood
  The half-chick
  How Glooskap made the birds
  The Indian Cinderella
  The judgment of the wind
  Kalamona and the winds
  The king who slept
  Land, water and wind
  Lionbruno
  Lost and found
  The maiden and the ratcatcher
  The man who could see everything
  The marriage of the mouse
  The master of the winds
  The match-making of a mouse
  A matter of importance
  The mole's bridegroom
  A mouse in search of a wife
  Musk and amber
  My boat
  My lady wind
  The night of the big wind
  Old mother wind
  A pound of tobacco
  The Prince of Coucy
  Princess Felicity

Wind (*Continued*)

The proud father
The rain, wind, and snow "Rhyme
  and reason"
Raising the wind
The rat's bridegroom
The rooster and the wind
The sage and the mouse
Segizbai and the little mouse-girl
The shepherd who fought the March
  wind
Sinko's luck
Sixpence for a breeze
Solomon and the four winds
Stine Bheag o' Tarbat
The stone crusher of Banjang
A story of the wind
The strongest
Sweet and low
The village of cream puffs
The wedding of the mouse
Whistle the wind(s)
The white wolf
Who has seen the wind?
Who is strongest?
Why an Illinoian wouldn't buy Idaho
  land
Why there are four seasons in the
  year
The young head of the Cheng family

, **East**
  The magic sandals
  The man who loved flowers
  No flowers

, **North**
  Awake, O north wind
  The lad and the north wind
  The lad who went to the north
    wind
  Little diamond and the north wind
  Per and the north wind
  The selfish giant
  Shingebiss
  The sun and the north wind
  The three princesses of Whiteland

, **Northwest**
  Lost and found

, **South**
  Drat the wind!
  Son of the south wind

, **Southeast**
  The city east of the moon and
    south of the sun

, **Southwest**
  The king of the Golden River, or
    The Black brothers
  The shepherd, the king, and the
    southwest wind

, **West**
  Gheeger Gheeger the cold west
    wind
  Heart of the west wind
  (The) Soria-Moria-castle

Wind and tempest
  LAWSON — STRANGE p155-163

The wind and the ant
  SERWER — LET'S p22-29

The wind and the sun
  ARBUTHNOT — TIME p206-207
  MY BOOK HOUSE v. 3 p196.
  STRONG — FAVORITE p96.

Wind and wave and wandering flame
  PILKINGTON — SHAM. p169-177

Wind bloweth where it listeth
  MY BOOK HOUSE v. 2 p79.

The wind-demon
  BUCK — FAIRY p306-320

Wind in the Black Hills
  JOHNSON — WHAT p226-227

Wind in the willows. *See* The open road

Wind people (wind folk)
  The theft of fire

Windmills
  Mother Codling and her family
  Surprising adventures of Don
    Quixote of La Mancha
  The two millers

Windows
  The penitent governor
  Stretch, Puff and Blazer
  The wind's eye

Winds and ogres
  GREEN — GREEKSp60-61

The wind's eye
  LEACH — SOUP p21-24

Wine
  Bastianelo
  The best wish
  Dwarf stories
  The game of chess in the mountains
  The grateful monkey's secret
  Hwan and Dang

Wine (*Continued*)
    Kralyevich Marko drinks wine during
    the Ramadhan
    The leopard's wine
    The magic amber
    Monkey-dance and sparrow-dance
    The philosophers of King Darius
    The pot of gold
    The son of the King of Spain
    The stolen wine
    Tavadan and the fire giant
    Tony Di-Moany

   —**Casks**
    Death of a prisoner

   —**Cellars**
    The blue cap

   , **Palm**
    Anansi steals the palm wine
    Catfish and his terrible end
    The man who learned the language
    of the animals
    Olode the hunter becomes an oba

Winged wonders
    McHARGUE – BEASTS p75-83

Wings
    The adventures of Magboloto
    Anansi and the alligator eggs
    Birdling
    The flying castle
    Growing wings
    How the animals made wings for bat
    and flying squirrel
    The little rabbit who wanted red
    wings

Winkelried, Arnold
    Arnold Winkelried

Winkle, Tinkle, and Twinkle
    MONTROSE – WINTER p67-80

A winky-tooden song
    MY BOOK HOUSE v. 1 p215.

Winnie the Pooh
    That is why he was always called Pooh

Winnie-the-Pooh
    MY BOOK HOUSE v. 5 p68-75

The winning of Gerd
    HOSFORD – THUNDER p65-72

Winter
    See also **Cold; Snows;** etc.
    A, B, C, Kitty's in the snow I see!
    The beacon light

    The bells
    The city of the winter sleep
    Cold moon
    Cold, son of wind and snow
    The fox and the hare in winter
    How Peary reached the north pole
    How summer came to Canada
    Hunger moon
    I-yay! I-yay! I-yay
    It is God that hath made us
    It snows and it blows
    Jack Frost
    Jingle bells, jingle bells
    Little diamond and the north wind
    Little Peppino
    Off we'll go
    Over the river and through the woods
    Peboan and Seegwun
    Prosperpine
    Pushing westward with Lewis and
    Clark
    The selfish giant
    Shingebiss
    Snow
    The snow man
    The snow-queen
    There were two little boys
    The three lemons
    Three old maids a-skating went
    White fields
    Why the woodchuck comes out in
    midwinter
    Willows in the snow
    The wise ant
    Wolf moon

Winter
    BUDD– FULL p66-79

The winter flower
    MONTROSE – WINTER p11-21

Winter rose
    LIN – MILKY p57-63

Wintering with Paul Bunyan
    IVES – TALES p261-276

The winter's tale
    MY BOOK HOUSE v. 7 p146-159

Winthrop, Edward
    Bride's brook

The Wi-oombeans and piggi-billa
    PARKER – AUSTRALIAN p184-188

Wisconsin
    Harvest moon
    How kingfisher got his necklace

Wisconsin (*Continued*)
Little bear
Odds and ends

Wisconsin
LEACH – RAINBOW p164-166

Wisdom
See also **Common sense; Knowledge;**
titles beginning with Wise, etc.
Akiba and the daughter of Kalba
Sabbu'a
All things wise and wonderful
A beautiful young woman as the head
of the family
The bird that told tales
The boy hero of Harlem
Buh rabbit's tail
The cat and the fox
The cat, the dog, and the mongoose
Chanticleer and Partlet
The charitable woman and the three
loaves
Charlotte's web; Wilbur's boast
The children who could do without
their elders
Cincinnatus; the man who would not
be king
The clever peasant girl
Coat o' clay
Conversation
Diogenes the wise man
The donkey, the ox and the farmer
Down by the River Avon
The eagle and the owl
The enchanted island
Finlay the giant killer
The fisherman and his soul
The five wise words
Gift of the unicorn
Goha the wise
The golden dolls
The golden peacock
The golden phoenix
The golden pitcher
The good judge
Grandfather's advice
The greedy rich man
Hansel and Grethel
Hodja and the jumbled job
How hare asked for wisdom
How Kwaku Ananse won a kingdom
with a grain of corn
How men learned about evil
How Ologbon-Ori sought wisdom
How the mosquitoes came to Oneata
How the peasants bought wisdom
How the turtle fooled the leopard
How the world got wisdom
How wisdom came to man
How wisdom was spread throughout
the world

In the beginning
Introduction (Tales of wit and wisdom)
Introduction (The wisdom and folly of
women)
The jewel of the fox's tongue
Joseph and his brethren
Joshua and the princess
Judge not the vessel
The judgements of a magistrate
Kantjil discovers the wisdom of Allah
The kelpie
Kilmeny
The king and the bishop
The king and the wise man
King Solomon and the Queen of Sheba
King Solomon's pupils
The land where there were no old men
The little-man-as-big-as-your-thumb-
with mustaches-seven-miles-long
The lost half-hour
The magic muntr
The merchant's wife
The mixed-up feet and the silly
bridegroom
Modesty and wisdom
Molla Nasreddin and his donkey
The mountain where old people were
abandoned
The mouse surrounded
The mystery of the scroll
Naba Zid-Wende
Njal the lawyer
Odin, the all-father
Odin . . . The price of wisdom
Ooka and the wasted wisdom
Patient Griselda
Poor old cricket!
The princess and Rabbit Joshuah
Robin Ddu
The royal banquet
The sack of corn
Saint Peter and his trombone
The salmon's revenge
The seven-year blessing
The shrewd peasant
Siengimieng, the minister
Snow in the mountains
The speech of beasts
The story of the smart parrot
The story of Wang Li
The straight and narrow way
Tales of wit and wisdom
Terrapin's pot of sense
This is how it began
The three brothers
Three fat ewes for three fine hounds
The three questions
Tim for wealth and happiness
The Tims
The traveler and the nut tree
The traveller and his host

Wisdom (*Continued*)

The treasure thief
The tsarino's greatest treasure
The turban
The two boxes
Vassillissa the wise
Watermelons, walnuts and the wisdom
   of Allah
Wen Yen-Poh, the thinker
Why the rabbit's nose twitches
Why wisdom is found everywhere
The will of the wise man
The woodcutter's daughter
The young Finn
The young fox and the old fox

The wisdom and folly of women
   NAHMAD – PORTION p85-106

The wisdom of Allah
   JUDA – WISE p66-70

The wise ant
   WILSON – GREEK p9-10

The wise bird and the hunter; an old
Hebrew fable
   STRONG – FAVORITE p72-74

The wise doctor
   BULATKIN – EURASIAN p124-125

The wise goat
   GILSTRAP – SULTAN'S p18-25

The wise judge
   ALEXANDER – PEBBLES p19.
   DAVIS – LION'S p108-112
   VITTORINI – OLD p14-18

The wise king and the little bee
   DOBBS – ONCE p19-23

The wise liar
   FOSTER – STONE p76-80

A wise man on a camel
   REED – TALK. p76.

The wise man's pillow
   WYNDHAM – CHINA p14-19

Wise men
   The bad prince
   How a man became unwitched
   The three suitors
   The will of the wise man

The wise men of Chelm
   DOBBS – MORE p45-48

The wise men of Gotham
   JACOBS – MORE p222-228
   LEACH – NOODLES p30-34
   MY BOOK HOUSE v. 6 p170-172

The wise men of Hebron
   JAGENDORF – NEW p190-194

The wise merchant
   FEINSTEIN – FOLK p73-78

The wise monkey
   BROWN – AROUND p99-109

The wise old camel
   KAULA – AFRICAN p146-154

The wise old woman
   UCHIDA – SEA p61-71

The wise owl
   GINSBURG – MASTER p19-26

The wise priest
   HARDENDORFF – TRICKY p93-96

A wise priest learns a lesson: Khaemwese
and Tabubu
   JAMES – MYTHS p148-156

A wise sentence
   VITTORINI – OLD p24-27

The wise wife
   BULATKIN – EURASIAN p27-38

The wise witness
   BORSKI – GOOD p75-77

The wise woodland maid
   TOOR – GOLDEN p39-46

The wish-hound
   MANNING – PETER p166-168

Wishbone
   BATCHELOR – SUPER. p109-110

Wishes
   Aunt Misery
   Baba Yaga
   Be careful!
   The beautiful blue jay
   Becky's garden
   The best wish
   The blacksmith and the devil
   The boy and the monk
   Cardiff town
   Cenerentola
   A Chinese cinderella
   Clever Carmelita

Wishes (*Continued*)

The clumber pup
The crow's pearl
A dead secret
The devil and the tailor
The devil to pay
Did the tailor have a nightmare?
Dookiram, the poor one
Fairy tricks
A flower to catch a thief
The four fishes
Freddy and his fiddle
Gigi and the magic ring
The golden snuff-box
The goldfish
The grateful beasts
The gudewife's midnight labours
Half a yard
The half-pint jinni
Hecho the lazy
Jack at Hell Gate
John Reid and the mermaid
The kindly ghost
Lady Melicent
The lady's quest
Lars, my lad!
The lazy boy
Lazy Hans
The little black box
The little duck
Little Freddie with his fiddle
The little grey man
Little one-inch
The little rabbit who wanted red
  wings
The magic fishbone
The maiden who did not get her wish
Make a wish
The man who had no wife
The man who sold magic
The master-smith
The old man of Cury
The old woman and the fish
Ooka and the wonderful wishes
Padre Ulivo and his guests
Phaeton; the boy who rode the chariot
  of the sun
The poor and the rich
The Prince Fernando
Prince Finn the fair
The raven's magic gem
Rich woman, poor woman
The ridiculous wishes
The search for the magic lake
The seven wishes
The shoemaker's apron
The soldier and the devil
The son of the baker of Barra
Star light, star bright
A story of three brothers

Stupid Peruonto
The sun, the moon and the star of
  morning
There was a little man and his name
  was Gice
The three brothers and the black hen
The three mermaids
Three pennyworth
The three petitions
The three wasted wishes
Three who found their hearts' desire
(The) three wishes
The tinder box
The tinker of Tamlacht
The twelve young men
The two millers
The two wishes
Volkh's journey to the East
The white parrot
The white unicorn
The wonderful knapsack

Wishes
  BATCHELOR — SUPER. p106-110
  JOHNSON — WHAT p46-47

The wishing chair of the Lord of Errigal
  MacMANUS — BOLD p193-207

The wishing cup
  HUME — FAVORITE p47-54

The wishing ring
  PROTTER — CHILD p199-202

The wishing star
  PICARD — MERMAID p29-47

Wishing trees
  Three little tales of Washington

A wisp of straw
  SPICER — WITCHES p38-42

Wit. *See* **Humor**

A wit to outwit wit
  HSIEH — CHINESE p39-40

The witch
  BUCK — FAIRY p162-167
  MELZACK — DAY p59-94

The witch and the earthen jar
  MANNING — GIANNI p86-94

The witch and her four sons
  MATSON — LONGHOUSE p49-59

The witch and the swan maiden
MANNING – GLASS p63-70

The witch aunts
PALMER – JOURNEY p68-81

Witch doctors
The castle in the lake
The good witch-doctor in the
mountains
The lion's whiskers
Omganda and the gold
The soothsayers
The witch who lived in a cave
The young hunter and the Juju man

Witch flights
HOPE-SIMPSON – CAVAL. p76-84

Witch hunts – the aftermath
HOPE-SIMPSON – CAVAL. p152-155

The witch in the hill
SPICER – WITCHES p72-79

The witch in the stone boat
HOKE – WITCHES p197-204

The witch of Berkeley
HOPE-SIMPSON – CAVAL. 128-
132

The witch of Endor
HOPE-SIMPSON – CAVAL. p168-
171

The witch of Fraddam
MANNING – PETER p72-76

The witch of Laggan
SHEPPARD – SCOT. p56-60

The witch of Lok Island
HOKE – WITCHES p206-218

The witch of Ohio
JAGENDORF – SAND p67-71

The witch of Wandaland
PALMER – JOURNEY p31-54

The witch! The witch!
HOKE – WITCHES p169-171

The witch tree of the North country
JAGENDORF – UPSTATE p64-66

The witch who lived in a cave
NORLEDGE – ABORIGINAL p32.

Witchcraft
See also Witch doctors; etc.
Bird of power
The blue lake
The boy who wanted to learn
witchcraft
The enchanted buck
Eterna
The goldspinners
The journey to the land of the dead
A letter to my love
The magic banana
The magic bed-knob
Mainly in moonlight
A message in a bottle
The parrot
Pietro Bailliardo
Revolt
The schoolmaster and the devil
The sorcerer's apprentice
The strange trial
The tale of the Balaton
The tale of the lay of the smithy
The whale and the sorcerer

Witches
See also Magic; Witchcraft; Wizards
About the good American witch
About witches, enchantments, and
spells
According to tradition
The adventures of Silvervit and
Lillvacker
Ah Tcha the sleeper
Aliosha's visit to the bald mountain
Alison Gros(s)
Anansi and five
Anansi and the old hag
The armless maiden
At Christmas
Baba Yaga
Baba Yaga and the little girl with the
kind heart
The bad baronets
A baker's dozen
The battle
The bean trees that are sacred to the
witches
The beekeeper and the bewitched
hare
Belief
Bergamot
Bewitched cream
The black cat of the witch-dance-
place
The black dog of the wild forest
The blackstairs mountain
Blanche's high-flying Halloween
Blodeuedd and the slaying of Llew
The blue cap
The blue foal

Witches (*Continued*)

Blue water
Bola Bola
The boy on a broomstick
The boy with the golden star
The brave little prince
The bride-price for Olwen
The broomstick train
Bukolla
Buttercup
Casi Lampu'a Lentemue
The castle of no return
A cat and a broom
The cat which lost a claw
A charm against witches
The children who lived in a tree-house
The city under the sea
Clach Mor and the witch of Badenoch
The competition of fools
The cowskin boat
The coyote and the evil witches
The czar's frog daughter
Damian and the dragon
The dancing feather
The dangers of sorcery
Dear-boy
The death watch
The devil's apprentice
The devil's bowling ball
Disbelief
The donkey lettuce
The double knights
The dough image
The downfall of witches
A dozen is thirteen
Duffy and the devil
The dwarf and the goose
East of the sun and west of the moon
The elephant's tail
The enchanted cow
Esben and the witch
Fair Vasilissa and Baba Yaga
Fairy Ilona and Argelus
Fereyel and Debbo(-Engal) the witch
Fiddler John and the devil
Finn MacCool, the giants and the
  small men
The first mosquito
The first witch's cat
The fisherman and his soul
The flight
Flying with witches
For a peaceful night
Foretelling the future
The forgotten bride
The friendly frog
The frog
The frog princess
The giant worm of the well
The girl out of the egg

The girl who met the witch of the
  woods
The girl who played a trick on the
  devil
Glooskap, the whale, and the sorcerer
The golden fleece
The golden-haired children
Golden hood
The great-aunt
The gull
Haddam witches
Haensel and Gretel
The hand of glory
Hansel and Gretel
Hansel and Grethel
Hardy Hardback
Heimdall, the watchmen of Asgard
Hereward the wake
Hooker and the witches
The horned witches
The horned woman
The horned women
How men learned to sing songs
How to kill a witch
The hungry old witch
I saw three witches
Ifor the scoffer
Italy
Ivashko and the witch
The ivory box
Jackal or tiger?
Jacob Heard and the golden horse
Jankyn and the witch
The Ji-jaller bag
Jip and the witch of Walgrave
Johnnie and Grizzle
Johnny and the witch-maidens
Jorinda and Joringel
Journey by broomstick
The jurga
King Bean
King Florimonde and the winged
  horse
Lady Melicent
The lady's quest
The Laidley worm of Spindlestone
  Heugh
The Lambton worm
Lancashire---?
Lancashire—fiction
Land of wonders
Lazy Hans
Leaving paradise
Legend of the witch of Cape Ann
The light princess
Lines written in dejection
The little birch tree
Little Capuchin monkey's story
The little creature
Little Firenko
The little fox

Witches (*Continued*)

Little Jip
Little Ros and Long Leda
Loki's monstrous brood
Lynx of the forest
MacCodrum of the seals
Madgy Figgey and the sow
The magic ball
The magic bed-knob
The magic carpet
The magic mango
The magic mountain
The magic storm
The magician's heart
The maiden in the country under-
   ground
Marya Morevna
Meg o' the moors
The melancholy prince and the girl
   of milk and blood
Memory
The miller and the water sprite
The monkey prince and the witch
Monsters, witches and giants
Morgan and the pot of brains
The mountain witch and the dragon-
   king
The mountain witch and the peddler
The mouse hole
Nagasramin and the witches
The necklace
A negro couple talks of witchcraft
A new way to cure old witch-hunting
Night
The night of four times
The nine peahens and the golden
   apples
The nine white sheep
Njord, Frey and Freya
Odysseus and Circe
Old Gally Mander
The old hag of the forest
The old hag's long leather bag
Old man knowall
Old Meg, the witch
Old Sal's curse
The old witch
Once in, never out again
One-eyed Likho
The origin of the coconut
Painted skin
Peahens and golden apples
The peeping servant
Pengersec and the witch of Fraddom
Peter and the witch of the wood
Pinkel
The poor girl who stepped out golden
   flowers
The power of thought
The power of witches

The powers of plants and trees to
   protect against witches
Prince Daniel
Prince Hat beneath the earth
Prince Ivan and the sun princess
Prince Lindworm
Protection against witches
Prunella
The queen of underland
The quest for Olwen
Rabbi Leib and the witch Cunegunde
Rabbit and the Indian chief
Rapunzel
Reaction
The Red Etin
The red king and the witch
Revenge (Theocritus)
The ride-by-night
Samson and the doll in green and
   brown
Scurvyhead
The secret-keeping boy
The seven ravens
The silver bell
Sister Alionushka, brother Ivanushka
The six brothers
The skipper and the witch
Some white witchcraft
The spell-song
Spin, weave, wear
The steers that wouldn't draw
Stine Bheag o' Tarbat
The stone king
The story of King Frost
The story of Maia
The story of Noschoy Datta of Ujjain
The story of the pig
The story of Zoulvisia
The student-witch
The sun-child
Suppose you met a witch
The swan princess
Sweden
The tale of the two cunning servants
The talking tree
Tam O' Shanter
Tatterhood
Tehi Tegi
The third witch
The three brothers and the marvelous
   things
The three brothers and the treacle
   toffee
The three clever brothers
Three eels
The three golden billy-goats
The three misty women
Three princes and their beasts
The three sisters and the old witch
A time of witches
The tinder box

Witches (*Continued*)

To cure a sudden stitch
To feed my people: The coming of
corn
To kill a king, from "News from
Scotland"
The toromiro of Rapa-Nui
The treasure under the tree
The trials of Conneda
Tropsyn
Tshikashi Tshikulu and the woman
The twin brothers
The twins
The twins and the snarling witch
The two girls and the iron-nose witch
Two poems
The two step-sisters
The two youths whose father was
under the sea
Uletka
Vasilia the beautiful
Vassilissa the beautiful
Weather witches; Two points of view
The weaver-woman's monument
The wedding of the dragon-god
The weird sisters (1) (2)
The well of D'yeree-in-Dowan
Which was witch?
The white bear
The white bride and the black bride
The white dove
The white hound
The white witch of Espeloo
The widow's daughter
The Wilbur witches
William Winter
Winkle, Tinkle, and Twinkle
With a wig, with a wag
The wonder ship and ship's crew
The yellow-haired witch
The youth who could become an
ant, a lion, or an eagle
Zini and the witches
Zohair and the witch

, **Sea**
The little mermaid

, **Signs of**
Memory

Witches and ghosts
JOHNSON – WHAT p219-224

Witches and witchcraft
BATCHELOR – SUPER. p126-129

The witches of Ascalon
SERWER – LET'S p3-8

The witches' reel
HOPE-SIMPSON – CAVAL. p113.

Witches' sabbats
HOPE-SIMPSON – CAVAL. p196-
202

Witches' song
HOKE – WITCHES p192-193
HOPE-SIMPSON – CAVAL. p76-77

The witching wood
FARJEON – SILVER p125-146

A witch's confession
HOPE-SIMPSON – CAVAL. p107-109

The witch's curse
HOPE-SIMPSON – CAVAL. p114-123

The witch's shoes
HOKE – WITCHES p219-220

The witch's skin
ALEGRIA – THREE p86-89

With a wig, with a wag
See also The old witch
COTHRAN – WITH p1-8

With and without
LEACH – NOODLES p56.

With tail-fans spread
REED – TALK. p40.

Withers, Carl
WITHERS – I SAW p160.
WITHERS – WORLD p118.

Withy (trees)
The bitter withy

The witless imitator
HSIEH – CHINESE p18-20

Witnesses
The wise witness

The witsduks
CURRY – DOWN p90-100

Wiverns. *See* **Wyverns**

Wives
See also titles beginning with **Wife**
Aniello
The animal languages

726

Wives (*Continued*)

Anpu and Bata
The bad-tempered wife
Bash Tchelik
Bluebeard
Chandasimha, his son and their two
 wives
The chatterbox
The child of death
Chin-Chin Kobakama
Clever Oonagh
The cobbler astrologer and the forty
 thieves
Conan's punishment
The contrary wife
The contrary woman
The cow maiden
The crane wife
The crane's feather
The curious wife
The czar's frog daughter
Daughter of the jade emperor
The devil's wife as godmother
Dobrynia and Alyosha
Doll i' the grass
The doll in the grass
The duck with red feet
Dunay
The encounter with death
The fairy wife
The faithful wife
The five eggs
Flash-of-the-paddle and Listener-to-
 the-heavenly voice
A flower to catch a thief
The frog-princess
Frog's wives make ndiba pudding
The gambler's wife
Giving away secrets
Gobborn seer
The goldfish
The guttonous wife
Gudbrand of the hillside
Hantsjc and the remarkable beast
The hardhearted rich man
The hare who had been married
Hereafterthis
How the devil married three sisters
How the half boys came to be
The hunter and the hind
The husband, the wife, and the devil
An Indian love story
The iron box
Jankyn and the witch
Juan and the helpful frog
Kamiyo of the river
King Solomon's pupils
Kralyevich Marko and Mina of
 Kostur
The language of animals

The lazy cat
Leave well enough alone
Little Radoyitsa
MacCodrum of the seals
The mad man, the dead man, and the
 devil
Male and female created he them:
 The river of separation
The man who fled a nagging wife
The man who had no wife
Mango mountain
The master of the winds
The moon and his frog-wife
Morgan and the pot of brains
The mosquitoes
The most obedient wife
The ogre courting
An old woman sows discord
Outlaw Vukossav's wife
A peasant tricks the devil
The peasant's strong wife
The prince and the Three Fates
The rabbit and the possum seek a
 wife
The raven's magic gem
The restless pigeon and his wife
Richmuth of Cologne
The robe
The royal monument pavilion
Samba the coward
A secret told to a stranger
The shepherd who understood the
 language of the animals
The shepherd with the curious wife
The six brothers
The skillful huntsman
The smart husband and the smarter
 wife
The snake and the toad
The snow wife
The spider
Spider's web
Stavr Godinovich and his clever wife
A story of three brothers
Stubborn husband, stubborn wife
A suspicious wife with an enforced
 extra husband
The tale of the two brothers
Think on four wives
Three foolish wives
Three fools
The three unmarried ministers
Three who found their hearts' desire
The three wishes
The town of fools
Tsimbarume, the hardened bachelor
Two out of the sack
Vassillissa the wise
What happened to six wives who ate
 onions
Where to lay the blame

Wives (*Continued*)

Which was witch?
Who is boss?
Who should get the neck ring?
Why the dog lost his wife
The wise wife
The wonders of the three donals

The wizard earl
    COLUM – STONE p108-115

The wizard king
    MANNING – PRINCES p40-48

The wizard of Oz. The cowardly lion
    MY BOOK HOUSE v. 6 p62-69

The wizard of Reay's book of magic
    SHEPPARD – SCOT. p61-63

The wizard of the Nile
    MOZLEY – EGYPT p19-23

A wizard of the twilight
    MY BOOK HOUSE v. 12 p55-63

Wizards

Aniello
Arnsy Maull, the conjure man
The bewitched court
The blue parrot
The boy who became king of the
    sharks
The broken box
Cannetella
The Carl of the drab coat
Childe Rowland
Childe Rowland and the King of
    Elfland
Cooked for fifteen
Farmer Weathersky
Gold
The golden bird
The golden carnation
The grateful prince
The heart of Princess Joan
The hunchback and the miser
The idle boy
Iron, steel and strongest-of-all
Jack and the wizard
John Gethin and the candle
Juan Cigarron
Kabadaluk
Kojata
The lass who went out at the cry of
    dawn
The little black book of magic
Little cricket
The little milleress
The little nag

Long, broad and sharpsight
Magic in Marblehead
The maiden, the knight, and the
    waterfall
Many moons
A message in a bottle
The mouse and the wizard
New lamps for old
Oh and alas
The old wizard and the children
The palace of the night
Popo and the princess
Prince Finn the fair
Prince Llewellyn and the red-haired
    man
The princess
The princess and the dwarf
Radowid
Recruits
The reluctant familiar
Rich woman, poor woman
Robin Ddu
Se-Osiris and the sealed letter
The silver penny
Sir Michael Scott
The slave of the lamp
The slave of the ring
The Somalis; wizards of lion country
The sorcerer's apprentice(s)
The stork caliph
Swen-Naba; king of the warlocks
The sword of light
The sword of the stone
The tale of Vassilissa the wise
Teutli, the mountain that is alive
The three enchanted maidens
Thunderbird
Tolkien's magic ring
Tom Thumb
A toy princess
Trim Tram Turvey
The two wizards
The underground palace
Vukub-Cakix
The whale that smoked a pipe
Winter rose
A wisp of straw
The would-be wizard

Wokun
    LEACH – RAINBOW p230-231

The wolf
    DEUTSCH – TALES p56-62

The wolf and the cat
    WYNDHAM – TALES p68-71

The wolf and the crane
    STRONG – FAVORITE p62.

The wolf and the dog
  LA FONTAINE – FABLES p48-49

The wolf and the fox
  BAMBERGER – FIRST p152-155
  LA FONTAINE – FABLES p36-37

The wolf and the lamb
  GREEN – BIG p189.

The wolf and the mouse
  KRYLOV – 15 p28-29

The wolf and the old woman
  GREEN – BIG p212.

The wolf and the ram
  DURHAM – TIT p43-45

The wolf and the seven kids
  BAMBERGER – FIRST p75-79
  ARBUTHNOT – TIME p32-33

The wolf and the stork
  LA FONTAINE – FABLES p20-21

The wolf and the watch-dog
  GREEN – BIG p90-91

The wolf-bride
  JAGENDORF – UPSTATE p196-202

The wolf in sheep's clothing
  ARBUTHNOT – TIME p208.

The wolf in the ram's skin
  COOPER – FIVE p41-57

"The wolf loses his prey". See The wolf
and the ram

Wolf moon
  BUDD – FULL p71-74

The wolf plays shepherd
  LA FONTAINE – FABLES p26-27

The wolf, the fox, and the jug of honey
  BELPRÉ – TIGER p43-47

The wolf, the goat, and the kid
  LA FONTAINE – FABLES p38-39

The wolf turned shepherd
  GREEN – BIG p224-225

The wolf wears a sheepskin
  WILSON – GREEK p180-181

Wolf wisdom
  LEEKLEY – WORLD p20-26

Wolfe, Humbert
  The blackbird

Wolfert Webber, or golden dreams
  MY BOOK HOUSE v. 11 p107-151

The wolf's food
  MAAS – MOON p99-103

The wolf's reward
  SEKI – FOLKTALES p20-22

Wolves
  About Jan the Prince, Princess
    Wonderface, and the flamebird
  The art of reading
  The ass gets the better of the wolf
  The baby camel
  Be careful what you say
  The beginning of the world and the
    making of California
  The boy who became a reindeer
  The boy who cried wolf
  The boy who was called "thick-head"
  Browny
  Brer wolf's little tar men
  The bun
  The cat and the fox
  The cat, the cock and the lamb
  The clever fox
  The cock who went traveling
  The crow and the whale
  The creation of the wolf
  The dervish and the wolf
  Dog luck
  The escape of the animals
  The fiddler going home
  The firebird
  The fishes and the wolf
  The flower of beauty
  The foolish dog
  The foolish man
  The foolish wolf
  The forest wolf and the prairie wolf
  The fox and the hare
  The fox and the wolf
  The fox and the wolf and the keg of
    butter
  The fox and the wolf at the wedding
  The fox as shepherd
  The fox, the wolf, and the horse
  Georgic and Merlin
  The giant of the hills
  The giant who had no heart in his
    body
  Glooskap's country
  The goat and her three kids
  The goat and the wolf
  The hare who was afraid of nothing
  Hecho the lazy

Wolves (*Continued*)

Hiram goes courting
A horned goat
The horse, the lion, and the wolf
The hound Gelert
How Brer rabbit met brer tar-baby
How death came
How Dounai won a bride for Prince
  Vladimir
How Fenris Wolf was bound
How the cardinal got his red feathers
How the groundhog lost his tail
How the redbird got his color
How the wolf lost his tail
How Ysengrin the wolf was taught
  to fish
A hungry wolf
The hunting cat
Itsayaya's revenge
Johnny and the three goats
Johnny-cake
Jonnikin and the flying basket
Journey in a well
The king who could not sleep
The lark, the wolf, and the fox
The lion-wolf
The lion's share
Little Red Riding Hood
Little Tom Thumb
Loki's monstrous brood
Manabozho's nephew
The marriage of Tom and the vixen
Mirabella
The miracle flame
Mr. Samson cat
Mrs. Fox's wedding
Mittens the cat
Mowgli's brothers
Nathlook: Susie, my name
The old dog and the gray wolf
The one who wasn't afraid
The out-foxed fox
The owl and the wolf
Owl with the great head and eyes
Peahens and golden apples
The plains' call
The poor wolf
Prince Ivan and the firebird
The proud goat
The rabbit and the tar wolf
Rabbit scratches buh elephant's back
The rain leak in an old house
The ram and the goat
The ram and the pig who went into
  the woods to live by themselves
Red Riding Hood
Reineke fox
Reynard the fox
St. Francis and the wolf
Saint Peter's horses

Salakhbai and the fox
Seerko
Shaydoola
Sheem
The shepherd's boy
The shepherd's dog and the wolf
The son of the King of Spain
The story of the three little pigs
The straw ox
The struggle between the wolf and the
  fox
The stupid wolf
The tailless jackal
The terrible leak
The theft of dawn
The theft of fire
The thirteen enchanted cats
The three cranberries
The three goslings
The three little pigs
Three princes and their beasts
The three princesses and the unclean
  spirit
Transportation problem
The troll who hid his life
The two-faces
Two pieces of meat confuse the mind
  of the fly
The vixen and the rooster
The werewolf
The white wolf
Why God made the dog
Why groundhog's tail is short
Why the animals have no fire
Why the terrapin's shell is scarred
The woodman and the fox

The woman and the mouse
  TRACEY – LION p118-121

The woman and the sacred bora ring
  NORLEDGE – ABORIGINAL p16-17

A woman had a rooster
  MY BOOK HOUSE v. 1 p73.

The woman in moon
  THOMPSON – HAWAII. p76-80

The woman in the chest
  RANKE – GERMANY p136-139

The woman of Llyn-y-fan (1) The meeting
    JONES – WELSH p182-189

The woman of Llyn-y-fan (2) The parting
  JONES – WELSH p190-193

The woman of Llyn-y-fan (3) The sequel
  JONES – WELSH p195.

The woman of peace and the kettle
BRIGGS – PERS. p106-108

The woman of rock
JORDAN – BURRO p46-47

The woman of the snow
LITTLEDALE – GHOSTS p157-164

The woman tribe
CARPENTER – SOUTH p100-107

The woman who came down from
heaven
SEKI – FOLKTALES p63-69

The woman who flummoxed the fairies
LEODHAS – HEATHER p35-43

The woman who raised a bear as a son
MELZACK – DAY p77-84

The woman who wanted to cook with
salt water
BERRY – MAGIC p50-55

The womb of the earth
MARRIOTT – AMER. p205-206

Women
    Akiba and the daughter of Kalba
        Sabbu'a
    Are there such women?
    The babymakers
    The cat who came indoors
    The charitable woman and the three
        loaves
    The clever peasant girl
    The first strawberries
    Frigg and the goddesses
    The goldsmith, the wood carver, the
        tailor, and the hermit who quarreled
        over a wooden woman
    How the parrots helped the women
    Introduction (The wisdom and folly
        of women)
    A legend of Knockmany
    The little birch tree
    Male and female created he them;
        The river of separation
    The marriage of Gawaine
    The marriage of Sir Gawain
    The merchant's wife
    Pandora . . . the fateful casket
    The philosophers of King Darius
    The pious washerwomen
    The time of deep darkness
    The whale and the sorcerer
    Who rules the roost

    Why cats live with women
    Why dog has a fur coat and woman
        has seven tempers
    Why women talk more than men
    Why women won't listen
    The wisdom and folly of women

, Western
    A few lost ladies

The wonder child
MOZLEY – EGYPT p44-57

The wonder of Skoupa
HAVILAND – GREECE p53-59

The wonder ship and ship's crew
MacMANUS – BOLD p101-119

The wonder-tree
LEEUW – INDO. p151-156

The wonderful bed
BELTING – THREE p146-156

The wonderful cake
PILKINGTON – SHAM p102-103

The wonderful horse
LAWSON – STRANGE p44-53

The wonderful knapsack
CHILD – CASTLES p97-107

The wonderful mare Khadra
DAVIS – TEN p81-92

The wonderful night
MINCIELI – TALES p32-34

The wonderful plow, The Little People
of the Island of Rugen
BELTING – ELVES p35-40

The wonderful talking bowl
UCHIDA – SEA p99-111

The wonderful tar-baby story
ARBUTHNOT – TIME p192-193;
194-196

The wonderful tree
HEADY – JAMBO p46-52
MANNING – GLASS p1-9

The wonderful tune
SHEAHAN – HENRY p109-128

The wonderful wooden peacock flying
machine
TOOZE – WONDER. p15-25

The wonderful world
MY BOOK HOUSE v. 3 p11.

The wonderland of an artist's workshop
MY BOOK HOUSE v. 6 p164-169

The wonders of the three donals
MacMANUS – HIBERIAN p185-201

The wonders seen by Wurrunna
PARKER – AUSTRALIAN p155-167

Wong Siang, the clever
ALEXANDER – PEBBLES p18.

Wood
The bobtail monkey
The cruel stepmother
Fate and the faggot gatherer
The goldsmith, the wood carver, the
tailor, and the hermit who quarreled
over a wooden woman
The house in the woods
It's all the fault of Adam
Knock on wood
Magic in Marblehead
The man in the moon
The mink and the weasel
Stupid Peruonto
The white dove
The witching wood

–**Birch**
The magic storm

, **Burnt**
The magical tune

–**Chips**
The three tasks

–**Firewood**
The cruel uncle
The three wishes

–**Ohia**
Fire magic and the mud hen

The wood carver of Ruteng
COURLANDER – KANT. p111-116

Wood-carvers and wood-carving
The beckoning cat
The goldsmith, the wood carver, the
tailor, and the hermit who quarreled
over a wooden woman
How Papantla got its patron saint
Kamiyo of the river
The legend of Pathasos
The luck boy of Toy Valley
The magic baby shoes
The singing fir-tree

The toromiro of Rapa-Nui
A voice from heaven
Whistle the winds
Wooden Peter

Wood cutters. *See* **Woodcutters**

The wood cutter's son and the two turtles
EELLS – SPAIN p25-35

The wood fairy
HAVILAND – CZECH. p35-47

The wood nymphs
BELTING – THREE p125-130

The wood of Tontla
MAAS – MOON p31-43

Wood-maidens
Smolicheck

Wood-spirits
Smart Dai-adalla
The wood nymphs

Woodchucks
The groundhog family
The hare and the tortoise
The little rabbit who wanted red
wings
Why groundhog's tail is short
Why the woodchuck comes out in
midwinter

–**Tails**
How the groundhog lost his tail
Why groundhog's tail is short

The woodcock and the fox
BUDBERG – RUSSIAN p241-242

Woodcocks
Coyote and the alder stump
The king of the demons and the worm
Shamir

The woodcutter and the water demon
WYNDHAM – TALES p43-46

The woodcutter of Gura
COURLANDER – FIRE p19-23

Woodcutters
Allah will provide
The ash lad who had an eating match
with the troll
The black-bearded Brownies of
Boneburg

Woodcutters (*Continued*)

Casperl
The child in the bamboo tree
The clever peasant girl
The clumber pup
Don't tease the tengu!
East of the sun and west of the moon
The enchanted waterfall
Fair wages for all
The fame of the princess
The faun and the woodcutter's
  daughter
The five tiger general
Four riddles
A fox in hiding
Gianni and the giant
The giant outwitted
The golden axe
Good luck and great riches
Haensel and Gretel
Hansel and Gretel
The heavenly maiden and the wood-
  cutter
The honest woodman
How the dotty Afghan woodman
  died
It's all the fault of Adam
Jacques the wood cutter
King Lindorm
The king of the wood
The lazy cat
The lion and the woodcutter
The little duck
Little Tom Thumb
Lost and found
The lost children
Mary-Ann and the cauld lady of
  Hylton
Mighty Mikko
Monkey-dance and sparrow-dance
More south than south, more north
  than north
Ooka and the barbered beast
Peach boy
The pheasants and the bell
The revenge of the serpent
The rich man and the poor man
The ridiculous wishes
The ring in the porridge bowl
Snake magic
The sticky-sticky pine
The sun-king's hair
The three enchanted mares
The three golden hairs of the king of
  the cave giants
The three wasted wishes
Through the eyes
The tree that shadowed the world
The ungrateful bear
Why the bear cannot play the kantele

The wild huntsman
The winter flower
The woman of the snow
The wood nymphs
The woodman and the fox

The woodcutter's daughter
  MASEY – STORIES p73-83

The wooden bowl
  HEARN – JAPANESE p60-68
  VITTORINI –OLD p86-91

The wooden horse
  GREEN – GREEKS p40-41

Wooden Peter
  ILLYES – ONCE p18-22

The woodman and the fox
  ALMEDINGEN – RUSS. p40-47

The woodpecker and the jade stone
  BOWES – BIRD p24-31

Woodpeckers
At the wedding of Miss Jenny Wren
The black giant of Luckless River
The black woodpecker
The boy who was lost
The case of the mouse-deer and the
  crocodile's eggs
The coomacka-tree
The deer and its friends
The elephant and the gnat
How maple sugar came
The mouse and the sun
The outwitted hunter
The rabbit prince
Sartak-Pai
Seven sons
The stork caliph
The three friends
The ungrateful lion
The sword of the stone
The wagtail and the rainbow
Why the woodpecker has a long nose

Woods. *See* **Forests**

The woodsman's daughter and the lion
  ALEGRIA´ – THREE p34-39

Woodsmen
See also **Woodcutters**
Adventuring: white man on the
  warpath
And upon the fourth bray
The cold heart–Part 1
The king and the monkey

Woodsmen (*Continued*)

The lazy maiden
The little snake
Luc, the king's woodsman

The wooing of Etain
MORAY — FAIR p3-16

The wooing of Lottie Moon
JAGENDORF — SAND p22-25

Wool

Baa, baa, black sheep
Hanging at Wessagrescus
Why sheep does not come in out of
the rain

A word from the author
FELTON — WORLD'S p9-14

The word of Igor's armament
MY BOOK HOUSE v. 10 p119-129

Wordplay riddles
LEACH — NOODLES p60-61

Words

Agayk and the strangest spear
The ferryman
It's been well used
Jack O'Leary's plow
King Matthias and the old man
A lie for a lie
The pillow
Some namesakes of the dragon
The story of the smart parrot
A time for everything
Wainamoinen finds the lost-words

Wordsworth, William
The cock is crowing
The kitten and falling leaves

Wordsworth, William

A boy of the Lake country

Work

See also **Superstitions—Work; Tests;**
Workers
The book of magic
The calm Brahman
The city mouse and the country
mouse
The donkey, the ox and the farmer
Fareedah's carpet
The grateful animals and the talisman
Ijapa and the oba repair a roof
It's all the fault of Adam

The Kildare pooka
The lazy gardener and the little red
man
The lazy man
The little brother of the sun
The little orphan
Live alone; die alone
The luck fairies
Master and man
Pa Grumble
Ruddy-my-beard
A rupee earned
The snow-wife
The spoiled daughter
The story of Li'l Hannibal
The ten dwarfs of Aunt Greenwater
The thirteen flies
Tim for wealth and happiness
The unwashed pot
Utzel and his daughter Poverty
The weary spirits of Lanai
Why cats and dogs are enemies
Yallery Brown

Work
BATCHELOR — SUPER. p56-59

Work-let-me-see
SHERLOCK — WEST p125-129

Workers

Fairy workmen
The Guragies: workmen of high
Africa
The hired man
Horns
The jurga
The learned young professor
The rich landowner and his worker
The talking cat
The unsmiling princess

World, End of

The old woman and her hominy pot

The world beyond
MARRIOTT — AMER. p196-200

The world is so full
MY BOOK HOUSE v. 1 p17.

A world of beauty: The Peyote religion
MARRIOTT — AMER. p171-176

A world of nonsense
WITHERS — WORLD p1.

The world of the gods
HOSFORD — THUNDER p1-5

World trees. *See* Trees, World

World, Beginning of. *See* Creation

The world's great epics
MY BOOK HOUSE v. 12 p221-225

The world's most truthful man
FELTON – WORLD'S p93-100

The world's smartest cat
MARGOLIS – IDY p45-50

Worm moon
BUDD – FULL p13-16

Worms
Alison Gross
The armadillos
The boy who was called "thick-head"
The clever earthworm
Dragons?
The fairyland of science
The giant worm of the well
The growing rock
How the great rocks grew
It
The king of the demons and the
worm Shamir
The Laidley worm of Spindlestone
Heugh
The Lambton worm
Old Shellover
The queen of the planets
Rabbit and the grain buyers
Who is the mightiest?
Why the cock eats worms
The witch of Wandaland
Worm moon

Worry
Clever Elsie
The emperor's questions
Mr. fox learns what trouble is
The old men who said "Why"
The seed of happiness

The worst spinster in Norfolk
FARJEON – SILVER p159-168

Worster, W.
Kagssagssuk, the homeless boy who
became a strong man

The worthless man of poverty
HOLLADAY – BANTU p15-23

Woswosim birds
The rescue of fire

The would-be wizard
CARPENTER – ELEPHANT'S p49-57

Would you like to see goats dance on
stilts
MY BOOK HOUSE v. 1p121.

The wounded archer
GREEN – GREEKS p34-35

Wousers (animals)
Pecos Bill
Pecos Bill and his bouncing bride

Wratislaw, A. H.
The lame vixen

Wreaths
White-bear-King-Valemon

The wreck of the Palatine
TAFT – PROFILE p59-66

The wren
GREEN – BIG p47-51

The wren and the bear
GREEN – BIG p226-229

Wrens
At the wedding of Miss Jenny Wren
The eagle and the wren
The fox and the heron
The king of the birds
The marriage of the robin and the
wren
Mr. wren borrows money of Mr.
buzzard
The princess and the vagabone
The robin and the wren
There was an old man with a beard
The tree that shadowed the world
Wee robin's Christmas song
Why wagtail wags her tail

—Feathers
How the little black wren got its
red feathers

The wrestler of Kyushu
COURLANDER – TIGER'S p83-86

The wrestlers
COURLANDER – OLODE p107-109

Wrestlers and wrestling
The boy and the water-sprite
The champion
The coming of the corn
The demon wrestler

Wrestlers and wrestling (*Continued*)

    Jean Britisse, the champion
    The king and the wrestler
    The lizard's lost meat
    Lord Krishna, or The eighth child
    The mighty wrestlers
    The origin of corn
    The peasant's strong wife
    Strong man
    Thor and the giants
    The twins

The wrestling match of the two Buddhas
    UCHIDA – MAGIC p23-31

Wright, Orville and Wilbur
    Wilbur Wright and Orville Wright

Writing
    Flyleaf scribblings
    The two boxes
    Why the cat and dog cannot live at
      peace

Written in the stars
    MINCIELI – TALES p111-120

The wrong man
    LEACH – NOODLES p25.

The wrong song
    RANKE – GERMANY p145.

Wu Meng, the thoughtful
    ALEXANDER – PEBBLES p9.

Wurrunna's trip to the sea
    PARKER – AUSTRALIAN p155-160

Wylie, Elinor
    To Llewelyn (who inquired concerning
      wyverns)

Wynken, Blynken, and Nod
    MY BOOK HOUSE v. 2 p24-25

Wynne, Annette
    In Columbus' time
    Indian children
    Little maid of far Japan

Wyoming
    Bowleg Bill

Wyoming
    LEACH – RAINBOW p166-167

Wyverns (wiverns, wyvers) (imaginary animals)
    To Llewelyn (who inquired
      concerning wyverns)

Y

Yakshas (desert tribe)
Rodents rampart on a field of azure
The story of Noschoy Datta of Ujjain

Yakuts (people)
The girl in the moon
The owl's punishment

Yale University
The ghostly hitchhiker

Yallery Brown
GARNER — GOBLINS p42-51
JACOBS — MORE p28-36

The yam child
ARNOTT — TALES p20-35

Yama and the poor man
KRUEGER — SERPENT p98-105

Yams
Anansi and five
Anansi and the elephant exchange
knocks
Anansi borrows money
Bouki buys a burro
The coming of the yams
A contest with skillful spirits
How yams got their eyes
Ijapa and the hot-water test
Ijapa and Yanrinbo swear an oath
Ijapa goes to the Osanyin shrine
Ticky-picky boom-boom
The war of the plants
Why yams and cassava hide in the
ground

Yankee Doodle
MY BOOK HOUSE v. 1 p101.

The Yankee peddler
MY BOOK HOUSE v. 5 p127a-127b

Yankees
LEACH — RAINBOW p257-258

Yanni
MANNING — DRAGONS p76-78

Yao, Emperor
The greatest archer

A yard of nose
BELTING — THREE p54-63

Yarn
The companion
The girl and the golden chair
The golden castle that hung in the air

Yawning
BATCHELOR — SUPER. p23-24

Ye merry doinges of Robin Hood
MY BOOK HOUSE v. 11 p49-72

The year of Nyangondhu's cattle
HARMAN — TALES p90-95

The year of the feast at Simbi
HARMAN — TALES p95-103

The year of the monkeys of Ramogi
HARMAN — TALES p103-108

"Year of the moon"
The animals' quarrel

The year with three names
HARMAN — TALES p89-108

The yellow dragon
HAMPDEN — GYPSY p45-50
MANNING — DRAGONS p55-61

Yellow hair: George Armstrong Custer
MARRIOTT — AMER. p155-160

The yellow-haired witch
SPICER — WITCHES p11-17

The yellow ribbon
LEACH — RAINBOW p203-204

Yells
Thorsteinn Shiver

Yemen
The horse without a master
Rescue from the fire worshippers
Saadia the potmender

Yes, that's the girl that struts about
MY BOOK HOUSE v. 3 p26.

Yeshivah
The saving of a soul
The story of Mordecai and Esther

Yet gentle will the griffin be
PALMER – DRAGONS p88.

Yew
The powers of plants and trees to
protect against witches

Ygg. *See* **Odin**

Yggdrasil, the world tree
AULAIRE – NORSE p31-35

Yi Chang and the haunted house
JEWETT – WHICH p16-28
LITTLEDALE – GHOSTS p45-59

Yiankos
MANNING – DAMIAN p75-86

Yodeling
How the Kuhreihen began

Yogesvara
The heron
The monsoon season

Yogi
The cat that went to heaven

Yoni and her stepmother
INS-SOB – FOLK p46-48

Yoro reveals himself as Gessar Khan
HAZELTINE – HERO p400-415

Yoruba
The king and kuffie

Yoruba proverb
COURLANDER – OLODE p9.

You are right
SUN – LAND p111-112

You can't hold it
LEACH – SOUP p107-108

You have a napkin
LEACH – SOUP p25-27

You must pay for the horse, Aga
URE – RUMANIAN p167-168

You'd scream too
LEACH – RAINBOW p218-219

Young, Ella
The lordship of the Fianna

Young Bekie
MANNING –ENGLISH p74-81

Young Charlotte
LEACH – RAINBOW p252-255

Young Conall of Howth
O'SULLIVAN – FOLK. p79-97

The young coyote's visit
HEADY – TALES p35-40

The young Finn
O'FAOLAIN – IRISH p125-133

The young fox and the old fox
GREEN – BIG p68-69

The young gentleman and the tiger
INS-SOB – FOLK. p160-162

The young giant
THOMPSON – ONE p286-292

Young Gim and the robbers
INS-SOB – FOLK. p62-65

The young girl and the devil
ALEGRIA – THREE p80-83

Young happy
HAMPDEN – GYPSY p67-68

The young head of the Cheng family
WYNDHAM – CHINA p25-33

Young hunter
RUSHMORE – DANCING p61-72

The young hunter and the Juju man
CARPENTER – AFRICAN p137-144

The young Irish lad from the hiring fair
LEODHAS – GHOSTS p113-124

Young John
JAGENDORF – UPSTATE p189-192

Young Kate
FARJEON – LITTLE p32-35

The young Lord of Lorn
MANNING – ENGLISH p5-16

The young man and the giant
NORLEDGE – ABORIGINAL p38-39

The young man and the kangaroo
NORLEDGE – ABORIGINAL p29.

The young man and the priest
INS-SOB – FOLK p73-75

The young man who married a fairy
SHEPPARD – WELSH p72-77

Young Michael and the uninvited guest
ALMEDINGEN – KNIGHTS p73-85

Young midshipman David Farragut
MY BOOK HOUSE v. 8 p82-90

Young Paul
JAGENDORF – NEW p3-7

The young piper, The Little People of
Ireland
BELTING – ELVES p55-60

Young Pollard and the brawn of Bishop
Auckland
FINLAY – FOLK p86-95

A young prince named Siegfried
HAZELTINE – HERO p252-268

A young Quaker of New England
MY BOOK HOUSE v. 12 p118-119

The young shepherd
MANNING – JONNIKIN p95-105

The young storyteller
FOSTER – STONE p81-82

The young Tamlin
MORAY – FAIR p47-57

The young Urashima
McALPINE – JAPAN. p106-120

The young widow
INS-SOB – FOLK p110-120

The young wife of Nam Xuong
SUN – LAND p91-96

The young witch-horse
JAGENDORF – UPSTATE p84-87

Your America
MY BOOK HOUSE v. 11 p216.

Your name
BATCHELOR – SUPER. p63-64

Youth
Fionn in search of his youth
Idunn's apples of youth
Teen-ager
Those young men

The three young men and death
The young Urashima

, Eternal (perpetual)
Alchemy: the magic science
The finch with the golden voice
The fountain of youth
The golden phoenix
The green isle
The knight and the naiad of the
lake
The land of youth
The legend of Urashima
Magicians of the way
Oisin in the land of the ever young
Oisin, son of Finn MacCool
Ossian in the land of eternal youth
The son of the King of Spain
The spell of the mermaid
The spring ay-petri
The spring of youth
The three golden hairs of Grandad
Sol
Tithonus, the grasshopper
True love in the Blue Mountains

The youth and the dog dance
MacMILLAN – GLOOS. p259-265

The youth impresses the devil in his iron
house. See The devil and the pit

The youth who could become an ant, a
lion, or an eagle
TOOR, – GOLDEN p67-79

The youth who made friends with the
beasts and the birds
CARPENTER – SOUTH p27-34

The youth who trusted in God
SPICER – LONG p73-91

The youth who wanted some fun
MY BOOK HOUSE v. 7 p20-25

Yu the Great
The quellers of the flood

Yudhisthir
This hound hath loved me

Yugoslavia
Bas Celik
Be careful what you say
The bee on the cap
The best wish
The big prescription
The child and the colt
The cock at the tsar's throne

740

Yugoslavia (*Continued*)

Ero and the kadi
Ero and the tsar
Ero from the other world
Fate
The frog-wife
"General" dog and his army
The giant who counted stones
How the gipsy sold his horse
How the peasants brought wisdom
I am not from Sarajevo
Kabadaluk: the little Arab boy
The king's vine
The lemon and his army
Lies for a wager
The little fairy
The magic ring
Nail soup
Nasradin Hodja returns a gift

St. Sava and the devil
Three eels
The traveller and his host
The Tsar Trajan's ears
The tsar's son and the swan-girl
The tsar's son-in-law and the winged
old woman
Two pennies
Vladimir's adventures in search of a
fortune
The wild dog and the king's son

— **Ballads.** *See* **Ballads-Yugoslavia**

Yuki-Onna
BUCK — FAIRY p251-256

Yung–Kyung–Pyung
SHERLOCK — ANANSI p59-63

Z

Zab
  MEHDEVI – PERSIAN p51-61

Zagloul, Ahmed
  ZAGLOUL – BLACK p161.

Zagloul, Zane
  ZAGLOUL – BLACK p161.

Zalewski, C. Stanley
  Polish rhymes

Zane, Elizabeth
  Beautiful doll

Zangwill, Israel
  The melting pot

Zebras
  Afar in the desert
  Colored coats
  The first zebra

Zeitlin, Ida
  Yoro reveals himself a Gessar Khan

Zeno, Nicolo and Antonio
  Lord Sinclair and the Zeno brothers

Zeus
  Bears in the sky
  The firebringer . . . Prometheus
  Why are giants so stupid?

Zeus and the horse
  GREEN – BIG p26.

Zezolla and the date-palm tree
  TOOR – GOLDEN p29-39

Zilioniene, Gala
  A ghost at the door

Zimmern, Helen
  Rustem and his rose-colored steed

Zimwis
  Little sister and zimwi

Zini and the witches
  HOPE-SIMPSON – CAVAL. p23-34

Zlateh the goat
  SINGER – ZLATEH p79-90

Zo Han-Zun, who became a stone
Buddha
  IN-SŎB – FOLK p75-77

Zodiac, Signs of
  Beasts of the zodiac
  Giants, dragons, and gods

Zohair and the witch
  NAHMAD – PEASANT p147-151

Zolo Dumah and the priest
  HASKETT – GRAINS p55-57

A zoo in the park
  MY BOOK HOUSE v. 1 p186.

Zoos
  All's well that ends well
  Deep insight
  Dream behind bars

Zoroaster, the Mystic
  Alchemy: the magic science